Prayer of the poor

Kabbalistic Sukkot Machzor

KABBALAH PUBLISHING

www.kabbalah.com™

Edited by YEHUDA BERG

The Kabbalah Centre
155 E. 48th St., New York, NY 10017
1062 S. Robertson Blvd., Los Angeles, CA 90035

First Edition
July 2012

Printed in the USA

ISBN13: 978-1-57189-861-6

I dedicate this Machzor with all my heart to my father

David Soleimanzadeh (David ben Yosef)

with gratitude for making my life
filled with Light and inspiration.

I hope, through his humor and strength, his
Light will continue to provide for the people of future generations.

Chag Sameach.

Have a nice day.

TABLE OF CONTENTS

TO THE GREATNESS OF THE VALUE OF THE ASHURIT FONT

And then you should open your mouth with wisdom and say *Keri'at Shema* with intention. This means you should understand the words you are saying and that when you recite the words of *Keri'at Shema* (from the Prayer Book) you should visualize in your mind the shape of each word and its letters. For example when you say the word "*Shema*" you should visualize the letters *Shin, Mem* and *Ayin* the way they are written in *Ashurit* font in front of your eyes. You should then visualize every word the same way until the end. You should visualize the vowels and the intonations that are above every letter, the same way as they are written in this Prayer Book and by doing so you should merit that each word will excel in its form to the Upper Worlds and every letter shall go to its place and to its root to activate miraculous actions and *tikkunim* (corrections) that are related to you. And by doing so [scanning the *Ashurit* font] on a daily basis, it will enable you (and it has been proven) to remove all negative thoughts and nonsense that interferes with the purity of your thought and intention in prayers. The more scanning of the *Ashurit* font a person does with the *Keri'at Shema* and any other part of the prayer will add purity to his thoughts during prayer. This meditation is a simple action and then you are promised to successfully educate yourself with your prayer and all will be desired by God just like the good scent. Amen so be it.

(*Seder HaYom* by Rav Yosef Chaim - the Ben Ish-Chai).

"When you go to sleep you should visualize the Tetragrammaton Name (יהוה), Blessed Be He, as if it was written in capital *Ashurit*. The eyes should always turn to God and God will protect him from falling into a trap".

(*Tziporen Shamir*, par. 68 v. 121 by Rav Chaim Yosef David Azulai - the Chida 1724-1806)

GENERAL GUIDANCE

According to Rav Isaac Luria (the Ari), and Rav Shalom Sharabi (the Rashash), all the words of intention, Holy Names and names of angels that are written in this book, even though they are a part of the text, should not be pronounced verbally. When you get to a word like this, you should scan it with your eyes and not say it.

IN THE MATTER OF SUKKOT
(FROM THE *GATE OF MEDITATIONS* AND *PRI ETZ CHAIM*)

MEDITATIONS OF THE MIKVEH FOR THE EVE OF YOM TOV (HOLIDAY)

On the Eve of the Holiday you need to do *Mikveh*. And you should meditate on the Names: יוד הי ויו הי אלף הי יוד הי, which together have the numerical value of the word Holiday (*Regel* =233), and you should meditate that *Mikveh* has the numerical value of the Name: אלף הה יוד הה, which is 151. And you should say the following verse and meditate on the Names that are derived from it:

ויקרא vayikra

אלף למד הי יוד מם

ע"ב יוד הי ויו הי

אלהים Elohim

אלף למד הי יוד מם

ס"ג יוד הי ואו הי

ליבשה layabasha

אלף למד הה יוד מם

מ"ה יוד הא ואו הא

ארץ eretz

אלף למד הא יוד מם

ב"ן יוד הה וו הה

ר"ת ולמקוה ulemikveh המים hamayim קרא kara ימים yamim

יהוה אלהים (with its nine letters =121)

THE SECRET OF THE HOLIDAY OF SUKKOT

As we have learned, the world was created on *Rosh Hashanah* and because of this, everything goes back to its original state at this time of *Rosh Hashanah* every year, which means that *Zeir* and *Nukva* are in the form of Back-to-Back. We need the process of the Sawing to bring them into Unification and Face-to-Face form, which happens during the time from *Rosh Hashanah* to *Simchat Torah*.

From *Rosh Hashanah* to *Yom Kippur*, the Ten *Sefirot* of *Nukva-Rachel* are being sawed from the back of *Zeir Anpin*, thus for the time being *Nukva-Rachel* is not ready for the Unification and during all these days (from *Rosh Hashanah* to *Simchat Torah*) the Unification is between *Yisrael* (or *Yaakov*) and *Leah*.

Accordingly all the days between *Rosh Hashanah* and *Yom Kippur* are in the secret of the verse "*His left arm is under my head*", which means the hug (the process of sweetening the Judgments) that comes from Left Column. As we know, the reason for the Sawing process is to transfer the harsh Judgment from the back of *Zeir Anpin* towards the *Nukva* so He (*Zeir Anpin*) will be left with only Mercies and She (*Nukva*) will be left with all of the Judgments. And in order to sweeten Her Judgments *Zeir Anpin* hugs Her with His left (*Gevurah*), because we know that the Judgments can be sweetened only by their root; and then it is the time for the Sawing. These three aspects (the transferring of the Judgments, the sweetening of the Judgments and the Sawing) are happening all at once by the process of the *Dormita* (sleeping). And this is called the Hugging of the Left.

During *Yom Kippur* the *Nukva* (where all of Her Judgments have been sawed), is elevated to Supernal *Ima* and receives Five Judgments *from* Ima Itself.

After *Yom Kippur* until the day before *Simchat Torah*, is the secret of the continuation of the verse "*and His right arm is hugging me*", which means that *Nukva* is now receiving Mercies (Right Column). There are two aspects of Mercies: One from Supernal *Ima* and the other aspect from *Zeir Anpin*. And in each of these two aspects of Mercies there are two Illuminations—Inner Light and Surrounding Light.

Drawing the Inner Light from Supernal *Ima* is accomplished (without any action) by the days from *Yom Kippur* to *Sukkot*. And drawing the Surrounding Light from Supernal *Ima* is done by the action of seating in the *Sukkah*.

Drawing the Inner Light from *Zeir Anpin* is accomplished by the action of the shaking of the *Lulav*. And the drawing of the Surrounding Light from *Zeir Anpin* is done by the action of circling the *bimah* with the *Lulav* (just to clarify, all the Mercies that enter *Nukva* are for her construction to become a complete *Partzuf*).

In General the expansion of the Mercies is always from Above to Below, meaning, first it will expand in *Chesed* and then in *Gevurah* etc. but during the days from *Yom Kippur* to *Sukkot* the Inner Light from Supernal *Ima* enters from the lowest to the highest. The reason for this change is:

As of now (on *Yom Kippur*), the *Nukva* is filled with Judgments and if the inner aspect of the Mercies will enter Her in the regular order, from Above to Below, they could be nullified (because each day, only one aspect of the Inner Light of Mercy enters the *Nukva*). And even if the highest and strongest aspect (*Chesed* of *Chesed*) would enter first, it would vanished because of the strong Judgments. And the reason for the Mercies to enter *Nukva* is to sweeten the Judgments, and that is why on the first day, we need that the lowest and weakest *Chesed* (the general illumination of the Mercies) to enter the *Nukva*; even though this *Chesed* will be nullified by the Judgments it still creates an impression of correction. And on the second day a higher *Chesed* enters *Nukva* and creates more impression until the last day, when the highest *Chesed* enters *Nukva* and then it has the power to overcome the Judgments and sweeten them.

This is the order of the entrance of the Mercies:
On the ninth and tenth days of *Tishrei*, the general Illumination of the Mercies enters *Malchut* and *Yesod* of *Nukva*. On the 11th day, the fifth *Chesed* enters to Her *Hod*. On the 12th day, the fourth *Chesed* enters Her *Netzach*. On the 13th day, the third *Chesed* enters Her *Tiferet*. On the 14th day, the second *Chesed* enters Her *Gevurah*.

On the 15th day, this is the first day of *Sukkot*, two aspects of the Mercies enter. From the aspect of the day, the highest *Chesed* (the first *Chesed* and the last from the Inner Light aspect of *Ima*) enters *Chesed* of *Nukva*. From the aspect of the *Sukkah*, the highest *Chesed* (first *Chesed* and first from the Surrounding Light aspect of *Ima*) also enters *Nukva*.

And this explains why the first day of *Sukkot* (the 15th day of *Tishrei*) is a Holiday. First, on this day all the Mercies aspects complete their entrance into *Nukva*. Second, the Supernal *Chesed* that is called *Yomam*, enters. Third, on this day, the entrance of the Mercies from the Surrounding Light (which are higher than the Mercies of the Inner Light aspect) begins. Fourth, as mentioned above, the highest aspect of the Mercy from the Surrounding Light enters.

And you should know that the aspect of "*and His right arm is hugging me*" starts only on the 15th day of *Tishrei*, the first day of *Sukkot*, as the essence of the correction of the *Nukva* is done by the Mercies, and especially by the Mercies that come from the Surrounding Light, which is called Hugging. So from the first day the Hugging begins and this is why it says "*And you shall take to yourself on the first day*," even though the spreading of the Mercies had already begun prior to *Yom Kippur*, the Surrounding Mercies have not entered yet. And that is why the 15th day of *Tishrei* is a complete Holiday. But on the days following (from the 16th of *Tishrei* until the 21st day of *Tishrei*), even though that the Surrounding Mercies continue and enter it is not considered a complete *Yom Tov* (Holiday) but only *Chol Hamo'ed*.

THE SECRET OF THE SUKKAH

The *Sukkah* represents the Surrounding Light of the *Nukva* from the aspect of the Mercies of *Ima*. And we (the Israelites that sit inside it and are called Sons of Kings—Sons of Kingdom, where *Malchut*-Kingdom is *Rachel-Nukva* of *Zeir Anpin*) who build the *Sukkah* sit in the shade of this Surrounding Light that is being disbursed in Her (the *Nukva*), circling and surrounding Her as a *Sukkah*, so we can draw from this Surrounding Light; as the sages say that the *Sukkah* is corresponds to the clouds of honor that were in the desert—a cloud corresponds to Mercy as in the verse "*And the cloud of the Lord was upon them by day*," where day is a code name for Mercy. And that is why the clouds of honor were connected to Aaron, (when he died they disappeared) man of Mercy. And there are seven clouds corresponding to the seven Surroundings of Mercy that enter the Seven Lower *Sefirot* of *Nukva*, from *Chesed* to *Malchut*, and also correspond to the seven days of *Sukkot*.

And the *Sukkah* is the aspect of Supernal *Ima* that covers and protects Her children (*Zeir Anpin* and *Nukva*) in three different kinds of Surrounding Light: One kind to *Zeir Anpin* Itself; one kind to Nukva Itself; and one kind to both of them. And this is why the word "*basukkot*" (in the *sukkot*) appears three times in the Torah (Leviticus 23;42-43) twice without the letter *Vav* (correspond to the Surrounding of *Zeir Anpin* by Itself and the Surrounding of *Nukva* by Itself) and the third time with the letter *Vav* (correspond to the Surrounding of both of them.)

The word *Sukkah* without *Vav* has the same numerical value to the Name אלהים (=86), which is a code name to *Zeir Anpin* or *Nukva* when They are by Themselves. And the word *Sukkah* with *Vav* has the same numerical value of the Names יהוה (*Zeir Anpin*) and אדני (*Nukva*) as They are together surrounded by Supernal *Ima*.

The walls of the *Sukkah* represent *Netzach*, *Hod* and *Yesod* of *Ima* from the Surrounding Light but the *sechach* (the roof of the *Sukkah*) is the aspect of the lower half of *Tiferet* of *Ima* (from Her Chest and below), which is like a roof over Her *Netzach*, *Hod* and *Yesod*. And we know that this aspect of *Tiferet* is the *Keter* (crown) of *Zeir Anpin* that stands on top of everything that is seated below It. And therefore the roof of the *Sukkah* cannot be higher than twenty *amah* (around 13 feet), as *Zeir Anpin* and *Nukva* Who stand below, each have Ten *Sefirot* (together twenty *amah*) including the roof, which is the *Keter* of *Zeir Anpin*.

It is known that the *Keter* includes all other nine *Sefirot* below Him. In the same manner *Tiferet* of *Ima*, where all the Illuminations come from, includes *Keter* of *Zeir Anpin*. Also it is known that one hundred Lights are drawn from *Ima* to *Zeir Anpin* (the secret of one hundred blessings that a person recites every day), which is drawn from the Name יוד הי וא הי (=63, from *Ima*) and Its *miluy* (=37. All together =100). And because these one hundred Lights are going through *Keter* of *Zeir Anpin* they leave an impression there and this is why the roof of the *Sukkah* is called *sechach*, as it equals 100.

THE SECRET OF THE LULAV

It was explained that by the shaking of the *Lulav* (palm frond) seven aspects of Mercies from the Inner Light of *Zeir Anpin* enter the Seven Lower *Sefirot* of *Rachel-Nukva*; one Mercy each day of the seven days of *Sukkot*. And even though each day we shake the *Lulav* fully (to six edges four times) to draw these Mercies into Her only one Mercy will enter. On the first day, the first Mercy will enter Her *Chesed*, on the second day, the second Mercy will enter Her *Gevurah* and so on until the seventh day (that is called *Hosha'ana Rabbah*), when the general aspect of the Mercies enter her *Malchut*. And the reason for the shaking of the *Lulav* is to draw the Mercies from *Da'at* of *Zeir Anpin* that are blocked by *Yesod* of *Ima*, and by the shaking, Their Illumination goes down with the Mercies that spread in the Seven Lower *Sefirot* of *Zeir Anpin* (the secret of the four species as will be explained later) and from there to *Nukva*. Then we circle the *bimah* (the podium we use to read the Torah on) once each day with the *Lulav* and its species to draw the Mercies (that are mentioned above) but now from the Surrounding Light aspect to the *Nukva* that is called *bimah*. We don't shake the *Lulav* while we circle the *bimah* because we want the Surrounding Light to be revealed. In the same way that the Mercies from the Inner Light aspects descend, there are also in the Surrounding Light seven aspects, and each day one Illumination descends and enters *Zeir Anpin* and then *Nukva*. And because in regular manner the Inner Light enters first, we shake the *Lulav* first and only then do we circle the *bimah*. We shake the *Lulav* and its species in four stages to six edges, three times each, which all together equals 72 shakings like the numerical value of the word *Chesed* (Mercy חסד) that spreads each day.

The four species correspond to the four letters of the Name יהוה, which is in *Zeir Anpin* as follows: The letter *Yud* י is *Chesed*, *Gevurah* and *Tiferet* of *Zeir Anpin* and corresponds to the three *hadasim* (myrtle brunches); The letter *Hei* ה is *Netzach* and *Hod* of *Zeir Anpin* and corresponds to the two *aravot* (willow branches); The letter *Vav* ו is *Yesod* of *Zeir Anpin* and corresponds to the *Lulav*; and the last letter *Hei* ה is *Malchut* of *Zeir Anpin* (the *Tiara* of the *Yesod* of *Zeir Anpin*—the Head of the Righteous, but not Its *Nukva*) and corresponds to the *Etrog* (citron).

The *Lulav* is the *Yesod* and therefore its shape is long and strait like the spinal cord (from *Da'at*—the brain to the *Yesod*—male reproductive organ). And that is why the connection point between the *Lulav* (*Yesod*) and the *Etrog* (the Tiara of the *Yesod*) will be at the end-bottom of the *Lulav*. Also, as it corresponds to the *Yesod*, the *Lulav* should be higher than the other species because it needs to reach the Brain and from there obtain the seed drop.

The three *hadasim* correspond to the three patriarchs and to *Chesed*, *Gevurah* and *Tiferet*, where each is inclusive of the others (three inclusive of three), which is why each myrtle has to have three leaves coming from the same steam.

The two *aravot* are *Netzach* and *Hod* (as mentioned).

And here we explained that the four species correspond to the seven aspects of Mercies that spread in the Seven Lower *Sefirot* of *Zeir Anpin*, (*Chesed*, *Gevurah*, *Tiferet*, *Netzach*, *Hod*, *Yesod* and the Tiara of *Yesod*), but they are not the Seven *Sefirot* themselves.

So when we shake the *Lulav* and its species forward (*holacha*—away from us), we elevate them to their root, which is in *Da'at* of *Zeir Anpin*, and they receive great Illumination. Then we shake the *Lulav* backward (*hava'a*—towards our chest) and we meditate to draw this Illumination to the *Nukva* to build in Her the aspect of the Seven Inner Mercies during the seven days of *Sukkot* (because the Head of the *Nukva* is in the Chest of *Zeir Anpin*, we need to bring the bottom end of the *Lulav* to touch the chest). And without the shaking They could not receive this Illumination because it is blocked, as mentioned above, and by the shaking it is awakened and Illuminates.

Da'at is encompassed Six Edges and (other) Six Edges are hold on to It. The Six Edges of *Da'at* are the six aspects of Mercies that are the root and source for the six Mercies that spread in *Tiferet* with the (other) Six Edges, which they are five Mercies from *Chesed* to *Hod* and another aspect of Mercy (the general aspect) in *Yesod*. And these lower Mercies are the *Lulav* and its species. And this is why we shake them towards the six directions (south, north, and east, up, down and west) that represent the Six Upper Edged of *Da'at* in order to draw Illuminations – from the Upper Six to the lower Six.

The order of the direction of the shaking of the *Lulav* is like the order of the Six Supernal Edges of *Da'at*. We begin toward the south-*Chesed*, then toward the north-*Gevurah*, then toward the east-*Tiferet*, and while we point east we shake upwards-*Netzach* and then downwards-*Hod*. Then we shake toward the west-*Yesod* as the general aspect of the Mercies. And the reason we shake three times in each direction is they correspond to the three *Mochin* that exist in the Head of *Zeir Anpin* (*Chochmah*, *Binah* and *Da'at*). There are eighteen shakings, and this is why *Yesod* is the last as It receives from the eighteen aspects of Mochin that exist in the Six Supernal Edges of *Da'at*, and *Yesod* is called *Chai Ha'olamim* (the Life of the Worlds - *chai* has the numerical value of 18).

The three *Mochin* are represented by the three letters יהו - Yud י in *Chochmah*, Hei ה in *Binah* and Vav ו in *Da'at*. And because each Edge of the Six Edges of *Da'at* is inclusive of the three *Mochin* it will also be called in the Name יהו but still with a different order as follows:

יהו with the *miluy* יוד הי ויו in the south; היו with the *miluy* ואו יוד הי in the north; ויה with the *miluy* ואו יוד הא in the east; יוה with the *miluy* יוד ויו הי upwards; היו with the *miluy* הי יוד ואו downwards and והי with the *miluy* ואו הא יוד in the west.

And meditate to draw Illumination from these eighteen letters of *Da'at*, which are the sequences of the Name יהו that goes to the *Nukva*, where She now stands in the Chest of *Zeir Anpin* (and to where we bring back the *Lulav*.) And also meditate to connect the letter Hei ה, which is the *Nukva*, to the three letters יהו and to complete the Name יהוה.

HOSHA'ANA RABBAH

On *Yom Kippur*, *Rachel* is taking Five *Gevurot* (Judgments) from *Ima* through the five prayers and not by *Zeir Anpin*. And in order that the external negative forces will not have any hold on these Judgments, because They are in the *Yesod* of the *Nukva*, She is sealed in her *Yesod* to protect these Judgments. And this sealing is the main and the essential וזותם—Sealing that is done by the three Names (הי יוד הי אלף—הא יוד הא אלף—הה יוד הה אלף, Who have the numerical value of the word Sealing—וזותם =454+1), Which are in *Netzach*, *Hod* and *Yesod* of *Ima*, and the external negative forces cannot hold onto *Ima* and they also cannot touch the Judgments.

And on the night of *Hosha'ana Rabbah* (the seventh day of *Sukkot*) another Sealing is done: The External Sealing in the secret of Sealing inside a Sealing, and it is given in Her *Malchut*, which is the Tiara of Her *Yesod*. Indeed this Sealing is lesser than the first Sealing and it is done by the *miluy* of the three Names (י וד כלף—א וד ה כלף—ה וד ה כלף, Which with the other three Names has the numerical value of the word "secondary"—משׁנה =395) as it is secondary to the main Sealing, because the main Sealing is in the *Yesod*. But, as it is also made from *Ima* it has the power to reject the external negative forces and that is why it will also be called also Sealing—וזותם. And as in the time of the Sealing of the *Yesod* the world was sentenced and people were judged and sealed to Life or death, so it is the same in the time of the second Sealing of *Malchut* where the world is sentenced and people are judged in the second time.

The difference is that in the time of the first and main Sealing it was the exact time of the Judgment, the decree and the verdict. But now (on *Hosha'ana Rabbah*) it is the external Sealing, meaning the notes with the verdict that was sealed on *Yom Kippur* are now given to the messengers to reprove with calamity on people. So the main aspect of the Judgment is done and finalized at midnight of *Hoasha'ana Rabbah* and only then the Sealing is finally sealed in her *Malchut*. And if someone (God forbid) is sentenced to death it can be shown through the shade of the moon light (the head of this person will be missing). And this is when we go and check our shadow in the moon light after midnight.

But still, even though the notes are given to the messengers at midnight, they cannot activate the verdict until after *Simchat Torah* and there is still time to change the verdict during the night of *Hosha'ana Rabbah*. This is why we study during this night, especially reading the Book of Deuteronomy, which is called the Secondary Torah, and to meditate that with this reading we create the secondary Sealing in Her *Malchut*, and by doing so can return the notes with the negative verdict. And that is why the day of *Hosha'ana Rabbah* is considered to be a day with some judgment even though the judgment ended during the night already. As we said previously, the messengers cannot activate the verdict until after *Simchat Torah*. And so a person should pay very close attention to his actions and thoughts during the prayers of *Hosha'ana Rabbah* because there is still an option to correct and change the verdict.

You should know that because the Sealing is done in the middle of the night and so the Judgment is activated, that is why looking at a shadow is done after midnight and specifically by the moon light and not by a candle. The reason is that the moon is the secret of the *Nukva* of *Zeir Anpin*, which is called *Rachel*, and the Sealing of Her *Malchut* is done in the middle of the night. Then it is the time of Her shining, and She goes to Illuminate the world through the Sealing that was given in Her, as it is known that the Judgments are like the judges that judge the world. And because the Judgment is given into Her hands, through Her government She notifies and shows the decrees in the world. And that is why the decree cannot be noticeable except by looking at it in the shadow with the moon light.

SHEMINI ATZERET AND SIMCHAT TORAH

As it has been explained already that in all days from *Rosh Hashanah* until now (*Shemini Atzeret*), all the Unifications are between *Yisrael* or *Yaakov* and *Leah*, but *Rachel* has been corrected and rebuilt step by step, slowly-slowly during these days (for the sin of Adam that occured in *Rosh Hashanah*). And now (on *Shemini Atzeret*) Her Body is corrected and built, and She was sawed and returned to the Face to Face form, and She received all the Mercy aspects of *Ima* and *Zeir Anpin* (for the correction of Her Body and for Unification reasons) and She had the two Sealings as mentioned. Also on *Hosha'ana Rabbah*, by the act of the beaten willows (whose custom was founded by the Prophets) we build for the *Nukva* a vessel with *Mayin Nukvin* (female water—awakened from Below), which are the Five Judgments of *Ima* and all of Her aspects are completed. And this is why on this day (*Shemini Atzeret*) different and Five new Judgments are given to *Rachel* in the secret of the Unification from *Zeir Anpin* (and not from *Ima*) and this is why these Five Judgments are sweetened more because They are from *Zeir Anpin* (in the secret of the Unification.) And this day is called *Simchat Torah* (the Happiness of the Torah) as *Zeir Anpin* is called Torah, and is happy to unify with His real and main mate, Who is *Rachel*, as it is known.

And these Five Judgments (the sweetened) are actually the *Mayin Nukvin* of *Nukva*, as the Five Judgments that She received on *Hosha'ana Rabbah* were only the Vessel for the *Mayin Nukvin* and that is why it (the Vessel) was completed by *Ima*. But the Judgments that are the actual *Mayin Nukvin* are from the actual Unification with *Zeir Anpin*, and then He gives Her (from the secret of the Unification) the drop of *Mayin Duchrin* (male water—awakened from Above). And in the *Musaf* prayer (and not before) of *Shemini Atzeret* it is the time of the Unification between *Zeir Anpin* and *Rachel*, as They are equals. And in this Unification *Zeir Anpin* gives Her Five Judgments (in the secret of the drop of the Unification, as there are male and female Judgments) and this is why we mention the rain (we change from summer connection to winter connection) in *Musaf* and say "Who causes wind to blow and rain to fall" as the Judgments are called rain (and then in *Pesach* He gives Her Mercies.)

THE ORDER OF THE PRAYERS AND THE ELEVATION OF THE WORLD ON HOLIDAYS

In *Minchah* of the Eve of the Holiday, meditate that *Malchut* elevates to its place before the accusation (before It fell from *Atzilut* to *Beriah*).

In every prayer of a Holiday – as we explained about the seven blessings in *Shabbat* prayers, you should meditate on the seven Names that come out from the seven letters of the Name: יהו אהי"ה. However, as we say, the Holidays are only *Mikra'ei Kodesh* (from *Ima*) and not *Kodesh* (from *Abba*), therefore, we meditate on the Names of אלהי"ם and אהי"ה, which are both in Supernal *Ima*, as follows:

In *Magen Avraham*, meditate on the Name: הי יוד הי אלף, (an *Alef* in the shape of *Yud-Vav-Yud*).

In *Mechayeh Hametim*, meditate on the Name: הי יוד הי אלף, (an *Alef* in the shape of *Yud-Vav-Dalet*).

In *Ha'El Hakadosh*, meditate on the Name: הא יוד הא אלף.

In *Mekadesh Israel*, meditate on the Name: הה יוד הה אלף.

In the *Avodah*, meditate on the Name: מם יוד הי למד אלף.

In the *Hoda'ah*, meditate on the Name: מם יוד הה למד אלף.

And in *Sim Shalom*, meditate on the Name: מם יוד הא למד אלף.

In the Arvit of the Holiday, meditate that *Netzach*, *Hod* and *Yesod* of *Ima* that are in *Netzach*, *Hod* and *Yesod* of *Zeir Anpin* are illuminating in *Nukva*.

In *Shacharit* of a Holiday, during the silent *Amidah*, you should meditate that *Chochmah*, *Binah*, and *Da'at* of *Zeir Anpin* elevate in *Netzach*, *Hod*, and *Yesod* of *Ima*, and *Keter*, *Chochmah*, *Binah* and *Da'at* of *Nukva* elevate to *Da'at* of *Chesed*, *Gevurah*, *Tiferet* of *Zeir Anpin*. **And in the repetition,** meditate that *Chochmah*, *Binah* and *Da'at* of *Zeir Anpin* elevate to *Chesed*, *Gevurah* and *Tiferet* of *Ima*; and *Keter*, *Chochmah*, *Binah* and *Da'at* of *Nukva* elevate to *Da'at* of *Chochmah*, *Binah* and *Da'at* of *Zeir Anpin*.

Then you should say the complete *Halel*, to receive the additional *Mochin* and to sweeten the Illumination of *Ima*.

Afterwards, when we take the Torah out, we say the 13 Attributes of Mercy, and we ask to go out of slavery to freedom, to have favor in the eyes of man and to have wealth. We also ask for vengeance against our internal enemies.

Five people go up to the Torah on the Holiday; as *Netzach*, *Hod* and *Yesod* of *Abba* are enclosed by *Netzach*, *Hod*, and *Yesod* of *Ima*, and the only revealed aspect is the two lower parts of *Netzach* of *Ima*, and the two lower parts of *Hod* of *Ima* (since the two upper parts of *Netzach* and *Hod* of *Ima* stay above in the head of *Zeir Anpin*, as *Mochin*, and *Yesod* of *Ima* is short and ends in the chest of *Zeir Anpin* and is not revealed outwards.) And *Yesod* of *Abba*, (which is in *Yesod* of *Ima*) is long and one part of It is revealed outside of *Yesod* of *Ima*. So together we have five parts that are revealed on the Holiday: Two lower parts of *Netzach*, and the two lower parts of *Hod*, of *Ima*, and one revealed part of the *Yesod* of *Abba*, and corresponding to them we have five people that are called to go up to the Torah on the Holiday. And since *Zeir Anpin* is unable to receive the illumination of *Yesod* of *Abba*, like in *Shabbat*, but rather He is able to receive the Tiara of *Yesod* of *Abba* and four parts of *Netzach* and *Hod* of *Ima*, therefore there are only five people who go up to the Torah, as the fifth one corresponds to the Tiara of *Yesod* of *Abba* and the other four correspond to the four parts of *Netzach* and *Hod* of *Ima*.

In *Musaf* of the Holiday you should meditate that *Chochmah*, *Binah* and *Da'at* of *Zeir Anpin* elevate into *Chochmah*, *Binah*, *Da'at* of *Ima*, and *Keter*, *Chochmah*, *Binah* and *Da'at* of *Nukva* elevate into *Netzach*, *Hod* and *Yesod* of *Ima*. **And in the Repetition,** since *Zeir Anpin* has no more elevation to *Keter* like on *Shabbat*, meditate that in "*Kadosh, Kadosh, Kadosh*," *Nukva* elevates to the three middle *Sefirot* and in "*Ayeh*" She elevates to the top three *Sefirot* of *Ima* (but She never rises to *Keter* of *Ima*.)

In *Mincha* of the Holiday you should meditate that *Zeir Anpin* elevates into the right side of *Keter* of *Ima* and *Nukva* elevates to the left side of *Keter* of *Ima*.

ERUV TAVSHILIN (MEALS MIX)

Eruv Tavshilin is a ceremony in which one makes minimum preparation for *Shabbat* on the night prior to the holiday. Although cooking food on a holiday for a holiday meal is permitted, cooking or preparing a meal on a holiday for *Shabbat* is not. When a holiday falls on Friday, the *Eruv Tavshilin* ceremony is performed to enable us to cook food for *Shabbat* during the holiday.

This is achieved by setting aside some bread (minimum of two ounces) and some cooked food—eggs, meat or fish (minimum of two ounces) for the *Shabbat* meal on Friday. The bread and the cooked food is lifted in the right hand and the blessing "*Al Mitzvat Eruv*" is recited.

We put the two cooked items together and say the following blessing:

baruch בָּרוּךְ Ata אַתָּה יְהֹוָה Adonai אֱלֹהֵינוּ Elohenu

melech מֶלֶךְ ha'olam הָעוֹלָם asher אֲשֶׁר kideshanu קִדְּשָׁנוּ

bemitzvotav בְּמִצְוֹתָיו vetzivanu וְצִוָּנוּ al עַל mitzvat מִצְוַת eruv עֵרוּב:

And then say:

beden בְּדֵין eruva עֵרוּבָא yehe יְהֵא share שָׁרֵא lana לָנָא

la'afuyei לְאֲפוּיֵי ulvishulei וּלְבַשּׁוּלֵי ulatmunei וּלְאַטְמוּנֵי

ultakunei וּלְתַקּוּנֵי (ulmishchat וּלְמִשְׁוַט) uladlukei וּלְאַדְלוּקֵי

sheraga שְׁרָגָא ulme'evad וּלְמֶעְבַּד kol כָּל tzarchana צָרְכָנָא

miyom מִיּוֹם tov טוֹב leShabbat לְשַׁבַּת lana לָנָא

ulchol וּלְכָל benei בְּנֵי ha'ir הָעִיר hazot הָזֹאת:

After saying it in Aramaic a person should say it in a language that he/she understands (below we have it in Hebrew and in English):

בְּעֵירוּב זֶה יִהְיֶה מוּתָּר לָנוּ לֶאֱפוֹת וּלְבַשֵּׁל וּלְהַדְלִיק הַנֵּר
וְלַעֲשׂוֹת כָּל צְרָכֵינוּ מִיּוֹ"ט לְשַׁבָּת לָנוּ וּלְכָל בְּנֵי הָעִיר הַזֹּאת:

"Through this [*eruv*] it shall be permissible for us to bake, cook, put away a dish [to preserve its heat], kindle a light, prepare, and do on the Holiday all that is necessary for *Shabbat*—for us and for all the people who dwell in this city."

The *Eruv* will be eaten in the Third Meal of *Shabbat* (we should make sure it is put somewhere safe during *the Holiday* and *Shabbat* - if it disappears it could be a problem).

ERUV TAVSHILIN (MEALS MIX)

Blessed are You, Lord, our God, King of the world,
Who has sanctified us with His commandments and obliged us with concerning the Precept of Eruv.
"Through this [eruv] it shall be permissible for us to bake, cook, put away a dish [to preserve its heat],
kindle a light, prepare, and do on the Holiday all that is necessary for Shabbat—
for us and for all the people who dwell in this city"

CANDLE LIGHTING

We light the candles to draw the spiritual Light into our personal lives. Every physical action in our world initiates a corresponding reaction in the Upper Worlds. By lighting the physical candles of the Holiday with the consciousness and intent to connect to the energy of the Holiday in the Upper Worlds, we arouse and draw spiritual Light into our physical world.

When a woman lights the candles, she is also helping to correct the sin of Eve, which was a Desire to Receive for the Self Alone. The action of lighting the candles becomes an act of sharing. Because the husband and children are closest to the woman, they receive the benefit of this action.

LeSHEM YICHUD

לְשֵׁם leshem   יִחוּד yichud   קוּדְשָׁא kudesha   בְּרִיךְ berich   הוּא hu

וּשְׁכִינְתֵּיהּ ushchintei   (יאהדונהי) bid'chilu בִּדְחִילוּ   ur'chimu וּרְחִימוּ

(יאהויהה), ur'chimu וּרְחִימוּ   ud'chilu וּדְחִילוּ   (איההויהה),

לְיַחֲדָא leyachda   שֵׁם shem   יוֹ"ד yud   קֵי kei   בּוא"ו bevav   קֵי kei

בְּיִחוּדָא beyichuda   שְׁלִים shelim   (יהוה)   בְּשֵׁם beshem   כָּל kol   ילי

יִשְׂרָאֵל, Yisrael   הֲרֵינִי hareni   בָּאָה va'a   לְקַיֵם lekayem

מִצְוַת mitzvat   עֲשֵׂה aseh   שֶׁל shel   הַצְּדָקָה hatzedakah   ע"ה ריבוע אלהים

וְהֲרֵינִי vahareni   נוֹתֶנֶת notenet   שְׁתֵּי shetei   פְּרוּטוֹת perutot

לִצְדָקָה litzdakah ריבוע אלהים ע"ה   וְעוֹד ve'od   הֲרֵינִי hareni   נוֹתֶנֶת notenet

פְּרוּטָה peruta   אַחַת achat   לִצְדָקָה litzdakah ע"ה ריבוע אלהים   לְתַקֵּן letaken

אֶת et   שֹׁרֶשׁ shoresh   מִצְוָה mitzva   זוֹ zo   וְכָל vechol ילי   תַּרְיָ"ג taryag

מִצְוֹת mitzvot   הַכְּלוּלוֹת hakelulot   בָּה ba   בְּמָקוֹם bemakom   עֶלְיוֹן elyon.

It is good for a woman to give three coins for charity before lighting the candles and then continue,

וְהֲרֵינִי vahareni   בָּאָה va'a   לְקַיֵם lekayem   מִצְוַת mitzvat   עֲשֵׂה ase

דְרַבָּנָן derabanan   לְהַדְלִיק lehadlik   נֵרוֹת nerot   לִכְבוֹד lichvod

---

CANDLE LIGHTING - LeSHEM YICHUD

For the sake of the unification between The Holy Blessed One and His Shechinah,
with fear and love and with love and fear, in order to unify the Name Yud-Kei and Vav-Kei in perfect unity, and in the name of all Israel, I am hereby prepared to fulfill the obligatory precept of charity, and hereby I'm giving two coins for charity and another one for charity to correct the root of the precept of charity with all the 613 other precepts which are included in it, in the supernal place,

(It is good for a woman to give three coins for charity before lighting the candles and then continue)

And I hereby prepare to fulfill the obligatory precept from the sages of lighting candles for the honor of Yom Tov

יוֹם yom ע"ה נגד, ז, זז, מזבוז, אל יהיה tov טוֹב והו letaken לְתַקֵּן shoresh שֹׁרֶשׁ

מִצְוָה mitzva זוֹ zo בְּמָקוֹם bemakom עֶלְיוֹן elyon וִיהִי vihi נֹעַם no'am

אֲדֹנָי Adonai ללה אֱלֹהֵינוּ Elohenu ילה עָלֵינוּ alenu וּמַעֲשֵׂה uma'ase יָדֵינוּ yadenu

כּוֹנְנָה konena עָלֵינוּ alenu וּמַעֲשֵׂה uma'ase יָדֵינוּ yadenu כּוֹנְנֵהוּ konenehu:

Then the woman lights the candles, covers her eyes with her hands and recites the following blessing:

בָּרוּךְ baruch אַתָּה Ata יְהֹוָאדֹנָיאהדונהי Adonai אֱלֹהֵינוּ Elohenu ילה

מֶלֶךְ melech הָעוֹלָם ha'olam אֲשֶׁר asher קִדְּשָׁנוּ kideshanu

בְּמִצְוֹתָיו bemitzvotav וְצִוָּנוּ vetzivanu לְהַדְלִיק lehadlik

נֵר ner יהוה אהיה יהוה אלהים יהוה יהוה אדני shel שֶׁל (On *Shabbat* add: שַׁבָּת shabbat וְשֶׁל veshel)

יוֹם yom ע"ה נגד, ז, זז, מזבוז, אל יהוה tov טוֹב והו:

בָּרוּךְ baruch אַתָּה Ata יְהֹוָאדֹנָיאהדונהי Adonai אֱלֹהֵינוּ Elohenu ילה

מֶלֶךְ melech הָעוֹלָם ha'olam שֶׁהֶחֱיָנוּ shehecheyanu

וְקִיְּמָנוּ vekiyemanu וְהִגִּיעָנוּ vehigi'anu לַזְּמַן lazman הַזֶּה hazeh והו:

YEHI RATZON

The power of righteous children and a righteous husband is given to us through this blessing. A woman's greatest opportunity for sharing is with her family, which is closest to her in her daily life. The definition of sharing with one's child or spouse takes on a whole new meaning when understood from a Kabbalistic point of view. To help us understand what sharing genuinely means, we must first comprehend what is *not* deemed sharing. Kabbalist Rav Berg explains that when parents raise their kids, most acts of sharing are considered part of one's duty as a loving parent. In other words, there are no "merit points" in the Upper Worlds when we share with our loved ones. Real sharing occurs only when it's difficult for us to give, when we go outside of ourselves and leave our comfort zones. We ordinarily play with or give to our children when doing so pleases us. We derive as much pleasure as they do. If we can learn to share, and give our time and attention to them when it is difficult for us, we will reap far greater benefits. Lighting the candles is considered to be a genuine act of sharing toward our family.

---

to correct the root of the precept in the Supernal Place. "May the pleasantness of the Lord, our God, be upon us and may He establish the work of our hands for us and may the work of our hands establish Him." (Psalms 90:17)

Blessed are You, Lord, our God, King of the world,
Who has sanctified us with His commandments and obliged us with lighting the candles of Yom Tov.

Blessed are You, Lord, our God, King of the world,
Who has kept us alive, sustained us, and brought us to this time.

יְהִי yehi רָצוֹן ratzon מהע ע"ה, ע"ב בריבוע קס"א ע"ה, אל שדי ע"ה

מִלְפָנֶיךָ milfanecha ס"ג מ"ה ב"ן יְהֹוָהאֲדֹנָי Adonai אֱלֹהַי Elohai

אֲבוֹתַי avotai ; דמב דע"ב, מילוי דע"ב, רמ"ב ; ילה לכב ; מילוי דע"ב, דמב, ילה וֵאלֹהֵי velohei

שֶׁתָחוֹס shetachus וּתְרַחֵם utrachem ג"פ רי"ו ; וז"פ אל, רי"ו ול"ב נתיבות החוכמה,

וְחַסְדְךָ chasdecha וְתַגְדִיל vetagdil, עָלַי alai רמ"ח (אברים), עסמ"ב וט"ז אותיות פשוטות

עִמָדִי imadi לָתֵת latet לִי li זֶרַע zera אֲנָשִׁים anashim עוֹשֵׂי osei

רְצוֹנֶךָ retzonecha, וְעוֹסְקִים ve'oskim בְּתוֹרָתְךָ betoratcha לִשְׁמָה lishma.

וְיִהְיוּ veyih'yu אל (יא"י מילוי דס"ג) מְאִירִים me'irim בְּתוֹרָה batorah

בִּזְכוּת bizchut נֵרוֹת nerot יוֹם yom ע"ה נגד, מזבוח, זן, אל יהוה tov טוֹב והו

הַלָלוּ halalu, כְּמוֹ kemo שֶׁנֶאֱמַר shene'emar כִּי ki נֵר ner מִצְוָה mitzvah

וְתוֹרָה vetorah אוֹר or רו, א"ס וְגַם vegam תָחוֹס tachos וּתְרַחֵם utrachem

אותיות פשוטות ט"ז עסמ"ב, (אברים) רמ"ח נתיבות החוכמה ל"ב רי"ו, אל, וז"פ ; ג"פ רי"ו

עַל al בַּעֲלִי ba'ali

(A woman should mention her husband's name and his father's name here)

וְתִתֵּן vetiten ב"פ כהת לוֹ lo אֹרֶךְ orech יָמִים yamim גלך

וּשְׁנוֹת ushnot וְחַיִּים chayim אהיה אהיה יהוה, בינה ע"ה

עִם im בְּרָכָה beracha וְהַצְלָוֹזָה vehatzlacha, וּתְסַיְעֵהוּ ut'saye'ehu

לַעֲשׂוֹת la'asot רְצוֹנְךָ retzoncha בִּשְׁלֵמוּת bishlemut. כֵּן ken יְהִי yehi

רָצוֹן ratzon אָמֵן amen ע"ה אל שדי ע"ה, וקס"א בריבוע ע"ב מהע ע"ה, יאהדונהי

(מ"ב אותיות בפסוק)

יִהְיוּ yih'yu אל (יא"י מילוי דס"ג) לְרָצוֹן leratzon מהע ע"ה, ע"ב בריבוע וקס"א ע"ה, אל שדי ע"ה

אִמְרֵי imrei פִי fi ר"ת אֶלֶף = אלף למד דלת יוד עין דלת ר"ת א"ה וְהֶגְיוֹן vehegyon לִבִּי libi

לְפָנֶיךָ lefanecha ס"ג מ"ה ב"ן יְהֹוָהאֲדֹנָי Adonai צוּרִי tzuri וְגֹאֲלִי vego'ali

---

YEHI RATZON

May it be pleasing before You, Lord, my God, and God of my forefathers, that You will take pity and be merciful to me, and may You increase Your compassion to me by granting me, for offspring, ones who do Your bidding and who occupy themselves in Your Torah for Its own sake. May they be resplendent in the Torah by virtue of these candles, as it was said: "Because the commandment is a candle and the Torah is Light." (Proverbs 6:23) May You also take pity and be merciful to my husband (A woman should mention her husband's name and his father's name here) *and may You grant him lengthy days and years of life, filled with blessings and success, and may You help him in doing Your bidding perfectly. May it so be Your desire, Amen. "May the words of my mouth and the thoughts of my heart be pleasing before You, Lord, my Rock and my Redeemer." (Psalms 19:15)*

MINCHAH OF EREV SUKKOT AND SIMCHAT TORAH

The purpose of the *Minchah* prayer is not simply to make a connection to the Light of the Creator, it is to quiet the energy of judgment in the world. The best time to do this is when the energy of judgment appears in its greatest number and intensity. Kabbalist Rav Isaac Luria (the Ari), would only recite *Minchah* when the sun was setting. He understood that the numerical value of the word *Minchah* (103) is also the number of sub-worlds (within the five major worlds), controlled by the Left Column energy of judgment.

The sin of the golden calf occurred during the time of *Minchah*, consequently becoming the seed that helped infuse the world with judgment in the late afternoon. Isaac the patriarch is our channel to overcome judgment. Isaac came to this world to create a path that would lead us to sweetening the judgment in our lives. We can choose to either continue creating difficult paths for ourselves or we can follow the path of sweetening judgment paved by Isaac.

LeSHEM YICHUD

hu הוּא berich בְּרִיךְ kudesha קוּדְשָׁא yichud יְוזוּד leshem לְשֵׁם

ur'chimu וּרְוזִימוּ bid'chilu בִּדְוזִילוּ (יאהדונהי) ush'chintei וּשְׁכִינְתֵּיהּ

leyachda לְיַוזְדָא (איההיוהה) ud'chilu וּדְוזִילוּ ur'chimu וּרְוזִימוּ (יאההויהה)

beyichuda בְּיִוזוּדָא kei קֵי bevav בְּוא"ו kei קֵי yud יו"ד shem שֵׁם

,Yisrael יִשְׂרָאֵל ילי kol כָּל beshem בְּשֵׁם (יהוה) shelim שְׁלִים

tefilat תְּפִלַּת lehitpalel לְהִתְפַּלֵל ba'im בָּאִים anachnu אֲנַוזְנוּ hine הִנֵּה

avinu אָבִינוּ ד"פ ב"ן Yitzchak יִצְוזָק shetiken שֶׁתִּקֵן ע"ה ב"פ ב"ן mincha מִנְוזָה

hamitzvot הַמִּצְוות ילי kol כָּל im עִם hashalom הַשָּׁלוֹם alav עָלָיו

shorsha שׁוֹרְשָׁהּ et אֶת letaken לְתַקֵן ba בָּהּ hakelulot הַכְּלוּלוֹת

ru'ach רוּוַז nachat נַוזַת la'asot לַעֲשׂוֹת elyon עֶלְיוֹן bemakom בִּמְקוֹם

ל"יוֹצְרֵנוּ retzon רְצוֹן vela'asot וְלַעֲשׂוֹת leyotzrenu לְיוֹצְרֵנוּ ע"ה,

ללה Adonai אֲדֹנָי no'am נֹעַם vihi וִיהִי •bor'enu בּוֹרְאֵינוּ אל שדי ע"ה

yadenu יָדֵינוּ uma'ase וּמַעֲשֵׂה alenu עָלֵינוּ ילה Elohenu אֱלֹהֵינוּ

‡konenehu כּוֹנְנֵהוּ yadenu יָדֵינוּ uma'ase וּמַעֲשֵׂה alenu עָלֵינוּ konena כּוֹנְנָה

MINCHAH OF EREV SUKKOT AND SIMCHAT TORAH
LESHEM YICHUD

For the sake of the unification of the Holy Blessed One and His Shechinah, with fear and love and with love and fear, in order to unify the Name Yud-Kei and Vav-Kei in perfect unity, and in the name of Israel, we have hereby come to recite the prayer of Minchah, established by Isaac, our forefather, may peace be upon him, With all its commandments, to correct its root in the supernal place, to bring satisfaction to our Maker, and to fulfill the wish of our Creator. "And may the pleasantness of the Lord, our God, be upon us and may He establish the work of our hands for us and may the work of our hands establish Him." (Psalms 90:17)

THE SACRIFICES – KORBANOT - THE TAMID – (DAILY) OFFERING

Moshe מֹשֶׁה el אֶל־ Adonai יְהֹוָה(אדני/אהדונהי) ra'ah ראה vaydaber וַיְדַבֵּר

benei בְּנֵי et אֶת־ tzav צַו lemor לֵאמֹר פוי, אל אדני מהטע, ע"ב בריבוע וקס"א, אל שדי

Yisrael יִשְׂרָאֵל alehem אֲלֵהֶם ve'amarta וְאָמַרְתָּ et אֶת־ korbani קָרְבָּנִי

lachmi לַחְמִי le'ishai לְאִשַּׁי re'ach רֵיחַ nichochi נִיחֹחִי tishmeru תִּשְׁמְרוּ

lahem לָהֶם ve'amarta וְאָמַרְתָּ bemo'ado בְּמוֹעֲדוֹ: li לִי lehakriv לְהַקְרִיב

ze זֶה ha'ishe הָאִשֶּׁה asher אֲשֶׁר takrivu תַּקְרִיבוּ ladonai לַיהֹוָה(אדני/אהדונהי)

kevasim כְּבָשִׂים benei בְּנֵי־ shana שָׁנָה temimim תְּמִימִם shenayim שְׁנַיִם

layom לַיּוֹם ola עֹלָה ע"ה גגד, מזבוי, ז, אל יהוה tamid תָּמִיד ע"ה קס"א קנ"א קמ"ג:

hakeves הַכֶּבֶשׂ echad אֶחָד אהבה, דאגה ta'ase תַּעֲשֶׂה vaboker בַבֹּקֶר et אֶת־

ve'et וְאֵת hakeves הַכֶּבֶשׂ hasheni הַשֵּׁנִי ta'ase תַּעֲשֶׂה ben בֵּין

ha'arbayim הָעַרְבָּיִם: va'asirit וַעֲשִׂירִת ha'efa הָאֵיפָה solet סֹלֶת

lemincha לְמִנְחָה ע"ה ב"פ ב"ן belula בְּלוּלָה beshemen בְּשֶׁמֶן

katit כָּתִית revi'it רְבִיעִת hahin הַהִין: olat עֹלַת ושיר, אבגיתץ

(Meditate here to surrender the *klipa* named *Tola* using the Name: אבגיתץ)

tamid תָּמִיד ע"ה קס"א קנ"א קמ"ג ha'asuya הָעֲשֻׂיָה

behar בְּהַר Sinai סִינַי נגמם, ה' הויות (ה' גבורות) lere'ach לְרֵיחַ nicho'ach נִיחֹחַ

ishe אִשֶּׁה ladonai לַיהֹוָה(אדני/אהדונהי) venisko וְנִסְכּוֹ revi'it רְבִיעִת

hahin הַהִין lakeves לַכֶּבֶשׂ ha'echad הָאֶחָד אהבה, דאגה bakodesh בַּקֹּדֶשׁ

hasech הַסֵּךְ nesech נֶסֶךְ shechar שֵׁכָר י"פ ב"ן ladonai לַיהֹוָה(אדני/אהדונהי):

THE SACRIFICES – KORBANOT - THE TAMID – (DAILY) OFFERING

"And God spoke to Moses and said, Command the children of Israel and say to them, My offering, the bread of My fire-offering, My pleasing fragrance, you shall take care to sacrifice to Me at its specified time. And you shall say to them: This is the fire-offering that you shall sacrifice to God, a perfect one-year-old sheep, two per day, as a regular daily offering; one sheep you shall do in the morning and the second sheep you shall do in the late afternoon. And one tenth of ephah of fine flour, for a meal-offering, mixed with one quarter of a hin of pressed oil. This is a regular burnt-offering that is made at Mount Sinai as a pleasing fragrance and as a fire-offering before God. Its libation is one quarter of a hin for the one sheep in the Sanctuary; pour a libation of old wine before God.

ben בֵּין ta'ase תַּעֲשֶׂה hasheni הַשֵּׁנִי hakeves הַכֶּבֶשׂ ve'et וְאֵת

uchnisko וּכְנִסְכּוֹ haboker הַבֹּקֶר keminchat כְּמִנְחַת ha'arbayim הָעַרְבַּיִם

(elevation to *Beriah*) re'ach רֵיחַ (elevation to *Yetzirah*) ishe אִשֶּׁה ta'ase תַּעֲשֶׂה

✢(elevation to the Endless World) ladonai לַיהוָֹאדְנִיָּאהדונהי (elevation to *Atzilut*) nicho'ach נִיחוֹחַ

THE INCENSE

These verses from the *Torah* and the *Talmud* speak about the 11 herbs and spices that were used in the Temple. These herbs and spices were used for one purpose: to help us remove the force of death from every area of our lives. This is one of the few prayers whose sole goal is the eradication of death. The *Zohar* teaches us that whoever has judgment pursuing him needs to connect to this incense. The 11 herbs and spices connect to 11 Lights that sustain the *klipot* (shells of negativity). When we uproot the 11 Lights from the *klipot* through the power of the incense, the *klipot* lose their life-force and die. In addition to bringing the 11 spices to the Temple, the people brought resin, wine, and other items with metaphysical properties to help battle the Angel of Death.

It says in the *Zohar*: "Come and see, whoever is pursued by judgment is in need of incense and must repent before his master, for incense helps judgment to disappear from him." The 11 herbs and spices correspond to the 11 Holy Illuminations that revive the *klipa*. By elevating them, the *klipa* will die. Through these 11 herbs, the *klipot* are pushed away and the energy-point that was giving them life is removed. And since the Pure Side and its livelihood disappear, the *klipot* is left with no life. Thus the secret of the incense is that it cleanses the force of plague and cancels it. The incense kills the Angel of Death and takes away his power to kill.

יכה Elohenu אֱלֹהֵינוּ Adonai יְהוָֹאדְנִיָּאהדונהי hu הוּא Ata אַתָּה

ב"ן מ"ה ס"ג lefanecha לְפָנֶיךָ avotenu אֲבוֹתֵינוּ shehiktiru שֶׁהִקְטִירוּ

(הַנּבְרָרִים מֵהַקְלִיפוֹת ע"י י"א הַסַּמָּנִים) י"א פְּעָמִים אַדְנֹי ketoret קְטֹרֶת et אֶת

קְטֹרֶת – הֹק' בְּאַתְבַּ"שׁ ד' = תרי"ג (מִצְוֹת) תרי"ג hasamim הַסַּמִּים ע"ה קנ"א, אַדְנֹי אֱלֹהִים

kayam קַיָּם hamikdash הַמִּקְדָּשׁ ב"פ ראה shebet שֶׁבֵּית bizman בִּזְמַן

מהש, Moshe מֹשֶׁה yad יַד al עַל otam אוֹתָם tzivita צִוִּיתָ ka'asher כַּאֲשֶׁר

✢betoratach בְּתוֹרָתֶךָ kakatuv כַּכָּתוּב nevia'ch נְבִיאָךְ ע"ב בריבוע וקס"א, אל שדי

The second sheep you shall do in the afternoon like the meal-offering of the morning; its libation you shall do as a fire-offering of a fragrance which is pleasing to God." (Numbers 28:1-8)
THE INCENSE
It is You, Lord, our God, before whom our forefathers burned the incense spices, during the time when the Temple existed, as You had commanded them through Moses, Your Prophet, and as it is written in Your Torah:

THE PORTION OF THE INCENSE

To raise the Sefirot *from all of* Nogah *of* Atzilut, *Beriah,* Yetzirah *and* Asiyah.

Moshe מֹשֶׁה el אֶל־ Adonai יְהֹוָאהֲדֹנָהִי vayomer וַיֹּאמֶר

(Tiferet, Netzach) samim סַמִּים lecha לְךָ kach קַח מהע, ע"ב ברבוע וקס"א, אל שדי

vechelbena וְחֶלְבְּנָה (Yesod) ushchelet וּשְׁחֵלֶת (Hod) | nataf נָטָף ע"ה קנ"א, אדני אלהים

(Keter, Chochmah, Binah, Chesed, Gevurah) samim סַמִּים אל אדני פו, ע"ה (Malchut)

bevad בָּד bad בַּד (Surrounding Light) zaka זַכָּה ulvona וּלְבֹנָה ע"ה קנ"א, אדני אלהים

yih'ye יִהְיֶה ketoret קְטֹרֶת ota אֹתָהּ ve'asita וְעָשִׂיתָ י"א (הנברים ארני פעמים) יי"י

ma'ase מַעֲשֵׂה rokach רֹקַח (מצוות) תרי"ג = ד' באתב"ש – הק' – קטרת ;(הסממנים י"א י"י מההקליפות

kodesh קָדֶשׁ tahor טָהוֹר memulach מְמֻלָּח roke'ach רוֹקֵחַ שדי אבא י"פ

veshachakta וְשָׁחַקְתָּ mimena מִמֶּנָּה ס"ת רוזו בכוחו לגרש החיצונים ויועיל לזכירה:

hadek הָדֵק venatata וְנָתַתָּה mimena מִמֶּנָּה lifnei לִפְנֵי ha'edut הָעֵדֻת

be'ohel בְּאֹהֶל mo'ed מוֹעֵד asher אֲשֶׁר iva'ed אִוָּעֵד lecha לְךָ shama שָׁמָּה

kodesh קֹדֶשׁ kadashim קָדָשִׁים tihye תִּהְיֶה lachem לָכֶם vene'emar וְנֶאֱמַר:

vehiktir וְהִקְטִיר alav עָלָיו Aharon אַהֲרֹן ketoret קְטֹרֶת י"א פעמים ארני

samim סַמִּים (מצוות) תרי"ג = ד' באתב"ש – הק' – קטרת ;(הסממנים י"א י"י מההקליפות (הנברים

baboker בַּבֹּקֶר baboker בַּבֹּקֶר behetivo בְּהֵיטִיבוֹ ע"ה קנ"א, אדני אלהים

et אֶת־ hanerot הַנֵּרֹת yaktirena יַקְטִירֶנָּה: uveha'alot וּבְהַעֲלֹת

Aharon אַהֲרֹן et אֶת־ hanerot הַנֵּרֹת ben בֵּין ha'arbayim הָעַרְבַּיִם

ketoret קְטֹרֶת yaktirena יַקְטִירֶנָּה ר"ת אהבה, דאגה, אוזר י"א פעמים ארני

tamid תָּמִיד (הנברים) קטרת – הק' – ד' באתב"ש = תרי"ג (מצוות) ;

lifnei לִפְנֵי Adonai יְהֹוָאהֲדֹנָהִי ledorotechem לְדֹרֹתֵיכֶם: ע"ה קס"א קנ"א קמ"ג

THE PORTION OF THE INCENSE

"And God said to Moses: Take for yourself spices, balsam sap, onycha, galbanum, and pure frankincense, each of equal weight. You shall prepare it as an incense compound; the work of a spice-mixer, well-blended, pure, and holy. You shall grind some of it fine and place it before the Testimony in the Tabernacle of Meeting, in which I shall meet with you. It shall be the Holy of Holies unto you." (Exodus 30:34-36) And God also said: "Aaron shall burn upon the Altar incense spices early each morning when he prepares the candles. And when Aaron raises the candles at sundown, he shall burn the incense spices as a continual incense-offering before God throughout all your generations." (Exodus 30:7-8)

THE WORKINGS OF THE INCENSE

The filling of the incense has two purposes: First, to remove the *klipot* in order to stop them from going up along with the elevation of the Worlds, and second, to draw Light to *Asiyah*. So meditate to raise the sparks of Light from all of the *Nogah* of *Azilut*, *Beriah*, *Yetzirah* and *Asiyah*.

Count the incense using your right hand, one by one, and don't skip even one, as it is said: "If one omits one of all the ingredients, he is liable to receive the penalty of death." And therefore, you should be careful not to skip any of them because reciting this paragraph is a substitute for the actual burning of the incense.

אדני פעמים י״א **הַקְּטֹרֶת** haketoret **פִּטּוּם** pitum **רַבָּנָן** rabanan **תָּנוּ** tanu

(הנבררים מהקליפות ע״י י״א הסממנים) קטרת – הק׳ באתב״ש ד׳ = תרי״ג (מצוות);

פטום הקטרת = יְהֹוָה יְהוָה מצפצ יה אדני אל אלהים מצפצ (ו מרגלאין דעובת)**:**

דיורין אלהים ,ע = המספר **מֵאוֹת** me'ot **שָׁלֹשׁ** shelosh ◆keitzad **כֵּיצַד**

hayu **הָיוּ** manim **מָנִים** ushmona **וּשְׁמֹנָה** (יין) = מילוי הע׳ המספר veshishim **וְשִׁשִּׁים** **וְשִׁשִּׁים**

veshishim **וְשִׁשִּׁים** me'ot **מֵאוֹת** המספר = ע, אלהים דיורין shelosh **שָׁלֹשׁ** va◆ **בָּה**

yemot **יְמוֹת** keminyan **כְּמִנְיַן** vachamisha **וַחֲמִשָּׁה** (יין) = מילוי הע׳ המספר

לכב ב״ן, **בְּכָל**‎-bechol אדני אל ,פוי, ע״ה mane **מָנֶה** hachama **הַחַמָּה** **הַחַמָּה**

baboker **בַּבֹּקֶר** machatzito **מַחֲצִיתוֹ** אל יהוה. ,ז, מזבח ,נגד ע״ה yom **יוֹם**

manim **מָנִים** ushlosha **וּשְׁלֹשָׁה** ba'erev◆ **בָּעֶרֶב** umachatzito **וּמַחֲצִיתוֹ**

מלה kohen **כֹּהֵן** machnis **מַכְנִיס** shemehem **שֶׁמֵּהֶם** קס״א, קנ״א וקמ״ג yeterim **יְתֵרִים**

mehem **מֵהֶם** venotel **וְנוֹטֵל** אום ,יזל ,מ=מבה, אותיות ד׳ עם ; להו gadol **גָּדוֹל**

hakipurim **הַכִּפּוּרִים** beyom **בְּיוֹם** אל יהוה ,ז, מזבח ,נגד ע״ה chofnav **חָפְנָיו** melo **מְלֹא**

be'erev **בָּעֶרֶב** lamachteshet **לַמַּכְתֶּשֶׁת** machaziran **מַחֲזִירָן** **מַחֲזִירָן**

lekayem **לְקַיֵּם** kedei **כְּדֵי** hakipurim **הַכִּפּוּרִים** אל יהוה ,ז, מזבח ,נגד ע״ה yom **יוֹם**

דאגה ,אהבה ve'achad **וְאֶחָד** hadaka◆ **הַדַּקָּה** min **מִן** daka **דַּקָּה** mitzvat **מִצְוַת**

hen **הֵן:** ve'elu **וְאֵלּוּ** va◆ **בָּה** hayu **הָיוּ** samanim **סַמָּנִים** asar **עָשָׂר**

THE WORKINGS OF THE INCENSE

Our Sages have taught: How was the compounding of the incense done? Three hundred and sixty-eight portions were contained therein. These corresponded to the number of days in the solar year, one portion for each day: Half of it in the morning and half at sundown. As for the remaining three portions, the High Priest (Kohen Gadol), on Yom Kippur, filled both his hands with them. On the Eve of Yom Kippur, he would take them back to the mortar to fulfill the requirement that they should be very finely ground. Each portion contained eleven spices:

(1 הַצֳּרִי haTzori (Keter) מצפצ, אלהים דיודין, י"פ ייי • 2) וְהַצִּפֹּרֶן vehaTziporen (Yesod)

(3 וְהַחֶלְבְּנָה vehaChelbena (Malchut) ע"ה פוי, אל אדני • יהוה אדני אהיה שדי •

(4 וְהַלְּבוֹנָה vehaLevona (Surounding Light – שהוא אור לבן והוא יוזדי הנקרא אדון יוזדי)

מִשְׁקָל mishkal שִׁבְעִים shiv'im שִׁבְעִים shiv'im מָנֶה mane ע"ה פוי, אל אדני •

(5 מּוֹר Mor (Chesed)• 6) וּקְצִיעָה uKtzi'ah (Gevurah – רהע "כי מצפון תפתוח הרעה",

(7 וְשִׁבֹּלֶת veShibolet נֵרְדְּ Nerd (Tiferet)• צפון) רווח סוד והגבורה

(8 וְכַרְכֹּם veCharkom (Netzach) בזכֹּר, סנדלפון, ערי • מִשְׁקָל mishkal עֲשָׂה shisha

עֲשָׂר asar עֲשָׂה shisha עֲשָׂר asar מָנֶה mane ע"ה פוי, אל אדני • 9) קֹשְׁטְ Kosht

(Chochmah) שְׁנַיִם sheneim עֲשָׂר asar • 10) קְלוּפָה Kilufa (Binah) שְׁלֹשָׁה shelosha•

(11 קִנָּמוֹן Kinamon (Hod) ר"ת ג"פ ק' (בסוד קדוש קדוש קדוש)• תִּשְׁעָה tish'ah•

בּוֹרִית borit כַּרְשִׁינָא karshina תִּשְׁעָה tish'ah קַבִּין kabin• יַיִן yen מיכ, י"פ האא

קַפְרִיסִין Kafrisin סְאִין se'in תְּלַת telat וְקַבִּין vekabin תְּלָתָא telata אהיה קבין

וְאִם ve'im יוהרך, מ"א אותיות דפשוט, דמילוי ודמילוי דמילוי דאהיה ע"ה לֹא lo מָצָא matza

יַיִן yen מיכ, י"פ האא קַפְרִיסִין Kafrisin מֵבִיא mevi וְזֶמַר chamar וְזִיּוּר chivar

עָתִיק atik• מֶלַח melach סְדוֹמִית Sedomit רוֹבַע rova• מַעֲלֶה ma'ale

עָשָׁן ashan כָּל kol ילי שֶׁהוּא shehu• רִבִּי Ribi נָתָן Natan הַבַּבְלִי haBavli

אוֹמֵר omer• אַף af הַיַּיּות וד' אותיות מִכְפַּת mikipat הַיַּרְדֵּן haYarden כָּל kol ילי

שֶׁהִיא shehi• אִם im יוהרך, מ"א אותיות דפשוט, דמילוי ודמילוי דמילוי דאהיה ע"ה נָתַן natan

בָּהּ ba דְּבַשׁ devash שׁוֹי (דעשׁוֹפר) וי"ד (האוֹזן) = ע"ך דינין דגדלות פְּסָלָהּ pesala•

וְאִם ve'im יוהרך, מ"א אותיות דפשוט, דמילוי ודמילוי דמילוי דאהיה ע"ה וְחִסֵּר chiser

אַחַת achat מִכָּל mikol ילי סַמְמָנֶיהָ samemaneha וְזַיָּיב chayav מִיתָה mita:

---

1) Balsam. 2) Onycha. 3) Galbanum. 4) Frankincense; the weight of seventy portions each. 5) Myrrh. 6) Cassia. 7) Spikenard. 8) And Saffron; the weight of sixteen portions each. 9) Twelve portions of Costus. 10) Three of aromatic Bark 11) Nine of Cinnamon. Further, nine kavs of Lye of Carsina. And three kavs and three se'ahs of Cyprus wine. And if one should not find any Cyprus wine, he should bring an old white wine. And a quarter of the salt of Sodom. And a small measure of a smoke raising herb. Rabbi Natan, the Babylonian, advised also, a small amount of Jordan resin. If he added to it honey, he would make it defective. If he omits even one of all its herbs, he would be liable to death.

רַבָּן Raban שִׁמְעוֹן Shimon בֶּן ben גַּמְלִיאֵל Gamli'el אוֹמֵר omer:

הַצֳּרִי haTzori מַצִפְצ. אלהים דיורין, י"פ ייי eno אֵינוּ ela אֶלָּא seraf שְׂרָף

הַנּוֹטֵף hanotef מֵעֲצֵי me'atzei הַקְּטָף haketaf◆ בּוֹרִית borit

כַּרְשִׁינָא karshina לָמָה lema הִיא hee בָּאָה va'a◆ כְּדֵי kedei

לְשָׁפוֹת leshapot בָּהּ ba אֶת et הַצִּפּוֹרֶן haTziporen יהוה אדני אהיה עדי

כְּדֵי kedei שֶׁתְּהֵא shetehe נָאָה na'a◆ יֵין yen ע' (כנגד ע' אומות העולם התלויים בסמאל), מיכ, י"פ האא

כַּפְרִיסִין Kafrisin לָמָה lema הוּא hu בָּא va◆ כְּדֵי kedei

לִשְׁרוֹת lishrot בּוֹ bo אֶת et הַצִּפּוֹרֶן haTziporen יהוה אדני אהיה עדי

כְּדֵי kedei שֶׁתְּהֵא shetehe עַזָּה aza◆ וַהֲלֹא vahalo מֵי mei רַגְלַיִם raglayim ילי

יָפִין yafin לָהּ la אֶלָּא ela שֶׁאֵין she'en מַכְנִיסִין machnisin מֵי mei ילי

רַגְלַיִם raglayim בַּמִּקְדָּשׁ bamikdash מִפְּנֵי mipenei הַכָּבוֹד hakavod לאו:

תַּנְיָא tanya◆ רִבִּי Ribi נָתָן Natan אוֹמֵר omer: כְּשֶׁהוּא keshehu

שׁוֹחֵק shochek אוֹמֵר omer הָדֵק hadek הֵיטֵב hetev◆ הֵיטֵב hetev

הָדֵק hadek◆ מִפְּנֵי mipenei שֶׁהַקּוֹל shehakol יָפֶה yafe לַבְּשָׂמִים labesamim◆

פִּטְּמָהּ pitema לַחֲצָאִין lachatza'in◆ כְּשֵׁרָה keshera◆ לְשָׁלִישׁ leshalish

וּלְרַבִיעַ ulravi'a לֹא lo שָׁמַעְנוּ shamanu◆ אָמַר amar רִבִּי Ribi

יְהוּדָה Yehuda: זֶה ze הַכְּלָל hakelal◆ אִם im יוהך, מ"א אותיות דפשוט, דמילוי

כְּמִדָּתָהּ kemidata ע"ה דאהיה דמילוי כְּשֵׁרָה keshera לַחֲצָאִין lachatza'in◆ ורדמילוי דמילוי

וְאִם ve'im יוהך, מ"א אותיות דפשוט, דמילוי ורדמילוי דמילוי דאהיה ע"ה חִסֵּר chiser

אַחַת achat מִכָּל mikol ילי סַמְמָנֶיהָ samemaneha וְחַיָּיב chayav מִיתָה mita:

Rabban Shimon ben Gamliel says: The balsam was a sap that only seeped from the balsam trees. For what purpose was the Lye of Carsina added? In order to rub the Onycha with it to make it pleasant looking. For what purpose was the Cyprus wine added? In order to steep in it the Onycha. Urine is more appropriate for this, but urine is not brought into the Temple out of respect. It was taught that Rabbi Natan said: When he ground, he said: 'Grind it fine, grind it fine.' This is because voice is beneficial to the spices. If he compounds half the amount it is still valid, yet regarding a third or a quarter, we have no information. Rabbi Yehuda said: This is the general rule: If it is in its correct proportions, then half is valid. Yet if he omits one of all its spices, he is liable to death.

אוֹ o   לְשִׁשִּׁים leshishim   אַוַּת achat   קַפְּרָא: Kapara   בַּר Var   תָּנֵי tanei

שֶׁל shel   בָּאָה va'a   הָיְתָה hayta   שָׁנָה shana   לְשִׁבְעִים leshiv'im

בַּר Var   תָּנֵי tanei   וְעוֹד ve'od   לוֹצְאָין lachatza'in◆   שִׁירַיִם shirayim   עִירִים

בָּהּ ba   נוֹתֵן noten יה‑ה   הָיָה haya   אִלּוּ ilu   Kapara :קַפְּרָא

= ע"ך דינין הגדלות (האוזו) וי' (דשופר) שוי   devash דְּבַשׁ   shel שֶׁל   kortov קוֹרְטוֹב

מִפְּנֵי mipenei   la'amod לַעֲמוֹד   yachol יָכוֹל   מ"ה adam אָדָם   en אֵין

דְּבַשׁ devash   בָּהּ ba   me'arvin מְעַרְבִין   en אֵין   velama וְלָמָה◆   recha◆ רֵיוְזֹה

שֶׁהַתּוֹרָה shehatorah   mipenei מִפְּנֵי = ע"ך דינין הגדלות (האוזו) וי' (דשופר) שוי

דאלהים דקטנות מוּוזין ג se'or שְׂאֹר ילי chol כָּל ki כִּי :amra אָמְרָה

devash דְּבַשׁ ילי vechol וְכָל = ר' = ריבוע אלהים ; א' = כללות שם אלהים ; ע' = אלהים דיודין (ע'

mimenu מִמֶּנּוּ taktiru תַּקְטִירוּ lo לֹא = ע"ך דינין הגדלות (האוזו) וי"ד (דשופר) שוי

ladonai :לַיהוה אדני/אהדונהי   ishe אִשֶּׁה שוכן הם בוזינת דינין דקטנות ודגדלות לכן נאסרה הקרבתן

Right

imanu עִמָּנוּ   שוכינה   פְּנֵי   Tzeva'ot צְבָאוֹת   Adonai יהוה אדני/אהדונהי

ריבוע דס"ג, קס"א ע"ה ו' אותיות משה, מהע, ע"ב בריבוע וקס"א, אל עדי, misgav מִשְׂגָּב

dp אלהים ע"ה ; יכה Elohei אֱלֹהֵי מילוי ע"ב, דמב ; יכה lanu לָנוּ אלהים, אהיה אדני, אלהים

sela :סֶלָה   אידהנויה   יאהדונהי   הויות,   ו   Yaakov יַעֲקֹב

Left

ashrei אַשְׁרֵי   שוכינה   פְּנֵי   Tzeva'ot צְבָאוֹת   Adonai יהוה אדני/אהדונהי

bote'ach בֹּטֵחַ תפארת = אדם אשרי צבאות יהוה ; מ"ה adam אָדָם

bach :בָּךְ אדם בוטוח ע"ה מילוי ע"ב ע"ה: = מילוי בך בוטוח ; (יאהדונהי) ע"ה ; בך בוטוח = אמן = (יאהדונהי) בך אדם

Bar Kappara taught that once every sixty or seventy years the leftovers would accumulate to half the measure. Bar Kappara also taught that if one would add to it a Kortov of honey, no man would withstand its smell. Why is honey not mixed with it? Because the Torah had stipulated: Because any leaven or honey, you must not burn any of it as burnt-offering to God. (Kritut 6; Yerushalmi, Yoma: ch.4) (Right) "The Lord of Hosts is with us, our strength is the God of Jacob, Selah." (Psalms 46:12) (Left) "The Lord of Hosts, joyful is one who trusts in You." (Psalms 84:13)

Central

יְהוּ אדני יאהדונהי רֹ"ת יהה   hamelech הַמֶּלֶךְ   יהוה ועו"ע נהורין hoshi'a הוֹשִׁיעָה   Adonai אדני יאהדונהי

יָ"ה, אֵל, יהוה   veyom בְּיוֹם   ע"ה, נְגֶד, מִזְבֵּחַ, זָן,   ya'anenu יַעֲנֵנוּ

kor'enu קָרְאֵנוּ   רֹ"ת יב"ק, אלהים יהוה, אהיה אדני יהוה ; ס"ת = בֹ"ן ועם כף דהמלך = ע"ב:

ladonai לַיהוּ אדני אהדונהי   ve'arva וְעָרְבָה

virushalaim וִירוּשָׁלַיִם   Yehuda יְהוּדָה   minchat מִנְחַת

kadmoniyot קַדְמֹנִיּוֹת: uch'shanim וּכְשָׁנִים   olam עוֹלָם   kimei כִּימֵי

ANA BEKO'ACH (an explanation about the *Ana Beko'ach* can be found on pages 222-224)

The *Ana Beko'ach* is perhaps the most powerful prayer in the entire universe. Second-century Kabbalist Rav Nachunya ben HaKana was the first sage to reveal this combination of 42 letters, which encompass the power of Creation.

Chesed, Sunday *(Alef Bet Gimel Yud Tav Tzadik)* אבג יתץ

♦yeminecha יְמִינֶךָ   gedulat גְּדוּלַת   ♦beko'ach בְּכֹחַ   ana אָנָּא

tzerura צְרוּרָה: tatir תַּתִּיר

Gevurah, Monday *(Kuf Resh Ayin Shin Tet Nun)* קרע שטן

♦sagevenu שַׂגְּבֵנוּ   amecha עַמְּךָ   ♦rinat רִנַּת   kabel קַבֵּל

nora נוֹרָא: taharenu טַהֲרֵנוּ

(Central) *"Lord save us. The King shall answer us the day we call."* (Psalms 20:10) *"May the Lord find the offering of Yehuda and Jerusalem pleasing as He had always done and as in the years of old."* (Malachi 3:4)

ANA BEKO'ACH
Chesed, Sunday אבג יתץ
We beseech You, with the power of Your great right, undo this entanglement.
Gevurah, Monday קרע שטן
Accept the singing of Your Nation. Strengthen and purify us, Awesome One.

Tiferet, Tuesday *(Nun Gimel Dalet Yud Kaf Shin)* נגד יכש

na נָא ‣gibor גִּבּוֹר dorshei דּוֹרְשֵׁי ‣yichudecha יְחוּדְךָ

kevavat כְּבָבַת ⁝shomrem שָׁמְרֵם

Netzach, Wednesday *(Bet Tet Resh Tzadik Tav Gimel)* בטר צתג

barchem בָּרְכֵם ‣taharem טַהֲרֵם rachamei רַחֲמֵי ‣tzidkatecha צִדְקָתְךָ

tamid תָּמִיד ⁝gomlem גָּמְלֵם

Hod, Thursday *(Chet Kuf Bet Tet Nun Ayin)* חקב טנע

chasin חֲסִין ‣kadosh קָדוֹשׁ berov בְּרוֹב ‣tuvcha טוּבְךָ

nahel נַהֵל ⁝adatecha עֲדָתְךָ

Yesod, Friday *(Yud Gimel Lamed Pei Zayin Kuf)* יגל פזק

yachid יָחִיד ‣ge'e גֵּאֶה le'amecha לְעַמְּךָ ‣pene פְּנֵה

zochrei זוֹכְרֵי ⁝kedushatecha קְדֻשָּׁתְךָ

Malchut, Saturday *(Shin Kuf Vav Tzadik Yud Tav)* שקו צית

shav'atenu שַׁוְעָתֵנוּ ‣kabel קַבֵּל ushma וּשְׁמַע ‣tza'akatenu צַעֲקָתֵנוּ

yode'a יוֹדֵעַ ⁝ta'alumot תַּעֲלוּמוֹת

BARUCH SHEM KEVOD
Whispering this final verse brings all the Light from the Upper Worlds into our physical existence.

baruch בָּרוּךְ shem שֵׁם kevod כְּבוֹד malchuto מַלְכוּתוֹ (Whisper): יוֹזוֹ אותיות

va'ed וָעֶד⁝ le'olam לְעוֹלָם ריבוע ס"ג וי' אותיות דס"ג

Tiferet, Tuesday נגד יכש
Please, Mighty One, those who seek Your unity, guard them like the pupil of the eye.

Netzach, Wednesday בטר צתג
Bless them. Purify them. Your compassionate righteousness always grant them.

Hod, Thursday חקב טנע
Invincible and Mighty One, with the abundance of Your goodness, govern Your congregation.

Yesod, Friday יגל פזק
Sole and proud One, turn to Your people, those who remember Your sanctity.

Malchut, Saturday שקו צית
Accept our cry and hear our wail, You that knows all that is hidden.

BARUCH SHEM KEVOD
"Blessed is the Name of Glory. His Kingdom is forever and for eternity." (Pesachim 56a)

THE ASHREI

Twenty-one of the twenty-two letters of the Aramaic alphabet are encoded in the *Ashrei* in their correct order from *Alef* to *Tav*. King David, the author, left out the Aramaic letter *Nun* from this prayer, because *Nun* is the first letter in the Aramaic word *nefilah*, which means "falling." Falling refers to a spiritual decline, as in falling into the *klipa*. Feelings of doubt, depression, worry, and uncertainty are consequences of spiritual falling. Because the Aramaic letters are the actual instruments of Creation, this prayer helps to inject order and the power of Creation into our lives, without the energy of falling.

In this Psalm there are ten times the Name: יהוה for the Ten *Sefirot*. This Psalm is written according to the order of the *Alef Bet*, but the letter *Nun* is omitted to prevent falling.

ראה ב"פ	vetecha בֵּיתֶךָ	yoshvei יוֹשְׁבֵי	(סוד הכתר)	ashrei אַשְׁרֵי
ha'am הָעָם	ashrei אַשְׁרֵי	sela סֶלָה:	yehalelucha יְהַלְלוּךָ	od עוֹד
lo כּוֹ	מהע, מעוה, ע"ב בריבוע וקס"א, אל שדי, ד"פ אלהים ע"ה	shekacha שֶׁכָּכָה
(Keter)	she'Adonai שֶׁיְהוָֹה לאה ר"ת	ha'am הָעָם	ashrei אַשְׁרֵי
leDavid לְדָוִד ז"פ ס"ג	tehila תְּהִלָּה: ע"ה אמת, אהיה פעמים אהיה, יכה:	Elohav אֱלֹהָיו
va'avarcha וַאֲבָרְכָה	hamelech הַמֶּלֶךְ	Elohai אֱלוֹהַי	aromimcha אֲרוֹמִמְךָ
va'ed וָעֶד:	ד"ס"ג רי אותיות ריבוע דס"ג	le'olam לְעוֹלָם	shimcha שִׁמְךָ
יהוה אל זן מזבוח, נגד, ע"ה לכב ב"ן,	yom יוֹם	bechol בְּכָל
shimcha שִׁמְךָ יהוה מ"ה	va'ahalela וַאֲהַלְלָה	avarcheka אֲבָרְכֶךָ
va'ed וָעֶד: דס"ג אותיות רי דס"ג ריבוע	le'olam לְעוֹלָם
אום יזל, מבה, = אותיות ד' עם ; לההו	gadol גָּדוֹל
כלה אדני, umhulal וּמְהֻלָּל (Chochmah)	Adonai יֱהוָֹה
cheker וֵחֶקֶר:	en אֵין והו	veligdulato וְלִגְדֻלָּתוֹ	me'od מְאֹד

THE ASHREI

"Joyful are those who dwell in Your House, they shall praise You, Selah." (Psalms 84:5) "Joyful is the nation that this is theirs and joyful the nation that the Lord is their God." (Psalms 145:15) "A praise of David:

א   *I shall exalt You, my God, the King, and I shall bless Your Name forever and for eternity.*

ב   *I shall bless You every day and I shall praise Your Name forever and for eternity.*

ג   *The Lord is great and exceedingly praised. His greatness is unfathomable.*

ר"ת דלים | מַעֲשֶׂיךָ ma'asecha | יְשַׁבַּח yeshabach | לְדוֹר ledor | דּוֹר dor

וּגְבוּרֹתֶיךָ ugvurotecha | יַגִּידוּ yagidu | יו', כ"ב אותיות פשוטות (=אכא) וה' אותיות סופיות מנצפ"ך

וְדִבְרֵי vedivrei | הוֹדֶךָ hodecha | כְּבוֹד kevod | הֲדַר hadar

אדני | אהיה | אלהים, | ר"ת | נִפְלְאֹתֶיךָ nifle'otecha

פ"ז | טהור | כתם | (בסוד | פ"ז | = | הפסוק | ר"ת | אָשִׂיחָה asicha

וּגְדֻלָּתְךָ ugdulatcha | נוֹרְאֹתֶיךָ no'rotecha | יֹאמֵרוּ yomeru | וֶעֱזוּז ve'ezuz

(כתיב: וגדלותיך) ר"ת | ס"ת = יא"י (מילוי דס"ג) | ע"ב, ריבוע יהוה | ס"ת = | אֲסַפְּרֶנָּה asaperena

יַבִּיעוּ yabi'u | לאו | טוּבְךָ tuvcha | רַב־ rav | זֵכֶר zecher

ס"ת = ב"ן, יבמ, לכב ; ר"ת הפסוק = רי"ו יהו"ה | יְרַנֵּנוּ yeranenu | וְצִדְקָתְךָ vetzidkatcha

(Binah) | Adonai | לַיְהֹוָ֥הֵאֱלֹהֵיאֲדֹנָֽי | וְרַחוּם verachum | חַנּוּן chanun

חנון ורחום יהוה = יהוה | ר"ת | apayim אַפַּיִם | ס"ג ב"ן | ס"ת = | ס"ג = | erech אֶרֶךְ | עשל = יהוה

יהוה | ריבוע | ע"ב, | חֶסֶד chased | וְחֶסֶד | (כתיב: וגדול) | ugdal וּגְדָל־

tov | והו | Adonai | לַיְהֹוָ֥הֵאֱלֹהֵיאֲדֹנָֽי | (Chesed) | טוֹב־ tov | לַכֹּל lakol

al עַל־ | verachamav וְרַחֲמָיו | (מילוי דס"ג) | ל"ז | ס"ת ; | ארני | יה

ma'asav מַעֲשָׂיו | ס"ת ריבוע ב"ן ע"ה | ע"ב, ריבוע יהוה | ; עמם ; ר"ת ריבוע ב"ן ע"ה | ילי ; | kol כֹּל

ד *One generation and the next shall praise Your deeds and tell of Your might.*

ה *The brilliance of Your splendid glory and the wonders of Your acts, I shall speak of.*

ו *They shall speak of the might of Your awesome acts and I shall tell of Your greatness.*

ז *They shall express the remembrance of Your abundant goodness, and Your righteousness they shall*
joyfully proclaim. ח *The Lord is merciful and compassionate, slow to anger and great in kindness.*

ט *The Lord is good to all, His compassion extends over all His acts.*

יוֹדוּךָ yoducha יְ־הֹוָ־ה (אדני/אהדונהי) Adonai (Gevurah) כָּל־ kol יל מַעֲשֶׂיךָ ma'asecha

וַחֲסִידֶיךָ vachasidecha ר"ת אלהים, אהיה אדני לְבָרְכוּכָה yevarchucha ס"ת = מ"ה:

כְּבוֹד kevod מַלְכוּתְךָ malchutcha יֹאמֵרוּ yomeru וּגְבוּרָתְךָ ugvuratcha

יְדַבֵּרוּ yedaberu ר"ת הפסוק = אלהים, אהיה אדני ; ס"ת = ב"ן, יבמ, לכב:

לְהוֹדִיעַ lehodi'a לִבְנֵי livnei הָאָדָם ha'adam ר"ת ללה, אדני

גְּבוּרֹתָיו gevurotav וּכְבוֹד uchvod הֲדַר hadar

מַלְכוּתוֹ malchuto ר"ת מ"ה וס"ת = רי"ו ; ר"ת הפסוק ע"ה = ק"כ צירופי אלהים:

מַלְכוּתְךָ malchutcha מַלְכוּת malchut כָּל־ kol יל עֹלָמִים olamim

וּמֶמְשַׁלְתְּךָ umemshaltecha בְּכָל־ bechol ב"ן, לכב דּוֹר dor וָדֹר vador רי"ו:

סוֹמֵךְ somech ריבוע אדני Adonai יְ־הֹוָ־ה (אדני/אהדונהי) (Tiferet)

לְכָל־ lechol הַנֹּפְלִים hanoflim יה אדני ; סומך אדני לכל ר"ת סאל, אבן (יאהדונהי)

וְזוֹקֵף vezokef לְכָל־ lechol יה אדני הַכְּפוּפִים hakefufim נמם:

עֵינֵי enei כֹל chol ריבוע דמ"ה אֵלֶיךָ elecha יל יְשַׂבֵּרוּ yesaberu וְאַתָּה veAta

נוֹתֵן noten אבגיתצ, ועיר לָהֶם lahem אֶת־ et אָכְלָם ochlam בְּעִתּוֹ be'ito:

POTE'ACH ET YADECHA

We connect to the letters *Pei, Alef,* and *Yud* by opening our hands and holding our palms skyward. Our consciousness is focused on receiving sustenance and financial prosperity from the Light through our actions of tithing and sharing, our Desire to Receive for the Sake of Sharing. In doing so, we also acknowledge that the sustenance we receive comes from a higher source and is not of our own doing. According to the sages, if we do not meditate on this idea at this juncture, we must repeat the prayer.

פּתֵחוֹ (ע"ע"וֹוֹ נֹהוֹרִיןֵ לִמֵ"ה ולֹס"ה)

פּוֹתֵחַוֹ אֶת יָדְךָ ר"ת פּאי	יוֹד הֵי וֵיו יוֹד הֵי וֵיו הֵי (וֹזֵ וֹזִיוּוֹרֵתֵי)
גִימֵ' יְאַהֹדֹנֹהֹי זוֹ"ןֵ	אַלֵף לַמֵד אַלֵף לַמֵד (ע"ע)
וֹחֲכֵמֹה דֹ"א וֹ"ק	יוֹד הֵא וֹאו הֵא (לֹ"א)
יֵסוֹד דֹנֵק	אֲדֹנֵי (וֹלֹנוֹקֹבֵא)

פּוֹתֵחַוֹ אֶת יָדְךָ pote'ach et yadecha ר"ת פּאי וֹס"ת וֹחֲתֵר עֵם ג' אוֹתֵיוֹת = דִיקַרֵנוֹסֵא

ובֵאַתֵבֵ"ע הוּא סאל, פּאי, אמןֵ, יְאַהֹדֹנֹהֹי ; וֹעוֹד יֵכֵויןֵ עֵם וֹחֲתֵר בֵעֵילוֹב יהוה – יָוֹזְהָתֻוֹכָה

אַלֵף לַמֵד הֵי יוֹד מֵם אַלֵף לַמֵד הֵי יוֹד מֵם מֵווֹחֵיןֵ דֹפֵנֵים דֹאַווֹר אֱלֹהֵים אֱלֹהֵים

לֵהַבֵעֵיר פֵ"ו אוֹרוֹת לֵכֵל מֵילוֹי דֹכֵל

	וֹזֵתֵר	
אוֹווֹר דֹפֵרֵצוֹפֵי נֹהֵ"י וֹזֵגֵ"ת		וֹאוֹווֹר דֹפֵרֵצוֹפֵי נֹהֵ"י וֹזֵגֵ"ת
דֹפֵרֵצוֹף וֹזֵ"ת דֹיֵצֵירֵה דֹ"א		דֹיֵצֵירֵה דֹרוֹזֵל הֹנֹקֵרֵאַת לֵאַה
לֵף מֵד י וֹד ם		לֵף מֵד י וֹד ם
אַלֵף לַמֵד הֵי יוֹד מֵם	סָאל יְאַהֹדֹנֹהֹי	אַלֵף לַמֵד הֵי יוֹד מֵם

וּמַשְׂבִּיעַ umasbi'a וֹחֲתֵר עֵם ג' אוֹתֵיוֹת = דִיקַרֵנוֹסֵא

ובֵא"ת בֵ"ע הוּא סאל, אמןֵ, יְאַהֹדֹנֹהֹי ; וֹעוֹד יֵכֵויןֵ עֵם וֹחֲתֵר בֵעֵילוֹב יהוה – יָוֹזְהָתֻוֹכָה

אַלֵף לַמֵד הֵי יוֹד מֵם אַלֵף לַמֵד הֵי יוֹד מֵם מֵווֹחֵיןֵ דֹפֵנֵים דֹאַווֹר אֱלֹהֵים אֱלֹהֵים

לֵהַבֵעֵיר פֵ"ו אוֹרוֹת לֵכֵל מֵילוֹי דֹכֵל

	וֹזֵתֵר	
אוֹווֹר דֹפֵרֵצוֹפֵי נֹהֵ"י וֹזֵגֵ"ת		וֹאוֹווֹר דֹפֵרֵצוֹפֵי נֹהֵ"י וֹזֵגֵ"ת
דֹפֵרֵצוֹף נֹהֵ"י דֹיֵצֵירֵה דֹ"א		דֹיֵצֵירֵה דֹרוֹזֵל הֹנֹקֵרֵאַת לֵאַה
לֵף מֵד י וֹד ם		לֵף מֵד י וֹד ם
אַלֵף לַמֵד הֵי יוֹד מֵם		אַלֵף לַמֵד הֵי יוֹד מֵם

לְכָל lechol יה אֲדֹנֵי (לֵהַבֵעֵיר מֵווֹחֵיןֵ דֹ-יֵה אַל הֹנוֹקֹבֵא שֵהֵיא אֲדֹנֵי)

חַי chai כֵל וֹזֵי = אהֵיה אהֵיה יהוה, בֵינֵה ע"ה, וֹזֵיים

רָצוֹן ratzon מֵהֵע ע"ה, ע"ב בֵרֵיבוֹע וֹקֹסֵ"א ע"ה, אַל שֵדֵי ע"ה ; ר"ת רוֹזֵל שֵהֵיא הֹמֵלֵכוֹת הֹצֵרֵיכֵה לֵשֵפֵע

יוֹד הֵי יוֹד הֵי וֵיו יוֹד הֵי וֵיו הֵי יֵסוֹד דֹאַבֵא

אַלֵף הֵי יוֹד הֵי יֵסוֹד דֹאֵימֵא

לֵהַמֵתֵיק רוֹזֵל ובֵ' רֵמֵעֵיןֵ שֹׂךְ פַּר

We should also meditate to draw abundance and sustenance and blessing to all the worlds from the *ratzon* mentioned above. We should meditate and focus on this verse because it is the essence of prosperity, and meditate that God is intervening and sustaining and supporting all of Creation.

POTE'ACH ET YADECHA

פ	*Open*	*Your*	*Hands*	*and*	*satisfy*	*every*	*living*	*thing*	*with*	*desire.*

צַדִּיק tzadik יְהוָאדֹנָי-אֱלֹהִים-אֲדֹנָי Adonai (Yesod) בְּכֹל bechol ב"ן, לכב

דְּרָכָיו derachav וְחָסִיד vechasid בְּכֹל bechol ב"ן, לכב בְּמַעֲשָׂיו ma'asav יבמ, ב"ן:

קָרוֹב karov יְהוָאדֹנָי-אֱלֹהִים-אֲדֹנָי Adonai (Malchut) לְכֹל lechol יה אֲדֹנָי

קֹרְאָיו kor'av לְכֹל lechol יה אֲדֹנָי אֲשֶׁר asher

יִקְרָאֻהוּ yikra'uhu בֶאֱמֶת ve'emet אהיה פעמים אהיה, ז"פ ס"ג:

רָצוֹן retzon מהטי ע"ה, ע"ב ברִיבוע וקס"א ע"ה, אל שדי ע"ה, יְרֵאָיו yere'av יַעֲשֶׂה ya'ase

וְאֶת ve'et שַׁוְעָתָם shav'atam יִשְׁמַע yishma ר"ת רי וְיוֹשִׁיעֵם veyoshi'em:

שׁוֹמֵר shomer כ"א הויות שובתפילין Adonai יְהוָאדֹנָי-אֱלֹהִים-אֲדֹנָי (Netzach)

אֶת et כֹּל kol ילי ohavav אֹהֲבָיו ר"ת אכא

וְאֵת ve'et כֹּל kol ילי haresha'im הָרְשָׁעִים יַשְׁמִיד yashmid:

תְּהִלַּת tehilat יְהוָאדֹנָי-אֱלֹהִים-אֲדֹנָי Adonai (Hod) יְדַבֶּר yedaber ראה פִּי pi

וִיבָרֵךְ vivarech ע"ב ס"ג מ"ה ב"ן, הברכה (למתק את ז' המלכים שמתו) כֹּל kol ילי

בָּשָׂר basar שֵׁם shem kodsho קָדְשׁוֹ רִיבוע ס"ג ו"י אותיות דס"ג לְעוֹלָם le'olam

וַאֲנַחְנוּ va'anachnu נְבָרֵךְ nevarech יָהּ Yah מֵעַתָּה me'ata וָעֶד va'ed:

וְעַד ve'ad עוֹלָם olam הַלְלוּיָהּ haleluya אלהים, אהיה אדני ; ללה:

צ *The Lord is righteous in all His ways and virtuous in all His deeds.*

ק *The Lord is close to all who call Him, and only to those who call Him truthfully.*

ר *He shall fulfill the will of those who fear Him; He hears their wailing and saves them.*

שׁ *The Lord protects all who love Him and He destroys the wicked.*

ת *My lips utter the praise of the Lord and all flesh shall bless His Holy Name, forever and for eternity."*

(Psalms 145) "And we shall bless the Lord forever and for eternity. Praise the Lord!" (Psalms 115:18)

ר"ת הפסוק = נפעל רווז נטעמה וזיה יוזידה ע"ה

ס"ג מ"ה ב"ן lefanecha לְפָנֶיךָ אדני פעמים י"א ketoret קְטֹרֶת tefilati תְפִלָתִי tikon תִכּוֹן

hakshiva הַקְשִׁיבָה :arev עֶרֶב minchat־ מִנְחַת kapai כַּפַּי mas'at מַשְׂאַת

ילה ; דמ"ב ,ע"ב מילוי ; לכב velohai וֵאלֹהַי malki מַלְכִּי shave'i שַׁוְעִי lekol לְקוֹל

:etpalal אֶתְפַּלָל elecha אֵלֶיךָ ki כִּי

HALF KADDISH

ו"ה כמנין אותיות י"א ; עדי ומילוי עדי veyitkadash וְיִתְקַדַשׁ yitgadal יִתְגַדַל

אדני, יהוה אלהים יהוה ,ב"ן קנ"א raba רַבָּא (דע"ב י"ה שֵׁם) shemei שְׁמֵיהּ

אידהנויה. amen אָמֵן :יב"ק ג"פ = ס"ת ; אלהים ו"פ = ר"ת ; ע"ה וע"ב ברבוע מ"ה ,וס"ג קס"א מילוי

kir'utei כִרְעוּתֵיהּ vera בְרָא di דִי be'alma בְעָלְמָא

veyatzmach וְיַצְמַח malchutei מַלְכוּתֵיהּ veyamlich וְיַמְלִיךְ

אידהנויה. amen אָמֵן :meshichei מְשִׁיחֵיהּ vikarev וִיקָרֵב purkanei פוּרְקָנֵיהּ

uvchayei וּבְחַיֵי uvyomechon וּבְיוֹמֵיכוֹן bechayechon בְחַיֵיכוֹן

ba'agala בַּעֲגָלָא Yisrael יִשְׂרָאֵל בּ"פ bet בֵּית יל dechol דְכָל

אידהנויה. amen אָמֵן :amen אָמֵן ve'imru וְאִמְרוּ kariv קָרִיב uvizman וּבִזְמַן

The congregation and the *chazan* say the following:

Twenty eight words (until *be'alma*), meditate: (יוד ויו דלת הי יוד ויו יוד ויו הי יוד) דע"ב דמילוי מילוי
Twenty eight letters (until *almaya*), meditate: (יוד ויו דלת הי יוד ויו יוד ויו הי יוד) דע"ב דמילוי מילוי

ב"ן, קנ"א raba רַבָּא (דס"ג י"ה שֵׁם) shemei שְׁמֵיהּ yehe יְהֵא

mevarach מְבָרֵךְ ע"ה וע"ב ברבוע מ"ה ,וס"ג קס"א מילוי ,אדני יהוה אלהים יהוה

yitbarach יִתְבָּרֵךְ almaya עָלְמַיָא le'almei לְעָלְמֵי le'alam לְעָלַם

"Let my prayer be set before You
as the incense offering, the lifting up of my hand as the afternoon meal offering." (Psalms 141:2)
"Listen to the sound of my outcry, my King, My God for it is to You I am praying." (Psalms 5:3)

HALF KADDISH
May His great Name be more exalted and sanctified. (Amen)
In the world that He created according to His will, and may His kingdom reign.
And may He cause His redemption to sprout and may He bring the Mashiach closer. (Amen) In your
lifetimes and in your days and in the lifetime of all the House of Israel, speedily and in the near future,
and you should say, Amen. (Amen) May His great Name be blessed forever and for all eternity blessed

Seven words with six letters each (שם בן מ"ב) meditate:

יהוה ـ יוד הי ויו הי ـ מילוי דמילוי דע"ב (יוד ויו דלת הי יוד הי ויו יוד הי הי יוד)

Also, seven times the letter *Vav* (שם בן מ"ב) meditate:

יהוה ـ יוד הי ויו הי ـ מילוי דמילוי דע"ב (יוד ויו דלת הי יוד הי ויו יוד הי הי יוד).

veyishtabach וְיִשְׁתַּבַּח ע"ב יהוה אל אבג יתץ

veyitpa'ar וְיִתְפָּאַר הי גו יה קרע שטן ـ veyitromam וְיִתְרֹמֵם וה כוזו נגד יכש

veyitnase וְיִתְנַשֵּׂא במוכסז בטר צתג ـ veyit'hadar וְיִתְהַדָּר כוזו יה וזקב טנע

veyit'ale וְיִתְעֲלֶה וה יוד ה יגל פזק ـ veyit'halal וְיִתְהַלָּל א ואו הא שקו צית

shemei שְׁמֵיהּ (שם י"ה דמ"ה) dekudsha דְּקוּדְשָׁא berich בְּרִיךְ hu הוּא:

amen אָמֵן אידהנויה

le'ela לְעֵלָּא min מִן kol כָּל ילי birchata בִּרְכָתָא shirata שִׁירָתָא

tishbechata תֻּשְׁבְּחָתָא venechamata וְנֶחֱמָתָא da'amiran דַּאֲמִירָן

be'alma בְּעָלְמָא ve'imru וְאִמְרוּ amen אָמֵן: amen אָמֵן אידהנויה.

THE AMIDAH

When we begin the connection, we take three steps backward, signifying our leaving this physical world. Then we take three steps forward to begin the *Amidah*. The three steps are:

1. Stepping into the land of Israel – to enter the first spiritual circle.
2. Stepping into the city of Jerusalem – to enter the second spiritual circle.
3. Stepping inside the Holy of Holies – to enter the innermost circle.

Before we recite the first verse of the *Amidah*, we ask: "*God, open my lips and let my mouth speak,*" thereby asking the Light to speak for us so that we can receive what we need and not just what we want. All too often, what we want from life is not necessarily the desire of the soul, which is what we actually need to fulfill us. By asking the Light to speak through us, we ensure that our connection will bring us genuine fulfillment and opportunities for spiritual growth and change.

---

and lauded, and glorified and exalted, And extolled and honored,
and uplifted and praised, be the Name of the Holy Blessed One. (Amen) Above all blessings,
songs, praises, and words of consolation that may be said in the world, and you shall say, Amen. (Amen)

> **When the Eve of the Holiday falls on the Eve of *Shabbat*:**
> You should meditate to elevate *Nefesh* of *Asiyah* by the Name: (ב"ן) יוד הה וו הה,
> and then to the *Ruach* of the world of *Yetzirah* by the Name: (מ"ה) יוד הא ואו הא,
> and then to the *Neshamah* of *Beriah* by the Name: (ס"ג) יוד הי ואו הי,
> and then to elevate all the above mentioned to *Nefesh* of *Atzilut*: (ע"ב) יוד הי ויו הי.

yagid יַגִּיד ufi וּפִי tiftach תִּפְתָּח sefatai שְׂפָתַי (pause here) ללה Adonai אֲדֹנָי

יןן (כ"ב אותיות פשוטות [=אכא] וה' אותיות סופיות סזזץ) tehilatecha תְּהִלָּתֶךָ ס"ת = בוכו:

THE FIRST BLESSING - INVOKES THE SHIELD OF ABRAHAM.

Abraham is the channel of the Right Column energy of positivity, sharing, and mercy. Sharing actions can protect us from all forms of negativity.

Chesed that becomes *Chochmah*

In this section there are 42 words, the secret of the 42-Letter Name of God and therefore it begins with the letter *Bet* (2) and ends with the letter *Mem* (40).

Bend your knees at "*baruch*," bow at "*Ata*" and straighten up at "*Adonai*."

ב   א

(אותיות הא"ב המסמלות את העשפע המגיע) לה' המלכות   א–ת   Ata אַתָּה baruch בָּרוּךְ

> **When the Eve of the Holiday falls on the Eve of *Shabbat*:**
> While **bending** you should meditate on the Name: אלף הי יוד הי in order to lower
> the *Neshamah* of the world of *Atzilut* to be as *Mayin Nukvin* in order to elevate the *Shechinah*.
> And while **straightening up** you should meditate on the Name: יוד הי ויו הי to elevate the
> *Shechinah* and to prepare the World of *Atzilut* to be able to receive the World of *Beriah*.

ילה   Elohenu אֱלֹהֵינוּ   (יא)   Adonai אדנויאהדונהי יְהֹוָה

♦avotenu אֲבוֹתֵינוּ   ;   ילה ;   דמב   ע"ב,   מילוי   ;   לכב   velohei וֵאלֹהֵי

(*Chochmah*) Avraham אַבְרָהָם   ;   ילה ;   דמב   ע"ב,   מילוי   Elohei אֱלֹהֵי

וז'פ אל, רי"ו ול"ב נתיבות הוכמה רמ"ח (אברים), עסמ"ב וט"ז אותיות פשוטות

THE AMIDAH
"My Lord, open my lips, and my mouth shall relate Your praise." (Psalms 51:17)
THE FIRST BLESSING
Blessed are You, Lord,
our God and God of our forefathers: the God of Abraham,

ד״פ ב״ן   (*Binah*)   Yitzchak   יִצְחָק ; ילה ; דמב , ע״ב מילוי   Elohei   אֱלֹהֵי

הֲוַיּוֹת, יאהדונהי אידהנויה ׳ו (*Da'at*)   Yaakov   יַעֲקֹב ; ילה ; דמב , ע״ב מילוי ; לכב   velohei   וֵאלֹהֵי

גדול = להו ; סיט = הגדול האל   hagadol   הַגָּדוֹל דס״ג) (מילוי יא״י ; לאה   haEl   הָאֵל

•vehanora   וְהַנּוֹרָא   hagibor   הַגִּבּוֹר ההה ר״ת   אום ,יזל , מבה = אותיות ד עם

•elyon   עֶלְיוֹן   יהוה ריבוע ע״ב ר״ת ; דס״ג) (מילוי יא״י   El   אֵל

ילי   hakol   הַכֹּל   kone   קוֹנֵה   •tovim   טוֹבִים   chasadim   וַחֲסָדִים   gomel   גּוֹמֵל

umevi   וּמֵבִיא   •avot   אָבוֹת   chasdei   וְזֹכֵר   vezocher   וְזוֹכֵר

lema'an   לְמַעַן   venehem   בְנֵיהֶם   livnei   לִבְנֵי   go'el   גּוֹאֵל

אוֹז, דאגה: be'ahava   בְּאַהֲבָה אל שדי ע״ה ע״ה, וקס״א ברביעו ע״ב מהע ע״ה,   shemo   שְׁמוֹ

When saying the word *"be'ahava"* you should meditate to devote your soul to sanctify the Holy Name and accept upon yourself the four forms of death.

umagen   וּמָגֵן   umoshi'a   וּמוֹשִׁיעַ   ozer   עוֹזֵר   melech   מֶלֶךְ

ג״פ אל (יא״י מילוי דס״ג) ; ר״ת מיכאל גבריאל נוריאל:

---

the God of Isaac, and the God of Jacob. The great, mighty and Awesome God.
The Supernal God, Who bestows beneficial kindness and creates everything.
Who recalls the kindness of the forefathers and brings a Redeemer to their descendants
for the sake of His Name, lovingly. King, Helper, Savior and Shield.

Bend your knees at "baruch," bow at "Ata" and straighten up at "Adonai."

 י
ק
Ata אַתָּה baruch בָּרוּךְ

When the Eve of the Holiday falls on the Eve of *Shabbat*:

While bending your knees you should meditate: אלף הי יוד הי in order to lower the *Neshamah* of *Beriah* to be as *Mayin Nukvin* in order to elevate the *Shechinah*. And **while straightening up** you should meditate: יוד הי ואו הי to elevate the *Shechinah* and to prepare the World of *Beriah* to be elevated to *Atzilut* and to be able to receive *Yetzirah*.

צ
(הוד) Adonai יאהדונהי(יְהֹוָאהדונהי)יְהֹוָה

ת
Avraham אַבְרָהָם גּוּריאל גַבריאל בּמיכאל ר״ת ; (דס״ג מילוי יי״א) אל ג״פ magen בְּמָגֵן

י

פשוטות אותיות וט״ז (אברים), עסמ״ב רמ״ז הַחוכמה, נתיבות ול״ב רי״ו אל, וז״פ

THE SECOND BLESSING
THE ENERGY OF ISAAC IGNITES THE POWER FOR THE RESURRECTION OF THE DEAD.

Whereas Abraham represents the power of sharing, Isaac represents the Left Column energy of Judgment. Judgment shortens the *tikkun* process and paves the way for our eventual resurrection.

Gevurah that becomes *Binah*.
In this section there are 49 words corresponding to the 49 Gates of the Pure System in *Binah*.

לללה Adonai אֲדֹנָי אותיות דס״ג וי׳ ס״ג ריבוע le'olam לְעוֹלָם gibor גִּבּוֹר Ata אַתָּה

(בוכו). אלד, ע״ה אויביו. על מתגבר יהודה היה ובו ואמיץ, גדול עם והוא אַגְלָא ר״ת)

lehoshi'a לְהוֹשִׁיעַ rav רַב Ata אַתָּה metim מֵתִים מְחַיֶּה ס״ג mechaye מְחַיֶּה

מ״ה ר״ת ; עסמ״ב דמילוי אותיות מספר כוזו, ואו, הא יוד hatal הַטַּל morid מוֹרִיד

If you mistakenly say *"Mashiv haru'ach,"* and realize this before the end of the blessing *"baruch Ata Adonai,"* you should return to the beginning of the blessing *"Ata gibor"* and continue as usual. But if you only realize this after the end of the blessing, you should start the *Amidah* from the beginning.

Blessed are You, Lord, the Shield of Abraham.
THE SECOND BLESSING
You are mighty forever, Lord.
You resurrect the dead and are very capable of redeeming.
Who causes dew to fall.

bechesed בְּחֶסֶד אהיה אהיה יהוה, בינה ע״ה chayim וְזָיִּים mechalkel מְכַלְכֵּל

berachamim בְּרַחֲמִים metim מֵתִים ס״ג mechaye מְחַיֶּה ◆ ע״ב, ריבוע יהוה.

somech סוֹמֵךְ ◆ (טלא דעתיק) rabim רַבִּים (במוכסז) מצפ״צ, אלהים דההין, י״פ יהוה

cholim חוֹלִים verofe וְרוֹפֵא (זו״ן) ◆ noflim נוֹפְלִים (אכדטם) כוזו, ריבוע אדני

umekayem וּמְקַיֵּם ◆ asurim אֲסוּרִים umatir וּמַתִּיר ◆ וזולה = מ״ה וד׳ אותיות.

chamocha כָמוֹךָ יכי mi מִי ◆ afar עָפָר lishenei לִישֵׁנֵי emunato אֱמוּנָתוֹ

gevurot גְּבוּרוֹת ba'al בַּעַל (you should enunciate the letter Ayin in the word "ba'al")

memit מֵמִית melech מֶלֶךְ ◆ lach לָךְ dome דּוֹמֶה יכי umi וּמִי

umchaye וּמְחַיֶּה ס״ג (יוד הי ואו הי) umatzmi'ach וּמַצְמִיחַ yeshu'a יְשׁוּעָה:

vene'eman וְנֶאֱמָן Ata אַתָּה lehachayot לְהַחֲיוֹת metim מֵתִים:

baruch בָּרוּךְ Ata אַתָּה יְהוָה(אַהדֹהֱ)(יֱהוֹאַהֵֹ)יאהדונהי Adonai

mechaye מְחַיֶּה ס״ג (יוד הי ואו הי) hametim הַמֵּתִים: ר״ת מ״ה וס״ת מ״ה:

You sustain life with kindness and resurrect the dead with great compassion.
You support those who have fallen, heal the sick, release the imprisoned, and fulfill Your faithful words to those who are asleep in the dust. Who is like You, Master of might, and Who can compare to You, King, Who causes death, Who gives life, and Who sprouts salvation? And You are faithful to resurrecting the dead. Blessed are You, Lord, Who resurrects the dead.

Saying the *Kedusha* (Holiness) we meditate to bring the Holiness of the Creator among us. As it says: *"Venikdashti betoch Benei Israel"* (God is hallowed among the children of Israel).

On *Shacharit* of *Chol Hamo'ed* You should meditate on the letters *Gimel* ג and *Yud* י from the Name: אבגיתץ (the initials of the first verse of the *Ana Beko'ach*), which helps spiritual remembering.

On *Minchah* You should meditate on the letters *Alef* א and *Bet* ב from the Name: אבגיתץ (the initials of the first verse of the *Ana Beko'ach*), which helps spiritual remembering.

נַקְדִּישָׁךְ nakdishach וְנַעֲרִיצָךְ vena'aritzach

כְּנֹעַם keno'am שִׂיחַ si'ach סוֹד sod האא י"פ מיכ, עֲרְפֵי sarfei

קֹדֶשׁ kodesh הַמְשַׁלְּשִׁים hameshaleshim לְךָ lecha קְדֻשָּׁה kedusha

וְכֵן vechen כָּתוּב katuv עַל al יַד yad נְבִיאָךְ nevi'ach וְקָרָא vekara

זֶה ze אֶל el זֶה ze י"ב פרקין דיעקב מאירים לי"ב פרקין דרחל וְאָמַר ve'amar

קָדוֹשׁ kadosh | קָדוֹשׁ kadosh קָדוֹשׁ kadosh (סוד ג' רישין דעתיקא קדישא)

יְהֹוָהאדנ"י Adonai צְבָאוֹת Tzeva'ot פני שכינה מָלֹא melo כָּל chol כל

הָאָרֶץ ha'aretz אלהים ההין ע"ה כְּבוֹדוֹ kevodo

וְאוֹמְרִים ve'omrim מְשַׁבְּחִים meshabechim לְעֻמָּתָם le'umatam

(או"א) בָּרוּךְ baruch כְּבוֹד kevod יְהֹוָהאדנ"י Adonai ; כבוד ה' = יוד הי ואו הה

בִּמְקוֹמוֹ mimekomo עסמ"ב, הברכה (למתק את ז' המלכים שמתו) ;ר"ת ע"ב, ריבוע יהוה ;ר"ת מיכ:

וּבְדִבְרֵי uvdivrei קָדְשָׁךְ kodshach כָּתוּב katuv לֵאמֹר lemor:

(וו"ן) יִמְלֹךְ yimloch קדוש ברוך ימלך ר"ת יב"ק, אלהים יהוה, אהיה אדנ"י יהוה

יְהֹוָהאדנ"י Adonai לְעוֹלָם le'olam ריבוע ס"ג ו"י אותיות דס"ג אֱלֹהַיִךְ Elohayich ילה

צִיּוֹן Tziyon יוסף, ו' הויות, קנאה לְדֹר ledor וָדֹר vador רי"ו ;ר"ת אצלו (מלכות אצל ז"א – ו)

הַלְלוּיָהּ haleluya אלהים, אהיה אדנ"י ; ללה:

NAKDISHACH

We sanctify You and we revere You,
*according to the pleasant words of the counsel of the Holy Angels, who recite Holy before You three times,
as it is written by Your Prophet: "And each called to the other and said: Holy, Holy, Holy, Is the Lord of Hosts,
the entire world is filled with His glory." (Isaiah 6:3) Facing them they give praise and say:
"Blessed is the glory of the Lord from His Place." (Ezekiel 3:12) And in Your Holy Words, it is written as follows:
"The Lord, your God, shall reign forever, for each and for every generation. Zion, Praise the Lord!" (Psalms 146:10)*

THE THIRD BLESSING

This blessing connects us to Jacob, the Central Column and the power of restriction. Jacob is our channel for connecting Mercy with Judgment. By restricting our reactive behavior, we are blocking our Desire to Receive for the Self Alone. Jacob also gives us the power to balance our acts of Mercy and Judgment toward other people in our lives.

Tiferet **that becomes** *Da'at* (14 words).

אַתָּה Ata קָדוֹשׁ kadosh וְשִׁמְךָ veshimcha קָדוֹשׁ kadosh ר"ת = אוּר, רו, אֵין סוף◆

וּקְדוֹשִׁים ukdoshim בְּכָל bechol ב"ן, לכב ע"ה נגד, מזבוח, זן, אל יהוה יוֹם yom

יְהַלְלוּךָ yehalelucha סֶלָה sela◆

בָּרוּךְ baruch אַתָּה Ata יְהֹוָ(אדני)(יהוה)(אדני)יאהדונהי Adonai

הָאֵל haEl לאה ; יי"א (מילוי דס"ג) ע"ה הַקָּדוֹשׁ hakadosh י"פ מ"ה (יוד הא ואו הא)◆

Meditate here on the Name: יאהדונהי, as it can help to remove anger.

THIRTEEN MIDDLE BLESSINGS

There are thirteen blessings in the middle of the *Amidah* that connect us to the Thirteen Attributes.

THE FIRST (FOURTH) BLESSING

This blessing helps us transform information into knowledge by helping us internalize everything that we learn.

Chochmah

In this blessing there are 17 words, the same numerical value as the word *tov* (good) in the secret of *Etz HaDa'at Tov vaRa*, (Tree of Knowledge Good and Evil), where we connect only to the *Tov*.

אַתָּה Ata חוֹנֵן chonen לְאָדָם le'adam מ"ה דַּעַת da'at◆

וּמְלַמֵּד umlamed לֶאֱנוֹשׁ le'enosh בִּינָה bina ע"ה אהיה אהיה יהוה, וחיים◆

וְוָגֵּנוּ vechonenu מֵאִתְּךָ me'itecha וְחָכְמָה chochma במילוי = תרי"ג (מצוות)

בִּינָה bina ע"ה אהיה אהיה יהוה, וחיים וָדַעַת vada'at ר"ת וחבו◆

בָּרוּךְ baruch אַתָּה Ata יְהֹוָ(אדני)(יהוה)יאהדונהי Adonai חוֹנֵן chonen הַדַּעַת hada'at◆

THE THIRD BLESSING

You are Holy, and Your Name is Holy, and the Holy Ones praise You every day, for you are God, the Holy King Selah. Blessed are You, Lord, the Holy God

THIRTEEN MIDDLE BLESSINGS - THE FIRST (FOURTH) BLESSING

You graciously grant knowledge to man and understanding to humanity. Graciously grant us, from Yourself, wisdom, understanding, and knowledge. Blessed are You, Lord, Who graciously grants knowledge.

THE SECOND (FIFTH) BLESSING

This blessing keeps us in the Light. Everyone at one time or another succumbs to the doubt and uncertainty that the Satan constantly implants in us. If we make the unfortunate mistake of stepping back and falling away from the Light, we do not want the Creator to mirror our actions and step away from us. Instead, we want Him to catch us. In the box below there are certain lines that we can recite and meditate on for others who may be stepping back. The war against the Satan is the oldest war known to man. And the only way to defeat the Satan is to unite, share, help and pray for each other.

Binah

In this blessing there are 15 words, as the powerful action of *teshuva* (repentance) raises 15 levels on the way to *Kise haKavod* (the Throne of Honor). It goes through seven *Reki'im* (Firmaments), seven *Avirim* (Air), and another Firmament on top of the Holy Animals (together this adds up to 15). Also, there are 15 words in the two main verses of Isaiah the Prophet and King David that speak of *teshuva* (*Isaiah 55:7; Psalms 32:5*). The number 15 is also the secret of the Name: יה.

◆(יְהֹוּ אֲדֹנָי אהדונהי – וֹסד שובה) letoratecha לְתוֹרָתֶךָ avinu אָבִינוּ hashivenu הֲשִׁיבֵנוּ◆

◆la'avodatecha לַעֲבוֹדָתֶךָ malkenu מַלְכֵּנוּ vekarvenu וְקָרְבֵנוּ

shelema שְׁלֵמָה bitshuva בִּתְשׁוּבָה vehachazirenu וְהַחֲזִירֵנוּ

lefanecha לְפָנֶיךָ ס"ג מ"ה ב"ן:

If you want to pray for another and help them in their spiritual process say:

ע"ה עוֹדִי אַל ע"ה, וּקס"א ברִיבוֹעַ ע"ב, ע"ה מהֹשֵׁי ratzon רָצוֹן yehi יְהִי

ילה; דמב ע"ב, מ"ה ב"ן מילוי יְהֹוּ אֲדֹנָי אהדונהי ס"ג מ"ה ב"ן Elohai אֱלֹהַי Adonai milfanecha מִלְפָנֶיךָ

shetachtor שֶׁתַּחְתוֹר avotai אֲבוֹתַי דמב, ; לכב מילוי ע"ב, ילה velohei וֵאלֹהֵי

utkabel וּתְקַבֵּל kevodecha כְּבוֹדֶךָ kise כִּסֵא mitachat מִתַּחַת chatira חֲתִירָה וְתִירָה

yemincha יְמִינְךָ ki כִּי (*the person's name and his/her father's name*) et אֶת bitshuva בִּתְשׁוּבָה

◆shavim שָׁבִים lekabel לְקַבֵּל peshuta פְּשׁוּטָה Adonai יְהֹוּ אֲדֹנָי אהדונהי

Adonai יְהֹוּ אֲדֹנָי אהדונהי Ata אַתָּה baruch בָּרוּךְ

bitshuva בִּתְשׁוּבָה: harotze הָרוֹצֶה

THE SECOND (FIFTH) BLESSING

Bring us back, our Father, to Your Torah,
and bring us close, our King, to Your service, and cause us to return with perfect repentance before You.

May it be pleasing before You, Lord, my God and God of my forefathers, that You shall dig deep beneath the Throne of Your Glory and accept as repentant (the person's name and his/her father's name) *because Your Right Hand, Lord, extends outwards to receive those who repent.*

Blessed are You, Lord, Who desires repentance.

THE THIRD (SIXTH) BLESSING

This blessing helps us achieve true forgiveness. We have the power to cleanse ourselves of our negative behavior and hurtful actions toward others through forgiveness. This blessing does not mean we plead for forgiveness and our slate is wiped clean. Forgiveness refers to the methodologies for washing away the residue that comes from our iniquities. There are two ways to wash away the residue: physical and spiritual. We collect physical residue when we are in denial of our misdeeds and the laws of cause and effect. We cleanse ourselves when we experience any kind of pain, whether it is financial, emotional, or physical. If we choose to cleanse spiritually, we forgo the physical cleansing. We do so by arousing the pain in ourselves that we caused to others. We feel the other person; and with a truthful heart, recite this prayer experiencing the hurt and heartache we inflicted on others. This form of spiritual cleansing prevents us from having to cleanse physically.

Chesed

In this blessing there are 21 words which is the numerical value of the Holy Name: אהיה.

(ר"ת סאל, אבן (יאהדונהי) avinu אָבִינוּ אהיה אדני אלהים, lanu לָנוּ יהוה ע"ב selach סְלַח

= מחול לנו ע"ה ; אלהים, אהיה אדני lanu לָנוּ mechol מָחוֹל ◆chatanu וְטָאנוּ ki כִּי

קס"א ו"י אותיות El אֵל ki כִּי ◆fashanu פָּשַׁעְנוּ ki כִּי malkenu מַלְכֵּנוּ

Ata אָתָּה baruch בָּרוּךְ Ata אָתָּה ע"ב יהוה vesalach וְסָלַח והו tov טוֹב

lislo'ach לִסְלוֹחַ hamarbe הַמַּרְבֶּה chanun וְחַנּוּן Adonai יאהדונהי

THE FOURTH (SEVENTH) BLESSING

This blessing helps us achieve redemption after we are spiritually cleansed.

Gevurah

(ר"ת רנ"ב (אברים באשה, כנגד הגבורה) ve'onyenu בְעָנְיֵנוּ na נָא ראה re'e רְאֵה

lega'olenu לְגָאֳלֵנוּ umaher וּמַהֵר ◆rivenu רִיבֵנוּ veriva וְרִיבָה

shemecha שְׁמֶךָ lema'an לְמַעַן shelema שְׁלֵמָה מ"ה ge'ula גְּאֻלָּה

Ata אָתָּה פהל chazak וְזָק go'el גּוֹאֵל (מילוי דס"ג יא"י El אֵל ki כִּי

Yisrael יִשְׂרָאֵל go'el גּוֹאֵל Adonai יהואדניאהדונהי Ata אָתָּה baruch בָּרוּךְ

THE FIFTH (EIGHTH) BLESSING

This blessing gives us the power to heal every part of our body. All healing originates from the Light of the Creator. Accepting and understanding this truth opens us to receive this Light. We should also think of sharing this healing energy with others.

THE THIRD (SIXTH) BBLESSING

Forgive us, our Father, for we have transgressed. Pardon us, our King, for we have sinned, because You are a good and forgiving God. Blessed are You, Lord, Who is gracious and forgives magnanimously.

THE FOURTH (SEVENTH) BLESSING

Behold our poverty and take up our fight; hurry to redeem us with a complete redemption for the sake of Your Name, because You are a powerful and a redeeming God. Blessed are You, Lord, Who redeems Israel.

Tiferet

רְפָאֵנוּ refa'enu יְהֹוָה Adonai וְנֵרָפֵא venerafe ר"ת רי"ו.

הוֹשִׁיעֵנוּ hoshi'enu וְנִוָּשֵׁעָה venivashe'a כִּי ki תְהִלָּתֵנוּ tehilatenu

אַתָּה Ata ר"ת = ב"פ רי"ו. וְהַעֲלֵה veha'ale אֲרוּכָה arucha וּמַרְפֵּא umarpe

לְכָל lechol יה אדני תַּחֲלוּאֵינוּ tachalu'enu וּלְכָל ulchol יה אדני

מַכְאוֹבֵינוּ mach'ovenu וּלְכָל ulchol יה אדני מַכּוֹתֵינוּ makotenu

---

To pray for healing for yourself and/or others add the following; and in the parentheses below, insert the names:

יְהִי yehi רָצוֹן ratzon מהש"ע ע"ה, ברבוע ע"ב, וקס"א ע"א אל שדי ע"ה

מִלְפָנֶיךָ milfanecha ס"ג מ"ה ב"ן יְהֹוָה Adonai אֱלֹהַי Elohai מילוי ע"ב, דמב ; ילה

וֵאלֹהֵי velohei ילה ; דמב ; מילוי ע"ב, לכב ; אֲבוֹתַי avotai שֶׁתְרַפֵּאֵנִי shetirpa'eni

(וְתְרַפֵּא vetirpa (insert the person's name) בֶּן ben (Women: בַּת bat) (insert their mother's name))

רְפוּאָה refu'a שְׁלֵמָה shelema רְפוּאַת refu'at הַנֶּפֶשׁ hanefesh

וּרְפוּאַת urfu'at הַגּוּף haguf, כְּדֵי kedei שֶׁאֶהְיֶה she'ehye וְזָק chazak פהל

(Women:) וְזָקָה chazaka (פהל) כֹּחַ ko'ach, בִּבְרִיאוּת bivri'ut, וְאָמִיץ ve'amitz

(Women:) וְאָמִיצַת (ve'amitzat) בְּמָאתַיִם bematayim וְאַרְבָּעִים ve'arba'im

וּשְׁמוֹנָה ushmona רמ"ח (אברים), אברהם, וז"ת אל, רי"ו ול"ב נתיבות החכמה, עסמ"ב וט"ז אותיות

(Women: וּשְׁנַיִם ushnayim) וַחֲמִשִּׁים vechamishim וּמָאתַיִם bematayim (Women:) פשוטות

אֵבָרִים evarim וּשְׁלֹשׁ ushlosh מֵאוֹת me'ot המספר = ש"י = אלהים דיודין

וְשִׁשִּׁים veshishim (י) וְשִׁבְעָה vachamisha גִּידִים gidim המספר = מילוי הע' שֶׁל shel

נִשְׁמָתִי nishmati וְגוּפִי vegufi, לְקִיּוּם lekiyum תּוֹרָתְךָ toratcha הַקְּדוֹשָׁה hakedosha.

כִּי ki אֵל El יא"י (מילוי דס"ג) רוֹפֵא rofe רַחֲמָן rachaman וְנֶאֱמָן vene'eman

:אַתָּה Ata בָּרוּךְ baruch אַתָּה Ata יְהֹוָה Adonai רוֹפֵא rofe

וְזוּלֵי cholei וזולה = מ"ה (יוד הא ואו הא) וד' אותיות וד' עַמּוֹ amo יִשְׂרָאֵל Yisrael

ר"ת רפ"וז (להעלות הניצוצות שנפלו לקליפה רמשם באים התחלואים):

THE FIFTH (EIGHTH) BLESSING

Heal us, Lord, and we shall heal. Save us and we shall be saved.
For You are our praise. Bring cure and healing to all our ailments, to all our pains, and to all our wounds.

May it be pleasing before You, Lord, my God and God of my forefathers, that You would heal me (and the person's name and their mother's name) completely with healing of the spirit and healing of the body, so that I shall be strong in health and vigorous in my strength in all 248 (a woman says: 252) organs and 365 sinews of my soul and my body, so that I shall be able to keep Your Holy Torah.

Because You are a healing,
compassionate, and trustworthy God, blessed are You, Lord, Who heals the sick of His People, Israel.

THE SIXTH (NINTH) BLESSING

This blessing draws sustenance and prosperity for the entire globe and provides us with personal sustenance. We would like all of our years to be filled with dew and rain, the sustaining lifeblood of our world.

Netzach

If you mistakenly say "*barech alenu*" instead of "*barchenu*," and realize this before the end of the *Amidah* ("*yihyu leratzon*" – the second one), then you should return and say "*barchenu*" and continue as usual. If you realize this later, you should start the *Amidah* from the beginning.

bechol בְּכָל ילה Elohenu אֱלֹהֵינוּ Adonai יְהֹוָה barchenu בָּרְכֵנוּ

shenatenu שְׁנָתֵנוּ uvarech וּבָרֵך ◆yadenu יָדֵינוּ ma'asei מַעֲשֵׂי ב"ן, לכב

betalelei בְּטַלְלֵי ratzon רָצוֹן מהע ע"ה, ע"ב בריבוע וקס"א ע"ה, אל שדי ע"ה

utehi וּתְהִי ◆ בינה (וע"ה אהיה אהיה יהוה, וזיים) undava וּנְדָבָה beracha בְּרָכָה

vesava וְשָׂבַע ע"ה בינה chayim וְחַיִּים acharita אַחֲרִיתָהּ

◆livracha לִבְרָכָה hatovot הַטּוֹבוֹת kashanim כַּשָּׁנִים veshalom וְשָׁלוֹם

To pray for sustenance for yourself and/or others add the following; and in the parentheses below, insert the names:

milfanecha מִלְּפָנֶיךָ ratzon רָצוֹן yehi יְהִי

velohei וֵאלֹהֵי Elohenu אֱלֹהֵינוּ Adonai יְהֹוָה

li לִי shetiten שֶׁתִּתֵּן avotenu אֲבוֹתֵינוּ

((insert their father's name) (bat בַּת :Women) ben בֶּן (insert the person's name) לְ vechen (וְכֵן)

hayom הַיּוֹם shulchani שׁוּלְחָנִי al עַל hasemuchim הַסְּמוּכִים ulchol וּלְכָל

velo וְלֹא bechavod בְּכָבוֹד umzonotehem וּמְזוֹנוֹתֵיהֶם mezonotai מְזוֹנוֹתַי uvchol וּבְכָל yom יוֹם

bizchut בִּזְכוּת be'isur בְּאִסּוּר velo וְלֹא beheter בְּהֶיתֵּר bevizui בְּבִזּוּי

hagadol הַגָּדוֹל shimcha שִׁמְךָ

דִּיקַרְנוֹסָא :Do not pronounce this name)

THE SIXTH (NINTH) BLESSING

During the summer:

Bless us, Lord, our God, in all our endeavors, and bless our years with the dews of good will, blessing, and benevolence. May its conclusion be life, contentment, and peace, as with other years for blessing,

May it be pleasing before You, Lord, my God and God of my forefathers, that You would provide for me and for my household, today and everyday, mine and their nourishment, with dignity and not with shame, in a permissible but not a forbidden manner, by virtue of Your great Name

lachem לָכֶם	vaharikoti וַהֲרִיקֹתִי	mipasuk מִפָּסוּק:	hayotze הַיּוֹצֵא
nesa נְסָה	umipasuk וּמִפָּסוּק:	dai דָּי	beli בְּלִי	ad עַד	beracha בְּרָכָה
Adonai יְהוָֹואדניהאהדונהי	panecha פָּנֶיךָ ס״ג מ״ה ב״ן, אין סוף רו, or אוֹר	alenu עָלֵינוּ
basar בָּשָׂר	matnot מַתְּנוֹת	lidei לִידֵי	tatzrichenu תַּצְרִיכֵנוּ	ve'al וְאַל
vadam וָדָם	ki כִּי	im אִם יוֹהֵך, מ״א אותיות אהיה בפשוטו ומילואו ומילוי דמילואו ע״ה	basar בָּשָׂר
miyadcha מִיָּדְךָ	hamele'a הַמְּלֵאָה	ume'otzar וּמֵאוֹצַר	matnat מַתְּנַת	chinam וְנָם
techalkelni תְּכַלְכְּלֵנִי	vetashpi'eni וְתַשְׁפִּיעֵנִי	amen אָמֵן יאהדונהי	sela סֶלָה.

El אֵל יא״י (במילוי דס״ג) tov טוֹב והו ki כִּי umetiv וּמֵטִיב

Ata אַתָּה umvarech וּמְבָרֵךְ hashanim הַשָּׁנִים: baruch בָּרוּךְ

Ata אַתָּה Adonai יְהוָֹואדניהאהדונהי mevarech מְבָרֵךְ hashanim הַשָּׁנִים:

THE SEVENTH (TENTH) BLESSING

This blessing gives us the power to positively influence all of humanity. Kabbalah teaches that each individual affects the whole. We affect the world, and the rest of the world affects us, even though we cannot perceive this relationship with our five senses. We call this relationship quantum consciousness.

Hod

teka תְּקַע ב״פ סוֹזֶף וי׳ אותיות = עם ד׳ אותיות beshofar בְּשׁוֹפָר gadol גָּדוֹל לְהוּ ; =

lecherutenu לְחֵרוּתֵנוּ מבה, יזל, אום מ״ה אדני vesa וְשָׂא nes נֵס lekabetz לְקַבֵּץ

galuyotenu גָּלֻיּוֹתֵינוּ vekabetzenu וְקַבְּצֵנוּ yachad יוֹד me'arba מֵאַרְבַּע

kanfot כַּנְפוֹת וּבוֹ (בסגולתו להוציא ניצוצות מן הקליפות) ויכוין וַזְבְּןֶ עם נקודותיו = ע״ב, ריבוע יהוה

ha'aretz הָאָרֶץ אלהים ההון ע״ה ; ר״ת = אדני le'artzenu לְאַרְצֵנוּ:

---

for You are a good
and a beneficent God and You bless the years. Blessed are You, Lord, Who blesses the years.

THE SEVENTH (TENTH) BLESSING

Blow a great Shofar for our freedom and
raise a banner to gather our exiles, and gather us speedily from all four corners of the Earth to our Land.

The following is recited throughout the entire year:

The following meditation helps us to release and redeem all the remaining sparks of Light we have lost through our irresponsible actions (especially sexual misconduct):

yehi יְהִי ratzon רָצוֹן מהע ע"ה, ע"ב בריבוע וקס"א ע"ה, אל שדי ע"ה milfanecha מִלְפָנֶיךָ

Adonai יהו‎אדנ‎יאהדונהי Elohai אֱלֹהַי מילוי ב"ן מ"ה ס"ג ; ילה דמב, ע"ב,

velohei וֵאלֹהֵי avotai אֲבוֹתַי ; ילה דמב, ע"ב מילוי לכב; shekol שֶׁכָל tipa טִיפָה ילי

vetipa וְטִיפָה shel שֶׁל keri קְרִי sheyatza שֶׁיָצָא mimeni מִמֶנִי levatala לְבַטָלָה tipa טִיפָה

umikol וּמִכָל ילי Yisrael יִשְׂרָאֵל bichlal בִּכְלָל uvifrat וּבִפְרָט shelo שֶׁלֹא

bimkom בִּמְקוֹם mitzva מִצְוָה בֵּין ben be'ones בְּאוֹנֶס בֵּין ben beratzon בְּרָצוֹן

bemezid בְּמֵזִיד, ben בֵּין beshogeg בְּשׁוֹגֵג בֵּין ben מהע ע"ה, ע"ב בריבוע וקס"א ע"ה, אל שדי ע"ה בֵּין

ben בֵּין begilgul בְּגִלְגוּל ze זֶה בֵּין ben בֵּין begilgul בְּגִלְגוּל behirhur בְּהִרְהוּר בֵּין ben acher אַחֵר, uven וּבֵין bema'ase בְּמַעֲשֶׂה,

venivla וְנִבְלַע bakelipot בַּקְלִיפוֹת, shetaki'a שֶׁתְּקִיעָא shetaki שֶׁתְּקִ hakelipot הַקְלִיפוֹת

hanitzotzot הַנִיצוֹצוֹת keri קְרִי shenivle'u שֶׁנִבְלְעוּ ba בָּה bizechut בִּזְכוּת

shimcha שִׁמְךָ hagadol הַגָדוֹל לְהוֹ ; עם ד' אותיות = מבה, יול, אום HaYotze הַיוֹצֵא hayotze

mipasuk מִפָסוּק: vayki'enu וַיְקִאֶנוּ ר"ת ותבו ו-ילי bala בָלַע ומב chayil חַיִל veyzil וָזִיל:

uvizechut וּבִזְכוּת mibitno מִבִטְנוֹ yorishenu יֹרִשֶׁנוּ El אֵל יא"י (מילוי דס"ג) ; ס"ת וול

shimcha שִׁמְךָ hagadol הַגָדוֹל לְהוֹ ; עם ד' אותיות = מבה, יול, אום יוֹ‎הַבֿוֹה

shetachazirem שֶׁתַּחֲזִירֵם limkom לִמְקוֹם kedusha קְדוּשָׁה

vehatov וְהַטוֹב be'enecha בְּעֵינֶיךָ יהו קס"א ע"ה ; ריבוע מ"ה ase עֲשֵׂה.

You should meditate to correct the thought that caused the loss of the sparks of Light. Also meditate on the Names that control our thoughts for each of the six days of the week as follows:

Sunday	יְהֹוָה	ועם: דמרגלא אהיה מן א טופטיה ואו זין ואו כף צבא עַל	*Beriah*
Monday	יְהֹוָה	ועם: דמרגלא אהיה מן ה טופטיה ואו זין ואו כף מגן עַל	*Yetzirah*
Tuesday	מצפץ	ועם: דמרגלא אהיה מן י טופטיה ואו זין ואו כף פוזד צוה	*Asiyah*
Wednesday	אל	ועם: דמרגלא יהו מן י טופטיה ואו זין ואו כף פוזד צוה	*Asiyah*
Thursday	אלהים	ועם: דמרגלא יהו מן ה טופטיה ואו זין ואו כף מגן עַל	*Yetzirah*
Friday	מצפץ	ועם: דמרגלא יהו מן ו טופטיה ואו זין ואו כף צבא עַל	*Beriah*

Each of these Names (עַל צבא, כף ואו זין ואו, טופטיה) adds up to 193, which is the same numerical value as the word *zokef* (raise). These Names raise the Holy Spark from the *Chitzoniyim*. Also, when you say the words *"mekabetz nidchei"* (in the continuation of the blessing), which adds up to 304 — the same numerical value of *Shin*, *Dalet* (demon), meditate to collect all the lost sparks and cancel out the power of the negative forces.

May it be pleasing before You, Lord, my God and God of my forefathers, that every single drop of keri that came out of me in vain, and from all of Israel in general, and especially not as a cause of precept, if it was coerced or willfully, with intention or without, by passing thought or by an action, in this lifetime or in previous, and it was swallowed by the klipa, that the klipa will vomit all the sparks of keri that was swolled by it, by virtue of Your great Name that comes from the verse:"He swallowed up wealth and vomited it out, and from his belly God will cast it." (Job 20:15), and by the virtue of Your great Name you will return them to the Holy Place, and do what is good in Your eyes.

בָּרוּךְ baruch אַתָּה Ata יְ‑הֹוָ‑ה אֲדֹנָי-אהדונהי Adonai ; יכוין וזבו בעילוב יהוה כזה: יְוֹהֶבוּוה

מְקַבֵּץ mekabetz ע"ב ס"ג מ"ה ב"ן, הַבְּרָכָה (למתק את ד' המלכים שמותו)

נִדְחֵי nidchei ע"ב, ריבוע יהוה עַמּוֹ amo וזבו עַמּוֹ יִשְׂרָאֵל: Yisrael

THE EIGHTH (ELEVENTH) BLESSING

This blessing helps us to balance Judgment with Mercy. As Mercy is time, we can use it to change ourselves before Judgment occurs.

Yesod

הָשִׁיבָה hashiva שׁוֹפְטֵינוּ shoftenu כְּבָרִאשׁוֹנָה kevarishona◆

וְיוֹעֲצֵינוּ veyo'atzenu כְּבַתְּחִלָּה kevatechila ר"ת עכ"ה (דינים זכרים עב'יסוד) ויהוה (הממותקם)◆

וְהָסֵר vehaser מִמֶּנּוּ mimenu יָגוֹן yagon (סמאל) וַאֲנָחָה va'anacha (לילית)◆

וּמְלוֹךְ umloch עָלֵינוּ aleinu מְהֵרָה mehera אַתָּה Ata

יְ‑הֹוָ‑ה אֲדֹנָי-אהדונהי Adonai לְבַדְּךָ levadcha◆ בְּחֶסֶד bechesed ע"ב, ריבוע יהוה

וּבְרַחֲמִים uvrachamim מצפצ, אלהים דיודין, י"פ יי' ; להמתיק ברוזמים דינ' צדק ומשפט

בְּצֶדֶק betzedek וּבְמִשְׁפָּט uvmishpat ע"ה = ה"פ אלהים: baruch בָּרוּךְ אַתָּה Ata

יוהווּאהדונהי-אהדונהי Adonai מֶלֶךְ melech אוֹהֵב ohev ממתיק דינ'

צְדָקָה tzedaka ע"ה ריבוע אלהים וּמִשְׁפָּט umishpat ע"ה ה"פ אלהים:

THE NINTH (TWELFTH) BLESSING

This blessing helps us remove all forms of negativity, whether it comes from people, situations or even the negative energy of the Angel of Death [(**do not pronounce these names**) *Sa-ma-el* (male aspect) and *Li-li-th* (female aspect), which are encoded here], by using the Holy Name: *Shadai* שׁדי, which is encoded mathematically into the last four words of this blessing and also appears inside a *Mezuzah* for the same purpose.

Blessed are You, Lord, Who gathers the displaced of His Nation, Israel.
THE EIGHTH (ELEVENTH) BLESSING
Restore our judges, as at first, and our mentors, as in the beginning. Remove from us sorrow and moaning. Reign over us soon, You alone, Lord, with kindness and compassion, with righteousness and justice. Blessed are You, Lord, the King Who loves righteousness and justice.

Keter

לַמִּינִים laminim וְלַמַּלְשִׁינִים velamalshinim אַל al תְּהִי tehi תִקְוָה tikva

וְכָל vechol הַזֵּדִים hazedim כְּרֶגַע kerega (ג"פ אלהים עם ט"ו אותיות פשוטות)

יֹאבֵדוּ yovedu◆ וְכָל vechol יכי וְכָל vechol אוֹיְבֶיךָ oyvecha (סמאל)

וְכָל vechol יכי שׂוֹנְאֶיךָ son'echa (לילית) מְהֵרָה mehera יִכָּרֵתוּ yikaretu◆

וּמַלְכוּת umalchut הָרִשְׁעָה harish'a מְהֵרָה mehera תְּעַקֵּר te'aker

וּתְשַׁבֵּר utshaber וּתְכַלֵּם utchalem וּתְכַנִּיעֵם vetachni'em בִּמְהֵרָה bimhera

בְיָמֵינוּ veyamenu◆ בָּרוּך baruch אַתָּה Ata יְהֹוָה(יְהֹוִה)(אֲדֹנָי)(אהדונהי) Adonai

שׁוֹבֵר shover אוֹיְבִים oyvim וּמַכְנִיעַ umachni'a זֵדִים zedim ר"ת = שדי◆

THE TENTH (THIRTEENTH) BLESSING

This blessing surrounds us with total positivity to help us always be at the right place at the right time. It also helps attract only positive people into our lives.

Yesod

עַל al הַצַּדִּיקִים hatzadikim צדיק יסוד עולם וְעַל ve'al הַחֲסִידִים hachasidim

וְעַל ve'al שְׁאֵרִית she'erit עַמְּךָ amecha בֵּית bet ב"פ ראה יִשְׂרָאֵל Yisrael◆

וְעַל ve'al פְּלֵיטַת peletat בֵּית bet ב"פ ראה סוֹפְרֵיהֶם sofrehem◆

וְעַל ve'al גֵּרֵי gerei הַצֶּדֶק hatzedek וְעָלֵינוּ ve'alenu◆ יֶהֱמוּ yehemu

נָא na רַחֲמֶיךָ rachamecha יְהֹוָה(אֲדֹנָי)(אהדונהי) Adonai אֱלֹהֵינוּ Elohenu יכה

וְתֵן veten שָׂכָר sachar י"פ ב"ן טוֹב tov והו לְכָל lechol יה אדני

הַבּוֹטְחִים habotchim בְּשִׁמְךָ beshimcha בָּאֱמֶת be'emet אהיה פעמים אהיה, ז"פ ס"ג◆

THE NINTH (TWELFTH) BLESSING

For the heretics and for the slanderers, let there be no hope.
Let all the wicked perish in an instant. And may all Your foes and all Your haters be speedily cut down.
And as for the evil government, may You quickly uproot and smash it, and may You destroy and humble it,
speedily in our days. Blessed are You, Lord, Who smashes foes and humbles the wicked.

THE TENTH (THIRTEENTH) BLESSING

On the righteous, on the pious, on the remnants of the House of Israel, on the remnants
of their writers' academies, on the righteous converts, and on us, may Your compassion be
stirred, Lord, our God. And give good reward to all those who truly trust in Your Name.

וְשִׂים vesim וְחֶלְקֵנוּ chelkenu עִמָּהֶם imahem וּלְעוֹלָם ul'olam רִיבוּעַ ס"ג וי' אותיות דס"ג

לֹא lo נֵבוֹשׁ nevosh כִּי ki בָּךְ vecha בָּטָחְנוּ batachnu◆

וְעַל ve'al וְחַסְדְּךָ chasdecha הַגָּדוֹל hagadol לְהוּ ; עם ד' אותיות = מבה, יזל, אום

בֶּאֱמֶת be'emet אהיה פעמים אהיה, אהיה, ז"פ ס"ג נִשְׁעָנּוּ nish'anenu:

בָּרוּךְ baruch אַתָּה Ata יְהוָואדניאהדונהי Adonai מִשְׁעָן mish'an

וּמִבְטָח umivtach לַצַּדִּיקִים latzadikim ר"ת ימול (כל מי שנימול נקרא צדיק):◆

THE ELEVENTH (FOURTEENTH) BLESSING

This blessing connects us to the power of Jerusalem, to the building of the Temple, and to the preparation for the *Mashiach*.

Hod

תִּשְׁכּוֹן tishkon בְּתוֹךְ betoch יְרוּשָׁלַיִם Yerushalayim עִירְךָ ircha

כַּאֲשֶׁר ka'asher דִּבַּרְתָּ dibarta ראה וְכִסֵּא vechise דָּוִד David

עַבְדְּךָ avdecha פוי, אל אדני מְהֵרָה mehera בְּתוֹכָהּ vetocha תָּכִין tachin

Meditate here that *Mashiach Ben Yosef* shall not be killed by the wicked *Armilos* (Do not pronounce).

וּבְנֵה uvne אוֹתָהּ ota בִּנְיַן binyan עוֹלָם olam בִּמְהֵרָה bimhera

בְּיָמֵינוּ veyamenu: בָּרוּךְ baruch אַתָּה Ata יְהוָואדניאהדונהי Adonai

בּוֹנֵה bone ס"ג יְרוּשָׁלַיִם Yerushalayim:

THE TWELFTH (FIFTEENTH) BLESSING

This blessing helps us achieve a personal state of *Mashiach* by transforming our reactive nature into becoming proactive. Just as there is a global *Mashiach*, each person has a personal *Mashiach* within. When enough people achieve their transformation, the way will be paved for the appearance of the global *Mashiach*.

---

and place our lot with them. And may we never be embarrassed, for it is in You that we place our trust; it is upon Your great compassion that we truly rely. Blessed are You, Lord, the support and security of the righteous.

THE ELEVENTH (FOURTEENTH) BLESSING

May You dwell in Jerusalem, Your City,
as You have promised. And may You establish the throne of David, Your servant, speedily within it and build it as an eternal structure, speedily in our days Blessed are You, Lord, Who builds Jerusalem.

Netzach

This blessing contains 20 words, which is the same number of words in the verse *"Ki nicham Adonai Tzion nicham kol chorvoteha..."* (Isaiah 51:3), a verse that speaks about the Final Redemption.

David דָּוִד   אדני   יהוה   אהיה   יהוה   tzemach צֶמַח   et אֶת

vekarno וְקַרְנוֹ   tatzmia'ch תַּצְמִיחַ   mehera מְהֵרָה   פיי, אל אדני   avdecha עַבְדְּךָ

lishu'atcha לִישׁוּעָתְךָ   ki כִּי   ♦bishu'atecha בִּישׁוּעָתֶךָ   tarum תָרוּם

kivinu קִוִּינוּ   hayom הַיּוֹם   ילי   kol כָּל־   ע"ה   נגד, מזבוח, זן, אל יהוה

You should meditate and ask here for the Final Redemption to occur right away.

Adonai יְהֹוָה(אדניאהדונהי)   Ata אַתָּה   baruch בָּרוּךְ

matzmi'ach מַצְמִיחַ   keren קֶרֶן   yeshu'a יְשׁוּעָה♦

THE THIRTEENTH (SIXTEENTH) BLESSING

This blessing is the most important of all blessings, because here we acknowledge all of our reactive behavior. We make reference to our wrongful actions in general, and we also specify a particular incident. The section inside the box provides us with an opportunity to ask the Light for personal sustenance. The Ari states that throughout this prayer, even on fast days, we have a personal angel accompanying us. If we meditate upon this angel, all our prayers must be answered. The Thirteenth Blessing is one above the twelve zodiac signs, and it raises us above the influence of the stars and planets.

Tiferet

(הֵה)   וָו   הֵה   (יוֹד)   Adonai יְהֹוָה(אדניאהדונהי)   kolenu קוֹלֵנוּ   shema שְׁמַע

rachem רַחֵם   harachaman הָרַחֲמָן   av אָב (אבג יתץ)♦   ילה Elohenu אֱלֹהֵינוּ

alenu עָלֵינוּ   אברהם, ווﬞפ אל, ריﬞו ולﬞב נתיבות הוכמה, רמﬞוז (אברים), עסמﬞב וטﬞז אותיות פשוטות

(קרע שטן)   berachamim בְּרַחֲמִים   vekabel וְקַבֵּל♦   מצפצ, אלהים דיורדין, יﬞפ יי

et אֶת   ע"ה   uvratzon וּבְרָצוֹן   מהשע ע"ה, ע"ב בריבוע וקסﬞא ע"ה, אל שדי ע"ה

tefilatenu תְּפִלָּתֵנוּ (נגד) יכשﬞ♦   ki כִּי   El אֵל   ייﬞא   (מילוי   דסﬞג)

shome'a שׁוֹמֵעַ tefilot תְּפִלּוֹת   vetachanunim וְתַחֲנוּנִים   Ata אַתָּה (בטר צתג)♦

THE TWELFTH (FIFTEENTH) BLESSING

The offspring of David, Your servant, may You speedily cause to sprout.
And may You raise their worth with Your salvation, because it is for Your salvation that we have hoped all day long. Blessed are You, Lord, Who sprouts out the worth of the salvation.

THE THIRTEENTH (SIXTEENTH) BLESSING

Hear our voice, Lord, our God. Merciful Father, have mercy over us.
Accept our prayer with compassion and favor, because You are God, Who hears prayers and supplications.

It is good for you to be aware, acknowledge and confess your prior negative actions and to ask for your livelihood here:

רִבּוֹנוֹ ribono שֶׁל shel עוֹלָם olam, וְחָטָאתִי chatati עָוִיתִי aviti

ס״ג מ״ה ב״ן לְפָנֶיךָ lefanecha יְהִי yehi רָצוֹן ratzon מהש״ע ע״ה, וּפָשַׁעְתִּי ufashati

ע״ב בריבוע וקס״א ע״ה, אל שדי ע״ה, מִלְפָנֶיךָ milfanecha ס״ג מ״ה ב״ן שֶׁתִּתְמוֹזֵל shetimchol

; עמם ילי יל" כָּל kol עַל al לִי li וּתְכַפֵּר utchaper יהוה ע״ב וְתִסְלַח vetislach

מ״ה ma מַה shechatati שֶׁחָטָאתִי veshe'aviti וְשֶׁעָוִיתִי veshepashati וְשֶׁפָּשַׁעְתִּי

אל יהוה זן, מזבח, נגד, ע״ה miyom מִיוֹם ב״ן מ״ה ס״ג lefanecha לְפָנֶיךָ

haze וה" הַזֶּה יהוה אל זן, מזבח, נגד, ע״ה hayom הַיוֹם ad עַד shenivreti שֶׁנִּבְרֵאתִי עַד־בְּרֵאתִי

וּבִפְרָט uvifrat (mention here a specific negative action or behavior you would like to ask forgiveness for)

ע״ה שדי אל ,ע״ה וקס״א בריבוע ע״ב, ע״ב, ע״ה מהש״ע ratzon רָצוֹן vihi וִיהִי

ילה Elohenu אֱלֹהֵינוּ Adonai יְהֹוָהאֲדֹנָיאהֲדֹנָהֵי ס״ג מ״ה ב״ן milfanecha מִלְפָנֶיךָ

shetazmin שֶׁתַּזְמִין avotenu אֲבוֹתֵינוּ ילה ; דמב ע״ב, מילוי לכב ; velohei וֵאלֹהֵי

אדני יה ulchol וּלְכָל li לִי umzonotenu וּמְזוֹנוֹתֵינוּ parnasatenu פַּרְנָסָתֵנוּ

אל יהוה זן, מזבח, נגד, ע״ה hayom הַיוֹם ראה ב״פ veti בֵּיתִי anshei אַנְשֵׁי

אל יהוה זן, מזבח, נגד, ע״ה yom יוֹם לכב ב״ן, uvchol וּבְכָל

velo וְלֹא berevach בְּרֵיוַוח אל יהוה זן, מזבח, נגד, ע״ה vayom וָיוֹם

,bevizui בְּבִזּוּי velo וְלֹא בוכו bechavod בְּכָבוֹד ,vetzimtzum וְצִמְצוּם

etztarech אֶצְטָרֵךְ velo וְלֹא ,vetza'ar וְצַעַר velo וְלֹא benachat בְּנַחַת

,lehalva'atam לְהַלְוָאָתָם velo וְלֹא vadam וְדָם basar בָּשָׂר lematenot לְמַתְּנוֹת

vehapetucha וְהַפְּתוּחָה harchava הָרְוָחָבָה miyadcha מִיָּדְךָ ela אֶלָּא

hagadol הַגָּדוֹל shimcha שִׁמְךָ uvizchut וּבִזְכוּת vehamele'a וְהַמְּלֵאָה

לחו; עם ד' אותיות = מבה, יזל, אום (Do not pronounce this Name:) דְּיִקְרְנוֹסָא וחתך עם ג' אותיות

:haparnasa הַפַּרְנָסָה al עַל hamemune הַמְּמוּנֶה (יאהדונהי, אמן, סאל = ובאתב״ע –

Master of the World!
I have transgressed. I have committed iniquity and I have sinned before You. May it be Your will that You would pardon, forgive and excuse all my transgressions, and all the iniquities that I have committed, and all the sins that I have sinned before You, ever since the day I was created and until this day (and especially...). May it be pleasing before You, Lord, our God and God of my forefathers, that You would provide for my livelihood and sustenance, and that of my household, today and each and every day, with abundance and not with meagerness; with dignity and not with shame; with comfort and not with suffering; and that I may not require the gifts of flesh and blood, nor their loans, but only from Your Hand, which is generous, open, and full, and by virtue of Your great Name, which is responsible for livelihood.

rekam רֵיקָם malkenu מַלְכֵּנוּ ב"ן מ"ה ס"ג umilfanecha וּמִלְּפָנֶיךָ

va'anenu וְעֵנֵנוּ chonenu וְחָנֵּנוּ (טוֹע) (וזקב) te'shivenu תְּשִׁיבֵנוּ al אַל

shome'a שׁוֹמֵעַ Ata אַתָּה ki כִּי tefilatenu תְּפִלָּתֵנוּ: ushma וּשְׁמַע

tefilat תְּפִלַּת kol כָּל־ pe פֶּה (פֶּה דו"א) ילי מילה ; וע"ה אלהים, אהיה אדני (יג"ל פוק)

baruch בָּרוּךְ Ata אַתָּה Adonai יְהֹוָה (יהוה)(יאהדונהי)

You should meditate here on the Holy Name: אראריתא

Rav Chaim Vital says: "I have found in the books of the kabbalists that the prayer of a person, who meditates on this Name in the blessing *shome'a tefila*, will never go unanswered."

שׁוֹמֵעַ shome'a תְּפִלָּה tefila (שׁקו ציית) אתב"ש אוכצ, ב"ן אדני וניקודה ע"ה = יוד הי וו הה:

THE FINAL THREE BLESSINGS

Through the merit of Moses, Aaron and Joseph, who are our channels for the final three blessings, we are able to bring down all the spiritual energy that we aroused with our prayers and blessings.

THE SEVENTEENTH BLESSING

During this blessing, referring to Moses, we should always meditate to try to know exactly what God wants from us in our life, as signified by the phrase, "Let it be the will of God." We ask God to guide us toward the work we came to Earth to do. The Creator cannot just accept the work that we want to do; we must carry out the work we were destined to do.

Netzach

You have made requests (of daily needs) to God. Now, after asking for your needs to be met, you should praise the Creator in the last three blessings. This is like a person who has received what he needs from his Master and departs from Him. You should say *"retze"* and meditate for the Supernal Desire (*Keter*) that is called *metzach haratzon* (Forehead of the Desire).

רְצֵה retze אלף למד הה יוד מם

Meditate here to transform misfortune and tragedy (צרה) into desire and acceptance (רצה).

Yisrael יִשְׂרָאֵל be'amecha בְּעַמְּךָ ילה Elohenu אֱלֹהֵינוּ Adonai יְהֹוָה Adonai

---

And from before You,
our King, do not turn us away empty-handed but be gracious, answer us, and hear our prayer.
Because You hear the prayer of every mouth. Blessed are You, Lord, Who hears prayers.

THE FINAL THREE BLESSINGS
THE SEVENTEENTH BLESSING

Find favor, Lord, our God, in Your People, Israel,

וְלִתְפִלָּתָם velitfilatam שְׁעֵה she'e◆ וְהָשֵׁב vehashev הָעֲבוֹדָה ha'avoda

לִדְבִיר lidvir רי"י בֵּיתֶךָ betecha ב"פ ראה. וְאִשֵּׁי ve'ishei יִשְׂרָאֵל Yisrael

וּתְפִלָּתָם utfilatam מְהֵרָה mehera בְּאַהֲבָה be'ahava אוזר, דאזה

תְּקַבֵּל tekabel בְּרָצוֹן beratzon מהס"ע ע"ה, ע"ב בריבוע וקס"א ע"ה, אל שדי ע"ה◆

וּתְהִי ut'hi לְרָצוֹן leratzon מהס"ע ע"ה, ע"ב בריבוע וקס"א ע"ה, אל שדי ע"ה

תָּמִיד tamid ע"ה קס"א קנ"א קמ"ג avodat עֲבוֹדַת Yisrael יִשְׂרָאֵל amecha עַמֶּךָ:

On *Chol Hamo'ed Sukkot* we add:

If you mistakenly forgot to say "*ya'ale veyavo*," and realize this before the end of the blessing ("*baruch Ata Adonai*"), you should return to say "*ya'ale veyavo*" and continue as usual. If you realize this after the end of the blessing ("*hamachazir shechinato leTziyon*") but before you start the next blessing ("*modim*") you should say "*ya'ale veyavo*" there and continue as usual. If you only realize this after you have started the next blessing ("*modim*") but before the second "*yih'yu leratzon*" (on pg. 50) you should return to "*retze*" (pg. 43) and continue from there. If you realize this after (the second "*yih'yu leratzon*") you should start the *Amidah* from the beginning.

avotenu אֲבוֹתֵינוּ ילה ; דמב =,ע"ב מילוי ; לכב velohei וֵאלֹהֵי ילה Elheinu אֱלֹהֵינוּ

veyeratze וְיֵרָצֶה רי"י veyera'e וְיֵרָאֶה veyagi'a וְיַגִּיעַ veyavo וְיָבֹא ya'ale יַעֲלֶה

(ו' פ') veyizacher וְיִזָּכֵר ר"ת מ"ב veyipaked וְיִפָּקֵד veyishama וְיִשָּׁמַע

◆avotenu אֲבוֹתֵינוּ ע"ב קס"א וגע"ב vezichron וְזִכְרוֹן zichronenu זִכְרוֹנֵנוּ

◆irach עִירָךְ Yerushalayim יְרוּשָׁלַיִם וגע"ב קס"א ע"ב zichron זִכְרוֹן

David דָוִד ben בֶּן Mashi'ach מְשִׁיחַ וגע"ב קס"א ע"ב vezichron וְזִכְרוֹן

ע"ב כהת ; בן דוד = אדנ"י ע"ה vezichron וְזִכְרוֹן◆ פוי, אל אדנ"י avdach עַבְדָּךְ ע"ב קס"א וגע"ב

Yisrael יִשְׂרָאֵל ב"פ ראה bet בֵּית amecha עַמֶּךָ ילי kol כָּל

◆אכא letova לְטוֹבָה lifleta לִפְלֵיטָה ב"ן מ"ה ס"ג lefanecha לְפָנֶיךָ

יהוה ריבוע ע"ב, lechesed לְחֶסֶד מוזי בריבוע דמ"ה מילוי lechen לְחֵן

◆ע"ה lechayim לְחַיִּים אהיה אהיה יהוה בינה, ◆ulrachamim וּלְרַחֲמִים

בוזוז, ז, אל יהוה: ע"ה נגד, beyom בְּיוֹם ◆ulshalom וּלְשָׁלוֹם tovim טוֹבִים

---

and turn to their prayer.

Restore the service to the inner sanctuary of Your Temple. Accept the offerings of Israel and their prayer with favor, speedily, and with love. May the service of Your People Israel always be favorable to You

On *Chol Hamo'ed* we add:

Our God and God of our forefathers,

may it rise, come, arrive, appear, find favor, be heard, be considered, and be remembered, our remembrance and the remembrance of our forefathers: the remembrance of Jerusalem, Your City, and the remembrance of Mashiach, Son of David, Your servant, and the remembrance of Your entire Nation, the House of Israel, before You for deliverance, for good, for grace, kindness, and compassion, for a good life, and for peace on the day of:

והו chag הַסֻכּוֹת haSukkot הַזֶּה hazeh וזֹג

בְּיוֹם beyom ע"ה נגד, מזבוח, ז', אל יהוה mikra מִקְרָא kodesh קֹדֶשׁ haze הַזֶּה והו•

לְרַחֵם lerachem אברהם, וז"פ אל, רי"ו ול"ב נתיבות החכמה, רמ"ח (אברים),

וּלְהוֹשִׁיעֵנוּ ulhoshi'enu אותיות פשוטות bo בּוֹ עָלֵינוּ alenu

זָכְרֵנוּ zochrenu יְהֹוָ... Adonai אֱלֹהֵינוּ Elohenu ילה bo בּוֹ

לְטוֹבָה letova אכא• וּפָקְדֵנוּ ufokdenu vo בּוֹ לִבְרָכָה livracha•

וְהוֹשִׁיעֵנוּ vehoshi'enu vo בּוֹ לְחַיִּים lechayim אהיה אהיה יהוה, בינה ע"ה

טוֹבִים tovim• bidvar בְּדְבַר ראה yeshu'a יְשׁוּעָה וְרַחֲמִים verachamim•

חוּס chus וְחָנֵּנוּ vechonenu וַחֲמוֹל vachamol וְרַחֵם verachem אברהם, וז"פ אל,

וְהוֹשִׁיעֵנוּ vehoshi'enu ki כִּי elecha אֵלֶיךָ enenu עֵינֵינוּ ki כִּי ריבוע מ"ה• alenu•

אֵל El יא"י (מילוי דס"ג) melech מֶלֶךְ chanun וְחַנּוּן verachum וְרַחוּם Ata אָתָּה•

וְאַתָּה veAta verachamecha בְּרַחֲמֶיךָ harabim הָרַבִּים• tachpotz תַּחְפֹּץ

בָּנוּ banu vetirtzenu וְתִרְצֵנוּ vetechezena וְתֶחֱזֶינָה enenu עֵינֵינוּ ריבוע מ"ה

בְּשׁוּבְךָ beshuvcha leTziyon לְצִיּוֹן יוסף, ו' הויות, קנאה berachamim בְּרַחֲמִים

בָּרוּךְ baruch Ata אָתָּה יְהֹוָ... Adonai יוד הא... יפ ייי•

הַמַּחֲזִיר hamachazir שְׁכִינָתוֹ shechinato leTziyon לְצִיּוֹן יוסף, ו' הויות, קנאה•

THE EIGHTEENTH BLESSING

This blessing is our thank you. Kabbalistically, the biggest "thank you" we can give the Creator is to do exactly what we are supposed to do in terms of our spiritual work.

This festival of Sukkot, on this Holy Day of Convocation.
To take pity on us and to save us.
Remember us, Lord, our God, on this day, for good; consider us on it for blessing; and deliver us on it for a good life, with the words of deliverance and mercy. Take pity and be gracious to us, have mercy and be compassionate with us, and save us, for our eyes turn to You, because You are God, the King Who is gracious and compassionate.

And You in Your great compassion take delight in us and are pleased with us. May our eyes witness Your return to Zion with compassion. Blessed are You, Lord, Who returns His Shechinah to Zion.

Hod
Bow your entire body at "*modim*" and straighten up at "*Adonai*."

מוֹדִ֫ים modim מאה ברכות שׁתיקן דוד לאמרם כל יום

> **When the Eve of the Holiday falls on the Eve of *Shabbat*:**
>
> **While bowing** you should meditate on the Name: אלף הא יוד הא in order to lower the *Ruach* of *Yetzirah*, to be as *Mayin Nukvin* in order to elevate the *Shechinah*. And **while straightening up** you should meditate on the Name: וד הא ואו הא, to elevate the *Shechinah* and to prepare the World of *Yetzirah* to be elevated to *Beriah* and to be able to receive *Asiyah*.

(וֹ) Adonai יְהֹוָ֫הֿﬡﬢﬨﬥﬡﬧﬨﬢﬨ hu הוּא sheAta שָׁאַתָּה֫ lach לָ֫ךְ anachnu אֲנַ֫חְנוּ

avotenu אֲבוֹתֵ֫ינוּ ; יֵלה ; מילוי ע"ב, דמב ; לכב velohei וֵאלֹהֵ֫י ילה Elohenu אֱלֹהֵ֫ינוּ

tzurenu צוּרֵ֫נוּ va'ed וָעֶ֫ד֫ דס"ג אותיות וי' ס"ג ריבוע le'olam לְעוֹלָם

; דס"ג) מילוי (ייא"י אל ג"פ umagen וּמָגֵ֫ן chayenu וְחַיֵּ֫ינוּ ע"ה הההין אלהים tzur צוּר

hu הוּא Ata אַתָּ֫ה yish'enu יִשְׁעֵ֫נוּ נוריאל גבריאל מיכאל ר"ת

unsaper וּנְסַפֵּר lecha לְךָ node נ֫וֹדֶה רי"ו vador וָד֫וֹר ledor לְדֹר

hamesurim הַמְּסוּרִים chayenu וְחַיֵּ֫ינוּ al עַל tehilatecha תְּהִלָּתֶ֫ךָ

hapekudot הַפְּקוּד֫וֹת nishmotenu נִשְׁמוֹתֵ֫ינוּ ve'al וְעַל beyadecha בְּיָדֶ֫ךָ

לכב ב"ן, shebechol שֶׁבְּכָל nisecha נִסֶּ֫יךָ ve'al וְעַל lach לָ֫ךְ

ve'al וְעַל ע"ה נגד, מזבח, זן, אל יהוה yom י֫וֹם imanu עִמָּ֫נוּ ריבוע ס"ג, קס"א ע"ה וד' אותיות

לכב ב"ן, shebchol שֶׁבְּכָל vetovotecha וְטוֹבוֹתֶ֫יךָ nifle'otecha נִפְלְאוֹתֶ֫יךָ

והו hatov הַטּוֹב vetzahorayim וְצָהֳרָ֫יִם vavoker וָבֹ֫קֶר erev עֶ֫רֶב et עֵת

hamerachem הַמְרַחֵם֫ rachamecha רַחֲמֶ֫יךָ chalu כָל֫וּ lo לֹא ki כִּי

lo לֹא ki כִּי אברהם, וז"פ אל, רי"ו ול"ב נתיבות החכמה, רמ"ח (אברים), עסמ"ב וט"ו אותיות פשוטות

lach לָ֫ךְ kivinu קִוִּ֫ינוּ me'olam מֵעוֹלָם ki כִּי chasadecha חֲסָדֶ֫יךָ tamu תַּ֫מּוּ

THE EIGHTEENTH BLESSING
We give thanks to You, for it is You, Lord, Who is our God and God of our forefathers, forever and for all eternity. You are our Rock, the Rock of our lives, and the Shield of our salvation. From one generation to another, we shall give thanks to You and we shall tell of Your praise. For our lives that are entrusted in Your hands, for our souls that are in Your care, for Your miracles that are with us every day, and for Your wonders and Your favors that are with us at all times: evening, morning and afternoon. You are the good One, for Your compassion has never ceased. You are the compassionate One, for Your kindness has never ended, for we have always placed our hope in You.

MODIM DERABANAN

This prayer is recited by the congregation in the repetition when the *chazan* says "*modim*."

In this section there are 44 words, which is the same numerical value as the Name:
ריבוע אהיה (א אה אהי אהיה).

מוֹדִים modim מאה ברכות עתיקן דוד לאמרם כל יום anachnu אֲנַחְנוּ לַך lach

שָׁאַתָּה sheAta הוּא hu יְהֹוָה (אדני יאהדונהי) Adonai אֱלֹהֵינוּ Elohenu ילה

וֵאלֹהֵי velohei לכב ; ע"ב, מילוי ; דמב, מילוי ; ילה avotenu אֲבוֹתֵינוּ

אֱלֹהֵי Elohei מילוי ע"ב, דמב ; ילה chol כָּל ילי בָּשָׂר basar. yotzrenu יוֹצְרֵנוּ

יוֹצֵר yotzer bereshit בְּרֵאשִׁית. berachot בְּרָכוֹת vehoda'ot וְהוֹדָאוֹת

לְשִׁמְךָ leshimcha הַגָּדוֹל hagadol לההו ; עם ד' אותיות = מבה, יזל, אום

וְהַקָּדוֹשׁ vehakadosh עַל al שֶׁהֶחֱיִיתָנוּ shehecheyitanu וְקִיַּמְתָּנוּ vekiyamtanu.

כֵּן ken techayenu תְּחַיֵּנוּ utchonenu וּתְחָנֵּנוּ. vete'esof וְתֶאֱסוֹף

גָּלֻיּוֹתֵינוּ galuyotenu לְחַצְרוֹת lechatzrot kodshecha קָדְשֶׁךָ. lishmor לִשְׁמוֹר

חֻקֶּיךָ chukecha וְלַעֲשׂוֹת vela'asot retzoncha רְצוֹנֶךָ. ul'ovdecha וּלְעָבְדְּךָ

belevav בְּלֵבָב בוכו shalem שָׁלֵם. al עַל she'anachnu שֶׁאֲנַחְנוּ

modim מוֹדִים לָך lach. baruch בָּרוּך El אֵל יא"י (מילוי דס"ג) hahoda'ot הַהוֹדָאוֹת:

וְעַל ve'al כֻּלָּם kulam יִתְבָּרֵך yitbarach וְיִתְרוֹמַם veyitromam

וְיִתְנַשֵּׂא veyitnase תָּמִיד tamid ע"ה קס"א קנ"א קס"א קמ"ג shimcha שִׁמְךָ

מַלְכֵּנוּ malkenu לְעוֹלָם le'olam ריבוע ס"ג וי' אותיות דס"ג וָעֶד va'ed.

וְכָל vechol hachayim הַחַיִּים ילי yoducha יוֹדוּךָ sela סֶלָה:
אהיה אהיה יהוה, בינה ע"ה

MODIM DERABANAN

We give thanks to You, for it is You Lord,
our God and God of our forefathers, the God of all flesh, our Maker and the Former of all Creation. Blessings and thanks to Your great and Holy Name for giving us life and for preserving us. So may You continue to give us life, be gracious to us, and gather our exiles to the courtyards of Your Sanctuary, so that we may keep Your laws, fulfill Your will, and serve You wholeheartedly. For this, we thank You. Bless the God of thanksgiving.

And for all those things, may Your Name be always blessed,
exalted and extolled, our King, forever and ever, and all the living shall thank You, Selah.

et אֶת־ מ"ה ריבוע יהוה ריבוע יהוה vivarchu וְיִבָרְכוּ vihalelu וִיהַלְלוּ

be'emet בֶּאֱמֶת hagadol הַגָּדוֹל לְהוֹ ; עם ד' אותיות = מבה, יזל, אום shimcha שִׁמְךָ

; והו tov טוֹב ki כִּי le'olam לְעוֹלָם ריבוע ס"ג ו' אותיות דס"ג ז"פ ס"ג, אהיה פעמים אהיה,

yeshu'atenu יְשׁוּעָתֵנוּ (מילוי דס"ג) יא"י ; לאה (מילוי דס"ג) haEl הָאֵל יזל, מבה, אום, אהיה יהוה = כי טוב

: והו hatov הַטּוֹב (מילוי דס"ג) יא"י ; לאה haEl הָאֵל sela• סֶלָה ve'ezratenu וְעֶזְרָתֵנוּ

Bend your knees at *"baruch,"* bow at *"Ata"* and straighten up at *"Adonai."*

Ata אַתָּה baruch בָּרוּךְ

When the Eve of the Holiday falls on the Eve of *Shabbat*:

While bending you should meditate on the Name: אלף הה יוד הה in order to lower the *Nefesh* of *Asiyah*, to be as *Mayin Nukvin* in order to elevate the *Shechinah*. And **while straightening up** meditate on the Name: יוד הה וו הה הה to elevate the *Shechinah* and to prepare *Asiyah* to be elevated to *Yetzirah*.

---

shimcha שִׁמְךָ והו hatov הַטּוֹב (הי) Adonai יאהדונהי ואהדונהי יהוה

: ע"ה דוד בן משיח ס"ת כהת, lehodot לְהוֹדוֹת na'e נָאֶה ulcha וּלְךָ

On Shcharit of Chol Hamo'ed we do the blessing of the *Kohanim* here (page 355).

THE FINAL BLESSING

We are emanating the energy of peace to the entire world. We also make it our intent to use our mouths only for good. Kabbalistically, the power of words and speech is unimaginable. We hope to use that power wisely, which is perhaps one of the most difficult tasks we have to carry out.

Yesod

uvracha וּבְרָכָה אכא tova טוֹבָה shalom שָׁלוֹם sim שִׂים

מוזי ברביע, דמ"ה מילוי chen חֵן ע"ה בינה אהיה, יהוה אהיה chayim וְחַיִּים

אלהים ריבוע ע"ה tzedaka צְדָקָה יהוה ריבוע ע"ב, vachesed וָחֶסֶד

עמם ; ילי kol כָּל־ ve'al וְעַל alenu עָלֵינוּ verachamim וְרַחֲמִים

kulanu כֻּלָּנוּ avinu אָבִינוּ uvarchenu וּבָרְכֵנוּ amecha עַמְּךָ Yisrael יִשְׂרָאֵל

מ"ה ב"ן ס"ג panecha פָּנֶיךָ רו, א"ס be'or בְּאוֹר דאגה אהבה, ke'echad כְּאֶחָד

And they shall praise and bless Your great Name,
sincerely and forever, for It is good, the God of our salvation and our help, Selah, the good God.
Blessed are You, Lord, whose Name is good and to You it is befitting to give thanks.

THE FINAL BLESSING

Place peace, goodness, blessing, life, grace, kindness, righteousness, and mercy upon us and upon all of Israel, Your People. Bless us all as one, our Father, with the Light of Your Countenance,

לָּנוּ lanu נָתַתָּ natata ב"ן מ"ה ס"ג א"ס, רו, panecha פָּנֶיךָ ve'or בְּאוֹר ki כִּי

תּוֹרָה torah ילה Elohenu אֱלֹהֵינוּ Adonai יְהֹוָואדניאהדונהי אדני אהיה אלהים,

וָחֶסֶד וָחֶסֶד vachesed דאגה אוזר, ahava אַהֲבָה ❖ ע"ה יהוה בינה אהיה אהיה vechayim וְחַיִּים

❖ verachamim וְרַחֲמִים אלהים אלהים ריבוע ע"ה tzedaka צְדָקָה ❖ יהוה ריבוע ע"ב,

be'enecha בְּעֵינֶיךָ והו vetov וְטוֹב ❖ veshalom וְשָׁלוֹם beracha בְּרָכָה

ילי kol כָּל et אֶת ulvarech וּלְבָרֵךְ levarchenu לְבָרְכֵנוּ מ"ה ריבוע ; קס"א ע"ה

❖ veshalom וְשָׁלוֹם oz עֹז אהיה פ"י berov בְּרוֹב Yisrael יִשְׂרָאֵל amecha עַמְּךָ

Adonai יוהווהאדניאהדונהי Ata אַתָּה baruch בָּרוּךְ

Yisrael יִשְׂרָאֵל amo עַמּוֹ et אֶת hamevarech הַמְבָרֵךְ

יאהדונהי amen אָמֵן ❖ bashalom בַּשָּׁלוֹם יב"ק = (אילההויהם) אלהים = ר"ת

When the Eve of the Holiday falls on the Eve of *Shabbat*:
Meditate here to elevate the Name: יהוה, as follow:
The letter ה and the Name ב"ן to the letter ו and to the Name מ"ה.
The letter ו and the Name מ"ה to the letter ה and to the Name ס"ג.
The letter ה and the Name ס"ג to the letter י and to the Name ע"ב.

YIH'YU LERATZON

There are 42 letters in the verse in the secret of *Ana Beko'ach*.

יִהְיוּ yih'yu (ייא"י מילוי דס"ג) אל מהט ע"ה, ע"ב בריבוע וקס"א ע"ה, אל עדוי ע"ה leratzon לְרָצוֹן

libi לִבִּי vehegyon וְהֶגְיוֹן = אלף למד שין דלת יוד ע"ה ר"ת אָלֶף fi פִי imrei אִמְרֵי

❖ vego'ali וְגֹאֲלִי tzuri צוּרִי Adonai יְהֹוָואדניאהדונהי ב"ן מ"ה ס"ג lefanecha לְפָנֶיךָ

---

because it is with the Light of Your Countenance that You, Lord, our God, have given us Torah and life, love and kindness, righteousness and mercy, blessing and peace. May it be good in Your Eyes to bless us and to bless Your entire Nation, Israel, with abundant power and with peace.

Blessed are You, Lord, Who blesses His Nation, Israel, with peace, Amen.

YIH'YU LERATZON

"May the utterances of my mouth and the thoughts of my heart find favor before You, Lord, my Rock and my Redeemer." (Psalms 19:15)

ELOHAI NETZOR

אֱלֹהַי Elohai ; נְצֹר netzor לְשׁוֹנִי leshoni מֵרָע mera

וְשִׂפְתוֹתַי vesiftotai מִדַּבֵּר midaber מִרְמָה mirma וְלִמְקַלְלַי velimkalelai

נַפְשִׁי nafshi תִדֹּם tidom וְנַפְשִׁי venafshi כֶּעָפָר ke'afar

לַכֹּל lakol תִּהְיֶה tihye פְּתַח petach לִבִּי libi בְּתוֹרָתֶךָ betoratecha

וְאַחֲרֵי ve'acharei מִצְוֹתֶיךָ mitzvotecha תִּרְדּוֹף tirdof נַפְשִׁי nafshi

וְכָל vechol הַקָּמִים hakamim עָלַי alai לְרָעָה lera'a מְהֵרָה mehera

הָפֵר hafer עֲצָתָם atzatam וְקַלְקֵל vekalkel מַחְשְׁבוֹתָם machshevotam

עֲשֵׂה ase לְמַעַן lema'an שְׁמֶךָ shemach עֲשֵׂה ase לְמַעַן lema'an

יְמִינֶךָ yeminach עֲשֵׂה ase לְמַעַן lema'an תּוֹרָתֶךָ toratach עֲשֵׂה ase

לְמַעַן lema'an קְדֻשָּׁתֶךָ kedushatach לְמַעַן lema'an

יֵחָלְצוּן yechaltzun יְדִידֶיךָ yedidecha הוֹשִׁיעָה hoshi'a

יְמִינְךָ yemincha וַעֲנֵנִי va'aneni

Before we recite the next verse *"Yih'yu leratzon"* we have an opportunity to strengthen our connection to our soul using our name. Each person has a verse in the *Torah* that connects to their name. Either their name is in the verse, or the first and last letters of the name correspond to the first or last letters of a verse. For example, the name Yehuda begins with a *Yud* and ends with a *Hei*. Before we end the *Amidah*, we state that our name will always be remembered when our soul leaves this world.

YIH'YU LERATZON (THE SECOND)

There are 42 letters in the verse in the secret of *Ana Beko'ach*.

יִהְיוּ yih'yu לְרָצוֹן leratzon

אִמְרֵי imrei פִי fi וְהֶגְיוֹן vehegyon לִבִּי libi

לְפָנֶיךָ lefanecha יְהוָה Adonai צוּרִי tzuri וְגֹאֲלִי vego'ali

---

ELOHAI NETZOR

My God, guard my tongue from evil and my lips from speaking deceit. To those who curse me, let my spirit remain silent, and let my spirit be as dust for everyone. Open my heart to Your Torah and let my heart pursue Your commandments. All those who rise against me to do me harm, speedily nullify their plans and disturb their thoughts. Do so for the sake of Your Name. Do so for the sake of Your Right. Do so for the sake of Your Torah. Do so for the sake of Your Holiness, "So that Your loved ones may be saved. Redeem Your right and answer me." (Psalms 60:7)

YIH'YU LERATZON (THE SECOND)

"May the utterances of my mouth and the thoughts of my heart find favor before You, Lord, my Rock and my Redeemer." (Psalms 19:15)

OSE SHALOM

We now take three steps backward to draw the Light of the Upper Worlds into our life. We bow to the Left, Right, and Center, and we should meditate that by taking these three steps backwards, that the Holy Temple that was destroyed should be built once again.

You take three steps backward;

עוֹשֶׂה שָׁלוֹם ose shalom

Left
You turn to the left and say:

בִּמְרוֹמָיו bimromav ר"ת ע"ב, ריבוע יהוה

Right
You turn to the right and say:

הוּא hu בְּרַחֲמָיו verachamav יַעֲשֶׂה ya'ase

שָׁלוֹם shalom עָלֵינוּ aleinu ר"ת ע"ע נהורין

Center
You face the center and say:

וְעַל ve'al כָּל kol ילי ; עמם amo עַמּוֹ amo יִשְׂרָאֵל Yisrael

וְאִמְרוּ ve'imru אָמֵן amen יאהדונהי:

יְהִי yehi רָצוֹן ratzon מהשי ע"ה, ע"ב, ברריבוע וקס"א ע"ה, אל שדי ע"ה

מִלְּפָנֶיךָ milfaneicha ס"ג מ"ה ב"ן יְהֹוָה אלה Adonai אֱלֹהֵינוּ eloheinu ילה

וֵאלֹהֵי velohei אֲבוֹתֵינוּ avoteinu ; ילה ; מילוי ע"ב, דמב ; לכב שֶׁתִּבְנֶה shetivne

בֵּית bet ב"פ ראה הַמִּקְדָּשׁ hamikdash בִּמְהֵרָה bimhera veyameinu בְיָמֵינוּ veyameinu

וְתֵן veten וְזַלְקֵנוּ chelkenu בְּתוֹרָתֶךָ betoratach לַעֲשׂוֹת la'asot וְזֻקֵּי chukei

רְצוֹנֶךָ retzonach וּלְעָבְדֶךָ ul'ovdach פוי, אל אדני בְּלֵבָב belevav בוכו שָׁלֵם shalem.

You take three steps forward.

On *Shacharit* of *Chol Hamo'ed* we continue with:

"The Order of the Shaking and Taking of the *Lulav*" on page 361, then say *Halel* on pages 375-400, then with the *Hosha'anot* (Circeling, according to the day, on pages 401-431) (On *Hosha'ana Rabbah* we continue with *Hosha'anot* on pages 432-478) then say *Kaddish Titkabal* on page 489, then we take the *Torah* out from page 491 and on, read the *Torah* from page 743 and on, say Half *Kaddish* on pages 501-502, and continue on page 663.

OSE SHALOM

He, Who makes peace in His High Places, He, in His compassion, shall make peace upon us. And upon His entire nation, Israel, and you shall say, Amen.

May it be pleasing before You, Lord, our God and God of our forefathers, that You shall rebuild the Temple speedily, in our days, and place our lot in Your Torah, so that we may fulfill the laws of Your desire and serve You wholeheartedly.

YEHI SHEM

ר"ת ריבוע ע"ב וריבוע ס"ג mevorach מְבֹרָךְ Adonai לַיהוָֹואהדונהי shem שֵׁם yehi יְהִי

me'ata מֵעַתָּה (להעלות רפ"ח ניצוצות ענפי לקליפה דמטם באים התולואים) רפ"ח = מברך יהוה

ve'ad וְעַד olam עוֹלָם mimizrach מִמִּזְרַח יל": shemesh שֶׁמֶשׁ ad עַד

Adonai לַיהוָֹואהדונהי: shem שֵׁם mehulal מְהֻלָּל mevo'o מְבוֹאוֹ קָדוֹשׁ ר"ת

al עַל Adonai לַיהוָֹואהדונהי goyim גּוֹיִם כל עמם ילי kol כָּל al עַל ram רָם

kevodo כְּבוֹדוֹ: ר"ת ; כחו י"פ טל, י"פ ועולמל hashamayim הַשָּׁמָיִם

הרי adir אַדִּיר מ"ה ma מָה adonenu אֲדֹנֵינוּ Adonai לַיהוָֹואהדילאיאהדונהי

ha'aretz הָאָרֶץ ; ומב לכב ב"ן, bechol בְּכָל shimcha שִׁמְךָ אלהים דההן ע"ה:

KADDISH TITKABAL

ש"א אותיות כמנין ו"ה ; veyitkadash וְיִתְקַדַּשׁ עדי ומילוי עדי ; yitgadal יִתְגַּדַּל

שֵׁם י"ה דע"ב) raba רַבָּא קנ"א ב"ן, יהוה אלהים יהוה אדני, shemei שְׁמֵהּ

מילוי קס"א וס"ג, מ"ה ברבוע וע"ב ע"ה ע"ה ; ר"ת = ו"פ אלהים ; ס"ת = ג"פ יב"ק] amen אָמֵן אידהנויה:

chir'utei כִרְעוּתֵיהּ vera בְּרָא di דִי be'alma בְּעָלְמָא

veyatzmach וְיַצְמַח malchutei מַלְכוּתֵהּ veyamlich וְיַמְלִיךְ

amen אָמֵן אידהנויה: meshichei מְשִׁיחֵיהּ vikarev וִיקָרֵב purkanei פֻּרְקָנֵהּ

uvchayei וּבְחַיֵי uvyomechon וּבְיוֹמֵיכוֹן bechayechon בְּחַיֵיכוֹן

ba'agala בַּעֲגָלָא Yisrael יִשְׂרָאֵל ב"פ ראה bet בֵּית ילי dechol דְכָל

amen אָמֵן אידהנויה: amen אָמֵן ve'imru וְאִמְרוּ kariv קָרִיב uvizman וּבִזְמַן

YEHI SHEM

"May the Name of the Lord be blessed from now till all eternity. From sunrise till sundown, may the Name of the Lord be praised and elevated. Above all nations is the Lord. His glory is above the Heavens." (Psalms 113:2-4) "The Lord, our Master, how tremendous is Your Name in all the Earth." (Psalms 8:10)

KADDISH TITKABAL

May His great Name be more exalted and sanctified. (Amen) In the world that He created according to His will, and may His Kingdom reign. And may He cause His redemption to sprout and may He bring the Mashiach closer. (Amen) In your lifetimes and in your days and in the lifetime of all the House of Israel, speedily and in the near future, and you shall say, Amen. (Amen)

The congregation and the *chazan* say the following:

Twenty eight words (until *be'alma*) – meditate:

מילוי דמילוי דע"ב (יוד ויו דלת הי יוד ויו יוד הי יוד)

Twenty eight letters (until *almaya*) - meditate:

מילוי דמילוי דע"ב (יוד ויו דלת הי יוד ויו יוד הי יוד)

בְּ"א קנ"א raba רַבָּא (שם י"ה דס"ג) shemei שְׁמֵיהּ yehe יְהֵא

mevarach, מְבָרַךְ יהוה אלהים אדני, מילוי קס"א וס"ג, מ"ה ברבוע וע"ב ע"ה

yitbarach ◆ יִתְבָּרֵךְ ◆almaya עָלְמַיָּא le'almei לְעָלְמֵי le'alam לְעָלַם

Seven words with six letters each (שם בן מ"ב) – meditate:

יהוה ◆ יוד הי ויו הי ◆ מילוי דמילוי דע"ב (יוד ויו דלת הי יוד ויו יוד הי יוד)

Also, seven times the letter *Vav* (שם בן מ"ב) – meditate:

יהוה ◆ יוד הי ויו הי ◆ מילוי דמילוי דע"ב (יוד ויו דלת הי יוד ויו יוד הי יוד).

י"פ ע"ב יהוה אל אבג יתץ ◆ veyishtabach וְיִשְׁתַּבַּח

veyitpa'ar וְיִתְפָּאַר הי גו יה קרע שטן (וה כוזו נגד יכש) veyitromam וְיִתְרֹמַם

veyit'hadar וְיִתְהַדָּר במוכסז בטר צתג veyitnase וְיִתְנַשֵּׂא כוזו יה וזקב טנע ◆

veyit'ale וְיִתְעַלֶּה וה יוד ה יוד ה יגל פזק. veyit'halal וְיִתְהַלָּל א ואו הא שקו צית.

hu הוּא verich בְּרִיךְ dekudsha דְּקוּדְשָׁא (שם י"ה דמ"ה) shemei שְׁמֵיהּ

amen אידהנויה ◆ אָמֵן

◆shirata שִׁירָתָא ◆birchata בִּרְכָתָא ילי kol כָּל min מִן le'ela לְעֵלָּא◆

da'amiran דַּאֲמִירָן ◆venechamata וְנֶחֱמָתָא tishbechata תֻּשְׁבְּחָתָא

amen אידהנויה. אָמֵן amen אָמֵן ve'imru וְאִמְרוּ be'alma בְּעָלְמָא

uva'utana וּבָעוּתָנָא tzelotana צְלוֹתָנָא titkabal תִּתְקַבַּל

ילי dechol דְּכָל uva'utehon וּבָעוּתְהוֹן tzelotehon צְלוֹתְהוֹן im עִם

avuna אֲבוּנָא kadam קֳדָם Yisrael יִשְׂרָאֵל ראה ב"פ beit בֵּית

amen אידהנויה ◆ אָמֵן amen אָמֵן ve'imru וְאִמְרוּ devishmaya דְּבִשְׁמַיָּא

May His great Name be blessed forever and for all eternity. Blessed and lauded, and glorified, and exalted, and extolled, and honored, and uplifted, and praised be the Name of the Holy Blessed One. (Amen) Above all blessings, songs, praises, and words of consolation that may be said in the world, and you shall say, Amen. (Amen) May our prayers and pleas be accepted, together with the prayers and pleas of the entire House of Israel, before our Father in Heaven, and you say, Amen. (Amen)

יְהֵא yehe שְׁלָמָא shelama רַבָּא raba קָנ"א ב"ן, יהוה אלהים יהוה אדני, מילוי קס"א וס"ג,

מִן min שְׁמַיָּא shemaya ◆ וְחַיִּים chayim אהיה אהיה יהוה, בינה ע"ה

וְשֵׂבַע vesava וִישׁוּעָה vishu'a וְנֶחָמָה venechama וְשֵׁיזָבָא vesheizava

וּרְפוּאָה urfu'a וּגְאֻלָּה ug'ula וּסְלִיחָה uslicha וְכַפָּרָה vechapara

וְרֶיוַח verevach וְהַצָּלָה vehatzala ◆ לָנוּ lanu אלהים, אהיה אדני וּלְכָל ulchol

עַמּוֹ amo יִשְׂרָאֵל Yisrael וְאִמְרוּ ve'imru אָמֵן amen ◆ אָמֵן amen איהנויה.

Take three steps backwards and say:

עוֹשֶׂה ose שָׁלוֹם shalom בִּמְרוֹמָיו bimromav ◆ ע"ב, ריבוע יהוה. הוּא hu

בְּרַחֲמָיו berachamav יַעֲשֶׂה ya'ase שָׁלוֹם shalom עָלֵינוּ alenu

וְעַל ve'al כָּל kol עַמּוֹ amo יִשְׂרָאֵל Yisrael וְאִמְרוּ ve'imru אָמֵן amen ◆

אָמֵן amen איהנויה.

LAMNATZE'ACH

When the Eve of the Holiday falls on the Eve of *Shabbat* we skip "*Lamnatzach*" and say "*Adonai Malach*" on page 57.

By meditating upon the *Magen David* (Shield of David), we harness the power, strength, and valor of King David so that we can defeat our personal enemies. Our real enemies are not found in the outside world, regardless of what our ego tells us. Our real enemy is our *Desire to Receive for the Self Alone*. When we defeat the enemy within, external enemies suddenly disappear from our lives.

God revealed this Psalm to King David by Divine Inspiration. It was written on a golden plate made in the shape of the *Menorah* (shown on page 54). God also showed it to Moses. King David carried this Psalm written and engraved on the gold plate on his shield, the Shield of David. When King David went to war, he would meditate on the secrets of the *Menorah* and the seven sentences of this Psalm engraved on it, and his enemies would literally fall in defeat before him. By meditating upon it (reading the letters without turning the image upside down), we harness that power (*Midbar Kdemot*, by the Chida and also in *Menorat Zahav*, by Rav Zusha.)

May there be abundant peace from Heaven. Life, contentment, salvation, consolation, deliverance, healing, redemption, pardon, atonement, comfort, and relief. For us and for His entire nation, Israel, and you shall say, Amen. (Amen) He, Who makes peace in His high places, He, in His compassion, shall make peace upon us And upon His entire nation, Israel, and you shall say, Amen. (Amen)

לַמְנַצֵּ֥חַ lamnatze'ach   בִּנְגִינֹת binginot   מִזְמוֹר mizmor   שִׁיר shir:

אֱלֹהִים Elohim   אהיה אדני ; ילה   יְחָנֵּ֥נוּ yechonenu   וִיבָרְכֵ֑נוּ vivarchenu

יָאֵ֤ר ya'er   כף ויו זן ויו (יאהדונהי) ר"ת פאי, אמן   פָּנָ֣יו panav   אִתָּ֣נוּ itanu   סֶֽלָה sela:

לָדַ֣עַת lada'at   ר"ת סאל, אמן (יאהדונהי)   בָּאָ֣רֶץ ba'aretz   דַּרְכֶּ֑ךָ darkecha

בְּכָל bechol   ב"ן, לכב   גּוֹיִ֥ם goyim   יְשׁוּעָתֶֽךָ yeshu'atecha:

יוֹד֣וּךָ yoducha   עַמִּ֥ים amim   אֱלֹהִ֑ים Elohim   אהיה אדני ; ילה   יוֹד֥וּךָ yoducha

עַמִּ֥ים amim   כֻּלָּֽם kulam: יִֽשְׂמְח֥וּ yismechu   וִֽירַנְּנ֗וּ viranenu

לְאֻמִּ֑ים le'umim   ר"ת ע"ה = איהיוהה   כִּֽי ki   תִשְׁפֹּ֣ט tishpot   עַמִּ֣ים amim

מִישֹׁ֑ר mishor   וּלְאֻמִּ֓ים ul'umim   בָּאָ֣רֶץ ba'aretz   תַּנְחֵ֣ם tanchem   סֶֽלָה sela:

יוֹד֣וּךָ yoducha   עַמִּ֥ים amim   אֱלֹהִ֑ים Elohim   אהיה אדני ; ילה   יוֹד֥וּךָ yoducha

עַמִּ֥ים amim   כֻּלָּֽם kulam: ר"ת יודוך ישמחו יודוך ארץ = יא"י (מילוי דס"ג)

אֶ֤רֶץ eretz   נָ֣תְנָה natna   נתה, קס"א קנ"א קמ"ג   וְעם ר"ת אלהים לדעת יברכנו = ע"ב, ריבוע יהוה

יְבוּלָ֑הּ yevula   ר"ת אני   יְבָרְכֵ֥נוּ yevarchenu   אֱלֹהִ֖ים Elohim   אהיה אדני ; ילה

אֱלֹהֵֽינוּ eloheinu   ילה: יְבָרְכֵ֥נוּ yevarchenu   אֱלֹהִ֥ים Elohim   אהיה אדני ; ילה

וְיִֽירְא֣וּ veyir'u   אֹת֑וֹ oto   כָּל kol   ילי   אַפְסֵי afsei   אָֽרֶץ aretz:

LAMNATZE'ACH

"For the Leader; with string-music: A Psalm, a Song. God be gracious unto us, and bless us; may He cause His face to shine toward us; Selah. That Your way may be known upon earth, Your salvation among all nations. Let the people give thanks to You, God; let the people give thanks to You, all of them. Let the nations be glad and sing for joy; for You will judge the people with equity, and lead the nations upon Earth. Selah Let the people give thanks to You, God; let the people give thanks to You, all of them. The earth has yielded her increase; may God, our own God, bless us. May God bless us; and let all the ends of the earth fear Him." (Psalms 67)

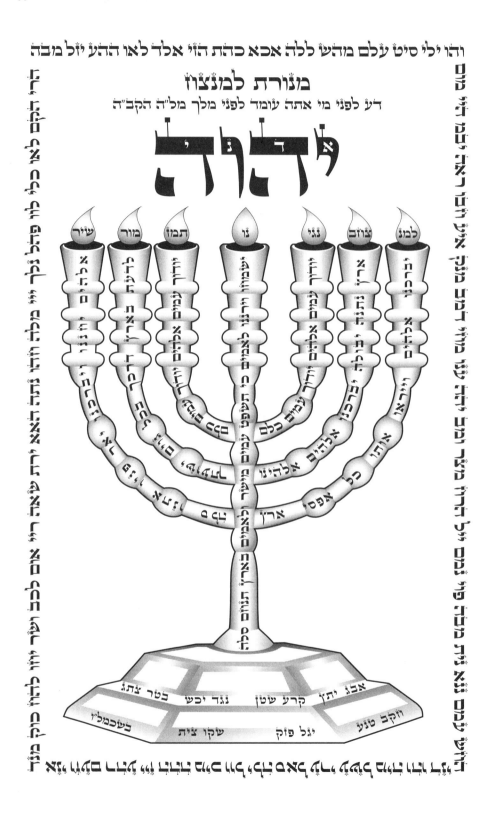

When the Eve of the Holiday falls on the Eve of *Shabbat* the following is recited instead of *"lamnatze'ach binginot"*:

יְהֹוָאדֹנָיאההֹדֹנַהי Adonai מָלָךְ malach גֵּאוּת ge'ut לָבֵשׁ lavesh לָבֵשׁ lavesh

יְהֹוָאדֹנָיאההֹדֹנַהי Adonai עֹז oz הִתְאַזָּר hit'azar אַף af, ר"ת = אלהים, אהיה אדני

תִּכּוֹן tikon תֵּבֵל tevel ב"פ ר"י: בַּל bal תִּמּוֹט timot: נָכוֹן nachon כִּסְאֲךָ kis'acha

מֵאָז me'az ומב מֵעוֹלָם me'olam אַתָּה Ata ר"ת הפסוק קנ"א, אדני אלהים: נָשְׂאוּ nas'u

נְהָרוֹת neharot יְהֹוָאדֹנָיאההֹדֹנַהי Adonai נָשְׂאוּ nas'u ר"ת = קין נְהָרוֹת neharot

קוֹלָם kolam יִשְׂאוּ yis'u נְהָרוֹת neharot דָּכְיָם dochyam ר"ת דנ"י:

מִקֹּלוֹת mikolot מַיִם mayim רַבִּים rabim אַדִּירִים adirim הרי

מִשְׁבְּרֵי mishberei יָם yam יְלִי ; ר"ת אמי אַדִּיר adir הרי

בַּמָּרוֹם bamarom יְהֹוָאדֹנָיאההֹדֹנַהי Adonai ; ר"ת אבי: עֵדֹתֶיךָ edoteicha

נֶאֶמְנוּ ne'emnu מְאֹד me'od ר"ת = קין לְבֵיתְךָ leveitcha ב"פ ראה

נָאֲוָה na'avah קֹדֶשׁ kodesh יְהֹוָאדֹנָיאההֹדֹנַהי Adonai לְאֹרֶךְ le'orech

יָמִים yamim נלך ; ר"ת ילי ; יהוה = אדני ; ס"ת = ע"ע נהורין עם י"ג אותיות:

KADDISH YEHE SHELAMA

יִתְגַּדַּל yitgadal וְיִתְקַדַּשׁ veyitkadash שׂדִי ומילוי שׂדי ; י"א אותיות כמנין ו"ה

שְׁמֵיהּ shemei (שם י"ה דע"ב) רַבָּא raba קנ"א ב"ן, יהוה אלהים יהוה אדני,

אָמֵן amen אידהנויה. מילוי קס"א וס"ג, מ"ה ברבוע וע"ב ע"ה ; ר"ת = ו"פ אלהים ; ס"ת = ג"פ יב"ק:

בְּעָלְמָא be'alma דִּי di בְּרָא vera כִּרְעוּתֵיהּ chir'utei.

וְיַמְלִיךְ veyamlich מַלְכוּתֵיהּ malchutei. וְיַצְמַח veyatzmach

פּוּרְקָנֵיהּ purkanei. וִיקָרֵב vikarev מְשִׁיחֵיהּ meshichei: אָמֵן amen אידהנויה.

"The Lord has reigned. He clothed Himself with pride. The Lord clothed Himself and girded Himself with might. He also established the world firmly, so that it would not collapse. Your Throne has been established. Ever since then, You have been forever. The rivers have lifted, Lord, the rivers have raised their voices. The rivers shall raise their powerful waves. More than the roars of many waters, and the powerful waves of the sea, You are immense in the high places, Lord. Your testimonies are extremely trustworthy. Your house is the holy sanctuary. The Lord shall be for the length of days." (Psalms 93)

KADDISH YEHE SHELAMA

May His great Name be more exalted and sanctified. (Amen)
In the world that He created according to His will, and may His kingdom reign.
And may He cause His redemption to sprout and may He bring the Mashiach closer. (Amen)

וּבְחַיֵּי uvchayei   וּבְיוֹמֵיכוֹן uvyomechon   בְּחַיֵּיכוֹן bechayechon

בַּעֲגָלָא ba'agala   יִשְׂרָאֵל Yisrael   ב"פ ראה   בֵּית bet   ילי   דְכָל dechol

וּבִזְמַן uvizman   קָרִיב kariv   וְאִמְרוּ ve'imru   אָמֵן amen   אמן amen אידהנויה.

The congregation and the *chazan* say the following:

Twenty Eight words (until *be'alma*) – meditate:
מילוי דבמילוי דס"ג (יוד ויו דלת הי ואו אלף ואו הי יוד)
Twenty Eight letters (until *almaya*) - meditate:
מילוי דבמילוי דמ"ה (יוד ואו דלת הא אלף ואו הי יוד).

יְהֵא yehe   שְׁמֵיהּ shemei   (שם י"ה דס"ג)   רַבָּא raba   קנ"א ב"ן,

יהוה אלהים יהוה אדני, מילוי קס"א וס"ג, מ"ה ברבוע וע"ב ע"ה   מְבָרַךְ mevarach,

לְעָלַם le'alam   לְעָלְמֵי le'almei   עָלְמַיָּא almaya   יִתְבָּרַךְ yitbarach

Seven words with six letters each (שם בן מ"ב) – meditate:
יהוה ♦ יוד הי ואו הי ♦ מילוי דמילוי דס"ג (יוד ויו דלת הי ואו אלף ואו הי יוד) ;
Also, seven times the letter *Vav* (שם בן מ"ב) – meditate:
יהוה ♦ יוד הא ואו הא ♦ מילוי דמילוי דמ"ה (יוד ואו דלת הא אלף ואו הי יוד).

וְיִשְׁתַּבַּח veyishtabach   י"פ ע"ב יהוה אל אבג יתץ.

וְיִתְפָּאַר veyitpa'ar   הי גו יה קרע שטן   וְיִתְרוֹמַם veyitromam   וה כוזו נגד יכש.

וְיִתְנַשֵּׂא veyitnase   במוכסז בטר צתג   וְיִתְהַדָּר veyit'hadar   כוזו יה וזקב טנע.

וְיִתְעַלֶּה veyit'ale   וה יוד ה יגל פזק   וְיִתְהַלָּל veyit'halal   א ואו הא שקו צית.

שְׁמֵיהּ shemei   (שם י"ה דמ"ה)   דְּקוּדְשָׁא dekudsha   בְּרִיךְ verich   הוּא hu:

אָמֵן amen אידהנויה.

לְעֵלָּא le'ela   מִן min   כָּל kol   ילי   בִּרְכָתָא birchata   שִׁירָתָא shirata

תֻּשְׁבְּחָתָא tishbechata   וְנֶחָמָתָא venechamata   דַּאֲמִירָן da'amiran

בְּעָלְמָא be'alma   וְאִמְרוּ ve'imru   אָמֵן amen   אָמֵן amen אידהנויה.

In your lifetimes and in your days and in the lifetime of all the House of Israel, speedily and in the near future, and you shall say, Amen. (Amen) May His great Name be blessed forever and for all eternity. Blessed and lauded, and glorified, and exalted, and extolled, and honored, and uplifted, and praised be the Name of the Holy Blessed One. (Amen) Above all blessings, songs, praises, and words of consolation that may be said in the world, and you shall say, Amen. (Amen)

יְהֵא yehe שְׁלָמָא shelama רַבָּא raba קס"א ב"ן, יהוה אלהים יהוה אדני, מילוי קס"א וס"ג,

מ"ה ברבוע וע"ב ע"ה min בֵּן shemaya שְׁמַיָּא chayim וְחַיִּים aהיה אהיה יהוה, בינה ע"ה

vesava וְשָׂבָע vishu'a וִישׁוּעָה venechama וְנֶחָמָה veshezava וְשֵׁיזָבָא

urefu'a וּרְפוּאָה uge'ula וּגְאֻלָּה uslicha וּסְלִיחָה vechapara וְכַפָּרָה

verevach וְרֵיוַוח vehatzala וְהַצָּלָה lanu לָנוּ alohim, אהיה אדני ulchol וּלְכֹל יה אדני

amo עַמּוֹ Yisrael יִשְׂרָאֵל ve'imru וְאִמְרוּ amen אָמֵן : amen אָמֵן אידהנויה.

Take three steps backwards and say:

ose עוֹשֶׂה shalom שָׁלוֹם bimromav בִּמְרוֹמָיו ע"ב, ריבוע יהוה. hu הוּא

berachamav בְּרַחֲמָיו ya'ase יַעֲשֶׂה shalom שָׁלוֹם alenu עָלֵינוּ ר"ת ש"ע נהורין.

ve'al וְעַל kol כֹּל יבי ; עמם amo עַמּוֹ Yisrael יִשְׂרָאֵל ve'imru וְאִמְרוּ amen אָמֵן :

amen אָמֵן אידהנויה.

ALENU

Alenu is a cosmic sealing agent. It cements and secures all of our prayers, protecting them from any negative forces such as the *klipot*. All prayers prior to *Alenu* drew down what the kabbalists call Inner Light. *Alenu*, however, attracts Surrounding Light, which envelops our prayers with a protective force-field to block out the *klipot*.

Drawing Surrounding Light in order to be protected from the *klipot* (negative side).

alenu עָלֵינוּ ריבוע דס"ג leshabe'ach לְשַׁבֵּחַ עלינו לשבוח = אבג יתץ, ועור

la'adon לַאֲדוֹן אני ; ס"ת ס"ג ע"ה hakol הַכֹּל ר"ת כללה, אדני

latet לָתֵת gedula גְּדֻלָּה leyotzer לְיוֹצֵר bereshit בְּרֵאשִׁית ר"ת גלב (בא"ר ב"י יג"ל)

shelo שֶׁלֹּא asanu עָשָׂנוּ kegoyei כְּגוֹיֵי ha'aratzot הָאֲרָצוֹת

velo וְלֹא samanu שָׂמָנוּ kemishpechot כְּמִשְׁפְּחוֹת ha'adama הָאֲדָמָה

May there be abundant peace from Heaven, life, contentment, salvation, consolation, deliverance, healing, redemption, pardon, atonement, comfort, and relief. For us and for His entire nation, Israel, and you shall say, Amen. (Amen) He, Who makes peace in His high places, with His compassion He shall make peace for us and for His entire nation, Israel. And you shall say, Amen. (Amen)

ALENU

It is incumbent upon us to give praise to the Master of all and to attribute greatness to the Molder of Creation, for He did not make us like the nations of the lands. He did not place us like the families of the Earth

שֶׁלֹּא shelo · שָׂם sam · חֶלְקֵנוּ chelkenu · כָּהֶם kahem · וְגוֹרָלֵנוּ vegoralenu

כְּכָל kechol · הֲמוֹנָם hamonam · שֶׁהֵם shehem · מִשְׁתַּחֲוִים mishtachavim

לְהֶבֶל lahevel · וָרִיק varik · וּמִתְפַּלְלִים umitpalelim · אֶל el · אֶל el

לֹא lo · Yoshi'a יוֹשִׁיעַ (pause here, and bow your entire body when you say "va'anachnu mishtachavim")

וַאֲנַחְנוּ va'anachnu · מִשְׁתַּחֲוִים mishtachavim · לִפְנֵי lifnei · מֶלֶךְ melech

מַלְכֵי malchei · הַמְּלָכִים hamelachim · הַקָּדוֹשׁ hakadosh · בָּרוּךְ baruch

הוּא hu · שֶׁהוּא shehu · נוֹטֶה note · שָׁמַיִם shamayim

וּמוֹשַׁב umoshav · אֶרֶץ aretz · וְיוֹסֵד veyosed

יְקָרוֹ yekaro · בַּשָּׁמַיִם bashamayim · מִמַּעַל mima'al

מְרוֹמִים meromim · בְּגָבְהֵי begovhei · עֻזּוֹ uzo · וּשְׁכִינַת ush'chinat

אַחֵר acher · עוֹד od · וְאֵין ve'ein · אֱלֹהֵינוּ eloheinu · הוּא hu

וְאֶפֶס ve'efes · מַלְכֵּנוּ malkenu · אֱמֶת emet

זוּלָתוֹ zulato · כַּכָּתוּב kakatuv · בַּתּוֹרָה batorah · וְיָדַעְתָּ veyadata

אֶל el · וַהֲשֵׁבֹתָ vahashevota · הַיּוֹם hayom

הוּא hu · Adonai לַיהֹוָה · כִּי ki · לְבָבֶךָ lvavecha

הָאֱלֹהִים haElohim

בַּשָּׁמַיִם bashamayim · מִמַּעַל mima'al

הָאָרֶץ ha'aretz · וְעַל ve'al

מִתָּחַת mitachat · אֵין en · עוֹד od

He did not make our lot like theirs and our destiny like that of their multitudes, for they prostrate themselves to futility and emptiness and they pray to a deity that does not help. But we prostrate ourselves before the King of all Kings, the Holy Blessed One. It is He Who spreads the Heavens and establishes the earth. The Seat of His glory is in the Heaven above and the Divine Presence of His power is in the Highest of Heights. He is our God and there is no other. Our King is true and there is none beside Him. As it is written in the Torah: "And you shall know today and you shall take it to your heart that it is the Lord Who is God in the Heavens above and upon the Earth below, and there is none other". (Deuteronomy 4:39)

עַל al כֵּן ken נְקַוֶּה nekave לָךְ lach יְהֹוָה Adonai אֱלֹהֵינוּ Elohenu

לִרְאוֹת lir'ot מְהֵרָה mehera בְּתִפְאֶרֶת betiferet עֻזָּךְ uzach

לְהַעֲבִיר leha'avir גִּלּוּלִים gilulim מִן min הָאָרֶץ ha'aretz

וְהָאֱלִילִים veha'elilim כָּרוֹת karot יִכָּרֵתוּן yikaretun לְתַקֵּן letaken

עוֹלָם olam בְּמַלְכוּת bemalchut שַׁדַּי Shadai וְכָל vechol בְּנֵי benei

בָשָׂר vasar יִקְרְאוּ yikre'u בְשִׁמְךָ vishmecha לְהַפְנוֹת lehafnot אֵלֶיךָ eleicha

כָּל kol רִשְׁעֵי rish'ei אָרֶץ aretz יַכִּירוּ yakiru וְיֵדְעוּ veyed'u כָּל kol

יוֹשְׁבֵי yoshvei תֵבֵל tevel כִּי ki לְךָ lecha תִּכְרַע tichra כָּל kol

בֶּרֶךְ berech תִּשָּׁבַע tishava כָּל kol לָשׁוֹן lashon לְפָנֶיךָ lefanecha

יְהֹוָה Adonai אֱלֹהֵינוּ Elohenu יִכְרְעוּ yichre'u וְיִפֹּלוּ veyipolu

וְלִכְבוֹד velichvod שִׁמְךָ shimcha יְקָר yekar יִתֵּנוּ yitenu וִיקַבְּלוּ vikabelu

כֻּלָּם chulam אֶת et עוֹל ol מַלְכוּתֶךָ malchutecha וְתִמְלוֹךְ vetimloch

עֲלֵיהֶם alehem מְהֵרָה mehera לְעוֹלָם le'olam וָעֶד va'ed

כִּי ki הַמַּלְכוּת hamalchut שֶׁלְּךָ shelcha הִיא hee וּלְעוֹלְמֵי ul'olmei

עַד ad תִּמְלוֹךְ timloch בְּכָבוֹד bechavod כַּכָּתוּב kakatuv

בְּתוֹרָתֶךָ betoratach יְהֹוָה Adonai יִמְלֹךְ yimloch לְעֹלָם le'olam

וָעֶד va'ed וְנֶאֱמַר vene'emar וְהָיָה vehaya

לְמֶלֶךְ lemelech Adonai עַל al כָּל kol

הָאָרֶץ ha'aretz בַּיוֹם bayom

הַהוּא hahu יִהְיֶה yih'ye יְהֹוָה Adonai אֶחָד echad

וּשְׁמוֹ ushmo אֶחָד echad

Consequently, we place our hope in You, Lord, our God, that we shall speedily see the glory of Your might, when You remove the idols from the earth and the deities shall be completely destroyed to correct the world with the kingdom of the Almighty. And all mankind shall then call out Your Name and You shall turn back to Yourself all the wicked ones of the earth. Then all the inhabitants of the world shall recognize and know that, for You, every knee bends and every tongue vows. Before You, Lord, our God, they shall kneel and fall and shall give honor to Your glorious Name. And they shall all accept the yoke of Your Kingdom and You shall reign over them, forever and ever. Because the kingdom is Yours. And forever and for eternity, You shall reign gloriously. As it is written in the Torah: "The Lord shall reign forever and ever," (Exodus 15:18) and it is also stated: "The Lord shall be King over the whole world and, on that day, the Lord shall be One and His Name One." (Zechariah 14:9)

When the Holiday falls on *Shabbat* (or on *Shabbat Chol Hamo'ed*) we begin here, otherwise we begin on page 79.

KABBALAT SHABBAT

You should go out to the field and if it is not possible it is good to go outside to a courtyard to a place which is empty and clear. And you should stand in a high place and turn to the west. At the time of sunset, close your eyes and put your hands on your chest, right hand over the left and stand with awe and fear as you stand in front of the King to receive the Holiness of *Shabbat*.

You should meditate that *Chakal* וֹקְ"ל (field), which is the numerical value of 138 equals: הַוָיָה אֶהְיֶה הַוָיָה אֲדֹנָי (יאהדונהי ★ יאהדונהי). Also it has the same numerical value of the *Milui* of the four Names (וד' י וי' ★ ★ וד' א או י ★ י ואו' וד' ★ י יו' וד') with the ten letters. And also ס"ג (יוד הי ואו הי) with its ten letters and the Name אֲדֹנָי have the numerical value of 138.

Now in the field (*Sade* שָׂדֶה) meditate that it is considered as the external part of the Four Worlds, and our goal, during *Kabbalat Shabbat* in the field, is to elevate this external part (the elevation is in the secret of the Internal Light of the external.)

You should visualize the Four Worlds in the following order, and meditate to elevate them as *Chochmah, Binah, Da'at* of the Lower World is entering into *Netzach, Hod, Yesod* of the Upper World. And later (when saying the word "*havu*" in Psalm 29) meditate on the elevation of the three Upper Levels of *Asiya* into *Netzach, Hod, Yesod* of *Yetzirah*.

Atzilut	יוד הי ויו הי
Beriah	יוד הי ואו הי
Yetzirah	יוד הא ואו הא
Asiyah	יוד הה וו הה

Say the following with all your force and might and with happiness:

leshem לְשֵׁם   yichud יִחוּד   kudsha קוּדְשָׁא   berich בְּרִיךְ   hu הוּא

ush'chintei וּשְׁכִינְתֵּיהּ   (יאהדונהי)   bid'chilu בִּדְחִילוּ   ur'chimu וּרְחִימוּ

ur'chimu וּרְחִימוּ (יאההויהה),   ud'chilu וּדְחִילוּ (איההויהה),   leyachda לְיַחֲדָא,

shem שֵׁם   yud יוֹ"ד   kei קֵי   bevav בְּוָא"ו   kei קֵי   beyichuda בְּיִחוּדָא

shelim שְׁלִים (יהוה)   beshem בְּשֵׁם   kol כָּל   י-   Yisrael יִשְׂרָאֵל,

bo'u בּוֹאוּ   venetze וְנֵצֵא   likrat לִקְרַאת   Shabbat שַׁבָּת   malketa מַלְכְּתָא,

lachakal לַחֲקַל   tapuchin תַּפּוּחִין   kadishin קַדִּישִׁין◆

KABBALAT SHABBAT
LESHEM YICHUD

For the sake of the unification of the Holy Blessed One and His Shechinah
with fear and love and with love and fear, in order to unify the Name Yud-Kei with Vav-Kei in perfect
unity and in the name of all Israel, let us go out towards the Queen Shabbat, to the field of the holy apples.

MIZMOR LEDAVID

In this Psalm the word *Kol* קוֹל which means voice, is used seven times. The voice is the Voice of the Creator—*Kol Adonai*. These seven voices represent seven dimensions of the Light. These seven dimensions express themselves through the seven verses of the *Ana Beko'ach*, the 42-Letter Name of God. Whenever we make a connection to the 42-Letter Name of God, we are tapping the primordial force of Creation. This kind of energy brings new life, rejuvenation, and total positivity to our lives. This helps awaken us to receive the Light of Shabbat.

In this Psalm we also find the Name: יהוה eighteen times. Eighteen is the same numerical value as the Armaic word *Chai* יי meaning life. Accordingly, we have 72 letters (4x18). These equate to the numerical value of the Armaic word *Chesed* חסד. *Chesed* represents the energy of mercy. The reasoning behind this construction of the prayer is to give us the ability to surround ourselves with the energy of Mercy that is now flowing into our world during *Shabbat*. Normally, at this time of day (sunset), the universe is filled with the energy of Judgment. On Shabbat, however, we are connecting only to Mercy, as *Shabbat* is a realm without Judgment. But there is a prerequisite: We have to be careful not to stand in judgment of others during the period just before Shabbat. During this time, the Satan always tries to incite hostilities and arguments between husbands and wives, families and friends. If the Satan succeeds and we are judgmental, we cannot connect to the Light of mercy. We must put ourselves into a frame of total happiness.

In this Psalm there are 18 times יהוה which adds up to 72 letters which is the numerical value of *Chesed*, for the Mercy that descends from the Upper World. There are 11 verses which is the same numerical value as ו"ה and 91 words, which is the numerical value for *Amen* אמן. Meditate that the three lower joints of the letter ל of *Tzelem* of *Abba* and *Ima* are entering *Zeir Anpin*.

מִזְמוֹר mizmor לְדָוִד leDavid

הָבוּ havu אוֹד, אהבה, דאגה

You should meditate to draw three times ב"ן from the Thirteen *Tikunei Dikna* of *Asiyah* to *Da'at* of *Asiyah* in order to elevate it to *Yesod* of *Yetzirah*.

לַיהוָֹהאדניאהדונהי ladonai בְּנֵי benei ר"ת הבל

You should meditate that your soul will be elevated with the soul of Abel during the night.

אֵלִים elim הבו יהוה בני אלים = יעקב

הָבוּ havu אוֹד, אהבה, דאגה

You should meditate to draw three times מ"ה from the Thirteen *Tikunei Dikna* of *Yetzirah* to *Binah* of *Asiyah* in order to elevate it to *Hod* of *Yetzirah*

לַיהוָֹהאדניאהדונהי la'donai כָּבוֹד kavod ר"ת כלה (ב"ן ג' ספירות) וָעֹז va'oz:

MIZMOR LEDAVID
A Psalm of David:
Render to the Lord, you sons of the powerful ones, render to the Lord honor and might.

הָבוּ havu אוֹד, אהבה, דאגה

You should meditate to draw three times ס"ג from the Thirteen *Tikunei Dikna* of *Beriah* to *Chochmah* of *Asiyah* in order to elevate it to *Netzach* of *Yetzirah*. Also, three times הָבוּ (=13), which equals to יוד הא ואו (=39), and the last הא (*Nukva*) of the Name יהוה, receives from the first three letters.

שְׁמוֹ shemo כְּבוֹד kevod ladonai ליהו̇ה־אדני־אהדונהי ר"ת כלה (ב"ן וג' ספירות)

ע"ב בריבוע וקס"א ע"ה, אל עֹדי ע"ה, מהע ע"ה ; הבו יהוה כבוד שמו = אדם דוד משיח

הִשְׁתַּחֲווּ hishtachavu

You should meditate to draw three times ע"ב from the Thirteen *Tikunei Dikna* of *Atzilut* to *Chochmah* of *Asiyah* in order for ס"ג to go to *Binah* and מ"ה and ב"ן will go to Da'at, as this is Their place in the secret of *Chasdim* and *Gevurot* as it is known.

בְּהַדְרַת behadrat ר"ת הבל ladonai ליהו̇ה־אדני־אהדונהי

You should meditate that your soul will be elevated with the soul of Abel during the night.

קֹדֶשׁ kodesh ר"ת למפרע קבלה (שביום שבת צריך ללמוד קבלה):

ז' קוֹלוֹת – Seven Voices

קוֹל kol (*Chesed*) ליהו̇ה־אדני־אהדונהי Adonai (אבגיתץ) – (ו)

עַל־ al הַמַּיִם hamayim ר"ת = אלף למד (וֹחסד – ואל עֹני רמוֹ במילה בהמשך)◆

אֵל־ El יא"י (מילוי דס"ג) הַכָּבוֹד hakavod לאו הִרְעִים hir'im

עַל־ al מַיִם mayim Adonai ליהו̇ה־אדני־אהדונהי (להמתיק שכ"ה דינים) ה"פ אדני

רַבִּים rabim ר"ת הרעים (שכ"ה דינים – ועני העשכ"ה דינים נמתקים ע"י עני שמות א"ל הרמוזים לעיל):

קוֹל־ kol (*Gevurah*) ליהו̇ה־אדני־אהדונהי Adonai (קרעשטן) – (ד)

בַּכּוֹחַ bako'ach ר"ת יב"ק, אלהים יהוה, אהיה אדני יהוה

קוֹל kol (*Tiferet*) ליהו̇ה־אדני־אהדונהי Adonai (נגדיכש) – (א)

בְּהָדָר behadar ר"ת יב"ק, אלהים יהוה, אהיה אדני יהוה:

Render to the Lord honor worthy of His Name, prostrate yourselves before the Lord in the glory of His Holiness. The voice of the Lord is upon the waters, The Lord of glory had thundered, the Lord is upon vast waters. The Voice of the Lord is powerful. The Voice of the Lord is majesty.

kol **קוֹל** (Netzach) **יְהֹוָאַדנּיאהדונהי** Adonai (בְּטִרְצָתֵגּ – א) **שֹׁבֵר** shover

arazim **אֲרָזִים** vayeshaber **וַיְשַׁבֵּר** Adonai **יְהֹוָאַדנּיאהדונהי** et **אֶת־** arzei **אַרְזֵי**

haLevanon **הַלְּבָנוֹן** ר״ת האא: vayarkidem **וַיַּרְקִידֵם** kemo **כְּמוֹ** egel **עֵגֶל**

Levanon **לְבָנוֹן** veSiryon **וְשִׂרְיוֹן** kemo **כְּמוֹ** ven **בֶּן־** ven **רְאֵמִים** re'emim:

kol **קוֹל־** (Hod) **יְהֹוָאַדנּיאהדונהי** Adonai (וֹזְקִבִטְנֵע – ו) **חֹצֵב** chotzev

lahavot **לַהֲבוֹת** (ס״ת הב״ל (כי עתה עולים בקדושה כל ניצוצות קין והבל עירדו בקליפות) **אֵשׁ** esh:

kol **קוֹל** (Yesod) **יוֹהוּוויאֲדנּיאהדונהי** Adonai (יוֹגוֹלוּפוּוּזוּקוּ – א)

yachil **יָחִיל** ס״ת ללה, אדני **מִדְבָּר** midbar **יָחִיל** yachil **יְהֹוָאַדנּיאהדונהי** Adonai

midbar **מִדְבָּר** kadesh **קָדֵשׁ** ר״ת קין: kol **קוֹל** (Malchut) **יְהֹוָאַדנּיאהדונהי** Adonai

(עֶקְצִית וּיכֵּון לכלול בו כל עשיה העשמות האוזרים – ודאאוא)

yecholel **יְחוֹלֵל** ayalot **אַיָּלוֹת** vayechesof **וַיֶּחֱשֹׂף** ye'arot **יְעָרוֹת**

uvhechalo **וּבְהֵיכָלוֹ** kulo **כֻּלּוֹ** omer **אֹמֵר** kavod **כָּבוֹד**:

יְהֹוָאַדנּיאהדונהי Adonai lamabul **לַמַּבּוּל** yashav **יָשָׁב** ר״ת ילי וס״ת הבל

le'olam **לְעוֹלָם** melech **מֶלֶךְ** Adonai **יְהֹוָאַדנּיאהדונהי** vayeshev **וַיֵּשֶׁב**

yiten **יִתֵּן** le'amo **לְעַמּוֹ** oz **עֹז** Adonai **יְהֹוָאַדנּיאהדונהי** ריבוע ס״ג י' אותיות דס״ג:

יְהֹוָאַדנּיאהדונהי Adonai yevarech **יְבָרֵךְ** עסמ״ב, הברכה (למתק את ז' המלכים שמתו)

et **אֶת־** amo **עַמּוֹ** vashalom **בַּשָּׁלוֹם** ר״ת ע״ב, ריבוע יהוה:

Meditate to raise *Chesed, Gevurah, Tiferet* to the place of *Chochmah, Binah, Da'at* and then to raise *Netzach, Hod, Yesod* to the place of *Chesed, Gevurah, Tiferet* and then to raise *Malchut* to the place of *Netzach, Hod, Yesod* by the seven voices (*kol*) and the seven **יהוה**.

The Voice of the Lord breaks cedars, the Lord breaks the cedars of Lebanon. He makes them dance around like a calf, Lebanon and Sirion like a wild young ox. The Voice of the Lord cleaves the flames of fire. The Voice of the Lord convulses the wilderness, the Lord convulses the wilderness of Kadesh. The Voice of the Lord frightens the hinds and strips the forests bare, and in His Temple all proclaim His glory. The Lord sat at the deluge, and the Lord sits as King forever. the Lord gives might to His people. The Lord will bless His people with peace. (Psalms 29)

ANA BEKO'ACH (An explanation and translation can be found on pages 222-224)

Chesed, Sunday (Alef Bet Gimel Yud Tav Tzadik) אבג יתץ

ana אָנָּא   beko'ach בְּכֹחַ   gedulat גְּדוּלַת   yeminecha יְמִינֶךָ

tatir תַּתִּיר   tzerura צְרוּרָה

Gevurah, Monday (Kuf Resh Ayin Sin Tet Nun) קרע שטן

kabel קַבֵּל   rinat רִנַּת   amecha עַמְּךָ   sagevenu שַׂגְּבֵנוּ

taharenu טַהֲרֵנוּ   nora נוֹרָא

Tiferet, Tuesday (Nun Gimel Dalet Yud Kaf Shin) נגד יכש

na נָא   gibor גִבּוֹר   dorshei דוֹרְשֵׁי   yichudecha יִחוּדֶךָ

kevavat כְּבָבַת   shomrem שָׁמְרֵם

Netzach, Wednesday (Bet Tet Resh Tzadik Tav Gimel) בטר צתג

barchem בָּרְכֵם   taharem טַהֲרֵם   rachamei רַחֲמֵי   tzidkatecha צִדְקָתֶךָ

tamid תָּמִיד   gomlem גָּמְלֵם

Hod, Thursday (Chet Kuf Bet Tet Nun Ayin) חקב טנע

chasin חֲסִין   kadosh קָדוֹשׁ   berov בְּרֹב   tuvcha טוּבְךָ

nahel נַהֵל   adatecha עֲדָתֶךָ

Yesod, Friday (Yud Gimel Lamed Pei Zayin Kuf) יגל פזק

yachid יָחִיד   ge'e גֵּאֶה   le'amecha לְעַמְּךָ   pene פְּנֵה

zochrei זוֹכְרֵי   kedushatecha קְדֻשָּׁתֶךָ

Malchut, Saturday (Shin Kuf Vav Tzadik Yud Tav) שקו צית

shav'atenu שַׁוְעָתֵנוּ   kabel קַבֵּל   ushma וּשְׁמַע   tza'akatenu צַעֲקָתֵנוּ

yode'a יוֹדֵעַ   ta'alumot תַּעֲלוּמוֹת

BARUCH SHEM KEVOD

Whispering this final verse brings all the Light from the Upper Worlds into our physical existence.

(Whisper): יוזו אותיות   baruch בָּרוּךְ   shem שֵׁם   kevod כְּבוֹד   malchuto מַלְכוּתוֹ

le'olam לְעוֹלָם   ריבוע ס"ג ו"י אותיות דס"ג   va'ed וָעֶד

LECHA DODI

This prayer was written by Kabbalist Rav Shlomo Elkabetz, and contains ten verses that connect us to the entire Ten *Sefirot*—the transmitters by which the Light of God animates our universe—including our souls. During the week, we encounter many challenges and opportunities that may disrupt and misalign these ten energy forces on both a personal and universal level. The level of disruption is based on our individual and collective actions. Consequently, the levels of energy in the world and in our soul can become disordered and in disarray. On a personal level this can manifest in overreacting and anger to situations to which we would normally respond with restraint and patience. Each of the ten verses in *Lecha Dodi* adjusts each level of the Ten *Sefirot*, rearranging them into their correct positions in the universe. It also realigns each *Sefira* within our body, putting us into proper emotional, physical, and spiritual balance.

The intention of *Lecha Dodi* is to elevate the ten *Sefirot* of *Yetzirah* to the Upper World (*Beriah*).

Keter

לְכָה lecha   דּוֹדִי dodi   לִקְרַאת likrat   כַּלָּה kalah•

פְּנֵי penei   וחכמה   בינה   שַׁבָּת Shabbat   נְקַבְּלָה nekabela:

Chochmah

שָׁמוֹר shamor   וְזָכוֹר vezachor   ע"ב   קס"א,   יהי   אור   ע"ה

אָוֶד echad bedibur בְּדִבּוּר (סוד המשוכת העפע מן ד' עומות ליסוד הנקרא זכור) אהבה, דאגה•

הַמְּיוּחָד hameyuchad (מילוי דס"ג) יא"י El אֵל hishmi'anu הִשְׁמִיעָנוּ•

יְהוֹ...אהיה...אהדונהי Adonai אֶחָד echad אהבה, דאגה וּשְׁמוֹ ushmo ע"ב בריבוע קס"א ע"ה,

לְשֵׁם leshem אֶחָד echad ע"ה מהע אהבה, דאגה•

וּלְתִפְאֶרֶת ultiferet וְלִתְהִלָּה velit'hila ע"ה אמת, אהיה פעמים אהיה, ד"פ ס"ג: Lecha

Binah

לִקְרַאת likrat שַׁבָּת Shabbat לְכוּ lechu וְנֵלְכָה venelcha•

כִּי ki הִיא hee מְקוֹר mekor הַבְּרָכָה haberacha•

מֵרֹאשׁ merosh ריבוע אלהים אלהים דיודין ע"ה מִקֶּדֶם mikedem נְסוּכָה nesucha•

סוֹף sof מַעֲשֶׂה ma'ase בְּמַחֲשָׁבָה bemachashava תְּחִלָּה techila: Lecha

---

LECHA DODI

Keter   *Go my beloved towards the bride, let us welcome the presence of the Shabbat!*

Chochmah   *"Safeguard" and "remember" as one utterance. The unique God made us hear. God is One and His Name is One, for renown, for splendor and for praise.*

Binah   *Come, let us go towards the Shabbat, for It is the source of blessing. From the beginning, from antiquity, It was honored. The end of deed was first in thought.*

Chesed

מְלוּכָה melucha • עֲרִי, סְנַדְלְפֹון, בֹּוזֹוֵר ir עִיר melech מֶלֶךְ mikdash מִקְדָּשׁ

הַהֲפֵכָה hahafecha • מִתֹּוךְ mitoch צְאִי tze'i קוּמִי kumi

הַבָּכָא habacha • בְּעֵמֶק be'emek שֶׁבֶת shevet לָךְ lach רַב rav

Lecha וְחֶמְלָה chemla ❖ עָלַיִךְ alayich יַחֲמֹול yachmol וְהוּא vehu

Gevurah

בִּגְדֵי bigdei לִבְשִׁי livshi • קוּמִי kumi מֵעָפָר me'afar הִתְנַעֲרִי hitna'ari

בֵּית bet יִשַׁי Yishai בֶּן ben יַד yad עַל al • עַמִּי ami תִּפְאַרְתֵּךְ tifartech

Lecha גְּאָלָה ge'ala ❖ נַפְשִׁי nafshi אֶל el קָרְבָה korva • הַלֹּוזֵמִי halachmi

Tiferet

קוּמִי kumi אֹורֵךְ orech בָא va כִּי ki • הִתְעֹורְרִי hit'oreri • הִתְעֹורְרִי hit'oreri

אֹורִי ori • דַּבֵּרִי daberi שִׁיר shir עוּרִי uri עוּרִי uri • כָּבֹוד kevod

Lecha נִגְלָה nigla ❖ עָלַיִךְ alayich Adonai יְהֹוָה

Netzach

תִּכָּלְמִי tikalmi • וְלֹא velo תֵבֹושִׁי tevoshi לֹא lo

תֶּהֱמִי tehemi • וּמַה uma תִּשְׁתֹּוחֲחִי tishtochachi מַה ma

עַמִּי ami • עֲנִיֵּי aniyei יֶחֱסוּ yechesu בָּךְ bach

Lecha תִּלָּה tila ❖ עַל al עֲרִי, סְנַדְלְפֹון, בֹּוזֹוֵר ir עִיר venivneta וְנִבְנְתָה

Chesed *Sanctuary of the King! royal city! Arise and depart from amidst the upheaval. For too long you have dwelt in the valley of weeping. He will bestow His compassion upon you.*

Gevurah *Shake off the dust, arise. Don your clothes of splendor, my people. Through the son of Ishai, from Bet Lechem, will the redemption draw close to my soul.*

Tiferet *Wake up! Wake up! For your Light has come, rise and shine. Awaken, awaken, and utter a song. The glory of God is revealed upon you.*

Netzach *Feel no shame, do not be humiliated. Why are you downcast? Why are you disconsolate? In you will My people's afflicted find shelter, as the city is built upon its hilltop.*

Hod

וְהָיוּ vehayu לִמְשִׁסָּה limshisa שׁוֹסָיִךְ shosayich ◆ וְרָחֲקוּ verachaku כָּל kol יִלֹי

כְּמְבַלְּעָיִךְ meval'ayich ◆ יָשִׂישׂ yasis עָלַיִךְ alayich אֱלֹהָיִךְ Elohayich יִלֹה ◆

כִּמְשׂוֹשׂ kimsos וְזָתָן chatan עַל al כַּלָּה kalah: Lecha

Yesod

יָמִין yamin וּשְׂמֹאל usmol תִּפְרוֹצִי tifrotzi ◆ וְאֶת ve'et

יְהֹוָה Adonai תַּעֲרִיצִי ta'aritzi ◆ עַל al יָד yad

אִישׁ ish בֶּן ben פַּרְצִי Partzi ◆ וְנִשְׂמְחָה venismecha וְנָגִילָה venagila: Lecha

Malchut

בּוֹאִי bo'i בְשָׁלוֹם veshalom עֲטֶרֶת ateret בַּעְלָה ba'la ◆

גַּם gam בְּשִׂמְחָה besimcha בְּרִנָּה berina וּבְצָהֳלָה uv'tzahola ◆

תּוֹךְ toch אֱמוּנֵי emunei עַם am סְגֻלָּה segula:

BO'I KALAH

When we utter the words *Bo'i Kalah*, which means "draw near bride," we receive an extra soul that comes to us every *Shabbat* to help us capture the extra energy that is being revealed. For example, an 8-ounce glass cannot contain ten ounces of water. The glass would need to be enlarged. When we receive the extra soul, this enlarges our soul, thereby, increasing its overall capacity to receive the additional Light of Shabbat. This is a golden opportunity to join our souls through the Light of *Shabbat*, with the Light of the Creator.

We learn from this verse, that to maximize our connection, we are supposed to treat the energy of *Shabbat* like a bride. After a man has been married for twenty years, he usually does not have the same feeling, passion, longing, and anticipation that he first had when his wife was still a bride, just a few brief moments before their wedding ceremony.

Hod   *May your oppressors be downtrodden, and may those who devoured you be driven far away. Your God will rejoice over you as a groom rejoices over a bride.*

Yesod   *To the right and to the left you shall spread, and you shall extol God through a man, a descendant of Perets. Then we shall be joyful and mirthful.*

Malchut   *Come in peace, crown of her husband. Even in joy, in song, and in cheer. Among the faithful of the treasured nation.*

You should meditate to elevate the World of *Yetzirah* (which means: *Malchut* is elevated to *Netzach*, *Hod*, *Yesod*, then *Netzach*, *Hod*, *Yesod* are elevated to *Chesed*, *Gevurah*, *Tiferet*, then *Chesed*, *Gevurah*, *Tiferet* are elevated to *Chochmah*, *Binah*, *Da'at*, and then *Chochmah*, *Binah* and *Da'at*, are elevated to *Netzach*, *Hod*, *Yesod* of *Beriah*.) Indeed, the Seven Lower *Sefirot* of *Yetzirah* are elevated by the Seven *Margela'in* and the Holy Names: אהי"ה יהו"ה, which equal 42:

א יְהֹוָה, ה אֵל, י יֱהֹוָה, ה אֱלֹהִים, ה אֲדֹנָי, יה ארדני, ה מצפצ, ו מצפצ

And the Three Upper *Sefirot* are elevated by the three times the word *Bo'i* which is equal to 13, like the words for "love," "unity" and "care" (אחד, אהבה, דאגה), and also equals יאא (13).

kalah כַּלָּה bo'i בּוֹאִי ג"פ באי = יוד הא ואו   **Bow to the Right**
Chochmah – Speach

בואי כלה = אכדטם (כי על ידי זה נמתקו הדינים)

kalah כַּלָּה bo'i בּוֹאִי ג"פ באי = יוד הא ואו   **Bow to the Left**
Binah – Action

בואי כלה = אכדטם (כי על ידי זה נמתקו הדינים)

toch תּוֹךְ emunei אֱמוּנֵי am עַם segula סְגֻלָּה:

Meditate to receive the extra soul called: *Nefesh*
from the aspect of the night of *Shabbat*

The third "*bo'i kalah*" should be said silently, as it corresponds to *Da'at* (and *Da'at* is not part of the Ten *Sefirot*).

kalah כַּלָּה bo'i בּוֹאִי ג"פ באי = יוד הא ואו   **Bow to the Center**
Da'at – Thought

ג"פ באי כלה = צדיק ; בואי כלה = אכדטם (כי על ידי זה נמתקו הדינים)

Shabbat שַׁבָּת malketa מַלְכְּתָא:

lecha לְכָה dodi דּוֹדִי likrat לִקְרַאת kalah כַּלָּה.

penei פְּנֵי חכמה בינה Shabbat שַׁבָּת nekabela נְקַבְּלָה:

MIZMOR SHIR LEYOM HASHABBAT
The initials are of: *LeMoshe* (for Moses) connects us to quantum consciousness.

After we sing the *Lecha Dodi*, we recite two paragraphs that were recited by Adam during the first *Shabbat* in the Garden of Eden. Adam signifies all the souls of humanity. At the time of Creation, all these souls that were and ever will be were unified as one entity, we call Adam. The Garden of Eden is a realm of pure Light and immortality. The Aramaic letters that compose this paragraph represent specific energy forces that nourish and fulfill this unified soul called Adam. The letters are a formula that acts as an antenna to draw these forces into our lives, thereby giving us a taste of the Garden of Eden.

(We bow to the Left) *Come Bride.*   (We bow to the Right) *Come, Bride,*
(We bow to the Center) *Among the faithful of the treasured nation, come Bride, Queen Sabbath.*
Go my beloved towards the bride; let us welcome the presence of the Sabbath!

haShabbat הַשַּׁבָּת ע"ה נגד, מזבח, זן, אל יהוה leyom לְיוֹם shir שִׁיר mizmor מִזְמוֹר

Initials of *LeMoshe* (למשה) —*Moshe* is a code name for the world of *Atzilut*, which is where we are now elevating *Beriah*, which gets illuminated from *Netzach, Hod, Yesod* of *Atzilut*. Also it is called *Moshe*, because now *Moshe* receives 1,000 illuminations (those he had lost because of the golden calf) and then gives us back what we lost. Also, *Moshe* with tens of thousands of righteous souls are descending in order to elevate all the Holy Sparks and the souls that are in the depths of the *klipa* and all the souls of the living and dead that cannot elevate on their own.

lehodot לְהֹדוֹת ר"ת ט"ל (ג"פ באי וג"פ הבו דלעיל) והו tov טוֹב

(ט"ל = יוד הא ואו, עוהם ג"ר (וזב"ד) דבריאה שיעלו כעת לאצילות)
Meditate to elevate the Three Upper *Sefirot* of *Beriah* to *Atzilut*

ladonai לַיהֹוָה אדנ"י אהדונה"י

Meditate on the Holy Name: יוד הי ויו הי which is *Malchut* of *Atzilut*.
Also meditate on the 42-Letter Name of *Mem Hei* of *Atzilut*:

יהוה, יוד הא ואו הא, יוד ואו דלת הא אלף ואו אלף ואו הא אלף

with this Name, the Seven Lower *Sefirot* of *Beriah* are going to be elevated to *Atzilut*.
Also meditate on the Holy Name: יוד הי ואו הי which is the secret of the world of *Beriah*
(which is now elevated to *Atzilut* by the 42-Letter Name mentioned above).

baboker בַּבֹּקֶר lehagid לְהַגִּיד elyon עֶלְיוֹן leshimcha לְשִׁמְךָ ulzamer וּלְזַמֵּר

alei עֲלֵי balelot בַּלֵּילוֹת ve'emunat'cha וֶאֱמוּנָתְךָ chasdecha חַסְדֶּךָ

bechinor בְּכִנּוֹר higayon הִגָּיוֹן alei עֲלֵי navel נָבֶל va'alei וַעֲלֵי asor עָשׂוֹר

befa'olecha בְּפָעֳלֶךָ Adonai יְהֹוָה אדנ"י אהדונה"י simachtani שִׂמַּחְתַּנִי ki כִּי

gadlu גָּדְלוּ מ"ה ma מַה aranen אֲרַנֵּן yadecha יָדֶיךָ bema'asei בְּמַעֲשֶׂיךָ

amku עָמְקוּ me'od מְאֹד Adonai יְהֹוָה אדנ"י אהדונה"י ma'asecha מַעֲשֶׂיךָ

ba'ar בַּעַר ish אִישׁ יחו" (Superior *Keter*) machshevotecha מַחְשְׁבֹתֶי(ו)ךָ

zot זֹאת et אֶת יָבִין yavin lo לֹא uchsil וּכְסִיל yeda יֵדַע lo לֹא

bifro'ach בִּפְרֹחַ כוחות הקדושה (ע"ב שמות) resha'im רְשָׁעִים kemo כְּמוֹ esev עֵשֶׂב

The souls of the wicked are judged now to see if they are worthy of being elevated from *Gehenom*.

MIZMOR SHIR LEYOM HASHABBAT
"A Psalm, a song for the day of Shabbat!
It is good to say thanks to You, the Lord, and to sing Your Name, Exalted One, And to relate Your kindness in the morning and Your faithfulness in the evenings, upon a ten-stringed instrument and lyre, with singing accompanied by a harp. Because You have made me happy, Lord, with Your deeds, for the work of Your hands, I shall sing joyously. How great are Your deeds, Lord, and how greatly profound are Your thoughts. A boor cannot know nor can a fool understand this. When the wicked bloom like grass

vayatzitzu וַיָּצִיצוּ kol כָּל־ ילי po'alei פֹּעֲלֵי aven אָוֶן

(the *klipa* that wants to be elevated with the Holiness) lehishamdam לְהִשָּׁמְדָם

adei עֲדֵי ad עַד (but it is not allowed to go up): veAta וְאַתָּה marom מָרוֹם

hine הִנֵּה ki כִּי: Adonai יְהֹוָה(אדני יאהדונהי) ריבוע דס"ג י' אותיות le'olam לְעֹלָם

oyvecha אֹיְבֶיךָ hine הִנֵּה ki כִּי־ Adonai יְהֹוָה(אדני יאהדונהי) oyvecha אֹיְבֶיךָ

(the *klipa*) aven אָוֶן po'alei פֹּעֲלֵי kol כָּל־ ילי yitpardu יִתְפָּרְדוּ yovedu יֹאבֵדוּ

baloti בַּלֹּתִי karni קַרְנִי kir'em כִּרְאֵים (the Holiness) vatarem וַתָּרֶם

eni עֵינִי ריבוע דמ"ה vatabet וַתַּבֵּט: ra'anan רַעֲנָן beshemen בְּשֶׁמֶן

mere'im מְרֵעִים alai עָלַי bakamim בַּקָּמִים beshurai בְּשׁוּרָי

The souls of the righteous that are elevated now: יוד הי ואו הה oznai אָזְנָי tishmana תִּשְׁמַעְנָה

tzadik צַדִּיק ג"פ באי כלה דלעיל katamar כַּתָּמָר yifrach יִפְרָח ס"ת קרח

(meditate to elevate the soul of *Korach*) ke'erez כְּאֶרֶז baLevanon בַּלְּבָנוֹן yisge יִשְׂגֶּה:

Adonai יְהֹוָה(אדני יאהדונהי) ראה ב"פ bevet בְּבֵית shetulim שְׁתוּלִים

od עוֹד yafrichu יַפְרִיחוּ: ילה Elohenu אֱלֹהֵינוּ bechatzrot בְּחַצְרוֹת

vera'ananim וְרַעֲנַנִּים deshenim דְּשֵׁנִים beseva בְּשֵׂיבָה yenuvun יְנוּבוּן

yashar יָשָׁר ki כִּי lehagid לְהַגִּיד: אל (יא"י מילוי דס"ג) yih'yu יִהְיוּ

bo בּוֹ: (כתיב: עלתה) avlata עַוְלָתָה velo וְלֹא־ tzuri צוּרִי Adonai יְהֹוָה(אדני יאהדונהי)

ADONAI MALACH

In this Psalm we have 45 words corresponding to the Holy Name: מ"ה (יוד הא ואו הא)

ge'ut גֵּאוּת malach מָלָךְ (*Zeir Anpin*) Adonai יְהֹוָה(אדני יאהדונהי)
(410 cords of *Arich Anpin* - where *Zeir Anpin* is elevated on *Shabbat* and He is clothing them)

hit'azar הִתְאַזָּר oz עֹז Adonai יְהֹוָה(אדני יאהדונהי) lavesh לָבֵשׁ lavesh לָבֵשׁ

---

and all doers of iniquity blossom in order to destroy them forever. And You are exalted forever, Lord. For behold, Your enemies, Lord! Your enemies shall perish and all the doers of iniquity shall be dispersed And You shall lift up my worth like an ox and I will be drenched with fresh oil. And my eyes will see my foes and my ears will hear those who rise up to harm me. A righteous man will flourish like a palm leaf, like a cedar in Lebanon he will grow tall. They are planted in the House of the Lord, they shall flourish in the courtyards of our God. They will still be fruitful in old age, vigorous and fresh they shall be to declare that the Lord is just, my Rock in whom there is no wrong." (Psalms 92)

ADONAI MALACH

"The Lord has reigned. He clothed Himself with pride. The Lord clothed and girded Himself with might.

ב"פ רי"ו   tevel תֵּבֵל   tikon תִּכּוֹן   אדני אהיה אלהים, = ר"ת   af אַף

ומב   me'az מֵאָז   kis'acha כִּסְאֲךָ   nachon נָכוֹן   timot תִּמּוֹט: bal בַּל

neharot נְהָרוֹת   nas'u נָשְׂאוּ:   אדני אלהים = קנ"א, ר"ת   Ata אַתָּה   me'olam מֵעוֹלָם

(410 cords of Arich Anpin -
Which draw Light from the sea of *Chochmah* -דא"ח סתימא מווזא- on *Shabbat* to *Zeir Anpin).*

Adonai יְהֹוָאדֹנָיאהדונהי

yis'u יִשְׂאוּ   kolam כּוֹלָם   neharot נְהָרוֹת   קין = ר"ת   nas'u נָשְׂאוּ

(Backwards, initials of the name Cain, as when Beriah is elevated his sparks are being corrected)

נְהָרוֹת neharot דָּכְיָם dochyam ר"ת דֹנָי:

Meditate that we are now in the World of *Atzilut* — and with the 42-Letter Name (the seven voices) that comes from *Abba* and *Ima*, we are elevating to the World of *Beriah.*

ערי, סנדלפון, בוזוּך, = ר"ת   rabim רַבִּים   mayim מַיִם   (410 cords)   mikolot מִקֹּלוֹת

ילי   yam יָ ם   mishberei מִשְׁבְּרֵי   adirim אַדִּירִים הרי   לעשות בה מן עוהם ה"ג - *Ima)*

Arich Anpin [has 221 *Ribo* (tens of thousands) illuminations],
He is giving 150 *Ribo* (tens of thousands) illuminations to *Zeir Anpin.*
Initials of אמי (my mother) because, *Zeir Anpin* first goes up and takes *Mochin* from *Ima* (mother).

Adonai יְהֹוָאדֹנָיאהדונהי bamarom בַּמָּרוֹם הרי adir אַדִּיר

Initials of אבי (my father) because, *Zeir Anpin* later goes up and takes *Mochin* from *Abba* (father).

levetcha לְבֵיתְךָ   קין = ר"ת   me'od מְאֹד   ne'emnu נֶאֶמְנוּ   edotecha עֵדֹתֶיךָ

le'orech לְאֹרֶךְ   Adonai יְהֹוָאדֹנָיאהדונהי   kodesh קֹדֶשׁ   na'ava נָאֲוָה ב"פ ראה

האותיות עם נהורים שע' = ימים לאורך ה' ; אדני ס"ת ; ילי ר"ת ; נלך   yamim יָמִים:

Meditate on the Name ילי to elevate the Name: אדני and the sparks of the souls of *Beriah* that are captured by the *klipa* and cannot elevate by the above mentioned 42-Letter Name. Then meditate on the Name: יוּד הֵי וָיו הֵי, which is the *Atzilut* (where everything is being elevated).

He also established the world firmly, so that it would not collapse. Your Throne has been established. Ever since then, You have been forever. The rivers have lifted, Lord, the rivers have raised their voices. The rivers shall raise their powerful waves. More than the roars of many waters, and the powerful waves of the sea, You are immense in the high places, The Lord. Your testimonies are extremely trustworthy. Your House is the holy Sanctuary. The Lord shall be for the length of days." (Psalms 93)

BAR YOCHAI

Kabbalists throughout history agree that a human being cannot overcome the force of negativity alone, without the teachings and knowledge of the *Zohar* and the technology of *Kabbalah*. Why is it that when we know that something is bad for us, we still engage in it? Why is it that when we know something is good for us, we abstain or procrastinate? Why do we forego positive actions in favor of negative ones nine times out of ten? The reason, according to Kabbalah, is that we constantly battle an opponent in the Game of Life. This opponent is called Satan. It ignites all of our reactive negative thoughts and actions. For 5,000 years, it has been beating us at this game that hovers on the narrow edge of life and death, pain and suffering, good and evil. The kabbalistic insight as to why our opponent has been so successful is that Satan convinces humankind that Satan does not even exist. Through the Light of the *Zohar*, Satan is exposed and once we know who the opponent really is, we have a chance of beating it. The *Zohar* not only exposes and identifies the real enemy, it also gives us the power to overtake and defeat him.

It is incumbent upon us to connect to the seed and origin of the *Zohar* itself—its author, *Rav Shimon bar Yochai*. And so each *Shabbat* we sing the song of *Bar Yochai* to make this vital connection.

בַּר Bar | יוֹחָאי Yochai | נִמְשַׁחְתָּ nimshachta | אַשְׁרֶיךָ ashrecha

שֶׁמֶן shemen | שָׂשׂוֹן sason | מֵחֲבֵרֶיךָ mechaverecha:

Malchut

בַּר Bar | יוֹחָאי Yochai | שֶׁמֶן shemen | מִשְׁחַת mishchat | קֹדֶשׁ kodesh,

נִמְשַׁחְתָּ nimshachta | מִמִּדַּת mimidat | הַקֹּדֶשׁ hakodesh

נָשָׂאתָ nasata | צִיץ tzitz | מנֵּזר | נֵזֶר nezer | הַקֹּדֶשׁ hakodesh,

חָבוּשׁ chavush | עַל al | רֹאשְׁךָ roshcha | פְּאֵרֶךָ pe'erecha: | *Yochai Bar*

Yesod

בַּר Bar | יוֹחָאי Yochai | מוֹשַׁב moshav | טוֹב tov | והו | יָשַׁבְתָּ yashavta,

יוֹם yom | ע"ה | נֶגֶד | מזבח, | זַ, | אל | יהוה | נָסַתָ nasta

יוֹם yom | ע"ה | נֶגֶד | מזבח, | זַ, | אל יהוה | אֲשֶׁר asher | בָּרַכְתָּ barachta

בִּמְעָרַת bim'arat | צוּרִים tzurim | שֶׁעָמַדְתָּ she'amadeta | שָׁם sham

קָנִיתָ kanita | הוֹדְךָ hodcha | וַהֲדָרֶךָ vahadarecha: | *Yochai Bar*

BAR YOCHAI

Bar Yochai, you are anointed and praises, drawing the oil of happiness from your friends.

Malchut   Bar Yochai holy oil anointed you from the holy tribute. You carried the tiara of the holy crown, on you head for beauty.

Yesod   Bar Yochai, you sat in good place, the day you run and escaped. In the cave of rock you stood, to obtain your majesty and glory.

Netzach Hod

בַּר Bar יוֹחַאי Yochai עֲצֵי atzei שִׁטִים shitim עוֹמְדִים omdim,

לִמוּדֵי limudei יְהֹוָה Adonai הֵם hem לוֹמְדִים lomdim, אוֹר or or רז, א"ס

מִפְלָא mufla אוֹר or or רז, א"ס הַיְקוֹד hayekod הֵם hem יוֹקְדִים yokdim,

הֲלֹא halo הֵמָה hema יוֹרוּךְ yorucha מוֹרֶךְ morecha: *Bar Yochai*

Tiferet

בַּר Bar יוֹחַאי Yochai וְלִשְׂדֵה velisde תַּפּוּחִים tapuchim,

עָלִיתָ alita לִלְקוֹט lilkot בּוֹ vo מֶרְקָחִים merkachim.

סוֹד sod מֵיכ, י"פ הַאא תּוֹרָה torah כְּצִיצִים ketzitzim וּפְרָחִים ufrachim,

נַעֲשֶׂה na'ase אָדָם adam נֶאֱמַר ne'emar בַּעֲבוּרֶךְ ba'avurecha: *Bar Yochai*

Gevurah

בַּר bar יוֹחַאי yochai נֶאֱזַרְתָּ ne'ezarta בִּגְבוּרָה bigvura רי"ו

וּבְמִלְחֶמֶת uvmilchemet אֵשׁ esh דָת dat הַשַּׁעְרָה hasha'ra.

וְחֶרֶב vecherev רי"ו הוֹצֵאתָ hotzeta מִתַּעְרָה mita'ra,

שָׁלַפְתָּ shalafta נֶגֶד neged מִזְבוּ, זן, אל יהוה צוֹרְרֶיךְ tzorerecha: *Bar Yochai*

Chesed

בַּר bar יוֹחַאי yochai לִמְקוֹם limkom אַבְנֵי avnei שַׁיִשׁ shayish,

הִגַּעְתָ higata לִפְנֵי lifnei וחכמה בינה אַרְיֵה arye לַיִשׁ layish.

גַּם gam גֻּלַת gulat כּוֹתֶרֶת koteret עַל al עַיִשׁ ayish,

תְּשׁוּרִי tashuri וּבְמִי umi ילי יְשׁוּרֶךְ yeshurecha: *Bar Yochai*

Netzach Hod	*Bar Yochai, the acacia wood stands for you to study God's teachings. A wonderful, shining light is a glow, as your teachers taught you.*
Tiferet	*Bar Yochai, you came to a field of apples to gather potions. The secret of Torah is like buds and blossoms; "Let us create man" was stated with you in mind.*
Gevura	*Bar Yochai, you take courage with vigor, and fight with fire. You drew a sword out of its sheath against your opponent.*
Chesed	*Bar Yochai, to the place of marble stones, you arrived with lion's face. We will see even the headstone of lions, but who will see you?*

Binah

Bar בַּר   Yochai יוֹחַאי   bekodesh בְּקֹדֶשׁ   hakodashim, הַקֳּדָשִׁים

kav קַו   yarok יָרֹק   mechadesh מְחַדֵּשׁ (י״ב הויות, קס״א קנ״א)   chodashim וְחֳדָשִׁים

sheva שֶׁבַע   shabatot שַׁבָּתוֹת   sod סוֹד (מ״כ, י״ף האא)   chamishim וַחֲמִשִּׁים,

kasharta קָשַׁרְתָּ   kishrei קִשְׁרֵי   shin שִׁי״ן   kesharecha קְשָׁרֶיךָ ✦ *Bar Yochai*

Chochmah

Bar בַּר   Yochai יוֹחַאי   yod יוּ״ד   chochmah וְחָכְמָה (במילוי = תרי״ג מצוות)

keduma, קְדוּמָה   hishkafta הִשְׁקַפְתָּ   lichvodo לִכְבוֹדוֹ   penima פְּנִימָה ◆

teruma, תְּרוּמָה   reshit רֵאשִׁית   netivot נְתִיבוֹת   lev ל״ב

at אֶת   keruv כְּרוּב   mimshach מִמְשַׁח   ziv זִיו   orecha אוֹרֶךָ ✦ *Bar Yochai*

Keter

bar בַּר   yochai יוֹחַאי   or אוֹר (רז, א״ס)   mufla מֻפְלָא   rom רוֹם   ma'la, מַעֲלָה

yareta יָרֵאתָ   milhabit מִלְהַבִּיט   ki כִּי   rav רַב   la לָהּ,

ta'aluma תַּעֲלוּמָה   ve'ayin וְאַיִן   kore קוֹרֵא   la לָהּ,

namta נַמְתָּ   ayin עַיִן (ריבוע דמ״ה)   lo לֹא   teshurecha תְּשׁוּרֶךָ ✦ *Bar Yochai*

Bar בַּר   Yochai יוֹחַאי   ashrei אַשְׁרֵי   yoladetecha, יוֹלַדְתֶּךָ

ashrei אַשְׁרֵי   ha'am הָעָם   hem הֵם   lomdecha לוֹמְדֶךָ ◆

ve'ashrei וְאַשְׁרֵי   ha'omdim הָעוֹמְדִים   al עַל   sodecha סוֹדֶךָ (מ״כ, י״ף האא)

levushei לְבוּשֵׁי   choshen וְחֹשֶׁן   tumeicha תֻּמֶּיךָ   ve'urecha וְאוֹרֶךָ ✦ *Bar Yochai*

shemen שֶׁמֶן   sason שָׂשׂוֹן   yochai יוֹחַאי   nimshachta נִמְשַׁחְתָּ   ashrecha, אַשְׁרֶיךָ

mechavereicha מֵחֲבֵרֶיךָ ✦

Binah	Bar Yochai, in the Holy of Holies, a green line renews the months. Seven Shabbats are the secret of fifty, the letter Shins for your own connections.
Chochmah	Bar Yochai, the ancient Yud of Chochmah, you observed its inner honor. 32 paths are the beginning of offering; you are the Cherub from which brilliant light anoints.
Keter	Bar Yochai, a wonderful light of highest greatness, you feared looking to her greatness. A mystery no one can read, you sleep, and no eye can see you.

Bar Yochai, praised be those who gave birth to you, praised be the people who study your writings. And praised be the people who can understand your secret, dress with armor of your breastplate and of your Urim and Tumim. Bar Yochai, you are anointed and praises, drawing the oil of happiness from your friends.

KEGAVNA

Kegavna is a passage from the *Zohar* that the sages tell us to read after the song of *Bar Yochai*, because it reveals a secret of *Shabbat*. It helps remove us from this physical world, acting as a rocket booster and escape the "gravitational pull" of our planet.

le'ela לְעֵילָא mityachadin מִתְיַחֲדִין de'inun דְּאִנּוּן kegavna כְּגַוְנָא

ityachadat אִתְיַחֲדַת ihi אִיהִי hachi הָכִי of אוֹף, דאנה. אהבה. be'echad בְּאֶחָד

lemehevei לְמֶהֱוֵי de'echad אהבה. דאנה. de'echad דְּאֶחָד א״ס רו, beraza בְּרָזָא letata לְתַתָּא

,chad וְחַד lakavel לְקָבֵל chad וְחַד le'ela לְעֵילָא imehon עִמְּהוֹן

דאנה. אהבה. echad אֶחָד hu הוּא berich בְּרִיךְ kudsha קוּדְשָׁא

,dikarei דִּיקְרֵיהּ kursaya כּוּרְסַיָּא al עַל yativ יָתִיב la לָא le'ela לְעֵילָא

א״ס רו, beraza בְּרָזָא it'avidat אִתְעֲבִידַת de'ihi דְּאִיהִי ad עַד

lemehevei לְמֶהֱוֵי ,dilei דִּילֵיהּ kegavna כְּגַוְנָא אהבה. דאנה. de'echad דְּאֶחָד

ukimna אוּקִימְנָא veha וְהָא אהבה. דאנה. be'echad בְּאֶחָד אהבה. דאנה. echad אֶחָד

דאנה. אהבה. echad אֶחָד dadonai דיי אלהינואהדונהי א״ס רו, raza רָזָא

ushmo ושמו מהשע ע״ה, ע״ב ברבוע קס״א ע״ה, אל שדי ע״ה echad אֶחָד אהבה. דאנה.

,Shabbat שַׁבָּת ihi אִיהִי ,deShabbat דְּשַׁבָּת א״ס רו, raza רָזָא

דאנה. de'echad דְּאֶחָד א״ס רו, beraza בְּרָזָא de'itachada דְּאִתְאַחֲדָא

דאנה. de'echad דְּאֶחָד א״ס רו, raza רָזָא ala עֲלַהּ lemishrei לְמִשְׁרֵי

deha דְּהָא ,shabeta שַׁבְּתָא dema'alei דִּמְעֲלֵי tzelota צְלוֹתָא

,kadisha קְדִישָׁא yakira יַקִּירָא kursaya כּוּרְסַיָּא itachadat אִתְאַחֲדַת

ve'itetakanat וְאִתְתַּקְנַת אהבה. דאנה. de'echad דְּאֶחָד א״ס רו, veraza בְּרָזָא

◆ila'a עִלָּאָה kadisha קְדִישָׁא malka מַלְכָּא ala עֲלַהּ lemishrei לְמִשְׁרֵי

KEGAVNA

She may join them above as one paralleling one. The Holy Blessed One is One above Who does not sit on the throne of glory until She also becomes as the secret of the one like Him so that She may be one within one. And we have established the secret of: The Lord is One and His Name is One. The secret of the Shabbat: She is called Shabbat when She is united in the secret of the one, so that He, being the secret of the one, may rest upon Her. This is the prayer of the evening of Shabbat, because then the holy Throne of Glory is unified in the secret of the one and is made prepared so that the supreme holy King may rest upon It.

kad כַּד   ayil עָיֵל   shabeta שַׁבְּתָא,   ihi אִיהִי   ityachadat אִתְיַחֲדַת

ve'itparshat וְאִתְפָּרְשַׁת   misitra מִסִּטְרָא   achara אוֹרָא,

vechol וְכֹל ילי   dinin דִּינִין   mit'aberin מִתְעַבְּרִין   mina מִנָּה,

ve'ihi וְאִיהִי   ishte'arat אִשְׁתָּאֲרַת   beyichuda בְּיִחוּדָא   dinhiru דִּנְהִירוּ

kadisha קַדִּישָׁא,   ve'itatrat וְאִתְעַטְּרַת   bechama בְּכַמָּה   itrin עִטְרִין

legabei לְגַבֵּי   malka מַלְכָּא   kadisha קַדִּישָׁא,   vechol וְכֹל ילי   shultanei שׁוּלְטָנֵי

rugzin רוּגְזִין   umarei וּמָארֵי   dedina דְדִינָא   kulhu כֻּלְּהוּ   arkin עֲרְקִין,

velet וְלֵית   shultana שׁוּלְטָנָא   achara אוֹרָא   bechulhu בְּכֻלְּהוּ   almin עָלְמִין.

ve'anpaha וְאַנְפָּהָא   nehirin נְהִירִין   binhiru בִּנְהִירוּ   ila'a עִלָּאָה,

veitatrat וְאִתְעַטְּרַת   letata לְתַתָּא   be'ama בְּעַמָּא   kadisha קַדִּישָׁא,

vechulhu וְכֻלְּהוּ   mit'atrin מִתְעַטְּרִין   benishmatin בְּנִשְׁמָתִין   chadetin וְזַדְתִּין.

keden כְּדֵין   sheruta שֵׁירוּתָא   ditzlota דְצְלוֹתָא,   levarcha לִבְרְכָא

la לָהּ   bechedva בְּחֶדְוָה,   binhiru בִּנְהִירוּ   de'anpin דְאַנְפִּין.

SHABBAT CANDLES CONNECTION

Look at the candles and meditate:

Zeir and **Nukva**	**Abba** and **Ima**
For the second candle:	For the first candle:
The three *Yichudim* of *Zeir* and *Nukva* that add up to 250 which is the numerical value of *Ner* (candle).	The three *Yichudim* of *Abba* and *Ima* that add up to 250 which is the numerical value of *Ner* (candle).
יאההויהה	יאההויהה
יאהלוההים	יאהלוההים
יאהדונהי	יאהדונהי

As they unite above to the One, so does She unite below in the secret of the One, so that When the Shabbat arrives, She unifies and divests herself of the other side and all the judgments are removed from Her and She remains in the oneness of the holy Light, and She crowns Herself with many crowns for the holy King. And all the wrathful dominions and the bearers of grievance flee together, and there remains no other power in all the worlds. And Her countenance shines with the supernal Light and She crowns Herself with the holy Nation below as they are all crowned with new souls. Then they begin by blessing her with joy and with radiant faces.

ARVIT OF SUKKOT AND SIMCHAT TORAH

In the evening prayer of *Arvit*, we connect to Jacob the Patriarch, who is the channel for Central Column energy. He helps us connect the two energies of Judgment and Mercy in a balanced way. It is said that the whole world was created only for Jacob, who embodies truth: "Give truth to Jacob" *(Michah 7:20)*. To activate the power of our prayer, and specifically the power of the prayer of *Arvit*, we must be truthful with others and, most importantly, with ourselves.

LeShem Yichud

hu הוּא   berich בְּרִיךְ   kudsha קוּדְשָׁא   yichud יְוֵוד   leshem לְשֵׁם

ur'chimu וּרְחִימוּ   bid'chilu בִּדְחִילוּ   (יאהדונהי)   ush'chintei וּשְׁכִינְתֵּיה

leyachda לְיַחֲדָא   (איההיוהה)   ud'chilu וּדְחִילוּ   ur'chimu וּרְחִימוּ   (יאההויהה)

beyichuda בְּיִחוּדָא   kei קֵי   bevav בְּוָא"ו   kei קֵי   yud יוּ"ד   shem שֵׁם

,Yisrael יִשְׂרָאֵל   kol כָּל   beshem בְּשֵׁם   (יהוה)   shelim שְׁלִים

tefilat תְּפִלַּת   lehitpalel לְהִתְפַּלֵּל   ba'im בָּאִים   anachnu אֲנַחְנוּ   hine הִנֵּה

(ve וְ)   kodesh קוֹדֶשׁ   Shabbat שַׁבָּת   :on *Shabbat* add)   shel שֶׁל   arvit עַרְבִית

◆(Atzeret עֲצֶרֶת   Shemini שְׁמִינִי   :on *Simchat-Torah* say)   (Sukkot סֻכּוֹת   :on *Sukkot* say)

alav עָלָיו   avinu אָבִינוּ   Yaakov יַעֲקֹב   shetiken שֶׁתִּקֵּן

hakelulot הַכְּלוּלוֹת   hamitzvot הַמִּצְוֹת   kol כָּל   im עִם   hashalom הַשָּׁלוֹם

elyon עֶלְיוֹן   bemakom בְּמָקוֹם   shorsha שׇׁרְשָׁהּ   et אֶת   letaken לְתַקֵּן   ba בָּהּ

vela'asot וְלַעֲשׂוֹת   leyotzrenu לְיוֹצְרֵנוּ   ru'ach רוּחַ   nachat נוֹחַ   la'asot לַעֲשׂוֹת

◆bor'enu בּוֹרְאֵנוּ   retzon רְצוֹן

◆vihi וִיהִי   no'am נֹעַם   Adonai אֲדֹנָי   Elohenu אֱלֹהֵינוּ

konena כּוֹנְנָה   yadenu יָדֵינוּ   uma'ase וּמַעֲשֵׂה   alenu עָלֵינוּ

:konenehu כּוֹנְנֵהוּ   yadenu יָדֵינוּ   uma'ase וּמַעֲשֵׂה   alenu עָלֵינוּ

ARVIT OF SUKKOT AND SIMCHAT TORAH - LESHEM YICHUD

For the sake of the unification of the Holy Blessed One and His Shechinah, with fear and love and with love and fear, in order to unify the Name Yud-Kei and Vav-Kei in perfect unity, and in the name of Israel, we have hereby come to recite the prayer of Arvit of (on Shabbat add: the Holy Sabbath and) (on Sukkot: Sukkot) (on Simchat Torah: Shmini Atzeret), established by Jacob, our forefather, may peace be upon him, With all its commandments, to correct its root in the supernal place, to bring satisfaction to our Maker, and to fulfill the wish of our Creator. "And may the pleasantness of the Lord, our God, be upon us and may He establish the work of our hands for us and may the work of our hands establish Him." (Psalms 90:17)

HALF KADDISH

ר״ה אותיות כמנין י״א ; עדי ובמילוי עדי veyitkadash וְיִתְקַדַּשׁ yitgadal יִתְגַּדַּל

אדני, יהוה אלהים יהוה קנ״א ב״ן, raba רַבָּא (דע״ב י״ה עם) shemei שְׁמֵיהּ

אידהנוייה. amen אָמֵן ג״פ יב״ק; ס״ת = ר״ת = ו״פ אלהים; ע״ה ברבוע מ״ה וס״ג, קס״א מילוי

kir'utei כִּרְעוּתֵיהּ   vera בְּרָא   di דִּי   be'alma בְּעָלְמָא

veyatzmach וְיַצְמַח   mal'chutei מַלְכוּתֵיהּ   veyamlich וְיַמְלִיךְ

purkanei פּוּרְקָנֵיהּ   vikarev וִיקָרֵב   meshichei מְשִׁיחֵיהּ   amen אָמֵן אידהנוייה.

bechayechon בְּחַיֵּיכוֹן   uvyomechon וּבְיוֹמֵיכוֹן   uvchayei וּבְחַיֵּי

dechol דְּכָל   bet בֵּית ראה ב״פ   Yisrael יִשְׂרָאֵל   ba'agala בַּעֲגָלָא

uvizman וּבִזְמַן   kariv קָרִיב   ve'imru וְאִמְרוּ   amen אָמֵן   amen אָמֵן אידהנוייה.

The congregation and the chazan say the following:
**Twenty eight words (until be'alma) and
twenty eight letters (until almaya)**

yehe יְהֵא   shemei שְׁמֵיהּ   (עם י״ה דס״ג) raba רַבָּא   קנ״א ב״ן,

mevarach מְבָרַךְ   ע״ה ברבוע מ״ה וס״ג, מילוי קס״א אדני, יהוה אלהים יהוה

yitbarach יִתְבָּרַךְ   almaya עָלְמַיָּא   le'almei לְעָלְמֵי   le'alam לְעָלַם

**Seven words with six letters each (עם בן מ״ב) – and also,
seven times the letter Vav (עם בן מ״ב)**

HALF KADDISH
May His great Name be more exalted and sanctified. (Amen)
In the world that He created according to His will, and may His Kingdom reign. And may He cause His redemption to sprout and may He bring the Mashiach closer. (Amen) In your lifetimes and in your days and in the lifetime of all the House of Israel, speedily and in the near future, and you should say, Amen. (Amen) May His great Name be blessed forever and for all eternity blessed and lauded,

וְיִשְׁתַּבַּח veyishtabach יִפ ע"ב יהוה אל אבג יתץ.

וְיִתְפָּאַר veyitpa'ar הי גו יה קרע סטן. וְיִתְרֹמֵם veyitromam וה כווו נגד יכש.

וְיִתְנַשֵּׂא veyitnase במוכסז בטר צתג. וְיִתְהַדָּר veyit'hadar כווו יה וזקב טנע.

וְיִתְעַלֶּה veyit'ale וה יוד ה יגל פזק. וְיִתְהַלָּל veyit'halal א ואו הא שקו ציֵת.

שְׁמֵיהּ shemei (שם י"ה דמ"ה) דְּקֻדְשָׁא dekudsha בְּרִיךְ verich הוּא hu:

אָמֵן amen אידהנויה.

לְעֵלָּא le'ela מִן min כָּל kol ילי מִן בִּרְכָתָא birchata שִׁירָתָא shirata.

תֻּשְׁבְּחָתָא tishbechata וְנֶחֱמָתָא venechamata. דַּאֲמִירָן da'amiran

בְּעָלְמָא be'alma וְאִמְרוּ ve'imru אָמֵן amen: אָמֵן amen אידהנויה.

BARCHU

The *chazan* says:

בָּרְכוּ barchu יהוה ריבוע יהוה ריבוע מ"ה אֶת et יְהֹוָאדֹנָיאהדונהי Adonai

הַמְּבֹרָךְ hamevorach ס"ת כהת, משיוז בן דוד ע"ה:

When the Holiday falls on *Shabbat* and on *Shabbat Chol Hamo'ed*:
Meditate to receive the extra soul called: *Ruach*
from the aspect of the night of *Shabbat*

First the congregation replies the following, and then the *chazan* repeats it:

Neshamah ..... *Ruach* ..... *Nefesh*

הַמְּבֹרָךְ hamevorach יְהֹוָאדֹנָיאהדונהי Adonai בָּרוּךְ baruch

Yechidah ..... *Chayah*

לְעוֹלָם le'olam ריבוע ס"ג וי' אותיות דס"ג וָעֶד va'ed:

---

and glorified and exalted,
and extolled and honored, and uplifted and praised be, the Name of the Holy Blessed One. (Amen) Above all
blessings, songs, praises, and words of consolation that may be said in the world, and you shall say, Amen. (Amen)
BARCHU
Bless the Lord, the Blessed One.
Blessed be the Lord, the Blessed One, forever and for eternity.

HaMa'ariv Aravim – First Chamber – Livnat Hasapir

In the time of *Arvit*, we have an opportunity to connect to four different "Chambers" in the House of the King - Chamber of Sapphire Stone (*Livnat Hasapir*), Chamber of Love (*Ahavah*), Chamber of Desire (*Ratzon*), and the Chamber of Holy of Holies (*Kodesh HaKodeshim*). Each Chamber connects us to another level in the spiritual plane. The blessing connecting us to the First Chamber, *Livnat Hasapir*, contains 53 words, which is also the numerical value of the word gan גן, meaning "garden," therefore connecting us to the Garden of Eden of our world.

Hechal Livnat Hasapir (the Chamber of Sapphire Stone) of *Nukva* in *Beriah*.

ילה Elohenu אֱלֹהֵינוּ Adonai יְהֹוָאדְנִיאהדונהי Ata אַתָּה baruch בָּרוּךְ

ma'ariv מַעֲרִיב bidvaro בִּדְבָרוֹ asher אֲשֶׁר ha'olam הָעוֹלָם melech מֶלֶךְ

(מצוות)◆ תרי"ג = במילוי (*Atzilut*) bechochmah בְּחָכְמָה aravim עֲרָבִים

◆(*Beriah*) bitvuna בִּתְבוּנָה כתר she'arim שְׁעָרִים pote'ach פּוֹתֵחַ

et אֶת umachalif וּמַחֲלִיף (*Yetzirah*) itim עִתִּים meshane מְשַׁנֶּה

hakochavim הַכּוֹכָבִים et אֶת umsader וּמְסַדֵּר (*Asiyah*) hazemanim הַזְּמַנִּים

baraki'a בָּרָקִיעַ bemishmerotehem בְּמִשְׁמְרוֹתֵיהֶם ◆(*The Seven Planets*)

golel גּוֹלֵל מלה.◆ valayla וְלָיְלָה yomam יוֹמָם bore בּוֹרֵא ◆kirtzono כִּרְצוֹנוֹ

אוֹר or רז, אין סוף שך נצוצות של ו' המלכים choshech חֹשֶׁךְ mipenei מִפְּנֵי

וְחֹשֶׁךְ or רז, אין סוף◆ שך נצוצות של ו' המלכים vechoshech mipenei מִפְּנֵי אוֹר or רז, אין סוף◆

layla לָיְלָה umevi וּמֵבִיא עז"ה נגד, מזבוח, זן, אל יהוה yom יוֹם hama'avir הַמַּעֲבִיר

uven וּבֵין עז"ה נגד, מזבוח, זן, אל יהוה yom יוֹם ben בֵּין umavdil וּמַבְדִּיל מלה.◆

shemo שְׁמוֹ פני שכינה Tzeva'ot צְבָאוֹת Adonai יְהֹוָאדְנִיאהדונהי מלה.◆ layla לָיְלָה

baruch בָּרוּךְ Adonai◆ יְהֹוָאדְנִיאהדונהי עז"ה, אל שדי עז"א וקס"א עז"ה, עז"ב בריבוע עז"ה מהטע

aravim◆ עֲרָבִים hama'ariv הַמַּעֲרִיב Adonai יְהֹוָאדְנִיאהדונהי Ata אַתָּה

HaMa'ariv Aravim – First Chamber – Livnat Hasapir

Blessed are You, Lord, our God, King of the universe,

Who brings with His words evenings with wisdom. He opens gates with understanding. He changes the seasons and varies the times and arranges the stars in their constellations in the sky, according to His will. He creates day and night and rolls Light away from before darkness, and darkness from before Light. He is the One Who causes the day to pass and brings on night and separates between day and night. Lord of Hosts, His Name is the Lord. Blessed are You, Lord, who brings on evenings.

AHAVAT OLAM – SECOND CHAMBER - LOVE

This blessing connects us to the Second Chamber, *Ahavah* (Love) and its purpose is to inspire us with a renewed love for others and for the world.

Hechal Ahavah (the Chamber of Love) of *Nukva* in *Beriah*.
The following paragraph has 50 words corresponding to the 50 Gates of *Binah*.

אַהֲבַת ahavat עוֹלָם olam בֵּית bet ב"פ ראה יִשְׂרָאֵל Yisrael עַמְּךָ amecha

אָהַבְתָּ ◆ahavta תּוֹרָה torah (*Atzilut*) וּמִצְוֹת umitzvot (*Beriah*) וְחֻקִּים chukim

◆לִמַּדְתָּ limadeta אוֹתָנוּ otanu (*Asiyah*) וּמִשְׁפָּטִים umishpatim (*Yetzirah*)

עַל al כֵּן ken יְהוָֹה Adonai אֱלֹהֵינוּ Elohenu יכה

בְּשָׁכְבֵנוּ beshochvenu וּבְקוּמֵנוּ uvkumenu נָשִׂיוַ nasi'ach בְּחֻקֶּיךָ bechukecha

וְנִשְׂמַח venismach וְנַעֲלֹז vena'aloz בְּדִבְרֵי bedivrei תַּלְמוּד talmud

תּוֹרָתֶךָ toratecha וּבְמִצְוֹתֶיךָ umitzvotecha וּבְחֻקּוֹתֶיךָ vechukotecha

לְעוֹלָם le'olam ריבוע דס"ג וי' אותיות דס"ג ◆וָעֶד va'ed כִּי ki הֵם hem

וְחַיֵּינוּ chayenu וְאֹרֶךְ ve'orech יָמֵינוּ yamenu וּבָהֶם uvahem נֶהֶגֶּה nehge

יוֹמָם yomam וְלַיְלָה valayla מלה◆ וְאַהֲבָתְךָ ve'ahavatcha לֹא lo תָסוּר tasur

מִמֶּנּוּ mimenu לְעוֹלָמִים ◆le'olamim בָּרוּךְ baruch אַתָּה Ata

יְהוָֹה Adonai אוֹהֵב ohev אֶת et עַמּוֹ amo יִשְׂרָאֵל Yisrael:

THE SHEMA (to learn more about the *Shema* go to page 330)

The *Shema* is one of the most powerful tools to draw the energy of healing to our lives. The true power of the *Shema* is unleashed when we recite this prayer while meditating on others who need healing energy.

1) In order to receive the Light of the *Shema*, you have to accept upon yourself the precept of: "Love your neighbor as yourself," and see yourself united with all the souls that comprise the Original Adam.
2) You need to meditate to connect to the precept of the Reciting of *Shema* twice a day.
3) Before saying the *Shema* you should cover your eyes with your right hand (saying the words "*Shema Yisrael … le'olam va'ed*"). And you should read the *Shema* with deep meditation, chanting it with the intonations. It is necessary to be careful with the pronunciation of all the letters.

(According to the Ramchal the elevation of the *Mochin* is as on the *Shema* of *Shacharit* on page 331).

AHAVAT OLAM – SECOND CHAMBER - LOVE

With eternal love, You have loved Your Nation, the House of Israel. Torah, commandments, statutes, and laws, You have taught us. Therefore, Lord, our God, when we lie down and when we rise up, we shall discuss Your statutes and we shall rejoice and exult in the words of the teachings of Your Torah, Your commandments, and Your statutes, forever and ever. They are our lifetimes and the length of our days; with them we shall direct ourselves day and night. And Your love, You shall never remove from us. Blessed are You, Lord, Who loves His Nation, Israel.

First, meditate in general, on the first *Yichud* of the four *Yichuds* of the Name: יהוה, and in particular, to awaken the letter ה, and then to connect it with the letter ו. Then connect the letter י and the letter ה together in the following order: *Hei* (ה), *Hei-Vav* (ה"ו), then *Yud-Hei* (י"ה), which adds up to 31, the secret of יא"ל of the Name ג"ס. It is good to meditate on this *Yichud* before reciting any *Shema* because it acts as a replacement for the times that you may have missed reading the *Shema*. This *Yichud* has the same ability to create a Supernal connection like the reading of the *Shema* - to raise *Zeir* and *Nukva* together for the *Zivug* of *Abba* and *Ima*.

Shema – שְׁמַע

General Meditation: שׁם ע — to draw the energy from the seven lower *Sefirot* of *Ima* to the *Nukva*, which enables the *Nukva* to elevate the *Mayin Nukvin* (awakening from Below).

Particular Meditation: שׁם = יהוה ـ שׂדי and five times the letters י and ד of ב"ן = ע [The letter *Hei* (ה) is formed by the letters *Dalet* (ד) and *Yud* (י), so in ב"ן we have four times the letter ה plus another time the letters י and ד from יוד of ב"ן.]. Also the three letters ו (18) - that are left from ב"ן, plus ב"ן itself (52) equals ע (70).

Yisrael – יִשְׂרָאֵל

General Meditation: שׂיר אל — to draw energy from *Chesed* and *Gevurah* of *Abba* to *Zeir Anpin*, to do his action in the secret of *Mayin Duchrin* (awakening from Above).

Particular Meditation: (the rearranged letters of the word *Yisrael*) – שׂר אלי

אלהים דיודין (אלף למד הי יוד מם) = ע',
רבוע אלהים (א אל אלה אלהי אלהים) = ר',
מ"א אותיות רבוע אלהים במילואו (אלף אלף למד למד הי אלף למד הי יוד אלף למד הי יוד מם) = אל"י.

Also meditate to draw the Inner *Mochin* of *Abba* of *Katnut* into *Zeir Anpin*.

Adonai Elohenu Adonai - יהוה אלהינו יהוה

General Meditation: to draw energy to *Abba*, *Ima* and *Da'at* from *Arich Anpin*,

Particular Meditation: (יוד הי וי הי) ע"ב (אלף הי יוד הי) קס"א (יוד הי ויו הי) ע"ב.

Echad – אֶחָד
(The secret of the complete *Yichud-Unification*)

The letters *Alef* א and *Chet* ח from *Echad* אֶחָד are *Zeir Anpin* and the letter *Dalet* ד is *Nukva*. **You should meditate** to devote your soul for the sanctification of the Holy Name, thereby elevating your *Nefesh*, *Ruach*, *Neshamah* and *Neshamah* of *Neshamah* with *Zeir Anpin* and *Nukva* (using the Names: ע"ב and ס"ג) to *Abba* and *Ima* as the secret of *Mayin Nukvin*, and by that energy, *Abba* and *Ima* will be unified in the secret of the Name: יאההויה"ה. **Also meditate** to draw out the Inner Six Edges of *Gadlut* of *Ima* into *Zeir Anpin*. The Drop, which is ע"ב, is drawn out from the external of *Arich Anpin,* and descends to *Yesod* of *Ima*, where it becomes: ע"ב ס"ג מ"ה ב"ן, and the four spelled out אהיה (אלף הי יוד הי, אלף הי יוד הי, אלף הא יוד הא, אלף הה יוד הה) become Her clothing. As a result, *Zeir Anpin* now has four spelled out יה"ו (יוד הי ויו, יוד הי ואו, יוד הא ואו, יוד הה וו), four spelled out אה"י (אלף הי יוד, אלף הי יוד, אלף הא יוד, אלף הה יוד) and the Inner Six Edges of *Gadlut* of *Ima*. **Also meditate** on the Name: אל"ף ה"י וי"י ה"י, which is the entire *Mochin* in the secret of *Da'at*. **And also meditate** (according to the Ramchal) on the four spelled out *Alef* (אלף=111) of the Name: אהי"ה that is equal to the word *Midat* (444), making the *Keter* for Leah.

Baruch Shem - בָּרוּךְ שֵׁם כְּבוֹד מַלְכוּתוֹ לְעוֹלָם וָעֶד

Baruch Shem Kevod – Chochmah, Binah, Da'at of Leah;
Malchuto — Her *Keter*; *Le'olam* – the rest of Her *Partzuf*;
Va'ed – the four היה (4 times 20 equal to *Va'ed*=80) will make the *Keter* for Rachel.
And the four spelled out היה (הי יוד הי, הי יוד הי, הא יוד הא, הה יוד הה) will make the rest of Her body.

שְׁמַע shema עֹ רבתי יִשְׂרָאֵל Yisrael יְהֹוָהֹאדנים־יאהדונהי Adonai

אֱלֹהֵינוּ Elohenu ילה ד׳ רבתי echad אֶחָד‎ | Adonai יְהֹוָהֹאדנים־יאהדונהי‎ ; אהבה, דאגה:

(: Whisper) יוזו אותיות baruch בָּרוּךְ shem שֵׁם kevod כְּבוֹד malchuto מַלְכוּתוֹ,

le'olam לְעוֹלָם ריבוע דס״ג וי׳ אותיות דס״ג va'ed וָעֶד:

Yud, Chochmah, head — 42 words corresponding to the Holy 42-Letter Name of God.

ב   א

et אֵת (ה׳ אהבת מ״ע על יכוין לקיים) ; ב״פ אין סוף, ב״פ רו, ב״פ אור, ve'ahavta וְאָהַבְתָּ

י   ג

ע״ה בן דוד משיחו Elohecha אֱלֹהֶיךָ ; ס״ת כהת, ילה Adonai יְהֹוָהֹאדנים־יאהדונהי

ר   ק   צ   ת

nafshecha נַפְשְׁךָ לכב, ב״ן uvchol וּבְכָל levavcha לְבָבְךָ לכב, ב״ן, bechol בְּכָל

כ   ט   ע

hadevarim הַדְּבָרִים vehayu וְהָיוּ me'odecha מְאֹדֶךָ: לכב ב״ן, uvchol וּבְכָל

כ   י   ד   נ

hayom הַיּוֹם metzavecha מְצַוְּךָ anochi אָנֹכִי asher אֲשֶׁר ha'ele הָאֵלֶּה

ט   ב   ש

veshinantam וְשִׁנַּנְתָּם levavecha לְבָבֶךָ: al עַל (pause here) ע״ה נגד, מזבוח, זן, אל יהוה

ת   צ

beshivtecha בְּשִׁבְתְּךָ מ״ב bam בָּם vedibarta וְדִבַּרְתָּ levanecha לְבָנֶיךָ

ב   ק   ח

vaderech בַּדֶּרֶךְ uvlechtecha וּבְלֶכְתְּךָ ראה ב״פ bevetecha בְּבֵיתֶךָ

נ   ט

uvkumecha וּבְקוּמֶךָ: uvshochbecha וּבְשָׁכְבְּךָ קס״א ס״ג ב״פ יב״ק,

ל   נ   י   ע

yadecha יָדֶךָ al עַל le'ot לְאוֹת ukshartam וּקְשַׁרְתָּם

THE SHEMA

"Hear Israel, the Lord our God. The Lord is One." (Deuteronomy 6:4)

"Blessed is the glorious Name, His Kingdom is forever and for eternity." (Pesachim 56a)

"And you shall love the Lord, your God, with all your heart and with all your soul and with all that you possess. Let those words that I command you today be upon your heart. And you shall teach them to your children and you shall speak of them while you sit in your home and while you walk on your way and when you lie down and when you rise. You shall bind them as a sign upon your hand

vehayu וְהָיוּ	letotafot לְטֹטָפֹת	ben בֵּין	enecha עֵינֶיךָ
ע"ה קס"א ; ריבוע מ"ה:	uchtavtam וּכְתַבְתָּם	al עַל-
mezuzot מְזֻזוֹת (זו מות) נית	betecha בֵּיתֶךָ ב"פ ראה	uvish'arecha וּבִשְׁעָרֶיךָ:

VEHAYA IM SHAMO'A

Hei, Binah, **arms and body** — 72 words corresponding to the 72 Names of God.

vehaya וְהָיָה יהוה ; יהה **im** אִם־ יוה"ך, מ"א אותיות דפשוט, דמילוי ודמילוי דמילוי דאהיה ע"ה

shamo'a שָׁמֹעַ tishme'u תִּשְׁמְעוּ el אֶל- mitzvotai מִצְוֹתַי asher אֲשֶׁר

anochi אָנֹכִי metzave מְצַוֶּה etchem אֶתְכֶם hayom הַיּוֹם ע"ה נגד, מזבח, זן, אל יהוה

(pause here) le'ahava לְאַהֲבָה אוזר, דאגה et אֶת- Adonai יְהֹוָה אדני יאהדונהי

Elohechem אֱלֹהֵיכֶם ul'ovdo וּלְעָבְדוֹ (enunciate the letter *Ayin* in the word "*ul'ovdo*")

bechol בְּכָל- ב"ן, לכב levavchem לְבַבְכֶם uvchol וּבְכָל-

nafshechem נַפְשְׁכֶם: venatati וְנָתַתִּי metar מְטַר- artzechem אַרְצְכֶם

be'ito בְּעִתּוֹ yore יוֹרֶה umalkosh וּמַלְקוֹשׁ ve'asafta וְאָסַפְתָּ deganecha דְגָנֶךָ

vetiroshcha וְתִירֹשְׁךָ veyitz'harecha וְיִצְהָרֶךָ: venatati וְנָתַתִּי esev עֵשֶׂב ע"ב שמות

---

and they shall be as frontlets between your eyes.
And you shall write them upon the doorposts of your house and your gates." (Deuteronomy 6:5-9)

VEHAYA IM SHAMO'A

"And it shall come to be that if you shall listen to My commandments that I am commanding you with today to love the Lord, your God, and to serve Him with all your heart and with all your soul, then I shall send rain upon your land in its proper time, both early rain and late rain. You shall then gather your grain and your wine and your oil. And I shall give grass

מנגד ・ כוק ・ לההו ・ יוזו
‏׃vesavata וְשָׂבָעְתָּ ・ ve'achalta וְאָכַלְתָּ ・ livhemtecha לִבְהֶמְתֶּךָ ・ besadcha בְּשָׂדְךָ

ההה ・ ייו ・ רהע ・ וזעם ・ אני
levavchem לְבַבְכֶם ・ yifte יִפְתֶּה ・ pen פֶּן ・ lachem לָכֶם ・ hishamru הִשָּׁמְרוּ

סאל ・ יכה ・ ווכ ・ מיכ
acherim אֲחֵרִים ・ elohim אֱלֹהִים ・ va'avadetem וַעֲבַדְתֶּם ・ vesartem וְסַרְתֶּם

עשׁל ・ ערי
‏׃lahem לָהֶם ・ vehishtachavitem וְהִשְׁתַּחֲוִיתֶם ・ (הקליפות) נגד (העומד) משה

הוזע ・ דני ・ והו ・ מיה
bachem בָּכֶם ・ Adonai יְהֹוָה ・ af אַף ・ (pause here) ・ vechara וְחָרָה

מבה ・ נית ・ גנא ・ עמם
velo וְלֹא ・ hashamayim הַשָּׁמַיִם ・ et אֶת ・ ve'atzar וְעָצַר

מצר ・ הרוח ・ ייל ・ גמם ・ פוי
titen תִתֵּן ・ lo לֹא ・ veha'adama וְהָאֲדָמָה ・ matar מָטָר ・ yihye יִהְיֶה ‏יי

דמב ・ מוזי ・ ענו ・ יהה ・ ומב
me'al מֵעַל ・ mehera מְהֵרָה ・ va'avadetem וַאֲבַדְתֶּם ・ yevula יְבוּלָהּ ・ et אֶת

וזבו ・ איע ・ מנק
asher אֲשֶׁר ・ hatova הַטֹּבָה ・ אלהים ע"ה ・ ha'aretz הָאָרֶץ

היי ・ יבם ・ ראה
Vav, Zeir Anpin ‏׃lachem לָכֶם ・ noten נֹתֵן ・ Adonai יְהֹוָה

מום
stomach — 50 words corresponding to the 50 Gates of *Binah* ・ vesamtem וְשַׂמְתֶּם

levavchem לְבַבְכֶם ・ al עַל ・ ele אֵלֶּה ・ devarai דְּבָרַי ・ et אֶת

otam אֹתָם ・ ukshartem וּקְשַׁרְתֶּם ・ nafshechem נַפְשְׁכֶם ・ ve'al וְעַל

---

in your field for your cattle. And you shall eat and you shall be satiated. Be careful lest your heart be seduced and you may turn away and serve alien deities and prostrate yourself before them. And the wrath of the Lord shall be upon you and He shall stop the Heavens and there shall be no more rain and the earth shall not give forth its crop. And you shall quickly perish from the good land that the Lord has given you. And you shall place those words of Mine upon your heart and upon your soul and you shall bind them

א   ה   י   ה

vehayu וְהָיוּ   yedchem יֶדְכֶם   al עַל־   לאו ר״ת   le'ot לְאוֹת

ה   י   ה

מ״הֵ: מ״הֵ   enechem עֵינֵיכֶם   ben בֵּין   letotafot לְטוֹטָפֹת

ה   י   ה   א

benechem בְּנֵיכֶם   et אֶת־   otam אֹתָם   velimadetem וְלִמַּדְתֶּם

י   ה   א

beshivtecha בְּשִׁבְתְּךָ   מ״ב בן שׂם   bam בָּם   ראה   ledaber לְדַבֵּר

ה   א   ה

ב״פ יב״ק, ס״ג קס״א vaderech בַּדֶּרֶךְ   uvlechtecha וּבְלֶכְתְּךָ ב״פ ראה   bevetecha בְּבֵיתֶךָ

ה   א   ה   י

al עַל־   uchtavtam וּכְתַבְתָּם   uvkumecha וּבְקוּמֶךָ:   uvshochbecha וּבְשָׁכְבְּךָ

ה   א   ה   י

lema'an לְמַעַן   uvish'arecha וּבִשְׁעָרֶיךָ:   betecha בֵּיתֶךָ ב״פ ראה   mezuzot מְזוּזוֹת

ה   א   ה   י

venechem בְּנֵיכֶם   vimei וִימֵי ייל   yemechem יְמֵיכֶם ר״ת   yirbu יִרְבּוּ

אהיה אהיה

(enunciate the letter *Ayin* in the word "*nishba*") asher אֲשֶׁר   ha'adama הָאֲדָמָה   al עַל

אהיה

Adonai יְהֹוָואֲדֹנָיֵאֱלֹהֵינוּ   המבול   לשבועת   יכוין   nishba נִשְׁבַּע

אהיה   אהיה   אהיה   אהיה

kimei כִּימֵי   lahem לָהֶם   latet לָתֵת   la'avotechem לַאֲבֹתֵיכֶם

אהיה אהיה   אהיה אהיה   אהיה

הַשָּׁמַיִם: אלהים דההין ע״ה ha'aretz הָאָרֶץ   al עַל־   י״פ טל, י״פ כוזו   hashamayim הַשָּׁמַיִם

as a sign upon your hands and they shall be as frontlets between your eyes. And you shall teach them to your children and speak of them while you sit at home and while you walk on your way and when you lie down and when you rise. You shall write them upon the doorposts of your house and upon your gates. This is so that your days shall be numerous and so shall the days of your children upon the Earth that the Lord had sworn to your fathers to give them as the days of the Heavens upon the Earth." (Deuteronomy 11:13-21)

VAYOMER

Hei, *Malchut*, legs and reproductive organs,

72 words corresponding to the 72 Names of God in direct order (according to the Ramchal).

You should meditate on the precept:
"not to follow negative sexual thoughts of the heart and the sights of the eyes for prostitution."

VAYOMER

"And the Lord spoke to Moses and said,
Speak to the Children of Israel and say to them that they should make for themselves Tzitzit,
on the corners of their garments, throughout all their generations. And they must place upon the Tzitzit,
of each corner, a blue strand. And this shall be to you as a Tzitzit: you shall see it and remember
the commandments of the Lord and fulfill them. And you shall not stray after your hearts and your eyes,

asher אֲשֶׁר־ atem אַתֶּם zonim זֹנִים acharehem אַחֲרֵיהֶם׃ lema'an לְמַעַן

tizkeru תִּזְכְּרוּ va'asitem וַעֲשִׂיתֶם et אֶת־ kol כָּל־ mitzvotai מִצְוֹתָי

vihyitem וִהְיִיתֶם kedoshim קְדֹשִׁים lelohechem לֵאלֹהֵיכֶם׃

ani אֲנִי Adonai יְהֹוָה Elohechem אֱלֹהֵיכֶם asher אֲשֶׁר

hotzeti הוֹצֵאתִי etchem אֶתְכֶם me'eretz מֵאֶרֶץ Mitzrayim מִצְרַיִם

You should meditate to remember the exodus from *Mitzrayim* (Egypt).

lihyot לִהְיוֹת lachem לָכֶם lelohim לֵאלֹהִים ;

ani אֲנִי Adonai יְהֹוָה Elohechem אֱלֹהֵיכֶם׃

Be careful to complete this paragraph together with the *chazan* and the congregation, and say the word "*emet*" out loud. The *chazan* should say the word "*emet*" in silence.

emet אֱמֶת אהיה פעמים אהיה, ז"פ ס"ג׃

The congregation should be silent, listen and hear the words "*Adonai Elohechem emet*" spoken by the *chazan*. If you did not complete the paragraph together with the *chazan* you should repeat the last three words on your own. With these three words the *Shema* is completed.

Adonai יְהֹוָה Elohechem אֱלֹהֵיכֶם׃

emet אֱמֶת אהיה פעמים אהיה, ז"פ ס"ג׃

after which you adulterate. This is so that you shall remember to fulfill all My ·commandments and thereby be holy before your God. I am the Lord, your God, Who brought you out of the land of Egypt to be your God. I, the Lord, your God, Is true." (Numbers 15:37-41) the Lord, your God, is true!

VE'EMUNA – THIRD CHAMBER – RATZON

Ve'emuna connects us to the Third Chamber in the House of the King: Ratzon, or desire. Before we can connect to any form of spiritual energy, we need to feel a want or desire. Desire is the vessel that draws spiritual Light. A small desire draws a small amount of Light. A large desire draws a large amount.

Hechal Ratzon (the Chamber of Desire) of *Nukva* in *Beriah*.

alenu עָלֵינוּ, vekayam וְקַיָּם zot זֹאת ילי kol כָּל (בוונת לילה) ve'emuna וֶאֱמוּנָה

ve'en וְאֵין ילה Elohenu אֱלֹהֵינוּ Adonai יְהֹוָה(אדניאהדונהי) hu הוּא ki כִּי

amo עַמּוֹ Yisrael יִשְׂרָאֵל va'anachnu וַאֲנַחְנוּ zulato זוּלָתוֹ

hago'alenu הַגּוֹאֲלֵנוּ melachim מְלָכִים miyad מִיַּד hapodenu הַפּוֹדֵנוּ

aritzim עָרִיצִים ילי kol כָּל mikaf מִכַּף malkenu מַלְכֵּנוּ

אדני אהיה, אלהים לאה ; (מילוי דס"ג) יא"י haEl הָאֵל lanu לָנוּ hanifra הַנִּפְרָע

אדני יה lechol לְכָל gemul גְּמוּל hameshalem הַמְשַׁלֵּם mitzarenu מִצָּרֵינוּ

nafshenu נַפְשֵׁנוּ hasam הַשָּׂם nafshenu נַפְשֵׁנוּ oyvei אוֹיְבֵי

lamot לַמּוֹט natan נָתַן velo וְלֹא אהיה אהיה יהוה, בינה ע"ה bachayim בַּחַיִּים

bamot בָּמוֹת al עַל hamadrichenu הַמַּדְרִיכֵנוּ raglenu רַגְלֵנוּ

עמם ; ילי kol כָּל al עַל karnenu קַרְנֵנוּ vayarem וַיָּרֶם oyvenu אוֹיְבֵינוּ

ha'ose הָעוֹשֶׂה (מילוי דס"ג) יא"י ; לאה haEl הָאֵל son'enu שׂוֹנְאֵינוּ

beFar'o בְּפַרְעֹה unkama וּנְקָמָה nisim נִסִּים אהיה אדני אלהים, lanu לָנוּ

benei בְּנֵי be'admat בְּאַדְמַת uvmoftim וּבְמוֹפְתִים be'otot בְּאוֹתוֹת

ילי kol כָּל ve'evrato בְּעֶבְרָתוֹ hamake הַמַּכֶּה Cham וְחָם

et אֵת vayotzi וַיּוֹצִא מצר Mitzrayim מִצְרָיִם bechorei בְּכוֹרֵי

olam עוֹלָם lecherut לְחֵרוּת mitocham מִתּוֹכָם Yisrael יִשְׂרָאֵל amo עַמּוֹ

VE'EMUNA – THIRD CHAMBER - RATZON

And trustworthy. All this and He are set upon us because He is the Lord, our God, and there is none other. And we are Israel, His Nation. He redeems us from the hands of kings. He is our King, Who delivers us from the reach of tyrants; The God, Who avenges us against our enemies. He pays our mortal enemies their due. He Who keeps us alive and does not allow our feet to falter; He Who lets us walk upon the plains of our foes. He Who raises our worth over all our enemies. He is God, Who wrought for us retribution against Pharaoh, with signs and wonders, in the land of the children of Cham. He Who struck down with His anger at the first-born of Egypt, and brought out His Nation, Israel, from amongst them to everlasting freedom.

הַמַּעֲבִיר hama'avir   בָּנָיו banav

בֵּין ben   גִּזְרֵי gizrei   יַם yam   סוּף Suf   וְאֶת ve'et   רוֹדְפֵיהֶם rodfehem

וְאֶת ve'et   שׂוֹנְאֵיהֶם son'ehem   בִּתְהוֹמוֹת bitehomot   טִבַּע tiba   רָאוּ ra'u

בָנִים vanim   אֶת et   גְּבוּרָתוֹ gevurato   שִׁבְּחוּ shibechu   וְהוֹדוּ vehodu

לִשְׁמוֹ lishmo   וּמַלְכוּתוֹ umalchuto

בְּרָצוֹן beratzon   קִבְּלוּ kibelu

עֲלֵיהֶם alehem   מֹשֶׁה Moshe

וּבְנֵי uvnei   יִשְׂרָאֵל Yisrael   לְךָ lecha   עָנוּ anu

שִׁירָה shira   בְּשִׂמְחָה besimcha   רַבָּה raba   וְאָמְרוּ ve'amru   כֻלָּם chulam

מִי mi   כָמֹכָה chamocha   בָּאֵלִם ba'elim   יְהֹוָה Adonai

מִי mi   כָּמֹכָה kamocha   נֶאְדָּר nedar

בַּקֹּדֶשׁ bakodesh   נוֹרָא nora   תְהִלֹּת tehilot

עֹשֵׂה ose   פֶלֶא fele   מַלְכוּתְךָ malchutcha   יְהֹוָה Adonai

אֱלֹהֵינוּ Elohenu   רָאוּ ra'u   בָנֶיךָ vanecha   עַל al   הַיָּם hayam

יַחַד yachad   כֻּלָּם kulam   הוֹדוּ hodu   וְהִמְלִיכוּ vehimlichu

וְאָמְרוּ ve'amru   יְהֹוָה Adonai | יִמְלֹךְ yimloch   לְעֹלָם le'olam

וָעֶד va'ed   וְנֶאֱמַר vene'emar   כִּי ki   פָדָה fada

אֶת et   Adonai יְהֹוָה   יַעֲקֹב Yaakov

וּגְאָלוֹ ug'alo   מִיָּד miyad   חָזָק chazak   מִמֶּנּוּ mimenu   בָּרוּךְ baruch

אַתָּה Ata   יְהֹוָה Adonai   גָּאַל ga'al   יִשְׂרָאֵל Yisrael

---

He Who caused His Children to pass between the sections of the Sea of Reeds, while their pursuers and their enemies, He drowned in the depths. The Children saw His might and they praised and gave thanks to His Name; they accepted His sovereignty over them willingly. Moses and the Children of Israel raised their voices in song to Him, with great joy, and they all said, as one "Who is like You among the gods, Lord? Who is like You, awesome in holiness, tremendous in praise and Who works wonders?" (Exodus 15:11) Our Children saw Your Kingdom, Lord, our God, upon the sea, and they all in unison gave thanks to You and accepted Your sovereignty and said: "The Lord shall reign forever and ever." (Exodus 15:18) And it is stated: "For the Lord has delivered Jacob and redeemed him from the hand of one that is stronger than he." (Jeremiah 31:10) Blessed are You, Lord, Who redeemed Israel.

HASHKIVENU – FOURTH CHAMBER – HOLY OF HOLIES

The Fourth Chamber is *Kodesh HaKodeshim,* the Holy of Holies, which is our link to the next level that we reach through the *Amidah.*

Hechal Kodesh HaKodashim (the Chamber of Holy of Holies) of *Nukva* in *Beriah.*

לאה ר"ת leshalom לְעוֹלָם avinu אָבִינוּ hashkivenu הַשְׁכִּיבֵנוּ

אהיה אהיה יהוה, בינה ע"ה lechayim לְחַיִּים malkenu מַלְכֵּנוּ veha'amidenu וְהַעֲמִידֵנוּ

alenu עָלֵינוּ ufros וּפְרוֹשׂ ulshalom וּלְשָׁלוֹם tovim טוֹבִים

(יאהדונהי) אמן סאל, = סוכה vetaknenu וְתַקְּנֵנוּ shelomecha שְׁלוֹמֶךָ sukat סֻכַּת

ס"ג מ"ה ב"ן milfanecha מִלְּפָנֶיךָ אכא tova טוֹבָה be'etza בְּעֵצָה malkenu מַלְכֵּנוּ

shemecha שְׁמֶךָ lema'an לְמַעַן mehera מְהֵרָה vehoshi'enu וְהוֹשִׁיעֵנוּ

(we don't ask for protection, as there is no need for protection from the *klipa* on *Shabbat* – וְהָגֵן בַּעֲדֵנוּ)

Meditate to include *Hechal Kodesh HaKodashim* of *Beriah* in *Atzilut* so it becomes as *Atzilut* itself.

When the Holiday falls on *Shabbat* and on *Shabbat Chol Hamo'ed*:
Meditate to receive the extra soul called: *Neshamah*
from the aspect of the night of *Shabbat*

---

ve'al וְעַל above *Yaakov* and *Rachel* alenu עָלֵינוּ partitions of *Yesod* in *Ima* ufros וּפְרוֹשׂ

(יאהדונהי) אמן = סאל = סוכה sukat סֻכַּת irach עִירָךְ Yerushalayim יְרוּשָׁלַיִם

Adonai יאהדונהי יְהֹוָה Ata אַתָּה baruch בָּרוּךְ •shalom שָׁלוֹם

= אדני ר"ת ; (יאהדונהי) אמן = סאל = סוכה sukat סֻכַּת hapores הַפּוֹרֵשׂ shalom שָׁלוֹם

And the partitions should become like the *Sukkah* roof in order to make room (inside *Zeir Anpin*) for the *Gevurot* to expand without going out to *Yaakov* and *Rachel*. So now They will receive Light from the *Chasadim* that were delayed from Their ascent.

Yisrael יִשְׂרָאֵל amo עַמּוֹ ; עמם ילי : kol כָּל ve'al וְעַל ר"ת ש"ע נהורין alenu עָלֵינוּ

amen יאהדונהי אָמֵן : Yerushalayim יְרוּשָׁלַיִם ve'al וְעַל

HASHKIVENU – FOURTH CHAMBER – HOLY OF HOLIES

Lay us down in peace, Father, and stand us up, our King, for good life and for peace. Spread over us Your protection of peace. Set us straight, with good counsel from You and save us speedily, for the sake of Your Name. And spread over us and over Jerusalem, Your city, a shelter of mercy and peace. Blessed are You, Lord, Who spreads the shelter of peace over us and over His entire nation, Israel, and over Jerusalem, Amen!

When the hilday falls on *Shabbat* and on *Shabbat Chol Hamo'ed* we add:

VESHAMRU

We have the ability to unite Heaven and Earth through the power of the *Alef-Hei-Vav-Hei* אהוה.

haShabbat הַשַּׁבָּת et אֶת־ Yisrael יִשְׂרָאֵל venei בְּנֵי veshamru וְשָׁמְרוּ

ledorotam לְדֹרֹתָם haShabbat הַשַּׁבָּת et אֶת־ la'asot לַעֲשׂוֹת ר״ת ביאה

beni בֵּינִי :olam עוֹלָם berit בְּרִית (וו אשתו, למשוך נשמה קדושה ולא מסט״א) ר״ת אהל :beni

le'olam לְעוֹלָם hee הִוא ר״ת ביאה ot אוֹת Yisrael יִשְׂרָאֵל benei בְּנֵי uven וּבֵין

asa עָשָׂה נלך yamim יָמִים sheshet שֵׁשֶׁת ki כִּי־ דס״ג אותיות י׳ רבוע

ve'et וְאֶת־ כזו יל, טל ש״פ hashamayim הַשָּׁמַיִם et אֶת־ Adonai יְהוָֹהאהדונהי

ha'aretz הָאָרֶץ אל יהוה זן, מזבוח, נגד, ע״ה uvayom וּבַיּוֹם ע״ה דההין אלהים

hashevi'i הַשְּׁבִיעִי shavat שָׁבַת :vayinafash וַיִּנָּפַשׁ

ELE MO'ADEI (on *Shabbat Chol Hamo'ed* we skip)

mikra'ei מִקְרָאֵי Adonai יְהוָֹהאהדונהי mo'adei מוֹעֲדֵי ele אֵלֶּה

kodesh קֹדֶשׁ asher אֲשֶׁר־ tikre'u תִּקְרְאוּ otam אֹתָם :bemo'adam בְּמוֹעֲדָם

vaydaber וַיְדַבֵּר ראה Moshe מֹשֶׁה מהע, ע״ב ברבוע וקס״א, אל שדי, ד״פ אלהים ע״ה

et אֶת־ Adonai יְהוָֹהאהדונהי mo'adei מוֹעֲדֵי el אֶל־ benei בְּנֵי Yisrael יִשְׂרָאֵל:

HALF KADDISH

yitgadal יִתְגַּדַּל veyitkadash וְיִתְקַדַּשׁ שדי ומילוי שדי ; י״א אותיות כמנין ו״ה

shemei שְׁמֵיהּ (שם י״ה דע״ב) raba רַבָּא קנ״א ב״ן, יהוה אלהים יהוה אדני,

amen אָמֵן :אידהנויה מילוי קס״א וס״ג, מ״ה ברבוע וע״ב ע״ה ; ר״ת = ו״פ אלהים ; ס״ת = ג״פ יב״ק

VESHAMRU

"And the children of Israel shall keep the Sabbath, to make the Sabbath an eternal covenant for all their generations. Between Me and the children of Israel, it is an eternal sign that in six days did the Lord make the Heavens and the Earth and on the Seventh day, He was refreshed." (Exodus 31:16-17)

ELE MO'ADEI

"Those are the holiday of the Lord, Holy Covenant you shall call them, on their time. And Moses declared the holidays of the Lord to the children of Israel" (Leviticus 23:44)

HALF KADDISH

May His great Name be more exalted and sanctified. (Amen)

be'alma בְּעָלְמָא di דִּי vera בְּרָא kir'utei כִּרְעוּתֵיה

veyamlich וְיַמְלִיךְ malchutei מַלְכוּתֵיה veyatzmach וְיַצְמַח

purkanei פּוּרְקָנֵיה vikarev וִיקָרֵב meshichei מְשִׁיחֵיה amen אָמֵן

bechayechon בְּחַיֵּיכוֹן uvyomechon וּבְיוֹמֵיכוֹן uvchayei וּבְחַיֵּי

dechol דְּכָל bet בֵּית Yisrael יִשְׂרָאֵל ba'agala בַּעֲגָלָא

uvizman וּבִזְמַן kariv קָרִיב ve'imru וְאִמְרוּ amen אָמֵן amen אָמֵן

The congregation and the chazan say the following:

Twenty eight words (until *be'alma*) and twenty eight letters (until *almaya*)

yehe יְהֵא shemei שְׁמֵיה raba רַבָּא

mevarach מְבָרַךְ

le'alam לְעָלַם le'almei לְעָלְמֵי almaya עָלְמַיָּא yitbarach יִתְבָּרַךְ

Seven words with six letters each (שם בן מ"ב) and also, seven times the letter *Vav* (שם בן מ"ב)

veyishtabach וְיִשְׁתַּבַּח

veyitpa'ar וְיִתְפָּאַר veyitromam וְיִתְרוֹמַם

veyitnase וְיִתְנַשֵּׂא veyit'hadar וְיִתְהַדָּר

veyit'ale וְיִתְעַלֶּה veyit'halal וְיִתְהַלָּל

shemei שְׁמֵיה dekudsha דְּקוּדְשָׁא verich בְּרִיךְ hu הוּא

amen אָמֵן

le'ela לְעֵלָּא min מִן kol כָּל birchata בִּרְכָתָא shirata שִׁירָתָא

tishbechata תֻּשְׁבְּחָתָא venechamata וְנֶחָמָתָא da'amiran דַּאֲמִירָן

be'alma בְּעָלְמָא ve'imru וְאִמְרוּ amen אָמֵן amen אָמֵן

In the world that He created according to His will, and may His kingdom reign.
And may He cause His redemption to sprout and may He bring the Mashiach closer. (Amen)
In your lifetimes and in your days and in the lifetime of all the House of Israel, speedily and in the near future, and you should say, Amen. (Amen) May His great Name be blessed forever and for all eternity blessed and lauded, and glorified and exalted, and extolled and honored, and uplifted and praised, be the Name of the Holy Blessed One. (Amen) Above all blessings, songs, praises, and words of consolation that may be said in the world, and you shall say, Amen. (Amen)

THE AMIDAH - GENERAL

When we begin the connection, we take three steps backward, signifying our leaving this physical world. Then we take three steps forward to begin the *Amidah*. The three steps are:
1. Stepping into the land of Israel – to enter the first spiritual circle.
2. Stepping into the city of Jerusalem – to enter the second spiritual circle.
3. Stepping inside the Holy of Holies – to enter the innermost circle.

Before we recite the first verse of the *Amidah*, we ask: "*God, open my lips and let my mouth speak,*" thereby asking the Light to speak for us so that we can receive what we need and not just what we want. All too often, what we want from life is not necessarily the desire of the soul, which is what we actually need to fulfill us. By asking the Light to speak through us, we ensure that our connection will bring us genuine fulfillment and opportunities for spiritual growth and change.

If the Holiday falls on weekdays we skip the meditaions below and continue with the *Amidah* on page 97.

If the Holiday falls on *Shabbat* we scan the meditaions below and continue with the *Amidah* on page 97.

On *Shabbat Chol Hamo'ed* we scan the meditaions below and we continue with the *Amidah* on page 686.

The Format of the Ascension in *Arvit* of *Shabbat*

When saying "*Baruch*" meditate to draw Netzach, Hod, Yesod and Chesed, Gevurah, Tiferet of Keter, Chochmah, Binah, Da'at of Netzach, Hod, Yesod of Chesed, Gevurah, Tiferet of the Internal of Tevunah (that were drawn during the recitation of the "*Shema*" to Keter, Chochmah, Binah, Da'at. And Chesed, Gevurah, Tiferet) **to** Chesed, Gevurah, Tiferet and Netzach, Hod, Yesod of Keter, Chochmah, Binah, Da'at of Netzach, Hod, Yesod and Chesed, Gevurah, Tiferet of Binah of the Internal of Zeir Anpin.

When saying "*Ata*" meditate to draw Keter, Chochmah, Binah of Keter, Chochmah, Binah of Tevuna to Keter, Chochmah, Binah of Zeir Anpin and push down the Six Edges (of Tevunah) to the Six Edges of Zeir Anpin.

When saying "*Adonai*" meditate to draw Netzach, Hod, Yesod and Chesed, Gevurah, Tiferet of Keter, Chochmah, Binah, Da'at of Netzach, Hod, Yesod of Chesed, Gevurah, Tiferet of the Internal of Israel Saba **to** Chesed, Gevurah, Tiferet and Netzach, Hod, Yesod of Zeir Anpin **and then draw** Keter, Chochmah, Binah of Israel Saba to Keter, Chochmah, Binah of Zeir Anpin and push down the Six Edges (of Israel Saba) to the Six Edges of Zeir Anpin.

yagid יַגִּיד ufi וּפִי tiftach תִּפְתָּח sefatai שְׂפָתַי (pause here) לללה Adonai אֲדֹנָי

(כ"ב אותיות פשוטות [=אכא] וה' אותיות סופיות בזו"ר) ייז תֵהִלָּתֶךָ tehilatecha ס"ת = בוכו:

THE FIRST BLESSING - INVOKES THE SHIELD OF ABRAHAM.

Abraham is the channel of the Right Column energy of positivity, sharing, and mercy. Sharing actions can protect us from all forms of negativity.

Chesed that becomes Chochmah

In this section there are 42 words, the secret of the 42-Letter Name of God and therefore it begins with the letter *Bet* (2) and ends with the letter *Mem* (40).

Bend your knees at "*baruch*," bow at "*Ata*" and straighten up at "*Adonai*."

בָּרוּךְ baruch (אותיות הא"ב המסמלות את השפע המגיע) לה' המלכות א-ת Ata אַתָּה

יְהֹוָה Adonai (יא) אֱלֹהֵינוּ Elohenu יֹלה

וֵאלֹהֵי velohei לכב ; ע"ב, מילוי ; דמב, ילה וַאֲבוֹתֵינוּ avotenu

אֱלֹהֵי Elohei ע"ב, מילוי ; דמב, ילה ; אַבְרָהָם Avraham (Chochmah)
ו"ף, אל, רי"ו ול"כ נתיבות הוחכמה, רמ"ח (אברים), עסמ"ב וט"ז אותיות פשוטות

אֱלֹהֵי Elohei ע"ב, מילוי ; דמב, ילה ; יִצְחָק Yitzchak (Binah) ב"ן ד"פ
וֵאלֹהֵי velohei לכב ; מילוי ע"ב, דמב, ילה ; יַעֲקֹב Yaakov (Da'at) ז' הויות, יאהדונהי אידהנויה

THE AMIDAH

"*My Lord, open my lips, and my mouth shall relate Your praise.*" (Psalms 51:17)

THE FIRST BLESSING

Blessed are You, Lord,
our God and God of our forefathers: the God of Abraham, the God of Isaac, and the God of Jacob.

הָאֵל haEl ; יא"י (מילוי דס"ג) ; האל הגדול = סיט ; גדול = להו ; לאה ‏הַגָּדוֹל hagadol

הַגִּבּוֹר hagibor ר"ת ההה ‏וְהַנּוֹרָא vehanora ◆ ‏עם ד' אותיות = מבה, יזל, אום

אֵל El ‏יא"י (מילוי דס"ג) ; ר"ת ע"ב, ריבוע יהוה ‏עֶלְיוֹן elyon ◆

גּוֹמֵל gomel ‏וַחֲסָדִים chasadim ‏טוֹבִים tovim ◆ ‏קוֹנֵה kone ‏הַכֹּל hakol

וְזוֹכֵר vezocher ‏חַסְדֵי chasdei ‏אָבוֹת avot ◆ ‏וּמֵבִיא umevi

גּוֹאֵל go'el ‏לִבְנֵי livnei ‏בְנֵיהֶם venehem ‏לְמַעַן lema'an

שְׁמוֹ shemo ‏בְּאַהֲבָה be'ahava ‏אותז, דאגה:

When saying the word "be'ahava" you should meditate to devote your soul to sanctify the Holy Name and accept upon yourself the four forms of death.

מֶלֶךְ melech ‏עוֹזֵר ozer ‏וּמוֹשִׁיעַ umoshi'a ‏וּמָגֵן umagen

ג"פ אל (יא"י מילוי דס"ג) ; ר"ת מיכאל גבריאל נוריאל:

Bend your knees at "baruch," bow at "Ata" and straighten up at "Adonai."

(on Shabbat) אהיה יהו אלף הי יוד הי :‏יְהֹוָה

בָּרוּךְ baruch ‏אַתָּה Ata ‏יְהֹוָה Adonai (הד)

מָגֵן magen ‏אַבְרָהָם Avraham ; ר"ת מיכאל גבריאל נוריאל:

ו"ה אל, רי"ו ול"ב נתיבות הוחכמה, רמ"ח (אברים), עסמ"ב וט"ז אותיות פשוטות:

The great, mighty and awesome God. The Supernal God, Who bestows beneficial kindness and creates everything. Who recalls the kindness of the forefathers and brings a Redeemer to their descendants for the sake of His Name, lovingly. King, Helper, Savior and Shield. Blessed are You, Lord, the shield of Abraham.

THE SECOND BLESSING

THE ENERGY OF ISAAC IGNITES THE POWER FOR THE RESURRECTION OF THE DEAD.

Whereas Abraham represents the power of sharing, Isaac represents the Left Column energy of judgment. Judgment shortens the *tikkun* process and paves the way for our eventual resurrection.

Gevurah that becomes *Binah*.

In this section there are 49 words corresponding to the 49 Gates of the Pure System in *Binah*.

לכלה Adonai אֲדֹנָי ס"ג ו"י אותיות דס"ג le'olam לְעוֹלָם ריבוע ס"ג גבור gibor Ata אַתָּה

(ר"ת אֲגְלָא והוא שם גדול ואמיץ, ובו היה יהודה מתגבר על אויביו. ע"ה אלד, בוכו).

lehoshi'a לְהוֹשִׁיעַ rav רַב Ata אַתָּה metim מֵתִים ס"ג mechaye מְחַיֵּה

hatal הַטָּל יוד הא ואו, כוזו, מספר אותיות דמילואי עסמ"ב ; ר"ת מ"ה morid מוֹרִיד

If you mistakenly say "*Mashiv haru'ach*," and realize this before the end of the blessing "*baruch Ata Adonai*," you should return to the beginning of the blessing "*Ata gibor*" and continue as usual. But if you only realize this after the end of the blessing, you should start the *Amidah* from the beginning.

bechesed בְּחֶסֶד אהיה אהיה יהוה, בינה ע"ה chayim חַיִּים mechalkel מְכַלְכֵּל

berachamim בְּרַחֲמִים metim מֵתִים ס"ג mechaye מְחַיֵּה ריבוע יהוה. ע"ב,

somech סוֹמֵךְ (טלא דעתיק). rabim רַבִּים י"פ ייי אלהים דההין, כ"ו (במ"ו כסו)

cholim חוֹלִים verofe וְרוֹפֵא (ו"ן). noflim נוֹפְלִים כוז, ריבוע אדני (אכדטם)

umekayem וּמְקַיֵּם asurim אֲסוּרִים umatir וּמַתִּיר אותיות ד"י מ"ה = וזוכה.

chamocha כָּמוֹךָ ילי mi מִי afar עָפָר lishenei לִישֵׁנֵי emunato אֱמוּנָתוֹ

gevurot גְּבוּרוֹת ba'al בַּעַל (you should enunciate the letter *Ayin* in the word "*ba'al*")

memit מֵמִית melech מֶלֶךְ lach לָךְ dome דוֹמֶה ילי umi וּמִי

yeshu'a יְשׁוּעָה umatzmi'ach וּמַצְמִיחַ (יוד הי ואו הי) ס"ג umchaye וּמְחַיֵּה

metim מֵתִים lehachayot לְהַחֲיוֹת Ata אַתָּה vene'eman וְנֶאֱמָן

(אהיה יהו אלף הי יוד הי :*on Shabbat*) יְהֹוָה:

Adonai יֱהֹוָה(יְהֹוָה)יאהדונהי Ata אַתָּה baruch בָּרוּךְ

mechaye מְחַיֵּה ס"ג (יוד הי ואו הי) hametim הַמֵּתִים ר"ת מ"ה וס"ת מ"ה.

THE SECOND BLESSING

You are mighty forever, Lord. You resurrect the dead and are very capable of redeeming. Who causes dew to fall. You sustain life with kindness and resurrect the dead with great compassion. You support those who have fallen, heal the sick, release the imprisoned, and fulfill Your faithful words to those who are asleep in the dust. Who is like You, Master of might, and Who can compare to You, King, Who causes death, Who gives life, and Who sprouts salvation? And You are faithful to resurrecting the dead. Blessed are You, Lord, Who resurrects the dead.

THE THIRD BLESSING

This blessing connects us to Jacob, the Central Column and the power of restriction. Jacob is our channel for connecting mercy with judgment. By restricting our reactive behavior, we are blocking our Desire to Receive for the Self Alone. Jacob also gives us the power to balance our acts of mercy and judgment toward other people in our lives.

Tiferet that becomes Da'at (14 words).

אַתָּה Ata קָדוֹשׁ kadosh וְשִׁמְךָ veshimcha קָדוֹשׁ kadosh ר"ת = אור, רז, אין סוף◆

וּקְדוֹשִׁים ukdoshim בְּכָל־ bechol ב"ן, לכב יוֹם yom ע"ה נגד, מזבוח, זן, אל יהוה

יְהַלְלוּךָ yehalelucha סֶלָה sela:

אהלה יהו אלף הא יוד הא (on Shabbat מצפצ)

בָּרוּךְ baruch אַתָּה Ata יְהֹוָ֯אֲדֹנָי(יֱהֹוִאֲדֹנָי)יאהדונהי Adonai

הָאֵל haEl הַקָּדוֹשׁ hakadosh י"פ מ"ה (יוד הא ואו הא): לאה ; ייא"י (מילוי דס"ג)

Meditate here on the Name: יאהדונהי, as it can help to remove anger.

THE MIDDLE BLESSING

The middle blessing connects us to the true power of *Sukkot* and *Simchat Torah*. *Sukkot* and *Simchat Torah* are the seed of the entire year for Mercy and Happiness. Just as an apple seed begets an apple tree, a negative seed begets a negative year. Likewise, a positive seed generates a positive year. *Sukkot* and *Simchat Torah* are our opportunity to choose the seed we wish to plant for our coming year. The power of the letters in this Fourth Blessing is in their ability to automatically choose the correct seed we need and not necessarily the seed we want.

אַתָּה Ata בְּחַרְתָּנוּ vechartanu מִכָּל mikol ילי הָעַמִּים ha'amim◆

אָהַבְתָּ ahavta אוֹתָנוּ otanu וְרָצִיתָ veratzita בָּנוּ banu◆

וְרוֹמַמְתָּנוּ veromamtanu מִכָּל mikol ילי הַלְּשׁוֹנוֹת haleshonot◆

וְקִדַּשְׁתָּנוּ vekidashtanu בְּמִצְוֹתֶיךָ bemitzvotecha◆ וְקֵרַבְתָּנוּ vekeravtanu

מַלְכֵּנוּ malkenu לַעֲבוֹדָתֶךָ la'avodatecha◆ וְשִׁמְךָ veshimcha הַגָּדוֹל hagadol

וְהַקָּדוֹשׁ vehakadosh עָלֵינוּ alenu קָרָאתָ karata: לההו ; ועם ד' אותיות = מבה, יזל, אום

THE THIRD BLESSING

You are Holy, and Your Name is Holy, and the Holy Ones praise You every day, for you are God, the Holy King Selah. Blessed are You, Lord, the Holy God.

THE MIDDLE BLESSING

You have chosen us from among all the nations. You have loved us and have found favor in us. You have exalted us above all the tongues and You have sanctified us with Your commandments. You draw us close, our King, to Your service and proclaimed Your great and Holy Name upon us.

When the Holliday falls on Saturday night then the following is said:

vatelamdenu וַתְּלַמְּדֵנוּ • tzidkecha צִדְקֶךָ mishpetei מִשְׁפְּטֵי vatodi'enu וַתּוֹדִיעֵנוּ

la'asot לַעֲשׂוֹת bahem בָּהֶם chukei וְחֻקֵּי retzonecha רְצוֹנֶךָ • vatiten וַתִּתֶּן ב״פ כהת

lanu לָנוּ Adonai יְהֹוָה אדני, אהיה אלהים, Elohenu אֱלֹהֵינוּ יֲלה

be'ahava בְּאַהֲבָה אוזר, דאגה • mishpatim מִשְׁפָּטִים yesharim יְשָׁרִים •

umitzvot וּמִצְוֹת chukim וְחֻקִּים ז״פ ס״ג, אהיה פעמים אהיה, emet אֱמֶת vetorot וְתוֹרוֹת

umo'adei וּמוֹעֲדֵי sason שָׂשׂוֹן zemanei וּזְמַנֵּי vatanchilenu וַתַּנְחִילֵנוּ • tovim טוֹבִים

vatorishenu וַתּוֹרִישֵׁנוּ • nedava נְדָבָה vechagei וְחַגֵּי kodesh קֹדֶשׁ

vachagigat וַחֲגִיגַת mo'ed מוֹעֵד uchvod וּכְבוֹד Shabbat שַׁבָּת kedushat קְדֻשַּׁת

likdushat לִקְדֻשַּׁת Shabbat שַׁבָּת kedushat קְדֻשַּׁת ben בֵּין • haregel הָרֶגֶל

hivdalta הִבְדַּלְתָּ והו tov טוֹב אל יהוה ז״ן, מזבוז, נגד ע״ה yom יוֹם

misheshet מִשֵּׁשֶׁת hashevi'i הַשְּׁבִיעִי אל יהוה ז״ן, מזבוז, נגד ע״ה yom יוֹם ve'et וְאֶת

vehivdalta וְהִבְדַּלְתָּ • kidashta קִדַּשְׁתָּ hama'ase הַמַּעֲשֶׂה yemei יְמֵי

bikdushatach בִּקְדֻשָּׁתָךְ: Yisrael יִשְׂרָאֵל amecha עַמְּךָ et אֶת vekidashta וְקִדַּשְׁתָּ

Adonai יְהֹוָה אדני, אהיה אלהים, lanu לָנוּ ב״פ כהת vatiten וַתִּתֶּן

דאגה אוזר, be'ahava בְּאַהֲבָה יֲלה Elohenu אֱלֹהֵינוּ

(u וּ limnucha לִמְנוּחָה shabbatot שַׁבָּתוֹת :On Shabbat add)

uzmanim וּזְמַנִּים chagim וְחַגִּים • lesimcha לְשִׂמְחָה mo'adim מוֹעֲדִים

:On Shabbat add) yom יוֹם ע״ה נגד, מזבוז, ז, אל יהוה et אֶת • lesason לְשָׂשׂוֹן

(אל יהוה ז, מזבוז, נגד ע״ה yom יוֹם ve'et וְאֶת • והו hazeh הַזֶּה haShabbat הַשַּׁבָּת

•(hazeh הַזֶּה haSukkot הַסֻּכּוֹת chag וְחַג :On Sukkot say)

•(hazeh הַזֶּה atzeret עֲצֶרֶת chag וְחַג shemini שְׁמִינִי :On Simchat Torah say)

mikra מִקְרָא והו tov טוֹב אל יהוה ז, מזבוז, נגד ע״ה yom יוֹם et אֶת

simchatenu שִׂמְחָתֵנוּ • zeman זְמַן והו hazeh הַזֶּה kodesh קֹדֶשׁ

You have informed us of Your righteous ordinances and You have taught us to do the decrees of Your will. May You give us, Lord, our God with love, fair ordinances and true teachings and good laws and commandments. And may You give us, as a heritage, seasons of joy and appointed festivals of Holiness and free willed festive-offerings. May You make us inherit the Shabbat Holiness and the glory of the Festival and the festive-offering of the Pilgrimage. You have distinguished between the sanctity of the Shabbat and the sanctity of the festival, and between the seventh day and the six working days, and have sanctified Your nation, Israel, with Your sanctity.

And may You give us, Lord, our God, with love (on Shabbat add: Sabbath for rest and) Holidays for happiness, Festivals and time of joy, this day (on Shabbat add: of Sabbath and this day) (on Sukkot: of Sukkot) (on Simchat Torah: of Shmini the Holiday of Atzeret) and this good day of Holy Convocation; the time of our happiness.

בְּאַהֲבָה be'ahava   אוֹד, דאגה   מִקְרָא mikra   קֹדֶשׁ kodesh•

זֵכֶר zecher   לִיצִיאַת litzi'at   מִצְרַיִם Mitzrayim   מצר•

אֱלֹהֵינוּ Elohenu ילה ; מילוי ע"ב, דמב ; ילה וֵאלֹהֵי velohei לכב ; מילוי ע"ב, דמב ; ילה avotenu אֲבוֹתֵינוּ

יַעֲלֶה ya'ale וְיָבֹא veyavo וְיַגִּיעַ veyagi'a וְיֵרָאֶה veyera'e רי"ו veyeratze וְיֵרָצֶה

veyizacher וְיִזָּכֵר veyipaked וְיִפָּקֵד veyishama וְיִשָּׁמַע מ"ב = ר"ת

זִכְרוֹנֵנוּ zichronenu וְזִכְרוֹן vezichron ע"ב קס"א ונש"ב avotenu אֲבוֹתֵינוּ•

זִכְרוֹן zichron ע"ב קס"א ונש"ב יְרוּשָׁלַיִם Yerushalayim עִירָךְ irach•

וְזִכְרוֹן vezichron ע"ב קס"א ונש"ב מָשִׁיחַ mashi'ach בֶּן ben

דָּוִד David ע"ה כהת ; בֶּן דוד = אדני ע"ה עַבְדָּךְ avdach פוי, אל אדני•

וְזִכְרוֹן vezichron ע"ב קס"א ונש"ב כָּל kol ילי עַמְּךָ amecha בֵּית bet ב"פ ראה

יִשְׂרָאֵל Yisrael ס"ג ; מ"ה בן לְפָנֶיךָ lefanecha לְפַלֵיטָה lifleta לְטוֹבָה letova אכא•

לְחֵן lechen מילוי דמ"ה בריבוע ; מוזי לְחֶסֶד lechesed ע"ב, ריבוע יהוה

וּלְרַחֲמִים ulrachamim• לְחַיִּים lechayim אהיה אהיה יהוה, בינה ע"ה

טוֹבִים tovim וּלְשָׁלוֹם ulshalom• בְּיוֹם beyom ע"ה נגד, מזבח, זן, אל יהוה

(On Shabbat add: הַשַּׁבָּת haShabbat הַזֶּה hazeh והו• וּבְיוֹם uvyom ע"ה נגד, מזבח, זן, אל יהוה)

(On Sukkot say: וְחַג chag הַסֻּכּוֹת haSukkot הַזֶּה hazeh)•

(On Simchat Torah say: שְׁמִינִי shemini וְחַג chag עֲצֶרֶת atzeret הַזֶּה hazeh)•

טוֹב tov beyom בְּיוֹם ע"ה נגד, מזבח, זן, אל יהוה והו

מִקְרָא mikra קֹדֶשׁ kodesh הַזֶּה hazeh והו•

---

with love, a Holy Convocation, a remembrance of the exit from Egypt.
Our God and the God of our fathers,
may it rise and come and arrive and appear and find favor and be heard and be considered
and be remembered, our remembrance and the remembrance of our fathers, the remembrance
of Jerusalem, Your city, and the remembrance of Mashiach Ben David, Your servant, and the remembrance
of Your entire Nation, the House of Israel, before You for deliverance, for good, for grace, kindness
and compassion, for a good life and for peace on this Day (**on Shabbat say:** *of Sabbath and on this Day*)
(**on Sukkot:** *of Sukkot*) (**on Simchat Torah:** *of Shmini the Holiday of Atzeret*)
on this good Day of Holy Convocation,

לְרַחֵם lerachem אברהם, ו"פ אל, רי"ו ול"ב נתיבות החוכמה, רמ"וז (אברים), עסמ"ב וט"ז אותיות פשוטות

בּוֹ bo עָלֵינוּ alenu וּלְהוֹשִׁיעֵנוּ ulhoshi'enu ◆ זָכְרֵנוּ zochrenu **(from** *Zeir Anpin***)**

יְהֹוָה(אדני/אהדונהי) Adonai אֱלֹהֵינוּ Elohenu ילה letova לְטוֹבָה letova בּוֹ bo אבא ◆

וּפָקְדֵנוּ ufokdenu **(from** *Nukva***)** בּוֹ vo לִבְרָכָה livracha ◆

וְהוֹשִׁיעֵנוּ vehoshi'enu **(from** *Da'at***)** בּוֹ vo לְחַיִּים lechayim אהיה אהיה יהוה, בינה ע"ה

טוֹבִים tovim ◆ בִּדְבַר bidvar ראה יְשׁוּעָה yeshu'a וְרַחֲמִים verachamim ◆

חוּס chus וְחָנֵּנוּ vechanenu וַחֲמוֹל vachamol וְרַחֵם verachem אברהם,

עָלֵינוּ alenu ◆ ו"פ אל, רי"ו ול"ב נתיבות החוכמה, רמ"וז (אברים), עסמ"ב וט"ז אותיות פשוטות

וְהוֹשִׁיעֵנוּ vehoshi'enu כִּי ki אֵלֶיךָ elecha עֵינֵינוּ enenu ריבוע מ"ה ◆

כִּי ki אֵל El יא"י מֶלֶךְ melech וְחַנּוּן chanun וְרַחוּם verachum אָתָּה Ata:

וְהוֹשִׁיעֵנוּ vehasi'enu יְהֹוָה(אדני/אהדונהי) Adonai אֱלֹהֵינוּ Elohenu ילה ◆

אֶת et בִּרְכַּת birkat מוֹעֲדֶיךָ mo'adecha לְחַיִּים lechayim אהיה אהיה יהוה, בינה ע"ה

בְּשִׂמְחָה besimcha וּבְשָׁלוֹם uvshalom ◆ כַּאֲשֶׁר ka'asher רָצִיתָ ratzita

וְאָמַרְתָ ve'amarta לְבָרְכֵנוּ levarchenu ◆ כֵּן ken תְּבָרְכֵנוּ tevarchenu

סֶלָה selah:

MEKADESH ISRAEL VEHAZEMANIM (THE TIMES)

)On *Shabbat* **add:** אֱלֹהֵינוּ Elohenu ילה וֵאלֹהֵי velohei לכב ; מילוי ע"ב, דמב ; ילה

אֲבוֹתֵינוּ avotenu רְצֵה retze נָא na בִּמְנוּחָתֵינוּ vimnuchatenu**(**

---

to take pity on us and to save us. Remember us, Lord,
our God, on it for good and consider us, on it, for blessing and deliver us on it for a good life with the words
of deliverance and mercy. Take pity and be gracious to us and have mercy and be compassionate with us and
save us, for our eyes turn to You because You are God, King Who is gracious and compassionate.
And give us, Lord, our God Your blessing of Your Holidays for happy and peaceful life.
As You desired and said to bless us. So You shall bless us Selah.

MEKADESH ISRAEL VEHAZEMANIM (THE TIMES)
(**on Shabbat:** *Our God and the God of our forefathers, please desire our rest.*)

קַדְּשֵׁנוּ kadeshenu — בְּמִצְוֹתֶיךָ vemitzvotecha◆ — תֵן ten — וְחֶלְקֵנוּ chelkenu

בְּתוֹרָתֶךָ vetoratach◆ — שַׂבְּעֵנוּ sabe'enu — מִטּוּבָךְ mituvach — לֹאוּ

שַׂמֵּחַ same'ach◆ — נַפְשֵׁנוּ nafshenu — בִּישׁוּעָתָךְ bishu'atach◆

וְטַהֵר vetaher — לִבֵּנוּ libenu — לְעָבְדְּךָ le'ovdecha — פוי, אל יהוה בֶּאֱמֶת ve'emet

אֱלֹהֵינוּ Elohenu — וְהַנְחִילֵנוּ vehanchilenu — ס"ג, ז"פ, ס'ג. — יְהֹוֹ ⁄אדני⁄אהדונהי Adonai

(add *Shabbat* *On*: יכה — be'ahava בְּאַהֲבָה — אוזד, דאגה

וּבְרָצוֹן uvratzon — מהש ע"ה, ע"ב ברוביע וקס"א ע"ה, אל עדי) — בְּשִׂמְחָה besimcha

וּבְשָׂשׂוֹן uvsason — (add *Shabbat* *On*: שַׁבָּתוֹת shabbatot (ו u) — מוֹעֲדֵי mo'adei

קָדְשֶׁךָ kodshecha◆ — וְיִשְׂמְחוּ veyismechu — בְךָ vecha — כָל kol — יִשְׂרָאֵל Yisrael

מְקַדְּשֵׁי mekadeshei — שְׁמֶךָ shemecha◆ — בָּרוּךְ baruch — אַתָּה Ata

יְהֹוֹ ⁄אדני⁄אהדונהי Adonai

(on *Shabbat*: יה אדני) אהיה יהו אלף הה יוד הה

מְקַדֵּשׁ mekadesh (add *Shabbat* On*: הַשַּׁבָּת haShabbat (ו ve) Yisrael יִשְׂרָאֵל

וְהַזְּמַנִּים vehazemanim:

THE FINAL THREE BLESSINGS

Through the merit of Moses, Aaron and Joseph, who are our channels for the final three blessings, we are able to bring down all the spiritual energy that we aroused with our prayers and blessings.

THE FIFTH BLESSING

During this blessing, referring to Moses, we should always meditate to try to know exactly what God wants from us in our life, as signified by the phrase, "Let it be the will of God." We ask God to guide us toward the work we came to Earth to do. The Creator cannot just accept the work that we want to do; we must carry out the work we were destined to do.

Sanctify us with Your commandments and place
our lot in Your Torah and satiate us from Your goodness
and gladden our spirits with Your salvation. And purify our heart
so as to serve You truly. And grant us, Lord, our God, (on Shabbat: with love and favor,) with happiness
and joy (on Shabbat: Sabbaths and) the Holidays, and all Israel, who sanctify Your Name will be joyful
with You. Blessed are You, Lord, who sanctifies (on Shabbat: the Sabbath) and Israel and the Times.

Netzach

Meditate for the Supernal Desire (*Keter*) that is called *Metzach HaRatzon* (Forehead of the Desire).

רְצֵה retze אלף למד הה יוד מם

Meditate here to transform misfortune and tragedy (צרה) into desire and acceptance (רצה).

יְהֹוָואדנהיאהדונהי Adonai אֱלֹהֵינוּ יכה Elohenu בְּעַמְּךָ be'amecha יִשְׂרָאֵל Yisrael

וְלִתְפִלָּתָם velitfilatam שְׁעֵה she'e ◆ וְהָשֵׁב vehashev הָעֲבוֹדָה ha'avoda

לִדְבִיר רי"ו lidvir בֵּיתֶךָ betecha ב"פ ראה ◆ וְאִשֵׁי ve'ishei יִשְׂרָאֵל Yisrael

וּתְפִלָּתָם utfilatam מְהֵרָה mehera בְּאַהֲבָה be'ahava אוזד, דאגה

תְקַבֵּל tekabel בְּרָצוֹן beratzon מהש׳ ע"ה, ע"ב בריבוע וקס"א ע"ה, אל שדי ע"ה ◆

וּתְהִי ut'hi לְרָצוֹן leratzon מהש׳ ע"ה, ע"ב בריבוע וקס"א ע"ה, אל שדי ע"ה

תָּמִיד tamid ע"ה קס"א קנ"א קמ"ג avodat עֲבוֹדַת Yisrael יִשְׂרָאֵל amecha עַמֶּךָ:

וְאַתָּה veAta בְּרַחֲמֶךָ verachamecha הָרַבִּים harabim ◆

תַּחְפֹּץ tachpotz בָּנוּ banu וְתִרְצֵנוּ vetirtzenu וְתֶחֱזֶינָה vetechezena

עֵינֵינוּ enenu ריבוע מ"ה beshuvcha בְּשׁוּבְךָ leTziyon לְצִיּוֹן יוסף, ו הויות, קנאה

בְּרַחֲמִים berachamim מצפצ, אלהים דיודין, י"פ ייי:

(on Shabbat: אל יוד הי למד אלף יהו אהיה)

בָּרוּךְ baruch אַתָּה Ata יְהֹוָואדנהיאהדונהי Adonai

הַמַּחֲזִיר hamachazir שְׁכִינָתוֹ shechinato לְצִיּוֹן leTziyon יוסף, ו הויות, קנאה:

THE FIFTH BLESSING

Find favor, Lord, our God,
in Your People, Israel, and turn to their prayer.

Restore the service to the inner sanctuary of Your Temple. Accept the offerings of Israel and their prayer with favor, speedily, and with love. May the service of Your People Israel always be favorable to You. And You in Your great compassion take delight in us and are pleased with us. May our eyes witness Your return to Zion with compassion. Blessed are You, Lord, Who returns His Shechinah to Zion.

THE SIXTH BLESSING

This blessing is our thank you. Kabbalistically, the biggest 'thank you' we can give the Creator is to do exactly what we are supposed to do in terms of our spiritual work.

Hod

Bow your entire body at "*modim*" and straighten up at "*Adonai.*"

lach כְּךָ anachnu אֲנַחְנוּ מאה ברכות עתיקן דוד לאמרם כל יום modim מוֹדִים

יכה Elohenu אֱלֹהֵינוּ (וּ) Adonai יְהֹוָהיאהדונהי hu הוּא sheAta שָׁאַתָּה

le'olam לְעוֹלָם avotenu אֲבוֹתֵינוּ יכה ; לכב ; מילוי ע"ב, דמב velohei וֵאלֹהֵי

ע"ה אלהים דההן tzur צוּר tzurenu צוּרֵנוּ va'ed וָעֶד דס"ג אותיות וי' ס"ג ריבוע

נוּריאל גַּבְריאל מיכאל ר"ת ; (ס"ג) מילוי (ייא"י אל ג"פ umagen וּמָגֵן chayenu חַיֵּינוּ וְזִוִּינוּ

node נוֹדֶה רי"ו vador וָדוֹר ledor לְדוֹר hu הוּא Ata אַתָּה yish'enu יִשְׁעֵנוּ

chayenu וְזִוִּינוּ al עַל tehilatecha תְּהִלָּתֶךָ unsaper וּנְסַפֵּר lecha לְךָ

nishmotenu נִשְׁמוֹתֵינוּ ve'al וְעַל beyadecha בְּיָדֶךָ hamesurim הַמְּסוּרִים

shebechol שֶׁבְּכָל nisecha נִסֶּיךָ ve'al וְעַל lach לָךְ hapekudot הַפְּקוּדוֹת

אותיות וד' ע"ה קס"א ס"ג, ריבוע אל יהוה זן, מזבח, נגד, ע"ה yom יוֹם imanu עִמָּנוּ

shebechol שֶׁבְּכָל vetovotecha וְטוֹבוֹתֶיךָ nifle'otecha נִפְלְאוֹתֶיךָ ve'al וְעַל

hatov הַטּוֹב vetzahorayim וְצָהֳרַיִם vavoker וָבֹקֶר erev עֶרֶב et עֵת לכב ב"ן,

hamerachem הַמְרַחֵם rachamecha רַחֲמֶיךָ chalu כָלוּ lo לֹא ki כִּי והו

lo לֹא ki כִּי אותיות פעוטות עסמ"ב וט"ז (אברים), רמ"ז נתיבות החכמה, רי"ו ול"ב אל, ח"פ אברהם,

lach לָךְ kivinu קִוִּינוּ me'olam מֵעוֹלָם ki כִּי chasadecha חֲסָדֶיךָ tamu תַמּוּ וְזֶסְדֶיךָ

THE SIXTH BLESSING

We give thanks to You, for it is You, Lord, Who is our God and God of our forefathers, forever and for all eternity. You are our Rock, the Rock of our lives, and the Shield of our salvation. From one generation to another, we shall give thanks to You and we shall tell of Your praise. For our lives that are entrusted in Your hands, for our souls that are in Your care, for Your miracles that are with us every day, and for Your wonders and Your favors that are with us at all times: evening, morning and afternoon. You are the good One, for Your compassion has never ceased. You are the compassionate One, for Your kindness has never ended, for we have always placed our hope in You.

veyitromam וְיִתְרוֹמַם yitbarach יִתְבָּרַךְ kulam כֻּלָּם ve'al וְעַל

shimcha שִׁמְךָ קמ"ג קנ"א קס"א ע"ה tamid תָּמִיד veyitnase וְיִתְנַשֵּׂא

va'ed וְעֵד ◆ אותיות דס"ג וי' ס"ג רִיבוּע le'olam לְעוֹלָם malkenu מַלְכֵּנוּ

sela סֶלָה : yoducha יוֹדוּךְ אהיה אהיה יהוה, בינה ע"ה ילי hachayim הַחַיִּים vechol וְכָל

et אֶת־ מ"ה ריבוע יהוה יהוה vivarchu וִיבָרְכוּ vihalelu וִיהַלְלוּ

be'emet בֶּאֱמֶת אום יכל, = אותיות ד' עם ; להו' hagadol הַגָּדוֹל shimcha שִׁמְךָ

וְהוּ ; tov טוֹב ki כִּי אותיות דס"ג וי' ס"ג רִיבוּע le'olam לְעוֹלָם אהיה פעמים אהיה, ז"פ ס"ג

yeshu'atenu יְשׁוּעָתֵנוּ לאה ; יא"י (מילוי דס"ג) יכל, מבה, אום, אהיה, יהוה = כי טוב haEl הָאֵל ◆

hatov הַטּוֹב וְהוּ : לאה ; יא"י (מילוי דס"ג) haEl הָאֵל sela סֶלָה ◆ ve'ezratenu וְעֶזְרָתֵנוּ

Bend your knees at "baruch," bow at "Ata" and straighten up at "Adonai."

(on Shabbat אֱלֹהִים:) אהיה יהו אלף למד הה יוד מם

hatov הַטּוֹב וְהוּ (הי) Adonai יְהֹוָהאדנייאהדונהי Ata אַתָּה baruch בָּרוּךְ

shimcha שִׁמְךָ ס"ת כהת, משיוו בן דוד ע"ה: lehodot לְהוֹדוֹת na'e נָאֶה ulcha וּלְךָ

The Final Blessing

We are emanating the energy of peace to the entire world. We also make it our intent to use our mouths only for good. Kabbalistically, the power of words and speech is unimaginable. We hope to use that power wisely, which is perhaps one of the most difficult tasks we have to carry out.

Yesod

shalom שָׁלוֹם sim שִׂים

chen וְחֵן אהיה אהיה יהוה, בינה ע"ה אכא chayim וְחַיִּים uvracha וּבְרָכָה tova טוֹבָה

מילוי דמ"ה בריבוע, מוזי ע"ב, ריבוע יהוה tzedaka צְדָקָה ע"ה ריבוע אלהים vachesed וָחֶסֶד

And for all those things, may Your Name be always blessed, exalted and extolled, our King, forever and ever, and all the living shall thank You, Selah. And they shall praise and bless Your great Name, sincerely and forever, for It is good, the God of our salvation and our help, Selah, the good God. Blessed are You, Lord, whose Name is good, and to You it is befitting to give thanks.

The Final Blessing
Place peace, goodness, blessing, life, grace, kindness, righteousness,

וְרַחֲמִים verachamim עָלֵינוּ alenu וְעַל־ ve'al כָּל־ kol

יִשְׂרָאֵל Yisrael עַמֶּךָ amecha וּבָרְכֵנוּ uvarchenu אָבִינוּ avinu כֻּלָּנוּ kulanu

כְּאֶחָד ke'echad פָּנֶיךָ panecha בְּאוֹר be'or כִּי ki

בְּאוֹר ve'or פָּנֶיךָ panecha נָתַתָּ natata לָּנוּ lanu

יְהֹוָה Adonai אֱלֹהֵינוּ Elohenu תּוֹרָה torah וְחַיִּים vechayim

אַהֲבָה ahava וָחֶסֶד vachesed

צְדָקָה tzedaka וְרַחֲמִים verachamim בְּרָכָה beracha

וְשָׁלוֹם veshalom וְטוֹב vetov בְּעֵינֶיךָ be'enecha

לְבָרְכֵנוּ levarchenu וּלְבָרֵךְ ulvarech אֶת et כָּל־ kol עַמֶּךָ amecha

יִשְׂרָאֵל Yisrael בְּרוֹב berov עֹז oz וּשָׁלוֹם veshalom:

(on Shabbat:)

בָּרוּךְ baruch אַתָּה Ata יְהֹוָה Adonai

הַמְבָרֵךְ hamevarech אֶת et עַמּוֹ amo יִשְׂרָאֵל Yisrael

בַּשָּׁלוֹם bashalom אָמֵן amen.

YIH'YU LERATZON

There are 42 letters in the verse in the secret of *Ana Beko'ach*.

יִהְיוּ yih'yu לְרָצוֹן leratzon

אִמְרֵי imrei פִי fi וְהֶגְיוֹן vehegyon לִבִּי libi

לְפָנֶיךָ lefanecha יְהֹוָה Adonai צוּרִי tzuri וְגֹאֲלִי vego'ali:

---

and mercy upon us and upon all of Israel, Your People. Bless us all as one, our Father, with the Light of Your Countenance, because it is with the Light of Your Countenance that You, Lord, our God, have given us Torah and life, love and kindness, righteousness and mercy, blessing and peace. May it be good in Your Eyes to bless us and to bless Your entire Nation, Israel, with abundant power and with peace. Blessed are You, Lord, Who blesses His Nation, Israel, with peace, Amen.

YIH'YU LERATZON
"May the utterances of my mouth and the thoughts of my heart find favor before You, Lord, my Rock and my Redeemer." (Psalms 19:15)

ELOHAI NETZOR

אֱלֹהַי Elohai מילוי ע"ב, רמב ; ילה ; נְצוֹר netzor לְשׁוֹנִי leshoni מֵרָע mera•

וְעֵפְתוֹתַי vesiftotai מִדַּבֵּר midaber ראה מִרְמָה mirma• וְלִמְקַלְלַי velimkalelai

נַפְשִׁי nafshi תִדּוֹם tidom• וְנַפְשִׁי venafshi כֶּעָפָר ke'afar

לַכֹּל lakol יה אדני תִּהְיֶה tih'ye• פָּתוֹחַ petach לִבִּי libi בְּתוֹרָתֶךָ betoratecha•

וְאַחֲרֵי ve'acharei מִצְוֹתֶיךָ mitzvotecha תִרְדּוֹף tirdof נַפְשִׁי nafshi•

וְכָל vechol יְלי הַקָּמִים hakamim עָלַי alai לְרָעָה lera'a רהע• מְהֵרָה mehera

הָפֵר hafer עֲצָתָם atzatam וְקַלְקֵל vekalkel מַחְשְׁבוֹתָם machshevotam•

עֲשֵׂה ase לְמַעַן lema'an שְׁמֶךָ shemach• עֲשֵׂה ase לְמַעַן lema'an

יְמִינֶךָ yeminach• עֲשֵׂה ase לְמַעַן lema'an תּוֹרָתֶךָ toratach• עֲשֵׂה ase

לְמַעַן lema'an קְדֻשָּׁתֶךָ kedushatach• ר"ת הפסוק = מ"ה יהוה lema'an לְמַעַן

יֵחָלְצוּן yechaltzun יְדִידֶיךָ yedidecha ר"ת ילי יהוה ועי"ע נהורין הוֹשִׁיעָה hoshi'a

יְמִינְךָ yemincha וַעֲנֵנִי va'aneni (כתיב: וַעֲנֵנוּ) ר"ת אל (ייא"י מילוי דס"ג):

Before we recite the next verse "Yih'yu leratzon" we have an opportunity to strengthen our connection to our soul using our name. Each person has a verse in the Torah that connects to their name. Either their name is in the verse, or the first and last letters of the name correspond to the first or last letters of a verse. For example, the name Yehuda begins with a *Yud* and ends with a *Hei*. Before we end the *Amidah*, we state that our name will always be remembered when our soul leaves this world.

YIH'YU LERATZON (THE SECOND)
There are 42 letters in the verse in the secret of *Ana Beko'ach*.

יִהְיוּ yih'yu אל (ייא"י מילוי דס"ג) לְרָצוֹן leratzon מהטע ע"ה, ע"ב בריבוע וקס"א ע"ה, אל שדי ע"ה

אִמְרֵי imrei פִי fi ר"ת אֶלֶף = אלף למד עין דלת יוד ע"ה וְהֶגְיוֹן vehegyon לִבִּי libi

לְפָנֶיךָ lefanecha ס"ג מ"ה בן יְהֹוָה Adonai צוּרִי tzuri וְגֹאֲלִי vego'ali:

ELOHAI NETZOR
My God, guard my tongue from evil and my lips from speaking deceit. To those who curse me, let my spirit remain silent, and let my spirit be as dust for everyone. Open my heart to Your Torah and let my heart pursue Your commandments. All those who rise against me to do me harm, speedily nullify their plans and disturb their thoughts. Do so for the sake of Your Name. Do so for the sake of Your Right. Do so for the sake of Your Torah. Do so for the sake of Your Holiness, "So that Your loved ones may be saved. Redeem Your right and answer me." (Psalms 60:7)

YIH'YU LERATZON (THE SECOND)
"May the utterances of my mouth and the thoughts of my heart find favor before You, Lord, my Rock and my Redeemer." (Psalms 19:15)

OSE SHALOM

You take three steps backward;

shalom עֹשֶׂה ose עֹשֶׂה שָׁלוֹם

Left
You turn to the left and say:

בִּמְרוֹמָיו bimromav ר"ת ע"ב, ריבוע יהוה

Right
You turn to the right and say:

ya'ase יַעֲשֶׂה verachamav בְּרַחֲמָיו hu הוּא

alenu עָלֵינוּ ר"ת ע"ע נהורין shalom שָׁלוֹם

Center
You face the center and say:

Yisrael יִשְׂרָאֵל amo עַמּוֹ ; עממ ילי kol כָּל ve'al וְעַל

amen אָמֵן יאהדונהי ve'imru וְאִמְרוּ

yehi יְהִי ratzon רָצוֹן מהש ע"ה, ע"ב, בריבוע וקס"א ע"ה, ע"ה שדי אל ע"ה

milfanecha מִלְּפָנֶיךָ ס"ג מ"ה ב"ן יְהֹוָה יאהדונהי Adonai אֱלֹהֵינוּ Elohenu ילה

velohei וֵאלֹהֵי ; מילוי ע"ב, דמב ; ילה avotenu אֲבוֹתֵינוּ shetivne שֶׁתִּבְנֶה

bet בֵּית ב"פ ראה hamikdash הַמִּקְדָּשׁ bimhera בִּמְהֵרָה veyamenu בְיָמֵינוּ

veten וְתֵן chelkenu וְחֶלְקֵנוּ betoratach בְּתוֹרָתֶךָ la'asot לַעֲשׂוֹת chukei וְחֻקֵּי

retzonach רְצוֹנֶךָ ul'ovdach וּלְעָבְדְּךָ פוי, אל אדני belevav בְּלֵבָב בוכו shalem שָׁלֵם.

You take three steps forward.

When the holiday falls on *Shabbat* we say "*Birkat Me'en Sheva*" on pages 111-114,
and then continue with *Kaddish Titkabal* on page 114.

Otherwise, wecontinue with *Kaddish Titkabal* onpage 114.

OSE SHALOM

He, Who makes peace in His High Places, He, in His compassion,
shall make peace upon us. And upon His entire nation, Israel, and you shall say, Amen.
May it be pleasing before You,
Lord, our God and God of our forefathers, that You shall rebuild the Temple speedily, in our days, and
place our lot in Your Torah, so that we may fulfill the laws of Your desire and serve You wholeheartedly.

When the Holiday falls on *Shabbat* we say *Birkat Me'en Sheva* here:

After the *Amidah*, the congregation should remain standing and say "*Vay'chulu*" out loud. And even when you pray alone you are obligated to say it. Since there is a deep secret about reciting it three times on Friday night (in the *Amidah*, here, and later in the *Kidush* over the wine.) Therefore you should not skip any of the three.

Do not speak while the congregation says "*Vay'chulu*" and not while the *chazan* says "*Birkat Me'en Sheva*."

VAY'CHULU

These verses from the Torah connect us to the very first *Shabbat* that occurred in the Garden of Eden. This *Shabbat* was the seed of the creation of our universe. By connecting ourselves to the original seed, we capture the force of Creation, bringing rejuvenation and renewal to our lives.

Meditate on the letter ק, from the Name: שׁקוֹציִת

Also, meditate that the three upper parts of the Surrounding *Mochin* of the letter *Lamed* (ל) of the *Tzelem* (צל״ם) of *Ima* are entering *Zeir Anpin* (as the head of *Zeir Anpin* is expanding).

The *Mochin* from *Abba* will enter *Zeir Anpin* later in the *Kidush*.

וַיְכֻלּוּ vay'chulu ... הַשָּׁמַיִם hashamayim ...

וְהָאָרֶץ veha'aretz ... וְכָל־ vechol ... צְבָאָם tzeva'am ...

וַיְכַל vay'chal ... אֱלֹהִים Elohim ... בַּיּוֹם bayom ...

הַשְּׁבִיעִי hashevi'i ... מְלַאכְתּוֹ melachto ... אֲשֶׁר asher ... עָשָׂה asa

וַיִּשְׁבֹּת vayishbot ... בַּיּוֹם bayom ... אֲשֶׁר asher ... יְהוָה

הַשְּׁבִיעִי hashevi'i ... מִכָּל־ mikol ... מְלַאכְתּוֹ melachto ... אֲשֶׁר asher

עָשָׂה asa ... וַיְבָרֶךְ vay'varech ...

אֱלֹהִים Elohim ... אֶת־ et ... יוֹם yom ...

הַשְּׁבִיעִי hashevi'i ... וַיְקַדֵּשׁ vay'kadesh ... אֹתוֹ oto ... כִּי ki ... בוֹ vo

שָׁבַת shavat ... מִכָּל־ mikol ... מְלַאכְתּוֹ melachto ... אֲשֶׁר asher

בָּרָא bara ...

אֱלֹהִים Elohim ... לַעֲשׂוֹת la'asot

VAY'CHULU

"And the Heavens and the Earth were completed and all their hosts. And God completed, on the seventh day, His work that He had done. And He abstained, on the seventh day, from all His work which He had done. And God blessed the seventh day and He sanctified it, for on it He had abstained from all His work which God had created to do". (Genesis 2:1-3)

BIRKAT ME'EN SHEVA

We are connecting ourselves to the founding Patriarchs, Abraham, Isaac, and Jacob. This connection works like a mini-*Amidah* prayer that occurs on *Shabbat*. Usually there is no repetition of the *Amidah* during *Arvit* (the evening connection), because it is night, a time of darkness, which signifies a lack of available spiritual Light. But on *Shabbat*, the Light floods our plane of existence. The following connection is our tool for capturing this additional Light.

According to Kabbalah, "*Birkat Me'en Sheva*" has a great importance as it's the secret of the Patriarchs—which means *Chesed*, *Gevurah* and *Tiferet*—that illuminate from Their places to the *Nukva* without Her going up to Them. That is why it's called "*Me'en Sheva*" (one blessing made from seven) and not a complete repetition (for all seven blessings). And therefore we say it even when praying in a place without a *Torah* scroll (like in the house of a groom or the house of a mourner).

בָּרוּךְ baruch אַתָּה Ata א-ת

(אותיות הא"ב המסמלות את השפע המגיע) לה המלכות

יְ֒הֹוָ֒ה Elohenu אֱלֹהֵינוּ Adonai אֱדֹנָיאהדונהי יְהֹוָ֒ה ילה

וֵאלֹהֵי velohei לכב ; מילוי ע"ב, דמב ; ילה אֲבוֹתֵינוּ avotenu◆

אֱלֹהֵי Elohei מילוי ע"ב = דמב ; ילה אַבְרָהָם Avraham וז"פ אל, רי"ו ול"ב נתיבות החכמה,

אֱלֹהֵי Elohei מילוי ע"ב, דמב ; ילה אותיות פשוטות. יִצְחָק Yitzchak ד"פ ב"ן רמ"ח, עסמ"ב וט"ז

וֵאלֹהֵי velohei לכב ; מילוי ע"ב, דמב ; ילה יַעֲקֹב Yaakov ו הויות, יאהדונהי אידהנויה

הָאֵל haEl לאה ; ייא"י ; (מילוי דס"ג) הַגָּדוֹל hagadol האל הגדול = סיט ;

אֱל El ; ר"ת, ע"ב, ריבוע יהוה עֶלְיוֹן elyon◆

וְהַנּוֹרָא vehanora◆ ר"ת ההה הגבור הַגִּבּוֹר hagibor אום, יזל, = מוכה = אותיות ד' עם ; לההו

קוֹנֵה kone בְּרוֹזְמָיו verachamav שָׁמַיִם shamayim י"פ טל, י"פ כוזו וָאָרֶץ va'aretz◆

If the *chazan* mistakenly continued the repetition as on weekdays, he should stop and return to the blessing of *Shabbat*.

BIRKAT ME'EN SHEVA

Blessed are You, Lord, our God and God of our forefathers:
The God of Abraham, the God of Isaac, and the God of Jacob. The great, mighty,
and Awesome God, the Supreme God, Who created with His compassion the Heavens and the Earth.

The congregation together with the *chazan*:

מָגֵן magen ג"פ אל (ייא"י מילוי דס"ג) ; ר"ת מיכאל גבריאל נוריאל

אָבוֹת avot בִּדְבָרוֹ bidvaro ♦

אהיה יהו יהוה

מְחַיֶּה mechaye ס"ג מֵתִים metim בְּמַאֲמָרוֹ bema'amaro ♦

אהיה יהו יהוה

הָאֵל haEl לאה ; אל (ייא"י מילוי דס"ג)

הַקָּדוֹשׁ hakadosh האל הקדוש = מ"ה י"פ שֶׁאֵין she'en כָּמוֹהוּ kamohu ♦

אהיה יהו מצפצ

הַמֵּנִיחַ hameni'ach לְעַמּוֹ le'amo בְּיוֹם beyom ע"ה נגד, מזבוח, זן, אל יהוה

שַׁבַּת Shabbat קָדְשׁוֹ kodsho ♦

אהיה יהו יה אדני

כִּי ki בָם vam מ"ב רָצָה ratza לְהָנִיחַ lehani'ach לָהֶם lahem ♦

אהיה יהו אל

לְפָנָיו lefanav נַעֲבוֹד na'avod בְּיִרְאָה beyir'a רי"ו וָפַחַד vafachad ♦

וְנוֹדֶה venode לִשְׁמוֹ lishmo מהע ע"ה, ע"ב בריבוע וקס"א ע"ה, אל שדי ע"ה

בְּכָל bechol ב"ן, לכב יוֹם yom ע"ה נגד, מזבוח, זן, אל יהוה ע"ה קס"א קנ"א קמ"ג תָּמִיד tamid

מֵעֵין me'en הַבְּרָכוֹת haberachot וְהַהוֹדָאוֹת vehahoda'ot ♦

אהיה יהו אלהים

לַאֲדוֹן la'adon אני הָעוֹלָם hashalom ♦

אהיה יהו מצפצ

מְקַדֵּשׁ mekadesh הַשַּׁבָּת haShabbat וּמְבָרֵךְ umvarech הַשְּׁבִיעִי hashevi'i ♦

וּמֵנִיחַ umeni'ach בִּקְדֻשָּׁה bikdusha לְעַם le'am עלם

מְדֻשְּׁנֵי medushenei עֹנֶג oneg ר"ת עדן נהר גן זֶכֶר zecher

לְמַעֲשֵׂה lema'ase בְרֵאשִׁית vereshit ר"ת מ"ב:

He Who hass shielded the forefathers with His Word, Who resurrects the dead with His Utterance, the King, the Holy One Who has no equal, Who grants rest to His people on His Holy Shabbat day. For it is them that He desired in order to grant them rest. Before Him, we will serve with awe and dread and we shall give thanks to His Name everyday, forever with appropriate blessings and thanks to the Master of peace, Who sanctifies the Shabbat, blesses the seventh day, and gives rest with Holiness to the people who are satiated with delight, in memory of the work of Creation.

The *chazan* continues alone:

אֱלֹהֵינוּ Elohenu ילה וֵאלֹהֵי velohei לכב ; מילוי דע"ב, דמב ; ילה אֲבוֹתֵינוּ avotenu

רְצֵה retze נָא na בִּמְנוּחָתֵנוּ vimnuchatenu◆ קַדְּשֵׁנוּ kadeshenu

בְּמִצְוֹתֶיךָ bemitzvotecha שִׂים sim וְתֵן חֶלְקֵנוּ chelkenu בְתוֹרָתֶךָ betoratach◆

שַׂבְּעֵנוּ sabe'enu מִטּוּבָךְ mituvach לאו◆ שַׂמֵּחַ same'ach נַפְשֵׁנוּ nafshenu

בִּישׁוּעָתֶךְ bishu'atach◆ וְטַהֵר vetaher לִבֵּנוּ libenu לְעָבְדְּךָ le'ovdecha

בֶּאֱמֶת be'emet אהיה פעמים אהיה, ז"פ ס"ג◆ וְהַנְחִילֵנוּ vehanchilenu פוי, אל אדני

יְהֹוָה Adonai Elohenu אֱלֹהֵינוּ ילה בְּאַהֲבָה be'ahava אוזר, דאגה

וּבְרָצוֹן uvratzon מהש ע"ה, ע"ב בריבוע וקס"א ע"ה, אל שדי ע"ה

שַׁבַּת Shabbat קָדְשֶׁךָ kodshecha◆ וְיָנוּחוּ veyanuchu בָה va כֹל kol יל

יִשְׂרָאֵל Yisrael מְקַדְּשֵׁי mekadshei שְׁמֶךָ shemecha◆ בָּרוּךְ baruch

אַתָּה Ata יְהֹוָה Adonai מְקַדֵּשׁ mekadesh הַשַּׁבָּת haShabbat:

KADDISH TITKABAL

יִתְגַּדַּל yitgadal וְיִתְקַדַּשׁ veyitkadash עדי ומילוי עדי ; י"א אותיות כמנין ו"ה

שְׁמֵהּ shemei (שם י"ה דע"ב) רַבָּא raba קנ"א ב"ן, יהוה אלהים יהוה אדני,

אמן amen אידהנויה. בְּעָלְמָא be'alma דִּי di בְּרָא vera כִּרְעוּתֵיהּ kir'utei◆

וְיַמְלִיךְ veyamlich מַלְכוּתֵיהּ malchutei◆ וְיַצְמַח veyatzmach

פּוּרְקָנֵיהּ purkanei◆ וִיקָרֵב vikarev מְשִׁיחֵיהּ meshichei: אמן amen אידהנויה.

Our God and God of our forefathers,
may You please desire our rest, sanctify us with Your commandments, place our lot in Your Torah, satiate us with Your goodness, gladden our souls with Your salvation, and purify our hearts to serve You sincerely. And grant us, Lord, our God, with love and favor, Your Holy Shabbat as a heritage. And may they rest in it, all of Israel, those who sanctify Your Name. Blessed are You, Lord, Who sanctifies the Shabbat.

KADDISH TITKABAL
May His great Name be more exalted and sanctified. (Amen)
In the world that He created according to His will, and may His Kingdom reign. And may He cause His redemption to sprout and may He bring the Mashiach closer. (Amen)

בְּחַיֵּיכוֹן bechayechon וּבְיוֹמֵיכוֹן uvyomechon וּבְחַיֵּי uvchayei

דְּכָל dechol ילי בֵּית bet ב"פ ראה בֵּית bet יִשְׂרָאֵל Yisrael בַּעֲגָלָא ba'agala

וּבִזְמַן uvizman קָרִיב kariv וְאִמְרוּ ve'imru אָמֵן amen : אָמֵן amen אידהנויה.

The congregation and the *chazan* say the following:

Twenty eight words (until *be'alma*) and twenty eight letters (until *almaya*)

יְהֵא yehe שְׁמֵיהּ shemei (שם י"ה דס"ג) ש"ם י"ה רַבָּא raba קנ"א ב"ן, ב"ן,

מְבָרַךְ mevarach יהוה אלהים יהוה אדנ"י, מילוי קס"א וס"ג, מ"ה ברבוע וע"ב ע"ה

לְעָלַם le'alam לְעָלְמֵי le'almei לְעָלְמֵי le'almei עָלְמַיָּא almaya◆ יִתְבָּרֵךְ yitbarach◆

Seven words with six letters each (שם בן מ"ב) – and also, seven times the letter *Vav* (שם בן מ"ב)

וְיִשְׁתַּבַּח veyishtabach יפ ע"ב יהוה אל אבג יתץ ◆

וְיִתְפָּאַר veyitpa'ar הי גו יה קרע שטן ◆ וְיִתְרוֹמַם veyitromam וה כוזו נגד יכש ◆

וְיִתְנַשֵּׂא veyitnase במוכסז בטר צתג ◆ וְיִתְהַדָּר veyit'hadar כוזו יה וזקב טנע ◆

וְיִתְעַלֶּה veyit'ale וה יוד ה יגל פזק ◆ וְיִתְהַלָּל veyit'halal א ואו הא שקו צית ◆

שְׁמֵיהּ shemei (שם י"ה דמ"ה) דְּקוּדְשָׁא dekudsha בְּרִיךְ verich הוּא hu :

אָמֵן amen אידהנויה ◆

לְעֵלָּא le'ela מִן min כָּל kol ילי בִּרְכָתָא birchata ◆ שִׁירָתָא shirata ◆

תִּשְׁבְּחָתָא tishbechata וְנֶחָמָתָא venechamata ◆ דַּאֲמִירָן da'amiran

בְּעָלְמָא be'alma וְאִמְרוּ ve'imru אָמֵן amen : אָמֵן amen אידהנויה.

תִּתְקַבַּל titkabal צְלוֹתָנָא tzelotana וּבָעוּתָנָא uva'utana

עִם im צְלוֹתְהוֹן tzelotehon וּבָעוּתְהוֹן uva'utehon דְּכָל dechol ילי

דְּבִשְׁמַיָּא devishmaya בֵּית bet ב"פ ראה יִשְׂרָאֵל Yisrael קָדָם kadam אֲבוּנָא avuna

וְאִמְרוּ ve'imru אָמֵן amen : אָמֵן amen אידהנויה ◆

In your lifetimes and in your days and in the lifetime of all the House of Israel, speedily and in the near future, and you shall say, Amen. (Amen) May His great Name be blessed forever and for all eternity. Blessed and lauded, and glorified, and exalted, and extolled, and honored, and uplifted, and praised be the Name of the Holy Blessed One. (Amen) Above all blessings, songs, praises, and words of consolation that may be said in the world, and you shall say, Amen. (Amen) May our prayers and pleas be accepted, together with the prayers and pleas of the entire House of Israel, before our Father in Heaven, and you say, Amen. (Amen)

קָנ"א ב"ק, יהוה אלהים יהוה ארני, מילוי קס"א וס"ג. raba רַבָּא shelama שְׁלָמָא yehe יְהֵא

מ"ה ברבוע וע"ב ע"ה chayim וְחַיִּים ◆ shemaya שְׁמַיָּא min מִן אהיה אהיה יהוה, בינה ע"ה

veshezava וְשֵׁיזָבָא venechama וְנֶחָמָה vishu'a וִישׁוּעָה vesava וְשָׂבָע

vechapara וְכַפָּרָה uslicha וּסְלִיחָה ug'ula וּגְאֻלָּה urfu'a וּרְפוּאָה

verevach וְרֵיוַח ◆ vehatzala וְהַצָּלָה lanu לָנוּ אלהים, אהיה ארני יה ארני ulchol וּלְכָל

amen אָמֵן ◆ amen אָמֵן ve'imru וְאִמְרוּ Yisrael יִשְׂרָאֵל amo עַמּוֹ אידהנויה.

Take three steps backwards and say:

shalom שָׁלוֹם ose עוֹשֶׂה

berachamav בְּרַחֲמָיו hu הוּא ◆ יהוה. ריבוע ע"ב, bimromav בִּמְרוֹמָיו

נהורין ◆ ע"ד ר"ת alenu עָלֵינוּ shalom שָׁלוֹם ya'ase יַעֲשֶׂה

amen אָמֵן ve'imru וְאִמְרוּ Yisrael יִשְׂרָאֵל amo עַמּוֹ ; עמם יל kol כָּל ve'al וְעַל

◆ אידהנויה amen אָמֵן

On **Simchat Torah** we do the *Hakafot* here on pages 759-802, and then read the Torah portion of *Vezot Haberacha* on pages 746-747, for five people, and then continue here (page 116).

When the Holiday falls on *Shabbat* or on *Shabbat Chol Hamo'ed* we say here *Mizmor LeDavid*:
MIZMOR LEDAVID
In "*Mizmor LeDavid*" there are 57 words as the numerical value of the word *Zan* זָן (sustenance). Reciting it will prevent lacking in both spiritual and physical sustenance.

lo לֹא ro'i רֹעִי Adonai יְהֹוָהאדניהי leDavid לְדָוִד mizmor מִזְמוֹר

mei מִי al עַל yarbitzeni יַרְבִּיצֵנִי deshe דֶּשֶׁא bine'ot בִּנְאוֹת echsar אֶחְסָר :

yeshovev יְשׁוֹבֵב nafshi נַפְשִׁי yenahaleni יְנַהֲלֵנִי עמם ר"ת menuchot מְנֻחוֹת יל

lema'an לְמַעַן tzedek צֶדֶק vema'gelei בְּמַעְגְּלֵי yancheni יַנְחֵנִי

ע"ה: שדי אל וקס"א ע"ה, בריבוע ע"ב ע"ה, מהשע shemo שְׁמוֹ

May there be abundant peace from Heaven, life, contentment, salvation, consolation, deliverance, healing, redemption, pardon, atonement, comfort, and relief. For us and for His entire nation, Israel, and you shall say, Amen. (Amen) He, Who makes peace in His High Places, With His compassion He shall make peace for us and for His entire nation, Israel. And you shall say, Amen. (Amen)

MIZMOR LEDAVID

"A Psalm of David: The Lord is my Shepherd, I shall not lack. In lush meadows He lays me down beside tranquil waters. He leads me. He restores my soul. He leads me on paths of justice for His Name's sake.

ra רַע ira אִירָא lo לֹא־ tzalmavet צַלְמָוֶת begei בְּגֵיא elech אֵלֵךְ ki כִּי־ gam גַּם

umish'antecha וּמִשְׁעַנְתֶּךָ shivtecha שִׁבְטְךָ imadi עִמָּדִי Ata אַתָּה ki כִּי־

shulchan שֻׁלְחָן lefanai לְפָנַי ta'aroch תַּעֲרֹךְ yenachamuni יְנַחֲמֻנִי hema הֵמָּה

vashemen בְּשֶׁמֶן dishanta דִשַּׁנְתָּ tzorerai צֹרְרָי neged נֶגֶד

roshi רֹאשִׁי kosi כּוֹסִי revaya רְוָיָה ach אַךְ tov טוֹב

vachesed וָחֶסֶד yirdefuni יִרְדְּפוּנִי

veshavti וְשַׁבְתִּי chayai חַיָּי yemei יְמֵי kol כָּל־

le'orech לְאֹרֶךְ Adonai יהואדהאהדונהי bevet בְּבֵית

yamim יָמִים

On *Shabbat Chol Hamo'ed* we skip this Psalm.

SHIR HAMA'ALOT LEDAVID

These verses connect us to the ancient Holy Temple. According to Kabbalah, the Holy Temple is the energy center and source of all spiritual Light for the whole world, similar to a nuclear power plant that provides electrical energy for an entire city. The land of Israel is the energy center of the planet; Jerusalem is the energy center of Israel; the physical Temple was the energy center of Jerusalem; and the Holy of Holies, inside the Temple, was the ultimate energy center for the Temple and thus for the entire physical world. When the Temple was standing, it acted as a generator that chugged along 24 hours a day to produce all the spiritual Light and energy we needed. With its destruction, the power lines were severed. The Aramaic letters in this connection re-establish the lines of communication with the spiritual essence of the Temple, giving us the ability to capture this energy for our personal lives.

This praise was said by King David for his kingdom, as everything was in one Unification – "Justice and Peace kissed each other." And that's the meaning of: "I shall request good for you."

samachti שָׂמַחְתִּי leDavid לְדָוִד hama'alot הַמַּעֲלוֹת shir שִׁיר

be'omrim בְּאֹמְרִים li לִי bet בֵּית Adonai יהואדהאהדונהי nelech נֵלֵךְ

bish'arayich בִּשְׁעָרָיִךְ raglenu רַגְלֵינוּ hayu הָיוּ omdot עֹמְדוֹת

Yerushalayim יְרוּשָׁלָיִם Yerushalayim יְרוּשָׁלָיִם habenuya הַבְּנוּיָה

ke'ir כְּעִיר shechubera שֶׁחֻבְּרָה la לָהּ yachdav יַחְדָּו

Though I walk in the valley overshadowed by death, I will fear no evil for You are with me. Your rod and Your staff, they comfort me. You prepare a table for me in full view of my tormentors. You anoint my head with oil, my cup overflows. May only goodness and kindness pursue me all the days of my life, and may I dwell in the House of the Lord for long days." (Psalms 23)

SHIR HAMA'ALOT LEDAVID

"A Song of Ascents by David: I rejoiced when they said to me: Let us go to the House of the Lord. Our legs stood immobile within your gates, Jerusalem. The built-up Jerusalem is like a city that has been united together.

עֵדֻת edut יָהּ Yah שִׁבְטֵי shivtei שְׁבָטִים shevatim עָלוּ alu שֶׁשָּׁם shesham

לְיִשְׂרָאֵל leYisrael לְהֹדוֹת lehodot לְשֵׁם leshem יְהֹוָה Adonai:

כִּי ki שָׁמָּה shama עֵ"ה ה"פ אלהים יָשְׁבוּ yashvu כִסְאוֹת chis'ot לְמִשְׁפָּט lemishpat

כִּסְאוֹת kis'ot לְבֵית levet ב"פ ראה דָּוִד David: שַׁאֲלוּ sha'alu שְׁלוֹם shelom

יְרוּשָׁלָיִם Yerushalayim יִשְׁלָיוּ yishlayu אֹהֲבָיִךְ ohavayich: יְהִי yehi

שָׁלוֹם shalom בְּחֵילֵךְ bechelech שַׁלְוָה shalva בְּאַרְמְנוֹתָיִךְ be'armenotayich:

לְמַעַן lema'an אַחַי achai וְרֵעָי vere'ai אֲדַבְּרָה adabera נָּא na שָׁלוֹם shalom

בָּךְ bach: לְמַעַן lema'an בֵּית bet ב"פ ראה יְהֹוָה Adonai

אֱלֹהֵינוּ Elohenu ילה אֲבַקְשָׁה avaksha טוֹב tov והי לָךְ lach:

KADDISH YEHE SHELAMA

יִתְגַּדַּל yitgadal וְיִתְקַדַּשׁ veyitkadash עדי ומילוי עדי ; י"א אותיות כמנין ו"ה

שְׁמֵיהּ shemei (עם י"ה דע"ב קנ"א ב"ן, יהוה אלהים יהוה אדני, רַבָּא raba

מילוי קס"א וס"ג, מ"ה ברבוע וע"ב ע"ה ; ר"ת = ו"פ אלהים ; ס"ת = ג"פ יב"ק) אָמֵן amen אידהנויה.

בְּעָלְמָא be'alma דִּי di בְּרָא vera כִרְעוּתֵיהּ kir'utei.

וְיַמְלִיךְ veyamlich מַלְכוּתֵיהּ malchutei. וְיַצְמַח veyatzmach

פוּרְקָנֵיהּ purkanei. וִיקָרֵב vikarev מְשִׁיחֵיהּ meshichei: אָמֵן amen אידהנויה.

בְּחַיֵּיכוֹן bechayechon וּבְיוֹמֵיכוֹן uvyomechon וּבְחַיֵּי uvchayei

דְכָל dechol ילי בֵּית bet ב"פ ראה יִשְׂרָאֵל Yisrael בַּעֲגָלָא ba'agala

וּבִזְמַן uvizman קָרִיב kariv וְאִמְרוּ ve'imru אָמֵן amen: אָמֵן amen אידהנויה.

---

and the hills like young lambs. What ails you sea that you flee? Jordan that you turn backward? Mountains that you skip like rams? Hills, like young lambs? Before the Lord tremble, Earth, before the God of Jacob, Who turns the rock into a lake of water, the flint into a flowing fountain." (Psalms 113)

KADDISH YEHE SHELAMA

May His great Name be more exalted and sanctified. (Amen) In the world that He created according to His will, and may His kingdom reign. And may He cause His redemption to sprout and may He bring the Mashiach closer. (Amen) In your lifetimes and in your days and in the lifetime of all the House of Israel, speedily and in the near future, and you shall say, Amen. (Amen)

The congregation and the *chazan* say the following:

Twenty eight words (until *be'alma*) and twenty eight letters (until *almaya*)

קנ"א ב"ן raba רַבָּא (שם י"ה דס"ג) שם י"ה shemei שְׁמֵיהּ yehe יְהֵא

יהוה אלהים יהוה אדני, מילוי קס"א וס"ג, מ"ה ברבוע וע"ב ע"ה mevarach מְבָרַךְ

◆yitbarach יִתְבָּרַךְ ◆almaya עָלְמַיָּא le'almei לְעָלְמֵי le'alam לְעָלַם

Seven words with six letters each (שם בן מ"ב) and also, seven times the letter *Vav* (שם בן מ"ב)

י"פ ע"ב יהוה אל אבג יתץ ◆ veyishtabach וְיִשְׁתַּבַּח

הי גו יה קרע שטן veyitpa'ar וְיִתְפָּאַר ◆ וְיִתְרֹמַם veyitromam וה כוזו נגד יכש ◆

במוכסז בטר צתג ◆ veyitnase וְיִתְנַשֵּׂא כוזו יה וזקב טנע ◆ וְיִתְהַדָּר veyit'hadar

א ואו הא שקו צית ◆ veyit'ale וְיִתְעַלֶּה וה יוד ה יגל פזק ◆ וְיִתְהַלָּל veyit'halal

:hu הוּא verich בְּרִיךְ dekudsha דְּקוּדְשָׁא (שם י"ה דמ"ה) shemei שְׁמֵיהּ

אידהנויה. amen אָמֵן

◆shirata שִׁירָתָא ◆birchata בִּרְכָתָא יכי kol כָּל min מִן le'ela לְעֵלָּא

da'amiran דַּאֲמִירָן ◆venechamata וְנֶחָמָתָא tishbechata תִּשְׁבְּחָתָא

אידהנויה. amen אָמֵן :amen אָמֵן ve'imru וְאִמְרוּ be'alma בְּעָלְמָא

מ"ה ברבוע וע"ב ע"ה, יהוה אלהים יהוה אדני, מילוי קס"א וס"ג, קנ"א ב"ן raba רַבָּא shelama שְׁלָמָא yehe יְהֵא

אהיה אהיה יהוה, בינה ע"ה chayim וְחַיִּים ◆shemaya שְׁמַיָּא min מִן

veshezava וְשֵׁיזָבָא venechama וְנֶחָמָה vishu'a וִישׁוּעָה vesava וְשָׂבַע

vechapara וְכַפָּרָה uslicha וּסְלִיחָה uge'ula וּגְאֻלָּה urefu'a וּרְפוּאָה

יה אדני ulchol וּלְכָל אלהים, אהיה אדני lanu לָנוּ ◆vehatzala וְהַצָּלָה verevach וְרֵיוַח

אידהנויה. amen אָמֵן :amen אָמֵן ve'imru וְאִמְרוּ Yisrael יִשְׂרָאֵל amo עַמּוֹ

May His great Name be blessed forever and for all eternity. Blessed and lauded, and glorified, and exalted, and extolled, and honored, and uplifted, and praised be the Name of the Holy Blessed One. (Amen) Above all blessings, songs, praises, and words of consolation that may be said in the world, and you shall say, Amen. (Amen) May there be abundant peace from Heaven, life, contentment, salvation, consolation, deliverance, healing, redemption, pardon, atonement, comfort, and relief. For us and for His entire nation, Israel, and you shall say,

Amen. (Amen)

Take three steps backwards and say:

עוֹשֶׂה ose שָׁלוֹם shalom בִּמְרוֹמָיו bimromav ע״ב, ריבוע יהוה. הוּא hu

בְּרַחֲמָיו berachamav יַעֲשֶׂה ya'ase שָׁלוֹם shalom עָלֵינוּ alenu ר״ת ש״ע נהורין.

וְעַל ve'al כָּל kol יל; עמם עַמּוֹ amo יִשְׂרָאֵל Yisrael וְאִמְרוּ ve'imru אָמֵן amen:

אָמֵן amen אידהנויה.

BARCHU

The *chazan* (or a person who said the *Kaddish Yehe Shelama*) says:

רַבָּנָן rabanan: בָּרְכוּ barchu יהוה ריבוע יהוה ריבוע מ״ה אֶת et

יְהֹוָאֱדִנִיאֱהדונהי Adonai ס״ת כהת, משיוח בן דוד ע״ה: הַמְּבוֹרָךְ hamevorach ס״ת כהת, משיוח בן דוד ע״ה:

First the congregation replies the following and then the *chazan* (or a person who said the *Kaddish Yehe Shelama*) repeats it:

Nefesh		Ruach		Neshamah	
בָּרוּךְ baruch	יְהֹוָאֱדִנִיאֱהדונהי Adonai		הַמְּבוֹרָךְ hamevorach		

	Chayah		Yechidah
לְעוֹלָם le'olam ריבוע ס״ג ו׳ אותיות דס״ג	וָעֶד va'ed:		

ALENU

Alenu is a cosmic sealing agent. It cements and secures all of our prayers, protecting them from any negative forces such as the *klipot*. All prayers prior to *Alenu* drew down what the kabbalists call Inner Light. *Alenu*, however, attracts Surrounding Light, which envelops our prayers with a protective force-field to block out the *klipot*.

Drawing Surrounding Light in order to be protected from the *klipot* (negative side).

עָלֵינוּ alenu ריבוע דס״ג לְשַׁבֵּוֹן leshabe'ach עלינו לשבוח = אבג יתץ, ושׁר

לַאֲדוֹן la'adon אני ; ס״ת ס״ג ע״ה הַכֹּל hakol ר״ת ללה, אדני

לָתֵת latet גְּדֻלָּה gedula לְיוֹצֵר leyotzer בְּרֵאשִׁית bereshit ר״ת גלב (באך ב״י יג״ל)

He, Who makes peace in His High Places, with His compassion
He shall make peace for us and for His entire nation, Israel. And you shall say, Amen. (Amen)

BARCHU

Masters: Bless the Lord, the Blessed One.
Blessed be the Lord, the Blessed One, forever and for eternity.

ALENU

It is incumbent upon us to give praise to the Master of all and to attribute greatness to the Molder of Creation,

וְלֹא velo — הָאֲרָצוֹת ha'aratzot — כְּגוֹיֵי kegoyei — עָשָׂנוּ asanu — שֶׁלֹּא shelo

שֶׁלֹּא shelo — הָאֲדָמָה ha'adama — כְּמִשְׁפְּחוֹת kemishpechot — שָׂמָנוּ samanu — שֶׁלֹּא shelo

כְּכָל kechol — וְגוֹרָלֵנוּ vegoralenu — כָּהֶם kahem — חֶלְקֵנוּ chelkenu — שָׂם sam

לְהֶבֶל lahevel — מִשְׁתַּחֲוִים mishtachavim — שֶׁהֵם shehem — ◆hamonam הֲמוֹנָם

◆Yoshi'a יוֹשִׁיעַ — לֹא lo — אֶל el — אֶל el — umitpalelim וּמִתְפַּלְלִים — varik וְרִיק

(pause here, and bow your entire body when you say "va'anachnu mishtachavim")

מֶלֶךְ melech — לִפְנֵי lifnei — מִשְׁתַּחֲוִים mishtachavim — va'anachnu וַאֲנַחְנוּ

baruch בָּרוּךְ — hakadosh הַקָּדוֹשׁ — hamelachim הַמְּלָכִים — malchei מַלְכֵי

◆hu הוּא שֶׁהוּא shehu — note נוֹטֶה — shamayim שָׁמַיִם

umoshav וּמוֹשַׁב — ◆aretz אֶרֶץ — veyosed וְיוֹסֵד — ush'chinat וּשְׁכִינַת

◆mima'al מִמַּעַל — bashamayim בַּשָּׁמַיִם — yekaro יְקָרוֹ

◆meromim מְרוֹמִים — begovhei בְּגָבְהֵי — uzo עֻזּוֹ — ush'chinat וּשְׁכִינַת

◆acher אַחֵר — od עוֹד — ve'en וְאֵין — Elohenu אֱלֹהֵינוּ — hu הוּא

ve'efes וְאֶפֶס — malkenu מַלְכֵּנוּ — emet אֱמֶת

veyadata וְיָדַעְתָּ — batorah בַּתּוֹרָה — kakatuv כַּכָּתוּב — ◆zulato זוּלָתוֹ

el אֶל — vahashevota וַהֲשֵׁבֹתָ — hayom הַיּוֹם

hu הוּא — Adonai יְהֹוָה — ki כִּי — levavecha לְבָבֶךָ

בַּשָּׁמַיִם bashamayim — mima'al מִמַּעַל — ;

הָאֱלֹהִים haElohim

ha'aretz הָאָרֶץ — ve'al וְעַל — mitachat מִתַּחַת

◆od עוֹד — en אֵין

---

for He did not make us like the nations of the lands. He did not place us like the families of the Earth He did not make our lot like theirs and our destiny like that of their multitudes, for they prostrate themselves to futility and emptiness and they pray to a deity that does not help. But we prostrate ourselves before the King of all Kings, the Holy Blessed One. It is He Who spreads the Heavens and establishes the Earth. The Seat of His glory is in the Heaven above and the Divine Presence of His power is in the Highest of Heights. He is our God and there is no other. Our King is true and there is none beside Him. As it is written in the Torah: "And you shall know today and you shall take it to your heart that it is the Lord Who is God in the Heavens above and upon the Earth below, and there is none other." (Deuteronomy 4:39)

עַל al — כֵּן ken — נְקַוֶּה nekave — לְךָ lach — יְהֹוָה Adonai

אֱלֹהֵינוּ Elohenu — לִרְאוֹת lir'ot — מְהֵרָה mehera — בְּתִפְאֶרֶת betiferet

עֻזֶּךָ uzach — לְהַעֲבִיר leha'avir — גִּלּוּלִים gilulim

מִן min — הָאָרֶץ ha'aretz — וְהָאֱלִילִים veha'elilim — כָּרוֹת karot

יִכָּרֵתוּן yikaretun — לְתַקֵּן letaken — עוֹלָם olam — בְּמַלְכוּת bemalchut

שַׁדַּי Shadai — וְכָל vechol — בְּנֵי benei — בָשָׂר vasar — יִקְרְאוּ yikre'u

בִשְׁמֶךָ vishmecha — לְהַפְנוֹת lehafnot — אֵלֶיךָ elecha — כָּל kol — רִשְׁעֵי rish'ei

אָרֶץ aretz — יַכִּירוּ yakiru — וְיֵדְעוּ veyed'u — כָּל kol — יוֹשְׁבֵי yoshvei

תֵבֵל tevel — כִּי ki — לְךָ lecha — תִכְרַע tichra — כָּל kol — בֶּרֶךְ berech

תִּשָּׁבַע tishava — כָּל kol — לָשׁוֹן lashon — לְפָנֶיךָ lefanecha

יְהֹוָה Adonai — אֱלֹהֵינוּ Elohenu — יִכְרְעוּ yichre'u — וְיִפֹּלוּ veyipolu

וְלִכְבוֹד velichvod — שִׁמְךָ shimcha — יְקָר yekar — יִתֵּנוּ yitenu

וִיקַבְּלוּ vikabelu — כֻלָּם chulam — אֶת et — עוֹל ol — מַלְכוּתֶךָ malchutecha

וְתִמְלוֹךְ vetimloch — עֲלֵיהֶם alehem — מְהֵרָה mehera — לְעוֹלָם le'olam

וָעֶד va'ed — כִּי ki — הַמַּלְכוּת hamalchut — שֶׁלְּךָ shelcha

הִיא hee — וּלְעוֹלְמֵי ul'olmei — עַד ad — תִּמְלוֹךְ timloch — בְּכָבוֹד bechavod

כַּכָּתוּב kakatuv — בְּתוֹרָתֶךָ betoratach — יְהֹוָה Adonai — יִמְלֹךְ yimloch

לְעֹלָם le'olam — וָעֶד va'ed

Consequently, we place our hope in You,
Lord, our God, that we shall speedily see the glory of Your might, when You remove the idols
from the Earth and the deities shall be completely destroyed to correct the world with the kingdom
of the Almighty. And all mankind shall then call out Your Name and You shall turn back to Yourself all
the wicked ones of the Earth. Then all the inhabitants of the world shall recognize and know that,
for You, every knee bends and every tongue vows. Before You, Lord, our God, they shall kneel and fall and
shall give honor to Your glorious Name. And they shall all accept the yoke of Your Kingdom and You
shall reign over them, forever and ever. Because the kingdom is Yours. And forever and for eternity, You
shall reign gloriously. As it is written in the Torah: "The Lord shall reign forever and ever" (Exodus 15:18)

Adonai יְהֹוָאדֹנָיאהֱדֹנֵהִי יהֹוה ; יהוה vehaya וְהָיָה :vene'emar וְנֶאֱמַר

ha'aretz הָאָרֶץ ; עמם יִלי kol כָּל al עַל lemelech לְמֶלֶךְ ha'aretz אלהים דההין ע"ה

hahu הַהוּא יהוה אל זֶן, מזבוֹה, נגד, ע"ה bayom בַּיוֹם

echad אֶחָד Adonai יְהֹוָאדֹנָיאהֱדֹנֵהִי יִיי yih'ye יִהְיֶה אהבה, דאגה

:echad אֶחָד מהשׂ ע"ה, ע"ב בריבוע וקס"א ע"ה, אל שׂדי ע"ה ushmo וּשְׁמוֹ אהבה, דאגה:

If you prayed alone recite the following before you start *Arvit* and before "*Alenu*" instead of "*Barchu*":

omedet עוֹמֶדֶת achat אַחַת chaya וְחַיָּה Akiva עֲקִיבָא Rabi רַבִּי amar אָמַר

al עַל vechakuk וְחָקוּק Yisrael יִשְׂרָאֵל ushma וּשְׁמָהּ baraki'a בָּרָקִיעַ

be'emtza בָּאֶמְצַע omedet עוֹמֶדֶת Yisrael יִשְׂרָאֵל mitzcha מִצְחָהּ

et אֶת יהוה ריבוע יהוה וריבוע מ"ה barchu בָּרְכוּ ve'omeret וְאוֹמֶרֶת haraki'a הָרָקִיעַ

vechol וְכָל ס"ת כהה, משיחו בן דוד ע"ה hamevorach הַמְבוֹרָךְ Adonai יְהֹוָאדֹנָיאהֱדֹנֵהִי

Adonai יְהֹוָאדֹנָיאהֱדֹנֵהִי baruch בָּרוּךְ :onim עוֹנִים mala מַעֲלָה gedudei גְּדוּדֵי יִלי

hamevorach הַמְבוֹרָךְ le'olam לְעוֹלָם ריבוע ס"ג וי' אותיות דס"ג va'ed וָעֶד.

THE BLESSING FOR THE CHILDREN

After the *Kidush,* the kabbalists recommend that each father will bless his children because it is a time of favor and blessings are abundant. As children are unable to draw blessings upon themselves through their own action, doing so by an adult, will be very effective. As the Light of abundance comes down from Above to cling onto the children and embrace them because they have not yet sinned, and through children, the blessings can better spread (However, even grown up children can receive blessings from their fathers).

---

and it is also stated: "The Lord shall be King over the whole world and, on that day, the Lord shall be One and His Name One." (Zechariah 14:9)

Rabbi Akiva said: Standing in Heaven, there is one animal named Israel, and Israel is engraved on her forehead, and she is standing in mid-Heaven saying: Bless the Lord, the Blessed One, and all of Heaven's armies are answering: Blessed be the Lord, the Blessed One, forever and for eternity.

For a son: אהיה אדני ; ילה ; Elohim אֱלֹהִים yesimcha יְשִׂימְךָ

Continue "yevarechecha" ◆vechiMenashe וְכִמְנַשֶּׁה keEfrayim כְּאֶפְרַיִם

For a daughter: אהיה אדני ; ילה ; Elohim אֱלֹהִים yesimech יְשִׂימֵךְ

◆veLeah וְלֵאָה Rachel רָחֵל Rivka רִבְקָה keSara כְּשָׂרָה

Right   veyishmerecha וְיִשְׁמְרֶךָ Adonai יְהוָֹה yevarechecha יְבָרֶכְךָ

ר"ת = יהוה ; וס"ת = מ"ה:

Left   elecha אֵלֶיךָ panav פָּנָיו | Adonai יְהוָֹה ya'er יָאֵר   כף ויו זין ויו

וִיחֻנֶּךָּ vichuneka מנצר ; יהה אותיות בפסוק:

Center   elecha אֵלֶיךָ panav פָּנָיו | Adonai יְהוָֹה yisa יִשָּׂא

וְיָשֵׂם veyasem לְךָ lecha שָׁלוֹם shalom האא תיבות בפסוק:

Yisrael יִשְׂרָאֵל benei בְּנֵי al עַל shemi שְׁמִי et אֶת vesamu וְשָׂמוּ

avarchem אֲבָרְכֵם אני va'ani וַאֲנִי:

ra רָע יל mikol מִכָּל oti אֹתִי hago'el הַגֹּאֵל פוי, אל אדני hamal'ach הַמַּלְאָךְ

hane'arim הַנְּעָרִים et אֶת (לבמתק את ז' המלכים עטמתו) עסמ"ב, הברכה yevarech יְבָרֵךְ

veshem וְשֵׁם shemi שְׁמִי vahem בָהֶם ב"פ קס"א = עם ה' אותיות veyikare וְיִקָּרֵא

avotai אֲבֹתַי וז"פ אל, רי"ו ול"ב נתיבות הוחכמה, רמ"ז (אברים), Avraham אַבְרָהָם

veyidgu וְיִדְגּוּ ד"פ בן אותיות פשוטות וט"ז עסמ"ב veYitzchak וְיִצְחָק

לרב larov בְּקֶרֶב bekerev אלהים הָאָרֶץ ha'aretz דהדהן ע"ה:

ben בֵּן פֹּרָת porat יוֹסֵף Yosef ציון, ו' הויות, קנאה Yosef פֹּרָת porat עֲלֵי alei

ayin עַיִן ריבוע מ"ה banot בָּנוֹת tza'ada צָעֲדָה alei עֲלֵי shur שׁוּר ושר:

THE BLESSING FOR THE CHILDREN

For a son: *"May God make you as Ephraim and as Menashe." (Genesis 48:20)*
For a daughter: *May God make you as Sarah, Rivkah, Rachel and as Leah.*
(Right) *"May the Lord bless you and safeguard you.*
(Left) *May the Lord shine His countenance for you and be gracious to you.*
(Central) *May the Lord lift His countenance to you and set peace on you.*
And they placed My Name on the Children of Israel and I shall bless them." (Numbers 6:24-27)
"The angel who redeemed me from all evil
will bless the lads, and may my name and the name of my forefathers, Abraham and Isaac,
be called upon them. And let them grow in multitude amidst the earth." (Genesis 48:16) "A fruitful bough
is Joseph. A fruitful bough by the well, and whose branches ran over the wall." (Genesis 49:22)

KIDDUSH FOR EREV SUKKOT AND SIMCHAT TORAH

VAY'CHULU
When the Holiday falls on Friday night then the following is said:

יוֹם yom ע"ה נגד, מזבוח, זן, אל יהוה הַשִּׁשִׁי hashishi:

וַיְכֻלּוּ vaychulu ע"ב, ריבוע יהוה (י יה יהו יהוה) הַשָּׁמַיִם hashamayim י"פ טל, י"פ כוזו

וְהָאָרֶץ veha'aretz אלהים דההין ע"ה ; ר"ת והו וְכָל־ vechol צְבָאָם tzeva'am ס"ת צלם:

וַיְכַל vaychal אֱלֹהִים Elohim אהיה אדני ע"ה נגד, מזבוח, זן, אל יהוה בַּיּוֹם bayom יכה

הַשְּׁבִיעִי hashevi'i מְלַאכְתּוֹ melachto אֲשֶׁר asher עָשָׂה asa וַיִּשְׁבֹּת vayishbot

בַּיּוֹם bayom ע"ה נגד, מזבוח, זן, אל יהוה הַשְּׁבִיעִי hashevi'i מִכָּל־ mikol יכי

מְלַאכְתּוֹ melachto אֲשֶׁר asher עָשָׂה asa: וַיְבָרֶךְ vayvarech עסמ"ב, הברכה (לבמתק

אֱלֹהִים Elohim אהיה אדני ; יכה אֶת־ et אֶת־ yom יוֹם ע"ה נגד, מזבוח, זן, אל את ז' המלכים שמתו)

וַיְקַדֵּשׁ vaykadesh hashevi'i הַשְּׁבִיעִי יהוה oto אֹתוֹ ki כִּי vo בּוֹ shavat שָׁבַת

מִכָּל־ mikol יכי מְלַאכְתּוֹ melachto אֲשֶׁר־ asher בָּרָא bara קנ"א ב"ן, יהוה אלהים יהוה

אֱלֹהִים Elohim אהיה אדני ; יכה לַעֲשׂוֹת la'asot: אדני, מילוי קס"א וס"ג, מ"ה ברבוע וע"ב ע"ה

אֵלֶּה ele מוֹעֲדֵי mo'adei Adonai יְהֹוָהוּאדנהיאהדונהי מִקְרָאֵי mikra'ei

קֹדֶשׁ kodesh אֲשֶׁר־ asher תִּקְרְאוּ tikre'u אֹתָם otam בְּמוֹעֲדָם bemo'adam:

וַיְדַבֵּר vaydaber מֹשֶׁה Moshe מהש, ע"ב ברבוע וקס"א, אל שדי, ד"פ אלהים ע"ה ראה

אֶת־ et מוֹעֲדֵי mo'adei Adonai יְהֹוָהוּאדנהיאהדונהי אֶל־ el בְּנֵי benei יִשְׂרָאֵל Yisrael:

סַבְרִי savri מָרָנָן maranan

(and the others reply) לְחַיִּים lechayim אהיה אהיה יהוה, בינה ע"ה

בָּרוּךְ baruch אַתָּה Ata Adonai יְהֹוָהוּאדנהיאהדונהי אֱלֹהֵינוּ Elohenu יכה

מֶלֶךְ melech הָעוֹלָם ha'olam בּוֹרֵא bore פְּרִי peri הַגָּפֶן hagefen:

KIDDUSH FOR EREV SUKKOT AND SIMCHAT TORAH
VAY'CHULU
"And the Heavens and the Earth were completed and all their hosts. And God completed, on the seventh day, His work that He had done. And He abstained, on the seventh day, from all His work which He had done. And God blessed the seventh day and He sanctified it, for on it He had abstained from all His work which God had created to do". (Genesis 2:1-3)

"Those are the holiday of the Lord, Holy Covenant you shall call them, on their time.
And Moses spoke the Holidays of the Lord to the children of Israel" (Leviticus 23:44)
With your permission, my masters. (And the others reply: To life!)
Blessed are You, Lord, our God, the King of the world, Who creates the fruit of the vine.

בָּרוּךְ baruch   אַתָּה Ata   יְהֹוָה Adonai   אֱלֹהֵינוּ Elohenu

מֶלֶךְ melech   הָעוֹלָם ha'olam   אֲשֶׁר asher   בּוֹחֵר bachar   בָּנוּ banu

מִכָּל mikol   עַם am   וְרוֹמְמָנוּ veromemanu   מִכָּל mikol   לָשׁוֹן lashon

וְקִדְּשָׁנוּ vekideshanu   בְּמִצְוֹתָיו vemitzvotav   וַתִּתֶּן vatiten   Elohenu אֱלֹהֵינוּ

לָנוּ lanu   אֱלֹהֵינוּ Elohenu   יְהֹוָה Adonai

בְּאַהֲבָה be'ahava   (On Shabbat add: שַׁבָּתוֹת shabbatot   לִמְנוּחָה limnucha

מוֹעֲדִים mo'adim   לְשִׂמְחָה lesimcha   וְחַגִּים chagim   וּזְמַנִּים uzmanim

לְשָׂשׂוֹן lesason   אֶת et   יוֹם yom   (On Shabbat add:

הַשַּׁבָּת haShabbat   הַזֶּה hazeh   וְאֶת ve'et   יוֹם yom)

(On Sukkot say: חַג chag   הַסֻּכּוֹת haSukkot   הַזֶּה hazeh)

(On Simchat Torah say: שְׁמִינִי shemini   חַג chag   עֲצֶרֶת atzeret   הַזֶּה hazeh)

אֶת et   יוֹם yom   טוֹב tov   מִקְרָא mikra   קֹדֶשׁ kodesh

הַזֶּה hazeh   זְמַן zeman   שִׂמְחָתֵנוּ simchateno   בְּאַהֲבָה be'ahava

מִקְרָא mikra   קֹדֶשׁ kodesh   זֵכֶר zecher   לִיצִיאַת litzi'at   מִצְרַיִם Mitzrayim

כִּי ki   בָּנוּ banu   בָחַרְתָּ bacharta   וְאוֹתָנוּ ve'otanu   קִדַּשְׁתָּ kidashta

מִכָּל mikol   הָעַמִּים ha'amim   (On Shabbat add: וְשַׁבָּתוֹת veshabbatot)

מוֹעֲדֵי mo'adei   קָדְשֶׁךָ kodshecha   (On Shabbat add: בְּאַהֲבָה be'ahava)

וּבְרָצוֹן uvratzon   בְּשִׂמְחָה vesimcha   וּבְשָׂשׂוֹן uvsason   הִנְחַלְתָּנוּ hinchaltanu

בָּרוּךְ baruch   אַתָּה Ata   יְהֹוָה Adonai   מְקַדֵּשׁ mekadesh

(On Shabbat add: הַשַּׁבָּת haShabbat וְ ve)   יִשְׂרָאֵל Yisrael   וְהַזְּמַנִּים vehazemanim

---

Blessed are You, Lord our God, King of the universe, who has chosen us from among all nations, exalted us above all tongues, and sanctified us with its communications. And You, Lord our God, have lovingly given us: (on Shabbat add: Sabbaths for rest) appointed times for gladness, feasts and times for joy, (on Shabbat add: this Sabbath and) (on Sukkot: this Sukkot) (on Simchat Torah: this Shmini the Holiday of Atzeret) and this good day of Holy Convocation; The time of our happiness; With love, a Holy Convocation, a remembrance of the exit from Egypt. For You have chosen and sanctified us above all peoples, (on Shabbat add: and Sabbaths and) Your holy festivals (on Shabbat add: in love and favor) in gladness and joy have You granted us. Blessed are You, Lord, who sanctifies (on Shabbat add: the Sabbath and) Israel and the times.

On *Sukkut* we say the blessing of "*Leshev BaSukkah*" and then the blessing of "*Shehecheyanu*".
On *Simchat Torah* we continue with the blessing of "*Shehecheyanu*" below.

LESHEV BASUKKAH

בָּרוּךְ baruch אַתָּה Ata יְהֹוָ(אדני)אהדונהי Adonai

יְהֹוָה יֵאֶהֱוִֹהַה :On the first night meditate

יְהֹוָה יֵאֶהֱוִֹהַה :On the second night meditate

יְהֹוָה יֵאֶהֱוִֹהַה :On the third night meditate

יְהֹוָה יֵאֶהֱוִֹהַה :On the fourth night meditate

יְהֹוָה יֵאֶהֱוִֹהַה :On the fifth night meditate

יהדֹווהֹו יואֹוהֹוהֹוֵויֹוהֹו :On the sixth night meditate

יְהֹוָה יֵאֶהֱוִֹהַה :On the seventh night meditate

אֱלֹהֵינוּ Elohenu ילה melech מֶלֶךְ ha'olam הָעוֹלָם

אֲשֶׁר asher קִדְּשָׁנוּ kideshanu בְּמִצְוֹתָיו bemitzvotav

וְצִוָּנוּ vetzivanu לֵישֵׁב leshev בַּסֻכָּה basuka סאל

SHEHECHEYANU

בָּרוּךְ baruch מֶלֶךְ melech אַתָּה Ata יְהֹוָ(אדני)אהדונהי Adonai אֱלֹהֵינוּ Elohenu ילה

שֶׁהֶחֱיָנוּ shehecheyanu הָעוֹלָם ha'olam

וְקִיְּמָנוּ vekiyemanu וְהִגִּיעָנוּ vehigi'anu לַזְּמַן lazeman הַזֶּה hazeh והו

LESHEV BASUKKAH
Blessed are You, Lord, our God, King of the universe,
who sanctified us with His precepts and command us to sit in the Sukkah.
SHEHECHEYANU
Blessed are You, Lord, our God, King of the universe,
Who has kept us alive, sustained us, and brought us to this time.

THE ORDER OF THE SEVEN USHPIZIN – FROM THE RAV

On each night, before entering the Sukkah one should say:

Another important aspect of the *Sukkah* is the custom of inviting a different biblical guest to our *Sukkah* on each day of *Sukkot*—a custom that originated with the Ari. The *Ushpizin* (special guests invited each day) are Abraham, Isaac, Jacob, Moses, Aaron, Joseph, and David. Each guest acts as a chariot for the energy of the particular *Sefirah* connected to each day. There is, in addition, an Aramaic prayer that is recited for each different visitor. Inviting the *Ushpizin* connects us to them, and with their assistance we better connect to the Light of the *Sefirot* and to the power of the Clouds of Honor. The *Ushpizim* help us build the vessel that contains the Light of the Creator, which we will need for an entire year.

לְשֵׁם leshem · יִחוּד yichud · קוּדְשָׁא kudesha · בְּרִיךְ berich · הוּא hu

וּשְׁכִינְתֵּיהּ ushchinte · בִּדְחִילוּ bidchilu · וּרְחִימוּ urchimu (יְאהֲדוֹנָהי), (יֱאֱהֱוֹהֱה),

וּרְחִימוּ urchimu · וּדְחִילוּ udchilu (אֱיֱהֱוֹיֱהֱה), לְיַחֲדָא leyachda · שֵׁם shem

יוּ"ד yud · קֵי kei · בְּוָא"ו bevav · קֵי kei · בְּיִחוּדָא beyichuda · שְׁלִים shelim (יְהֹוָה)

בְּשֵׁם beshem · כָּל kol · יִשְׂרָאֵל Yisrael, · וּבְשֵׁם uvshem · כָּל kol

הַנְּפָשׁוֹת hanefashot · וְהָרוּחוֹת veharuchot · וְהַנְּשָׁמוֹת vehaneshamot

הַמִּתְיַחֲסִים hamityachasim · אֶל el · שָׁרְשֵׁי shorshei · נַפְשֵׁנוּ nafshenu

רוּחֵנוּ ruchenu · וְנִשְׁמָתֵנוּ venishmatenu, · וּמַלְבּוּשֵׁיהֶם umalbushehem

וְהַקְּרוֹבִים vehakerovim · לָהֶם lahem · שֶׁבַּמִּכְלָלוּת shemiklalut · אֲצִילוּת Atzilut

בְּרִיאָה Beri'a · יְצִירָה Yetzira · עֲשִׂיָּה Asiya, · וּמִכָּל umikol · פְּרָטֵי peratei

אֲצִילוּת Atzilut · בְּרִיאָה Beri'a · יְצִירָה Yetzira · עֲשִׂיָּה Asiya

דְּכֹל dechol · פַּרְצוּף partzuf · וּסְפִירָה usfira · דִּפְרָטֵי difratei

אֲצִילוּת Atzilut · בְּרִיאָה Beri'a · יְצִירָה Yetzira · עֲשִׂיָּה Asiya◆

הִנֵּה hineh · אֲנַחְנוּ anachnu · בָּאִים va'im · לְקַיֵּם lekayem · מִצְוַת mitzvat

עֲשֵׂה aseh · לֵישֵׁב leshev · בְּסֻכָּה basuka (אמן), (יְאהֲדוֹנָהי, סְאל◆)

כְּמוֹ kemo · שֶׁצִּוָּנוּ shetzivanu · יְהוָֹואֲדֹנָהֽיֱאֱהֱדֹוֹנָהֽי Adonai · אֱלֹהֵינוּ Elohenu

---

THE ORDER OF THE SEVEN USHPIZIN

For the sake of the unification between the Holy Blessed One and His Shechinah, with fear and love and with love and fear, in order to unify the Name Yud-Kei and Vav-Kei in perfect unity, and in the name of all Israel, and in the name of all the Nefashot (lower souls) Ruchot (spirits) and Neshamot (higher souls) that give attribute to the root of our Nefashot Ruchot and Neshamot, and their clothing and all that is associated with it from the generality of Azilut, Beriah, Yetzirah, and Asiyah and from all of the specific of Azilut, Beriah, Yetzirah, and Asiyah, of each Partzuf and Sefirah of the specific of Azilut, Beriah, Yetzirah, and Asiyah, we hereby fulfill the obligatory precept of sitting in the Sukkah, as the Lord, our God commanded us

בְּתוֹרָתוֹ betorato — הַקְּדוֹשָׁה hakedosha — עַל al — יְדֵי yedei — מֹשֶׁה Moshe — מהע,

עָלָיו alav — הַשָּׁלוֹם hasalom: — רַבֵּנוּ rabenu — ע"ב בריבוע קס"א, אל שדי, ד"פ אלהים ע"ה

בַּסֻּכֹּת basukot — אמן, יאהדונהי, סאל — תֵּשְׁבוּ teshvu — שִׁבְעַת shiv'at — יָמִים yamim — נלך

יֵשְׁבוּ yeshvu — בְּיִשְׂרָאֵל beYisrael — הָאֶזְרָח ha'ezrach — ילי — כָּל kol

בַּסֻּכֹּת basukot — אמן, יאהדונהי, סאל: — לְמַעַן lema'an — יֵדְעוּ yed'u

אֶת et — הוֹשַׁבְתִּי hoshavti — בַסֻּכּוֹת vasukot — כִּי ki — דֹרֹתֵיכֶם dorotechem

בְּנֵי benei — יִשְׂרָאֵל Yisrael — בְּהוֹצִיאִי behotzi'i — אוֹתָם otam — מֵאֶרֶץ me'eretz

מִצְרָיִם Mitzrayim — מצר: — לְתַקֵּן letaken — שֹׁרֶשׁ shoresh — מִצְוָה mitzva — זוֹ zo

בְּמָקוֹם bemakom — עֶלְיוֹן elyon — לַעֲשׂוֹת la'asot — כַּוָּנַת kavanat — יוֹצְרֵנוּ yotzrenu

שֶׁצִּוָּנוּ shetzivanu — לַעֲשׂוֹת la'asot — מִצְוָה mitzva — זוֹ zo — לְהַשְׁלִים lehashlim

אִילָן ilan — הָעֶלְיוֹן ha'elyon — וּלְהָקִים ulhakim — סֻכַּת sukat — אמן, יאהדונהי, סאל

דָּוִד David — לְהַחֲזִיר lehachazir — הָעֲטָרָה ha'atara — לְיָשְׁנָה leyoshna

וּלְהַשְׁלִים ulhashlim — שְׁלֵמוּת shelemut — תִּקּוּן tikun — הַנְּפָשׁוֹת hanefashot

וְהָרוּחוֹת varuchot — וְהַנְּשָׁמוֹת vehaneshamot — שֶׁמִּכְּלָלוּת shemiklalut

אֲצִילוּת Atzilut — בְּרִיאָה Beri'a — יְצִירָה Yetzira — עֲשִׂיָּה Asiya — וּמִכָּל umikol

פְּרָטֵי peratei — אֲצִילוּת Atzilut — בְּרִיאָה Beri'a — יְצִירָה Yetzira — עֲשִׂיָּה Asiya

וִיהִי vihi — רָצוֹן ratzon — מהע ע"ה, ע"ב בריבוע וקס"א ע"ה, אל שדי ע"ה

מִלְּפָנֶיךָ milfanecha — ס"ג מ"ה ב"ן — יְהֹוָה Adonai — אֱלֹהֵינוּ Elohenu — ילה

וֵאלֹהֵי velohei — לכב ; מילוי ע"ב, דמב ; ילה — אֲבוֹתֵינוּ avotenu — שֶׁיְהֵא sheyhe — עַתָּה ata

עֵת et — רָצוֹן ratzon — מהע ע"ה, ע"ב בריבוע וקס"א ע"ה, אל שדי ע"ה; עת רצון = י' הויות וי' אהיה

לִהְיוֹת lihyot — עוֹלָה ola — מִצְוָה mitzva — זוֹ zo — לְפָנֶיךָ lefanecha — ס"ג מ"ה ב"ן:

---

in His Holy Torah by Moses our teacher, may peace be upon him: "You shall dwell in booths seven days; all that are born in Israel shall dwell in booths; that your generations may know that I made the children of Israel to dwell in booths, when I brought them out of the land of Egypt" to correct the root of this precept in the Supernal Place, and to follow the intention of our Creator Who commanded us to do this precept. To complete the Supernal Tree, to erect the Sukkah of David, to restore the Tiara to its former place, and to complete the total correction of the Nefashot Ruchot and Neshamot, from the generality of Azilut, Beriah, Yetzirah, and Asiyah and from all of the specific of Azilut, Beriah, Yetzirah, and Asiyah. And May it be pleasing before You, Lord, my God, and God of my forefathers, that this hour will be a time of favor that this precept ascend before you.

On the first night:

וּבְכֹחַ (uvcho'ach) מִצְוָה (mitzva) זוֹ (zo) יִמְשֵׁךְ (yimashech) הַחֶסֶד (haChesed)

הַפְּנִימִי (hapenimi) הָעֶלְיוֹן (ha'elyon) הַנִּקְרָא (hanikra) יוֹמָם (yomam) [ע"ב, ריבוע יהוה]

יוֹמָא (yoma) דְּכָלִיל (dechalil) לְכֻלְּהוּ (lechulehu) יוֹמֵי (yomei) שֶׁהוּא (shehu)

הַחֶסֶד (haChesed) [ע"ב, ריבוע יהוה] שֶׁבַּחֶסֶד (shebaChesed) [ע"ב, ריבוע יהוה] הַחֶסֶד

מֵאִמָּא (meIma) עִלָּאָה (ila'a) לְרָחֵל (leRachel) אִמֵּנוּ (imenu) וְגַם (vegam)

תְּקַבֵּל (tekabel) עוֹד (od) רָחֵל (Rachel) אִמֵּנוּ (imenu) הַחֶסֶד (haChesed) [ע"ב, ריבוע יהוה]

הָעֶלְיוֹן (ha'elyon) שֶׁבְּכָל (shebchol) [בן, לכב] הַחֲסָדִים (haChasadim) דְּאוֹר (de'or) [רו, א"ס]

מַקִּיף (makif) מֵאִמָּא (meIma) עִלָּאָה (ila'a) קַדִּישָׁא (kadisha) שֶׁהוּא (shehu)

הַחֶסֶד (haChesed) [ע"ב, ריבוע יהוה] שֶׁבַּחֶסֶד (shebaChesed) [ע"ב, ריבוע יהוה] שֶׁבָּהּ (sheba)

On the second night:

וּבְכֹחַ (ubcho'ach) מִצְוָה (mitzva) זוֹ (zo) יִמְשֵׁךְ (yimashech) לְרָחֵל (leRachel)

אִמֵּנוּ (imenu) אוֹר (or) [רו, א"ס] הַמַּקִּיף (hamakif) הַחֶסֶד (haChesed) [ע"ב, ריבוע יהוה]

שֶׁבַּגְּבוּרָה (shebaGevura) [רי"ו] מֵאִמָּא (meIma) עִלָּאָה (ila'a) קַדִּישָׁא (kadisha)

On the third night:

וּבְכֹחַ (uvcho'ach) מִצְוָה (mitzva) זוֹ (zo) יִמְשֵׁךְ (yimashech) לְרָחֵל (leRachel)

אִמֵּנוּ (imenu) אוֹר (or) [רו, א"ס] הַמַּקִּיף (hamakif) הַחֶסֶד (haChesed) [ע"ב, ריבוע יהוה]

שֶׁבַּתִּפְאֶרֶת (shebaTiferet) מֵאִמָּא (meIma) עִלָּאָה (ila'a) קַדִּישָׁא (kadisha)

On the fourth night:

וּבְכֹחַ (uvcho'ach) מִצְוָה (mitzva) זוֹ (zo) יִמְשֵׁךְ (yimashech) לְרָחֵל (leRachel)

אִמֵּנוּ (imenu) אוֹר (or) [רו, א"ס] הַמַּקִּיף (hamakif) הַחֶסֶד (haChesed) [ע"ב, ריבוע יהוה]

שֶׁבַּנֶּצַח (shebaNetzach) מֵאִמָּא (meIma) עִלָּאָה (ila'a) קַדִּישָׁא (kadisha)

On the first night: *And with the power of this precept the Supernal and Internal Mercy (that is called day, a day that is including all the other days, which is the Mercy of Chesed) will be drawn from Supernal Ima to Rachel the matriarch. And more, Rachel the matriarch will receive the Supernal Mercy of all Mercies of the Surrounding Light of Supernal Holy Ima, which is the Mercy of Chesed in Her.*

On the second night: *And with the power of this precept the Surrounding Light of Mercy of Gevurah will be drawn from Supernal Holy Ima to Rachel the matriarch.*

On the third night: *And with the power of this precept the Surrounding Light of Mercy of Tiferet will be drawn from Supernal Holy Ima to Rachel the matriarch.*

On the fourth night: *And with the power of this precept the Surrounding Light of Mercy of Netzach will be drawn from Supernal Holy Ima to Rachel the matriarch.*

On the fifth night:

וּבְכֹחַ uvcho'ach מִצְוָה mitzva זוֹ zo יִמָּשֵׁךְ yimashech לְרָחֵל leRachel

אִמֵּנוּ imenu אוֹר or רו, א"ס רוּ, ע"ב, ריבוע יהוה הַמַּקִיף hamakif הַחֶסֶד haChesed

שֶׁבַּהוֹד shebaHod ההה מֵאִימָא meIma עִלָּאָה ila'a קָדִישָׁא kadisha:

On the sixth night:

וּבְכֹחַ uvcho'ach מִצְוָה mitzva זוֹ zo יִמָּשֵׁךְ yimashech לְרָחֵל leRachel

אִמֵּנוּ imenu אוֹר or רו, א"ס הַמַּקִיף hamakif כְּלָלוּת kelalut

הַחֲמִשָּׁה hachamisha וְחֲסָדִים Chasadim שֶׁבַּיְסוֹד shebaYesod ההע

מֵאִימָא meIma עִלָּאָה ila'a קָדִישָׁא kadisha:

On the seventh night:

וּבְכֹחַ uvcho'ach מִצְוָה mitzva זוֹ zo יִמָּשֵׁךְ yimashech לְרָחֵל leRachel

אִמֵּנוּ imenu אוֹר or רו, א"ס הַמַּקִיף hamakif כְּלָלוּת kelalut

הַחֲמִשָּׁה hachamisha וְחֲסָדִים Chasadim שֶׁבַּמַּלְכוּת shebaMalchut

מֵאִימָא meIma עִלָּאָה ila'a קָדִישָׁא kadisha:

וְהוּכַן vehuchan בְּוֶחֶסֶד bachesed ע"ב, ריבוע יהוה כִּסֵּא kiseh

וְיִתְמַתְקוּ veyitmateku הַגְּבוּרוֹת hagevurot וְיִתְבַּסְּמוּ veyitbasemu•

וּכְמוֹ uchmo שֶׁנֶּאֱמַר shene'emar: וִימִינוֹ vimino תּוֹזַבְּקֵנִי techabekeni•

וְהִנֵּה vehineh אֲנַחְנוּ anachnu יִשְׂרָאֵל Yisrael בְּנֵי benei הַמַּלְכוּת hamalchut

רָחֵל Rachel עֲקֶרֶת akeret הַבַּיִת habayit ב"פ ראה• עָשִׂינוּ asinu הַסֻּכָּה hasuka

כְּמִצְוַת kemitzvat יְהוָֹה Adonai אֱלֹהֵינוּ Elohenu יכה

אֲשֶׁר asher הִיא hi כְּנֶגֶד keneged זֹן, מזבוה, אל יהוה עֲנָנֵי anenei כָּבוֹד chavod•

On the fifth night: *And with the power of this precept the Surrounding Light of Mercy of Hod will be drawn from Supernal Holy Ima to Rachel the matriarch.*
On the sixth night: *And with the power of this precept the Surrounding Light of Mercy of Yesod will be drawn from Supernal Holy Ima to Rachel the matriarch.*
On the seventh night: *And with the power of this precept the Surrounding Light of Mercy of Malchut will be drawn from Supernal Holy Ima to Rachel the matriarch.*
And a Thorn will be established with Mercy and the Judgments will be sweetened, as it says: "And His right will hug me." And here we, Israel, the sons of Malchut, Rachel the mistress of the house, built the Sukkah as your command Lord our God, as the Sukkah corresponds to the clouds of honor

kakatuv כַּכָּתוּב: va'anan וְעָנַן Adonai יְהֹוָה/אדנילאהדונהי alehem עֲלֵיהֶם

yomam יוֹמָם: vehem וְהֵם shiva שִׁבְעָה ananim עֲנָנִים, uchnegdam וּכְנֶגְדָם

hem הֵם shiv'at שִׁבְעַת yemei יְמֵי hasuka הַסֻּכָּה אמן, יאהדונהי, סאל.

vehineh וְהִנֵּה anachnu אֲנַחְנוּ yoshvim יוֹשְׁבִים betzel בְּצֵל or אוֹר רו, א"ס

hamakif הַמַּקִּיף hamitpashet הַמִּתְפַּשֵּׁט aleha עָלֶיהָ פהל hamakif הַמַּקִּיף

vesovev וְסוֹבֵב ota אוֹתָה. uvishivatenu וּבִישִׁיבָתֵנוּ ba בָּהּ yimashech יִמָּשֵׁךְ

elenu אֵלֵינוּ min מִן ha'or הָאוֹר רו, א"ס hamakif הַמַּקִּיף hahu הַהוּא:

avinu אָבִינוּ av אָב harachaman הָרַחֲמָן, peros פְּרוֹשׂ alenu עָלֵינוּ

sukat סֻכַּת אמן, יאהדונהי, סאל shelomecha שְׁלוֹמֶךָ. vetakenenu וְתַקְּנֵנוּ

ve'etza בְּעֵצָה tova טוֹבָה אבא ס"ג מ"ה ב"ן. milfanecha מִלְפָנֶיךָ uvtzel וּבְצֵל

kenafecha כְּנָפֶיךָ tastirenu תַּסְתִּירֵנוּ. ushmor וּשְׁמוֹר tzetenu צֵאתֵנוּ

uvo'enu וּבוֹאֵנוּ lechayim לְחַיִּים אהיה אהיה יהוה, בינה ע"ה tovim טוֹבִים

ulshalom וּלְשָׁלוֹם. veyitkayem וְיִתְקַיֵּם banu בָּנוּ mikra מִקְרָא

shekatuv שֶׁכָּתוּב al עַל yedei יְדֵי David דָוִד melech מֶלֶךְ Yisrael יִשְׂרָאֵל:

Adonai יְהֹוָה/אדנילאהדונהי shomrecha שֹׁמְרֶךָ Adonai יְהֹוָה/אדנילאהדונהי

tzilecha צִלְּךָ al עַל yad יַד yeminecha יְמִינֶךָ: ki כִּי hayita הָיִיתָ

ezrata עֶזְרָתָה li לִּי uvtzel וּבְצֵל kenafecha כְּנָפֶיךָ aranen אֲרַנֵּן:

veyitkayem וְיִתְקַיֵּם banu בָּנוּ mikra מִקְרָא shekatuv שֶׁכָּתוּב al עַל

yedei יְדֵי Hoshe'a הוֹשֵׁעַ hanavi הַנָּבִיא: yashuvu יָשֻׁבוּ yoshvei יֹשְׁבֵי

vetzilo בְצִלּוֹ yechayu יְחַיּוּ dagan דָגָן veyifrechu וְיִפְרְחוּ chagafen כַגָּפֶן:

---

as it is written: "And the cloud of the Lord was upon them by day" (Numbers 10:14); seven clouds as for them we sit seven days in the Sukkah. And here we sit in the shadow of the Surrounding Light that spreads over the Sukkah, surrounds and circles it. And by us sitting in it [Illumination] from this Surrounding light will be drawn on us. Our Father, Merciful Father, Spread over us Your protection of peace. Set us straight, with good counsel from You and hide us in the shade of Your Wings and watch over our goings and our comings, for a good life and for peace. And may it be fulfilled in us, the verse written by David, King of Israel: "The Lord is your protective shade at your right hand" (Psalms 121:5) "For You have been my help, and in the shadow of Your wings do I rejoice." (Psalms 63:8) And may it be fulfilled in us, the verse written by the prophet Hosea: "They that dwell under his shadow shall again make corn to grow, and shall blossom as the vine." (Hosea 14:8)

veyitkayem וְיִתְקַיֵּם | banu בָּנוּ | mikra מִקְרָא | shekatuv שֶׁכָּתוּב

va'asim וָאָשִׂם | hanavi הַנָּבִיא: | Yeshaya יְשַׁעְיָה | yedei יְדֵי | al עַל

devarai דְּבָרַי | ראה beficha בְּפִיךָ | uvtzel וּבְצֵל | yadi יָדִי | kisiticha כִּסִּיתִיךָ

linto'a לִנְטֹעַ | shamayim שָׁמַיִם י"פ טל, י"פ כוזו | velisod וְלִיסֹד | aretz אָרֶץ

velemor וְלֵאמֹר | leTziyon לְצִיּוֹן יוסף, ר"פ יהוה, קנאה | ami עַמִּי | ata אַתָּה:

Initials of the Name יהוה

yomam יוֹמָם | yetzave יְצַוֶּה יְהֹוָהאדנ־יאהדונהי Adonai | chasdo וְחַסְדּוֹ ג' | היות

uvalayla וּבַלַּיְלָה א"ח ב"ע אוכצ | shiro שִׁירוֹ (כתיב שירה) מלה | imi עַמִּי | tefila תְּפִלָּה

leEl לְאֵל | chayai וְזִיּי: | har'enu הַרְאֵנוּ | Adonai יְהֹוָהאדנ־יאהדונהי

chasdecha וְחַסְדֶּךָ | veyesh'acha וְיֶשְׁעֲךָ | titen תִּתֶּן ב"פ כהת | lanu לָנוּ מום:

vechesed וָחֶסֶד ע"ב, ריבוע יהוה | Adonai יְהֹוָהאדנ־יאהדונהי | me'olam מֵעוֹלָם | ve'ad וְעַד

olam עוֹלָם | al עַל | yere'av יְרֵאָיו | vetzidkato וְצִדְקָתוֹ | livnei לִבְנֵי | vanim בָנִים:

hodu הוֹדוּ | la'adonai לַיהֹוָהאדנ־יאהדונהי | ki כִּי | tov טוֹב | והו אום

ki כִּי | le'olam לְעוֹלָם ריבוע ס"ג עם י' אותיות | chasdo וְחַסְדּוֹ ג' היות, מזלא:

Initials of the Name אהיה

ohev אֹהֵב | tzedaka צְדָקָה ע"ה אלהים בריבוע | umishpat וּמִשְׁפָּט ע"ה ה"פ אלהים

chesed חֶסֶד ע"ב | Adonai יְהֹוָהאדנ־יאהדונהי | mal'a מָלְאָה | ha'aretz הָאָרֶץ מילוי אלהים ע"ה:

hodu הוֹדוּ אהיה | leEl לְאֵל ייא"י (מילוי דס"ג) | hasamayim הַשָּׁמַיִם י"פ טל, י"פ כוזו | ki כִּי

le'olam לְעוֹלָם ריבוע ס"ג עם י' אותיות | chasdo וְחַסְדּוֹ ג' היות: | yehi יְהִי | chasdecha וְחַסְדֶּךָ

Adonai יְהֹוָהאדנ־יאהדונהי | alenu עָלֵינוּ | ka'asher כַּאֲשֶׁר | yichalnu יִחַלְנוּ | lach לָךְ:

And may it be fulfilled in us, the verse written by the prophet Isaiah: "And I have put My words in your mouth, and have covered you in the shadow of My hand, that I may plant the Heavens, and lay the foundations of the Earth, and say to Zion: 'you are My people.'" (Isaiah 51:16) יהוה *"During the day may the Lord command his kindness and during the night may His dwelling be with me—prayer to God for my life. Show us Your kindness, Lord, and grant us Your salvation." (Psalms 85:8) "The kindness of the Lord from ever and forever, upon those who fear Him and His righteousness upon his children's children." (Psalms 103:17) "Give thanks to the Lord for He is good, for His kindness is forever." (Psalms 118:1)* אהיה *"He loves righteousness and justice; the kindness of the Lord fills the world." (Psalms 33:5) "Give thanks to God of the Heavens for His kindness is forever." (Psalms 136:26) "Lord, may Your kindness be upon us as we have placed our hope in You."*

הִנֵּה hineh   עֵין en   רִיבוּעַ   מ"ה   יְהֹוָ֗ה Adonai   אֵל el

יְרֵאָיו yere'av   לַמְיַחֲלִים lamyachalim   כֻּחַסְדּוֹ lechasdo   ג'   הויות,   מזלא:

Initials of the Name אדנ"י

אַתָּה Ata   יְהֹוָ֗ה Adonai   לֹא lo   תִכְלָא tichla

רַחֲמֶיךָ rachamecha   מִמֶּנִּי mimeni   וַחַסְדְּךָ chasdecha   וַאֲמִתְּךָ va'amitcha

תָּמִיד tamid   ע"ה קמ"ג קנ"א קס"א קס"א ע"ה   נתה   יִצְּרוּנִי yitzeruni: לְד"בּמיו diminu

אֱלֹהִים Elohim   יכה   וְחַסְדְּךָ chasdecha   בְּקֶרֶב bekerev   הֵיכָלֶךָ hechalecha:

נָחִיתָ nachita   בְוֹחַסְדְּךָ vechasdecha   עַם am   זוּ zu   גָּאָלְתָּ ga'alta   נֵהַלְתָּ nehalta

בְעָזְּךָ ve'azcha   אֵל el   נְוֵה neve   קׇדְשֶׁךָ kodshecha: יְהֹוָ֗ה Adonai

יִגְמֹר yigmor   בַּעֲדִי ba'adi   יְהֹוָ֗ה Adonai   וְחַסְדְּךָ chasdecha

לְעוֹלָם le'olam   רִיבוע ס"ג עם י' אותיות   מַעֲשֵׂי ma'asei   יָדֶיךָ yadecha   אַל al   תֶּרֶף teref:

אֵל El יָיא"י (מילוי דס"ג)   מָלֵא maleh   רַחֲמִים rachamim◆

פְּרוֹס peros   עָלֵינוּ alenu   סֻכַּת sukat   אמן, יאהדונהי, סאל   רַחֲמִים rachamim

וְשָׁלוֹם veshalom◆   כִּי ki   אַתָּה Ata   יְהֹוָ֗ה Adonai   הַפּוֹרֵשׂ hapores

סֻכַּת sukat   אמן, יאהדונהי, סאל   שָׁלוֹם shalom   עָלֵינוּ alenu

וְעַל ve'al   יִשְׂרָאֵל Yisrael   עמם; ילי kol   כָּל kol   וְעַל ve'al   יְרוּשָׁלַיִם Yerushalayim

עִיר ir   מזוזר, סנדלפון, ערי   הַקֹּדֶשׁ hakodesh   תִּבָּנֶה tibane

וְתִכּוֹנֵן vetikonen   כוק   בִּמְהֵרָה bimhera   בְיָמֵינוּ veyamenu   אָמֵן amen יאהדונהי:

"Behold the eye of the Lord is upon those who fear Him; upon those who hope for His kindness." (Psalms 33:18) אדנ"י *"You, Lord, do not withhold Your mercy from me; may Your kindness and faithfulness always protect me." (Psalms 40:12) "God, we had hoped for Your kindness in the midst of Your sanctuary." (Psalms 48:10) "In Your kindness You guided this people that You redeemed, You led them with Your strength to Your Holy Sanctuary." (Exodus 15:13) "The Lord shall complete on my behalf. Lord, Your kindness is forever; allow Your handiwork not to become weak." (Psalms 138:8)*

God, Who is full of compassion, spread over us Your shelter of compassion and peace;
for You are the Lord, Who spreads a shelter of peace over us and over all Israel,
and over Jerusalem, the Holy City, may it be built and established speedily in our days, Amen.

אֲזַמִין azamin — לִסְעוּדָתִי lis'udati — אֻשְׁפִּיזִין ushpizin — עִלָּאִין ila'in

קַדִּישִׁין kadishin — אַבְרָהָם Avraham — יִצְחָק Yitzchak — וְיַעֲקֹב, veYa'akov

מֹשֶׁה Moshe — וְאַהֲרֹן, veAharon — יוֹסֵף Yosef — דָּוִד: David

On the first night:

בְּמָטֵי bemati — מִינָךְ minach

אַבְרָהָם Avraham — אֻשְׁפִּיזִי ushpizi — עִלָּאִי ila'i — דְּיִתְבֵי deyatvei — עִימִי imi

וְעִימָךְ ve'imach — כֹּל kol — אֻשְׁפִּיזִין ushpizin — עִלָּאִין ila'in — יִצְחָק Yitzchak

וְיַעֲקֹב, veYa'akov — מֹשֶׁה Moshe — וְאַהֲרֹן, veAharon — יוֹסֵף Yosef — דָּוִד: David

On the second night:

בְּמָטֵי bemati — מִינָךְ minach — יִצְחָק Yitzchak — אֻשְׁפִּיזִי ushpizi — עִלָּאִי ila'i

דְּיִתְבֵי deyatvei — עִימִי imi — וְעִימָךְ ve'imach — כֹּל kol

אֻשְׁפִּיזִין ushpizin — עִלָּאִין ila'in — אַבְרָהָם Avraham — וְיַעֲקֹב, veYa'akov

מֹשֶׁה Moshe — וְאַהֲרֹן, veAharon — יוֹסֵף Yosef — דָּוִד: David

On the third night:

בְּמָטֵי bemati — מִינָךְ minach — יַעֲקֹב Ya'akov — אֻשְׁפִּיזִי ushpizi — עִלָּאִי ila'i

דְּיִתְבֵי deyatvei — עִימִי imi — וְעִימָךְ ve'imach — כֹּל kol

אֻשְׁפִּיזִין ushpizin — עִלָּאִין ila'in — אַבְרָהָם Avraham — יִצְחָק, Yitzchak

מֹשֶׁה Moshe — וְאַהֲרֹן, veAharon — יוֹסֵף Yosef — דָּוִד: David

---

I invite to my meal the exalted guests: Abraham, Isaac, Jacob, Moses, Aaron, Joseph, and David.
On the first day: *May it please you, Abraham, my exalted guest, that all the other exalted guests dwell here with me and with you—Isaac, Jacob, Moses, Aaron, Joseph, and David.*
On the second day: *May it please you, Isaac, my exalted guest, that all the other exalted guests dwell here with me and with you—Abraham, Jacob, Moses, Aaron, Joseph, and David.*
On the third day: *May it please you, Jacob, my exalted guest, that all the other exalted guests dwell here with me and with you—Abraham, Isaac, Moses, Aaron, Joseph, and David.*

On the fourth night:

בְּמָטֵי bemati   מִינָךְ minach   מֹשֶׁה Moshe   אֻשְׁפִּיזִי ushpizi   עִלָּאִי ila'i

דְּיִתְבֵי deyatvei   עִימִי imi   וְעִימָךְ ve'imach   כֹּל kol

אֻשְׁפִּיזִין ushpizin   עִלָּאִין ila'in   אַבְרָהָם Avraham   יִצְחָק Yitzchak

וְיַעֲקֹב, veYa'akov   אַהֲרֹן Aharon   יוֹסֵף Yosef   דָוִד: David

On the fifth night:

בְּמָטֵי bemati   מִינָךְ minach   אַהֲרֹן Aharon   אֻשְׁפִּיזִי ushpizi   עִלָּאִי ila'i

דְּיִתְבֵי deyatvei   עִימִי imi   וְעִימָךְ ve'imach   כֹּל kol

אֻשְׁפִּיזִין ushpizin   עִלָּאִין ila'in   אַבְרָהָם Avraham   יִצְחָק Yitzchak

וְיַעֲקֹב, veYa'akov   מֹשֶׁה Moshe   יוֹסֵף Yosef   דָוִד: David

On the sixth night:

בְּמָטֵי bemati   מִינָךְ minach   יוֹסֵף Yosef   אֻשְׁפִּיזִי ushpizi   עִלָּאִי ila'i

דְּיִתְבֵי deyatvei   עִימִי imi   וְעִימָךְ ve'imach   כֹּל kol

אֻשְׁפִּיזִין ushpizin   עִלָּאִין ila'in   אַבְרָהָם Avraham   יִצְחָק Yitzchak

וְיַעֲקֹב, veYa'akov   מֹשֶׁה Moshe   וְאַהֲרֹן veAharon   דָוִד: David

On the seventh night:

בְּמָטֵי bemati   מִינָךְ minach   דָוִד David   אֻשְׁפִּיזִי ushpizi   עִלָּאִי ila'i

דְּיִתְבֵי deyatvei   עִימִי imi   וְעִימָךְ ve'imach   כֹּל kol

אֻשְׁפִּיזִין ushpizin   עִלָּאִין ila'in   אַבְרָהָם Avraham   יִצְחָק Yitzchak

וְיַעֲקֹב, veYa'akov   מֹשֶׁה Moshe   וְאַהֲרֹן veAharon   יוֹסֵף: Yosef

---

On the fourth day: *May it please you, Moses, my exalted guest, that all the other exalted guests dwell here with me and with you—Abraham, Isaac, Jacob, Aaron, Joseph, and David.*

On the fifth day: *May it please you, Aaron, my exalted guest, that all the other exalted guests dwell here with me and with you—Isaac, Jacob, Moses, Joseph, and David.*

On the sixth day: *May it please you, Joseph, my exalted guest, that all the other exalted guests dwell here with me and with you—Isaac, Jacob, Moses, Aaron, and David.*

On the seventh day: *May it please you, David, my exalted guest, that all the other exalted guests dwell here with me and with you—Isaac, Jacob, Moses, Aaron, and Joseph.*

Each night, after inviting the *Ushpizin*, one should dedicate a chair and say:
"This chair is dedicated for the Seven Holy *Ushpizin*, their merit will protect us all, Amen".

נלך • yamim יָמִים shiv'at שִׁבְעַת teshvu תֵּשְׁבוּ סאל, יאהדונהי, אמן basukot בַּסֻכֹּת

• kadishin קָדִישִׁין ila'in עִלָּאִין ushpizin אֻשְׁפִּיזִין tivu תִּיבוּ

kadishin קָדִישִׁין ila'in עִלָּאִין avahan אֲבָהָן tivu תִּיבוּ

ila'a עִלָּאָה dimhemnuta דִּמְהֵימְנוּתָא betzila בְּצִלָּא lemitav לְמֵיתַב

zaka'a זַכָּאָה • hu הוּא berich בְּרִיךְ dekudsha דְּקוּדְשָׁא betzila בְּצִלָּא

• deYisrael דְּיִשְׂרָאֵל chulakhon חוּלָקְהוֹן vezaka'a וְזַכָּאָה chulakana חוּלָקָנָא

amo עַמּוֹ Adonai יְהֹוָאדניאהדונהי chelek וְזֵלֶק ki כִּי dichtiv דִּכְתִיב

• nachalato נַחֲלָתוֹ chevel וְזֶבֶל אידהנויה יאהדונהי, ד"פ יהוה, Ya'akov יַעֲקֹב

On the first night (Abraham—Chesed):

vadonai וַיהֹוָאדניאהדונהי נלך bayamim בְּיָמִים ba בָּא zaken זָקֵן רמ"ח veAvraham וְאַבְרָהָם

7X לכב: bakol בַּכֹּל רמ"ח Avraham אַבְרָהָם et אֶת berach בֵּרַךְ

hoshi'eni הוֹשִׁיעֵנִי nafshi נַפְשִׁי chaltza וְזִלְּצָה Adonai יְהֹוָאדניאהדונהי החיל shuva שׁוּבָה

Adonai יְהֹוָאדניאהדונהי chasdecha וְזַסְדֶּךָ yehi יְהִי chasdecha זַסְדֶּךָ: lema'an לְמַעַן

kuma קוּמָה lach לָךְ: yichalnu יִחַלְנוּ ka'asher כַּאֲשֶׁר alenu עָלֵינוּ

chasdecha וְזַסְדֶּךָ: lema'an לְמַעַן ufdenu וּפְדֵנוּ מום lanu לָנוּ ezrata עֶזְרָתָה

On the second night (Isaac—Gevurah):

hahi הַהוּא ba'aretz בָּאָרֶץ ב"ן ד"פ Yitzchak יִצְחָק vayizra וַיִּזְרַע

me'a מֵאָה hahi הַהוּא basana בַּשָּׁנָה vayimtza וַיִּמְצָא

7X Adonai יְהֹוָאדניאהדונהי: vayvarachehu וַיְבָרֲכֵהוּ כתר she'arim שְׁעָרִים

מום: lanu לָנוּ lishu'ata לִישׁוּעָתָה ulcha וּלְכָה gevuratecha גְּבוּרָתְךָ et אֶת orera עוֹרְרָה

al אַל יל ה Elohim אֱלֹהִים veseva וְשֵׂיבָה zikna זִקְנָה ad עַד vegam וְגַם

יה אדני lechol לְכָל ledor לְדוֹר zero'acha זְרוֹעֲךָ agid אַגִּיד ad עַד ta'azveni תַעַזְבֵנִי

רי"ו gevura גְּבוּרָה im עִם zero'a זְרוֹעַ lecha לְךָ: gevuratecha גְּבוּרָתְךָ yavo יָבוֹא

yadati יָדַעְתִּי ata עַתָּה: yeminecha יְמִינְךָ tarum תָּרוּם yadcha יָדְךָ ta'oz תָּעֹז

"In Sukkot shall you dwell seven days." Be seated, exalted and holy guests, be seated, our exalted holy fathers; to sit in the shade of exalted faith; in the shade of the Holy One, blessed by He. Fortunate is our portion and fortunate is the portion of Israel. As is written: "For the portion of the Lord is His people; Jacob is the lot of His inheritance." (Deuteronomy 32:9)

כִּי ki הוֹשִׁיעַ hoshi'a יהוה Adonai מְשִׁיחוֹ meshicho יַעֲנֵהוּ ya'anehu

מִשְּׁמֵי mismei קָדְשׁוֹ kodsho בִּגְבֻרוֹת bigvurot יֵשַׁע yesha יְמִינוֹ yemino׃

On the third night (Jacob—Tiferet):

מַה ma טֹבוּ tovu יַעֲקֹב Ya'akov אֹהָלֶיךָ ohalecha

מִשְׁכְּנֹתֶיךָ mishkenotecha יִשְׂרָאֵל Yisrael ×7

תִּתֵּן titen לְרֹאשְׁךָ lerosh'cha לִוְיַת livyat וְחֵן chen עֲטֶרֶת ateret

תִּפְאָרֶת tiferet תְּמַגְּנֶךָ temageneka׃ כִּי ki תִּפְאֶרֶת tiferet עֻזָּמוֹ uzamo אָתָּה Ata

וּבִרְצוֹנְךָ uvirtzoncha תָּרוּם tarum (כתיב תרים) קַרְנֵנוּ karnenu׃ עוּרִי uri עוּרִי uri

לִבְשִׁי livshi עֻזֵּךְ uzech צִיּוֹן Tziyon לִבְשִׁי livshi בִּגְדֵי bigdei

תִּפְאַרְתֵּךְ tif'artech יְרוּשָׁלַיִם Yerushalayim עִיר ir

הַקֹּדֶשׁ hakodesh׃ וּלְתִתְּךָ ultitcha עֶלְיוֹן elyon עַל al כֹּל kol

הַגּוֹיִם hagoyim אֲשֶׁר asher עָשָׂה asa לִתְהִלָּה lit'hila וּלְשֵׁם ulshem

וּלְתִפְאָרֶת ultif'aret וְלִהְיֹתְךָ velihyotcha עַם am קָדֹשׁ kadosh

לַיהוה ladonai אֱלֹהֶיךָ Elohecha כַּאֲשֶׁר ka'asher דִּבֵּר diber׃

On the fourth night (Moses—Netzach):

תּוֹרָה tora צִוָּה tziva לָנוּ lanu מֹשֶׁה Moshe

מוֹרָשָׁה morasha קְהִלַּת kehilat יַעֲקֹב Ya'akov ×3

וְהָאִישׁ vehaish מֹשֶׁה Moshe עָנָו anav מְאֹד me'od מִכֹּל mikol

הָאָדָם ha'adam אֲשֶׁר asher עַל al פְּנֵי penei הָאֲדָמָה ha'adama ×3

וְלֹא velo קָם kam נָבִיא navi עוֹד od בְּיִשְׂרָאֵל beYisrael כְּמֹשֶׁה keMoshe

אֲשֶׁר asher יְדָעוֹ yeda'o יהוה Adonai פָּנִים panim אֶל el פָּנִים panim ×3

יהוה Adonai אֱלֹהִים Elohim צְבָאוֹת Tzeva'ot הֲשִׁיבֵנוּ hashivenu

הָאֵר ha'er פָּנֶיךָ panecha וְנִוָּשֵׁעָה venivashe'a׃ תּוֹדִיעֵנִי todi'eni

אֹרַח orach חַיִּים chayim שֹׂבַע sova שְׂמָחוֹת semachot אֶת et

פָּנֶיךָ panecha נְעִמוֹת ne'imot בִּימִינְךָ bimincha נֶצַח netzach׃

On the fifth night (Aaron—Hod):

וַיְדַבֵּר vaydaber יהוה Adonai אֶל el מֹשֶׁה Moshe לֵּאמֹר lemor׃

דַּבֵּר daber אֶל el אַהֲרֹן Aharon וְאֶל ve'el בָּנָיו banav לֵאמֹר lemor

כֹּה ko תְבָרֲכוּ tevarachu אֶת et

בְּנֵי benei יִשְׂרָאֵל Yisrael אָמוֹר amor לָהֶם lahem׃ יְבָרֶכְךָ yevarechecha

יהוה Adonai וְיִשְׁמְרֶךָ veyishmerecha׃ יָאֵר ya'er

יהוה Adonai פָּנָיו panav אֵלֶיךָ elecha וִיחֻנֶּךָּ vichuneka׃

yisa יִשָּׂא Adonai יְהֹוָהאלהיםיאהדונהי panav פָּנָיו elecha אֵלֶיךָ veyasem וְיָשֵׂם
lecha לְךָ shalom שָׁלוֹם: vesamu וְשָׂמוּ et אֶת shemi שְׁמִי al עַל benei בְּנֵי
Yisrael יִשְׂרָאֵל va'ani וַאֲנִי avarachem אֲבָרְכֵם: 3X (from 'vaydaber')

Adonai יְהֹוָהאלהיםיאהדונהי adonenu אֲדֹנֵינוּ ma מָה ma מ"ה adir אַדִּיר הרי shimcha שִׁמְךָ
bechol בְּכָל ha'aretz הָאָרֶץ לכב אלהים דההין ע"ה asher אֲשֶׁר tena תְּנָה נתה
hodcha הוֹדְךָ al עַל hasamayim הַשָּׁמָיִם י"פ טל: gadol גָּדוֹל להו, מובה עד"א
kevodo כְּבוֹדוֹ bishu'atecha בִּישׁוּעָתֶךָ hod הוֹד ההה vehadar וְהָדָר
teshave תְּשַׁוֶּה alav עָלָיו: vehishmi'a וְהַשְׁמִיעַ Adonai יְהֹוָהאלהיםיאהדונהי
et אֶת hod הוֹד ההה kolo קוֹלוֹ venachat וְנָחַת zero'o זְרֹעוֹ yar'e יִרְאֶה רי"ו:

On the sixth night (Joseph—Yesod):

vayitzbor וַיִּצְבֹּר Yosef יוֹסֵף ציון bar בָּר kechol כַּחוֹל hayam הַיָּם harbe הַרְבֵּה ילי
me'od מְאֹד ad עַד chadal וְחָדַל כי ki לִסְפֹּר lispor ki כִּי en אֵין mispar בְּמִסְפָּר: 3X
ben בֵּן porat פֹּרָת Yosef יוֹסֵף ציון ben בֵּן porat פֹּרָת alei עֲלֵי ayin עָיִן מ"ה בריבוע
banot בָּנוֹת tza'ada צָעֲדָה alei עֲלֵי shur שׁוּר אבג יתץ, ושר, אהבת חנם: 3X
ulYosef וּלְיוֹסֵף ציון amar אָמַר mevorechet מְבֹרֶכֶת Adonai יְהֹוָהאלהיםיאהדונהי
artzo אַרְצוֹ mimeged מִמֶּגֶד shamayim שָׁמָיִם י"פ mital מִטָּל טל כוזו
umitehom וּמִתְּהוֹם rovetzet רֹבֶצֶת tachat תָּחַת: umimeged וּמִמֶּגֶד
tevu'ot תְּבוּאֹת shamesh שָׁמֶשׁ umimeged וּמִמֶּגֶד geresh גֶּרֶשׁ yerachim יְרָחִים:
umerosh וּמֵרֹאשׁ hararei הַרְרֵי kedem קֶדֶם umimeged וּמִמֶּגֶד
giv'ot גִּבְעוֹת olam עוֹלָם: umimeged וּמִמֶּגֶד eretz אֶרֶץ umlo'a וּמְלֹאָה
urtzon וּרְצוֹן מהע shochni שֹׁכְנִי sene סְנֶה tavota תְּבוֹאתָה lerosh לְרֹאשׁ
Yosef יוֹסֵף ציון ulkodkod וּלְקָדְקֹד nezir נְזִיר echav אֶחָיו: 3X (from 'ulYosef amar')
nichsefa נִכְסְפָה vegam וְגַם kalta כָּלְתָה nafshi נַפְשִׁי lechatzrot לְחַצְרוֹת
Adonai יְהֹוָהאלהיםיאהדונהי libi לִבִּי uvsari וּבְשָׂרִי yeranenu יְרַנְּנוּ el אֶל El אֵל יא"י
chai חָי: vo וֹ yatzata יָצָאתָ leyesha לְיֵשַׁע amecha עַמֶּךָ leyesha לְיֵשַׁע derachav הֲרִכוֹ
et אֶת meshichecha מְשִׁיחֶךָ machatzta מָחַצְתָּ rosh רֹאשׁ mibet מִבֵּית ב"פ ראה
rasha רָשָׁע arot עָרוֹת yesod יְסוֹד ההע ad עַד tzavar צַוָּאר sela סֶלָה:

On the seventh night (David—Malchut):

vay'hi וַיְהִי David דָוִד lechol לְכָל יה אדני derachav דְרָכָיו 3X
maskil מַשְׂכִּיל vadonai וַיְהֹוָהאלהיםיאהדונהי imo עִמּוֹ: 3X
migdol מִגְדּוֹל (כתיב מגדיל) yeshu'ot יְשׁוּעוֹת malko מַלְכּוֹ פי"ו ve'ose וְעֹשֶׂה chesed חֶסֶד
limshicho לִמְשִׁיחוֹ ע"ב ledavid לְדָוִד ulzaro וּלְזַרְעוֹ ad עַד olam עוֹלָם: 3X

כִּי Ata אַתָּה Adonai אֲדֹנָי tov טוֹב יהוה vesalach וְסָלֹוּ ע״ב יהוה verav וְרַב

וְחֶסֶד chesed ע״ב יה lechol לְכֹל אדני korecha קֹרְאֶיךָ malchutcha מַלְכוּתְךָ

מַלְכוּת malchut kol כָּל ילי olamim עֹלָמִים umemshaltecha וּמֶמְשַׁלְתְּךָ

בְּכֹל bechol לכב dor דּוֹר vador וָדֹר רי״ו vehaya וְהָיָה יהה יהוה ha'aretz הָאָרֶץ

Adonai יְהֹוָ‌ה‌אדנ‌יאהד‌ונהי lemelech לְמֶלֶךְ al עַל kol כָּל ילי עמם ha'aretz הָאָרֶץ

bayom בַּיּוֹם גגד, זן hahu הַהוּא יי״י yih'ye יִהְיֶה Adonai יְהֹוָ‌ה‌אדנ‌יאהד‌ונהי אלהים דההין ע״ה

echad אֶחָד אהבה ushmo וּשְׁמוֹ מהשע ע״ה echad אֶחָד ע״ה אֶחָד אהבה:

לְךָ lecha יְהֹוָ‌ה‌אדנ‌יאהד‌ונהי Adonai hagdula הַגְּדֻלָּה vehagvura וְהַגְּבוּרָה רי״ו

וְהַתִּפְאֶרֶת vehatiferet וְהַנֵּצַח vehanetzach וְהַהוֹד vehahod ההה ki כִּי chol כָּל ילי

בַּשָּׁמַיִם basamayim יפ טל uva'aretz וּבָאָרֶץ lecha לְךָ יְהֹוָ‌ה‌אדנ‌יאהד‌ונהי Adonai

הַמַּמְלָכָה hamamlacha וְהַמִּתְנַשֵּׂא vehamitnase lechol לְכֹל יה אדני lerosh לְרֹאשׁ:

FAREWELL TO THE SUKKAH
Before leaving the *Sukkah* for the last time, one should recite the following:

יְהִי yehi רָצוֹן ratzon מהשע ע״ה, ע״ב בריבוע וקס״א ע״ה, אל שדי ע״ה milfanecha מִלְּפָנֶיךָ ס״ג

יְהֹוָ‌ה‌אדנ‌יאהד‌ונהי Adonai Elohenu אֱלֹהֵינוּ ילה velohei וֵאלֹהֵי לכב ; מילוי ע״ב, מ״ה ב״ן

avotenu אֲבוֹתֵינוּ ילה ; דמב shebizchut שֶׁבִּזְכוּת kiyum קִיּוּם mitzvat מִצְוַת

suka סֻכָּה אמן, יאהדונהי, סאל zot זֹאת shekiyamnu שֶׁקִּיַּמְנוּ, nizke נִזְכֶּה

venichye וְנִחְיֶה leshana לְשָׁנָה haba'a הַבָּאָה lishev לֵישֵׁב besuka בְּסֻכָּה אמן,

hatmale הִתְמַלֵּא vesukot בְּשֻׂכּוֹת oro עֹרוֹ, shene'emar שֶׁנֶּאֱמַר: יאהדונהי

ken כֵּן יְהִי yehi רָצוֹן ratzon מהשע ע״ה, ע״ב בריבוע וקס״א ע״ה, אל שדי ע״ה: amen אָמֵן, יאהדונהי

FAREWELL TO THE SUKKAH
And May it be pleasing before You,

Lord, my God, and God of my forefathers, that in the merit of the fulfillment of this precept of Sukkah that we have fulfilled, may we merit and live in the coming year to sit in the Sukkah of the Leviathan. As it is stated: "May its skin be filled with sukkot." (Job 40:31) Amen; so may it be His will.

SPECIAL MEDITATION FOR SPIRITUAL MEMORY

Rav Chaim Vital writes (Gate of Divine Inspiration, pg. 87), "One *Yichud* (unification) that augments the memory of every person is the secret of the two Names of *Yud* and *Hei* spelled out with *Yud* and with *Hei*. Their letters are combined together, one letter from each at a time, as follows:

The time for this meditation is every morning at dawn.

MORNING BLESSINGS

You should say the Morning Blessings from midnight onward. And you should be aware to say all of the blessings as soon as you rise after midnight, and if you don't say them completely upon rising after midnight you are preventing the abundance of the Upper World and the *Mochin* from infusing the Upper *Partzufim*. And you also cause the *klipot* to remain attached in the Upper Places. Also, the *klipot's* power spreads into your *Nefesh, Ruach, Neshamah, Chaya, Yechida*, and your senses. Using your senses now, together with the *klipot*, attached, you become drained of energy instead of grasping the opportunity to use the power to remove and cancel the *klipot*. And this is one of the reasons that other kinds of misfortune and chaos occur in our lives, Heaven Forbid, and for this reason it is important to say all the Morning Blessings when you rise at midnight, even if you plan to go to sleep afterwards, this does not apply to sleeping during the day – as there is no negative energy attached to daytime sleep. When you rise after midnight, or do not sleep at all and begin studying after midnight, you should also say the Morning Blessings (excluding the Torah Blessings, which will be said at dawn). As it is mentioned in the *Zohar, Vayakhel* 14-25: "Rav Elazar and Rav Yossi were studying from the beginning of the night, when midnight came they heard the cry of the rooster and they did say the Morning Blessings." (*Nahar Shalom*, pg. 88)

MODEH ANI

Every night, when our souls ascend to the Upper Worlds, a powerful force attempts to stop us from awakening and seeing the light of a new day. This force resides within each one of us. It is our negative side, or what the kabbalists call our "Evil Inclination," fueled by our negative behavior from the previous day. However, the Creator gives us another chance each day to change and reveal the Light that we failed to reveal the day before. The connection of *Modeh Ani* allows us to take advantage of this opportunity. This sequence of Aramaic letters arouses our appreciation for the return of our soul to our body. This act of appreciation helps to strengthen and protect all the blessings we receive.

When you wake up, even though your hands are not clean, you can still say the verse *"modeh ani"* since it does not contain one of the Holy Names.

בֵּ"ן מֵ"ה ס"ג lefanecha לְפָנֶיךָ אני אֲנִי (moda מוֹדָה :Women say) modeh מוֹדָה

bi בִּי shehechezarta שֶׁהֶחֱזַרְתָּ vekayam וְקַיָּם chai וְחַי melech מֶלֶךְ

emunatecha אֱמוּנָתֶךָ: raba רַבָּה bechemla בְּחֶמְלָה nishmati נִשְׁמָתִי

MORNING BLESSINGS
MODEH ANI
I give thanks before You, living and existing King,
for restoring my soul to me, compassionately. Great is Your trustworthiness. (Beresheet Rabba, Ch 68)

WASHING OF THE HANDS

When we sleep at night, many negative forces latch onto our body. When our soul returns and reconnects with our body, it removes most of that negativity, but not from our hands. By washing our hands each morning upon waking, we accomplish three important objectives:
1) To cleanse and wash away all negative forces that cling to our hands during the night;
2) To connect ourselves to the cause and seed level of reality (proactive) and not just the effect (reactive);
3) To detach ourselves from the energy of *ani* (poor) and connect ourselves to the energy of *ashir* (rich).

Wash your hands in the water of *Chesed* (mercy) to remove the filth of the *klipa* that is attached to the Five *Gevurot* (judgments) מנצפ״ך that are revealed by the ten fingers of the hands of *Zeir Anpin* of *Asiyah*. **First**, hold the washing vessel in your right hand and fill it with water, and then hand it over to the left hand. **Then**, pour the water from the left onto the right and then pour water from the right onto the left. This process should be repeated a second and a third time. In a way that every hand would be washed three times. You should not wash one hand three times in a row, but alternate between right and left and in doing so the impure spirit that is called "*Shiv'ta* (do not pronounce this name) the daughter of a king" jumps from one hand to the other until it is completely removed from the hands. And if you don't follow this order, this impure spirit is not removed. Before the blessing you should open the palms of your hands like someone who wants to receive something and meditate to raise *Asiyah* by the 42-Letter Name of *Yetzirah*, which is the numerical value of three hands:

Right hand (*HaGedola*) יהוה אלהינו יהוה, the secret of the first half of the Name יוד ואו דלת הא אלף

Left hand (*HaChazaka*) כוזו במוכסז כוזו, the secret of the last half of the Name ואו אלף הא ואו הא אלף

Middle Hand (*Rama*) יהוה יוד הא ואו הא Is the root of the Name itself and from it spreads those three hands and therefore it is in the middle. And by these three hands of *Yetzirah* we raise *Asiyah*.

The washing of the hands is the *tikkun* of the Inner Light, its interior and exterior (*Netzach, Hod, Yesod*) of *Asiyah*. **The blessing** is the *tikkun* of the Surrounding Light of the exterior (*Netzach, Hod, Yesod*) of *Asiyah*. 13 words correspond to the Thirteen Attributes of *Asiyah*.

Wash your hands, go to the bathroom as necessary, and then wash your hands again. The way to wash our hands: Hold the washing vessel in your right hand and fill it with water, and then hand it over to your left hand. Then, pour the water from the left over the right and then pour water from the right onto the left. That process should be repeated a second and a third time. You should not wash them three times in a row, but alternate between right and left. Rub your hands together 3 times and raise them to the level of the eyes and say the blessing before drying the hands.

(וושון) Adonai לַיהוֹ־וָ־ה (רוום) Ata אַתָּה (אל) baruch בָּרוּךְ

(חסד) (ורב) ha'olam הָעוֹלָם (אפים) melech מֶלֶךְ (ארך) ילה Elohenu אֱלֹהֵינוּ

(לאלפים) bemitzvotav בְּמִצְוֹתָיו (נצר) (חסד) kideshanu קִדְּשָׁנוּ (ואמת) asher אֲשֶׁר

(ונקה) yadayim יָדָיִם (וושטאה) netilat נְטִילַת (ופשע) al עַל (נשא עון) vetzivanu וְצִוָּנוּ

The last three words of this blessing are *Al Netilat Yadayim*: The first letter from each of these three words spells *ani* עֲנִי, Aramaic for "a poor person," and has the numerical value as the Holy Name *Mem Hei* (יוד הא ואו הא). The last two letters of each of these three words, *Ayin Lamed* עַל, *Lamed Tav* לת, and *Yud Mem* ים, have the same numerical value as the word *ashir* עָשִׁיר, meaning "a rich person."

WASHING OF THE HANDS
Blessed are You, Lord, our God, the King of the world,
Who has sanctified us with His commandments and obliges us with the washing of the hands.

ASHER YATZAR

Reciting *Asher Yatzar* after each time we have been to the bathroom connects us to the original spiritual DNA and blueprint of a human being. We may wake up in the morning feeling depleted of spiritual energy, depressed, fearful, moody, or even full of dread for the day to come. Through the power of *Asher Yatzar*, we inject the Light of Creation into our immune system; strengthening and boosting it so that we become filled with Light and spiritually recharged for the entire day.

In this section, there are 45 words, which are equal to the numerical value of the word *Adam* (human being) and the same numerical value of the name *Mem-Hei*, which was created by *Chochmah*. The word *Chochmah* is divided into two other words that mean strength (*Ko'ach*) to the *Mem-Hei*. You should meditate on the Holy Name *Mem-Hei*:

יוד הא ואו הא

The blessing is the *tikkun* of Surrounding Light of the interior (*Netzach, Hod, Yesod*) of *Asiyah*.

(*Abba* of *Asiyah*) baruch בָּרוּךְ Ata אַתָּה יְדֹוָד‎/אהדונהי Adonai

אֱלֹהֵינוּ Elohenu יל"ה melech מֶלֶךְ ha'olam הָעוֹלָם asher אֲשֶׁר yatzar יָצַר

אֶת et הָאָדָם ha'adam מ"ה בְּחָכְמָה bechochma במילוי תרי"ג (מצוות)♦

וּבָרָא uvara קנ"א ב"ן, יהוה אלהים אדני, מילוי קס"א וס"ג, מ"ה ברבוע וע"ב ע"ה

בּוֹ vo נְקָבִים nekavim נְקָבִים nekavim♦ וַחֲלוּלִים chalulim

וַחֲלוּלִים chalulim אברהם, וז"פ אל, רי"ו ול"ב נתיבות הוחכמה, רמ"ח (אברים), עסמ"ב וט"ו אותיות

גָּלוּי galuy♦ וְיָדוּעַ veyadu'a לִפְנֵי lifnei כִסֵּא chise כְבוֹדֶךָ chevodecha פשוטות.

שֶׁאִם she'im ב"ן, לכב יוהך, מ"א אותיות דפשוט,, דמילוי ודמילוי דמילוי דאהיה ע"ה

יִסָּתֵם yisatem אֶחָד echad אהבה, דאגה מֵהֶם mehem oh אוֹ im אִם יוהך, מ"א

יִפָּתֵוּ‎/יִפָּתֵוחַ yipate'ach דאהיה ע"ה דמילוי ודמילוי דמילוי echad אֶחָד אהבה, דאגה

מֵהֶם mehem ei אִי efshar אֶפְשָׁר lehitkayem לְהִתְקַיֵּם afilu אֲפִלּוּ

שָׁעָה sha'a אֶחָת echat♦ baruch בָּרוּךְ Ata אַתָּה יְדֹוָד‎/אהדונהי Adonai

רוֹפֵא rofe chol כָּל ילי basar בָּשָׂר umafli וּמַפְלִיא la'asot לַעֲשׂוֹת‼

ASHER YATZAR

Blessed are You, Lord, our God, the King of the world, Who made man with wisdom and created in him many openings and many cavities. It is obvious and known before Your Throne of Glory that should any one of them become blocked or should any one of them break open, then it would be impossible to remain alive for even one hour. Blessed are You, Lord, the Healer of all flesh and Who amazes by what He does.

ELOHAI NESHAMAH: CONNECTING WITH OUR SOUL

Kabbalah teaches us that there are five main levels of our soul: *Nefesh, Ruach, Neshamah, Chaya* and *Yechida*. In our day-to-day lives, most of us are not fully connected to all five levels. An umbilical-like cord constantly runs through the five levels of the soul, feeding us the minimum amount of Light we need to keep the "pilot light" glimmering in our soul. We recite *Elohai Neshamah* every morning to connect our conscious mind to the five levels of our soul so that we can awaken our true purpose and meaning in life.

The name of a person is not merely a word; it is also the spiritual connection to the soul. Each letter of a name is part of the spiritual genetic alphabet that infuses the soul with the particular form of energy that the name creates. The power of this blessing is that it tunnels through the Upper Worlds and creates a connection to all five parts of our soul. We deepen our connection to this prayer by combining our Hebrew name with the word *Neshamah* (soul). To merge your name with *Neshamah*, from right to left; **On weekdays,** insert the first letter of your name followed by the first letter of *Neshamah*. Then insert the second letter of your name followed by the second letter of *Neshamah,* and so on. **On Shabbat**, insert the first letter of *Neshamah* followed by the first letter of your name. Then insert the second letter of your *Neshamah* followed by the second letter of name, and so on. Meditate on the entire sequence of letters before connecting to the prayer. For example, with the name *Yehuda*, the combinations will look as follows:

Not every person merits the part of the soul called *Neshamah*, however, we all still have a part of the soul of Adam (the first man) that encompasses all of Creation. In this blessing, there are 47 words, which are equal to the numerical value of:

יאהדוניהה

(Pause here) יְלָה ; דמ"ב ,ע"ב, מילוי Elohai אֱלֹהַי *(Ima of Asiyah)*

(five aspects of the collective *Atzilut, Beriah, Yetzirah* and *Asiyah*) neshama נְשָׁמָה

◆*(Chayah from Atzilut)* tehora טְהוֹרָה (in the soul of *Adam*) bi בִּי shenatata שֶׁנָּתַתָּ

Ata אַתָּה ◆*(Neshamah from Beriah)* verata בְרָאתָהּ Ata אַתָּה

nefachta נְפַחְתָּהּ Ata אַתָּה ◆*(Ruach from Yetzirah)* yetzarta יְצַרְתָּהּ

meshamera מְשַׁמְּרָהּ veAta וְאַתָּה ◆*(Nefesh from Asiyah)* bi בִּי

litela לִטְּלָהּ atid עָתִיד veAta וְאַתָּה ◆עֲדֵי bekirbi בְּקִרְבִּי

◆lavo לָבֹא le'atid לֶעָתִיד bi בִּי ulhachazira וּלְהַחֲזִירָהּ mimeni מִמֶּנִּי

ELOHAI NESHAMAH
My God,
the soul that You have given in me is pure. You have formed it. You have created it. You have breathed it into me and You preserve it within me. You shall eventually take it away from me yet return it to me in the coming future.

שׁדי vekirbi בְּקִרְבִּי shehaneshamah שֶׁהַנְּשָׁמָה zeman זְמַן ילי kol כָּל

ב"ן מ"ה ס"ג lefanecha לְפָנֶיךָ אני ani אֲנִי modeh מוֹדֶה

velohei וֵאלֹהֵי ילה ; דמב ע"ב, מילוי Elohai אֱלֹהַי Adonai יְהֹוָאדְנִיאהדונהי

לכב ; מילוי ע"ב, דמב ; ילה יהוה ribon רִבּוֹן avotai אֲבוֹתַי ב"ן מ"ה ס"ג

ילי kol כָּל אני adon אֲדוֹן hama'asim הַמַּעֲשִׂים ילי kol כָּל

Adonai יְהֹוָאדְנִיאהדונהי Ata אַתָּה baruch בָּרוּךְ haneshamot הַנְּשָׁמוֹת

metim מֵתִים lifgarim לִפְגָרִים neshamot נְשָׁמוֹת hamachazir הַמַּחֲזִיר

THE EIGHTEEN BLESSINGS

The purpose of the Eighteen Blessings is to reconnect our soul to our physical body after it has been almost totally disconnected during the previous night's sleep. All of us are blessed with various gifts that, most of the time we do not appreciate, such as the connection of our soul to our body. Unfortunately, most of us only start to appreciate our gifts once we have lost them. Through the power of these Eighteen Blessings, we can inject a proactive energy force of appreciation, which, in turn, protects and preserves all that we hold dear.

The Eighteen Blessings correspond to *Yesod* of *Asiyah*. With these blessings, we draw great abundance and great illumination to the Three Upper *Sefirot* of *Asiyah*, and by that, their external part is blessed and receives this great Light and the external becomes equal to the internal.

THE FIRST BLESSING - DISTINGUISHES BETWEEN DAY AND NIGHT

The greatest gift we have as human beings is the power of free will. The phrase "distinguishing between day and night" refers to the ability we have to choose the Light of the Creator over darkness or good over evil. By saying this blessing, we are given clarity to see these two opposing forces that are usually concealed from us.

The First Blessing is in the three *Partzufim* of *Keter*: external, middle and internal of Direct Light of the middle *Partzuf* of *Zeir Anpin* of *Asiyah* of *Atzilut*, and of Lower *Asiyah*.

ילה Elohenu אֱלֹהֵינוּ Adonai יְהֹוָאדְנִיאהדונהי Ata אַתָּה baruch בָּרוּךְ

ושר אבג"יתץ, hanoten הַנּוֹתֵן ha'olam הָעוֹלָם melech מֶלֶךְ

; יהוה אהיה אהיה ע"ה וזיים, vina בִינָה גבריאל מלאך = ע"ה שכוי lasechvi לַשֶּׂכְוִי

lehavchin לְהַבְחִין אדני ,ללה = וס"ת (sweetening the night's judgment) ס"ג ר"ת מילוי

ben בֵּין yom יוֹם ע"ה נגד, מזבוח, וז, אל יהוה uven וּבֵין layla לַיְלָה מלה ; ר"ת = ג"פ יהוה

As long as the soul is within me, I am grateful to You, Lord, my God and the God of my fathers, the Governor of all actions. The Master of all souls. Blessed are You, Lord, Who restores souls to dead corpses.

THE EIGHTEEN BLESSINGS - THE FIRST BLESSING

Blessed are You, Lord, our God,
the King of the world, Who gives the rooster the understanding to distinguish between day and night.

THE SECOND BLESSING - GIVES SIGHT TO THE BLIND

King David said: *"We have eyes, but see not. We have ears, but hear not."* Too often, we are blinded by a lucrative opportunity or we fail to anticipate the chaos of an impending situation. The real power of this blessing is that it helps heighten our senses of perception and intuition so that we can see the truths that are normally concealed from us.

The Second Blessing is in the three *Partzufim* of *Keter*: external, middle and internal of Returning Light of the middle *Partzuf* of *Zeir Anpin* of *Asiyah* of *Atzilut*, and of Lower *Asiyah*.

יכה Elohenu אֱלֹהֵינוּ Adonai יְהֹוָאֵדְנֵיאֵהרוּנֵהי Ata אַתָּה baruch בָּרוּךְ

ivrim עִוְרִים poke'ach פּוֹקֵחַ ha'olam הָעוֹלָם melech מֶלֶךְ

THE THIRD BLESSING - RELEASES THOSE WHO ARE BOUND

Often we become prisoners of our jobs, our mortgage payments, our relationships, our careers, or even other people's perceptions of us. In essence, to one degree or another, everyone is a prisoner, held captive by his Desire to Receive for the Self Alone. The energy that emanates from this blessing has the power to release us from the clutches of this powerful and self-destructive desire.

The Third Blessing is in the three of *Partzufim* of *Chochmah*: external, middle and internal of Direct Light of the middle *Partzuf* of *Zeir Anpin* of *Asiyah* of *Atzilut*, and of Lower *Asiyah*.

יכה Elohenu אֱלֹהֵינוּ Adonai יְהֹוָאֵדְנֵיאֵהרוּנֵהי Ata אַתָּה baruch בָּרוּךְ

asurim אֲסוּרִים matir מַתִּיר ha'olam הָעוֹלָם melech מֶלֶךְ

THE FOURTH BLESSING – STRAIGHTENS THOSE WHO ARE BENT OVER

The inner meaning of this blessing pertains to the often skewed view we have of the world and the people around us. Our self-centered ego distorts our perception of reality to the point where everyone else appears crooked, imperfect, and wrong. This particular sequence of Aramaic letters has the power to imbue us with acceptance and understanding so that we can transform the negative part of our character which perceives others as bent.

The Fourth Blessing is in the three *Partzufim* of *Chochmah*: external, middle and internal of Returning Light of the middle *Partzuf* of *Zeir Anpin* of *Asiyah* of *Atzilut*, and of Lower *Asiyah*.

יכה Elohenu אֱלֹהֵינוּ Adonai יְהֹוָאֵדְנֵיאֵהרוּנֵהי Ata אַתָּה baruch בָּרוּךְ

kefufim כְּפוּפִים zokef זוֹקֵף ha'olam הָעוֹלָם melech מֶלֶךְ

THE SECOND BLESSING
Blessed are You, Lord, our God, King of the world, Who gives sight to the blind.
THE THIRD BLESSING
Blessed are You, Lord, our God, King of the world, Who releases those who are bound.
THE FOURTH BLESSING
Blessed are You, Lord, our God, King of the world, Who straightens those who are bent over.

THE FIFTH BLESSING - CLOTHES THE NAKED

Kabbalah explains that the body is the clothing of the soul. Just as a negative person cannot change his character by donning an expensive suit, we cannot bring about personal change or lasting fulfillment without connecting to a world beyond our body consciousness. The sequence of letters in this blessing gives us the power to rise above our body consciousness and connect with our soul consciousness.

The Fifth Blessing is in the three *Partzufim* of *Binah*: External, middle and internal of Direct Light of the middle *Partzuf* of *Zeir Anpin* of *Asiyah* of *Atzilut*, and of Lower *Asiyah*. At the end of the blessing meditate to draw 378 illuminations from the Face of *Arich Anpin* to the Face of *Chashmal* of *Zeir* and *Nukva* of *Atzilut*, which is the secret of *malbush*

(*Malbush* means clothing which has the same numerical value of *Chashmal* – electricity).

יכה ׀ Elohenu אֱלֹהֵינוּ ׀ Adonai יְהֹוָאדְנִיאהדונהי ׀ Ata אַתָּה ׀ baruch בָּרוּךְ

‡arumim עֲרוּמִּים ׀ malbish מַלְבִּישׁ ׀ ha'olam הָעוֹלָם ׀ melech מֶלֶךְ

THE SIXTH BLESSING - GIVES STRENGTH TO THE WEARY

We often try to affect positive change within ourselves. We attempt to face down our fears, rid ourselves of anger, and overcome our jealousies. But Satan, a negative intelligence, battles us from the inside, and can prevent these changes from happening. The sequence of letters in this blessing gives us that extra help and energy we need to defeat Satan.

The Sixth Blessing is in the three *Partzufim* of *Binah*: External, middle and internal of Returning Light of the middle *Partzuf* of *Zeir Anpin* of *Asiyah* of *Atzilut*, and of Lower *Asiyah*. At the end of the blessing meditate to draw 378 illuminations from the Face of *Arich Anpin* to the Face of *Chashmal* of *Zeir* and *Nukva* of *Atzilut*, which is the secret of *malbush*

(*Malbush* means clothing which has the same numerical value of *Chashmal* – electricity).

melech מֶלֶךְ יכה Elohenu אֱלֹהֵינוּ Adonai יְהֹוָאדְנִיאהדונהי Ata אַתָּה baruch בָּרוּךְ

‡נלך ko'ach כֹּחַ laya'ef לַיָּעֵף ויסר ,אבגיתץ, hanoten הַנּוֹתֵן ha'olam הָעוֹלָם

THE SEVENTH BLESSING - KEEPS THE LAND OVER THE WATER

The kabbalists teach that before the creation of the world, water filled all of reality and existence. Water is a physical expression of the energy force of mercy and the Lightforce of the Creator, also known as the Desire to Share. Physical matter has the inherent essence of the Desire to Receive, represented by the creation of the land on our planet. God created a delicate balance between the Desire to Share and the Desire to Receive, manifested in the balance between the water and the land. This blessing helps us achieve and maintain this balance.

THE FIFTH BLESSING
Blessed are You, Lord, our God, King of the world, Who clothes the naked.

THE SIXTH BLESSING
Blessed are You, Lord, our God, King of the world, Who gives strength to the weary.

The **Seventh Blessing** is in the three *Partzufim* of *Chesed*: External, middle and internal of Direct Light of the middle *Partzuf* of *Zeir Anpin* of *Asiyah* of *Atzilut*, and of Lower *Asiyah*.

ילה   Elohenu אֱלֹהֵינוּ   Adonai יְהֹוָואדנילאהדונהי   Ata אַתָּה   baruch בָּרוּךְ

ע״ה דההין אלהים   ha'aretz הָאָרֶץ   roka רוֹקַע   ha'olam הָעוֹלָם   melech מֶלֶךְ

al עַל   hamayim הַמָּיִם:

THE EIGHTH BLESSING - PROVIDES FOR THE FOOTSTEPS OF MAN

When a person embarks on a spiritual path, he or she will inevitably face obstacles and challenges along the way. This particular sequence of Aramaic letters gives us the power of certainty, to know that the spiritual path we are on is the correct one, even when the road before us is temporarily dim.

The **Eighth Blessing** is in the three *Partzufim* of *Chesed*: External, middle and internal of Returning Light of the middle *Partzuf* of *Zeir Anpin* of *Asiyah* of *Atzilut*, and of Lower *Asiyah*.

ילה   Elohenu אֱלֹהֵינוּ   Adonai יְהֹוָואדנילאהדונהי   Ata אַתָּה   baruch בָּרוּךְ

gaver גָּבֶר: mitz'adei מִצְעֲדֵי   hamechin הַמֵּכִין   ha'olam הָעוֹלָם   melech מֶלֶךְ

THE NINTH BLESSING - PROVIDES FOR ALL MY NEEDS

This ancient sequence of letters ensures that we receive what our soul truly desires and not what our short-term reactive impulses cause us to crave.

The **Ninth Blessing** is in the Three *Partzufim* of *Gevurah*: External, middle and internal of Direct Light of the middle *Partzuf* of *Zeir Anpin* of *Asiyah* of *Atzilut*, and of Lower *Asiyah*.

ילה   Elohenu אֱלֹהֵינוּ   Adonai יְהֹוָואדנילאהדונהי   Ata אַתָּה   baruch בָּרוּךְ

(ע״ע נהורין דפנים עליונים) שֶׁע (ע״ע   she'asa שֶׁעָשָׂה   ha'olam הָעוֹלָם   melech מֶלֶךְ

להמתיק דיני ע״ה דלהון) = אלף למד אלף אלף למד [אל א' = יהוה ד' = אותיות והכולל ואל ב' = ייא״י דס״ג]

tzorki צָרְכִּי: ילי   kol כָּל   li לִי   אותיות ו״ה דיורין אלהים = עָשָׂה

THE SEVENTH BLESSING
Blessed are You, Lord, our God, King of the world, Who keeps land over the water.

THE EIGHTH BLESSING
Blessed are You, Lord, our God, King of the world, Who provides for the footsteps of man.

THE NINTH BLESSING
Blessed are You, Lord, our God, King of the world, Who provides for all my needs.

THE TENTH BLESSING - STRENGTHENS ISRAEL WITH MIGHT

In Aramaic, the word for "strength" is *Gevurah*. *Gevurah* has the same numerical value (216) as the three-letter sequences of the 72 Names of God (72 x 3 = 216), which helps us achieve mind over matter and overcome our reactive nature. Another secret can be found in the last three words of the blessing. The first three letters of the last three words (*Alef* א, *Yud* י, and *Bet* ב) have the same numerical value (13) as the Aramaic word for *Ahavah* (אהבה) which means "love." If we have love in our lives, we will always have the ability to tap into the power of the 72 Names of God.

The Tenth Blessing is in the three *Partzufim* of *Gevurah*: External, middle and internal of Returning Light of the middle *Partzuf* of *Zeir Anpin* of *Asiyah* of *Atzilut*, and of Lower *Asiyah*.

בָּרוּך baruch   אַתָּה Ata   יְהֹוָאדְנִיאהדונהי Adonai   אֱלֹהֵינוּ Elohenu   יל״ה

מֶלֶךְ melech   הָעוֹלָם ha'olam   אוֹזֵר ozer   יִשְׂרָאֵל Yisrael

בִּגְבוּרָה bigvura   רי״ו ; ר״ת = אהבה, אוזר, דאגה:

THE ELEVENTH BLESSING - CROWNS ISRAEL WITH SPLENDOR

The word for "splendor" in Aramaic is *Tifara*, from the root *Tiferet*. *Tiferet* is the *Sefirah* or the specific dimension that connects the Upper Worlds to our physical world. The sequence of letters that make up this blessing gives us the ability to capture and store the Light—like a portable battery that can fuel us—even after we close the Siddur.

The Eleventh Blessing is in the three *Partzufim* of *Tiferet*: External, middle and internal of Direct Light of the middle *Partzuf* of *Zeir Anpin* of *Asiyah* of *Atzilut*, and of Lower *Asiyah*.

בָּרוּך baruch   אַתָּה Ata   יְהֹוָאדְנִיאהדונהי Adonai   אֱלֹהֵינוּ Elohenu   יל״ה

מֶלֶךְ melech   הָעוֹלָם ha'olam   עוֹטֵר oter   יִשְׂרָאֵל Yisrael   בְּתִפְאָרָה betifara:

THE TWELFTH BLESSING - DID NOT MAKE ME A GENTILE/GENTILE WOMAN

On the surface level, this blessing appears to be discriminatory. Kabbalistically, the word gentile has nothing to do with a person's religious affiliation. Rather, it is a code word which represents someone who does not have a powerful and intense Desire to Receive. This blessing ignites our desire for spiritual growth, inner change, and positive transformation.

THE TENTH BLESSING

Blessed are You, Lord, our God, King of the world, Who strengthens Israel with might.

THE ELEVENTH BLESSING

Blessed are You, Lord, our God, King of the world, Who crowns Israel with splendor.

The Twelfth Blessing is in the three *Partzufim* of *Tiferet*: External, middle and internal of Returning Light of the middle *Partzuf* of *Zeir Anpin* of *Asiyah* of *Atzilut*, and of Lower *Asiyah*.

יל־ה Elohenu אֱלֹהֵינוּ Adonai יְהֹוָה Ata אַתָּה baruch בָּרוּךְ

goi :גּוֹי asani עָשַׂנִי shelo שֶׁלֹּא ha'olam הָעוֹלָם melech מֶלֶךְ

Women say: יל־ה Elohenu אֱלֹהֵינוּ Adonai יְהֹוָה Ata אַתָּה baruch בָּרוּךְ

goya :גּוֹיָה asani עָשַׂנִי shelo שֶׁלֹּא ha'olam הָעוֹלָם melech מֶלֶךְ

THE THIRTEENTH BLESSING -DID NOT MAKE ME A SLAVE/MAIDSERVANT
This blessing gives us the support we need so that we are not governed and held captive by our reactive nature and the material world.

The Thirteenth Blessing is in the three *Partzufim* of *Netzach*: External, middle and internal of Direct Light of the middle *Partzuf* of *Zeir Anpin* of *Asiyah* of *Atzilut*, and of Lower *Asiyah*.

יל־ה Elohenu אֱלֹהֵינוּ Adonai יְהֹוָה Ata אַתָּה baruch בָּרוּךְ

aved :עֶבֶד asani עָשַׂנִי shelo שֶׁלֹּא ha'olam הָעוֹלָם melech מֶלֶךְ

Women say: יל־ה Elohenu אֱלֹהֵינוּ Adonai יְהֹוָה Ata אַתָּה baruch בָּרוּךְ

shifcha :שִׁפְחָה asani עָשַׂנִי shelo שֶׁלֹּא ha'olam הָעוֹלָם melech מֶלֶךְ

THE FOURTEENTH BLESSING –
DID NOT MAKE ME A WOMAN/ MADE ME ACCORDING TO HIS WILL
Although this blessing appears to be chauvinistic, it is not. Kabbalistically, the inherent energy of the dimension of *Zeir Anpin* (comprising the *Sefirot* of *Chesed* to *Yesod*)—the pipeline through which the Light flows from the Upper Worlds into our world—is masculine. *Malchut*, our world has an inherent feminine energy. This prayer ignites appreciation for our ability to generate spiritual Light through the two energy forces of male and female, and helps the two halves of the soul—male and female—to unite.

The Fourteenth Blessing is in the three *Partzufim* of *Netzach*: External, middle and internal of Returning Light of the middle *Partzuf* of *Zeir Anpin* of *Asiyah* of *Atzilut*, and of Lower *Asiyah*.

יל־ה Elohenu אֱלֹהֵינוּ Adonai יְהֹוָה Ata אַתָּה baruch בָּרוּךְ

isha :אִשָּׁה asani עָשַׂנִי shelo שֶׁלֹּא ha'olam הָעוֹלָם melech מֶלֶךְ

Women say: kirtzono :כִּרְצוֹנוֹ she'asani שֶׁעָשַׂנִי baruch בָּרוּךְ

THE TWELFTH BLESSING
Blessed are You, Lord, our God, King of the world, Who did not make me a gentile / gentile woman.
THE THIRTEENTH BLESSING
Blessed are You, Lord, our God, King of the world, Who did not make me a slave / maidservant.
THE FOURTEENTH BLESSING
Blessed are You, Lord, our God, King of the world, Who did not make me a woman. /
Blessed is He Who made me according to His Will.

THE FIFTEENTH BLESSING - REMOVES THE BOND OF SLEEP FROM MY EYES

Kabbalists have said that humanity has been asleep for 2000 years. Unfortunately, some people live their entire lives asleep. They never raise their level of consciousness, and fail to affect true inner change. The Aramaic letters in this blessing help to awaken us from that coma.

The Fifteenth Blessing is in the three Partzufim of Hod: External, middle and internal of Direct Light of the middle Partzuf of Zeir Anpin of Asiyah of Atzilut, and of Lower Asiyah.

יכה Elohenu אֱלֹהֵינוּ Adonai יְהֹוָאדְנָיאהדונהי Ata אַתָּה baruch בָּרוּךְ

chevlei וְּבְלֵי hama'avir הַמַּעֲבִיר ha'olam הָעוֹלָם melech מֶלֶךְ

me'afapai מֵעַפְעַפָּי utnuma וּתְנוּמָה רֵיבוּע מ"ה me'enai מֵעֵינָי shena שֵׁנָה

This blessing does not end here but in the end of the next section ("*gomel chasadim tovim le'amo Yisrael*"), so that is why we don't answer *AMEN* here.

VIHI RATZON

This prayer helps us to remove the forces of negativity that lie within us.

Vihi Ratzon removes the control of the chitzoniyim (negative external forces) from the internal aspect.

milfanecha מִלְּפָנֶיךָ מהש ע"ה, ע"ב בריבוע קס"א ע"ה, אל שדי ע"ה ratzon רָצוֹן vihi וִיהִי

ס"ג מ"ה ב"ן Elohai אֱלֹהַי מילוי ע"ב, דמב ; יכה Adonai יְהֹוָאדְנָיאהדונהי

shetargileni שֶׁתַּרְגִּילֵנִי avotai אֲבוֹתַי יכה ; דמב ; מילוי ע"ב ; לכב velohei וֵאלֹהֵי

bemitzvoteicha בְּמִצְוֹתֶיךָ vetadbikeni וְתַדְבִּיקֵנִי betoratecha בְּתוֹרָתֶךָ

lidei לִידֵי velo וְלֹא chet חֵטְא lidei לִידֵי tevi'eni תְבִיאֵנִי ve'al וְאַל

lidei לִידֵי velo וְלֹא nisayon נִסָּיוֹן lidei לִידֵי velo וְלֹא avon עָוֹן

hara הָרָע miyetzer מִיֵּצֶר vetarchikeni וְתַרְחִיקֵנִי vizayon בִּזָּיוֹן

et אֶת vechof וְכוֹף והו hatov הַטּוֹב beyetzer בְּיֵצֶר vetadbikeni וְתַדְבִּיקֵנִי

hayom הַיּוֹם utneni וּתְנֵנִי lach לָךְ lehisht'abed לְהִשְׁתַּעְבֵּד yitzri יִצְרִי

ע"ה נגד, מזבוח, זְ, אל יהוה yom יוֹם לכב ב"ן uvchol וּבְכָל ע"ב, אל יהוה, זְ, מזבוח, נגד ע"ה

THE FIFTEENTH BLESSING

Blessed are You, Lord,
our God, King of the world, Who removes the bonds of sleep from my eyes and slumber from my eyelids.

VIHI RATZON

And may it be Your will, Lord, our God and God of our fathers, that You accustom me to Your Torah and cause me to cleave to Your precepts, and do not bring me to the hands of sin, iniquity, temptation, nor shame. And cause me to distance myself from the Evil Inclination, and cling me to the Good Inclination, and compel my will to be subservient to You. Grant me this day and every day,

יהוה ריבוע ע"ב, ulchesed וּלְחֶסֶד בריבוע ע"ב, מ"ה מילוי מוזי, lechen לְחֵן

מ"ה ריבוע ; קס"א ע"ה be'enecha בְּעֵינֶיךָ ulrachamim וּלְרַחֲמִים

vegomleni וְגָמְלֵנִי ro'ai רוֹאִי ילי chol כָּל מ"ה ריבוע uv'enei וּבְעֵינֵי

Adonai יְהֹוָאדֹנָהיאהדונהי Ata אַתָּה baruch בָּרוּךְ tovim טוֹבִים chasadim וַחֲסָדִים

Yisrael יִשְׂרָאֵל le'amo לְעַמּוֹ tovim טוֹבִים chasadim וַחֲסָדִים gomel גּוֹמֵל

YEHI RATZON

Too often we attract negative people and unfavorable situations into our lives. We find ourselves in the wrong place at the wrong time. We do business with the wrong people. Here, we gain the ability to remove all external negative events from intruding into our lives. We also remove eleven distinct areas of negativity that can invade our environment.

Yehi Ratzon removes the control of the *chitzoniyim* (negative external forces) from the external aspect. In this section we mention 11 aspects corresponding to the 11 incenses of the *Ketoret*.

milfanecha מִלְּפָנֶיךָ מהש ע"ה, ע"ב בריבוע קס"א ע"ה, אל שדי ע"ה ratzon רָצוֹן yehi יְהִי

velohei וֵאלֹהֵי מילוי ע"ב, דמב ; ילה Elohai אֱלֹהַי Adonai יְהֹוָאדֹנָהיאהדונהי ס"ג מ"ה ב"ן

hayom הַיּוֹם shetatzileni שֶׁתַּצִּילֵנִי avotai אֲבוֹתַי ילה ; דמב, מילוי לכב

yom יוֹם ע"ה לכב ב"ן, uvchol וּבְכָל ב"ן, אל יהוה זו, מזבוח, נגד ע"ה

vayom וְיוֹם ע"ה נגד, מזבוח, זו, אל יהוה me'azei מֵעַזֵּי אלהים ע"ה, אהיה אדני ע"ה

ra רָע me'adam מֵאָדָם panim פָּנִים ume'azut וּמֵעַזּוּת fanim פָּנִים

ra רָע mishachen מִשָּׁכֵן ra רָע mechaver מֵחָבֵר ra רָע miyetzer מִיֵּצֶר

hara הָרָע מ"ה ריבוע me'ayin מֵעַיִן ra רָע mipega מִפֶּגַע

kashe קָשֶׁה midin מִדִּין hara הָרָע umilashon וּמִלָּשׁוֹן

shehu שֶׁהוּא ben בֵּין kashe קָשֶׁה din דִּין umiba'al וּמִבַּעַל

berit בְּרִית ven בֶּן she'eno שֶׁאֵינוֹ uven וּבֵין berit בְּרִית ven בֶּן

---

grace, loving kindness, and mercy in Your sight and in the sight of all that behold me, and bestow upon me loving kindness. Blessed are You, Lord, Who bestows loving kindness on His people Israel.

YEHI RATZON

May it be Your will, Lord our God and God of our forefathers, to save me this day and every day from an arrogant man and from arrogance, from an evil man, from the Evil Inclination, from an evil companion, from an evil neighbor, from an evil happening, from evil eye, and from evil speech, from harsh judgment, and a harsh opponent, whether he be a son of the covenant or not a son of the covenant.

BLESSINGS OF THE TORAH
The next three blessings are known as *Birkot haTorah* (Blessings of the Torah).

THE SIXTEENTH BLESSING -TEACHINGS OF THE TORAH
The kabbalists teach that without a connection to the Torah, we do not stand a chance affecting genuine positive change in our lives or in the world around us. According to Kabbalah, reference to the Torah refers to spiritual work and spiritual study, and to using spiritual tools. This blessing connects us to the inner essence of the Torah giving us the energy and fuel we need to ignite all the other blessings we have recited, and to imbue our lives with passion and spiritual energy.

The Sixteenth Blessing has two aspects:
1) The aspect of the *Mitzva* of *Esek* ("involved") of the Torah, which is in *Zeir Anpin* of *Atzilut*.
2) The aspect that is in the three *Partzufim* of *Hod*: The external, middle and internal of Returning Light of the middle *Partzuf* of *Zeir Anpin* of *Asiyah* of *Atzilut*, and of Lower *Asiyah* (as in the other blessings). While saying this blessing, you should meditate on both aspects, and while saying the words *"asher kideshanu..."* you should also meditate to draw the *Tzelems* into *Chochmah*, *Binah*, *Da'at* of *Zeir Anpin* of *Atzilut*, as we meditate on the other precepts of the *Torah*.

יל׳ Elohenu אֱלֹהֵינוּ Adonai יְהֹוָואֲדֹנָיאַהדֹונָהי Ata אַתָּה baruch בָּרוּךְ

kideshanu קִדְּשָׁנוּ asher אֲשֶׁר ha'olam הָעוֹלָם melech מֶלֶךְ

torah תּוֹרָה ראה divrei דִּבְרֵי al עַל vetzivanu וְצִוָּנוּ bemitzvotav בְּמִצְוֹתָיו

According to the Ari:
We answer AMEN after this blessing, as this is a separate blessing from the next one.

THE SEVENTEENTH BLESSING - TEACHES TORAH TO THE NATION
We say this blessing with the consciousness to help everyone make a connection to the energy of the Torah. This is our opportunity to genuinely care about others and to share the Light of the Creator—one of the most powerful ways to transform our reactive nature into a proactive one.

The Seventeenth Blessing is in the three *Partzufim* of *Yesod*: External, middle and internal of Direct Light of the middle *Partzuf* of *Zeir Anpin* of *Asiyah* of *Atzilut*, and of Lower *Asiyah*.

יל׳ Elohenu אֱלֹהֵינוּ Adonai יְהֹוָואֲדֹנָיאַהדֹונָהי na נָא veha'arev וְהַעֲרֶב

befinu בְּפִינוּ toratcha תוֹרָתְךָ ראה divrei דִּבְרֵי et אֶת

Yisrael יִשְׂרָאֵל ראה ב״פ bet בֵּית amecha עַמְּךָ uv'fifiyot וּבְפִיפִיּוֹת

BLESSINGS OF THE TORAH
THE SIXTEENTH BLESSING
Blessed are You, Lord, our God, King of the world,
Who has sanctified us with His commandments and obliged us regarding the teachings of the Torah.
THE SEVENTEENTH BLESSING
And sweeten for us, Lord,
our God, the words of Your Torah in our mouths and the mouths of Your Nation, the House of Israel.

venih'ye וְנִהְיֶה   anachnu אֲנַחְנוּ   vetze'etza'enu וְצֶאֱצָאֵינוּ

(You should meditate for your children to be righteous, connected to the Torah and to the Light)

vetze'etza'ei וְצֶאֱצָאֵי   tze'etza'enu צֶאֱצָאֵינוּ   vetze'etza'ei וְצֶאֱצָאֵי

amecha עַמְּךָ   bet בֵּית   בּ"פ   ראה   Yisrael יִשְׂרָאֵל   kulanu כֻּלָּנוּ

yod'ei יוֹדְעֵי   shemecha שְׁמֶךָ   velomdei וְלוֹמְדֵי   toratcha תוֹרָתְךָ

lishma לִשְׁמָהּ◆   baruch בָּרוּךְ   Ata אַתָּה   Adonai יְהֹוָ֣ואדנייאהדונהי

hamelamed הַמְּלַמֵּד   torah תוֹרָה   le'amo לְעַמּוֹ   Yisrael יִשְׂרָאֵל:

THE EIGHTEENTH BLESSING - GIVES THE TORAH

The Aramaic word *chai* וזי ("life") has the numerical value of 18. This blessing connects us to the Tree of Life, (*Etz HaChayim* – עֵץ הַחַיִּים) the dimension where only fulfillment, order, and endless bliss exist.

The Eighteenth Blessing is in the three *Partzufim* of *Yesod*: external, middle and internal of Returning Light of the middle *Partzuf* of *Zeir Anpin* of *Asiyah* of *Atzilut*, and of Lower *Asiyah*.

baruch בָּרוּךְ   Ata אַתָּה   Adonai יְהֹוָ֣ואדנייאהדונהי   Elohenu אֱלֹהֵינוּ   ילה

melech מֶלֶךְ   ha'olam הָעוֹלָם   asher אֲשֶׁר   bachar בָּחַר

banu בָּנוּ   mikol מִכָּל   יכי   ha'amim הָעַמִּים   venatan וְנָתַן

lanu לָנוּ   אלהים, אהיה   ארני   et אֶת   torato תוֹרָתוֹ◆   baruch בָּרוּךְ

Ata אַתָּה   Adonai יְהֹוָ֣ואדנייאהדונהי   noten נוֹתֵן   אבגיתץ, ושר   hatorah הַתּוֹרָה:

THE BLESSING OF THE *KOHANIM*

Finishing the Eighteen Blessings, we make an immediate connection to the *Torah*. The verses that we recite are the blessings of the priests (*Kohanim*). In ancient times, when the *Kohen* blessed the congregation in the Temple, he used the formula *Yud, Yud, Yud* ייי one of the 72 Names of God. Each of the following three sentences begins with a *Yud*. When we recite this prayer, we activate and reveal tremendous powers of healing in our lives.

And may we and our offspring, and the offspring of our offspring, and the offspring of all Your Nation, the House of Israel, all of us know Your Names and be learners of Your Torah for its own sake. Blessed are You, Lord, Who teaches the Torah to His Nation, Israel.

THE EIGHTEENTH BLESSING

Blessed are You, Lord, our God, King of the world, Who has chosen us from among all the nations and has given us His Torah. Blessed are You, Lord, Who gives the Torah.

וַיְדַבֵּר vaydaber — ראה — יְהֹוָה Adonai — אֶל־ el — מֹשֶׁה Moshe

אֶל־ el — אַהֲרֹן Aharon — וְאֶל־ ve'el — בָּנָיו banav — לֵאמֹר lemor — דַּבֵּר daber ראה — לֵאמֹר lemor

כֹּה ko — הי — תְּבָרְכוּ tevarchu — יהוה — ריבוע — יהוה — ריבוע מ"ה

אֶת־ et — בְּנֵי benei — יִשְׂרָאֵל Yisrael — אָמוֹר amor — לָהֶם lahem

The initials of the three verses give us the Holy Name: ""'.
In this section there are 15 words, which are equal to the numerical value of the Holy Name: הֹהֹ.

(Right – *Chesed*)

יְבָרֶכְךָ yevarechecha — יְהֹוָה Adonai — וְיִשְׁמְרֶךָ veyishmerecha

ר"ת = יהוה ; וס"ת = מ"ה:

(Left - *Gevurah*)

יָאֵר ya'er — כף — ויו — זין — ויו — יְהֹוָה Adonai — פָּנָיו panav

אֵלֶיךָ elecha — וִיחֻנֶּךָּ vichuneka — מנד — ; — יהוה — אותיות — בפסוק:

(Central – *Tiferet*)

יִשָּׂא yisa — יְהֹוָה Adonai — פָּנָיו panav — אֵלֶיךָ elecha

וְיָשֵׂם veyasem — לְךָ lecha — שָׁלוֹם shalom — האא — תיבות — בפסוק:

(*Malchut*)

וְשָׂמוּ vesamu — אֶת־ et — שְׁמִי shemi — עַל־ al — בְּנֵי benei — יִשְׂרָאֵל Yisrael

וַאֲנִי va'ani אני — אֲבָרְכֵם avarchem:

Shacharit Prayer can be found on page 181 and *Talit* order can be found on page 187.

THE BLESSING OF THE *KOHANIM*
"And the Lord spoke to Moses and said:
Speak to Aaron and his sons saying: So shall you bless the Children of Israel,
Say to them: May the Lord bless you and protect you.
May the Lord enlighten His countenance for you and give you grace.
May the Lord lift His countenance towards you and give you peace.
And they shall place My Name upon the Children of Israel and I shall bless them." (Numbers 6:22-27)

TIKKUN CHATZOT – TIKKUN LEAH

Kabbalah teaches us that our negative actions create space (represented by the destruction of the Holy Temple) between the physical reality and the spiritual reality, and that chaos has domain in this space. This gap causes the *Shechinah* (our spiritual protection shield and sustainer) some pain as She cannot nourish us. Reciting *Tikkun Chatzot* helps to restore this gap and remove the separation between us, the *Shechinah* and the Creator.

1. *Tikkun Chatzot* is recited only after the cosmic midnight until dawn.
2. *Tikkun Leah* is recited on *Sukkot Chol Hamo'ed*.

leshem לְשֵׁם   yichud יְוֹוֹד   kudsha קוּדְשָׁא   berich בְּרִיךְ   hu הוּא

ush'chintei וּשְׁכִינְתֵּיהּ   (יאהדונהי),   bid'chilu בִּדְחִילוּ   ur'chimu וּרְחִימוּ

(איההויהה),   ud'chilu וּדְחִילוּ   ur'chimu וּרְחִימוּ   (יאההויהה),

leyachada לִיַחֲדָא   shem שֵׁם   yud יוּ"ד   kei קֵי   bevav בְּוָא"ו   kei קֵי

beyichuda בְּיִחוּדָא   shelim שְׁלִים   (יהוה)   beshem בְּשֵׁם   kol כָּל ילי

Yisrael יִשְׂרָאֵל   hareni הֲרֵינִי   muchan מוּכָן   lomar לוֹמַר:

tikkun תִּקּוּן   Leah לֵאָה

kemo כְּמוֹ   shesidru שֶׁסִּדְּרוּ   lanu לָנוּ   אלהים, אהיה ארני   rabotenu רַבּוֹתֵינוּ

zichronam זִכְרוֹנָם   livracha לִבְרָכָה   letaken לְתַקֵּן   et אֶת   shorsham שָׁרְשָׁם

bemakom בִּמְקוֹם   elyon עֶלְיוֹן   la'asot לַעֲשׂוֹת   nachat נַחַת   ru'ach רוּחַ

leyotzrenu לְיוֹצְרֵנוּ   vela'asot וְלַעֲשׂוֹת   retzon רְצוֹן   מהש ע"ה, ע"ב בריבוע וקס"א ע"ה,

בּוֹרְאֵנוּ bor'enu•   וִיהִי vihi   נֹעַם no'am   אֲדֹנָי Adonai   ע"ה אל שדי   ללה

yadenu יָדֵינוּ   uma'ase וּמַעֲשֵׂה   alenu עָלֵינוּ   ילה   Elohenu אֱלֹהֵינוּ

konenehu כּוֹנְנֵהוּ:   yadenu יָדֵינוּ   uma'ase וּמַעֲשֵׂה   alenu עָלֵינוּ   konena כּוֹנְנָה

TIKKUN CHATZOT – TIKKUN LEAH

For the sake of unification between the Holy Blessed One and His Shechinah, with fear and love and with love and fear, in order to unify the Name Yud, Kei and Vav, Kei in perfect unity, and in the name of all Israel, I hereby pray Tikkun Leah that was established by our sages of blessed memory, to correct its root in the Supernal Place to bring satisfaction to our Maker, and to fulfill the wish of our Creator "May the pleasantness of the Lord our God be upon us and may He establish the work of our hands for us and may the work of our hands establish Him." (Psalms 90:17)

Meditate here to connect to the moment (cosmic midnight) when the Creator enters the Garden of Eden to joyously unite with all the righteous souls (as is mentioned in the *Zohar*).

se'u שְׂאוּ she'arim שְׁעָרִים כתר rashechem רָאשֵׁיכֶם vehinase'u וְהִנָּשְׂאוּ

melech מֶלֶךְ veyavo וְיָבוֹא olam עוֹלָם pitchei פִּתְחֵי (מלכות) נשאו (ל"א) וה' ו'

hakavod הַכָּבוֹד mi מִי ze זֶה melech מֶלֶךְ ר"ת = פ"ו בסוד כתם טהור פו

hakavod הַכָּבוֹד Adonai יְהֹוָה ; כבוד יהוה = יוד הי ואו הה izuz עִזּוּז

vegibor וְגִבּוֹר Adonai יְהֹוָה gibor גִּבּוֹר milchama מִלְחָמָה:

use'u וּשְׂאוּ she'arim שְׁעָרִים כתר rashechem רָאשֵׁיכֶם

melech מֶלֶךְ veyavo וְיָבוֹא olam עוֹלָם pitchei פִּתְחֵי נשא ת"ת שהוא עילאה ו'

hakavod הַכָּבוֹד melech מֶלֶךְ ze זֶה hu הוּא mi מִי ; לאו hakavod הַכָּבוֹד

tzeva'ot צְבָאוֹת הה ואו הי יוד = יהוה כבוד ; Adonai יְהֹוָה לאו

sela סֶלָה: לאו hakavod הַכָּבוֹד melech מֶלֶךְ hu הוּא שכינה פני:

This Psalm and the following one are based on the yearning of *Malchut* to be elevated with her mate, *Zeir Anpin*.

lam'natze'ach לַמְנַצֵּחַ maskil מַשְׂכִּיל livnei לִבְנֵי Korach קֹרַח:

ke'ayal כְּאַיָּל ta'arog תַּעֲרֹג al עַל afikei אֲפִיקֵי mayim מָיִם ken כֵּן

nafshi נַפְשִׁי ta'arog תַּעֲרֹג elecha אֵלֶיךָ Elohim אֱלֹהִים ; אהיה אדני ילה:

tzam'a צָמְאָה nafshi נַפְשִׁי lelohim לֵאלֹהִים אהיה אדני ; ילה leEl לְאֵל

matai מָתַי avo אָבוֹא ve'era'e וְאֵרָאֶה penei פְּנֵי ראה chai וָי (מילוי דס"ג) ייא"י

Elohim אֱלֹהִים אהיה אדני ; ילה: hayta הָיְתָה li לִי dim'ati דִמְעָתִי וחכמה בינה

lechem לֶחֶם יום ג' הויות yomam יוֹמָם valayla וְלַיְלָה מלה be'emor בֶּאֱמֹר elai אֵלַי

kol כָּל hayom הַיּוֹם ע"ה נגד, מזבוח, זך, אל יהוה ayeh אַיֵּה Elohecha אֱלֹהֶיךָ ילה:

"Lift up your heads gates, and be lifted up, everlasting doors; that the King of glory may come in. 'Who is the King of glory?' 'The Lord strong and mighty, 'The Lord mighty in battle. Lift up your heads gates, lift them up, everlasting doors; that the King of Glory may come in. 'Who then is the King of Glory?' 'Lord of Hosts; He is the King of Glory.' Selah." (Psalms 24:7-10).

"For the Leader; Maschil of the sons of Korach: As the hart pants after the water brooks, so pants my soul after You, God. My soul thirsts for God, for the living God: 'When shall I come and appear before God?' My tears have been my food day and night, while they say unto me all the day: 'Where is your God?'"

ele אֵלֶּה   ezkera אֶזְכְּרָה   ve'eshpecha וְאֶשְׁפְּכָה   alai עָלַי

nafshi נַפְשִׁי   ki כִּי   e'evor אֶעֱבֹר   basach בַּסָּךְ   edadem אֶדַּדֵּם

ad עַד־   bet בֵּית ב"פ ראה   Elohim אֱלֹהִים אהיה אדני ; ילה   bekol בְּקוֹל־   rina רִנָּה

vetoda וְתוֹדָה   hamon הָמוֹן   chogeg וְחוֹגֵג ר"ת וזהו׃   ma מַה־ מ"ה

tishtochachi תִּשְׁתּוֹחֲחִי   nafshi נַפְשִׁי   vatehemi וַתֶּהֱמִי   alai עָלַי

hochili הוֹחִילִי   lelohim לֵאלֹהִים אהיה אדני ; ילה   ki כִּי־   od עוֹד   odenu אוֹדֶנּוּ

yeshu'ot יְשׁוּעוֹת   panav פָּנָיו׃   Elohai אֱלֹהַי מילוי ע"ב, דמב ; ילה   alai עָלַי

nafshi נַפְשִׁי   tishtochach תִּשְׁתּוֹחָח   al עַל־   ken כֵּן   ezkorcha אֶזְכָּרְךָ

me'eretz מֵאֶרֶץ   Yarden יַרְדֵּן י' הויות יוד אותיות יהוה   veChermonim וְחֶרְמוֹנִים

mehar מֵהַר   Mitz'ar מִצְעָר׃   tehom תְּהוֹם־   el אֶל־   tehom תְּהוֹם

kore קוֹרֵא   lekol לְקוֹל   tzinorecha צִנּוֹרֶיךָ   kol כָּל־ ילי

mishbarecha מִשְׁבָּרֶיךָ   vegalecha וְגַלֶּיךָ   alai עָלַי   avaru עָבָרוּ׃

yomam יוֹמָם   yetzave יְצַוֶּה   Adonai יְהֹוָאַדֹנָיֱהֹוִהַדֹנָי   chasdo וְחַסְדּוֹ

shiro שִׁירוֹ   uvalayla וּבַלַּיְלָה מלה (להמשיך הארה ממזלא עילאה) ג' הויות = מזלא

(ketiv כתיב׃ שִׁירֹה)   imi עִמִּי ס"ת יהוה   tefila תְּפִלָּה אתב"ש אוכצ, ב"ן אדני

leEl לְאֵל י"א = יוד הי ו הה   chayai וְחַיָּי (מילוי דס"ג)   omra אוֹמְרָה וניקודה ע"ה =

lama לָמָה   sal'i סַלְעִי (מילוי דס"ג)   leEl לְאֵל י"א (מילוי דס"ג)   shechachtani שְׁכַחְתָּנִי

lama לָמָה   koder קֹדֵר   elech אֵלֵךְ   belachatz בְּלַחַץ   oyev אוֹיֵב׃

These things I remember, and pour out my soul within me, how I passed on with the throng, and led them to the House of God, with the voice of joy and praise, a multitude keeping holyday. Why are you cast down, my soul? And why moan you within me? Hope you in God; for I shall yet praise Him for the salvation of His Countenance. My God, my soul is cast down within me; therefore do I remember You from the land of Jordan, and the Hermons, from the hill Mizar. Deep calls unto deep at the voice of Your cataracts; all Your waves and Your billows are gone over me. By day the Lord will command His loving kindness, and in the night His song shall be with me, even a prayer unto the God of my life. I will say to God my Rock: 'Why have You forgotten me? Why go I mourning under the oppression of the enemy?'

בְּרְצֵח beretzach בְּעַצְמוֹתַי be'atzmotai וְחֶרְפּוּנִי cherfuni צוֹרְרָי tzorerai

בְּאָמְרָם be'omram אֵלַי elai כָּל־ kol יִלי הַיּוֹם hayom ע"ה נגד, מזבח, זן, אל יהוה

אַיֵּה aye אֱלֹהֶיךָ elohecha יל-ה׃ מַה־ ma מ"ה תִּשְׁתּוֹחֲחִי tishtochachi

נַפְשִׁי nafshi וּמַה־ uma מ"ה תֶּהֱמִי tehemi עָלָי alai הוֹזִילִי hochili

לֵאלֹהִים lelohim אהיה אדני ; יל-ה כִּי־ ki עוֹד od אוֹדֶנּוּ odenu

יְשׁוּעֹת yeshu'ot פָּנַי panai וחכמה בינה ; מילוי ע"ב, דמב ; יל-ה׃ וֵאלֹהַי velohai לכב

שָׁפְטֵנִי shofteni אֱלֹהִים Elohim אהיה אדני ; יל-ה וְרִיבָה veriva

רִיבִי rivi מִגּוֹי migoy לֹא־ lo וְחָסִיד chasid מֵאִישׁ me'ish

מִרְמָה mirma וְעַוְלָה ve'avla תְּפַלְּטֵנִי׃ tefalteni כִּי־ ki אַתָּה Ata

אֱלֹהֵי Elohei מָעוּזִּי ma'uzi מילוי ע"ב, דמב ; יל-ה לָמָה lama זְנַחְתָּנִי zenachtani

לָמָה lama קֹדֵר koder אֶתְהַלֵּךְ et'halech בְּלַחַץ belachatz אוֹיֵב׃ oyev

שְׁלַח shelach אוֹרְךָ orcha וַאֲמִתְּךָ va'amitecha הֵמָּה hema יַנְחוּנִי yanchuni

יְבִיאוּנִי yevi'uni אֶל־ el הַר har קָדְשְׁךָ kodshecha וְאֶל ve'el

מִשְׁכְּנוֹתֶיךָ׃ mishkenotecha וְאָבוֹאָה ve'avoa אֶל־ el מִזְבַּח mizbach

אֱלֹהִים Elohim אהיה אדני ; יל-ה אֶל־ el אֵל El יי-א"י (מילוי דס"ג) נגד, זן, אל יהוה

שִׂמְחַת simchat גִּילִי gili וְאוֹדְךָ ve'odcha בְכִנּוֹר vechinor אֱלֹהִים Elohim

אֱלֹהָי Elohai יל-ה ; מילוי ע"ב, דמב אהיה אדני מַה־ ma מ"ה

תִּשְׁתּוֹחֲחִי tishtochachi נַפְשִׁי nafshi וּמַה־ uma מ"ה תֶּהֱמִי tehemi עָלָי alai

הוֹזִילִי hochili לֵאלֹהִים lelohim אהיה אדני ; יל-ה כִּי־ ki עוֹד od אוֹדֶנּוּ odenu

יְשׁוּעֹת yeshu'ot פָּנַי panai וחכמה בינה ; מילוי ע"ב, דמב ; יל-ה׃ וֵאלֹהַי velohai לכב

---

*As with a crushing in my bones, my adversaries taunt me; while they say to me all the day:
'Where is your God?' Why are you cast down, my soul? And why moan you within me?
Hope you in God; for I shall yet praise Him, the salvation of my countenance, and my God." (Psalms 42).*

*"Be You my judge, God, and plead my cause against an ungodly nation; deliver me from the deceitful and
unjust man. For You are the God of my strength; why have You cast me off? Why go I mourning under the
oppression of the enemy? Send out Your light and Your truth; let them lead me; let them bring me to Your
Holy Mountain, and to Your Dwelling-Places. Then will I go to the altar of God, to God, my exceeding joy; and
praise You upon the harp, God, my God. Why are you cast down, my soul? And why moan you within me?
Hope in God; for I shall yet praise Him, the salvation of my countenance, and my God." (Psalms 43)*

ha'aretz הָאָרֶץ ladonai לַיהֹוָ֑ה (pause here) mizmor מִזְמ֥וֹר leDavid לְדָוִ֗ד

va בָ֥ה veyoshvei וְֽיֹשְׁבֵי tevel תֵּ֝בֵ֗ל umlo'a וּ֝מְלוֹאָ֗ה

ve'al וְעַל־ yesada יְסָדָ֑הּ yamim יַמִּ֣ים al עַל־ hu ה֭וּא ki כִּי־

ya'ale יַֽעֲלֶ֥ה mi מִֽי־ yechoneneha יְכֽוֹנְנֶֽהָ neharot נְהָר֥וֹת

yakum יָקוּם umi וּמִי־ Adonai יְהֹוָ֑ה vehar בְהַר־

bimkom בִּמְק֥וֹם kodsho קָדְשֽׁוֹ

chapayim כַּפַּ֗יִם neki נְקִ֥י

uvar וּבַר־ levav לֵ֫בָ֥ב

asher אֲשֶׁ֤ר lo לֹא־ nasa נָשָׂ֣א lashav לַשָּׁ֣וְא

nafshi נַפְשִׁ֑י velo וְלֹ֖א nishba נִשְׁבַּ֣ע lemirma לְמִרְמָֽה

yisa יִשָּׂ֣א veracha בְ֭רָכָה me'et מֵאֵ֣ת Adonai יְהֹוָ֑ה

utz'daka וּ֝צְדָקָ֗ה meElohei מֵאֱלֹהֵ֥י

yish'o יִשְׁעֽוֹ ze זֶ֭ה dor דּ֣וֹר dorshav דֹּרְשָׁ֑יו

mevakshei מְבַקְשֵׁ֨י fanecha פָנֶ֖יךָ

Ya'akov יַֽעֲקֹ֣ב sela סֶֽלָה se'u שְׂא֤וּ she'arim שְׁעָרִ֨ים

rashechem רָֽאשֵׁיכֶ֗ם vehinase'u וְֽ֭הִנָּשְׂאוּ

pitchei פִּתְחֵ֣י olam עוֹלָ֑ם veyavo וְ֝יָב֗וֹא melech מֶ֣לֶךְ hakavod הַכָּבֽוֹד

mi מִ֥י ze זֶה֮ melech מֶ֢לֶךְ

hakavod הַכָּב֥וֹד Adonai יְהֹוָה֮ izuz עִזּ֪וּז

vegibor וְגִבּ֥וֹר Adonai יְהֹוָ֗ה gibor גִּבּ֥וֹר milchama מִלְחָמָֽה

"A Psalm of David: The Earth is the Lord's, and the fullness thereof; the world, and they that dwell therein. For He has founded it upon the seas, and established it upon the floods. Who shall ascend into the Mountain of the Lord? And who shall stand in His Holy Place? He that has clean hands, and a pure heart; who has not taken My Name in vain, and has not sworn deceitfully. He shall receive a blessing from the Lord and righteousness from the God of his salvation. Such is the generation of them that seek after Him that seek Your Face, even Jacob. Selah. Lift up your heads gates, and be lifted up, everlasting doors; that the King of Glory may come in. 'Who is the King of Glory?' The Lord strong and mighty, the Lord mighty in battle.

שְׂאוּ se'u שְׁעָרִים she'arim כתר רָאשֵׁיכֶם rashechem וּשְׂאוּ use'u

מֶלֶךְ melech וְיָבֹא veyavo עוֹלָם olam פִּתְחֵי pitchei נשא ת״ת שהוא עילאה ו

הַכָּבוֹד hakavod מִי mi ילי :לאו הוּא hu זֶה ze מֶלֶךְ melech

צְבָאוֹת tzeva'ot הַכָּבוֹד hakavod לאו יְהֹוָה Adonai כבוד יהוה כ= יוד הי ואו הה ואהדנהי

:סֶלָה sela לאו הַכָּבוֹד hakavod מֶלֶךְ melech הוּא hu פני שכינה צְבָאוֹת tzeva'ot

LAMNATZE'ACH (an explanation about the "lamnatze'ach" can be found on page 54).

לַמְנַצֵּחַ lam'natze'ach בִּנְגִינֹת binginot מִזְמוֹר mizmor שִׁיר shir:

אֱלֹהִים Elohim אהיה אדני ; ילה יְחָנֵּנוּ yechonenu וִיבָרְכֵנוּ vivarchenu

יָאֵר ya'er כף ויו זין ויו = ר״ת פ.א.י, אמן (יאהדונהי) אִתָּנוּ itanu פָּנָיו panav סֶלָה sela:

לָדַעַת lada'at ר״ת ס.א.ל, אמן (יאהדונהי) בָּאָרֶץ ba'aretz דַּרְכֶּךָ darkecha

בְּכָל bechol ב״ן לכב גּוֹיִם goyim יְשׁוּעָתֶךָ yeshu'atecha:

יוֹדוּךָ yoducha עַמִּים amim אֱלֹהִים Elohim אהיה אדני ; ילה

יוֹדוּךָ yoducha עַמִּים amim כֻּלָּם kulam יִשְׂמְחוּ yismechu וִירַנְּנוּ viranenu

לְאֻמִּים le'umim איהיוהה = ע״ה ר״ת כִּי ki תִשְׁפֹּט tishpot עַמִּים amim

מִישׁוֹר mishor וּלְאֻמִּים ul'umim בָּאָרֶץ ba'aretz תַּנְחֵם tanchem סֶלָה sela:

יוֹדוּךָ yoducha עַמִּים amim אֱלֹהִים Elohim אהיה אדני ; ילה יוֹדוּךָ yoducha

עַמִּים amim כֻּלָּם kulam: ר״ת יודוך ישמחו יודוך ארץ = יא״י (מילוי דס״ג)

אָרֶץ eretz נָתְנָה natna נתה, = ע״ב, ריבוע יהוה קס״א קנ״א קמ״ג ועם ר״ת אלהים לדעת יברכנו

יְבוּלָהּ yevula ר״ת אני יְבָרְכֵנוּ yevarchenu אֱלֹהִים Elohim אהיה אדני ; ילה

אֱלֹהֵינוּ Elohenu ילה:יהל יְבָרְכֵנוּ yevarchenu אֱלֹהִים Elohim אהיה אדני ; ילה

וְיִירְאוּ veyir'u אֹתוֹ oto כֹּל kol ילי אַפְסֵי afsei אָרֶץ aretz:

---

*Lift up your heads, gates, lift them up, everlasting doors; that the King of Glory may come in.
'Who then is the King of Glory?' Lord of Hosts; He is the King of Glory.' Selah." (Psalms 24)*

LAMNATZE'ACH

*"For the Leader; with string-music: A Psalm, a Song. God be gracious unto us, and bless us; may He cause His
face to shine toward us; Selah. That Your way may be known upon earth, Your salvation among all nations.
Let the people give thanks to You, God; let the people give thanks to You, all of them. Let the nations be glad
and sing for joy; for You will judge the people with equity, and lead the nations upon earth. Selah Let the people
give thanks to You, God; let the people give thanks to You, all of them. The earth has yielded her increase; may
God, our own God, bless us. May God bless us; and let all the ends of the earth fear Him." (Psalms 67)*

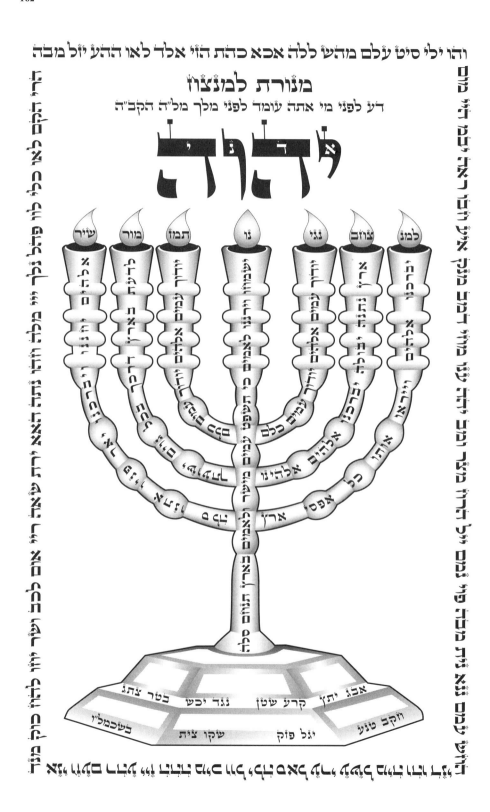

HALELUYAH

Reciting this Psalm is for the *Zivug* (unification) of *Leah* and her connection.

הַלְלוּיָהּ haleluya אלהים, אהיה ארני ; אהיה ארני ; יה ; ללה ; אֹֽודֶה ode יְהֹוָֹה Adonai

בְּכָל bechal בּ"ן, לבב לבב levav בּוֹכוּ בְּסוֹד besod מיכ, י"פ האא

יְשָׁרִים yesharim וְעֵדָה ve'eda סיט: גְּדֹלִים gedolim מַעֲשֵׂי ma'asei

יְהֹוָֹה Adonai דְּרוּשִׁים derushim לְכָל lechol יה ארני

וְחֶפְצֵיהֶם cheftzehem: הֹוד hod ההה וְהָדָר vehadar פָּעֳלוֹ pa'olo

וְצִדְקָתֹו vetzidkato עֹמֶדֶת omedet לָעַד la'ad ב"פ ב"ן: זֵכֶר zecher

עָשָׂה asa לְנִפְלְאֹתָיו lenifle'otav רַזוּן chanun וְרַחוּם verachum

יְהֹוָֹה Adonai וחנן ורחום יהוה = עשל: טֶרֶף teref natan נָתַן לִירֵאָיו lire'av

יִזְכֹּר yizkor לְעֹולָם le'olam ריבוע דס"ג ו"י אותיות דס"ג בְּרִיתֹו berito:

כֹּחַ ko'ach מַעֲשָׂיו ma'asav הִגִּיד higid לְעַמֹּו le'amo לָתֵת latet לָהֶם lahem

נַחֲלַת nachalat גֹּויִם goyim: מַעֲשֵׂי ma'asei יָדָיו yadav אֱמֶת emet

נֶאֱמָנִים ne'emanim umishpat וּמִשְׁפָּט ע"ה ה"פ ס"ג, ז"פ ס"ג אלהים אהיה פעמים אהיה

כָּל kol יל"י פִּקּוּדָיו pikudav מנק: סְמוּכִים semuchim לָעַד la'ad ב"פ ב"ן

לְעֹולָם le'olam ריבוע דס"ג ו"י אותיות דס"ג עֲשׂוּיִם asuyim בֶּאֱמֶת be'emet

לְעַמֹּו le'amo שָׁלַח shalach פְּדוּת pedut וְיָשָׁר veyashar: ז"פ ס"ג אהיה פעמים אהיה

צִוָּה tziva לְעֹולָם le'olam ריבוע דס"ג ו"י אותיות דס"ג בְּרִיתֹו berito

קָדֹושׁ kadosh וְנֹורָא venora שְׁמֹו shemo ע"ב בריבוע קס"א ע"ב עסל ע"ב, אל שדי ע"ה, מהש ע"ה:

HALELUYAH
'Praise the Lord!

א *I will give thanks to the Lord with my whole heart,* ב *in the council of the upright, and in the congregation.* ג *The works of the Lord are great,* ד *sought out of all them that have delight therein.* ה *His work is glory and majesty;* ו *and His righteousness endures forever.* ז *He has made a memorial for His wonderful works;* ח *the Lord is gracious and full of compassion.* ט *He has given food to those that fear Him;* י *He will ever be mindful of His covenant.* כ *He has declared to His people the power of His works,* ל *in giving them the heritage of the nations.* מ *The works of His hands are truth and justice;* נ *all His precepts are sure.* ס *They are established for ever and ever,* ע *they are done in truth and uprightness.* פ *He has sent redemption unto His people;* צ *He has commanded His covenant for ever;* ק *Holy and awesome is His Name.*

reshit רֵאשִׁית chochmah וָזְכְמָה במילוי = תרי"ג (מצוות) yir'at יִרְאַת

Adonai יְהֹוָה(אדני-אלהים-יאהדונהי) sechel שֵׂכֶל tov טוֹב והו lechol לְכָל־ יה אדני

osehem עֹשֵׂיהֶם tehilato תְּהִלָּתוֹ omedet עֹמֶדֶת la'ad לָעַד ב"פ ב"ן:

You should meditate on the five final letters — מנצפ"ך — in order to complete the 27 letters which are the illustration of the newborn. You should also meditate: כל"ך סעפ"ה יאעוצ"ה. Then, meditate on: אלד (this Name is the secret of the birth of *Leah* and has the same numerial value of *Leah*).

no'a נוֹעַ tanu'a תָּנוּעַ eretz אֶרֶץ kashikor כַּשִּׁכּוֹר vehitnodeda וְהִתְנוֹדֲדָה

kameluna כַּמְּלוּנָה vechavad וְכָבַד aleha עָלֶיהָ פהל pish'a פִּשְׁעָה

venafla וְנָפְלָה velo וְלֹא־ tosif תֹסִיף kum קוּם vehaya וְהָיָה יהוה ; יהה

bayom בַּיּוֹם ע"ה נגד, מזבוח, זך, אל יהוה hahu הַהוּא yifkod יִפְקֹד

Adonai יְהֹוָה(אדני-אלהים-יאהדונהי) al עַל־ tzeva צְבָא hamarom הַמָּרוֹם bamarom בַּמָּרוֹם

ve'al וְעַל־ malchei מַלְכֵי ha'adama הָאֲדָמָה al עַל־ ha'adama הָאֲדָמָה:

Before reciting the following Psalm,
you should cry for your negative actions and ask for forgiveness:

lam'natze'ach לַמְנַצֵּחַ mizmor מִזְמוֹר leDavid לְדָוִד: bevo בְּבוֹא־ elav אֵלָיו

Natan נָתָן hanavi הַנָּבִיא ka'asher כַּאֲשֶׁר ba בָּא el אֶל־ Batshava בַּת־שֶׁבַע:

choneni וָחָנֵּנִי Elohim אֱלֹהִים אהיה אדני ; ילה kechasdecha כְּחַסְדֶּךָ kerov כְּרֹב

rachamecha רַחֲמֶיךָ meche מְחֵה fesha'ai פְּשָׁעָי: herev הֶרֶב (כתיב : הרבה)

kabeseni כַּבְּסֵנִי me'avoni מֵעֲוֹנִי umechatati וּמֵחַטָּאתִי tahareni טַהֲרֵנִי:

ר *The fear of the Lord is the beginning of wisdom;*
שׂ *a good understanding have all they that do thereafter;* ת *His praise endures for ever."* (Psalms 111)

"The earth reels to and fro like a drunken man, and sways to and from as a lodge; and the transgression thereof is heavy upon it, and it shall fall, and not rise again. And it shall come to pass in that day, that Lord will punish the host of the high heaven on high, and the kings of the earth upon the earth." (Isaiah 24:20-21)

"For the Leader: A Psalm of David; When Nathan the prophet came to him, after he had gone in to Bathsheba. Be gracious unto me, God, according to Your mercy; according to the multitude of Your compassions blot out my transgressions. Wash me thoroughly from mine iniquity, and cleanse me from my sin.

כִּי ki fesha'ai פְשָׁעַי ani אֲנִי eda אֵדָע eda וְחַטָּאתִי vechatati

נֶגְדִּי negdi מזבוח, זן, אל יהוה ע"ה tamid תָמִיד קס"א קנ"א קמ"ג:

לְךָ lecha levadecha לְבַדְּךָ chatati וְחָטָאתִי vehara וְהָרַע be'enecha בְעֵינֶיךָ

titzdak תִּצְדַּק lema'an לְמַעַן asiti עָשִׂיתִי מ"ה ריבוע ; קס"א ע"ה

בְּדָבְרֶךָ bedovrecha tizke תִזְכֶּה veshoftecha בְשָׁפְטֶךָ: hen הֵן

בְעָווֹן be'avon cholalti וְחוֹלָלְתִּי uv'chet וּבְחֵטְא yechematni יֶחֱמַתְנִי imi אִמִּי:

הֵן hen emet אֱמֶת אהיה פעמים אהיה, ז"פ ס"ג chafatzta וְחָפַצְתָּ vatuchot בַטֻּחוֹת

וּבְסָתֻם uvsatum chochmah וְחָכְמָה במילוי = תרי"ג (מצות) todi'eni תוֹדִיעֵנִי:

תְחַטְּאֵנִי techat'eni ve'ezov בְאֵזוֹב ve'et'har וְאֶטְהָר techabseni תְכַבְּסֵנִי

וּמִשֶּׁלֶג umisheleg אלף אלף אלף (רג' אהיה) albin אַלְבִּין: tashmi'eni תַּשְׁמִיעֵנִי

שָׂשׂוֹן sason vesimcha וְשִׂמְחָה tagelna תָּגֵלְנָה atzamot עֲצָמוֹת dikita דִּכִּיתָ:

הַסְתֵּר haster mechata'ai מֵחֲטָאָי מ"ה בן ב"פ מצר ס"ג panecha פָנֶיךָ מ"ה בן:

וְכָל vechol ילי avonotai עֲוֹנֹתַי meche מְחֵה: lev לֵב tahor טָהוֹר י"פ אכא

בְּרָא bera קנ"א ב"ן, יהוה אלהים יהוה אדני, מילוי קס"א וס"ג, מ"ה ברבוע וע"ב ע"ה ;
לב טהור ברא = קס"א קנ"א קמ"ג li לִי Elohim אֱלֹהִים אהיה אדני ; ילה ; לי אלהים = ריבוע אדני

וְרוּחַ veru'ach nachon נָכוֹן chadesh וְחַדֵּשׁ י"ב הויות, קס"א קנ"א bekirbi בְּקִרְבִּי עדי:

אַל al tashlicheni תַּשְׁלִיכֵנִי milfanecha מִלְּפָנֶיךָ ס"ג מ"ה בן verua'ch וְרוּחַ

קָדְשְׁךָ kodshecha al אַל tikach תִּקַּח mimeni מִמֶּנִי: hashiva הָשִׁיבָה li לִי

שָׂשׂוֹן sason yish'echa יִשְׁעֶךָ veru'ach וְרוּחַ nediva נְדִיבָה tismecheni תִסְמְכֵנִי:

For I know my transgressions; and my sin is ever before me. Against You, You only, have I sinned, and done that which is evil in Your sight; that You may be justified when You speak, and be in the right when You judge. Behold, I was brought forth in iniquity, and in sin did my mother conceive me. Behold, You desire truth in the inward parts; make me, therefore, to know wisdom in my inmost heart. Purge me with hyssop, and I shall be clean; wash me, and I shall be whiter than snow. Make me to hear joy and gladness; that the bones which You have crushed may rejoice. Hide Your Face from my sins, and blot out all my iniquities. Create me a clean heart, God; and renew a steadfast spirit within me. Cast me not away from Your presence; and take not Your Holy Spirit from me. Restore unto me the joy of You salvation; and let a willing spirit uphold me.

alamda אֲלַמְּדָה fosh'im פֹשְׁעִים derachecha דְּרָכֶיךָ vechata'im וְחַטָּאִים

elecha אֵלֶיךָ yashuvu: יָשׁוּבוּ hatzileni הַצִּילֵנִי midamim מִדָּמִים

Elohim אֱלֹהִים יכה ; אהיה אדני Elohei אֱלֹהֵי מילוי ע"ב, דמב ; יכה

teshu'ati תְּשׁוּעָתִי teranen תְּרַנֵּן leshoni לְשׁוֹנִי tzidkatecha: צִדְקָתֶךָ

Adonai אֲדֹנָי יכה sefatai שְׂפָתַי tiftach תִּפְתָּח ufi וּפִי

yagid יַגִּיד יוד (כ"ב אותיות [=אכא] ה-ה אותיות מזוֹזְךָ) tehilatecha תְּהִלָּתֶךָ ס"ת = בוכו:

ki כִּי lo לֹא tachpotz תַחְפֹּץ zevach זֶבַח ve'etena וְאֶתֵּנָה נתה, קס"א קנ"א קמ"ג

ola עוֹלָה lo לֹא tirtze תִרְצֶה: zivchei זִבְחֵי Elohim אֱלֹהִים אהיה אדני ; יכה

ru'ach רוּחַ nishbara נִשְׁבָּרָה ר"ת = ג"פ אלהים (יומתיקם בשם ס"ג עובס"ת)

lev לֵב- nishbar נִשְׁבָּר venidke וְנִדְכֶּה ר"ת = אלהים, אהיה אדני Elohim אֱלֹהִים

lo לֹא tivze תִבְזֶה ר"ת = ה"פ אלהים ע"ה ; וס"ת מילוי ע"ב: אהיה אדני ; יכה

hetiva הֵיטִיבָה virtzoncha בִרְצוֹנְךָ et אֶת־ Tziyon צִיּוֹן יוסף, ו' הויות, קנאה

tivne תִבְנֶה chomot חוֹמוֹת ע"ה קס"א קנ"א קמ"ג Yerushalayim: יְרוּשָׁלָיִם

az אָז tachpotz תַחְפֹּץ zivchei זִבְחֵי tzedek צֶדֶק ola עוֹלָה

vechalil וְכָלִיל az אָז ya'alu יַעֲלוּ al עַל- mizbachacha מִזְבְּחֶךָ farim: פָרִים

While reciting these verses, one should meditate that the word *Tzion* corresponds to *Rachel* and the word *Yerushalayim* corresponds to *Leah*, and ask the Creator to raise them up from their fall.

ad עַד ana אָנָה ריבוע מ"ה bichya בְּכִיָּה מילוי דס"ג veTziyon בְּצִיּוֹן **(Rachel)**

umisped וּמִסְפָּד ריבוע ע"ב birushalayim בִּירוּשָׁלַיִם: **(Leah)** יוסף, ו' הויות, קנאה

Then will I teach transgressors Your ways; and sinners shall return unto You. Deliver me from blood guiltiness, God, You are God of my salvation; so shall my tongue sing aloud of Your righteousness. God, open You my lips; and my mouth shall declare Your praise. For You delight not in sacrifice, else would I give it; You have no pleasure in burnt-offering. The sacrifices of God are a broken spirit; a broken and a contrite heart, God, You will not despise. Do good in Your favour unto Zion; build You the walls of Jerusalem. Then will You delight in the sacrifices of righteousness, in burnt-offering and whole offering; then will they offer bullocks upon Your altar." (Pslams 51)

How long it will be crying in Zion and mourning in Jerusalem?

תָּקוּם takum כ"א הויות שבתפילין ג"פ רי"ו ; אברהם, וז"פ אל, רי"ו ול"ב נתיבות תְּרוּחֵם terachem

צִיּוֹן Tziyon (Rachel) יוסף, ו' הויות, קְנְאָה הוֹכמה, רמ"ח (אברים), עסמ"ב וט"ז אותיות פשוטות

תִּבְנֶה tivne חוֹמוֹת chomot ע"ה קס"א קנ"א קמ"ג יְרוּשָׁלַיִם Yerushalayim (Le'ah):

אֱלֹהֵינוּ Elohenu ילה וֵאלֹהֵי velohei לכב ; מילוי ע"ב, דמב ; ילה אֲבוֹתֵינוּ avotenu

מֶלֶךְ melech רַחֲמָן rachaman רַחֵם rachem אברהם, וז"פ אל, רי"ו ול"ב נתיבות הוֹכמה,

טוֹב tov והו אלנו alenu עסמ"ב וט"ז אותיות פשוטות רמ"ח (אברים), וּמֵטִיב umetiv

שׁוּבָה shuva החזו אהיה ארני, אלהים, לָנוּ lanu הִדָּרֶשׁ hidaresh עָלֵינוּ alenu

בִּגְלַל biglal רַחֲמֶיךָ rachamecha בַּהֲמוֹן bahamon אֲבוֹת avot שֶׁעָשׂוּ she'asu

בֵּיתְךָ vetcha ב"פ ראה כְּבַתְּחִלָּה kevatechila בְּנֵה bene רְצוֹנֶךָ retzonecha

בֵּית bet ב"פ ראה כוכ konen מִקְדָּשְׁךָ mikdashcha עַל al מְכוֹנוֹ mechono כּוֹנֵן

שִׂמְחֵנוּ samchenu בְּבִנְיָנוֹ bevinyano הַרְאֵנוּ har'enu בְּתִקּוּנוֹ betikuno

שְׁכִינָתְךָ shechinatcha וְהָשֵׁב vehashev לְתוֹכוֹ letocho

לַעֲבוֹדָתָם la'avodatam כֹּהֲנִים kohanim וְהָשֵׁב vehashev וּלְוִיִּם uleviyim

לְדוּכָנָם leduchanam לְשִׁירָם leshiram וּלְזִמְרָם ulzimram וְהָשֵׁב vehashev

יִשְׂרָאֵל Yisrael לִנְוֵיהֶם linvehem וְשָׁם vesham נַעֲלֶה na'ale

וְנִרְאֶה venerae ראה וְנִשְׁתַּחֲוֶה venishtachave לְפָנֶיךָ lefanecha ס"ג מ"ה ב"ן:

You shal redeem us, and be mercifull to Zion, and You shal build Jerusalem's walls.

Our God and God of our fathers, Compassionate King,
have mercy upon us. Good and Kind, seek us. Return to us with Your mass compassion.
Because of Your fathers who obeyed Your will. Build Your house as before. And bring back
the Temple to its place. Show us its rebuilding. Let us be happy with its restoration. Bring Your Shechinah
and bring back the Kohanim to their works, the Levites to their stand, their singing and chanting. Bring
Israel back to their dwelling place. And there we will ascend and appear prostrate ourselves before you.

עודי ע"ה אֵל עודי ע"ה בריבוע וקס"א ע"ה, ע"ב מהש"ע ע"ה ratzon רָצוֹן yehi יְהִי

ילה Elohenu אֱלֹהֵינוּ Adonai יְהוָֹה ב"ן מ"ה ס"ג milfanecha מִלְּפָנֶיךָ

sheta'alenu שֶׁתַּעֲלֵנוּ avotenu אֲבוֹתֵינוּ ; דמב, ע"ב מילוי לכב ; ילה velohei וֵאלֹהֵי

◆bigvulenu בִּגְבוּלֵנוּ vetita'enu וְתִטָּעֵנוּ le'artzenu לְאַרְצֵנוּ besimcha בְּשִׂמְחָה

ב"ן מ"ה ס"ג lefanecha לְפָנֶיךָ na'ase נַעֲשֶׂה vesham וְשָׁם

temidim תְּמִידִים chovotenu וְחוֹבוֹתֵינוּ korbenot קָרְבְּנוֹת et אֶת

kehilchatam כְּהִלְכָתָם umusafim וּמוּסָפִים kesidram כְּסִדְרָם

et אֶת־ Adonai יְהוָֹה beshuv בְּשׁוּב hama'alot הַמַּעֲלוֹת shir שִׁיר

kecholmim כְּחוֹלְמִים hayinu הָיִינוּ יוסף, ו' הויות, קנאה Tziyon צִיּוֹן shivat שִׁיבַת

rina רִנָּה ulshonenu וּלְשׁוֹנֵנוּ pinu פִּינוּ sechok שְׂחוֹק yimale יִמָּלֵא az אָז

Adonai יְהוָֹה higdil הִגְדִּיל vagoyim בַּגּוֹיִם yomru יֹאמְרוּ az אָז

Adonai יְהוָֹה higdil הִגְדִּיל ele אֵלֶּה im עִם־ la'asot לַעֲשׂוֹת

hayinu הָיִינוּ אותיות וד' קס"א ע"ה, דס"ג, ריבוע imanu עִמָּנוּ la'asot לַעֲשׂוֹת

et אֶת־ Adonai יְהוָֹה shuva שׁוּבָה הוזע semechim שְׂמֵחִים

banegev בַּנֶּגֶב ka'afikim כַּאֲפִיקִים (שְׁבוּתֵנוּ : כתיב) shevitenu שְׁבִיתֵנוּ

yiktzoru יִקְצֹרוּ berina בְּרִנָּה bedim'a בְּדִמְעָה hazor'im הַזֹּרְעִים

meshech מֶשֶׁךְ nose נֹשֵׂא uvacho וּבָכֹה כלי yelech יֵלֵךְ haloch הָלוֹךְ

alumotav אֲלֻמֹּתָיו nose נֹשֵׂא verina בְרִנָּה yavo יָבֹא bo בֹּא־ hazara הַזָּרַע

May it be pleasing before You, Lord, our God and God of our forefathers, that You will take us up joyfully to our land and plant us within our boundaries, and there we will perform before You the rites of our compulsory offerings, the Tamid-offerings, in their order, and the Musaf-offerings, according to their laws.

"A Song of Ascents. When Lord brought back those that returned to Zion, we were like unto them that dream. Then was our mouth filled with laughter; and our tongue with singing; then said they among the nations: 'The Lord has done great things with these.' The Lord has done great things with us; we are rejoiced. Turn our captivity, Lord, as the streams in the dry land. They that sow in tears shall reap in joy. Though he goes on his way weeping that bears the measure of seed, he shall come home with joy, bearing his sheaves." (Psalms 126)

AMAR RABBI SHIMON

The essence of this passage from the *Zohar, Noah,* 122-127 concerns the hands. Since the hands are the tools with which we carry out life's actions, the forces of darkness latch onto them in order to influence our deeds. We can infuse our hands with the positive energy that dwells in the Upper Worlds so that they bring blessing and good fortune to all our endeavors.

אֲמַר amar רַבִּי Rabbi שִׁמְעוֹן Shimon אֲרֵימַת aremat יְדַאי yedai

בִּצְלוֹתִין bitzlotin לְעֵילָא le'ela דְּכַד dechad רְעוּתָא re'uta עִלָּאָה ila'a,

לְעֵילָא le'ela לְעֵילָא le'ela, קָיְימָא kayma עַל al הַהוּא hahu

רְעוּתָא re'uta, דְּלָא dela אִתְיְדַע ityeda, וְלָא velo אִתְפַּס itpas כְּלָל kelal

לְעָלְמִין le'almin, רֵישָׁא reisha דְּסְתִים desatim יַתִּיר yatir לְעֵילָא le'eila,

וְהַהוּא vehahu רֵישָׁא resha אַפֵּיק apek מַאי mai דְּאַפֵּיק de'apek, וְלָא vela

יְדִיעַ yedi'a, וְנָהִיר venaher מַאי mai דְּנָהֵיר denaher, כְּלָא kola

בִּסְתִימוּ bistimu. רְעוּ re'o דְּמַחֲשָׁבָה demachashava עִלָּאָה ila'a

לְמִרְדַף lemirdaf אֲבַתְרֵיהּ avatrei, וּלְאִתְנַהֲרָא ule'itnehara מִנֵּיהּ minei.

וְזַד chad פְּרִיסוּ perisu אִתְפְּרֵיס itpereis, וּמִגּוֹ umigo הַהוּא hahu

פְּרִיסָא perisa, בִּרְדִיפוּ birdifu דְּהַהִיא dehahi מַחֲשָׁבָה machashava

עִלָּאָה ila'a, מְטֵי matei וְלָא vela מְטֵי matei. עַד ad

הַהוּא hahu פְּרִיסָא perisa נָהֵיר naher מַה ma דְּנָהֵיר denaher.

וּכְדֵין uchden אִיהוּ ihu מַחֲשָׁבָה machashava עִלָּאָה ila'a,

נָהֵיר naher בִּנְהִירוּ binhiru סְתִים satim דְּלָא dela יְדִיעַ yedi'a,

וְהַהוּא vehahu מַחֲשָׁבָה machashava לָא la יָדַע yada.

AMAR RABBI SHIMON

Rav Shimon said: "I raise my hands on high to pray. When the Supernal Desire at the highest point Above, is established upon the forever unknown and ungraspable desire, it becomes the most concealed Head Above. And that Head emanates all that He emanates and all that is unknown. And He illuminates all that he illuminates in a concealed manner. The desire of the Supernal Thought runs after it to be illuminated from it. But a veil spreads and from its spreading and the running after it, it is allowed to reach, and to not reach, the Light. The Light shines upward toward the veil. Therefore the Supernal Thought shines with Unrevealed Illumination, and with Light unknown to the 'Mind (Moach) of air.' And the Thought itself is considered unknown.

כְּדֵין keden בָּטַשׁ batash הַאי hai נְהִירוּ nehiru דְּמַוֹזְשַׁבָה demachashava

דְּלָא dela אִתְיָידַע ityeda, בִּנְהִירוּ binhiru דְּפַרְסָא defarsa

דְּקָיְימָא dekayma, דְּנָהִיר denaheir מִמַה mima דְּלָא dela יְדִיע yedi'a

וְלָא vela ,ityeda אִתְגַּלְיָיא itgalya• uchden וּכְדֵין da דָּא

נְהִירוּ nehiru דְּמַוֹזְשַׁבָה demachashava דְּלָא dela אִתְיָידַע ityeda

בָּטַשׁ batash בִּנְהִירוּ binhiru דִּפְרִיסָא difrisa, וְנָהֲרִין venaharin

כַּוְזדָא kachada, וְאִתְעֲבִידוּ ve'it'avidu תֵּשַׁע tesha הֵיכָלִין hechalin•

וְהֵיכָלִין vehechalin, לָאו lav אִינוּן inun נְהוֹרִין nehorin, וְלָאו velav

אִינוּן inun רוּוזִין ruchin, וְלָאו velav אִינוּן inun נִשְׁמָתִין nishmatin וְלָא vela

אִית it מָאן man דְּקָיְימָא dekayma בְּהוֹ beho• רְעוּתָא re'uta, דְּכָל dechol

תֵּשַׁע tesha נְהוֹרִין nehorin, דְּקָיְימֵי dekaymei כֻּלְּהוֹ kolho

בְּמַוֹזְשַׁבָה bemachashava, דְּאִיהוּ de'ihu וַזד chad מִנַּיְיהוּ minayhu

בְּוזוּשְׁבְּנָא bechushbena כֻּלְּהוֹ kolho לְמִרְדַּף lemirdaf בַּתְרַיְיהוּ, batrayhu

בְּשַׁעֲתָא besha'ata דְּקָיְימֵי dekaymei בְּמַוֹזְשַׁבָה bemach'shava וְלָא vela

מִתְדַּבְּקָן mitdabkan וְלָא vela אִתְיָידְעוּ, ityeda'u וְאִלֵּין ve'ilen לָא la

קָיְימֵי kaymei לָא la בִּרְעוּתָא, bir'uta וְלָא vela בְּמַוֹזְשַׁבָה bemachashava

עִלָּאָה ila'a תָּפְסִין tafsin בָּה ba וְלָא vela תָּפְסִין tafsin•

Then, the Illumination of the Unknown Thought hits upon the Illumination of the veil that stands and shines of what is unknown, what is not known, and what is unrevealed. Thus, the Illumination of the Thought that is not known hits upon the veil's Illumination, and they shine together. And from them, nine Chambers are made. These Chambers are not Light. And they are neither Ruchot nor Neshamot, and nobody can understand what they are. The desire of all nine Lights is standing in the Thought and is also considered one of Them. And all desire to pursue them while the nine Lights are located in the Thought. Nevertheless, the Chambers are not attained and not known because they are not established as either an aspect of desire or as an aspect of Supernal Thought. They grasp and do not grasp.

בְּאִלֵּין be'ilen קָיְימֵי kaymei כָּל kol רָזֵי razei דִּמְהֵימְנוּתָא dim'hemenuta,

וְכָל vechol אִינוּן inun נְהוֹרִין nehorin מֵרָזָא meraza

דְּמַחֲשָׁבָה demachashava עִלָּאָה ila'a כֻּלְּהוּ kolho אִקְרוּן ikrun אֵין en

סוֹף sof. עַד ad הָכָא hacha בְּטוֹ mato נְהוֹרִין nehorin וְלָא vela

בְּטוֹן maton, וְלָא vela אִתְיְידְעוּ ityeda'u, לָאו lav הָכָא hacha

רְעוּתָא re'uta, וְלָא vela מַחֲשָׁבָה machashava. כַּד kad נָהִיר naher

מַחֲשָׁבָה machashava, וְלָא vela אִתְיְידַע ityeda בְּמַּאן miman

דְּנָהִיר denaher, כְּדֵין keden אִתְלַבַּשׁ itlabesh וְאַסְתִּים ve'astim גּוֹ go

בִּינָה bina, וְנָהִיר venaher לְמַאן leman דְּנָהִיר denaher וְאָעִיל ve'ael דָּא da

בְּדָא beda, עַד ad דְּאִתְכְּלִילוּ de'itkelilu כֻּלְּהוּ kolho כַּחֲדָא kachada.

וּבְרָזָא uv'raza דְּקָרְבָּנָא dekorbana כַּד kad סָלִיק salek, כֹּלָּא kola

אִתְקְשַׁר itkashar דָּא da בְּדָא beda, וְנָהִיר venaher דָּא da בְּדָא beda,

כְּדֵין keden קָיְימֵי kaymei כֻּלְּהוּ kolho בִּסְלִיקוּ bisliku,

וּמַחֲשָׁבָה umachashava אִתְעַטַּר it'atar בְּאֵין be'en סוֹף sof.

הַהוּא hahu נְהִירוּ nehiru דְּאִתְנְהִיר de'itneher מִנֵּיהּ minei

מַחֲשָׁבָה machashava עִלָּאָה ila'a, אִקְרֵי ikrei אֵין en סוֹף sof.

וּמִנֵּיהּ uminei אַשְׁתְּכַח ishtechach וְקָיְימָא vekayma וְנָהִיר venaher

לְמַאן leman דְּנָהִיר denaher, וְעַל ve'al דָּא da כֹּלָּא kola

קָאִים ka'em. זַכָּאָה zaka'a וְחוּלְקֵידוֹן chulakehon דְּצַדִּיקַיָּיא detzadikaya

בְּעָלְמָא be'alma דֵּין den וּבְעָלְמָא uve'alma דְּאָתֵי de'atei.

With these all the secrets of Faith are based upon. And all of these Lights come from the secret of the Supernal Thought and all are called the Ein Sof. Because the Lights reach and do not reach, and are not known, there is neither desire nor thought at this point. When Unknown Thought shines from its source, it shines upon whom She shines, and They enter each other until They are as one. Returning to the secret of the sacrifice: When it is raised, all are enmeshed within one another and shine one upon the other. Now all the stages are in the secret of the Ascending and, when it ascends to the Unknown Head, Thought is crowned by the Ein Sof. This Illumination that the Supernal Thought illuminates from is called Ein Sof. And from there it comes. It is established and shines upon Whom It shines. And all is based upon this. Happy are the righteous in this world and the World to Come.

PETICHAT ELIYAHU HANAVI – THE OPENING OF ELIJAH THE PROPHET

Reciting these paragraphs can help you open your heart to spiritual wisdom.

וִיהִי vihi נֹעַם no'am אֲדֹנָי Adonai ללה אֱלֹהֵינוּ Elohenu ילה עָלֵינוּ alenu

וּמַעֲשֵׂה uma'ase יָדֵינוּ yadenu כּוֹנְנָה konena עָלֵינוּ alenu

וּמַעֲשֵׂה uma'ase יָדֵינוּ yadenu כּוֹנְנֵהוּ konenehu׃

פָּתַח patach אֵלִיָּהוּ Eliyahu ע"ב קס"א, לכב הַנָּבִיא hanavi, זָכוּר zachur

לְטוֹב letov (סוד המעלכת העשפע מן ד' עצמות ליסוד הנקרא זכור) יהי אור ע"ה והו ;

וְאָמַר ve'amar׃ זכור לטוב = בוזר"ך, סנדלפון, ערי ; אליהו הנביא זכור לטוב = ת' כנגד ת' כוחות הס"א

רִבּוֹן ribon יהוה ע"ב ס"ג מ"ה ב"ן עָלְמִין almin דְּאַנְתְּ de'ant הוּא hu וְחָד chad

וְלָא vela בְּחֻשְׁבָּן bechushban, אַנְתְּ ant הוּא hu עִלָּאָה ila'a עַל al כָּל kol

עַל al סְתִימָא setima סְתִימָאָ setima עלמם ; ילי עִלָּאִין ila'in, עמם ; עָל al כָּל kol ילי ; עמם סְתִימִין setimin,

לֵית let מַחֲשָׁבָה machashava תְּפִיסָא tefisa בָּךְ bach כְּלָל kelal ▪ אַנְתְּ ant

הוּא hu דְּאַפֵּקְתְּ de'apakt עֶשֶׂר eser תִּקּוּנִין tikunin, וְקָרֵינָן vekarenan

לוֹן lon עֶשֶׂר eser סְפִירָן sefiran, לְאַנְהָגָא le'anhaga בְּהוֹן behon

עָלְמִין almin סְתִימִין setimin דְּלָא dela אִתְגַּלְיָן itgalyan וְעָלְמִין ve'almin

דְּאִתְגַּלְיָן de'itgalyan ▪ וּבְהוֹן uv'hon אִתְכַּסִּיאַת itkasi'at מִבְּנֵי mibenei

נָשָׁא nasha ▪ וְאַנְתְּ ve'ant הוּא hu דְּקָשִׁיר dekashir לוֹן lon וּמְיַחֵד umyached

לוֹן lon ▪ וּבְגִין uvgin דְּאַנְתְּ de'ant מִלְגָּאו milgav כָּל kol ילי מַאן man

דְּאַפְרִישׁ de'afrish וְחָד chad מִן min וְחַבְרֵיהּ chavrei מֵאִלֵּין me'ilen

עֶשֶׂר eser, אִתְחֲשִׁיב itchashiv לֵיהּ lei כְּאִלּוּ ke'ilu אַפְרִישׁ afrish בָּךְ bach ▪

PETICHAT ELIYAHU HANAVI

"And may the pleasantness of the Lord, our God, be upon us and may He establish the workof of our hands for us and may the work of our hands establish Him" (Psalms 90:17). Elijah opened, saying: Master of the worlds, You are One without enumeration. You are above all high ones, the most concealed of all. No thought can grasp You at all. You are the one that produced the Ten Emanations. And we named them Ten Sefirot, to conduct with them obscure worlds that are not revealed, and revealed worlds. And through them, You are screened from human beings. And You are the One who connects them and unites them. And because you are from within, thus, anyone who separates these ten one from the other, to give dominance to that one alone, it is considered for him, as if he separates in You.

וְאִלֵּין (ve'ilen) עֶשֶׂר (eser) סְפִירָן (sefiran) אִינוּן (inun) אַזְלִין (azlin)

כְּסִדְרָן (kesidran), חַד (chad) וְחַד (vechad) אֲרִיךְ (arich), וְחַד (vechad) קָצֵר (katzer),

וְחַד (vechad) בֵּינוֹנִי (benoni). וְאַנְתְּ (ve'ant) הוּא (hu) דְּאַנְהִיג (de'anhig) לוֹן (lon),

וְלֵית (velet) מָאן (man) דְּאַנְהִיג (de'anhig) לָךְ (lach). לָא (la) לְעֵילָא (le'ela),

וְלָא (vela) לְתַתָּא (letata), וְלָא (vela) מִכָּל (mikol) ילי סִטְרָא (sitra).

לְבוּשִׁין (levushin) תַּקָּנַת (takant) לוֹן (lon), דְּמִנַּיְהוּ (deminayhu) פַּרְחִין (farchin)

נִשְׁמָתִין (nishmatin) לִבְנֵי (livnei) נָשָׁא (nasha). וְכַמָּה (vechama) גּוּפִין (gufin)

תַּקָּנַת (takant) לוֹן (lon), דְּאִתְקְרִיאוּ (de'itkeri'u) גּוּפָא (gufa) לְגַבֵּי (legabei)

לְבוּשִׁין (levushin) דִּמְכַסְיָן (dim'chasyan) עֲלֵיהוֹן (alehon). וְאִתְקְרִיאוּ (ve'itkeri'u)

בְּתִקּוּנָא (betikuna) דָא (da), חֶסֶד (Chesed) ע"ב, ריבוע יהוה דְּרוֹעָא (dero'a)

יְמִינָא (yemina), גְּבוּרָה (Gevurah) רי"ו דְּרוֹעָא (dero'a) שְׂמָאלָא (semala),

תִּפְאֶרֶת (Tiferet) גּוּפָא (gufa), נֶצַח (Netzach) וְהוֹד (veHod) ההה תְּרֵין (teren)

שׁוֹקִין (shokin), יְסוֹד (Yesod) ההע סִיּוּמָא (siyuma) דְּגוּפָא (degufa) אוֹת (ot)

בְּרִית (berit) קֹדֶשׁ (kodesh). מַלְכוּת (Malchut) פֶּה (pe) מילה ; וע"ה אלהים, ואהיה אדני בְּרִית (berit)

תּוֹרָה (torah) שֶׁבְּעַל (shebe'al) פֶּה (pe) מילה ; וע"ה אלהים, אהיה אדני קָרֵינָן (karenan)

וְחָכְמָה (Chochmah) במילוי = תרי"ג (מצוות) לַהּ (la). מוֹחָא (mocha), אִיהוּ (ihu)

מַחֲשָׁבָה (mach'shava) מִלְגָּאו (milgav), בִּינָה (Binah) ע"ה וזיים, אהיה אהיה יהוה

לִבָּא (liba) וּבָהּ (uva) הַלֵּב (halev) מֵבִין (mevin) וְעַל (ve'al) אִלֵּין (ilen) תְּרֵין (teren)

כְּתִיב (ketiv): הַנִּסְתָּרֹת (hanistarot) לַיהֹוָה (ladonai) אֱלֹהֵינוּ (Elohenu) יל"ה

And these Ten Sefirot follow their order, the one is long, and one, is short. And the one is average. And You conduct them, and there is no other who will lead You, neither Above, nor Below, nor in any other side. You prepared garments, from which the Neshamot fly to the human beings and you prepared several bodies. And they are named bodies in relation to the clothing, in which they are attired. The Sefirot are named by this emendation, Chesed being the right arm, Gevurah being the left arm. Tiferet means the body. Netzach and Hod, the two thighs, Yesod the final part of the body, the sign of the Holy Covenant, Malchut, the mouth, we call it the Oral Torah. Chochmah is the brain, the thought within. Binah is the heart, and through it, the heart understands. And about these two, it is written, "The secret things belong to the Lord our God" (Deuteronomy 29:28).

כֶּתֶר Keter יהוה מלך יהוה מלך יהוה ימלוך לעולם ועד (באתב"ש ע גאל) עֶלְיוֹן elyon, אִיהוּ ihu

כֶּתֶר keter יהוה מלך יהוה מלך יהוה ימלוך לעולם ועד (באתב"ש ע גאל) מַלְכוּת malchut◆

וַעֲלֵיה ve'alei מֵרֵאשִׁית mereshit מַגִּיד magid אַתְמַר itmar: פהל ve'alei

אַחֲרִית acharit◆ וְאִיהוּ ve'ihu קַרְקַפְתָּא karkafta דִּתְפִלֵּי ditfilei◆

מִלְּגָאו milgav אִיהוּ ihu אוֹת ot יו"ד Yud וְאוֹת ve'ot ה"א He ה"א He וְאוֹת ve'ot

וָא"ו Vav וְאוֹת ve'ot ה"א He, דְּאִיהוּ de'ihu אֹרַח orach אֲצִילוּת atzilut,

אִיהוּ ihu שַׁקְיוּ shakyu דְּאִילָנָא de'ilana בִּדְרוֹעֵי bidro'oy וְעַנְפוֹי ve'anpoy,

כְּמַיָּא kemaya דְּאַשְׁקֵי de'ashkei לְאִילָנָא le'ilana וְאִתְרַבֵּי ve'itrabei

בְּהַהוּא behahu שַׁקְיוּ shakyu◆ רִבּוֹן ribon יהוה ע"ב ס"ג מ"ה ב"ן עָלְמִין almin,

אַנְתְּ ant הוּא hu עִלַּת ilat הָעִלּוֹת ha'ilot, וְסִבַּת vesibat הַסִּבּוֹת hasibot,

דְּאַשְׁקֵי de'ashkei לְאִילָנָא le'ilana בְּהַהוּא behahu נְבִיעוּ nevi'u,

וְהַהוּא vehahu נְבִיעוּ nevi'u אִיהוּ ihu כְּנִשְׁמְתָא kenishmeta לְגוּפָא legufa,

דְּאִיהִי de'ihi וְחַיִּים chayim אהיה אהיה יהוה, בינה ע"ה לְגוּפָא legufa◆ וּבָךְ uvach

לֵית let דִּמְיוֹן dimyon, וְלֵית velet דִּיּוּקְנָא diyukna, מִכָּל mikol ילי

מַה ma מ"ה דִּלְגָאו dilgav וּלְבַר ulvar◆ וּבְרֵאת uvarata שְׁמַיָּא shemaya

וְאַרְעָא ve'ar'a, וְאַפֵּקְת ve'apakt מִנְּהוֹן minehon שִׁמְשָׁא shimsha

וְסִיהֲרָא vesihara וְכֹכְבַיָּא vechochvaya וּמַזָּלֵי umazalei◆ וּבְאַרְעָא uve'ar'a,

אִילָנִין ilanin וּדְשָׁאִין udsha'in וְגִנְּתָא veginta דְּעֵדֶן de'eden וְעִשְׂבִּין ve'isbin

וְחֵיוָן vechevan וְנוּנִין venunin וְעוֹפִין ve'ofin וּבְעִירִין uv'irin וּבְנֵי uvnei

נָשָׁא nasha◆ לְאִשְׁתְּמוֹדְעָא le'ishtemode'a בְּהוֹן behon עִלָּאִין ila'in,

וְאֵיךְ ve'ech יִתְנַהֲגוּן yitnahagun בְּהוֹן behon עִלָּאִין ila'in וְתַתָּאִין vetata'in◆

The Supernal Keter is the Crown of Malchut. And about this is said, "Declaring the end from the beginning" (Isaiah 46:10). And that is the skull of the Tefilin. Within is Yud-Vav-Dalet, Hei-Alef, Vav-Alef-Vav, Hei-Alef, which is in the path of Atzilut. It is the watering of the tree in its arms and branches, as waters that water that tree and it multiplies by this watering. Master of the Worlds, You are the Cause of all Causes, and the Reason for all Reasons, that waters the tree by that stream, and that spring is like a soul to the body, that is the life of the body. And to Yourself there is no likeness nor form inside or outside. And You created Heavens and Earth and produced from them sun and moon and stars and constellations. And in the earth, trees and grasses, and the Garden of Eden, and plants, and animals and fowl and fish and human beings, through them to acknowledge the high ones, and how the higher and lower ones behave.

וְאֵיךְ ve'ech אַשְׁתְּמוֹדְעָן ishtemode'an מֵעִלָּאֵי me'ila'ei וְתַתָּאֵי vetata'ei♦

וְלֵית velet דְּיָדַע deyada בָּךְ bach כְּלָל kelal, וּבַר uvar [יצחק, ד"פ ב"ן]

מִנָּךְ minach לֵית let יְחוּדָא yichuda בְּעִלָּאֵי be'ila'ei וְתַתָּאֵי vetata'ei,

וְאַנְתְּ ve'ant אִשְׁתְּמוֹדְעָ ishtemoda אֲדוֹן adon [אני] עַל al כֹּלָּא kola♦

וְכָל vechol סְפִירָן sefiran [יל], כָּל kol [יל וזד] חַד chad אִית it לֵיהּ lei שֵׁם shem

יְדִיעַ yedi'a, וּבְהוֹן uvhon אִתְקְרִיאוּ itkeri'u מַלְאֲכַיָּא mal'achaya♦

וְאַנְתְּ ve'ant לֵית let לָךְ lach שֵׁם shem יְדִיעַ yedi'a, דְּאַנְתְּ de'ant הוּא hu

מְמַלֵּא memale כָּל kol [יל] שְׁמָהָן shemahan, וְאַנְתְּ ve'ant הוּא hu

שְׁלִימוּ shelimu דְּכֻלְּהוּ dechulhu, וְכַד vechad אַנְתְּ ant תִּסְתַּלַּק tistalak

מִנְּהוֹן minehon אִשְׁתְּאָרוּ ishte'aru כֻּלְּהוּ kulehu שְׁמָהָן shemahan

כְּגוּפָא kegufa בְּלָא bela נִשְׁמָתָא nishmata♦ אַנְתְּ ant וְזַכִּים chakim

וְלָאו velav בְּחָכְמָה beChochmah [במילוי = תרי"ג (מצוות)] יְדִיעָא yedi'a♦ אַנְתְּ ant

הוּא hu מֵבִין mevin, וְלָאו velav מִבִּינָה miBinah [ע"ה וזיים, אהיה יהוה אהיה אהיה]

יְדִיעָא yedi'a♦ לֵית let לָךְ lach אֲתַר atar יְדִיעָא yedi'a♦

אֶלָּא ela לְאִשְׁתְּמוֹדְעָא le'ishtemode'a תֻּקְפָּךְ tukfach וְוֵזָךְ vechelach

לִבְנֵי livnei נָשָׁא nasha, וּלְאַחֲזָאָה ule'achza'a לוֹן lon, אֵיךְ ech

אִתְנְהִיג itnehig עָלְמָא alma בְּדִינָא vedina וּבְרַחֲמֵי uvrachamei,

דְּאִינוּן de'inun צֶדֶק tzedek וּמִשְׁפָּט umishpat [ע"ה ה"פ אלהים]

כְּפוּם kefum עוֹבְדֵיהוֹן ovadehon דִּבְנֵי divnei נָשָׁא nasha♦

And how the lower ones recognize to attain from the higher ones; and in you, there is absolutely nobody who is knowledgeable. And besides your unification, there is no such unique unity in the Upper and Lower ones, and You are recognized as the Master over all. Each of the Sefirot has a recognizable name, of its own. And by them the angels are named. Yet you have no known name, You are He, who fills all the names. And it is You who completes them all. And when You are gone from them, all the names remain as body without a soul. You are wise, but not with known wisdom. You understand, but not with any known understanding. And You do not occupy any known place so that human beings should perceive His strength and might and to show them how the world conducted with justice and mercy that are righteousness and just trial, according to the deeds of the lower ones.

דִּין din, אִיהוּ ihu, גְּבוּרָה gevurah רי"ו, מִשְׁפָּט mishpat ע"ה ה"פ אלהים

עַמּוּדָא amuda, מַלְכוּתָא malchuta, צֶדֶק tzedek, דְּאֶמְצָעִיתָא de'emtza'ita

קַדִּישָׁא kadisha, מֹאזְנֵי moznei, צֶדֶק tzedek, תְּרֵין teren, סַמְכֵי samchei

קְשׁוֹט keshot, הִין hin, צֶדֶק tzedek, אוֹת ot, בְּרִית berit, כֹּלָּא kula

לְאַחֲזָאָה le'achza'a, אֵיךְ ech, אִתְנְהִיג itnehig, עָלְמָא alma, אֲבָל aval

לָאו lav, דְּאִית de'it, לָךְ lach, צֶדֶק tzedek, יְדִיעָא yedi'a, דְּאִיהוּ de'ihu

דִּין din, מִשְׁפָּט mishpat ע"ה ה"פ אלהים, יְדִיעָא yedi'a, וְלָאו velav, דְּאִיהוּ de'ihu

רַחֲמֵי rachamei, וְלָאו velav, מִכֹּל mikol ילי, אִלֵּין ilen, מִדּוֹת midot

כְּלָל kelal, קוּם kum, רִבִּי Ribi, שִׁמְעוֹן Shimon, וְיִתְחַדְּשׁוּן veyitchadeshun

מִלִּין milin, עַל al, דְּהָא deha, יְדָךְ yedach, אִית it, לָךְ lach

לְגַלָּאָה legala'a, רָזִין razin, טְמִירִין temirin, עַל al, יְדָךְ yedach, מַה ma מ"ה

דְּלָא dela, אִתְיְהִיב ityehiv, רְשׁוּ reshu, לְגַלָּאָה legala'a, לְשׁוּם leshum

בַּר bar, נָשׁ nash, עַד ad, כְּעַן ke'an, קָם kam, רִבִּי Ribi, שִׁמְעוֹן Shim'on,

פָּתַח patach, וְאָמַר ve'amar, לְךְ lecha, יְהֹוָה Adonai, הַגְּדֻלָּה haGedula

וְהַגְּבוּרָה vehaGevurah רי"ו, וְהַתִּפְאֶרֶת vehaTiferet, וְהַנֵּצַח vehaNetzach

וְהַהוֹד vehaHod ההה, כִּי ki, כֹל chol ילי, בַּשָּׁמַיִם bashamayim י"פ טל, י"פ כוזו

וּבָאָרֶץ uva'aretz, לְךְ lecha, יְהֹוָה Adonai, הַמַּמְלָכָה hamamlacha

וְגוֹ' vegomer, (On chol Hamo'ed you should give here three coins to charity), עִלָּאִין ila'in

שִׁמְעוּ shema'u, אִינוּן inun, דְּמִיכִין demichin, דְּחֶבְרוֹן deChevron

וְרַעְיָא veRaya, מְהֵימְנָא Mehemna, אִתְעָרוּ it'aru, מִשֵּׁנַתְכוֹן mishenatchon

---

Judgement is Gevurah, judicial trial is the Central Column, Righteousness—the Holy Malchut; just scales are two supports of truth. A truly measured hin is this sign of the covenant of Yesod. All to show the leadership of the world, but it is not as if there is certain justice that is strictly judgmental, and not a certain just trial that is strictly of mercy, and or of any of these attributes, at all. Rise, Rabbi Shimon and let new ideas come through you, as you have permission, that through you obscure mysteries will be revealed, because permission was not granted to any person until now to reveal them. Rabbi Shimon rose, opened and said, "Yours, Lord, is the greatness, and the power..." (I Chronicles 29:11). Listen, Supreme Ones, they who rest in Chevron, and the Faithful Shepherd, be shaken off from your sleep.

hakitzu הָקִיצוּ veranenu וְרַנְּנוּ shochnei שֹׁכְנֵי afar עָפָר, ilen אֵלִין inun אִנּוּן

tzadikaya צַדִּיקַיָא, de'inun דְּאִנּוּן misitra מִסִּטְרָא dehahu דְּהַהוּא

de'itmar דְּאִתְּמַר ba בָּהּ: ani אֲנִי yeshena יְשֵׁנָה velibi וְלִבִּי er עֵר,

velav וְלָאו inun אִנּוּן metim מֵתִים, uvgin וּבְגִין da דָא

itmar אִתְּמַר vehon בְּהוֹן hakitzu הָקִיצוּ veranenu וְרַנְּנוּ vegomer וְגוֹ'

Raya רַעְיָא Mehemna מְהֵימְנָא, ant אַנְתְּ va'avahan וַאֲבָהָן, hakitzu הָקִיצוּ

veranenu וְרַנְּנוּ le'it'aruta לְאִתְעָרוּתָא dish'chinta דִּשְׁכִינְתָּא de'ihi דְּאִיהִי

yeshena יְשֵׁנָה vegaluta בְּגָלוּתָא. de'ad דְּעַד ke'an כְּעַן tzadikaya צַדִּיקַיָא

kulhu כֻּלְּהוּ demichin דְּמִיכִין veshinta וְשִׁנְתָּא vechorehon בְּחוֹרֵיהוֹן.

miyad מִיָּד yahivat יְהִיבַת shechinta שְׁכִינְתָּא telat תְּלַת kalin קָלִין

legabei לְגַבֵּי Raya רַעְיָא Meheimna מְהֵימְנָא veyima וְיֵימָא lei לֵיהּ

kum קוּם Raya רַעְיָא Mehemna מְהֵימְנָא, deha דְּהָא alach עֲלָךְ

itmar אִתְּמַר kol קוֹל | dodi דּוֹדִי dofek דוֹפֵק מנק legabai לְגַבַּאי,

be'arba בְּאַרְבַּע atvan אַתְוָן dilei דִּילֵיהּ. veyima וְיֵימָא vehon בְּהוֹן

pitchi פִּתְחִי li לִי achoti אֲחוֹתִי rayati רַעְיָתִי yonati יוֹנָתִי tamati תַמָּתִי.

deha דְּהָא tam תַּם avonech עֲוֹנֵךְ bat בַּת Tziyon צִיּוֹן יוסף, ר' הויות, קנאה

lo לֹא yosif יוֹסִיף lehaglotech לְהַגְלוֹתֵךְ. sheroshi שְׂרֹאשִׁי nimla נִמְלָא

tal טָל nimla נִמְלָא mai מַאי כוזו, או, וא, הא יוד tal טָל יוד הא ואו, כוזו.

"Awake and sing, you, that dwell in dust" (Isaiah 26:19). It is those righteous that are from this aspect about which is said, *"I sleep, but my heart wakes"* (Song of Songs 5:2). And they are not dead, therefore it says about them, *"Awake and sing..."* Faithful Shepherd, you and the Patriarchs, awake and sing to the waking of the Shechinah that sleeps in exile, as up to now all the righteous are sleeping, and the sleep is in the caverns. Instantly, the Shechinah emits three sounds towards the Faithful Shepherd, and says to him 'Rise, faithful Shepherd. As about you it was said, *"hark, my beloved is knocking"* (Ibid.) by me, with His four letters. And he will say with them, *"Open to me, my sister, my love, my dove, my undefiled"* (Ibid.). Since, *"The punishment of your iniquity is accomplished, daughter of Zion; he will no more carry you away into exile"* (Lamentations 4:22). *"For my head is filled with dew"* (Song of Songs 5:2). He asks, 'What is that which means 'Filled with dew'?

אֶלָּא ela, אָמַר amar, קֻדְשָׁא kudsha, בְּרִיךְ berich, הוּא ,hu

אַנְתְּ ant, וְחָשַׁבְתְּ chashavt, דְּמִיּוֹמָא demiyoma, דְּאִתְחָרַב de'itcharav

בֵּי bei, מַקְדְּשָׁא makdesha, דְּעָאלְנָא de'alna, בְּבֵיתָא beveta, דִּילִי dili

וְעָאלְנָא ve'alna, בְּיִשּׁוּבָא veyishuva, לָאו lav, הָכִי ,hachi, דְּלָא dela

עָאלְנָא alna, כָּל kol, יְלִי, זִמְנָא zimna, דְּאַנְתְּ de'ant, בְּגָלוּתָא ,begaluta

הֲרֵי harei, לָךְ lach, סִימָנָא simana, שֶׁרָאשִׁי sheroshi, נִמְלָא nimla

טַל tal, יוד הא ואו, כווו He א"הֵ, שְׁכִינְתָּא shechinta, בְּגָלוּתָא ,begaluta

שְׁלִימוּ shelimu, דִּילָהּ dila, וְחַיִּים vechayim אהיה אהיה יהוה, בינה ע"ה אדנה, דִּילָהּ ,dila

אִיהוּ ihu, טַל tal יוד הא ואו, כווו, וְדָא veda, אִיהוּ ihu, אוֹת ot, יוֹ"ד Yod

וְאוֹת ve'ot, הֵ"א He, וְאוֹת ve'ot, וָא"ו Vav, וְאוֹת ve'ot, הֵ"א He, אִיהִי ihi

שְׁכִינְתָּא shechinta, דְּלָא dela, מְחֻשְׁבַּן mechushban, טַ"ל tal יוד הא ואו, כווו

אֶלָּא ela, יוֹ"ד Yod, הֵ"א He, וָא"ו ,Vav, דְּסַלְּיקוּ disliku, אַתְוָן atvan

לְחֻשְׁבַּן lechushban, טַ"ל tal יוד הא ואו, כווו, דְּאִיהוּ de'ihu, מַלְיָא malya

לִשְׁכִינְתָּא ,lishchinta, מִנְבִּיעוּ minevi'u, דְּכֹל dechol יְלִי, מְקוֹרִין mekorin

עִלָּאִין ,ilai'n, מִיָּד miyad, קָם kam, רַעְיָא Raya, מְהֵימְנָא ,Mehemna

וַאֲבָהָן va'avahan, קַדִּישִׁין kadishin, עִמֵּיהּ imei, עַד ad, כָּאן kan, רָזָא raza

דְּיִחוּדָא ,deyichuda, בָּרוּךְ baruch, יְהֹוָה Adonai, לְעוֹלָם le'olam

אָמֵן amen, וְאָמֵן ve'amen רִיבּוֹעַ דְּס"ג ו' אוֹתִיּוֹת דְּס"ג ; ר"ת לאוּ:

But the Holy One, blessed be He, said, You think that from the day of the Temple's destruction, I entered My own abode, and I entered the settlement? Not so, as I have not entered as you are in exile. And here is your proof, "For my head is filled with dew". Hei-Alef is the Shechinah, and she is in exile. Her perfection, and her life is dew (Heb. tal = 39), and that is Yud-Vav-Dalet, Hei-Alef, Vav-Alef-Vav numerically tal (= 39). And the Hei-Alef, the Shechinah, was not in the reckoning of tal, only the Yud-Vav-Dalet, Hei-Alef, Vav-Alef-Vav, which amount to tal. And it is He, who fills the Shechinah from the fountain of all the Supernal Sources. The Faithful Shepherd immediately rose up, and the holy Patriarchs with him. Up to here the mysteries of unification. "Blessed be the Lord forever, Amen and Amen!" (Psalms 89:53)

וִיהֵא רַעֲוָא מִן קֳדָם עַתִּיקָא
veyehe ra'ava min kodam atika

קַדִּישָׁא דְּכָל ילי קַדִּישִׁין טְמִירָא
kadisha dechol kadishin temira

דְּכָל ילי טְמִירִין סְתִימָא דְּכֹלָּא,
dechol temirin setima dechola,

דְּיִתְמְשַׁח טַלָּא עִלָּאָה מִנֵּיהּ לְמַלְיָא
deyitmeshach tala ila'a minei lemalya

רֵישֵׁיהּ דִּזְעֵיר אַנְפִּין וּלְהַטִּיל לַחֲקַל
reshei dize'ir anpin ulehatil lachakal

תַּפּוּחִין קַדִּישִׁין (שמו של מט"ט) אהיה יהוה יהוה אדני, מנוזם
tapuchin kadishin

בִּנְהִירוּ דְּאַנְפִּין בְּרַעֲוָא וּבְחֶדְוָתָא
binhiru de'anpin bera'ava ubchedvata

דְּכֹלָּא. וְיִתְמְשַׁח מִן קֳדָם עַתִּיקָא
dechola. veyitmeshach min kodam atika

קַדִּישָׁא דְּכָל ילי קַדִּישִׁין טְמִירָא
kadisha dechol kadishin temira

דְּכָל ילי טְמִירִין סְתִימָא דְּכֹלָּא.
dechol temirin setima dechola.

רְעוּתָא וְרַחֲמֵי וְחִנָּא וְחִסְדָּא
re'uta verachamei china vechisda

בִּנְהִירוּ עִלָּאָה בִּרְעוּתָא וְחֶדְוָה
binhiru ila'a bire'uta vechedva

עֲלַי וְעַל ב"פ ראה veti בֵּיתִי benei בְּנֵי עמם ; ילי kol כָּל ve'al alai
alai ve'al kol benei veti ve'al

כָּל ילי kol ; עמם בְּנֵי Yisrael יִשְׂרָאֵל עַמֵּיהּ amei. וְיִפָרְקִנָן
kol benei Yisrael amei. veyifrekinan

מִכָּל mikol ילי עֲקָתִין aktin בִּישִׁין bishin דְּיֵיתוּן deyetun לְעָלְמָא le'alma.
mikol aktin bishin deyetun le'alma.

וְיַזְמִין veyazmin וְיִתְיְהִיב veyityehiv לָנָא lana וּלְכָל ulchol יה ארני
veyazmin veyityehiv lana ulchol

נַפְשָׁתָנָא nafshatana חִנָּא china וְחִסְדָּא vechisda וְחַיֵּי vechayei
nafshatana china vechisda vechayei

אֲרִיכֵי arichei וּמְזוֹנֵי umzonei רְוִיחֵי revichei וְרַחֲמֵי verachamei מִן min
arichei umzonei revichei verachamei min

קֳדָמֵיהּ kodamei. אָמֵן יאהדונהי amen כֵּן ken יְהִי yehi רָצוֹן ratzon
kodamei. amen ken yehi ratzon

אָמֵן יאהדונהי amen וְאָמֵן יאהדונהי ve'amen מוהע ע"ה, ע"ב ברבוע וקס"א ע"ה, אל שדי ע"ה
amen ve'amen

And may it be pleasing before the Holy of Holiest Atika, the hidden of all and the most concealed, that a Supernal Dew will be drawn from him to fulfill the head of Zeir Anpin, and to drop to Chakal Tapuchin Kadishin from this shining face with desire and happiness for all. And also will be drawn from the Holy of Holiest Atika, the hidden of all and the most concealed willingly, mercy, grace, kindness, with supernal illumination with desire and happiness, for me and for my household, and for all of Your people, Israel. And he will save us from all negative incidents that exist in our world. And he will bring and give us and all the rest of the people, grace and kindness, long life and sustenance, welfare and mercy from before him. Amen shall it be. Amen and Amen.

יְדִיד yedid   נֶפֶשׁ nefesh   אָב av   הָרַחֲמָן harachaman ◆   מְשׁוֹךְ meshoch

עַבְדָּךְ avdach   פוי, אל אדני el   אֶל ◆   רְצוֹנָךְ retzonach ◆   יָרוּץ yarutz

עַבְדָּךְ avdach   פוי, אל אדני kemo   כְּמוֹ kemo   אַיָּל ayal ◆   יִשְׁתַּחֲוֶה yishtachave   אֵל el

הֲדָרָךְ hadarach   ב"פ יבק, ס"ג קס"א◆   מוּל mul   לוֹ lo   יֶעֱרַב ye'erav

יְדִידוּתָךְ yedidutach   ר"ת ילי◆   מִנּוֹפֶת minofet   צוּף tzuf   וְכָל vechol   טָעַם: ta'am

הָדוּר hadur   נָאֶה na'e   זִיו ziv   הָעוֹלָם ha'olam ◆   נַפְשִׁי nafshi

חוֹלַת cholat   אַהֲבָתָךְ ahavatach ◆   אָנָּא ana   ב"ן   אֵל El   (מילוי דס"ג) יא"י

נָא na   רְפָא refa   נָא na   לָהּ la   ◆ (11-Letter Name for healing)

בְּהַרְאוֹת behar'ot   לָהּ la   נֹעַם no'am   זִיוָךְ zivach ◆   אָז az   תִּתְחַזֵּק titchazek

וְתִתְרַפֵּא vetitrape ◆   וְהָיְתָה vehayta   לָהּ la   שִׂמְחַת simchat   עוֹלָם olam:

וָתִיק vatik   יֶהֱמוּ yehemu   רַחֲמֶיךָ rachamecha ◆   וְחוּסָה vechusa

נָא na   עַל al   בֵּן ben   אֲהוּבָךְ ahuvach ◆   כִּי ki   זֶה ze

כַּמָּה chame   נִכְסוֹף nichsof   נִכְסַף nichsaf ◆   לִרְאוֹת lir'ot

בְּתִפְאָרֶת betiferet   עֻזָּךְ uzach ◆   אָנָּא ana   ב"ן   אֵלִי Eli   וְחֶמְדַּת chemdat

לִבִּי libi ◆   וְחוּסָה chusha   נָא na   וְאַל ve'al   תִּתְעַלָּם: tit'alam

הִגָּלֶה higale   נָא na   וּפְרוֹשׂ ufros   חָבִיב chaviv הוּ ◆   עָלַי alai   אֵת et   סֻכַּת sukat

שְׁלוֹמָךְ shelomach ◆   תָּאִיר ta'ir   אֶרֶץ eretz   מִכְּבוֹדָךְ mikevodach   ב"ן, לכב ◆

נָגִילָה nagila   וְנִשְׂמְחָה venismecha   בָּךְ vach ◆   מַהֵר maher   אָהוּב ahuv

כִּי ki   בָא va   מוֹעֵד mo'ed ◆   וְחָנֵּנוּ vechonenu   כִּימֵי kimei   עוֹלָם olam:

ᵃ Beloved of the soul, Compassionate Father, draw Your servant to Your desire. Your servant will run like a hart, he will bow before Your majesty. Your friendship will be sweeter than the dripping of the honeycomb and any taste. ה Majestic, Beautiful, Radiance of the world, my soul pines for Your love. Please, God, heal her, by showing her the pleasantness of Your radiance. Then she will be strengthened and healed, and she will have the gladness of the world. ו All Worthy One, may Your mercy be aroused and please take pity on the sons of Your beloved, because it is so very long that I have yearned intensely, speedily to see the splendor of Your strength. Only these my heart desired, so please take pity and do not conceal Yourself. ה Reveal and spread upon me, my Beloved, the shelter of Your peace. Illuminate the world with Your glory that we may rejoice and be glad with You. Hasten, show love, for time has come, and show us grace as in day of old.

LeShem Yichud

לְשֵׁם יִחוּד קוּדְשָׁא בְּרִיךְ הוּא

וּשְׁכִינְתֵּיה (יאהדונהי) בִּדְחִילוּ וּרְחִימוּ

וּרְחִימוּ וּדְחִילוּ (איההיוהה), לְיַחֲדָא (יאההויהה)

שֵׁם יוּ"ד קֵי בְּוָא"ו קֵי בְּיִחוּדָא

שָׁלִים (יהוה) בְּשֵׁם כָּל יִשְׂרָאֵל,

הֲרֵינִי מְקַבֵּל עָלַי אֱלָהוּתוֹ יִתְבָּרֵךְ

וְיִרְאָתוֹ וְאַהֲבָתוֹ וְהִנְנִי עֶבֶד

לְהַשֵּׁם יִתְבָּרֵךְ, וְהֲרֵינִי מְקַיֵּם

מִצְוַת וְאָהַבְתָּ ב"פ אור, ב"פ רו, ב"פ א"ס לְרֵעֲךָ

כָּמוֹךָ וַהֲרֵינִי אוֹהֵב אֶת כָּל אָדָם

מִיִשְׂרָאֵל כְּנַפְשִׁי, וַהֲרֵינִי מְכַוֵּן

לְקַיֵּם מִצְוַת צִיצִית וּמִצְוַת תַּלְמוּד

תּוֹרָה, וַהֲרֵינִי מְכַוֵּן לְקַיֵּם

מִצְוַת קְרִיאַת שְׁמַע וּתְפִלַּת שַׁחֲרִית,

הֵם וְהַמִּצְוֹת הַנִּלְוֹת וְהַכְּלוּלוֹת

בָּהֶם, וַאֲנִי אני מְכַוֵּן בְּכֹל ב"י, לכב

לַעֲשׂוֹת נַחַת רוּחַ לְיוֹצְרֵנוּ שֶׁלֹּא

עַל מְנַת לְקַבֵּל פְּרָס בְּשׁוּם צַד,

וַאֲנִי אני מְכַוֵּן בְּכֹל ב"י, לכב לְדַעַת

רַבִּי שִׁמְעוֹן בֶּן יוֹחַאי הַקָּדוֹשׁ,

LeShem Yichud

For the sake of the unification between the Holy Blessed One and His Shechinah, with fear and love and with love and fear, in order to unify the Name Yud-Kei and Vav-Kei in perfect unity, and in the name of all Israel, I hereby accept upon myself His Divinity, blessed be He, and the love of Him and the fear of Him, and I hereby declare myself a servant to God blessed be He. And I hereby accept upon myself the obligatory commandment of "Love your fellow as you do yourself." And I hereby declare that I love each one of Israel with my soul. And I am hereby prepared to fulfill the obligatory precept of wearing the Tzitzit, Studying Torah. And I am hereby prepared to fulfill the obligatory precept of the Shema and the prayer of Shacharit and all the precepts that are concerned with it. And I meditate to bring satisfaction to our maker, not for the sake of receiving any prize. And all my intention is according to the holy Rabbi Shimon bar Yochai.

וְהֲרֵינִי vehareni מְקַבֵּל mekabel עָלַי alai כָּל kol יל״י תרי״ג taryag

מִצְוֹת mitzvot דְּאוֹרַיְיתָא de'orayta וּמִצְוֹת umitzvot דְּרַבָּנָן derabanan

הֵם hem וְעַנְפֵיהֶם ve'anfehem ♦ וְאַתָּה veAta הָאֵל haEl לאה ; יא״י (מילוי דס״ג)

הַטּוֹב hatov והו בְּרוֹב berov י״פ אהיה רַחֲמֶיךָ rachamecha

תַּצִּילֵנוּ tatzilenu מִיֵּצֶר miyetzer הָרָע hara וּתְזַכֵּנוּ ut'zakenu

לְעָבְדֶךָ le'ovdecha בֶּאֱמֶת be'emet פו', אל אדני אהיה פעמים אהיה, ז״פ ס״ג

אָמֵן amen יאהדונהי כֵּן ken יְהִי yehi רָצוֹן ratzon מהטע ע״ה, ע״ב בריבוע וקס״א ע״ה,

וִיהִי vihi נֹעַם no'am אֲדֹנָי Adonai ללה אֱלֹהֵינוּ Elohenu ילה אל עדי ע״ה.

עָלֵינוּ alenu וּמַעֲשֵׂה uma'ase יָדֵינוּ yadenu כּוֹנְנָה konena

עָלֵינוּ alenu וּמַעֲשֵׂה uma'ase יָדֵינוּ yadenu כּוֹנְנֵהוּ konenehu:

יְהִי yehi רָצוֹן ratzon מהטע ע״ה, ע״ב בריבוע וקס״א ע״ה, אל עדי ע״ה

מִלְּפָנֶיךָ milfanecha ס״ג מ״ה ב״ן יְהוָֹה Adonai יאהדונהי

אֱלֹהֵינוּ Elohenu ילה וֵאלֹהֵי velohei לכב ; מילוי ע״ב, דמב ; ילה

אֲבוֹתֵינוּ avotenu שֶׁתַּכְנִיעַ shetachni'a כָּל kol יל״י

הַמְקַטְרְגִים hamekatregim וְכֹל vechol יל״י הַקְּלִיפּוֹת hakelipot

הַחִיצוֹנִים hachitzonim הַמְשׁוֹטְטִים hameshotetim בָּעוֹלָם ba'olam

וּמְעַכְּבִים ume'akvim תְּפִלָּתִי tefilati לַעֲלוֹת la'alot לְפָנֶיךָ lefanecha ס״ג מ״ה ב״ן

כִּי ki אַתָּה Ata יוֹדֵעַ yode'a שֶׁרְצוֹנִי shertzoni לַעֲשׂוֹת la'asot

רְצוֹנֶךָ retzoncha, אַךְ ach אהיה שְׂאוֹר se'or שֶׁבְּעִיסָה shebe'isa

מְעַכֵּב me'akev אוֹתִי oti, לְכֵן lachen גְּעוֹר ge'or בָּהֶם bahem שָׁאַל she'al

יְזִיקוּנִי yezikuni וְאַל ve'al יְעַכְּבוּ ye'akvu אֶת et תְּפִלָּתִי tefilati

---

And I hereby accept upon myself all the 613 precepts of the Torah and the sages and its outcomes. And You, the good God, with your mighty mercy will save us from the evil inclination and allow us the privilege of serving you with truth Amen, so may His will be. "May the pleasantness of the Lord, our God, be upon us and may He establish the work of our hands for us and may the work of our hands establish Him." (Psalms 90:17)

May it be pleasing before You, Lord, my God and God of my forefathers, that You would subjugate all the denouncers and the external klipot that exist in the world, and they deferred my prayer to come before You. And You know that my only desire is to follow your desire, but the leaven in the dough deferred me. So castigate them so they would not harm me and they would not defer my prayer,

ve'al וְאַל umkubelet וּמְקוֹבֶּלֶת lefanecha לְפָנֶיךָ ס״ג מ״ה ב״ן יאהדונהי amen אָמֵן ken כֵּן

ve'al וְאַל yishletu יִשְׁלְטוּ bi בִּי lo לֹא begufi בְּגוּפִי velo וְלֹא

benishmati בְּנִשְׁמָתִי, veshetehe וְשֶׁתְהֵא tefilati תְּפִלָּתִי retzuya רְצוּיָה

yehi יְהִי ratzon רָצוֹן מהש״ו ע״ה, ע״ב וקס״א ע״ה, בריבוע אל שדי ע״ה:

hareni הֲרֵינִי mechaven מְכַוֵּין bitfilati בְּתְפִלָּתִי ke'ilu כְּאִלּוּ

ani אֲנִי omed עוֹמֵד birushalayim בִּירוּשָׁלַיִם bevet בְּבֵית ב״פ ראה

hamikdash הַמִּקְדָּשׁ umchaven וּמְכַוֵּין keneged כְּנֶגֶד מזבוח, זן, אל יהוה bet בֵּית

kodesh קֹדֶשׁ hakodashim הַקֳּדָשִׁים kemo כְּמוֹ shene'emar שֶׁנֶּאֱמַר ב״פ ראה:

vehitpalelu וְהִתְפַּלְלוּ el אֶל hamakom הַמָּקוֹם haze הַזֶּה והו:

yehi יְהִי ratzon רָצוֹן מהש״ו ע״ה, ע״ב וקס״א ע״ה, בריבוע אל שדי ע״ה

milfanecha מִלְּפָנֶיךָ ס״ג מ״ה ב״ן Adonai יְהֹוָֹאדֹנָיֹ אהדונהי Elohenu אֱלֹהֵינוּ ילה

velohei וֵאלֹהֵי מילוי ע״ב, דמב ; ילה avotenu אֲבוֹתֵינוּ sheyehe שֶׁיְּהֵא libi לִבִּי

nachon נָכוֹן umasur וּמָסוּר beyadi בְּיָדִי shelo שֶׁלֹּא eshkachecha אֶשְׁכָּחֶךָ:

RIBON ALMA

Rabbi Shimon says in the Zohar, Idra Rabba 303: "The soul of man is taken from the higher levels downward to Malchut. By that, it causes everything to be in single union. Whoever interrupts this union from the world is as if he severs the above mentioned soul, and indicates that another soul exists besides this one. As a result he and his memory will disappear from this world for generations upon generations." Saying "Ribon Alma" before the prayer protects us from doing intellectual mistakes throughout our spiritual work.

ribon רִבּוֹן alma עָלְמָא yehe יְהֵא ra'ava רַעֲוָא kamach קָמָּךְ lemehav לְמֶיהַב

lan כֵּן veziela וְזֵילָא chela חֵילָא le'it'ara לְאִתְעָרָא vikarach בִּיקָרָךְ ulme'ebad וּלְמֶעֱבַד

re'utach רְעוּתָךְ ulesadara וּלְסַדְּרָא chola כֹּלָא kedeka כְּדְקָא ya'ut יָאוּת.

---

and they would not control me, not my body and not my soul.
And my prayer would be accepted by You, Amen, so may His will be.

I hereby meditate in my prayer
as if I am standing in the Temple in Jerusalem, and tuned against the Holy of Holies. As it says: "and they shall pray toward this place" (1 kings 8:35). May it be pleasing before You, Lord, my God and God of my forefathers, that my heart will be founded and devoted by me so I will not forget You.

RIBON ALMA

Master of the World, may it be pleasing before You
to give us strength, to stir ourself to honor You, to do Your will and to put everything in the right direction.

וְאַף al עַל gav גַּב delet דְּלֵית anan אֲנַן yad'in יָדְעִין leshava'a לְשַׁוָּאָה

רְעוּתָא re'uta veliba וְלִבָּא letakana לְתַקָּנָא chola כֹּלָא, yehe יְהֵא ra'ava רַעֲוָא

קָמָךְ kamach detitre'ei דְּתִתְרְעֵי vemilin בְּמִלִּין utzelota וּצְלוֹתָא dilan דִּילָן

לְתַקָּנָא letakana tikuna תִּקּוּנָא dil'ela דִּלְעֵלָּא kideka כִּדְקָא ya'ut יָאוּת

וְלֶהֱוֵי ulehevo hechalin הֵיכָלִין ila'in עִלָּאִין veruchin וְרוּוִזין ila'in עִלָּאִין

עֵילֵי ayle hechala הֵיכָלָא behechala בְּהֵיכָלָא verucha וְרוּוָזא verucha בְּרוּוָזא

עַד ad demitchaberan דְּמִתְווַזבְּרָן beduchtayho בְּדוּכְתֵּיהוֹ kideka כִּדְקָא

וֹזֵי chazei, שִׁיפָא sheyafa besheyafa בְּשִׁיפָא, ve'ishtelimu וְאִשְׁתְּלִימוּ da דָא

בְדָא veda ve'ityachadu וְאִתְיַוֹזֶדוּ da דָא veda בְדָא ad עַד inun אִנּוּן chad וַד,

וְנַהֲרִין venaharin da דָא veda בְדָא. ucheden וּכְדֵין nishmeta נִשְׁמָתָא

לוֹן lon venaher וְנָהֵר mile'ela מִלְעֵלָּא atya אַתְיָא dechola דְּכֹלָא ila'a עִלָּאָה

וְלֶהֱוּוּ velehevu nehirin נְהִירִין kolehu כֻּלְּהוּ vutzinin בּוּצִינִין bishlemu בְּשְׁלִימוּ

כִּדְקָא kideka, chazei וֹזֵי ad עַד dehahu דְּהַהוּא nehora נְהוֹרָא ila'a עִלָּאָה

אִתְּעַר ite'ar, vechola וְכֹלָא a'el אָעֵיל legabei לְגַבֵּי kodesh קֹדֶשׁ

קָדָשִׁים kodashim ve'itbarcha וְאִתְבָּרְכָא ve'itmalya וְאִתְמַלְיָא kevera כְּבֵירָא

דְּמַיִין demayin nav'in נָבְעִין vela וְלָא faskin פָּסְקִין vecholho וְכֻלְּהוּ

מִתְבָּרְכָן mitbarchan le'ela לְעֵלָּא vetata וְתַתָּא. vehahu וְהַהוּא dela דְּלָא

אִתְיְדַע ityeda vela וְלָא a'el אָעֵיל bechushbena בְּוֹשְׁבְּנָא, re'uta רְעוּתָא

דְּלָא dela itpas אִיתְפַּס le'almin לְעָלְמִין, basim בָּסִים lego לְגוֹ lego לְגוֹ

בְּגַוַּיְהוֹ, vela וְלָא ityeda אִתְיְדַע hahu הַהוּא re'uta רְעוּתָא

And although we do not know how to be mindful and to direct our heart, to correct everything, may it be pleasing before You, that our words and prayer will be accepted to correct the Supernal Tikkun in the right direction, so the Supernal Chambers and the Supernal Souls are elevated, one chamber penetrates the other, and one soul the other, until they all rest in their proper places as is suitable. One organ is within the other and one complements the other. The elements merge until they become one and shine within each other. Consequently, this most Supernal Soul descends and shines on them, and all the candles (Sefirot) are becomingly lit in all their perfection, until this Supernal Light is aroused and all the chambers enter the Holy of Holies, and it is blessed and filled like a well of spring water that never ceases to flow, and all the Upper and Lower are blessed. The innermost of secrets that cannot be conceived and is taken account, it is a desire that can never be grasped, is sweetened deep within the Sefirot, and its desire cannot be conceived

re'uta רְעוּתָא kola כֹּלָּא ucheden וּכְדֵין, leminda לְמִנְדַּע itpas אִיתְפַס vela וְלֹא

vishlemu בְּשֵׁלִימוּ ihu אִיהוּ vechola וְכֹלָּא sof סוֹף en אֵין ad עַד chada חֲדָא וְזֵדָּא

kola כֹּלָּא de'it'aved דְּאִתְעֲבֵד ad עַד lego לְגוֹ umigo וּמִגּוֹ miletata מִלְּתָתָא

kola כֹּלָּא ve'ashlem וְאַשְׁלֵם kola כֹּלָּא ve'itmali'a וְאִתְמַלְיָאה chad וְזַד,

ya'ut יָאוּת kideka כִּדְקָא kola כֹּלָּא ve'itbasem וְאִתְבַּסֵּם ve'itnahir וְאִתְנְהֵר.

amach עַמָּך im עִם re'utach רְעוּתָך yehe יְהֵא alma עָלְמָא ribon רִבּוֹן

achazei אֲחֲזֵי yeminach יְמִינָך ufurkan וּפֻרְקָן le'alam לְעָלַם. Yisrael יִשְׂרָאֵל

ule'amtuyei וּלְאַמְטוּיֵי makdeshach מַקְדְּשָׁך bevet בְּבֵית le'amach לְעַמָּך

tzelotana צְלוֹתָנָא ulekabela וּלְקַבְּלָא nehorach נְהוֹרָך mituv מִטּוּב lana לָנָא

detehevei דְּתֶהֱוֵי kamach קָמָך ra'ava רַעֲוָא yehe יְהֵא berachmei בְּרַחֲמֵי.

be'orach בְּאֹרַח milin מִלִּין denema דְּנֵימָא lan לָן vesmech וְסָמֵך sa'ed סָעֵד

betikunin בְּתִקּוּנִין dil'ela דִּלְעֵלָּא betikuna בְּתִקּוּנָא mishor מִישׁוֹר.

kadisha קַדִּישָׁא umatronita וּמַטְרוּנִיתָא kadisha קַדִּישָׁא demalka דְּמַלְכָּא

le'ashalfa לְאַשְׁלָפָא shelim שְׁלִים yichuda יִחוּדָא uleme'ebad וּלְמֶעְבַּד

midarga מִדַּרְגָּא chayei וְחַיֵּי dechol דְּכָל nishmeta נִשְׁמְתָא lehahi לְהַהִיא

dargin דַּרְגִּין. dechol דְּכָל sofa סוֹפָא ad עַד ledarga לְדַרְגָּא

nishmeta נִשְׁמְתָא hahi הַהִיא dihevei דִּיהֱוֵי begin בְּגִין

umitpasheta וּמִתְפַּשְּׁטָא bechola בְּכֹלָּא mishtechacha מִשְׁתְּכַוָּא

telayin תַּלְיָן vetata וְתַתָּא ela עֵלָּא deha דְּהָא bechola בְּכֹלָּא

va בֵּה: umitkayemei וּמִתְקַיְּמֵי nishmeta נִשְׁמְתָא behai בְּהַאי

---

or directed at knowing him. Thus, all the levels up to Ein Sof (The Endless World) unite into one, and everything is perfected from Above, Below, and within. All the levels are filled with his Light, all reach completion and all shine because of him and are suitably sweetened as it should be.

Master of the World, May Your desire be with Your nation Israel forever. The redemption of Your Right may You show to Your nation in Your Temple. May You fill us with the best of Your enlightenment and may You receive our prayers with mercy. May it be pleasing before You to assist and support us to say the words in the right way, for the Supernal Tikkun and the Tikkun of the Holy King and the Holy Matron. So it will create a complete unification which will draw out this soul which gives life to all from one height to another, all the way to the end of all levels. Because of the existence of this soul in everything and its extention in everything, Above and Below depend on this soul and exist because of it.

ADON OLAM

The two words *Adon Olam* (אדון עולם) are equal to the numerical value of the Aramaic words *Ein Sof* (207), meaning the "Endless World"—our true origin. *Adon Olam* is also the numeric value of the Aramaic word *Or*, which means "Light." The actual words *Adon Olam* translate into English as "Master of the Universe." Through this prayer, we want to arouse a sense of awe and wonderment toward the knowledge and understanding of the spiritual system and the order and perfection of the world and of the Light of the Creator.

מֶלֶךְ malach◆ אֲשֶׁר asher א"ס, רז, אור, אֵנִי olam עוֹלָם adon אֲדוֹן

נַעֲשָׂה na'asa לְעֵת le'et נִבְרָא nivra◊ יְצִיר yetzir ילי kol כָּל beterem בְּטֶרֶם

מהיצ ע"ה, shemo שְׁמוֹ melech מֶלֶךְ azai אֲזַי ילי kol כָּל vecheftzo בְּחֶפְצוֹ

ע"ב בריבוע וקס"א ע"ה, אל שדי ע"ה kichlot כִּכְלוֹת ve'acharei וְאַחֲרֵי nikra נִקְרָא◊

נוֹרָא nora◊ yimloch יִמְלוֹךְ מ"ב levado לְבַדּוֹ ילי◆ hakol הַכֹּל

יהוה yihye יִהְיֶה vehu וְהוּא hove הֹוֶה◆ vehu וְהוּא haya הָיָה vehu וְהוּא

בְּתִפְאָרָה betifara◊ echad אֶחָד vehu וְהוּא◊ ve'en וְאֵין אהבה, דאגה sheni שֵׁנִי◆

רֵאשִׁית resheet beli בְּלִי ulhachbira וּלְהַחְבִּירָה◊ lehamshilo לְהַמְשִׁילוֹ

beli בְּלִי vehamisra וְהַמִּשְׂרָה◊ ha'oz הָעֹז velo וְלוֹ tachlit תַּכְלִית◆ beli בְּלִי

utmura וּתְמוּרָה◊ shinuy שִׁנּוּי beli בְּלִי dimyon דִּמְיוֹן◆ beli בְּלִי erech עֵרֶךְ

עם ד' אותיות = ; להו gedol גָּדוֹל perud פֵּרוּד◆ beli בְּלִי chibur וְחִבּוּר beli בְּלִי

מבה, יזל, אום ko'ach כֹּחַ ugvurah וּגְבוּרָה◊ רי"ו vehu וְהוּא◆ Eli אֵלִי vechai וָחַי

ע"ה נגד, beyom בְּיוֹם chevli וְחֶבְלִי ע"ה אלהים דההין vetzur וְצוּר go'ali גֹּאֲלִי◆

מזבוז, זן, אל יהוה umanusi וּמָנוּסִי nisi נִסִּי vehu וְהוּא◊ אלהים דההין tzara צָרָה אל יהוה

ekra אֶקְרָא◊ אל יהוה ,זן ,מזבוז ,נגד ע"ה beyom בְּיוֹם kosi כּוֹסִי menat מְנָת

ADON OLAM

Master of the Universe, Who reigned before any form was created and, when everything was made according to His will, His Name was proclaimed as King. And after everything has expired, He, the Awesome One, shall reign alone. He was, He is, and He shall remain in splendor. He is One and there is no other to compare to Him or to declare as His equal. Without beginning, without conclusion, His is the power and dominion, unfathomable and unimaginable, unchanging and irreplaceable. He is without connections or separation. His strength and valor are great. He is my God and my living Redeemer; the forbearance of pain in time of distress. He is my banner, my refuge, and the portion of my cup on the day that I call out.

vehu וְהוּא rofe רוֹפֵא vehu וְהוּא marpe מַרְפֵּא vehu וְהוּא tzofe צוֹפֶה

vehu וְהוּא ezra עֶזְרָה beyado בְּיָדוֹ afkid אַפְקִיד ruchi רוּוְזִי

be'et בְּעֵת ר״ת = קנ״א ב״ן, יהוה אלהים יהוה אדני, מילוי קס״א וס״ג, מ״ה ברבוע וע״ב ע״ה

ishan אִישָׁן ve'a'ira וְאָעִירָה ve'im וְעִם ruchi רוּוְזִי geviyati גְוִיָּתִי

Adonai אֲדֹנָי li לִי velo וְלֹא ira אִירָא bemikdasho בְּמִקְדָּשׁוֹ

tagel תָּגֵל nafshi נַפְשִׁי meshichenu מְשִׁיוֵזנוּ yishlach יִשְׁלַוֹז mehera מְהֵרָה

ve'az וְאָז nashir נָשִׁיר bevet בְּבֵית kodshi קָדְשִׁי

amen אָמֵן amen אָמֵן shem שֵׁם hanora הַנּוֹרָא

THE SMALL TALIT

The connection of the small *Talit* (*Talit katan* or *Tzitzit*) refers to a garment worn underneath the shirt. The small *Talit* creates a protective security shield around the wearer's skin and body so that evil forces cannot infiltrate or penetrate them. Our skin has the energy of *Malchut*, which is connected to the one percent realm. The small *Talit* controls the energy field around the skin and protects it.

It says in the *Zohar* that the *Tzitzit* is a talisman that covers and protects the wearer from all evil spirits and negative angels. Rabbenu Bachye says that the precept of the *Tzitzit* is linked to the Resurrection of the Dead. The *Tzitzit* represents the Surrounding Light, and for that reason, the *Talit* needs to be large in order to cover the head and the body, back and front, all the way down to the chest. The small *Talit* represents the Surrounding Light of *Katnut*.

If you do not use a *Talit* for the prayers you should only recite this blessing.
If you slept with a small *Talit* you should touch the *Tzitzit* first.

baruch בָּרוּךְ Ata אַתָּה Adonai יְהֹוָאדֹנָיאָהדֹנֹהִי Elohenu אֱלֹהֵינוּ

melech מֶלֶךְ ha'olam הָעוֹלָם asher אֲשֶׁר kideshanu קִדְּשָׁנוּ

bemitzvotav בְּמִצְוֹתָיו vetzivanu וְצִוָּנוּ al עַל mitzvat מִצְוַת tzitzit צִיצִית

He is a healer and a remedy. He watches and He helps. In His Hands, I surrender my spirit when I sleep and when I awaken. With my spirit shall my body remain. The Lord is with me, I shall not fear. In His Temple shall my spirit rejoice. He shall send our Mashiach speedily. Then we shall sing in His Temple: Amen, Amen, the Awesome Name.

THE SMALL TALIT

Blessed are You, Lord, our God, the King of the Earth,
Who has sanctified us with His commandments and obliged us with the commandment of Tzitzit.

THE TALIT

The *Talit* is a shawl that is draped over the shoulders of the wearer, over his clothes. It surrounds him with a spiritual protective layer of illumination. The four corners of the *Talit*, with their tassels, connect us to the four corners of the universe and to the quantum level of our world, helping us gain control over our lives. The *Talit* connects us to the Surrounding Light—our soul's potential. Generally, only married men wear it, because the energy awakened by the *Talit* is manifested through the man's connection with his wife.

LeSHEM YICHUD

LeShem Yichud is a spark plug that activates the next series of prayers and actions, joining the Upper Worlds with our physical world.

leshem **לְשֵׁם** yichud **יִחוּד** kudsha **קוּדְשָׁא** berich **בְּרִיךְ** hu **הוּא**

ush'chintei **וּשְׁכִינְתֵּיהּ** (**יאהדונהי**) bid'chilu **בִּדְחִילוּ** ur'chimu **וּרְחִימוּ**

ur'chimu **וּרְחִימוּ** ud'chilu **וּדְחִילוּ** (**איההיוהה**) leyachada **לְיַחֲדָא**

shem **שֵׁם** yud **יוּ"ד** kei **קֵי** bevav **בְּוָא"ו** kei **קֵי** beyichuda **בְּיִחוּדָא**

hareni **הֲרֵינִי** Yisrael **יִשְׂרָאֵל** kol **כָּל** beshem **בְּשֵׁם** (**יהוה**) shelim **שְׁלִים**

metzuyetzet **מְצוּיֶצֶת** talit **טַלִּית** lilvosh **לִלְבּוֹשׁ** muchan **מוּכָן**

Adonai **יְהֹוָהּ** shetzivanu **שֶׁצִּוָּנוּ** kemo **כְּמוֹ** kehilchata **כְּהִלְכָתָה**

ve'asu **וְעָשׂוּ** hakedosha **הַקְּדוֹשָׁה** vetorato **בְּתוֹרָתוֹ** Elohenu **אֱלֹהֵינוּ**

kedei **כְּדֵי** vigdehem **בְגְדֵיהֶם** kanfei **כַּנְפֵי** al **עַל** tzitzit **צִיצִת** lahem **לָהֶם**

vela'asot **וְלַעֲשׂוֹת** leyotzri **לְיוֹצְרִי** ru'ach **רוּחַ** nachat **נַחַת** la'asot **לַעֲשׂוֹת**

vehareni **וְהֲרֵינִי** bor'i **בּוֹרְאִי** retzon **רְצוֹן**

hatalit **הַטַּלִית** atifat **עֲטִיפַת** al **עַל** levarech **לְבָרֵךְ** muchan **מוּכָן**

liftor **לִפְטוֹר** mechaven **מְכַוֵּין** vehareni **וְהֲרֵינִי** razal **רַזַ"ל** ketikkun **כְּתִקּוּן**

she'alai **שֶׁעָלַי** hakatan **הַקָּטָן** talit **טַלִּית** gam **גַּם** zo **זוֹ** bivracha **בְּבְרָכָה**

THE TALIT
LeSHEM YICHUD

For the sake of the unification between the Holy Blessed One and His Shechinah, with fear and love and with love and fear, in order to unify the Name Yud-Kei and Vav-Kei in perfect unity, and in the name of all Israel, I am hereby prepared to wear a Talit with Tzitzit, according to the law and as we were commanded by the Lord, our God, in His Holy Torah: "And they made for themselves Tzitzit on the corners of their clothes." (Numbers 15:38) In order to give pleasure to my Maker and to fulfill the wish of my Creator, I am hereby prepared to bless upon the enwrapping with the Talit, as was established by our Sages of blessed memory. I hereby intend to exempt the small Talit that I am wearing, with this blessing.

וִיהִי vihi   נֹעַם no'am   אֲדֹנָי Adonai ללה   אֱלֹהֵינוּ Elohenu ילה

עָלֵינוּ alenu   וּמַעֲשֵׂה uma'ase   יָדֵינוּ yadenu   כּוֹנְנָה konena

עָלֵינוּ alenu   וּמַעֲשֵׂה uma'ase   יָדֵינוּ yadenu   כּוֹנְנֵהוּ konenehu:

WRAPPING THE TALIT: After the blessing, you wrap the *Talit* over your head, leaving your face uncovered and the four corners falling on your chest. Then you grab the two right side *Tzitzits* and throw them over your left shoulder so they drape down your back. Pause for a moment and then take hold of the two left side *Tzitzits* and throw them over your left shoulder, draping them down your back in such a way that the four *Tzitzits* will be hanging over your left shoulder towards and down the back. You should pause for about four seconds, before allowing the *Talit* to drop down, so it can hang comfortably and loosely over both shoulders with two *Tzitzits* in the front and two in the back.

> The *Talit* is the aspect of the Surrounding Light of *Gadlut*.
> The *Talit* is the *tikkun* of the external part (*Netzach, Hod, Yesod*) of *Yetzirah*.
> **The blessing** is the *tikkun* of the Surrounding Light, and
> **The wearing** of the *Talit* is the *tikkun* of the Inner Light.

מֶלֶךְ melech   אֱלֹהֵינוּ Eelohenu ילה   יְהֹוָאדְנִיאהדונהי Adonai   אַתָּה Ata   בָּרוּךְ baruch

בְּמִצְוֹתָיו bemitzvotav   קִדְּשָׁנוּ kideshanu   אֲשֶׁר asher   הָעוֹלָם ha'olam

בְּצִיצִת betzitzit ר"ת ל"ב נתיבות החכמה: לְהִתְעַטֵּף lehit'atef   וְצִוָּנוּ vetzivanu

Yichud of the *Talit*: At first, you should meditate on the *Yichud* (unification) of *Zeir Anpin*, which is: יהוה, which has the numerical value of 32 paths of wisdom (ל"ב נתיבות החכמה). In particular, you should meditate to connect the letters יה, which are *Abba* and *Ima*, with the letter ו, which is *Zeir Anpin*, so that it becomes the Surrounding Light which is the *Talit*. Then, you should meditate to connect the letter ו (*Zeir Anpin*) with the last letter ה, to draw the Surrounding Light to the letter ה, which is the *Tzitzit*.

VA'ANI
COMMUNICATING WITH THE THREE PILLARS OF PRAYER (ABRAHAM, ISAAC AND JACOB)

There are three forces present in the universe that are required to generate power, be it physical or spiritual. These forces are the Right Column positive, sharing energy of which Abraham is the channel; the Left Column receiving, negative energy, of which Isaac is the channel, and the Central Column of balance, resistance, of which Jacob is the channel. The ancient kabbalists explain that Abraham, Isaac and Jacob are the foundation of every prayer. Their names are transmitters that activate and give power to all blessings and prayers that we perform throughout this *Siddur*.

"May the pleasantness of the Lord our God be upon us and may He establish the work of our hands for us and may the work of our hands establish Him." (Psalms 90:17)
Blessed are You, Lord, our God, the King of the World,
Who has sanctified us with His commandments and obliged us with enwrapping ourselves with Talit.

You should say the verse below while entering the temple, standing at the doorpost:

Abraham (Right)

אבֹגיתֵץ   chasdecha וַחַסְדְּךָ   אהיה י"פ   berov בְּרֹב   אני   va'ani וַאֲנִי

ב"פ ראה   vetecha בֵיתֶךָ   avo אָבוֹא

Isaac (Left)

יהוה = ר"ת ; אדני, כללה,   hechal הֵיכַל   el אֶל־   ע"ב י"פ   eshtachave אֶשְׁתַּחֲוֶה

kodshecha קָדְשְׁךָ

Jacob (Central)

beyir'atecha בְּיִרְאָתֶךָ:

Then bow down and enter.

Right

imanu עִמָּנוּ   שכינה   פני   Tzeva'ot צְבָאוֹת   Adonai יְהֹוָה‏אדני‏יאהדונהי

ריבוע ס"ג, קס"א, אותיות ו"ד, מ"ה‏, ע"ה מ"ה, ריבוע ע"ב וקס"א, אל שדי,   misgav מִשְׂגָּב

ד"פ אלהים ע"ה   מילוי ע"ב, דמב ; ילה   Elohei אֱלֹהֵי   אדני אהיה אלהים,   lanu לָנוּ

sela סֶלָה: אידהנויה   יאהדונהי   הויות,   י   Ya'akov יַעֲקֹב

Left

ashrei אַשְׁרֵי   שכינה   פני   Tzeva'ot צְבָאוֹת   Adonai יְהֹוָה‏אדני‏יאהדונהי

bote'ach בֹּטֵחַ   תפארת =   אדם אשרי צבאות ה' ; מ"ה   adam אָדָם

בך ע"ב ע"ה: מילוי = בך בוטח   (יאהדונהי) ע"ה ;   אמן = בך בוטח   אדם בוטח בך   bach בָּךְ

Central

ר"ת יהה   hamelech הַמֶּלֶךְ   יהוה וש"ע נהורין יהוה   hoshi'a הוֹשִׁיעָה   Adonai יְהֹוָה‏אדני‏יאהדונהי

kor'enu קָרְאֵנוּ   אל יהוה ע"ה   נגד, מזבח, זך,   veyom בְיוֹם   ya'anenu יַעֲנֵנוּ

ע"ב: דהמלך כ' אות ועם = ב"ן ; ס"ת = ב"ן ; אהיה אדני יהוה, אלהים   ר"ת יב"ק,

---

VA'ANI

"And I, with the profusion of Your kindness,
come to Your House and bow towards Your Holy Ark, in awe of You." (Psalms 5:8)

"The Lord of Hosts, joyful is one who trusts in You." (Psalms 84:13)
"The Lord of Hosts is with us. The God of Jacob is a refuge for us, Selah.
Lord redeem us. The King shall answer us on the day we call Him." (Psalms 46:12)

ESH TAMID - MEDITATION TO CONTROL OUR THOUGHTS

Our brain is a receiver and there are two transmitting stations that send signals/thoughts to our brain. One source is the Light and the other is Satan. These verses disrupt and override any negative thoughts that might enter our minds.

Each verse is recited seven times:

אֵשׁ esh תָּמִיד tamid ע"ה קס"א קנ"א קמ"ג תּוּקַד tukad עַל־ al

הַמִּזְבֵּחַ hamizbe'ach נגד, זין, אל יהוה לֹא lo תִכְבֶּה tichbe:

Recite seven times

סְעַפִּים se'afim שָׂנֵאתִי saneti וְתוֹרָתְךָ vetoratcha אָהָבְתִּי ahavti:

Recite seven times

לֵב lev טָהוֹר tahor י"פ אכא בְּרָא־ bera:

קנ"א ב"ן, יהוה אלהים יהוה אדני, מילוי קס"א וס"ג, מ"ה ברבוע וע"ב ע"ה

לב טהור ברא = קס"א קנ"א קמ"ג

לִי li אֱלֹהִים Elohim אהיה אדני ; ילה ; לי אלהים = ריבוע אדני

וְרוּחַ veru'ach נָכוֹן nachon וְחַדֵּשׁ chadesh י"ב הויות, קס"א קנ"א בְּקִרְבִּי bekirbi שדי:

Recite seven times

AYIN LAMED MEM

This three-letter combination of the 72 Names of God gives us control over unwanted thoughts such as worry, pessimism, and obsessive or compulsive ideas. Besides using this meditation in the morning prayers, we can use it throughout the day as needed.

You should meditate on the Holy Name:

עלם

This helps to control your thoughts.

ESH TAMID

"And the Eternal Fire shall burn upon the Altar and shall never extinguish." (Leviticus 6:6)
"I hate scattered thoughts but Your Torah, I love." (Psalms 119:113)
"Create for me a pure heart, God, and renew a correct spirit within me." (Psalms 51:12)

THE MORNING PRAYER

You should be very careful not to speak, even a single word, during the prayers and meditations.

According to Kabbalah, there are three distinct energy forces that govern three specific times of the day: Right Column (Abraham): morning, Left Column (Isaac): afternoon, and Central Column (Jacob): evening. The prayers of *Shacharit* correspond to the Right Column (Abraham)—sharing, merciful, positive energy. Too often we awake in a bad mood, and this negative state of mind remains with us throughout the day. To counteract this negativity, we have the connection of *Shacharit*, which imbues us with the energy of happiness and vitality, motivating us to reveal Light throughout the day.

LeSHEM YICHUD

לְשֵׁם leshem   יְוֹוּד yichud   קוּדְשָׁא kudsha   בְּרִיךְ berich   הוּא hu

וּשְׁכִינְתֵּיה ush'chintei   (יאהדונהי)   בִּדְחִילוּ bid'chilu   וּרְחִימוּ ur'chimu

וּרְחִימוּ (יאההויהה) ur'chimu   וּדְחִילוּ ud'chilu   (איההיוהה)   לְיַחֲדָא leyachda

שֵׁם shem   יוּ"ד yud   קֵי kei   בְּוָא"ו bevav   קֵי kei   בְּיִחוּדָא beyichuda

שְׁלִים shelim   (יהוה)   בְּשֵׁם beshem   כָּל kol   יְ׳   יִשְׂרָאֵל Yisrael,

הִנֵּה hine   אֲנַחְנוּ anachnu   בָּאִים ba'im   לְהִתְפַּלֵּל lehitpalel   תְּפִלַת tefilat

שַׁחֲרִית shacharit   שֶׁל shel   (On *Shabbat* Add:) שַׁבָּת Shabbat   קוֹדֶשׁ kodesh   וְ ve)

(on *Sukkot* say: סֻכּוֹת Sukkot) (on *Simchat-Torah* say: שְׁמִינִי Shemini   עֲצֶרֶת Atzeret).♦

שֶׁתִּקֵן shetiken   אַבְרָהָם Avraham   וז"פ אל, רי"י, ול"ב נתיבות החכמה.

הַשָׁלוֹם hashalom   עָלָיו alav   אָבִינוּ avinu   רמ"ז (אברים), עסמ"ב וט"ז אותיות פשוטות

הַכְּלוּלוֹת hakelulot   הַמִּצְוֹת hamitzvot   יְ׳ kol כָּל   עִם im

בְּמָקוֹם bemakom   שָׁרְשָׁהּ shorsha   אֶת et   לְתַקֵן letaken   בָּהּ ba

לְיוֹצְרֵנוּ leyotzrenu   רוּחַ ru'ach   נוֹחַת nachat   לַעֲשׂוֹת la'asot   עֶלְיוֹן elyon

וְלַעֲשׂוֹת vela'asot   רָצוֹן retzon   מהש ע"ה, ע"ב ברבוע וקס"א ע"ה, אל שדי ע"ה

בּוֹרְאֵנוּ bor'enu♦   וִיהִי vihi   נֹעַם no'am   אֲדֹנָי Adonai   לכה

אֱלֹהֵינוּ elohenu   יכה עָלֵינוּ alenu   וּמַעֲשֵׂה uma'ase   יָדֵינוּ yadenu   כּוֹנְנָה konena

עָלֵינוּ alenu   וּמַעֲשֵׂה uma'ase   יָדֵינוּ yadenu   כּוֹנְנֵהוּ konenehu ‡

THE MORNING PRAYER -LeSHEM YICHUD

For the sake of the unification of The Holy Blessed One and His Shechinah, with fear and love and with love and fear, in order to unify the Name Yud-Kei and Vav-Kei in perfect unity, and in the name of Israel, we have hereby come to recite the Morning prayer of (on Shabbat add: the Holy Sabbath and) (on Sukkot: Sukkot) (on Simchat Torah: Shmini Atzeret), established by Abraham, our forefather, may peace be upon him, with all its commandments, to correct its root in the supernal place, to bring satisfaction to our Maker, and to fulfill the wish of our Creator. "And the pleasantness of the Lord, our God, be upon us and may He establish the work of our hands for us and may the work of our hands establish Him." (Psalms 90:17)

A COMMITMENT FOR LOVE AND UNITY - ELEVATING OUR CONSCIOUSNESS

A thin, weak string cannot lift a treasure chest. However, when we weave together many thin strings, we form a rope. By uniting ourselves with the rest of the world through making a Commitment for Love, we can pull down the greatest spiritual treasures, even though we might not be worthy or strong enough to accomplish this individually.

Regarding the danger of deviation, the Kaf-Hachayim says: "In a place of deviation, the blessing removes itself, and people who had disagreements end up with damage and accidents to their bodies as well as their wealth. Those who care for themselves should stay away from any deviation."

The *Ari* writes in the Gate of Meditations: before you start your connections and prayers, you should accept within yourself the precept of "love your fellow as you do yourself." Meaning, you must meditate to love all people who are doing spiritual work as if they are part of your soul, so that your prayers will be included and elevated with the universal prayer and bring results. It is especially important to have love for the *Chaverim* (people who dedicate their lives to spiritual work) and to recognize that praying for others enables and allows our prayers to be accepted.

הֲרֵינִי hareni מְקַבֵּל mekabel עָלַי alai מִצְוַת mitzvat עֲשֵׂה ase שֶׁל shel

וְאָהַבְתָּ ve'ahavta ב"פ אור, ב"פ רו, ב"פ א"ס לְרֵעֲךָ lere'acha כָּמוֹךָ kamocha◆

וְהֲרֵינִי vehareni אוֹהֵב ohev אֶת et כָּל kol יל' אֶחָד echad אהבה, דאגה

מִבְּנֵי mibenei יִשְׂרָאֵל Yisrael כְּנַפְשִׁי kenafshi וּמְאוֹדִי◆ ume'odi

וְהֲרֵינִי vehareni מְזַמֵּן mezamen פֶּה pe מ'לה ; ע"ה אלהים, אהיה אדנ'

שֶׁלִּי sheli לְהִתְפַּלֵל lehitpalel לִפְנֵי lifnei מֶלֶךְ melech מַלְכֵי malchei

הַמְּלָכִים hamelachim הַקָּדוֹשׁ hakadosh בָּרוּךְ baruch הוּא hu◆

THE BINDING OF ISAAC

By reciting this verse, which describes Abraham binding Isaac, we connect to the power of mercy. Simultaneously, we bind our judgment as part of our internal cleansing, and we receive help to bind the negative thoughts of people who come against us in judgment.

A COMMITMENT FOR LOVE
ELEVATING OUR CONSCIOUSNESS

I hereby accept upon myself the obligatory commandment of "Love your fellow as you do yourself." I hereby declare that I love each one of Israel with my soul and my strength. And I hereby prepare my mouth to pray before the King of all Kings, the Holy Blessed One.

avotenu אֲבוֹתֵינוּ ; יכה ; מילוי ע"ב, דמב ; לכב velohei וֵאלֹהֵי Elohenu אֱלֹהֵינוּ

והו tov טוֹב ונש"ב קס"א ע"ב bezichron בְּזִכְרוֹן zochrenu זָכְרֵנוּ

bifkudat בִּפְקֻדַת ufokdenu וּפָקְדֵנוּ בן מ"ה ס"ג milfanecha מִלְפָנֶיךָ

shemei שְׁמֵי mishmei מִשְׁמֵי verachamim וְרַחֲמִים yeshu'a יְשׁוּעָה

Adonai יְהֹוָאדֹנָיהּ אהיה אדני אלהים, lanu לָנוּ uzchor וּזְכָר ◆kedem קֶדֶם

hakadmonim הַקַדְמוֹנִים ahavat אַהֲבַת יכה Elohenu אֱלֹהֵינוּ

ו"פ אל, רי"ו ול"ב נתיבות החכמה, רמ"ח (אברים), עסמ"ב וט"ז אותיות פשוטות Avraham אַבְרָהָם

◆avadecha עֲבָדֶיךָ veYisrael וְיִשְׂרָאֵל בן ד"פ Yitzchak יִצְחָק

ריבוע יהוה ע"ב, hachesed הַחֶסֶד ve'et וְאֶת haberit הַבְּרִית et אֶת

le'Avraham לְאַבְרָהָם shenishbata שֶׁנִשְׁבַּעְתָּ hashevu'a הַשְׁבוּעָה ve'et וְאֶת

ו"פ אל, רי"ו ול"ב נתיבות החכמה, רמ"ח (אברים), עסמ"ב וט"ז אותיות פשוטות

ha'akeda הָעֲקֵדָה ve'et וְאֶת ◆haMoriya הַמוֹרִיָה behar בְּהַר avinu אָבִינוּ

gabei גַבֵּי al עַל beno בְּנוֹ בן ד"פ Yitzchak יִצְחָק et אֶת she'akad שֶׁעָקַד

◆betoratach בְּתוֹרָתֶךָ kakatuv כַּכָּתוּב אל יהוה גגד, ז, hamizbe'ach הַמִזְבֵּחַ

THE PORTION CONCERNING THE BINDING

Reciting the portion concerning the Binding of Isaac every day allows us to atone for all our sins and create a shield of protection against all sickness, which cancels death from humanity.

THE BINDING OF ISAAC

Our God and the God of our forefathers, remember us favorably before You, and evoke for us the remembrance of salvation and mercy, from the earliest and the highest Heavens. And remember, for our sake, Lord, our God, the love of the ancients: Your servants, Abraham, Isaac, and Israel. And remember, also the Covenant, the compassion, and the oath that You pledged to Abraham, our forefather, on Mount Moriah, when he bound his son, Isaac, upon the altar, as it is related in Your Torah:

vayehi וַיְהִ֗י achar אַחַר֙ hadevarim הַדְּבָרִ֣ים ha'ele הָאֵ֔לֶּה

vehaElohim וְהָ֣אֱלֹהִ֔ים ; אהיה אדני ; nisa נִסָּ֖ה et אֶת־ Avraham אַבְרָהָ֑ם

ח"פ אל, רי"ו ול"ב נתיבות החוכמה, רמ"ח (אברים), עסמ"ב וט"ז אותיות פשוטות וַיֹּ֣אמֶר vayomer

elav אֵלָ֔יו Avraham אַבְרָהָ֖ם ח"פ אל, רי"ו ול"ב נתיבות החוכמה, רמ"ח (אברים),

עסמ"ב וט"ז אותיות פשוטות vayomer וַיֹּ֥אמֶר hineni הִנֵּֽנִי׃ vayomer וַיֹּ֡אמֶר kach קַח־

na נָ֠א et אֶת־ bincha בִּנְךָ֨ et אֶת־ yechidcha יְחִֽידְךָ֤ asher אֲשֶׁר־

ahavta אָהַ֙בְתָּ֙ et אֶת־ Yitzchak יִצְחָ֔ק ד"פ ב"ן velech וְלֶ֨ךְ־ lecha לְךָ֔

el אֶל־ eretz אֶ֖רֶץ haMoriya הַמֹּרִיָּ֑ה veha'alehu וְהַעֲלֵ֤הוּ sham שָׁ֙ם

le'ola לְעֹלָ֔ה al עַ֚ל achad אַחַ֣ד אהבה, דאגה heharim הֶֽהָרִ֔ים asher אֲשֶׁ֖ר

omar אֹמַ֥ר ח"פ אל, Avraham אֵלֶֽיךָ׃ elecha אֵלֶֽיךָ vayashkem וַיַּשְׁכֵּ֨ם

baboker בַּבֹּ֜קֶר רי"ו ול"ב נתיבות החוכמה, רמ"ח (אברים), עסמ"ב וט"ז אותיות פשוטות

vayachavosh וַֽיַּחֲבֹשׁ֙ et אֶת־ חמם chamoro חֲמֹר֔וֹ vayikach וַיִּקַּ֞ח et אֶת־

shenei שְׁנֵ֤י ne'arav נְעָרָיו֙ ito אִתּ֔וֹ ve'et וְאֵ֖ת Yitzchak יִצְחָ֣ק ד"פ ב"ן beno בְּנ֑וֹ

vayevaka וַיְבַקַּע֙ atzei עֲצֵ֣י ola עֹלָ֔ה vayakom וַיָּ֣קָם vayelech וַיֵּ֔לֶךְ כלי

el אֶל־ hamakom הַמָּק֖וֹם asher אֲשֶׁר־ amar אָֽמַר־ lo ל֥וֹ

haElohim הָאֱלֹהִֽים׃ ; אהיה אדני bayom בַּיּ֣וֹם ע"ה נגר, מזבח, זו, אל יהוה

hashelishi הַשְּׁלִישִׁ֗י vayisa וַיִּשָּׂ֨א Avraham אַבְרָהָ֧ם ח"פ אל, רי"ו ול"ב נתיבות החוכמה,

רמ"ח (אברים), עסמ"ב וט"ז אותיות פשוטות et אֶת־ enav עֵינָ֛יו ריבוע מ"ה

vayar וַיַּ֛רְא et אֶת־ hamakom הַמָּק֖וֹם merachok מֵרָחֹֽק׃ שדי:

THE PORTION CONCERNING THE BINDING

"And it came to be that after those events, God tested Abraham and said to him: 'Abraham' and he replied: 'Here I am'. And He said: 'Please take your son, your only one, whom you love; Isaac, and go to the land of Moriah. Place him as a burnt-offering upon one of the mountains that I shall tell you.' And Abraham rose early in the morning, saddled his donkey, and took two lads with him, together with his son, Isaac. Abraham split wood for the offering then got up and went towards the place of which God told him. On the third day, Abraham lifted his eyes and saw the place from afar.

וַיֹּאמֶר vayomer אַבְרָהָם avraham וז"פ אל, רי"ו ול"ב נתיבות החוכמה, רמ"ח (אברים),

אֶל el נְעָרָיו ne'arav שְׁבוּ shevu לָכֶם lachem פֹּה po עסמ"ב וט"ז אותיות פשוטות

עִם im הַחֲמוֹר hachamor מילה (להכניע הקליפות בסוד החומר) ; ע"ה אלהים, אהיה אדני,

וַאֲנִי va'ani וְהַנַּעַר vehana'ar נֵלְכָה nelcha עַד ad כֹּה ko אני

וְנִשְׁתַּחֲוֶה venishtachave וְנָשׁוּבָה venashuva אֲלֵיכֶם alechem וַיִּקַּח vayikach

אַבְרָהָם Avraham וז"פ אל, רי"ו ול"ב נתיבות החוכמה, רמ"ח (אברים), עסמ"ב וט"ז אותיות פשוטות

אֶת et עֲצֵי atzei הָעֹלָה ha'ola וַיָּשֶׂם vayasem עַל al יִצְחָק Yitzchak ד"פ ב"ן

בְּנוֹ beno וַיִּקַּח vayikach וזם בְּיָדוֹ beyado אֶת et הָאֵשׁ ha'esh שאה

וְאֶת ve'et הַמַּאֲכֶלֶת hama'achelet וַיֵּלְכוּ vayelchu שְׁנֵיהֶם sheneihem

יַחְדָּו yachdav וַיֹּאמֶר vayomer יִצְחָק Yitzchak ד"פ ב"ן אֶל el

אַבְרָהָם Avraham וז"פ אל, רי"ו ול"ב נתיבות החוכמה, רמ"ח (אברים), עסמ"ב וט"ז אותיות פשוטות

אָבִיו aviv וַיֹּאמֶר vayomer אָבִי avi הִנֶּנִּי hineni בְּנִי veni

וַיֹּאמֶר vayomer הִנֵּה hine הָאֵשׁ ha'esh שאה וְהָעֵצִים veha'etzim וְאַיֵּה ve'aye

הַשֶּׂה hase לְעֹלָה le'ola וַיֹּאמֶר vayomer אַבְרָהָם Avraham וז"פ אל, רי"ו ול"ב

אֱלֹהִים Elohim נתיבות החוכמה, רמ"ח (אברים), עסמ"ב וט"ז אותיות פשוטות אהיה אדני ; ילה

יִרְאֶה yir'eh רי"ו לוֹ lo הַשֶּׂה hase לְעֹלָה le'ola בְּנִי beni ר"ת הבל (למתק או"ז

וַיֵּלְכוּ vayelchu בראיה) ע"מ לתקן עון הבל שחטא שְׁנֵיהֶם sheneihem יַחְדָּו yachdav

וַיָּבֹאוּ vayavo'u אֶל el הַמָּקוֹם hamakom אֲשֶׁר asher אָמַר amar לוֹ lo

הָאֱלֹהִים haElohim אהיה אדני ; ילה וַיִּבֶן vayiven שָׁם sham אַבְרָהָם Avraham

אֶת et וז"פ אל, רי"ו ול"ב נתיבות החוכמה, רמ"ח (אברים), עסמ"ב וט"ז אותיות פשוטות

הַמִּזְבֵּחַ hamizbe'ach נגד, זן, אל יהוה וַיַּעֲרֹךְ vaya'aroch אֶת et הָעֵצִים ha'etzim

וַיַּעֲקֹד vaya'akod אֶת et יִצְחָק Yitzchak ד"פ ב"ן בְּנוֹ beno וַיָּשֶׂם vayasem

---

And Abraham said to his lads: Stay here with the donkey, while I and my son go until there, where we shall prostrate ourselves then return to you. And Abraham took the wood for the burnt-offering and placed it upon Isaac, his son. He took in his hand the fire and the knife as they went together. And Isaac said to his father: 'My father.' and he said: 'Here I am, my son.' And Isaac said: 'Behold the fire and the wood, but where is the lamb for the burnt-offering?' And Abraham said: 'God shall show the lamb for the burnt-offering, my son.' And they went together. And they came to the place God showed him, There, Abraham built an Altar and arranged the wood. He bound his son, Isaac, and placed

עלם mima'al מִמַּעַל אֶל יהוה, זָ, נגר, hamizbe'ach הַמִּזְבֵּחַ al עַל־ oto אֹתוֹ

ל"ב נתיבות רי"ו אל, וז"פ Avraham אַבְרָהָם vayishlach וַיִּשְׁלַח la'etzim לָעֵצִים

וזעם vayikach וַיִּקַּח yado יָדוֹ et אֶת־ אותיות פשוטות עסמ"ב וט"ז (אברים), רמ"ח הוזכמה,

beno בְּנוֹ et אֶת־ lishchot לִשְׁחֹט hama'achelet הַמַּאֲכֶלֶת et אֶת־

mal'ach מַלְאַךְ elav אֵלָיו קס"א ב"פ = אותיות עם ה' vayikra וַיִּקְרָא

ר"ת מ"ה כוזו, י"פ טל, י"פ hashamayim הַשָּׁמַיִם min מִן־ Adonai יאההויהה

(אברים), רמ"ח הוזכמה ל"ב נתיבות וז"ו רי"ו אל, וז"פ Avraham אַבְרָהָם | vayomer וַיֹּאמֶר

(אברים), רמ"ח הוזכמה ל"ב נתיבות רי"ו Avraham אַבְרָהָם אותיות פשוטות עסמ"ב וט"ז

al אֶל־ vayomer וַיֹּאמֶר hineni הִנֵּנִי vayomer וַיֹּאמֶר אותיות פשוטות עסמ"ב וט"ז

ta'as תַּעַשׂ ve'al וְאַל־ hana'ar הַנַּעַר el אֶל־ yadcha יָדְךָ tishlach תִּשְׁלַח

yere יָרֵא ki כִּי yadati יָדַעְתִּי ata עַתָּה | ki כִּי me'uma מְאוּמָה lo לוֹ

et אֶת־ chasachta חָשַׂכְתָּ velo וְלֹא Ata אַתָּה אהיה אדני ; Elohim אֱלֹהִים

vayisa וַיִּשָּׂא mimeni מִמֶּנִּי yechidcha יְחִידְךָ et אֶת־ bincha בִּנְךָ

אותיות פשוטות עסמ"ב וט"ז (אברים), רמ"ז הוזכמה נתיבות ל"ב ורי"ו אל, וז"פ Avraham אַבְרָהָם

achar אַחַר ayil אַיִל vehine וְהִנֵּה vayar וַיַּרְא רביע מ"ה enav עֵינָיו et אֶת־

בקרניו בסבך נאחז כשאומר bekarnav בְּקַרְנָיו basevach בַּסְּבַךְ ne'echaz נֶאֱחַז

יצזק שיעזוט כדי האיל, מרוזיק היה העגל קיטרוג בעבור והשטן עגל, הם סבך שאומר לתיבות יכוין
השטן את הכניע הקטורת) סממני עס"ז (= בקרניו נאחז אור נגא, איל, הנה (= ומיכאל

הוזכמה נתיבות ל"ב רי"י אל, וז"פ Avraham אַבְרָהָם כלי vayelech וַיֵּלֶךְ

et אֶת־ (אברים), עסמ"ב וט"ז אותיות פשוטות vayikach וַיִּקַּח רמ"ז

beno בְּנוֹ tachat תַּחַת le'ola לְעֹלָה vaya'alehu וַיַּעֲלֵהוּ ha'ayil הָאַיִל

וז"פ אל, רי"י ל"ב נתיבות Avraham אַבְרָהָם ב"פ קס"א = אותיות עם ה' vayikra וַיִּקְרָא

hamakom הַמָּקוֹם shem שֵׁם־ אותיות פשוטות וט"ז עסמ"ב (אברים), רמ"ז הוזכמה,

---

him upon the altar, on top of the wood. And Abraham reached out with his hand and took the knife to slaughter his son. The Angel of the Lord called to him from the Heavens and said: 'Abraham, Abraham.' And he said: 'Here I am.' And He said: 'Do not send your hand forth against the lad and do not do anything to him, for I now know that you fear God and you did not withhold your son from Me.' And Abraham lifted his eyes and saw and beheld a ram, entangled in a bush by his horns. Abraham went forth and took the ram; he burnt it as an offering, instead of his son. And Abraham called the name of this place

הַהוּא hahu | יְהֹוָה Adonai | יִרְאֶה yir'e | רי"ו | אֲשֶׁר asher

יֹּאמֶר ye'amer | הַיּוֹם hayom | ע"ה נגד, מזבח, זן, אל יהוה | בְּהַר behar

יְהֹוָה Adonai | יֵרָאֶה yera'e | רי"ו | וַיִּקְרָא vayikra | עם ה' אותיות = ב"פ קס"א

מַלְאַךְ mal'ach | יְהֹוָה Adonai | אֶל el | אַבְרָהָם Avraham | וז"פ אל,

מִן min | שֵׁנִית shenit | רי"ו ול"ב נתיבות החכמה, רמ"ח (אברים), עסמ"ב וט"ז אותיות פשוטות

הַשָּׁמָיִם hashamayim | י"פ כוזו ; ר"ת מ"ה: | וַיֹּאמֶר vayomer | בִּי bi

יַעַן ya'an | כִּי ki | יְהֹוָה Adonai | נְאֻם ne'um | נִשְׁבַּעְתִּי nishbati | י"פ טל, י"פ כוזו

אֲשֶׁר asher | עָשִׂיתָ asita | אֶת et | הַדָּבָר hadavar | ראה הזה | הַזֶּה haze | והו | וְלֹא velo

כִּי ki | יְחִידְךָ yechidecha | אֶת et | בִּנְךָ bincha | אֶת et | חָשַׂכְתָּ chasachta | וְשַׂכְתָּ

בָּרֵךְ varech | אֲבָרֶכְךָ avarechecha | וְהַרְבָּה veharba | אַרְבֶּה arbe | יצחק, ד"פ ב"ן | בָרֵךְ

אֶת et | זַרְעֲךָ zar'acha | כְּכוֹכְבֵי kechochvei | הַשָּׁמָיִם hashamayim | י"פ טל, י"פ כוזו

וְכַחוֹל vechachol | אֲשֶׁר asher | עַל al | שְׂפַת sefat | הַיָּם hayam | ילי

וְיִרַשׁ veyirash | זַרְעֲךָ zar'acha | אֵת et | שַׁעַר sha'ar | אֹיְבָיו oyvav:

וְהִתְבָּרְכוּ vehitbarchu | יהוה ריבוע | ריבוע יהוה מ"ה | בְּזַרְעֲךָ vezaracha

כֹּל kol | ילי | גוֹיֵי goyei | הָאָרֶץ ha'aretz | ע"ה דההין אלהים | עֵקֶב ekev | ב"פ מום

אֲשֶׁר asher | שָׁמַעְתָּ shamata | בְּקֹלִי bekoli: | וַיָּשָׁב vayashov

אַבְרָהָם Avraham | וז"פ אל, רי"ו ול"ב נתיבות החכמה, רמ"ח (אברים), עסמ"ב וט"ז אותיות פשוטות

אֶל el | נְעָרָיו ne'arav | וַיָּקֻמוּ vayakumu | וַיֵּלְכוּ vayelchu | יַחְדָּו yachdav

אֶל el | בְּאֵר Be'er | קנ"א ב"ן, יהוה אלהים יהוה אדני, מילוי קס"א וס"ג, מ"ה ברבוע וע"ב ע"ה

שָׁבַע Shava | וַיֵּשֶׁב vayeshev | אַבְרָהָם Avraham | וז"פ | אל,

בִּבְאֵר biVe'er | רי"ו ול"ב נתיבות החכמה, רמ"ח (אברים), עסמ"ב וט"ז אותיות פשוטות

שָׁבַע Shava: | קנ"א ב"ן, יהוה אלהים אדני, מילוי קס"א וס"ג, מ"ה ברבוע וע"ב ע"ה

---

as: Lord shall see, when what is said on the Mount of the Lord shall be seen. Then the Angel of the Lord called to Abraham a second time from the Heavens, and said: 'I have sworn upon My Being, proclaimed the Lord, that since you have done this thing and you did not withhold your son, your only one, I shall surely bless you and I shall greatly multiply your seed, like the stars of the sky and the sand upon the seashore. Your seed shall inherit the gate of his enemies. All nations of the world shall be blessed by your seed, because you have listened to My Voice.' And Abraham returned to his lads. They got up and went to Be'er Sheva. And Abraham resided in Be'er Sheva." (Genesis 22:1-19)

RIBONO SHEL OLAM

Light can never be revealed without a Vessel. *Ribono Shel Olam* helps us build our personal Vessel to draw all the Light that Abraham generated by virtue of his actions.

רִבּוֹנוֹ shel שֶׁל olam עוֹלָם kemo כְּמוֹ shekavash שֶׁכָּבַשׁ

Avraham אַבְרָהָם וז"פ אל, רי"ו ול"ב נתיבות החכמה, רמ"ח (אברים), עסמ"ב וט"ו אותיות פשוטות

אָבִינוּ avinu אֶת et רַחֲמָיו rachamav לַעֲשׂוֹת la'asot רְצוֹנְךָ retzoncha

בְּלֵבָב belevav בוכו שָׁלֵם shalem ◆ כֵּן ken יִכְבְּשׁוּ yichbeshu

רַחֲמֶיךָ rachamecha אֶת et כַּעַסְךָ ka'asecha ◆ וְיִגוֹלוּ veyigolu

רַחֲמֶיךָ rachamecha עַל al מִדוֹתֶיךָ midotecha ◆ וְתִתְנַהֵג vetitnaheg

Elohenu אֱלֹהֵינוּ Adonai יְהֹוָה ריבוע דס"ג, קס"א ע"ה וד' אותיות imanu עִמָנוּ

uvmidat וּבְמִדַת יֵלה bemidat בְּמִדַת hachesed הַחֶסֶד ע"ב, ריבוע יהוה

אדני אהיה, אלהים, לנו lanu וְתִכָּנֵס vetikanes ◆ הָרַחֲמִים harachamim

לאו lifnim לִפְנִים mishurat מִשׁוּרַת hadin הַדִין ◆ וּבְטוּבְךָ uvtuvcha

charon וְחָרוֹן yashuv יָשׁוּב ◆ עם ד' אותיות = מבה, יזל, אום hagadol הַגָדוֹל לְהוֹ ;

ume'artzach וּמֵאַרְצָךְ ume'irach וּמֵעִירָךְ me'amach מֵעַמָךְ apach אַפָּךְ

אדני אהיה, אלהים, לנו lanu וְקַיֵם vekayem ◆ uminachalatach וּמִנַחֲלָתָךְ

ראה hadavar הַדָבָר et אֶת יֵלה Elohenu אֱלֹהֵינוּ Adonai יְהֹוָה

yedei יְדֵי al עַל betoratach בְּתוֹרָתָךְ shehivtachtanu שֶׁהִבְטַחְתָנוּ

avdach עַבְדָךְ פוי, אל אדני Moshe מֹשֶׁה מהשע, ע"ב בריבוע וקס"א, אל שדי, ד"פ אלהים ע"ה

beriti בְּרִיתִי et אֶת vezacharti וְזָכַרְתִי ka'amur כָּאָמוּר

beriti בְּרִיתִי et אֶת ve'af וְאַף הויות, יאהדונהי אידהנויה Yaakov יַעֲקוֹב

RIBONO SHEL OLAM

Master of the Universe, just as Abraham, our father, suppressed his compassion to wholeheartedly fulfill Your will, so may Your compassion suppress Your wrath and may Your compassion reveal itself above Your other attributes. Behave with us, Lord, our God, according to the attributes of kindness and of compassion; for our sake, act towards us from beyond the framework of strict judgment. By Your great benevolence, Your anger shall be retracted from Your Nation, Your City, Your Land, and Your Heritage. Fulfill for us, Lord, our God, what You have promised to us in Your Torah, through Moses, Your servant, as it states: "I shall remember My Covenant with Jacob and My Covenant

יִצְחָק Yitzchak · ד"פ · ב"ן · וְאַף ve'af · אֶת־ et · בְּרִיתִי beriti

אַבְרָהָם Avraham · ו"פ אל, רי"ו ול"ב נתיבות החכמה, רמ"ח (אברים), עסמ"ב וט"ז אותיות פשוטות

אֹזְכֹּר ezkor · וְהָאָרֶץ veha'aretz · אלהים דההין ע"ה · אֶזְכֹּר ezkor · וְנֶאֱמַר vene'emar

בְּאֶרֶץ be'eretz · בִּהְיוֹתָם bihyotam · זֹאת zot · גַּם־ gam · וְאַף־ ve'af

אֹיְבֵיהֶם oyvehem · לֹא־ lo · מְאַסְתִּים me'astim · וְלֹא־ velo · גְּעַלְתִּים ge'altim

לְכַלֹּתָם lechalotam · לְהָפֵר lehafer · בְּרִיתִי beriti · אֹתָם itam · כִּי ki · אֲנִי ani

יְהֹוָה Adonai · אֱלֹהֵיהֶם Elohehem · יל"ה · וְזָכַרְתִּי vezacharti

לָהֶם lahem · בְּרִית berit · רִאשֹׁנִים rishonim · אֲשֶׁר asher · הוֹצֵאתִי hotzeti

אֹתָם otam · מֵאֶרֶץ me'eretz · מִצְרַיִם Mitzrayim · לְעֵינֵי le'enei · ריבוע מ"ה

הַגּוֹיִם hagoyim · לִהְיוֹת lihyot · לָהֶם lahem · לֵאלֹהִים lelohim · אהיה אדני; יל"ה

אֲנִי ani · אֲנִי · יְהֹוָה Adonai · וְנֶאֱמַר vene'emar · וְשָׁב veshav

יְהֹוָה Adonai · אֱלֹהֶיךָ Elohecha · יל"ה · אֶת־ et · שְׁבוּתְךָ shevutcha

וְרִחֲמֶךָ verichamecha · וְשָׁב veshav · וְקִבֶּצְךָ vekibetzcha · מִכָּל mikol · ילי

הָעַמִּים ha'amim · אֲשֶׁר asher · הֱפִיצְךָ hefitz'cha · יְהֹוָה Adonai

אֱלֹהֶיךָ Elohecha · יל"ה · שָׁמָּה shama · אִם־ im · יוהך, מ"א אותיות דפשוטות,

בִּקְצֵה biktze · נִדַּחֲךָ nidachacha · יי · יִהְיֶה yih'ye · ע"ה דאהיה דמילוי דמילוי

הַשָּׁמָיִם hashamayim · כוזו י"פ טל, י"פ · מִשָּׁם misham · יְקַבֶּצְךָ yekabetzcha

וּמִשָּׁם umisham · יל"ה · אֱלֹהֶיךָ Elohecha · יְהֹוָה Adonai

יְהֹוָה Adonai · וֶהֱבִיאֲךָ vehevi'acha · יִקָּחֶךָ yikachecha

אֱלֹהֶיךָ Elohecha · יל"ה · אֶל־ el · הָאָרֶץ ha'aretz · אלהים דההין ע"ה · אֲשֶׁר asher

---

*with Isaac and even My Covenant with Abraham, I shall remember, and also the Land, I shall remember."
(Leviticus 26:42) And as it also states: "And despite Israel's inequities, when they were to be in
the land of their enemies, I did not despise them nor loathe them such as to destroy them and nullify
My Covenant with them, because I am the Lord, their God. And for their sake, I shall remember
the covenant of the first generation that I had brought out of the land of Egypt for the nations to behold,
in order to be God unto them. I am the Lord." (Leviticus 26:44-45) And as it also states:
"And the Lord shall bring you back from captivity and shall have mercy upon you. And He shall
again gather you from among all nations where the Lord, your God, had dispersed you.
If you have been forsaken at the end of the Heavens, then from there the Lord, your God, shall gather
you and, from there, He shall fetch you. And the Lord, your God, shall lead you to the Land which*

יָרְשׁוּ yarshu אֲבֹתֶיךָ avotecha וִירִשְׁתָּהּ virishta וְהֵיטִבְךָ vehetivcha

וְהִרְבְּךָ vehirbecha מֵאֲבֹתֶיךָ me'avotecha: וְנֶאֱמַר vene'emar עַל al

יְדֵי yedei נְבִיאֶךָ nevi'echa: יְהֹוָה Adonai וְחָנֵּנוּ chonenu

לָךְ lecha קִוִּינוּ kivinu הֱיֵה heye זְרֹעָם zero'am לַבְּקָרִים labekarim

אַף־ af יְשׁוּעָתֵנוּ yeshu'atenu (reference to the "Ten martyrs of the kingdom")

בְּעֵת be'et צָרָה tzara אלהים הההן: וְנֶאֱמַר vene'emar: וְעֵת־ ve'et

צָרָה tzara אלהים הההן הִיא hee לְיַעֲקֹב leYaakov הויות, יאהדונהי אידהנויה

וּמִמֶּנָּה umimena יִוָּשֵׁעַ yivashe'a: וְנֶאֱמַר vene'emar: בְּכָל־ bechol ב"כ, לכב

צָרָתָם tzaratam | לוֹ lo (כתיב: לֹא) צָר tzar וּמַלְאַךְ umal'ach

פָּנָיו panav הוֹשִׁיעָם hoshi'am בְּאַהֲבָתוֹ be'ahavato וּבְחֶמְלָתוֹ uvchemlato

הוּא hu גְּאָלָם ge'alam וַיְנַטְּלֵם vaynatlem וַיְנַשְּׂאֵם vaynas'em

כָּל־ kol ילי יְמֵי yemei עוֹלָם olam: וְנֶאֱמַר vene'emar:

THE THIRTEEN ATTRIBUTES

The *Thirteen Attributes* are 13 virtues or properties that reflect the 13 different aspects of our daily relationship with the Creator. They work like a mirror. If we perform a negative action in our world, the mirror reflects this negative energy back onto us. As we attempt to transform our reactive nature into a proactive one, this direct feedback from the world of *Yetzirah* helps to guide and correct us. The number 13 also represents "one above the 12 signs of the zodiac." The 12 astrological signs dictate our instinctive, reactive behaviors. The number 13 gives us control over the 12 signs, thus giving us control over our reactive nature.

An astrological chart is best understood as a DNA blueprint of a person's soul, revealing what the person came into this world to do, and what he or she needs to correct and transform in this lifetime. We are supposed to use the positive aspects of our astrological sign to overcome and transform all the negative aspects imbued in our inner character. It is important to understand that our personal astrological profile is not the *cause* of our nature; it is the *effect*. We are handed a particular DNA blueprint based on our past-life track record. This past-life behavior—and the subsequent spiritual credits and debits that it produced—dictated the time and sign under which we were born. Astrology is merely the mechanism by which we acquire the required traits necessary for our inner growth and change.

---

your forefathers have inherited, and you shall inherit it. He shall benefit you and multiply your numbers over that of your forefathers." (Deuteronomy 30:3-5) And it is also said, through Your prophets: "Lord, be gracious to us, for we have hoped for You. Be their strong Arm in the mornings and also our salvation in times of trouble." (Isaiah 33:2) And as it is said: "It is a time of trouble for Jacob, but he shall be saved from it." (Jeremiah 30:7) Also: "God was distressed by their distress, so the angels that are before Him, redeemed them. With His love and His compassion, He had saved them. He took them and carried them throughout eternity." (Isaiah 33:9) And it is said:

(1) אל   מִי mi   אֵל El   (מילוי) (דס"ג) (יא"י)   כָּמוֹךָ kamocha

(2) רוזם   נֹשֵׂא nose   עָוֺן avon

(3) ווזנון   וְעֹבֵר ve'over   עַל־ al   פֶּשַׁע pesha

(4) ארך   לִשְׁאֵרִית lish'erit   נַחֲלָתוֹ nachalato

(5) אפים   לֹא־ lo   הֶחֱזִיק hechezik   לָעַד la'ad   ב"פ ב"ן   אַפּוֹ apo

(6) ורב וחסד   כִּי־ ki   חָפֵץ chafetz   וָחֶסֶד chesed   ע"ב, ריבוע יהוה   הוּא hu:

(7) ואמת   יָשׁוּב yashuv   יְרַחֲמֵנוּ yerachamenu

(8) נצר וחסד   יִכְבֹּשׁ yichbosh   עֲוֺנֹתֵינוּ avonotenu

(9) לאלפים   וְתַשְׁלִיךְ vetashlich   בִּמְצֻלוֹת bimtzulot

יָם yam   ילי   כָּל־ kol   ילי   חַטֹּאותָם chatotam:

(10) נשא עון   תִּתֵּן titen   ב"פ כהת   אֱמֶת emet   אהיה פעמים אהיה, ז"פ ס"ג   לְיַעֲקֹב leYaakov   ז' הויות, יאהדונהי אידהנויה (וזיבור ז"א ומלכות)

(11) ופשע   חֶסֶד chesed   ע"ב, ריבוע יהוה   לְאַבְרָהָם leAvraham   ח"פ אל, רי"ו ול"ב נתיבות החכמה, רמ"ח (אברים), עסמ"ב וט"ז אותיות פשוטות

(12) ווזטאה   אֲשֶׁר־ asher   נִשְׁבַּעְתָּ nishbata   לַאֲבֹתֵינוּ la'avotenu

(13) ונקה   מִימֵי mimei   קֶדֶם kedem:

THE THIRTEEN ATTRIBUTES
"1) Who is a God like You? 2) Who bears iniquity. 3) And overlooks sin. 4) For the remnant of His heritage. 5) He did not retain His anger forever. 6) For He desires kindness. 7) He shall again have mercy over us. 8) And suppress our iniquities. 9) You shall cast into the depths of the sea all their sins. 10) You grant truth to Jacob. 11) and kindness to Abraham. 12) As You have vowed to our forefathers. 13) From the earliest days." (Micah 7:18-20)

וְנֶאֱמַר vene'emar: וַהֲבִיאוֹתִים vahavi'otim אֶל el הָר har

קָדְשִׁי kodshi בְּבֵית bevet ב״פ ראה וְשִׂמַּחְתִּים vesimachtim

תְּפִלָּתִי tefilati עוֹלֹתֵיהֶם olotehem וְזִבְחֵיהֶם vezivchehem לְרָצוֹן leratzon

כִּי ki מִזְבְּחִי mizbechi עַל al מהע ע״ה, ע״ב בריבוע וקס״א ע״ה, אל שדי ע״ה,

בֵּיתִי veti ב״פ ראה בֵּית bet תְּפִלָּה tefila באתב״ש אוכבי אוכצ, ב״ן אדני

לְכָל lechol הָעַמִּים ha'amim יה אדני יִקָּרֵא yikare ונקודה ע״ה = יוד הי וו הה ר״ת ילה:

ELU DEVARIM

אֵלּוּ elu דְּבָרִים devarim ראה שֶׁאֵין she'en לָהֶם lahem שִׁעוּר shi'ur:

הַפֵּאָה hape'a וְהַבִּכּוּרִים vehabikurim וְהָרֵאָיוֹן vehare'ayon וּגְמִילוּת ugmilut

וַחֲסָדִים chasadim וְתַלְמוּד vetalmud תּוֹרָה torah. אֵלּוּ elu

דְּבָרִים devarim ראה שֶׁאָדָם she'adam מ״ה עוֹשֶׂה ose אוֹתָם otam, והו

אוֹכֵל ochel מִפֵּרוֹתֵיהֶם miperotehem בָּעוֹלָם ba'olam הַזֶּה haze והו

וְהַקֶּרֶן vehakeren ריבוע דס״ג ו׳ אותיות דס״ג קַיֶּמֶת kayemet לוֹ lo לְעוֹלָם le'olam

הַבָּא haba. וְאֵלּוּ ve'elu הֵן hen. כָּבוֹד kibud אָב av וָאֵם va'em,

וּגְמִילוּת ugmilut חֲסָדִים chasadim. וּבִקּוּר uvikur חוֹלִים cholim וכולה =

וְהַכְנָסַת vehachnasat אוֹרְחִים orchim. וְהַשְׁכָּמַת vehashkamat מ״ה עם ד׳ אותיות,

בֵּית bet ב״פ ראה הַכְּנֶסֶת hakeneset. וַהֲבָאַת vahava'at שָׁלוֹם shalom בֵּין ben

אָדָם adam מ״ה לַחֲבֵירוֹ lachavero. וּבֵין uven אִישׁ ish לְאִשְׁתּוֹ le'ishto.

וְתַלְמוּד vetalmud תּוֹרָה torah כְּנֶגֶד keneged מזבוה, ז, אל יהוה כֻּלָּם kulam:

And it is also said: "I have brought them to My Holy Mountain and have rejoiced them in My House of Prayer. Their burnt-offerings and their sacrifices shall be accepted upon My Altar, for My House shall be called: 'My House of Prayer' for all nations." (Isaiah 56:7)

ELU DEVARIM

"The following items have no set measure: the corner of the field, the first fruit, the viewing-offering, giving kindness, and the study of Torah. The following things one person can do and benefit from their fruit, both in this world and, as the capital remains intact for him, in the World to Come. And these are: Honoring the father and mother, Bestowing kindness, Visiting the sick, Showing hospitality to guests, Arriving early at the synagogue, Bringing peace between man and his fellow and between man and his wife, and the study of Torah is equivalent to them all." (Pe'ah Ch.1:1, Shabbat 127a)

LE'OLAM YEHE ADAM

It is important to maintain a sense of awe of the Creator and to have a healthy fear of disconnecting from the Light by behaving dishonestly, whether we are alone or among others. Awe helps us realize that it is our opponent—*Satan*—who is attempting to control our behavior, and not our true nature.

לְעוֹלָם le'olam רִיבוּעַ דס"ג וי' אותיות דס"ג yehe יְהֵא אָדָם adam אָדָם yere יְרֵא

שָׁמַיִם shamayim יִ"פ טל, יִ"פ כוזו baseter בַּסֵּתֶר ב"פ מצר kevagalui כְּבַגָּלוּי◆

וּמוֹדֶה umode עַל al הָאֱמֶת ha'emet אהיה פעמים אהיה, ז"פ ס"ג◆

וְדוֹבֵר vedover אֱמֶת emet אהיה פעמים אהיה, ז"פ ס"ג bilvavo בִּלְבָבוֹ◆

וְיַשְׁכֵּם veyashkim וְיֹאמַר veyomar: רִבּוֹן ribon יהוה ע"ב ס"ג מ"ה ב"ן

הָעוֹלָמִים ha'olamim וַאֲדוֹנֵי va'adonei הָאֲדוֹנִים ha'adonim◆ לֹא lo אַל al

צִדְקוֹתֵינוּ tzidkotenu אֲנַחְנוּ anachnu מַפִּילִים mapilim תַחֲנוּנֵינוּ tachanunenu

לְפָנֶיךָ lefanecha ס"ג מ"ה ב"ן ki כִּי עַל al רַחֲמֶיךָ rachamecha הָרַבִּים harabim:

אֲדֹנָי Adonai | ללה שְׁמָעָה shema'a Adonai | ללה סְלָחָה selacha

אֲדֹנָי Adonai ללה הַקְשִׁיבָה hakshiva וַעֲשֵׂה va'ase אַל al תְּאַחַר te'achar

לְמַעַנְךָ lema'ancha Elohai אֱלֹהַי מילוי ע"ב, דמב ; ילה ki כִּי שִׁמְךָ shimcha

נִקְרָא nikra עַל al עִירְךָ ircha וְעַל ve'al עַמֶּךָ amecha: מַה ma מ"ה

אֲנַחְנוּ anachnu מַה ma מ"ה chayenu וְחַיֵּינוּ◆ מַה ma מ"ה וְחַסְדֵּנוּ chasdenu מ"ה

מַה ma מ"ה tzidkotenu צִדְקוֹתֵינוּ◆ מַה ma מ"ה kochenu כּוֹחֵנוּ מַה ma מ"ה

גְּבוּרָתֵנוּ gevuratenu◆ מַה ma מ"ה nomar נֹאמַר לְפָנֶיךָ lefanecha ס"ג מ"ה ב"ן

יְהֹוָ◌אדניאהיאהרונהי Adonai אֱלֹהֵינוּ Elohenu ילה וֵאלֹהֵי velohei לכב ; מילוי ע"ב, דמב ; ילה

אֲבוֹתֵינוּ avotenu הֲלֹא halo כָּל kol הַגִּבּוֹרִים hagiborim יכי hagiborim כְּאַיִן ke'ayin

לְפָנֶיךָ lefanecha ס"ג מ"ה ב"ן◆ וְאַנְשֵׁי ve'anshei הַשֵּׁם hashem כְּלֹא kelo הָיוּ hayu◆

LE'OLAM YEHE ADAM

You should always have fear of the Heavens in private and in public and should admit to truth and speak truth in your heart. You should rise early and say: Ruler of the worlds, Master of all Masters, "do not present our pleas before You because of our righteousness but because of Your abundant compassion. Lord, hear us. Lord, forgive us. Lord, listen and act and do not delay. My God, do so for Your sake, for Your Name is invoked upon Your City and upon Your Nation." (Daniel 9:18-19) What is our worth and to what avail are our lives, our righteousness, our strength, and our valor? What can we say before You, Lord, our God and the God of our forefathers? All the powerful ones are as nothing before You. Those men of fame are now as if they had never existed.

וַחֲכָמִים vachachamim · כִּבְלִי kivli · מַדָּע mada · וּנְבוֹנִים unvonim

כִּבְלִי kivli · הַשְׂכֵּל haskel ♦ · כִּי ki · כָּל chol · מַעֲשֵׂינוּ ma'asenu

תֹהוּ tohu · וִימֵי vimei · וְחַיֵּינוּ chayenu · הֶבֶל hevel

לְפָנֶיךָ lefanecha · וּמוֹתַר umotar · הָאָדָם ha'adam · מִן min

הַבְּהֵמָה habehema · אַיִן ayin · כִּי ki · הַכֹּל hakol · הָבֶל havel׃

LEVAD HANESHAMAH (EXEPT FOR THAT PURE SOUL)

The only thing of genuine value and importance is our soul, for the soul is an actual part of God. If we make the mistake of forgetting that everyone around us is also part of the Creator,we immediately disconnect ourselves from the Light. *Levad HeNeshamah* helps us value and appreciate the Godliness in all creatures and respect the spiritual essence of our world.

לְבַד levad · הַנְּשָׁמָה haneshamah · הַטְּהוֹרָה hatehora · שֶׁהִיא shehi

עֲתִידָה atida · לִתֵּן liten · דִין din · וְחֶשְׁבּוֹן vecheshbon · לִפְנֵי lifnei · כִסֵּא chise

כְּבוֹדֶךָ chevodecha · וְכָל vechol · הַגּוֹיִם hagoyim · כְּאַיִן ke'ayin

נֶגְדְּךָ negdecha · הֵן hen · גּוֹיִם goyim · שֶׁנֶּאֱמַר shene'emar׃

כְּמַר kemar · מִדְּלִי midli · וּכְשַׁחַק uch'shachak · מֹאזְנָיִם moznayim

נֶחְשָׁבוּ nechshavu · הֵן hen · אִיִּים iyim · כַּדַּק kadak · יִטּוֹל yitol׃

AVAL

We are all descendants of Abraham, Isaac, and Jacob. These great biblical patriarchs came into this world and created a spiritual architecture with them as conduits, connecting with specific aspects of the Light, so that you and I and all the people of the world can tap into the same energy that they themselves embodied. It is because of the merit of these spiritual giants that we may now make the highest possible spiritual connections.

All the wise men are as if without any knowledge and all the sensible ones, as if without intelligence. All of our deeds are chaotic and the days of our lives are vain before You. (Tana Devei Rabbi Eliezar Ch. 21) *And man is not superior to beasts, for all is vanity.* (Ecclesiastes 3:19)

LEVAD HaNeshamah

Except For that pure soul

that is destined to stand in judgment and be accountable before Your Throne of Glory. The nations are as nothing before You, as it is said: "Truly all nations are as a drop in a bucket and are considered as the dust upon the scales. He removes the lands as easily as dust." (Isaiah 40:15)

אֲבָל aval   אֲנַֽחְנוּ anachnu   עַמְּךָ amecha   בְּנֵי benei   בְּרִיתֶֽךָ veritecha   בְּנֵי benei

אַבְרָהָם Avraham   ו״פ אל, רי״ו ול״ב נתיבות החכמה, רמ״ח (אברים), עסמ״ב וט״ז אותיות פשוטות

אֹהַבְךָ ohavecha   שֶׁנִּשְׁבַּֽעְתָּ shenishbata   לוֹ lo   בְּהַר behar

הַמּוֹרִיָּה haMoriya   זֶֽרַע zera   יִצְחָק Yitzchak   ד״פ ב״ן   עֲקֵדְךָ akedecha

שֶׁנֶּעֱקַד shene'ekad   עַל al   גַּבֵּי gabei   הַמִּזְבֵּֽחַ hamizbe'ach   נגד, ז״ן, אל יהוה

עֲדַת adat   יַעֲקֹב Yaakov   י הויות, יאהדונהי איהדנויה   בִּנְךָ bincha

בְּכוֹרֶֽךָ vechorecha   שֶׁמֵּאַהֲבָתְךָ sheme'ahavatcha   שֶׁאָהַֽבְתָּ she'ahavta

אוֹתוֹ oto   וּמִשִּׂמְחָתְךָ umisimchatcha   שֶׁשָּׂמַֽחְתָּ shesamachta   בּוֹ bo

קָרָֽאתָ karata   אוֹתוֹ oto   יִשְׂרָאֵל Yisrael   וִישֻׁרוּן vishurun:

LEFICHACH

Lefichach awakens a sense of appreciation, ensures our good fortune, and protects all that we hold dear. There is nothing spiritually wrong with striving for bigger and better things in life, but it is our soul consciousness, not our body consciousness, that will determine whether we receive inner happiness and contentment or dissatisfaction and frustration. The deeper message is that we must be happy with our lot in life whatever it may look like, because that experience of happiness and appreciation is exactly what we need to achieve our spiritual growth.

לְפִיכָךְ lefichach   אֲנַֽחְנוּ anachnu   וְחַיָּבִים chayavim   לְהוֹדוֹת lehodot   לָךְ lach

וּלְשַׁבֵּחֲךָ ulshabechach   וּלְפָאֶרְךָ ulfa'arach   וּלְרוֹמְמָךְ ulromemach

וְלִתֵּן veliten   שִׁיר shir   שֶֽׁבַח shevach   וְהוֹדָאָה vehoda'a   לְשִׁמְךָ leshimcha

הַגָּדוֹל hagadol   להוו ; עם ד׳ אותיות = מכה, יזל, אום   וְחַיָּבִים vechayavim

אֲנַֽחְנוּ anachnu   לוֹמַר lomar   לְפָנֶֽיךָ lefanecha   ס״א מ״ה ב״ן   שִׁירָה shira

בְּכָל bechol   ב״ן, לכב   יוֹם yom   ע״ה נגד, מזבוח, ז״ן, אל יהוה   תָּמִיד tamid   ע״ה קס״א קנ״א קמ״ג

AVAL

But we are Your Nation, the members of Your Covenant: the children of Abraham, who had loved You and to whom You had sworn upon Mount Moriah; the offspring of Isaac, Your bound one, who was bound upon the altar; and the Congregation of Jacob, Your son, Your firstborn, that out of the love and joy You had for him, You had rejoiced in him and called him Israel and also Yeshurun.

LEFICHACH

Consequently, we have an obligation to give thanks to You, to praise, glorify, and exalt You, and give a song of praise and gratitude to Your great Name. We are obligated to say before You, daily and forever,

אַשְׁרֵנוּ ashrenu מַה ma מ"ה טוֹב tov והו וְחֶלְקֵנוּ chelkenu

וּמַה uma מ"ה נָּעִים na'im גּוֹרָלֵנוּ goralenu◆ וּמַה uma מ"ה

יָּפָה yafa מְאֹד me'od יְרֻשָׁתֵנוּ yerushatenu◆ אַשְׁרֵנוּ ashrenu

שֶׁאֲנַחְנוּ she'anachnu מַשְׁכִּימִים mashkimim וּמַעֲרִיבִים uma'arivim

בְּבָתֵּי bevatei כְנֵסִיּוֹת chenesiyot וּבְבָתֵּי uvevatei מִדְרָשׁוֹת midrashot◆

וּמְיַחֲדִים umyachadim שִׁמְךָ shimcha בְּכָל bechol ב"ן, לכב

יוֹם yom ע"ה נגד, זן, אל יהוה תָּמִיד tamid ע"ה נתה, קס"א קנ"א קמ"ג

אוֹמְרִים omrim פַּעֲמַיִם pa'amayim בְּאַהֲבָה be'ahava אהוד, דאגה ♦

SMALL SHEMA

This version of the *Shema* acts as a rocket booster, helping to launch us into *Shacharit*, the morning connection. First we scan the meditations that precede the *Shema* to prepare our internal Vessel. When we recite the *Shema*, we unite the Upper Worlds with the physical world. We acknowledge that there is only one Creator, one Source, and that the past, the present and the future are one. We overlay our physical reality with the Tree of Life Reality, creating a bridge with your consciousness, meditating that all is one.

Inside the *Shema* are two large Aramaic letters: *Ayin* ע and *Dalet* ד. Together, they spell the Aramaic word for "witness," עד. The Light is a witness to all we do, and we are always accountable for our actions, even if we think nobody saw us perform them. This is the law of Cause and Effect.

On *Shabbat* we skip the medition and continue on page 209.

First, meditate in general, on the first *Yichud* of the four *Yichuds* of the Name: יהוה, and in particular, to awaken the letter ה, and then to connect it with the letter ו. Then connect the letter י and the letter ה together in the following order: Hei (ה), Hei-Vav (ו"ה), then Yud-Hei (י"ה), which adds up to 31, the secret of יא"ל of the Name ס"ג. It is good to meditate on this *Yichud* before reciting any *Shema* because it acts as a replacement for the times that you may have missed reading the *Shema*. This *Yichud* has the same ability to create a Supernal connection like the reading of the *Shema* - to raise *Zeir* and *Nukva* together for the *Zivug* of *Abba* and *Ima*.

how fortunate we are; how good is our lot; how pleasant is our destiny; and how beautiful is our inheritance. We are joyful for being able to rise early and return late, in and from the synagogues and houses of study, and to proclaim the unity of Your Name, daily and forever, and we say twice, lovingly:

Shema - שְׁמַע

General Meditation: שָׁם עַ — to draw the energy from the Seven Lower *Sefirot* of *Ima* to the *Nukva*, which enables the *Nukva* to elevate the *Mayin Nukvin* (awakening from Below).

Particular Meditation: שָׁם = יְהֹוָה ← שַׁדַּי and five times the letters י and ה of בְּ"ן = עַ [The letter *Hei* (ה) is formed by the letters *Dalet* (ד) and *Yud* (י), so in בְּ"ן we have four times the letter ה plus another time the letters י and ה from יוֹד of בְּ"ן.]. Also the three letters ו (18) that are left from בְּ"ן, plus בְּ"ן itself (52) equals עַ (70).

Yisrael – יִשְׂרָאֵל

General Meditation: שִׁיר אֵל — to draw energy from *Chesed* and *Gevurah* of *Abba* to *Zeir Anpin*, to do his action in the secret of *Mayin Duchrin* (awakening from Above).

Particular Meditation: (the rearranged letters of the word *Yisrael*) – שׁר אֵלִי

עַ"ר = מִילוּי דְעַדַּ"י (יוֹד לָת וד),

אֵלִי = מ"א אוֹתִיוֹת שֶׁבְּאֵהיָה דְאַלְפִין פָּשׁוּט וּמֵלֵא וּמֵלָא דְמֵלָא

(אֵהיָה אָלֶף הֵא יוֹד הֵא אָלֶף לָמֵד פָּא הֵא אָלֶף יוֹד וָאוֹ דָלֶת הֵא אָלֶף).

Meditate to draw the Surrounding Light of *Ima* and the Inner Light of *Abba* of *Katnut* into *Zeir Anpin*.

Adonai Elohenu Adonai - יְהֹוָה אֱלֹהֵינוּ יְהֹוָה

General Meditation: to draw energy to *Abba*, *Ima* and *Da'at* from *Arich Anpin*,

Particular Meditation: עַ"ב (יוֹד הִי וִיו הִי) קְסַ"א (אַלֶף הִי יוֹד הִי) עַ"ב (יוֹד הִי וִי הִי)

Echad – אֶחָד

(The secret of the complete *Yichud-Unification*)

The letters *Alef* א and *Chet* ח from *Echad* אֶחָד are *Zeir Anpin* and the letter *Dalet* ד is *Nukva*. **You should meditate** to devote your soul for the sanctification of the Holy Name, thereby elevating your *Nefesh*, *Ruach*, *Neshamah* and *Neshamah* of *Neshamah* with *Zeir Anpin* and *Nukva* (using the Names: עַ"ב and ס"ג) to *Abba* and *Ima* as the secret of *Mayin Nukvin*, and by that energy, *Abba* and *Ima* will be unified in the secret of the Name: יְאֱהֹדוּנְהִי. **Also meditate** to draw out the Surrounding Light of *Katnut* of *Abba* and the Inner Six Edges of *Gadlut* of *Ima* into *Zeir Anpin*. The Drop, which is עַ"ב, is drawn out from the Internal of *Arich Anpin*, and descends to *Yesod* of *Ima*, where it becomes: עַ"ב ס"ג מ"ה בְּן, and the four spelled out אֱהיָה (אַלֶף הִי יוֹד הִי, אַלֶף הִי יוֹד הִי, אַלֶף הֵא יוֹד הֵא, אַלֶף הֵה יוֹד הֵה) become Her clothing. As a result, *Zeir Anpin* now has four spelled out יְהֹ"ו (יוֹד הִי וִיו, יוֹד הִי וָאוֹ, יוֹד הֵא וָאוֹ, יוֹד הֵה וָ), four spelled out אֱהֹ"י (אַלֶף הִי יוֹד, אַלֶף הִי יוֹד, אַלֶף הֵא יוֹד, אַלֶף הֵה יוֹד) and the Inner Six Edges of *Gadlut* of *Ima*. **Also meditate** on the Name: אַלֶ"ף הֵ"י וִ"ו הֵ"י, which is the entire *Mochin* in the secret of *Da'at*. **And also meditate** (according to the Ramchal) on the four spelled out *Alef* (אַלֶף=111) of the Name: אֱהיָה that is equal to the word *Midat* (444), making the *Keter* for *Leah*.

Baruch Shem Kevod Malchuto Le'olam Va'ed
בָּרוּךְ שֵׁם כְּבוֹד מַלְכוּתוֹ לְעוֹלָם וָעֶד

Baruch Shem Kevod — *Chochmah*, *Binah*, *Da'at* of *Leah*;
Malchuto — Her *Keter*; *Le'olam* — the rest of Her *Partzuf*;

Va'ed — the four הֵיָה (4 times 20 equal to *Va'ed*=80) will make the *Keter* for *Rachel*.

And the four spelled out הֵיָה (הִי יוֹד הִי, הִי יוֹד הִי, הֵא יוֹד הֵא, הֵה יוֹד הֵה) will make the rest of Her body.

שְׁמַע shema ע' רבתי יִשְׂרָאֵל Yisrael יְהֹוָה‎אדניאהדונהי Adonai

אֱלֹהֵינוּ Elohenu יְהֹוָה‎אדניאהדונהי Adonai | יכֹלֹה ד' רבתי echad אֶחָד‎ ; אהבה, דאגה:

(Whisper :) יחו אותיות בָּרוּךְ baruch שֵׁם shem כְּבוֹד kevod מַלְכוּתוֹ malchuto,

לְעוֹלָם le'olam ריבוע דס"ג וי' אותיות דס"ג וָעֶד va'ed:

ATA HU

The following *Ata Hu* occupies the metaphysical realm—*Ein Sof* (the Endless World)—that existed before our world was created. The second *Ata Hu* dwells in our physical world, which, was created after the universe came into being. This knowledge helps to reinforce that there is only one Light that encompasses both the spiritual and physical domains.

אַתָּה Ata הוּא hu אֶחָד‎ echad אהבה, דאגה kodem קֹדֶם‎ עָמם

שֶׁבָּרָאתָ shebarata הָעוֹלָם ha'olam וְאַתָּה veAta הוּא hu אֶחָד‎ echad

אַתָּה Ata ha'olam• הָעוֹלָם shebarata שֶׁבָּרָאתָ le'achar לְאַחַר‎ אהבה, דאגה

וְאַתָּה veAta והו haze הֹזֶה ba'olam בָּעוֹלָם (מילוי דס"ג) יא"י El אֵל hu הוּא

וְאַתָּה veAta haba• הַבָּא ba'olam בָּעוֹלָם (מילוי דס"ג) יא"י El אֵל hu הוּא

kadesh קָדֵשׁ yitamu• יִתַּמּוּ lo לֹא ushnotecha וּשְׁנוֹתֶיךָ hu הוּא

mekadshei מְקַדְּשֵׁי am עַם al עַל be'olamach בְּעוֹלָמָךְ shemach שְׁמָךְ

tarum תָּרוּם malkenu מַלְכֵּנוּ uvishu'atcha וּבִישׁוּעָתְךָ shemecha• שְׁמָךְ

vekarov בְּקָרוֹב vetoshi'enu וְתוֹשִׁיעֵנוּ karnenu• קַרְנֵנוּ vetagbiha וְתַגְבִּיהַ

hamekadesh הַמְקַדֵּשׁ baruch בָּרוּךְ shemecha• שְׁמֶךָ lema'an לְמַעַן

varabim בָּרַבִּים מהשע ע"ה, ע"ב בריבוע וקס"א ע"ה, אל שדי ע"ה shemo שְׁמוֹ:

SMALL SHEMA
"Hear Israel, the Lord our God, The Lord is One." (Deuteronomy 6:4)
"Blessed is the Name of Glory, whose Kingdom is forever and for eternity." (Pesachim 56a)

ATA HU
You are One before You had created the world and You are One after You had created the world. You are Divine in this world and You are Divine in the World to Come. It is You, and Your years are Endless. (Psalms 102:28) Sanctify Your Name, in Your world, upon the nation which sanctifies Your Name. With Your salvation, our King, You shall raise and exalt our worth. Redeem us soon for the sake of Your Name. Blessed is He, Who sanctifies His Name upon the masses.

אַתָּה Ata — הוּא hu — יְהֹוָה Adonai — הָאֱלֹהִים haElohim

בַּשָּׁמַיִם bashamayim — מִמַּעַל mima'al

וְעַל ve'al — הָאָרֶץ ha'aretz — מִתַּחַת mitachat — בִּשְׁמֵי bishmei

הַשָּׁמַיִם hashamayim — הָעֶלְיוֹנִים ha'elyonim

וְהַתַּחְתּוֹנִים vehatachtonim — אַתָּה Ata — הוּא hu — רִאשׁוֹן rishon — וְאַתָּה veAta

אַחֲרוֹן acharon — וּמִבַּלְעָדֶיךָ umibal'adecha — אֵין en — אֱלֹהִים Elohim — הוּא hu

קַבֵּץ kabetz — נְפוּצוֹת nefutzot — קֹוֶיךָ kovecha — מֵאַרְבַּע me'arba

כַּנְפוֹת kanfot — הָאָרֶץ ha'aretz — יַכִּירוּ yakiru

וְיֵדְעוּ veyedu — כָל chol — בָּאֵי ba'ei — עוֹלָם olam — כִּי ki — אַתָּה Ata — הוּא hu

הָאֱלֹהִים haElohim — לְבַדְּךָ levadecha — לְכֹל lechol

מַמְלְכוֹת mamlechot — הָאָרֶץ ha'aretz — אַתָּה Ata — עָשִׂיתָ asita

אֶת et — הַשָּׁמַיִם hashamayim — וְאֶת ve'et — הָאָרֶץ ha'aretz

אֶת et — הַיָּם hayam — וְאֶת ve'et — כָּל kol — אֲשֶׁר asher

בָּם bam — וּמִי umi — בְּכֹל vechol — מַעֲשֵׂה ma'ase — יָדֶיךָ yadecha

בָּעֶלְיוֹנִים ba'elyonim — וּבַתַּחְתּוֹנִים uvatachtonim — שֶׁיֹּאמַר sheyomar — לְךָ lach

מַה ma — תַּעֲשֶׂה ta'ase — וּמַה uma — תִּפְעָל tif'al — אָבִינוּ avinu

שֶׁבַּשָּׁמַיִם shebashamayim — חַי chay — וְקַיָּם vekayam — עֲשֵׂה ase

עִמָּנוּ imanu — חֶסֶד chesed

בַּעֲבוּר ba'avur — כְּבוֹד kevod — שִׁמְךָ shimcha — הַגָּדוֹל hagadol

הַגִּבּוֹר hagibor — וְהַנּוֹרָא vehanora — שֶׁנִּקְרָא shenikra — עָלֵינוּ alenu

---

You are the Lord, the God in the Heavens Above and upon the Earth Below. In the lights of the Heavens Above and the Earth Below, You are first and You are last and apart from You there is no other God. Gather the dispersed of those who have hope in You from the four corners of the Earth. Let all humanity come to recognize and to know that it is You alone Who is God of all the kingdoms of the Earth. You have made the Heavens, the Earth, the sea, and all that they contain. And who among all those who Your hands have made Above and Below can tell You what to do and how to perform? Our Father in the Heavens, Who lives and Who exists, bestow kindness to us for the sake of the glory of Your great, powerful, and awesome Name, that has been invoked upon us.

וְקַיֶּם vekayem לָנוּ lanu אלהים, אלֹהים, אהיה אֲדֹנִי יְהוָֹואדניאהדונהי Adonai

אֱלֹהֵינוּ Elohenu ילה אֶת et הַדָּבָר hadavar ראה שֶׁהִבְטַוְזְתָּנוּ shehivtachtanu

עַל al יְדֵי yedei צְפַנְיָה Tzefanya וֹזְוֹךְ chozach כָּאָמוּר ka'amur בָּעֵת: ba'et

הַהִיא hahi אָבִיא avi אֶתְכֶם etchem וּבָעֵת uva'et קַבְּצִי kabetzi

אֶתְכֶם etchem כִּי ki אֶתֵּן eten אֶתְכֶם etchem לְשֵׁם leshem

הָאָרֶץ ha'aretz בְּשׁוּבִי beshuvi אֶת־ et שְׁבוּתֵיכֶם shevutechem

לְעֵינֵיכֶם le'enechem ריבוע דמ"ה אָמַר amar יְהוָֹואדניאהדונהי Adonai:

THE SACRIFICES – KORBANOT

The word *Korbanot* means "sacrifices." *Korbanot* comes from the Aramaic word *krav*, meaning "war," and also from the Aramaic word *kiruv*, meaning "to bring close." Obviously, we no longer bring physical sacrifices to a Temple, but through this connection, we can still go to war against Satan and bring ourselves closer to the Upper Worlds. By reciting the *Korbanot* prayers with an open mind and trusting heart, we are generating the same amount of power as if we were carrying out all the proper actions in the Temple.

THE OLAH (GRAIN) SACRIFICE

According to the *Zohar* (*Zohar Chadash* 41d), we say this section to cleanse the night of negative thoughts.

וַיְדַבֵּר vaydaber ראה יְהוָֹואדניאהדונהי Adonai אֶל־ el מֹשֶׁה Moshe

אֶת־ et צַו tzav לֵּאמוֹר: lemor

וְאֶת־ ve'et בָּנָיו banav לֵאמוֹר lemor זֹאת zot תּוֹרַת torat אַהֲרֹן Aharon

הָעֹלָה ha'ola הִוא hee הָעֹלָה ha'ola עַל al מוֹקְדָה mokda עַל al

הַמִּזְבֵּחַ hamizbe'ach כָּל kol הַלַּיְלָה halayla עַד ad

May You fulfill for us, Lord, our God, what You have promised us through Tzefaniah, Your seer, as it was said: "At that time, I shall bring you and, at that time, I shall gather you. Because I shall give you fame and praise from among all the nations of the world. I shall return you from captivity before your own eyes. says the Lord." (Tzefaniah 3:20)

THE SACRIFICES – KORBANOT - THE OLAH (GRAIN) SACRIFICE

"And the Lord spoke to Moses and said: Command Aaron and his sons, saying, this is the law of the burnt-offering. It is the burnt-offering that is burnt upon the Altar, throughout the night until

tukad תּוּקַד, אַל יְכֻבֶּה נְגד, זן, hamizbe'ach הַמִּזְבֵּחַ ve'esh וְאֵשׁ haboker הַבֹּקֶר

vad בָּד mido מִדּוֹ מלה hakohen הַכֹּהֵן velavash וְלָבַשׁ :bo בּוֹ

besaro בְּשָׂרוֹ al עַל־ yilbash יִלְבַּשׁ vad בַד umichnesei וּמִכְנְסֵי־

tochal תֹּאכַל asher אֲשֶׁר hadeshen הַדֶּשֶׁן et אֶת־ veherim וְהֵרִים

hamizbe'ach הַמִּזְבֵּחַ al עַל־ ha'ola הָעֹלָה et אֶת־ ha'esh שאה ha'esh הָאֵשׁ

נְגד, זן, אַל יְכֻבֶּה: hamizbe'ach הַמִּזְבֵּחַ etzel אֵצֶל vesamo וְשָׂמוֹ

begadim בְּגָדִים velavash וְלָבַשׁ begadav בְּגָדָיו et אֶת־ ufashat וּפָשַׁט

el אֶל־ hadeshen הַדֶּשֶׁן et אֶת־ vehotzi וְהוֹצִיא acherim אֲחֵרִים

tahor טָהוֹר makom מָקוֹם el אֶל־ lamachane לַמַּחֲנֶה michutz מִחוּץ י"פ אכא:

tukad תּוּקַד, אַל יְכֻבֶּה נְגד, זן, hamizbe'ach הַמִּזְבֵּחַ al עַל־ veha'esh וְהָאֵשׁ שאה

hakohen הַכֹּהֵן פהל aleha עָלֶיהָ uvi'er וּבִעֵר tichbe תִכְבֶּה lo לֹא bo בּוֹ מלה

aleha עָלֶיהָ פהל ve'arach וְעָרַךְ baboker בַּבֹּקֶר baboker בַּבֹּקֶר etzim עֵצִים

chelvei וְחֶלְבֵי פהל aleha עָלֶיהָ vehiktir וְהִקְטִיר ha'ola הָעֹלָה

(מילואי אהיה) tamid תָּמִיד ע"ה קס"א קנ"א קמ"ג esh אֵשׁ :hashelamim הַשְּׁלָמִים

tukad תּוּקַד al עַל־ hamizbe'ach הַמִּזְבֵּחַ נְגד, זן, אַל יְכֻבֶּה lo לֹא tichbe תִכְבֶּה:

THE TAMID – (DAILY) OFFERING

The second sacrifice is the daily offering. The Aramaic word *olat* עוֹלַת, meaning "elevated," can be rearranged to spell *tola* תּוֹלַע, a negative force that is awakened each morning. By adding the word *olat*, as in *Olat Tamid*, we uproot and nullify the negative forces of the morning. *Olat* has the same numeric value (506) as the first sentence in the *Ana Beko'ach*, which corresponds to the *Sefirah* of *Chesed*, which is Mercy. It also represents the seed level of our soul - a realm where separation and negativity do not exist. By changing the letters in *tola* to *olat* and meditating on the first sentence of the *Ana Beko'ach,* we remove the negative force and return to the seed of unconditional love and oneness.

By saying this section, we raise the inner part of the three Upper Sefirot of *Asiyah* to the Upper Level. This is the secret of the *Tamid* Offering, to bring closer the Upper and the Lower, and to elevate the Lower all the way up (*Writings of the Ari: Gates of Meditation* Vol. 1 Ch. 3).

---

the morning, and the fire of the Altar shall be kept burning thereon. The Kohen shall put on his linen garment; his linen trousers he shall wear on his flesh. He shall remove the ashes when the fire has consumed the offering on the Altar; he shall place them beside it. He shall then take off his clothes, put on other garments, and carry the ashes outside the camp to a clean place. And the fire on the Altar shall remain burning and shall not be extinguished. The Kohen shall place wood upon it early in the morning. He shall lay the offering upon it and shall burn the fat as incense of the peace-offerings. The eternal fire shall burn upon the Altar and not be extinguished." (Leviticus 6:1-6)

There is a *tola'at* (worm) in the Holy Side which is the secret of *Chesed* that increases and reveals and shines every morning. And similar to that, there is another *Tola* in the *klipa* (The Impure Side). This negative worm awakens every morning to destroy the world, and God, with Mercy, reveals the worm of the Pure Side which is the Light of *Chesed* (that is mentioned above). And this is the secret of the *Tamid* (Daily Offering) that is called "*Olat HaTamid*," as the word *olat* has the same letters as *tola*, just in a different order. Through the *Olat HaTamid* that is recited every morning, the *tola* of the Impure Side will surrender. In this section you should meditate to purify the Worlds and to prepare them to receive the abundance from the aspect of *Shabbat*, even though they are purified from the aspect of the weekdays.

וַיְדַבֵּר vaydaber רָאה יְהֹוָה Adonai אֶל el מֹשֶׁה Moshe

לֵּאמֹר lemor צַו tzav אֶת־ et בְּנֵי benei

יִשְׂרָאֵל Yisrael וְאָמַרְתָּ ve'amarta אֲלֵהֶם alehem אֶת־ et קָרְבָּנִי korbani

לַחְמִי lachmi לְאִשַּׁי le'ishai רֵיחַ re'ach נִיחֹחִי nichochi תִּשְׁמְרוּ tishmeru

לְהַקְרִיב lehakriv לִי li בְּמוֹעֲדוֹ bemo'ado וְאָמַרְתָּ ve'amarta לָהֶם lahem

זֶה ze הָאִשֶּׁה ha'ishe אֲשֶׁר asher תַּקְרִיבוּ takrivu לַיהֹוָה ladonai

כְּבָשִׂים kevasim בְּנֵי benei שָׁנָה shana תְמִימִם temimim שְׁנַיִם shenayim

לַיּוֹם layom ola עֹלָה תָמִיד tamid

אֶת־ et הַכֶּבֶשׂ hakeves אֶחָד echad ta'ase תַּעֲשֶׂה בַבֹּקֶר vaboker

וְאֵת ve'et הַכֶּבֶשׂ hakeves הַשֵּׁנִי hasheni תַּעֲשֶׂה ta'ase בֵּין ben

הָעַרְבָּיִם ha'arbayim וַעֲשִׂירִית va'asirit הָאֵיפָה ha'efa סֹלֶת solet

לְמִנְחָה lemincha בְּלוּלָה belula בְּשֶׁמֶן beshemen

כָּתִית katit רְבִיעִת revi'it הַהִין hahin עֹלַת olat

(Meditate here to surrender the *klipa* named *Tola* using the Name: אבגיתץ)

תָּמִיד tamid הָעֲשֻׂיָה ha'asuya בְּהַר behar סִינַי Sinai

לְרֵיחַ lere'ach נִיחֹחַ nicho'ach אִשֶּׁה ishe לַיהֹוָה ladonai

---

THE TAMID – (DAILY) OFFERING

"And the Lord spoke to Moses and said: Command the children of Israel and say to them, My offering, the bread of My fire-offering, My pleasing fragrance, you shall take care to sacrifice to Me at its specified time. And you shall say to them: This is the fire-offering that you shall sacrifice to God, perfect one-year-old sheep, two per day, as a regular daily offering; one sheep you shall do in the morning and the second sheep you shall do in the late afternoon. And one tenth of ephah of fine flour, for a meal-offering, mixed with one quarter of a hin of pressed oil. This is a regular burnt-offering that is made at Mount Sinai as a pleasing fragrance and as a fire-offering before the Lord.

veniskó וְנִסְכּוֹ   revi'it רְבִיעִת   hahin הַהִין   lakeves לַכֶּבֶשׂ

ha'echad הָאֶחָד   אהבה, דאגה   bakodesh בַּקֹּדֶשׁ   hasech הַסֵּךְ

nesech נֶסֶךְ   shechar שֵׁכָר   י"פ ב"ן   ladonai לַיהֹוָה:

ve'et וְאֵת   hakeves הַכֶּבֶשׂ   hasheni הַשֵּׁנִי   ta'ase תַּעֲשֶׂה   ben בֵּין

ha'arbayim הָעַרְבָּיִם   keminchat כְּמִנְחֹת   haboker הַבֹּקֶר   uchnisko וּכְנִסְכּוֹ

ta'ase תַּעֲשֶׂה   ishe אִשֵּׁה   (elevation to *Yetzirah*) re'ach רֵיחַ   (elevation to *Beriah*)

nicho'ach נִיחֹוֹחַ   (elevation to *Atzilut*) ladonai לַיהֹוָה   (elevation to the Endless World):

THE INCENSE

These verses from the *Torah* and the *Talmud* speak about the 11 herbs and spices that were used in the Temple. These herbs and spices were used for one purpose: To help us remove the force of death from every area of our lives. This is one of the few prayers whose sole goal is the eradication of death. The *Zohar* teaches us that whoever has judgment pursuing him needs to connect to this incense. The 11 herbs and spices connect to 11 Lights that sustain the *klipot* (shells of negativity). When we uproot the 11 Lights from the *klipot* through the power of the incense, the *klipot* lose their life-force and die. In addition to bringing the 11 spices to the Temple, the people brought resin, wine, and other items with metaphysical properties to help battle the Angel of Death.

It says in the *Zohar*: "Come and see, whoever is pursued by judgment is in need of incense and must repent before his master, for incense helps judgment to disappear from him." The 11 herbs and spices correspond to the 11 holy illuminations that revive the *klipa*. By elevating them, the *klipa* will die. Through these 11 herbs, the *klipot* are pushed away and the energy-point that was giving them life is removed. And since the Pure Side and its livelihood disappear, the *klipot* is left with no life. Thus the secret of the incense is that it cleanses the force of plague and cancels it. The incense kills the Angel of Death and takes away his power to kill.

Ata אַתָּה   hu הוּא   Adonai יְהֹוָה   Elohenu אֱלֹהֵינוּ יל>   shehiktiru שֶׁהִקְטִירוּ

avotenu אֲבוֹתֵינוּ   lefanecha לְפָנֶיךָ ס"ג מ"ה ב"ן   et אֶת   ketoret קְטֹרֶת

קְטֹרֶת – הַק' בְּאַתְבַּ"שׁ ד' = תרי"ג (מצוות) ; י"א פְּעָמִים אֲדֹנָי (הַנְּבְרָרִים מֵהַקְּלִיפוֹת עַ"י י"א הַסַּמְמָנִים)

hasamim הַסַּמִּים   ע"ה   קָנָ"א,   אֲדֹנָי   אלהים   bizman בִּזְמָן

shebet שֶׁבֵּית   ב"פ   ראה   hamikdash הַמִּקְדָּשׁ   kayam קָיָם

ka'asher כַּאֲשֶׁר   tzivita צִוִּיתָ   otam אוֹתָם   al עַל־   yad יַד   Moshe מֹשֶׁה מהע,

nevia'ch נְבִיאָךְ אל עדי   kakatuv כַּכָּתוּב   betoratach בְּתוֹרָתָךְ: ע"ב בָּרִיבוּעַ וקס"א,

---

Its libation is one quarter of a hin for the one sheep in the Sanctuary, pour a libation of old wine before the Lord. The second sheep you shall do in the afternoon like the meal-offering of the morning; its libation you shall do as a fire-offering of a fragrance which is pleasing to the Lord." (Numbers 28:1-8)

THE INCENSE

It is You, Lord, our God, before whom our forefathers burned the incense spices, during the time when the Temple existed, as You had commanded them through Moses, Your Prophet, and as it is written in Your Torah:

THE PORTION OF THE INCENSE

To raise the Sefirot from all of Nogah of Atzilut, Beriah, Yetzirah and Asiyah.

וַיֹּאמֶר vayomer · יְהֹוָה Adonai · אֶל el · מֹשֶׁה Moshe

קַח kach · לְךָ lecha · סַמִּים samim (Tiferet, Netzach)

נָטָף nataf (Hod) | וּשְׁחֵלֶת ushchelet (Yesod) · וְחֶלְבְּנָה vechelbena

(Malchut) סַמִּים samim (Keter, Chochmah, Binah, Chesed, Gevurah)

וּלְבֹנָה ulvona zaka זַכָּה (Surrounding Light) · בַּד bad · בְּבַד bevad

יִהְיֶה yih'ye · קְטֹרֶת ketoret · אֹתָהּ ota · וְעָשִׂיתָ ve'asita

רֹקַח rokach · מַעֲשֵׂה ma'ase

רוֹקֵחַ roke'ach · מְמֻלָּח memulach · טָהוֹר tahor · קֹדֶשׁ kodesh

וְשָׁחַקְתָּ veshachakta · מִמֶּנָּה mimena

הָדֵק hadek · וְנָתַתָּה venatata · מִמֶּנָּה mimena · לִפְנֵי lifnei · הָעֵדֻת ha'edut

בְּאֹהֶל be'ohel · מוֹעֵד mo'ed · אֲשֶׁר asher · אוּעֵד iva'ed · לְךָ lecha · שָׁמָּה shama

קֹדֶשׁ kodesh · קָדָשִׁים kadashim · תִּהְיֶה tihye · לָכֶם lachem · וְנֶאֱמַר vene'emar

וְהִקְטִיר vehiktir · עָלָיו alav · אַהֲרֹן Aharon · קְטֹרֶת ketoret

סַמִּים samim

בַּבֹּקֶר baboker · בַּבֹּקֶר baboker · בְּהֵיטִיבוֹ behetivo

אֶת et · הַנֵּרֹת hanerot · יַקְטִירֶנָּה yaktirena · וּבְהַעֲלֹת uveha'alot

אַהֲרֹן Aharon · אֶת et · הַנֵּרֹת hanerot · בֵּין ben · הָעַרְבַּיִם ha'arbayim

יַקְטִירֶנָּה yaktirena · קְטֹרֶת ketoret

תָּמִיד tamid

לִפְנֵי lifnei · יְהֹוָה Adonai · לְדֹרֹתֵיכֶם ledorotechem

THE PORTION OF THE INCENSE

"And the Lord said to Moses: Take for yourself spices, balsam sap, onycha, galbanum, and pure frankincense, each of equal weight. You shall prepare it as an incense compound: The work of a spice-mixer, well-blended, pure, and holy. You shall grind some of it fine and place it before the Testimony in the Tabernacle of Meeting, in which I shall meet with you. It shall be the Holy of Holies unto you." (Exodus 30:34-36) And God also said: "Aaron shall burn upon the Altar incense spices early each morning when he prepares the candles. And when Aaron raises the candles at sundown, he shall burn the incense spices as a continual incense-offering before the Lord throughout all your generations." (Exodus 30:7-8)

THE WORKINGS OF THE INCENSE

The filling of the incense has two purposes: First, to remove the *klipot* in order to stop them from going up along with the elevation of the Worlds, and second, to draw Light to *Asiyah*. So meditate to raise the sparks of Light from all of the *Nogah* of *Azilut*, *Beriah*, *Yetzirah* and *Asiyah*.

Count the incense using the fingers of your right hand, one by one, and don't skip even one, as it is said: "If one omits one of all the ingredients, he is liable to receive the penalty of death." And therefore, you should be careful not to skip any of them, because reciting this paragraph is a substitute for the actual burning of the incense.

אַדֹנִי י"א פְּעָמִים haketoret הַקְּטֹרֶת pitum פִּטּוּם rabanan רַבָּנָן tanu תָּנוּ

(מִצְוֹת) תרי"ג = ד' ד' באתב"ע הַקּ - קְטֹרֶת (הַסַּמָּנִים י"א ע"י (הַנִּבְרָרִים

(דְשַׁבָּת מַרְגְלָאֵין ו') מְצַפְצֵף אֱלֹהִים אֵל אֲדֹנִי יָהּ מְצַפְצֵף יְהֹוָה יְהֹוָה = הַקְּטֹרֶת פִּטּוּם

דְיוֹדִין אֱלֹהִים ,ע = הַמִּסְפָּר me'ot מֵאוֹת shelosh שְׁלֹשׁ ketzad כֵּיצַד

hayu הָיוּ manim מָנִים ushmona וּשְׁמוֹנָה (י') הָעֵ' מִילּוּי = הַמִּסְפָּר veshishim וְשִׁשִּׁים

veshishim וְשִׁשִּׁים דְיוֹדִין אֱלֹהִים ,ע = הַמִּסְפָּר me'ot מֵאוֹת shelosh שְׁלֹשׁ va וָ bah בָּהּ

yemot יְמוֹת keminyan כְּמִנְיָן vachamisha וַחֲמִשָּׁה (י') הָעֵ' מִילּוּי = הַמִּסְפָּר

לכב ,ב"ז bechol בְּכָל אֲדֹנִי אֶל ,פוי ,ע"ה mane מָנֶה hachama הַחַמָּה הַוֹּזָּמָה

baboker בַּבֹּקֶר machatzito מַחֲצִיתוֹ יְהֹוָה אֶל ,ז ,נֶגֶד מֹזְבֵּחַ ,ע"ה yom יוֹם

manim מָנִים ushlosha וּשְׁלֹשָׁה ba'erev בָּעֶרֶב umachatzito וּמַחֲצִיתוֹ

מלה kohen כֹּהֵן machnis מַכְנִיס shemehem שֶׁמֵּהֶם קנ"א וקמ"ג ,קס"א קס"א yeterim יְתֵרִים

mehem מֵהֶם venotel וְנוֹטֵל ,אום ,יזל ,מבה = אוֹתִיּוֹת ד' עִם ; לְהוּו gadol גָּדוֹל

hakipurim הַכִּפּוּרִים chofnav חָפְנָיו melo מְלֹא יְהֹוָה אֶל ,מֹזְבֵּחַ ,ז ,נֶגֶד ע"ה beyom בְּיוֹם

be'erev בָּעֶרֶב lamachteshet לַמַּכְתֶּשֶׁת machaziran מַחֲזִירָן

lekayem לְקַיֵּם kedei כְּדֵי hakipurim הַכִּפּוּרִים יְהֹוָה אֶל ,ז ,מֹזְבֵּחַ ,נֶגֶד ע"ה yom יוֹם

דָאגָה ,אַהֲבָה ve'achad וְאֶוָד hadaka הַדַּקָּה min מִן daka דַּקָּה mitzvat מִצְוֹת

hen הֵן ve'elu וְאֵלּוּ va וָ bah בָּהּ hayu הָיוּ samanim סַמָּנִים asar עֲשַׂר

THE WORKINGS OF THE INCENSE

Our Sages have taught: How was the compounding of the incense done? Three hundred and sixty-eight portions were contained therein. These corresponded to the number of days in the solar year, one portion for each day: Half of it in the morning and half at sundown. As for the remaining three portions, the High Priest, on Yom Kippur, filled both his hands with them. On the Eve of Yom Kippur, he would take them back to the mortar to fulfill the requirement that they should be very finely ground. Each portion contained eleven spices:

1) הַצֳּרִי haTzori (Keter) מצפצ, אלהים דיודין, י"פ יי"י ♦ 2) וְהַצִּפּׂרֶן vehaTziporen (Yesod)

3) וְהַחֶלְבְּנָה vehaChelbena (Malchut) ע"ה פוי, אל אדני♦ יהוה אדני אהיה ע"ה פוי, אל אדני♦

4) וְהַלְּבוֹנָה vehaLevona – Surrounding Light) שהוא אור לבן והוא יוזיד"י הנקרא אדון יוזיד)

מִשְׁקָל mishkal שִׁבְעִים שִׁבְעִים shiv'im shiv'im מָנֶה mane ע"ה פוי, אל אדני♦

5) מוֹר Mor (Chesed)♦ 6) וּקְצִיעָה uKtzi'ah רהע (Gevurah – "כי מצפון תפתח הרעה",

7) וְשִׁבּוֹלֶת veShibolet נֵרְדְּ Nerd (Tiferet)♦ צפון רוח סוד והגבורה

8) וְכַרְכּוֹם veCharkom (Netzach) בזְׇהר, סנדלפון, ערי♦ מִשְׁקָל mishkal שִׁשָּׁה shisha

עָשָׂר asar שִׁשָּׁה shisha עָשָׂר asar מָנֶה mane ע"ה פוי, אל אדני♦ 9) קֹשְׁטְ Kosht

(Chochmah) שְׁנַיִם sheneim עָשָׂר asar♦ 10) קְלוּפָה Kilufa (Binah) שְׁלֹשָׁה shelosha♦

11) קִנָּמוֹן Kinamon (Hod) (בסוד קדוש קדוש קדוש) ר"ת ג"פ ק♦ תִּשְׁעָה tish'ah♦

בּוֹרִית borit כַּרְשִׁינָא karshina תִּשְׁעָה tish'ah קַבִּין kabin♦ יַיִן yen מיכ, י"פ האא♦

קַפְרִיסִין Kafrisin סְאִין se'in תְּלַת telat וְקַבִּין vekabin תְּלָתָא telata אהיה קבין

וְאִם ve'im יוהר, מ"א אותיות דפשוט, דמילוי ודמילוי דמילוי דאהיה ע"ה לֹא lo מָצָא matza

יַיִן yen מיכ, י"פ האא כַּפְרִיסִין Kafrisin מֵבִיא mevi וְחֶמַר chamar וִיּׄוֹר chivar

עָתִיק atik♦ רוּבַע rova♦ סְדוֹמִית Sedomit מֶלַח melach מָלֵוֹּ ma'ale מַעֲלֶה ma'ale

עָשָׁן ashan כֹּל kol שֶׁהוּא shehu♦ רִבִּי Ribi נָתָן Natan הַבַּבְלִי haBavli

אוֹמֵר omer: אַף af מִכְפַּת mikipat הַיַּרְדֵּן haYarden י היוית וד' אותיות כֹּל kol יל

שֶׁהִיא shehi♦ אִם im יוהר, מ"א אותיות דפשוט, דמילוי ודמילוי דמילוי דאהיה ע"ה נָתַן natan

בָּה ba דְּבַשׁ devash שׇׁ (דעופר) וי"ד (האווזו) = ש"ך דינין דגדלות פְּסָלָה pesala♦

וְאִם ve'im יוהר, מ"א אותיות דפשוט, דמילוי ודמילוי דמילוי דאהיה ע"ה וְחִסֵּר chiser

אַחַת achat מִכָּל mikol יל סַמְמָנֶיהָ samemaneha וְחַיָּיב chayav מִיתָה mita:

---

1) Balsam. 2) Onycha. 3) Galbanum. 4) Frankincense; the weight of seventy portions each. 5) Myrrh. 6) Cassia. 7) Spikenard. 8) And Saffron; the weight of sixteen portions each. 9) Twelve portions of Costus. 10) Three of aromatic Bark 11) Nine of Cinnamon. Further, nine kavs of Lye of Carsina. And three kavs and three se'ehs of Cyprus wine. And if one should not find any Cyprus wine, he should bring an old white wine. And a quarter of the salt of Sodom. And a small measure of a smoke raising herb. Rabbi Natan, the Babylonian, advised also, a small amount of Jordan resin. If he added to it honey, he would make it defective. If he omits even one of all its herbs, he would be liable to death.

רַבָּן Raban שִׁמְעוֹן Shimon בֶּן ben גַּמְלִיאֵל Gamli'el אוֹמֵר omer:

הַצֳּרִי haTzori אלהים דיודין, י"פ ייי מצפצ, אֵינוֹ eno אֶלָּא ela שְׂרָף seraf

הַנּוֹטֵף hanotef מֵעֲצֵי me'atzei הַקְּטָף haketaf◆ בּוֹרִית borit

כַּרְשִׁינָא karshina לָמָה lema הִיא hee בָּאָה va'a◆ כְּדֵי kedei

לְשַׁפּוֹת leshapot בָּהּ ba אֶת et הַצִּפֹּרֶן haTziporen יהוה אדני אהיה עדי

כְּדֵי kedei שֶׁתְּהֵא shetehe נָאָה na'a◆ יַיִן yen ע' (כנגד ע' אומות העולם התלויים בסמאל),

קַפְרִיסִין Kafrisin לָמָה lema הוּא hu בָּא va◆ כְּדֵי kedei מיכ, י"פ האא

לִשְׁרוֹת lishrot בּוֹ bo אֶת et הַצִּפֹּרֶן haTziporen יהוה אדני אהיה עדי

כְּדֵי kedei שֶׁתְּהֵא shetehe עַזָּה aza◆ וַהֲלֹא vahalo בְּמֵי mei יְלִי רַגְלַיִם raglayim

יָפִין yafin לָהּ la אֶלָּא ela שֶׁאֵין she'en מַכְנִיסִין machnisin בְּמֵי mei יְלִי

רַגְלַיִם raglayim בַּמִּקְדָּשׁ bamikdash מִפְּנֵי mipenei הַכָּבוֹד hakavod לאו:

תַּנְיָא tanya◆ רִבִּי Ribi נָתָן Natan אוֹמֵר omer: כְּשֶׁהוּא keshehu

שׁוֹחֵק shochek אוֹמֵר omer הָדֵק hadek הֵיטֵב hetev◆ הֵיטֵב hetev

הָדֵק hadek◆ מִפְּנֵי mipenei שֶׁהַקּוֹל shehakol יָפֶה yafe לַבְּשָׂמִים labesamim◆

פִּטְּמָהּ pitema לַחֲצָאִין lachatza'in כְּשֵׁרָה keshera◆ לִשְׁלִישׁ leshalish

וְלִרְבִיעַ ulravi'a לֹא lo שָׁמַעְנוּ shamanu◆ אָמַר amar רִבִּי Ribi

יְהוּדָה Yehuda: זֶה ze הַכְּלָל hakelal◆ אִם im יוהך, מ"א אותיות דפשוט, דמילוי

כְּמִדָּתָהּ kemidata כְּשֵׁרָה keshera לַחֲצָאִין lachatza'in◆ ורמילוי דמילוי דאהיה ע"ה

וְאִם ve'im יוהך, מ"א אותיות דפשוט, דמילוי ורמילוי דמילוי דאהיה ע"ה וְחָסֵר chiser

אַחַת achat מִכָּל mikol יְלִי סַמְמָנֶיהָ samemaneha וְחַיָּיב chayav מִיתָה mita:

Rabban Shimon ben Gamliel says: The balsam was a sap that only seeped from the balsam trees. For what purpose was the lye of Carsina added? In order to rub the Onycha with it to make it pleasant looking. For what purpose was the Cyprus wine added? In order to steep in it the Onycha. Urine is more appropriate for this, but urine is not brought into the Temple out of respect. It was taught that Rabbi Natan said: When he ground, he said: 'Grind it fine, grind it fine.' This is because voice is beneficial to the spices. If he compounds half the amount it is still valid, yet regarding a third or a quarter, we have no information. Rabbi Yehuda said: This is the general rule: If it is in its correct proportions, then half is valid. Yet if he omits one of all its spices, he is liable to death.

o **או** leshishim **לְשָׁשִׁים** achat **אֲוַת** Kapara: **קָפָּרָא** Var **בַּר** tanei **תָּנֵי**

shel **שֶׁל** va'a **בָּאָה** hayta **הָיְתָה** shana **שָׁנָה** leshiv'im **לְשִׁבְעִים**

Var **בַּר** tanei **תָּנֵי** ve'od **וְעוֹד** lachatza'in **לַחֲצָאִין** shirayim **שִׁירַיִם**

ba **בָּהּ** noten **נוֹתֵן** haya **הָיָה** ilu **אִלּוּ** Kapara: **קָפָּרָא**

devash **דְּבַשׁ** shel **שֶׁל** kortov **קָרְטוֹב**

en **אֵין** adam **אָדָם** yachol **יָכוֹל** la'amod **לַעֲמוֹד** mipenei **מִפְּנֵי**

devash **דְּבַשׁ** ba **בָּהּ** me'arvin **מְעָרְבִין** en **אֵין** velama **וְלָמָּה** recha **רֵיחָהּ**

shehatorah **שֶׁהַתּוֹרָה** mipenei **מִפְּנֵי**

amra **אָמְרָה** ki **כִּי** chol **כָּל** se'or **שְׂאֹר**

devash **דְּבַשׁ** vechol **וְכָל**

mimenu **מִמֶּנּוּ** taktiru **תַקְטִירוּ** lo **לֹא**

ladonai: **לַיהוה** ishe **אִשֶּׁה**

Right

imanu **עִמָּנוּ** Tzeva'ot **צְבָאוֹת** Adonai **יהוה**

misgav **מִשְׂגָּב**

Elohei **אֱלֹהֵי** lanu **לָנוּ**

sela: **סֶלָה** Yaakov **יַעֲקֹב**

Left

ashrei **אַשְׁרֵי** Tzeva'ot **צְבָאוֹת** Adonai **יהוה**

bote'ach **בֹּטֵחַ** adam **אָדָם**

bach: **בָּךְ**

Bar Kappara taught that once every sixty or seventy years the leftovers would accumulate to half the measure. Bar Kappara also taught that if one would add to it a Kortov (liquid messurment) of honey, no man would withstand its smell. Why is honey not mixed with it? Because the Torah had stipulated: Because any leaven or honey, you must not burn any of it as burnt-offering to the Lord. *(Kritut 6; Yerushalmi, Yoma: ch.4)*
(Right) *"The Lord of Hosts is with us, our strength is the God of Jacob, Selah." (Psalms 46:12)*
(Left) *"The Lord of Hosts, joyful is one who trusts in You." (Psalms 84:13)*

Central

יְהוֹ(אדני־יאהדונהי) ר"ת יהה hamelech הַמֶּלֶךְ יהוה וש"ע נהורין ע"ה hoshi'a הוֹשִׁיעָה יהוה וש"ע נהורין Adonai יהוה

יְעֲנֵנוּ yaʼanenu בְּיוֹם veyom ע"ה נגד, מזבח, זן, אל יהוה ya'anenu

קָרְאֵנוּ kor'enu ר"ת יב"ק, אלהים יהוה, אהיה אדני יהוה; ס"ת = ב"ן ועם כף דהמלך = ע"ב:

וְעָרְבָה ve'arva לַיהוֹ(אדני־יאהדונהי) ladonai

מִנְחַת minchat יְהוּדָה Yehuda וִירוּשָׁלָ͏ִם virushalaim

כִּימֵי kimei עוֹלָם olam וּכְשָׁנִים uch'shanim קַדְמֹנִיּוֹת: kadmoniyot

THE ORDER OF THE ALTAR SERVICE RITUAL

We recite all the activities and actions that were performed in the Temple. Utilizing the energy transference of the Aramaic letters, it is as though we are actually performing these rites and rituals ourselves. The organs of the animals that were used as sacrifices in the Temple represent our internal organs and when we recite the words of these specific sacrifices, we bring healing and order to our lives.

אַבַּיֵי ◆Abayei (pause   here) הֲוָה hava מְסַדֵּר mesader סֵדֶר seder

הַמַּעֲרָכָה hama'aracha מִשְׁמָא mishema דִּגְמָרָא digmara וְאַלִּבָּא ve'aliba

דְּאַבָּא deAba שָׁאוּל Sha'ul◆ מַעֲרָכָה ma'aracha גְּדוֹלָה gedola

קוֹדֶמֶת kodemet לְמַעֲרָכָה lema'aracha שְׁנִיָּה sheniya שֶׁל shel

קְטֹרֶת ketoret = ד' באתב"ע הק' – קְטֹרֶת; הסממנים א"י י"א ע"י מהקליפות (הנבררים) אדני פעמים י"א

וּמַעֲרָכָה uma'aracha שְׁנִיָּה sheniya שֶׁל shel קְטֹרֶת ketoret תרי"ג (מצוות) ◆

קוֹדֶמֶת kodemet לְסִדּוּר lesidur שְׁנֵי shenei גְּזִירֵי gezirei עֵצִים etzim◆ תרי"ג = ד' באתב"ע הק' – קְטֹרֶת; הסממנים א"י י"א ע"י מהקליפות (הנבררים) אדני פעמים י"א (מצוות)

(Central) *"Lord save us. The King shall answer us the day we call."* (Psalms 20:10) *"May the Lord find the offering of Yehuda and Jerusalem pleasing as He had always done and as in the years of old."* (Malachi 3:4)

THE ORDER OF THE ALTAR SERVICE RITUAL

Abayei, he listed the order of the ritual according to the Gemara and Abba Shaul. The large pyre order preceded the second pyre order of incense. The second pyre of incense preceded the arrangement of the two wooden logs.

וְסִדּוּר (vesidur) שְׁנֵי (shenei) גְזִירֵי (gezirei) עֵצִים (etzim) קוֹדֵם (kodem) עמם

לְדִשּׁוּן (ledishun) מִזְבֵּחַ (mizbe'ach) גגר, זן, אל יהוה הַפְּנִימִי (hapenimi)◆

וְדִשּׁוּן (vedishun) מִזְבֵּחַ (mizbe'ach) גגר, זן, אל יהוה הַפְּנִימִי (hapenimi)

קוֹדֵם (kodem) עמם לַהֲטָבַת (lahatavat) חָמֵשׁ (chamesh) נֵרוֹת (nerot)◆

וַהֲטָבַת (vahatavat) חָמֵשׁ (chamesh) נֵרוֹת (nerot) קוֹדֶמֶת (kodemet)

לְדַם (ledam) הַתָּמִיד (hatamid) ע"ה קס"א קס"א קמ"ג◆ וְדָם (vedam)

הַתָּמִיד (hatamid) ע"ה קס"א קס"א קמ"ג קוֹדֵם (kodem) עמם

לַהֲטָבַת (lahatavat) שְׁתֵּי (shetei) נֵרוֹת (nerot)◆ וַהֲטָבַת (vahatavat)

שְׁתֵּי (shetei) נֵרוֹת (nerot) י"א פעמים אדני קוֹדֶמֶת (kodemet) לִקְטֹרֶת (liktoret)

(הנבררים מהקליפות ע"י י"א הסממנים ; קטרת – הק' באתב"ש ד' = תרי"ג (מצוות)◆ וּקְטֹרֶת (uktoret)

י"א פעמים אדני (הנבררים מהקליפות ע"י י"א הסממנים ; קטרת – הק' באתב"ש ד' = תרי"ג (מצוות)

לְאֵבָרִים (le'evarim)◆ וְאֵבָרִים (ve'evarim) לְמִנְחָה (leminchah) ע"ה ב"פ ב"ן

וּמִנְחָה (uminchah) ע"ה ב"פ ב"ן לַחֲבִתִּין (lachavitin)◆ וַחֲבִתִּין (vachavitin)

לִנְסָכִין (linsachin)◆ וּנְסָכִין (unsachin) לְמוּסָפִין (lemusafin)◆ וּמוּסָפִין (umusafin)

לְבָזִיכִין (levazichin)◆ וּבָזִיכִין (uvazichin) קוֹדְמִין (kodmin) לְתָמִיד (letamid)

ע"ה קס"א קס"א קמ"ג שֶׁל (shel) בֵּין (ben) הָעַרְבַּיִם (ha'arbayim)◆ שֶׁנֶּאֱמַר (shene'emar):

וְעָרַךְ (ve'arach) עָלֶיהָ (aleha) פהל הָעֹלָה (ha'ola) וְהִקְטִיר (vehiktir):

עָלֶיהָ (aleha) פהל חֶלְבֵי (chelvei) הַשְּׁלָמִים (hashelamim)◆ עָלֶיהָ (aleha) פהל

הַשְׁלֵם (hashlem) כָּל (kol) יכי הַקָּרְבָּנוֹת (hakorbanot) כֻּלָּם (kulam):

The arrangement of two wooden logs preceded the removal of ashes from the inner Altar. The removal of ashes from the inner Altar preceded the preparation of the five candles. The preparation of the five candles preceded the blood of the daily offering. The blood of the daily offering preceded the preparation of the two candles. The preparation of the two candles preceded the incense. The incense preceded the limbs and the limbs preceded the meal-offerings. The meal-offerings preceded the baked-offerings. The baked-offerings preceded the wine libations. The wine libations preceded the Musaf sacrifices. The Musaf sacrifices preceded the daily offering at sundown. As was said, He set the burnt-offerings on it as incense. And upon it, you shall complete all of the sacrifices. (Yoma 33a)

ANA BEKO'ACH

The *Ana Beko'ach* is perhaps the most powerful prayer in the entire universe. Second-century Kabbalist Rav Nachunya ben HaKana was the first sage to reveal this combination of 42 letters, which encompass the power of Creation.

The *Ana Beko'ach* is a unique formula, built of 42 letters written in seven sentences, that gives us the ability to transcend this physical world with all its limitations. It is known as the 42-letter Name of God. The *Ana Beko'ach* can literally remove all friction, barriers, and obstacles associated with our physical existence. It injects order into chaos, removes Satan's influence from our nature, generates financial sustenance, arouses unity with and love for others, and provides healing energy to the body and soul. We recite or scan the *Ana Beko'ach* every day, as many times as we want.

There are four elements that we connect to, using the *Ana Beko'ach*. They are:

1) **SEVEN SENTENCES** - The seven sentences correspond to the Seven *Sefirot*, from *Chesed* to *Malchut*. Although there are Ten *Sefirot* in total, only the Lower Seven exert influence in our physical world. By connecting to these Seven, we seize control over this physical world.

2) **LETTERS OF THE MONTH** - Abraham the Patriarch revealed the astrological secrets of the Aramaic letters and of the signs of the zodiac in his kabbalistic treatise, *The Book of Formation* (*Sefer Yetzirah*). Each month of the year is governed by a planet, and each planet has a corresponding verse in the *Ana Beko'ach*; therefore, we also meditate upon the planet and the Aramaic letter that created both the planet and the zodiac sign of that month. In doing so, we connect to the positive energy of each planet and not to its negative influence. For example, the Aramaic letter *Lamed* created the sign of Libra, *Tishrei*. Libra is governed by the planet Venus. The Aramaic letter that gave birth to Venus is *Pei*; therefore, each day during the month of *Tishrei*, we meditate upon the the letters *Lamed* and *Pei* following the recital and meditation of the fifth verse of the *Ana Beko'ach*.

The Month and the Letters		The Astrological Sign And the Letter		The Planet And the Letter		Ana Beko'ach meditation
Tishrei	פּל	Libra	ל	Venus	פ	וּקרבטנע

3) **CORRECTION OF THE SOUL - TIKKUN HANEFESH** - Throughout history, kabbalists have used this healing meditation twice a day, seven days a week, to regenerate and revitalize all the organs of the body. When we reach the sentence in the *Ana Beko'ach* that governs the particular month we are in, we stop and meditate on the letters of the month, and then do the *Tikkun HaNefesh*. (See page 803) Using the chart as a guide, hold your right hand over the particular part of the body to which you are channeling energy. Look at the Aramaic letter combination for the specific area of the body that you are focusing on, and allow the Light to penetrate through your right hand, into that part of the body.

4) **ANGELS OF THE DAY** - Angels are distinct packets of spiritual energy that act as a transportation system for our prayers. They carry our words and thoughts to the Upper Worlds. There is a line of *Ana Beko'ach* for each day of the week, and there are unique angels that govern each day. (See pages 804-806)

Chesed, Sunday *(Alef Bet Gimel Yud Tav Tzadik)* אבג יתץ

אָנָּא ana ✦בְּכֹחַ beko'ach גְּדוּלַת gedulat יְמִינֶךָ yeminecha✦

תַּתִּיר tatir צְרוּרָה tzerura⬧

Gevurah, Monday *(Kuf Resh Ayin Sin Tet Nun)* קרע שטן

קַבֵּל kabel ✦רִנַּת rinat עַמְּךָ amecha שַׂגְּבֵנוּ sagevenu✦

טַהֲרֵנוּ taharenu נוֹרָא nora⬧

Tiferet, Tuesday *(Nun Gimel Dalet Yud Kaf Shin)* נגד יכש

נָא na ✦גִּבּוֹר gibor דּוֹרְשֵׁי dorshei יִחוּדֶךָ yichudecha✦

כְּבָבַת kevavat שָׁמְרֵם shomrem⬧

Netzach, Wednesday *(Bet Tet Resh Tzadik Tav Gimel)* בטר צתג

בָּרְכֵם barchem טַהֲרֵם taharem✦ רַחֲמֵי rachamei צִדְקָתְךָ tzidkatecha✦

תָּמִיד tamid גָּמְלֵם gomlem⬧

Hod, Thursday *(Chet Kuf Bet Tet Nun Ayin)* וזקב טנע

חֲסִין chasin ✦קָדוֹשׁ kadosh בְּרוֹב berov טוּבְךָ tuvcha✦

נַהֵל nahel עֲדָתֶךָ adatecha⬧

ANA BEKO'ACH

Chesed, Sunday אבג יתץ
We beseech You, with the power of Your great right, undo this entanglement.

Gevurah, Monday קרע שטן
Accept the singing of Your Nation. Strengthen and purify us, Awesome One.

Tiferet, Tuesday נגד יכש
Please, Mighty One, those who seek Your unity, guard them like the pupil of the eye.

Netzach, Wednesday בטר צתג
Bless them. Purify them. Your compassionate righteousness always grant them.

Hod, Thursday וזקב טנע
Invincible and Mighty One, with the abundance of Your goodness, govern Your congregation.

Yesod, Friday (Yud Gimel Lamed Pei Zayin Kuf) יגל פזק

יָחִיד yachid   גֵּאֶה ge'e◆   לְעַמְּךָ le'amecha   פְּנֵה pene◆

זוֹכְרֵי zochrei   קְדֻשָּׁתֶךָ kedushatecha:

Malchut, Saturday (Shin Kuf Vav Tzadik Yud Tav) שקו צית

שַׁוְעָתֵנוּ shav'atenu   קַבֵּל kabel◆   וּשְׁמַע ushma   צַעֲקָתֵנוּ tza'akatenu◆

יוֹדֵעַ yode'a   תַּעֲלוּמוֹת ta'alumot:

BARUCH SHEM KEVOD

Whispering this final verse brings all the Light from the Upper Worlds into our physical existence.

(Whisper): יו"ו אותיות   בָּרוּךְ baruch   שֵׁם shem   כְּבוֹד kevod   מַלְכוּתוֹ malchuto

וָעֶד va'ed: לְעוֹלָם le'olam   ריבוע ס"ג וי' אותיות דס"ג

RIBON HAOLAMIM

God has given us specific instructions regarding the sacrifices that were to be carried out in the *Beit HaMikdash* (Holy Temple of Jerusalem). Because of the destruction of the Temple, we are not able to carry out those instructions. Here, we ask God to allow us to use the power of these Aramaic letters as a replacement for those sacrifices.

רִבּוֹן ribon   יהוה ע"ב ס"ג מ"ה ב"ן   הָעוֹלָמִים ha'olamim   אַתָּה Ata   צִוִּיתָנוּ tzivitanu

לְהַקְרִיב lehakriv   קָרְבָּן korban   הַתָּמִיד hatamid   ע"ה   קס"א קנ"א קמ"ג

בְּמוֹעֲדוֹ bemo'ado◆   וְלִהְיוֹת velihiyot   כֹּהֲנִים Kohanim

בַּעֲבוֹדָתָם ba'avodatam   וּלְוִיִּם uLeviyim   בְּדוּכָנָם beduchanam

וְיִשְׂרָאֵל veYisrael   בְּמַעֲמָדָם bema'amadam◆   וְעַתָּה ve'ata

בַּעֲוֹנוֹתֵינוּ ba'avonoteinu   חָרֵב charev   בֵּית bet   ב"פ ראה   הַמִּקְדָּשׁ hamikdash

---

Yesod, Friday יגל פזק
Sole and proud One, turn to Your people, those who remember Your sanctity.

Malchut, Saturday שקו צית
Accept our cry and hear our wail, You that knows all that is hidden.

BARUCH SHEM KEVOD
"Blessed is the Name of Glory. His Kingdom is forever and for eternity." (Pesachim 56a)

RIBON HAOLAMIM
Master of all Worlds, You have commanded us to sacrifice the daily offering at its appointed time, that the Kohens shall do their service, the Levites shall be on their platforms, and the Israelites shall be in their situations. Yet now, due to our sins, the Temple has been destroyed

וְאֵין ve'en   קמ"ג קנ"א קס"א ע"ה   הַתָּמִיד hatamid   וּבְטַל uvutal

מלה   כֹּהֵן Chohen   לֹא lo   ארני אהיה, אלהים,   לָנוּ lanu

בְּדוּכָנוֹ beduchano◆   לֵוִי Levi   וְלֹא velo   ◆בַּעֲבוֹדָתוֹ ba'avodato

וְאַתָּה veAta   בְּמַעֲמָדוֹ◆ bema'amado   יִשְׂרָאֵל Yisrael   וְלֹא velo

שְׂפָתֵינוּ sefatenu✦   פָרִים farim   וּנְשַׁלְּמָה un'shalma   אָמַרְתָּ✦ amarta

לָכֵן lachen   יְהִי yehi   רָצוֹן ratzon   מהע ע"ה, ע"ב ברבוע וקס"א ע"ה, אל סודי ע"ה   מִלְּפָנֶיךָ milfanecha

ילה   אֱלֹהֵינוּ Elohenu   יְהֹוָהֵ Adonai   ס"ג מ"ה ב"ן   מִלְּפָנֶיךָ milfanecha

וֵאלֹהֵי velohei   אֲבוֹתֵינוּ avotenu   ילה ; דמב ע"ב, מילוי ; לכב   שֶׁיְּהֵא sheyehe

זֶה ze   שִׂיחַ si'ach   שִׂפְתוֹתֵינוּ siftotenu   וְחָשׁוּב chashuv   וּמְקֻבָּל um'kubal

וּמְרוּצֶה um'rutze   לְפָנֶיךָ lefanecha   ס"ג מ"ה ב"ן   כְּאִלּוּ ke'ilu   הִקְרַבְנוּ hikravnu

קָרְבַּן korban   הַתָּמִיד hatamid   ע"ה קס"א קנ"א קמ"ג   בְּמוֹעֲדוֹ bemo'ado

וְעָמַדְנוּ✦ ve'amadnu   עַל al   מַעֲמָדוֹ ma'amado   כְּמוֹ kemo   שֶׁנֶּאֱמַר shene'emar✦

וְנֶאֱמַר vene'emar✦   פָרִים farim   un'shalma וּנְשַׁלְּמָה   שְׂפָתֵינוּ sefatenu◆

וְשָׁחַט veshachat   אֹתוֹ oto   עַל al   יֶרֶךְ yerech   הַמִּזְבֵּחַ hamizbe'ach   נגד, זז, אל יהוה

צָפוֹנָה tzafona   (מכוון למאמרם ז"ל הרוצה להעשיר יצפין) הברכה, מ"ה ב"ן ס"ג ע"ב יה וע"ה יה פעמים יה

לִפְנֵי lifnei   יְהֹוָהֵ Adonai   וְזָרְקוּ vezarku   ס"ת   יהוה

בְּנֵי benei   אַהֲרֹן Aharon   הַכֹּהֲנִים hakohanim   אֶת et   דָּמוֹ damo

עַל al   הַמִּזְבֵּחַ hamizbe'ach   נגד, זז, אל יהוה   סָבִיב saviv✦

וְנֶאֱמַר vene'emar✦   זֹאת zot   הַתּוֹרָה hatorah   לָעֹלָה la'ola

לַמִּנְחָה lamincha   ע"ה   ב"ן   וְלַחַטָּאת velachatat   וְלָאָשָׁם vela'asham

וְלַמִּלּוּאִים velamilu'im   וּלְזֶבַח ulzevach   הַשְּׁלָמִים hashelamim✦

---

and the daily offering has ceased. We now have no Kohen to do his service; No Levite to stand his platform; and no Israelite in his situation. But we asked: "May we compensate for the bull-offerings with our lips?" (Hosea 14:3) Therefore, may it be Your will, Lord, our God and the God of our fathers, that those words that come out of our lips shall be worthy, acceptable and favorable before You, as if we had sacrificed our daily offering at its appointed time and as if we had stood at that occasion, as it was said: "May we compensate for the bull-offerings with our lips?" (Hosea 14:3) And as it was also said: "And he shall slaughter it on the northern side of the Altar before the Lord. Aaron's sons, the Kohens, shall sprinkle its blood upon the Altar, all around." (Leviticus 1:11) And: "This is the law regarding the burnt-offering, the meal-offering, the sin-offering, the guilt-offering, the inauguration-offering, and the peace-offering." (Leviticus 1:11)

THE POWER OF PEACE

It is important to connect to all levels of the Torah during the day; therefore, we read these verses from the *Mishnah*, followed by verses from the *Gemara* (both are aspects of the *Talmud*). This specific section from the *Talmud* helps to imbue us with the power of truth, unity and peace because it is the only chapter containing no debate or opposing views about the interpretations of the Torah.

Meditate here to elevate, *Netzach, Hod, Yesod* of *Asiyah* into *Chesed, Gevurah, Tiferet;* and then to elevate *Malchut* into *Netzach, Hod, Yesod;* and then to elevate the Sparks of Light that are in the *klipa* into *Malchut.*

We say this section here because it is the only chapter in the entire *Mishnah* where all the opinions are in agreement, and is why this chapter is called: "*Halacha Pesuka,*" meaning unargumental law. Now, while the worlds are elevated, we need the power of peace, not of disagreement.

FIRST MISHNAH

By saying this *Mishnah*, the Internal aspect of *Netzach* of *Asiyah* rises and becomes External to the External part of *Chesed* of *Asiyah*.

אֵיזֶהוּ ezehu מְקוֹמָן mekoman שֶׁל shel זְבָחִים zevachim• קָדְשֵׁי kodshei

קָדָשִׁים kodashim שׁוֹחֲטָתָן shechitatan בַּצָּפוֹן batzafon• פָּר par

שֶׁל shel יוֹם yom הַכִּפּוּרִים hakipurim וְשָׂעִיר vesa'ir

שׁוֹחֲטָתָן shechitatan בַּצָּפוֹן batzafon וְקִבּוּל vekibul דָּמָן daman בִּכְלֵי bichlei

שָׁרֵת sharet בַּצָּפוֹן batzafon• וְדָמָן vedaman טָעוּן ta'un הַזָּיָה hazaya עַל al

בֵּין ben הַבַּדִּים habadim וְעַל ve'al הַפָּרֹכֶת haparochet וְעַל ve'al

מִזְבֵּחַ mizbach הַזָּהָב hazahav• וּמַתָּנָה matana אַחַת achat מֵהֶן mehen מְעַכֶּבֶת me'akevet• שְׁיָירֵי shiyerei הַדָּם hadam

הָיָה haya שׁוֹפֵךְ shofech עַל al יְסוֹד yesod מַעֲרָבִי ma'aravi

שֶׁל shel מִזְבֵּחַ mizbe'ach הַחִיצוֹן hachitzon• אִם im

לֹא lo נָתַן natan לֹא lo עִכֵּב ikev:

THE POWER OF PEACE
FIRST MISHNAH

Where is the location of sacrifices? The most holy are slaughtered on the North side. The bull and male goat of Yom Kippur are slaughtered on the North side; their blood is received in service vessels on the North side. Their blood is required to be sprinkled between the poles, on the curtain, and on the Golden Altar. The absence of one of them hinders. He pours the leftover blood on the Western foundation of the outer Altar; if he does not pour, he did not hinder.

SECOND MISHNAH

By saying this *Mishnah*, the Internal aspect of *Hod* of *Asiyah* rises and becomes External to the External part of *Gevurah* of *Asiyah*.

hanisrafim הַנִּשְׂרָפִים us'irim וּשְׂעִירִים hanisrafim הַנִּשְׂרָפִים parim פָּרִים

daman דָּמָן vekibul וְקִבּוּל ◆batzafon בַּצָּפוֹן shechitatan שְׁחִיטָתָן

ta'un טָעוּן vedaman וְדָמָן ◆batzafon בַּצָּפוֹן sharet שָׁרֵת bichlei בִּכְלֵי

hazaya הַזָּיָה al עַל haparochet הַפָּרֹכֶת ve'al וְעַל mizbach מִזְבּוֹן נגד, זו, אל יהוה

hazahav הַזָּהָב ◆וזהו matana מַתָּנָה נתה, קס"א קנ"א קמ"ג achat אוֹזֵת

mehen מֵהֶן me'akevet מְעַכֶּבֶת shiyrei שְׁיָירֵי hadam הַדָּם haya הָיָה יהה

shofech שׁוֹפֵךְ al עַל yesod יְסוֹד השע ma'aravi מַעֲרָבִי shel שֶׁל

mizbe'ach מִזְבּוֹן נגד, זו, אל יהוה ◆hachitzon הַחִיצוֹן im אִם יוהר,

◆ikev עִכֵּב lo לֹא natan נָתַן lo לֹא מ"א אותיות דפשוט, דמילוי ודמילוי דמילוי דאהיה ע"ה

elu אֵלוּ va'elu וְאֵלוּ nisrafin נִשְׂרָפִין bevet בְּבֵית ב"פ ראה hadeshen הַדֶּשֶׁן:

THIRD MISHNAH

By saying this *Mishnah*, the Internal aspect of *Yesod* of *Asiyah* rises and becomes External to the External part of *Tiferet* of *Asiyah*. Here, we complete *Chesed, Gevurah, Tiferet* of *Asiyah*.

hen הֵן elu אֵלוּ vehayachid וְהַיָּחִיד hatzibur הַצִּבּוּר chatot וְטֹּאת

rashei רָאשֵׁי se'irei שְׂעִירֵי hatzibur הַצִּבּוּר: chatot וְטֹּאת

shechitatan שְׁחִיטָתָן ◆mo'adot מוֹעֲדוֹת veshel וְשֶׁל chodashim וְדָשִׁים

sharet שָׁרֵת bichlei בִּכְלֵי daman דָּמָן vekibul וְקִבּוּל ◆batzafon בַּצָּפוֹן

matanot מַתָּנוֹת arba אַרְבַּע ta'un טָעוּן vedaman וְדָמָן ◆batzafon בַּצָּפוֹן

SECOND MISHNAH

Bulls and male goats that are to be burned
are slaughtered on the North side. Their blood is received in service vessels on the North side. Their blood requires sprinkling upon the curtain and upon the Golden Altar. The absence of one of them hinders. He pours the leftover blood upon the Western foundation of the outer Altar; if he did not pour, he did not hinder. These and the preceding offerings are burned in ash repositories.

THIRD *MISHNAH*

The communal and the personal sin-offerings are the communal sin-offerings:
The male goats of Rosh Chodesh and of the festivals: these are slaughtered on the North side. And their blood is received in service vessels in the North side. Their blood requires four poured portions

עַל al   אַרְבַּע arba   קְרָנוֹת keranot◆   כֵּיצַד keitzad◆   עָלָה ala

בַּכֶּבֶשׁ bakevesh   וּפָנָה ufana   לַסּוֹבֵב lasovev   וּבָא uva   לוֹ lo

לַקֶּרֶן lekeren   דְּרוֹמִית deromit   מִזְרָחִית mizrachit◆   מִזְרָחִית mizrachit

צְפוֹנִית tzefonit◆   צְפוֹנִית tzefonit   מַעֲרָבִית ma'aravit◆   מַעֲרָבִית ma'aravit

דְּרוֹמִית deromit◆   שְׁיָּרֵי shiyrei   הַדָּם hadam   הָיָה haya

שׁוֹפֵךְ shofech   עַל al   יְסוֹד yesod   הַדְּרוֹמִי haderomi◆

וְנֶאֱכָלִין vene'echalin   לִפְנִים lifnim   מִן min   הַקְּלָעִים hakela'im

לְזִכְרֵי lezichrei   כְּהֻנָּה chehuna   בְּכָל bechol   מַאֲכָל ma'achal◆

לְיוֹם leyom   וְלַיְלָה valayla   עַד ad   וְצוֹת chatzot

FOURTH MISHNAH - THE OLAH (BURNT) OFFERING
You say this *Mishnah* for the entirety of *Asiyah*.

הָעוֹלָה ha'ola   קֹדֶשׁ kodesh   קָדָשִׁים kodashim   שְׁחִיטָתָהּ shechitata

בַּצָּפוֹן batzafon◆   וְקִבּוּל vekibul   דָּמָהּ dama   בִּכְלֵי bichlei

שָׁרֵת sharet   בַּצָּפוֹן batzafon◆   וְדָמָהּ vedama   טָעוּן ta'un   שְׁתֵּי shetei

מַתָּנוֹת matanot   שֶׁהֵן shehen   אַרְבַּע arba◆   וּטְעוּנָה ute'una

הֶפְשֵׁט hefshet   וְנִתּוּחַ venitu'ach   וְכָלִיל vechalil   לָאִשִּׁים la'ishim

FIFTH MISHNAH - THE ASHAM (GUILT) OFFERINGS
By saying this *Mishnah*, the Internal aspect of the Right Column of *Malchut* of *Asiyah* rises and becomes External to the External aspect of *Netzach* of *Asiyah*.

זִבְחֵי zivchei   שַׁלְמֵי shalmei   צִבּוּר tzibur   וַאֲשָׁמוֹת va'ashamot◆

אֵלּוּ elu   הֵן hen   אֲשָׁמוֹת ashamot   אָשָׁם asham   גְּזֵלוֹת gezelot◆

---

upon the four corners of the Altar. How: He ascends the ramp, then turns to the Surrounding ledge; then goes to the Southeastern corner, the Northeastern, the Northwestern, and the Southwestern corner. He pours the leftover blood on the Southern foundation. These are eaten within the curtains by the males of the Kohens, in every meal for one day and one night, until midnight.

FOURTH MISHNAH - THE OLAH (BURNT) OFFERING
The burnt-offering belongs to the most holy.
It is slaughtered in the North and its blood is received in service vessels in the North. Its blood requires two four-part portions. It requires flaying, dismemberment, and complete consumption by fire.

FIFTH MISHNAH - THE ASHAM (GUILT) OFFERINGS
The communal peace-offerings and guilt-offerings; These are the guilt-offerings: The guilt-offerings for thefts,

אָשָׁם asham מֵעִילוֹת me'ilot • אָשָׁם asham שְׁפוּחָה shifcha וַחֲרוּפָה charufa•

אָשָׁם asham נָזִיר nazir • אָשָׁם asham מְצוֹרָע metzora• אָשָׁם asham

תָּלוּי taluy • שְׁוִזיטָתָן shechitatan בַּצָפוֹן batzafon • וְקִבּוּל vekibul דָּמָן daman

בִּכְלֵי bichlei שָׁרֵת sharet בַּצָפוֹן batzafon • וְדָמָן vedaman

טָעוּן ta'un שְׁתֵּי shetei מַתָּנוֹת matanot שֶׁהֵן shehen אַרְבַּע arba•

וְנֶאֱכָלִין vene'echalin לִפְנִים lifnim מִן min הַקְּלָעִים hakela'im

לְזִכְרֵי lezichrei כְּהֻנָה chehuna בְּכָל bechol ב"ן, לכב ma'achal מַאֲכָל

לְיוֹם leyom ע"ה גנר, מזבוח, זן, אל יהוה valayla וְלַיְלָה מלה ad עַד וְוְצוֹת chatzot:

SIXTH MISHNAH - THE TODA (THANKS) OFFERINGS

By saying this *Mishnah*, the Internal aspect of the Left Column of *Malchut* of *Asiyah* rises and becomes External to the External aspect of *Hod* of *Asiyah*.

הַתּוֹדָה hatoda וְאֵיל ve'el נָזִיר nazir קָדָשִׁים kodashim קַלִּים kalim•

שְׁוִזיטָתָן shechitatan בְּכָל bechol ב"ן, לכב מָקוֹם makom בְּעֶזְרָה ba'azara

וְדָמָן vedaman טָעוּן ta'un שְׁתֵּי shetei מַתָּנוֹת matanot שֶׁהֵן shehen

אַרְבַּע arba• וְנֶאֱכָלִין vene'echalin בְּכָל bechol ב"ן, לכב הָעִיר ha'ir

לְכֹל lechol יה ארני עָרי אָדָם adam מ"ה בְּכָל bechol ב"ן, לכב סֹזְוְֹּף, סנדלפון,

מַאֲכָל ma'achal לְיוֹם leyom ע"ה גנר, מזבוח, זן, אל יהוה valayla וְלַיְלָה מלה עַד ad

וְוְצוֹת chatzot• הַמּוּרָם hamuram מֵהֶם mehem כַּיּוֹצֵא kayotze בָּהֶם vahem

אֶלָא ela שֶׁהַמּוּרָם shehamuram נֶאֱכָל ne'echal לַכֹּהֲנִים lakohanim

לִנְשֵׁיהֶם linshehem וְלִבְנֵיהֶם velivnehem וּלְעַבְדֵיהֶם ul'avdehem:

---

for misuses of sacred objects, for being with a married maid servant, of the Nazir, of a leper, and of a doubtful transgression. These are slaughtered on the North side and their blood is received in service vessels on the North side. Their blood requires two four-part portions. They are eaten within the curtains by the male Kohens, in every meal for one day and for one night, until midnight.

SIXTH MISHNAH - THE TODA (THANKS) OFFERINGS

The thanks-offering and the Nazir's ram are of minor sanctity. They are slaughtered anywhere in the courtyard. Their blood requires two four-part portions. They are eaten throughout the city by any person, in every meal for one day and for one night until midnight. That part which is set aside is treated in the same manner, except that this portion is eaten by the Kohens, their wives, their sons, and their slaves.

SEVENTH MISHNAH - THE SHELAMIM (PEACE) OFFERINGS

By saying this *Mishnah*, the Internal aspect of the Central Column of *Malchut* of *Asiyah* rises and becomes External to the External aspect of *Yesod* of *Asiyah*.

שְׁלָמִים shelamim קָדָשִׁים kodashim קַלִּים kalim◆ שׁוֹחֲטָתָן shechitatan

בְּכֹל bechol ב"ז, לכב בָּעֲזָרָה ba'azara◆ מָקוֹם makom וְדָמָן vedaman

טָעוּן ta'un שְׁתֵּי shetei מַתָּנוֹת matanot שֶׁהֵן shehen אַרְבַּע arba◆

וְנֶאֱכָלִין vene'echalin בְּכֹל bechol ב"ז, לכב הָעִיר ha'ir בֹּזְזֹּר, סנדלפון, עֲרִי

לְכָל lechol יה אדֹני אָדָם adam מ"ה בְּכֹל bechol ב"ז, לכב מַאֲכָל ma'achal

לִשְׁנֵי lishnei יָמִים yamim נלך וְלַיְלָה velayla מלה אֶחָד echad אהבה, דאגה◆

הַמּוּרָם hamuram מֵהֶם mehem כַּיּוֹצֵא kayotze בָּהֶם vahem

אֶלָּא ela שֶׁהַמּוּרָם shehamuram נֶאֱכָל ne'echal לַכֹּהֲנִים lakohanim

לִנְשֵׁיהֶם linshehem וְלִבְנֵיהֶם velivnehem וּלְעַבְדֵּיהֶם ul'avdehem׃

THE FINAL MISHNAH

With this final *Mishnah*, we have the power to elevate the entire world of *Asiyah*. Any souls, or Light, that are trapped inside the *klipot* are also elevated by this verse. Because this specific section contains no debate or opposing views, it creates a thread of unity; it is only through this unity that we have the ability to elevate to the World of Formation (*Yetzirah*).

By saying this *Mishnah*, the Internal aspect (which was in the *klipa*) rises and becomes External to the External aspect of *Malchut* of *Asiyah*. And with this, you complete all of *Asiyah*.

הַבְּכוֹר habechor וְהַמַּעֲשֵׂר vehama'aser וְהַפֶּסַח vehapesach קָדָשִׁים kodashim

בָּעֲזָרָה ba'azara וְדָמָן vedaman טָעוּן ta'un מַתָּנָה matana נתה, קס"א קנ"א קמ"ג שׁוֹחֲטָתָן shechitatan בְּכֹל bechol ב"ז, לכב מָקוֹם makom קַלִּים kalim◆

הַיְסוֹד hayesod ההע◆ עֻנָּה shina בָּאֲכִילָתָן va'achilatan◆

אֶחָת echat◆ וּבִלְבַד uvilvad שֶׁיִּתֵּן sheyiten כְּנֶגֶד keneged מזבוו, זו, אל יהוה

SEVENTH MISHNAH - THE SHELAMIM (PEACE) OFFERINGS

The peace-offerings are of lesser sanctity. They are slaughtered anywhere in the courtyard. Their blood requires two four-part portions. They are eaten throughout the city by any person, in every meal, for two days and one night. That part which is set aside is treated in the same manner, except that this portion is eaten by the Kohens, their wives, their sons, and their slaves.

THE FINAL MISHNAH

The firstborn animal, the tithes of cattle, and the Pesach-offering are of minor sanctity. They are slaughtered anywhere in the courtyard. Their blood requires one poured portion, provided that this is poured against the base of the Altar. They differ in the way that they are eaten:

וְהַמַּעֲשֵׂר vehama'aser ◆ לַכֹּהֲנִים lakohanim נֶאֱכָל ne'echal הַבְּכוֹר habechor

וְנֶאֱכָלִין vene'echalin ◆ מ״ה. אָדָם adam ארני יה לְכָל lechol

עָרִי, סַנְדַּלְפוֹן, בּוֹזָּך, הָעִיר ha'ir לכב ב״ו, בְּכָל bechol

נֶּלֶך יָמִים yamim לִשְׁנֵי lishnei מַאֲכָל ma'achal לכב ב״ו, בְּכָל bechol

אֵינוֹ eno הַפֶּסַח hapesach ◆ דאגה. אהבה, אֶחָד echad מלה וְלַיְלָה velayla

נֶאֱכָל ne'echal וְאֵינוֹ ve'eno ◆ מלה. בְּלַיְלָה valayla אֶלָא ela נֶאֱכָל ne'echal

אֶלָא ela נֶאֱכָל ne'echal וְאֵינוֹ ve'eno ◆ חֲצוֹת chatzot עַד ad אֶלָא ela

צָלִי: tzali אֶלָא ela נֶאֱכָל ne'echal וְאֵינוֹ ve'eno ◆ לִמְנוּיָיו limnuyav

---

RIBI YISHMAEL

Ribi Yishmael acts as a link in the chain of Sefirot. It connects us to 13 Sefirot—ten in the World of Action (Asiyah) and three in the next level up, the World of Formation (Yetzirah). It is good to count the 13 Sefirot of Asiyah with the fingers of the right hand.

רִבִּי Ribi יִשְׁמָעֵאל Yishmael אוֹמֵר omer, בְּשָׁלֹשׁ bish'losh עֶשְׂרֵה esre

נגמם מִדּוֹת midot הַתּוֹרָה hatorah נִדְרֶשֶׁת nidreshet ◆ (1 מִקַּל mikal נגמם

וָחֹמֶר vachomer ◆ (2 מִגְּזֵרָה migezera שָׁוָה shava ◆ (3 מִבִּנְיָן mibinyan אָב av

וְכָתוּב vechatuv אֶחָד echad אהבה, דאגה. ◆ וּמִבִּנְיָן umibinyan אָב av

וּשְׁנֵי ushenei כְתוּבִים chetuvim ◆ (4 מִכְּלָל mikelal וּפְרָט ufrat ◆

(5 מִפְּרָט miperat וּכְלָל uchlal ◆ (6 כְּלָל kelal וּפְרָט ufrat וּכְלָל uchlal

אִי ei אַתָּה Ata דָן dan אֶלָא ela כְּעֵין ke'en הַפְּרָט haperat ◆

The firstborn animal may be eaten by the Kohen, and the tithe may be eaten by anyone. They are eaten throughout the city, in any meal for two days and one night. The Pesach-offering may be eaten only during that night, only until midnight, and may only be eaten by those who contributed to it. It may only be eaten roasted.

RIBI YISHMAEL

"Rabbi Yishmael says: By thirteen attributes is the Torah taught: 1) From lenient law and from strict law. 2) From similarity of words. 3) From a general principle derived from one verse and from a general principle derived from two verses. 4) From a general statement followed by a specific statement. 5) From a specific statement followed by a generality. 6) From a general statement, followed by a specific statement, followed by a generally: then you may only infer what is similar to the specification.

(7) מִכְּלָל mikelal   שֶׁהוּא shehu   צָרִיךְ tzarich   לִפְרָט lifrat.

וּמִפְּרָט umiperat   שֶׁהוּא shehu   צָרִיךְ tzarich   לִכְלָל lichlal.

(8) וְכֹל vechol   יְלִי דָּבָר davar   שֶׁהָיָה shehaya   בִּכְלָל bichlal

מִן min   הַכְּלָל hakelal   לְלַמֵּד lelamed   לֹא lo   לְלַמֵּד lelamed.

אַצְמוֹ atzmo   יָצָא yatza   אֶלָּא ela   לְלַמֵּד lelamed   עַל al   הַכְּלָל hakelal

יָצָא yatza.   כֻּלּוֹ kulo   (9) וְכֹל vechol   יְלִי דָּבָר davar   שֶׁהָיָה shehaya

בִּכְלָל bichlal.   וְיָצָא veyatza   לִטְעוֹן lit'on   טַעַן ta'un   אַחֵר acher

שֶׁהוּא shehu   כְּעִנְיָנוֹ che'inyano.   יָצָא yatza   לְהָקֵל lehakel   וְלֹא velo

לְהַחְמִיר lehachmir: (10) וְכֹל vechol   יְלִי דָּבָר davar   שֶׁהָיָה shehaya

בִּכְלָל bichlal   וְיָצָא veyatza   לִטְעוֹן lit'on   טַעַן ta'un   אַחֵר acher   שֶׁלֹּא shelo

כְּעִנְיָנוֹ che'inyano   יָצָא yatza   לְהָקֵל lehakel   וּלְהַחְמִיר ul'hachmir:

(11) וְכֹל vechol   יְלִי דָּבָר davar   שֶׁהָיָה shehaya   בִּכְלָל bichlal

וְיָצָא veyatza   לִדּוֹן lidon   בְּדָבָר bedavar   וְחָדָשׁ chadash   י"ב הויות, קס"א קנ"א

אִי ei   אַתָּה Ata   יָכוֹל yachol   לְהַחֲזִירוֹ lehachaziro   לִכְלָלוֹ lichlalo   עַד ad

שֶׁיַּחֲזִירֶנּוּ sheyachazirenu   הַכָּתוּב hakatuv   לִכְלָלוֹ lichlalo   בְּפֵירוּשׁ beferush:

(12) וְדָבָר vedavar   הַלָּמֵד halamed   מֵעִנְיָנוֹ me'inyano   וְדָבָר vedavar

הַלָּמֵד halamed   מִסּוֹפוֹ misofo: (13) וְכֵן vechan   (וְכָאן)   שְׁנֵי shenei

כְתוּבִים chetuvim   הַמַּכְחִישִׁים hamach'chishim   זֶה ze   אֶת et   זֶה ze

עַד ad   שֶׁיָּבֹא sheyavo   הַכָּתוּב hakatuv   הַשְּׁלִישִׁי hashelishi

וְיַכְרִיעַ veyachri'a   בֵּינֵיהֶם benehem:

---

7) From a general statement that requires a specific statement that, in turn, requires a general statement to explain it. 8) Anything that was part of a general statement which was then singled out from the general statement, to teach something. It was not to teach about itself that it was singled out, but to teach about the entire general statement. 9) Anything that was part of a general statement, which was later singled outto discuss another claim to its context. It was singled out in order to be more lenient and not more stringent. 10) Anything that was part of a general statement and was later singled out in order to discuss another claim out of its context. It was singled out in order to be more lenient and not more stringent. 11) Anything that was part of a general statement and was singled out in order to discuss a new concept, you cannot return it to its general context, unless the text returns it, explicitly, to its general context. 12) A matter that is learned from its context and a matter that is derived from its end. 13) And also from two verses that contradict each other, until a third one comes along and reconciles them. (Torat Kohanim Portion of Vayikra.)

Yehuda יְהוּדָה ven בֶּן Tema תֵּימָא :omer אוֹמֵר hevei הֱוֵי az עַז

kanamer כַּנָּמֵר vekal וְקַל (עוהם ה' גבורות) kanesher כַּנֶּשֶׁר veratz וְרָץ

katzevi כַּצְּבִי vegibor וְגִבּוֹר ka'ari כָּאֲרִי la'asot לַעֲשׂוֹת retzon רְצוֹן

avicha אָבִיךָ מהע ע"ה, ע"ב בריבוע וקס"א ע"ה, אל שדי ע"ה shebashamayim שֶׁבַּשָּׁמָיִם

hu הוּא haya הָיָה יהה :omer אוֹמֵר az עַז panim פָּנִים

laGehinom לַגֵּיהִנֹּם uvoshet וּבֹשֶׁת panim פָּנִים leGan לְגַן Eden: עֵדֶן

YEHI RATZON

Even though, according to Kabbalah, the Temple still exists in the spiritual reality of the Endless World, its physical structure is missing, leaving our physical world incomplete. This prayer helps set in motion and accelerate the eventual reconstruction of the physical Temple.

yehi יְהִי ratzon רְצוֹן מהע ע"ה, ע"ב, בריבוע וקס"א ע"ה, אל שדי ע"ה

milfanecha מִלְּפָנֶיךָ ס"ג מ"ה ב"ן יְהֹוָה Adonai Elohenu אֱלֹהֵינוּ ילה

velohei וֵאלֹהֵי לכב מילוי ע"ב, דמב ; avotenu אֲבוֹתֵינוּ

shetivne שֶׁתִּבְנֶה bet בֵּית ב"פ ראה hamikdash הַמִּקְדָּשׁ

bim'hera בִּמְהֵרָה ◆veyamenu בְיָמֵינוּ veten וְתֵן chelkenu וְחֶלְקֵנוּ

betoratach בְּתוֹרָתֶךָ la'asot לַעֲשׂוֹת chukei וְחֻקֵּי retzonach רְצוֹנֶךָ

ul'ovdach וּלְעָבְדְּךָ פוי, אל אדני belevav בְּלֵבָב בוכו shalem: שָׁלֵם

You should be careful not to speak or even to pause too long here, and you should proceed to *Hodu* right after the *Kaddish*.

KADDISH AL YISRAEL

Kaddish, in general, means to elevate the Worlds in the secret of the Column. There is one column that connects the worlds to each other and stands in the middle of each palace. And by this column, each palace rises to the upper one and becomes one with it (as is mentioned in the *Zohar*). This column is the *Kaddish*. The secret of *Kaddish Al Yisrael* is that it elevates us from the World of *Asiyah* (ב"ן) to the World of *Yetzirah* (מ"ה).

Yehuda Ben Tema says: Be courageous like a tiger and light as an eagle and run like a deer and be strong like a lion to thus fulfill the will of Your Father in Heaven. He used to frequently say: An insolent person goes to Hell and a modest person to the Garden of Eden. (Avot Ch. 5)

YEHI RATZON

May it be Your will, Lord, our God and the God of our forefathers,
that You shall build the Temple speedily in our days. And that You may place our lot
in Your Torah, so that we may fulfill the laws of Your desires and worship You wholeheartedly.

יִתְגַּדֵּל וְיִתְקַדַּשׁ yitgadal veyitkadash שְׂדִי וּמִלּוּי שְׂדִי ; י"א אוֹתִיּוֹת כְּמִנְיַן ו"ה

שְׁמֵהּ shemei (שֵׁם י"ה דע"ב) רַבָּא raba קנ"א ב"ן, יהוה אלהים יהוה אדני,

מִלּוּי קס"א וס"ג, מ"ה בְּרָבוּעַ וע"ב ע"ה ; ר"ת = ו"פ אלהים ; ס"ת = ג"פ יב"ק אָמֵן amen אידהנויה.

בְּעָלְמָא be'alma דִּי di דְּבָרָא vera בְרָא chir'utei כִרְעוּתֵיהּ.

וְיַמְלִיךְ veyamlich מַלְכוּתֵהּ malchutei. וְיַצְמַח veyatzmach

פּוּרְקָנֵהּ purkanei. וִיקָרֵב vikarev מְשִׁיחֵהּ meshichei: אָמֵן amen אידהנויה.

בְּחַיֵּיכוֹן bechayechon וּבְיוֹמֵיכוֹן uvyomeichon וּבְחַיֵּי uvchayei

דְּכָל dechol יֵלי bet בֵּית רַאה דּ"פ יִשְׂרָאֵל Yisrael בַּעֲגָלָא ba'agala

וּבִזְמַן uvizman קָרִיב kariv וְאִמְרוּ ve'imru אָמֵן amen: אָמֵן amen אידהנויה.

The congregation and the *chazan* say the following:

מִלּוּי דְמִלּוּי דס"ג (יוד ויו דלת הי ויו אלף ואו הי יוד) Twenty eight words (until *be'alma*) meditate:
מִלּוּי דְמִלּוּי דמ"ה (יוד ואו דלת הא אלף ואו הא אלף) Twenty eight letters (until *almaya*) meditate:

יְהֵא yehe שְׁמֵהּ shemei (שֵׁם י"ה דס"ג) רַבָּא raba קנ"א ב"ן,

יהוה אלהים יהוה אדני, מִלּוּי קס"א וס"ג, מ"ה בְּרָבוּעַ וע"ב ע"ה מְבָרַךְ mevarach,

לְעָלַם le'alam לְעָלְמֵי le'almei עָלְמַיָּא almaya. יִתְבָּרַךְ yitbarach.

Seven words with six letters each (שֵׁם בֶּן מ"ב) meditate:
יהוה ↑ יוד הי ויו הי ↓ מִלּוּי דְמִילּוּי דס"ג (יוד ויו דלת הי ואו אלף ואו הי יוד)
Also, seven times the letter *Vav* (שֵׁם בֶּן מ"ב) meditate:
יהוה ↑ יוד הי ואו הי ↓ מִלּוּי דְמִילּוּי דמ"ה (יוד ואו דלת הא אלף ואו הא אלף ואו הא אלף).

וְיִשְׁתַּבַּח veyishtabach י"פ ע"ב יהוה אל אבג יתץ.

וְיִתְפָּאַר veyitpa'ar הִי גּוֹ יה הִי קָרַע שָׂטָן. וְיִתְרוֹמַם veyitromam וה כוזו נגד יכש.

וְיִתְנַשֵּׂא veyitnase בְּמוּכְסוּ בְּטַר צָתָג. וְיִתְהַדָּר veyit'hadar כוזו יה וזקב טנע.

וְיִתְעַלֶּה veyit'ale וה יוד ה יגל פזק. וְיִתְהַלָּל veyit'halal א ואו הא שקו צית.

שְׁמֵהּ shemei (שֵׁם י"ה דמ"ה) דְּקוּדְשָׁא dekudsha בְּרִיךְ verich הוּא hu:

אָמֵן amen אידהנויה.

KADDISH AL YISRAEL

May His great Name be more exalted and sanctified. (Amen) In the world that He created according to His will, and may His Kingdom reign. And may He cause His redemption to sprout and may He bring the Mashiach closer. (Amen) In your lifetimes and in your days and in the lifetime of all the House of Israel, speedily and in the near future, and you shall say Amen. (Amen) May His great Name be blessed forever and for all eternity. Blessed and lauded, and glorified, and exalted, and extolled, and honored, and uplifted, and praised be the Name of the Holy Blessed One. (Amen)

shirata שִׁירָתָא♦ birchata בִּרְכָתָא♦ kol כָּל יכי min מִן le'ela לְעֵלָּא

da'amiran דַּאֲמִירָן venechamata וְנֶחֱמָתָא♦ tishbechata תֻּשְׁבְּחָתָא

amen אָמֵן אידהנויה. :amen אָמֵן ve'imru וְאִמְרוּ be'alma בְּעָלְמָא

ve'al וְעַל rabanan רַבָּנָן ve'al וְעַל Yisrael יִשְׂרָאֵל al עַל

talmidei תַּלְמִידֵי kol כָּל יכי עמם ; ve'al וְעַל talmidehon תַּלְמִידֵיהוֹן

be'orayta בְּאוֹרַיְתָא de'askin דְּעָסְקִין talmidehon תַּלְמִידֵיהוֹן♦

vedi וְדִי haden הָדֵין ve'atra בְּאַתְרָא di דִּי kadishta קַדִּישְׁתָּא♦

yehe יְהֵא ve'atar וְאַתָר♦ atar אֲתַר ב"כ vechol בְּכָל

vechisda וְחִסְדָּא china חִנָּא ul'chon וּלְכוֹן ul'hon וּלְהוֹן lana לָנָא

shemaya שְׁמַיָּא marei מָארֵי kadam קָדָם min מִן verachamei וְרַחֲמֵי♦

amen אָמֵן אידהנויה. :amen אָמֵן ve'imru וְאִמְרוּ ve'ar'a וְאַרְעָא

yehe יְהֵא shelama שְׁלָמָא raba רַבָּא קנ"א ב"ק, יהוה אלהים יהוה אדני, מילוי קס"א וס"ג,

chayim וְחַיִּים♦ shemaya שְׁמַיָּא min מִן מ"ה ברבוע וע"ב ע"ב אהיה אהיה יהוה, בינה ע"ה

veshezava וְשֵׁיזָבָא venechama וְנֶחֱמָה vishu'a וִישׁוּעָה vesava וְסָבַע

vechapara וְכַפָּרָה uslicha וּסְלִיחָה ug'ula וּגְאֻלָּה urfu'a וּרְפוּאָה

ulchol וּלְכָל יה אדני lanu לָנוּ אלהים, אהיה אדני vehatzala וְהַצָּלָה♦ verevach וְרֵיוַח

amen אָמֵן אידהנויה. :amen אָמֵן ve'imru וְאִמְרוּ Yisrael יִשְׂרָאֵל amo עַמּוֹ

Take three steps backwards and say:

hu הוּא♦ ע"ב, ריבוע יהוה. bimromav בִּמְרוֹמָיו shalom שָׁלוֹם ose עוֹשֶׂה

berachamav בְּרַחֲמָיו♦ ר"ת ש"ע נהורין alenu עָלֵינוּ shalom שָׁלוֹם ya'ase יַעֲשֶׂה

:amen אָמֵן ve'imru וְאִמְרוּ Yisrael יִשְׂרָאֵל amo עַמּוֹ יכי ; עמם kol כָּל ve'al וְעַל

amen אָמֵן אידהנויה♦

Above all blessings, songs, praises, and words of consolation that may be said in the world, and you shall say, Amen. (Amen) Upon Israel, His Sages, their disciples, and all the students of their disciples who occupy themselves with the Holy Torah, in this place and in each and every location, may there be for us, for them, and for all, grace, kindness, and compassion from the Master of the Heavens and Earth, and you shall say Amen. (Amen) May there be abundant peace from Heaven, life, contentment, salvation, consolation, deliverance, healing, redemption, pardon, atonement, comfort, and relief for us and for His entire Nation, Israel, and you shall say, Amen. (Amen) He, Who makes peace in His High Places, with His compassion He shall make peace for us and for His entire Nation, Israel. And you shall say, Amen. (Amen)

HODU, EL NEKAMOT AND AROMIMCHA

The power of the *Kaddish* lies in its ability to elevate us to the Upper Worlds. But the initial launch from our physical world—*Asiyah*—requires an additional thrust. The ancient sages gave us three prayers, *Hodu*, *El Nekamot* and *Aromimcha*, for this purpose. This initial launch stage occurs in the World of Action (*Asiyah*).

HODU

Our *klipot's* sole nourishment comes from our world (*Malchut* or *Asiyah*), and consequently, the *klipot* try to prevent our world of *Malchut*, the World of Action (*Asiyah*), from rising to the World of Formation (*Yetzirah*), because that movement would disconnect them from their only source of Light. *Hodu* cuts off the *klipot's* oxygen supply, helping us break away from the *klipot's* gravitational pull.

We say *Hodu* to empower *Malchut* of *Yetzirah,* which is included in *Hechal Kodesh HaKodashim* of *Asiyah* in order to break the power of the *klipot* that prevents *Asiyah* from rising to *Yetzirah*. From *Hodu* to *baruch Elohim* (pg.253), there are 295 words which is the numerical value of *Elohim* spelled out with *Hei* (אלף למד הה יוד מם). And therefore, you should not add or omit any of the words. This prayer praises the sun on its trail when it comes to shine upon the world. So is *Yisrael* praising God with the sun, as it says: "You should be seen together with the sun" (Psalms 72:5).

הוֹדוּ hodu אהיה לַיהֹוָאדְנִיאהדונהי ladonai קִרְאוּ kir'u בִּשְׁמוֹ vishmo מהש ע"ה,

ע"ב בריבוע וקס"א, אל שדי ע"ה ; לאו הוֹדִיעוּ hodi'u בָּעַמִּים va'amim

עֲלִילֹתָיו :alilotav שִׁירוּ shiru לוֹ lo זַמְּרוּ zameru לוֹ lo שִׂיחוּ sichu

בְּכָל bechol ב"ן, לכב נִפְלְאֹתָיו nifle'otav: הִתְהַלְלוּ hit'halelu בְּשֵׁם beshem

קָדְשׁוֹ kodsho יִשְׂמַח yismach משיוו לֵב lev מְבַקְשֵׁי mevakshei

יְהֹוָאדְנִיאהדונהי Adonai: דִּרְשׁוּ dirshu יְהֹוָאדְנִיאהדונהי Adonai וְעֻזּוֹ ve'uzo

בַּקְּשׁוּ bakeshu פָּנָיו fanav תָּמִיד tamid ע"ה קס"א קנ"א קמ"ג:

זִכְרוּ zichru נִפְלְאֹתָיו nifle'otav אֲשֶׁר asher עָשָׂה asa מֹפְתָיו moftav

וּמִשְׁפְּטֵי umishpetei פִּיהוּ :fihu זֶרַע zera יִשְׂרָאֵל Yisrael

עַבְדּוֹ avdo בְּנֵי benei יַעֲקֹב Yaakov ' היות, יאהדונהי אידהנויה

בְּכָל bechol הוּא hu יְהֹוָאדְנִיאהדונהי Adonai אֱלֹהֵינוּ Elohenu יכה בְּחִירָיו:bechirav

בְּכָל bechol ב"ן, לכב הָאָרֶץ ha'aretz אלהים דההין ע"ה מִשְׁפָּטָיו:mishpatav

---

HODU, EL NEKAMOT AND AROMIMCHA
HODU

"Be grateful to the Lord. Call out His Name and make His deeds known among nations. Sing to Him, chant to Him, and speak of all His wonders. Be proud of His Holy Name. The heart of those who seek the Lord and His power shall rejoice. Constantly seek His presence. Remember the wonders that He has performed, His miracles, and the law that He uttered. You are the seed of Israel, His servant, and the sons of Jacob, His Chosen Ones. He is the Lord, our God. His judgments cover the whole Earth.

זִכְרוּ לְעוֹלָם le'olam בְּרִיתוֹ berito דְּבָר davar ראה

צִוָּה tziva דּוֹר dor לְאֶלֶף le'elef asher אֲשֶׁר

כָּרַת karat אֶת־ et אַבְרָהָם Avraham

וּשְׁבוּעָתוֹ ush'vu'ato לְיִצְחָק leYitzchak

וַיַּעֲמִידֶהָ vaya'amideha לְיַעֲקֹב leYaakov לְחֹק lechok

לְיִשְׂרָאֵל leYisrael בְּרִית berit עוֹלָם olam לֵאמֹר lemor לָךְ lecha

אֶתֵּן eten אֶרֶץ eretz כְּנָעַן Kena'an וְחֶבֶל chevel נַחֲלַתְכֶם nachalatchem

בִּהְיוֹתְכֶם bih'yotchem מְתֵי metei מִסְפָּר mispar כִּמְעָט kim'at

וְגָרִים vegarim בָהּ ba וַיִּתְהַלְּכוּ vayit'halchu מִגּוֹי migoi אֶל־ el

גּוֹי goi וּמִמַּמְלָכָה umimamlacha אֶל־ el עַם am אַחֵר acher לֹא־ lo

הִנִּיחַ hini'ach לְאִישׁ le'ish לְעָשְׁקָם le'oshkam וַיּוֹכַח vayochach

עֲלֵיהֶם alehem מְלָכִים melachim אַל־ al תִּגְּעוּ tige'u בִּמְשִׁיחָי bimshichai

וּבִנְבִיאַי uvinvi'ai אַל־ al תָּרֵעוּ tare'u שִׁירוּ shiru לַיהֹוָה ladonai

כָּל־ kol הָאָרֶץ ha'aretz בַּשְּׂרוּ baseru מִיּוֹם miyom

אֶל־ el יוֹם yom יְשׁוּעָתוֹ yeshu'ato

סַפְּרוּ saperu בַגּוֹיִם vagoyim (properly enunciate the letter *Alef* in the word "et") אֶת־ et

כְּבוֹדוֹ kevodo בְּכָל bechol הָעַמִּים ha'amim נִפְלְאֹתָיו nifle'otav

כִּי ki גָּדוֹל gadol יְהֹוָה Adonai

וּמְהֻלָּל um'hulal מְאֹד me'od וְנוֹרָא venora הוּא hu עַל־ al

כָּל־ kol כִּי ki אֱלֹהִים Elohim כָּל־ kol

אֱלֹהֵי elohei הָעַמִּים ha'amim אֱלִילִים elilim (pause here)

Remember His Covenant always. That which He concluded with Abraham, vowed to Isaac, established for Jacob as a statute, and for Israel as an eternal Covenant: To you I give the land of Canaan, the share of your heritage, where you were only a few and were lost strangers in it. They wandered from one nation to another and from one kingdom to another. Yet He did not allow any one to harm them; He admonished kings because of them: Do not touch My anointed ones and do not cause distress to My prophets. Sing to the Lord all of Earth and proclaim daily His salvation. Relate His glory among the nations and His wonders among all peoples: For the Lord is great and most praised; He is awesome above and beyond all deities. For the gods of all nations are only deities

ההה hod הוֹד **asa** עָשָׂה י"פ טל, י"פ כוזו shamayim שָׁמַיִם vadonai וַיהֹוָהאלהיאהדונהי

bimkomo בִּמְקֹמוֹ vechedva וְחֶדְוָה oz עֹז lefanav לְפָנָיו vehadar וְהָדָר

mishpechot מִשְׁפְּחוֹת ladonai לַיהֹוָהאדניאהדונהי דאגה, אהבה, אוזר, havu הָבוּ

kavod כָּבוֹד ladonai לַיהֹוָהאדניאהדונהי דאגה, אהבה, אוזר, havu הָבוּ amim עַמִּים

kevod כָּבוֹד ladonai לַיהֹוָהאדניאהדונהי דאגה, אהבה, אוזר, havu הָבוּ va'oz וָעֹז

shemo שְׁמוֹ מהיו ע"ה, ע"ב בריבוע וקס"א ע"ה, אל עדי ע"ה ; הבו יהוה כבוד שמו = אדם דוד משיחו

se'u שְׂאוּ mincha מִנְחָה ע"ה ב"ן uvo'u וּבֹאוּ ב"פ lefanav לְפָנָיו

behadrat בְּהַדְרַת ladonai לַיהֹוָהאדניאהדונהי hishtachavu הִשְׁתַּחֲווּ

kodesh קֹדֶשׁ ר"ת למפרע קבלה (היינו שביום שבת צריך ללמוד קבלה)

chilu חִילוּ milfanav מִלְּפָנָיו kol כָּל־ יל ha'aretz הָאָרֶץ אלהים דההין ע"ה

af אַף־ tikon תִּכּוֹן tevel תֵּבֵל ב"פ רי"ו bal בַּל־ timot תִּמּוֹט

yismechu יִשְׂמְחוּ hashamayim הַשָּׁמַיִם י"פ טל, י"פ כוזו vetagel וְתָגֵל אותיות גלות

ha'aretz הָאָרֶץ אלהים דההין ע"ה ; ר"ת יהוה ; ס"ת = ריבוע דס"ג (שכעתהתהיה גאולה תהא שמוזה)

veyomru וְיֹאמְרוּ vagoyim בַּגּוֹיִם Adonai יְהֹוָהאדניאהדונהי malach מָלָךְ

yir'am יִרְעַם hayam הַיָּם יל umlo'o וּמְלֹאוֹ ר"ת יהו, אהיה ; ר"ת יבמ, ב"ן ;

ya'alotz יַעֲלֹז hasade הַשָּׂדֶה אהיה אלהים, אלהים, מום ס"ת ; vechol וְכָל־ יל

asher אֲשֶׁר bo בּוֹ az אָז yeranenu יְרַנְּנוּ atzei עֲצֵי haya'ar הַיָּעַר

va בָא ki כִּי־ milifnei מִלִּפְנֵי Adonai יְהֹוָהאדניאהדונהי ערי מזוזפך, סנדלפון,

hodu הוֹדוּ ha'aretz הָאָרֶץ אלהים דההין ע"ה ; ר"ת לאה אהיה et אֶת־ lishpot לִשְׁפּוֹט

ki כִּי ladonai לַיהֹוָהאדניאהדונהי tov טוֹב ki כִּי והו ; כי טוב = יהוה אהיה, אום, מבה, יזל ki כִּי

le'olam לְעוֹלָם chasdo וְחַסְדּוֹ ג' הויות (מזלא עילאה) ; ר"ת = נגה אותיות דס"ג ו' ריבוע דס"ג

---

and the Lord made the Heavens. Majesty and magnificence are His presence; power and joy are His place. Render the Lord you families of nations, render the Lord honor and power. Render the Lord honor befitting His Name, bring a gift and come before Him with splendor of holiness. Tremble before Him, all dwellers of Earth, so that the world will be built and will not collapse. Heaven will rejoice and the Earth will be happy. Let the nations say: the Lord reigns! Let the sea and all therein roar; let the field and all therein exult. Then shall the forest sing before the Lord, because He has come to judge the Earth. Be grateful to the Lord for He is good; for His kindness goes on forever.

וְאָמְרוּ ve'imru הוֹשִׁיעֵנוּ hoshi'enu אֱלֹהֵי Elohei מילוי ע"ב, דמב ; ילה

יִשְׁעֵנוּ yish'enu וְקַבְּצֵנוּ vekabetzenu וְהַצִּילֵנוּ vehatzilenu מִן min

הַגּוֹיִם hagoyim לְהֹדוֹת lehodot לְשֵׁם leshem קָדְשֶׁךָ kodshecha

לְהִשְׁתַּבֵּחַ lehishtabe'ach בִּתְהִלָּתֶךָ bit'hilatecha: בָּרוּךְ baruch

יְהֹוָ(אדני אהדונהי) Adonai אֱלֹהֵי Elohei מילוי ע"ב, דמב ; ילה יִשְׂרָאֵל Yisrael

מִן min הָעוֹלָם ha'olam וְעַד ve'ad יהוה אלהי ישראל = תרי"ג (מצוות) ; ס"ת = אדני

הָעֹלָם ha'olam וַיֹּאמְרוּ vayomru כָּל־ chol ילי הָעָם ha'am אָמֵן amen יאהדונהי

וְהַלֵּל vehalel ללה, אדני לַיהֹוָ(אדני אהדונהי) ladonai: רוֹמְמוּ romemu

יְהֹוָ(אדני אהדונהי) Adonai אֱלֹהֵינוּ Elohenu ילה וְהִשְׁתַּחֲווּ vehishtachavu

לַהֲדֹם lahadom רַגְלָיו raglav קָדוֹשׁ kadosh הוּא hu: רוֹמְמוּ romemu

יְהֹוָ(אדני אהדונהי) Adonai אֱלֹהֵינוּ Elohenu ילה וְהִשְׁתַּחֲווּ vehishtachavu

לְהַר lehar קָדְשׁוֹ kodsho כִּי ki קָדוֹשׁ kadosh יְהֹוָ(אדני אהדונהי) Adonai

אֱלֹהֵינוּ Elohenu ילה: וְהוּא vehu רַחוּם rachum לְכַפֵּר yechaper ר"ת רי"ו

עָוֹן avon (Abba of the klipa) וְלֹא־ velo יַשְׁחִית yashchit (Ima of the klipa)

וְהִרְבָּה vehirba לְהָשִׁיב lehashiv אַפּוֹ apo (Zeir of the klipa) וְלֹא־ velo

יָעִיר ya'ir כָּל־ kol ילי חֲמָתוֹ chamato (Nukva of the klipa): אַתָּה Ata

יְהֹוָ(אדני אהדונהי) Adonai לֹא־ lo תִכְלָא tichla רַחֲמֶיךָ rachamecha מִמֶּנִּי mimeni

וַחַסְדְּךָ chasdecha ר"ת = אברהם, וז"פ אל, רי"ו ול"ב נתיבות החכמה, רמ"ח (אברים), עסמ"ב וט"ז

וַאֲמִתְּךָ va'amitecha תָמִיד tamid ע"ה קס"א קנ"א קמ"ג אותיות פשוטות יִצְּרוּנִי yitzeruni:

זְכֹר zechor ע"ב קס"א, יהי אור ע"ה (סוד המעשכת העפע מן ד' שמות ליסוד הנקרא זכור)

רַחֲמֶיךָ rachamecha יְהֹוָ(אדני אהדונהי) Adonai וַחֲסָדֶיךָ vachasadecha כִּי ki

---

And say: Save us, God of our salvation; gather us and save us from all nations, to give thanks to Your Holy Name, and to be glorified in saying Your praise. Blessed is the Lord, the God of Israel, from this world to the world to come! The whole nation says 'Amen' and gives praise to the Lord." (1 Chronicles 16:8-36) "Exult the Lord, our God, and prostrate yourselves at His footrest, for He is sacred." (Psalms 99:5) "Exult the Lord, our God, and prostrate yourselves at His Holy Mountain, for the Lord, our God, is Holy." (Psalms 99:9) "He is merciful, forgives iniquities, and does not destroy. He frequently contains His anger and does not release all His Wrath." (Psalms 78:38) "And You, Lord, do not withhold Your mercy from me. May Your kindness and truth always protect me." (Psalms 40:12) "Remember Your mercy and kindness, Lord,

מֵעוֹלָם me'olam הֵמָּה hema עֻמְםׂ׃ תְּנוּ tenu עֹז oz לֵאלֹהִים lelohim אֱלֹהִים אֶהְיֶה אֲדֹנָי ; יְלָה

עַל־ al יִשְׂרָאֵל Yisrael גַּאֲוָתוֹ ga'avato וְעֻזּוֹ ve'uzo בַּשְּׁחָקִים bashechakim׃

נוֹרָא nora אֱלֹהִים Elohim אֲדֹנָי אֶהְיֶה ; יְלָה ; מִמִּקְדָּשֶׁיךָ mimikdashecha

אֵל El יִשְׂרָאֵל Yisrael (מִלּוּי דס״ג) יא״י אל ישראל = כ״ב הויות (כ״א דתפילין וא׳ דטלית)

הוּא hu נֹתֵן noten אבגיתץ, ישר, עֹז oz וְתַעֲצֻמוֹת veta'atzumot לָעָם la'am עלם

בָּרוּךְ baruch אֱלֹהִים Elohim אֲדֹנָי אֶהְיֶה ; יְלָה ; ס״ת מילוי עֹז׳ד (יֹן לֹת וד) ; ברוך אלהים = עֹד׳י׃

EL NEKAMOT

The Name Yud, Hei, Vav, and Hei appear in this connection eleven times. The power of eleven removes the dominance of the klipot. There are Ten Sefirot between our world and the Endless World. The eleventh connection is designed to give the klipot their nourishment so they won't try to rob us of ours. When we initiate this giving of Light, we gain control over the klipot. Additional support is available to us by virtue of ten spiritual giants who lived and died so they could assist us. These ten righteous souls were the incarnation of the ten brothers who sold Joseph (son of the biblical Patriarch Jacob), into slavery. In their last incarnation, Joseph's brothers were brutally murdered, but they possessed the power to leave the confines of their physical bodies so they suffered no pain. By reflecting on their actions, we can get an additional surge of power to help us lift off from the physical world.

From here until the *Aromimcha*, the Holy Name: יהוה appears eleven times in order to sort the *klipot* that are attached to the 11 curtains. When you say *El Nekamot*, you should meditate that God should avenge (*Nekama* - but the deeper meaning is to elevate, which comes from the same root - *Lehakim*) the deaths of the Ten Martyrs. When we recite *El Nekamot* it gives the Ten Martyrs' souls strength to be able to collect the sparks of the souls that are captured inside the *klipa* of *Asiyah*.

אֵל El יא״י (מִלּוּי דס״ג) נְקָמוֹת nekamot יְהֹוָה Adonai רֹת אֲנִי

אֵל El יא״י (מִלּוּי דס״ג) נְקָמוֹת nekamot מִנֹק ; רֹת = יבֹק, אלהים יהוה, אהיה אדני יהוה

הוֹפִיעַ hofi'a׃ הִנָּשֵׂא hinase שֹׁפֵט shofet הָאָרֶץ ha'aretz אלהים דההן עֹה

הָשֵׁב hashev רֹת = עֹה שֹדי גְּמוּל gemul עֹה עַל־ al גֵּאִים ge'im׃

---

for they are eternal." (Psalms 25:6)

"*Give power to God, for His majesty is over Israel and His power is in the Heavens. God, You are awesome in Your Temples, God of Israel. He gives powers and might to the nation, blessed is God.*" (Psalms 68:35-36)

EL NEKAMOT

"*You are the God of retributions, Lord.*
God of retributions appear. Arise, Judge of the world. Repay the arrogant with their due." (Psalms 94:1-2)

amecha עַמְּךָ al עַל hayeshu'a הַיְשׁוּעָה ladonai לַיהֹוָהאדני־יאהדונהי

virchatecha בִּרְכָתֶךָ sela סֶּלָה Adonai יְהֹוָהאדני־יאהדונהי: Tzeva'ot צְבָאוֹת פני שכינה

imanu עִמָּנוּ ריבוע ס"ג, קס"א ע"ה ו"ד אותיות misgav מִשְׂגָּב משה, מהע, ע"ב בריבוע וקס"א,

Elohei אֱלֹהֵי אהיה אדני, אלהים, ע"ה lanu לָנוּ אל עדי, ד"פ אלהים ע"ה מילוי ע"ב, דמב ; ילה

Ya'akov יַעֲקֹב ז הויות, יאהדונהי אידהנויה sela סֶּלָה: יְהֹוָהאדני־יאהדונהי Adonai

Tzeva'ot צְבָאוֹת פני שכינה ; יהוה צבאות אשרי אדם = התפארת adam אָדָם ashrei אַשְׁרֵי מ"ה

bote'ach בֹּטֵחַ bach בָּךְ אדם בוטח בך = אמן ע"ה ; יאהדונהי ע"ה ; בוטח בך = מילוי ע"ב ע"ה:

Adonai יְהֹוָהאדני־יאהדונהי hoshi'a הוֹשִׁיעָה יהוה ועי"ע נהורין hamelech הַמֶּלֶךְ ר"ת יהה

ya'anenu יַעֲנֵנוּ veyom בְיוֹם ע"ה נגד, מזבח, זן, אל יהוה kore'nu קָרְאֵנוּ ר"ת יב"ק,

hoshi'a הוֹשִׁיעָה: ע"ב = דהמלך כ' ועם ב"ן ס"ת ; אלהים יהוה, אהיה אדני יהוה ; יהוה ועי"ע נהורין

et אֶת־ amecha עַמְּךָ ס"ת כהת, משיוו בן דוד ע"ה uvarech וּבָרֵךְ et אֶת־

nachalatecha נַחֲלָתֶךָ ur'em וּרְעֵם venas'em וְנַשְּׂאֵם ad עַד ha'olam הָעוֹלָם:

nafshenu נַפְשֵׁנוּ (properly enunciate the letter Chet in the word "chiketa") chiketa וְזִכְּתָה

ladonai לַיהֹוָהאדני־יאהדונהי (יוד הה וו הה) ; ר"ת שם נוזל משיוו בן דוד ע"ה כהת,

ezrenu עֶזְרֵנוּ umaginenu וּמָגִנֵנוּ hu הוּא ki כִּי vo בוֹ yismach יִשְׂמַח משיוו

libenu לִבֵּנוּ ki כִּי veshem בְשֵׁם kodsho קָדְשׁוֹ vatachnu בָטַחְנוּ: yehi יְהִי

chasdecha וְזַסְדְּךָ Adonai יְהֹוָהאדני־יאהדונהי alenu עָלֵינוּ ka'asher כַּאֲשֶׁר

yichalnu יוִֹּלְנוּ lach לָךְ: (יאהדונהי) סאל, אמן har'enu הַרְאֵנוּ יְהֹוָהאדני־יאהדונהי Adonai

chasdecha וְזַסְדְּךָ veyesh'acha וְיֶשְׁעֲךָ titen תִּתֶּן־ ב"פ כהת lanu לָנוּ אלהים, אהיה אדני:

Salvation belongs to the Lord and Your blessing is upon Your Nation, Selah." (Psalms 3:9)
"The Lord of Hosts is with us, and our strength is the God of Jacob, Selah." (Psalms 46:12)
"The Lord of Hosts, joyful is the man that trusts in You." (Psalms 84:13) "Lord, redeem us.
The King shall answer us upon the day we call Him." (Psalms 20:10) "Redeem Your Nation and
bless Your inheritance, provide for them and uplift them forever." (Psalms 28:9) "Our soul
has awaited Lord. He is our help and our shield. God, in Him our heart rejoices because
we have trusted in His Holy Name. Lord, may Your kindness be upon us for we have placed our trust
in You." (Psalms 33:20-22) "Show us Your kindness, Lord, and grant us Your salvation." (Psalms 85:8)

קוּמָה kuma   (מקוה) קנ"א   עֶזְרָתָה ezrata   לָנוּ lanu   אלהים, אהיה אדני   וּפְדֵנוּ ufdenu

לְמַעַן lema'an   וְחַסְדֶּךָ chasdecha: אָנֹכִי anochi   יְהֹוָ֑ה(אדני אהדונהי) Adonai

אֱלֹהֶיךָ Elohecha יה   הַמַּעַלְךָ hama'alcha   מֵאֶרֶץ me'eretz   מִצְרָיִם mitz'rayim

הַרְחֶב־ harchev   פִּיךָ picha   וַאֲמַלְאֵהוּ va'amal'ehu: מצר   אַשְׁרֵי ashrei

הָעָם ha'am   שֶׁכָּכָה shekacha   מעה, מהע, ע"ב בריבוע וקס"א, אל שדי, ד"פ אלהים ע"ה

לוֹ lo   אַשְׁרֵי ashrei   הָעָם ha'am   ר"ת לאה   שֶׁיְהֹוָה(אדני אהדונהי) sheAdonai

אֱלֹהָיו Elohav יֹלה: וַאֲנִי va'ani אני   בְּחַסְדְּךָ bechasdecha   בָטַחְתִּי vatachti

יָגֵל yagel לֹהי   לִבִּי libi   בִּישׁוּעָתֶךָ bishu'atecha   ר"ת = ב"ן   אָשִׁירָה ashira

לַיהֹוָה(אדני אהדונהי) ladonai   כִּי ki   גָּמַל gamal   עָלָי alai   ס"ת   ילה:

AROMIMCHA

When we do negative actions, we give our Light to the *klipa* – especially those in *Asiyah* - thereby preventing *Asiyah* from elevating. Because of this spiritual heaviness, we need to get rid of the *klipa* so *Asiyah* will be able to ascend to the World of Formation. Whereas the prayer *Hodu* disconnects us from the *klipa*, *Aromimcha* helps to retrieve and elevate the sparks of Light that are still trapped inside the *klipa*. When we separate these sparks of Light from the *klipa*, the *klipa* loses all its power and let go of *Asiyah*. The word *aromimcha* means "praise" but also "raise up," in reference to the lifting up of the sparks from the *klipa*. *Aromimcha* contain 92 words, which connects us to the power of the word "*Amen*" (equals 91 plus 1 for the word itself).

In this Psalm there are ten times the Name: יהוֹה which correspond to the Ten *Sefirot*. And there are 92 words, which is the numerical value of יהוה אדני (plus 1 for the word itself). *Aromimcha* is comprised of words of gratitude of the souls and the sparks of *Asiyah* that were saved and rose from the *klipot* of *Asiyah*, to become *Mayin Nukvin*. These souls thank God for raising them from *She'ol*.

אֲרוֹמִמְךָ aromimcha

עִנְיַן נִצּוֹצֵי הַקְּדוּשָׁה הָעוֹלִים וְיוֹצְאִים מִקְּלִיפּוֹת דְּעֲשִׂיָּה הַנִּקְרָא נֶפֶשׁ   יְהֹוָ֑ה(אדני אהדונהי) Adonai (Keter)

כִּי ki   דִלִּיתָנִי dilitani   וְלֹא־ velo   שִׂמַּחְתָּ simach'ta   אֹיְבַי oyvai   לִי li:

"Arise and help us! Redeem us for the sake of Your kindness!" (Psalms 44:27) "I am the Lord, your God, Who took you out of the land of Egypt. Open your mouth wide and I shall fill it." (Psalms 81:11) "Joyful is the nation for whom all this is true; happy is the nation that the Lord is their God." (Psalms 144:15) "And I have trusted in Your kindness, therefore my heart shall rejoice in Your salvation. I shall sing for the Lord, for He has rewarded me." (Psalms 13:6)

AROMIMCHA

"I exalt You, Lord, for having uplifted me and did not rejoice my enemies on my account.

יְהֹוָאדֹנָיאהדונהי *(Chochmah)* Adonai מילוי ע"ב, רמב ; ילה אֱלֹהַי Elohai שִׁוַּעְתִּי shivati

אֵלֶיךָ elecha וַתִּרְפָּאֵנִי vatirpa'eni‪:‬ יְהֹוָאדֹנָיאהדונהי Adonai *(Binah)*

הֶעֱלִיתָ he'elita מִן־ min שְׁאוֹל she'ol נַפְשִׁי nafshi (elevation of the souls from *Asiyah*)

חִיִּיתַנִי chiyitani ס"ת ילי מִיָּרְדִי miyordi (כתיב: מיורדי) בּוֹר vor‪:‬ זַמְּרוּ zameru

לַיהֹוָאדֹנָיאהדונהי ladonai *(Chesed)* חֲסִידָיו chasidav וְהוֹדוּ vehodu אהיה

לְזֵכֶר lezecher קָדְשׁוֹ kodsho‪:‬ כִּי ki רֶגַע rega ג"פ אלהים וה' אותיות שבכל שם אלהים

בְּאַפּוֹ be'apo ס"ת = אלהים, אהיה אדני ; ועם ם דחיים = ריבוע אדני

וְחַיִּים chayim אהיה אהיה יהוה, בינה ע"ה כי רגע באפו וחיים ברצונו = עין דלת יוד בִּרְצוֹנוֹ birtzono

בָּעֶרֶב ba'erev יָלִין yalin בֶּכִי bechi ר"ת י"ד (כנגד מספר אותיות יהוה אלהינו יהוה,

וְלַבֹּקֶר velaboker רִנָּה rina בערב ילין בכי ולבקר רנה = וכן מספר האותיות כוזו במוכסז כוזו)

בַּל־ bal בְּשַׁלְוִי veshalvi אָמַרְתִּי amarti אֲנִי va'ani מטטרון שר הפנים

אֶמּוֹט emot לְעוֹלָם le'olam ריבוע ס"ג ו' אותיות דס"ג‪:‬ יְהֹוָאדֹנָיאהדונהי Adonai *(Gevurah)*

בִּרְצוֹנְךָ birtzoncha הֶעֱמַדְתָּה he'emadeta לְהַרְרִי lehareri עֹז oz

הִסְתַּרְתָּ histarta פָּנֶיךָ fanecha ס"ג מ"ה ב"ן הָיִיתִי hayiti נִבְהָל nivhal‪:‬

אֵלֶיךָ elecha יְהֹוָאדֹנָיאהדונהי Adonai *(Tiferet)* אֶקְרָא ekra וְאֶל ve'el

יְהֹוָאדֹנָיאהדונהי Adonai *(Netzach)* אֶתְחַנָּן etchanan‪:‬ מָה ma מ"ה בֶּצַע betza

בְּדָמִי bedami בְּרִדְתִּי berideti אֶל el ס"ת ילי שָׁחַת shachat הַיוֹדְךָ hayodcha

עָפָר afar הֲיַגִּיד hayagid יו, כ"ב אותיות פשוטות (= אכא) וה' אותיות סופיות (מנצפ"ך)

אֲמִתֶּךָ amitecha‪:‬ שְׁמַע shema יְהֹוָאדֹנָיאהדונהי Adonai *(Hod)* וְחָנֵּנִי vechoneni

יְהֹוָואדֹנָיאהדונהי Adonai *(Yesod)* הֱיֵה heyeh יהה עֹזֵר ozer כִּי־ li‪:‬ מוזיי

Lord, my God, I cried out to You, and You healed me. Lord, You raised my spirit from She'ol (Hell), and kept me alive when I sunk into the pit. Sing to the Lord, you, His pious ones, and give thanks to His Holy Name. For there is quietude in His anger and there is life in His will. In the evening, one may lie down crying yet be singing in the morning. When I was tranquil, I said that I shall never fall. Lord, You supported my mountain with strength; when You hid Your countenance, I was frightened. It is to You, Lord, that I call, and to the Lord that I plead. What gain is there in spilling my blood; to be lowered into my grave? Does the dust give thanks to You, does it proclaim Your Truth? Lord, hear me and be gracious to me. Lord, be my helper.

ילי ס"ת li לִי lemachol לְמָחוֹל mispedi מִסְפְּדִי hafachta הָפַכְתָּ

simcha שִׂמְחָה: vate'azreni וַתְּאַזְּרֵנִי saki שַׂקִּי pitachta פִּתַּחְתָּ

(pause) yidom יִדֹּם velo וְלֹא chavod כָּבוֹד yezamercha יְזַמֶּרְךָ lema'an לְמַעַן

Elohai אֱלֹהַי אדני אהיה, אלהים = ר"ת (Malchut) Adonai יהוה/אדני/אהדונהי

odeka אוֹדֶךָ: מילוי ע"ב, דמב ; ילה ; le'olam לְעוֹלָם אותיות דס"ג וי' ס"ג ריבוע

We recite the following only on *Hosha'ana Rabbah*.

THE LORD IS THE GOD

The Name *Yud, Hei, Vav,* and *Hei* יהוה corresponds to the Upper Worlds. The Name *Elohim* אלהים refers both to the concept of Judgment and to the physical world. During *Hosha'ana Rabbah*, the Upper and Lower Worlds are joined. This prayer helps us to transform any judgments decreed against us into Mercy. It is important to understand that when life appears to be judging us harshly, there is always a reason.

יהוה/אדני/אהדונהי Adonai הוּא hu הָאֱלֹהִים haElohim אדני אהיה ; ילה ;

הוּא hu יהוה/אדני/אהדונהי Adonai ר"ת ; יהה. עוֹ עג"כ = האלהים הוא יהוה

הָאֱלֹהִים haElohim אהיה אדני ; ילה ; יהוה הוא האלהים = עוֹ עג"כ ; ר"ת ; יהה.

Recite this verse twice.

THE LORD IS KING

This prayer transcends the concept of time, space, and motion, as well as the illusions of the five senses. The phrase "The Lord is King, the Lord has reigned, the Lord shall reign forever and for eternity" unifies past, present, and future, into one whole, so that when we recite *Adonai Melech* (The Lord is King) with the consciousness of transformation, we can correct mistakes we made in the past, while creating a better future and accomplishing it in the present. When we live in the present, we can correct the past and affect our future.

Angels are distinct energy forces that act as a transportation system for our prayers. This connection is so powerful that even the angels remain and sing along with us, instead of just carrying our words and thoughts to the Upper Worlds.

According to the Book of *Hechalot*: "There is one angel that stands every morning in the middle of Heaven, and sings the verses of '*Adonai Melech*,' and all the troops in the Upper Worlds sing with him all the way until *Barechu*." Because the angels sing *Adonai Melech* while standing, so do we.

You have turned my mourning into a celebration for me.
You have undone my sackcloth and have girded me with joy. So that
grace shall sing for You and never be silenced, Lord, my God, I shall forever thank You." (Psalms 30:2-13)

THE LORD IS THE GOD
The Lord is the God! The Lord is the God! (1 Kings 18:39)

Say these verses while standing.

חכמה–וחסד · בינה–גבורה · ם ן ·
malach מֶלֶךְ Adonai יְהֹוָאדֹנָיאהדֹונֹהי melech מֶלֶךְ Adonai יְהֹוָאדֹנָיאהדֹונֹהי

דעת–תפארת · פ ר
yimloch יִמְלֹךְ | Adonai יְהֹוָאדֹנָיאהדֹונֹהי (מֶלֶךְ מָלַךְ יִמְלֹךְ = מנֹזֶרֶף, סנֹדֹלפֹון, ערי)

דעת–תפארת · יהוה
va'ed וָעֶד וְעֹל רֹ"ת ייל ; דס"ג אותיות וי' דס"ג ריבוע le'olam לְעֹלָם

נצוֹ · ם ן · הוֹד · ז
malach מֶלֶךְ Adonai יְהֹוָאדֹנָיאהדֹונֹהי melech מֶלֶךְ Adonai יְהֹוָאדֹנָיאהדֹונֹהי

יסוֹד · פ ר
yimloch יִמְלֹךְ | Adonai יְהֹוָאדֹנָיאהדֹונֹהי (מֶלֶךְ מָלַךְ יִמְלֹךְ = מנֹזֶרֶף, סנֹדֹלפֹון, ערי)

יהוה · יסוֹד
va'ed וָעֶד וְעֹל רֹ"ת ייל ; דס"ג אותיות וי' דס"ג ריבוע le'olam לְעֹלָם

lemelech לְמֶלֶךְ Adonai יְהֹוָאדֹנָיאהדֹונֹהי יהה ; יהוה vehaya וְהָיָה

bayom בַּיּוֹם עֹ"ה אלהים דההין עֹ"ה ha'aretz הָאָרֶץ עמם ; ילי kol כָּל al עַל

Adonai יְהֹוָאדֹנָיאהדֹונֹהי ייי yih'ye יִהְיֶה hahu הַהוּא אל יהה זֹ, מזבוֹ, נגד עֹ"ה

echad אֶחָד אהבה, דאגה מהשֹע עֹ"ה, עֹ"ב בריבוע וקסֹ"א, אל שֹדֹי עֹ"ה ushmo וּשְׁמוֹ

echad אֶחָד אהבה, דאגה (בסוֹד אבא ואמא ואריך אנפין דעוֹלם העשֹיֹה)

hoshi'enu הוֹשִׁיעֵנוּ | Adonai יְהֹוָאדֹנָיאהדֹונֹהי Elohenu אֱלֹהֵינוּ ילה

vekabetzenu וְקַבְּצֵנוּ min מִן hagoyim הַגּוֹיִם lehodot לְהוֹדוֹת

leshem לְשֵׁם kodshecha קָדְשֶׁךָ lehishtabe'ach לְהִשְׁתַּבֵּחַ

bit'hilatecha בִּתְהִלָּתֶךָ

baruch בָּרוּךְ Adonai יְהֹוָאדֹנָיאהדֹונֹהי | Elohei אֱלֹהֵי מילוי עֹ"ב, דמב ; ילה

Yisrael יִשְׂרָאֵל ס"ת = ארנֹי ; יהוה אלהי ישראל = תרי"ג (מצווֹת) min מִן ha'olam הָעוֹלָם

THE LORD IS KING

The Lord is King, the Lord has reigned, the Lord shall reign forever and for eternity.
The Lord is King, the Lord has reigned, the Lord shall reign forever and for eternity.
"And the Lord has always been King over the whole earth. And upon that day, the Lord shall be One and His Name One." (Zecharyah 14:9) "Save us, Lord, our God, and gather us from amongst the nations to give thanks to Your Holy Name and be glorified in Your praise. Blessed is the Lord, the God of Israel, from this world to the World to Come,

ha'am הָעָם ילי kol כָּל־ ve'amar וְאָמַר ha'olam הָעוֹלָם ve'ad וְעַד

amen אָמֵן יאהדונהי haleluya הַלְלוּיָהּ אלהים, אהיה אדני ; ללהּ:

kol כָּל ילי haneshama הַנְּשָׁמָה tehalel תְּהַלֵּל ר"ת כהת, משיחו בן דוד ע"ה

Yah יָהּ haleluya הַלְלוּיָהּ אלהים, אהיה אדני ; ללהּ:

On the Holiday and on *Shabbat* continue on page 248.

On *Chol Hamo'ed* (not on *Shabbat*) we say here "*Lamnatze'ach*" (pages 246-247) and then continue with "*Baruch She'amar*" on page 274.

LAMNATZE'ACH

Elohim אֱלֹהִים shir שִׁיר mizmor מִזְמוֹר binginot בִּנְגִינֹת lam'natze'ach לַמְנַצֵּחַ

אהיה אדני ; ילה ya'er יָאֵר vivarchenu וִיבָרְכֵנוּ yechonenu יְחָנֵּנוּ ילה כף ויו זן ויו

panav פָּנָיו itanu אִתָּנוּ ר"ת פאי, אמן (יאהדונהי) sela סֶלָה: lada'at לָדַעַת ר"ת סאל,

goyim גּוֹיִם bechol בְּכָל darkecha דַּרְכֶּךָ ba'aretz בָּאָרֶץ ב"ן, לכב (יאהדונהי) אמן

yeshu'atecha יְשׁוּעָתֶךָ Elohim אֱלֹהִים amim עַמִּים yoducha יוֹדוּךָ: אהיה אדני ; ילה

yoducha יוֹדוּךָ amim עַמִּים kulam כֻּלָּם: yismechu יִשְׂמְחוּ viranenu וִירַנְּנוּ

le'umim לְאֻמִּים ki כִּי־ = איההוויהה ע"ה ר"ת amim עַמִּים tishpot תִּשְׁפֹּט

mishor מִישׁוֹר ul'umim וּלְאֻמִּים ba'aretz בָּאָרֶץ tanchem תַּנְחֵם sela סֶלָה:

yoducha יוֹדוּךָ amim עַמִּים Elohim אֱלֹהִים אהיה אדני ; ילה yoducha יוֹדוּךָ

amim עַמִּים kulam כֻּלָּם: ר"ת יודוך ישמחו יודוך ארץ = יא"י (מילוי דס"ג)

eretz אֶרֶץ natna נָתְנָה נתה, קס"א קנ"א קמ"ג = ע"ב, ריבוע יהוה לדעת יברכנו אלהים ר"ת ועם

yevula יְבוּלָהּ yevarchenu יְבָרְכֵנוּ ר"ת אני Elohim אֱלֹהִים אהיה אדני ; ילה

Elohenu אֱלֹהֵינוּ ילה: yevarchenu יְבָרְכֵנוּ Elohim אֱלֹהִים אהיה אדני ; ילה

veyir'u וְיִירְאוּ oto אוֹתוֹ kol כָּל ילי afsei אַפְסֵי־ aretz אָרֶץ:

Continue with "*Baruch She'amar*" on page 274.

---

and the whole nation said: Amen, Praise the Lord." (Psalms 106:47-48)
"Every soul will praise the Lord, Praise the Lord!" (Psalms 150:6)

LAMNATZE'ACH

"For the Musician, a melodious Psalm and a Song: May God give us favor and bless us. May He shine His Countenance upon us, Selah! To make known Your ways to the world and Your salvation among the nations. The nations shall give thanks to You, God. All the nations shall give thanks to You. The peoples shall rejoice and sing because You judge nations with fairness, and You guide peoples on earth. Selah. The nations shall give thanks to You, God. All nations shall give thanks to You. The earth has given its yield. May the Lord, our God, bless us. May God bless us and may all fear Him from all the ends of the earth." (Psalms 67)

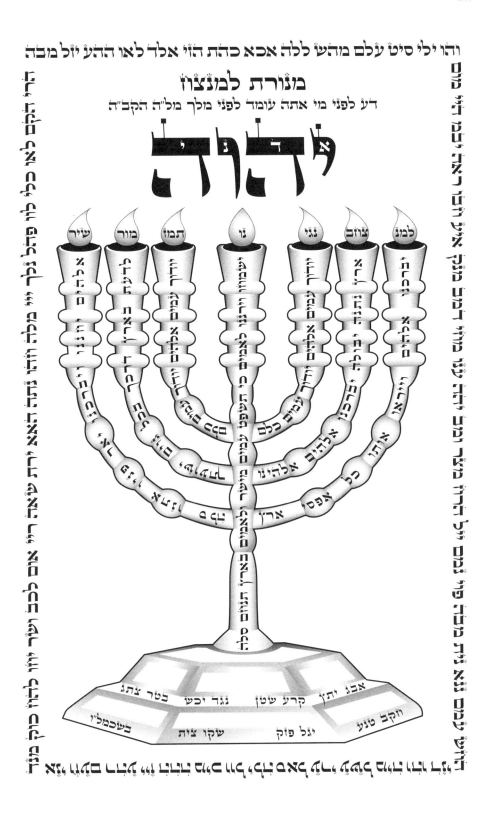

LAMNATZE'ACH

In this Psalm there are 13 verses corresponding to the Thirteen Atributes of Mercy and, six times the Name: יהוה corresponding to the Six Edges of *Zeir Anpin*. Meditate for the first *Ma'amar* (Utterance) of Creation: בְּרֵאשִׁית בָּרָא אֱלֹהִים אֵת הַשָּׁמַיִם וְאֵת הָאָרֶץ.

(א-אל) לַמְנַצֵּחַ lamnatze'ach מִזְמוֹר mizmor לְדָוִד leDavid:

(ב-רחום) הַשָּׁמַיִם hashamayim י״פ טל, י״פ כוזו מְסַפְּרִים mesaperim כְּבוֹד kevod

אל El ייא״י (מילוי דס״ג) ; ר״ת מכאל (מיכאל = גגא) ; כבוד אל = ס״ג (יוד הי ואו הי – דעת דנוקבא)

uma'ase וּמַעֲשֵׂה yadav יָדָיו magid מַגִּיד הָרָקִיעַ haraki'a:

(ג-וחנון) yom יוֹם ע״ה נגד, מזבוח, זן, אל יהוה leyom לְיוֹם ע״ה נגד, מזבוח, זן, אל יהוה

yabi'a יַבִּיעַ omer אֹמֶר velayla וְלַיְלָה מלה lelayla לְלַיְלָה מלה

yechave יְחַוֶּה (ד-וארך) דַּעַת da'at: en אֵין omer אֹמֶר ve'en וְאֵין

devarim דְּבָרִים ראה beli בְּלִי nishma נִשְׁמָע kolam קוֹלָם:

(ה-אפים) בְּכָל bechol ב״ן, לכב ב״ן הָאָרֶץ ha'aretz אלהים דההין ע״ה

yatza יָצָא רי״ו kavam קַוָּם uviktze וּבִקְצֵה tevel תֵּבֵל ב״פ

milehem מִלֵּיהֶם lashemesh לַשֶּׁמֶשׁ sam שָׂם ohel אֹהֶל bahem בָּהֶם:

(ו-ורב חסד) vehu וְהוּא kechatan כְּחָתָן yotze יֹצֵא mechupato מֵחֻפָּתוֹ

yasis יָשִׂישׂ kegibor כְּגִבּוֹר larutz לָרוּץ orach אֹרַח:

(ז-ואמת) מִקְצֵה miktze הַשָּׁמַיִם hashamayim י״פ טל, י״פ כוזו

motza'o מוֹצָאוֹ utkufato וּתְקוּפָתוֹ al עַל ketzotam קְצוֹתָם

ve'en וְאֵין nistar נִסְתָּר ב״פ מצר mechamato מֵחַמָּתוֹ:

LAMNATZE'ACH

"1) To the conductor, a song of David:
2) The Heavens declare the glory of God and the expanse of the sky tells of His handiwork.
3) Day following day brings expressions of praise, and night following night bespeaks wisdom.
4) There is no speech and there are no words, their sound is unheard. 5) Their line goes forth throughout the earth, and their words reach the farthest ends of the land. He had set up a tent in their midst.
6) And He is like a groom coming forth from his bridal tent, rejoicing like a warrior to run the course.
7) The end of the Heavens is its source and its circuit is to their other end. Nothing is hidden from its heat.

The kabbalists wrote: This Psalm has a great and magnificent ability of protection. From here on we have six consecutive verses of five words each, and the second word of each verse is: יְהוָֹה. You should count the words with your right hand fingers in the following way: say the first word and put your thumb down, then say the second word which is יְהוָֹה and keep the index finger up, then say the third word and put the middle finger down, then the fourth word and put the ring finger down, and while saying the fifth word put the little finger down. And while doing so meditate that the Creator will straighten those who are bent over and also, that all your spiritual enemies will surrender and you would defeat them.

temima תְּמִימָה (Chesed) Adonai יְהֹוָאֱדנִיֱאהדוֹנֵי torat תּוֹרַת (ו-נֵצר וֶחֶסד)

(Gevurah) Adonai יְהֹוָאֱדנִיֱאהדוֹנֵי edut עֵדוּת nefesh נָפֶשׁ meshivat מְשִׁיבַת

נֶאֱמָנָה ne'emana מַחְכִּימַת machkimat פֶּתִי peti (ט-לאלפים) פְּקוּדֵי pikudei מֹנךּ

mesamchei מְשַׂמְּחֵי yesharim יְשָׁרִים (Tiferet) Adonai יְהֹוָאֱדנִיֱאהדוֹנֵי

bara בָּרָה (Netzach) Adonai יְהֹוָאֱדנִיֱאהדוֹנֵי mitzvat מִצְוַת lev לֵב

yir'at יִרְאַת (עֵין) (י-נֹשׂא) מ"ה: ריבוע enayim עֵינָיִם me'irat מְאִירַת

omedet עוֹמֶדֶת tehora טְהוֹרָה (Hod) Adonai יְהֹוָאֱדנִיֱאהדוֹנֵי

(Yesod) Adonai יְהֹוָוֹהֱאֱדנִיֱאהדוֹנֵי mishpetei מִשְׁפְּטֵי ב"פ ב"ן la'ad לָעַד

אֱמֶת emet אהיה פעמים אהיה, ז"פ ס"ג tzadku צָדְקוּ yachdav יַחְדָּו:

rav רָב umipaz וּמִפָּז mizahav מִזָּהָב hanechemadim הַנֶּחֱמָדִים (י"א-ופשע)

וּמְתוּקִים umtukim מִדְּבַשׁ midevash שׁרי דֵשוֹפר ועם י"ד האווזֹ הרי עיֶ"ך דיֵנין הגדלות

venofet וְנֹפֶת tzufim צוּפִים: gam גַּם avdecha עַבְדְּךָ פוֹי, אל אדֹני

nizhar נִזְהָר bahem בָּהֶם beshomram בְּשָׁמְרָם ekev עֵקֶב ב"פ מום rav רָב:

---

8) The Torah of the Lord (Chesed) *is perfect and restores the soul.*
The testimony of the Lord (Gevurah) *is trustworthy, making the simple wise.*
9) The orders of the Lord (Tiferet) *are upright and they gladden the heart.*
The commandment of the Lord (Netzach) *is clear and enlightens the eyes.*
10) The fear of the Lord (Hod) *is pure and endures forever.*
The judgments of the Lord (Yesod) *are true and altogether righteous.*

11) *They are more desirable than gold and many precious stones, and sweeter than honey and the dripping of the combs. Even Your servant is careful of them, for in observing them there is great reward.*

ministarot מִנִּסְתָּרוֹת yavin יָבִין ילי mi מִי־ shegi'ot שְׁגִיאוֹת (י"ב-מזמיאה)

nakeni נַקֵּנִי (י"ג-ונקה) gam גַּם mizedim מִזֵּדִים chasoch וְשֹׂךְ

yimshelu יִמְשְׁלוּ al אַל־ פוי, אל אדני avdecha עַבְדֶּךָ שׁךְ נְצוֹצוֹת עַל וֹ' הַמְּלָכִים

vi בִי az אָז etam אֵיתָם veniketi וְנִקֵּיתִי mipesha מִפֶּשַׁע rav רָב׃

מ"ב אותיות בפסוק

yih'yu יִהְיוּ (ייא"י מילוי דס"ג) אל leratzon לְרָצוֹן מהש עה"ה, עה"ב ברבוע וקס"א וקס"א עה"ה, אל עדי עה"ה

imrei אִמְרֵי־ fi פִי ר"ת המספר אֶלֶף = אלף למד שׁין דלת יוד עה"ה

vehegyon וְהֶגְיוֹן libi לִבִּי lefanecha לְפָנֶיךָ ס"ג מ"ה ב"ן יְהֹוָ (אהדיאיאהדינהי) Adonai

tzuri צוּרִי vego'ali וְגֹאֲלִי׃

RANENU

There are 22 verses in this Psalm, indicating a connection to the 22 letters of the Aramaic alphabet. Because the Aramaic letters are the actual instruments of Creation, this prayer helps to inject order and the power of Creation into chaotic areas in our lives that need rejuvenation. Human beings are built from a four-letter genetic alphabet (A, T, C, and G) found in our DNA, with each letter representing a different chemical. The letters combine to create a set of instructions to build a human being. According to Kabbalah, the universe is built from the 22-letter genetic alphabet of the Aramaic letters, with each of the 22 letters representing a particular energy force; these forces combine in various sequences to create our universe.

In the next two Psalms there are great and deep secrets, so be cautious to say them meticulously. Because if one of the words is missing or is swallowed one would lose great goodness.

In this Psalm there are 161 words like the numerical value of the Name: אלף הי יוד הי. Also there are 22 verses corresponding to the 22 letters of the Aramaic alphabet, which is the numerical value of the Name: אכא from the 72 Names of God.

Also meditate for the second *Ma'amar* (Utterance) of Creation: יהי אור ("and God said: Let there be light" - The Light was first created for the righteous and then concealed for the future to come.)

12) *Yet, You, Who can discern mistakes, from unperceived faults cleanse me.*
13) *And, also from intentional sins, restrain Your servant. Let them not control me; then I shall be perfect and cleansed of great transgressions. May the words of my mouth and the thoughts of my heart find favor before You, Lord, my Rock and my Redeemer." (Psalms 19)*

רַנְּנוּ ranenu צַדִּיקִים tzadikim

Meditate on the Name: אֶהְיֶה דְיוֹדִין (אלף הי יוד הי), because it is a correction to remove anger.

בַּיהוה badonai לַיְשָׁרִים laysharim נָאוָה nava תְהִלָּה tehila

הוֹדוּ hodu לַיהוה ladonai

בְּכִנּוֹר bechinor בְּנֵבֶל benevel עָשׂוֹר asor

זַמְּרוּ zameru לוֹ lo

שִׁירוּ shiru לוֹ lo שִׁיר shir וְחַדֵּשׁ chadash

הֵיטִיבוּ hetivu נַגֵּן nagen בִּתְרוּעָה bitru'a כִּי ki יָשָׁר yashar

דְבַר devar Adonai יהוה וְכָל vechol מַעֲשֵׂהוּ ma'asehu

בֶּאֱמוּנָה be'emuna אֹהֵב ohev צְדָקָה tzedaka

וּמִשְׁפָּט umishpat חֶסֶד chesed יהוה Adonai

מָלְאָה mal'a הָאָרֶץ ha'aretz בִּדְבַר bidvar

יהוה Adonai שָׁמַיִם shamayim נַעֲשׂוּ na'asu

וּבְרוּחַ uvru'ach פִּיו piv כָּל kol צְבָאָם tzeva'am כֹּנֵס kones כַּנֵּד kaned

מֵי mei הַיָּם hayam נֹתֵן noten בָּאוֹצָרוֹת be'otzarot

תְּהוֹמוֹת tehomot יִירְאוּ yir'u מֵיהוה meAdonai כָּל kol

הָאָרֶץ ha'aretz מִמֶּנּוּ mimenu יָגוּרוּ yaguru כָּל kol

יוֹשְׁבֵי yoshvei תֵבֵל tevel כִּי ki הוּא hu אָמַר amar וַיֶּהִי vayehi

הוּא hu צִוָּה tziva וַיַּעֲמֹד vaya'amod יהוה Adonai הֵפִיר hefir

עֲצַת atzat גּוֹיִם goyim הֵנִיא heni מַחְשְׁבוֹת machshevot עַמִּים amim

---

RANENU

"Sing joyfully, righteous ones for the Lord, because it is for the upright that praise is fitting. Give thanks to the Lord with a harp, and with the ten-stringed lyre play melodies to Him. Sing a new song to Him and play well with the sound of trumpets, for the word of the Lord is upright and, all His deeds He did with faithfulness. He loves charity and justice, and the kindness of the Lord fills the Earth. By the Word of the Lord, the Heavens were made, by the Breath of His Mouth, all their hosts. He gathers the waters of the sea like a wall and He places the deep waters in vaults. All the Earth will be fearful of the Lord and of Him will be, in dread, all the inhabitants of the world. For He spoke and it came to be, He commanded and it stood firm. The Lord annuls the counsel of the nations and He balks the designs of peoples.

עֲצַת atzat   יְהֹוָה Adonai   לְעוֹלָם le'olam   ס"ג י' אותיות דס"ג ריבוע

תַּעֲמֹד ta'amod   מַחְשְׁבוֹת machshevot   לִבּוֹ libo   לְדֹר ledor   וָדֹר vador ריי:

אַשְׁרֵי ashrei   הַגּוֹי hagoi   asher אֲשֶׁר   יְהֹוָה Adonai

אֱלֹהָיו Elohav ילה   הָעָם ha'am   בָּחַר bachar   לְנַחֲלָה lenachala   לוֹ lo:

מִשָּׁמַיִם mishamayim י"פ טל, י"פ כוזו   הִבִּיט hibit   יְהֹוָה Adonai

רָאָה ra'a מ"ה: אֶת et   כָּל kol ילי   בְּנֵי benei   הָאָדָם ha'adam

מִמְּכוֹן mimechon   שִׁבְתּוֹ shivto   הִשְׁגִּיחַ hishgi'ach   אֶל el   כָּל kol ילי

יֹשְׁבֵי yoshvei   הָאָרֶץ ha'aretz אלהים דההין ע"ה: הַיֹּצֵר hayotzer   יַחַד yachad

לִבָּם libam   הַמֵּבִין hamevin   אֶל el   כָּל kol ילי   מַעֲשֵׂיהֶם ma'asehem:

אֵין en   הַמֶּלֶךְ hamelech   נוֹשָׁע nosha   בְּרָב berov   וְזִיל chayil ומב   גִּבּוֹר gibor

לֹא lo   יִנָּצֵל yinatzel   בְּרָב berov   כֹּחַ ko'ach: שֶׁקֶר sheker   הַסּוּס hasus

לֹא lo   וְזִילוֹ chelo אהיה י"פ   וּבְרֹב uvrov   לִתְשׁוּעָה litshu'a כוק, ריבוע אדני

יְמַלֵּט yemalet: הִנֵּה hine   עֵין en ריבוע מ"ה   יְהֹוָה Adonai

אֶל el גגא   יְרֵאָיו yere'av   לַמְיַחֲלִים lamyachalim   לְחַסְדּוֹ lechasdo ג' הויות = מלא

(להמשיך הארה ממולא עילאה)   לְהַצִּיל lehatzil   מִמָּוֶת mimavet   נַפְשָׁם nafsham

וּלְחַיּוֹתָם ulchayotam   בְּרָעָב bara'av: נַפְשֵׁנוּ nafshenu (צריך להדגיע ההויות)

וְזָכְתָה chiketa כהת, משיחו בן דוד ע"ה   לַיהֹוָה ladonai (יוד הה וו הה) ;

עֶזְרֵנוּ ezrenu נוזל שם רית   וּמָגִנֵּנוּ umaginenu   הוּא hu: כִּי ki   בוֹ vo

יִשְׂמַח yismach משיחו   לִבֵּנוּ libenu   כִּי ki   בְשֵׁם veshem   קָדְשׁוֹ kodsho

בָּטָחְנוּ vatachnu: יְהִי yehi   חַסְדְּךָ chasdecha   יְהֹוָה Adonai

עָלֵינוּ alenu: כַּאֲשֶׁר ka'asher   יִחַלְנוּ yichalnu   סאל, אמן (יאהדונהי)   לָךְ lach:

The counsel of the Lord will endure forever and the designs of His heart throughout the generations. Praiseworthy is the nation whose God is the Lord, the people whom He chose for His own heritage. From His dwelling place, the Lord looks down and He sees all the inhabitants of the Earth. He fashions their hearts into oneness and He comprehends all their deeds. A king is not saved by a great army nor is a hero rescued by great strength. A horse is a false savior, despite its great strength, it provides no escape. Behold, the Eye of the Lord is on those who fear Him, upon those who await His kindness. to rescue their soul from death and to sustain them in famine. Our soul waited for the Lord for He is our help and our shield; for, in Him, will our hearts be glad; for in His Holy Name, we trusted. May Your kindness, Lord, be upon us just as we awaited You." (Psalms 33).

LeDavid

In this Psalm there are 161 words like the numerical value of the Name: אלף הי יוד הי. Also there are 22 verses correspond to the 22 letters of the Aramaic alphabet which is the numerical value of the Name: אכא from the 72 Names of God. And each verse begins with one of the letters of the alphabet in consecutive order (with one exception, the letter ו *Vav* does not appear. Instead, at the end there is an extra verse starting with the letter פ *Pei* which in *Atbash* is the letter *Vav*).

Also meditate for the third *Ma'amar* (Utterance) of Creation: יהי רקיע ("and God said: Let there be an expanse" - The expanse separated the water under the expanse from the water above it.)

לְדָוִד leDavid

בְּשַׁנּוֹתוֹ beshanoto אֶת־ et טַעְמוֹ ta'mo לִפְנֵי lifnei אֲבִימֶלֶךְ Avimelech

(שבשמים אבינו) וַיְגָרְשֵׁהוּ vay'garshehu (לסמא''ל) וַיֵּלַךְ vayelach כלי׃

אֲבָרְכָה avarcha אֶת־ et יְהֹוָה Adonai בְּכָל־ bechol עֵת et

תָּמִיד tamid ע''ה קס''א קנ''א קמ''ג תְּהִלָּתוֹ tehilato בְּפִי befi׃

בַּיהֹוָה badonai תִּתְהַלֵּל tit'halel נַפְשִׁי nafshi

יִשְׁמְעוּ yishme'u עֲנָוִים anavim וְיִשְׂמָחוּ veyismachu׃

גַּדְּלוּ gadelu לַיהֹוָה ladonai אִתִּי iti וּנְרוֹמְמָה unromema

שְׁמוֹ shemo ע''ה שדי אל ע''ה, וקס''א ע''ב בריבוע מהש יַחְדָּו yachdav׃

דָּרַשְׁתִּי darashti אֶת־ et יְהֹוָה Adonai וְעָנָנִי ve'anani

ר''ת ורדאי, אהיה (ובשם זה עלה משה למרום והוא מזן ממלאכי וזבלה) ; ס''ת = כהת, משיוזזי בן דוד ע''ה

וּמִכָּל umikol יכי מְגוּרוֹתַי megurotai הִצִּילָנִי hitzilani נוהנ׃

הִבִּיטוּ hibitu אֵלָיו elav וְנָהָרוּ venaharu

וּפְנֵיהֶם ufnehem אַל־ al יֶחְפָּרוּ yechparu׃

זֶה ze עָנִי ani ריבוע מ''ה קָרָא kara וַיהֹוָה vadonai

שָׁמֵעַ shame'a וּמִכָּל umikol יכי צָרוֹתָיו tzarotav הוֹשִׁיעוֹ hoshi'o׃

LeDavid

"From David, when he disguised his sanity before Abimelech, who drove him out and he left. I bless the Lord at all times; His praise is always in my mouth. In God does my soul glory, may humble ones hear and be glad. Declare the greatness of the Lord with me and let us exalt His Name together. I sought out the Lord and He answered me and from all my fears, He delivered me. They look to Him and become radiant and their faces were not shamed. This poor man calls and the Lord hears and from all his troubles He saved him.

חֹנֶה chone   מַלְאַךְ mal'ach   יְהֹוָה Adonai

סָבִיב saviv   לִירֵאָיו lire'av   וַיְחַלְּצֵם vay'chaletzem

טַעֲמוּ ta'amu   וּרְאוּ ur'u   כִּי ki   טוֹב tov

אַשְׁרֵי ashrei   הַגֶּבֶר hagever   יֶחֱסֶה yechese   בּוֹ bo

יְראוּ yir'u   אֶת et   יְהֹוָה Adonai   קְדֹשָׁיו kedoshav

כִּי ki   אֵין en   מַחְסוֹר machsor   לִירֵאָיו lire'av

כְּפִירִים kefirim   רָשׁוּ rashu   וְרָעֵבוּ vera'evu   וְדֹרְשֵׁי vedorshei

יְהֹוָה Adonai   לֹא lo   יַחְסְרוּ yachseru   כָל chol   טוֹב tov

לְכוּ lechu   בָנִים vanim   שִׁמְעוּ shim'u   לִי li

יִרְאַת yir'at   יְהֹוָה Adonai   אֲלַמֶּדְכֶם alamedchem

מִי mi   הָאִישׁ ha'ish   הֶחָפֵץ hechafetz   חַיִּים chayim   אֹהֵב ohev   יָמִים yamim   לִרְאוֹת lir'ot   טוֹב tov

נְצֹר netzor   לְשׁוֹנְךָ leshoncha   מֵרָע mera

וּשְׂפָתֶיךָ usfatecha   מִדַּבֵּר midaber   מִרְמָה mirma

סוּר sur   מֵרָע mera   וַעֲשֵׂה va'aseh   טוֹב tov

בַּקֵּשׁ bakesh   שָׁלוֹם shalom   וְרָדְפֵהוּ verodfehu

עֵינֵי enei   יְהֹוָה Adonai   אֶל el   צַדִּיקִים tzadikim

וְאָזְנָיו ve'oznav   אֶל el   שַׁוְעָתָם shavatam

The angel of the Lord encamps around those who fear Him and releases them. Taste and see that the Lord is good; joyful is the man who takes refuge in Him. Fear the Lord all His Holy Ones, for those who fear Him shall not lack anything. Young lions may want and hunger, but those who seek the Lord shall not lack any good. Go, sons, heed me and I shall teach you the fear of the Lord. Who is the man who desires life and who loves days of seeing good? Guard your tongue from evil and your lips from speaking deceit. Turn away from evil and do good, seek peace and pursue it. The Eyes of the Lord are toward the righteous and His Ears to their cry.

פָּנֵי penei וְחָכְמָה בִּינָה (the face of anger) יְהֹוָאדְנִיָאהדונהי Adonai

בְּעֹשֵׂי be'osei רָע ra לְהַכְרִית lehachrit מֵאֶרֶץ me'eretz זִכְרָם zichram מֵזֵּר

‡(including the everlasting Luz bone, while He saves all the bones of the righteous)

שָׁמֵעַ shame'a   וַיְהֹוָאדְנִיָאהדונהי vadonai   צָעֲקוּ tza'aku

וּמִכָּל־ umikol־ יְלֹי   צָרוֹתָם tzarotam   הִצִּילָם hitzilam‡

קָרוֹב karov   יְהֹוָאדְנִיָאהדונהי Adonai   לְנִשְׁבְּרֵי־ lenishberei־   לֵב lev

(the seven kings who died) וְאֶת־ ve'et   דַּכְּאֵי־ dakei־   רוּחַ ru'ach   יוֹשִׁיעַ yoshia‡

רַבּוֹת rabot   רָעוֹת ra'ot   צַדִּיק tzadik

וּמִכֻּלָּם umikulam   יַצִּילֶנּוּ yatzilenu   יְהֹוָאדְנִיָאהדונהי Adonai‡

שֹׁמֵר shomer   כָּל־ kol   יְלֹי   עַצְמוֹתָיו atzmotav

אַחַת achat   מֵהֵנָּה mehena   לֹא lo   נִשְׁבָּרָה nishbara‡

תְּמוֹתֵת temotet   רָשָׁע rasha   רָעָה ra'a   רהע

וְשֹׂנְאֵי veson'ei   צַדִּיק tzadik   יֶאְשָׁמוּ yeshamu‡

פּוֹדֶה pode   יְהֹוָאדְנִיָאהדונהי Adonai   נֶפֶשׁ nefesh   עֲבָדָיו avadav

וְלֹא velo   יֶאְשְׁמוּ ye'eshemu   כָּל־ kol   יְלֹי   הַחוֹסִים hachosim   בּוֹ bo‡

TEFILA LEMOSHE

This prayer gives us the ability to connect to the consciousness of Moses, the greatest prophet that ever lived. Moses was the epitome of pure sharing, with unconditional love and caring for others. It was this attribute, along with his close, profound relationship with God that gave him all his power.

The Face (the Face of anger) of the Lord is against evildoers, to cut off their memory from the Earth (including the everlasting Luz bone, while He saves all the bones of the righteous). They cried out and the Lord heeds; from all their troubles, He rescued them. The Lord is close to the brokenhearted (the seven kings who died) and He saves those who are crushed in spirit. Many are the mishaps of the righteous, but, from them all, the Lord rescues him. He guards all His bones such that not even one of them was broken. You shall bring an evil death-blow upon the wicked and those who hate the righteous shall be condemned. The Lord redeems the souls of His servants, and all those who seek refuge in Him shall not be condemned." (Psalms 34)

Meditate for the fourth *Ma'amar* (Utterance) of Creation:

יִקָּווּ הַמַּיִם מִתַּחַת הַשָּׁמַיִם אֶל מָקוֹם אֶחָד וְתֵרָאֶה הַיַּבָּשָׁה ("and God said: Let the water under the sky be gathered to one place, and let dry ground appear" – as it says (hereinafter): "May Your works be seen upon Your servants" – "Your Works," meaning the revelation of the land.)

בא"ת ב"ש אוֹכֵץ = בָּ"ן אֲדֹנָי וְנִיקוּדָה ע"ה יוֹד הֵי וָו הֵה   tefila תְּפִלָּה   לְמֹשֶׁה leMoshe

מהע', ע"ב בריבוע וקס"א, אֵל שַׁדַּי, ד"פ אלהים ע"ה   ish אִישׁ הָאֱלֹהִים haElohim   ילה ;

ר"ת לאה (רומז לו"א כבוד יִשְׂרָאֵל הַמְזֻוָּוג עִם לאה) ; ס"ת מֹשֶׁה (כלת מֹשֶׁה)

אֲדֹנָי Adonai ללה   ma'on מָעוֹן   Ata אַתָּה הָיִיתָ hayita   lanu לָּנוּ אלהים, אהיה אדני

בְּדֹר bedor ר"ת הבל (שהוא משה גלגול הבל שמתגלגל בכל דור להורות בני דורו)   וָדֹר vador רי"ו :

beterem בְּטֶרֶם   harim הָרִים   yuladu יֻלָּדוּ   vatecholel וַתְּחוֹלֵל   eretz אֶרֶץ

vetevel וְתֵבֵל ב"פ רי"ו   ume'olam וּמֵעוֹלָם   ad עַד   olam עוֹלָם

Ata אַתָּה el אֵל יא"י (מילוי דס"ג): tashev תָּשֵׁב   enosh אֱנוֹשׁ   ad עַד

daka דַּכָּא מ"ה: vatomer וַתֹּאמֶר   shuvu שׁוּבוּ   venei בְּנֵי   adam אָדָם

ki כִּי   elef אֶלֶף מספר אֶלֶף = אלף למד פה עין דלת יוד ע"ה   shanim שָׁנִים

be'enecha בְּעֵינֶיךָ ע"ה קס"א ; ריבוע מ"ה ע"ה נגד, מזבוח, זן, אל יהוה   keyom כְּיוֹם   etmol אֶתְמוֹל ki כִּי ya'avor יַעֲבֹר   ve'ashmura וְאַשְׁמוּרָה   valayla בַלָּיְלָה מלה:

zeramtam זְרַמְתָּם   shena שֵׁנָה   yih'yu יִהְיוּ אל (יא"י מילוי דס"ג)

baboker בַּבֹּקֶר   kechatzir כֶּחָצִיר   yachalof יַחֲלֹף: baboker בַּבֹּקֶר   yatzitz יָצִיץ

vechalaf וְחָלָף   la'erev לָעֶרֶב   yemolel יְמוֹלֵל   veyavesh וְיָבֵשׁ: ki כִּי

chalinu כָלִינוּ   ve'apecha בְאַפֶּךָ   uvachamat'cha וּבַחֲמָתְךָ   nivhalnu נִבְהָלְנוּ:

TEFILA LeMoshe

"A prayer of Moses, the man of God:
God, You have been a dwelling place for us in all generations, before the mountains were born and You had not yet fashioned the earth and the inhabited land. Forever and for eternity, You are God. You reduce man to a pulp and You say: Repent you sons of man. Because a thousand years in Your eyes are but a bygone yesterday and like a watch in the night. You flood them away and they become sleep-like, by morning they are like grass that withers. In the morning it blossoms and becomes rejuvenated, by evening it is cut down and brittle. We are consumed by Your fury and we are confounded by Your wrath.

שַׁתָּ (shata) (כתיב עה) avonotenu עֲוֹנֹתֵינוּ lenegdecha לְנֶגְדֶּךָ alumenu עֲלֻמֵנוּ

לִמְאוֹר lim'or panecha פָּנֶיךָ מ״ה ס״ג ב״ן ki כִּי chol כָל yamenu יָמֵינוּ ילו

פָּנוּ panu ve'evratecha בְּעֶבְרָתֶךָ kilinu כִלִּינוּ shanenu שָׁנֵינוּ chemo כְּמוֹ

הֶגֶה hege יְמֵי yemei shenotenu שְׁנוֹתֵינוּ vahem בָּהֶם shiv'im שִׁבְעִים

שָׁנָה shana ve'im וְאִם יוֹהך, מ״א אותיות דפשוט, דמילוי ודמילוי דמילוי דאתיה ע״ה

בִּגְבוּרֹת bigvurot shemonim שְׁמוֹנִים shana שָׁנָה verahbam וְרָהְבָּם

עָמָל amal va'aven וָאָוֶן ki כִּי gaz גָּז chish וָחִישׁ vana'ufa וַנָּעֻפָה mi בְּ־ ילו

יוֹדֵעַ yode'a oz עֹז apecha אַפֶּךָ uch'yir'atcha וּכְיִרְאָתְךָ evratecha עֶבְרָתֶךָ

לִמְנוֹת limnot yamenu יָמֵינוּ ken כֵּן hoda הוֹדַע venavi וְנָבִא levav לְבַב בוכו

וְחָכְמָה chochma במילוי = תרי״ג (מצוות) shuva שׁוּבָה החוֹ יְהֹוָה אדניאהדונהי Adonai

עַד ad מָתַי matai vehinachem וְהִנָּחֵם al עַל avadecha עֲבָדֶיךָ למב, מילוי דע״ב

שַׂבְּעֵנוּ sabe'enu vaboker בַבֹּקֶר chasdecha וַסְדֶּךָ unranena וּנְרַנְּנָה

וְנִשְׂמְחָה venismecha bechol בְּכָל ב״ן, לכב yamenu יָמֵינוּ samchenu שַׂמְּחֵנוּ

כִּימוֹת kimot initanu עִנִּיתָנוּ shenot שְׁנוֹת ra'inu רָאִינוּ ra'a רָעָה רהעו

יֵרָאֶה yera'e רי״ו el אֶל avadecha עֲבָדֶיךָ fa'olecha פָעֳלֶךָ vahadarcha וַהֲדָרְךָ

עַל al benehem בְּנֵיהֶם vihi וִיהִי no'am נֹעַם (נעם עליון) Adonai אֲדֹנָי כלה

אֱלֹהֵינוּ Elohenu ילה alenu עָלֵינוּ uma'ase וּמַעֲשֵׂה yadenu יָדֵינוּ

כּוֹנְנָה konena alenu עָלֵינוּ uma'ase וּמַעֲשֵׂה yadenu יָדֵינוּ konenehu כּוֹנְנֵהוּ

You have set our iniquities before Yourself, our immaturity before the Light of Your countenance. For all our days passed by because of Your anger. We consumed our years like a fleeting thought. The days of our years among them are seventy years, and if with strength, eighty years, their proudest success is but toil and pain, for it is cut off swiftly and we fly away. Who knows the power of Your fury? As You are feared, so is Your anger. According to the count of our days so may You teach us, and then we shall acquire a heart of wisdom. Return Lord, for how much longer? Relent concerning Your servants. Satisfy us in the morning with Your kindness, then we shall sing out and rejoice throughout our days. Gladden us according to the day that You had afflicted us, the years when we saw evil. May Your works be seen upon Your servants and Your majesty upon their children. And may the pleasantness of the Lord, our God, be upon us and may He establish the work of our hands for us and may the work of our hands establish Him." (Psalms 90)

YOSHEV

Every positive action creates positive angels, and every negative action creates negative angels. Angels are distinct forces of spiritual energy. Negative angels or energy forces disrupt our lives in many ways. For example, oftentimes people do not understand what we are trying to say to them, or we do not fully understand what is being said to us. It is as though an unseen interference creates confusion and sends mixed signals. Miscommunication eventually leads to misunderstanding, which in turn can lead to fights, arguments, and, all too often, a lot of pain. At other times, things go wrong; no matter what we do, nothing seems to turn things around.

Meditate for the fifth *Ma'amar* (Utterance) of Creation: תַּדְשֵׁא הָאָרֶץ דֶּשֶׁא ("and God said: Let the land produce vegetation" — vegetation was created to sustain all creatures and they should dwell in its shade.)

Shadai שַׁדַּי betzel בְּצֵל elyon עֶלְיוֹן ב״פ מצר beseter בְּסֵתֶר yoshev יֹשֵׁב

machsi מַחְסִי ladonai לַיהֹוָה omar אֹמַר :yitlonan יִתְלוֹנָן

וּמְצוּדָתִי umtzudati מילוי דע״ב, דמב ; ילה ; ר״ת אום, מובה, יזל Elohai אֱלֹהַי

yatzilcha יַצִּילְךָ hu הוּא ki כִּי :bo בּוֹ סיט evtach אֶבְטַח

:havot הַוּוֹת midever מִדֶּבֶר yakush יָקוּשׁ מיה ר״ת mipach מִפַּח

kenafav כְּנָפָיו vetachat וְתַחַת lach לָךְ yasech יָסֶךְ be'evrato בְּאֶבְרָתוֹ

tira תִירָא lo לֹא :amito אֲמִתּוֹ vesochera וְסֹחֵרָה tzina צִנָּה techse תֶּחְסֶה

:yomam יוֹמָם ya'uf יָעוּף mechetz מֵחֵץ מלה layla לַיְלָה mipachad מִפַּחַד

yashud יָשׁוּד miketev מִקֶּטֶב yahaloch יַהֲלֹךְ ba'ofel בָּאֹפֶל midever מִדֶּבֶר

צָהֳרָיִם :tzahorayim yipol יִפֹּל mitzidecha מִצִּדְּךָ elef אֶלֶף מספר אֶלֶף = אלף למד עין

:yigash יִגַּשׁ lo לֹא elecha אֵלֶיךָ miminecha מִימִינֶךָ urvava וּרְבָבָה דלת יוד ע״ה

YOSHEV

"One who finds refuge in the Supreme One and dwells in the shade of Shaddai, I say of the Lord: He is my refuge and my fortress, my God in Whom I put my trust. For He shall rescue you from the snare of the trap and from destructive pestilence. He shall cover you with his pinion and you shall find refuge under his wings. His truth is a shield and armor. You shall not fear the terror of the nights, of the arrow that flies by day, of pestilence that moves in the darkness or of the destruction that strikes at noon. A thousand will fall at your side and ten thousand at your right, yet they will not approach you.

veshilumat וְשִׁלֻּמַת tabit תַּבִּיט ע"ה קס"א ; ריבוע מ"ה be'enecha בְּעֵינֶיךָ rak רַק

Adonai יְהוָֹה(אדני-אהיה) Ata אַתָּה ki כִּי tir'e תִרְאֶה resha'im רְשָׁעִים

me'onecha מְעוֹנֶךָ samta שַׂמְתָּ elyon עֶלְיוֹן machsi מַחְסִי וֹעֹם

veNega וְנֶגַע ra'a רָעָה elecha אֵלֶיךָ te'une תְאֻנֶּה lo לֹא

mal'achav מַלְאָכָיו ki כִּי be'aholecha בְּאָהֳלֶךָ yikrav יִקְרַב lo לֹא

lishmorcha לִשְׁמָרְךָ lach לָךְ yetzave יְצַוֶּה

derachecha דְּרָכֶיךָ bechol בְּכָל

pen פֶּן yisa'uncha יִשָּׂאוּנְךָ kapayim כַּפַּיִם al עַל

shachal שַׁחַל al עַל raglecha רַגְלֶךָ ba'even בָּאֶבֶן tigof תִּגֹּף

kefir כְּפִיר tirmos תִּרְמֹס tidroch תִּדְרֹךְ vafeten וָפֶתֶן

va'afaltehu וַאֲפַלְּטֵהוּ chashak חָשַׁק vi בִי ki כִּי vetanin וְתַנִּין

asagvehu אֲשַׂגְּבֵהוּ

shemi שְׁמִי yada יָדַע ki כִּי

anochi אָנֹכִי imo עִמּוֹ ve'e'enehu וְאֶעֱנֵהוּ yikra'eni יִקְרָאֵנִי

va'achabdehu וַאֲכַבְּדֵהוּ achaltzehu אֲחַלְּצֵהוּ vetzara בְצָרָה

We say the last verse of this Psalm twice in order to have 130 words,
which is the numerical value of the Name: יוֹד הא ואו הא יוֹד הא ואו יוֹד הא ואו הא,
which has the power to chase those negative entities (that are mentioned here) away.

yamim יָמִים orech אֹרֶךְ

orech אֹרֶךְ bishu'ati בִּישׁוּעָתִי ve'arehu וְאַרְאֵהוּ asbi'ehu אַשְׂבִּיעֵהוּ

bishu'ati בִּישׁוּעָתִי ve'arehu וְאַרְאֵהוּ asbi'ehu אַשְׂבִּיעֵהוּ yamim יָמִים

You shall merely look with your eyes and see the retribution of the wicked. Because You are, Lord, my refuge. You have placed Your dwelling place in the highest Place. No evil will befall you nor will any plague come near your tent. He will charge His angels to you to protect you in all your ways. They will carry you on their palms lest you strike your foot against a stone. You will tread upon the lion and the viper, you will trample the young lion and the serpent. For he has yearned for Me and I will deliver him. I will elevate him because he knows My Name. He will call upon Me and I will answer him. I am with him in distress. I will release him and I will honor him. With long life I will satiate him and I will show him My salvation. With long life I will satiate him and I will show him My salvation." (Psalms 91)

MIZMOR SHIRU

According to Kabbalah, people will sometimes reincarnate into animals as part of their *tikkun* (correction) process. By reciting this Psalm with that in mind, we are helping to elevate their souls.

Meditate for the seventh *Ma'amar* (Utterance) of Creation: יִשְׁרְצוּ הַמַּיִם ("and God said: Let the water teem" — as it says in this Psalm: "The sea in its fullness will roar".)

מִזְמוֹר mizmor שִׁירוּ shiru לַיהוָֹה ladonai שִׁיר shir וְזָדָשׁ chadash

כִּי־ ki נִפְלָאוֹת nifla'ot עָשָׂה asa

הוֹשִׁיעָה hoshi'a לּוֹ lo יְמִינוֹ yemino וּזְרוֹעַ uzro'a

קָדְשׁוֹ kodsho: הוֹדִיעַ hodi'a יְהוָֹה Adonai יְשׁוּעָתוֹ yeshu'ato

לְעֵינֵי le'enei הַגּוֹיִם hagoyim גִּלָּה gila צִדְקָתוֹ tzidkato: זָכַר zachar

וְחַסְדּוֹ chasdo וֶאֱמוּנָתוֹ ve'emunato

לְבֵית levet רָאוּ ra'u כָּל־ chol אַפְסֵי afsei

אָרֶץ aretz אֵת et יְשׁוּעַת yeshu'at אֱלֹהֵינוּ Elohenu הָרִיעוּ hari'u:

לַיהוָֹה ladonai כָּל־ kol הָאָרֶץ ha'aretz;

פִּצְחוּ pitzchu וְרַנְּנוּ veranenu וְזַמֵּרוּ vezameru:

זַמְּרוּ zameru לַיהוָֹה ladonai בְּכִנּוֹר bechinor בְּכִנּוֹר bechinor

וְקוֹל vekol זִמְרָה zimra: בַּחֲצֹצְרוֹת bachatzotzrot וְקוֹל vekol שׁוֹפָר shofar

הָרִיעוּ hari'u לִפְנֵי lifnei הַמֶּלֶךְ hamelech יְהוָֹה Adonai:

יִרְעַם yir'am הַיָּם hayam וּמְלֹאוֹ umlo'o תֵּבֵל tevel וְיֹשְׁבֵי veyoshvei

בָהּ va: נְהָרוֹת neharot יִמְחֲאוּ yimcha'u כָף chaf יַחַד yachad

הָרִים harim יְרַנֵּנוּ yeranenu: לִפְנֵי lifnei יְהוָֹה Adonai

כִּי ki בָא va לִשְׁפֹּט lishpot הָאָרֶץ ha'aretz יִשְׁפֹּט yishpot

תֵּבֵל tevel בְּצֶדֶק betzedek וְעַמִּים ve'amim בְּמֵישָׁרִים bemesharim:

MIZMOR SHIRU

"A Psalm; Sing to the Lord a new song for He has done wonders. His right Hand and His Holy Arm helped Him. The Lord had made known His salvation; in sight of the nations He revealed His righteousness. He recalled His kindness and faithfulness to the House of Israel. All the ends of the Earth have seen the salvation of our God. Call out to the Lord all the inhabitants of the Earth. Open your mouths in joyous songs and play melodies. Play melodies to the Lord on a harp. With harp and sound of chanted praise. With trumpets and Shofar sounds, call out before the King, the Lord. The sea in its fullness will roar, the world and those who dwell therein. Rivers will clap hands, mountains will exult together before the Lord, for He will have arrived to judge the earth. He will judge the world with righteousness and peoples with fairness." (Psalms 98)

SHIR LAMA'ALOT

This configuration of Aramaic letters helps to awaken an inner realization that nothing of substance can be achieved in this physical world without the help of the Creator. Alone, we can do nothing. The Satan, our ego, will do everything in its power to convince us that we are the sole architects of our success. This connection helps us recognize the profound truth that the Creator's hand can always be found within our good fortune.

In this praise, the word *Shomer* (guard, or derivatives of it) is mentioned six times. This stands for the letter *Vav* (ו=6) of the Name: יהוה. Also, meditate for the eighth *Ma'amar* (Utterance) of Creation: תוצא הארץ נפש וזיה ("and God said: Let the land produce living creatures").

esa אֶשָּׂא (מעלות) בכל נקנית שמלכות (מלמד) lama'alot לַמַּעֲלוֹת shir שִׁיר

(הרים שנקראים האבות) heharim הֶהָרִים el אֶל־ מ"ה ריבוע enai עֵינַי

me'im מֵעָם ezri עֶזְרִי :ezri עֶזְרִי yavo יָבֹא (א"א) me'ayin מֵאַיִן

va'aretz: וָאָרֶץ כוו י"פ ,טל י"פ shamayim שָׁמַיִם ose עֹשֵׂה Adonai יְהוֹוָהדִיהֵאדְנִיהֵ

yanum יָנוּם al אַל־ raglecha רַגְלֶךָ lamot לַמּוֹט yiten יִתֵּן al אַל־

ר"ת = דמב, מילוי דע"ב velo וְלֹא yanum יָנוּם lo לֹא־ hine הִנֵּה :shomrecha שֹׁמְרֶךָ

Yisrael: יִשְׂרָאֵל כ"א נהורין שבתפילין ההויות ע"ע da'a דא"א shomer שׁוֹמֵר yishan יִישָׁן

tzilecha צִלְּךָ Adonai יְהוֹוָהדִיהֵאדְנִיהֵ shomrecha שֹׁמְרֶךָ Adonai יְהוֹוָהדִיהֵאדְנִיהֵ

hashemesh הַשֶּׁמֶשׁ yomam יוֹמָם :היי yeminecha יְמִינֶךָ yad יַד־ al עַל־

:מלה balayla בַּלָּיְלָה veyare'ach וְיָרֵחַ יכה ר"ת yakeka יַכֶּכָּה lo לֹא־

ילי mikol מִכָּל־ yishmorcha יִשְׁמָרְךָ Adonai יְהוֹוָהדִיהֵאדְנִיהֵ

מ"כ: nafshecha נַפְשֶׁךָ et אֶת־ yishmor יִשְׁמֹר ra רָע

uvo'echa וּבוֹאֶךָ tzet'cha צֵאתְךָ yishmor יִשְׁמָר־ Adonai יְהוֹוָהדִיהֵאדְנִיהֵ

וכל: olam עוֹלָם ve'ad וְעַד־ me'ata מֵעַתָּה

SHIR LAMA'ALOT

"A Song of Acents: I raise my eyes to the mountains, where will my help come from? My help comes from the Lord, Who made the Heavens and the Earth. He will not allow your foot to be moved. Your Keeper will not slumber. Behold, He neither slumbers nor sleeps, the Keeper of Israel. The Lord is your Keeper. The Lord is your shade upon your right hand. By day the sun will not harm you, nor will the moon at night. The Lord will protect you from all evil. He will keep your soul. The Lord will guard your departure and your arrival, from now till eternity." (Psalms 121)

SHIR HAMA'ALOT LEDAVID

These verses connect us to the ancient Holy Temple. According to Kabbalah, the Holy Temple is the energy center and source of all spiritual Light for the whole world, similar to a nuclear power plant that provides electrical energy for an entire city. The land of Israel is the energy center of the planet; Jerusalem is the energy center of Israel; the physical Temple was the energy center of Jerusalem; and the Holy of Holies, inside the Temple, was the ultimate energy center for the Temple and thus for the entire physical world. When the Temple was standing, it acted as a generator that chugged along 24 hours a day to produce all the spiritual Light and energy we needed. With its destruction, the power lines were severed. The Aramaic letters in this connection re-establish the lines of communication with the spiritual essence of the Temple, giving us the ability to capture this energy for our personal lives.

This praise was said by King David for his kingdom, as everything was in one unification – "justice and peace kissed each other." And that's the meaning of: "I shall request good for you."

shir שִׁיר   hama'alot הַמַּעֲלוֹת   leDavid לְדָוִד   samachti שָׂמַחְתִּי

בְּאֹמְרִים be'omrim   לִי li   בֵּית bet ב״פ ראה   יְהֹוָאדֹנָיאהדונהי Adonai   נֵלֵךְ nelech נלך׃

עֹמְדוֹת omdot   הָיוּ hayu   רַגְלֵינוּ raglenu ר״ת רהע   בִּשְׁעָרָיִךְ bish'arayich

יְרוּשָׁלָיִם Yerushalayim׃   יְרוּשָׁלַם Yerushalayim   הַבְּנוּיָה habenuya   כְּעִיר ke'ir

שֶׁשָּׁם shesham   יַחְדָּו yachdav׃   לָהּ la   שֶׁחֻבְּרָה shechubera סנדלפון, ערי   בזוזך,

עָלוּ alu   שְׁבָטִים shevatim   שִׁבְטֵי shivtei   יָהּ Yah   עֵדוּת edut

לְיִשְׂרָאֵל leYisrael   לְהֹדוֹת lehodot   לְשֵׁם leshem   יְהֹוָאדֹנָיאהדונהי Adonai׃

כִּי ki   שָׁמָּה shama ע״ה ה״פ אלהים   יָשְׁבוּ yashvu   כִסְאוֹת chis'ot   לְמִשְׁפָּט lemishpat

כִּסְאוֹת kis'ot   לְבֵית levet ב״פ ראה   דָּוִיד David׃   שַׁאֲלוּ sha'alu   שְׁלוֹם shelom

יְרוּשָׁלָם Yerushalayim   יִשְׁלָיוּ yishlayu   אֹהֲבָיִךְ ohavayich׃   יְהִי yehi

שָׁלוֹם shalom   בְּחֵילֵךְ bechelech   שַׁלְוָה shalva   בְּאַרְמְנוֹתָיִךְ be'armenotayich׃

לְמַעַן lema'an   אַחַי achai   וְרֵעָי vere'ai   אֲדַבְּרָה adabera   נָא na   שָׁלוֹם shalom

בָּךְ bach׃   לְמַעַן lema'an   בֵּית bet ב״פ ראה   יְהֹוָאדֹנָיאהדונהי Adonai

אֱלֹהֵינוּ Elohenu ילה   אֲבַקְשָׁה avaksha   טוֹב tov והו   לָךְ lach׃

SHIR HAMA'ALOT LEDAVID

"A Song of Ascents by David: I rejoiced when they said to me: Let us go to the House of the Lord. Our legs stood immobile within your gates, Jerusalem. The built-up Jerusalem is like a city that has been united together. For there the tribes ascend the tribes of God, who are testimony for Israel, to give thanks to the Name of the Lord. For there sat thrones of judgments, thrones of the House of David, they have prayed for the peace of Jerusalem, those who love you will be serene. May there be peace within your walls, and serenity within your palaces. For the sake of my brothers and my comrades, I shall speak of peace on your behalf. For the sake of the House of the Lord, I shall request good for you." (Psalms 122)

SHIR HAMA'ALOT ELECHA

All of humanity is considered to be one unified soul, which has the nature of receiving. The Light of the Creator has many dimensions, one of which expresses itself in our physical realm as the *Shechinah*, which has the nature of sharing and imparting. Joining the unified soul with the *Shechinah* is like the union of a bride and groom. The words that compose this Psalm help us to unite with the *Shechinah* and thereby to reach ultimate fulfillment.

This praise is said by the lower *Yisrael* for the sake of the Bride. Therefore, in the word *"hayoshevi"* there is an extra letter *Hei* (ה - *Malchut*) as it is the last letter of the Name: יהוה - which is the Bride.

אֶת־ et נָשָׂאתִי nasati אֵלֶיךָ eleicha הַמַּעֲלוֹת hama'alot שִׁיר shir

עֵינַי einai הַיֹּשְׁבִי hayoshvi בַּשָּׁמָיִם bashamayim

הִנֵּה hine כְּעֵינֵי che'enei עֲבָדִים avadim אֶל־ el יַד yad

אֲדוֹנֵיהֶם adonehem כְּעֵינֵי ke'enei שִׁפְחָה shifcha אֶל־ el יַד yad

גְּבִרְתָּה gevirta כֵּן ken עֵינֵינוּ enenu אֶל־ el יְהֹוָה Adonai

אֱלֹהֵינוּ Elohenu עַד ad שֶׁיְּחָנֵּנוּ sheyechonenu וְחָנֵּנוּ chonenu

רַבַּת rabat שָׂבְעָה sav'a לָּהּ la נַפְשֵׁנוּ nafshenu הַלַּעַג hala'ag

הַשַּׁאֲנַנִּים hasha'ananim הַבּוּז habuz לִגְאֵי lige'ei יוֹנִים yonim (כתיב לגאיונים)

SHIR HAMA'ALOT LeDAVID

Here we make our connection to the Final Redemption – the end of all chaos and spiritual darkness. Two thousand years ago, Kabbalist Rav Shimon bar Yochai said that when the wisdom of the *Zohar* becomes the property of the people (as it is now) and the secrets of the Torah are learned by everyone, young and old (as you are doing now), it will be the sign that the age of the Final Redemption is upon us.

This following praise speaks of The Final Redemption. It is also connects us to the above mentioned Bride that escapes its distress that were pursueing her from the Other Side, and entered the Holy Side, when *Shabbat* starts.

SHIR HAMA'ALOT ELECHA

"A Song of Ascents: To You I raised my eyes, You Who dwell in the Heavens. Behold! Like the eyes of servants unto their master's hand, Like the eyes of a maid unto her mistress's hand, so are our eyes unto the Lord, our God, until He will favor us. Favor us, Lord, favor us, for we are fully sated with contempt. Our soul is fully sated with the mockery of the complacent ones, with the contempt of the arrogant." (Psalms 123)

Meditate for the ninth *Ma'amar* (Utterance) of Creation: נֵעֲשֶׂה אָדָם ("and God said: Let us make man" – as it says in this Psalm "had the Lord not been with us" – God image is within us).

Adonai יְהֹוָֹה(אַדְנִי־אַהֲדֹנָהי) lulei לוּלֵי leDavid לְדָוִד hama'alot הַמַּעֲלוֹת shir שִׁיר

na נָא yomar יֹאמַר lanu לָנוּ shehaya שֶׁהָיָה

Yisrael יִשְׂרָאֵל: shehaya שֶׁהָיָה Adonai יְהֹוָֹה lulei לוּלֵי

adam אָדָם alenu עָלֵינוּ bekum בְּקוּם lanu לָנוּ:

bacharot בַּחֲרוֹת bela'unu בִּלְעוּנוּ chayim וָחַיִּים azai אֲזַי

shetafunu שְׁטָפוּנוּ hamayim הַמַּיִם azai אֲזַי: banu בָנוּ apam אַפָּם

azai אֲזַי: nafshenu נַפְשֵׁנוּ al עַל־ avar עָבַר nachla נַחְלָה

hazeidonim הַזֵּידוֹנִים hamayim הַמַּיִם nafshenu נַפְשֵׁנוּ al עַל־ avar עָבַר

netananu נְתָנָנוּ shelo שֶׁלֹּא Adonai יְהֹוָֹה baruch בָּרוּךְ

ketzipor כְּצִפּוֹר nafshenu נַפְשֵׁנוּ leshinehem לְשִׁנֵּיהֶם: teref טֶרֶף

nishbar נִשְׁבָּר hapach הַפַּח yokshim יוֹקְשִׁים mipach מִפַּח nimleta נִמְלְטָה

beshem בְּשֵׁם ezrenu עֶזְרֵנוּ nimlatnu נִמְלָטְנוּ: va'anachnu וַאֲנַחְנוּ

va'aretz וָאָרֶץ: shamayim שָׁמַיִם ose עֹשֵׂה Adonai יְהֹוָֹה

HALELUYA

King David says, "We have eyes, but see not. We have ears, but hear not." (*Psalms* 115:6) Far too often, our five senses and rational mind provide us with only a limited view of reality. Even science tells us that we utilize less than 10 percent of our brain capacity. Kabbalah asks, "Where is the remaining 90 percent?" This prayer helps to awaken our dormant capacities and strengthens our perception. We achieve a heightened sense of awareness and superior intuition.

In the following Psalm we have 20 verses for the 13 Attributes and the seven voices, and we also have 165 words for the Name: (וד' אותיות השורש) אלף הי יוד הי. Meditate for the sixth *Ma'amar* (Utterance) of Creation: יְהִי מְאוֹרֹת ("and God said: Let there be lights" – the stars were created to serve God in His courtyards – the world).

SHIR HAMA'ALOT LEDAVID

"A Song of Ascents by David: Had the Lord not been with us, let Israel declare now! Had the Lord not been with us when a man rises up against us, then they would have swallowed us up alive when their anger was kindled against us. Then the waters would have washed us away, the currents would have surged against our soul, then they would have surged across our soul, the treacherous waters. Blessed is the Lord, Who did not allow us to be as prey for their teeth. Our soul escaped like a bird from the hunters' snare. The snare broke and we escaped. Our help is from the Name of the Lord, Maker of the Heavens and the Earth." (Psalms 124)

הַלְלוּיָהּ haleluya אֱלֹהִים, אֲהָיָה אֲדֹנָי ; ללה ; הַלְלוּ halelu שֵׁם shem אֶת־ et

יְהֹוָ֒אדנ֒יאהדונהי Adonai הַלְלוּ halelu עַבְדֵי avdei יְהֹוָ֒אדנ֒יאהדונהי Adonai:

עֹמְדִים she'omdim בְּבֵית bevet ראה ב״פ יְהֹוָ֒אדנ֒יאהדונהי Adonai

בְּחַצְרוֹת bechatzrot בֵּית bet ב״פ ראה אֱלֹהֵינוּ Elohenu ילה: הַלְלוּיָהּ haleluya

טוֹב tov כִּי ki ללה ; וְהוּ יהוה אֲהָיָה, אֲדֹנָי אֱלֹהִים, אום, מבה, יזל

יְהֹוָ֒אדנ֒יאהדונהי Adonai זַמְּרוּ zameru לִשְׁמוֹ lishmo מהש ע״ה, ע״ב בריבוע וקס״א ע״ה, אל עדי ע״ה

כִּי ki נָעִים na'im כִּי ki יַעֲקֹב Yaakov ז הויות, יאהדונהי איההויה

בָּחַר bachar לוֹ lo יָהּ Yah יָהּ Yisrael יִשְׂרָאֵל lisgulato לִסְגֻלָּתוֹ: כִּי ki

אֲנִי ani אני יָדַעְתִּי yadati כִּי־ ki גָּדוֹל gadol להו, עם ד׳ אותיות – מבה, יזל, אום

יְהֹוָ֒אדנ֒יאהדונהי Adonai וַאֲדֹנֵינוּ va'adonenu מִכָּל־ mikol ילי

אֱלֹהִים Elohim ילה: ; אֲדֹנָי כָּל kol ילי אֲשֶׁר־ asher וָפֵץ chafetz

יְהֹוָ֒אדנ֒יאהדונהי Adonai עָשָׂה asa בַּשָּׁמַיִם bashamayim י״פ טל, י״פ כוזו

וּבָאָרֶץ uva'aretz בַּיַּמִּים bayamim נלך וְכָל־ vechol תְּהוֹמוֹת tehomot:

מַעֲלֶה ma'ale נְשִׂאִים nesi'im מִקְצֵה miktze הָאָרֶץ ha'aretz אלהים דהין ע״ה

בְּרָקִים berakim לַמָּטָר lamatar עָשָׂה asa מוֹצֵא־ motze רוּחַ rua'ch

מֵאוֹצְרוֹתָיו me'otzrotav: שֶׁהִכָּה shehika בְּכוֹרֵי bechorei מִצְרַיִם Mitzrayim

אָדָם me'adam מ״ה עַד־ ad בְּהֵמָה behema ב״ן: שָׁלַח shalach אֹתוֹת otot

וּמֹפְתִים umoftim בְּתוֹכֵכִי betochechi מִצְרַיִם Mitzrayim מצר בְּפַרְעֹה beFar'o

וּבְכָל־ uvchol ב״ן, לכב עֲבָדָיו avadav: שֶׁהִכָּה shehika גּוֹיִם goyim

רַבִּים rabim וְהָרַג veharag מְלָכִים melachim עֲצוּמִים atzumim:

HALELUYA

"Praise the Lord! Praise the Name of the Lord, praise the Name of the Lord, you servants of the Lord, you who stand in the House of the Lord, in the courtyards of the House of our God. Praise God, for the Lord is good. Sing to His Name for it is pleasant, for God selected Jacob for His own, Israel as His treasure. For I know that the Lord, our God, is greater than all heavenly powers. Whatever the Lord wished for, He did in the Heavens and the Earth, in the seas and all the depths. He raises clouds from the ends of the Earth; He made lightning bolts for the rain; He brings forth winds from His treasuries. It was He Who smote the firstborn of Egypt, from man to beast. He sent signs and wonders into your midst, Egypt, upon Pharaoh and upon all his servants. It was He Who smote many nations and slew mighty kings:

לְסִיחוֹן leSichon מֶלֶךְ melech הָאֱמֹרִי haEmori וּלְעוֹג ul'Og מֶלֶךְ melech

הַבָּשָׁן haBashan וּלְכֹל ulchol יה אדני מַמְלְכוֹת mamlechot כְּנָעַן Kena'an:

וְנָתַן venatan אַרְצָם artzam נַחֲלָה nachala נַחֲלָה nachala לְיִשְׂרָאֵל leYisrael

עַמּוֹ amo: יְהֹוָה/אדניאהדונהי Adonai שִׁמְךָ shimcha לְעוֹלָם le'olam

ר"ת יזל רביע דס"ג ג' אותיות דס"ג יְהֹוָה/אדניאהדונהי Adonai זִכְרְךָ zichrecha לְדֹר־ ledor

וָדֹר vador ר"י: כִּי ki יָדִין yadin יְהֹוָה/אדניאהדונהי Adonai עַמּוֹ amo

וְעַל־ ve'al עֲבָדָיו avadav יִתְנֶחָם yitnecham: עֲצַבֵּי atzabei הַגּוֹיִם hagoyim

כֶּסֶף kesef וְזָהָב vezahav מַעֲשֵׂה ma'ase יְדֵי yedei אָדָם adam:

פֶּה pe מילה, וע"ה אלהים, אהיה אדני לָהֶם lahem וְלֹא velo יְדַבֵּרוּ yedaberu

עֵינַיִם enayim ריבוע מ"ה לָהֶם lahem וְלֹא velo יִרְאוּ yir'u: אָזְנַיִם oznayim

יֵשׁ־ yesh יוד הי ואו הה אֵין en אַף af יַאֲזִינוּ ya'azinu וְלֹא velo לָהֶם lahem

רוּחַ ru'ach בְּפִיהֶם befihem: כְּמוֹהֶם kemohem יִהְיוּ yih'yu אל (ייא"י מילוי דס"ג)

עֹשֵׂיהֶם osehem כֹּל kol ילי אֲשֶׁר־ asher בֹּטֵחַ bote'ach בָּהֶם bahem:

בֵּית bet ב"פ ראה יהוה ריבוע יהוה ריבוע מ"ה יִשְׂרָאֵל Yisrael בָּרְכוּ barchu אֶת־ et

יְהֹוָה/אדניאהדונהי Adonai בֵּית bet ב"פ ראה אַהֲרֹן Aharon בָּרְכוּ barchu יהוה ריבוע

הַלֵּוִי haLevi בֵּית bet ב"פ ראה יְהֹוָה/אדניאהדונהי Adonai: אֶת־ et מ"ה ריבוע יהוה

בָּרְכוּ barchu יהוה ריבוע יהוה אֶת־ et מ"ה ריבוע יְהֹוָה/אדניאהדונהי Adonai

יִרְאֵי yir'ei יהוה ריבוע יהוה מ"ה בָּרְכוּ barchu Adonai יְהֹוָה/אדניאהדונהי Adonai

אֶת־ et יְהֹוָה/אדניאהדונהי Adonai: בָּרוּךְ baruch יְהֹוָה/אדניאהדונהי Adonai

מִצִּיּוֹן miTziyon יוסף, ו' הויות, קנאה שֹׁכֵן shochen יְרוּשָׁלַיִם Yerushalayim

הַלְלוּיָהּ haleluya אלהים, אהיה אדני ; ללה:

Sichon, the king of the Emorites, Og, the king of the Bashan, and all the kingdoms of Canaan and presented their land as a heritage, a heritage for Israel, His nation. The Lord is Your Name forever. The Lord is your memorial throughout the generations. When the Lord will judge the nations, He will relent concerning His servants. The idols of the nations are silver and gold, human handiwork. They have mouths, but they do not speak. They have eyes, but they do not see. They have ears, but they do not heed; neither is there any breath in their mouths. Like them shall their makers become and everyone who trusts in them. House of Israel, bless the Lord. House of Aaron, bless the Lord. House of Levi, bless the Lord. Those who fear the Lord, bless the Lord. Blessed is the Lord from Zion, He who dwells in Jerusalem, Praise the Lord!" (Psalms 135)

HODU

The following Psalm has 26 verses that connect us to the Name: יהוה. It also connects us to the 26 Angels (one for each verse – in consecutive order of the Aramaic alphabet). Meditate for the tenth *Ma'amar* (Utterance) of Creation: פרו ורבו ("and God said: Be fruitful and become numerous" – for the righteous to be born and thank the Creator.

ל'

אדריאל

הוֹדוּ hodu אהיה לַיהוָהואהדונהי ladonai כִּי־ ki טוֹב tov והו ;

כי טוב = יהוה אהיה = אום, מובה, יזל

כִּי ki לְעוֹלָם le'olam ריבוע דס״ג ו׳ אותיות דס״ג וְחַסְדּוֹ chasdo

ג׳ הויות, מזלא (להמשיך הארה ממזלא עילאה) ; ר״ת = נגה : יוֹד

ברכיאל

הוֹדוּ hodu אהיה לֵאלֹהֵי lelohei מילוי דע״ב, דמב ; ילה

הָאֱלֹהִים haElohim אהיה אדני ; ילה

כִּי ki לְעוֹלָם le'olam ריבוע דס״ג ו׳ אותיות דס״ג וְחַסְדּוֹ chasdo

ג׳ הויות, מזלא (להמשיך הארה ממזלא עילאה) ; ר״ת = נגה : יוֹד

גועיאל

הוֹדוּ hodu אהיה לַאֲדֹנֵי la'adonei הָאֲדֹנִים ha'adonim

כִּי ki לְעוֹלָם le'olam ריבוע דס״ג ו׳ אותיות דס״ג וְחַסְדּוֹ chasdo

ג׳ הויות, מזלא (להמשיך הארה ממזלא עילאה) ; ר״ת = נגה : יוֹד

דורעיאל

לְעֹשֵׂה le'ose נִפְלָאוֹת nifla'ot גְּדֹלוֹת gedolot לְבַדּוֹ levado מ״ב בסוד שם בן מ״ב

כִּי ki לְעוֹלָם le'olam ריבוע דס״ג ו׳ אותיות דס״ג וְחַסְדּוֹ chasdo

ג׳ הויות, מזלא (להמשיך הארה ממזלא עילאה) ; ר״ת = נגה : יוֹד

הדריאל

לְעֹשֵׂה le'ose הַשָּׁמַיִם hashamayim י״פ טל, י״פ כוזו בִּתְבוּנָה bitvuna

כִּי ki לְעוֹלָם le'olam ריבוע דס״ג ו׳ אותיות דס״ג וְחַסְדּוֹ chasdo

ג׳ הויות, מזלא (להמשיך הארה ממזלא עילאה) ; ר״ת = נגה : יוֹד

HODU

"Give thanks to the Lord for He is good, for His kindness endures forever.
Give thanks to the Lord of all the heavenly powers, for His kindness endures forever.
Give thanks to the Master of all masters, for His kindness endures forever.
To the One Who alone performs great wonders, for His kindness endures forever.
To the One Who made the heavens with understanding, for His kindness endures forever.

וועדיאל

hamayim הַמָּיִם al עַל־ אלהים דההין ע"ה ha'aretz הָאָרֶץ leroka לְרֹקַע

chasdo וְחַסְדּוֹ אותיות דס"ג ו"י ריבוע דס"ג le'olam לְעוֹלָם ki כִּי

ג' הויות = מזלא (להמשיך הארה ממזלא עילאה) ; ר"ת = נגה : יוֹד

וזבדיאל

gedolim גְּדֹלִים אין סוף רז, orim אוֹרִים le'ose לְעֹשֵׂה

chasdo וְחַסְדּוֹ אותיות דס"ג ו"י ריבוע דס"ג le'olam לְעוֹלָם ki כִּי

ג' הויות = מזלא (להמשיך הארה ממזלא עילאה) ; ר"ת = נגה : יוֹד

וחניאל

hashemesh הַשֶּׁמֶשׁ et אֶת־

למֶמְשֶׁלֶת בַּיּוֹם bayom ע"ה נגד, מזבוז, זן, אל יהוה lememshelet בַּיּוֹם bayom lememshelet לְמֶמְשֶׁלֶת

chasdo וְחַסְדּוֹ אותיות דס"ג ו"י ריבוע דס"ג le'olam לְעוֹלָם ki כִּי

ג' הויות, מזלא (להמשיך הארה ממזלא עילאה) ; ר"ת = נגה : יוֹד

טהוריאל

vechochavim וְכוֹכָבִים et hayare'ach הַיָּרֵחַ אֶת־

מלה balayla בַּלַּיְלָה lememshelot לְמֶמְשָׁלוֹת

chasdo וְחַסְדּוֹ אותיות דס"ג ו"י ריבוע דס"ג le'olam לְעוֹלָם ki כִּי

ג' הויות, מזלא (להמשיך הארה ממזלא עילאה) ; ר"ת = נגה : יוֹד

ידידיאל

bivchorehem בִּבְכוֹרֵיהֶם מצר Mitzrayim מִצְרַיִם lemake לְמַכֵּה

chasdo וְחַסְדּוֹ אותיות דס"ג ו"י ריבוע דס"ג le'olam לְעוֹלָם ki כִּי

ג' הויות, מזלא (להמשיך הארה ממזלא עילאה) ; ר"ת = נגה : יוֹד

To the One Who spreads out the earth upon the waters, for His kindness endures forever.
To the One Who made great Lights, for His kindness endures forever.
The sun for the reign of the day, for His kindness endures forever.
The moon and the stars for the reign of the night, for His kindness endures forever.
To the One Who smote Egypt through their firstborn, for His kindness endures forever.

ה

כרוביאל

וַיּוֹצֵא vayotze יִשְׂרָאֵל Yisrael מִתּוֹכָם mitocham

כִּי ki לְעוֹלָם le'olam רִיבּוּעַ דס״ג ו״י אותיות דס״ג וְחַסְדּוֹ chasdo

ג׳ הויות, מזלא (להמשיך הארה ממזלא עילאה) ; ר״ת = נגה : הָיָ

להטיאל

בְּיָד beyad חֲזָקָה chazaka וּבִזְרוֹעַ uvizro'a נְטוּיָה netuya

כִּי ki לְעוֹלָם le'olam רִיבּוּעַ דס״ג ו״י אותיות דס״ג וְחַסְדּוֹ chasdo

ג׳ הויות, מזלא (להמשיך הארה ממזלא עילאה) ; ר״ת = נגה : הָיָ

מהגביאל

לְגֹזֵר legozer יַם־ yam יל׳ סוּף Suf לִגְזָרִים ligzarim

כִּי ki לְעוֹלָם le'olam רִיבּוּעַ דס״ג ו״י אותיות דס״ג וְחַסְדּוֹ chasdo

ג׳ הויות, מזלא (להמשיך הארה ממזלא עילאה) ; ר״ת = נגה : הָיָ

נוריאל

וְהֶעֱבִיר vehe'evir יִשְׂרָאֵל Yisrael בְּתוֹכוֹ betocho

כִּי ki לְעוֹלָם le'olam רִיבּוּעַ דס״ג ו״י אותיות דס״ג וְחַסְדּוֹ chasdo

ג׳ הויות, מזלא (להמשיך הארה ממזלא עילאה) ; ר״ת = נגה : הָיָ

נוצציאל

וְנִעֵר veni'er פַּרְעֹה Par'o וְחֵילוֹ vecheilo בְיַם־ veyam יל׳ סוּף Suf

כִּי ki לְעוֹלָם le'olam רִיבּוּעַ דס״ג ו״י אותיות דס״ג וְחַסְדּוֹ chasdo

ג׳ הויות, מזלא (להמשיך הארה ממזלא עילאה) ; ר״ת = נגה : הָיָ

And Who took Israel out of their midst, for His kindness endures forever. With a strong Hand and with an outstretched Arm, for His kindness endures forever. To the One Who divided the Sea of Reeds into parts, for His kindness endures forever. And Who caused Israel to pass through It, For His kindness endures forever. And threw Pharaoh and his army into the Sea of Reeds, for His kindness endures forever.

נוֹדִיאֵל

לְמוֹלִיךְ lemolich עַמּוֹ amo בַּמִּדְבָּר bamidbar

כִּי ki לְעוֹלָם le'olam ריבוע דס"ג וי' אותיות דס"ג וְחַסְדּוֹ chasdo

ג' הויות, מזלא (להמשיך הארה ממזלא עילאה) ; ר"ת = נגה : וְיו

סַרְעִיאֵל

לְמַכֵּה lemake מְלָכִים melachim גְּדֹלִים gedolim

כִּי ki לְעוֹלָם le'olam ריבוע דס"ג וי' אותיות דס"ג וְחַסְדּוֹ chasdo

ג' הויות, מזלא (להמשיך הארה ממזלא עילאה) ; ר"ת = נגה : וְיו

עֲשָׂאֵל

וַיַּהֲרֹג vayaharog מְלָכִים melachim אַדִּירִים adirim הרי

כִּי ki לְעוֹלָם le'olam ריבוע דס"ג וי' אותיות דס"ג וְחַסְדּוֹ chasdo

ג' הויות, מזלא (להמשיך הארה ממזלא עילאה) ; ר"ת = נגה : וְיו

פְּקְדִיאֵל

לְסִיחוֹן leSichon מֶלֶךְ melech הָאֱמֹרִי haEmori

כִּי ki לְעוֹלָם le'olam ריבוע דס"ג וי' אותיות דס"ג וְחַסְדּוֹ chasdo

ג' הויות, מזלא (להמשיך הארה ממזלא עילאה) ; ר"ת = נגה : וְיו

צְרוּפִיאֵל

וּלְעוֹג ulOg מֶלֶךְ melech הַבָּשָׁן haBashan

כִּי ki לְעוֹלָם le'olam ריבוע דס"ג וי' אותיות דס"ג וְחַסְדּוֹ chasdo

ג' הויות, מזלא (להמשיך הארה ממזלא עילאה) ; ר"ת = נגה : וְיו

קְדוֹשִׁיאֵל

וְנָתַן venatan אַרְצָם artzam לְנַחֲלָה lenachala

כִּי ki לְעוֹלָם le'olam ריבוע דס"ג וי' אותיות דס"ג וְחַסְדּוֹ chasdo

ג' הויות, מזלא (להמשיך הארה ממזלא עילאה) ; ר"ת = נגה : וְיו

To the One Who led His nation, through the wilderness, for His kindness endures forever.
To the One Who smite kings, for His kindness endures forever.
And slew mighty kings, for His kindness endures forever.
Sichon, the king of the Emorites, for His kindness endures forever.
And to Og, the king of Bashan, for His kindness endures forever.
And presented their land as a heritage, for His kindness endures forever.

ה

רוממיאל

avdo עַבְדוֹ leYisrael לְיִשְׂרָאֵל nachala נַחֲלָה

chasdo וְחַסְדּוֹ le'olam לְעוֹלָם ריבוע דס"ג ו' אותיות דס"ג ki כִּי

ג' הויות, מזלא (להמשיך הארה ממזלא עילאה) ; ר"ת = נגה : הָיָ

שׁוֹמְרִיאֵל

lanu לָנוּ zachar זָכַר shebshiflenu שֶׁבְּשִׁפְלֵנוּ אלהים, אהיה אדני עֶ"בְּשֶׁ"פְלֵנוּ

chasdo וְחַסְדּוֹ le'olam לְעוֹלָם ריבוע דס"ג ו' אותיות דס"ג ki כִּי

ג' הויות, מזלא (להמשיך הארה ממזלא עילאה) ; ר"ת = נגה : הָיָ

שׁמְרִיאֵל

mitzarenu מִצָּרֵינוּ vayifrekenu וַיִּפְרְקֵנוּ

chasdo וְחַסְדּוֹ le'olam לְעוֹלָם ריבוע דס"ג ו' אותיות דס"ג ki כִּי

ג' הויות, מזלא (להמשיך הארה ממזלא עילאה) ; ר"ת = נגה : הָיָ

תּוּמְכִּיאֵל

basar בָּשָׂר יה אדני lechol לְכָל ג' הויות lechem לֶחֶם , וְעֹד אבג יתץ noten נֹתֵן

ר"ת = יב"ק, אלהים יהוה, אהיה אדני יהוה

chasdo וְחַסְדּוֹ le'olam לְעוֹלָם ריבוע דס"ג ו' אותיות דס"ג ki כִּי

ג' הויות, מזלא (להמשיך הארה ממזלא עילאה) ; ר"ת = נגה : הָיָ

תּהְפִּיאֵל

hashamayim הַשָּׁמָיִם (מילוי דס"ג) ייא"י leEl לָאֵל אהיה hodu הוֹדוּ י"פ טל, י"פ כוזו

chasdo וְחַסְדּוֹ le'olam לְעוֹלָם ריבוע דס"ג ו' אותיות דס"ג ki כִּי

ג' הויות, מזלא (להמשיך הארה ממזלא עילאה) ; ר"ת = נגה : הָיָ

LeChai Olamiim

This prayer contains 22 sentences, each starting with one of the 22 Aramaic letters in alphabetical order. Whenever we find a connection to the number 22, it is our opportunity to draw upon the creative and DNA-like powers of the Aramaic letters to transform our reactive nature and become proactive, creating order out of chaos.

A heritage for Israel, His servant, for His kindness endures forever.
In our lowliness He remembered us, for His kindness endures forever.
And released us from our tormentors, for His kindness endures forever.
He gives nourishment to all flesh, For His kindness endures forever.
Give thanks to the God of the Heavens, for His kindness endures forever." (Psalms 136)

olamim עוֹלָמִים lechai לְחַי	veha'emuna וְהָאֱמוּנָה		ha'aderet הָאַדֶּרֶת
olamim עוֹלָמִים lechai לְחַי	vehaberacha וְהַבְּרָכָה		habina הַבִּינָה
	בינה ע״ה = אהיה אהיה יהוה = וזיים		
olamim עוֹלָמִים lechai לְחַי	vehagedula וְהַגְּדֻלָּה		haga'ava הַגַּאֲוָה
olamim עוֹלָמִים lechai לְחַי	vehadibur וְהַדִּבּוּר		hade'a הַדֵּעָה
olamim עוֹלָמִים lechai לְחַי	vehehadar וְהֶהָדָר	ההה	hahod הַהוֹד
olamim עוֹלָמִים lechai לְחַי	vehavatikut וְהַוָתִיקוּת		hava'ad הַוַעַד
olamim עוֹלָמִים lechai לְחַי	vehazohar וְהַזוֹהַר	ייי	hazach הַזָךְ
olamim עוֹלָמִים lechai לְחַי	vehachosen וְהַחוֹסֶן	ומב	hachayil הַחַיִל
olamim עוֹלָמִים lechai לְחַי	vehatohar וְהַטוֹהַר		hateches הַטֶכֶס
olamim עוֹלָמִים lechai לְחַי	vehayir'a וְהַיִרְאָה	רי״ו	hayichud הַיִחוּד
olamim עוֹלָמִים lechai לְחַי	vehakavod וְהַכָּבוֹד	לאו	haketer הַכֶּתֶר
	כתר = ה׳ מלך ה׳ מלך ה׳ ימלוך לעולם ועד ובאתב״ש גאל		
olamim עוֹלָמִים lechai לְחַי	vehalibuv וְהַלִבּוּב		halekach הַלֶקַח
olamim עוֹלָמִים lechai לְחַי	vehamemshala וְהַמֶּמְשָׁלָה		hamelucha הַמְּלוּכָה
olamim עוֹלָמִים lechai לְחַי	vehanetzach וְהַנֶצַח		hanoy הַנוֹי

LeChai Olamim

The strength and faithfulness	to the One Who lives eternally
The discernment and blessing	to the One Who lives eternally
The grandeur and greatness	to the One Who lives eternally
The wisdom and speech	to the One Who lives eternally
The glory and majesty	to the One Who lives eternally
The convocation and authority	to the One Who lives eternally
The refinement and radiance	to the One Who lives eternally
The accomplishment and power	to the One Who lives eternally
The adornment and purity	to the One Who lives eternally
The oneness and reverence	to the One Who lives eternally
The crown and honor	to the One Who lives eternally
The study and insight	to the One Who lives eternally
The kingship and dominion	to the One Who lives eternally
The beauty and triumph	to the One Who lives eternally

olamim עוֹלָמִים lechai לְחַי   וְהַשֵּׂגֶב vehasegev   הַסֵּגוּי hasiguy

olamim עוֹלָמִים lechai לְחַי   וְהָעֲנָוָה veha'anava   הָעֹז ha'oz

olamim עוֹלָמִים lechai לְחַי   וְהַפְּאֵר vehape'er   הַפְּדוּת hapedut

olamim עוֹלָמִים lechai לְחַי   וְהַצֶּדֶק vehatzedek   הַצְּבִי hatzevi

olamim עוֹלָמִים lechai לְחַי   וְהַקְּדֻשָׁה vehakedusha   הַקְּרִיאָה hakeri'a

olamim עוֹלָמִים lechai לְחַי   וְהָרוֹמְמוֹת veharomemot   הָרֹן haron

olamim עוֹלָמִים lechai לְחַי   וְהַשֶּׁבַח hashevach   הַשִּׁיר hashir

olamim עוֹלָמִים lechai לְחַי   וְהַתְּפָאֶרֶת vehatiferet   הַתְּהִלָּה hatehila

תהלה ע"ה = אמת, אהיה פעמים אהיה, ז"פ ס"ג

ki כִּי gavar גָּבַר alenu עָלֵינוּ chasdo וְחַסְדּוֹ ³ הַוָיות, מזלא (להמשיך האָרה ממזלא עילאה)

ve'emet וֶאֱמֶת אהיה פעמים אהיה, ז"פ ס"ג Adonai יְהֹ־וָ־ה אהיהאדנֹ־ה־י

le'olam לְעוֹלָם ריבוע דס"ג וי' אותיות דס"ג haleluya הַלְלוּיָה אלהים, אהיה אדני ; כלה:

baruch בָּרוּךְ shenatan שֶׁנָּתַן le'amo לְעַמוֹ Yisrael יִשְׂרָאֵל et אֶת

yom יוֹם ע"ה נגד, מזבח, זן, אל יהוה haShabbat הַשַּׁבָּת (On Shabbat add:) hazeh הַזֶּה והו

ve'et וְאֶת yom יוֹם ע"ה נגד, מזבח, זן, אל יהוה) (on Sukkot say:) סֻכּוֹת Sukkot)

(on Simchat-Torah say:) Shemini שְׁמִינִי Atzeret עֲצֶרֶת) hazeh הַזֶּה והו ◆

et אֶת yom יוֹם ע"ה נגד, מזבח, זן, אל יהוה

tov טוֹב והו mikra מִקְרָא kodesh קֹדֶשׁ hazeh הַזֶּה והו ◆

The eminence and supremacy	*to the One Who lives eternally*
The might and modesty	*to the One Who lives eternally*
The redemption and splendor	*to the One Who lives eternally*
The desire and righteousness	*to the One Who lives eternally*
The summons and sanctity	*to the One Who lives eternally*
The exultation and exaltation	*to the One Who lives eternally*
The song and praise	*to the One Who lives eternally*
The lauding and magnificence	*to the One Who lives eternally*

"For His compassion has overwhelmed us and the truth of the Lord is forever. Praise the Lord!" (Psalms 117:2)
Blessed is the One who gave His nation Israel this day of (on **Shabbat:** *Sabbath and the day of*)
(on **Sukkot:** *Sukkot*) (on **Simchat Torah:** *Shmini Atzeret*) *holiday, and this good day of Holy Convocation.*

BARUCH SHE'AMAR

From here ("*Baruch She'amar*") until "*Chei Ha'olamim*" (pg. 312) you are in the World of *Yetzirah*.

When saying *Baruch She'amar* you should stand and hold the two front *Tzitziot* and meditate to create equality between *Asiyah* and *Yetzirah* since the purification of *Yetzirah* is done by the *Talit*. Thirteen times the word "*Baruch*" corresponding to the Thirteen Attributes of *Yetzirah*.

(1) אֵל   (Keter) בָּרוּךְ baruch שֶׁאָמַר she'amar וְהָיָה vehaya יהה

Olam Asiyah is now equal to *Olam Yetzirah* – בְּשָׁוֶה ♦ha'olam הָעוֹלָם

(2) רוזם   (Chochmah) בָּרוּךְ baruch הוּא♦hu

(3) וחנון   (Binah) בָּרוּךְ baruch אוֹמֵר omer וְעֹשֶׂה ve'ose♦

(4) ארך   בָּרוּךְ baruch גוֹזֵר gozer וּמְקַיֵּם umkayem♦

(5) אפים   בָּרוּךְ baruch עֹשֶׂה ose בְּרֵאשִׁית vereshit♦

(6) ורב וחסד   בָּרוּךְ baruch מְרַחֵם merachem אברהם, וז"פ אל, רי"ו ול"ב נתיבות החכמה, עַל al הָאָרֶץ ha'aretz רמ"ח (אברים), עסמ"ב וט"ז אותיות פשוטות אלהים דההין ע"ה

(7) ואמת   בָּרוּךְ baruch מְרַחֵם merachem אברהם, וז"פ אל, רי"ו ול"ב נתיבות החכמה, עַל al הַבְּרִיּוֹת haberiyot♦ רמ"ח (אברים), עסמ"ב וט"ז אותיות פשוטות

(8) נצר וחסד   בָּרוּךְ baruch מְשַׁלֵּם meshalem שָׂכָר sachar ב"ן י"פ

   טוֹב tov והו לִירֵאָיו lire'av♦

(9) לאלפים   בָּרוּךְ baruch וָחַי chai לָעַד la'ad ב"ן ב"פ

   וְקַיָּם vekayam לָנֶצַח lanetzach♦

(10) נשא עון   בָּרוּךְ baruch פּוֹדֶה pode וּמַצִּיל umatzil♦

(11) ופשע   בָּרוּךְ baruch שְׁמוֹ shemo מהש ע"ה, ע"ב בריבוע וקס"א ע"ה, אל שדי ע"ה♦

BARUCH SHE'AMAR

1) Blessed is the One Who spoke and the world came into being.
2) Blessed be He. 3) Blessed is the One Who says and does.
4) Blessed is the One Who decrees and fulfills. 5) Blessed is the One Who instigates Creation.
6) Blessed is the One Who is compassionate to the world. 7) Blessed is the One Who is compassionate to all creatures. 8) Blessed is the One Who repays well those who fear Him. 9) Blessed is the One Who lives forever and exists for eternity. 10) Blessed is the One Who redeems and saves. 11) Blessed is His Name.

(12) ווזטאה   baruch בָּרוּךְ   Ata אַתָּה   Adonai יְהֹו(אֲדֹנָי)אֲהדוֹנֲהי

Elohenu אֱלֹהֵינוּ   ילה   melech מֶלֶךְ   ha'olam הָעוֹלָם

haEl הָאֵל   לאה   ;   יייי   (מילוי)   (דס"ג)   av אָב

harachman הָרַחֲמָן   hamehulal הַמְהֻלָּל   befe בְּפֶה   פ"ו

(מנין התיבות בברוך שאמר – בסוד "כתם טהור פ"ו)   amo עַמּוֹ•

meshubach מְשֻׁבָּח   umfo'ar וּמְפֹאָר   bilshon בִּלְשׁוֹן

chasidav חֲסִידָיו   va'avadav וַעֲבָדָיו•   uvshirei וּבְשִׁירֵי

David דָּוִד   avdach עַבְדָּךְ   פוי, אל אדני   nehalelach נְהַלֶּלְךָ

Adonai יְהֹו(אֲדֹנָי)אהדונהי   Elohenu אֱלֹהֵינוּ ילה   bishvachot בִּשְׁבָחוֹת

uvizmirot וּבִזְמִירוֹת•   ungadelach וּנְגַדֶּלְךָ   unshabchach וּנְשַׁבֵּחֲךָ

unfa'arach וּנְפָאָרְךָ   venamlichach וְנַמְלִיכְךָ   venazkir וְנַזְכִּיר

shimcha שִׁמְךָ   malkenu מַלְכֵּנוּ   Elohenu אֱלֹהֵינוּ ילה

yachid יָחִיד   chei וְחֵי   (לפי האריז"ל, וְחַי לפי הרשב"י)

ha'olamim הָעוֹלָמִים•   melech מֶלֶךְ   meshubach מְשֻׁבָּח

um'fo'ar וּמְפֹאָר   adei עֲדֵי־   ad עַד

shemo שְׁמוֹ   מהשׁי ע"ה, ע"ב ברִיבּוֹע וקס"א ע"ה, אל שׁדי ע"ה

hagadol הַגָּדוֹל   לההו ;   עם ד' אותיות = מבה, יזל, אום•

(13) ונקה   baruch בָּרוּךְ   Ata אַתָּה   Adonai יְהֹו(אֲדֹנָי)(יְהֹו(אֲדֹנָי))אהדונהי

melech מֶלֶךְ   mehulal מְהֻלָּל   batishbachot בַּתִּשְׁבָּחוֹת:

---

12) Blessed are You, Lord, our God, the King of the world. The God, the compassionate Father, Who is lauded by the mouths of His Nation and Who is praised and glorified by the tongues of His righteous and His servants. With the songs of David, Your servant, We shall laud You, Lord, our God. With praises and songs, we shall exult and praise You, glorify You, and proclaim You, King. We shall mention Your Name our King, our God, Unique One and life of the worlds; the King Who is praised and glorified. And forever is His Name great. 13) Blessed are You, Lord, the King Who is extolled with praises.

On *Chol Hamo'ed* (not on *Shabbat*) we recite this Psalm instead of "*Mizmor shir leyom hashabbat*" and "*Adonai malach*" (pages 277-280), and continue with "*Yehi Chevod*" on page 280.

The Ari says to recite this Psalm while sitting down.

MIZMOR LETODA

The essence of this prayer is appreciation for the unseen miracles that occur in our life. There are 42 words in this prayer, connecting us to the *Ana Beko'ach*, the 42-Letter Name of God. Each word connects to one of the 42 letters.

Mizmor LeToda is the *tikkun* of *Yetzirah* in *Yetzirah* and corresponds to *Abba* and *Ima* of *Yetzirah*.

א

letoda לְתוֹדָה   (מ"ב)   בֶּן   שֵׁם   —   תֵּבוֹת   (מ"ב)   mizmor מִזְמוֹר

ב

הָרִיעוּ hari'u   יהוה למד אלף ע"ה ס"ת ; דיודין אלהים   ladonai לַיהוָֹה(אדנ"י ואהדונהי) יל"י

'

כָּל־ kol יל"י   ha'aretz הָאָרֶץ   אלהים ההוין ע"ה ; ר"ת הלכה ; ס"ת ע"ה כוק, ריבוע אדני

ר   ק   צ

Adonai לַיהֹוָֹה(אדנ"י ואהדונהי)   et אֶת־   ivdu עִבְדוּ

ט   ע   ע

lefanav לְפָנָיו עָ"עָל   bo'u בֹּאוּ   ר"ת = אהבה, אוזר, דאגה   besimcha בְּשִׂמְחָה

ד   ג   ג   ג

Adonai לַיהֹוָֹה(אדנ"י ואהדונהי)   ki כִּי־   de'u דְּעוּ   birnana בִּרְנָנָה:

ב   ע   '

asanu עָשָׂנוּ   hu הוּא־   ילה ; אדנ"י אהיה   Elohim אֱלֹהִים   hu הוּא

ג   ת   צ   ר   ט

mar'ito מַרְעִיתוֹ:   vetzo וְצֹאן   amo עַמּוֹ   anachnu אֲנַוְזְנוּ (ולא : כתיב)   velo וְלוֹ

MIZMOR LETODA

"A song of thanks giving:
Sing joyfully to the Lord, all of the Earth. Serve the Lord with happiness. Come before Him with song.
Know that the Lord is God. He made us and we are His. We are His nation, the flock of His pasture.

betoda בְּתוֹדָה	she'arav שְׁעָרָיו	bo'u בֹּאוּ
ז"פ ס"ג, אֲהֵיֶה פַּעֲמִים אֲהֵיֶה ע"ה אֱמֶת, bit'hila בִּתְהִלָּה	chatzerotav וְצֵרֹתָיו	
מ"ה רִיבּוּעַ יְהֹוָה רִיבּוּעַ יְהֹוָה רִיבּוּעַ barchu בָּרְכוּ	lo לוֹ אֲהֵיֶה	hodu הֹודוּ
ע"ה:. עֹדִי אֵל מַהַשׁ ע"ה, וקס"א בְּרִיבּוּעַ ע"ב ע"ה, מַהַשׁ shemo שְׁמֹו		
Adonai יְהֹוָה(וַאֲדֹנִיאָאֲהֹדֹנֹהֹי) יֹל מִבָּה, אוֹם, = יְהֹוָה אֲהֵיֶה וְהוּ ; טֹוב כִּי tov טֹוב ki כִּי		
(לְהַמְשִׁיךְ מִזְלָא, הֲוָיֹות, ג chasdo וְסַדֹּו אוֹתִיֹות וי' ס"ג רִיבּוּעַ le'olam לְעֹולָם		
emunato אֱמוּנָתֹו:. גְבוּרָה רי"ו, vador וָדֹר dor דֹר ve'ad וָעַד (הָאָרָה מִמֹּזְלָא עִילָאָה)		

Continue with "Yehi Chevod" on page 280.

MIZMOR SHIR LEYOM HASHABBAT

The *Zohar* says that the following two paragraphs were recited by Adam during the first Shabbat in the Garden of Eden. The terms *Adam* and *Garden of Eden* are code words. Adam is the name given to the one unified soul that encompasses all the souls of humanity that have ever or will ever come to this world. The Garden of Eden was a realm of pure Light and positive energy. The Aramaic letters that compose this paragraph represent specific energy forces that nourished and fulfilled this unified soul called Adam. This paragraph is merely the "formula" that defines these forces. The letters also act as antennas that draw these forces into our lives, thereby giving us a taste of the "Garden of Eden."

The first paragraph connects to the realm of *Malchut*, our physical universe of chaos and darkness. The second refers to the level of *Zeir Anpin*, the Upper Worlds of pure positivity and fulfillment. The sole purpose of joining these two worlds is to remove all the chaos and darkness from our existence.

In the first paragraph we have 112 words (יְהֹוָה ← יְהֹוָה, אֲהֵיֶה ← אֲדֹנִי ← יְהֹוָה ← אֱלֹהִים, יב"ק) and 16 verses – corresponding to the nine dots of *Malchut* (as *Malchut* does not have a consistent dot but She is included in all the other nine dots) and the seven voices of the given *Torah*.

Come to His gates with gratitude
and to His courtyards with praise. Give thanks to Him; bless His Name. Because the Lord is good,
His kindness is eternal, and His faithfulness is for each and every generation." (Psalms 100)

haShabbat הַשַּׁבָּת ע"ה נגד, מזבוח, חן, אל יהוה leyom לְיוֹם shir שִׁיר mizmor מִזְמוֹר

Initials of *LeMoshe* (למשה)

ladonai לַיהֹוָהאדנייאהדונהי ר"ת ט"ל lehodot לְהֹדוֹת וְהוּ tov טוֹב

baboker בַּבֹּקֶר lehagid לְהַגִּיד elyon עֶלְיוֹן leshimcha לְשִׁמְךָ ulzamer וּלְזַמֵּר

alei עֲלֵי balelot בַּלֵּילוֹת ve'emunat'cha וֶאֱמוּנָתְךָ chasdecha חַסְדְּךָ

bechinor בְּכִנּוֹר higayon הִגָּיוֹן alei עֲלֵי navel נָבֶל va'alei וַעֲלֵי asor עָשׂוֹר

befa'olecha בְּפָעֳלֶךָ Adonai יְהֹוָהאדנייאהדונהי simachtani שִׂמַּחְתַּנִי ki כִּי

gadlu גָּדְלוּ מ"ה ma מַה aranen אֲרַנֵּן yadecha יָדֶיךָ bema'asei בְּמַעֲשֵׂי

amku עָמְקוּ me'od מְאֹד Adonai יְהֹוָהאדנייאהדונהי ma'asecha מַעֲשֶׂיךָ

ba'ar בַּעַר ish אִישׁ יחו (Superiour *Keter*) machshevotecha מַחְשְׁבֹתֶיךָ

zot זֹאת et אֶת yavin יָבִין lo לֹא uchsil וּכְסִיל yeda יֵדַע lo לֹא

bifro'ach בִּפְרֹחַ resha'im רְשָׁעִים kemo כְּמוֹ esev עֵשֶׂב כוונות הקדושה (ע"ב שמות)

(The souls of the wicked are judged now to see if they are worthy to be elevated from *Gehenom*)

aven אָוֶן po'alei פֹּעֲלֵי ילי kol כָּל vayatzitzu וַיָּצִיצוּ

lehishamdam לְהִשָּׁמְדָם (The *klipa* that wants to be elevated with the Holiness)

marom מָרוֹם ve'ata וְאַתָּה (but it is not allowed to go up) ad עַד adei עֲדֵי

hine הִנֵּה ki כִּי Adonai יְהֹוָהאדנייאהדונהי ריבוע דס"ג י' אותיות דס"ג le'olam לְעֹלָם

oyvecha אֹיְבֶיךָ hine הִנֵּה ki כִּי Adonai יְהֹוָהאדנייאהדונהי oyvecha אֹיְבֶיךָ

yovedu יֹאבֵדוּ yitpardu יִתְפָּרְדוּ kol כָּל ילי po'alei פֹּעֲלֵי aven אָוֶן (The *klipa*)

MIZMOR SHIR LEYOM HASHABBAT

"A Psalm, a song for the day of Shabbat: It is good to say thanks to You, the Lord, and to sing Your Name, Exalted One. To relate Your kindness in the morning and Your faithfulness in the evenings upon ten-stringed instrument and lyre, with singing accompanied by a harp. Because You have made me happy, Lord, with Your deeds, for the work of Your Hands, I shall sing joyously. How great are Your deeds, Lord, and how greatly profound are Your thoughts. A boor cannot know nor can a fool understand this. When the wicked bloom like grass and all doers of iniquity blossom in order to destroy them forever. And You are exalted forever, Lord. For behold, Your enemies, Lord! For behold, Your enemies shall perish and all the doers of iniquity shall be dispersed.

baloti בַּלֹּתִי — karni קַרְנִי — kir'em כִּרְאֵים — (The Holiness) — vatarem וַתָּרֶם

[דמ"ה ריבוע] — eni עֵינִי — vatabet וַתַּבֵּט — ra'anan רַעֲנָן — beshemen בְּשֶׁמֶן

mere'im מְרֵעִים — alai עָלַי — bakamim בַּקָּמִים — beshurai בְּשׁוּרָי

(The soul of the righteous that is elevated now) [יוד הי ואו הה] oznai אָזְנָי — tishmana תִּשְׁמַעְנָה

[ס"ת קרחו] yifrach יִפְרָח — katamar כַּתָּמָר — [ג"פ בא כלה דלעיל] tzadik צַדִּיק

:yisge יִשְׂגֶּה — baLevanon בַּלְּבָנוֹן — ke'erez כְּאֶרֶז — (meditate to elevate the soul of *Korach*)

Adonai יְהוָֹ(אדני־אהדונהי) — [ב"פ] ראה bevet בְּבֵית — shetulim שְׁתוּלִים

od עוֹד — :yafrichu יַפְרִיחוּ — [ילה] Elohenu אֱלֹהֵינוּ — bechatzrot בְּחַצְרוֹת

vera'ananim וְרַעֲנַנִּים — deshenim דְּשֵׁנִים — beseva בְּשֵׂיבָה — yenuvun יְנוּבוּן

yashar יָשָׁר — ki כִּי — lehagid לְהַגִּיד — [(ייא"י) מילוי דס"ג] אל yih'yu יִהְיוּ

:bo בּוֹ (כתיב: עלתה) avlata עַוְלָתָה — velo- וְלֹא — tzuri צוּרִי — Adonai יְהוָֹ(אדני־אהדונהי)

ADONAI MALACH

In this Psalm there are 45 words corresponding to the Holy Name: מ"ה (יוד הא ואו הא)

ge'ut גֵּאוּת — malach מָלָךְ — (*Zeir Anpin*) — Adonai יְהוָֹ(אדני־אהדונהי)

(410 cords of *Arich Anpin* - where *Zeir Anpin* is elevated on *Shabbat* and he is clothing them)

hit'azar הִתְאַזָּר — oz עֹז — Adonai יְהוָֹ(אדני־אהדונהי) — lavesh לָבֵשׁ — lavesh לָבֵשׁ

af- אַף־ [ר"ת] = אלהים, אהיה אדני [ב"פ רי"ו] — tikon תִּכּוֹן — tevel תֵּבֵל

kis'acha כִּסְאֲךָ — nachon נָכוֹן — :timot תִּמּוֹט — bal בַּל־

me'az מֵאָז ומב — me'olam מֵעוֹלָם — Ata אַתָּה [ר"ת] = [קנ"א] ארני, אלהים:

And You shall lift up my worth like an ox and I will be drenched with fresh oil. And my eyes will see my foes and my ears will hear those who rise up to harm me. A righteous man will flourish like a palm leaf, like a cedar in the Lebanon, he will grow tall. They are planted in the House of the Lord, they shall flourish in the courtyards of our God. They will still be fruitful in old age, vigorous and fresh they shall be. To declare that the Lord is just, my rock in Whom there is no wrong." (Psalms 92).

ADONAI MALACH
*The Lord has reigned. He clothed Himself with pride.
The Lord clothed Himself and girded Himself with might. He also established the world firmly so that it will not collapse. Your throne has been established ever since, You have been forever.*

neharot **נְהָרוֹת** nas'u **נָשְׂאוּ**

(410 cords of *Arich Anpin* -

which draw Light from the sea of *Chochmah* -**דא"א** **מוזא סתימא**- on *Shabbat* to *Zeir Anpin*)

neharot **נְהָרוֹת**   קין   =   ר"ת   nas'u **נָשְׂאוּ**   Adonai **יְהֹוָ[אדני]אהדונהי**

:דנ[י]   ר"ת   dochyam **דָכְיָם**   neharot **נְהָרוֹת**   yis'u **יִשְׂאוּ**   kolam **קוֹלָם**

יְלִי עָרִי, סנדלפון, בזכור = ר"ת rabim **רַבִּים**   mayim **מַיִם**   (410 cords) mikolot **מִקֹּלוֹת**

יְלִי יְלִי yam **יָם**   mishberei **מִשְׁבְּרֵי**   הרי adirim **אַדִּירִים**   (ג"ה עולה בה מן לעשׂות – *Ima*)

Arich Anpin [has 221 *Ribo* (tens of thousands) Illuminations],

He is giving 150 *Ribo* (tens of thousands) Illuminations to *Zeir Anpin*.

Initials of **אמ"י** (my mother) because, *Zeir Anpin* first goes up and takes *Mochin* from *Ima* (mother).

Adonai **יְהֹוָ[אדני]אהדונהי**:   bamarom **בַּמָּרוֹם**   הרי   adir **אַדִּיר**

Initials of **אב"י** (my father), because *Zeir Anpin* later goes up and takes *Mochin* from *Abba* (Father).

levetcha **לְבֵיתְךָ**   קין = ר"ת   me'od **מְאֹד**   ne'emnu **נֶאֶמְנוּ**   edotecha **עֵדֹתֶיךָ**

le'orech **לְאֹרֶךְ**   Adonai **יְהֹוָ[אדני]אהדונהי**   kodesh **קֹדֶשׁ**   na'ava **נָאֲוָה** ראה ב"פ

:האותיות עם נהורים שׂע' = לאורך ה'; ס"ת אדנ"י ; ר"ת ילי ; גלך ; yamim **יָמִים**

YEHI CHEVOD

We find 18 verses in this connection, with 18 times the power of *Yud, Hei, Vav,* and *Hei.* The significance of 18 is found within the power of the *Mezuzah.* The kabbalists teach that the *Mezuzah,* which contains a piece of parchment bearing the Aramaic letters *Shin, Dalet, Yud* שׂד"י, or *Shaddai* - a powerful Name of God that brings us protection from negative forces, should be placed at each doorway. A doorway or entranceway is the beginning, or seed level of a room. Negative forces cling to all entryways, infecting the seed with negativity. The *Mezuzah* not only cancels this negative force but also transforms the negative energy into positive energy.

Another secret of *Shin, Dalet, Yud* is its a connection to another 72 Name of God, one that gives us the ability to eradicate all forms of negativity: The next letter after *Shin* שׂ in the Aramaic alphabet is *Tav* ת. The next letter to *Dalet* ד is *Hei* ה. The next letter after *Yud* י is *Kaf* כ. Placed side by side and in reverse order, these letters spell *Kaf, Hei, Tav* כהת. This three-letter sequence has the power to defuse negative energy, and was used to destroy the evil *Haman* in Persia during Purim, 2500 years ago.

The rivers have lifted the Lord,
the rivers have raised their voices. The rivers will raise their powerful waves. More than the roars of many waters and the powerful waves of the sea, You are immense in the High Places, Lord. Your testimonies are extremely trustworthy. Your House is the Holy Sanctuary. The Lord will be there for long days." (Psalms 93)

When you say the 18 verses of *Yehi Chevod*, you should meditate on the 18 letters of the six combinations of the Name *Shaddai* שד"י that exist in the central Vessels of *Zeir Anpin* of *Yetzirah*, and also meditate on the 18 times the Name: יהוה appears in this section, because they are equal to the two letters *Tet* ט in the Name of the Angel *Ma-tat-ron* מטטרו"ן (**Do not pronounce**) which is in *Zeir Anpin* of *Yetzirah*. You should meditate that the *Tet* (9) corresponds to *Tikkunei Dikna* of *Zeir Anpin* of *Yetzirah* (nine of Direct Light and nine of Returning Light).

The numerical value of the acronym of the 18 verses of *Yehi Chevod* adds up to 686. The numerical value of the last letter of each of the 18 verses is 602, plus 18 (*Yesod – Chai - וח"י*) adds up to 620. The number of words in *Yehi Chevod* is 138 (with the *Kolel*). You should also meditate to draw קס"א, קמ"ג, קנ"א with ע"ב, מ"ה, ב"ן (which adds up to 686 – with the *Kolel* - and is equal to the numerical value of the word *Porat*), to "Ben Porat Yosef " which is *Yesod – Chai* (18) *Almin*. Thereby creating the *Keter* (620) of *Nukva* (which is called: *Chakal* חק"ל, which adds up to 138).The *Keter* itself will be built later by the 22 letters of the *Ashrei*.

(אָרֶךְ) Adonai יְהֹוָה chevod כְּבוֹד yehi יְהִי (Keter–ע')

yismach יִשְׂמַח le'olam לְעוֹלָם

bema'asav בְּמַעֲשָׂיו (אָפִים) Adonai יְהֹוָה yehi יְהִי (Keter–ד')

shem שֵׁם (וְרַב וָחֶסֶד) Adonai יְהֹוָה mevorach מְבֹרָךְ

olam עוֹלָם ve'ad וְעַד me'ata מֵעַתָּה

ad עַד shemesh שֶׁמֶשׁ mimizrach מִמִּזְרַח (Chochmah–י')

shem שֵׁם Adonai יְהֹוָה mehulal מְהֻלָּל mevo'o מְבוֹאוֹ (נִשָּׂא עָוֹן)

goyim גּוֹיִם kol כָּל al עַל ram רָם (Chochmah–ע')

hashamayim הַשָּׁמַיִם al עַל (וּפֶשַׁע) Adonai יְהֹוָה

shimcha שִׁמְךָ (וְנַקֵּה) Adonai יְהֹוָה (Binah–י') kevodo כְּבוֹדוֹ

le'olam לְעוֹלָם Adonai יְהֹוָה (פּוֹקֵד)

zichrecha זִכְרְךָ ledor לְדֹר vador וָדֹר

YEHI CHEVOD

"May the glory of the Lord last forever. May the Lord rejoice in His works." (Psalms 104:31)
"May the Name of the Lord be blessed from now and for all eternity. From the sun's rising until its setting the Lord's Nameis praised. The Lord is high above all nations. His glory is above the heavens." (Psalms 113:2-4)
"Lord, Your Name is forever. Lord, Your fame is for every generation." (Psalms 135:13)

(ד–Binah) יְהֹוָה Adonai (עַל עוֹלָמִים) bashamayim בַּשָּׁמַיִם י"פ טל, י"פ כוזו

hechin הֵכִין kis'o כִּסְאוֹ umalchuto וּמַלְכוּתוֹ

bakol בַּכֹּל ב"ן, לכב mashala מָשָׁלָה מבה: (ד–Chesed) yismechu יִשְׂמְחוּ

hashamayim הַשָּׁמַיִם י"פ טל, י"פ כוזו vetagel וְתָגֵל אותיות גלות (כעתהיה גאולה תהא שמחה)

ha'aretz הָאָרֶץ אלהים דההין ע"ה ; ר"ת יהוה וס"ת ריבוע דס"ג veyomru וְיֹאמְרוּ

vagoyim בַגּוֹיִם Adonai יְהֹוָה (וְעַל רבעים) malach מָלָךְ ר"ת יבם, ב"ן:

(ע–Chesed) Adonai יְהֹוָה (ארך) melech מֶלֶךְ

יְהֹוָה Adonai (אפים) Adonai יְהֹוָה malach מָלָךְ (ורב וחסד) |

yimloch יִמְלֹךְ מלך מלך ימלך = מזוזך, סנדלפון, ערי ריבוע ס"ג ו"י אותיות דס"ג le'olam לְעֹלָם

(י–Gevurah) Adonai יְהֹוָה va'ed וָעֶד: ר"ת ייל (נושא) עוֹן

melech מֶלֶךְ olam עוֹלָם va'ed וָעֶד ר"ת = כוק, ריבוע ריבוע אדני

avdu אָבְדוּ goyim גוֹיִם me'artzo מֵאַרְצוֹ ס"ת = ב"ן:

(ד–Gevurah) Adonai יְהֹוָה (ופשע) hefir הֵפִיר atzat־עֲצַת

goyim גוֹיִם heni הֵנִיא machshevot מַחְשְׁבוֹת amim עַמִּים:

(י–Tiferet) rabot רַבּוֹת machashavot מַחֲשָׁבוֹת belev בְּלֶב־ ish אִישׁ

va'atzat וַעֲצַת Adonai יְהֹוָה (ונקה) hee הִיא takum תָקוּם כ"א היות:

"The Lord established His Throne in the Heavens, and His kingdom rules over everything." (Psalms 103:19) "Let the Heavens rejoice and let the Earth be glad and let them proclaim among the nations: The Lord has reigned. (1 Chronicles 16:31) "The Lord reigns, the Lord has reigned. The Lord shall reign forever and ever. The Lord is King forever and ever. Nations have perished from His land." (Psalms 10:16) "The Lord has disrupted the conspiracy of peoples and thwarted the plans of nations." (Psalms 33:10) "Many are the thoughts in the heart of man, but it is the purpose of the Lord that takes place." (Proverbs 19:21)

(*Tiferet*–ש׳) עֲצַת atzat יְהֹוֽאדֹנֵיאהדוֹנֵהי Adonai (פּוּקִד) le'olam לְעוֹלָם

ריבוע ס״ג ו״י אותיות דס״ג ta'amod תַּעֲמֹד machshevot מַחְשְׁבוֹת libo לִבּוֹ

hu הוּא ki כִּי (*Netzach*–י׳) רי״ו: vador וָדֹר ledor לְדֹר

vaya'amod וַיַּעֲמֹד: tziva צִוָּה hu הוּא vayehi וַיְהִי amar אָמַר

(על שלשים) Adonai יְהֹוֽאדֹנֵיאהדוֹנֵהי vachar בָּחַר ki כִּי (*Netzach*–ש׳)

lo לוֹ: lemoshav לְמוֹשָׁב חוֹבּוֹ iva אִוָּה קִנְאָה, הֱיוֹת, ו יוֹסֵף, beTziyon בְּצִיּוֹן

Yah יָהּ lo לוֹ bachar בָּחַר בָּחַר הֱיוֹת, יאהדונהי איהדונהי Yaakov יַעֲקֹב ז ki כִּי (*Hod*–ד׳)

yitosh יִטֹשׁ lo לֹא ki כִּי (*Hod*–י׳) lisgulato לִסְגֻלָּתוֹ: Yisrael יִשְׂרָאֵל

lo לֹא venachalato וְנַחֲלָתוֹ amo עַמּוֹ (וְעל רבעים) Adonai יְהֹוֽאדֹנֵיאהדוֹנֵהי

ר״ת רי״ו yechaper יְכַפֵּר rachum רַחוּם vehu וְהוּא (*Yesod*–ד׳) ya'azov יַעֲזֹב:

(*Ima* of the *klipa*) yashchit יַשְׁחִית velo וְלֹא (*Abba* of the *klipa*) avon עָוֹן

(*Zeir* of the *klipa*) apo אַפּוֹ lehashiv לְהָשִׁיב vehirba וְהִרְבָּה

(*Nukva* of the *klipa*) chamato וַחֲמָתוֹ: יל kol כָּל ya'ir יָעִיר velo וְלֹא:

(ע׳–יסוד) יְהֹוֽאדֹנֵיאהדוֹנֵהי Adonai hoshi'a הוֹשִׁיעָה יהוה וע״ע נהורין

הַמֶּלֶךְ hamelech ר״ת יהוה ya'anenu יַעֲנֵנוּ veyom בְּיוֹם ע״ה נגד, מזבח, זן אל יהוה

קָרְאֵנוּ kor'enu ר״ת יב״ק, אלהים יהוה, אהיה אדני יהוה ; ס״ת ב״ן ועם כ׳ דהמלך = ע״ב:

Then without any interruption you should immediately start the two verses of *Ashrei* to make *Keter* to *Nukva* from the 22 letters of *Ashrei* (as mentioned before *Yehi Chevod*).

"The purpose of the Lord shall endure forever and the thoughts of His Heart, for all generations." (Psalms 33:11) *"Because He said and it came to be, He commanded and it was established."* (Psalms 33:9) *"For the Lord chose Zion as His desired dwelling place."* (Psalms 132:13) *"For God chose Jacob for Himself and Israel as His treasure."* (Psalms 135:4) *"For the Lord shall not forsake His people nor shall He abandon His heritage."* (Psalms 94:14) *"And He is merciful, forgivesiniquity, and does not destroy; He frequently diverts His anger and does not arouse all His Wrath."* (Psalms 70:38) *"Lord save us. The King shall answer on the day that we call Him."* (Psalms 20:10)

THE ASHREI

Twenty-one of the twenty-two letters of the Aramaic alphabet are encoded in the *Ashrei* in their correct order from *Alef* to *Tav*. King David, the author, left out the Aramaic letter *Nun* from this prayer, because *Nun* is the first letter in the Aramaic word *nefilah*, which means "falling." Falling refers to a spiritual decline, as in falling into the *klipa*. Feelings of doubt, depression, worry, and uncertainty are consequences of spiritual falling. Because the Aramaic letters are the actual instruments of Creation, this prayer helps to inject order and the power of Creation into our lives, without the energy of falling.

In this Psalm there are ten times the Name: יהוה for the Ten *Sefirot*. This Psalm is written according to the order of the *Alef Bet*, but the letter *Nun* is omitted to prevent falling.

ראה ב"פ vetecha בֵּיתֶךָ yoshvei יוֹשְׁבֵי (סוד הכתר) ashrei אַשְׁרֵי

ha'am הָעָם ashrei אַשְׁרֵי sela סֶלָה: yehalelucha יְהַלְלוּךָ od עוֹד

lo לֹא מהטע, משה, ע"ב בריבוע וקס"א, אל שדי, ד"פ אלהים ע"ה shekacha שֶׁכָּכָה

(*Keter*) she'Adonai שֶׁיְהוָה ר"ת לאה ha'am הָעָם ashrei אַשְׁרֵי

leDavid לְדָוִד ילה ע"ה אמת, אהיה פעמים אהיה, ז"פ ס"ג tehila תְּהִלָּה: Elohav אֱלֹהָיו

va'avarcha וַאֲבָרְכָה hamelech הַמֶּלֶךְ Elohai אֱלוֹהַי aromimcha אֲרוֹמִמְךָ

va'ed וָעֶד: דס"ג אותיות וי' דס"ג ריבוע le'olam לְעוֹלָם shimcha שִׁמְךָ

יהוה אל זן מזבוח, נגד, ע"ה לכב ב"ן, yom יוֹם bechol בְּכָל

va'ed וָעֶד: דס"ג אותיות וי' ריבוע דס"ג le'olam לְעוֹלָם avarcheka אֲבָרְכֶךָ va'ahalela וַאֲהַלְלָה מ"ה יהוה shimcha שִׁמְךָ

אום יזל, מבה, = אותיות ד' עם ; להו gadol גָּדוֹל

כלה אדני, umhulal וּמְהֻלָּל (*Chochmah*) Adonai יְהוָה מאד me'od

cheker וְחֵקֶר: en אֵין והו veligdulato וְלִגְדֻלָּתוֹ me'od מְאֹד

THE ASHREI

"Joyful are those who dwell in Your House, they shall praise You, Selah." (Psalms 84:5) "Joyful is the nation that this is theirs and joyful the nation that the Lord is their God." (Psalms 145:15) "A Praise of David:
א *I shall exalt You, my God, the King, and I shall bless Your Name forever and for eternity.*
ב *I shall bless You every day and I shall praise Your Name forever and for eternity.*
ג *The Lord is great and exceedingly praised. His greatness is unfathomable.*

ר"ת דלים   ma'asecha מַעֲשֶׂיךָ   yeshabach יְשַׁבַּח   ledor לְדוֹר   dor דּוֹר

יָ"ז, כ"ב אותיות פשוטות (=אכא) וה' אותיות סופיות מנצפ"ך: yagidu יַגִּידוּ   ugvurotecha וּגְבוּרֹתֶיךָ

vedivrei וְדִבְרֵי   hodecha הוֹדֶךָ   kevod כְּבוֹד   hadar הֲדַר

אדנ"י   אהיה   אלהים,   ר"ת   nifle'otecha נִפְלְאֹתֶיךָ

פ"ז: טהור   כתם   (בסוד   פ"ז   =   הפסוק   ר"ת   asicha אָשִׂיחָה

ugdulatcha וּגְדוּלָּתְךָ   yomeru יֹאמֵרוּ   no'rotecha נוֹרְאֹתֶיךָ   ve'ezuz וֶעֱזוּז

ס"ת = יא"י (מילוי דס"ג):   asaperena אֲסַפְּרֶנָּה   ר"ת = ע"ב, ריבוע יהוה   ס"ת =   (כתיב: וּגְדֻלוֹתֶיךָ)

yabi'u יַבִּיעוּ   לאו   tuvcha טוּבְךָ   rav רַב   zecher זֵכֶר

ס"ת = ב"ן, יבמ, לכב ; ר"ת הפסוק = רי"ו יהוה: yeranenu יְרַנֵּנוּ   vetzidkatcha וְצִדְקָתְךָ

(Binah)   Adonai יְהֹוָ֒אהדונהי   verachum וְרַחוּם   chanun וְחַנּוּן

ר"ת = יהוה   apayim אַפַּיִם   ס"ת = ס"ג ב"ן   ס"ת = עאל   erech אֶרֶךְ   חנון ורחום יהוה

יהוה: ריבוע   ע"ב,   chased וְחֶסֶד   (כתיב: וְגָדוֹל)   ugdal וּגְדָל

lakol לַכֹּל   (Chesed)   Adonai יְהֹוָ֒אהדונהי   והו   tov טוֹב

al עַל   verachamav וְרַחֲמָיו   (מילוי דס"ג)   ל"ו ;   ס"ת ;   אדנ"י   יה

ס"ת ריבוע ב"ן ע"ב, ריבוע יהוה: ma'asav מַעֲשָׂיו   ס"ת ריבוע ב"ן ע"ה ;   ר"ת ; עמם ;   ילי   kol כֹּל

ד   *One generation and the next shall praise Your deeds and tell of Your might.*

ה   *The brilliance of Your splendid glory and the wonders of Your acts, I shall speak of.*

ו   *They shall speak of the might of Your awesome acts and I shall tell of Your greatness.*

ז   *They shall express the remembrance of Your abundant goodness, and Your righteousness they shall joyfully proclaim.* ח *The Lord is merciful and compassionate, slow to anger and great in kindness.*

ט   *The Lord is good to all, His compassion extends over all His acts.*

yoducha יוֹדוּךָ (Gevurah) Adonai יְהֹוָ(אדני)הֹוִה kol יֵלִי כָּל ma'asecha מַעֲשֶׂיךָ

vachasidecha לְבָרְכוּכָה ר"ת אלהים, אהיה אדני yevarchucha ס"ת = מ"ה: וַחֲסִידֶיךָ

kevod כְּבוֹד malchutcha מַלְכוּתְךָ yomeru יֹאמֵרוּ ugvuratcha וּגְבוּרָתֶךָ

yedaberu יְדַבֵּרוּ ר"ת הפסוק = אלהים, אהיה אדני ; ס"ת = ב"ן, יבמ, לכב:

lehodi'a לְהוֹדִיעַ livnei לִבְנֵי ha'adam הָאָדָם ר"ת כלה, אדני

gevurotav גְּבוּרֹתָיו uchvod וּכְבוֹד hadar הֲדַר

malchuto מַלְכוּתוֹ ר"ת מ"ה וס"ת = רי"ו ; ר"ת הפסוק ע"ה = רי"ו = ק"כ צירופי אלהים:

malchutcha מַלְכוּתְךָ malchut מַלְכוּת kol יֵלִי כָּל olamim עֹלָמִים

umemshaltecha וּמֶמְשַׁלְתְּךָ bechol בְּכָל ב"ן, לכב dor דּוֹר vador וָדֹר רי"ו:

somech סוֹמֵךְ ריבוע אדני Adonai יְהֹוָ(אדני)הֹוִה (Tiferet)

lechol לְכָל יה אדני ; סומך אדני לכל ר"ת סאל, אמן (יאהדונהי) hanoflim הַנֹּפְלִים

vezokef וְזוֹקֵף lechol לְכָל יה אדני hakefufim הַכְּפוּפִים נמם:

enei עֵינֵי ריבוע דמ"ה chol כֹּל יֵלִי elecha אֵלֶיךָ yesaberu יְשַׂבֵּרוּ veAta וְאַתָּה

noten נוֹתֵן אבגית"ן, ועיר lahem לָהֶם et אֶת ochlam אָכְלָם be'ito בְּעִתּוֹ:

י   *All that You have made shall thank You, God, and Your pious ones shall bless You.*

כ   *They shall speak of the glory of Your Kingdom and talk of Your mighty deeds.*

ל   *His mighty deeds He makes known to man and the glory of His splendid Kingdom.*

מ   *Yours is the Kingdom of all worlds and Your reign extends to each and every generation.*

ס   *The Lord supports all those who fell and holds upright all those who are bent over.*

ע   *The eyes of all look hopefully towards You, and You give them their food at its proper time.*

POTE'ACH ET YADECHA

We connect to the letters *Pei, Alef,* and *Yud* by opening our hands and holding our palms skyward. Our consciousness is focused on receiving sustenance and financial prosperity from the Light through our actions of tithing and sharing, our Desire to Receive for the Sake of Sharing. In doing so, we also acknowledge that the sustenance we receive comes from a higher source and is not of our own doing. According to the sages, if we do not meditate on this idea at this juncture, we must repeat the prayer.

פתחו (שע"ז נהורין למ"ה ולס"ה)

פותחו את ידך ר"ת פאי
גימ' יאהדונהי ז"ן
וחכמה דו"א ו"ק
יסוד דנוק'

יוד הי ויו הי יוד הי ויו הי (וי' וזוורתי)
אלף למד אלף למד (ע"ע)
יוד הא ואו הא (לו"א)
אדני (ולנוקבא)

פּוֹתֵוֹן pote'ach **אֶת** et **יָדֶךְ** yadecha ר"ת פאי וס"ת וזתך עם ג' אותיות = **דִיקְרְנוֹסָא**

ובאתב"ע הוא סאל, פאי, אמן, יאהדונהי ; ועוד יכוין שם וזתך בעילוב יהוה – **יוֹזְהַתוֹכָה**

מצפץ מצפץ מוזוין דפנים דאוזור אלהים אלהים
להמעליך פ"ו אורות לכל מילוי דכל

ואוזור דפרצופי נה"י וזג"ת
דיצירה דרוזל הנקראת לאה
לף מד י וד ם
אלף למד הי יוד מם

וזתך

סאל יאהדונהי

אוזור דפרצופי נה"י וזג"ת
דפרצוף וזג"ת דיצירה דו"א
לף מד י וד ם
אלף למד הי יוד מם

וּמַשְׂבִּיעַ umasbi'a וזתך עם ג' אותיות = **דִיקְרְנוֹסָא**

ובא"ת ב"ע הוא סאל, אמן, יאהדונהי ; ועוד יכוין שם וזתך בעילוב יהוה – **יוֹזְהַתוֹכָה**

מצפץ מצפץ מוזוין דפנים דאוזור אלהים אלהים
להמעליך פ"ו אורות לכל מילוי דכל

ואוזור דפרצופי נה"י וזג"ת
דיצירה דרוזל הנקראת לאה
לף מד י וד ם
אלף למד הי יוד מם

וזתך

אוזור דפרצופי נה"י וזג"ת
דפרצוף נה"י דיצירה דו"א
לף מד י וד ם
אלף למד הי יוד מם

לְכָל lechol יה אדני (להמעליך מוזוין ד-יה אל הנוקבא שהיא אדני)

וָזִי chai כל וזי = אהיה אהיה יהוה, בינה ע"ה, וזיים

רָצוֹן ratzon מהע' ע"ה, ע"ב בריבוע וקס"א ע"ה, אל שדי ע"ה ; ר"ת רווזל שהיא המלכות הצריכה לשפע

יוד יוד הי יוד הי ויו יוד הי ויו הי יסוד דאבא
אלף הי יוד הי יסוד דאימא
להמתיק רווזל וב' דמעין שך פר

Also meditate to draw abundance and sustenance and blessing to all the worlds from the *ratzon* mentioned above. You should meditate and focus on this verse because it is the essence of prosperity, and that God is intervening and sustaining and supporting all of Creation.

POTE'ACH ET YADECHA

פ   *Open   Your   Hands   and   satisfy   every   living   thing   with   desire.*

לכב ב"ן, bechol **בְּכָל** (Yesod) Adonai יהווהו אדנ"י אהדונהי **צַדִּיק** tzadik

יבמ, ב"ן **מַעֲשָׂיו** ma'asav ב"ן, לכב bechol **בְּכָל** vechasid **וְחָסִיד** derachav **דְּרָכָיו**

אדנ"י יה lechol **לְכָל** (Malchut) Adonai יהו אדנ"י אהדונהי karov **קָרוֹב**

asher **אֲשֶׁר** אדנ"י יה lechol **לְכָל** kor'av **קֹרְאָיו**

ז"פ ס"ג אהיה, פעמים אהיה ve'emet **בֶּאֱמֶת** yikra'uhu **יִקְרָאֻהוּ**

ya'ase **יַעֲשֶׂה** yere'av **יְרֵאָיו** מהשע ע"ה, ע"ב בריבוע וקס"א ע"ה, אל שדי ע"ה retzon **רָצוֹן**

veyoshi'em **וְיוֹשִׁיעֵם** yishma **יִשְׁמַע** shav'atam **שַׁוְעָתָם** ve'et **וְאֶת** ר"ת ריי

(Netzach) Adonai יהו אדנ"י אהדונהי שבתפילין הויות כ"א shomer **שׁוֹמֵר**

אכא ר"ת ohavav **אֹהֲבָיו** ילי kol **כָּל** et **אֶת**

yashmid **יַשְׁמִיד** haresha'im **הָרְשָׁעִים** ילי kol **כָּל** ve'et **וְאֵת**

pi **פִּי** ראה yedaber **יְדַבֶּר** (Hod) Adonai יהו אדנ"י אהדונהי tehilat **תְּהִלַּת**

ילי kol **כָּל** ע"ב ס"ג מ"ה ב"ן, הברכה (למתק את ז' המלכים שמתו) vivarech **וִיבָרֵךְ**

אותיות דס"ג ריבוע ס"ג וי le'olam **לְעוֹלָם** kodsho **קָדְשׁוֹ** shem **שֵׁם** basar **בָּשָׂר**

me'ata **מֵעַתָּה** ya **יָהּ** nevarech **נְבָרֵךְ** va'anachnu **וַאֲנַחְנוּ** va'ed **וָעֶד**

ללה: haleluya **הַלְלוּיָהּ** אלהים, אהיה אדנ"י olam **עוֹלָם** ve'ad **וְעַד**

THE FIVE PSALMS

At the beginning and end of each Psalm, we find the word *Haleluyah*, meaning "Praise the Lord." As Kabbalah always says, God does not need our praise. The word is a code; these ten *Haleuyahs* link us to the Ten *Sefirot*. They help us ascend to the top of the World of Formation, *Yetzirah*.

צ   *The Lord is righteous in all His ways and virtuous in all His deeds.*

ק   *The Lord is close to all who call Him, and only to those who call Him truthfully.*

ר   *He shall fulfill the will of those who fear Him; He hears their wailing and saves them.*

ש   *The Lord protects all who love Him and He destroys the wicked.*

ת   *My lips utter the praise of the Lord and all flesh shall bless His Holy Name, forever and for eternity."*

(Psalms 145) "And we shall bless the Lord forever and for eternity. Praise the Lord!" (Psalms 115:18)

Ten times *Haleluyah* is the *tikkun* of the Ten *Sefirot* of *Beriah* in *Yetzirah*

THE FIRST PSALM – MALCHUT AND YESOD

This first Psalm contains *Yud, Hei, Vav,* and *Hei,* the Tetragrammaton (יהוה), nine times. This nine is linked to the upper nine *Sefirot*, from *Yesod* to *Keter*. The energy of our realm, the World of *Malchut*, is receiving. Like the moon, *Malchut* has no Light of its own and draws its Light from the upper nine dimensions through our spiritual actions of transformation.

haleli הַלְלִי ; ללה : אהיה אדני , אהיה, אלהים haleluya הַלְלוּיָהּ (*Malchut* of *Yetzirah*)

נַפְשִׁי nafshi אֶת־ et יְהוָה (אדני יאהדונהי) Adonai (*Keter*): אֲהַלְלָה ahalela מ״ה יהוה

יְהוָה (אדני יאהדונהי) Adonai (*Chochmah*) בְּחַיָּי bechayai אֲזַמְּרָה azamra

לֵאלֹהַי lelohai מילוי ע״ב, דמב ; ילה בְּעוֹדִי be'odi ר״ת וס״ת הפסוק = אמן (יאהדונהי):

אַל־ al תִּבְטְחוּ tivtechu בִנְדִיבִים vindivim בְּבֶן־ beven אָדָם adam

שֶׁאֵין she'en לוֹ lo תְשׁוּעָה teshu'a: תֵּצֵא tetze רוּחוֹ rucho יָשֻׁב yashuv

לְאַדְמָתוֹ le'admato בַּיּוֹם bayom ע״ה נגד, מזבח, זן אל יהוה ההוּא hahu

אָבְדוּ avdu עֶשְׁתֹּנֹתָיו eshtonotav: אַשְׁרֵי ashrei שֶׁאֵל sheEl יא״י (מילוי דס״ג)

יַעֲקֹב Ya'akov י הויות, יאהדונהי אידהנויה בְּעֶזְרוֹ be'ezro שִׂבְרוֹ sivro

עַל al יְהוָה (אדני יאהדונהי) Adonai (*Binah*) אֱלֹהָיו Elohav ילה: עֹשֶׂה ose

שָׁמַיִם shamayim י״פ טל, י״פ כוזו וָאָרֶץ va'aretz אֶת־ et הַיָּם hayam ילי

וְאֶת־ ve'et כָּל־ kol ילי אֲשֶׁר asher בָּם bam עם בן מ״ב הַשֹּׁמֵר hashomer

אֱמֶת emet אהיה פעמים אהיה, ז״פ ס״ג, ד״פ ס״ג ריבוע ס״ג ו׳ אותיות דס״ג: לְעוֹלָם le'olam

עֹשֶׂה ose מִשְׁפָּט mishpat ע״ה ה״פ אלהים לַעֲשׁוּקִים la'ashukim נֹתֵן noten

לֶחֶם lechem ג הויות אבניתא, ושר לָרְעֵבִים lare'evim יְהוָה (אדני יאהדונהי) Adonai

מַתִּיר matir (*Chesed*) אֲסוּרִים asurim: יְהוָה (אדני יאהדונהי) Adonai (*Gevurah*)

פֹּקֵחַ poke'ach מ״ה קמ״ג עִוְרִים ivrim יְהוָה (אדני יאהדונהי) Adonai (*Tiferet*) זֹקֵף zokef

כְּפוּפִים kefufim יְהוָה (אדני יאהדונהי) Adonai (*Netzach*) אֹהֵב ohev צַדִּיקִים tzadikim:

THE FIVE PSALMS - THE FIRST PSALM

"Praise the Lord! My soul praises the Lord! I shall praise the Lord while I am still alive; I shall play melodies to my God while I exist. Do not place your trust in nobles; not in a man who has no means of salvation. His breath leaves him and he returns to his earth. Upon that day, his plans perish. Fortunate is the one whom the God of Jacob comes to his aid, and who rests his hope on the Lord, his God. He creates the Heavens and the earth, the sea, and all that they contain. The One Who guards truth forever; Who acts justly toward the oppressed; Who gives bread to the hungry. The Lord releases those who are imprisoned. The Lord gives sight to the blind. The Lord stands upright those who are bent over. The Lord loves the righteous.

שׁדי = ר"ת gerim גֵּרִים et אֶת־ shomer שֹׁמֵר (Hod) Adonai יְהֹוָאדנָיאהדונהי

ve'almana וְאַלְמָנָה (וִיהִי מראה) ויפה תואר יפה יוסף (וִיהִי) יוסף yatom יָתוֹם

resha'im רְשָׁעִים קס"א ע"ב יב"ק, ב"פ vederech וְדֶרֶךְ יהוה = ר"ת ye'oded יְעוֹדֵד

(Yesod) Adonai יְהֹוָואדנָיאהדונהי yimloch יִמְלֹךְ רי"ו ר"ת ye'avet יְעַוֵּת

Tziyon צִיּוֹן ילה Elohayich אֱלֹהַיִךְ דס"ג ו"י אותיות רביע ס"ג ו"י le'olam לְעוֹלָם

ז"א אצל שמלכות (רמז אצלו ר"ת ; רי"ו vador וָדֹר ledor לְדֹר קנאה, הויות, ו יוסף,

כנגדה) הויה היה שאין אע"פ haleluya הַלְלוּיָהּ (Yesod of Yetzirah) אלהים, אהיה אדני ; ללה:

THE SECOND PSALM – THE NEXT TWO SEFIROT

The power of this Psalm helps us balance our acts of judgment and mercy towards other people.

This Psalm contains the Name: יהוה five times, which corresponds to the five *Chasadim* (mercy) through which the five *Gevurot* (judgment) are sweetened. This Psalm contains 139 words (with the *Kolel*) which adds up to the numerical value of *ko'ach* (strength), and *Yabok* (יב"ק = יהוה ▲ אלהים - a code for sweetening judgment).

וְהוּ ; כי טוב = tov טוֹב ki כִּי־ ללה ; אדני אהיה, אלהים haleluya הַלְלוּיָהּ

ki כִּי־ (Hod) ילה Elohenu אֱלֹהֵינוּ zamera זַמְּרָה (Yesod) יול, מבה, אום, אהיה, יהוה

na'im נָעִים (Netzach) ז"פ ס"ג:, אהיה פעמים אהיה, אמת, ע"ה tehila תְהִלָּה nava נָאוָה

bone בּוֹנֵה ס"ג Yerushalayim יְרוּשָׁלַיִם Adonai יְהֹוָואדנָיאהדונהי (First Chesed)

nidchei נִדְחֵי ע"ב, רביע יהוה Yisrael יִשְׂרָאֵל yechanes יְכַנֵּס:

harofe הָרֹפֵא lishvurei לִשְׁבוּרֵי lev לֵב ר"ת ללה, אדני

The Lord watches over the converts and gives encouragement to the orphan and the widow, But He twists the way of the wicked. The Lord shall reign forever, your God, for each and every generation, Zion. Praise the Lord!" (Psalms 146)

THE SECOND PSALM

"Praise the Lord! For it is good to play melodies to our God, for it is pleasant and beautiful to praise Him. The Lord builds Jerusalem. He shall gather the scattered of Israel. He is healer of the brokenhearted

UMECHABESH LE'ATZVOTAM

According to the *Zohar*, this verse releases the energy of immortality, hastening its arrival. By releasing the energy of immortality into our spiritual atmosphere, we are helping to empower medical researchers, biologists, geneticists, and all other scientists in their quest to find the secrets to longevity, anti-aging, and the regeneration of human cells and organs.

וּמְוַזֵבֵשׁ umechabesh לְעַצְּבוֹתָם le'atzvotam:

מוֹנֶה mone מִסְפָּר mispar לַכּוֹכָבִים lakochavim לְכֻלָּם lechulam

שֵׁמוֹת shemot gadol גָּדוֹל לְהוֹ ; עִם ד' אותיות = מובה, יזל, אום yikra יִקְרָא

אֲדוֹנֵינוּ adonenu וְרַב verav ko'ach כּוֹחַ ע"ב ס"ג מ"ה ב"ן, וד' כוללים

לִתְבוּנָתוֹ litvunato אֵין en מִסְפָּר mispar: מְעוֹדֵד me'oded עֲנָוִים anavim

יְהוֹוָהּאהדונהי Adonai (*Second Chesed*) מַשְׁפִּיל mashpil רְשָׁעִים resha'im

עֲדֵי adei אָרֶץ aretz: עֱנוּ enu לַיְהוֹוָהּאהדונהי ladonai (*Third Chesed*)

בְּתוֹדָה betoda זַמְּרוּ zameru לֵאלֹהֵינוּ lelohenu ילה בְּכִנּוֹר vechinor:

הַמְכַסֶּה ham'chase שָׁמַיִם shamayim י"פ, טל, כוזו be'avim בְּעָבִים

הַמֵּכִין hamechin לָאָרֶץ la'aretz מָטָר matar ר"ת מלה הַמַּצְמִיוֹן hamatzmi'ach

הָרִים harim וְחָצִיר chatzir: נֹתֵן noten אבגיתץ, ושר לִבְהֵמָה livhema ב"ן

לַחְמָהּ lachma עֹרֶב orev לִבְנֵי livnei אֲשֶׁר asher יִקְרָאוּ yikra'u:

לֹא lo בִּגְבוּרַת vigvurat הַסּוּס hasus ריבוע ארני, כוק יֶחְפָּץ yechpatz

לֹא־ lo בְּשׁוֹקֵי veshokei הָאִישׁ ha'ish (*Netzach and Hod*) יִרְצֶה yirtze:

UMECHABESH LE'ATZVOTAM

And He tends to their grief. He sets the numbers of stars and calls them by their names. Our Master is great and exceedingly powerful. His understanding is limitless. The Lord gives strength to the humble, and lowers the wicked down to Earth. Raise your voices to the Lord with gratitude. Play melodies with a harp to our God. He covers the Heavens with clouds. He prepares rain for the earth; He causes mountains to grow grass. He provides the beasts with food and for the young ravens that call out. He does not desire the strength of the horse nor does He want the thighs of man.

rotze רוֹצֶה Adonai יְהֹוָה (Fourth Chesed) et אֶת־ yere'av יְרֵאָיו

ham'yachalim הַמְיַחֲלִים et אֶת־ lechasdo לְחַסְדּוֹ

et אֶת־ Yerushalayim יְרוּשָׁלַיִם shabechi שַׁבְּחִי

haleli הַלְלִי (Fifth Chesed) Adonai יְהֹוָה Elohayich אֱלֹהַיִךְ

Tziyon צִיּוֹן ki כִּי chizak וְחִזַּק berichei בְּרִיחֵי

she'arayich שְׁעָרָיִךְ berach בֵּרַךְ banayich בָּנַיִךְ bekirbech בְּקִרְבֵּךְ

hasam הַשָּׂם gevulech גְּבוּלֵךְ shalom שָׁלוֹם chelev חֵלֶב chitim וְחִטִּים

yasbi'ech יַשְׂבִּיעֵךְ hashole'ach הַשֹּׁלֵחַ imrato אִמְרָתוֹ aretz אָרֶץ

ad עַד mehera מְהֵרָה yarutz יָרוּץ devaro דְּבָרוֹ

hanoten הַנֹּתֵן sheleg שֶׁלֶג katzamer כַּצָּמֶר

kefor כְּפוֹר ka'efer כָּאֵפֶר mashlich מַשְׁלִיךְ yefazer יְפַזֵּר karcho קַרְחוֹ

chefitim כְּפִתִּים lifnei לִפְנֵי karato קָרָתוֹ mi מִי ya'amod יַעֲמֹד

yishlach יִשְׁלַח devaro דְּבָרוֹ veyamsem וְיַמְסֵם yashev יַשֵּׁב rucho רוּחוֹ

yizelu יִזְּלוּ mayim מָיִם magid מַגִּיד devarav דְּבָרָיו

leYaakov לְיַעֲקֹב chukav וְחֻקָּיו umishpatav וּמִשְׁפָּטָיו

leYisrael לְיִשְׂרָאֵל (Hod) lo לֹא asa עָשָׂה chen כֵּן lechol לְכָל

goy גּוֹי umishpatim וּמִשְׁפָּטִים bal בַּל

(Hod) yeda'um יְדָעוּם haleluya הַלְלוּיָהּ

The Lord only wants those who fear Him and those who place their hopes in His kindness. Praise the Lord, Jerusalem, and laud your God, Zion, for He has strengthened the bolts of your gates and blessed your children within. He sets peace at your borders. He satiates you with the best of wheat. He sends out His messages to the earth and His words travel very fast. He sends down snow as if it was wool and He scatters frost as if ash. He tosses His hail as if crumbs of bread. Who can stand up to His cold? He sends forth His word and melts it. He makes His wind blow and His waters to flow. He teaches His words to Jacob; His statutes and laws to Israel. He has not done so for any other nation. He informed them not of the laws. Praise the Lord!" (Psalms 147)

THE THIRD PSALM (DAILY HALEL) – TIFERET AND GEVURAH

In this Psalm, we offer thanks to the Creator, but what we are actually doing is acknowledging that we are not really entitled to anything - that our gifts in this life far outweigh our efforts. This does not come from the standpoint of having low self-worth, but rather from a combined sense of humility and appreciation for everything we receive in life.

You should be very careful with this Psalm and say it slowly with genuine deep meditation because here the sages said: "My part should be with those who say the *Halel* everyday." There are 14 verses for the word *yad* (hand) whose numerical value is 14, connecting us to *Yad Rama* (Central Column) and *Yad Chazaka* (Left Column).

(Tiferet of Yetzirah) הַלְלוּיָהּ haleluya אלהים, אהיה אדני ; ללה הַלְלוּ halelu (Asiyah)

אֶת־ et אהיה ר״ת Adonai יְהֹוָאדֹנִיאהדונהי min מִן־ אהיה ר״ת הַשָּׁמַיִם hashamayim

הַלְלוּהוּ haleluhu (Yetzirah) ; ר״ת מ״ה כוו , י״פ טל, י״פ בַּמְּרוֹמִים bameromim:

הַלְלוּהוּ haleluhu (Beriah) chol כָּל יל״י מַלְאָכָיו mal'achav הַלְלוּהוּ haleluhu

(Atzilut) כָּל kol יל״י צְבָאָו tzeva'av ר״ת הפסוק = ע״ב ס״ג מ״ה ; ס״ת הפסוק = אהיה ס״ג:

הַלְלוּהוּ haleluhu shemesh שֶׁמֶשׁ veyare'ach וְיָרֵחַ haleluhu הַלְלוּהוּ כָּל kol יל״י

כּוֹכְבֵי kochvei or אוֹר רו, ין סוף: haleluhu הַלְלוּהוּ shemei שְׁמֵי

הַשָּׁמַיִם hashamayim י״פ טל, י״פ כוו vehamayim וְהַמַּיִם asher אֲשֶׁר me'al מֵעַל

אֶת־ et עלם yehalelu יְהַלְלוּ ר״ת מ״ה: ; ר״ת כוו , י״פ טל, י״פ hashamayim הַשָּׁמַיִם

שֵׁם shem יְהֹוָאדֹנִיאהדונהי Adonai ki כִּי hu הוּא tziva צִוָּה venivra'u וְנִבְרָאוּ:

וַיַּעֲמִידֵם vaya'amidem la'ad לָעַד ב״ן ב״פ le'olam לְעוֹלָם ריבוע ס״ג וי אותיות דס״ג

וְחָק־ chok נָתַן natan velo וְלֹא ס״ת קנ״א (אלף הה יוד הה, מקוה), אדני אלהים

יַעֲבוֹר ya'avor רפ״ח (להעלות רפ״ח ניצוצות שנפלו לקליפה דמשם באים התחלואים:)

THE THIRD PSALM

"Praise the Lord! Praise the Lord from the Heavens; praise Him in the high places; praise Him, all His angels; praise Him, all His Hosts. Praise Him, sun and moon; praise Him, all stars of Light; praise Him, the Highest Heavens, and the water that is above the Heavens. They praise the Name of the Lord, for He commanded and they were created. And He erected them forever and ever; He set laws that cannot be transgressed.

הַלְלוּ halelu אֶת־ et יְהֹוָואהדניהאהדונהי Adonai מִן min הָאָרֶץ ha'aretz אלהים דודהין ע"ה

תַּנִּינִים taninim וְכָל־ vechol ילי תְּהֹמוֹת tehomot: אֵשׁ esh וּבָרָד uvarad

שֶׁלֶג sheleg אלף אלף אלף דג אהיה וְקִיטוֹר vekitor רוּחַ ru'ach סְעָרָה se'ara

עֹשָׂה osa דְבָרוֹ devaro ראה: הֶהָרִים heharim וְכָל־ vechol ילי גְּבָעוֹת geva'ot

עֵץ etz פְּרִי peri וְכָל־ vechol ילי הָעֵצִים arazim: הַחַיָּה hachaya וְכָל־ vechol ילי

בְּהֵמָה behema רֶמֶשׂ remes בין vetzipor וְצִפּוֹר kanaf כָּנָף ע"ה קנ"א, אדני אלהים:

מַלְכֵי malchei אֶרֶץ eretz וְכָל־ vechol ילי לְאֻמִּים le'umim שָׂרִים sarim

וְכָל־ vechol ילי שֹׁפְטֵי shoftei אָרֶץ aretz: בַּחוּרִים bachurim וְגַם־ vegam

בְּתוּלוֹת betulot זְקֵנִים zekenim עִם־ im נְעָרִים ne'arim: יְהַלְלוּ yehalelu

אֶת־ et שֵׁם shem יְהֹוָואהדניהאהדונהי Adonai כִּי ki נִשְׂגָּב nisgav

שְׁמוֹ shemo מהש ע"ה, ע"ב בריבוע וקס"א ע"ה, אל שדי ע"ה לְבַדּוֹ levado שם בן מ"ב

הוֹדוֹ hodo אהיה עַל־ al אֶרֶץ eretz וְשָׁמָיִם veshamayim י"פ טל, י"פ כוזו:

וַיָּרֶם vayarem קֶרֶן keren לְעַמּוֹ le'amo תְּהִלָּה tehila ע"ה אמת, אהיה פעמים אהיה, ז"פ ס"ג

לְכָל lechol יה ארני חֲסִידָיו chasidav לִבְנֵי livnei יִשְׂרָאֵל Yisrael

עַם־ am קְרֹבוֹ kerovo (Gevurah of Yetzirah) הַלְלוּיָהּ haleluya אלהים, אהיה ארני ; ללה:

THE FOURTH PSALM (SHIRU) - CHESED

This Psalm is comprised of nine verses referring to nine "skies" that separate the Upper Worlds from the Lower World. This idea of separation is a direct reference to the concept of time and its relationship to Cause and Effect. Through these verses, we manipulate time and shorten the distance between Cause and Effect.

To allow us to express our uniquely human trait of free will, time is inserted into the Cause and Effect process. This space gives Satan, our ego, and our limiting selfish thoughts the opportunity to challenge us. Satan makes us believe that we get away with our negative actions. He makes us believe that life is unfair and that good behavior goes unrewarded. Changing ourselves and our belief systems becomes more challenging. Now that we are approaching the end of days, the Final Correction, we can shorten the separation between Cause and Effect and reap the rewards of our positive behavior much more quickly. Likewise, our negative actions will produce a much quicker payback. The result in both situations is accelerated change on our part.

Praise the Lord from the Earth. Great fish and depths, fire and hail, snow and steam, and stormy wind do His bidding. The mountains and the hills, fruit trees and all the cedars, wild beasts and all cattle, creeping things and winged birds; Kings of the Earth and all nations, princes and all the judges of the Earth; Young men and maidens, old along with the young: they all praise the Name of the Lord, for His Name alone is powerful; His splendor is over the Earth and Heavens. And He praises the word of His nation, a praise for all His pious ones, for the children of Israel, the nation that is close to Him. Praise the Lord!" (Psalm 148)

There are 61 words in this Psalm like the numerical value of the Names: *Alef Gimel Lamed Alef* (אגלא) (35, also equals to *Alef Lamed Dalet* אלד) plus יהוה (26), to give us protection from Evil Eye.

הַלְלוּיָה (*Chesed of Yetzirah*) haleluya אלהים, אהיה ארני ; לכה ; shiru שִׁירוּ

לַיהֹוָה ladonai שִׁיר shir וְחָדָשׁ chadash י"ב הויות, קס"א קנ"א

תְּהִלָּתוֹ tehilato בִּקְהַל bik'hal וַחֲסִידִים :chasidim יִשְׂמַח yismach מושיזו

יִשְׂרָאֵל Yisrael בְּעֹשָׂיו be'osav בְּנֵי benei צִיּוֹן Tziyon יוסף, ו הויות, קנאה

יָגִילוּ yagilu בְּמַלְכָּם :vemalkam יְהַלְלוּ yehalelu שְׁמוֹ shemo מהש ע"ה,

וְכִנּוֹר vechinor בְּתֹף betof בְּמָחוֹל vemachol ע"ב בריבוע וקס"א ע"ה, אל שדי ע"ה

יְזַמְּרוּ yezameru לוֹ :lo כִּי ki רוֹצֶה rotze יְהוָה Adonai

בְּעַמּוֹ be'amo ר"ת = ע"ב ס"ג מ"ה ב"ן, הברכה (למתק את ז המלכים עמתו) ; ס"ת יהוה

יְפָאֵר yefa'er עֲנָוִים anavim בִּישׁוּעָה bishu'a פוי, אל ארני ; ר"ת הפסוק = שדי:

יַעְלְזוּ yalezu וַחֲסִידִים chasidim ג"פ אם (אותיות דפשוט, דמילוי ורדמילוי דמילוי דג"פ אהיה)

בְּכָבוֹד bechavod בוכו, ובאתב"ש הוא אם שם שלשופ"ק הממתק את ג' אם דלעיל (והוא עולה למנין

יְרַנְּנוּ yeranenu עַל al מִשְׁכְּבוֹתָם :mishkevotam עסמ"ב קס"א קנ"א קמ"ג וג"פ אם הנ"ל)

רוֹמְמוֹת romemot אֵל El (מילוי דס"ג) יא"י bigronam בִּגְרוֹנָם

וְחֶרֶב vecherev רי"ו pifiyot פִּיפִיּוֹת בְּיָדָם :beyadam לַעֲשׂוֹת la'asot ר"ת = קנ"א ב"ן, מילוי יהוה אלהים יהוה קס"א וס"ג, מ"ה ברבוע וע"ב ע"ה

נְקָמָה nekama מנק בַּגּוֹיִם bagoyim תּוֹכֵחוֹת tochechot בַּלְאֻמִּים :bale'umim

לֶאְסֹר lesor מַלְכֵיהֶם malchehem בְּזִקִּים bezikim וְנִכְבְּדֵיהֶם venichbedehem

בְּכַבְלֵי bechavlei בַּרְזֶל varzel ר"ת בלהה רוזל זלפה לאה: la'asot לַעֲשׂוֹת

בָּהֶם bahem מִשְׁפָּט mishpat ע"ה ה"פ אלהים katuv כָּתוּב hadar הָדָר hu הוּא

לְכָל lechol וַחֲסִידָיו chasidav יה ארני הַלְלוּיָה haleluya אלהים, אהיה ארני ; לכה:

THE FOURTH PSALM

"Praise the Lord! Sing to the Lord a new song. His praise is in the gathering of the pious. Israel shall rejoice with its Maker, the children of Zion shall exult with their King. They shall praise His Name with dance. With drum and harp they shall play melodies to Him. For the Lord favors His nation; He glorifies the humble with redemption. The pious shall be merry with His Glory and shall joyously sing upon their beds. The high praises of God are in their thoughts and a double-edged sword is in their hands to bring vengeance upon the nations, retributions upon the peoples, to bind their kings in chains, and their nobles in iron shackles, to administer to them justice that is written. Glory for all His pious ones, Praise the Lord!" (Psalms 149)

THE FIFTH PSALM (HALELU EL) – THE THREE UPPER SEFIROT

The six verses found here connect us to Ma-tat-ron (**do not pronounce**), the highest of all the angels. The Aramaic word for Ma-tat-ron contains six letters—*Mem, Tet, Tet, Reish, Vav,* final *Nun.* Each verse in this connection helps form the name. Because Ma-tat-ron controls all the angels in the spiritual world, he can help give us control over our physical world and assist us in accomplishing our spiritual work.

This Psalm has six verses for the six letters of the Angel מטטרו"ן (do not pronounce) of *Yetzirah* to raise *Asiyah* in it. The Angel סנדלפו"ן (do not pronounce) has seven letters and for this reason we repeat the sixth verse to complete the seventh. Also we say this Psalm to connect to the three Upper *Sefirot* of *Yetzirah*. It includes all the Ten *Sefirot* of *Yetzirah* with the secret of the Ten *Haleluyas*.

אל (יא"י מילוי דס"ג) אותיות בפסוק (*Keter*) haleluya הַלְלוּיָהּ אלהים, אהיה אדני ; ללה :

הַלְלוּ- halelu אַל El יא"י (מילוי) דס"ג bekodsho בְּקָדְשׁוֹ

הַלְלוּהוּ haleluhu (*Chochmah*) birki'a בִּרְקִיעַ uzo עֻזּוֹ ס"ת = ע"ב בֶּן :

הַלְלוּהוּ haleluhu (*Binah*) vigvurotav בִּגְבוּרֹתָיו הַלְלוּהוּ haleluhu (*Chesed*)

kerov כְּרֹב gudlo גָּדְלוֹ: הַלְלוּהוּ haleluhu (*Gevurah*) beteka בְּתֵקַע

שׁוֹפָר shofar הַלְלוּהוּ haleluhu (*Tiferet*) benevel בְּנֵבֶל benevel vechinor וְכִנּוֹר:

בְּמִנִּים haleluhu (*Netzach*) betof בְּתֹף umachol וּבְמָחוֹל הַלְלוּהוּ haleluhu (*Hod*)

שָׁמַע shama הַלְלוּהוּ haleluhu (*Yesod*) beminim בְּמִנִּים ve'ugav וְעֻגָב: הַלְלוּהוּ haleluhu (*Yesod*) vetziltzelei בְּצִלְצְלֵי

כֹּל kol יכלי hanshamah הַנְּשָׁמָה tehalel תְּהַלֵּל ר"ת כהת, משיזו בן דוד ע"ה betziltzelei בְּצִלְצְלֵי teru'a תְּרוּעָה: (*Malchut*) haleluhu הַלְלוּהוּ shama

יָהּ Yah הַלְלוּיָהּ haleluya אלהים, אהיה אדני ; ללה :

כֹּל kol יכלי hanshamah הַנְּשָׁמָה tehalel תְּהַלֵּל ר"ת כהת, משיזו בן דוד ע"ה

יָהּ Yah הַלְלוּיָהּ haleluya אלהים, אהיה אדני ; ללה :

THE FIFTH PSALM

"Praise the Lord! Praise Him in His Sanctuary; praise Him in the firmaments of His might; praise Him by His valorous deeds; praise Him according to His bountiful greatness; praise Him with blowing the Shofar; praise Him with lyre and harp; praise Him with drum and dance; praise Him with instruments and pipe; Praise Him with the sound of cymbals; praise Him with reverberating sounds. All the souls praise God. Praise Him! All the souls praise God. Praise Him!" (Psalms 150)

BARUCH

Each of these four verses is a conduit to the four letters in *Yud, Hei, Vav*, and *Hei* (יהוה), helping us make the jump to the upper part of the World of Formation – *Atzilut* of *Yetzirah*.

י

בָּרוּךְ baruch יְהֹוָה Adonai לְעוֹלָם le'olam רִיבוּעַ דס״ג ו״י אותיות דס״ג

אָמֵן amen יאהדונהי ; וְאָמֵן ve'amen יאהדונהי ר״ת ; לאו:

ה

בָּרוּךְ baruch יְהֹוָה Adonai מִצִּיּוֹן miTziyon יוסף, ו׳ הויות, קנאה

שֹׁכֵן shochen יְרוּשָׁלָיִם Yerushalayim הַלְלוּיָהּ haleluya אלהים, אהיה אדני ; ללה:

ו

בָּרוּךְ baruch יְהֹוָה Adonai אֱלֹהִים Elohim אהיה אדני ; ילה

אֱלֹהֵי Elohei מילוי דע״ב, דמב ; ילה יִשְׂרָאֵל Yisrael

עֹשֵׂה ose נִפְלָאוֹת nifla'ot לְבַדּוֹ levado שם בן מ״ב:

ה

וּבָרוּךְ uvaruch שֵׁם shem כְּבוֹדוֹ kevodo לְעוֹלָם le'olam רִיבוּעַ דס״ג ו״י אותיות דס״ג

וְיִמָּלֵא veyimale כְבוֹדוֹ chevodo אֶת־ et כָּל־ kol ילי

הָאָרֶץ ha'aretz אלהים דההין ע״ה amen אָמֵן יאהדונהי ve'amen וְאָמֵן יאהדונהי:

VAY'VARECH DAVID - THE HIGHEST POINT OF THE WORLD OF FORMATION (YETZIRAH)

The kabbalists teach us that there are two prerequisites for activating the power of a prayer:
1) Understanding the inner significance of the prayer, and
2) Certainty that the prayer will produce the Light and energy that it is designed to generate.

This next prayer imbues us with the power of certainty. *Vadai* ודאי (certainty) is created by the first letter of each of the first four words of this prayer. Everyone who recites this prayer arouses an intense feeling of certainty in their life. If we are not certain that the prayer will work, it won't. Satan's job is to fill us with uncertainty every chance he gets, even as we read these words. This prayer combats our doubts and uncertainties, and fills us with conviction and certitude.

Tikkun of Atzilut of Yetzirah.

Until the Song of the Sea we have ten times the Name: יהוה, five for *Chasadim* and five for *Gevurot.*

Stand when reciting "*vayvarech David.*"

וַיְבָרֶךְ vay'varech ע"ב מ"ה ב"ן, הברכה (למתק את ז' המלכים שמותו) David דָּוִד

אֶת־ et (בשם זה עלה משה למרום) ר"ת ודאי (=אהיה) (אדני•יאהדונהי) Adonai (First Chesed) לַיהֹוָ֨ה

הַקָּהָל hakahal ילי kol כָּל le'enei לְעֵינֵי (וזולתה ממלאכי מגן והוא) ריבוע מ"ה לְעֵינֵי

וַיֹּאמֶר vayomer David דָּוִד ר"ת = אדני baruch בָּרוּךְ Ata אַתָּה

אֱלֹהֵי Elohei (Second Chesed) Adonai (אדני•יאהדונהי) יְהֹוָ֨ה מילוי ע"ב, דמב ; ילה

יִשְׂרָאֵל Yisrael יהוה אלהי ישראל = תרי"ג (מצוות) avinu אָבִינוּ me'olam מֵעוֹלָם

וְעַד־ ve'ad olam עוֹלָם lecha לְךָ (אדני•יאהדונהי) יְהֹוָ֨ה Adonai (Third Chesed)

הַגְּדֻלָּה hagedula vehagevura וְהַגְּבוּרָה רי"ו vehatiferet וְהַתִּפְאֶרֶת

וְהַנֵּצַח vehanetzach vehahod וְהַהוֹד יהוה ki כִּי chol כָּל ילי

הַמַּמְלָכָה hamamlacha (Fourth Chesed) Adonai (אדני•יאהדונהי) יְהֹוָ֨ה bashamayim בַּשָּׁמַיִם י"פ טל, י"פ י"פ כוזו uva'aretz וּבָאָרֶץ lecha לְךָ

וְהַמִּתְנַשֵּׂא vehamitnase lechol לְכֹל יה אדני lerosh לְרֹאשׁ ריבוע אלהים ואלהים דיודין

וְהָעֹשֶׁר veha'osher עיה: vehakavod וְהַכָּבוֹד לאו milfanecha מִלְּפָנֶיךָ ס"ג מ"ה ב"ן

VAY'VARECH DAVID

"Then David blessed the Lord before the eyes of the whole congregation. David said: Blessed are You, Lord, the God of Israel, our Father, forever until eternity. Yours, Lord, are the greatness, the power, the glory, the victory, and the splendor. Everything in the Heavens and Earth is Yours. Yours, Lord, is the kingship; You are over all those who ascend to lead. The riches and honors are before You;

וְאַתָּה veAta מוֹשֵׁל moshel בַּכֹּל bakol   ב"ן, לכב ; ר"ת ומב

> On *Chol Hamo'ed* one should give here three coins to charity. The first coin corresponds to *Leah*, the second coin corresponds to *Malchut* of *Binah* which is in the head of *Zeir Anpin* (where *Leah* comes from) and the third coin corresponds to *Rachel*, the lower *Nukva*.

וּבְיָדְךָ uvyadcha כֹּחַ ko'ach וּגְבוּרָה ugvura   רי"ו ; ר"ת בוכו (אהיה)

וּבְיָדְךָ uvyadcha לְגַדֵּל legadel וּלְחַזֵּק ulchazek לְכֹל lakol   פהל   יה אדני:

וְעַתָּה ve'ata אֱלֹהֵינוּ Elohenu מוֹדִים modim   ילה כנגד מאה ברכות שתיקן דוד

אֲנַחְנוּ anachnu לָךְ lach וּמְהַלְלִים um'halelim לְשֵׁם leshem   לאמרם כל יום

תִּפְאַרְתֶּךָ tifartecha וִיבָרְכוּ vivarchu שֵׁם shem   יהוה ריבוע יהוה ריבוע מ"ה

כְּבוֹדֶךָ kevodecha וּמְרוֹמֵם umromam עַל al כָּל kol   ב"ן, לכב ; ילי ; עמם

בְּרָכָה beracha וּתְהִלָּה ut'hila   ע"ה אמת, אהיה פעמים אהיה, ז"פ ס"ג:

אַתָּה Ata הוּא hu יְהֹוָה Adonai (Fifth Chesed) לְבַדֶּךָ levadecha

אַתָּה ata עָשִׂיתָ asita אֶת et הַשָּׁמַיִם hashamayim שָׁמֵי shemei   י"פ טל, י"פ כוזו

הַשָּׁמַיִם hashamayim וְכָל vechol צְבָאָם tzeva'am   י"פ טל, י"פ כוזו ; ילי

הָאָרֶץ ha'aretz וְכָל vechol אֲשֶׁר asher עָלֶיהָ aleha   אלהים דההין ע"ה ; ילי ; פהל

הַיָּמִים hayamim וְכָל vechol אֲשֶׁר asher בָּהֶם bahem   נלך ; ילי

וְאַתָּה veAta מְחַיֶּה mechaye אֶת et כֻּלָּם kulam וּצְבָא utzva   ס"א

הַשָּׁמַיִם hashamayim לְךָ lecha מִשְׁתַּחֲוִים mishtachavim   י"פ טל, י"פ כוזו ; ר"ת מלה:

אַתָּה Ata הוּא hu יְהֹוָה Adonai (First Gevurah) הָאֱלֹהִים haElohim

אֲשֶׁר asher (stand until here) בָּחַרְתָּ bacharta   אהיה אדני ; ילה ; ר"ת אהיה

You rule over everything. In Your Hand are powers and might. And it is in Your Hand to make great and to give strength to all. Now, our God, we are grateful to You and praise the Name of Your splendors." (1 Chronicles 29:10-13) "And they shall bless the Name of Your glory, which is exalted above all blessing and praise. It is You, alone, Who is the Lord. You made the Heavens, the highest Heavens and all their hosts, the Earth and all that is upon it, the seas and all that they contain, and You sustain life in them all. And the hosts of the Heavens prostrate themselves before You It is You, Lord, the God, Who chose

Kasdim כַּשְׂדִּים   meUr מֵאוּר   vehotzeto וְהוֹצֵאתוֹ   beAvram בְּאַבְרָם

וְשַׂמְתָּ vesamta   שְׁמוֹ shemo   מהש ע"ה, ע"ב בריבוע וקס"א ע"ה, אל שדי ע"ה

אַבְרָהָם Avraham   וז"פ אל, רי"ו ול"ב נתיבות החכמה, רמ"ח (אברים), עסמ"ב וט"ז אותיות פשוטות:

lefanecha לְפָנֶיךָ   ne'eman נֶאֱמָן   levavo לְבָבוֹ   et אֶת   umatzata וּמָצָאתָ

et אֶת   latet לָתֵת   haberit הַבְּרִית   imo עִמּוֹ   vecharot וְכָרוֹת   ס"ג מ"ה ב"ן

haEmori הָאֱמֹרִי   haChiti הַחִתִּי   haKena'ani הַכְּנַעֲנִי   eretz אֶרֶץ

latet לָתֵת   vehaGirgashi וְהַגִּרְגָּשִׁי   vehaYevusi וְהַיְבוּסִי   vehaPerizi וְהַפְּרִזִּי

ki כִּי   ראה   devarecha דְּבָרֶיךָ   et אֶת   vatakem וַתָּקֶם   lezar'o לְזַרְעוֹ

צַדִּיק tzadik   אָתָּה: Ata   וַתֵּרֶא vatere   אֶת et   עֳנִי oni   ריבוע מ"ה

za'akatam זַעֲקָתָם   ve'et וְאֶת   מצר   beMitzrayim בְּמִצְרָיִם   avotenu אֲבֹתֵינוּ

ב"פ כהת   vatiten וַתִּתֵּן   Suf סוּף: Yam יָם ילי   al עַל   shamata שָׁמַעְתָּ

ב"ן, לכב   uvchol וּבְכָל   beFar'oh בְּפַרְעֹה   umoftim וּמֹפְתִים   otot אֹתֹת

yadata יָדָעְתָּ   ki כִּי   artzo אַרְצוֹ   am עַם   ב"ן, לכב uvchol וּבְכָל   avadav עֲבָדָיו

shem שֵׁם   lecha לְךָ   vata'as וַתַּעַשׂ   alehem עֲלֵיהֶם   hezidu הֵזִידוּ   ki כִּי

ילי vehayam וְהַיָּם   והו haze הַזֶּה: ע"ה נגד, מזבוז, זך אל יהוה   kehayom כְּהַיּוֹם

vetoch בְּתוֹךְ   vaya'avru וַיַּעַבְרוּ   lifnehem לִפְנֵיהֶם   bakata בָּקַעְתָּ

rodfehem רֹדְפֵיהֶם   ve'et וְאֶת   bayabasha בַּיַּבָּשָׁה   ילי hayam הַיָּם

kemo כְּמוֹ   (שרו של מצרים) ר"ת רהב vimtzolot בִּמְצוֹלֹת   hishlachta הִשְׁלַכְתָּ

אֶבֶן even   ר"ת = אהיה   bemayim בְּמַיִם   עַזִּים azim   ר"ת ע"ב, ריבוע יהוה:

Abram and brought him out of Ur of the Chaldeans and made his name Abraham. You found his heart faithful before You, and You established the Covenant with him to give the land of the Canaanite, the Hittite, the Amorite, the Perizzite, the Jebusite, and the Girgashite - to give it to his descendants. You have kept Your promise, for You are righteous. You saw the afflictions of our forefathers in Egypt and You heard their cries at the Sea of Reeds. You performed signs and wonders against Pharaoh, all his servants, and all the people of his land, for You knew that they had sinned willfully against our forefathers. You thereby made for Yourself a Name as it is to this day. You then split the sea before them so that they crossed mid-sea, on dry land; their pursuers You cast into the depths, like a stone in turbulent waters." (Nechamiah 9:5-11)

VAYOSHA

When said with enormous happiness, "vayosha" has the power to remove negativity and make our tikkun process much easier. The tikkun process refers to the personal corrections that each person has come into this world to make. The corrections we must make are based on our negative, reactive behavior from this life and from past lives. Tikkun can include areas of finance, relationships, and health among others. We can identify our tikkun in all areas of our life by noticing where we experience the most difficulties.

bayom בַּיּוֹם (Second Gevurah) Adonai יְהוָֹאדניּיאהדונהי vayosha וַיּוֹשַׁע

Yisrael יִשְׂרָאֵל et אֶת־ hahu הַהוּא ר"ת ; = וז"י אל יהוה זְָ, מוֹבוֹ, נֶגֶר, ע"ה

vayar וַיַּרְא (יאהדונהי) אמן = ר"ת ; מצר Mitzrayim מִצְרַיִם miyad מִיַּד

al עַל־ met מֵת מצר Mitzrayim מִצְרַיִם et אֶת־ Yisrael יִשְׂרָאֵל

et אֶת־ Yisrael יִשְׂרָאֵל vayar וַיַּרְא ילי: hayam הַיָּם sefat שְׂפַת

asa עָשָׂה asher אֲשֶׁר אהיה ר"ת hagedola הַגְּדֹלָה וזהו hayad הַיָּד

מצר beMitzrayim בְּמִצְרָיִם (Third Gevurah) Adonai יְהוָֹאדניּיאהדונהי

(Fourth Gevurah) Adonai יְהוָֹאדניּיאהדונהי et אֶת־ ha'am הָעָם vayir'u וַיִּירְאוּ

ר"ת ; איוב (Fifth Gevurah) badonai בַּיהוָֹאדניּיאהדונהי vaya'aminu וַיַּאֲמִינוּ

uvMoshe וּבְמֹשֶׁה מהש, ע"ב בריבוע וקס"א, אל שדי, ד"פ אלהים ע"ה avdo עַבְדּוֹ:

THE 72 NAMES OF GOD

This chart shows the 72 Names of God. Moses used these sequences and formulas to connect to the true laws of nature—miracles and wonders—and remove all the obstacles that prevent mankind from connecting to them. This is how the Red Sea was split (Exodus 14:19-21). The splitting of the Red Sea is an expression of connection to the 99 Percent Realm where miracles are the norm. Simply by scanning these configurations of letters, we connect to our true nature and power. We become more proactive and move closer to the true purpose of our soul.

VAYOSHA

"And on that day, the Lord saved Israel from the hand of Egypt, and Israel saw the Egyptians dead at the seashore. Israel beheld the great Hand that the Lord had wrought against Egypt; and the people feared the Lord; they believed in the Lord and in Moses, His servant." (Exodus 14:30-31)

To scan: Begin at upper right (A-1) and scan each row right to left, ending in lower left (I-8).

←

8	7	6	5	4	3	2	1	
כהת	אכא	ללה	מהש	עלם	סיט	ילי	והו	A
הקם	הרי	מבה	יזל	ההע	לאו	אלד	הזי	B
וזהו	מלה	ייי	נלך	פהל	לוו	כלי	לאו	C
ועשר	לכב	אום	ריי	שאה	ירת	האא	נתה	D
ייז	רהע	וועם	אני	מנד	כוק	להוו	ויוו	E
מיה	עעל	ערי	סאל	ילה	וול	מיכ	ההה	F
פוי	מבה	נית	נגא	עמם	הוע	דני	והו	G
מוזי	ענו	יהה	ומב	מצר	הרוו	ייל	נמם	H
מום	היי	יבמ	ראה	וזבו	איע	מנק	דמב	I

SONG OF THE SEA - AZ YASHIR MOSHE

Moses and the Israelites sang this song after the splitting of the Red Sea. It is the song of the soul. Unfortunately, we lose touch with our soul when we are caught up in the material world. This prayer helps to awaken the memory and power of the original song that resides in the depths of our soul; because when we are connected to our soul, we can achieve anything.

Eighteen times the Name of God (יהוה or אדני) for the eighteen blessings of the Worlds of *Yetzirah*. You should meditate that these eighteen are the numerical value of the two letters *Tet* ט in Ma-tat-ron (**do not pronounce**) which is in *Zeir Anpin* of *Yetzirah*, as well as meditate on the nine *tikkuns* of *Zeir Anpin* of *Yetzirah*, nine of Direct Light and nine of Returning Light. (The same way we meditated in *Yehi Chevod* on pg. 137) You should also imagine that you crossed the Red Sea on that day. Saying it with happiness will cleanse all of our transgressions.

אָז yashir יָשִׁיר־ Moshe מֹשֶׁה מהע, ע"ב בריבוע וקס"א, אל עדי, אל אלהים ע"ה

וּבְנֵי uvnei יִשְׂרָאֵל Yisrael ר"ת ע"ה נגד, מזבוח, זן אל יהוה et אֶת־ הַשִּׁירָה hashira

הַזֹּאת hazot ladonai לַיהֹוָהֵי וַיֹּאמְרוּ vayomru (ארך) לַאמֹר lemor

אָשִׁירָה ashira ladonai לַיהֹוָהֵי (אפים) כִּי־ ki גָּאֹה ga'o גָּאָה ga'a

סוּס sus ריבוע אדני, כוק וְרֹכְבוֹ verochvo רָמָה rama בַיָּם vayam יל"י:

עָזִּי ozi אלהים ע"ה, אהיה אדני ע"ה וְזִמְרָת vezimrat יָהּ Yah וַיְהִי־ vayehi לִי li

לִישׁוּעָה lishu'a זֶה ze אֵלִי Eli וְאַנְוֵהוּ ve'anvehu (Meditate on the Holy Name: יהואל)

אֱלֹהֵי Elohei מילוי ע"ב, דמב; ילה אָבִי avi וַאֲרֹמְמֶנְהוּ va'aromemenhu: יהואל, לכב

SONG OF THE SEA - AZ YASHIR MOSHE

Moses and the Children of Israel sang this song to the Lord: I sing to the Lord because He became most exalted and flung the horse and its rider into the sea. My strength and my praise are God; He became my salvation. This is my God and I shall glorify Him, the God of my father; and I shall exalt Him

יְהֹוָהִאדְנֵיאהדונהי Adonai (וזסד) (ורב) אִישׁ ish מִלְחָמָה milchama

יְהֹוָהִאדְנֵיאהדונהי Adonai (נשא עון) שְׁמוֹ shemo מהטע ע"ה, ע"ב בריבוע וקס"א ע"ה, אל שדי ע"ה:

מַרְכְּבֹת markevot פַּרְעֹה Par'oh וְחֵילוֹ vechelo יָרָה yara בַיָּם vayam יל"י

וּמִבְחַר umivchar שָׁלִשָׁיו shalishav טֻבְּעוּ tube'u בְיַם־ veYam יל"י סוּף Suf:

תְּהֹמֹת tehomot יְכַסְיֻמוּ yechasyumu יָרְדוּ yardu בִמְצוֹלֹת vimtzolot

כְּמוֹ־ kemo אָבֶן aven ר"ת = אהיה: יְמִינְךָ yemincha יְהֹוָהִאדְנֵיאהדונהי Adonai

(ופשע) נֶאְדָּרִי ne'edari בַּכֹּחַ bako'ach ר"ת = ע"ב, ריבוע יהוה וס"ת = יגל

יְמִינְךָ yemincha יְהֹוָהִאדְנֵיאהדונהי Adonai (ונקה) תִּרְעַץ tir'atz אוֹיֵב oyev

גְּאוֹנְךָ ge'oncha י"פ אהיה (בזמנא דמלכא משיחא) וּבְרֹב uvrov (בומנא דמלכא איוב צרעת

תַּהֲרֹס taharos קָמֶיךָ kamecha (ביומי גוג ומגוג) תְּשַׁלַּח te'shalach

וַחֲרֹנְךָ charoncha יֹאכְלֵמוֹ yochlemo כַּקַּשׁ kakash (בעת תחיית המתים):

וּבְרוּחַ uvru'ach אַפֶּיךָ apecha נֶעֶרְמוּ ne'ermu מַיִם mayim ר"ת אמן (יאהדונהי):

נִצְּבוּ nitzevu כְמוֹ־ chemo נֵד ned ר"ת ק"כ צירופי אלהים נֹזְלִים nozlim

קָפְאוּ kaf'u תְהֹמֹת tehomot בְּלֶב־ belev יָם yam יל"י אָמַר amar אוֹיֵב oyev

אֶרְדֹף erdof אַשִּׂיג asig אֲחַלֵּק achalek שָׁלָל shalal תִּמְלָאֵמוֹ timla'emo

נַפְשִׁי nafshi אָרִיק arik חַרְבִּי charbi תּוֹרִישֵׁמוֹ torishemo יָדִי yadi:

נָשַׁפְתָּ nashafta בְרוּחֲךָ veruchacha ר"ת ב"ן כִּסָּמוֹ kisamo יָם yam יל"י

צָלֲלוּ tzalelu כַּעוֹפֶרֶת ka'oferet בְּמַיִם bemayim אַדִּירִים adirim הרי ; ר"ת קמ"ג:

The Lord is the Master of war – The Lord is His Name. The chariots of Pharaoh and his army, He cast into the sea and his select officers were sunk into the Sea of Reeds. The deep waters covered them and they sunk into the depths like a stone. Your right, Lord, is immensely powerful; Your right, Lord, smashes the enemy. With Your great ingenuity, You demolish those who rise against You. You send forth Your wrath and it consumes them like straw. And with the wing of Your anger, the waters were filled up; the flowing waters stood like a wall and the deep waters froze in the heart of the sea. The enemy said: I shall pursue, overtake, and divide the spoils. I shall satisfy my desires with them. I shall unsheathe my sword and my hand shall impoverish them. You blew with Your wind and the sea covered them. They sank like lead in the mighty waters.

(פוקד) Adonai יְהֹוָֹה/אֲדֹנָיֵאהדונהי ba'elim בָּאֵלִם chamocha כָּמֹכָה יְלִי mi מִי

ne'edar נֶאְדָּר kamocha כָּמֹכָה יְלִי mi מִי ; ס"ת מ"ה, ריבוע יהוה, ע"ב, = ר"ת

tehilot תְּהִלֹּת nora נוֹרָא bakodesh בַּקֹּדֶשׁ = יבק, אלהים יהוה, אהיה אדני יהוה = ר"ת

ose עֹשֵׂה fele פֶלֶא: natita נָטִיתָ yemincha יְמִינְךָ tivla'emo תִּבְלָעֵמוֹ

am עַם ר"ת ב"ן vechasdecha בְחַסְדְּךָ nachita נָחִיתָ aretz (זו מות) ר"ת נית

neve נְוֵה el אֶל ve'ozcha בְעָזְּךָ nehalta נֵהַלְתָּ ga'alta גָּאָלְתָּ zu זוּ

kodshecha קָדְשֶׁךָ ר"ת קנ"א ב"ן, יהוה אלהים יהוה אדני, מילוי קס"א וס"ג, מ"ה ברבוע וע"ב ע"ה:

achaz אָחַז ומב chil וָחִיל yirgazun יִרְגָּזוּן amim עַמִּים sham'u שָׁמְעוּ

nivhalu נִבְהֲלוּ az אָז (כוונות ישמעאל) Pelashet פְּלָשֶׁת yoshvei יֹשְׁבֵי

Mo'av מוֹאָב elei אֵילֵי (כוונות עשו) Edom אֱדוֹם alufei אַלּוּפֵי

(כוונות שאר כל השרים שהם נכנעים תחתיהם) ra'ad רָעַד yochazemo יֹאחֲזֵמוֹ

Chena'an כְּנָעַן: yoshvei יֹשְׁבֵי יְלִי kol כָּל namogu נָמֹגוּ

תִּפֹּל tipol alehem עֲלֵיהֶם emata אֵימָתָה vafachad וָפַחַד ר"ת שם קדוע תעא"י

bigdol בִּגְדֹל zero'acha זְרוֹעֲךָ yidemu יִדְּמוּ ka'aven כָּאָבֶן ר"ת = טל (יוד הא ואו)

ad עַד ya'avor יַעֲבֹר amecha עַמְּךָ Adonai יְהֹוָֹה/אֲדֹנָיֵאהדונהי (על עולמים)

tevi'emo תְּבִאֵמוֹ: kanita קָנִיתָ zu זוּ am עַם ya'avor יַעֲבֹר ad עַד

machon מָכוֹן nachalatcha נַחֲלָתְךָ ר"ת ב"ן behar בְּהַר vetita'emo וְתִטָּעֵמוֹ

leshivtecha לְשִׁבְתְּךָ pa'alta פָּעַלְתָּ Adonai יְהֹוָֹה/אֲדֹנָיֵאהדונהי (ועל רבעים) ר"ת

yadecha יָדֶיךָ: konenu כּוֹנְנוּ (ארך) Adonai אֲדֹנָי mikedash מִקְּדָשׁ ע"ה = קס"א

Who among the deities is like You, Lord; Who is like You, awesome in holiness, tremendous in praise, and Who works wonders! You stretched out Your right and the earth swallowed them. With Your kindness, You governed this nation that You redeemed. You led them with Your strength to Your holy Sanctuary. Nations heard and trembled. Terror seized the dwellers of Philistia. Then the leaders of Edom were frightened. The mighty ones of Moab were panic-stricken and the dwellers of Canaan withered away. Dread and fear fell upon them, by the greatness of Your arm. They became still, like stones, until Your nation crossed over, the Lord, until the nation that You adopted crossed over Bring them and settle them in the mountains of Your heritage, in that place of Your dwelling which You have made, Lord. Your Hands established the Temple of the Lord.

A 72 Name of God is encoded in this connection: *Yud, Yud, Lamed* ייל. This formula gives us the power of certainty and us the ability to let go, especially in the face of adversity. When things are going well, most of us find it easy to accept the idea of a Creator and a Cause and Effect principle at work in our universe. But when we face a sudden obstacle or stressful situation, we just as readily doubt the existence of a Creator and the teachings of Kabbalah. The kabbalists teach us that absolutely everything is a test. If we can maintain certainty in the Light when adversity strikes, we will pass the test and the Light will work for us 100% of the time. Satan's mission is to flood our minds with uncertainty. The *Yud, Yud, Lamed* wipes out all uncertainties, giving us the strength to recognize and pass our tests. A test will produce negative consequences only if we fail to recognize that the hardship is a test—and if we doubt the existence of the Creator.

le'olam לְעֹלָם	yimloch יִמְלֹךְ		(אפים) Adonai יְהֹוָ	
	ריבוע ס"ג ו' אותיות דס"ג ; ר"ת ייל	va'ed וָעֶד	(ורב וזסד) Adonai יְהֹוָ	
va'ed וָעֶד	ריבוע ס"ג ו' אותיות דס"ג ; ר"ת ייל	le'olam לְעֹלָם	yimloch יִמְלֹךְ
ka'em קָאִם	malchutei מַלְכוּתֵיהּ	(נשא עון) Adonai יְהֹוָ	
ul'almei וּלְעָלְמֵי le'alam לְעָלַם	al-maya עָלְמַיָּא	ki כִּי	va בָא sus סוּס ריבוע
bayam בַיָּם יֵלִי	uvfarashav וּבְפָרָשָׁיו	berichbo בְרִכְבּוֹ	Par'oh פַּרְעֹה אדני, כוך
mei מֵי et-אֶת alehem עֲלֵהֶם	(ופשע) Adonai יְהֹוָ	vayashev וַיָּשֶׁב
vayabasha בַיַּבָּשָׁה halchu הָלְכוּ	Yisrael יִשְׂרָאֵל	uvnei וּבְנֵי יֵלִי	hayam הַיָּם יֵלִי
betoch בְּתוֹךְ	hayam הַיָּם יֵלִי	ki כִּי	ladonai לַיְהֹוָ (ונקה)
umoshel וּמֹשֵׁל (הכלה שהיא למלכות רמו) כלה ר"ת	hamelucha הַמְּלוּכָה
Tziyon צִיּוֹן behar בְּהַר	moshi'im מוֹשִׁעִים	ve'alu וְעָלוּ	bagoyim בַּגּוֹיִם
vehayta וְהָיְתָה Esav עֵשָׂו	har הַר et אֶת lishpot לִשְׁפֹּט	יוסף, ו' הויות, קנאה
vehaya וְהָיָה יהוה ; יהה hamelucha הַמְּלוּכָה (פוקד) ladonai לַיְהֹוָ
kol כָּל עמם ; יֵלִי al-עַל lemelech לְמֶלֶךְ (על שלשים) Adonai יְהֹוָ
hahu הַהוּא אלהים ההון ז, אל יהוה עה"ה, מזבוח, גגד, עה"ה bayom בַּיּוֹם ha'aretz הָאָרֶץ
echad אֶחָד אהבה, דאגה (ועל רבעים) Adonai יְהֹוָ yihye יִהְיֶה ייי
echad אֶחָד אהבה, דאגה ushmo וּשְׁמוֹ מהש עה"ה, עה"ב בריבוע וקס"א עה"ה, אל שדי עה"ה

The Lord shall reign forever and for eternity. The Lord shall reign forever and for eternity." (Exodus 15:1-18) Lord your kingdom will reign forever and eternity. "For when Pharaoh's horses, chariots, and cavalry came into the sea, Lord turned the water upon them; and the children of Israel walked upon the dry land within the sea." (Exodus 15:19) "For the Kingdom belongs to the Lord and He rules over the nations." (Psalms 22:29) "And deliverers shall ascend Mount Zion to seek retribution from Mount Esav, and then the entire universe shall recognize the Kingship of the Lord." (Obadiah 1:21) "And the Lord shall then be King over the whole Earth and upon that day the Lord shall be One and His Name One." (Zechariah 14:9)

On Chol Hamo'ed (not on *Shabbat*) continue with *"Yishtabach"* on page 311.

NISHMAT KOL CHAI

There is always extra energy being released into our physical world during a holiday or on Shabbat. This particular connection builds up our internal Vessel so that we have both the capability to draw in this extra force and the capacity to handle what we draw in.

This praise is precious and exalted and you should say it in a pleasant manner. The kabbalists say that when a person goes through some trouble, problem or any danger - making a vow to say *"Nishmat Kol Chai"* will give that person great assistance.

If you forget and skip *"Nishmat Kol Chai"* and already say the blessing of *"Yishtabach,"* as long as you didn't start the next blessing *"Yotzer Or,"* you can go back and say *"Nishmat Kol Chai."* But if you start *"Yotzer Or,"* you should complete it after the end of the prayer without the blessing of *"Yishtabach."*

נִשְׁמַת nishmat כָּל kol וְזִי ילי chai

ר"ת נכוז כמס' ג' הויות יהוה יהוה יהוה

On *Shabbat* meditate to receive the extra soul called: *Nefesh*

from the aspect of the day of *Shabbat*, and scan the following meditations:

The three above mentioned יהוה are the three *Mochin - Chochmah, Binah, Da'at -* that are in the Surrounding of the letter *Mem* (מ) of the *Tzelem* (צל"ם) of *Abba*, as the *Mochin* from *Ima* already entered *Zeir Anpin*. So right now *Zeir Anpin* has all his Surrounding for *Abba* and *Ima* [of the letter *Mem* (מ) of the *Tzelem* (צל"ם)] and that is why we can now receive the extra soul of *Shabbat*.

כָּל וְזִי = וְזִיים, אהיה אהיה יהוה

תמורת תפילין הנקרא וזי המלך, והוא נשמה, כי בינה הוא בוחינת נשמה.

אטמון = ק"ו, ב"פ ב"ן (יוד הה וו הה) עם ב' כוללים.

קול = ר"ת ועשה לו כתנת פסים (להתיר הקול).

אלף הי יוד הי   אלף הא יוד הא   אלף הה יוד הה

ס"ת ועשה לו כתנת פסים עולה למנין קס"א קמ"ג קס"א קנ"א (עם ד' תיבות ועשה לו כתנת פסים).

גם יכוין: פסי"ם נוטריקון פסקו"ן סגרו"ן להוא'ל בטטרו"ן

פַּסְקוֹן (בניקוד ה' שפתי תפתוח)

סַגְרוֹן (יכוין ס"ג ורנו כנפי הוויות וניקו' ניקו' רנו שמים)

יְהוֹאֵל (according to the Rashash) לכב (יוצא מפסוק זה אלי ואנוהו הוא וניקודו)

בטטרו"ן (בניקוד ר"ת הנה הנה אנכי שולח מלאך לפניך)

תְּבָרֵךְ tevarech אֶת et שִׁמְךָ shimcha יְהוֹהָ (אדני אלהים אהיה) Adonai אֱלֹהֵינוּ Elohenu ילה

וְרוּחַ veru'ach כָּל kol יל בָּשָׂר basar תְּפָאֵר tefa'er וּתְרוֹמֵם utromem

זִכְרְךָ zichrecha מַלְכֵּנוּ malkenu תָּמִיד tamid ע"ה קס"א קס"א קנ"א קמ"ג (מילואי אהיה)

NISHMAT KOL CHAI

The soul of every living thing shall bless Your Name Lord, our God, and the spirit of all flesh shall always glorify and exalt Your remembrance, our King.

מִן min הָעוֹלָם ha'olam וְעַד ve'ad הָעוֹלָם ha'olam אַתָּה ata

אֵל El (מילוי דס״ג) יא״י אֵין en לָנוּ lanu אלהים, אהיה אדני וּמִבַּלְעָדֶיךָ umibal'adecha

מֶלֶךְ melech גּוֹאֵל go'el וּמוֹשִׁיעַ umoshi'a פּוֹדֶה pode וּמַצִּיל umatzil

וְעוֹנֶה ve'one וּמְרַחֵם umrachem אברהם, וז״פ אל, רי״ו ול״ב נתיבות החכמה, רמ״ח (אברים), (עסמ״ב וט״ז אותיות פשוטות)

בְּכָל bechol ב״ן, לכב עֵת et צָרָה tzara אלהים דההין

וְצוּקָה vetzuka אֵין en לָנוּ lanu אלהים, אהיה אדני מֶלֶךְ melech

עוֹזֵר ozer וְסוֹמֵךְ vesomech ריבוע אדני, כוק אֶלָּא ela אַתָּה ata:

אֱלֹהֵי Elohei מילוי דע״ב, דמב ; ילה הָרִאשׁוֹנִים harishonim

וְהָאַחֲרוֹנִים veha'acharonim מ״ב Eloha אֱלוֹהַּ ילי kol כָּל בְּרִיּוֹת beriyot

אֲדוֹן adon אני kol כָּל ילי תּוֹלָדוֹת toladot הַמְהֻלָּל hamehulal

בְּכָל bechol ב״ן, לכב הַתִּשְׁבָּחוֹת hatishbachot הַמְנַהֵג hamenaheg

עוֹלָמוֹ olamo בְּחֶסֶד bechesed ע״ב, ריבוע יהוה וּבְרִיּוֹתָיו uvriyotav

בְּרַחֲמִים berachamim מצפצ, אלהים דיודין, י״פ יייי וַיְיָ ויאהדונהיאדני vadonai

אֱלֹהִים Elohim אהיה אדני ; ילה אֱמֶת emet אהיה פעמים אהיה, ז״פ ס״ג

לֹא lo דא״א נהורין ש״ע יָנוּם yanum וְלֹא velo יִישָׁן yishan

הַמְּעוֹרֵר hame'orer יְשֵׁנִים yeshenim וְהַמֵּקִיץ vehamekitz נִרְדָּמִים nirdamim

מְחַיֶּה mechaye ס״ג מֵתִים metim וְרוֹפֵא verofe חוֹלִים cholim חזלה =

פּוֹקֵחַ poke'ach מה עם ד׳ אותיות וְזוֹקֵף vezokef עִוְרִים ivrim כְּפוּפִים kefupim

הַמֵּשִׂיחַ hamesi'ach אִלְּמִים ilmim וְהַמְפַעֲנֵחַ vehamfa'ane'ach

נֶעְלָמִים ne'elamim וּלְךָ ulcha לְבַדְּךָ levadcha אֲנַחְנוּ anachnu

מוֹדִים modim כנגד מאה ברכות שתיקן דוד לאמרם כל יום:

From this world to the World to Come, You are God. And apart from You, we have no king, redeemer, or savior. He Who liberates, rescues, sustains, answers and is merciful in every time of distress and anguish, we have no king, helper or supporter but You, God of the first and of the last, God of all creatures, Master of all generations, Who is extolled through a multitude of praises, and Who guides His world with kindness and His creatures with mercy. And the Lord, God, is true and He neither slumbers nor sleeps. He Who arouses the ones who sleep, and awakens the slumberers. He Who resurrects the dead, and heals the sick. He gives sight to the blind and straightens the ones who are bent. He makes the mute speak and uncovers the hidden. And to You alone, we give thanks.

וְאִלּוּ ve'ilu   פִינוּ finu   מָלֵא male   שִׁירָה shira   כַּיָּם kayam   יל"י

וּלְשׁוֹנֵנוּ ulshonenu   רִנָּה rina   כַּהֲמוֹן kahamon   גַּלָּיו galav

וְשִׂפְתוֹתֵינוּ vesiftoteinu   שֶׁבַח shevach   כְּמֶרְחֲבֵי kemerchavei   רָקִיעַ raki'a

וְעֵינֵינוּ ve'enenu   רִיבוע מ"ה   מְאִירוֹת me'irot   כַּשֶּׁמֶשׁ kashemesh

וְכִירוֹן kenishrei   כְּנִשְׁרֵי   פְרוּשׂוֹת ferusot   וְיָדֵינוּ veyadenu   וְכַיָּרֵחַ vechayare'ach

שָׁמָיִם shamayim   י"פ טל, י"פ כוזו   וְרַגְלֵינוּ veragleinu   קָלוֹת kalot

כָּאַיָּלוֹת ka'ayalot   אֵין en   אֲנַחְנוּ anachnu   מַסְפִּיקִין maspikin

לְהוֹדוֹת lehodot   לְךָ lecha   יְהֹוָה Adonai   אֱלֹהֵינוּ Elohenu   יל"ה

וּלְבָרֵךְ ulvarech   אֶת et   שִׁמְךָ shimcha   מַלְכֵּנוּ malkenu   עַל al

אַחַת achat   מֵאֶלֶף me'elef   מספר אֶלֶף = אלף למד פא ה"ה יוד יוד דלת דלת ע"ה   אַלְפֵי alfei

הַטּוֹבוֹת hatovot   אֲלָפִים alafim   וְרוֹב verov   רִבֵּי ribei   רְבָבוֹת revavot   פְּעָמִים pe'amim

עִמָּנוּ imanu   רִיבוע קס"א, ע"ב, וד' אותיות   וְעִם ve'im   אֲבוֹתֵינוּ avotenu

מִלְּפָנִים milfanim   בְּמִצְרַיִם miMitzrayim   מצר   גְּאַלְתָּנוּ ge'altanu

יְהֹוָה Adonai   אֱלֹהֵינוּ Elohenu   יל"ה   מִבֵּית mibet   ב"פ ראה

עֲבָדִים avadim   פְּדִיתָנוּ peditanu   בְּרָעָב bera'av   זַנְתָּנוּ zantanu

וּבְשָׂבָע uvsava   כִּלְכַּלְתָּנוּ kilkaltanu   מֵחֶרֶב mecherev   הִצַּלְתָּנוּ hitzaltanu

מִדֶּבֶר midever   מִלַּטְתָּנוּ milatetanu   וּמֵחֳלָאִים umechola'im   רָעִים ra'im

וְרַבִּים verabim   דִּלִּיתָנוּ dilitanu   עַד ad   הֵנָּה hena   עֲזָרוּנוּ azarunu

רַחֲמֶיךָ rachamecha   וְלֹא velo   עֲזָבוּנוּ azavunu   וַחֲסָדֶיךָ chasadecha

---

Were our mouth as full of song as the sea and our tongue as full of joyous song as its multitude of waves, and our lips as full of praise as the breadth of the firmament, and our eyes as brilliant as the sun and the moon, and our hands as outspread as eagles of the skies and our legs as swift as hinds, We still cannot thank You enough, Lord, our God, and bless Your Name, our King, for even one of the thousands upon thousands of thousands and of the myriad upon myriad of myriad of favors, miracles and wonders that You performed for our ancestors and for us. From within Egypt, You have redeemed us, Lord, our God, and liberated us from the house of bondage. In famine You nourished us and in plenty, You sustained us. From the sword You saved us and from plague You let us escape and from severe numerous and enduring diseases, You spared us. Until now Your mercy has helped us and Your kindness has not forsaken us.

עַל al — כֵּן ken — אֵבָרִים evarim — שֶׁפִּלַּגְתָּ shepilagta — בָּנוּ banu

וְרוּחַ veru'ach — וּנְשָׁמָה unshama — שֶׁנָּפַחְתָּ shenafachta — בְּאַפֵּינוּ be'apenu

וְלָשׁוֹן velashon — אֲשֶׁר asher — שַׂמְתָּ samta — בְּפִינוּ befinu

הֵן hen — הֵם hem — יוֹדוּ yodu — וִיבָרְכוּ vivarchu

וִישַׁבְּחוּ vishabechu — וִיפָאֲרוּ vifa'aru — אֶת et — שִׁמְךָ shimcha — מַלְכֵּנוּ malkenu

תָּמִיד tamid — פֶּה pe — כָּל chol — כִּי ki

לְךָ lecha — יוֹדֶה yode — וְכָל vechol — לָשׁוֹן lashon — לְךָ lecha

תְּשַׁבֵּחַ te'shabe'ach — וְכָל vechol — עַיִן ayin — לְךָ lecha — תְּצַפֶּה tetzape

וְכָל vechol — בֶּרֶךְ berech — לְךָ lecha — תִכְרַע tichra

וְכָל vechol — קוֹמָה koma — לְפָנֶיךָ lefanecha — תִּשְׁתַּחֲוֶה tishtachave

וְהַלְּבָבוֹת vehalevavot — יִירָאוּךָ yira'ucha — וְהַקֶּרֶב vehakerev

וְהַכְּלָיוֹת vehakelayot — יְזַמְּרוּ yezameru — לִשְׁמֶךָ lishmecha — כַּדָּבָר kadavar

שֶׁנֶּאֱמַר shene'emar — כָּל kol — עַצְמוֹתַי atzmotai — תֹּאמַרְנָה tomarna

יְהֹוָה Adonai — מִי mi — כָמוֹךָ chamocha — מַצִּיל matzil — עָנִי ani

מֵחָזָק mechazak — מִמֶּנּוּ mimenu — וְעָנִי ve'ani — וְאֶבְיוֹן ve'evyon

מִגֹּזְלוֹ migozlo — שַׁוְעַת shavat — עֲנִיִּים aniyim — עַיִן ayin — אַתָּה ata

תִּשְׁמַע tishma — צַעֲקַת tza'akat — הַדַּל hadal — תַּקְשִׁיב takshiv — וְתוֹשִׁיעַ vetoshi'a

וְכָתוּב vechatuv — רַנְּנוּ ranenu — צַדִּיקִים tzadikim — בַּיהֹוָה badonai

לַיְשָׁרִים laysharim — נָאוָה nava — תְהִלָּה tehila

Therefore, organs that You have spread within us, and spirit and soul that You have breathed into our nostrils, and the tongue that You placed in our mouth, it is they that shall thank, bless, praise, and glorify Your Name, our King, forever. For every mouth shall offer thanks to You and every tongue shall say praise to You, And every eye shall look towards You. And every knee shall bend to You. And every erect form shall prostrate itself before You. And the hearts shall fear You. And the inner organs and the kidneys shall sing to Your Name, as it is written: All my bones shall say. Lord, who is like You? "You save the poor man from one stronger than he, and the poor and the destitute from one who wants to rob him." (Psalms 35:10) *You hear the outcry of the poor and You listen to the screams of the destitute and You save. And it is written: "Sing joyfully, righteous ones, before the Lord, for the upright praise is befitting."* (Psalms 33:1)

ISAAC AND RIVKAH

Isaac the Patriarch successfully prayed for his wife Rivkah to have a baby. All of us, especially at this juncture, pray for others who are in need of financial, health, personal, or emotional sustenance. The only way our own prayers will be answered is for us to pray for others with a genuine heart.

The next four verses correspond to the four pillars that carry the Throne of *Beriah* which the Ten *Sefirot* of *Atzilut* stand on. Also, the four verses stand for the Throne of *Beriah* itself which includes the three Patriarchs (*Chesed, Gevurah, Tiferet*) and King David (*Malchut*).

פדאל	קדמיאל	מיכאל	
titromam תִּתְרוֹמָם	yesharim יְשָׁרִים	befi בְּפִי	**Right** *Avraham*
וסדיאל	צדקיאל	גבריאל	
titbarach תִּתְבָּרֵךְ	tzadikim צַדִּיקִים	uvsiftei וּבְשִׂפְתֵי	**Left** *Yitzchak*
סטטרויה	רזיאל	רפאל	
titkadash תִּתְקַדֵּשׁ	chasidim וַחֲסִידִים	uvilshon וּבִלְשׁוֹן	**East** *Yaakov*
ענאל	יופיאל	נוריאל	
tit'halal תִּתְהַלָּל	kedoshim קְדוֹשִׁים	uvkerev וּבְקֶרֶב	**Fourth** *David*

bet בֵּית ב"פ ראה amcha עַמְּךָ rivevot רִבְבוֹת bemikhalot בְּמִקְהֲלוֹת
hayetzurim הַיְצוּרִים ילי kol כָּל chovat וְחוֹבַת sheken שֶׁכֵּן Yisrael יִשְׂרָאֵל
Elohenu אֱלֹהֵינוּ ילה Adonai יְהֹוָה ב"ן מ"ה ס"ג lefanecha לְפָנֶיךָ
avotenu אֲבוֹתֵינוּ ילה ; דמ"ב, דע"ב, מילוי ; לכב velohei וֵאלֹהֵי
leshabe'ach לְשַׁבֵּחַ ללה, אדני, lehalel לְהַלֵּל lehodot לְהוֹדוֹת
ulnatze'ach וּלְנַצֵּחַ lehader לְהַדֵּר leromem לְרוֹמֵם lefa'er לְפָאֵר
vetishbachot וְתִשְׁבָּחוֹת shirot שִׁירוֹת ראה divrei דִּבְרֵי עמם ילי kol כָּל al עַל
meshichecha מְשִׁיחֶךָ אל אדני פוי avdecha עַבְדְּךָ Yishai יִשַׁי ben בֶּן David דָּוִד

ISAAC AND RIVKAH

By the mouths of the upright, You shall be exalted.
And by the lips of the righteous, You shall be blessed.
And by the tongues of the pious, You shall be sanctified.
And among the holy ones, You shall be lauded.

And in the assemblies of the myriad of Your nation, the House of Israel, for such is the duty of all the creatures before You, Lord, our God and the God of our forefathers, to thank and to laud, to praise, glorify, exalt, adore and to render triumphant even beyond all expressions of the songs and praises of David, the son of Ishai, Your servant, Your anointed.

YISHTABACH

Now that we have split the Red Sea, our next level of connection is the World of Creation (*Beriah*). The first word, *Yishtabach* יִשְׁתַּבַּח has a numerical value of 720, or ten times the 72 Names of God (10 x 72). By reciting *Yishtabach,* we receive the power of King Solomon, that of wisdom. Solomon שְׁלֹמֹה is encoded in the next group of words and letters as shown below. Also, the first letters of each of the last five lines of this prayer spell out the name Abraham. Abraham denotes the power of sharing. We use the power of Solomon and Abraham—wisdom and sharing—to help us make the jump to the World of Creation.

The praise of *Yishtabach* is immense and awesome. It consists of 13 praises for the 13 Attributes of *Beriah* and the 13 *Sefirot* of *Yetzirah*. You should say the words slowly and gently and count them with the fingers of your right hand. Be careful not to stop between counting the 13 for any reason. And if you have to stop for any reason, you should go back and count them again from the beginning ("*ki lecha na'e*") in order to say them in one breath as mentioned in the *Zohar*.

On *Chol Hamo'ed* (not on *Shabbat*) we skip the word "*uvchen*" and start from the word "*Yishtabach*."

עְ"ב, רִיבּוּעַ יְהוה uvchen וּבְכֵן

malkenu מַלְכֵּנוּ בּ"פ בּ"ן la'ad לָעַד shimcha שִׁמְךָ יְ"פ עְ"ב yishtabach יִשְׁתַּבַּח

(King Solomon) hamelech הַמֶּלֶךְ (מִילוּי דס"ג) יְיא"י ; לאה haEl הָאֵל

vehakadosh וְהַקָּדוֹשׁ אום, יזל, מבה = אוֹתִיּוֹת ד' עִם ; לְהוּ hagadol הַגָּדוֹל

na'e נָאֶה lecha לְךָ ki כִּי uva'aretz וּבָאָרֶץ יְ"פ כוזו, יְ"פ טל, יְ"פ bashamayim בַּשָּׁמַיִם

יְהֹוהִאדְנֹיאהדונהי ; מִילוּי עְ"ב, דמב ; ילה velohei וֵאלֹהֵי ילה Elohenu אֱלֹהֵינוּ Adonai אֲדֹנָי

va'ed וָעֶד דס"ג אוֹתִיּוֹת וי, ס"ג רִיבּוּעַ le'olam לְעוֹלָם avotenu אֲבוֹתֵינוּ

אדני, (וּוֹזָוֹן) halel הַלֵּל (3 (רוֹזָוֹם) ushvacha וּשְׁבָחָה (2 (אל) shir שִׁיר (1

(וְרַב וָחֶסֶד) umemshala וּמֶמְשָׁלָה (6 (אפּים) oz עֹז (5 (ארך) vezimra וְזִמְרָה (4

gevura גְּבוּרָה (9 (נצר וָחֶסֶד) gedula גְּדֻלָּה (8 (ואמת) netzach נֶצַח (7

ז"פ ס"ג, אהיה פְּעָמִים אהיה אמת, עְ"ה (נשא עון) tehila תְּהִלָּה (10 רְיו"י (לאלפים)

YISHTABACH

And so, may Your Name be praised forever,
our King, the God, the great and Holy King, Who is in the Heavens and on the Earth. For to You are befitting, Lord, our God and the God of our forefathers, 1) song 2) and praise 3) exultation 4) and melody 5) power 6) and dominion 7) eternity 8) greatness 9) valor 10) praise

(11 וְתִפְאֶרֶת vetif'eret   (וּפֶשַׁע)•   (12 קְדֻשָׁה kedusha   (וְחֵטְא)•

(13 וּמַלְכוּת umalchut   (וּנְקֵה)•   בְּרָכוֹת berachot   וְהוֹדָאוֹת vehoda'ot

לְשִׁמְךָ leshimcha הַגָּדוֹל hagadol לְהוּ ; עִם ד' אוֹתִיּוֹת = מבה, יזל, אום

וְהַקָּדוֹשׁ vehakadosh•   וּמֵעוֹלָם ume'olam וְעַד ve'ad עוֹלָם olam

אַתָּה Ata   אֵל El   יא"י (מִלוּי דס"ג)• בָּרוּךְ baruch   אַתָּה Ata

יְהֹוָה(אדני)(יְהֹוָה)(אדני)אהדונהי Adonai מֶלֶךְ melech גָּדוֹל gadol לְהוּ ; עִם ד' אוֹתִיּוֹת =

מבה, יזל, אום יא"י (מִלוּי דס"ג) אֵל El• בַּתִּשְׁבָּחוֹת batishbachot וּמְהֻלָּל umehulal

בּוֹרֵא bore   הַנִּפְלָאוֹת hanifla'ot• אני אָדוֹן adon הַהוֹדָאוֹת• hahoda'ot

כָּל kol ילי הַנְּשָׁמוֹת haneshamot• רִבּוֹן ribon יהוה ע"ב ס"ג מ"ה ב"ן כָּל kol ילי

הַמַּעֲשִׂים hama'asim• הַבּוֹחֵר habocher בְּשִׁירֵי beshirei זִמְרָה zimra•

מֶלֶךְ melech (Abraham) אֵל El יא"י (מִלוּי) דס"ג

וְזִי chei (לְפִי הָאֲרִיז"ל, וְזִי לְפִי הָרש"ע) הָעוֹלָמִים ha'olamim: אָמֵן amen• יאהדונהי

---

11) and glory 12) holiness 13) and sovereignty. Blessings and thanksgiving to Your great and Holy Name from this world to the World to Come. You are God. Blessed are You, Lord, King, Who is great and lauded with praise. God of thanksgiving. Master of the wonders. Creator of the souls. Master of all deeds. One Who chooses melodious songs of praise. The King, the God Who gives life to all the worlds, Amen.

HALF KADDISH

The secret of this half *Kaddish* is that it elevates us from *Yetzirah* (מ"ה) to *Beriah* (ס"ג).

יתגד״ל וְיִתְקַדַּשׁ veyitkadash שׂדי ומילוי שׂדי ; י"א אותיות כמנין ו"ה yitgadal יִתְגַּדַּל

(עם י"ה דע"ב) רַבָּא raba קנ"א ב"ן, יהוה אלהים יהוה אדני, shemei שְׁמֵיהּ

מילוי קס"א וס"ג, מ"ה ברבוע וע"ב ע"ה ; ר"ת = ו"פ אלהים ; ס"ת = ג"פ יב"ק: amen אָמֵן אידהנויה.

be'alma בְּעָלְמָא di דִּי vera בְּרָא chir'utei כִרְעוּתֵיהּ

veyamlich וְיַמְלִיךְ mal'chutei מַלְכוּתֵיהּ veyatzmach וְיַצְמַח

purkanei פוּרְקָנֵיהּ vikarev וִיקָרֵב meshichei מְשִׁיחֵיהּ amen אָמֵן אידהנויה.

bechayechon בְּחַיֵּיכוֹן uvyomechon וּבְיוֹמֵיכוֹן uvchayei וּבְחַיֵּי

dechol דְּכָל bet בֵּית ילי ב"פ ראה Yisrael יִשְׂרָאֵל ba'agala בַּעֲגָלָא

uvizman וּבִזְמַן kariv קָרִיב ve'imru וְאִמְרוּ amen אָמֵן :amen אָמֵן אידהנויה.

The congregation and the *chazan* say the following:

Twenty eight words (until *be'alma*), meditate: מילוי דמילוי דע"ב (יוד ויו דלת הי יוד ויו יוד ויו הי יוד)
Twenty eight letters (until *almaya*), meditate: מילוי דמילוי דס"ג (יוד ויו דלת הי יוד ואו אלף ואו הי יוד)

yehe יְהֵא shemei שְׁמֵיהּ (עם י"ה דס"ג) raba רַבָּא קנ"א ב"ן,

mevarach מְבָרַךְ יהוה אלהים יהוה אדני, מילוי קס"א וס"ג, מ"ה ברבוע וע"ב ע"ה

le'alam לְעָלַם le'almei לְעָלְמֵי almaya עָלְמַיָּא yitbarach יִתְבָּרַךְ

Seven words with six letters each (עם בן מ"ב) meditate:
יהוה + יוד הי ויו הי + מילוי דמילוי דע"ב (יוד ויו דלת הי יוד ויו יוד ויו הי יוד)
Also, seven times the letter *Vav* (עם בן מ"ב) meditate:
יהוה + יוד הי ואו הי + מילוי דמילוי דס"ג (יוד ויו דלת הי יוד ואו אלף ואו הי יוד).

veyishtabach וְיִשְׁתַּבַּח י"פ ע"ב יהוה אל אבג יתץ.

veyitpa'ar וְיִתְפָּאַר הי גו יה קרע שטן. veyitromam וְיִתְרֹמַם וה כוזו נגד יכש.

veyitnase וְיִתְנַשֵּׂא במוכסז בטר צתג. veyit'hadar וְיִתְהַדָּר כוזו יה וזקב טנע.

veyit'ale וְיִתְעַלֶּה וה יוד ה יגל פזק. veyit'halal וְיִתְהַלָּל א ואו הא שקו צית.

shemei שְׁמֵיהּ (עם י"ה דמ"ה) dekudsha דְּקוּדְשָׁא verich בְּרִיךְ hu הוּא:

amen אָמֵן אידהנויה.

HALF KADDISH

May His great Name be more exalted and sanctified. (Amen) In the world that He created according to His will, and may His Kingdom reign. And may He cause His redemption to sprout and may He bring the Mashiach closer. (Amen) In your lifetimes and in your days and in the lifetime of all the House of Israel, speedily and in the near future, and you should say, Amen. (Amen) May His great Name be blessed forever and for all eternity blessed and lauded, and glorified and exalted, and extolled and honored, and uplifted and praised be, the Name of the Holy Blessed One. (Amen)

לְעֵלָּא le'ela מִן min כָּל ילי kol כֹּל בִּרְכָתָא birchata שִׁירָתָא shirata

תֻּשְׁבְּחָתָא tishbechata וְנֶחָמָתָא venechamata דַּאֲמִירָן da'amiran

בְּעָלְמָא be'alma וְאִמְרוּ ve'imru אָמֵן amen אָמֵן amen אידהנויה.

BARCHU

When we enter the World of Creation *(Beriah)*, we recite the *Barchu* (you should bless). This powerful connection brings back the part of our soul that left us while we slept. Even if a person remains awake, a part of his soul still leaves during the night. There are five words in the *Barchu* that connect us to the five parts of our soul. Each part of the soul is connected to one of the five worlds.

The *chazan* says:

בָּרְכוּ barchu יהוה ריבוע יהוה ריבוע מ"ה אֶת et יְהֹוָאֲדֹנִיאהדונהי Adonai

הַמְּבֹרָךְ hamevorach ס"ת כהת, מש"ויו בן דוד ע"ה:

While the *chazan* says the verse "*barchu*," the congregation says "*yishtabach*" as follows
(The *chazan* will say "*yishtabach*" as the congregation replies "*baruch*" as below):

יִשְׁתַּבַּח yishtabach י"פ ע"ב ברתיבוע וקס"א ע"ה, שְׁמוֹ shemo מהש ע"ב, ע"ב ברתיבוע וקס"א ע"ה,

הַקָּדוֹשׁ hakadosh בָּרוּךְ baruch הוּא hu שֶׁהוּא shehu רִאשׁוֹן rishon וְהוּא vehu אל שדי ע"ה

אַחֲרוֹן acharon וּמִבַּלְעָדָיו umibal'adav אֵין en אֱלֹהִים Elohim אהיה אדני ; ילה.

יְהִי yehi שֵׁם shem יְהֹוָאֲדֹנִיאהדונהי Adonai מְבֹרָךְ mevorach ר"ת ריבוע ע"ב וריבוע ס"ג

מֵעַתָּה me'ata וְעַד ve'ad עוֹלָם olam ייל: וּמְרוֹמָם umromam עַל al יהוה מברך = רפ"ח (להעלות רפ"ח ניצוצות שנפלו לקליפה דמשם באים התולדות)

כָּל kol ילי ; עמם בְּרָכָה beracha ע"ה אמת, אהיה פעמים אהיה, ז"פ ס"ג: וּתְהִלָּה ut'hila

When we reply "*baruch Adonai hamevorach le'olam va'ed*" we receive the five parts of the soul (*Nefesh, Ruach, Neshamah, Chayah* and *Yechidah*) that left us during the last night's sleep.

First the congregation replies the following, and then the *chazan* repeats it:

Neshamah	Ruach	Nefesh

בָּרוּךְ baruch יְהֹוָאֲדֹנִיאהדונהי Adonai הַמְּבוֹרָךְ hamevorach

Yechidah	Chayah

לְעוֹלָם le'olam ריבוע ס"ג ו' אותיות דס"ג וָעֶד va'ed:

Above all blessings,
songs, praises, and words of consolation that may be said in the world, and you shall say, Amen. (Amen)

BARCHU

Bless the Lord, the Blessed One.
Praised and exalted is the Name of the King of all Kings, the Holy Blessed One, Who is first and Who is last and without Whom, there is no God. Let the Name of the Lord be blessed from now till all eternity, above all blessings and praise. Blessed be the Lord, the Blessed One, forever and for eternity.

THE WORLD OF CREATION – *BERIAH*

The beginning verse states: *yotzer or uvore choshech* (forms light and creates darkness). This refers to the concept of Light and darkness, good and evil. A 50/50 split between good and evil gives us the free will to choose either Light or darkness.

From here (*"yotzer or"*) until *"ga'al Yisrael"* (page 342) you are in the World of *Beriah*.

Hechal Livnat Hasapir (the Chamber of Sapphire Stone)—*Yesod* of *Zeir Anpin* in *Beriah*.

ילה Elohenu **אֱלֹהֵינוּ** Adonai יְהֹוָהאהדונהי Ata **אַתָּה** baruch **בָּרוּךְ**

סוף אין רו, or **אוֹר** yotzer **יוֹצֵר** ha'olam **הָעוֹלָם** melech **מֶלֶךְ**

shalom **שָׁלוֹם** ose **עֹשֶׂה** • המלכים וו׳ על נצוצות שך choshech **וְחֹשֶׁךְ** uvore **וּבוֹרֵא**

uvore **וּבוֹרֵא** et **אֶת** הַכֹּל hakol יליי׳

On the Holiday and on *Shabbat* continue with *"hakol yoducha"* on page 317.

On *Chol Hamo'ed* (not on *Shabbat*) we say the following:

פהל aleha **עָלֶיהָ** veladarim **וְלַדָּרִים** la'aretz **לָאָרֶץ** hame'ir **הַמֵּאִיר**

גוו אור החוסד (שהוא uvtuvo **וּבְטוּבוֹ** • יי״י יפ׳ דיודין, אלהים מצפ״ץ, berachamim **בְּרַחֲמִים**

לכב ב״ן, bechol **בְּכָל** קנ״א קס״א הויות, י״ב mechadesh **מְחַדֵּשׁ** (בו

קמ״ג קנ״א קס״א קס״א ע״ה tamid **תָּמִיד** יהוה אל זן, מזבח, נגד, ע״ה yom **יוֹם**

מ״ה ma **מַה** מ״ב: ר״ת vereshit **בְּרֵאשִׁית** ma'ase **מַעֲשֵׂה**

kulam **כֻּלָּם** Adonai יְהֹוָהאדנילאהדונהי ma'asecha **מַעֲשֶׂיךָ** rabu **רַבּוּ**

asita **עָשִׂיתָ** (מצוות) תרי״ג = במילוי bechochmah **בְּחָכְמָה**

All the actions come (as potential of potential) from *Abba* which encloses the Endless Light, and done (as actual of potential) by *Ima* which encloses *Abba* - *Abba* says and *Ima* does.

kinyanecha **קִנְיָנֶךָ** ע״ה דההין אלהים ha'aretz **הָאָרֶץ** mal'a **מָלְאָה**

THE WORLD OF CREATION

Blessed are You, Lord, our God, King of the Universe,
"Who forms Light and creates darkness, makes peace, and creates everything." (Isaiah 45:7)

He Who shines upon the Earth and upon those who inhabit it, with compassion. And with His goodness, He renews, every day and always, the works of Creation. How manifold are Your works, Lord! *"You have made them all with wisdom, and the world is filled with Your possessions." (Psalms 104:24)*

מ"ב בן שם   levado לְבַדּוֹ   hameromam הַמְרוֹמָם   hamelech הַמֶּלֶךְ

hameshubach הַמְשֻׁבָּח   (יאהדונהי) = אמן ; ע"ה מאז לבדו : ומב   me'az מֵאָז

:olam עוֹלָם   mimot מִימוֹת   vehamitnase וְהַמִּתְנַשֵּׂא   vehamefo'ar וְהַמְפוֹאָר

אֱלֹהֵי Elohei   מילוי ע"ב, דמב ; ילה   olam עוֹלָם   berachamecha בְּרַחֲמֶיךָ

,(אברים) רמ"ח, נתיבות החכמה ול"ב רי"ו, אל וז"פ אברהם, rachem רַחֵם   harabim הָרַבִּים

עֻזֵּנוּ uzenu   אני   adon אָדוֹן   alenu עָלֵינוּ   אותיות פשוטות   עסמ"ב וט"ו

misgabenu מִשְׂגַּבֵּנוּ   ע"ה   דההין   אלהים   tzur צוּר

yish'enu יִשְׁעֵנוּ   נוריאל גבריאל מיכאל ר"ת ; (דס"ג מילוי יא"י) אל ג"פ   magen מָגֵן

:ba'adenu בְּעַדֵנוּ   משה, מהע, ע"ב בריבוע וקס"א, אל עדי, ד"פ אלהים ע"ה   misgav מִשְׂגָּב

EL BARUCH

The first letter of each word in this prayer follows the order of the 22 letters of the Aramaic alphabet. These 22 letters connect us to the metaphysical building blocks of the universe, providing us with an opportunity to take control over our world and over our destiny.

Hechal Etzem Hashamayim (the Heaven's Embodiment Chamber)—*Hod* of *Zeir Anpin* in *Beriah*. In this *Hechal* there are *Seraphim* with wings that are called *Chashmalim* and here is the secret of *chashmal* (electricity). אורפניאל — *Or-pnei-El* (**do not pronounce this name** - The Light of God's face) is the angel that ministers this *Hechal*. And this *Hechal* is called אלהים צבאות - *Elohim Tzeva'ot*, which is called *Hod* (*Elohim Tzeva'ot* with its ten letters adds up to 595, which is *Etzem Hashamayim*).

יזל, אום = מבה, אותיות עם ד' ; להו (דס"ג מילוי) יא"י El אֵל   gedol גָּדוֹל   baruch בָּרוּךְ

והו   tov טוֹב   chama חַמָּה   zahorei זָהֳרֵי   ufa'al וּפָעַל   hechin הֵכִין   de'a דֵּעָה

ע"ה עדי אל ע"ה, וקס"א בריבוע ע"ב ע"ה, מהע   lishmo לִשְׁמוֹ   kavod כָּבוֹד   yatzar יָצַר

uzo עֻזּוֹ   sevivot סְבִיבוֹת   natan נָתַן   me'orot מְאוֹרוֹת

You are the King, and You alone are the exalted One from the beginning; You, Who is praised, glorified, and exalted from the beginning of time. God of the World, take pity over us with Your plentiful compassions, Master of our strength, Rock of our stronghold. Shield of our redemption, Who is our stronghold.

EL BARUCH

God, blessed and great in knowledge, He prepared and generated the splendor of the sun. The good One, Who created glory for His Name, He set luminaries around His power.

פִּנּוֹת pinot צִבְאוֹת tziv'ot קְדוֹשִׁים kedoshim רוֹמְמֵי romemei

שַׁדַּי Shadai תָּמִיד tamid ע"ה קס"א קנ"א קמ"ג (ג' מילואי אהיה)

מְסַפְּרִים mesaprim, כְּבוֹד kevod אֵל El יא"י (מילוי דס"ג) ;

וּקְדוּשָׁתוֹ ukdushato (Da'at of Nukva) כבוד אל = ס"ג ; ר"ת מכאל (מיכאל = גוא)

תִּתְבָּרַךְ titbarach יְהֹוָה Adonai אֱלֹהֵינוּ Elohenu יכה

בַּשָּׁמַיִם bashamayim מִמַּעַל mima'al וְעַל ve'al

הָאָרֶץ ha'aretz מִתַּחַת mitachat עַל al כָּל kol

שֶׁבַח shevach מַעֲשֵׂי ma'asei יָדֶיךָ yadecha וְעַל ve'al מְאוֹרֵי me'orei

אוֹר or שֶׁיָּצַרְתָּ sheyatzarta הֵמָּה hema יְפָאֲרוּךָ yefa'arucha

סֶלָה sela

Continue with "*titbarach lanetzach*" on page 323.

הַכֹּל hakol יוֹדוּךָ yoducha וְהַכֹּל vehakol יְשַׁבְּחוּךָ yeshabechucha

וְהַכֹּל vehakol יֹאמְרוּ yomru אֵין en קָדוֹשׁ kadosh

כַּיְהֹוָה kadonai יְרוֹמְמוּךָ yeromemucha הַכֹּל hakol סֶלָה sela

יוֹצֵר yotzer הַכֹּל hakol הָאֵל haEl לאה ; אל (יא"י מילוי דס"ג)

הַפּוֹתֵחַ hapote'ach בְּכָל bechol יוֹם yom ע"ה נגד, מזבוח, זן, אל יהוה

דַּלְתוֹת daltot שַׁעֲרֵי sha'arei מִזְרָח mizrach וּבוֹקֵעַ uvoke'a

וְחַלּוֹנֵי chalonei רְקִיעַ raki'a מוֹצִיא motzi חַמָּה chama

מִמְּקוֹמָהּ mimekoma וּלְבָנָה ulvana מִמְּכוֹן mimechon שִׁבְתָּהּ shivta

וּמֵאִיר ume'ir לְעוֹלָם le'olam כֻּלּוֹ kulo וּלְיוֹשְׁבָיו ulyoshvav

שֶׁבָּרָא shebara קנ"א ב"ן, יהוה אלהים יהוה אדני, מילוי קס"א וס"ג, מ"ה ברבוע ע"ב ע"ה

May You be blessed, Lord, our God in Heavens Above and upon the Earth Below, and upon all Your magnificent handiwork and upon all the luminaries that You have made. They shall glorify You, Selah.

Everything gives thanks to You. Everything praises You. Everyone says that there is none as Holy as the Lord. Everyone exalts You, Selah! He, Who forms everything. The God Who opens daily the doors of the gateways of the east and Who splits the windows of the firmament. Who removes the sun from its place and the moon from the place of its rest. Who illuminates the whole world and its inhabitants which He created

la'aretz לָאָרֶץ hame'ir הַמֵּאִיר harachamim הָרַחֲמִים bemidat בְּמִדַּת

veladarim וְלַדָּרִים berachamim בְּרַחֲמִים מצפ״צ, אלהים דיודין, י״פ יי׳ aleha עָלֶיהָ פהל

uvtuvo וּבְטוּבוֹ (שהוא החסד אור גנוז בו) mechadesh מְחַדֵּשׁ י״ב הויות, קס״א קנ״א

bechol בְּכָל ב״ן, לכב ע״ה נגד, מזבוז, זן, אל יהוה yom יוֹם

tamid תָּמִיד ע״ה קס״א קנ״א קמ״ג ma'ase מַעֲשֵׂה vereshit בְרֵאשִׁית ר״ת מ״ב:

ma מָה ma רַבּוּ ma'asecha מַעֲשֶׂיךָ Adonai יְהֹוָה אדנייאהדונהי

kulam כֻּלָּם bechochma בְּחָכְמָה במילוי = תרי״ג (מצוות) asita עָשִׂיתָ

All the actions come (as potential of potential) from *Abba* which encloses the Endless Light, and done (as actual of potential) by *Ima* which encloses *Abba* - *Abba* says and *Ima* does.

mal'a מָלְאָה ha'aretz הָאָרֶץ אלהים דההין ע״ה kinyanecha קִנְיָנֶךָ hamelech הַמֶּלֶךָ

hameromam הַמְרוֹמָם levado לְבַדּוֹ me'az מֵאָז מ״ב ומב ; לבדו מאו ע״ה = אמן (יאהדונהי)

hameshubach הַמְשֻׁבָּח vehamefo'ar וְהַמְפֹאָר vehamitnase וְהַמִּתְנַשֵּׂא

mimot מִימוֹת olam עוֹלָם Elohei אֱלֹהֵי מילוי דע״ב, דמב ; ילה olam עוֹלָם

berachamecha בְּרַחֲמֶיךָ harabim הָרַבִּים rachem רַחֵם אברהם, וז״פ אל, רי״ו ול״ב

adon אֲדוֹן אני alenu עָלֵינוּ נתיבות החוכמה, רמ״ח (אברים), עסמ״ב וט״ז אותיות פעוtות

uzenu עֻזֵּנוּ tzur צוּר אלהים דההין ע״ה misgabenu מִשְׂגַּבֵּנוּ

yish'enu יִשְׁעֵנוּ magen מָגֵן ג״פ אל (ייא״י מילוי דס״ג) ; ר״ת בֹמיכאל גבריאל נוריאל

ba'adenu בַּעֲדֵנוּ: misgav מִשְׂגָּב מֹשֶׁה, מהש, ע״ב בריבוע קס״א, אל שדי, ד״פ אלהים ע״ה

On Shabbat - Hechal Ratzon (the Chamber of Desire) - *Tiferet* of *Zeir Anpin* in *Beriah*.

en אֵין aroch עֲרוֹךָ lecha לְךָ ve'en וְאֵין zulatach זוּלָתֶךָ efes אֶפֶס

biltach בִּלְתֶּךָ umi וּמִי ילי dome דוֹמֶה lach לָךָ: en אֵין aroch עֲרוֹךָ lecha לְךָ

Adonai יְהֹוָה ואדני Elohenu אֱלֹהֵינוּ ילה ba'olam בָּעוֹלָם haze הַזֶּה והו

---

with His attribute of mercy. And, with His goodness, He renews, every day and always, the works of Creation. How manifold are Your works, Lord, You have made them all with wisdom and the world is filled with Your possessions. The King, Who was exalted alone from the beginning. The One Who is praised, glorified and extolled from the beginning of time. God of the world, with Your plentiful compassions take pity over us. Master of our strength, shield of our redemption and Who is strength for us. There is no comparison to You, there is nothing except for You, for who is like You? There is no comparison to You, Lord, our God, in this world

ve'en וְאֵין | zulatach זוּלָתֶךָ | malkenu מַלְכֵּנוּ | lechayei לְחַיֵּי

ha'olam הָעוֹלָם | haba הַבָּא: | efes אֶפֶס | biltach בִּלְתֶּךָ | go'alenu גּוֹאֲלֵנוּ

limot לִימוֹת | hamashi'ach הַמָּשִׁיחַ◆ | umi וּמִי יִלִי | dome דוֹמֶה

lach לָךְ | moshi'enu מוֹשִׁיעֵנוּ | lit'chiyat לִתְחִיַּת | hametim הַמֵּתִים:

EL ADON

We find the 22 letters of the Aramaic alphabet encoded into this prayer. The first letter in each of the first 22 words is the alphabet in its correct order. Because the Aramaic letters are the actual instruments of Creation, this prayer helps to inject order and the power of Creation into our lives.

On *Shabbat*:

Meditate to draw additional Holiness of *Shabbat* (from the aspect of the day – male) to *Nukva* of *Zeir Anpin* of *Beriah* so She will have a new Name: אל אלף דלת נון יוד (702=*Shabbat*). Also **Meditate** to elevate "*Hechal Ahavah*" (*Chesed*) of *Zeir Anpin* of *Beriah* to the Upper "*Hechal Ahavah*" (*Chesed*) of *Abba* and *Ima* of *Beriah*, in order to draw the extra Holiness of *Shabbat*.

Hechal Ahavah (the Love Chamber) - *Chesed* of *Zeir Anpin* in *Beriah*.

Hechal Etzem Hashamayim (the Heaven's Embodiment Chamber)—*Hod* of *Zeir Anpin* in *Beriah*.

ב | | | | א

אֲנִי | adon אֲדוֹן | (דס"ג) | (מילוי) | יי"א"י | El אֵל

ה | | | ד | | ג

hama'asim◆ הַמַּעֲשִׂים | עמם ; יִלִי | kol כָּל | al עַל

ז | | | ו

umvorach וּמְבוֹרָךְ | | baruch בָּרוּךְ

י | | | ט | | ח

haneshama◆ הַנְּשָׁמָה | עמם ; יִלִי | chol כָּל | befi בְּפִי

עלם | | סיט | | יִלִי | | וֹהוּ

olam◆ עוֹלָם | male מְלֵא | vetuvo וְטוּבוֹ | godlo גָּדְלוֹ

And there will be nothing except for You, our King, in the life of the World to Come. There will be nothing without You, our Redeemer in the days of the Mashiach. And who will be like You, our Savior, at the resurrection of the dead?

EL ADON

א *God, Master over all the works.*
ב *Blessed One Who is blessed by the mouth of every soul.* ג *His greatness and His goodness fill the world.*

מהעי   da'at דַּעַת   ללה   utvuna וּתְבוּנָה   אכא   sovevim סוֹבְבִים   כהת   hodo הוֹדוֹ אהיה:

הזי   hamitga'e הַמִּתְגָּאֶה   אלד   al עַל   לאו   chayot וְזִיּוֹת   ההע   hakodesh הַקֹּדֶשׁ◆

יזל   venehdar וְנֶהְדָּר   מבה   bechavod בִּכְבוֹד בוכו   הרי   al עַל   הקם   hamerkava הַמֶּרְכָּבָה◆

לאו   zechut זְכוּת   כלי   umishor וּמִישׁוֹר   לוו   lifnei לִפְנֵי   פהל   chis'o כִּסְאוֹ◆

נלך   chesed וְחֶסֶד   יייי   verachamim וְרַחֲמִים ע״ב, ריבוע יהוה   מלה   male מָלֵא   וזהו   chevodo כְּבוֹדוֹ:

נתה   tovim טוֹבִים   האא   me'orot מְאוֹרוֹת   ירת   shebera'am שֶׁבְּרָאָם   שאה   Elohenu אֱלֹהֵינוּ ילה◆

ריי   yetzaram יְצָרָם   אום   beda'at בְּדַעַת

לכב   bevina בְּבִינָה ע״ה אהיה אהיה יהוה, וזיים   ושר   uv'haskel וּבְהַשְׂכֵּל◆

יוזו   ko'ach כֹּחַ   להוו   ugvura וּגְבוּרָה רי״ו   כוק   natan נָתַן   מגד   bahem בָּהֶם◆

אני   lih'yot לִהְיוֹת   וזעם   moshlim מוֹשְׁלִים   רהע   bekerev בְּקֶרֶב   ייי   tevel תֵּבֵל ב״פ רי״ו:

ההה   mele'im מְלֵאִים   מיכ   ziv זִיו   וול   umfikim וּמְפִיקִים   ילה   noga נֹגַהּ דניי◆

ד *Wisdom and insight surround His glory.* ה *He Who is exalted over the holy Beasts.*
ו *And splendors in glory over the Chariot.* ז *Merit and fairness are before His Throne.*
ח *Kindness and mercy fill His glory.* ט *Good are the luminaries that our God had created.*
י *With insight, and with discernment. He had fashioned them with knowledge.* כ *He bestowed upon them strength and power,* ל *To be dominant within the world.* מ *They are full of brilliance and radiate brightness.*

נָּאֶה na'e   זִיוָם zivam   בְּכָל bechol   ב"ן,   לכב   הָעוֹלָם ha'olam◆

שְׂמֵוִזִים semechim   בְּצֵאתָם betzetam   שָׂשִׂים sasim   בְּבוֹאָם bevo'am◆

עוֹשִׂים osim   בְּאֵימָה be'ema   ר"ת ע"ב (יוד הי ויו הי), ריבוע יהוה (י יה יהו יהוה)

רָצוֹן retzon   מהש ע"ה, ע"ב בריבוע וקס"א ע"ה, אל שדי ע"ה   קוֹנֵיהֶם konehem:

פְּאֵר pe'er   וְכָבוֹד vechavod   נוֹתְנִים notnim   לִשְׁמוֹ lishmo
מהש ע"ה, ע"ב בריבוע וקס"א ע"ה, אל שדי ע"ה

צָהֳלָה tzahola   וְרִנָּה verina   לְזֵכֶר lezecher   מַלְכוּתוֹ malchuto◆

קָרָא kara   לַשֶּׁמֶשׁ lashemesh   וַיִּזְרַח vayizrach   אוֹר or   רז,   אֵין סוֹף◆

רָאָה ra'a   רֹאֶה   וְהִתְקִין vehitkin   צוּרַת tzurat   הַלְּבָנָה halevana:

שֶׁבַח shevach   נוֹתְנִים notnim   לוֹ lo   כָל kol   יְלִי   צְבָא tzeva   מָרוֹם marom◆

תִּפְאֶרֶת tiferet   וּגְדוּלָּה ugdula   (Beriah)   שְׂרָפִים serafim

הַקֹּדֶשׁ hakodesh: וְאוֹפַנֵּי ve'ofanei   (Asiyah)   וְחַיּוֹת vechayot   וְזִיּוֹת (Yetzirah)

א Their brilliance is beautiful all around the world.
ס Glad as they go forth and exultant as they return. ע They do with awe their Creator's will.
פ All the hosts above bestow praise to Him. צ Jubilation and merry song upon the mention of His reign.
ק He called out to the sun and it glowed with light. ר He saw and fashioned the form of the moon. ש Splendor and glory they give to His Name. ת Splendor and greatness by the Seraphs, Beasts And the Holy Ofans.

On *Shabbat* we add the following:

LaEl Asher

Each of us is imbued with the Creator's DNA. These verses help us awaken all of the Godlike features within us so that we can achieve fulfillment and control over our lives.

לְאֵל laEl יא"י (מילוי) דס"ג אֲשֶׁר asher שָׁבַת shavat מִכָּל mikol

הַמַּעֲשִׂים hama'asim ✦ וּבַיּוֹם uvayom ע"ה נגד, מזבוו, זן, אל יהוה הַשְּׁבִיעִי hashevi'i

נִתְעַלָּה nit'ala

> Meditate that *Zeir Anpin* that was "sitting" in *Yetzirah*, is now elevating to *Beriah*.
>
> As for now, the five *Tzelem* (of *Netzach, Hod, Yesod* of *Yisrael Saba* and *Tevunah*) which is called צ,
> the five *Tzelem* (of *Chesed, Gevurah, Tiferet* of *Yisrael Saba* and *Tevunah*) which is called ל,
> and the five *Tzelem* (of *Chochmah, Binah, Da'at* of *Yisrael Saba* and *Tevunah*) which is called ם,
> (and is also called: *Nefesh, Ruach, Neshamah, Chayah, Yechidah*, of *Neshamah*), already entered
> to the five *Partzufim* of *Netzach, Hod, Yesod*, and to the five *Partzufim* of *Chesed, Gevurah, Tiferet*
> and to the five *Partzufim* of *Chochmah, Binah, Da'at* of *Binah* of *Zeir Anpin* — which is called —
> *Gadlut Alef* (First Adulthood - which is not considered as an elevation for *Zeir Anpin*).
> **Also meditate** for *Yaakov* and *Rachel* that They are now enclosing *Netzach, Hod, Yesod*
> of *Binah* of *Zeir Anpin* (which is *Netzach, Hod, Yesod* of *Yisrael Saba* and *Tevunah*).

וַיֵּשֶׁב veyashav עַל al כִּסֵּא kise כְּבוֹדוֹ chevodo ✦ תִּפְאֶרֶת tiferet

עָטָה ata לְיוֹם leyom ע"ה נגד, מזבוו, זן, אל יהוה הַמְּנוּחָה hamenucha ✦

עֹנֶג oneg ר"ת עדן נהר גן kara קָרָא לְיוֹם leyom ע"ה נגד, מזבוו, זן, אל יהוה

הַשַּׁבָּת haShabbat: זֶה ze שִׁיר shir שֶׁבַח shevach שֶׁל shel

יוֹם yom ע"ה נגד, מזבוו, זן, אל יהוה הַשְּׁבִיעִי hashevi'i שֶׁבּוֹ shebo שָׁבַת shavat

אֵל El יא"י (מילוי) דס"ג מִכָּל mikol ילי מְלַאכְתּוֹ melachto ✦

וְיוֹם veyom ע"ה נגד, מזבוו, זן, אל יהוה הַשְּׁבִיעִי hashevi'i מְשַׁבֵּחַ meshabe'ach

וְאוֹמֵר ve'omer: בְּמִזְמוֹר mizmor שִׁיר shir לְיוֹם leyom ע"ה נגד, מזבוו, זן, אל יהוה

הַשַּׁבָּת haShabbat ר"ת למשה: לְפִיכָךְ lefichach יְפָאֲרוּ yefa'aru

לְאֵל laEl יא"י (מילוי) דס"ג כָּל kol ילי יְצוּרָיו yetzurav ✦

LaEl Asher
To the God

Who rested from all the works and Who, on the Seventh Day, was elevated and sat on the Throne of His glory. With splendor He enwrapped the Day of Rest, He declared the Shabbat Day a delight. This is the song of praise of the Shabbat Day on which God rested from all His work. And the Seventh Day praises and says: A psalm, a song for the Shabbat Day. Therefore, let all that He had fashioned glorify God.

yitenu יִתֵּנוּ vechavod וְכָבוֹד ugdula וּגְדֻלָּה vikar וִיקָר shevach שֶׁבַח

menucha מְנוּחָה hamanchil הַמַּנְחִיל kol כָּל yotzer יוֹצֵר lamelech לַמֶּלֶךְ

Yisrael יִשְׂרָאֵל beyom בְּיוֹם le'amo לְעַמּוֹ

kodesh קֹדֶשׁ Shabbat שַׁבַּת

yitkadash יִתְקַדֵּשׁ Elohenu אֱלֹהֵינוּ Adonai יְהֹוָה shimcha שִׁמְךָ

malkenu מַלְכֵּנוּ yitpa'ar יִתְפָּאַר vezichrecha וְזִכְרְךָ

ve'al וְעַל mima'al מִמַּעַל bashamayim בַּשָּׁמַיִם

kol כָּל al עַל mitachat מִתַּחַת ha'aretz הָאָרֶץ

me'orei מְאוֹרֵי ve'al וְעַל yadecha יָדֶיךָ ma'ase מַעֲשֵׂה shevach שֶׁבַח

or אוֹר yefa'arucha יְפָאֲרוּךָ hema הֵמָּה sheyatzarta שֶׁיָּצַרְתָּ sela סֶלָה

TITBARACH LANETZACH

The last Name of the 72 Names of God—*Mem, Vav, final Mem* מום appears in this connection. This Name means "blemish" or "imperfection." If we are on this planet, we still have at least one imperfection, if not countless more. This connection helps us to correct these blemishes.

malkenu מַלְכֵּנוּ tzurenu צוּרֵנוּ lanetzach לָנֶצַח titbarach תִּתְבָּרַךְ

kedoshim קְדוֹשִׁים bore בּוֹרֵא vego'alenu וְגוֹאֲלֵנוּ

shimcha שִׁמְךָ yishtabach יִשְׁתַּבַּח

meshartim מְשָׁרְתִים yotzer יוֹצֵר malkenu מַלְכֵּנוּ la'ad לָעַד

kulam כֻּלָּם meshartav מְשָׁרְתָיו va'asher וַאֲשֶׁר

omdim עוֹמְדִים olam עוֹלָם berum בְּרוּם

Praise, honor, greatness and glory, let them render to God, the King, Who fashioned everything. He Who gives a heritage of contentment to His People, Israel, in His holiness, on the Day of Shabbat.

May Your Name, Lord, our God, be sanctified and may Your remembrance, our King, be glorified in the heaven above and upon the earth below. May You be blessed, our Savior, beyond all the praises of Your handiwork. And beyond the brilliant luminaries that You had formed, may they glorify You, Selah!

TITBARACH LANETZACH

May You be eternally blessed,
our Rock, our King, and our Redeemer, Creator of the Holy Angels. May Your Name be praised forever, our King, Who forms Ministering Angels. And Whose Ministering Angels stand in the heights of the world

בְּקוֹל ,bekol — יַחַד yachad — רי"י — בִּירְאָה beyir'a — וּמַשְׁמִיעִים umashmi'im

אֱלֹהִים Elohim — אהיה אדני ; ילה וַיַּיִם chayim — אהיה אהיה יהוה, בינה ע"ה — רָאה דִּבְרֵי divrei

כֻּלָּם kulam — אֲהוּבִים ahuvim — כֻּלָּם kulam — עוֹלָם olam — וּמֶלֶךְ umelech

כֻּלָּם kulam — ר"ת אבג" — גִּבּוֹרִים giborim — כֻּלָּם kulam — בְּרוּרִים berurim

קְדוֹשִׁים kedoshim — כֻּלָּם kulam — עוֹשִׂים osim — בְּאֵימָה be'ema — ר"ת ע"ב, ריבוע יהוה

וּבִירְאָה uvyir'a — רי"י רָצוֹן retzon — מהש ע"ה, ע"ב בר'בוע וקס"א ע"ה, אל שדי ע"ה

קוֹנֵיהֶם konehem — וְכֻלָּם vechulam — פּוֹתְחִים potchim — אֶת et — פִּיהֶם pihem

בִּקְדוּשָׁה bikdusha — וּבְטָהֳרָה uvtahora — בְּשִׁירָה beshira — וּבְזִמְרָה uvzimra

וּמְבָרְכִין umvarchin — וּמְשַׁבְּחִין umshabechin — וּמְפָאֲרִין umfa'arin

וּמַקְדִּישִׁין umakdishin — וּמַעֲרִיצִין uma'aritzin — וּמַמְלִיכִין umamlichin

ר"ת ז' ווין בסוד שם מ"ב בן ס"ת ; = מצפצ, אלהים דיודין, י"פ ייי.

ET SHEM

The word reshut רעות is found inside this connection. Reshut has the same numerical value (906) as the initials of the words comprising the last sentence in the Ana Beko'ach (Shav'atenu Kabel Ushma Tza'akatenu Yode'a Ta'alumot) - עיקו ציח. This specific sequence correlates to our physical world, Malchut.

אֶת-et — שֵׁם shem — הָאֵל haEl — (יא"י מילוי דס"ג) אל ; לאה — הַמֶּלֶךְ hamelech

הַגָּדוֹל hagadol — לההו ; עם ד' אותיות = מבה, יזל, אום — הַגִּבּוֹר hagibor

וְהַנּוֹרָא vehanora — ר"ת = יהוה — קָדוֹשׁ kadosh — הוּא hu

וְכֻלָּם vechulam — מְקַבְּלִים mekabelim — עֲלֵיהֶם alehem — עוֹל ol

מַלְכוּת malchut — שָׁמַיִם shamayim — י"פ טל, י"פ כוזו — זֶה ze — מִזֶּה mize

וְנוֹתְנִים venotnim — רְשׁוּת reshut — עיקו ציח — זֶה ze — לָזֶה laze

---

and loudly proclaim, with reverence and in unison, the words of the living God and the King of the Universe. They are all-beloved. They are all-pure. They are all-powerful. They are all-holy. They all execute, with reverence and with awe, the will of their Maker. They all open their mouths with holiness and with purity, and give song and melody. They bless, praise, glorify, sanctify, revere, and enthrone.

ET SHEM

The Name of God, the King, the great, powerful and awesome One, for He is Holy. They all accept upon themselves the yoke of the Heavenly Kingdom, one from another. And they give leave to one another lehakdish לְהַקְדִּישׁ leyotzram לְיוֹצְרָם benachat בְּנַחַת ru'ach רוּחַ◆

besafa בְּשָׂפָה verura בְּרוּרָה uvin'ima וּבִנְעִימָה◆

kedusha קְדוּשָׁה kulam כֻּלָּם ke'echad כְּאֶחָד

onim עוֹנִים be'ema בְּאֵימָה◆ ve'omrim וְאוֹמְרִים beyir'a בְּיִרְאָה

KADOSH, KADOSH, KADOSH

This phrase translates into "Holy, Holy, Holy," but it does not refer to what we normally consider the word "holy" to mean (sacred, blessed, or sanctified). Rather, it signifies the concept of *whole* or "wholly," as in the quantum wholeness of reality that is unified and interconnected. Repeating the word "holy" three times also connects us to the Right (positive), Left (negative), and Central Columns (neutral). This prayer instills within us the awareness that although we may have imperfections, we still have the Divine Spark of Light within us. Our soul is part of God.

It is good to recite this verse according to its intonations (*te'amim*).

(Central) kadosh קָדוֹשׁ (Left) kadosh קָדוֹשׁ (Right) | kadosh קָדוֹשׁ

Adonai יְהֹוָה Tzeva'ot צְבָאוֹת

melo מְלֹא chol כָּל ha'aretz הָאָרֶץ kevodo כְּבוֹדוֹ

veha'ofanim וְהָאוֹפַנִּים vechayot וְחַיּוֹת hakodesh הַקֹּדֶשׁ

bera'ash בְּרַעַשׁ gadol גָּדוֹל mitnase'im מִתְנַשְּׂאִים

haserafim הַשְּׂרָפִים le'umat לְעֻמַּת le'umatam לְעֻמָּתָם

ve'omrim וְאוֹמְרִים meshabchim מְשַׁבְּחִים

baruch בָּרוּךְ kevod כְּבוֹד Adonai יְהֹוָה

mimekomo מִמְּקוֹמוֹ

LaEl Baruch

Hechal Nogah (the Chamber of Brightness)—*Netzach* of *Zeir Anpin* in *Beriah*.

laEl לָאֵל baruch בָּרוּךְ◆ ne'imot נְעִימוֹת yitenu יִתֵּנוּ◆

---

and they consent to sanctify their Creator. And in a calm spirit, with a clear expression, and pleasantly, they proclaim sanctity, with reverence. And they all say in unison and in awe:

KADOSH, KADOSH, KADOSH

"Holy, Holy, Holy Is the Lord of Hosts. The world is full with His glory." (Isaiah 6:3)
"The Offanim and all the Holy Beasts soar with thunderous voice toward the Seraphs who stand opposite them, and give praise and say: Blessed is the glory of the Lord from His place." (Ezekiel 3:12)

LaEl Baruch

To the blessed God, they give their melodies.

♦vekayam וְקַיָּם   chai וָזֵי (דס"ג) (מילוי) יא"ר   El אֵל   lamelech לְמֶלֶךְ

♦yashmi'u יַשְׁמִיעוּ   vetishbachot וְתִשְׁבָּחוֹת   ♦yomeru יֹאמְרוּ   zemirot זְמִירוֹת

SEVEN VERSES

Each of these seven verses connects to a different heavenly body. Four thousand years ago, Abraham the Patriarch revealed that there were seven key heavenly bodies that could be seen with the naked eye - the sun, the moon, Mars, Mercury, Saturn, Venus and Jupiter. These are the ones with a direct influence over our physical world and they correspond to the Seven Lower *Sefirot*. According to Abraham, the Upper Three dimensions (*Sefirot*) do not directly influence our world.

מ"ב levado לְבַדּוֹ hu הוּא ki כִּי

♦vekadosh וְקָדוֹשׁ (*Chochmah*) marom מָרוֹם (*Keter*)

corresponding to the seven planets – כְּנֶגֶד ז' כּוֹכְבֵי לֶכֶת:

(Sun)	gevurot גְּבוּרוֹת	po'el פּוֹעֵל	(Binah)
(Moon)	chadashot וַחֲדָשׁוֹת	ose עוֹשֶׂה	(Chesed)
(Mars)	milchamot מִלְחָמוֹת	ba'al בַּעַל	(Gevurah)
(Mercury)	tzedakot צְדָקוֹת	zore'a זוֹרֵעַ	(Tiferet)
(Saturn)	yeshu'ot יְשׁוּעוֹת	matzmi'ach מַצְמִיחַ	(Netzach)
(Venus)	refu'ot רְפוּאוֹת	bore בּוֹרֵא	(Hod)

(*Pei Resh Tav Bet Gimel Dalet Kaf*) כ ד ג ב ת ר פ

(Jupiter)	tehilot תְּהִלּוֹת	nora נוֹרָא	(Yesod)
	♦hanifla'ot הַנִּפְלָאוֹת אני	adon אָדוֹן	(Malchut)

MA'ASE BERESHEET

Hechal Zechut (the Chamber of Merit)—*Gevurah* of *Zeir Anpin* in *Beriah*.

Be aware at all times that every new day is a renewal of all of Creation. Too often, we live life either in the past or the future, letting the present slip away. Real spiritual growth occurs in the present. This prayer helps to instill this consciousness within us. In the present, we proactively deal with the effects we have created in the past and through our actions, we plant seeds for our future. If we miss the opportunities that the present offers us, we will find ourselves on a reactive wheel with no control over our lives.

To the King, the living and everlasting God, they shall sing hymns and proclaim praises.

SEVEN VERSES

(Keter) *For He above is lofty* (Chochmah) *and Holy.*

(Binah)	*He performs mighty deeds.*	(Sun)	(Chesed)	*Makes new things.*	(Moon)
(Gevurah)	*Master of wars.*	(Mars)	(Tiferet)	*Sows righteousness.*	(Mercury)
(Netzach)	*Brings about salvation.*	(Saturn)	(Hod)	*Creates remedies.*	(Venus)
(Yesod)	*Awesome in praises.*	(Jupiter)	(Malchut)	*Lord of wonders*	

הַמְוֹחַדֵּשׁ hamechadesh קס״א קנ״א, קס״א קנ״א הוית, י״ב betuvo בְּטוּבוֹ bechol לכב ב״ן, בְּכָל־

יוֹם yom ע״ה קס״א קנ״א קמ״ג. אל יהוה זן, מזכוז, נגד, ע״ה tamid תָּמִיד

מַעֲשֵׂה ma'ase בְּרֵאשִׁית vereshit ר״ת מ״ב. כָּאמוּר ka'amur

לְעֹשֵׂה le'ose אוֹרִים orim רו, אין סוף גְּדֹלִים gedolim כִּי ki

לְעוֹלָם le'olam חַסְדּוֹ chasdo ג הוית, מזלא, אותיות דס״ג ו״י ס״ג ריבוע = נגה: ; ר״ת

בָּרוּךְ baruch אַתָּה Ata יְהוִֹאַדניהיאהדונהי Adonai יוֹצֵר yotzer הַמְּאוֹרוֹת hame'orot:

AHAVAT OLAM (AHAVA RABA)

Hechal Ahavah (the Love Chamber)—*Chesed* of *Zeir Anpin* in *Beriah*.

The purpose of this prayer is to inspire within us a love for the world and for other people.

אַהֲבַת ahavat עוֹלָם olam ("Ahava Raba" instead of "Ahavat Olam") **on** *Shabbat* we say

אַהֲבָה ahava אוֹר, דאגה, רַבָּה (raba ahavtanu אֲהַבְתָּנוּ ר״ת ע״ב, ריבוע יהוה

יְהוָֹאַדניהיאהדונהי Adonai אֱלֹהֵינוּ Elohenu ילה וְחֶמְלָה chemla גְּדוֹלָה gedola

וִיתֵרָה vitera וְחָמַלְתָּ chamalta עָלֵינוּ alenu. אָבִינוּ avinu מַלְכֵּנוּ malkenu

בַּעֲבוּר ba'avur שִׁמְךָ shimcha הַגָּדוֹל hagadol לוֹהוֹ ; עם ד' אותיות = מבה, יזל, אום

וּבַעֲבוּר uva'avur אֲבוֹתֵינוּ avotenu שֶׁבָּטְחוּ shebatchu בְּךָ vach

וַתְּלַמְּדֵמוֹ vatelamdemo וְחֻקֵּי chukei חַיִּים chayim אהיה אהיה יהוה, בינה ע״ה

לַעֲשׂוֹת la'asot רְצוֹנְךָ retzoncha בְּלֵבָב belevav בוכו עָלֵם shalem.

כֵּן ken תְּחָנֵּנוּ techonenu אָבִינוּ avinu אָב av הָרַחֲמָן harachaman.

MA'ASE BERESHEET

He, in His goodness, renews, every day and forever, the work of Creation as it is stated: "To the One Who makes the great luminaries, for His kindness is forever." (Psalms 136:7) Blessed are You, Lord, Maker of luminaries.

AHAVAT OLAM (AHAVA RABA)

You have loved us an abundant love, Lord, our God.

Great and abundant compassion You have bestowed upon us. our Father, our King, for the sake of Your great Name and for the sake of our forefathers who trusted in You. Teach life-giving precepts so we may fulfill Your will, wholeheartedly, so shall you be gracious to us, our Father, merciful Father.

הַמְרַחֵם hamerachem   אברהם, וז"פ אל, רי"ו ול"ב נתיבות החוכמה, רמ"ח (אברים),

רֻחֵם rachem   עסמ"ב וט"ו אותיות פשוטות   אברהם, וז"פ אל, רי"ו ול"ב נתיבות החוכמה, רמ"ח (אברים),

belibenu בְּלִבֵּנוּ   veten וְתֵן   alenu עָלֵינוּ   na נָא   עסמ"ב וט"ו אותיות פשוטות

בִּינָה vina   ע"ה אהיה אהיה יהוה, וחיים   •lehavin לְהָבִין   •lehaskil לְהַשְׂכִּיל

•lishmo'a לִשְׁמוֹעַ   lilmod לִלְמוֹד   •ulelamed וּלְלַמֵּד   lishmor לִשְׁמוֹר

vela'asot וְלַעֲשׂוֹת   ulkayem וּלְקַיֵּם   et אֶת־   kol כָּל־ יכי   divrei דִּבְרֵי ראה

talmud תַּלְמוּד   toratecha תּוֹרָתֶךָ   be'ahava בְּאַהֲבָה   •veha'er וְהָאֵר אזר, דאגה

enenu עֵינֵינוּ   ריבוע מ"ה   •betoratecha בְּתוֹרָתֶךָ   vedabek וְדַבֵּק

libenu לִבֵּנוּ   •vemitzvotecha בְּמִצְוֹתֶיךָ   veyached וְיַחֵד   levavenu לְבָבֵנוּ

le'ahava לְאַהֲבָה אזר, דאגה   ulyir'a וּלְיִרְאָה רי"ו   et אֶת־   •shemecha שְׁמֶךָ

velo וְלֹא   nevosh נֵבוֹשׁ   velo וְלֹא   nikalem נִכָּלֵם   velo וְלֹא   nikashel נִכָּשֵׁל

le'olam לְעוֹלָם ריבוע ס"ג וי' אותיות דס"ג   •va'ed וָעֶד   ki כִּי   veshem בְשֵׁם

kodshecha קָדְשְׁךָ   hagadol הַגָּדוֹל לההו ; עם ד' אותיות = מבה, יזל, אום

vehanora וְהַנּוֹרָא   •vatachnu בָטָחְנוּ   nagila נָגִילָה   venismecha וְנִשְׂמְחָה

•vishu'atecha בִּישׁוּעָתֶךָ   verachamecha וְרַחֲמֶיךָ   Adonai יְהֹוָ(אדני)אהדונהי

Elohenu אֱלֹהֵינוּ יכה   vachasadecha וַחֲסָדֶיךָ   harabim הָרַבִּים

al אַל   ya'azvunu יַעַזְבוּנוּ   netzach נֶצַח   sela סֶלָה   •va'ed וָעֶד

Gather the four corners of the *Talit* in your left hand and hold them against your heart until after reciting the words "la'ad ule'olmei olamim" on page 338.

maher מַהֵר   vehave וְהָבֵא   alenu עָלֵינוּ   beracha בְּרָכָה

veshalom וְשָׁלוֹם   mehera מְהֵרָה   me'arba מֵאַרְבַּע   kanfot כַּנְפוֹת

ha'aretz הָאָרֶץ   אלהים   דההין   ע"ה   ;   ר"ת   =   •אדני

Be merciful to us, merciful One. Place understanding in our hearts so we may understand, discern, hear, study, teach, keep, do, and fulfill all the words of the teachings of Your Torah in love. Enlighten our eyes with Your Torah. Bond our hearts with Your commandments. Unify our hearts to love and fear Your Name; then we shall be neither ashamed nor humiliated; nor shall we fail ever and for all eternity. Because we have placed our trust in Your great and awesome Name. May we rejoice and be happy in Your salvation. May Your compassion never leave us, Lord, our God, nor Your many kindnesses, Selah, forever. Hurry and bring upon us blessing and peace, speedily, from the four corners of the Earth.

tzavarenu צַוָּארֵנוּ עלם me'al מֵעַל hagoyim הַגּוֹיִם ol עוֹל ushvor וּשְׁבוֹר

◆le'artzenu לְאַרְצֵנוּ komemiyut קוֹמְמִיּוּת mehera מְהֵרָה veholichenu וְהוֹלִיכֵנוּ

ר"ת פאי, אמן Ata אַתָּה yeshu'ot יְשׁוּעוֹת po'el פּוֹעֵל (מילוי הס"ג) ייא"י El אֵל ki כִּי

◆velashon וְלָשׁוֹן am עָם ילי mikol מִכָּל vacharta בָּחַרְתָּ uvanu וּבָנוּ (יאהדונהי)

VEKERAVTANU MALKENU

Saying *Vekeravtanu Malkenu* reminds us of and gives us a direct connection to Mount Sinai and the energy of immortality.

malkenu מַלְכֵּנוּ vekeravtanu וְקֵרַבְתָּנוּ

LESHIMCHA HAGADOL

This phrase gives us the power to remove all doubt and uncertainty from our lives.

Without the power of certainty, all our prayers are rendered ineffective. The kabbalists explain that uncertainty is the seed of all evil in the world: about us, about the existence of God, about our destiny and about our ability to overcome challenges. Because our consciousness creates our reality, our uncertainty inevitably leads to chaos. When we destroy our doubt, all that can remain is positivity and certainty in the Light. The word *Amalek* עֲמָלֵק has the same numerical value as the Aramaic word for "uncertainty" and "doubt," ספק (240). *Amalek* refers to the doubts and uncertainties that infect us, causing disunity and hatred among people. A story in the Bible recounts how God ordered the Israelites to go and slaughter all the men, women, and children of the nation of *Amalek*. The *Zohar* explains that in this passage is a code for the key to destroying our doubt. God was really telling the Israelites to slaughter the uncertainty within them.

עם ד' אותיות = מבה, יזל, אום ; להוֹ hagadol הַגָּדוֹל leshimcha לְשִׁמְךָ

BE'AHAVA LEHODOT LACH

We are now gaining the strength to refrain from any kind of evil speech or gossip about other people.

Spiritually, evil speech is considered one of the most serious negative actions a person can commit— even more serious than murder. With murder, say the sages, one person only dies once. When we gossip about someone spiritually, three people die – the speaker, the listener and whoever is spoken of. And not only that, every time the gossip spreads from one person to another we kill that person again. Speech has tremendous power. When we speak ill of others, not only do we hurt and damage their lives, but the harm spills over into the person listening to the gossip, as well as into our own lives. The *Talmud* teaches that the destruction of the Temple occurred because of evil speech and hatred between people. If we do not refrain from speaking ill about our fellow man, others will not be able to refrain from speaking ill of us. The kabbalists teach us that evil speech is one of the spiritual causes of the most negative force in our physical world, *hatred for no reason*.

lach לָךְ lehodot לְהוֹדוֹת אוזר, ראגה be'ahava בְּאַהֲבָה

Break the yoke of the nations from our necks and quickly lead us, proudly upright, to our land. For You are God, Who works salvation. You chose us from among all nations and tongues.

VEKERAVTANU MALKENU - *And brought us close, our King,*

LESHIMCHA HAGADOL - *To Your great Name*

BE'AHAVA LEHODOT LACH - *To lovingly express our gratitude,*

:shimcha שִׁמְךָ et אֶת־ אוֹר, דאגה ul'ahava וּלְאַהֲבָה ulyachedcha וּלְיַחֶדְךָ

ר"ת הברכה עולה למנין ל"ב נתיבות החכמה

Adonai יְהֹוָאדֹנָיאהדונהי Ata אַתָּה baruch בָּרוּךְ

be'ahava בְּאַהֲבָה אוֹר, דאגה Yisrael יִשְׂרָאֵל be'amo בְּעַמּוֹ habocher הַבּוֹחֵר

ר"ת שם קדוש ביב (באתב"ע שמעו):

THE SHEMA

The *Shema* is one of the most powerful tools to draw the energy of healing to our lives. The true power of the *Shema* is unleashed when we meditate upon others who need healing energy while reciting it.

The first verse of the *Shema* channels the energy of *Zeir Anpin,* or the Upper Worlds.

The second verse refers to our world, the World of *Malchut.*

There is a total of 248 words in this prayer, and these 248 words transmit healing energy to the 248 parts of the human body and its soul. The first paragraph of the *Shema* is built of 42 words, connecting us to the 42-Letter Name of God in the *Ana Beko'ach*. The second paragraph is composed of 72 words that connect us to The 72 Names of God. The third paragraph contains 50 words that link us to The 50 Gates of Binah, which helps us rise above the 50 Gates of Negativity. The final paragraph of the *Shema* has 72 words, which also connects us to The 72 Names of God, but through a different letter combination than that which is used in the second paragraph.

1) In order to receive the Light of the *Shema,* you have to accept upon yourself the precept of: "Love your neighbor as yourself," and see yourself together with all the souls that are part of the original Adam.

2) You need to meditate to connect to the precept of the Reading of *Shema* twice a day.

3) Before saying the *Shema* you should cover your eyes with the right hand (while saying the words "*Shema Yisrael ... le'olam va'ed,*") and hold the four *tzitziot* with the left hand and place them on your heart.

4) You should read the *Shema* with deep meditation, saying it with the intonations. It is necessary to be careful with the pronunciation of all the letters. Every word that ends with the same letter that the next word begins with must be pronounced on its own and not lead into the next word e.g. *bechol levavcha*. *Bechol* ends with a *Lamed* and *levavcha* begins with a *Lamed*. Each of these words must be pronounced separately so that both *Lameds* are heard. And therefore we add a special symbol (˙) on top of each place.

First, meditate in general on the first *Yichud* of the four *Yichuds* of the Name: יהוה, and in particular to awaken the letter ה, and then to connect it with the letter ו. Then connect the letter י and the letter ה together in the following order: *Hei* (ה), *Hei-Vav* (ה"ו), then *Yud-Hei* (י"ה), which adds up to 31, the secret of יא"י of the Name ס"ג. It is good to meditate on this *Yichud* before reciting any *Shema* because it acts as a replacement for the times that you may have missed reading the *Shema*. This *Yichud* has the same ability to create a Supernal connection like the reading of the *Shema* - to raise *Zeir* and *Nukva* together for the *Zivug* of *Abba* and *Ima*.

to unify You, and to love Your Name.
Blessed are You, Lord, Who has chosen His Nation Israel, with love.

(According to the Ramchal, the elevation of the *Mochin* during this *Shema* is the same as during the *Shema* of *Shacharit* of weekdays, except that *Zeir Anpin* is elevated to *Netzach, Hod, Yesod* of *Ima*.)

Shema – שָׁמַע

The reason for saying the *Shema* here is to awaken the *Mochin* (brains/energy) for *Ze'ir Anpin*. We need to do so in *Beriah*, because in *Atzilut* we are not able to do that anymore.

General Meditation: עֹ שֹׁם — to draw the energy from the Seven Lower *Sefirot* of *Ima* to the *Nukva*, which enables the *Nukva* to elevate the *Mayin Nukvin* (awakening from Below).

Particular Meditation: שְׁרֹי ▴ יהוה = שֹׁם = שׁם and five times the letters י and ד of בֹ"ן = עֹ [The letter *Hei* (ה) is formed by the letters *Dalet* (ד) and *Yud* (י), so in בֹ"ן we have four times the letter ה plus another time the letters י and ד from יוד of בֹ"ן.]. Also the three letters ו (18) that are left from בֹ"ן, plus בֹ"ן itself (52) equals עֹ (70).

Yisrael – יִשְׂרָאֵל

General Meditation: שֹׁיר אֵל — to draw energy from *Chesed* and *Gevurah* of *Abba* to *Zeir Anpin*, to do his action in the secret of *Mayin Duchrin* (awakening from Above).

Particular Meditation: (the rearranged letters of the word *Yisrael*) – שֹׁר אֵלִי

י"ה דְאלֹהִים דְמוֹ וְכמה בהכאה (יו"ד פֿעמים ה"י) = שֹׁ',

י"ה דְאלֹהִים דְמוֹ בִינָה בהכאה (יו"ד פֿעמים ה"ה) = ר',

י"ה דְאלֹהִים דְמוֹ דְחוֹסדים דְדעת (יו"ד ה"א), וי"ה, דְאלֹהִים דְמוֹ דְגְבוֹרות דְדעת (י"ה) = אלֹי'.

Also meditate to draw the Surrounding Light of *Abba* of *Katnut* into *Zeir Anpin*.

Adonai Elohenu Adonai - יהוה אלֹהֵינוּ יהוה

General Meditation: to draw energy to *Abba*, *Ima* and *Da'at* from *Arich Anpin*,

Particular Meditation: (יוד הי וי הי) ע"ב (אלף הי יוד הי) קס"א (יוד הי ויו הי) ע"ב.

Echad – אֶחָד

(The secret of the complete Yichud-Unification)

The letters *Alef* א and *Chet* ח from *Echad* אֶחָד are *Zeir Anpin* and the letter *Dalet* ד is *Nukva*. **You should meditate** to devote your soul for the sanctification of the Holy Name, thereby elevating your *Nefesh*, *Ruach*, *Neshamah* and *Neshamah* of *Neshamah* with *Zeir Anpin* and *Nukva* (using the Names: ע"ב and ס"ג) to *Abba* and *Ima* as the secret of *Mayin Nukvin*, and by that energy, *Abba* and *Ima* will be unified in the secret of the Name: יאהדוֹנהי. **Also meditate** to draw out the Inner Six Edges of *Gadlut* of *Ima* into *Zeir Anpin*. The Drop, which is ע"ב, is drawn out from the external of *Atik*, and descends to *Yesod* of *Ima*, where it becomes: ע"ב ס"ג מ"ה בֹ"ן, and the four spelled out אהיה (אלף הי יוד הי, אלף הי יוד הי, אלף הא יוד הא, אלף הה יוד הה) become Her clothing. As a result, *Zeir Anpin* now has four spelled out יהֹ"ו (יוד הי ויו, יוד הי ואו, יוד הא ואו, יוד הה וו), four spelled out אהֹי"ה (אלף הי יוד, אלף הי יוד, אלף הא יוד, אלף הה יוד) and the Inner Six Edges of *Gadlut* of *Ima*. **Also meditate** on the Name: אלֹ"ף ה"י וי"ו ה"י, which is the entire *Mochin* in the secret of *Da'at*. **And also meditate** (according to the Ramchal) on the four spelled out *Alef* (אלף=111) of the Name: אהֹי"ה that is equal to the word *Midat* (444), making the *Keter* for Leah.

Baruch Shem - בָּרוּךְ שֵׁם כְּבוֹד מַלְכוּתוֹ לְעוֹלָם וָעֶד

Baruch Shem Kevod – *Chochmah, Binah, Da'at of Leah;*
Malchuto – *Her Keter;* **Le'olam** – *the rest of Her Partzuf;*
Va'ed – *the four* הוֹה (4 times 20 equal to *Va'ed*=80) will make the *Keter* for Rachel.

And the four spelled out הוֹה (הי יוד הי, הי יוד הי, הא יוד הי, הה יוד הה) will make the rest of Her body.

שְׁמַע shema עָ׳ רבתי יִשְׂרָאֵל Yisrael יְהֹוָ֥ה Adonai

אֱלֹהֵינוּ Elohenu יְהֹוָ֥ה Adonai | אֶחָֽד echad ד׳ רבתי

בָּרוּךְ baruch שֵׁם shem כְּבוֹד kevod מַלְכוּתוֹ malchuto, (Whisper :)

לְעוֹלָם le'olam וָעֶֽד va'ed

Yud, Chochmah, head — 42 words corresponding to the Holy 42-Letter Name of God.

אֵת et וְאָ֣הַבְתָּ֔ ve'ahavta

יְהֹוָ֖ה Adonai אֱלֹהֶ֑יךָ Elohecha

בְּכָל־ bechol לְבָבְךָ֥ levavcha וּבְכָל־ uvchol נַפְשְׁךָ֖ nafshecha

וּבְכָל־ uvchol מְאֹדֶֽךָ me'odecha וְהָי֞וּ vehayu הַדְּבָרִ֣ים hadevarim

הָאֵ֗לֶּה ha'ele אֲשֶׁ֨ר asher אָֽנֹכִ֧י anochi מְצַוְּךָ֛ metzavecha הַיּ֖וֹם hayom

עַל־ al (pause here) לְבָבֶֽךָ levavecha וְשִׁנַּנְתָּ֣ם veshinantam

לְבָנֶ֔יךָ levanecha וְדִבַּרְתָּ֖ vedibarta בָּ֑ם bam בְּשִׁבְתְּךָ֤ beshivtecha

בְּבֵיתֶ֨ךָ bevetecha וּבְלֶכְתְּךָ֤ uvlechtecha בַדֶּ֔רֶךְ vaderech

וּֽבְשָׁכְבְּךָ֖ uvshochbecha וּבְקוּמֶֽךָ uvkumecha

וּקְשַׁרְתָּ֥ם ukshartam לְא֖וֹת le'ot עַל־ al יָדֶ֑ךָ yadecha

---

THE SHEMA

"Hear Israel, the Lord our God. The Lord is One." (Deuteronomy 6:4)

"Blessed is the glorious Name, His Kingdom is forever and for eternity." (Pesachim 56a)

"And you shall love the Lord, your God, with all your heart and with all your soul and with all that you possess. Let those words that I command you today be upon your heart. And you shall teach them to your children and you shall speak of them while you sit in your home and while you walk on your way and when you lie down and when you rise. You shall bind them as a sign upon your hand

שי עֵינֶֽיךָ enecha   ק בֵּין ben   ז לְטֹֽטָפֹת letotafot   פ וְהָיוּ vehayu

י עַל־ al   ק וּכְתַבְתָּם uchtavtam   מ"ה: רִיבוּעַ ; א קס"א ע"ה

ת ׃וּבִשְׁעָרֶֽיךָ uvish'arecha   ב"פ ראה בֵּיתֶֽךָ betecha   (זז מות) נית mezuzot מְזֻזוֹת צ

VEHAYA IM SHAMO'A

Hei, Binah, arms and body — 72 words corresponding to the 72 Names of God.

וָהוּ   ילי
יהוה ; יהה im אִם־ יוה"ך, מ"א אותיות דפשוטו, דמילוי ודמילוי דמילוי דאהיה ע"ה vehaya וְהָיָה ע"ה

אכא   ללה   מהש   עלם   סיט
asher אֲשֶׁר   mitzvotai מִצְוֹתַי   el אֶל־   tishme'u תִּשְׁמְעוּ   shamo'a שָׁמֹֽעַ

כהת   הזי   אלד   לאו
anochi אָֽנֹכִי   metzave מְצַוֶּה   etchem אֶתְכֶם   hayom הַיּוֹם ע"ה נגד, מזבוז, זן, אל יהוה

מבה   יזל   ההע
Adonai יְהֹוָה‎(ואהדונהי)‎אהדונהי   et אֶת־ דאגה, אוזר, le'ahava לְאַהֲבָה (pause here)

הקם   הרי
ul'ovdo וּלְעָבְדוֹ (enunciate the letter *Ayin* in the word "ul'ovdo") ילה Elohechem אֱלֹהֵיכֶם

לאו   כלי   לוו
bechol בְּכָל־ ב"ן, לכב   levavchem לְבַבְכֶם לכב   uvchol וּבְכָל־ ב"ן, לכב

פהל   נלך   ייי   מלה
nafshechem נַפְשְׁכֶם׃   venatati וְנָתַתִּי   metar מְטַר־   artzechem אַרְצְכֶם

וזהו   נתה   האא   ירת   שאה
be'ito בְּעִתּוֹ   yore יוֹרֶה   umalkosh וּמַלְקוֹשׁ   ve'asafta וְאָסַפְתָּ   deganecha דְגָנֶֽךָ

ריי   אום   לכב   ועיר
vetiroshcha וְתִירֹֽשְׁךָ   veyitz'harecha וְיִצְהָרֶֽךָ׃   venatati וְנָתַתִּי   esev עֵֽשֶׂב ע"ב שמות

---

and they shall be as frontlets between your eyes.
And you shall write them upon the doorposts of your house and your gates." (Deuteronomy 6:5-9)

VEHAYA IM SHAMO'A

"And it shall come to be that if you shall listen to My commandments that I am commanding you with today to love the Lord, your God, and to serve Him with all your heart and with all your soul, then I shall send rain upon your land in its proper time, both early rain and late rain. You shall then gather your grain and your wine and your oil. And I shall give grass

בְּשָׂדְךָ besadcha לִבְהֶמְתֶּךָ livhemtecha וְאָכַלְתָּ ve'achalta וְשָׂבָעְתָּ vesavata

הִשָּׁמְרוּ hishamru לָכֶם lachem פֶּן pen יִפְתֶּה yifte לְבַבְכֶם levavchem

וְסַרְתֶּם vesartem וַעֲבַדְתֶּם va'avadetem אֱלֹהִים elohim אֲחֵרִים acherim

מֹשֶׁה (הָעוֹמֵד) נֶגֶד (הַקְּלִיפוֹת) וְהִשְׁתַּחֲוִיתֶם vehishtachavitem לָהֶם lahem

וְחָרָה vechara (pause here) אַף af יְהוָֹה Adonai בָּכֶם bachem

וְעָצַר ve'atzar אֶת et הַשָּׁמַיִם hashamayim וְלֹא velo

יִהְיֶה yihye מָטָר matar וְהָאֲדָמָה veha'adama לֹא lo תִתֵּן titen

אֶת et יְבוּלָהּ yevula וַאֲבַדְתֶּם va'avadetem מְהֵרָה mehera מֵעַל me'al

הָאָרֶץ ha'aretz הַטֹּבָה hatova אֲשֶׁר asher

יְהוָֹה Adonai נֹתֵן noten לָכֶם lachem *Vav, Zeir Anpin*

וְשַׂמְתֶּם vesamtem **stomach** – 50 words corresponding to the 50 Gates of *Binah* אֶת et

דְּבָרַי devarai אֵלֶּה ele עַל al לְבַבְכֶם levavchem וְעַל ve'al

נַפְשְׁכֶם nafshechem וּקְשַׁרְתֶּם ukshartem אֹתָם otam לְאוֹת le'ot

---

in your field for your cattle. And you shall eat and you shall be satiated. Be careful lest your heart be seduced and you may turn away and serve alien deities and prostrate yourself before them. And the wrath of the Lord shall be upon you and He shall stop the Heavens and there shall be no more rain and the earth shall not give forth its crop. And you shall quickly perish from the good land that the Lord has given you. And you shall place those words of Mine upon your heart and upon your soul and you shall bind them as a sign

עַל־ al   יֶדְכֶם yedchem   וְהָיוּ vehayu

לְטוֹטָפֹת letotafot   בֵּין ben   עֵינֵיכֶם enechem   ריבוע   מ"ה:

וְלִמַּדְתֶּם velimadetem   אֹתָם otam   אֶת־ et   בְּנֵיכֶם benechem

לְדַבֵּר ledaber   ראה   בָּם bam   שם   בן   מ"ב   בְּשִׁבְתְּךָ beshivtecha

בְּבֵיתֶךָ bevetecha ב"פ ראה   וּבְלֶכְתְּךָ uvlechtecha   בַדֶּרֶךְ vaderech ב"פ יב"ק, ס"ג קס"א   בְּבֵיתֶךָ

וּבְשָׁכְבְּךָ uvshochbecha   וּבְקוּמֶךָ: uvkumecha   וּכְתַבְתָּם uchtavtam   עַל־ al

מְזוּזוֹת mezuzot   בֵּיתֶךָ betecha ב"פ ראה   וּבִשְׁעָרֶיךָ: uvish'arecha   לְמַעַן lema'an

יִרְבּוּ yirbu   יְמֵיכֶם yemechem   ר"ת   יי"ל   וִימֵי vimei   בְּנֵיכֶם venechem

עַל־ al   הָאֲדָמָה ha'adama   אֲשֶׁר asher (enunciate the letter *Ayin* in the word *"nishba"*)

נִשְׁבַּע nishba   יכין   לשבועת   המבול   יְהֹוָאֲדֹנָי Adonai

לַאֲבֹתֵיכֶם la'avotechem   לָתֵת latet   לָהֶם lahem   כִּימֵי kimei

הַשָּׁמַיִם hashamayim   יי"פ טל, יי"פ כוזו   עַל־ al   הָאָרֶץ ha'aretz   אלהים דההין ע"ה:

---

upon your hands and they shall be as frontlets between your eyes. And you shall teach them to your children and speak of them while you sit at home and while you walk on your way and when you lie down and when you rise. You shall write them upon the doorposts of your house and upon your gates. This is so that your days shall be numerous and so shall the days of your children upon the Earth that the Lord had sworn to your fathers to give them as the days of the Heavens upon the Earth." (Deuteronomy 11:13-21)

VAYOMER

Hei, Malchut, legs and reproductive organs,

72 words corresponding to the 72 Names of God in direct order (according to the Ramchal).

עאם   סטב   ייי   ווו

Moshe מֹשֶׁה   el אֶל־   Adonai יְהֹוָאדְנִיאהדונהי   vayomer וַיֹּאמֶר

אוא   ליה   מבטע

el אֶל־ ראה   daber דַּבֵּר : lemor לֵאמֹר   מהטע, ע"ב בריבוע וקס"א, אל שדי, ד"פ אלהים ע"ה

הבמע   להו   אנד   הוי   כמת

ve'asu וְעָשׂוּ   alehem אֲלֵהֶם   ve'amarta וְאָמַרְתָּ   Yisrael יִשְׂרָאֵל   benei בְּנֵי

לוו   המם   היי   מרה   יצל

vigdehem בִּגְדֵיהֶם   kanfei כַּנְפֵי   al עַל־   tzitzit צִיצִת   lahem לָהֶם

נמר   פגל   לוו   כבי

tzitzit צִיצִת   al עַל־   venatnu וְנָתְנוּ   ledorotam לְדֹרֹתָם

וזהו   מנה   יוזי

techelet תְּכֵלֶת : petil פְּתִיל י"פ ב"ן   אלהים אדני קנ"א, ע"ה   hakanaf הַכָּנָף

רלי   שאה   שעת   השא   ניה

oto אֹתוֹ   ur'item וּרְאִיתֶם   letzitzit לְצִיצִת   lachem לָכֶם   ; יהוה יהה   vehaya וְהָיָה

You should pass the *tzitziot* over the eyes and kiss them, then repeat this procedure.

להו   ייו   והר   ליב   אום

Adonai יְהֹוָאדְנִיאהדונהי   mitzvot מִצְוֹת ילי   kol כָּל־   et אֶת־   uzchartem וּזְכַרְתֶּם

רהע   וזם   אני   מנד   כעק

acharei אַחֲרֵי   taturu תָתוּרוּ   velo וְלֹא־   otam אֹתָם   va'asitem וַעֲשִׂיתֶם

מכך   העה   יוזי

מ"ה ריבוע   enechem עֵינֵיכֶם   ve'acharei וְאַחֲרֵי   levavchem לְבַבְכֶם

You should pass the *Tzitziot* over the eyes and then kiss them.

Doing so (kissing the *tzitzit* and passing it over the eyes), is a great support and assistance for the soul to be protected from any transgression. And you should meditate on the precept: "not to follow negative sexual thoughts of the heart and the sights of the eyes for prostitution."

VAYOMER

"And the Lord spoke to Moses and said: Speak to the children of Israel and say to them that they should make for themselves Tzitzit, on the corners of their garments, throughout all their generations. And they must place upon the Tzitzit, of each corner, a blue strand. And this shall be to you as a Tzitzit: you shall see it and remember the commandments of the Lord and fulfill them. And you shall not stray after your hearts and your eyes,

lema'an לְמַעַן ∶acharehem אַחֲרֵיהֶם zonim זֹנִים atem אַתֶּם asher ־אֲשֶׁר

mitzvotai מִצְוֹתָי kol כָּל ־et אֶת va'asitem וַעֲשִׂיתֶם tizkeru תִּזְכְּרוּ∶

∶lelohechem לֵאלֹהֵיכֶם kedoshim קְדֹשִׁים vihyitem וִהְיִיתֶם

asher אֲשֶׁר Elohechem אֱלֹהֵיכֶם Adonai יְהֹוָה(אֲדֹנָי-אֲהדֹנֹהִי) ani אֲנִי

Mitzrayim מִצְרַיִם me'eretz מֵאֶרֶץ etchem אֶתְכֶם hotzeti הוֹצֵאתִי

You should meditate to remember the exodus from *Mitzrayim* (Egypt).

lelohim לֵאלֹהִים lachem לָכֶם lihyot לִהְיוֹת

∶Elohechem אֱלֹהֵיכֶם Adonai יְהֹוָה(אֲדֹנָי-אֲהדֹנֹהִי) ani אֲנִי

Be careful to complete this paragraph together with the *chazan* and the congregation, and say the word "emet" out loud. The *chazan* should say the word "emet" in silence.

יוד הי ויו אֱמֶת emet אהיה פעמים אהיה, ז"פ ס"ג∙

The congregation should be silent, listen and hear the words "Adonai Elohechem emet" spoken by the *chazan*. If you did not complete the paragraph together with the *chazan* you should repeat the last three words on your own. With these three words the *Shema* is completed.

∶Elohechem אֱלֹהֵיכֶם Adonai יְהֹוָה(אֲדֹנָי-אֲהדֹנֹהִי)

אֱמֶת emet אהיה פעמים אהיה, ז"פ ס"ג∙

VEYATZIV

Before the *Amidah*, signifying the World of Emanation *(Atzilut)*, we come across various connections. The Aramaic word *Emet* אמת appears four times on two occasions. The Ari says that the four appearances of the word *emet*, occuring on two occasions, for a total of eight times, refers to the four Exiles and to the four Redemptions of the Israelites that have occurred in history. This word means "truth." When a small degree of untruthfulness lies in our hearts, it is difficult to succeed in our spiritual work. This prayer has the power to remove all falsehoods and open our hearts to truth.

---

after which you adulterate. This is so that you shall remember to fulfill all My commandments and thereby be holy before your God. I am the Lord, your God, Who brought you out of the land of Egypt to be your God. I, the Lord, your God, Is true." (Numbers 15:37-41) the Lord, your God, is true!

We find another code in the word *Emet* אמת:

In Aramaic, this word begins with the letter *Alef* א, the first letter of the alphabet. The second letter in *Emet* is *Mem* מ, the middle of the alphabet. The last letter in *Emet* is *Tav* ת, the last letter of the alphabet. A person of truth has the power of the entire alphabet, which, in essence, is the power of the entire universe.

Hechal Ratzon (the Chamber of the Desire)—*Tiferet* of *Zeir Anpin* in *Beriah*.

א' עיל אמת וי"ה ווין (יאהדונהי) = אמן (יאהדונהי) • veyatziv וְיַצִּיב • venachon וְנָכוֹן • vekayam וְקַיָּם•

וְיָשָׁר veyashar • וְנֶאֱמָן vene'eman • וְאָהוּב ve'ahuv • וְחָבִיב vechaviv הזיי•

וְנֶחְמָד venechmad • וְנָעִים vena'im • וְנוֹרָא venora • וְאַדִּיר ve'adir הרי•

וּמְתֻקָּן umtukan • וּמְקֻבָּל umkubal • וְטוֹב vetov והו• • וְיָפֶה veyafe•

ראה hadavar הַדָּבָר הוי"ה וכו' יכוון ט"ו ווין גימ' יה, הויין עצמן ו, ור"ת הדבר הרי יהוה

haze הֲזֶה alenu עָלֵינוּ והו le'olam לְעוֹלָם ריבוע ס"ג וי' אותיות דס"ג va'ed וְעֶד:

emet אֱמֶת אהיה פעמים אהיה, ז"פ ס"ג Elohei אֱלֹהֵי מילוי ע"ב, דמב ל; ילה; יוד הי ואו

olam עוֹלָם • malkenu מַלְכֵּנוּ tzur צוּר אלהים דההין ע"ה Ya'akov יַעֲקֹב

magen מָגֵן ג"פ אל (ייא"י מילוי דס"ג); ר"ת מיכאל גבריאל נוריאל יִשְׁעֵנוּ

• yish'enu ledor לְדוֹר vador וְדוֹר רי"ו hu הוּא kayam קַיָּם וְשְׁמוֹ ushmo

vechis'o וְכִסְאוֹ kayam קַיָּם נְכוֹן nachon umalchuto וּמַלְכוּתוֹ ve'emunato וְאֱמוּנָתוֹ la'ad לְעַד ב"פ ב"ן; ר"ת לו

kayemet קַיֶּמֶת: udvarav וּדְבָרָיו chayim וְחַיִּים אהיה אהיה יהוה, בינה ע"ה

וְקַיָּמִים vekayamim וְנֶאֱמָנִים vene'emanim וְנֶחְמָדִים venechemadim la'ad לְעַד

ul'olmei וּלְעוֹלְמֵי olamim עוֹלָמִים• (kiss the *Tzitziot*, pass them over the eyes then release) ב"פ ב"ן•

VEYATZIV

And He is established, and correct, and lasting and straightforward, and trustworthy, and beloved, and dear, and desirable, and pleasant, and awesome, and powerful and proper, and accepted, and good, and beautiful. This is to us, forever and ever. It is true that the God of the World is our King, the Rock of Jacob and the Shield of our salvation. For every generation He endures and His Name endures. His Throne is established; His sovereignty and His faithfulness endure forever. His words are alive, enduring, trustworthy and pleasant for all eternity.

עַל al ◆avotenu אֲבוֹתֵינוּ alenu עָלֵינוּ ve'al וְעַל ve'al וְעַל banenu בָּנֵינוּ ve'al וְעַל

דּוֹרוֹתֵינוּ dorotenu ve'al וְעַל kol- כָּל־ ; עמם יִלי zera זֶרַע dorot דּוֹרוֹת

יִשְׂרָאֵל Yisrael עֲבָדֶיךָ avadecha: al עַל הָרִאשׁוֹנִים harishonim ve'al וְעַל

הָאַחֲרוֹנִים ha'acharonim דָּבָר davar ראה tov טוֹב והו vekayam וְקָיָם◆

וְזוּק chok uve'emuna וּבֶאֱמוּנָה אהיה פעמים אהיה, ז"פ ס"ג be'emet בֶּאֱמֶת ואו הא יוד

וְלֹא velo יַעֲבוֹר ya'avor רפ"ח (להעלות רפ"ח ניצוצות שנפלו לקליפה דמשם באים התחלואים)◆

שְׁאַתָּה sheAta ז"פ ס"ג אהיה פעמים אהיה emet אֱמֶת ואו הה יוד

הוּא hu Adonai יְהֹוָה(אדני אהדונהי) Elohenu אֱלֹהֵינוּ יֶלֹה

וֵאלֹהֵי velohei לכב ; מילוי ע"ב, דמב ; יֶלֹה avotenu אֲבוֹתֵינוּ◆

מַלְכֵּנוּ malkenu melech מֶלֶךְ avotenu אֲבוֹתֵינוּ go'alenu גּוֹאֲלֵנוּ

גּוֹאֵל go'el avotenu אֲבוֹתֵינוּ◆ yotzrenu יוֹצְרֵנוּ tzur צוּר אלהים דההין ע"ה

יְשׁוּעָתֵנוּ yeshu'atenu◆ podenu פּוֹדֵנוּ וּמַצִּילֵנוּ umatzilenu ר"ת = אלהים, אהיה אדני

MEM, HEI, SHIN

The letters *Mem* מ, *Hei* ה, and *Shin* שׁ unleash the force of healing. When we close our eyes and visualize these three letters emitting rays of Light, we awaken healing energy from the Upper Worlds and from within ourselves. We can meditate to bathe our entire body in a flood of white Light and to send this energy to others in need of healing. These letters, rearranged, spell out the name of Moses מֹשֶׁה = משׁה, who reached the highest level of connection to the Light of the Creator.

שֶׁמְךָ shemecha הוּא hu me'olam מֵעוֹלָם

ר"ת מהשע, משׂה, ע"ב בריבוע וקס"א, אל עדי

עוֹד od אדני אהיה אלהים, lanu לָנוּ ve'en וְאֵין

אֱלֹהִים Elohim אהיה אדני ; יֶלֹה זוּלָתְךָ zulatcha sela סֶלָה:

This is upon us and upon our sons and upon our future generations and upon all the future generations of the descendants of Israel, Your servants. Upon the earlier and upon the later ones, this is a good and an everlasting thing. With truth and with faith, this is an unbreakable decree. It is true that You are the Lord, our God and the God of our fathers, our King and the King of our fathers, our Redeemer and the Redeemer of our fathers, our Maker and the Rock of our salvation. Our Redeemer and Rescuer.

MEM HEI SHIN

Your Name is of eternity, and we have no other God but You. Selah.

EZRAT

Ayin, Alef, and *Alef,* עאא, the first letters of the first three words of this prayer, have a numerical value of 72. The number 72 is also a code for the concept of mercy and the *Sefirah* of *Chesed.* We learn from this connection that we were meant to live our lives with genuine mercy for others in order to activate the power of the 72 Names of God. If, for some reason, we are not generating results from our prayers, it is only for one reason: We are not treating the people in our life with true mercy. Kabbalah teaches us that even if we are justified in our anger and our refusal to forgive, we must have mercy in our hearts and in our actions towards both our friends and our enemies.

Ata אַתָּה avotenu אֲבוֹתֵינוּ ezrat עֶזְרַת

hu הוּא me'olam מֵעוֹלָם magen מָגֵן

velivnehem וְלִבְנֵיהֶם lahem לָהֶם umoshi'a וּמוֹשִׁיעַ

acharehem אַחֲרֵיהֶם bechol בְּכֹל dor דּוֹר vador וָדוֹר

berum בְּרוּם olam עוֹלָם

umishpatecha וּמִשְׁפָּטֶיךָ moshavecha מוֹשָׁבֶךָ

vetzidkatcha וְצִדְקָתְךָ ad עַד afsei אַפְסֵי aretz אָרֶץ

emet אֱמֶת ashrei אַשְׁרֵי

ish אִישׁ sheyishma שֶׁיִּשְׁמַע lemitzvotecha לְמִצְוֹתֶיךָ

vetoratcha וְתוֹרָתְךָ udvarcha וּדְבָרֶךָ yasim יָשִׂים al עַל libo לִבּוֹ

emet אֱמֶת sheAta שֶׁאַתָּה hu הוּא

adon אָדוֹן le'amecha לְעַמֶּךָ umelech וּמֶלֶךְ gibor גִּבּוֹר

lariv לָרִיב rivam רִיבָם le'avot לָאָבוֹת uvanim וּבָנִים

EZRAT

You have always been the aid for our forefathers, a shield and a savior for them and their children after them in every generation. In the heights of the world is Your abode and Your laws and justice extend to the ends of the Earth. It is true that a man who abides by Your commandments is joyful while he sets Your Torah and Your teachings upon his heart. It is true that You are a Master of Your people and a valorous King, Who fights for their cause, be it the fathers or the sons.

rishon רִאשׁוֹן hu הוּא הוּא Ata אַתָּה, ז"פ ס"ג אהיה פעמים אהיה emet אֱמֶת אהיה

en אֵין umibal'adecha וּמִבַּלְעָדֶיךָ ◆acharon אַחֲרוֹן hu הוּא veAta וְאַתָּה

◆umoshi'a וּמוֹשִׁיעַ go'el גּוֹאֵל melech מֶלֶךְ אדני אהיה אלהים, lanu לָּנוּ

miMitzrayim מִמִּצְרַיִם מצר, ז"פ ס"ג אהיה פעמים אהיה emet אֱמֶת אהיה

mibet מִבֵּית ◆יכה Elohenu אֱלֹהֵינוּ Adonai יְהֹוָה ge'altanu גְּאַלְתָּנוּ

bechorehem בְּכוֹרֵיהֶם יכי kol כָּל ◆peditanu פְּדִיתָנוּ avadim עֲבָדִים ב"פ ראה

◆ga'alta גָּאַלְתָּ Yisrael יִשְׂרָאֵל uvchorcha וּבְכוֹרְךָ haragta הָרַגְתָּ

vezedim וְזֵדִים ◆bakata בָּקַעְתָּ lahem לָהֶם Suf סוּף יכי veYam וְיָם

vayechasu וַיְכַסּוּ ◆יכי yam יָם avru עָבְרוּ vididim וִידִידִים ◆tibata טִבַּעְתָּ

lo לֹא mehem מֵהֶם דאגה אהבה, echad אֶחָד tzarehem צָרֵיהֶם mayim בַּיִם

ahuvim אֲהוּבִים shibechu שִׁבְּחוּ zot זֹאת al עַל ◆notar נוֹתַר

yedidim יְדִידִים venatnu וְנָתְנוּ (מילוי דס"ג) יא"י laEl לָאֵל veromemu וְרוֹמְמוּ

berachot בְּרָכוֹת vetishbachot וְתִשְׁבָּחוֹת shirot שִׁירוֹת zemirot זְמִירוֹת

◆vekayam וְקַיָּם chai וַזֹי (מילוי דס"ג) יא"י El אֵל lamelech לַמֶּלֶךְ vehoda'ot וְהוֹדָאוֹת

◆venora וְנוֹרָא gadol גָּדוֹל לְהֹוּ ; עם ד' אותיות = מובה, יז"ל, אום venisa וְנִשָּׂא ram רָם

magbiha מַגְבִּיהַּ ◆aretz אָרֶץ adei עֲדֵי ge'im גֵּאִים mashpil מַשְׁפִּיל

◆asirim אֲסִירִים motzi מוֹצִיא ◆marom מָרוֹם ad עַד shefalim שְׁפָלִים

ha'one הָעוֹנֶה dalim דַּלִּים ozer עוֹזֵר ◆anavim עֲנָוִים pode פּוֹדֶה

◆elav אֵלָיו shave'am שַׁוְּעָם be'et בְּעֵת Yisrael יִשְׂרָאֵל le'amo לְעַמּוֹ

Ozer Dalim: poverty removes the transgressions of a person and through that the Creator gives mercy to His creation. And therefore you should meditate to make yourself poor in the eyes of the *Shechinah* and be concerned that the *Shechinah* is in exile together with the Children of Israel.

It is true that You are first and You are last and apart from You we have no King Who redeems and saves. It is true that You have redeemed us from Egypt, Lord, our God, and from a house of slaves did You redeem us. You killed all their firstborn and You saved Your firstborn Israel. You split the Sea of Reeds for them. And You drowned the tyrants while Your beloved crossed the sea. The waters then covered their enemies and not one of them was spared. For this, the beloved ones praised and exalted God. And the dear ones offered melodies, songs, lyrics and praises, blessings and thanks to the King, to the living and lasting God. Who is Supernal and uplifted, powerful and awesome and Who degrades the arrogant to the ground; Who raises the meek to great heights; Who frees the imprisoned, redeems the humble and helps the needy; He, Who answers the children of Israel when they cry out to Him.

TEHILOT

We now begin to elevate to the World of Emanation (*Atzilut*). Accordingly, we rise and stand to ignite the engines of our soul. To prepare ourselves for this launch, we must eliminate any hatred or ill feelings that we harbor for others from our minds.

Hechal Kodesh HaKodashim (the Chamber of the Holy of Holies)—of *Zeir Anpin* in *Beriah*.

go'alam גּוֹאֲלָם   elyon עֶלְיוֹן   (מילוי דס״ג) יי״א   laEl לָאֵל   tehilot תִּהִלּוֹת

א, ע״ב ברִבוע וקס״א Moshe מֹשֶׁה   umvorach וּמְבֹרָךְ   hu הוּא   baruch בָּרוּךְ

אל שדי, ד״פ אלהים ע״ה Yisrael יִשְׂרָאֵל   uvnei וּבְנֵי

ve'amru וְאָמְרוּ   raba רַבָּה   besimcha בְּשִׂמְחָה   shira שִׁירָה   anu עָנוּ   lecha לְךָ

ba'elim בָּאֵלִים   chamocha כָּמֹכָה   ילי   mi מִי   chulam: כֻּלָּם

kamocha כָּמֹכָה ילי   mi מִי   Adonai יְהֹוָאדְנָיאהדונהי

nora נוֹרָא   bakodesh בַּקֹּדֶשׁ   ne'edar נֶאְדָּר

chadasha וְדָשָׁה   shira שִׁירָה   fele: פֶּלֶא   ose עֹשֵׂה   tehilot תִּהִלּוֹת

hagadol הַגָּדוֹל   leshimcha לְשִׁמְךָ   ge'ulim גְּאוּלִים   shibechu שִׁבְּחוּ

kulam כֻּלָּם   yachad יַוֹחַד   hayam הַיָּם   sefat שְׂפַת   al עַל

Adonai | יְהֹוָאדְנָיאהדונהי   ve'amru: וְאָמְרוּ   vehimlichu וְהִמְלִיכוּ   hodu הוֹדוּ

va'ed: וָעֶד   le'olam לְעֹלָם   yimloch יִמְלֹךְ

Tzeva'ot צְבָאוֹת   Adonai יְהֹוָאדְנָיאהדונהי   go'alenu גֹּאֲלֵנוּ   vene'emar וְנֶאֱמַר

Yisrael: יִשְׂרָאֵל   kedosh קְדוֹשׁ   shemo שְׁמוֹ

Yisrael: יִשְׂרָאֵל   ga'al גָּאַל   Adonai יְהֹוָאדְנָיאהדונהי   Ata אַתָּה   baruch בָּרוּךְ

Begin the *Amidah* immediately without any interruption, not even one breath. Doing so prevents separation between *Yesod* (awakened by the words *"ga'al Yisrael"*) and *Malchut* (awakened by the word *"Adonai"*). Your reward is great. You receive protection from negativity and from making mistakes. This action also helps to correct the transgression of spilling one's seed.

TEHILOT

Praises to the Supreme God, Who is their redeemer. Blessed is He Who is blessed. Moses and the Children of Israel raised their voice in song to You, with great joy, and they all said: "Who is like You among the deities, Lord? Who is like You, mighty in holiness, awesome in praises, and Who works wonders?" (Exodus 15:11) With a new song did the redeemed praise Your great Name by the seashore. All of them in unison gave thanks and accepted Your sovereignty and they said, "the Lord shall reign forever and ever." (Exodus 15:18) And it is said: "Our redeemer, the Lord of hosts is His Name, the holy One of Israel." (Isaiah 47:4) Blessed are You, Lord, Who redeemed Israel.

Malchut of *Atzilut* is included now in *Hechal Kodesh HaKodashim* of *Beriah*.

When the Holiday falls on *Shabbat* or on *Shabbat Chol Hamo'ed* scan the following:

The Format of the Ascension in *Shacharit* of *Shabbat*

In the silent connection of *Shachrit* of *Shabbat,* the *Mochin* from the Supernal *Abba* and *Ima* are starting to enter into *Zeir Anpin*. **Meditate**, that the letter **צ** of the *Tzelem* enter the five *Partzufim* of *Netzach, Hod, Yesod* of *Chochmah* of *Zeir Anpin* (which is called: *Nefesh, Ruach, Neshamah, Chayah, Yechidah* of *Nefesh* of *Chayah*).**So now,** *Keter, Chochmah, Binah, Da'at* of *Zeir Anpin* are elevated to *Netzach, Hod, Yesod* of the Supernal *Abba* and *Ima*, and *Chesed, Gevurah, Tiferet* of *Zeir Anpin* are elevated to *Chochmah, Binah, Da'at* of *Yisrael Saba* and *Tevunah* and *Netzach, Hod, Yesod* of *Zeir Anpin* are elevated to *Chesed, Gevurah, Tiferet* of *Yisrael Saba* and *Tevunah*, and *Yaakov* and *Rachel* (that are standing in *Netzach, Hod, Yesod* of *Binah* of *Zeir Anpin*, which means, *Netzach, Hod, Yesod* of *Yisrael Saba* and *Tevunah*) are elevated to *Chesed, Gevurah, Tiferet* of *Binah* of *Zeir Anpin* (which means *Chesed, Gevurah, Tiferet* of *Yisrael Saba* and *Tevunah*). **So now**, *Netzach, Hod, Yesod* of *Zeir Anpin* become *Mochin* (*Keter, Chochmah, Binah, Da'at*) for *Yaakov* and *Rachel*.

In the Silent connection - when saying "*Baruch*" meditate to draw the Six Edges (*Chesed, Gevurah, Tiferet, Netzach, Hod, Yesod* of *Keter, Chochmah, Binah, Da'at* of *Netzach, Hod, Yesod* of the Internal of Supernal *Ima*) that were drawn by the *Shema* (to *Keter, Chochmah, Binah, Da'at, Chesed, Gevurah, Tiferet* of *Zeir Anpin*); **to** *Chesed, Gevurah, Tiferet, Netzach, Hod, Yesod* of *Keter, Chochmah, Binah, Da'at* of *Netzach, Hod, Yesod* of *Chochmah* of the Internal of *Zeir Anpin*. **When saying "*Ata*" meditate to draw** *Keter, Chochmah, Binah, Da'at* of *Keter, Chochmah, Binah, Da'at* to the Three Upper *Sefirot* of *Zeir Anpin* and push down the Six Edges (of *Tevunah*) to the Six Edges of *Zeir Anpin*. **When saying "*Adonai*" meditate to draw** *Chochmah, Chesed, Netzach, Binah, Gevurah, Hod, Da'at, Tiferet, Yesod* (in three columns) of *Keter, Chochmah, Binah, Da'at* of *Netzach, Hod, Yesod* of the Internal of Supernal *Abba* to *Zeir Anpin* by the two stages of standing upright.

In the repetition of *Shachrit* of *Shabbat,* *Zeir Anpin* and *Leah* rise in *Chesed, Gevurah, Tiferet* of Supernal *Abba* and *Ima*. **Meditate**, that the letter **ל** of the *Tzelem* (five *Tzelamim* of *Chesed, Gevurah, Tiferet* of the Supernal *Abba* and *Ima*) enters the five *Partzufim* of *Chesed, Gevurah, Tiferet* of *Chochmah* of *Zeir Anpin* (which is called: *Nefesh, Ruach, Neshamah, Chayah, Yechidah* of *Ruach* of *Chayah*). **So now**, *Keter, Chochmah, Binah, Da'at* of *Zeir Anpin* are elevated to *Chesed, Gevurah, Tiferet* of the Supernal *Abba* and *Ima*, and *Chesed, Gevurah, Tiferet* of *Zeir Anpin* are elevated to *Netzach, Hod, Yesod* of the Supernal *Abba* and *Ima*, and *Netzach, Hod, Yesod* of *Zeir Anpin* are elevated to *Keter, Chochmah, Binah, Da'at* of *Yisrael Saba* and *Tevunah*, and *Yaakov* and *Rachel* (that are standing in *Chesed, Gevurah, Tiferet* of *Binah* of *Zeir Anpin*, which means, *Chesed, Gevurah, Tiferet* of *Yisrael Saba* and *Tevunah*) are elevated to *Keter, Chochmah, Binah, Da'at* of *Binah* of *Zeir Anpin* (which means *Keter, Chochmah, Binah, Da'at* of *Yisrael Saba* and *Tevunah*). **So now**, *Netzach, Hod, Yesod* of *Binah Zeir Anpin* become *Mochin* - *Keter, Chochmah, Binah, Da'at* – for *Yaakov* and *Rachel*.

In the repetition - when saying "*Baruch*" meditate to draw the Six Edges (*Chesed, Gevurah, Tiferet, Netzach, Hod, Yesod* of *Keter, Chochmah, Binah, Da'at* of *Chesed, Gevurah, Tiferet* of the Internal of Supernal *Ima*) that were drawn by the *Shema* (to *Keter, Chochmah, Binah, Da'at, Chesed, Gevurah, Tiferet* of *Zeir Anpin*); **to** *Chesed, Gevurah, Tiferet, Netzach, Hod, Yesod* of *Keter, Chochmah, Binah, Da'at* of *Chesed, Gevurah, Tiferet* of *Chochmah* of the Internal of *Zeir Anpin*. **When saying "*Ata*" meditate to draw** *Keter, Chochmah, Binah, Da'at* of *Keter, Chochmah, Binah, Da'at* to the Three Upper *Sefirot* of *Zeir Anpin* and push down the Six Edges (of *Tevunah*) to the Six Edges of *Zeir Anpin*. **When saying "*Adonai*" meditate to draw** *Chochmah, Chesed, Netzach,* and *Binah, Gevurah, Hod,* and *Da'at, Tiferet, Yesod* (in three columns) of *Keter, Chochmah, Binah, Da'at* of *Chesed, Gevurah, Tiferet* of the Internal of Supernal *Abba* to *Zeir Anpin* by the two stages of standing upright.

Meditate to receive the extra soul called: *Ruach*
from the aspect of the day of *Shabbat*.

On *Shabbat Chol Hamo'ed* continue with the *Amidah* on page 700.

On *Chol Hamo'ed* continue with the *Amidah* on page 26.

yagid יַגִּיד ufi וּפִי tiftach תִּפְתָּח sefatai שְׂפָתַי (pause here) ללה Adonai אֲדֹנָי

יזו (כ"ב אותיות פשוטות [=אכא] וה' אותיות סופיות בזוהר) ס"ת = בוכו: tehilatecha תְּהִלָּתֶךָ

THE FIRST BLESSING - INVOKES THE SHIELD OF ABRAHAM.

Abraham is the channel of the Right Column energy of positivity, sharing, and mercy. Sharing actions can protect us from all forms of negativity.

Chesed that becomes *Chochmah*

In this section there are 42 words, the secret of the 42-Letter Name of God and therefore it begins with the letter *Bet* (2) and ends with the letter *Mem* (40).

Bend your knees at "*baruch*," bow at "*Ata*" and straighten up at "*Adonai*."

א   ב

המלכות לה' (אותיות הא"ב המסמלות את העפוע המגיע) א–ת Ata אַתָּה baruch בָּרוּךְ

י

ילה Elohenu אֱלֹהֵינוּ (יא) Adonai יהוה/אהדונהי/אדני

ת   צ

avotenu אֲבוֹתֵינוּ ילה ; דמב ע"ב, מילוי ; לכב velohei וֵאלֹהֵי

ק   ר

(*Chochmah*) Avraham אַבְרָהָם ילה ; דמב ע"ב, מילוי Elohei אֱלֹהֵי

אותיות פשוטות וט"ז רי"ו אל, וז"פ (אברים), עסמ"ב רמ"וז החכמה, נתיבות ול"ב רי"ו אל,

ע   ש

ב"ן ד"פ (*Binah*) Yitzchak יִצְחָק ילה ; דמב ע"ב, מילוי Elohei אֱלֹהֵי

ט   י

איההויה יאהדונהי הויות, ו' (*Da'at*) Yaakov יַעֲקֹב ילה ; דמב ע"ב, מילוי ; לכב velohei וֵאלֹהֵי

THE AMIDAH
"My Lord, open my lips, and my mouth shall relate Your praise." (Psalms 51:17)

THE FIRST BLESSING
Blessed are You, Lord,
our God and God of our forefathers: the God of Abraham, the God of Isaac, and the God of Jacob.

גָּדוֹל = לְהוֹ ; סִיט = הָאֵל הַגָּדוֹל ; יא"י (מילוי דס"ג) לאה ; haEl **הָאֵל** hagadol **הַגָּדוֹל**

עם ד' אותיות = מבה, יזל, אום ר"ת ההה hagibor **הַגִּבּוֹר** vehanora ◆**וְהַנּוֹרָא**

רִיבּוּעַ יהוה ; ר"ת ע"ב, (מילוי דס"ג) יא"י El **אֵל** elyon ◆**עֶלְיוֹן**

hakol **הַכֹּל** kone **קוֹנֵה** tovim ◆**טוֹבִים** chasadim **וַחֲסָדִים** gomel **גּוֹמֵל**

umevi **וּמֵבִיא** avot ◆**אָבוֹת** chasdei **וַחַסְדֵי** vezocher **וְזוֹכֵר**

lema'an **לְמַעַן** venehem **בְּנֵיהֶם** livnei **לִבְנֵי** go'el **גּוֹאֵל**

אוֹזֵר, דאגה ✦ be'ahava **בְּאַהֲבָה** ע"ה מהש ע"ה, ע"ב בריבוע וקס"א ע"ה, אל שדי ע"ה shemo **שְׁמוֹ**

When saying the word "be'ahava" you should meditate to devote your soul to sanctify the Holy Name and accept upon yourself the four forms of death.

umagen **וּמָגֵן** umoshi'a **וּמוֹשִׁיעַ** ozer **עוֹזֵר** melech **מֶלֶךְ**

ג"פ אל (יא"י מילוי דס"ג) ; ר"ת מיכאל גבריאל נוריאל ✦

Bend your knees at "baruch," bow at "Ata" and straighten up at "Adonai."

(on *Shabbat*) **יֱהֹוֶה:** אהיה יהו אלף הי יוד הי

(הד) Adonai **יֲהֹוֶאדֹנָי**(יֱהֹוֶה)(יֱהֹוֶה)אהדונהי Ata **אַתָּה** baruch **בָּרוּךְ**

Avraham **אַבְרָהָם** ; ר"ת מיכאל גבריאל נוריאל ; ג"פ אל (יא"י מילוי דס"ג) magen **מָגֵן**

פשוטות ✦ אותיות וט"ז עסמ"ב (אברים), רמ"ח נתיבות החכמה, ול"ב ורי"ו אל, וז"פ

The great, mighty and awesome God.
The Supernal God, Who bestows beneficial kindness and creates everything.
Who recalls the kindness of the forefathers and brings a Redeemer to their descendants for the sake of His Name, lovingly. King, Helper, Savior and Shield. Blessed are You, Lord, the shield of Abraham.

THE SECOND BLESSING

THE ENERGY OF ISAAC IGNITES THE POWER FOR THE RESURRECTION OF THE DEAD.

Whereas Abraham represents the power of sharing, Isaac represents the Left Column energy of judgment. Judgment shortens the *tikkun* process and paves the way for our eventual resurrection.

Gevurah that becomes *Binah*.

In this section there are 49 words corresponding to the 49 Gates of the Pure System in *Binah*.

אַתָּה Ata גִּבּוֹר gibor לְעוֹלָם le'olam ס"ג וי' אותיות דס"ג אֲדֹנָי Adonai ללה

(ר"ת אַגְלָא והוא עם גדול ואמיץ, ובו היה יהודה מתגבר על אויביו. ע"ה אלד, בוכו).

מְחַיֵּה mechaye ס"ג מֵתִים metim אַתָּה Ata רַב rav לְהוֹשִׁיעַ lehoshi'a

מוֹרִיד morid הַטַּל hatal יוד הא ואו, כוזו, מספר אותיות דמילואי עסמ"ב ; ר"ת מ"ה:

If you mistakenly say "*Mashiv haru'ach*," and realize this before the end of the blessing "*baruch Ata Adonai*," you should return to the beginning of the blessing "*Ata gibor*" and continue as usual. But if you only realize this after the end of the blessing, you should start the *Amidah* from the beginning.

מְכַלְכֵּל mechalkel וְחַיִּים chayim אהיה אהיה יהוה, בינה ע"ה בְּחֶסֶד bechesed

בְּרַחֲמִים berachamim מֵתִים metim מְחַיֵּה mechaye ס"ג יהוה, ע"ב, ריבוע ס"ג

סוֹמֵךְ somech רַבִּים rabim (טלא דעתיקא) י"פ יהוה אלהים הההין (במוכסז) מצפצ,

וְזוֹלִים cholim וְרוֹפֵא verofe (זו"ן) נוֹפְלִים noflim ריבוע אדני כוך, (אכדטם)

וּמְקַיֵּם umekayem אֲסוּרִים asurim וּמַתִּיר umatir אותיות ודי מ"ה = וזולה

אֱמוּנָתוֹ emunato לִישֵׁנֵי lishenei עָפָר afar בְּמִי mi כָּמוֹךָ chamocha ילי

בַּעַל ba'al גְּבוּרוֹת gevurot (you should enunciate the letter *Ayin* in the word "*ba'al*")

וּמִי umi ילי דּוֹמֶה dome לָךְ lach מֶלֶךְ melech מֵמִית memit

וּמְחַיֵּה umchaye ס"ג (יוד הי ואו הי) וּמַצְמִיחַ umatzmi'ach יְשׁוּעָה yeshu'a

וְנֶאֱמָן vene'eman אַתָּה Ata לְהַחֲיוֹת lehachayot מֵתִים metim

(on *Shabbat*: יהוה אלף הי יוד הי אהיה יהו)

בָּרוּךְ baruch אַתָּה Ata יְהֹוָה (יְהֹוִ)(יֶאֱהֹדֹנָה)(יֶהֹוִה)(יַאהדונהי) Adonai

מְחַיֵּה mechaye ס"ג (יוד הי ואו הי) הַמֵּתִים hametim ר"ת מ"ה וס"ת מ"ה:

THE SECOND BLESSING

You are mighty forever, Lord. You resurrect the dead and are very capable of redeeming. Who causes dew to fall. You sustain life with kindness and resurrect the dead with great compassion. You support those who have fallen, heal the sick, release the imprisoned, and fulfill Your faithful words to those who are asleep in the dust. Who is like You, Master of might, and Who can compare to You, King, Who causes death, Who gives life, and Who sprouts salvation? And You are faithful to resurrecting the dead. Blessed are You, Lord, Who resurrects the dead.

NAKDISHACH – THE KEDUSHA

The congregation recites this prayer together.

Saying the *Kedusha* (Holiness) we meditate to bring the holiness of the Creator among us. As it says: *"Venikdashti betoch Benei Israel"* (God is hallowed among the children of Israel).

vena'aritzach וְנַעֲרִיצָךְ nakdishach נַקְדִּישָׁךְ

sarfei שַׂרְפֵי האא י"פ מ"כ, sod סוֹד si'ach שִׂיחַ keno'am כְּנוֹעַם

kedusha קְדֻשָּׁה lecha לְךְ hameshaleshim הַמְשַׁלְּשִׁים kodesh קֹדֶשׁ

vekara וְקָרָא nevi'ach נְבִיאָךְ yad יַד al עַל katuv כָּתוּב vechen וְכֵן

ve'amar וְאָמַר ze זֶה el אֶל ze זֶה י"ב פרקין דיעקב מאירים לי"ב פרקין דרחל

kadosh קָדוֹשׁ | kadosh קָדוֹשׁ kadosh קָדוֹשׁ (סוד ג' רישׁין דעתיקא קדישׁא)

Adonai יְהֹוָאֵדֹנָיֵאֱלֹהֶיֹנּוּ Tzeva'ot צְבָאוֹת פני שׁכינה melo מְלֹא chol כָּל ילי

ha'aretz הָאָרֶץ אלהים דההן ע"ה kevodo כְּבוֹדוֹ:

ve'omrim וְאוֹמְרִים meshabechim מְשַׁבְּחִים le'umatam לְעֻמָּתָם:

(או"א) בָּרוּךְ baruch kevod כְּבוֹד Adonai יְהֹוָאֵדֹנָיֵאֱלֹהֶיֹנּוּ ; כבוד ה' = יוד הי ואו הה

mimekomo מִמְּקוֹמוֹ עסמ"ב, הברכה (למתק את ז' המלכים עמתו) ; ר"ת ע"ב, ריבוע יהוה ; ר"ת מיכ:

uvdivrei וּבְדִבְרֵי kodshach קָדְשְׁךָ katuv כָּתוּב lemor לֵאמֹר:

(זו"ן) יִמְלֹךְ yimloch קָדוֹשׁ בָּרוּךְ ר"ת ימלך יב"ק, אלהים יהוה, אהיה אדני יהוה

Adonai יְהֹוָאֵדֹנָיֵאֱלֹהֶיֹנּוּ le'olam לְעוֹלָם ריבוע ס"ג ו' אותיות דס"ג Elohayich אֱלֹהַיִךְ ילה

Tziyon צִיּוֹן יוסף, ו' הויות, קנאה, קֹנָאה ; ר"ת אצלו (מלכות אצל ז"א – ו) ledor לְדֹר vador וָדֹר רי"ו

haleluya הַלְלוּיָהּ אלהים, אהיה אדני ; ללה:

NAKDISHACH – THE KEDUSHA

We sanctify You and we revere You, according to the pleasant words of the counsel of the Holy Angels, who recite Holy before You three times, as it is written by Your Prophet: "And each called to the other and said: Holy, Holy, Holy, Is the Lord of Hosts, the entire world is filled with His glory." (Isaiah 6:3) Facing them they give praise and say: "Blessed is the glory of the Lord from His Place." (Ezekiel 3:12) And in Your Holy Words, it is written as follows: "The Lord, your God, shall reign forever, for each and for every generation. Zion, Praise the Lord!" (Psalms 146:10)

THE THIRD BLESSING

This blessing connects us to Jacob, the Central Column and the power of restriction. Jacob is our channel for connecting mercy with judgment. By restricting our reactive behavior, we are blocking our Desire to Receive for the Self Alone. Jacob also gives us the power to balance our acts of mercy and judgment toward other people in our lives.

Tiferet that becomes Da'at (14 words).

אַתָּה Ata   קָדוֹשׁ kadosh   וְשִׁמְךָ veshimcha   קָדוֹשׁ kadosh ר"ת = אור, רז, אין סוף

וּקְדוֹשִׁים ukdoshim   בְּכָל bechol ב"ן, לכב   יוֹם yom ע"ה נגד, מזבח, זן, אל יהוה

יְהַלְלוּךָ yehalelucha   סֶלָה sela

(on Shabbat: אהלה יהו אלף הא יוד הא במצפצ)

בָּרוּךְ baruch   אַתָּה Ata   יְהוָֹה Adonai (יֱהֹוִה)(יֱהֹוִה)יאהדונהי

הָאֵל haEl לאה ;   הַקָּדוֹשׁ hakadosh יפ מ"ה (יוד הא ואו הא) ;   (מילוי דס"ג) ייא"י

Meditate here on the Name: יאהדונהי, as it can help to remove anger.

THE MIDDLE BLESSING

The middle blessing connects us to the true power of *Sukkot* and *Simchat Torah*. *Sukkot* and *Simchat Torah* are the seed of the entire year for Mercy and Happiness. Just as an apple seed begets an apple tree, a negative seed begets a negative year. Likewise, a positive seed generates a positive year. *Sukkot* and *Simchat Torah* are our opportunity to choose the seed we wish to plant for our coming year. The power of the letters in this Fourth Blessing is in their ability to automatically choose the correct seed we need and not necessarily the seed we want.

אַתָּה Ata   בְּחַרְתָּנוּ vechartanu   מִכָּל mikol   יל   הָעַמִּים ha'amim

אָהַבְתָּ ahavta   אוֹתָנוּ otanu   וְרָצִיתָ veratzita   בָּנוּ banu

וְרוֹמַמְתָּנוּ veromamtanu   מִכָּל mikol   יל   הַלְּשׁוֹנוֹת haleshonot

וְקִדַּשְׁתָּנוּ vekidashtanu   בְּמִצְוֹתֶיךָ bemitzvotecha   וְקֵרַבְתָּנוּ vekeravtanu

מַלְכֵּנוּ malkenu   לַעֲבוֹדָתֶךָ la'avodatecha   וְשִׁמְךָ veshimcha   הַגָּדוֹל hagadol

וְהַקָּדוֹשׁ vehakadosh   עָלֵינוּ alenu   קָרָאתָ karata לההו ; ועם ד' אותיות = מבה, יזל, אום

THE THIRD BLESSING

You are Holy, and Your Name is Holy, and the Holy Ones praise You every day, for you are God, the Holy King Selah. Blessed are You, Lord, the Holy God.

THE MIDDLE BLESSING

You have chosen us from among all the nations. You have loved us and have found favor in us. You have exalted us above all the tongues and You have sanctified us with Your commandments. You draw us close, our King, to Your service and proclaimed Your great and Holy Name upon us.

וַתִּתֶּן vatiten ב״פ כהת כָּנוּ lanu אלהים, אהיה אדני יְהֹוָה ‏אדני‏אהדונהי Adonai

אֱלֹהֵינוּ Elohenu יכה בְּאַהֲבָה be'ahava אוזר, דאגה

(וּ u) לִמְנוּחָה limnucha שַׁבָּתוֹת shabbatot :On Shabbat add)

מוֹעֲדִים mo'adim לְשִׂמְחָה lesimcha ◆ חַגִּים chagim וּזְמַנִּים uzmanim

לְשָׂשׂוֹן lesason ◆ אֶת et יוֹם yom ע״ה נגד, מזבוז, זן, אל יהוה :On Shabbat add)

הַשַּׁבָּת haShabbat הַזֶּה hazeh והו ◆ וְאֶת ve'et יוֹם yom ע״ה נגד, מזבוז, זן, אל יהוה)

:On Sukkot say) וְחַג chag הַסֻּכּוֹת haSukkot הַזֶּה hazeh◆

:On Simchat Torah say) שְׁמִינִי shemini וְחַג chag עֲצֶרֶת atzeret הַזֶּה hazeh◆

אֶת et יוֹם yom ע״ה נגד, מזבוז, זן, אל יהוה והו tov טוֹב mikra מִקְרָא kodesh קֹדֶשׁ

הַזֶּה hazeh והו◆ זְמַן zeman שִׂמְחָתֵנוּ simchatenu◆ בְּאַהֲבָה be'ahava אוזר, דאגה

מִקְרָא mikra קֹדֶשׁ kodesh◆ זֵכֶר zecher לִיצִיאַת litzi'at מִצְרָיִם Mitzrayim ◆מצר

אֱלֹהֵינוּ avotenu יכה◆ וֵאלֹהֵי vElohei לכב ; מילוי ע״ב, דמב ; יכה elhenu אלהינו

יַעֲלֶה ya'ale וְיָבֹא veyavo וְיַגִּיעַ veyagi'a וְיֵרָאֶה veyera'e רי׳׳י veyera'e וְיֵרָצֶה veyeratze

וְיִשָּׁמַע veyishama veyipaked וְיִפָּקֵד veyizacher וְיִזָּכֵר ר׳׳ת = מ׳׳ב

זִכְרוֹנֵנוּ zichronenu וְזִכְרוֹן vezichron ע״ב קס״א ונ׳׳ע׳׳ב avotenu אֲבוֹתֵינוּ◆

זִכְרוֹן zichron ע״ב קס״א ונ׳׳ע׳׳ב Yerushalayim יְרוּשָׁלַיִם עִירָךְ irach◆

וְזִכְרוֹן vezichron ע״ב קס״א ונ׳׳ע׳׳ב mashi'ach מָשִׁיחַ ben בֶּן David דָּוִד ע״ה כהת ;

עַבְדָּךְ avdach ע״ה = אדני ע״ה פוי, אל אדני◆ וְזִכְרוֹן vezichron ע״ב קס״א ונ׳׳ע׳׳ב

כָּל kol ילי עַמְּךָ amecha בֵּית bet ב״פ ראה Yisra'el יִשְׂרָאֵל

לְפָנֶיךָ lefanecha ס״ג מ״ה ב״ן lifleta לִפְלֵיטָה letova לְטוֹבָה◆ אכא

לְחֵן lechen מילוי דמ״ה בריבוע ; מוזי לְחֶסֶד lechesed ע״ב, ריבוע יהוה

And may You give us, Lord, our God, with love (**on Shabbat add:** Sabbath for rest and)
Holidays for happiness, Festivals and time of joy, this day (**on Shabbat add:** of Sabbath and this day)
(**on Sukkot:** of Sukkot) (**on Simchat Torah:** of Shmini the Holiday of Atzeret)
and this good day of Holy Convocation; The time of our happiness.
with love, a Holy Convocation, a remembrance of the exit from Egypt.
Our God and the God of our fathers, may it rise and come and arrive and appear and find favor and be heard
and be considered and be remembered, our remembrance and the remembrance of our fathers, the remembrance
of Jerusalem, Your city, and the remembrance of Mashiach Ben David, Your servant, and the remembrance
of Your entire Nation, the House of Israel, before You for deliverance, for good, for grace, kindness

tovim טוֹבִים אהיה אהיה יהוה, בינה ע"ה lechayim לְחַיִּים ◆ulrachamim וּלְרַחֲמִים

יהוה אל זן, מזבח, נגד ע"ה beyom בְּיוֹם ◆ulshalom וּלְשָׁלוֹם

(On *Shabbat* add: הַשַּׁבָּת haShabbat וְהוּ uvyom וּבְיוֹם ע"ה נגד, מזבח, זן, אל יהוה)

◆(hazeh הַזֶּה haSukkot הַסֻּכּוֹת chag וְזֶה :On *Sukkot* say)

◆(hazeh הַזֶּה atzeret עֲצֶרֶת chag וְזֶה shemini שְׁמִינִי :On *Simchat Torah* say)

בְּיוֹם beyom ע"ה נגד, מזבח, זן, אל יהוה והו tov טוֹב

◆והו hazeh הַזֶּה kodesh קֹדֶשׁ mikra מִקְרָא

(אברים), רמ"ח הַחָכְמָה נתיבות ול"ב רי"ו אל, וז"פ אברהם, lerachem לְרַחֵם

◆ulhoshi'enu וּלְהוֹשִׁיעֵנוּ alenu עָלֵינוּ bo בּוֹ פשוטות אותיות וט"ז עסמ"ב

ילה Elohenu אֱלֹהֵינוּ Adonai יְהֹוָואדֹנָיאהדונהי (from *Zeir Anpin*) zochrenu זְכְרֵנוּ

bo בּוֹ (from *Nukva*) ufokdenu וּפָקְדֵנוּ אכא◆ letova לְטוֹבָה bo בּוֹ

lechayim לְחַיִּים vo בּוֹ (from *Da'at*) vehoshi'enu וְהוֹשִׁיעֵנוּ ◆livracha לִבְרָכָה

yeshu'a יְשׁוּעָה ראה bidvar בִּדְבַר ◆tovim טוֹבִים אהיה אהיה יהוה, בינה ע"ה

vachamol וְחֲמוֹל vechanenu וְחָנֵּנוּ chus וְחוּס ◆verachamim וְרַחֲמִים

אותיות פשוטות וט"ז עסמ"ב (אברים), רמ"ח הַחָכְמָה נתיבות ול"ב רי"ו אל, וז"פ אברהם, verachem וְרַחֵם

◆alenu עָלֵינוּ enenu עֵינֵינוּ elecha אֵלֶיךָ ki כִּי vehoshi'enu וְהוֹשִׁיעֵנוּ

:Ata אַתָּה verachum וְרַחוּם chanun וְחַנּוּן melech מֶלֶךְ יאא El אֵל ki כִּי

◆ילה Elohenu אֱלֹהֵינוּ Adonai יְהֹוָואדֹנָיאהדונהי vehashsyenu וְהוֹשִׁיעֵנוּ

lechayim לְחַיִּים אהיה אהיה יהוה, בינה ע"ה mo'adecha מוֹעֲדֶיךָ birkat בִּרְכַּת et אֶת

ratzita רָצִיתָ ka'asher כַּאֲשֶׁר ◆uvshalom וּבְשָׁלוֹם besimcha בְּשִׂמְחָה

:selah סֶלָה tevarchenu תְּבָרְכֵנוּ ken כֵּן ◆levarchenu לְבָרְכֵנוּ ve'amarta וְאָמַרְתָּ

---

*and compassion, for a good life and for peace on this Day (on **Shabbat** say: of Sabbath and on this Day) (on **Sukkot**: of Sukkot) (on **Simchat Torah**: of Shmini the Holiday of Atzeret) on this good Day of Holy Convocation,, to take pity on us and to save us. Remember us, Lord, our God, on it for good and consider us, on it, for blessing and deliver us on it for a good life with the words of deliverance and mercy. Take pity and be gracious to us and have mercy and be compassionate with us and save us, for our eyes turn to You, because You are God, King Who is gracious and compassionate.*

And give us, Lord, our God Your blessing of Your holidays for happy and peaceful life.

As You desired and said to bless us. So You shall bless us Selah.

MEKADESH ISRAEL VEHAZEMANIM (THE TIMES)

אֱלֹהֵינוּ Elohenu וְאֱלֹהֵי velohei (On *Shabbat* add: יֵלֵה לְכב ; מ״כ, דמב ; ילה

אֲבוֹתֵינוּ avotenu רְצֵה retze נָא na בִּמְנוּחָתֵנוּ (vimnuchatenu)

קַדְּשֵׁנוּ kadshenu בְּמִצְוֹתֶיךָ vemitzvotecha• תֵּן ten וְלֵקֵנוּ chelkenu

בְּתוֹרָתֶךָ vetoratach• שַׂבְּעֵנוּ sabe'enu מִטּוּבֶךָ mituvach לְאוּ•

שַׂמְּחֵ same'ach נַפְשֵׁנוּ nafshenu בִּישׁוּעָתֶךָ bishu'atach•

וְטַהֵר vetaher לִבֵּנוּ libenu לְעָבְדְּךָ le'ovdecha פוי, אל יהה בֶּאֱמֶת ve'emet

אֲהֶיה פעמים אהיה, ד״פ ס״ג• וְהַנְחִילֵנוּ vehanchilenu יְהֹוָה Adonai

אֱלֹהֵינוּ Elohenu יֵלֵה (On *Shabbat* add: בְּאַהֲבָה be'ahava אווֹד, דאֲה

וּבְרָצוֹן uvratzon בְּשִׂמְחָה vesimcha

וּבְשָׂשׂוֹן uvsason שַׁבָּתוֹת shabatot (ו) (On *Shabbat* add: מוֹעֲדֵי mo'adei

קָדְשֶׁךָ kodshecha, וְיִשְׂמְחוּ veyismechu בְךָ vecha כָּל kol יִשְׂרָאֵל Yisrael

מְקַדְּשֵׁי mekadshei שְׁמֶךָ shemecha• בָּרוּךְ baruch אַתָּה Ata

יְהֹוָה Adonai

(on *Shabbat*: יה אדֹנִי) אֲהֶיה יהו אכף הה יוד הה

מְקַדֵּשׁ mekadesh (On *Shabbat* add: הַשַּׁבָּת hashabat ו ve) יִשְׂרָאֵל Yisrael

וְהַזְּמַנִּים vehazemanim•

THE FINAL THREE BLESSINGS

Through the merit of Moses, Aaron and Joseph, who are our channels for the final three blessings, we are able to bring down all the spiritual energy that we aroused with our prayers and blessings.

THE FIFTH BLESSING

During this blessing, referring to Moses, we should always meditate to try to know exactly what God wants from us in our life, as signified by the phrase, "Let it be the will of God." We ask God to guide us toward the work we came to Earth to do. The Creator cannot just accept the work that we want to do; we must carry out the work we were destined to do.

MEKADESH ISRAEL VEHAZEMANIM (THE TIMES)

(on Shabbat: *Our God and the God of our forefathers, please desire our rest.)*

Sanctify us with Your commandments and place our lot in Your Torah and satiate us from Your goodness and gladden our spirits with Your salvation. And purify our heart so as to serve You truly. And grant us, Lord, our God, (**on Shabbat:** *with love and favor,)* *with happiness and joy* (**on Shabbat:** *Sabbaths and) the Holidays, and all Israel, who sanctify Your Name will be joyful with You. Blessed are You, Lord, who sanctifies* (**on Shabbat:** *the Sabbath) and Israel and the Times.*

Netzach

Meditate for the Supernal Desire (*Keter*) that is called *Metzach HaRatzon* (Forehead of the Desire).

רְצֵה retze אלף למד הה יוד מם

Meditate here to transform misfortune and tragedy (צרה) into desire and acceptance (רצה).

Yisrael יִשְׂרָאֵל be'amecha בְּעַמְּךָ ילה Elohenu אֱלֹהֵינוּ Adonai יהואדני Adonai יְהֹוָאדנֹהי

ha'avoda הָעֲבוֹדָה vehashev וְהָשֵׁב ♦she'e שְׁעֵה velitfilatam וְלִתְפִלָּתָם

Yisrael יִשְׂרָאֵל ve'ishei וְאִשֵּׁי ♦ ב"פ ראה betecha בֵּיתֶךָ רי"ו lidvir לִדְבִיר

דאגה אוזר, be'ahava בְּאַהֲבָה mehera מְהֵרָה utfilatam וּתְפִלָּתָם

♦ע"ה ע"ה אל שדי אל קס"א ע"ה ברבוע ע"ב מהש ע"ה beratzon בְּרָצוֹן tekabel תְּקַבֵּל

ע"ה שדי אל ע"ה קס"א ברבוע ע"ב ע"ה מהש leratzon לְרָצוֹן ut'hi וּתְהִי

♦amecha עַמְּךָ Yisrael יִשְׂרָאֵל avodat עֲבוֹדַת קמ"ג קנ"א קס"א ע"ה tamid תָּמִיד

♦harabim הָרַבִּים verachamecha בְּרַחֲמֶךָ veAta וְאַתָּה

vetechezena וְתֶחֱזֶינָה vetirtzenu וְתִרְצֵנוּ banu בָּנוּ tachpotz תַּחְפֹּץ

קנאה הויות, ו יוסף, leTziyon לְצִיּוֹן beshuvcha בְּשׁוּבְךָ ריבוע מ"ה enenu עֵינֵינוּ

י"פ יי" דיודין, אלהים מצפצ, berachamim בְּרַחֲמִים

(אל on Shabbat:) אהיה יהו אלף למד הי יוד מם

Adonai יְהֹוָאדנֹהי Ata אַתָּה baruch בָּרוּךְ

♦קנאה הויות, ו יוסף, leTziyon לְצִיּוֹן shechinato שְׁכִינָתוֹ hamachazir הַמַּחֲזִיר

THE FINAL THREE BLESSINGS
THE FIFTH BLESSING

Find favor, Lord, our God,
in Your People, Israel, and turn to their prayer.

Restore the service to the inner sanctuary of Your Temple. Accept the offerings of Israel and their prayer with favor, speedily, and with love. May the service of Your People Israel always be favorable to You. And You in Your great compassion take delight in us and are pleased with us. May our eyes witness Your return to Zion with compassion. Blessed are You, Lord, Who returns His Shechinah to Zion.

THE SIXTH BLESSING

This blessing is our thank you. Kabbalistically, the biggest "thank you" we can give the Creator is to do exactly what we are supposed to do in terms of our spiritual work.

Hod

Bow your entire body at "*modim*" and straighten up at "*Adonai*."

מוֹדִים modim מֵאָה בְּרָכוֹת עֲתִיקָן דָּוִד לְאָמְרָם כָּל יוֹם anachnu אֲנַחְנוּ lach לָךְ

שְׁאַתָּה sheAta הוּא hu יְהֹוָה Adonai (וֹ) אֱלֹהֵינוּ Elohenu

וֵאלֹהֵי velohei אֲבוֹתֵינוּ avotenu לְעוֹלָם le'olam

צוּר tzur צוּרֵנוּ tzurenu וָעֶד va'ed

וּמָגֵן umagen chaycnu וַחַיֵּינוּ

אַתָּה Ata הוּא hu לְדֹר ledor וָדֹר vador נוֹדֶה node yish'enu יִשְׁעֵנוּ

לְךָ lecha וּנְסַפֵּר unsaper תְּהִלָּתֶךָ tehilatecha עַל al וַחַיֵּינוּ chayenu

הַמְּסוּרִים hamesurim בְּיָדֶךָ beyadecha וְעַל ve'al נִשְׁמוֹתֵינוּ nishmotenu

הַפְּקוּדוֹת hapekudot לָךְ lach וְעַל ve'al נִסֶּיךָ nisecha שֶׁבְּכָל shebechol

עִמָּנוּ imanu yom יוֹם

וְעַל ve'al נִפְלְאוֹתֶיךָ nifle'otecha וְטוֹבוֹתֶיךָ vetovotecha שֶׁבְּכָל shebechol

עֵת et וָבֹקֶר vavoker עֶרֶב erev וְצָהֳרָיִם vetzahorayim הַטּוֹב hatov

כִּי ki לֹא lo כָלוּ chalu רַחֲמֶיךָ rachamecha הַמְרַחֵם hamerachem

כִּי ki לֹא lo

וְחַסְדֶיךָ chasadecha ki כִּי מֵעוֹלָם me'olam קִוִּינוּ kivinu לָךְ lach: תַּמּוּ tamu

---

THE SIXTH BLESSING

We give thanks to You, for it is You, Lord, Who is our God and God of our forefathers, forever and for all eternity. You are our Rock, the Rock of our lives, and the Shield of our salvation. From one generation to another, we shall give thanks to You and we shall tell of Your praise. For our lives that are entrusted in Your hands, for our souls that are in Your care, for Your miracles that are with us every day, and for Your wonders and Your favors that are with us at all times: evening, morning and afternoon. You are the good One, for Your compassion has never ceased. You are the compassionate One, for Your kindness has never ended, for we have always placed our hope in You.

MODIM DeRABANAN

This prayer is recited by the congregation in the repetition when the *chazan* says "*modim*."

In this section there are 44 words which is the same numerical value as the Name:
רִיבּוּעַ אֶהְיֶה (א אה אהי אהיה).

lach כָּךְ anachnu אֲנַחְנוּ　　מאה ברכות עתיקן דוד לאמרם כל יום　modim מוֹדִים

ילה Elohenu אֱלֹהֵינוּ　　Adonai יְהֹוָהאֲדֹנָיאֲדֹנָי hu הוּא　sheAta שָׁאַתָּה

avotenu אֲבוֹתֵינוּ ילה ; דמב ע"ב, מילוי ; לכב velohei וֵאלֹהֵי

yotzrenu יוֹצְרֵנוּ .basar בָּשָׂר ילי chol כָּל ; ילה דמב, ע"ב מילוי Elohei אֱלֹהֵי

vehoda'ot וְהוֹדָאוֹת berachot בְּרָכוֹת .bereshit בְּרֵאשִׁית yotzer יוֹצֵר

לְהוּ ; עם ד' אותיות = מבה, יזל, אום hagadol הַגָּדוֹל leshimcha לְשִׁמְךָ

.vekiyamtanu וְקִיַּמְתָּנוּ shehecheyitanu שֶׁהֶחֱיִיתָנוּ al עַל vehakadosh וְהַקָּדוֹשׁ

vete'esof וְתֶאֱסוֹף .utchonenu וּתְחָנֵּנוּ techayenu תְּחַיֵּינוּ ken כֵּן

lishmor לִשְׁמֹר .kodshecha קָדְשֶׁךָ lechatzrot לְחַצְרוֹת galuyoteinu גָּלֻיּוֹתֵינוּ

ul'ovdecha וּלְעָבְדֶּךָ .retzoncha רְצוֹנֶךָ vela'asot וְלַעֲשׂוֹת chukecha חֻקֶּיךָ

she'anachnu שֶׁאֲנַחְנוּ al עַל .shalem שָׁלֵם בוכו belevav בְּלֵבָב פוי, אל אדני

:hahoda'ot הַהוֹדָאוֹת (מילוי דס"ג) יא"י El אֵל baruch בָּרוּךְ .lach כָּךְ modim מוֹדִים

veyitromam וְיִתְרוֹמַם yitbarach יִתְבָּרַךְ kulam כֻּלָּם ve'al וְעַל

shimcha שִׁמְךָ קמ"ג קנ"א קס"א קס"א ע"ה tamid תָּמִיד veyitnase וְיִתְנַשֵּׂא

.va'ed וָעֶד דס"ג אותיות ו' ריבוע ס"ג le'olam לְעוֹלָם malkenu מַלְכֵּנוּ

:sela סֶלָה yoducha יוֹדוּךָ אהיה אהיה יהוה, בינה ע"ה hachayim הַחַיִּים ילי vechol וְכָל

וְיִהַלְלוּ vihalelu vivarchu וִיבָרְכוּ יהוה ריבוע יהוה ריבוע יהוה מ"ה

לְהוּ ; עם ד' אותיות = מבה, יזל, אום hagadol הַגָּדוֹל shimcha שִׁמְךָ et אֶת

MODIM DeRABANAN

We give thanks to You, for it is You Lord,
our God and God of our forefathers, the God of all flesh, our Maker and the Former of all Creation. Blessings and
thanks to Your great and Holy Name for giving us life and for preserving us. So may You continue
to give us life, be gracious to us, and gather our exiles to the courtyards of Your Sanctuary, so that we may keep Your
laws, fulfill Your will, and serve You wholeheartedly. For this, we thank You. Bless the God of thanksgiving.

And for all those things, may Your Name be always blessed, exalted and extolled, our King, forever
and ever, and all the living shall thank You, Selah. And they shall praise and bless Your Great Name,

בְּאֱמֶת be'emet אהיה פעמים אהיה, ז"פ ס"ג ריבוע ס"ג וי' אותיות דס"ג le'olam לְעוֹלָם

כִּי ki טוֹב tov והו ; כי = טוב = יהוה, אהיה, אום, מבה, יזל.

הָאֵל haEl לאה ; יא"י (מילוי דס"ג) יְשׁוּעָתֵנוּ yeshu'atenu וְעֶזְרָתֵנוּ ve'ezratenu

סֶלָה sela. הָאֵל haEl לאה ; יא"י (מילוי דס"ג) הַטּוֹב hatov והו:

Bend your knees at "baruch," bow at "Ata" and straighten up at "Adonai."

(on Shabbat: אלהים) אהיה יהו אלף למד הה יוד מם

בָּרוּךְ baruch אַתָּה Ata יְהוָֹהאדנילאידהרונהי Adonai (הי) הַטּוֹב hatov והו

שִׁמְךָ shimcha וּלְךָ ulcha נָאֶה na'e לְהוֹדוֹת lehodot ס"ת כהת, משיחין בן דוד ע"ה:

BLESSING OF THE KOHANIM

During the repetition we say the blessing of the *Kohanim*. The Kohen is a channel for the Right Column energy of sharing and therefore also for healing. Because the Light revealed through this blessing is stronger than we can handle, we cover our eyes to prevent looking directly at this awesome healing Light.

If there is no Kohen present, the chazan should say:

אֱלֹהֵינוּ Elohenu ילה וֵאלֹהֵי velohei לכב ; מילוי ע"ב, דמב ; ילה אֲבוֹתֵינוּ avotenu,

בָּרְכֵנוּ barchenu בַּבְּרָכָה baberacha הַמְשֻׁלֶּשֶׁת hameshuleshet בַּתּוֹרָה batora

הַכְּתוּבָה haketuva עַל al יְדֵי yedei משה מהע, ע"ב בריבוע וקס"א, אל שדי, Moshe

עַבְדֶּךָ avdecha פוי, אל אדני הָאֲמוּרָה ha'amura מִפִּי mipi אַהֲרֹן Aharon ד"פ אלהים ע"ה

וּבָנָיו uvanav כֹּהֲנִים kohanim עַם am קְדוֹשֶׁךָ kedoshecha, כָּאָמוּר ka'amur:

Then the chazan will continue from "yevarechecha Adonai…" until "veyasem lecha Shalom" on page 356.

After the congregation answers Amen, the chazan will say "Kohanim". Then the Kohanim will recite the following in silence:

יְהִי yehi רָצוֹן ratzon מהע ע"ה, ע"ב בריבוע וקס"א ע"ה, אל שדי ע"ה מִלְּפָנֶיךָ milfanecha

יְהוָֹהאדנילאידהרונהי Adonai ס"ג מ"ה ב"ן אֱלֹהֵינוּ Elohenu ילה וֵאלֹהֵי velohei

לכב ; מילוי ע"ב, דמב ; ילה אֲבוֹתֵינוּ avotenu, שֶׁתִּהְיֶה shetihye בְּרָכָה beracha זוֹ zo

שֶׁצִּוִּיתָנוּ shetzivitanu לְבָרֵךְ levarech אֶת et עַמְּךָ amecha יִשְׂרָאֵל Yisrael

בְּרָכָה beracha שְׁלֵמָה shelema וְלֹא velo יִהְיֶה yihye יי בָּהּ ba

מִכְשׁוֹל michshol וְעָוֹן ve'avon מֵעַתָּה me'ata וְעַד ve'ad עוֹלָם olam:

---

sincerely and forever, for It is good, the God of our salvation and our help, Selah, the good God. Blessed are You, Lord, whose Name is good, and to You it is befitting to give thanks.

BLESSING OF THE KOHANIM

Our God and the God of our forefathers, bless us with the triple blessing written in the Torah by Moses, Your servant, and said by Aaron and his sons the Kohanim, Your Holy People, as it says: May it be your will Lord, our God and the God of our forefathers, that this blessing with which You commanded us to bless Your People, Israel, be a perfect blessing, and may it not contain any hindrance or iniquity from now until eternity.

The *Kohanim* say the following blessing facing the Ark and when they reach the word "*vetzivanu*," they should turn clockwise and face the congregation and continue the blessing. If there is only one *Kohen*, the *chazan* should not call him but instead the *Kohen* should say the following blessing right away.

יכֹה Elohenu אֱלֹהֵינוּ Adonai יְהֹוָאֲדֹנִיאהדונהי Ata אַתָּה baruch בָּרוּךְ

kideshanu קִדְּשָׁנוּ asher אֲשֶׁר ha'olam הָעוֹלָם melech מֶלֶךְ

vetzivanu וְצִוָּנוּ Aharon אַהֲרֹן shel שֶׁל bikdushato בִּקְדֻשָּׁתוֹ

אוזר, דאגה: be'ahava בְּאַהֲבָה Yisrael יִשְׂרָאֵל amo עַמּוֹ et אֶת levarech לְבָרֵךְ

The *chazan* prompts the *Kohanim* by reciting one word at a time (even if there is only one *Kohen* present). And the congregation answers: "*Amen*" (or "*ken yehi ratzon*" in case the *chazan* reciting it) after each verse.

The initials of the three verses give us the Holy Name: יי׳.
In this section, there are 15 words, which are equal to the numerical value of the Holy Name: ההה

(Right — *Chesed*)

veyishmerecha וְיִשְׁמְרֶךָ Adonai יְהֹוָאֲדֹנִיאהדונהי yevarechecha יְבָרֶכְךָ

ר״ת = יהוה ; וס״ת = מ״ה:

(Left - *Gevurah*)

elecha אֵלֶיךָ panav פָּנָיו | Adonai יְהֹוָאֲדֹנִיאהדונהי ya'er יָאֵר כף ויו זין ויו

vichuneka וִיחֻנֶּךָ מונד ; יהה אותיות בפסוק:

(Central — *Tiferet*)

elecha אֵלֶיךָ panav פָּנָיו | Adonai יְהֹוָאֲדֹנִיאהדונהי yisa יִשָּׂא

veyasem וְיָשֵׂם lecha לְךָ shalom שָׁלוֹם הֵאא תיבות בפסוק:

(*Malchut*)

Yisrael יִשְׂרָאֵל benei בְּנֵי al עַל shemi שְׁמִי et אֶת vesamu (וְשָׂמוּ

va'ani וַאֲנִי avarchem אֲבָרֲכֵם:)

The *Kohanim* add in silence:

ha'olamim הָעוֹלָמִים ribon רִבּוֹן יהוה ע״ב ס״ג מ״ה ב״ן,

Ata אַתָּה ase עֲשֵׂה, alenu עָלֵינוּ shegazarta שֶׁגָּזַרְתָּ מ״ה ma מַה asinu עָשִׂינוּ

mime'on מִמְּעוֹן hashkifa הַשְׁקִיפָה shehivtachtanu שֶׁהִבְטַחְתָּנוּ מ״ה ma מַה

hashamayim הַשָּׁמַיִם min מִן kodshecha קָדְשְׁךָ י״פ טל, י״פ כוזו ; ר״ת מ״ה

Yisrael יִשְׂרָאֵל: et אֶת amecha עַמְּךָ et אֶת uvarech וּבָרֵךְ

Blessed are You, Lord, our God, King of the universe,
Who has sanctified us with the sanctity of Aaron, and has commanded us to bless His People, Israel, with love.
(Right) May the Lord bless you and protect you. (Amen)
(Left) May the Lord shine His Countenance upon you and be gracious to you. (Amen).
(Central) May the Lord lift His Face towards you and give you peace. (Amen)
(And they shall place My Name upon the children of Israel and I shall bless them). (Numbers 6:24-27)
Master of the world, we have done what you have decreed for us. Now, You do as you promised us:
"Gaze down from your Holy Abode, from the Heaven, and bless your people, Israel" (Devarim 26,15)

In this section there are 22 words, which is the numerical value of the Holy Name: **אכא** You should medidtate on the following when the *chazan* says the first word of each verse:

Yevarechecha (first verse): אֵל נָא קָרֵב תְּשׁוּעַת בַּמְצַפִּיךָ (ר"ת אנקתם)

Ya'er (second verse): פּוֹדְךָ סַר תּוֹצִיאֵם בַּמֵּאַסֵר (ר"ת פסתם)

Yisa (third verse): פַּדֵה סוֹעִים פַּתּוֹ סוֹמִים יַעַר בַּוֹצְפִים (ר"ת פספסים)

דְּלֵה יוֹקְשִׁים וְקַבֵּץ נְפוּצִים סָמוּךְ יָהּ בְּמַפְלָתֵנוּ (ר"ת דיונסים)

(whisper:) יוֹ"ו אותיות בפסוק זה **malchuto מַלְכוּתוֹ kevod כְּבוֹד shem שֵׁם baruch בָּרוּךְ**

רִיבוע ס"ג ו"ו אותיות דס"ג **va'ed וָעֶד le'olam לְעוֹלָם**

If you had a bad dream that is causing you distress, say the following while the *Kohanim* say their blessing:

vechalomotai וְחֲלוֹמוֹתַי shelcha שֶׁלְּךָ ani אֲנִי olam עוֹלָם shel שֶׁל ribono רִבּוֹנוֹ שֶׁלְּךָ. **shelcha ma מַה yode'a יוֹדֵעַ ve'eni וְאֵינִי chalamti וְחָלַמְתִּי chalom חֲלוֹם** מ"ה **hu הוּא. ben בֵּן shechalamti שֶׁחֲלַמְתִּי ani אֲנִי le'atzmi לְעַצְמִי uven וּבֵין** **shechalmu שֶׁחֲלְמוּ li לִי acherim אֲחֵרִים, uven וּבֵין she'ani שֶׁאֲנִי chalamti וְחָלַמְתִּי** **al עַל acherim אֲחֵרִים, im אִם hem הֵם tovim טוֹבִים chazkem וְזַקְּמֵם ve'amtzem וְאַמְּצֵם kachalomotav כַּחֲלוֹמוֹתָיו** **shel שֶׁל Yosef יוֹסֵף hatzadik הַצַּדִּיק, ve'im וְאִם tzerichim צְרִיכִים refu'a רְפוּאָה refa'em רְפָאֵם** **kemei כְּמֵי mara מָרָה al עַל yedei יְדֵי Moshe מֹשֶׁה** **rabenu רַבֵּנוּ alav עָלָיו hashalom הַשָּׁלוֹם, uchmei וּכְמֵי** **Yericho יְרִיחוֹ al עַל yedei יְדֵי Elisha אֱלִישָׁע, ucheMiryam וּכְמִרְיָם** **mitzarata מִצָּרַעְתָּהּ ucheNa'aman וּכְנַעֲמָן mitzarato מִצָּרַעְתּוֹ ucheChizkiyahu וּכְחִזְקִיָּהוּ** **mecholyo מֵחָלְיוֹ. uchshem וּכְשֵׁם shehafachta שֶׁהָפַכְתָּ kilelat קִלְלַת Bil'am בִּלְעָם** **harasha הָרָשָׁע livracha לִבְרָכָה, ken כֵּן hafoch הֲפוֹךְ kol כָּל chalomotai וְחֲלוֹמוֹתַי** **alai עָלַי ve'al וְעַל kol כָּל Yisrael יִשְׂרָאֵל letova לְטוֹבָה** **velivracha וְלִבְרָכָה vetirtzeni וְתִרְצֵנִי berachamecha בְּרַחֲמֶיךָ harabim הָרַבִּים.**

מ"ב אותיות בפסוק זה **yihyu יְהְיוּ leratzon לְרָצוֹן** **fi פִּי imrei אִמְרֵי** **vehegyon וְהֶגְיוֹן libi לִבִּי lefanecha לְפָנֶיךָ Adonai יְהוָה tzuri צוּרִי vego'ali וְגוֹאֲלִי.**

Master of the World! I am Yours and my dreams are Yours. I had a dream, but I do not know its meaning: whether I had dreamt about myself, or whether others dreamt about me, or whether I had dreamt about others. If they [my dreams] are good, then strengthen them and invigorate them, like the dreams of Joseph, the righteous one. If they require healing, then remedy them like the waters of Marah at the hands of Moses, our master, may peace be upon him, like the waters of Jericho at the hands of Elisha and like Miriam from her leprosy, like Na'aman from his leprosy, and like Chizkiyahu from his illness. And just as You have converted the curse of the wicked Bilaam into blessings, so, too, change my dreams, for my sake and for the sake of all Israel, into good and into blessing. Favor me with Your bountiful compassions. "May the utterances of my mouth and the thoughts oef my heart find favor before You, Lord, my Rock and my Redeemer." (Psalms 19:15)

THE FINAL BLESSING

We are emanating the energy of peace to the entire world. We also make it our intent to use our mouths only for good. Kabbalistically, the power of words and speech is unimaginable. We hope to use that power wisely, which is perhaps one of the most difficult tasks we have to carry out.

Yesod

shalom שָׁלוֹם sim שִׂים

chen וְחֵן אהיה אהיה יהוה, בינה ע"ה chayim וְחַיִּים uvracha וּבְרָכָה אכא tova טוֹבָה

מילוי דמ"ה בריבוע, מוזי ע"ה ריבוע יהוה tzedaka צְדָקָה ע"ב, ריבוע יהוה vachesed וָחֶסֶד ע"ה ריבוע אלהים

עמם ; ילי kol כָּל ve'al וְעַל alenu עָלֵינוּ verachamim וְרַחֲמִים

kulanu כֻּלָּנוּ avinu אָבִינוּ uvarchenu וּבָרְכֵנוּ amecha עַמְּךָ Yisrael יִשְׂרָאֵל

ki כִּי ke'echad כְּאֶחָד אהבה, דאגה panecha פָּנֶיךָ ס"ג מ"ה ב"ן, א"ס רו, be'or בְּאוֹר

ve'or רו, א"ס panecha פָּנֶיךָ ס"ג מ"ה ב"ן natata נָתַתָּ lanu לָנוּ אלהים, אהיה אדני ve'or בְּאוֹר

vechayim וְחַיִּים torah תּוֹרָה ילה Elohenu אֱלֹהֵינוּ Adonai יְהֹוָאדֹנָהי אהיה אהיה יהוה, בינה ע"ה

ahava אַהֲבָה אוזר, דאגה בינה ע"ה vachesed וָחֶסֶד ע"ב, ריבוע יהוה

beracha בְּרָכָה verachamim וְרַחֲמִים ע"ה ריבוע אלהים tzedaka צְדָקָה

be'enecha בְּעֵינֶיךָ והו ע"ה קס"א ; ריבוע מ"ה vetov וְטוֹב veshalom וְשָׁלוֹם

amecha עַמְּךָ ילי kol כָּל et אֶת ulvarech וּלְבָרֵךְ levarchenu לְבָרְכֵנוּ

veshalom וְשָׁלוֹם oz עֹז אהיה י"פ berov בְּרוֹב Yisrael יִשְׂרָאֵל

(*on Shabbat*: מצפצ) אהיה יהו אלף למד הא יוד מם

Adonai יְהֹוָוהֹיאהדונהי Ata אַתָּה baruch בָּרוּךְ

Yisrael יִשְׂרָאֵל amo עַמּוֹ et אֶת hamevarech הַמְבָרֵךְ

amen אָמֵן יאהדונהי bashalom בַּשָּׁלוֹם (יב"ק) = (אילההוידם) אלהים = ר"ת

THE FINAL BLESSING

Place peace, goodness, blessing, life, grace, kindness, righteousness, and mercy upon us and upon all of Israel, Your People. Bless us all as one, our Father, with the Light of Your Countenance, because it is with the Light of Your Countenance that You, Lord, our God, have given us Torah and life, love and kindness, righteousness and mercy, blessing and peace. May it be good in Your Eyes to bless us and to bless Your entire Nation, Israel, with abundant power and with peace. Blessed are You, Lord, Who blesses His Nation, Israel, with peace, Amen.

YIH'YU LERATZON

There are 42 letters in the verse in the secret of *Ana Beko'ach*.

יִהְיוּ (יא"י מילוי דס"ג) אל yih'yu לְרָצוֹן leratzon מהשע ע"ה, ע"ב ברריבוע וקס"א ע"ה, אל שדי ע"ה

אִמְרֵי imrei פִּי fi ר"ת אֶלֶף = אלף למד שין דלת יוד ע"ה וְהֶגְיוֹן vehegyon לִבִּי libi

לְפָנֶיךָ lefanecha ס"ג מ"ה ב"ן יְהֹוָהאדנ־ילי־אהדונה־י Adonai צוּרִי tzuri וְגֹאֲלִי vego'ali:

ELOHAI NETZOR

אֱלֹהַי Elohai מילוי ע"ב, דמב ; ילה נְצוֹר netzor לְשׁוֹנִי leshoni מֵרָע mera◆

וּשְׂפָתוֹתַי vesiftotai מִדַּבֵּר midaber ראה מִרְמָה mirma◆ וְלִמְקַלְלַי velimkalelai

נַפְשִׁי nafshi תִדּוֹם tidom◆ וְנַפְשִׁי venafshi כֶּעָפָר ke'afar

לַכֹּל lakol תִּהְיֶה tih'ye◆ יה אדני פְּתַח pctach לִבִּי libi בְּתוֹרָתֶךָ betoratecha◆

וְאַחֲרֵי ve'acharei מִצְוֹתֶיךָ mitzvotecha תִּרְדּוֹף tirdof נַפְשִׁי nafshi◆

וְכֹל vechol ילי הַקָּמִים hakamim עָלַי alai לְרָעָה lera'a רהע◆ מְהֵרָה mehera

הָפֵר hafer עֲצָתָם atzatam וְקַלְקֵל vekalkel מַחְשְׁבוֹתָם machshevotam◆

עֲשֵׂה ase לְמַעַן lema'an שְׁמֶךָ shemach◆ עֲשֵׂה ase לְמַעַן lema'an

יְמִינֶךָ yeminach◆ עֲשֵׂה ase לְמַעַן lema'an תּוֹרָתֶךָ toratach◆ עֲשֵׂה ase

לְמַעַן lema'an קְדֻשָּׁתֶךָ kedushatach◆ ר"ת הפסוק = מ"ה יהוה לְמַעַן lema'an

יֵחָלְצוּן yechaltzun יְדִידֶיךָ yedidecha ר"ת ילי הוֹשִׁיעָה hoshi'a יהוה ועי"ע נהורין

יְמִינְךָ yemincha וַעֲנֵנִי va'aneni (כתיב: וַעֲנֵנוּ) ר"ת אל (יא"י מילוי דס"ג)◆

Before we recite the next verse *"Yih'yu leratzon"* we have an opportunity to strengthen our connection to our soul using our name. Each person has a verse in the *Torah* that connects to their name. Either their name is in the verse, or the first and last letters of the name correspond to the first or last letters of a verse. For example, the name Yehuda begins with a *Yud* and ends with a *Hei*. Before we end the *Amidah*, we state that our name will always be remembered when our soul leaves this world.

YIH'YU LERATZON

"May the utterances of my mouth
and the thoughts of my heart find favor before You, Lord, my Rock and my Redeemer." (Psalms 19:15)

ELOHAI NETZOR

My God, guard my tongue from evil and my lips from speaking deceit. To those who curse me, let my spirit remain silent, and let my spirit be as dust for everyone. Open my heart to Your Torah and let my heart pursue Your commandments. All those who rise against me to do me harm, speedily nullify their plans and disturb their thoughts. Do so for the sake of Your Name. Do so for the sake of Your Right. Do so for the sake of Your Torah. Do so for the sake of Your Holiness, "So that Your loved ones may be saved. Redeem Your right and answer me." (Psalms 60:7)

YIH'YU LERATZON (THE SECOND)

There are 42 letters in the verse in the secret of *Ana Beko'ach*.

יִהְיוּ yih'yu אל (ייא"י מילוי דס"ג) לְרָצוֹן leratzon מהטע ע"ה, ע"ב בריבוע וקס"א ע"ה, אל שדי ע"ה

אִמְרֵי־ imrei פִי fi ר"ת אֶלֶף = אלף למד מם דלת שין יוד ע"ה וְהֶגְיוֹן vehegyon לִבִּי libi

לְפָנֶיךָ lefanecha יְהֹוָאדֹנָיאהדונהי Adonai ס"ג מ"ה ב"ן צוּרִי tzuri וְגֹאֲלִי vego'ali:

OSE SHALOM

You take three steps backward;

עוֹשֶׂה ose שָׁלוֹם shalom

Left
You turn to the left and say:

בִּמְרוֹמָיו bimromav ר"ת ע"ב, ריבוע יהוה

הוּא hu בְּרַחֲמָיו verachamav יַעֲשֶׂה ya'ase

Right
You turn to the right and say:

שָׁלוֹם shalom עָלֵינוּ alenu ר"ת ש"ע נהורין

וְעַל ve'al כָּל־ kol יל; עמם יְלי; עָמוֹ amo יִשְׂרָאֵל Yisrael

Center
You face the center and say:

וְאִמְרוּ ve'imru אָמֵן amen יאהדונהי:

יְהִי yehi רָצוֹן ratzon מהטע ע"ה, ע"ב בריבוע וקס"א ע"ה, אל שדי ע"ה

מִלְּפָנֶיךָ milfanecha יְהֹוָאדֹנָיאהדונהי Adonai ס"ג מ"ה ב"ן אֱלֹהֵינוּ Elohenu יכה

וֵאלֹהֵי velohei אֲבוֹתֵינוּ avotenu, יכה ; דמב, דמב ; ע"ב, מילוי שֶׁתִּבְנֶה shetivne

בֵּית bet ב"פ ראה הַמִּקְדָּשׁ hamikdash בִּמְהֵרָה bimhera בְיָמֵינוּ veyamenu

וְתֵן veten וְזַלְקֵנוּ chelkenu בְּתוֹרָתָךְ betoratach לַעֲשׂוֹת la'asot וְחֻקֵּי chukei

רְצוֹנָךְ retzonach וּלְעָבְדָךְ ul'ovdach פוי, אל אדני בְּלֵבָב belevav בוכו שָׁלֵם shalem.

You take three steps forward.

YIH'YU LERATZON (THE SECOND)

*"May the utterances of my mouth
and the thoughts of my heart find favor before You, Lord, my Rock and my Redeemer." (Psalms 19:15)*

OSE SHALOM

*He, Who makes peace in His high places, He,
in His compassion, shall make peace upon us And upon His entire nation, Israel, and you shall say, Amen.
May it be pleasing before You,
Lord, our God and God of our forefathers, that You shall rebuild the Temple speedily, in our days, and
place our lot in Your Torah, so that we may fulfill the laws of Your desire and serve You wholeheartedly.*

THE ORDER OF THE TAKING AND THE SHAKING OF THE LULAV – FROM THE RAV

After the *Sukkah* the next important aspect of the Holiday is the Four Species. In *Leviticus 23:40*, it is said, "And you shall take to yourself on the first day the fruit of goodly trees, branches of palm trees, and boughs of thick trees, and willow of the brook, and you shall rejoice before the Lord, your God seven days."

The fruit of goodly trees (citrus) is the *Etrog*; the boughs of thick trees are the *Hadasim*; the branch of a palm tree is the *Lulav*; and the willows of the brook are the *Aravot*. But why must we take the Four Species, and why must we rejoice with them? From a technical perspective, the Four Species must be held in the hands of the person during the *Halel* service, which is taken from the *Book of Psalms*, Chapters 113 through 118. The *Lulav* is to be held in the right hand together with the three *Hadasim* and two Aravot, and the *Etrog* is to be held in the left hand.

The entire process is called *Netilat HaLulav*, or the Taking of the *Lulav*. Why this the process not named after the other plants? Are the others secondary in importance? The *Zohar* tells how Rav Shimon's pupils met a man in the field who had come to pick a *Lulav* for *Sukkot*. They asked him about the purpose of the Four Species and the man replied that his teacher, Rav Isaac, had taught him that *Sukkot* is a time for one to become stronger and reinforced in the face of the forces of darkness that have taken over all nations of the world.

But what is the purpose of the Four Species? Why were these particular plants chosen and not others? The Four Species are a symbolic representation of the Holy Name of the Creator יהוה, and only through them can one achieve control. We activate the software, which is the *Lulav*, so that we are able to connect to the hardware that is *Zeir Anpin*, which is the energy reservoir in the personal aspect of the DNA for genetic and spiritual purposes. This form of activation is achieved by "shaking" the bundle of software. These shakings receive messages that are transmitted into space, as would occur with a satellite or an antenna. Through the shakings we improve the reception of our antenna, which is the Four Species.

When the shakings are performed with the meditations outlined by Rav Isaac Luria (the Ari) the required connection may be achieved. And there are six directions in which we point the software: South, north, east, up, down and west. It should be noted that when we discuss directions, we are referring to the thought consciousness that begins and extends in these directions. Therefore, when we speak of the direction of south, we are discussing not only the physical direction, but also the "south" that according to the portion of *Va'era* of the *Zohar* is the origin of the thought consciousness called *Chesed*.

Thus, as long as our connection to the energy called *Zeir Anpin* includes six *Sefirot* or energies, then by means of the shakings the software will be activated. In our minds the shakings are guided by the thought that in the south we are able to tap into the thought conscious called *Chesed*.

We must perform these six cycles, for they represent the composition of *Zeir Anpin*, and our objective is to connect to *Zeir Anpin* and to receive the immense energy. Since *Zeir Anpin* contains these six thought energies, we must direct the physical and metaphysical antennae accordingly.

How we perform the appropriate connection with *Zeir Anpin*:

We start by directing our software toward the south, while our thoughts are tuned in to Abraham and *Chesed*. Next we turn to the north, which is Isaac and *Gevurah*, then to the east with our thoughts tuned in to the central column, Jacob and *Tiferet*. These three *Sefirot*, or energies, form the potential of the Upper Triangle of the *Magen David* (Star of David), and a protective shield is created. With the software of the four Kingdoms of Life, we have connected to the "Light of *Chasidim*," which will now be connected to us not only in a metaphysical way, but also on a physical level to protect our physical lives. And even though it is called "potential thought," we must still introduce this thought into our reality.

The fourth shaking, which is directed upward, will be directed with the thought that one must connect to Moses and *Netzach*. When the shakings are directed downward, while the tip of the *Lulav* still points upward, we connect to Aaron and *Hod*. The last shaking is to the west, connecting us to *Yesod* and to the chariot of Joseph the Righteous.

We shake the Lulav three times in each direction, where each act of shaking includes an outward extension of the *Lulav* and its return. These sets of three shakes are in accordance with the basic structure of the Three Column System. The thought consciousness required for the use of the Four Species contains an additional dimension that makes use of the letters of the Explicit Name (יהוה) in order to reinforce the action of the Four Species. The first three letters (יהו) denote Right, Left, and Central Columns.

This whole system was designed by Rav Isaac Luria, who studied and extracted it from the *Zohar* to help us reach our goal of "therefore choose life." Using the *Yud, Hei, Vav,* and *Hei* enables us to harness the power of *Zeir Anpin* so that we may remove any obstacle in our physical system and recompose the DNA to ensure that the future is without destruction, despair, or grief. At the same time, however, it is necessary for us to understand how we arrive at each letter and combination, because the greater our knowledge the better will be our channel to *Zeir Anpin*.

There are two additional aspects of the shakings. One is that the execution of three shakes in each of the six directions creates a set of 18 shakings in total. In numerology, 18 equals *chai* (חי), which means life. These sets of shakings inject us with the Life-force and connect us to the Tree of Life. The second aspect is the integration of the shakings into the *Halel* service; *Halel* הלל equals *Adonai* אדני in numerology (=65), which relates to *Malchut*. The *Halel* is also composed of Psalms written by King David (the chariot to the *Sefirah* of *Malchut*).

The combination of the shakings of the *Lulav* (the communication channel to *Zeir Anpin*) with the *Halel* service (the communication channel to *Malchut*) offers us a great opportunity to unite *Zeir Anpin* and *Malchut* and, having done so, to establish within ourselves the Creator's Lightforce. This effort is like metaphysical surgery that is performed to remove spiritual viruses, open up energy blockages, and repair defects that have developed over the past year in our spiritual and physical DNA.

The Four Species can help us as well as all of mankind. According to the *Zohar*, the Four Species are a way in which to receive blessings for the entire year. And if we do not take advantage of this once-yearly opportunity to attract energy, the *Zohar* specifically notes that we will not be able to introduce this energy into our lives.

לְשֵׁם leshem · יִחוּד yichud · קֻדְשָׁא kudesha · בְּרִיךְ berich · הוּא hu

וּשְׁכִינְתֵּיהּ ushchinte (יאהדונהי) · בִּדְחִילוּ bidchilu · וּרְחִימוּ urchimu (ואההויהה),

וּרְחִימוּ urchimu (איההויהה) · וּדְחִילוּ udchilu · לְיַחֲדָא leyachda · שֵׁם shem

יוּ"ד yud · קֵי kei · בְּוָא"ו bevav · קֵי kei · בְּיִחוּדָא beyichuda · שְׁלִים shelim (יהוה)

בְּשֵׁם beshem · כָּל kol · יְׄ · יִשְׂרָאֵל Yisrael · וּבְשֵׁם uvshem · כָּל kol · יְׄ

הַנְּפָשׁוֹת hanefashot · וְהָרוּחוֹת veharuchot · וְהַנְּשָׁמוֹת vehaneshamot

הַמִּתְיַחֲסִים hamityachasim · אֶל el · שָׁרְשֵׁי shorshei · נַפְשֵׁנוּ nafshenu · רוּחֵנוּ ruchenu

וְנִשְׁמָתֵנוּ venishmatenu, · וּמַלְבּוּשֵׁיהֶם umalbushehem · וְהַקְּרוֹבִים vehakerovim

כֻּלָּם lahem · שֶׁמִּכְּלָלוּת shemiklalut · אֲצִילוּת Atzilut · בְּרִיאָה Beri'a

יְצִירָה Yetzira · עֲשִׂיָּה Asiya, · וּמִכָּל umikol יְׄ · פְּרָטֵי peratei · אֲצִילוּת Atzilut

בְּרִיאָה Beri'a · יְצִירָה Yetzira · עֲשִׂיָּה Asiya · דְּכָל dechol · פַּרְצוּף partzuf

וּסְפִירָה usfira · דִּפְרָטֵי difratei · אֲצִילוּת Atzilut · בְּרִיאָה Beri'a · יְצִירָה Yetzira

עֲשִׂיָּה Asiya · הִנֵּה hineh · אֲנַחְנוּ anachnu · בָּאִים va'im · לְקַיֵּם lekayem:

On the first day of Sukkot add:

מִצְוַת mitzvat · עֲשֵׂה aseh · דְּאוֹרַיְתָא de'orayta · שֶׁל shel · נְטִילַת netilat

לוּלָב lulav · אהיה אהיה יהוה, וזים, בינה ע"ה, · הֲדַס hadas

עֲרָבָה arava · זרע · וְאֶתְרוֹג ve'etrog · ירת · בַּיּוֹם bayom · גבר, מזבוז, ז, אל יהוה

הָרִאשׁוֹן harishon · שֶׁל shel · וְזג chag · הַסֻּכּוֹת haSukkot◆

כְּמוֹ kemo · שֶׁצִּוָּנוּ shetzivanu · יְהֹוָ Adonai · אֱלֹהֵינוּ Elohenu יְׄ

בְּתוֹרָתוֹ betorato · הַקְּדוֹשָׁה hakedosha:

THE ORDER OF THE TAKING AND THE SHAKING OF THE LULAV

For the sake of the unification between the Holy Blessed One and His Shechinah, with fear and love and with love and fear, in order to unify the Name Yud-Kei and Vav-Kei in perfect unity, and in the name of all Israel, and in the name of all the Nefashot (lower souls) Ruchot (spirits) and Neshamot (higher souls) that give attribute to the root of our Nefashot Ruchot and Neshamot, and their clothing and all that is associated with it from the generality of Azilut, Beriah, Yetzirah, and Asiyah and from all of the specifics of Azilut, Beriah, Yetzirah, and Asiyah, of each Partzuf and Sefirah of the specifics of Azilut, Beriah, Yetzirah, and Asiyah, we hereby fulfill: On the first day of *Sukkot*: *the obligatory precept from the Torah of taking lulav, mirtle, wilow and citron, on the first day of the Holiday of Sukkot, as the Lord, our God commanded us in his Holy Torah:*

וּלְקַחְתֶּם ulkachtem לָכֶם lachem בַּיּוֹם bayom נגד, מזבוח, זן, אל יהוה

הָרִאשׁוֹן harishon פְּרִי peri עֵץ etz הָדָר hadar כַּפֹּת kapot תְּמָרִים temarim

וַעֲנַף va'anaf עֵץ etz עָבֹת avot וְעַרְבֵי ve'arvei נָחַל nachal:

And continue with "*letaken*" below:

On *Chol Hamo'ed* of Sukkot add:

מִצְוָה mitzva דְּרַבָּנָן derabanan שֶׁל shel נְטִילַת netilat לוּלָב lulav

הֲדַס hadas אהיה אהיה אהיה יהוה, וזיים, בינה ע״ה, וזיים ע״ה, ערבה arava זרע

וְאֶתְרוֹג ve'etrog ירה בַּמּוֹעֵד bamo'ed שֶׁל shel וְזֶ chag הַסֻּכּוֹת haSukkot:

And continue with "*letaken*" below:

לְתַקֵּן letaken אֶת et שָׁרָשִׁים shorsham בִּמְקוֹם bemakom עֶלְיוֹן elyon

בְּשִׁעוּר beshi'ur קוֹמָה koma, לַעֲשׂוֹת la'asot אֶת et כַּוָּנַת kavanat

יוֹצְרֵנוּ yotzrenu שֶׁצִּוָּנוּ shetzivanu לַעֲשׂוֹת la'asot מִצְוָה mitzva זוֹ zo,

לְהַשְׁלִים lehashlim אִילָן ilan הָעֶלְיוֹן ha'elyon וּלְהַשְׁלִים ulhashlim

אָדָם adam מ״ה הָעֶלְיוֹן ha'elyon, וּלְהָקִים ulhakim אֶת et

סֻכַּת sukat אמן, יאהדונהי, סאל דָּוִד David לְהַחֲזִיר lehachazir הָעֲטָרָה ha'atara

לְיוֹשְׁנָה leyoshna, לְבָרֵר levarer וּלְתַקֵּן ultaken וּלְהַעֲלוֹת ulha'alot כָּל kol ילי

הַנְּפָשׁוֹת hanefashot וְהָרוּחוֹת veharuchot וְהַנְּשָׁמוֹת vehaneshamot

וְנִיצוֹצֵי venitzotzei הַקְּדֻשָׁה hakedusha שֶׁנָּפְלוּ shenaflu בַּקְּלִפָּה bakelipa

עַל al יְדֵי ydei אָדָם Adam מ״ה הָרִאשׁוֹן harishon וְעַל ve'al

יָדֵינוּ yadenu, בְּגִלְגּוּלִים begilgulim אֵלוּ elu וּבְגִלְגּוּלִים uvgilgulim

אֲחֵרִים acherim, וּשְׁאֵרִית ush'erit הָרפ״ח harapach נִיצוֹצִין nitzotzin

"*And you shall take for yourself on the first day the fruit of goodly trees, branches of palm-trees, and boughs of thick trees, and willows of the brook*" (*Leviticus 23:40*),
On *Chol Hamo'ed* of Sukkot: *the precept from the our sages of taking lulav, mirtle, wilow and citron, in the time of the Holiday of Sukkot,*
to correct their root in the Supernal Place with its level of stature, and to follow the intention of our Creator Who commanded us to do this precept, to complete the Supernal Tree, to complete the Supernal Adam, to erect the Sukkah of David and to restore the Tiara to its former place. And to sort, to correct and to elevate all of the Nefashot, Ruchot and Neshamot, and the Holy sparks that fell into the klipa because of the first Adam and because of us, in this life time or in previous life times, and what's left from the 288 sparks.

וּלְהַשְׁלִים ulhashlim שְׁלֵמוּת shelemut תִּקּוּן tikun נַפְשֵׁנוּ nafshenu

רוּחֵנוּ ruchenu שֶׁבְּמִכְלָלוּת shemiklalut וְנִשְׁמָתֵנוּ venishmatenu אֲצִילוּת Atzilut

בְּרִיאָה Beri'a יְצִירָה Yetzira עֲשִׂיָּה Asiya, וּמִכָּל umikol פַּרְטֵי pirtei

אֲצִילוּת Atzilut בְּרִיאָה Beri'a יְצִירָה Yetzira עֲשִׂיָּה Asiya דְּכָל dechol

פַּרְצוּף partzuf וּסְפִירָה usfira דִּפְרָטֵי defirtei אֲצִילוּת Atzilut בְּרִיאָה Beri'a

יְצִירָה Yetzira עֲשִׂיָּה Asiya הַמִּתְיַחֲסִים hamityachasim אֶל el תִּקּוּן tikun

מִצְוָה mitzva זוֹ zo וְגַם vegam לְהַשְׁלִים lehashlim שְׁלֵמוּת shelemut

תִּקּוּן tikun אֵיבְרֵי evrei נְפָשׁוֹת nefashot רוּחוֹת ruchot וּנְשָׁמוֹת unshamot

שֶׁל shel כָּל kol יִשְׂרָאֵל yisrael הַחַיִּים hachayim

וְהַמֵּתִים vehametim הַחֲסֵרִים hachaserim מִתִּקּוּן mitikun מִצְוָה mitzva זוֹ zo

וִיהִי vihi רָצוֹן ratzon

מִלְּפָנֶיךָ milfanecha יְהֹוָה Adonai אֱלֹהֵינוּ Elohenu

וֵאלֹהֵי velohei אֲבוֹתֵינוּ avotenu, שֶׁיְּהֵא sheyhe

עַתָּה ata עֵת et רָצוֹן ratzon

לְפָנֶיךָ lefanecha לִהְיוֹת lihyot עוֹלָה ola

מִצְוָה mitzva זוֹ zo, לְתַקֵּן letaken אֶת et כָּל kol פְּגָמֵינוּ pegamenu

וּפִגְמֵי ufigmei אָדָם Adam הָרִאשׁוֹן harishon, אֲשֶׁר asher

פָּגַמְנוּ pagamnu בִּכְלָלוּת bichlalut אֲצִילוּת Atzilut בְּרִיאָה Beri'a

יְצִירָה Yetzira עֲשִׂיָּה Asiya, וּלְצָרֵף ultzaref וּלְבָרֵר ulvarer וּלְהַסִיר ulhasir

הַסִיגִים hasigim מִצַּלְמֵי mitzalmei לְבוּשֵׁי levushei נְפָשׁוֹת nefashot

רוּחוֹת ruchot וּנְשָׁמוֹת unshamot וְחַיּוֹת chayot יְחִידוֹת yechidot,

---

And to complete the total correction of our Nefashot, our Ruchot and our Neshamot, from the generality of Azilut, Beriah, Yetzirah, and Asiyah and from all of the specifics of Azilut, Beriah, Yetzirah, and Asiyah of each Partzuf and Sefirah of the specifics of Azilut, Beriah, Yetzirah, and Asiyah, which relate to the correction of this precept. And to complete the total correction of the organs of the Nefashot, Ruchot and Neshamot of all Israel, the living and the deceased, which are missing the correction of this precept. And May it be pleasing before You, Lord, my God, and God of my forefathers, that this hour will be a time of favor before you so this precept ascend and correct all of our blemishes and the blemishes of the first Adam, which we caused in the generality of Azilut, Beriah, Yetzirah, and Asiyah and to refine, to sort and to remove the slags from the images of the clothing of our Nefashot, our Ruchot, our Neshamot, our Chayot (the second highest level of the soul) and our Yechidot (the highest level of the soul)

דְּכִלְלוּת dichlalut וּפְרָטוּת ufratut דַּאֲצִילוּת daAtzilut בְּרִיאָה Beri'a

יְצִירָה Yetzira עֲשִׂיָּה Asiya, וּלְבָרֵר ulvarer וְחֶלְקֵי chelkei

הַנֶּפֶשׁ hanefesh שֶׁנִּפְגְּמוּ shenifgemu וְנָפְלוּ venaflu בְּנֹגַהּ benoga מוזי

דַּאֲצִילוּת daAtzilut בְּרִיאָה Beri'a יְצִירָה Yetzira עֲשִׂיָּה Asiya,

וְנֹגַהּ venoga מוזי כָּאוֹר ka'or רז, א"ס תִּהְיֶה tihye אֶל el מְקוֹם mekom

הַקֹּדֶשׁ hakodesh. וְהַפְרֵד vehafred נָא na מֵעָלֵינוּ me'alenu צַד tzad

הָרַע hara שֶׁבַּיֵּצֶר shebayetzer הָרַע hara, וּתְזַכְּכֵנוּ utzakchenu

וּתְלַבְּבֵנוּ utlabvenu בְּכֹחַ becho'ach הַיֵּצֶר hayetzer הַטּוֹב hatov והו:

וְעַל ve'al יְדֵי yedei מַעֲשֵׂה ma'ase הַמִּצְוָה hamitzva הַזֹּאת hazot

שֶׁל shel נְטִילַת netilat לוּלָב lulav אהיה אהיה יהוה, וויים, בינה ע"ה,

הֲדַס hadas עֲרָבָה arava אהיה אהיה יהוה ע"ה, וויים ע"ה וְאֶתְרוֹג ve'etrog ירת

יְתַקְּנוּ yetukno כָּל kol ילי בְּחִינַת bechinat שֵׁשׁ shesh קְצָווֹת ketzavot,

וְכָל vechol ילי צַלְמֵי tzalmei לְבוּשֵׁי levushei ה' Hei אַחֲרוֹנָה acharona

דַּהֲוָיָ"ה daHavaya, נֶפֶשׁ nefesh שֶׁל shel כְּלָלוּת kelalut אֲצִילוּת Atzilut

בְּרִיאָה Beri'a יְצִירָה Yetzira עֲשִׂיָּה Asiya, וְשֶׁל veshel כָּל kol ילי

פְּרָטֵי pirtei אֲצִילוּת Atzilut בְּרִיאָה Beri'a יְצִירָה Yetzira עֲשִׂיָּה Asiya:

וְעַל ve'al יְדֵי yedei הַדִּבּוּר hadibur שֶׁל shel הַמִּצְוָה hamitzva הַזֹּאת hazot,

כַּכָּתוּב kakatuv בַּתּוֹרָה batorah: וּלְקַחְתֶּם ulkachtem לָכֶם lachem בַּיּוֹם bayom

הָרִאשׁוֹן harishon נגד, מזבח, ז, אל יהוה פְּרִי peri עֵץ etz הָדָר hadar כַּפֹּת kapot

תְּמָרִים temarim וַעֲנַף va'anaf עֵץ etz עָבֹת avot עֵץ עֲרְבֵי ve'arvei נָחַל nachal:

---

of the generality and of the specific of Azilut, Beriah, Yetzirah, and Asiyah. And to sort the parts of the Nefesh that was damaged and fell into Nogah (brightness) of Azilut, Beriah, Yetzirah, and Asiyah, brightness appears as the Light [and return] to the Holy Place. And please, separate from us the evil side of the evil inclination and purify us and hearten us with the power of the good inclination.

And by the action of this precept

of taking lulav, mirtle, wilow and citron, all the aspects of the Six Edges and all the images of the clothing of the last Hei of the Havayah, Nefesh of the generality of Azilut, Beriah, Yetzirah, and Asiyah and the specifics of Azilut, Beriah, Yetzirah, and Asiyah.

And by the speech of this precept

as it is written in the Torah: "And you shall take for yourself on the first day the fruit of goodly trees, branches of palm-trees, and boughs of thick trees, and willows of the brook" (Leviticus 23:40),

יִתָּקְנוּ yetuknu · כָּל kol · ילי · בְּחִינַת bechinat · דַּעַת Da'at,

וְכָל vechol · ילי · צַלְמֵי tzalmei · לְבוּשֵׁי levushei · ו' v' · דַּהֲוָי"ה dahavaya,

רוּחַ ruach · שֶׁל shel · כְּלָלוּת kelalut · אֲצִילוּת Atzilut · בְּרִיאָה Beri'a

יְצִירָה Yetzira · עֲשִׂיָּה Asiya, · וְשֶׁל veshel · כָּל kol · ילי · פְּרְטֵי pirtei

אֲצִילוּת Atzilut · בְּרִיאָה Beri'a · יְצִירָה Yetzira · עֲשִׂיָּה Asiya:

וְעַל ve'al · יְדֵי yedei · הַכַּוָּנָה hakavana · שֶׁל shel · הַמִּצְוָה hamitzva

הַזֹּאת hazot · יִתָּקְנוּ yetuknu · כָּל kol · ילי · בְּחִינַת bechinat · בִּינָה Binah

וְכָל vechol · ילי · צַלְמֵי tzalmei · לְבוּשֵׁי levushei · ה' Hei (ע"ה אהיה אהיה יהוה, ע"ה וזיים,)

דַּהֲוָי"ה daHavaya, · נְשָׁמָה neshama · שֶׁל shel · כְּלָלוּת kelalut · אֲצִילוּת Atzilut

בְּרִיאָה Beri'a · יְצִירָה Yetzira · עֲשִׂיָּה Asiya, · וְשֶׁל veshel · כָּל kol · ילי

פְּרְטֵי pirtei · אֲצִילוּת Atzilut · בְּרִיאָה Beri'a · יְצִירָה Yetzira · עֲשִׂיָּה Asiya:

וְעַל ve'al · יְדֵי yedei · הַמַּוְזְשָׁבָה hamachshava · יִתָּקְנוּ yetuknu · כָּל kol · ילי

בְּחִינַת bechinat · וְזָכְמָה Chochma (במילוי = תרי"ג (מצוות,)) · וְכָל vechol · ילי

צַלְמֵי tzalmei · לְבוּשֵׁי levushei · יוּ"ד Yod · דַּהֲוָי"ה daHavaya,

וְזָיה chaya · שֶׁל shel · כְּלָלוּת kelalut · אֲצִילוּת Atzilut · בְּרִיאָה Beri'a

יְצִירָה Yetzira · עֲשִׂיָּה Asiya, · וְשֶׁל veshel · כָּל kol · ילי · פְּרְטֵי pirtei

אֲצִילוּת Atzilut · בְּרִיאָה Beri'a · יְצִירָה Yetzira · עֲשִׂיָּה Asiya:

---

all the aspects of Da'at
and all the images of the clothing of the Vav of the Havayah, Ruach of the generality of Azilut, Beriah, Yetzirah, and Asiyah and the specifics of Azilut, Beriah, Yetzirah, and Asiyah.
And by the intention of this precept, all the aspects of Binah
and all the images of the clothing of the Hei of the Havayah, Neshamah of the generality of Azilut, Beriah, Yetzirah, and Asiyah and the specifics of Azilut, Beriah, Yetzirah, and Asiyah.
And by the thought, all the aspects of Chochmah
and all the images of the clothing of the Yud of the Havayah, Chayah of the generality of Azilut, Beriah, Yetzirah, and Asiyah and the specifics of Azilut, Beriah, Yetzirah, and Asiyah.

וְעַל ve'al יְדֵי yedei רְעוּתָא re'uta דְלִבָּא deliba יִתְקָנוּ yetuknu

כָּל kol בְּוִזִינַת bechinat כֶּתֶר keter וְכָל vechol צַלְמֵי tzalmei

לְבוּשֵׁי levushei קוֹץ kotz הַיּ"וּד haYod דַּהֲוָי"ה dahavaya, יְוֹזִידָה yechida

שֶׁל shel כָּל kol כְּלָלוּת kelalut אֲצִילוּת Atzilut בְּרִיאָה Beri'a

יְצִירָה Yetzira עֲשִׂיָּה Asiya, וְשֶׁל veshel כָּל kol פְּרָטֵי pirtei

אֲצִילוּת Atzilut בְּרִיאָה Beri'a יְצִירָה Yetzira עֲשִׂיָּה Asiya:

וְיִתְיַוְזֹדֹוּ veyityachadu אַרְבַּע arba אוֹתִיּוֹת otiyot הַוָי"ה Havaya, שֶׁהֵם shehem

נֶפֶשׁ Nefesh רוּוַז Ruach וּנְשָׁמָה uNshama וְזַיָּה Chaya יְוֹזִידָה Yechida,

דִּכְלָלוּת dichlalut וּפְרָטוּת ufratut אֲצִילוּת Atzilut בְּרִיאָה Beri'a

יְצִירָה Yetzira עֲשִׂיָּה Asiya, בְּיִוֹזוּדָא beyichuda שָׁלִים shelim (יהוה)

וְיִהְיוּ veyihyu אל el כִּסֵּא kiseh שָׁלֵם shalem אֲשֶׁר asher בָּהֶם bahem

יִתְפַּשֵּׁט yitpashet שֶׁפַע shefa אוֹר or וְיִתְיַוְזֹדֹוּ veyityachadu

וְזָכְמָה Chochmah וּבִינָה uVinah

בְּיִוֹזוּדָא beyichuda שָׁלִים shelim (יאהדוי"ה) וְיִזְדַּוְגוּ veyizdavgu תִּפְאֶרֶת Tiferet

וּמַלְכוּת uMalchut זִוּוּגָא zivuga שָׁלִים shelim בְּשֵׁם beshem (יאהדונהי)

וּמִשָּׁם umisham יִמָּשֵׁךְ yimashech שֶׁפַע shefa וּבְרָכָה uvracha

בְּכָל bechol הָעוֹלָמוֹת ha'olamot, לְזַכֵּךְ lezakech

נַפְשֵׁנוּ nafshenu רוּוֹזֵנוּ ruchenu וְנִשְׁמָתֵנוּ venishmatenu שֶׁיִּהְיוּ sheyih'yu אל el

רְאוּיִים re'uyim לְעוֹרֵר le'orer מַיִּן mayin נֻקְבִין nukvin

וּלְהַמְשִׁיךְ ulhamshich אוֹר or מַיִּן mayin דְּכוּרִין dechurin,

---

And by the desire of the heart, all the aspects of Keter and all the images of the clothing of the thorn of the Yud of the Havayah, Yechidah of the generality of Azilut, Beriah, Yetzirah, and Asiyah and the specifics of Azilut, Beriah, Yetzirah, and Asiyah.And the four letters of Havayah, which are the Nefesh, Ruach, Neshamah, Chayah and Yechidah of the generality and of the specific of Azilut, Beriah, Yetzirah, and Asiyah, will be unified in perfect unity and they will be a complete chair and from them an abundance of Light will be spread. And Chochmah and Binah will be unified in perfect unity. And Tiferet and Malchut will joined in perfect unity by the Name. And abundance and blessing will be drawn from there into all the Worlds in order to purify our Nefasot, Rucuot and Neshamot, so they will be suitable to awaken the Female Water and to draw the Light of the Male Water.

וְאַל יְעַכֵּב שׁוּם חֵטְא וְעָוֹן וְהִרְהוּר
רַע אֶת הַמִּצְוָה הַזֹּאת, וְתַעֲלֶה
לְרָצוֹן לְרִיחַ
נִיחוֹחַ לְפָנֶיךָ יְהֹוָה
אֱלֹהֵינוּ וֵאלֹהֵי אֲבוֹתֵינוּ׃
וַהֲרֵינִי מוּכָן לְנַעֲנֵעַ הַלּוּלָב
עֲרָבָה הֲדַס
וְאֶתְרוֹג לְצַד דָּרוֹם שֶׁהוּא בְּחֶסֶד
שָׁלֹשׁ פְּעָמִים בְּהוֹלָכָה
וְהַבָאָה אֶל הֶחָזֶה׃ וּלְצַד צָפוֹן,
שֶׁהוּא בִּגְבוּרָה שָׁלֹשׁ פְּעָמִים
בְּהוֹלָכָה וְהַבָאָה אֶל הֶחָזֶה׃ וּלְצַד
מִזְרָח, שֶׁהוּא בְּתִפְאֶרֶת שָׁלֹשׁ
פְּעָמִים בְּהוֹלָכָה וְהַבָאָה אֶל הֶחָזֶה׃
וּלְצַד מַעְלָה, שֶׁהוּא בְּנֶצַח שָׁלֹשׁ
פְּעָמִים בְּהוֹלָכָה וְהַבָאָה אֶל הֶחָזֶה׃
וּלְצַד מַטָּה, שֶׁהוּא בְּהוֹד שָׁלֹשׁ
פְּעָמִים בְּהוֹלָכָה וְהַבָאָה אֶל הֶחָזֶה׃
וּלְצַד מַעֲרָב, שֶׁהוּא בִּיסוֹד שָׁלֹשׁ
פְּעָמִים בְּהוֹלָכָה וְהַבָאָה אֶל הֶחָזֶה׃

And no sin nor iniquity nor evil thought will delay this precept,
so it should ascend in favorable and pleasant fregnance before you Lord our God and the God of our fathers.
And herby I'm ready to shake the lulav, myrtle, willow and citron

towards   the   south,   which   is   Chesed,   three   times,   away   and   back   towards   the   chest.
And   towards   the   north,   which   is   Gevurah,   three   times   away   and   back   towards   the   chest.
And   towards   the   east,   which   is   Tiferet,   three   times   away   and   back   towards   the   chest.
And   towards   up,   which   is   Netzach,   three   times   away   and   back   towards   the   chest.
And   towards   down,   which   is   Hod,   three   times   away   and   back   towards   the   chest.
And   towards   the   west,   which   is   Yesod,   three   times   away   and   back   towards   the   chest.

וִיהִי רָצוֹן מִלְּפָנֶיךָ יְהֹוָה אֱלֹהֵינוּ
וֵאלֹהֵי אֲבוֹתֵינוּ שֶׁתְּהֵא שָׁעָה זוֹ שְׁעַת רָצוֹן
לְפָנֶיךָ וְתִהְיֶה עוֹלָה לְפָנֶיךָ מִצְוָה זוֹ שֶׁל
נְטִילַת הַלּוּלָב הֲדַס עֲרָבָה וְאֶתְרוֹג וְסֵדֶר
הַנְּעְנוּעִים לְהַמְשִׁיךְ הַחֲסָדִים הָרְאוּיִים לְהִמָּשֵׁךְ עַל
יָדָם בַּיּוֹם זֶה, וְיַעֲלֶה לְפָנֶיךָ כְּאִלּוּ כִּוַּנְתִּי
בְּכָל הַכַּוָּנוֹת שֶׁצָּרִיךְ לְכַוֵּן בַּלּוּלָב הֲדַס עֲרָבָה
וְאֶתְרוֹג שֶׁהֵם רוֹמְזִים אֶל אַרְבַּע אוֹתִיוֹת שֵׁם הוי"ה בְּמִלּוּי
הֵהִין שֶׁהֵם (יוד הה וו הה) וּכְאִלּוּ כִּוַּנְתִּי בְּסֵדֶר הַנְּעְנוּעִים שֶׁלָּהֶם וְיִמָּשֵׁךְ
וְחֶסֶד מֵחֲסָדִים בְּאוֹר פְּנִימִי כָּרָאוּי לִהְיוֹת נִמְשָׁךְ
בַּיּוֹם זֶה ◆ וִיהִי נֹעַם אֲדֹנָי אֱלֹהֵינוּ עָלֵינוּ וּמַעֲשֵׂה יָדֵינוּ
כּוֹנְנָה עָלֵינוּ וּמַעֲשֵׂה יָדֵינוּ כּוֹנְנֵהוּ:

And May it be pleasing before You, Lord, my God, and God of our forefathers, that this hour will be a time of favor before you so this precept of taking the lulav, myrtle, willow and citron and the order of shaking will ascend before You and draw the Mercies that suitable to be drawn by them on this day. And it will ascend before You as if I have intended all the meditations that are needed for the lulav, myrtle, willow and citron, which indicate the four letters of the Havayah filled with the letter Hei. And as I have intended in the order of the shaking so Mercy of Mercies from the Inner Light will be drawn as it should be drawn on this day. "May the pleasantness of the Lord our God be upon us and may He establish the work of our hands for us and may the work of our hands establish Him." (Psalms 90:17)

(Chesed) Ata אַתָּה (Yesod of Abba and Ima that influence) baruch בָּרוּךְ

(Tiferet) Adonai יְהֹוָֹאהדונהי

:On the first day meditate יְהֶוֶה יֶאֱהֱוֶיֱהֱ

Inner and Surrounding of Chesed of Chesed of Zeir Anpin to Nukva

:On the second day meditate יְהֹוָה יֶאֱהֱוֶיֱהֱ

Inner and Surrounding of Chesed of Gevurah of Zeir Anpin to Nukva

:On the third day meditate יְהֹוֹה יֶאֱהֱוֹיֱהֱ

Inner and Surrounding of Chesed of Tiferet of Zeir Anpin to Nukva

:On the fourth day meditate יְהֹוֶה יֶאֱהֱוֶיֱהֱ

Inner and Surrounding of Chesed of Netzach of Zeir Anpin to Nukva

:On the fifth day meditate יְהֹוֶה יֶאֱהֱוֶיֱהֱ

Inner and Surrounding of Chesed of Hod of Zeir Anpin to Nukva

:On the sixth day meditate יוֹהוּווֹהוּ יוּאאֱהוּווֹהוּיוֹהוּ

Inner and Surrounding of Chesed of Yesod of Zeir Anpin to Nukva

:On the seventh day meditate יהֹוה יאהֱהוֹיהֱה

Inner and Surrounding of Chesed of Malchut of Zeir Anpin to Nukva

(Malchut) ha'olam הָעוֹלָם (Binah) melech מֶלֶךְ (Gevurah) ילה Elohenu אֱלֹהֵינוּ

Meditate to devote your soul to sanctify the Holy Name and accept upon yourself
the four forms of death (stoning, burning, decapitation and strangulation.)

יאא יוד הי ויו הי ע"ב - stoning

הדה יוד הי ואו הי ס"ג - burning

וני יוד הא ואו הא מ"ה- decapitation

היה יוד הה וו הה ב"ן - strangulation

(Da'at and Tiferet) kidshanu קִדְּשָׁנוּ (Binah that confirms) asher אֲשֶׁר

(in Yesod) vetzivanu וְצִוָּנוּ (Netzach and Hod) bemitzvotav בְּמִצְוֹתָיו

✤(Malchut) ע"ה בינה, יהוה אהיה אהיה וחיים, lulav לוּלָב netilat נְטִילַת al עַל

On the first day one takes the lulav and say:

(Chesed) Ata אַתָּה (Yesod of Abba and ima that influence to) baruch בָּרוּךְ

(Gevurah) ילה Elohenu אֱלֹהֵינוּ (יוד הא ואו הא) (Tiferet) Adonai יְהֹוָֹאהדונהי

(in Yesod) shehecheyanu שֶׁהֶחֱיָנוּ (Malchut) ha'olam הָעוֹלָם (Binah) melech מֶלֶךְ

lazman לַזְּמַן vehigi'anu וְהִגִּיעָנוּ (Netzach and Hod) vekiyemanu וְקִיְּמָנוּ

✤(Malchut) והו hazeh הַזֶּה

Blessed are You, Lord, our God, King of the World,
Who has sanctified us with His commandments and obliged us with the Taking of the Lulav.
Blessed are You, Lord, our God, King of the world,
Who has kept us alive, sustained us, and brought us to this time.

Chesed—South—Abraham

Meditate to draw Mercies (from the three *Mochin*: *Chochmah*—*Binah*—*Da'at*),

to the clothing הא יוד הא אלף, which is in *Yesod* of *Tevunah*

(inside it is the *Moach* of *Da'at* of *Zeir Anpin*—יוד הי ויו), from *Chesed* of *Chesed* of

On the first day: *Chesed*;	On the second day: *Gevurah*;	On the third day: *Tiferet*;
On the fourth day: *Netzach*;		On the fifth day: *Hod*;
On the sixth day:		On the seventh day:
the Generality of the Five Mercies in *Yesod*;	the Generality of the Five Mercies in *Malchut*;	

Of *Da'at* of *Zeir Anpin*. And from the generality of יהו, which is:

Back to the chest	Away from the chest	
Moach of *Da'at*—הֵא	יוֹד הָא וָאו	1
Moach of *Binah*—הֵי	יוד הֵי וָאו	2
Moach of *Chochmah*—הֵי	יוד הֵי וִיו	3

To *Chesed* of *Chesed* of

On the first day: *Chesed*;	On the second day: *Gevurah*;	On the third day: *Tiferet*;
On the fourth day: *Netzach*;		On the fifth day: *Hod*;
On the sixth day:		On the seventh day:
the Generality of the Five Mercies in *Yesod*;	the Generality of the Five Mercies in *Malchut*;	

To His *Six Edges*; And from there to *Nukva* יוֹד הֵה וו הֵה

And when the *Lulav* and its species arrive to the chest we complete the *Hei* 'ה of the Name ע"ב.

Gevurah—North—Isaac

Meditate to draw Mercies (from the three *Mochin*: *Chochmah*—*Binah*—*Da'at*),

to the clothing הא יוד הא אלף, which is in *Yesod* of *Tevunah*

(inside it is the *Moach* of *Da'at* of *Zeir Anpin*—יוד הי ויו), from *Gevurah* of *Chesed* of

On the first day: *Chesed*;	On the second day: *Gevurah*;	On the third day: *Tiferet*;
On the fourth day: *Netzach*;		On the fifth day: *Hod*;
On the sixth day:		On the seventh day:
the Generality of the Five Mercies in *Yesod*;	the Generality of the Five Mercies in *Malchut*;	

Of *Da'at* of *Zeir Anpin*. And from the generality of יהו, which is:

Back to the chest	Away from the chest	
Moach of *Da'at*—אָה	הָא וְאו יוד	1
Moach of *Binah*—הִי	הִי וְאו יוד	2
Moach of *Chochmah*—הִי	הִי ויו יוד	3

To *Gevurah* of *Chesed* of

On the first day: *Chesed*;	On the second day: *Gevurah*;	On the third day: *Tiferet*;
On the fourth day: *Netzach*;		On the fifth day: *Hod*;
On the sixth day:		On the seventh day:
the Generality of the Five Mercies in *Yesod*;	the Generality of the Five Mercies in *Malchut*;	

To His *Six Edges*; And from there to *Nukva* יוד הֵה וו הֵה

And when the *Lulav* and its species arrive to the chest we complete the *Hei* 'ה of the Name ס"ג.

Tiferet—East—Jacob

Meditate to draw Mercies (from the three *Mochin: Chochmah—Binah—Da'at*),

to the clothing אלף הא יוד הא, which is in *Yesod* of *Tevunah*

(inside it is the *Moach* of *Da'at* of *Zeir Anpin*—יוד הי ויו), from *Tiferet* of *Chesed* of

On the first day: *Chesed*;	On the second day: *Gevurah*;	On the third day: *Tiferet*;
On the fourth day: *Netzach*;		On the fifth day: *Hod*;
On the sixth day: the Generality of the Five Mercies in *Yesod*;		On the seventh day: the Generality of the Five Mercies in *Malchut*;

Of *Da'at* of *Zeir Anpin*. And from the generality of יהו, which is:

Back to the chest	Away from the chest	
Moach of *Da'at*—הא	וֹאוֹ יוֹד הא	1
Moach of *Binah*—הִי	וֹאוֹ יוֹד הִי	2
Moach of *Chochmah*—הִי	וִיוֹ יוֹד הִי	3

To *Tiferet* of *Chesed* of

On the first day: *Chesed*;	On the second day: *Gevurah*;	On the third day: *Tiferet*;
On the fourth day: *Netzach*;		On the fifth day: *Hod*;
On the sixth day: the Generality of the Five Mercies in *Yesod*;		On the seventh day: the Generality of the Five Mercies in *Malchut*;

To His *Six Edges*; And from there to *Nukva* יוד הה וו הה

And when the *Lulav* and its species arrive to the chest we complete the *Hei* 'ה of the Name מ"ה.

Netzach—Up—Moses

Meditate to draw Mercies (from the three *Mochin: Chochmah—Binah—Da'at*),

to the clothing אלף הא יוד הא, which is in *Yesod* of *Tevunah*

(inside it is the *Moach* of *Da'at* of *Zeir Anpin*—יוד הי ויו), from *Netzach* of *Chesed* of

On the first day: *Chesed*;	On the second day: *Gevurah*;	On the third day: *Tiferet*;
On the fourth day: *Netzach*;		On the fifth day: *Hod*;
On the sixth day: the Generality of the Five Mercies in *Yesod*;		On the seventh day: the Generality of the Five Mercies in *Malchut*;

Of *Da'at* of *Zeir Anpin*. And from the generality of יהו, which is:

Back to the chest	Away from the chest	
Moach of *Da'at*—הא	יוֹד וְאוֹ הא	1
Moach of *Binah*—הִי	יוד וְאוֹ הִי	2
Moach of *Chochmah*—הִי	יוד וִיוּ הִי	3

To *Netzach* of *Chesed* of

On the first day: *Chesed*;	On the second day: *Gevurah*;	On the third day: *Tiferet*;
On the fourth day: *Netzach*;		On the fifth day: *Hod*;
On the sixth day: the Generality of the Five Mercies in *Yesod*;		On the seventh day: the Generality of the Five Mercies in *Malchut*;

To His *Six Edges*; And from there to *Nukva* יוד הה וו הה

And when the *Lulav* and its species arrive to the chest we complete the *Hei* 'ה of the Name ע"ב.

Hod—Down—Aaron

Meditate to draw Mercies (from the three *Mochin: Chochmah—Binah—Da'at*),

to the clothing אלף הא יוד הא, which is in *Yesod* of *Tevunah*

(inside it is the *Moach* of *Da'at* of *Zeir Anpin*—יוד הי ויו), from *Hod* of *Chesed* of

On the first day: *Chesed*;	On the second day: *Gevurah*;	On the third day: *Tiferet*;
On the fourth day: *Netzach*;		On the fifth day: *Hod*;
On the sixth day:		On the seventh day:
the Generality of the Five Mercies in *Yesod*;	the Generality of the Five Mercies in *Malchut*;	

Of *Da'at* of *Zeir Anpin*. And from the generality of יה, which is:

Back to the chest	Away from the chest	
Moach of *Da'at*—הָא	הָא יוד ואו	1
Moach of *Binah*—הָי	הָי יוֹד ואו	2
Moach of *Chochmah*—הָי	הָי יוד ויו	3

To *Hod* of *Chesed* of

On the first day: *Chesed*;	On the second day: *Gevurah*;	On the third day: *Tiferet*;
On the fourth day: *Netzach*;		On the fifth day: *Hod*;
On the sixth day:		On the seventh day:
the Generality of the Five Mercies in *Yesod*;	the Generality of the Five Mercies in *Malchut*;	

To His *Six Edges*; And from there to *Nukva* יוד הה וו הה

And when the *Lulav* and its species arrive to the chest we complete the *Hei* ה of the Name ס״ג.

Yesod—West—Joseph

Meditate to draw Mercies (from the three *Mochin: Chochmah—Binah—Da'at*),

to the clothing אלף הא יוד הא, which is in *Yesod* of *Tevunah*

(inside it is the *Moach* of *Da'at* of *Zeir Anpin*—יוד הי ויו), from *Yesod* of *Chesed* of

On the first day: *Chesed*;	On the second day: *Gevurah*;	On the third day: *Tiferet*;
On the fourth day: *Netzach*;		On the fifth day: *Hod*;
On the sixth day:		On the seventh day:
the Generality of the Five Mercies in *Yesod*;	the Generality of the Five Mercies in *Malchut*;	

Of *Da'at* of *Zeir Anpin*. And from the generality of יה, which is:

Back to the chest	Away from the chest	
Moach of *Da'at*—הואי	וואוו הואו יווודו	1
Moach of *Binah*—הוֹיי	וואוו הוֹיי יווודו	2
Moach of *Chochmah*—הוֹיי	וויוו הויו לוווֹדו	3

To *Yesod* of *Chesed* of

On the first day: *Chesed*;	On the second day: *Gevurah*;	On the third day: *Tiferet*;
On the fourth day: *Netzach*;		On the fifth day: *Hod*;
On the sixth day:		On the seventh day:
the Generality of the Five Mercies in *Yesod*;	the Generality of the Five Mercies in *Malchut*;	

To His *Six Edges*; And from there to *Nukva* יווודו הוֹדו ווו הוֹדו

And when the *Lulav* and its species arrive to the chest we complete the *Hei* ה of the Name מ״ה.

THE HALEL

The word *Halel* has the same numerical value (65) as *Lamed, Lamed, Hei* ללה, the 72 Name of God for dreams. Sixty-five is also the numerical value of both the word *hakeli* הכלי, which means the Vessel, and the Aramaic word אדני *Adonai*, the Name of God that corresponds to our physical world of *Malchut*. The *Halel* helps us lift off from this physical world to make our connections to the Holidays. The seven parts of the *Halel* correspond to the seven *Sefirot* that directly influence our world.

יכה   Elohenu אֱלֹהֵינוּ   Adonai יְהֹוָאדֹנִיאהדונהי   Ata אַתָּה   baruch בָּרוּךְ

kideshanu קִדְּשָׁנוּ   asher אֲשֶׁר   ha'olam הָעוֹלָם   melech מֶלֶךְ

et אֶת   ligmor לִגְמוֹר   vetzivanu וְצִוָּנוּ   bemitzvotav בְּמִצְוֹתָיו

הַהַלֵּל hahalel   לכה, אדני ; ר"ת לאה:

CHESED – HALELUYA

"God lifts me up from dust." This verse signifies the ability for positive change to occur at any moment. The first step is letting go of our ego. If we tune out those whispers and maintain total certainty that the Light can dramatically alter our situation instantly, we will ignite the power of this connection.

In this Psalm there are 58 words, which is the numerical value of the Holy Name: אל יהוה ע"ה.

avdei עַבְדֵי   halelu הַלְלוּ   לכה ; אלהים, אהיה ארני   haleluya הַלְלוּיָהּ

יְהֹוָאדֹנִיאהדונהי Adonai   shem שֵׁם   et אֶת   halelu הַלְלוּ   Adonai יְהֹוָאדֹנִיאהדונהי

ר"ת ריבוע ע"ב ריבוע ס"ג mevorach מְבֹרָךְ   Adonai יְהֹוָאדֹנִיאהדונהי   shem שֵׁם   yehi יְהִי

me'ata מֵעַתָּה (להעלות רפ"ח ניצוצות שנפלו לקליפה דמשם באים התולדים) רפ"ח = מברך יהוה

ad עַד   shemesh שֶׁמֶשׁ   mimizrach מִמִּזְרַח   יכל: olam עוֹלָם   ve'ad וְעַד

Adonai יְהֹוָאדֹנִיאהדונהי   shem שֵׁם   mehulal מְהֻלָּל   mevo'o מְבוֹאוֹ   ר"ת קדיש

THE HALEL
Blessed are You, Lord, our God, King of the world,
Who has sanctified us with His commandments and obliged us to complete the Halel.
CHESED – HALELUYA
"Praise the Lord, You servants of the Lord. Praise the Name of the Lord. May the Name of the Lord
be blessed from now and forever. From the rising of the sun until its setting, God's Name is praised.

ram רָם al עַל־ kol כָּל־ goyim גּוֹיִם ; עמם ילי Adonai יְהֹוָה

mi מִי al עַל הַשָּׁמַיִם hashamayim י"פ טל, י"פ כוזו ; ר"ת וזעמל kevodo כְּבוֹדוֹ:

hamagbihi הַמַּגְבִּיהִי lashavet לָשֶׁבֶת: hamashpili הַמַּשְׁפִּילִי lir'ot לִרְאוֹת

bashamayim בַּשָּׁמַיִם י"פ טל, י"פ כוזו uva'aretz וּבָאָרֶץ:

mekimi מְקִימִי me'afar מֵעָפָר dal דָּל me'ashpot מֵאַשְׁפֹּת yarim יָרִים

evyon אֶבְיוֹן: lehoshivi לְהוֹשִׁיבִי im עִם־ nedivim נְדִיבִים im עִם

nedivei נְדִיבֵי amo עַמּוֹ: moshivi מוֹשִׁיבִי akeret עֲקֶרֶת habayit הַבַּיִת

em אֵם־ ... עקרת הבית היא רחל ...

habanim הַבָּנִים semecha שְׂמֵחָה haleluya הַלְלוּיָהּ:

GEVURAH - BETZET YISRAEL

"Yehuda was holy," refers to the head of the Tribe of Yehuda, a man named Nachshon ben Aminadav. Nachshon was the first person to demonstrate complete certainty when he entered the Red Sea during the Exodus. He overcame his reactive fears and doubts and continued into the water until it reached his nostrils, whereupon it rushed into his throat and began choking him. At that precise moment, Satan attempted to bombard him with fear and uncertainty. Even when miracles are supposed to happen, the slightest doubt can prevent them from occurring. But Nachshon ben Aminadav didn't waver. A split second later, he was breathing fresh air as the waters of the Red Sea climbed toward the Heavens.

In this Psalm there are 52 words which correspond to the Holy Name: יוד הה וו הה (בהינת נוקבא).

betzet בְּצֵאת Yisrael יִשְׂרָאֵל miMitzrayim מִמִּצְרָיִם bet בֵּית

Yaakov יַעֲקֹב me'am מֵעַם lo'ez לֹעֵז: hayta הָיְתָה

Yehuda יְהוּדָה lekadsho לְקָדְשׁוֹ Yisrael יִשְׂרָאֵל mamshelotav מַמְשְׁלוֹתָיו:

God is high above all nations, His glory is above the Heavens. Who is like the Lord, our God, Who dwells so high, Who looks down upon the Heavens and the Earth? He raises the poor from the dust and uplifts the pauper from the trash heap. He seats them together with the noblemen, with the nobility of His Nation. He seats the mistress of the house, the mother of the children, happily. Praise the Lord!" (Psalms 113)

GEVURAH - BETZET YISRAEL

"When Israel left Egypt and the House of Jacob
from among a foreign nation, Judah then became sanctified to Him and Israel was His Dominion.

הַיָּם hayam יְלִי רָאָה ra'a וַיָּנֹס vayanos haYarden הַיַּרְדֵּן יְ הַיּוֹת וד' אותיות

יָסֹב yisov :le'achor לְאָחוֹר heharim הֶהָרִים רָקְדוּ rakdu כְאֵילִים che'elim

גְּבָעוֹת geva'ot כִּבְנֵי kivnei צֹאן tzon: מַה־ ma מ"ה לְךָ lecha הַיָּם hayam יְלִי

כִּי ki תָנוּס tanus הַיַּרְדֵּן haYarden יְ הַיּוֹת וד' אותיות תִּסֹּב tisov לְאָחוֹר :le'achor

הֶהָרִים heharim תִּרְקְדוּ tirkedu כְאֵילִים che'elim גְּבָעוֹת geva'ot

כִּבְנֵי kivnei צֹאן tzon: מִלְּפָנֵי milifnei אָדוֹן adon אני וְזוּלִי chuli אֶרֶץ aretz

מִלְּפָנֵי milifnei אֱלוֹהַּ Eloha שם בן מ"ב יַעֲקֹב Yaakov ו' הַיּוֹת, יאהדונהי אידהנויה:

הַהֹפְכִי hahofchi הַצוּר hatzur אלהים דההין ע"ה אֲגַם־ agam אהיה ריבוע אהיה = דם

(ומהפכו למים) מַיִם mayim וְזַלְמִישׁ chalamish לְמַעְיְנוֹ lema'yno מָיִם mayim:

TIFERET - LO LANU

Rav Yehuda Ashlag reminds us that despite whatever we are able to achieve spiritually on our own, we still can never truly earn or merit the Light that glimmers within us. Our physical body may not deserve anything in this world, but the Creator gave us the spark of Light that sustains our soul and is our essence. This spark of Light is known by the code word "Name," from the verse: *"Do it for Your Name!"* In reality, we are asking the Creator to give us Light for the God-like part of us—our soul. To ensure that we receive the Creator's Light with this prayer, we must mirror our request through actions. We do that when we recognize the spark of Light within others. Even our worst enemy is imbued with a spark of the Light of God. The more we recognize this, the more blessings and good fortune we receive in our own life.

לֹא lo Adonai יְהֹוָאדְנִיאהדונהי אדני אהיה אלהים לָנוּ lanu לֹא lo

לָנוּ lanu אלהים אהיה אדני כִּי ki לִשְׁמְךָ leshimcha תֵּן ten כָּבוֹד kavod

עַל־ al חַסְדְּךָ chasdecha עַל al אֲמִתֶּךָ amitecha: לָמָּה lama

יֹאמְרוּ yomru הַגּוֹיִם hagoyim אַיֵּה־ aye נָא na אֱלֹהֵיהֶם Elohehem ילה:

The sea saw and fled, the Jordan turned backward. The mountains skipped like rams, and the hills like young lambs. What ails you sea that you flee? Jordan that you turn backward? Mountains that you skip like rams? Hills, like young lambs? Before the Lord tremble, Earth, before the God of Jacob, Who turns the rock into a lake of water, the flint into a flowing fountain." (Psalms 113)

TIFERET - LO LANU

Not for our sake, Lord, not for our sake, but for the sake of Your Name give glory, for the sake of Your kindness and Your truth. Why should the nations say: Where is their God?

יכי kol כֹּל כוזו י״פ טל, י״פ vashamayim בַּשָּׁמַיִם ילה velohenu וֵאלֹהֵינוּ

kesef כֶּסֶף atzabehem עֲצַבֵּיהֶם asa עָשָׂה: chafetz וְחָפֵץ asher אֲשֶׁר

ע״ה ; מילה pe פֵּה: מ״ה adam אָדָם yedei יְדֵי ma'ase מַעֲשֵׂה vezahav וְזָהָב

אלהים, אהיה אדני ריבוע דמ״ה enayim עֵינַיִם yedaberu יְדַבֵּרוּ velo וְלֹא lahem לָהֶם

lahem לָהֶם ואו הי יוד oznayim אָזְנַיִם yir'u יִרְאוּ: velo וְלֹא lahem לָהֶם

yerichun יְרִיחוּן: velo וְלֹא lahem לָהֶם af אַף yishma'u יִשְׁמָעוּ velo וְלֹא

raglehem רַגְלֵיהֶם yemishun יְמִישׁוּן velo וְלֹא yedehem יְדֵיהֶם

bigronam בִּגְרוֹנָם: yehgu יֶהְגּוּ lo לֹא- yehalechu יְהַלֵּכוּ velo וְלֹא

osehem עֹשֵׂיהֶם (דס״ג) (מילוי) יא״י yih'yu יִהְיוּ kemohem כְּמוֹהֶם

Yisrael יִשְׂרָאֵל bahem בָּהֶם: bote'ach בֹּטֵחַ asher- אֲשֶׁר- יכי kol כֹּל

umaginam וּמָגִנָּם ezram עֶזְרָם badonai בַּיהֹוָאדְנִיאהדונהי betach בֹּטַח

bitchu בִּטְחוּ Aharon אַהֲרֹן ראה ב״פ bet בֵּית: hu הוּא

yir'ei יִרְאֵי hu הוּא umaginam וּמָגִנָּם ezram עֶזְרָם badonai בַּיהֹוָאדְנִיאהדונהי

ezram עֶזְרָם badonai בַּיהֹוָאדְנִיאהדונהי bitchu בִּטְחוּ Adonai יְהֹוָאדְנִיאהדונהי

hu הוּא: umaginam וּמָגִנָּם (כ״ב אותיות פשוטות (=אכא) ועוד ה׳ אותיות מנצפ״ך) ייז

NETZACH – ADONAI ZECHARANU

"The Heavens were given to God, but the land was given to the people." The Creator separated from this world so that we could become creators and express the godliness that is part of all of us. This paragraph gives us the strength to become true creators in our own lives. A tiny candle glimmering on a blazing sunlit day contributes little. But even the darkness of a large stadium responds to the light of a single candle. In this realm of darkness in which we find ourselves, one candle takes on tremendous value and worth.

When our own actions are those of sharing and revealing Light we achieve oneness with the Creator through similarity of form. This oneness enables us to become true creators in our own lives.

Our God is in the Heavens. He formed all that He desired. Their idols are of silver and gold, the work of the hands of man. They have mouths but cannot speak. They have eyes but cannot see. They have noses but cannot smell. Their hands cannot touch, their legs cannot walk. They utter no sounds from their throats. May their makers be like them and whoever trusts in them. Israel, place your trust in the Lord. He is your Helper and Protector. House of Aaron, place your trust in the Lord. He is your Helper and Protector. Those who fear the Lord, place your trust in the Lord. He is your Helper and Protector." (Psalms 115:1-11)

יְהֹוָֿאֲדֹנָיאהדונהי Adonai זְכָרָנוּ zecharanu יְבָרֵךְ yevarech עסמ"ב, הברכה

(למתק את ז' המלכים שמתו) עסמ"ב, הברכה (למתק את ז' המלכים שמתו) ; ר"ת ייי yevarech יְבָרֵךְ

אֶת־ et בֵּית bet ב"פ ראה Yisrael יִשְׂרָאֵל yevarech יְבָרֵךְ עסמ"ב, הברכה

Aharon: אַהֲרֹן ב"פ ראה bet בֵּית et אֶת־ (למתק את ז' המלכים שמתו)

yir'ei יִרְאֵי yevarech יְבָרֵךְ עסמ"ב, הברכה (למתק את ז' המלכים שמתו)

יְהֹוָֿאֲדֹנָיאהדונהי Adonai ר"ת ייי הַקְּטַנִּים haketanim עִם im הַגְּדֹלִים hagedolim:

yosef יֹסֵף Adonai יְהֹוָֿאֲדֹנָיאהדונהי alechem עֲלֵיכֶם alechem עֲלֵיכֶם

ve'al וְעַל benechem בְּנֵיכֶם: beruchim בְּרוּכִים atem אַתֶּם

ladonai לַיהֹוָֿאֲדֹנָיאהדונהי ose עֹשֵׂה shamayim שָׁמַיִם י"פ טל, י"פ כוזו

va'aretz וָאָרֶץ: hashamayim הַשָּׁמַיִם י"פ כוזו, י"פ טל, shamayim שָׁמַיִם י"פ טל, י"פ כוזו

ladonai לַיהֹוָֿאֲדֹנָיאהדונהי veha'aretz וְהָאָרֶץ אלהים דההין ע"ה natan נָתַן

livnei לִבְנֵי adam אָדָם מ"ה: lo לֹא hametim הַמֵּתִים yehalelu יְהַלְלוּ

Yah יָּה velo וְלֹא kol כָּל יֹ׳ yordei יֹרְדֵי duma דוּמָה: va'anachnu וַאֲנַֿחְנוּ

nevarech נְבָרֵךְ Yah יָּה me'ata מֵעַתָּה ve'ad וְעַד־ olam עוֹלָם

haleluya הַלְלוּיָֿה אלהים, אהיה אדני ; ללה:

HOD— AHAVTI

Rav Elimelech, a great 18th century Kabbalist, teaches us that while we pray, Satan, our Opponent, often comes to us to say: "Why are you bothering to stand here and pray? You don't really want to change. It's too difficult. So why bother with all this complicated spiritual work? Given all the negative actions you have already performed, your personal situation is hopeless." This prayer shuts down Satan's negative and destructive influence and helps us understand that it doesn't matter what we did previously. From this moment forward, we can change and transform our nature if we really want to.

NETZACH – ADONAI ZECHARANU

"The Lord Who remembers us, blesses. He blesses the House of Israel. He blesses the House of Aaron. He blesses those who fear the Lord, the small as well as the great. May the Lord increase you more and more, you and your children. Blessed are you Lord, Creator of Heaven and Earth. The Heavens are the Heavens of the Lord, and the Earth He gave to mankind. The dead do not praise the Lord, nor do those who descend to the grave. But we will bless the Lord from now and forever. Praise the Lord." (Psalms 115:12-end)

"God protects and saves the fools." The smartest men can make the biggest mistakes. If we think we really know it all, if our egos tell us that we are brilliant people, then we really are fools and the Light will never reach us. But those people who can admit that there is always something to learn are acknowledging that we are all fools, in a proactive manner. God will protect them and take them to even higher levels of fulfillment.

אָהַבְתִּי ahavti   כִּי ki   יִשְׁמַע yishma   יְהֹוָ Adonai

אֶת־ et   קוֹלִי koli   תַּחֲנוּנַי tachanunai: כִּי ki   הִטָּה hita

אָזְנוֹ ozno   לִי li   וּבְיָמַי uvyamai   אֶקְרָא ekra:

אֲפָפוּנִי afafuni   חֶבְלֵי chevlei   מָוֶת mavet   וּמְצָרֵי umtzarei   שְׁאוֹל she'ol

מְצָאוּנִי metza'uni   צָרָה tzara   וְיָגוֹן veyagon   אֶמְצָא emtza:

וּבְשֵׁם uvshem   יְהֹוָ Adonai   אֶקְרָא ekra

אָנָּה ana   יְהֹוָ Adonai   מַלְּטָה maleta   נַפְשִׁי nafshi:

חַנּוּן chanun   יְהֹוָ Adonai   וְצַדִּיק vetzadik   וֵאלֹהֵינוּ velohenu

מְרַחֵם merachem   שֹׁמֵר shomer   פְּתָאִים peta'im   יְהֹוָ Adonai   דַּלּוֹתִי daloti

וְלִי veli   יְהוֹשִׁיעַ yehoshi'a: שׁוּבִי shuvi   נַפְשִׁי nafshi   לִמְנוּחָיְכִי limnuchaychi

כִּי ki   יְהֹוָ Adonai   גָּמַל gamal   עָלָיְכִי alaychi:

וְחִלַּצְתָּ chilatzta   נַפְשִׁי nafshi   מִמָּוֶת mimavet   אֶת־ et   עֵינִי eni

מִן min   דִּמְעָה dim'a   אֶת־ et   רַגְלִי ragli   מִדֶּחִי midechi:

אֶתְהַלֵּךְ ethalech   לִפְנֵי lifnei   יְהֹוָ Adonai   בְּאַרְצוֹת be'artzot

הֶחַיִּים hachayim   הֶאֱמַנְתִּי he'emanti   כִּי ki

אֲדַבֵּר adaber   אֲנִי ani   עָנִיתִי aniti   מְאֹד me'od: אֲנִי ani

אָמַרְתִּי amarti   בְחָפְזִי vechofzi   כָּל kol   הָאָדָם ha'adam   כֹּזֵב kozev:

HOD– AHAVTI

"I wanted that the Lord would listen to my voice and to my supplications and turn His Ear towards me and that all my days I would call upon Him. Pangs of death have surrounded me and the misery of the grave has found me. I found trouble and sorrow. Then I called the Name of the Lord: Please, God, rescue my soul. For our Lord is gracious and righteous; our Lord is merciful. The Lord watches over the simple people. I became destitute and He saved me. Return, my soul, to your peacefulness, for the Lord has dealt kindly with you. For You have salvaged my soul from death, my eyes from tears, and my feet from stumbling. I shall walk before the Lord in the land of the living. I believed even as I spoke, when I was greatly impoverished, and I said in my haste, all men are treacherous." (Psalms 116:1-11)

YESOD - MA ASHIV

In the following paragraph, we find the verse *Ana Hashem*, which acknowledges that the Creator is our only true spiritual master and asks the Creator to give us signs, teachers, directions, and pathways that will lead us to the Light.

ילי kol כָּל ladonai לַיהֹוָואהדונהי ashiv אָשִׁיב מ"ה ma מָה

אדני אהיה אלהים, kos כּוֹס alai עָלָי tagmulohi תַּגְמוּלוֹהִי

yeshu'ot יְשׁוּעוֹת (כף וו סמך) = עסמ"ב, הברכה (למתק את ז' המלכים שמתו) במילוי

esa אֶשָּׂא uvshem וּבְשֵׁם Adonai יְהֹוָואהדונהי ekra אֶקְרָא

nedarai נְדָרַי ladonai לַיהֹוָואהדונהי ashalem אֲשַׁלֵּם negda נֶגְדָה

yakar יָקָר amo עַמּוֹ אדני יה lechol לְכָל na נָא נגד, מזבח, זן, אל יהוה

be'enei בְּעֵינֵי ריבוע דמ"ה Adonai יְהֹוָואהדונהי hamavta הַמָּוְתָה

ani אֲנִי אני ki כִּי Adonai יְהֹוָואהדונהי ana אָנָּה lachasidav לַחֲסִידָיו

אדני אל avdecha עַבְדֶּךְ ani אֲנִי אני אדני אל avdecha עַבְדְּךָ פוי, אל אדני

lecha לָךְ lemoserai לְמוֹסֵרָי pitachta פִּתַּחְתָּ amatecha אֲמָתֶךָ ben בֶּן

Adonai יְהֹוָואהדונהי uvshem וּבְשֵׁם toda תּוֹדָה zevach זֶבַח ezbach אֶזְבַּח

ashalem אֲשַׁלֵּם ladonai לַיהֹוָואהדונהי nedarai נְדָרַי ekra אֶקְרָא

amo עַמּוֹ אדני יה lechol לְכָל na נָא נגד, מזבח, זן, אל יהוה negda נֶגְדָה

betochechi בְּתוֹכֵכִי Adonai יְהֹוָואהדונהי ראה ב"פ bet בֵּית bechatzrot בְּחַצְרוֹת

לכה ; ארני אהיה אלהים, haleluya הַלְלוּיָהּ Yerushalayim יְרוּשָׁלָיִם

YESOD - MA ASHIV

"How can I repay the Lord
for all that He has bestowed upon me? I raise a cup of salvation and call out in the Name of the Lord.
I shall pay my vows to the Lord before all His People. It is difficult in the Eyes of the Lord,
the death of His pious ones. Please, Lord, I am Your servant. I am Your servant,
then a son of Your handmaid. You have untied my bonds. To You I shall sacrifice
a thanksgiving-offering and call out in the Name of the Lord. I shall pay my vows to the Lord, before all
His People, in the courtyards of the Lord, within Jerusalem. Praise the Lord." (Psalms 116:12-end)

MALCHUT - HALELU

"All the nations of the world should praise God." Each nation, according to Kabbalah, has its own path to the Light. But there is only one Creator who gives Light to all of us. For this reason, *"Love your neighbor as yourself"* applies to all the nations of the world. We must treat all people with dignity. There is war between nations and chaos in society only because of the lack of compassion and sensitivity between people.

goyim גּוֹיִם יִלי kol כָּל־ Adonai יְהֹוָ(אדני־אהדונהי) et־ אֶת־ halelu הַלְלוּ

gavar גָּבַר ki כִּי ha'umim: הָאֻמִּים יִלי kol כָּל־ shabechuhu שַׁבְּחוּהוּ

(להמשיך הארה ממזלא עילאה) מזלא, הויות, ג׳ chasdo חַסְדּוֹ alenu עָלֵינוּ

Adonai יְהֹוָ(אדני־אהדונהי) ס״ג פ״ז אהיה, אהיה פעמים אהיה ve'emet וֶאֱמֶת־

(ללה ; אהיה אדני, אהיה, אלהים,) haleluya הַלְלוּיָהּ דס״ג אותיות וי׳ ריבוע le'olam לְעוֹלָם

MALCHUT – HODU

The next four verses connect us to the four spiritual worlds, represented by the four different combinations of the *Yud, Hei, Vav,* and *Hei.* Each of these different combinations of letters is a transformer that channels currents of spiritual energy from various levels of the *Ten Sefirot* to our physical realm. Spiritually speaking, some people are connected to the Highest Worlds, while others are connected to the Middle and Lower Realms. The only way for humanity to achieve true unity is for each of us to let go of our ego and accept the fact that no one is higher or lower than anyone else; only our connections are different.

The *Talmud* reinforces this concept. We learn that a mosquito is actually on a much higher spiritual level than a man who isn't pursuing his spiritual work. A mosquito comes into this world to bite. As we all know, the mosquito does his job quite effectively. We came here to achieve a spiritual transformation. We give too much importance to a person's physical status in this world. However, whether one is an executive or a factory worker – if they are both doing their spiritual work, they are on the same level according to the Creator. Some people are never happy with where they are. Part of their work is to appreciate that they are doing their spiritual work. They should realize that they're on the same spiritual level as not only the people they envy but also the people they consider to be on a lower level than themselves. They are all working on spiritual tranformation.

Chochmah (ע״ב–יוד הי ויו הי, קס״א–אלף הי יוד הי)

והו tov טוֹב ki כִּי־ ladonai לַיהֹוָ(אדני־אהדונהי) אהיה hodu הוֹדוּ

כי טוב = יהוה אהיה, אום, מובה, יזל

chasdo וְחַסְדּוֹ le'olam לְעוֹלָם ki כִּי

ג׳ הויות, מזלא (להמשיך הארה ממזלא עילאה) ; ר״ת = גנה:

During *Sukkot* we shake the Lulav according the meditation charts on pages 383-385.
On *Simchat Torah* we skip the charts on pages 383-385, and continue with *"yomar na"* on page 386.

MALCHUT - HALELU
"Praise the Lord, all you people, Exalt Him, all you people. For His kindness has overwhelmed us and the truth of the Lord is eternal, Praise the Lord." (Psalms 117)
MALCHUT – HODU
"Give thanks to the Lord for He is good, for His kindness is forever.

Chesed—South—Abraham (ladonai לַיהוה(אדני יאהדונהי) hodu הוֹדוּ)

Meditate to draw Mercies (from the three *Mochin: Chochmah—Binah—Da'at*),

to the clothing אלף הא יוד הא, which is in *Yesod* of *Tevunah*

(inside it is the *Moach* of *Da'at* of *Zeir Anpin*—יוד הי ויו), from *Chesed* of *Chesed* of

On the first day: *Chesed*;	On the second day: *Gevurah*;	On the third day: *Tiferet*;
On the fourth day: *Netzach*;		On the fifth day: *Hod*;
On the sixth day: the Generality of the Five Mercies in *Yesod*;		On the seventh day: the Generality of the Five Mercies in *Malchut*;

Of *Da'at* of *Zeir Anpin*. And from the generality of יה, which is:

Back to the chest	Away from the chest	
Moach of *Da'at*—הָא	יוֹד הָא וָאו	1
Moach of *Binah*—הִי	יוֹד הִי וָאו	2
Moach of *Chochmah*—הִי	יוֹד הִי וִיו	3

To *Chesed* of *Chesed* of

On the first day: *Chesed*;	On the second day: *Gevurah*;	On the third day: *Tiferet*;
On the fourth day: *Netzach*;		On the fifth day: *Hod*;
On the sixth day: the Generality of the Five Mercies in *Yesod*;		On the seventh day: the Generality of the Five Mercies in *Malchut*;

To His *Six Edges*; And from there to *Nukva* יוֹד הֵה וָו הֵה

And when the *Lulav* and its species arrive to the chest we complete the *Hei* 'ה of the Name ע"ב.

Gevurah—North—Isaac (ki כִּי)

Meditate to draw Mercies (from the three *Mochin: Chochmah—Binah—Da'at*),

to the clothing אלף הא יוד הא, which is in *Yesod* of *Tevunah*

(inside it is the *Moach* of *Da'at* of *Zeir Anpin*—יוד הי ויו), from *Gevurah* of *Chesed* of

On the first day: *Chesed*;	On the second day: *Gevurah*;	On the third day: *Tiferet*;
On the fourth day: *Netzach*;		On the fifth day: *Hod*;
On the sixth day: the Generality of the Five Mercies in *Yesod*;		On the seventh day: the Generality of the Five Mercies in *Malchut*;

Of *Da'at* of *Zeir Anpin*. And from the generality of יה, which is:

Back to the chest	Away from the chest	
Moach of *Da'at*—הָא	הָא וָאו יוֹד	1
Moach of *Binah*—הִי	הִי וָאו יוֹד	2
Moach of *Chochmah*—הִי	הִי וִיו יוֹד	3

To *Gevurah* of *Chesed* of

On the first day: *Chesed*;	On the second day: *Gevurah*;	On the third day: *Tiferet*;
On the fourth day: *Netzach*;		On the fifth day: *Hod*;
On the sixth day: the Generality of the Five Mercies in *Yesod*;		On the seventh day: the Generality of the Five Mercies in *Malchut*;

To His *Six Edges*; And from there to *Nukva* יוֹד הֵה וָו הֵה

And when the *Lulav* and its species arrive to the chest we complete the *Hei* 'ה of the Name ס"ג.

Tiferet—East—Jacob (tov טוב)

Meditate to draw Mercies (from the three *Mochin: Chochmah—Binah—Da'at*),

to the clothing אלף הא יוד הא, which is in *Yesod* of *Tevunah*

(inside it is the *Moach* of *Da'at* of *Zeir Anpin*—יוד הי ויו), from *Tiferet* of *Chesed* of

On the first day: *Chesed*;	On the second day: *Gevurah*;	On the third day: *Tiferet*;
On the fourth day: *Netzach*;		On the fifth day: *Hod*;
On the sixth day:		On the seventh day:
the Generality of the Five Mercies in *Yesod*;		the Generality of the Five Mercies in *Malchut*;

Of *Da'at* of *Zeir Anpin*. And from the generality of יהו, which is:

Back to the chest	Away from the chest	
Moach of *Da'at*—הא	וְאוֹ יוד הֹא	1
Moach of *Binah*—הֹי	וְאוֹ יוֹד הֹי	2
Moach of *Chochmah*—הֹי	וִיוֹ יוֹד הֹי	3

To *Tiferet* of *Chesed* of

On the first day: *Chesed*;	On the second day: *Gevurah*;	On the third day: *Tiferet*;
On the fourth day: *Netzach*;		On the fifth day: *Hod*;
On the sixth day:		On the seventh day:
the Generality of the Five Mercies in *Yesod*;		the Generality of the Five Mercies in *Malchut*;

To His *Six Edges*; And from there to *Nukva* יוד הה וו הה

And when the *Lulav* and its species arrive to the chest we complete the *Hei* הֹ of the Name מ"ה.

Netzach—Up—Moses (ki כי)

Meditate to draw Mercies (from the three *Mochin: Chochmah—Binah—Da'at*),

to the clothing אלף הא יוד הא, which is in *Yesod* of *Tevunah*

(inside it is the *Moach* of *Da'at* of *Zeir Anpin*—יוד הי ויו), from *Netzach* of *Chesed* of

On the first day: *Chesed*;	On the second day: *Gevurah*;	On the third day: *Tiferet*;
On the fourth day: *Netzach*;		On the fifth day: *Hod*;
On the sixth day:		On the seventh day:
the Generality of the Five Mercies in *Yesod*;		the Generality of the Five Mercies in *Malchut*;

Of *Da'at* of *Zeir Anpin*. And from the generality of יהו, which is:

Back to the chest	Away from the chest	
Moach of *Da'at*—הא	יוֹד וְאוֹ הֹא	1
Moach of *Binah*—הֹי	יוֹד וְאוֹ הֹי	2
Moach of *Chochmah*—הֹי	יוֹד וִיוֹ הֹי	3

To *Netzach* of *Chesed* of

On the first day: *Chesed*;	On the second day: *Gevurah*;	On the third day: *Tiferet*;
On the fourth day: *Netzach*;		On the fifth day: *Hod*;
On the sixth day:		On the seventh day:
the Generality of the Five Mercies in *Yesod*;		the Generality of the Five Mercies in *Malchut*;

To His *Six Edges*; And from there to *Nukva* יוד הה וו הה

And when the *Lulav* and its species arrive to the chest we complete the *Hei* הֹ of the Name ע"ב.

Hod—Down—Aaron (le'olam לְעוֹלָם)

Meditate to draw Mercies (from the three *Mochin: Chochmah—Binah—Da'at*),

to the clothing אלף הא יוד הא, which is in *Yesod* of *Tevunah*

(inside it is the *Moach* of *Da'at* of *Zeir Anpin*—יוד הי ויו), from *Hod* of *Chesed* of

On the first day: *Chesed*;	On the second day: *Gevurah*;	On the third day: *Tiferet*;
On the fourth day: *Netzach*;		On the fifth day: *Hod*;
On the sixth day:		On the seventh day:
the Generality of the Five Mercies in *Yesod*;	the Generality of the Five Mercies in *Malchut*;	

Of *Da'at* of *Zeir Anpin*. And from the generality of יהו, which is:

Back to the chest	Away from the chest	
Moach of *Da'at*—הָא	הָא יוד ואו	1
Moach of *Binah*—הָי	הָי יוד ואו	2
Moach of *Chochmah*—הָי	הָי יוד ויו	3

To *Hod* of *Chesed* of

On the first day: *Chesed*;	On the second day: *Gevurah*;	On the third day: *Tiferet*;
On the fourth day: *Netzach*;		On the fifth day: *Hod*;
On the sixth day:		On the seventh day:
the Generality of the Five Mercies in *Yesod*;	the Generality of the Five Mercies in *Malchut*;	

To His *Six Edges*; And from there to *Nukva* יוד הה וו הה

And when the *Lulav* and its species arrive to the chest we complete the *Hei* 'ה of the Name ס"ג.

Yesod—West—Joseph (chasdo וְחַסְדוֹ)

Meditate to draw Mercies (from the three *Mochin: Chochmah—Binah—Da'at*),

to the clothing אלף הא יוד הא, which is in *Yesod* of *Tevunah*

(inside it is the *Moach* of *Da'at* of *Zeir Anpin*—יוד הי ויו), from *Yesod* of *Chesed* of

On the first day: *Chesed*;	On the second day: *Gevurah*;	On the third day: *Tiferet*;
On the fourth day: *Netzach*;		On the fifth day: *Hod*;
On the sixth day:		On the seventh day:
the Generality of the Five Mercies in *Yesod*;	the Generality of the Five Mercies in *Malchut*;	

Of *Da'at* of *Zeir Anpin*. And from the generality of יהו, which is:

Back to the chest	Away from the chest	
Moach of *Da'at*—הואו	ואווו הואו יווודו	1
Moach of *Binah*—הויו	ואווו הויו יווודו	2
Moach of *Chochmah*—הויו	ויווו הויו לוווד	3

To *Yesod* of *Chesed* of

On the first day: *Chesed*;	On the second day: *Gevurah*;	On the third day: *Tiferet*;
On the fourth day: *Netzach*;		On the fifth day: *Hod*;
On the sixth day:		On the seventh day:
the Generality of the Five Mercies in *Yesod*;	the Generality of the Five Mercies in *Malchut*;	

To His *Six Edges*; And from there to *Nukva* הוהו ווו הוהו יוווד

And when the *Lulav* and its species arrive to the chest we complete the *Hei* 'ה of the Name מ"ה.

(ס"ג – יוד הי ואו הי, קס"א – אלף הי יוד הי) **Binah**

יֹאמַר־ Yisrael נָא יִשְׂרָאֵל na yomar

chasdo וְחַסְדּוֹ ki כִּי לְעוֹלָם le'olam ריבוע ס"ג ו"י אותיות דס"ג

ג' הויות, מזלא (להמשיך הארה ממזלא עילאה) ; ר"ת = נגה:

(מ"ה – יוד הא ואו הא, קמ"ג – אלף הא יוד הא) **Zeir Anpin**

יֹאמְרוּ־ Aharon אַהֲרֹן ב"פ ראה vet בֵית־ na נָא yomru

chasdo וְחַסְדּוֹ ki כִּי לְעוֹלָם le'olam ריבוע ס"ג ו"י אותיות דס"ג

ג' הויות, מזלא (להמשיך הארה ממזלא עילאה) ; ר"ת = נגה:

(ב"ן – יוד הה וחו הה, קנ"א – אלף הה יוד הה) **Malchut**

יֹאמְרוּ־ Adonai יֱהֹוָאהדונהי יְהוָה yir'ei יִרְאֵי na נָא yomru

chasdo וְחַסְדּוֹ ki כִּי לְעוֹלָם le'olam ריבוע ס"ג ו"י אותיות דס"ג

ג' הויות, מזלא (להמשיך הארה ממזלא עילאה) ; ר"ת = נגה:

MIN HAMETZAR

"From the straits I called upon God." Unfortunately, most of us call upon the Creator when we are in dire straits. Kabbalah teaches that we also need to call upon the Creator during good times and recognize the Light's influence in all of our good fortune. The *Zohar* teaches us that if we create a spiritual opening within ourselves no wider than the eye of a needle, God will answer us and open the Supernal Gates for us. Whatever its size, this opening for spirituality must be a complete opening where there can be no doubt or uncertainty.

Yah יָה karati קָרָאתִי מצר hametzar הַמֵּצַר min מִן־ א' ארך

Yah יָה: vamerchav בַמֶּרְחָב anani עָנָנִי ב' אפים

ira אִירָא lo לֹא li לִי Adonai יֱהֹוָאהדונהי ג' ורב חסד

adam אָדָם מ"ה: li לִי ya'ase יַעֲשֶׂה מ"ה ma מַה־ ד' נשא עון

be'ozrai בְּעֹזְרִי li לִי Adonai יֱהֹוָאהדונהי ה' ופשע

veson'ai בְשֹׂנְאָי: er'e אֶרְאֶה אני va'ani וַאֲנִי ו' ונקה

Let Israel say so now, for His kindness is forever.
Let the House of Aaron say so now, for His kindness is forever.
Let those who fear the Lord say so now, for His kindness is forever.

MIN HAMETZAR

Greatly from my distress I called out to the Lord. Patient Lord answered me in His expansiveness. The Lord is with me, I shall not fear those who bear iniquities. What can man do to me? And sins, the Lord shall come to my rescue and cleanses. And I shall look upon my enemies.

badonai בַּיהֹוָואדניאהדונהי lachasot לַחֲסוֹת והו tov טוֹב ז׳ פוקד

מ"ה: ba'adam בָּאָדָם mibetoach מִבְּטֹחַ וו על שלשים

badonai בַּיהֹוָואדניאהדונהי lachasot לַחֲסוֹת והו tov טוֹב ט׳ ועל רבעים

goyim גּוֹיִם ילי kol כָּל־ bindivim בִּנְדִיבִים mibetoa'ch מִבְּטֹחַ

amilam אֲמִילַם: ki כִּי Adonai יְהֹוָואדניאהדונהי beshem בְּשֵׁם sevavuni סְבָבוּנִי

Adonai יְהֹוָואדניאהדונהי beshem בְּשֵׁם sevavuni סְבָבוּנִי gam גַּם־ sabuni סַבּוּנִי

do'achu דֹּעֲכוּ chidvorim כִּדְבוֹרִים sabuni סַבּוּנִי amilam אֲמִילַם: ki כִּי

Adonai יְהֹוָואדניאהדונהי beshem בְּשֵׁם kotzim קוֹצִים ke'esh כְּאֵשׁ

linpol לִנְפֹּל dechitani דְחִיתַנִי dacho דָּחֹה amilam אֲמִילַם: ki כִּי

ozi עָזִּי azarani עֲזָרָנִי vadonai וַיהֹוָואדניאהדונהי אלהים ע"ה, אהיה אדני ע"ה

lishu'a לִישׁוּעָה: li לִי vay'hi וַיְהִי־ Yah יָהּ vezimrat וְזִמְרָת

tzadikim צַדִּיקִים be'aholei בְּאָהֳלֵי vishua וִישׁוּעָה rina רִנָּה kol קוֹל

chayil חָיִל: osa עֹשָׂה Adonai יְהֹוָואדניאהדונהי yemin יְמִין

yemin יְמִין romema רוֹמֵמָה Adonai יְהֹוָואדניאהדונהי yemin יְמִין

amut אָמוּת lo לֹא chayil חָיִל osa עֹשָׂה Adonai יְהֹוָואדניאהדונהי

Yah יָהּ: ma'asei מַעֲשֵׂי va'asaper וַאֲסַפֵּר echye אֶחְיֶה ki כִּי

lo לֹא velamavet וְלַמָּוֶת Yah יָהּ yisrani יִסְּרַנִּי yasor יַסֹּר

avo אָבֹא tzedek צֶדֶק sha'arei שַׁעֲרֵי־ li לִי pitchu פִּתְחוּ netanani נְתָנָנִי:

hasha'ar הַשַּׁעַר zeh זֶה Yah יָהּ: ode אוֹדֶה vam בָם

vo בוֹ: yavo'u יָבֹאוּ tzadikim צַדִּיקִים ladonai לַיהֹוָואדניאהדונהי

It is good to take refuge in the Lord rather than to trust in man. It is better to take refuge in the Lord than to trust in noblemen. All the nations surrounded me. In the Name of the Lord, I shall cut them down. They surrounded me again and again. In the Name of the Lord, I shall cut them down. They surrounded me like bees, but are extinguished like a fire on thorns. With the Name of the Lord, I shall cut them down. They pushed me time and again to fall and the Lord came to my aid. The strength and cutting power of God were for me a salvation. The sound of song and salvation is in the tents of the righteous. The right of the Lord does mighty things. The right of the Lord is raised. The right of the Lord does mighty things. I shall not die, but rather I shall live and tell of the deeds of God. God has chastised me again and again, but He has not surrendered me to death. Open for me the gates of righteousness. I will go through them and give thanks to God. This is the Gate of the Lord, the righteous may go through It.

ODCHA

We have four verses that connect us to the four letters of the Tetragrammaton. Each verse is recited twice.

Yud – Chochmah – י

2x ‎:lishua לִישׁוּעָה li לִי vatehi וַתְּהִי־ anitani עֲנִיתָנִי ki כִּי odcha אוֹדְךָ

Hei – Binah – ה

hayta הָיְתָה habonim הַבּוֹנִים ma'asu מָאֲסוּ even אֶבֶן

2x ‎ר"ת פהלב: ; ע"ב ס"ג pina פִּנָּה ע"ה דיורין ואלהים אלהים ריבוע lerosh לְרֹאשׁ

Vav – Zeir Anpin – ו

zot זֹאת hayta הָיְתָה Adonai יְהֹוָהאדניאהדונהי me'et מֵאֵת

2x ‎דמ"ה: ריבוע be'enenu בְּעֵינֵינוּ niflat נִפְלָאת hee הִיא

Hei – Malchut – ה

Adonai יְהֹוָהאדניאהדונהי asa עָשָׂה אל יהוה זן, מזבוז, נגד, ע"ה hayom הַיּוֹם ze זֶה־

2x ‎:vo בוֹ מלה venismecha וְנִשְׂמְחָה nagila נָגִילָה

ANA

These four verses offer us a different pathway to connect to the Light. The numeric equivalent of the word אנא (Ana) is 52, which is also the numerical value of the Name of God that connects to our physical realm of *Malchut*.

You should meditate that *Malchut*, which is: ב"ן, receives from *Chochmah* which is: ע"ב.

(יוד הי ויו הי) Adonai יְהֹוָהאדניאהדונהי (יוד הה וו הה) ב"ן ana אָנָּא

‎:na נָּא hoshi'a הוֹשִׁיעָה נהורין וש"ע יהוה

During *Sukkot* we shake the Lulav according the meditation charts on pages 389-391.

On *Simchat Torah* we skip the charts on pages 389-391, and continue with "*ana*" on page 392.

ODCHA

I am grateful to You, for You have answered me and have become my salvation.
The stone that was rejected by the builders has become the main cornerstone.
This came about from the Lord, it is wondrous in our eyes.
The Lord has made this day let us be glad and rejoice in it.

ANA

We beseech You, Lord, save us now.

Chesed—South—Abraham

Meditate to draw Mercies (from the three *Mochin*: *Chochmah—Binah—Da'at*),

to the clothing אלף הא יוד הא, which is in *Yesod* of *Tevunah*

(inside it is the *Moach* of *Da'at* of *Zeir Anpin*—יוד הי ויו), from *Chesed* of *Chesed* of

On the first day: *Chesed*;	On the second day: *Gevurah*;	On the third day: *Tiferet*;
On the fourth day: *Netzach*;		On the fifth day: *Hod*;
On the sixth day:		On the seventh day:
the Generality of the Five Mercies in *Yesod*;	the Generality of the Five Mercies in *Malchut*;	

Of *Da'at* of *Zeir Anpin*. And from the generality of יהו, which is:

Back to the chest	Away from the chest	
Moach of *Da'at*—הָא	יוּד הָא וָאו	1
Moach of *Binah*—הִי	יוּד הִי וָאו	2
Moach of *Chochmah*—הִי	יוּד הִי וִיו	3

To *Chesed* of *Chesed* of

On the first day: *Chesed*;	On the second day: *Gevurah*;	On the third day: *Tiferet*;
On the fourth day: *Netzach*;		On the fifth day: *Hod*;
On the sixth day:		On the seventh day:
the Generality of the Five Mercies in *Yesod*;	the Generality of the Five Mercies in *Malchut*;	

To His *Six Edges*; And from there to *Nukva* יוּד הֵה וֵו הֵה

And when the *Lulav* and its species arrive to the chest we complete the *Hei* 'ה of the Name ע"ב.

Gevurah—North—Isaac (Adonai יאהדונהי יְהֹוָה ana אָנָּא)

Meditate to draw Mercies (from the three *Mochin*: *Chochmah—Binah—Da'at*),

to the clothing אלף הא יוד הא, which is in *Yesod* of *Tevunah*

(inside it is the *Moach* of *Da'at* of *Zeir Anpin*—יוד הי ויו), from *Gevurah* of *Chesed* of

On the first day: *Chesed*;	On the second day: *Gevurah*;	On the third day: *Tiferet*;
On the fourth day: *Netzach*;		On the fifth day: *Hod*;
On the sixth day:		On the seventh day:
the Generality of the Five Mercies in *Yesod*;	the Generality of the Five Mercies in *Malchut*;	

Of *Da'at* of *Zeir Anpin*. And from the generality of יהו, which is:

Back to the chest	Away from the chest	
Moach of *Da'at*—הָא	הָא וָאו יוד	1
Moach of *Binah*—הִי	הִי וָאו יוד	2
Moach of *Chochmah*—הִי	הִי וִיו יוד	3

To *Gevurah* of *Chesed* of

On the first day: *Chesed*;	On the second day: *Gevurah*;	On the third day: *Tiferet*;
On the fourth day: *Netzach*;		On the fifth day: *Hod*;
On the sixth day:		On the seventh day:
the Generality of the Five Mercies in *Yesod*;	the Generality of the Five Mercies in *Malchut*;	

To His *Six Edges*; And from there to *Nukva* יוּד הֵה וֵו הֵה

And when the *Lulav* and its species arrive to the chest we complete the *Hei* 'ה of the Name ס"ג.

Tiferet—East—Jacob

Meditate to draw Mercies (from the three *Mochin*: *Chochmah—Binah—Da'at*),

to the clothing אלף הא יוד הא, which is in *Yesod* of *Tevunah*

(inside it is the *Moach* of *Da'at* of *Zeir Anpin*—יוד הי ויו), from *Tiferet* of *Chesed* of

On the first day: *Chesed*;	On the second day: *Gevurah*;	On the third day: *Tiferet*;
On the fourth day: *Netzach*;		On the fifth day: *Hod*;
On the sixth day: the Generality of the Five Mercies in *Yesod*;		On the seventh day: the Generality of the Five Mercies in *Malchut*;

Of *Da'at* of *Zeir Anpin*. And from the generality of יהו, which is:

Back to the chest	Away from the chest	
Moach of *Da'at*—הא	וָאוֹ יוד הא	1
Moach of *Binah*—הי	וָאוּ יוד הי	2
Moach of *Chochmah*—הי	וִיוֹ יוד הִי	3

To *Tiferet* of *Chesed* of

On the first day: *Chesed*;	On the second day: *Gevurah*;	On the third day: *Tiferet*;
On the fourth day: *Netzach*;		On the fifth day: *Hod*;
On the sixth day: the Generality of the Five Mercies in *Yesod*;		On the seventh day: the Generality of the Five Mercies in *Malchut*;

To His *Six Edges*; And from there to *Nukva* יוד הה וו הה.

And when the *Lulav* and its species arrive to the chest we complete the *Hei* ה of the Name מ"ה.

Netzach—Up—Moses (hoshi'a הוֹשִׁיעָה)

Meditate to draw Mercies (from the three *Mochin*: *Chochmah—Binah—Da'at*),

to the clothing אלף הא יוד הא, which is in *Yesod* of *Tevunah*

(inside it is the *Moach* of *Da'at* of *Zeir Anpin*—יוד הי ויו), from *Netzach* of *Chesed* of

On the first day: *Chesed*;	On the second day: *Gevurah*;	On the third day: *Tiferet*;
On the fourth day: *Netzach*;		On the fifth day: *Hod*;
On the sixth day: the Generality of the Five Mercies in *Yesod*;		On the seventh day: the Generality of the Five Mercies in *Malchut*;

Of *Da'at* of *Zeir Anpin*. And from the generality of יהו, which is:

Back to the chest	Away from the chest	
Moach of *Da'at*—הא	יוֹד ואו הא	1
Moach of *Binah*—הי	יוד וָאוּ הי	2
Moach of *Chochmah*—הי	יוד ויו הִי	3

To *Netzach* of *Chesed* of

On the first day: *Chesed*;	On the second day: *Gevurah*;	On the third day: *Tiferet*;
On the fourth day: *Netzach*;		On the fifth day: *Hod*;
On the sixth day: the Generality of the Five Mercies in *Yesod*;		On the seventh day: the Generality of the Five Mercies in *Malchut*;

To His *Six Edges*; And from there to *Nukva* יוד הה וו הה.

And when the *Lulav* and its species arrive to the chest we complete the *Hei* ה of the Name ע"ב.

Hod—Down—Aaron

Meditate to draw Mercies (from the three *Mochin*: *Chochmah—Binah—Da'at*),

to the clothing אלף הא יוד הא, which is in *Yesod* of *Tevunah*

(inside it is the *Moach* of *Da'at* of *Zeir Anpin*—יוד הֹי ויו), from *Hod* of *Chesed* of

On the first day: *Chesed*;	On the second day: *Gevurah*;	On the third day: *Tiferet*;
On the fourth day: *Netzach*;		On the fifth day: *Hod*;
On the sixth day:		On the seventh day:
the Generality of the Five Mercies in *Yesod*;	the Generality of the Five Mercies in *Malchut*;	

Of *Da'at* of *Zeir Anpin*. And from the generality of יהֹ, which is:

Back to the chest	**Away from the chest**	
Moach of *Da'at*—הָא	הָא יוד ואו	1
Moach of *Binah*—הֹי	הֹי יוד ואו	2
Moach of *Chochmah*—הֹי	הֹי יוד ויו	3

To *Hod* of *Chesed* of

On the first day: *Chesed*;	On the second day: *Gevurah*;	On the third day: *Tiferet*;
On the fourth day: *Netzach*;		On the fifth day: *Hod*;
On the sixth day:		On the seventh day:
the Generality of the Five Mercies in *Yesod*;	the Generality of the Five Mercies in *Malchut*;	

To His *Six Edges*; And from there to *Nukva* יוד הֹה וֹ הֹה הֹה

And when the *Lulav* and its species arrive to the chest we complete the *Hei* הֹ of the Name ס"ג.

Yesod—West—Joseph (na נָא)

Meditate to draw Mercies (from the three *Mochin*: *Chochmah—Binah—Da'at*),

to the clothing אלף הא יוד הא, which is in *Yesod* of *Tevunah*

(inside it is the *Moach* of *Da'at* of *Zeir Anpin*—יוד הֹי ויו), from *Yesod* of *Chesed* of

On the first day: *Chesed*;	On the second day: *Gevurah*;	On the third day: *Tiferet*;
On the fourth day: *Netzach*;		On the fifth day: *Hod*;
On the sixth day:		On the seventh day:
the Generality of the Five Mercies in *Yesod*;	the Generality of the Five Mercies in *Malchut*;	

Of *Da'at* of *Zeir Anpin*. And from the generality of יהֹ, which is:

Back to the chest	**Away from the chest**	
Moach of *Da'at*—הֹאוֹ	וֹאָווֹ הֹואוֹ יוֹוֹדוֹ	1
Moach of *Binah*—הֹוִיוֹ	וֹאָווֹ הֹוִיוֹ יוֹוֹדוֹ	2
Moach of *Chochmah*—הֹוִיוֹ	וֹיוֹוֹו הֹוִיוֹ יוֹוֹדוֹ	3

To *Yesod* of *Chesed* of

On the first day: *Chesed*;	On the second day: *Gevurah*;	On the third day: *Tiferet*;
On the fourth day: *Netzach*;		On the fifth day: *Hod*;
On the sixth day:		On the seventh day:
the Generality of the Five Mercies in *Yesod*;	the Generality of the Five Mercies in *Malchut*;	

To His *Six Edges*; And from there to *Nukva* יוֹוֹדוֹ הֹוֹדוֹ ווֹו הֹוֹדוֹ

And when the *Lulav* and its species arrive to the chest we complete the *Hei* הֹ of the Name מ"ה.

You should meditate that *Malchut*, which is: ב"ן, receives from *Binah* which is: ס"ג.

אָנָּא ana ב"ן (יוד הה וו הה) יְהֹוָאדֹנָ֣יאההדונהי (אדני) Adonai (יוד הי ואו הי)

הוֹשִׁ֒יעָה hoshi'a יהוה וע"ע נהורין נָ֣א na:

During *Sukkot* we shake the Lulav according the meditation charts on pages 393-395.

On *Simchat Torah* we skip the charts on pages 393-395, and continue with "*ana*" on page 396.

We beseech You, Lord, save us now.

Chesed—South—Abraham

Meditate to draw Mercies (from the three *Mochin*: *Chochmah—Binah—Da'at*),

to the clothing יוד הא אלף, which is in *Yesod* of *Tevunah*

(inside it is the *Moach* of *Da'at* of *Zeir Anpin*—יוד הי ויו), from *Chesed* of *Chesed* of

On the first day: *Chesed*;	On the second day: *Gevurah*;	On the third day: *Tiferet*;
On the fourth day: *Netzach*;		On the fifth day: *Hod*;
On the sixth day:		On the seventh day:
the Generality of the Five Mercies in *Yesod*;	the Generality of the Five Mercies in *Malchut*;	

Of *Da'at* of *Zeir Anpin*. And from the generality of יה, which is:

Back to the chest	Away from the chest	
Moach of *Da'at*—הָא	יוֹד הָא וְאוֹ	1
Moach of *Binah*—הָי	יוֹד הָי וְאוֹ	2
Moach of *Chochmah*—הָי	יוֹד הִי וִיוֹ	3

To *Chesed* of *Chesed* of

On the first day: *Chesed*;	On the second day: *Gevurah*;	On the third day: *Tiferet*;
On the fourth day: *Netzach*;		On the fifth day: *Hod*;
On the sixth day:		On the seventh day:
the Generality of the Five Mercies in *Yesod*;	the Generality of the Five Mercies in *Malchut*;	

To His *Six Edges*; And from there to *Nukva* יוֹד הֵה וָו הֵה

And when the *Lulav* and its species arrive to the chest we complete the *Hei* הֵ of the Name ע"ב.

Gevurah—North—Isaac (Adonai יְהֹוָה/אדני/אהדונהי ana אָנָּא)

Meditate to draw Mercies (from the three *Mochin*: *Chochmah—Binah—Da'at*),

to the clothing יוד הא אלף, which is in *Yesod* of *Tevunah*

(inside it is the *Moach* of *Da'at* of *Zeir Anpin*—יוד הי ויו), from *Gevurah* of *Chesed* of

On the first day: *Chesed*;	On the second day: *Gevurah*;	On the third day: *Tiferet*;
On the fourth day: *Netzach*;		On the fifth day: *Hod*;
On the sixth day:		On the seventh day:
the Generality of the Five Mercies in *Yesod*;	the Generality of the Five Mercies in *Malchut*;	

Of *Da'at* of *Zeir Anpin*. And from the generality of יה, which is:

Back to the chest	Away from the chest	
Moach of *Da'at*—הָא	הָא וְאוֹ יוֹד	1
Moach of *Binah*—הָי	הָי וְאוֹ יוֹד	2
Moach of *Chochmah*—הָי	הִי וִיוֹ יוֹד	3

To *Gevurah* of *Chesed* of

On the first day: *Chesed*;	On the second day: *Gevurah*;	On the third day: *Tiferet*;
On the fourth day: *Netzach*;		On the fifth day: *Hod*;
On the sixth day:		On the seventh day:
the Generality of the Five Mercies in *Yesod*;	the Generality of the Five Mercies in *Malchut*;	

To His *Six Edges*; And from there to *Nukva* יוֹד הֵה וָו הֵה

And when the *Lulav* and its species arrive to the chest we complete the *Hei* הֵ of the Name ס"ג.

Tiferet—East—Jacob

Meditate to draw Mercies (from the three *Mochin*: Chochmah—Binah—Da'at),

to the clothing אלף הא יוד הא, which is in *Yesod* of *Tevunah*

(inside it is the *Moach* of Da'at of Zeir Anpin—יוד הי ויו), from *Tiferet* of *Chesed* of

On the first day: *Chesed*;	On the second day: *Gevurah*;	On the third day: *Tiferet*;
On the fourth day: *Netzach*;		On the fifth day: *Hod*;
On the sixth day: the Generality of the Five Mercies in *Yesod*;	On the seventh day: the Generality of the Five Mercies in *Malchut*;	

Of *Da'at* of *Zeir Anpin*. And from the generality of יהו, which is:

Back to the chest	Away from the chest	
Moach of Da'at—הא	וְאו יוד הא	1
Moach of Binah—הי	וְאו יוד הי	2
Moach of Chochmah—הי	ויו יוד הי	3

To *Tiferet* of *Chesed* of

On the first day: *Chesed*;	On the second day: *Gevurah*;	On the third day: *Tiferet*;
On the fourth day: *Netzach*;		On the fifth day: *Hod*;
On the sixth day: the Generality of the Five Mercies in *Yesod*;	On the seventh day: the Generality of the Five Mercies in *Malchut*;	

To His *Six Edges*; And from there to *Nukva* יוד הה וו הה

And when the *Lulav* and its species arrive to the chest we complete the *Hei* 'ה of the Name מ"ה.

Netzach—Up—Moses (hoshi'a הוֹשִׁיעָה)

Meditate to draw Mercies (from the three *Mochin*: Chochmah—Binah—Da'at),

to the clothing אלף הא יוד הא, which is in *Yesod* of *Tevunah*

(inside it is the *Moach* of Da'at of Zeir Anpin—יוד הי ויו), from *Netzach* of *Chesed* of

On the first day: *Chesed*;	On the second day: *Gevurah*;	On the third day: *Tiferet*;
On the fourth day: *Netzach*;		On the fifth day: *Hod*;
On the sixth day: the Generality of the Five Mercies in *Yesod*;	On the seventh day: the Generality of the Five Mercies in *Malchut*;	

Of *Da'at* of *Zeir Anpin*. And from the generality of יהו, which is:

Back to the chest	Away from the chest	
Moach of Da'at—הא	יוד ואו הא	1
Moach of Binah—הי	יוד ואו הי	2
Moach of Chochmah—הי	יוד ויו הי	3

To *Netzach* of *Chesed* of

On the first day: *Chesed*;	On the second day: *Gevurah*;	On the third day: *Tiferet*;
On the fourth day: *Netzach*;		On the fifth day: *Hod*;
On the sixth day: the Generality of the Five Mercies in *Yesod*;	On the seventh day: the Generality of the Five Mercies in *Malchut*;	

To His *Six Edges*; And from there to *Nukva* יוד הה וו הה

And when the *Lulav* and its species arrive to the chest we complete the *Hei* 'ה of the Name ע"ב.

Hod—Down—Aaron

Meditate to draw Mercies (from the three *Mochin*: *Chochmah*—*Binah*—*Da'at*),

to the clothing אלף הא יוד הא, which is in *Yesod* of *Tevunah*

(inside it is the *Moach* of *Da'at* of *Zeir Anpin*—יוד הי ויו), from *Hod* of *Chesed* of

On the first day: *Chesed*;	On the second day: *Gevurah*;	On the third day: *Tiferet*;
On the fourth day: *Netzach*;		On the fifth day: *Hod*;
On the sixth day:		On the seventh day:
the Generality of the Five Mercies in *Yesod*;	the Generality of the Five Mercies in *Malchut*;	

Of *Da'at* of *Zeir Anpin*. And from the generality of יה, which is:

Back to the chest	Away from the chest	
Moach of *Da'at*—הָא	הָא יוד ואו	1
Moach of *Binah*—הָי	הִי יוד ואו	2
Moach of *Chochmah*—הִי	הִי יוד ויו	3

To *Hod* of *Chesed* of

On the first day: *Chesed*;	On the second day: *Gevurah*;	On the third day: *Tiferet*;
On the fourth day: *Netzach*;		On the fifth day: *Hod*;
On the sixth day:		On the seventh day:
the Generality of the Five Mercies in *Yesod*;	the Generality of the Five Mercies in *Malchut*;	

To His *Six Edges*; And from there to *Nukva* יוד הה וו הה

And when the *Lulav* and its species arrive to the chest we complete the *Hei* ה of the Name ס"ג.

Yesod—West—Joseph (na נָ֫א)

Meditate to draw Mercies (from the three *Mochin*: *Chochmah*—*Binah*—*Da'at*),

to the clothing אלף הא יוד הא, which is in *Yesod* of *Tevunah*

(inside it is the *Moach* of *Da'at* of *Zeir Anpin*—יוד הי ויו), from *Yesod* of *Chesed* of

On the first day: *Chesed*;	On the second day: *Gevurah*;	On the third day: *Tiferet*;
On the fourth day: *Netzach*;		On the fifth day: *Hod*;
On the sixth day:		On the seventh day:
the Generality of the Five Mercies in *Yesod*;	the Generality of the Five Mercies in *Malchut*;	

Of *Da'at* of *Zeir Anpin*. And from the generality of יהו, which is:

Back to the chest	Away from the chest	
Moach of *Da'at*—הואו	ואווו הואו יוווֹדו	1
Moach of *Binah*—הויו	ואווו הֹוִלוּ יוווֹדו	2
Moach of *Chochmah*—הויו	וויוווּ הֹויוּ לְוֹוֹדוּ	3

To *Yesod* of *Chesed* of

On the first day: *Chesed*;	On the second day: *Gevurah*;	On the third day: *Tiferet*;
On the fourth day: *Netzach*;		On the fifth day: *Hod*;
On the sixth day:		On the seventh day:
the Generality of the Five Mercies in *Yesod*;	the Generality of the Five Mercies in *Malchut*;	

To His *Six Edges*; And from there to *Nukva* יוווֹדו הֹודוּ ווו הֹודוּ

And when the *Lulav* and its species arrive to the chest we complete the *Hei* ה of the Name מ"ה.

You should meditate that *Malchut*, which is ב"ן, receives from *Zeir Anpin* which is: מ"ה.

אָנָּא ana ב"ן (יוד הה וו הה) יְהֹוָואַדְנִיליאהדונהי Adonai (יוד הא ואו הא)

הַצְלִיחָה hatzlicha נָּא na:

Meditate that *Malchut*, which is ב"ן, receives from all the above mentioned: ע"ב, ס"ג, מ"ה.

אָנָּא ana ב"ן (יוד הה וו הה) יְהֹוָואַדְנִיליאהדונהי Adonai

(יוד הי ויו הי, יוד הי ואו הי, יוד הא ואו הא) הַצְלִיחָה hatzlicha נָּא na:

BARUCH HABA

We have four verses that connect us to the four letters of the Tetragrammaton. Each verse is recited twice.

Yud – Chochmah – י

בָּרוּךְ baruch   הַבָּא haba   בְּשֵׁם beshem   יְהֹוָואַדְנִיליאהדונהי Adonai

בֵּרַכְנוּכֶם berachnuchem   מִבֵּית mibet   ב"פ ראה   יְהֹוָואַדְנִיליאהדונהי Adonai: 2x

Hei – Binah – ה

אֵל El   (מילוי דס"ג)   יא"י (מילוי)   וַיָּאֶר vaya'er   כף   ויו   זין   ויו   יְהֹוָואַדְנִיליאהדונהי Adonai

לָנוּ lanu   אלהים,   אהיה,   אדני   אָסְרוּ isru   וְחָג chag   בַּעֲבֹתִים ba'avotim

עַד ad   קַרְנוֹת karnot   הַמִּזְבֵּחַ hamizbe'ach   נגד,   זין,   אל   יהוה: 2x

Vav – Zeir Anpin – ו

אֵלִי Eli   אַתָּה Ata   וְאוֹדֶךָּ ve'odeka

אֱלֹהַי Elohai   מילוי דע"ב,   דמב   ;   ילה   אֲרוֹמְמֶךָּ aromemeka: 2x

Hei – Malchut – ה

הוֹדוּ hodu   אהיה   לַיְהֹוָואַדְנִיליאהדונהי ladonai   כִּי ki   טוֹב tov   והו

כי טוב = יהוה אהיה, אום, מבה, יזל

כִּי ki   לְעוֹלָם le'olam   ריבוע   ס"ג   וי   אותיות   דס"ג   וְחַסְדּוֹ chasdo

ג' הויות, מזלא (להמשיך הארה ממזלא עילאה) ; ר"ת = נגה :

During *Sukkot* we shake the Lulav according the meditation charts on pages 397-399.

On *Simchat Torah* we skip the charts on pages 397-399, and continue with "*hodu*" on page 400.

We beseech You, Lord, give us success now. We beseech You, Lord, give us success now.

BARUCH HABA

Blessed is the one who comes
in the Name of the Lord. We bless you from The House of the Lord. The Lord is God, He illuminates
for us. Tie the holiday-offering with ropes till the corners of the Altar. You are my God and I thank You,
my God, and I shall exalt You. Be grateful to the Lord for He is good. For His kindness is forever.

Chesed—South—Abraham (ladonai ליהוﬣﬡﬢﬤﬨﬤ hodu הוֹדוּ)

Meditate to draw Mercies (from the three _Mochin_: _Chochmah—Binah—Da'at_),

to the clothing אלף הא יוד הא, which is in _Yesod_ of _Tevunah_

(inside it is the _Moach_ of _Da'at_ of _Zeir Anpin_—יוד הי ויו), from _Chesed_ of _Chesed_ of

On the first day: _Chesed_;	On the second day: _Gevurah_;	On the third day: _Tiferet_;
On the fourth day: _Netzach_;		On the fifth day: _Hod_;
On the sixth day:		On the seventh day:
the Generality of the Five Mercies in _Yesod_;		the Generality of the Five Mercies in _Malchut_;

Of _Da'at_ of _Zeir Anpin_. And from the generality of יהו, which is:

Back to the chest	Away from the chest	
Moach of _Da'at_—הֵא	יוֹד הֵא וָאוֹ	1
Moach of _Binah_—הִי	יוֹד הִי וָאוֹ	2
Moach of _Chochmah_—הִי	יוֹד הִי וִיו	3

To _Chesed_ of _Chesed_ of

On the first day: _Chesed_;	On the second day: _Gevurah_;	On the third day: _Tiferet_;
On the fourth day: _Netzach_;		On the fifth day: _Hod_;
On the sixth day:		On the seventh day:
the Generality of the Five Mercies in _Yesod_;		the Generality of the Five Mercies in _Malchut_;

To His _Six Edges_; And from there to _Nukva_ יוֹד הֵה וו הֵה

And when the _Lulav_ and its species arrive to the chest we complete the _Hei_ 'ה of the Name ע"ב.

Gevurah—North—Isaac (ki כִּי)

Meditate to draw Mercies (from the three _Mochin_: _Chochmah—Binah—Da'at_),

to the clothing אלף הא יוד הא, which is in _Yesod_ of _Tevunah_

(inside it is the _Moach_ of _Da'at_ of _Zeir Anpin_—יוד הי ויו), from _Gevurah_ of _Chesed_ of

On the first day: _Chesed_;	On the second day: _Gevurah_;	On the third day: _Tiferet_;
On the fourth day: _Netzach_;		On the fifth day: _Hod_;
On the sixth day:		On the seventh day:
the Generality of the Five Mercies in _Yesod_;		the Generality of the Five Mercies in _Malchut_;

Of _Da'at_ of _Zeir Anpin_. And from the generality of יהו, which is:

Back to the chest	Away from the chest	
Moach of _Da'at_—הֵא	הֵא וָאו יוֹד	1
Moach of _Binah_—הִי	הִי וָאוֹ יוֹד	2
Moach of _Chochmah_—הִי	הִי וִיו יוֹד	3

To _Gevurah_ of _Chesed_ of

On the first day: _Chesed_;	On the second day: _Gevurah_;	On the third day: _Tiferet_;
On the fourth day: _Netzach_;		On the fifth day: _Hod_;
On the sixth day:		On the seventh day:
the Generality of the Five Mercies in _Yesod_;		the Generality of the Five Mercies in _Malchut_;

To His _Six Edges_; And from there to _Nukva_ יוֹד הֵה וו הֵה

And when the _Lulav_ and its species arrive to the chest we complete the _Hei_ 'ה of the Name ס"ג.

Tiferet—East—Jacob (tov טוֹב)

Meditate to draw Mercies (from the three *Mochin: Chochmah—Binah—Da'at*),

to the clothing אלף הא יוד הא, which is in *Yesod* of *Tevunah*

(inside it is the *Moach* of *Da'at* of *Zeir Anpin*—יוד הי ויו), from *Tiferet* of *Chesed* of

On the first day: *Chesed*;	On the second day: *Gevurah*;	On the third day: *Tiferet*;
On the fourth day: *Netzach*;		On the fifth day: *Hod*;
On the sixth day: the Generality of the Five Mercies in *Yesod*;		On the seventh day: the Generality of the Five Mercies in *Malchut*;

Of *Da'at* of *Zeir Anpin*. And from the generality of יוד, which is:

Back to the chest	Away from the chest	
Moach of *Da'at*—הָא	וָאו יוד הָא	1
Moach of *Binah*—הִי	וָאו יוֹד הִי	2
Moach of *Chochmah*—הִי	וִיו יוֹד הִי	3

To *Tiferet* of *Chesed* of

On the first day: *Chesed*;	On the second day: *Gevurah*;	On the third day: *Tiferet*;
On the fourth day: *Netzach*;		On the fifth day: *Hod*;
On the sixth day: the Generality of the Five Mercies in *Yesod*;		On the seventh day: the Generality of the Five Mercies in *Malchut*;

To His *Six Edges*; And from there to *Nukva* יוד הה וו הה

And when the *Lulav* and its species arrive to the chest we complete the *Hei* ה' of the Name בו"ה.

Netzach—Up—Moses (ki כִּי)

Meditate to draw Mercies (from the three *Mochin: Chochmah—Binah—Da'at*),

to the clothing אלף הא יוד הא, which is in *Yesod* of *Tevunah*

(inside it is the *Moach* of *Da'at* of *Zeir Anpin*—יוד הי ויו), from *Netzach* of *Chesed* of

On the first day: *Chesed*;	On the second day: *Gevurah*;	On the third day: *Tiferet*;
On the fourth day: *Netzach*;		On the fifth day: *Hod*;
On the sixth day: the Generality of the Five Mercies in *Yesod*;		On the seventh day: the Generality of the Five Mercies in *Malchut*;

Of *Da'at* of *Zeir Anpin*. And from the generality of יוד, which is:

Back to the chest	Away from the chest	
Moach of *Da'at*—הָא	יוֹד וָאו הָא	1
Moach of *Binah*—הִי	יוֹד וָאו הִי	2
Moach of *Chochmah*—הִי	יוֹד וִיו הִי	3

To *Netzach* of *Chesed* of

On the first day: *Chesed*;	On the second day: *Gevurah*;	On the third day: *Tiferet*;
On the fourth day: *Netzach*;		On the fifth day: *Hod*;
On the sixth day: the Generality of the Five Mercies in *Yesod*;		On the seventh day: the Generality of the Five Mercies in *Malchut*;

To His *Six Edges*; And from there to *Nukva* יוד הה וו הה

And when the *Lulav* and its species arrive to the chest we complete the *Hei* ה' of the Name ע"ב.

<u>Hod—Down—Aaron</u> (le'olam לְעוֹלָם)

Meditate to draw Mercies (from the three *Mochin: Chochmah—Binah—Da'at*),

to the clothing אלף הא יוד הא, which is in *Yesod* of *Tevunah*

(inside it is the *Moach* of *Da'at* of *Zeir Anpin*—יוד הי ויו), from *Hod* of *Chesed* of

On the first day: *Chesed*;	On the second day: *Gevurah*;	On the third day: *Tiferet*;
On the fourth day: *Netzach*;		On the fifth day: *Hod*;
On the sixth day:		On the seventh day:
the Generality of the Five Mercies in *Yesod*;		the Generality of the Five Mercies in *Malchut*;

Of *Da'at* of *Zeir Anpin*. And from the generality of הי, which is:

Back to the chest	Away from the chest	
Moach of *Da'at*—הָא	הָא יוֹד וָאו	1
Moach of *Binah*—הִי	הִי יוֹד וָאו	2
Moach of *Chochmah*—הִי	הִי יוֹד וִלִיו	3

To *Hod* of *Chesed* of

On the first day: *Chesed*;	On the second day: *Gevurah*;	On the third day: *Tiferet*;
On the fourth day: *Netzach*;		On the fifth day: *Hod*;
On the sixth day:		On the seventh day:
the Generality of the Five Mercies in *Yesod*;		the Generality of the Five Mercies in *Malchut*;

To His *Six Edges*; And from there to *Nukva* יוד הה וו הה

And when the *Lulav* and its species arrive to the chest we complete the *Hei* ה of the Name ס"ג.

<u>Yesod—West—Joseph</u> (chasdo וְחַסְדוֹ)

Meditate to draw Mercies (from the three *Mochin: Chochmah—Binah—Da'at*),

to the clothing אלף הא יוד הא, which is in *Yesod* of *Tevunah*

(inside it is the *Moach* of *Da'at* of *Zeir Anpin*—יוד הי ויו), from *Yesod* of *Chesed* of

On the first day: *Chesed*;	On the second day: *Gevurah*;	On the third day: *Tiferet*;
On the fourth day: *Netzach*;		On the fifth day: *Hod*;
On the sixth day:		On the seventh day:
the Generality of the Five Mercies in *Yesod*;		the Generality of the Five Mercies in *Malchut*;

Of *Da'at* of *Zeir Anpin*. And from the generality of הי, which is:

Back to the chest	Away from the chest	
Moach of *Da'at*—הואו	וואוו הואו יווודו	1
Moach of *Binah*—הויו	וואוו הויו יווודו	2
Moach of *Chochmah*—הויו	וליוו הויו לווודו	3

To *Yesod* of *Chesed* of

On the first day: *Chesed*;	On the second day: *Gevurah*;	On the third day: *Tiferet*;
On the fourth day: *Netzach*;		On the fifth day: *Hod*;
On the sixth day:		On the seventh day:
the Generality of the Five Mercies in *Yesod*;		the Generality of the Five Mercies in *Malchut*;

To His *Six Edges*; And from there to *Nukva* יווודו הודו ווו הודו

And when the *Lulav* and its species arrive to the chest we complete the *Hei* ה of the Name מ"ה.

וה׳   tov **טוֹב**   ki **כִּי**   ladonai **לַיהֹוָ֜ה**   אהיה   hodu **הוֹדוּ**

כי טוב = יהוה אהיה, אום, מבה, יזל

chasdo **וְחַסְדּוֹ**   דס״ג   אותיות   וי   ס״ג   ריבוע   le'olam **לְעוֹלָם**   ki **כִּי**

ג׳ הויות, מזלא (להמשיך הארה ממזלא עילאה) ; ר״ת = נגה :

יְלֵי   kol **כָּל**   ילה   Elohenu **אֱלֹהֵינוּ**   Adonai **יְהֹוָ֜ה**   yehalelucha **יְהַלְלוּךָ**

osei **עוֹשֵׂי**   vetzadikim **וְצַדִּיקִים**   vachasidecha **וַחֲסִידֶיךָ**   ma'asecha **מַעֲשֶׂיךָ**

Yisrael **יִשְׂרָאֵל**   ב״פ ראה   bet **בֵּית**   ve'amcha **וְעַמְּךָ**   retzonecha **רְצוֹנֶךָ**

יהוה ריבוע יהוה ריבוע מ״ה   vivarchu **וִיבָרְכוּ**   yodu **יוֹדוּ**   berina **בְּרִנָּה**   kulam **כֻּלָּם**

לכב, ב״ן   kevodecha **כְּבוֹדֶךָ**   shem **שֵׁם**   et **אֶת**   vifa'aru **וִיפָאֲרוּ**   vishabchu **וִישַׁבְּחוּ**

na'im **נָעִים**   ulshimcha **וּלְשִׁמְךָ**   lehodot **לְהוֹדוֹת**   וה׳   tov **טוֹב**   lecha **לְךָ**   ki **כִּי**

Ata **אַתָּה**   olam **עוֹלָם**   ve'ad **וָעַד**   ume'olam **וּמֵעוֹלָם**   lezamer **לְזַמֵּר**

Adonai **יְהֹוָ֜ה**   Ata **אַתָּה**   baruch **בָּרוּךְ**   :   דס״ג (מילוי)   El **אֵל**   יא״י

amen **אָמֵן**   batishbachot **בַּתִּשְׁבָּחוֹת**   mehulal **מְהֻלָּל**   melech **מֶלֶךְ**   יאהדונהי

Recite this verse three times to connect to the Light of protection.

וז״פ אל, רי״ו ול״ב נתיבות החכמה, רמ״ח (אברים), עסמ״ב וט״ו אותיות פשוטות   veAvraham **וְאַבְרָהָם**

et **אֶת**   berach **בֵּרַךְ**   vadonai **וַיהֹוָ֜ה**   גלך   bayamim **בַּיָּמִים**   ba **בָּא**   zaken **זָקֵן**

וז״פ אל, רי״ו ול״ב נתיבות החכמה, רמ״ח (אברים), עסמ״ב וט״ו אותיות פשוטות   Avraham **אַבְרָהָם**

לכב, ב״ן   bakol **בַּכֹּל**

Meditate on the Name of the Angel (וּבְדִיָה) derived from the above mentioned verse.

ratzon **רָצוֹן**   yehi **יְהִי**   ken **כֵּן**   viychayeni **וִיחַיֵּינִי**   yishmereni **יִשְׁמְרֵנִי**

מהע ע״ה, ע״ב בריבוע וקס״א ע״ה, אל שדי ע״ה   milfanecha **מִלְּפָנֶיךָ**   ס״ג מ״ה ב״ן

umelech **וּמֶלֶךְ**   אהיה אדני ; ילה   chayim **וְחַיִּים**   אהיה אהיה יהוה, בינה ע״ה   Elohim **אֱלֹהִים**

amen **אָמֵן**   chai **וַי**   ילי   kol **כָּל**   nefesh **נֶפֶשׁ**   beyado **בְּיָדוֹ**   asher **אֲשֶׁר**   olam **עוֹלָם**

יאהדונהי   ratzon **רָצוֹן**   מהע ע״ה, ע״ב בריבוע וקס״א ע״ה, אל שדי ע״ה   yehi **יְהִי**   ken **כֵּן**

On *Simchat Torah* we continue with *Kaddish Titkabal* on page 489.

Be grateful to the Lord for He is good. For His kindness is forever." (Psalms 118) All Your deeds and all Your pious ones shall praise You, Lord, our God, and the righteous ones who do Your will, as well as Your nation, the House of Israel. They shall all joyously give thanks, bless, praise and glorify the Name of Your glory, because to You it is good to give thanks, and to Your Name, it is pleasing to sing. And from this world until the next, You are God. Blessed are You, Lord, a King Who is extolled in praises. Amen. "And Abraham was old, and ripe in age, and God has blessed Abraham with everything." (Genesis 24:1) May He preserve me and enliven me. And may it so be pleasing before the God of life and the King of the world, in Whose Hands lie the spirit of all that lives. Amen, may it so be His pleasure.

THE HOSHA'ANOT – FROM THE RAV

As we explained, during *Sukkot* we connect to the Light of *Chasadim* (Mercy), which is the ultimate Vessel for the Endless Light of the Creator, and by the power of the *Sukkah* we can draw an unlimited amount of this Light. The Light of *Chasadim* is responsible for breaking the power of Satan and its limiting servants, time, space, and motion. The amount of Light of *Chasadim* we will draw on *Sukkot* is how much power we will have to defeat the negative forces in our life.

During the year, we can connect to the Light of *Chasadim* only partially, with effort and actions of uncomfortable sharing. During *Sukkot,* the Light of *Chasadim* is available without limit.

There are two aspects of Mercies (*Chasadim*): One from Supernal *Ima* that comes from the *Sukkah*, and the other aspect from *Zeir Anpin* that comes from the *Lulav* and its species. And in each of these two aspects of Mercies there are two Illuminations—Inner Light and Surrounding Light.

According to the Ari, each day after the Halel and the connection of the Shaking of the *Lulav*, we still hold the *Lulav* and its species and begin the *Hosha'anot*, where we walk around the *bimah* in circles inside the *Sukkah* while reciting verses arranged in alphabetical order. This action connects us to the Surrounding Light from the aspect of *Zeir Anpin* and the verses we recite encrypt the power of the *Yud, Hei, Vav,* and *Hei*, completing the action of healing the DNA and reinforcing the immune system. The *Hosha'anot* is a process which by it we conclude our communication with the Four Species. We do so to connect to the root of the things in our life and to control them

The Four Species can help us as well as all of mankind. According to the *Zohar*, the Four Species are a way in which to receive blessings for the entire year. And if we do not take advantage of this once-yearly opportunity to attract energy, the *Zohar* specifically notes that we will not be able to introduce this energy into our lives.

Each day, we circle the *bimah*, once for each of the six Sefirot to connect to the energy from *Chesed* to *Yesod*, while holding the Four Species. On the seventh day, *Hosha'ana Rabbah* (the Great Salvation), we circle the *bimah* seven times to connect to the energy of *Malchut* but also to be able to collect all the energy of the Light of *Chasadim* of the previous days of *Sukkot*, as this day of *Hosha'anah Rabbah* is like the rear guard that collects what is left behind.

By the Light of Chasadim we can illuminate all the limitations of time, space, and motion, and see past, present, and future here now. Every action, word, or moment that we experience while we are in the *Sukkah*, draws from the Light of *Chasadim*, what a gift!

HOSHA'ANOT (CIRCLING) FOR THE FIRST DAY OF SUKKOT

Meditate to draw the Surrounding of Chesed of Chesed of Zeir Anpin

אלף הי יוד הי   אלף הי יוד הי   אלף הי יוד הי

And these three Names (אהיה=21) equal the Name יוד הי ואו הי (=63), and from the letters (י"א=31) comes the Name אל. And from the body of *Zeir Anpin* (His Six Edeges) it is all drawn to *Nukva*. During the circling one should meditate to draw Inner Light to *Leah* and *Rachel* and to be protected from one of the cosmic ministers (that is included with ten ministers of the nations).

אֶרְחַץ erchatz   בְּנִקָּיוֹן benikayon   כַּפַּי kapai   וַאֲסֹבְבָה va'asoveva   אֶת et

מִזְבַּחֲךָ mizbachacha נגד, זך, אל יהוה   יְהֹוָה Adonai אהדונהיאהדונהי: לַשְׁמִעַ lashmi'a

בְּקוֹל bekol   תּוֹדָה toda   וּלְסַפֵּר ulsaper   כָּל kol ילי   נִפְלְאוֹתֶיךָ nifle'otecha:

הוֹשַׁעְנָא hosha'ana • הוֹשַׁעְנָא hosha'ana:

לְמַעַנְךָ lema'anach   אֱלֹהֵינוּ Elohenu ילה: לְמַעַנְךָ lema'anach   בּוֹרְאֵנוּ bor'enu:

לְמַעַנְךָ lema'anach   גּוֹאֲלֵנוּ go'alenu: לְמַעַנְךָ lema'anach   דּוֹרְשֵׁנוּ dorshenu:

לְמַעַנְךָ lema'anach   אַדִּיר adir הרי   אַדִּירִים adirim הרי: לְמַעַנְךָ lema'anach

בּוֹרֵא bore   רוּחַ ru'ach   וְיוֹצֵר veyotzer   הָרִים harim: לְמַעַנְךָ lema'anach

גָּדוֹל gedol לההו, ועם ד' אותיות מבה, יזל, אום   הָעֵצָה ha'etza • מַשְׁפִּיל mashpil

וּמֵרִים umerim: לְמַעַנְךָ lema'anach   דּוֹבֵר dover   צֶדֶק tzedek   מַגִּיד magid

מֵישָׁרִים mesharim: לְמַעַנְךָ lema'anach   הַיּוֹדֵעַ hayode'a   וָעֵד va'ed

אִם im יוהך, מ"א אותיות דפשוט, דמילוי ודמילוי דמילוי דאהיה ע"ה   לְסַתֵּר yisater ב"פ מצר

אִישׁ ish   בַּמִּסְתָּרִים bamistarim: לְמַעַנְךָ lema'anach   וְהוּא vehu

בְּאֶחָד be'echad אהבה, דאגה ילי   וּמִי umi ילי   יְשִׁיבֶנּוּ yeshivenu   אֲמָרִים amarim:

HOSHA'ANOT (CIRCLING) FOR THE FIRST DAY OF SUKKOT

"I shall wash my hands in purity and I shall circle around Your altar, Lord.
To proclaim in a voice of thankfulness, and to relate all Your wonders." (Psalms 26:6-7)
Please save now. Please save now.

For Your sake, our God. For Your sake, our Creator. For Your sake, our Redeemer. For Your sake, our Seeker. For Your sake, the Mightiest of the mighty. For Your sake, Creator of the wind and Former of the mountains. For Your sake, Great One of counsel, Who humbles and uplifts. For Your sake, Speaker of righteousness, Teacher of upright principles. For Your sake, He Who knows and is witness, if a man would conceal himself in hidden places. For Your sake, He Who is One, and who can possibly respond to Him.

im עִם umitbarer וּמִתְבָּרֵר venaki וְנַקִי׳ zach זָךְ lema'anach לְמַעַנְךָ

matzpun מַצְפּוּן chofes וְחוֹפֵשׂ lema'anach לְמַעַנְךָ barim בָּרִים:

vechoker וְחוֹקֵר kol כָּל׳ chadarim וְחֲדָרִים: lema'anach לְמַעַנְךָ

tipcha טִפְחָה yemino יְמִינוֹ shamayim שָׁמַיִם ve'asa וְעָשָׂה

me'orim מְאוֹרִים: lema'anach לְמַעַנְךָ yasad יָסַד eretz אָרֶץ

batzurot בְּצֻרוֹת bike'a בִּקֵעַ ye'orim יְאוֹרִים: lema'anach לְמַעַנְךָ kabir כַּבִּיר

ko'ach כֹּחַ mechubad מְכֻבָּד ba'urim בָּאוּרִים: lema'anach לְמַעַנְךָ

lo לֹא yitamu יִתַּמּוּ shenotav שְׁנוֹתָיו ledor לְדוֹר dorim דּוֹרִים:

hosha'ana הוֹשַׁעְנָא hosha'ana הוֹשַׁעְנָא:

ana אָנָּא El אֵל echad אֶחָד ahavah, da'agah

ushmo וּשְׁמוֹ echad אֶחָד ahavah, da'agah

umi וּמִי yeshivenu יְשִׁיבֶנּוּ vehu וְהוּא be'echad בְּאֶחָד ahavah, da'agah

kara קָרָא shamayim שָׁמַיִם va'aretz וְאָרֶץ vaya'amdu וַיַּעַמְדוּ

ke'echad כְּאֶחָד ahavah, da'agah hoshi'enu הוֹשִׁיעֵנוּ bachagigat בַּחֲגִיגַת

yom יוֹם echad אֶחָד ahavah, da'agah:

ana אָנָּא zechor זְכֹר av אָב yarash יָרַשׁ et אֶת

ha'aretz הָאָרֶץ vehaya וְהָיָה echad אֶחָד ahavah, da'agah hechin הֵכִין

lamordim לַמּוֹרְדִים lev לֵב echad אֶחָד ahavah, da'agah vederech וְדֶרֶךְ

echad אֶחָד ahavah, da'agah likro לִקְרֹא kulam כֻּלָּם beshem בְּשֵׁם

Adonai יְהֹוָה ul'ovdo וּלְעָבְדוֹ shechem שְׁכֶם echad אֶחָד ahavah, da'agah:

For Your sake, Pure and Immaculate One, Who acts with integrity with those who are faithful. For Your sake, Searcher of the hidden and Prober of all chambers. For Your sake, He Whose right palm created the Heavens, and Who made the luminaries. For Your sake, He Who founded the earth; He Who is powerful with might, glorified by those residing in the valleys. For Your sake, He Whose years will not end for endless generations.
Please save now. Please save now.
Please One God, Whose Name is One, and can possibly respond to Him, He being the only One. He designated Heaven and Earth and they stood as one; save us on the celebration of one day. Please remember the patriarch (Abraham) who inherited the land when he was but one. He set up for the rebellious ones, one heart and one way so that they would all pray in God's Name, and to serve Him with one mind,

נגד, מזבח, ז, אל יהוה   hoshi'enu הוֹשִׁיעֵנוּ   bachagigat בַּחֲגִיגַת   yom יוֹם

ben בֵּן   zechor זְכוֹר לכב, ב״ן   ana אָנָּא: דאגה, אהבה   echad אֶחָד   ע״ב קס״א, יהי אור ע״ה

yachid יָחִיד   haya הָיָה יהה   lifnei לִפְנֵי   aviv אָבִיו   echad אֶחָד אהבה, דאגה.

shenehem שְׁנֵיהֶם   benisayon בְּנִסָּיוֹן   halchu הָלְכוּ   ke'echad כְּאֶחָד אהבה, דאגה.

natata נָתַתָּ   kofer כֹּפֶר   tachtav תַּחְתָּיו   ayil אַיִל   echad אֶחָד אהבה, דאגה:

hoshi'enu הוֹשִׁיעֵנוּ   bachagigat בַּחֲגִיגַת   yom יוֹם נגד, מזבח, ז, אל יהוה

av אָב   zechor זְכוֹר לכב, ב״ן ana אָנָּא: דאגה, אהבה   echad אֶחָד ע״ב קס״א, יהי אור ע״ה

kiva קִוָּה. דאגה, אהבה   echad אֶחָד   shechem שֶׁכֶם   chelek חֵלֶק   hosif הוֹסִיף

asaf אָסַף. דאגה, אהבה   ha'echad הָאֶחָד   hamachane הַמַּחֲנֶה   lehaflit לְהַפְלִיט

shamayim שָׁמַיִם י״פ טל, י״פ כוזו   malchut מַלְכוּת   lekabel לְקַבֵּל   banav בָּנָיו

bachagigat בַּחֲגִיגַת   hoshi'enu הוֹשִׁיעֵנוּ: דאגה, אהבה   echad אֶחָד   pe פֶּה ע״ה מום

ana אָנָּא: ב״ן לכב   echad אֶחָד אהבה, דאגה: yom יוֹם נגד, מזבח, ז, אל יהוה

uvrakim וּבְרָקִים   bekolot בְּקוֹלוֹת   shetayim שְׁתַּיִם   hamashmi'enu הַמַּשְׁמִיעֵנוּ

achat אַחַת   torah תּוֹרָה   hamanchilenu הַמַּנְחִילֵנוּ. דאגה, אהבה   ke'echad כְּאֶחָד

hoshi'enu הוֹשִׁיעֵנוּ. דאגה, אהבה   echad אֶחָד   umishpat וּמִשְׁפָּט ה״פ אלהים

bachagigat בַּחֲגִיגַת   echad אֶחָד אהבה, דאגה: yom יוֹם נגד, מזבח, ז, אל יהוה

(X2) hosha'ana הוֹשַׁעֲנָא: hosha'ana הוֹשַׁעֲנָא.

(X2) na נָא   hoshi'a הוֹשִׁיעָה ב״ן לכב   ana אָנָּא יהוה ש״ע נהורין

acharon אַחֲרוֹן   (דס״ג   מילוי)   ייא״י   El אֵל   לכב ב״ן   ana אָנָּא

ke'ishon כְּאִישׁוֹן.   netzurim נְצוּרִים   am עַם   ametz אַמֵּץ   verishon וְרִאשׁוֹן.

velachshon בְּלַחֲשׁוֹן.   hosha'ana הוֹשַׁעֲנָא   betza'akatam בְּצַעֲקָתָם

---

save us on the celebration of one day. Please remember the only son (Isaac), who was to his father one. Both of them went test as one. You allowed as substitute in his stead, one ram, save us on the celebration of one day. Please remember the patriarch (Jacob) who added a portion of one. He hoped to secure deliverance from one camp, gathered his children to accept the Kingdom of Heaven as one, save us on the celebration of one day. Please, One Who proclaims to us two, amidst thunder and lightning, as one; Who bequeathed to us one Torah and one Law, save us on the celebration of one day.

Please save now. Please save now. (X2)
Please bring salvation now. (X2)
Please God Who is last and first, give strength to the people guarded
like the pupil of the eye, in their cry of "Please save now" in silent [prayer];

אֶל יהוה ,זֶן ,מזבח ,נֶגֶד beyom בְּיוֹם אֶל יהוה ,זֶן ,מזבח ,נֶגֶד hayom הַיּוֹם

:na נָא נהורין ש"ע יהוה hoshi'a הוֹשִׁיעָה rishon רִאשׁוֹן

(X2) :na נָא נהורין ש"ע יהוה hoshi'a הוֹשִׁיעָה לכב בי"ן ana אָנָּא

בא"ת ב"ע כתר ge'al גְּאַל dishon דִּישׁוֹן ninei נִינֵי geda גְּדַע לכב בי"ן ana אָנָּא

אלהים ,אהיה אדני lanu לָנוּ unte וּנְטֵה belachashon בְּלַחֲשׁוֹן meyachadecha מְיַחֲדֶיךָ

אֶל יהוה ,זֶן ,מזבח ,נֶגֶד hayom הַיּוֹם fishon פִּישׁוֹן kememei כְּמֵימֵי shalom שָׁלוֹם

:na נָא נהורין ש"ע יהוה hoshi'a הוֹשִׁיעָה rishon רִאשׁוֹן beyom בְּיוֹם ,זֶן ,מזבח ,נֶגֶד

(X2) :na נָא נהורין ש"ע יהוה hoshi'a הוֹשִׁיעָה לכב בי"ן ana אָנָּא

(X2) :na נָא נהורין ש"ע יהוה hoshi'a הוֹשִׁיעָה והו Vahu אֲנִי אֲנִי Ani

hana'or הַנָּאוֹר be'uzcha בְּעֻזְךָ haye'or הַיְאוֹר yeruyei יְרוּיֵי kehoshata כְּהוֹשַׁעְתָּ

ke'ishon כָּאִישׁוֹן la'alutim לַעֲלוּטִים ma'or מָאוֹר רו, א"ס vetavrik וְתַבְרִיק

shachak שׁוֹחַק (מילוי דס"ג) יאָ"י El אֵל chen כֵּן kemo כְּמוֹ ata עַתָּה gam גַּם

nehalelach נְהַלְלֶךָ hachen הָכֵן le'amecha לְעַמֶּךָ pedut פְּדוּת shochen שׁוֹכֵן

:hosha'ana הוֹשַׁעְנָא ken כֵּן rishon רִאשׁוֹן ,זֶן ,מזבח ,נֶגֶד beyom בְּיוֹם

(X2) :na נָא נהורין ש"ע יהוה hoshi'a הוֹשִׁיעָה והו Vahu אֲנִי אֲנִי Ani

degel דֶּגֶל לאו mul מוּל לאו degel דֶּגֶל segel סֶגֶל kehoshata כְּהוֹשַׁעְתָּ

regel רֶגֶל mo'adei מוֹעֲדֵי ע"ה דיודין ואלהים אלהים ריביע verosh וְרֹאשׁ

nekuvei נְקוּבֵי aviv אָבִיב peduyei פְּדוּיֵי dishon דִּישׁוֹן dishanta דִּשַׁנְתָּ

nehalelach נְהַלְלֶךָ saviv סָבִיב dat דָּת sovevei סוֹבְבֵי הזו chaviv וְחָבִיב am עַם

:hosha'ana הוֹשַׁעְנָא ken כֵּן rishon רִאשׁוֹן ,זֶן ,מזבח ,נֶגֶד beyom בְּיוֹם

Today on the first day. Please save now.
Please bring salvation now. (X2)
Please cut down the descendants of Dishon, redeem those who unify You in silent [prayer],
extend to us peace as the waters of the Pishon, today on the first day. Please save now.
Please bring salvation now. (X2)
Ani Vahu (of the 72 Names of God) please bring salvation now. (X2)
As You saved those cast into the river with Your cataclysmic might, and You flashed illumination
to those enveloped (as) in darkness; so, too, now as well. Almighty Who dwells in the High
Heavens, prepare redemption for Your people; let us praise You on the first day. So please save now!
Ani Vahu (of the 72 Names of God) please bring salvation now. (X2)
As you saved the treasure, banner opposite banner, and chief among those of unsteady footy,
You did verily invigorate; redeemed in the spring, who were named the beloved people, who
circle the Law round and round, let us praise You on the first day. So please save now.

(X2) •na נָא יהוה ע"ע נהורין hoshi'a הוֹשִׁיעָה והו Vahu וָהוּ אני Ani אֲנִי

•emunai אֱמוּנַי הוֹשִׁיעַ hoshi'a ,chosim וְחוֹסִים moshi'a מוֹשִׁיעַ

•etanai אֵיתָנַי zera זֶרַע ,dorshim דּוֹרְשִׁים bedat'cha בְּדָתֶךְ am עַם

Adonai יְהֹוָ(אדני־אהדונהי) et אֶת odeh אוֹדֶה hazot הַזֹּאת מנק hapa'am הַפַּעַם

na נָא she'e שְׁעֵה •shav'atam שַׁוְעָתָם na נָא retze רְצֵה

heye יהוה הֱיֵה rishona רִאשׁוֹנָה מנק bapa'am בַּפַּעַם •letefilatam לִתְפִלָּתָם

na נָא אֶל יהוה זן, מזבח, נגד, beyom בְּיוֹם asher אֲשֶׁר am עַם •eyalutam אֱיָלוּתָם

omrim אוֹמְרִים :peditam פְּדִיתָם mipesha מִפֶּשַׁע Kipur כִּפּוּר

•kadonai כַּיְהֹוָ(אדני־אהדונהי) kadosh קָדוֹשׁ en אֵין •um'halelim וּמְהַלְלִים

:Adonai יְהֹוָ(אדני־אהדונהי) et אֶת ode אוֹדֶה hazot הַזֹּאת מנק hapa'am הַפַּעַם

ken כֵּן ,adatecha עֲדָתֶךָ ומב me'az מֵאָז kehoshata כְּהוֹשַׁעְתָּ

הוֹשִׁיעָה hoshi'a יהוה ע"ע נהורין et אֶת amecha עַמֶּךָ ס"ת כהת, משיוז בן דוד ע"ה

nehalelach נְהַלֶּלְךָ •nachalatecha נַחֲלָתֶךָ et אֶת uvarech וּבָרֵךְ

:hosha'ana הוֹשַׁעְנָא ken כֵּן rishon רִאשׁוֹן נגד, מזבח, זן, אל יהוה beyom בְּיוֹם

(X2) •na נָא יהוה ע"ע נהורין hoshi'a הוֹשִׁיעָה והו Vahu וָהוּ אני Ani אֲנִי

:kakatuv כְּכָתוּב

הוֹשִׁיעָה hoshi'a יהוה ע"ע נהורין et אֶת amecha עַמֶּךָ ס"ת כהת, משיוז בן דוד ע"ה

nachalatecha נַחֲלָתֶךָ et אֶת uvarech וּבָרֵךְ

:ha'olam הָעוֹלָם ad עַד venase'em וְנַשְּׂאֵם ur'em וּרְעֵם

Continue with *Kaddish Titkabal* on Page 489.

Ani Vahu (of the 72 Names of God) please bring salvation now. (X2)
Who saves those who seek refuge, save the believers, the people who delve into Your Law,
the descendants of the mighty ones. This time do I praise the Lord. Please favor their outcry,
please turn to their prayer at the first time, be their strength, a people who on the Day of Atonement
from sin did You redeem them; they say and give praise: There is none as Holy as the Lord.
This time do I praise the Lord. As You have saved Your congregation since the days of yesteryear,
so save Your people and bless Your heritage. Let us praise You on the first day. So please save now.
Ani Vahu (of the 72 Names of God) please bring salvation now. (X2) As is written:
"Redeem Your Nation and bless Your inheritance, provide for them and uplift them forever." (Psalms 28:9)

HOSHA'ANOT (CIRCLING) FOR THE SECOND DAY OF SUKKOT

Meditate to draw the Surrounding of Chesed of Gevurah of Zeir Anpin

אלף הה יוד הה · אלף הה יוד הה · אלף הה יוד הה · אלף הה יוד הה

And these three Names (אהיה=21) equal the Name יוד הי ואו הי (=63), and from the letters (יי"א=31) comes the Name אל. And from the body of *Zeir Anpin* (His Six Edges) it is all drawn to *Nukva*. During the circling one should meditate to draw Inner Light to *Leah* and *Rachel* and to be protected from one of the cosmic ministers (that is included with ten ministers of the nations).

אֶרְחַץ erchatz בְּנִקָּיוֹן benikayon כַּפָּי kapai וַאֲסֹבְבָה va'asoveva אֶת et

מִזְבַּחֲךָ mizbachacha נגד, זן, אל יהוה יְהֹוָאֲדֹנִיִּאֲהֹדֹנָהִי Adonai: לַשְׁמִעַ lashmi'a

בְּקוֹל bekol תּוֹדָה toda וּלְסַפֵּר ulsaper כָּל kol ילי נִפְלְאוֹתֶיךָ nifle'otecha:

הוֹשַׁעְנָא hosha'ana ◆ הוֹשַׁעְנָא hosha'ana:

לְמַעַנְךָ lema'anach אֱלֹהֵינוּ Elohenu ילה : לְמַעֲנָךְ lema'anach בּוֹרְאֵנוּ bor'enu:

לְמַעַנְךָ lema'anach גּוֹאֲלֵנוּ go'alenu: לְמַעֲנָךְ lema'anach דּוֹרְשֵׁנוּ dorshenu:

לְמַעַנְךָ lema'anach אַדִּיר adir הרי אַדִּירִים adirim: לְמַעֲנָךְ lema'anach

בּוֹרֵא bore רוּחַ ru'ach וְיוֹצֵר veyotzer הָרִים harim: לְמַעֲנָךְ lema'anach

גָּדוֹל gedol להו, ועם ד' אותיות מבה, יזל, אום הָעֵצָה haetza ◆ מַשְׁפִּיל mashpil

וּמֵרִים umerim: לְמַעֲנָךְ lema'anach דּוֹבֵר dover צֶדֶק tzedek מַגִּיד magid

מֵישָׁרִים mesharim: לְמַעֲנָךְ lema'anach הַיּוֹדֵעַ hayode'a וָעֵד va'ed

אִם im יוהך, מ"א אותיות דפשוט, דמילוי ודמילוי דמילוי דאהיה ע"ה יִסָּתֵר yisater ב"פ מצר

וְהוּא vehu לְמַעֲנָךְ lema'anach בַּמִּסְתָּרִים bamistarim: אִישׁ ish

בְּאֶחָד be'echad אהבה, ראגה וּמִי umi ילי יְשִׁיבֶנּוּ yeshivenu אֲמָרִים amarim:

HOSHA'ANOT (CIRCLING) FOR THE SECOND DAY OF SUKKOT

"I shall wash my hands in purity and I shall circle around Your altar, Lord.
To proclaim in a voice of thankfulness, and to relate all Your wonders." (Psalms 26:6-7)
Please save now. Please save now.

For Your sake, our God. For Your sake, our Creator. For Your sake, our Redeemer. For Your sake, our Seeker. For Your sake, the Mightiest of the mighty. For Your sake, Creator of the wind and Former of the mountains. For Your sake, Great One of counsel, Who humbles and uplifts. For Your sake, Speaker of righteousness, Teacher of upright principles. For Your sake, He Who knows and is witness, if a man would conceal himself in hidden places. For Your sake, He Who is One, and who can possibly respond to Him.

לְמַעַנְךָ lema'anach זָךְ zach קס"א ע"ה וְנָקִי venaki ייי וּמִתְבָּרֵר umitbarer עִם im

בָּרִים barim: לְמַעַנְךָ lema'anach וְחוֹפֵשׂ chofes מַצְפּוּן matzpun♦

וְחוֹקֵר vechoker כָּל kol ילי וְחַדָרִים chadarim: לְמַעַנְךָ lema'anach

טִפְּחָה tipcha יְמִינוֹ yemino שָׁמַיִם shamayim יפ טל, יפ כוזו וְעָשָׂה ve'asa♦

מְאוֹרִים me'orim: לְמַעַנְךָ lema'anach יָסַד yasad אֶרֶץ eretz♦

בַּצֻּרוֹת batzurot בִּקֵעַ bike'a יְאוֹרִים ye'orim: לְמַעַנְךָ lema'anach כָּבִיר kabir

כֹּחַ ko'ach♦ מְכֻבָּד mechubad בָּאוּרִים ba'urim: לְמַעַנְךָ lema'anach

לֹא lo יִתַּמּוּ yitamu שְׁנוֹתָיו shenotav לְדוֹר ledor דּוֹרִים dorim:

הוֹשַׁעְנָא hosha'ana♦ הוֹשַׁעְנָא hosha'ana:

אָנָּא ana בן, לכב אֶל El ייא"י (מילוי דס"ג) אֱזֹד echad אהבה, דאגה וּמְבַיֵּשׁ umvayesh

אוֹמְרִים omrim שְׁנַיִם shenayim♦ בַּחֲצִי bachatzi הַשֵּׁם hashem בָּרָא bara קנ"א

עוֹלָמוֹת olamot בן, יהוה אלהים יהוה אדני, מילוי קס"א וס"ג, מ"ה ברבוע וע"ב ע"ה

בְּאוֹתִיּוֹת be'otiyot שְׁנַיִם shenayim♦ יָצַר yatzar הַכֹּל hakol ילי בַּעֲבוּר ba'avur

אָדָם Adam מ"ה וְעֶזְרוֹ ve'ezro שְׁנַיִם shenayim♦ הוֹשִׁיעֵנוּ hoshi'enu

בַּחֲגִיגַת bachagigat יָמִים yamim נלך שְׁנַיִם shenayim: אָנָּא ana בן, לכב

זְכוֹר zechor ע"ב קס"א, יהי אור ע"ה אָב av בָּנָה bana בְּבֵית bevet ב"פ ראה

אֵל El ייא"י (מילוי דס"ג) מִזְבְּחוֹת mizbechot שְׁנַיִם shenayim♦ בְּנִסָּיוֹן benisayon

הָלַךְ halach מ"ה עִם im נְעָרִים ne'arim שְׁנַיִם shenayim♦ וּקְרָאתוֹ ukrato מִן min

הַשָּׁמַיִם hashamayim יפ טל, יפ כוזו ; ר"ת מ"ה פְּעָמִים pe'amim שְׁנַיִם shenayim♦

הוֹשִׁיעֵנוּ hoshi'enu בַּחֲגִיגַת bachagigat יָמִים yamim נלך שְׁנַיִם shenayim:

For Your sake, Pure and Immaculate One, Who acts with integrity with those who are faithful. For Your sake, Searcher of the hidden and Prober of all chambers. For Your sake, He Whose right palm created the Heavens, and Who made the luminaries. For Your sake, He Who founded the earth; He Who is powerful with might, glorified by those residing in the valleys. For Your sake, He Whose years will not end for endless generations. Please save now. Please save now.

Please God, Who is One, Who shames those who say Two, with half of the Name did He create words; with letters that were two, He formed everything for the sake of man and his helpmate, two, save us on the celebration of two days. Please remember the patriarch (Abraham) who built in Bel El two altars. For the Test, he traveled with young men who were two, and You called to him from the Heavens, totaling two times, save us on the celebration of two days.

hichmir הַכְמִיר ben בֶּן זְכוֹר ע"ב קס"א, יהי אור ע"ה לכב ב"ן zechor ana אָנָּא

chananto וְחֲנַנְתּוֹ shenayim שְׁנַיִם ba'amirot בַּאֲמִירוֹת av אָב rachamei רַחֲמֵי

shenayim שְׁנַיִם ulumim וּלְאֻמִּים shenayim שְׁנַיִם goyim גּוֹיִם

gevir גְּבִיר heve הֱוֵה (לכמתק ז' מלכים עמהתו) הברכה, עסמ"ב, vayvarech וַיְבָרֶךְ

bachagigat בַּחֲגִיגַת hoshi'enu הוֹשִׁיעֵנוּ shenayim שְׁנַיִם pe'amim פְּעָמִים

yamim יָמִים נלך shenayim שְׁנַיִם ana אָנָּא ב"ן, לכב זְכוֹר zechor ע"ב קס"א, יהי אור ע"ה

shenayim שְׁנַיִם pi פִּי venachal וְנָחַל tzair צָעִיר יהה haya הָיָה

avar עָבַר bemaklo בְּמַקְלוֹ et אֶת haYarden הַיַּרְדֵּן י' הויות ור' אותיות

shenayim שְׁנַיִם lemachanot לְמַחֲנוֹת יהה יהה vehaya וְהָיָה

shenayim שְׁנַיִם נלך yamim יָמִים bachagigat בַּחֲגִיגַת hoshi'enu הוֹשִׁיעֵנוּ

yedei יְדֵי al עַל torah תּוֹרָה hamashmi'enu הַמַּשְׁמִיעֵנוּ ana אָנָּא ב"ן, לכב

aseret עֲשֶׂרֶת hamanchilenu הַמַּנְחִילֵנוּ shenayim שְׁנַיִם ro'im רוֹעִים

shenayim שְׁנַיִם luchot לוּחוֹת al עַל ראה devarim דְּבָרִים

shenayim שְׁנַיִם edim עֵדִים banu בָּנוּ ume'id וּמֵעִיד hama'azin הַמַּאֲזִין

shenayim שְׁנַיִם נלך yamim יָמִים bachagigat בַּחֲגִיגַת hoshi'enu הוֹשִׁיעֵנוּ

(X2) hosha'ana הוֹשַׁעְנָא hosha'ana הוֹשַׁעְנָא

(X2) na נָא hoshi'a הוֹשִׁיעָה יהוה ע"ע נהורין לכב ב"ן ana אָנָּא

olam עוֹלָם vechimei וְכִימֵי dorsheni דָּרְשֵׁנִי yotzri יוֹצְרִי לכב ב"ן ana אָנָּא

talbisheni תַּלְבִּישֵׁנִי hodcha הוֹדְךָ umadei וּמַדֵּי chofsheni חָפְשֵׁנִי וּפְשָׁעֵנִי

sheni עֵנִי beyom בְּיוֹם נגד, מזבוז, זן, אל יהוה hayom הַיּוֹם נגד, מזבוז, זן, אל יהוה

na נָא hoshi'a הוֹשִׁיעָה יהוה ע"ע נהורין

Please remember the son (Isaac)

who aroused the compassion of his father through sayings that were two, You granted him nations that were two and kingdoms that were two; and he blessed, "Be a lord," totaling two times, save us on the celebration of two days. Please remember the one (Jacob) who was younger yet inherited the portion of two; he prepared savory dishes of kids that were two; he crossed the Jordan with his staff and became camps totaling two; save us on the celebration of two days. Please, He Who proclaimed to us the Torah through shepherds who were two; Who has bequeathed to us ten pronouncements upon Tablets that were two; Who summons to listen and calls for testimony for us witnesses who are two; save us on the celebration of two days.

Please save now. Please save now. (X2)

(X2) :na נָּא יהוה ע"ע נהורין ב"ן לכב הוֹשִׁיעָה hoshi'a ana אָנָּא

◆vehanfisheni וְהַנְפִישֵׁנִי   na נָּא   sov סוֹב   לכב ב"ן   ana אָנָּא

ס"ג ע"ב pene פְנֵה ◆hamsheni הַמְשֵׁנִי metzula מְצוּלָה umimemei וּמִמֵּימֵי

אֵלַי ve'al וְאַל elai אֵלַי נגד, מזבח, זך, אל יהוה hayom הַיוֹם ◆tevisheni תְּבִישֵׁנִי

:na נָּא יהוה ע"ע נהורין hoshi'a הוֹשִׁיעָה ◆sheni שֵׁנִי אל יהוה נגד, מזבח, זך, beyom בְּיוֹם

(X2) ◆na נָּא יהוה ע"ע נהורין hoshi'a הוֹשִׁיעָה Vahu וְהוּ Ani אֲנִי אָנִי

כְּהוֹשַׁעְתָּ kehoshata yegi'ei יְגִיעֵי ◆neshem נֶשֶׁם umukei וּמֻכֵּי gev גֵּו

atzim אָצִים ◆ashem אָשָׁם vaye'eshmu וַיֶּאֱשָׁמוּ אל י"פ vegeshem וְגֶשֶׁם

lecha לָך petzot פְצוֹת ◆filul פִּלּוּל sochachei סוֹחֲחֵי ◆lenaksheni לְנַקְשֵׁנִי

nehalelach נְהַלֶּלָך ◆bemilul בְּמִלּוּל lesalselach לְסַלְסְלָך ◆hilul הִלּוּל

:hosha'ana הוֹשַׁעְנָא ken כֵּן ◆sheni שֵׁנִי אל יהוה נגד, מזבח, זך, beyom בְּיוֹם

(X2) :na נָּא יהוה ע"ע נהורין ב"ן לכב hoshi'a הוֹשִׁיעָה ana אָנָּא

(X2) ◆na נָּא יהוה ע"ע נהורין hoshi'a הוֹשִׁיעָה Vahu וְהוּ Ani אֲנִי אָנִי

◆vanes וְנֵס bemofet בְּמוֹפֵת ◆chanes וְחָנֵס yotz'ei יוֹצְאֵי kehoshata כְּהוֹשַׁעְתָּ

◆lechabesheni לְכַבְּשֵׁנִי choshek וְחוֹשֶׁך ◆ones אוֹנֵס veshichata וְשִׁיחַת

◆te'udatecha תְּעוּדָתְך sovevei סוֹבְבֵי ◆adatecha עֲדָתְך seridei שְׂרִידֵי

nehalelach נְהַלֶּלָך ◆afudatecha אֲפוּדָתְך potzchei פּוֹצְחֵי

:hosha'ana הוֹשַׁעְנָא ken כֵּן ◆sheni שֵׁנִי אל יהוה נגד, מזבח, זך, beyom בְּיוֹם

(X2) ◆na נָּא יהוה ע"ע נהורין hoshi'a הוֹשִׁיעָה Vahu וְהוּ Ani אֲנִי אָנִי

Please bring salvation now. (X2)
Please, my Maker, look after me and as days of yesteryear, release me and in Your splendid vestments,
lothe me; today, on the second day. Please save now.
Please bring salvation now. (X2)
Please, turn now and grant me tranquility and from the watery depths draw me out,
turn to heed me and let me not be humiliated today, on the second day. Please save now.
Please bring salvation now. (X2)
Ani Vahu (of the 72 Names of God) please bring salvation now. (X2)
Just as You have saved those of labored breath, as well
as those afflicted bodily who were totally decimated by those who press to ensnare me; who utter prayers,
who open to praise You to exalt You with words. Let us praise You on the second day; so please save now.
Ani Vahu (of the 72 Names of God) please bring salvation now. (X2)

וְזֻלָּתָה chilta פְּנֵי penei ע"ב ס"ג ◆adoneha אֲדוֹנֶיהָ עַם am עָצוּר atzur

בְּרֹב berov bevet בְּבֵית vesoveva וְסוֹבְבָה ◆pachad פַּחַד יפ אהיה בּ"פ ראה

אֱלֹהֶיהָ ◆Eloheha shetei שְׁתֵּי pe'amim פְּעָמִים belev בְּלֵב יוֹחֵד yachad

וְעָנְתָה ve'anta ki כִּי tovim טוֹבִים hashenayim הַשְׁנַיִם min מִן haechad הָאֶחָד

אהבה, דאגה: tov טוֹב וְהוּ tikach תִּקַּח mimenu מִמֶּנּוּ ◆yadcha יָדְךָ

תַּעַצְמֵנוּ te'atzmenu. miyomayim מִיּוֹמַיִם techayenu תְּחַזֵּינוּ techayenu. uvashelishi וּבַשְׁלִישִׁי

תְּקִימֵנוּ tekimenu. haEl הָאֵל לאה asher אֲשֶׁר mimenu◆ מִמֶּנּוּ

כֹּל kol davar דָּבָר יפי lo לֹא ראה nichchad נִכְחַד: ve'anta וְעָנְתָה ki כִּי

טוֹבִים tovim hashenayim הַשְׁנַיִם min מִן haechad הָאֶחָד אהבה, דאגה:

כְּהוֹשַׁעְתָּ kehoshata me'az מֵאָז ומב ,adatecha עֲדָתֶךָ, ken כֵּן

הוֹשִׁיעָה hoshi'a יהוה ש"ע נהורין et אֶת amecha עַמֶּךָ ס"ת כהת, משיזו בן דוד ע"ה

וּבָרֵךְ uvarech et אֶת nachalatecha נַוְלָתֶךָ◆ nehalelach נְהַלְלָךְ

בְּיוֹם beyom נגה, מזבוז, ז, אל יהוה sheni שֵׁנִי◆ ken כֵּן הוֹשַׁעְנָא hosha'ana:

אֲנִי Ani וְהוּ Vahu וְהוּ hoshi'a הוֹשִׁיעָה יהוה ש"ע נהורין ◆na נָא (X2)

כַּכָּתוּב kakatuv:

הוֹשִׁיעָה hoshi'a יהוה ש"ע נהורין et אֶת amecha עַמֶּךָ ס"ת כהת, משיזו בן דוד ע"ה

וּבָרֵךְ uvarech et אֶת נַוְלָתֶךָ nachalatecha

וּרְעֵם ur'em venase'em וְנַשְּׂאֵם ad עַד הָעוֹלָם ha'olam:

Continue with *Kaddish Titkabal* on Page 489.

Just as You saved those who left Ha'nes amid wonder and miracle, and You destroyed the despot who wanted to subdue me; the remnants of Your congregation who circle around Your Testament, who burst into the song of Your Ephod. Let us praise You on the second day; so please save now.
Ani Vahu (of the 72 Names of God) please bring salvation now. (X2)
She prays before her Master, the nation frozen in abundant terror.
And she circles around in the House of her God two times with a unified heart, and she shall proclaim: "Two are better than one". As You have saved Your congregation since the days of yesteryear, so save Your people and bless Your heritage. Let us praise You on the second day; please save now.
Ani Vahu (of the 72 Names of God) please bring salvation now. (X2) As is written:
"Redeem Your Nation and bless Your inheritance, provide for them and uplift them forever." (Psalms 28:9)

HOSHA'ANOT (CIRCLING) FOR THE THIRD DAY OF SUKKOT

Meditate to draw the Surrounding of Chesed of Tiferet of Zeir Anpin

אלף הא יוד הא   אלף הא יוד הא   אלף הא יוד הא

And these three Names (אהיה=21) equal the Name יוד הי ואו הי (=63), and from the letters (יא"י=31) comes the Name אל. And from the body of *Zeir Anpin* (His Six Edeges) it is all drawn to *Nukva*. During the circling one should meditate to draw Inner Light to *Leah* and *Rachel* and to be protected from one of the cosmic ministers (that is included with ten ministers of the nations).

אֶרְחַץ erchatz בְּנִקָּיוֹן benikayon כַּפָּי kapai וַאֲסֹבְבָה va'asoveva אֶת et

מִזְבַּחֲךָ mizbachacha נגד, זן, אל יהוה, יְהֹוָה Adonai לַשְׁמִיעַ lashmi'a

בְּקוֹל bekol תּוֹדָה toda וּלְסַפֵּר ulsaper כָּל kol נִפְלְאוֹתֶיךָ nifle'otecha

הוֹשַׁעְנָא hosha'ana ◆ הוֹשַׁעְנָא hosha'ana

לְמַעַנְךָ lema'anach אֱלֹהֵינוּ Elohenu לְמַעַנְךָ lema'anach בּוֹרְאֵנוּ bor'enu

לְמַעַנְךָ lema'anach גּוֹאֲלֵנוּ go'alenu לְמַעַנְךָ lema'anach דּוֹרְשֵׁנוּ dorshenu

לְמַעַנְךָ lema'anach אַדִּיר adir אַדִּירִים adirim לְמַעַנְךָ lema'anach

בּוֹרֵא bore רוּחַ ruach וְיוֹצֵר veyotzer הָרִים harim לְמַעַנְךָ lema'anach

גָּדוֹל gedol הָעֵצָה ha'etza ◆ מַשְׁפִּיל mashpil

וּמֵרִים umerim לְמַעַנְךָ lema'anach דּוֹבֵר dover צֶדֶק tzedek מַגִּיד magid

מֵישָׁרִים mesharim לְמַעַנְךָ lema'anach הַיּוֹדֵעַ hayode'a וָעֵד va'ed

אִם im יִסָּתֵר yisater

אִישׁ ish בַּמִּסְתָּרִים bamistarim לְמַעַנְךָ lema'anach וְהוּא vehu

בְּאֶחָד be'echad וּמִי umi יְשִׁיבֶנּוּ yeshivenu אֲמָרִים amarim

---

HOSHA'ANOT (CIRCLING) FOR THE THIRD DAY OF SUKKOT

"I shall wash my hands in purity and I shall circle around Your altar, Lord.
To proclaim in a voice of thankfulness, and to relate all Your wonders." (Psalms 26:6-7)
Please save now. Please save now.

For Your sake, our God. For Your sake, our Creator. For Your sake, our Redeemer. For Your sake, our Seeker. For Your sake, the Mightiest of the mighty. For Your sake, Creator of the wind and Former of the mountains. For Your sake, Great One of counsel, Who humbles and uplifts. For Your sake, Speaker of righteousness, Teacher of upright principles. For Your sake, He Who knows and is witness, if a man would conceal himself in hidden places. For Your sake, He Who is One, and who can possibly respond to Him.

עִם im — וּמִתְבָּרֵר umitbarer — עה קס״א — וְנַקִי venaki — יי — זָךְ zach — לְמַעַנְךָ lema'anach

מַצְפּוּן matzpun — וְחוֹפֵשׂ chofes — לְמַעַנְךָ lema'anach — בָּרִים barim

לְמַעַנְךָ lema'anach — וְחַדָרִים chadarim — ילי — כָּל kol — וְחוֹקֵר vechoker

וְעָשָׂה ve'asa — ע״פ טל, י״פ כוז״ו — שָׁמַיִם shamayim — יְמִינוֹ yemino — טִפְּחָה tipcha

אֶרֶץ eretz — יָסַד yasad — לְמַעַנְךָ lema'anach — מְאוֹרִים me'orim

כַּבִּיר kabir — לְמַעַנְךָ lema'anach — יְאוֹרִים ye'orim — בִּקַע bike'a — בַּצֻרוֹת batzurot

לְמַעַנְךָ lema'anach — בָּאוּרִים ba'urim — מְכֻבָּד mechubad — כוֹחַ ko'ach

דוֹרִים dorim — לְדוֹר ledor — שְׁנוֹתָיו shenotav — יִתַּמּוּ yitamu — לֹא lo

הוֹשַׁעְנָא hosha'ana — הוֹשַׁעְנָא hosha'ana

בִּקְדֻשּׁוֹת bikdushot — הַנִּקְדָּשׁ hanikdash — לאה — הָאֵל haEl — ב״ן, לכב — אָנָא ana

יוֹם yom — ב״ן, לכב — בְּכָל bechol — בְּרֵאשִׁית vereshit — בְּמַעֲשֵׂה bema'ase — קנ״א ב״ן, יהוה אלהים יהוה אדני, מילוי קס״א וס״ג, מ״ה ברבוע וע״ב ע״ה — בָּרָא bara — שְׁלֹשָׁה shelosha

בְּוַחֲגִיגַת bachagigat — הוֹשִׁיעֵנוּ hoshi'enu — שְׁלֹשָׁה shelosha — שְׁלֹשָׁה shelosha — נגד, מזבוז, זן, אל יהוה — וּבַשִּׁשִּׁי uvashishi — וּבַשְּׁבִיעִי uvashvi'i

זְכוֹר zechor — ע״ב קס״א, יהי אור ע״ה — אָנָא ana — ב״ן, לכב — שְׁלֹשָׁה shelosha — נלך — יָמִים yamim

שְׁלֹשָׁה shelosha — מַלְאָכִים malachim — ראה — רָאָה ra'a — אָב av

שְׁלֹשָׁה shelosha — סְאִים se'im — לְהַסְעִידָם lehas'idam — וַיְמַהֵר vaymaher

שְׁלֹשָׁה shelosha — בְּרִית berit — בַּעֲלֵי ba'alei — אִתּוֹ ito — הָלְכוּ halchu

שְׁלֹשָׁה shelosha — נלך — יָמִים yamim — בְּוַחֲגִיגַת bachagigat — הוֹשִׁיעֵנוּ hoshi'enu

---

For Your sake, Pure and Immaculate One, Who acts with integrity with those who are faithful. For Your sake, Searcher of the hidden and Prober of all chambers. For Your sake, He Whose right palm created the Heavens, and Who made the luminaries. For Your sake, He Who founded the earth; He Who is powerful with might, glorified by those residing in the valleys. For Your sake, He Whose years will not end for endless generations.

Please save now. Please save now.

Please, God, Who is sanctified by three sanctifications;

Who brought into being at Creation three each day, and on the sixth and seventh, three, three, save us on the celebration of three days. Please remember the patriarch (Abraham) who saw angels three, and he hurried to feed them three se'im, who was joined by treaty partners, three; save us on the celebration of three days.

אָנָּא (ana) ב"ן, לכב זְכוֹר (zechor) ע"ב קס"א, יהי אור ע"ה בֵּן (ben) הוּכַן (huchan)

לַעֲקֵדָה (la'akeda) לְיָמִים (leyamim) נלך שְׁלשָׁה (shelosha)• כָּרַת (karat)

בְּרִית (berit) עִם (im) מֶלֶךְ (melech) וּמֵרֵעֵהוּ (umere'ehu) וְשַׂר (vesar) צְבָאוֹ (tzeva'o)

שְׁלשָׁה (shelosha)• בִּזְכוּתוֹ (bizchuto) נָחֲלוּ (nachalu) בָּנָיו (vanav) כְּתָרִים (ketarim)

שְׁלשָׁה (shelosha): הוֹשִׁיעֵנוּ (hoshi'enu) בַּחֲגִיגַת (bachagigat) יָמִים (yamim) נלך

שְׁלשָׁה (shelosha): אָנָּא (ana) ב"ן, לכב זְכוֹר (zechor) ע"ב קס"א, יהי אור ע"ה אָב (av)

וְזֶה (vezeh) שְׁלשָׁה (shelosha)• וְיוֹרְדִים (veyordim) בְּעוֹלִים (be'olim) סֻלָּם (sulam) חָזָה (chaza)

וּפִצֵּל (ufitzel) שְׁלשָׁה (shelosha)• מַקְלוֹת (maklot) בְּרְהָטִים (barhatim)

וַיְשַׁלַּח (vayshalach) בָּנָיו (banav) לְצֹעַן (letzo'an) פְּעָמִים (pe'amim) שְׁלשָׁה (shelosha)•

הוֹשִׁיעֵנוּ (hoshi'enu) בַּחֲגִיגַת (bachagigat) יָמִים (yamim) נלך שְׁלשָׁה (shelsha):

אָנָּא (ana) ב"ן, לכב הַגּוֹאֲלֵנוּ (hago'alenu) עַל (al) יְדֵי (yedei) אַחִים (achim)

שְׁלשָׁה (shelosha)• הַשָּׂם (hasam) בָּנוּ (banu) מַעֲלוֹת (ma'alot) כֹּהֲנִים (Kohanim)

לְוִיִּם (Leviyim) וְיִשְׂרָאֵל (veYisrael) שְׁלשָׁה (shelosha)• הַמַּנְחִילֵנוּ (hamanchilenu)

תּוֹרָה (torah) נְבִיאִים (nevi'im) וּכְתוּבִים (uchtuvim) שְׁלשָׁה (shelosha)•

הוֹשִׁיעֵנוּ (hoshi'enu) בַּחֲגִיגַת (bachagigat) יָמִים (yamim) נלך שְׁלשָׁה (shelosha):

הוֹשַׁעְנָא (hosha'ana)• הוֹשַׁעְנָא (hosha'ana): (X2)

אָנָּא (ana) ב"ן לכב הוֹשִׁיעָה (hoshi'a) יהוה ש"ע נהורין נָא (na): (X2)

אָנָּא (ana) ב"ן לכב יַסֵּד (yased) יְסוֹד (yesod) ההע מִקְדָּשִׁי (mikdashi)• לַעֲרֹב (la'arov)

בּוֹ (bo) נִיחוֹחִי (nichochei) אִשִּׁי (isi)• וְתַזְרִיחַ (vetazriach) אוֹר (or) רז, א"ס

שִׁמְשִׁי (shimshi)• הַיּוֹם (hayom) נגד, מזבח, זך, אל יהוה בְּיוֹם (beyom) נגד, מזבח, זך, מזבח, זך, אל יהוה

שְׁלִישִׁי (shelishi)• הוֹשִׁיעָה (hoshi'a) יהוה ש"ע נהורין נָא (na):

Please remember the son (Isaac) who was prepared for the Binding after three days, he established a covenant with a king, his associates and his general, who were three; in his merit did his children inherit three crowns; save us on the celebration of three days. Please remember the patriarch (Jacob) who beheld a ladder with ascending and descending, three, who peeled at the watering troughs sticks which were three, and who sent his children to Tzo'an on three occasions, save us on the celebration of three days. Please, Who redeems us through siblings three; Who instituted among us levels: Kohanim, Levites and Israelites, three; Who has bequeathed to us Torah, Prophets and Writings, three; save us on the celebration of three days.

Please save now. Please save now. (X2)

Please bring salvation now. (X2)

Please re-establish the foundation of my Sanctuary, to make sweet in it the aroma of my burnt-offering, and let shine the light of my sun; today, on the third day. Save now.

אָנָּא ana בין לכב הוֹשִׁיעָה יהוה ש״ע נהורין hoshi'a נָא na (X2)

אָנָּא ana בין לכב סוֹחֵ seche נָא na מוֹקְשִׁי mokshi וְשׁוֹבֵב veshovev

מֵעוֹן me'on מִקְדָּשִׁי mikdashi פְּדֵה pede בְּשָׁלוֹם beshalom נַפְשִׁי nafshi

הַיּוֹם hayom נגד, מזבח, זן, אל יהוה בְּיוֹם beyom נגד, מזבח, זן, אל יהוה שְׁלִישִׁי shelishi

הוֹשִׁיעָה יהוה ש״ע נהורין hoshi'a נָא na

אָנָּא ana בין לכב הוֹשִׁיעָה יהוה ש״ע נהורין hoshi'a נָא na (X2)

אֲנִי Ani וְהוּ Vahu הוֹשִׁיעָה יהוה ש״ע נהורין hoshi'a נָא na (X2)

כְּהוֹשַׁעְתָּ kehoshata יְדִידִים yedidim מִכַּף mikaf מַעֲבִידִים ma'avidim

וַתִּמְחַץ vatimchatz לוּדִים ludim בַּעֲלוֹת ba'alot לָךְ lecha רוּזְיִי rachshi

סְגֻלָּה segula מְאַשֶּׁרֶת me'usheret אֲשֶׁר asher לָךְ lecha סוֹבֶרֶת soveret

פּוֹצָחַת potzachat לָךְ lecha עֲטֶרֶת ateret נְהַלֶּלָךְ nehalelach

בְּיוֹם beyom נגד, מזבח, זן, אל יהוה שְׁלִישִׁי shelishi כֵּן ken הוֹשַׁעְנָא hosha'ana

אֲנִי Ani וְהוּ Vahu הוֹשִׁיעָה יהוה ש״ע נהורין hoshi'a נָא na (X2)

כְּהוֹשַׁעְתָּ kehoshata יְפֵה yefe נוֹף nof מִמִּכְלְאֵי mimichle'ei נוֹף nof

וַתֶּאֱנַף vate'enaf אָנוֹף anof עַד ad צֵאתִי tzeti וְזָפְשִׁי chafshi

שְׂרִידֵי seridei הָעֶדֶר haeder מֵאַדְרִים me'adrim אֶדֶר eder

פִּצוֹת petzot לָךְ lecha הוֹד hod יהה וְהֶדֶר vaheder נְהַלֶּלָךְ nehalelach

בְּיוֹם beyom נגד, מזבח, זן, אל יהוה שְׁלִישִׁי shelishi כֵּן ken הוֹשַׁעְנָא hosha'ana

אֲנִי Ani וְהוּ Vahu הוֹשִׁיעָה יהוה ש״ע נהורין hoshi'a נָא na (X2)

Please bring salvation now. (X2)
Please move away my obstacle now, and return my holy dwelling place;
redeem my soul in peace; today, on the third day. Save now.
Please bring salvation now. (X2)
Ani Vahu (of the 72 Names of God) please bring salvation now. (X2)
Just as You saved the dear friends from the clutches of the enslavers; and You smote the Ludim
when my stirrings went up before You; the fortunate chosen one, which looks to You with hope,
opens its mouth to You in supplication—let us praise You on the third day; so please save now.
Ani Vahu (of the 72 Names of God) please bring salvation now. (X2)
As You saved the beautiful of branches from the prisons of Nof, and You released Your full wrath
until I departed to freedom; the remnants of the flock who glorify the glorious, open their
mouths to You in exultation and splendor: let us praise You on the third day; so please save now.
Ani Vahu (of the 72 Names of God) please bring salvation now. (X2)

מְיַחֲדִים meyachadim שֵׁם shem הָאֵל haEl לאה ; יי״י (מילוי דס״ג)

הַיּוֹם hayom נגד, מזבח, זן, אל יהוה בְּשִׁירָה beshira עֲרוּכָה arucha.

וּבְבִיאַת uvevi'at הַגּוֹאֵל hago'el, הַעֲלֵה ha'ale לָנוּ lanu אלהים, אהיה אדני

אֲרוּכָה arucha. מְשׁוֹרְרִים meshorerim אֵין en כָּאֵל kaEl יי״י (מילוי דס״ג),

עַם am לוֹ lo תֵּאוֹת te'ot מְלוּכָה melucha. יְהְיֶה yihye יי לְיִשְׂרָאֵל leyisrael,

שְׁלִישִׁיָּה shelishiya בְּרָכָה beracha: סוֹבְבֵי sovevei תְּעוּדָתְךָ te'udatecha,

הָאֵר haer אֲפֵלָתָם afelatam. הַיּוֹם hayom נגד, מזבח, זן, אל יהוה

בְּבֵיתְךָ bevetecha ב״פ ראה, תַּקְשִׁיב takshiv תְּחִנָּתָם techinatam. לְדִין ledin

בְּשִׁבְתְּךָ beshivtecha, הַעֲבֵר ha'aver וְחַטָּאתָם chatatam. הָשִׁיבֵם hashivem

לְקַדְמוּתָם lekadmutam. מַעֲרָכָה ma'aracha לִקְרַאת likrat מַעֲרָכָה ma'aracha:

אֲנִי Ani וָהוּ Vahu אני יהוה ע״ע נהורין הוֹשִׁיעָה hoshi'a נָא na (X2)

כְּהוֹשַׁעְתָּ kehoshata מֵאָז me'az ומב עֲדָתְךָ adatecha, כֵּן ken

הוֹשִׁיעָה hoshia יהוה ש״ע נהורין אֶת et עַמֶּךָ amecha ס״ת כהת, משיוו בן דוד ע״ה

וּבָרֵךְ uvarech אֶת et נַחֲלָתְךָ nachalatecha. נְהַלֶּלְךָ nehalelach

בְּיוֹם beyom נגד, מזבח, זן, אל יהוה שְׁלִישִׁי shelishi. כֵּן ken הוֹשַׁעְנָא hosha'ana:

אֲנִי Ani וָהוּ Vahu אני יהוה ש״ע נהורין הוֹשִׁיעָה hoshi'a נָא na (X2)

כַּכָּתוּב kakatuv:

הוֹשִׁיעָה hoshi'a יהוה ש״ע נהורין אֶת et עַמֶּךָ amecha ס״ת כהת, משיוו בן דוד ע״ה

וּבָרֵךְ uvarech אֶת et נַחֲלָתְךָ nachalatecha

ur'em וּרְעֵם venase'em וְנַשְּׂאֵם ad עַד ha'olam הָעוֹלָם:

Continue with *Kaddish Titkabal* on Page 489.

They unify God's Name today, with an arranged song; and with the coming of the Redeemer bring us relief. They sing, "There are none like God," (Deuteronomy 33:26) a people to whom royalty is befitting; may there be for Israel the threefold blessing. Those who circle Your Testament, illuminate their darkness; today in Your House, hearken to their prayer. When You preside at judgment remove their sin; return them to their earlier army arranged attains army. Just as You saved Your congregation since days of yesteryear, so save Your people and bless Your heritage. Let us praise You on the third day; so please save now. Ani Vahu (of the 72 Names of God) please bring salvation now. (X2) As is written: "Redeem Your Nation and bless Your inheritance, provide for them and uplift them forever." (Psalms 28:9)

Hosha'anot (Circling) for the Fourth Day of Sukkot

Meditate to draw the Surrounding of Chesed of Netzach of Zeir Anpin

אלף הי יוד הא   אלף הי יוד הא   אלף הי יוד הא

And these three Names (אהיה=21) equal the Name יוד הי ואו הי (=63), and from the letters (יי"א=31) comes the Name אל. And from the body of *Zeir Anpin* (His Six Edeges) it is all drawn to *Nukva*. During the circling one should meditate to draw Inner Light to *Leah* and *Rachel* and to be protected from one of the cosmic ministers (that is included with ten ministers of the nations).

et אֶת va'asoveva וַאֲסֹבְבָה kapai כַּפַּי benikayon בְּנִקָּיוֹן erchatz אֶרְחַץ

mizbachacha מִזְבַּחֲךָ ,זַ ,גַּד, יְהֹוָה אֵל יהוה יֱהֹוִאדְנִיאהדונהי Adonai: lashmi'a לַשְׁמִעַ

bekol בְּקוֹל toda תּוֹדָה ulsaper וּלְסַפֵּר kol כָּל יְלִי נִפְלְאוֹתֶיךָ nifle'otecha:

hosha'ana הוֹשַׁעְנָא. hosha'ana הוֹשַׁעְנָא:

lema'anach לְמַעַנְךָ Elohenu אֱלֹהֵינוּ יֱלֹה: lema'anach לְמַעַנְךָ bor'enu בּוֹרְאֵנוּ:

lema'anach לְמַעַנְךָ go'alenu גּוֹאֲלֵנוּ: lema'anach לְמַעַנְךָ dorshenu דּוֹרְשֵׁנוּ:

lema'anach לְמַעַנְךָ adir אַדִּיר הרי adirim אַדִּירִים הרי: lema'anach לְמַעַנְךָ

bore בּוֹרֵא ru'ach רוּחַ veyotzer וְיוֹצֵר harim הָרִים: lema'anach לְמַעַנְךָ

gedol גָּדוֹל לֶהוּ, וְעַם ד' אוֹתִיוֹת מִבֵּה, יֶזֶל, אֹם ha'etza הָעֵצָה. mashpil מַשְׁפִּיל

umerim וּמֵרִים: lema'anach לְמַעַנְךָ dover דּוֹבֵר tzedek צֶדֶק magid מַגִּיד

mesharim מֵישָׁרִים: lema'anach לְמַעַנְךָ hayode'a הַיּוֹדֵעַ va'ed וָעֵד

im אִם יוהך, מ"א אוֹתִיוֹת דְּפָשׁוּט, דְּמִילּוּי וּדְמִילּוּי דְּמִילּוּי דַּאֲהִיה ע"ה אהיה yisater יִסָּתֵר בְּ"פ מֵצֵר

ish אִישׁ bamistarim בַּמִּסְתָּרִים: lema'anach לְמַעַנְךָ vehu וְהוּא

be'echad בְּאֶחָד אהבה, דָּאגָה יְלִי umi וּמִי yeshivenu יְשִׁיבֶנּוּ amarim אֲמָרִים:

Hosha'anot (Circling) for the Fourth Day of Sukkot

"I shall wash my hands in purity and I shall circle around Your altar, Lord.
To proclaim in a voice of thankfulness, and to relate all Your wonders." (Psalms 26:6-7)
Please save now. Please save now.
For Your sake, our God. For Your sake, our Creator. For Your sake, our Redeemer. For Your sake, our Seeker. For Your sake, the Mightiest of the mighty. For Your sake, Creator of the wind and Former of the mountains. For Your sake, Great One of counsel, Who humbles and uplifts. For Your sake, Speaker of righteousness, Teacher of upright principles. For Your sake, He Who knows and is witness, if a man would conceal himself in hidden places. For Your sake, He Who is One, and who can possibly respond to Him.

עִם im | וּמִתְבָּרֵר umitbarer | וְנַקִי יי ע"ה קס"א venaki | זַךְ zach | לְמַעַנְךָ lema'anach

בְּצָפוּן matzpun | וְחֹפֵשׂ chofes | לְמַעַנְךָ lema'anach | בָּרִים barim

לְמַעַנְךָ lema'anach | וַחֲדָרִים chadarim | כָּל יל"י kol | וְחוֹקֵר vechoker

וְעָשָׂה ve'asa | שָׁמַיִם י"פ טל, י"פ כוזו shamayim | יְמִינוֹ yemino | טִפְּחָה tipcha

אֶרֶץ eretz | יָסַד yasad | לְמַעַנְךָ lema'anach | מְאוֹרִים me'orim

כַּבִּיר kabir | לְמַעַנְךָ lema'anach | יְאוֹרִים ye'orim | בִּקֵּעַ bike'a | בְּצֻרוֹת batzurot

לְמַעַנְךָ lema'anach | בָּאוּרִים ba'urim | מְכֻבָּד mechubad | כֹּחַ ko'ach

דּוֹרִים dorim | לְדוֹר ledor | שְׁנוֹתָיו shenotav | יִתַּמּוּ yitamu | לֹא lo

הוֹשַׁעְנָא hosha'ana | הוֹשַׁעְנָא hosha'ana

בִּיסוֹדוֹת bisodot | עוֹלָמוֹ olamo | הַבּוֹרֵא habore | ב"ן לכב | אָנָּא ana

כִּסְאוֹ kiso | נוֹשְׂאֵי nosei | אבגיתצ, ושר, אהבת וחם הַנּוֹתֵן hanoten | אַרְבָּעָה arba'a

אַרְבָּעָה arba'a | פִּנּוֹת pinot | הַמַּצִּיב hamatziv | אַרְבָּעָה arba'a | חַיּוֹת chayot | וְזִיּוֹת

בַּחֲגִיגַת bachagigat | הוֹשִׁיעֵנוּ hoshi'enu | אַרְבָּעָה arba'a | וּתְקוּפוֹת utkufot

זְכוֹר zechor | ב"ן לכב | אָנָּא ana | אַרְבָּעָה arba'a | גלך yamim יָמִים

א"ס רז, | בְּאוֹר be'or | מִמִּזְרָח mimizrach | הֵעִיר he'ir | אָב av

וַיְּחָלֵק vayechalek | רָדַף radaf | אַרְבָּעָה arba'a | גלך leyamim לְיָמִים

בִּשַּׂרְתּוֹ bisarto | אַרְבָּעָה arba'a | מְלָכִים melachim | עַל al

אַרְבָּעָה arba'a | לְדוֹרוֹת ledorot | זַרְעוֹ zaro | לָשׁוּב lashuv

אַרְבָּעָה arba'a | גלך yamim יָמִים | בַּחֲגִיגַת bachagigat | הוֹשִׁיעֵנוּ hoshi'enu

---

For Your sake, Pure and Immaculate One, Who acts with integrity with those who are faithful. For Your sake, Searcher of the hidden and Prober of all chambers. For Your sake, He Whose right palm created the Heavens, and Who made the luminaries. For Your sake, He Who founded the earth; He Who is powerful with might, glorified by those residing in the valleys. For Your sake, He Whose years will not end for endless generations.

Please save now. Please save now.

Please, He Who created His world with four elements,
Who appointed as bearers of His Throne four angels; Who established four corners, as well as four seasons, save us on the celebration of four days. Please remember the patriarch (Abraham) who was roused from the with the light of day four; who pursued and was divided against kings that were four; You foretold him that his descendants would return after four generations; save us on the celebration of four days.

HOSHA'ANOT (CIRCLING) FOR SUKKOT

hugash הֻגַּשׁ ben בֶּן ע"ב קס"א, יהי אור ע"ה zechor זְכוֹר ב"ן לכב ana אָנָּא

chafar וְזָפַר ◆arba'a אַרְבָּעָה karnot קַרְנוֹת al עַל la'akeda לָעֲקֵידָה

vayetek וַיַּעְתֵּק ◆arba'a אַרְבָּעָה borot בּוֹרוֹת biFleshet בִּפְלֶשֶׁת

hoshi'enu הוֹשִׁיעֵנוּ ❖arba'a אַרְבָּעָה kiryat קִרְיַת lechevron לְחֶבְרוֹן

ב"ן לכב ana אָנָּא ❖arba'a אַרְבָּעָה נלך yamim יָמִים bachagigat בַּחֲגִיגַת

be'imahot בְּאִמָּהוֹת ne'ezar נֶעֱזַר tam תָּם ע"ב קס"א, יהי אור ע"ה zechor זְכוֹר

◆arba'a אַרְבָּעָה mishfatim מִשְׁפָּטִים lehinatzel לְהִנָּצֵל chinen וְחֹנֵן ◆arba'a אַרְבָּעָה

bidvarim בִּדְבָרִים banav בָּנָיו kilkalta כִּלְכַּלְתָּ bitfilato בִּתְפִלָּתוֹ

נלך yamim יָמִים bachagigat בַּחֲגִיגַת hoshi'enu הוֹשִׁיעֵנוּ ❖arba'a אַרְבָּעָה

bamidbar בַּמִּדְבָּר hamolichenu הַמּוֹלִיכֵנוּ ב"ן לכב ana אָנָּא ❖arba'a אַרְבָּעָה

lemalot לְמַלֹּאת tziva צִוָּה ◆arba'a אַרְבָּעָה bidgalim בִּדְגָלִים

hamtzavenu הַמְצַוֵּנוּ ◆arba'a אַרְבָּעָה turim טוּרִים bachoshen בַּחֹשֶׁן

❖arba'a אַרְבָּעָה beminim בְּמִינִים bechag בֶּחָג lehalelo לְהַלְלוֹ

❖arba'a אַרְבָּעָה נלך yamim יָמִים bachagigat בַּחֲגִיגַת hoshi'enu הוֹשִׁיעֵנוּ

(X2) ❖hosha'ana הוֹשַׁעְנָא ◆hosha'ana הוֹשַׁעְנָא

(X2) ❖na נָא יהוה ע"ע נהורין hoshi'a הוֹשִׁיעָה ב"ן לכב ana אָנָּא

◆shav'i שַׁוְעִי lecha לְךָ ye'erav יֶעֱרַב לכב ב"ן ana אָנָּא

מנק ketz קֵץ na נָא vekarev וְקָרֵב ◆bena'ane'i בְּנַעֲנֻעִי belulavi בְּלוּלָבִי

יִשְׁעִי yish'i ◆יהוה, אל יהוה beyom בְּיוֹם נגד, מזבוז, זן, אל יהוה hayom הַיּוֹם ◆yish'i יִשְׁעִי

❖na נָא נהורין ע"ע יהוה hoshi'a הוֹשִׁיעָה ◆revi'i רְבִיעִי

Please remember the son (Isaac) who was brought near for the Binding upon four corners; who dug in the land of the Pelishitines four wells; and who relocated to Hebron, city of four; save us on the celebration of four days. Please remember the perfect one (Jacob) who was assisted by four matriarchs; who pleaded to be saved from four tribulations; due to his prayer You sustained his descendants with things totaling four; save us on the celebration of four days. Please, He Who lead us in the wilderness under four banners; He Who commanded that the breastplate be filled with four rows; He Who has commanded us to praise Him on the Festival with four species; save us on the celebration of four days.

Please save now. Please save now. (X2)

Please bring salvation now. (X2)

Please, let my plea be pleasant to You when I wave my Lulav, and please bring near my final salvation; today on the fourth day. Please save now.

אָנָּא ana ב"ן לכב הוֹשִׁיעָה hoshi'a יהוה ע"ע נהורין נָא na: (X2)

אָנָּא ana ב"ן לכב סוֹב sov נָא na לְהַרְגִּיעִי lehargi'i◆

וְכוֹנֵן vechonen כוק אָרוֹזִי orchi וְרָבִעִי veriv'i◆ פָּעֳלִי pa'oli שֵׁעָה she'e

הַיוֹם hayom נגד, מזבוז, זין, אל יהוה beyom בַּיוֹם נגד, מזבוז, זין, אל יהוה רְבִיעִי revi'i◆

בְּהִשְׁתַּעַשְׁעִי behishta'ashe'i◆ נַהֵל nahel לְנָוֶה linve מַרְגּוֹעִי margo'i◆

הוֹשִׁיעָה hoshia יהוה ע"ע נהורין נָא na:

אָנָּא ana ב"ן לכב הוֹשִׁיעָה hoshi'a יהוה ע"ע נהורין נָא na: (X2)

אֲנִי Ani וָהוּ Vahu והו הוֹשִׁיעָה hoshi'a יהוה ע"ע נהורין נָא na◆ (X2)

כְּהוֹשַׁעְתָּ kehoshata יַקִיר yakir◆ מִשּׁוֹד mishod מְקַרְקֵר mekarker קִיר kir◆

וְתָךְ vatach וַתַּעֲקִיר vata'akir◆ שׁוֹקֵק shokek שִׁקּוּעִי shiku'i:

גַּם gam עַתָּה ata וְזָךְ chaletz◆ אָלוּץ alutz מִמַּאֲלֵץ mime'aletz◆

וּמַדְוֵי umadvei לֵב lev תַּעֲלֵץ te'aletz◆ נְהַלֶּלְךָ nehalelach

בַּיוֹם beyom נגד, מזבוז, זין, אל יהוה רְבִיעִי revi'i◆ כֵּן ken הוֹשַׁעֲנָא hosha'ana:

אֲנִי Ani וָהוּ Vahu והו הוֹשִׁיעָה hoshi'a יהוה ע"ע נהורין נָא na◆ (X2)

כְּהוֹשַׁעְתָּ kehoshata שׁוֹרֵק sorek◆ מִכַּף mikaf צַר tzar שׁוֹרֵק shorek◆

אֲשֶׁר asher שִׁנָּיו shinav וְזוֹרֵק chorek◆ לְקַצֵּץ lekatzetz אֶת et גִּזְעִי giz'i◆

פֶּתַע peta פִּתְאֹם pit'om◆ נָאַמְתָּ na'amta נְאֻם na'om◆

לְהַשְׁבִּיתוֹ lehashbito מִלְּאֹם mile'om◆ נְהַלֶּלְךָ nehalelach

בַּיוֹם beyom נגד, מזבוז, זין, אל יהוה רְבִיעִי revi'i◆ כֵּן ken הוֹשַׁעֲנָא hosha'ana:

Please bring salvation now. (X2)
Please turn now to calm me and set firm my journey and my repose.
Turn to my action in my joy; lead to my tranquil dwelling; today on the fourth day. Please save now.
Please bring salvation now. (X2)
Ani Vahu (of the 72 Names of God) please bring salvation now. (X2)
Just as You saved the dear one from the plunder of the smasher of walls
and You smote and You vanquished the one who desired my sinking; now, too, release the oppressed form
the oppressor and to the heartsick bring joy; let us praise You on the fourth day. So please save now!
Ani Vahu (of the 72 Names of God) please bring salvation now. (X2)
Just as You saved the vine from the hands of the contemptuous enemy,
who gnashes his teeth while cutting down my shoots; suddenly, You issued a statement,
to put an end to his nationhood, let us praise You on the fourth day. So please save now.

(X2) •na נָּא הוֹשִׁיעָה יהוה ש"ע נהורין hoshi'a והו Vahu אני Ani אֲנִי וְהוֹ

(מילוי דס"ג) ;יא"י לאה haEl הָאֵל •Ya יָהּ har'eh הַרְאֵה yish'acha יִשְׁעֲךָ

מנק ketz קֵץ maher מַהֵר •de'a דֵעָה להו, ועם ד' אותיות מבה, יזל, אום gedol גְּדוֹל

toratcha תּוֹרָתְךָ sovevei סוֹבְבֵי •nivashe'a נִוָשֵׁעָה le'om לְאוֹם pedut פְּדוּת

יהה heye הֱיֵה •Yisrael יִשְׂרָאֵל go'el גּוֹאֵל :arba'a אַרְבָּעָה pe'amim פְּעָמִים

na נָּא moshi'am מוֹשִׁיעָם na נָּא heye הֱיֵה •ka'el כָּאֵל uv'itot וּבְעִתּוֹת •moshi'am

ulcha וּלְךָ •yisham יִשָׁם מנק ketz קֵץ galeh גַּלֵּה •margo'am מַרְגֹּעָם

ken כֵּן ,adatecha עֲדָתְךָ ומב me'az מֵאָז kehoshata כְּהוֹשַׁעְתָּ :lishu'a לִישׁוּעָה

amecha עַמֶּךָ et אֶת hoshi'a יהוה ש"ע נהורין משיוז בן דוד ע"ה ס"ת כהת, hoshi'a הוֹשִׁיעָה

nehalelach נְהַלְּלָךְ •nachalatecha נַחֲלָתְךָ et אֶת uvarech וּבָרֵךְ

:hosha'ana הוֹשַׁעְנָא ken כֵּן •revi'i רְבִיעִי נגד, מזבח, זן, אל יהוה beyom בְּיוֹם

(X2) •na נָּא הוֹשִׁיעָה יהוה ש"ע נהורין hoshi'a והו Vahu אני Ani אֲנִי וְהוֹ

:kakatuv כַּכָּתוּב

amecha עַמֶּךָ et אֶת hoshi'a יהוה ש"ע נהורין ס"ת כהת, משיוז בן דוד ע"ה hoshi'a הוֹשִׁיעָה

nachalatecha נַחֲלָתְךָ et אֶת uvarech וּבָרֵךְ

:ha'olam הָעוֹלָם ad עַד venase'em וְנַשְּׂאֵם ur'em וּרְעֵם

Continue with *Kaddish Titkabal* on Page 489.

Ani Vahu (of the 72 Names of God) please bring salvation now. (X2)
Show your salvation, God, the Almighty, great in knowledge, hasten the Final Redemption, to a redeemed people, those who circle Your Torah four times. Redeemer of Israel, please become their savior and at times such as these please be their comforter, reveal their Final Redemption, and it is for You to save. Just as You saved Your congregation since days of yesteryear, so save Your people now, and bless Your heritage. Let us praise You on the fourth day; So please save now.
Ani Vahu (of the 72 Names of God) please bring salvation now. (X2) As is written:
"Redeem Your Nation and bless Your inheritance, provide for them and uplift them forever." (Psalms 28:9)

HOSHA'ANOT (CIRCLING) FOR THE FIFTH DAY OF SUKKOT

Meditate to draw the Surrounding of Chesed of Hod of Zeir Anpin

אלף הה יוד הא   אלף הה יוד הא   אלף הה יוד הא

And these three Names (אהיה=21) equal the Name יוד הי ואו הי (=63), and from the letters (יא"י=31) comes the Name אל. And from the body of *Zeir Anpin* (His Six Edeges) it is all drawn to *Nukva*. During the circling one should meditate to draw Inner Light to *Leah* and *Rachel* and to be protected from one of the cosmic ministers (that is included with ten ministers of the nations).

אֶרְחַץ erchatz בְּנִקָּיוֹן benikayon כַּפָּי kapai וַאֲסֹבְבָה va'asoveva אֶת et

מִזְבַּחֲךָ mizbachacha גּגּד, זֹ, אל יהוה יְהֹוָה/אֲדֹנָיֵאֱלֹהִים/אֲדֹנָי Adonai: לַשְׁמִעַ lashmi'a

בְּקוֹל bekol תּוֹדָה toda וּלְסַפֵּר ulsaper כָּל kol יל' נִפְלְאוֹתֶיךָ nifle'otecha:

הוֹשַׁעֲנָא hosha'ana ◆ הוֹשַׁעֲנָא hosha'ana:

לְמַעַנְךָ lema'anach אֱלֹהֵינוּ Elohenu יל"ה: לְמַעַנְךָ lema'anach בּוֹרְאֵנוּ bor'enu:

לְמַעַנְךָ lema'anach גּוֹאֲלֵנוּ go'alenu: לְמַעַנְךָ lema'anach דּוֹרְשֵׁנוּ dorshenu:

לְמַעַנְךָ lema'anach אַדִּיר adir הר' אַדִּירִים adirim: לְמַעַנְךָ lema'anach

בּוֹרֵא bore רוּחַ ru'ach וְיוֹצֵר veyotzer הָרִים harim: לְמַעַנְךָ lema'anach

גָּדוֹל gedol להו, ועם ד' אותיות מבה, יזל, אום הָעֵצָה haetza ◆ מַשְׁפִּיל mashpil

וּמֵרִים umerim: לְמַעַנְךָ lema'anach דּוֹבֵר dover צֶדֶק tzedek מַגִּיד magid

מֵישָׁרִים mesharim: לְמַעַנְךָ lema'anach הַיּוֹדֵעַ hayode'a וָעֵד va'ed

אִם im יוהך, מ"א אותיות דפשוט, דמילוי ודמילוי דמילוי דאהיה ע"ה יִסָּתֵר yisater ב"פ מצר

אִישׁ ish בַּמִּסְתָּרִים bamistarim: לְמַעַנְךָ lema'anach וְהוּא vehu

בְּאֶחָד be'echad אהבה, דאגה יל' וּמִי umi יְשִׁיבֶנּוּ yeshivenu אֲמָרִים amarim:

HOSHA'ANOT (CIRCLING) FOR THE FIFTH DAY OF SUKKOT

"I shall wash my hands in purity and I shall circle around Your altar, Lord.
To proclaim in a voice of thankfulness, and to relate all Your wonders." (Psalms 26:6-7)
Please save now. Please save now.

For Your sake, our God. For Your sake, our Creator. For Your sake, our Redeemer. For Your sake, our Seeker. For Your sake, the Mightiest of the mighty. For Your sake, Creator of the wind and Former of the mountains. For Your sake, Great One of counsel, Who humbles and uplifts. For Your sake, Speaker of righteousness, Teacher of upright principles. For Your sake, He Who knows and is witness, if a man would conceal himself in hidden places. For Your sake, He Who is One, and who can possibly respond to Him.

עִם im וּמִתְבָּרֵר umitbarer ע"ה קס"א וְנַקִי venaki יְיָ זַךְ zach לְמַעַנְךָ lema'anach

בְּצִפּוּן matzpun• וְחֹפֵשׂ chofes לְמַעַנְךָ lema'anach :בָּרִים barim

לְמַעַנְךָ lema'anach :וְחַדָרִים chadarim ילי כָּל kol וְחוֹקֵר vechoker

וְעָשָׂה ve'asa• ל"פ טל, יפ כוזו שָׁמַיִם shamayim יְמִינוֹ yemino טִפְחָה tipcha

אֶרֶץ eretz• יָסַד yasad לְמַעַנְךָ lema'anach :מְאוֹרִים me'orim

כַּבִּיר kabir לְמַעַנְךָ lema'anach בִּקַע bike'a :יְאוֹרִים ye'orim בַּצֻּרוֹת batzurot

לְמַעַנְךָ lema'anach :בְּאוּרִים ba'urim מְכֻבָּד mechubad כּוֹן ko'ach•

:דוֹרִים dorim לְדוֹר ledor שְׁנוֹתָיו shenotav יִתַּמּוּ yitamu לֹא lo

:הוֹשַׁעְנָא hosha'ana• הוֹשַׁעְנָא hosha'ana

שֵׁמוֹת shemot לִכְבוֹדוֹ lichvodo הַמְיַחֵד hameyached בן לכב אָנָא ana

קִנְיָנִים kinyanim בְּעוֹלָמוֹ be'olamo הַקוֹנֶה hakone וַחֲמִשָׁה chamisha•

גִּבּוֹרִים giborim בִּבְרִיּוֹתָיו bivriyotav הַיוֹצֵר hayotzer וַחֲמִשָׁה chamisha•

נלך יָמִים yamim בַּחֲגִיגַת bachagigat הוֹשִׁיעֵנוּ hoshi'enu וַחֲמִשָׁה chamisha•

אָב av ע"ב קס"א, יהי אור ע"ה זְכוֹר zechor בן לכב אָנָא ana :וַחֲמִשָׁה chamisha

וַחֲמִשָׁה chamisha• בִּבְתָרִים bivtarim בְּרִית berit כָּרַת karat

וַחֲמִשָׁה chamisha• לִמְלָכִים limlachim רְכוּשׁ rechush וְהֵשִׁיב veheshiv

:וַחֲמִשָׁה chamisha עָרִים arim הֲפִיכַת hafichat עַל al וְחָנַן vechanan

:וַחֲמִשָׁה chamisha נלך יָמִים yamim בַּחֲגִיגַת bachagigat הוֹשִׁיעֵנוּ hoshi'enu

---

For Your sake, Pure and Immaculate One, Who acts with integrity with those who are faithful. For Your sake, Searcher of the hidden and Prober of all chambers. For Your sake, He Whose right palm created the Heavens, and Who made the luminaries. For Your sake, He Who founded the earth; He Who is powerful with might, glorified by those residing in the valleys. For Your sake, He Whose years will not end for endless generations.
Please save now. Please save now.
Please, He Who has set aside for His glory five Names; Who owns in His world possessions live; Who formed among His creatures five mighty ones; save us on the celebration of five days. Please remember the patriarch (Abraham) who established a covenant with halves from five, and who returned the booty of five kings, and who beseeched regarding the destruction of five cities; save us on the celebration of five days.

behar בְּהַר hane'ekad הַנֶּעֱקָד ע״ב קס״א, יהי אור ע״ה zechor זְכוֹר ana אָנָּא בֵּ״ן לכב

mehoro מֵהוֹרוֹ yarash יָרַשׁ כתר chamisha וַחֲמִשָּׁה sh'arim שְׁעָרִים mor מוֹר

nefesh נֶפֶשׁ vehishlim וְהִשְׁלִים chamisha וַחֲמִשָּׁה berachot בְּרָכוֹת

hoshi'enu הוֹשִׁיעֵנוּ chamisha וַחֲמִשָּׁה beshemot בְּשֵׁמוֹת nekuva נְקוּבָה

bachagigat בַּחֲגִיגַת yamim יָמִים נלך chamisha וַחֲמִשָּׁה ana אָנָּא בֵּ״ן לכב

nisim נִסִּים lo לוֹ na'asu נַעֲשׂוּ tam תָּם ע״ה, יהי אור קס״א, ע״ב zechor זְכוֹר

achim אַחִים mibanav מִבָּנָיו vayatzeg וַיַּצֵּג chamisha וַחֲמִשָּׁה

hamachalif הַמַּחֲלִיף lenazir לְנָזִיר shat שָׁת kafro כִּפְּרוֹ chamisha וַחֲמִשָּׁה

yamim יָמִים נלך bachagigat בַּחֲגִיגַת hoshi'enu הוֹשִׁיעֵנוּ chamisha וַחֲמִשָּׁה

dat דַּת hamanchilenu הַמַּנְחִילֵנוּ ana אָנָּא בֵּ״ן לכב chamisha וַחֲמִשָּׁה

hamashmi'enu הַמַּשְׁמִיעֵנוּ chamisha וַחֲמִשָּׁה sefarim סְפָרִים

haktuvim הַכְּתוּבִים chamisha וַחֲמִשָּׁה bekolot בְּקוֹלוֹת dibrotav דִּבְּרוֹתָיו al עַל

chamisha וַחֲמִשָּׁה chamisha וַחֲמִשָּׁה haluchot הַלּוּחוֹת al עַל

chamisha וַחֲמִשָּׁה yamim יָמִים נלך bachagigat בַּחֲגִיגַת hoshi'enu הוֹשִׁיעֵנוּ

(X2) hosha'ana הוֹשַׁעְנָא hosha'ana הוֹשַׁעְנָא

(X2) na נָּא יהוה ש״ע נהורין hoshi'a הוֹשִׁיעָה ana אָנָּא בֵּ״ן לכב

lach'shi לַוְשִׁי she'e שְׁעֵה ukdoshi וּקְדוֹשִׁי yotzri יוֹצְרִי ana אָנָּא בֵּ״ן לכב

yokshi יוֹקְשִׁי veha'aver וְהַעֲבֵר umche וּמְחֵה verachshi וְרִחְשִׁי

chamishi וַחֲמִישִׁי hayom נגד, מזבח, זן, אל יהוה beyom בְּיוֹם נגד, מזבח, זן, אל יהוה hayom הַיּוֹם

Please remember the bound one (Isaac) on Mount Moriah with five gates, who inherited form his father five blessings, and whose perfected soul is described by five names; save us on the celebration of five days. Please remember the perfect one (Jacob) form whom were performed five miracles, and who presented from his sons five brothers; he transmitted his gifts to the one set apart who granted give outfits; save us on the celebration of five days. Please He Who bequeathed to us the Law, Five Books; Who proclaimed to us His commandments through five sounds, which were written upon the Tablets upon each five; save us on the celebration of five days.

Please save now. Please save now. (X2)

Please bring salvation now. (X2)

Please, my Creator and my Holy One, heed my silent prayer and my utterance, and erase and remove my trap; today on the fifth day. Please save now.

הוֹשִׁיעָה יהוה ע״ע נהורין hoshi'a נָא na׃

(X2) אָנָא ב״ן לכב hoshi'a הוֹשִׁיעָה יהוה ע״ע נהורין נָא na׃ ana

ana אָנָא ב״ן לכב seche סֻוֹכֶה na נָא mokshi מוֹקְשִׁי ve'al וְאַל

tizkor תִּזְכֹּר onshi עָנְשִׁי pene פְּנֵה elai אֵלַי ס״ג ע״ב dorshi דוֹרְשִׁי

hayom הַיּוֹם נגד, מזבח, זן, אל יהוה beyom בְּיוֹם chamishi וַחֲמִישִׁי

הוֹשִׁיעָה יהוה ע״ע נהורין hoshi'a נָא na׃

(X2) אָנָא ב״ן לכב hoshi'a הוֹשִׁיעָה יהוה ע״ע נהורין נָא na׃ ana

(X2) אֲנִי Ani וָהוֹ Vahu והו hoshi'a הוֹשִׁיעָה יהוה ע״ע נהורין נָא na׃

kehoshata כְּהוֹשַׁעְתָּ yekushei יְקוּשֵׁי malben מַלְבֵּן merimsat מֵרִמְסַת

hateven הַתֶּבֶן uchhidush וּכְהִדּוּשׁ matben מַתְבֵּן dishashta דְּשָׁשְׁתָּ

dosheshi דוֹשֵׁשִׁי׃ sefurei סְפוּרֵי eser עֶשֶׂר yatzu יָצְאוּ

mima'asar מִמַּאֲסָר petzem פְּצֶם na נָא mechoser מְחוֹסֶר nehalelach נְהַלְלָךְ

beyom בְּיוֹם נגד, מזבח, זן, אל יהוה chamishi וַחֲמִישִׁי ken כֵּן הוֹשַׁעְנָא hosha'ana׃

(X2) אֲנִי Ani וָהוֹ Vahu והו hoshi'a הוֹשִׁיעָה יהוה ע״ע נהורין נָא na׃

kehoshata כְּהוֹשַׁעְתָּ Yeshurun יְשֻׁרוּן migoy מִגּוֹי yetzirun יְצִירוּן

ulcha וּלְךָ yeshorerun יְשׁוֹרְרוּן El אַל ייא״י (מילוי דס״ג) merim מֵרִים

roshi רֹאשִׁי׃ siftei שְׂפָתֵי renanot רְנָנוֹת patzu פָּצוּ lecha לָךְ

neginot נְגִינוֹת betoda בְּתוֹדָה uvitchinot וּבִתְחִנּוֹת nehalelach נְהַלְלָךְ

beyom בְּיוֹם נגד, מזבח, זן, אל יהוה chamishi וַחֲמִישִׁי׃ ken כֵּן הוֹשַׁעְנָא hosha'ana׃

Please bring salvation now. (X2)
Please remove now my ensnaring trap and do not remember my punishment;
turn to me, He Who seeks me; today, on the fifth day. Please save now.
Please bring salvation now. (X2)
Ani Vahu (of the 72 Names of God) please bring salvation now. (X2)
Just as You saved those tortured in brickwork, those downtrodden by straw,
and as straw is trampled so did You crush those who would crush me. Those counted ten times, who left their
imprisonment, redeem them now from want; let us praise You on the fifth day. so please save now.
Ani Vahu (of the 72 Names of God) please bring salvation now. (X2)
Just as you saved Yeshurun from the nation
that oppressed them and to You do they sing praises, God, Who lifts up my head. Joyful lips burst out
in songs to You with thanks and supplications; let us praise You on the fifth day. so please save now.

(X2) •na נָא hoshi'a הוֹשִׁיעָה יהוה ע"ע נהורין והו Vahu אני Ani אֲנִי

•bikdusha בִּקְדֻשָׁה na'aratz נַעֲרָץ ad עַד shochen שׁוֹכֵן marom מָרוֹם

ram רָם (מילוי דס"ג) ב"פ ב"ן el אֵל יא"י shem שֵׁם la'ad לָעַד titbarach תִּתְבָּרַךְ

beshira בְּשִׁירָה umhalelim וּמְהַלְלִים meshorerim מְשׁוֹרְרִים •venisa וְנִשָׂא

pe'amim פְּעָמִים toratcha תּוֹרָתְךָ sovevei סוֹבְבֵי •chadasha חֲדָשָׁה וְחִדְּשָׁה

(מילוי דס"ג) יא"י el אֵל •seridecha שְׂרִידֶיךָ hoshia הוֹשִׁיעַ chamisha חֲמִשָׁה וְחִמְשָׁה

na נָא rachum רַחוּם •emunim אֱמוּנִים יהוה כ"א shomer שׁוֹמֵר

יהי ע"ב קס"א, uzchor וּזְכוֹר •le'etanim לָאֵיתָנִים chish חִישׁ וְחִישׁ, chasadecha חֲסָדֶיךָ וְחַסְדֶּיךָ

velivnei וְלִבְנֵי אהיה אדני אלהים, lanu לָנוּ •beritcha בְּרִיתְךָ et אֵת אור ע"ה

even אֶבֶן •lehargi'ah לְהַרְגִּיעָה lehoshi'ah לְהוֹשִׁיעָה יהוה ע"ע נהורין •vanim וָנִים בָּנִים

pe'amim פְּעָמִים toratcha תּוֹרָתְךָ sovevei סוֹבְבֵי :harosha הָרֹאשָׁה

,adatecha עֲדָתְךָ ומב me'az מֵאָז kehoshata כְּהוֹשַׁעְתָּ :chamisha חֲמִשָׁה וְחִמְשָׁה

amecha עַמְּךָ et אֵת hoshi'a הוֹשִׁיעָה יהוה ע"ע נהורין ס"ת כהת, משיחו בן דוד ken כֵּן

ע"ה uvarech וּבָרֵךְ et אֵת nachalatecha נַחֲלָתְךָ •nachalatecha נַחֲלָתְךָ nehalelach נְהַלְלָךְ

:hosha'ana הוֹשַׁעְנָא ken כֵּן •chamishi חֲמִישִׁי וַחֲמִישִׁי נגד יהוה אל, זן, מזבחו, beyom בְּיוֹם

(X2) •na נָא hoshi'a הוֹשִׁיעָה יהוה ע"ע נהורין והו Vahu אני Ani אֲנִי

:kakatuv כַּכָּתוּב

hoshi'a הוֹשִׁיעָה יהוה ע"ע נהורין ס"ת כהת, משיחו בן דוד ע"ה et אֵת amecha עַמְּךָ

uvarech וּבָרֵךְ et אֵת nachalatecha נַחֲלָתְךָ

:ha'olam הָעוֹלָם ad עַד venase'em וְנַשְׂאֵם ur'em וּרְעֵם

Continue with *Kaddish Titkabal* on Page 489.

Ani Vahu (of the 72 Names of God) please bring salvation now. (X2)
Save your remnants, God,
Who guards promises, Compassionate One, Your kindnesses, please hasten to the people standing firm, and recall Your covenant, for us and for our descendants, to save and bring tranquility, the pinnacle stone, who circle Your Torah five times. As You have saved Your congregation since days of yesteryear, so save Your people now, and bless Your heritage. Let us praise You on the fifth day; please save now. Ani Vahu (of the 72 Names of God) please bring salvation now. (X2) As is written: "Redeem Your Nation and bless Your inheritance, provide for them and uplift them forever." (Psalms 28:9)

HOSHA'ANOT (CIRCLING) FOR THE SIXTH DAY OF SUKKOT

Meditate to draw the Surrounding of Chesed of Tiferet of Zeir Anpin

אלף הא יוד הי   אלף הא יוד הי   אלף הא יוד הי

And these three Names (אהיה=21) equal the Name יוד הי ואו הי (=63), and from the letters (י"א=31) comes the Name אל. And from the body of *Zeir Anpin* (His Six Edeges) it is all drawn to *Nukva*. During the circling one should meditate to draw Inner Light to *Leah* and *Rachel* and to be protected from one of the cosmic ministers (that is included with ten ministers of the nations).

אֶרְחַץ erchatz בְּנִקָּיוֹן benikayon כַּפָּי kapai וַאֲסוֹבְבָה va'asoveva אֶת et

מִזְבַּחֲךָ mizbachacha נגד, ז, יְהֹוָהאאדהיהיאהדונהי Adonai: לַשְׁמִעַ lashmi'a

בְּקוֹל bekol תּוֹדָה toda וּלְסַפֵּר ulsaper כָּל kol ילי נִפְלְאוֹתֶיךָ nifle'otecha:

הוֹשַׁעְנָא hosha'ana ◆ הוֹשַׁעְנָא hosha'ana:

לְמַעַנְךָ lema'anach אֱלֹהֵינוּ Elohenu להי :לְמַעַנְךָ lema'anach בּוֹרְאֵנוּ bor'enu:

לְמַעַנְךָ lema'anach גּוֹאֲלֵנוּ go'alenu :לְמַעַנְךָ lema'anach דּוֹרְשֵׁנוּ dorshenu:

לְמַעַנְךָ lema'anach אַדִּיר adir הרי אַדִּירִים adirim :לְמַעַנְךָ lema'anach

בּוֹרֵא bore רוּחַ ruach וְיוֹצֵר veyotzer הָרִים harim :לְמַעַנְךָ lema'anach

גָּדוֹל gedol להו, ועם ד' אותיות מבה, יזל, אום ◆ הָעֵצָה ha'etza מַשְׁפִּיל mashpil

וּמֵרִים umerim :לְמַעַנְךָ lema'anach דּוֹבֵר dover צֶדֶק tzedek מַגִּיד magid

מֵישָׁרִים mesharim: לְמַעַנְךָ lema'anach הַיּוֹדֵעַ hayode'a וָעֵד va'ed

אִם im יוהרך, מ"א אותיות דפשוט, דמילוי ודמילוי דמילוי דאהיה ע"ה יְסָתֵר yisater ב"פ מצר

אִישׁ ish בַּמִּסְתָּרִים bamistarim: לְמַעַנְךָ lema'anach וְהוּא vehu

בְּאֶחָד be'echad אהבה, דאגה יְלי וּמִי umi יְשִׁיבֶנּוּ yeshivenu אֲמָרִים amarim:

HOSHA'ANOT (CIRCLING) FOR THE SIXTH DAY OF SUKKOT

"I shall wash my hands in purity and I shall circle around Your altar, Lord.
To proclaim in a voice of thankfulness, and to relate all Your wonders." (Psalms 26:6-7)
Please save now. Please save now.

For Your sake, our God. For Your sake, our Creator. For Your sake, our Redeemer. For Your sake, our Seeker. For Your sake, the Mightiest of the mighty. For Your sake, Creator of the wind and Former of the mountains. For Your sake, Great One of counsel, Who humbles and uplifts. For Your sake, Speaker of righteousness, Teacher of upright principles. For Your sake, He Who knows and is witness, if a man would conceal himself in hidden places. For Your sake, He Who is One, and who can possibly respond to Him.

עִם im וּמִתְבָּרֵר umitbarer וְנַקִי venaki זָךְ zach לְמַעַנְךָ lema'anach

בָּרִים barim לְמַעַנְךָ lema'anach וְחֹפֵשׂ chofes מַצְפּוּן matzpun

לְמַעַנְךָ lema'anach וְחַדָרִים chadarim כָּל kol וְחוֹקֵר vechoker

וְעָשָׂה ve'asa שָׁמַיִם shamayim יְמִינוֹ yemino טִפְּחָה tipcha

אָרֶץ eretz לָסַד yasad לְמַעַנְךָ lema'anach מְאוֹרִים me'orim

כָּבִּיר kabir לְמַעַנְךָ lema'anach יְאוֹרִים ye'orim בָּקַע bike'a בְּצוּרוֹת batzurot

לְמַעַנְךָ lema'anach בָּאוּרִים ba'urim מְכֻבָּד mechubad כֹּחַ ko'ach

דוֹרִים dorim לְדוֹר ledor שְׁנוֹתָיו shenotav יִתַּמּוּ yitamu לֹא lo

הוֹשַׁעְנָא hosha'ana הוֹשַׁעְנָא hosha'ana

אָנָּא ana הַבּוֹרֵא habore עוֹלָמוֹ olamo בְּיָמִים beyamim

עָשָׂה shisha הַבּוֹנֶה habone שֵׁשׁ shesh צְלָעוֹת tzela'ot

שְׂרָפִים serafim הַיוֹצֵר hayotzer שִׁשָּׁה shisha לִצְדָדִים litzdadim

בַּחֲגִיגַת bachagigat הוֹשִׁיעֵנוּ hoshi'enu שִׁשָּׁה shisha בִּכְנָפַיִם bichnafayim

יָמִים yamim שִׁשָּׁה shisha אָנָּא ana זְכוֹר zechor

אָב av זָנַח zanach תּוֹעֵבוֹת to'evot שִׁשָּׁה shisha אַחֲרֵי acharei

וּזְקָנָיו zekunav נוֹלְדוּ noldu לוֹ lo בָּנִים banim שִׁשָּׁה shisha נָטַע nata

אֵשֶׁל eshel וּבֹרַךְ uvorach בְּקֵץ beketz שָׁנִים shanim שִׁשָּׁה shisha

הוֹשִׁיעֵנוּ hoshi'enu בַּחֲגִיגַת bachagigat יָמִים yamim שִׁשָּׁה shisha

אָנָּא ana זְכוֹר zechor

הַנֶּעֱקַד hane'ekad בִּמְקוֹם bimkom מַעֲרָכוֹת ma'arachot שִׁשָּׁה shisha

---

For Your sake, Pure and Immaculate One, Who acts with integrity with those who are faithful. For Your sake, Searcher of the hidden and Prober of all chambers. For Your sake, He Whose right palm created the Heavens, and Who made the luminaries. For Your sake, He Who founded the earth; He Who is powerful with might, glorified by those residing in the valleys. For Your sake, He Whose years will not end for endless generations.

Please save now. Please save now.

Please, He Who created His world in six days; Who built six sides in six directions; Who formed the Serafim with six wings; save us on the celebration of six days. Please remember the patriarch (Abraham) who abandoned six abominations; after his old age there were born to him six sons; he planted an eshel tree and was blessed at the end of six years; save us on the celebration of six days. Please remember the one (Isaac) bound in the place of six arrangements;

kara כָּרָה ◦shisha שִׁשָּׁה mitzrot מִצָּרוֹת umilateto וּמִלַּטְתּוֹ gonanto גּוֹנַנְתּוֹ

ma'alot מַעֲלוֹת מ"ב bam בָּם ledorshei לְדוֹרְשֵׁי mikva'ot מִקְוָאוֹת

נלך yamim יָמִים bachagigat בַּחֲגִיגַת hoshi'enu הוֹשִׁיעֵנוּ ⁖shisha שִׁשָּׁה

tam תָּם ע"ה אור יהי קס"א ע"ב בֵ"ן לכב zechor זְכוֹר ana אָנָּא ⁖shisha שִׁשָּׁה

vetziva וְצִוָּה ◦shisha שִׁשָּׁה habchira הַבְּכִירָה min מִן holid הוֹלִיד

vehigbir וְהִגְבִּיר ◦shisha שִׁשָּׁה miminim מִמִּינִים mincha מִנְחָה kachat קַחַת

⁖beshisha בְּשִׁשָּׁה hamvorachim הַמְבוֹרָכִים shisha שִׁשָּׁה avi אֲבִי

⁖shisha שִׁשָּׁה נלך yamim יָמִים bachagigat בַּחֲגִיגַת hoshi'enu הוֹשִׁיעֵנוּ

◦shisha שִׁשָּׁה shemot שֵׁמוֹת la'efod לָאֵפוֹד hamechaber הַמְּחֻבָּר לכב בֵ"ן ana אָנָּא

◦shisha שִׁשָּׁה miklat מִקְלָט be'arei בְּעָרֵי nefashot נְפָשׁוֹת hamatzil הַמַּצִּיל

⁖shisha שִׁשָּׁה sedarim סְדָרִים chochmat וְחָכְמַת hamorishenu הַמּוֹרִישֵׁנוּ

⁖shisha שִׁשָּׁה נלך yamim יָמִים bachagigat בַּחֲגִיגַת hoshi'enu הוֹשִׁיעֵנוּ

(X2) ⁖hosha'ana הוֹשַׁעֲנָא ◦hosha'ana הוֹשַׁעֲנָא

(X2) ⁖na נָא יהוה ע"ע נהורין hoshi'a הוֹשִׁיעָה לכב בֵ"ן ana אָנָּא

vehayshar וְהַיְשַׁר ◦ma'arachi מַעֲרָכִי hayshar הַיְשַׁר לכב בֵ"ן ana אָנָּא

lalechet לָלֶכֶת ◦darki דַּרְכִּי et אֶת vechonena וְכוֹנְנָה ◦mahalachi מַהֲלָכִי

lirvuyei לִרְוֻיֵּי ◦deror דְּרוֹר na נָא ukra וּקְרָא ◦kodshi קָדְשִׁי har הַר el אֶל

mor מוֹר kemo כְּמוֹ ye'erav יֶעֱרַב vesicham וְשִׂיחָם ◦mamror מַמְרוֹר

deror דְּרוֹר ◦ נגד, מזבוח, ז, אל יהוה hayom הַיּוֹם נגד, מזבוח, ז, אל יהוה beyom בְּיוֹם

⁖na נָא נהורין ע"ע יהוה hoshia הוֹשִׁיעָה ◦shishi שִׁשִּׁי

(X2) ⁖na נָא יהוה ע"ע נהורין hoshi'a הוֹשִׁיעָה לכב בֵ"ן ana אָנָּא

You shielded him and You protected him from six difficulties; he dug pools of water for they who expounded upon them six levels; save us on this celebration of six days. Please remember the perfect one (Jacob) who begot from the six eldest; and who commanded to bring a gift of six species; and gave might to he who fathered six; who are blessed with six; save us on the celebration of six days. Please, He Who attached to the ephod the six Names; He Who saves lives through cities of refuge that were six; He Who bequeathed to us the wisdom of six orders; save us on the celebration of six days.
Please save now. Please save now. (X2) Please bring salvation now. (X2)
Please put in order my plan, and straighten out my journey,
and set firm my way to go to my Holy Mountain. Please proclaim liberty for those filled with bitterness, and let their utterances be as sweet as fragrant myrrh; today on the sixth day. Save please. Please save now.
Please bring salvation now. (X2)

וְקַבֵּץ vekabetz • סְגֻלָּתֶךָ segulatecha • סַגֵּל sagel | ב"ן לכב | אָנָּא ana

מְקוֹם mekom • נַחֲלָתֶךָ nachalatecha • לְהַר lehar • קְהִלָּתֶךָ kehilatecha

מַרְבֵּץ marbetz • לִנְוֵה linve • תְּקַבֵּץ tekabetz • פְּזוּרִים pezurim מִקְדָּשִׁי mikdashi

וְתַלְבִּישֵׁם vetalbishem • תְּשַׁבֵּץ tashbetz • הַיּוֹם hayom נגד, מזבח, זן, אל יהוה

בַּיּוֹם beyom נגד, מזבח, זן, אל יהוה • שִׁשִׁי shishi • הוֹשִׁיעָה hoshia יהוה ע"ע נהורין • נָּא na

הוֹשִׁיעָה hoshi'a יהוה ע"ע נהורין • נָּא na

אָנָּא ana | ב"ן לכב | הוֹשִׁיעָה hoshi'a יהוה ע"ע נהורין • נָּא na (X2)

אֲנִי Ani • וָהוּ Vahu • הוֹשִׁיעָה hoshi'a יהוה ע"ע נהורין • נָּא na (X2)

כְּהוֹשַׁעְתָּ kehoshata • יְלִידֵי yelidei • אָהַב ahav • מֵאוּר me'ur • הַלָּהַב halahav

וּמְוֻצֶּצֶת umachatzta • רַהַב rahav • לְכַלּוֹת lechalot • עַם am • קָדְשִׁי kodshi

סָלוּל salul • וּמְסַלּוּל umaslul • פִּתַּוְתָ pitachta • בְּמַצְלוּל bematzlul

לַעֲבֹר la'avor • עַם am • כָּלוּל kalul • נְהַלֶּלָךְ nehalelach

בַּיּוֹם beyom נגד, מזבח, זן, אל יהוה • שִׁשִׁי shishi • כֵּן ken • הוֹשַׁעְנָא hosha'ana

אֲנִי Ani • וָהוּ Vahu • הוֹשִׁיעָה hoshi'a יהוה ע"ע נהורין • נָּא na (X2)

כְּהוֹשַׁעְתָּ kehoshata • יְחִילֵי yechilei • תּוֹר tor • מֵאֶרֶץ me'eretz

כַּפְתּוֹר kaftor • וַתָּשֶׂם vatasem • מִסְתּוֹר mastor • עֲלֵימוֹ alemo

קְדוֹשִׁי kedoshi • סִגַּפְתָּ sigafta • פּוּט put • בִּשְׁוָזִין bishchin • נָפוּט nafut

לוֹזֵלֶץ lechaletz • עַם am • שָׁפוּט shafut • נְהַלֶּלָךְ nehalelach

בַּיּוֹם beyom נגד, מזבח, זן, אל יהוה • שִׁשִׁי shishi • כֵּן ken • הוֹשַׁעְנָא hosha'ana

אֲנִי Ani • וָהוּ Vahu • הוֹשִׁיעָה hoshi'a יהוה ע"ע נהורין • נָּא na (X2)

Please gather Your treasured ones, and assemble Your congregation to the mountain of Your heritage the place of the Sanctuary. Assemble the dispersed ones to the abode place of stratum, and dress them in knitted patterns; today on the sixth day. Please save now.

Please bring salvation now. (X2)

Ani Vahu (of the 72 Names of God) please bring salvation now. (X2)

Just as You saved the children of Your beloved one, from the burning flames, and You struck the Haughty ones to destroy my holy people. A straight and direct path did You provide in the depths to allow an entire people to pass; let us praise You on the sixth day. So please save now.

Ani Vahu (of the 72 Names of God) please bring salvation now. (X2)

Just as You saved those yearning for the era of redemption from the land of Kaftor and You placed a protective shield around them, my Holy One. You afflicted Put with the plague of boils to save a people ruled; let us praise You on the sixth day. So please save now.

Ani Vahu (of the 72 Names of God) please bring salvation now. (X2)

שֵׁעֵה she'e עֶלְיוֹן elyon לְוֹשִׁי lachshi נַעֲרָץ na'aratz בְּקֻדְשָׁה bikdusha◆

הַיּוֹם hayom נגד, מזבוז, זז, אל יהוה לְךָ lecha בְּדָרְשִׁי bedarshi◆ בְּשִׁירָה beshira

וְחֲדָשָׁה chadasha◆ וּכְבוֹשׁ uchvosh נָא na אֶת et כּוֹבְשִׁי kovshi, רְפָא refa

מַכֶּה maka אֲנוּשָׁה anusha◆ סוֹבְבֵי sovevei תּוֹרָתֶךָ toratcha זֹאת zot

הַפַּעַם hapa'am מנק שִׁשָּׁה shisha: הַקְשֵׁב hakshev נָא na קוֹל kol אֶבְיוֹן evyon,

בְּקָרְאוֹ bekor'o הוֹמֶה homeh עַם am◆ מצר־ מִן min מִצְרִים metzarim הוֹמֶה

בְּצִיּוֹן betzayon, בִּידֵי bidei עַמִּים amim וְצָרִים vetzarim◆ וְוִישׁ vechish

יֵשַׁע yesha וּפִדְיוֹן ufidyon, לְעַם le'am עלם בְּלֹא belo הוֹן hon נִמְכָּרִים nimkarim◆

וּשְׁבוּת ushvut גָּאַלְתָּם ge'ulatam תְּמַהֵר temaher תְּחִישָׁה tachisha:

סוֹבְבֵי sovevei תּוֹרָתֶךָ toratcha זֹאת zot הַפַּעַם hapa'am מנק שִׁשָּׁה shisha:

אֲנִי Ani אני וָהוּ Vahu והו יהוה ס"ע נהורין הוֹשִׁיעָה hoshi'a נָא na◆ (X2)

כְּהוֹשַׁעְתָּ kehoshata מֵאָז me'az ומב עֲדָתֶךָ adatecha, כֵּן ken

הוֹשִׁיעָה hoshia יהוה ס"ע נהורין ס"ת כהת, משיוו בן דוד ע"ה עֲמֶּךָ amecha אֶת et וּבָרֵךְ uvarech

אֶת et נַחֲלָתֶךָ nachalatecha◆ נְהַלְלֶךָ nehalelach

בְּיוֹם beyom נגד, מזבוז, זז, אל יהוה שִׁשִּׁי shishi◆ כֵּן ken הוֹשַׁעְנָא hosha'ana:

אֲנִי Ani אני וָהוּ Vahu והו יהוה ס"ע נהורין הוֹשִׁיעָה hoshi'a נָא na◆ (X2)

כַּכָּתוּב kakatuv:

הוֹשִׁיעָה hoshi'a יהוה ס"ע נהורין ס"ת כהת, משיוו בן דוד ע"ה עֲמֶּךָ amecha אֶת et

וּבָרֵךְ uvarech אֶת et נַחֲלָתֶךָ nachalatecha

וּרְעֵם ur'em וְנַשְּׂאֵם venase'em עַד ad הָעוֹלָם ha'olam:

Continue with *Kaddish Titkabal* on Page 489.

Heed my silent prayer, Supreme One, Who is revered in sanctity, today when I seek You with a new song; suppress those who suppress me, heal the mortal wound of those who circle Your Torah now for the sixth time. Hearken to the voice of the destitute one, as he calls out his distress, a people that stirs in a desolate land, in the hands of nations and oppressors, and hurry salvation and redemption, for a people that is sold for a pittance, and the redemption of the captivity, rush and hurry; Those who circle Your Torah now for the sixth time.
Ani Vahu (of the 72 Names of God) please bring salvation now. (X2)
so save Your people and bless Your heritage. Let us praise You on the third day; so please save now.
Ani Vahu (of the 72 Names of God) please bring salvation now. (X2) As is written:
"Redeem Your Nation and bless Your inheritance, provide for them and uplift them forever." (Psalms 28:9)

THE FIRST HAKAFAH (CIRCLING)—ABRAHAM—CHESED

The speech of the *Hakafah* connects to *Binah* (the Surrounding of *Ima*) אל יוד הי ואו הי – ייא"י דס"ג.

The action of the *Hakafah* connects to Mercies of *Da'at* אל יוד הי ויו יוד הי ואו יוד הא ואו (ג' יודין ע"ה).

And the man that circles (אדם=45) connects to the Six Edges of *Zeir Anpin*:

אל יוד הא ואו הא (45=מ"ה) (קס"א קס"א קס"א היוצאים מג' אלפין דמ"ה).

Meditate to connect to energy of protection (מגן =93) through the three Names אל (=31).

אֶרְחַץ erchatz בְּנִקָּיוֹן benikayon כַּפַּי kapai וַאֲסֹבְבָה va'asoveva אֶת et

מִזְבַּחֲךָ mizbachacha נגד, זן, אל יהוה יְהֹוָאֲדֹנָהִיאֲהֹדֹנָהִי Adonai לַשְׁמִעַ lashmi'a

בְּקוֹל bekol תוֹדָה toda וּלְסַפֵּר ulsaper כָּל kol יל' נִפְלְאוֹתֶיךָ nifle'otecha:

הוֹשַׁעְנָא hosha'ana • הוֹשַׁעְנָא hosha'ana:

לְמַעַנְךָ lema'anach אֱלֹהֵינוּ Elohenu ילה: לְמַעַנְךָ lema'anach בּוֹרְאֵנוּ bor'enu:

לְמַעַנְךָ lema'anach גּוֹאֲלֵנוּ go'alenu: לְמַעַנְךָ lema'anach דּוֹרְשֵׁנוּ dorshenu:

לְמַעַנְךָ lema'anach אַדִּיר adir הר' אַדִּירִים adirim הר': לְמַעַנְךָ lema'anach

בּוֹרֵא bore רוּחַ ru'ach וְיוֹצֵר veyotzer הָרִים harim: לְמַעַנְךָ lema'anach

גָּדוֹל gedol להוו, ועם ד' אותיות מבה, יזל, אום הָעֵצָה ha'etza • מַשְׁפִּיל mashpil

וּמֵרִים umerim: לְמַעַנְךָ lema'anach דּוֹבֵר dover צֶדֶק tzedek מַגִּיד magid

מֵישָׁרִים mesharim: לְמַעַנְךָ lema'anach הַיּוֹדֵעַ hayode'a וָעֵד va'ed

אִם im יוהך, מ"א אותיות דפשוט, דמילוי ודמילוי דמילוי דאהיה ע"ה יִסָּתֵר yisater ב"פ מצר

אִישׁ ish בַּמִּסְתָּרִים bamistarim: לְמַעַנְךָ lema'anach וְהוּא vehu

בְּאֶחָד be'echad אהבה, דאגה ובְּמִי umi יל' יְשִׁיבֶנּוּ yeshivenu אֹמְרִים amarim:

THE FIRST HAKAFAH (CIRCLING)—ABRAHAM—CHESED

"I shall wash my hands in purity and I shall circle around Your altar, Lord.
To proclaim in a voice of thankfulness, and to relate all Your wonders." (Psalms 26:6-7)
Please save now. Please save now.

For Your sake, our God. For Your sake, our Creator. For Your sake, our Redeemer. For Your sake, our Seeker. For Your sake, the Mightiest of the mighty. For Your sake, Creator of the wind and Former of the mountains. For Your sake, Great One of counsel, Who humbles and uplifts. For Your sake, Speaker of righteousness, Teacher of upright principles. For Your sake, He Who knows and is witness, if a man would conceal himself in hidden places. For Your sake, He Who is One, and who can possibly respond to Him.

לְמַעַנְךָ lema'anach זָךְ zach וְנַקִי יי עדה קסא venaki וּמִתְבָּרֵר umitbarer עִם im

בָּרִים barim לְמַעַנְךָ lema'anach וְחוֹפֵשׂ chofes מַצְפּוּן matzpun◆

וְחוֹקֵר vechoker כֹּל ילי kol וְחַדָרִים chadarim לְמַעַנְךָ lema'anach

טִפֻחָה tipecha יְמִינוֹ yemino שָׁמַיִם שׁפ טל ייפ כוזו shamayim וְעָשָׂה ve'asa

מְאוֹרִים me'orim לְמַעַנְךָ lema'anach יִסַּד yasad אָרֶץ eretz◆

בַּצוּרוֹת batzurot בִּקַּע bike'a יְאוֹרִים ye'orim לְמַעַנְךָ lema'anach כָּבִיר kabir

כּוֹחַ ko'ach◆ מְכֻבָּד mechubad בָּאוּרִים ba'urim לְמַעַנְךָ lema'anach

לֹא lo יִתַּמּוּ yitamu שְׁנוֹתָיו shenotav לְדוֹר ledor דוֹרִים dorim

הוֹשַׁעְנָא hosha'ana◆ הוֹשַׁעְנָא hosha'ana

אָנָּא בן, לכב יריא (מילוי דסג) ana אֵל El אוֹזֵד echad אהבה, דאגה

וְשָׂמוּ vesamu מהשע עה, עב בריבוע וקסא עה, אל שדי עה echad אוֹזֵד ushmo אהבה, דאגה◆

וּמִי ילי umi יְשִׁיבֶנּוּ yeshivenu וְהוּא vehu בְּאוֹזֵד be'echad אהבה, דאגה◆

קָרָא kara שָׁמַיִם ייפ טל, ייפ כוזו shamayim וָאָרֶץ va'aretz וַיַּעֲמֹדוּ vaya'amdu

כְּאוֹזֵד ke'echad אהבה, דאגה◆ הוֹשִׁיעֵנוּ hoshi'enu בְּהַקָּפַת behakafat

פַּעַם pa'am מנק אוֹזַת echat◆ אָנָּא ana בן, לכב עב קסא, יהי אור עה zechor זְכֹר

אָב av יָרַשׁ yarash אֶת et הָאָרֶץ ha'aretz וְהָיָה יהה יהוה vehaya

אוֹזֵד echad אהבה, דאגה◆ הֵכִין hechin לַמּוֹרְדִים lamordim לֵב lev

אוֹזֵד echad אהבה בפ יבק vederech וְדֶרֶךְ echad אוֹזֵד אהבה, דאגה◆

לִקְרֹא likro כֻּלָּם kulam בְּשֵׁם beshem יְהֹוָ אדניאהדונהי Adonai

---

For Your sake, Pure and Immaculate One, Who acts with integrity with those who are faithful. For Your sake, Searcher of the hidden and Prober of all chambers. For Your sake, He Whose right palm created the Heavens, and Who made the luminaries. For Your sake, He Who founded the earth; He Who is powerful with might, glorified by those residing in the valleys. For Your sake, He Whose years will not end for endless generations.

Please save now. Please save now.

Please One God, Whose Name is One, and can possibly respond to Him, He being the only One. He designated Heaven and Earth and they stood as one; save us at the first circling. Please remember the patriarch (Abraham) who inherited the land when he was but one. He set up for the rebellious ones, one heart and one way so that they would all pray in the Lord's Name,

וּלְעָבְדוֹ ul'ovdo שְׁכֶם shechem אֶחָד echad   אהבה, דאגה:

הוֹשִׁיעֵנוּ hoshi'enu בְּהַקָּפַת behakafat פַּעַם pa'am מנק אֶוֶת echat:

אָנָּא ana ב"ן, לכב זְכוֹר zechor ע"ב קס"א, יהי אור ע"ה בֶּן ben יָחִיד yachid

הָיָה haya יהה לִפְנֵי lifnei אָבִיו aviv אֶחָד echad   אהבה, דאגה.

שְׁנֵיהֶם shenehem בְּנִסָּיוֹן benisayon הָלְכוּ halchu כְּאֶחָד ke'echad אהבה, דאגה.

נָתַתָּ natata כֹּפֶר kofer תַּחְתָּיו tachtav אַיִל ayil אֶחָד echad   אהבה, דאגה:

הוֹשִׁיעֵנוּ hoshi'enu בְּהַקָּפַת behakafat פַּעַם pa'am מנק אֶוֶת echat:

אָנָּא ana ב"ן, לכב זְכוֹר zechor ע"ב קס"א, יהי אור ע"ה אָב av

הוֹסִיף hosif וְחֵלֶק chelek שְׁכֶם shechem אֶחָד echad   אהבה, דאגה.

קִוָּה kiva לְהַפְלִיט lehaflit הַמַּחֲנֶה hamachane הָאֶחָד ha'echad אהבה, דאגה.

אָסַף asaf בָּנָיו banav לְקַבֵּל lekabel מַלְכוּת malchut

שָׁמַיִם shamayim י"פ טל, כוו י"פ מום ע"ה פֶּה pe אֶחָד echad   אהבה, דאגה:

הוֹשִׁיעֵנוּ hoshi'enu בְּהַקָּפַת behakafat פַּעַם pa'am מנק אֶוֶת echat:

אָנָּא ana ב"ן לכב הַמַּשְׁמִיעֵנוּ hamashmi'enu שְׁתַּיִם shetayim בְּקוֹלוֹת bekolot

וּבְרָקִים uvrakim כְּאֶחָד ke'echad אהבה, דאגה. הַמַּנְחִילֵנוּ hamanchilenu

תּוֹרָה torah אַחַת achat וּמִשְׁפָּט umishpat ה"פ אלהים אֶחָד echad אהבה, דאגה.

הוֹשִׁיעֵנוּ hoshi'enu בְּהַקָּפַת behakafat פַּעַם pa'am מנק אֶוֶת echat:

הוֹשַׁעְנָא hosha'ana. הוֹשַׁעְנָא hosha'ana:

יָהּ Yah אָיוֹם ayom זְכוֹר zechor ע"ב קס"א, יהי אור ע"ה הַיּוֹם hayom נגד, מזבח, ז, אל יהוה

בְּרִית berit שִׁבְעַת shivat תְּמִימֶיךָ temimecha. בְּרִית berit אֶזְרָח ezrach,

אֲשֶׁר asher אֲרֻו arach, בְּחֻקּוֹת bechukot דָּת dat נְאוּמֶיךָ ne'umecha:

---

and to serve Him with one mind, save us at the first circling. Please remember the only son (Isaac), who was to his father one. Both of them went test as one. You allowed as substitute in his stead, one ram, save us at the first circling. Please remember the patriarch (Jacob) who added a portion of one. He hoped to secure deliverance from one camp, gathered his children to accept the Kingdom of Heaven as one, save us at the first circling. Please, One Who proclaims to us two, amidst thunder and lightning, as one; Who bequeathed to us one Torah and one Law, save us at the first circling. Please save now. Please save now. Awesome God, recall today the covenant of Your seven perfect ones, the covenant with the one who travelled the path of the statutes of the Law that You proclaimed.

אָב av, רַחֲמָן rachman, קָרֵב karev, זְמַן zeman, פְּדוּתֵנוּ pedutenu

בְּרַחֲמֶיךָ berachamecha◆ זָכְרֵנוּ zochrenu יְהֹוָה Adonai

בִּרְצוֹן birtzon עָ"ה, ע"ב בְּרִבּוּעַ וְקָ"סֹא ע"ה, מהש"ע עָמֶּךָ amecha:

מְחוֹלֵל mecholel כֹּל kol יל וְכֹל vechol ילי יָכֹל yachol, הָיָה heye יהה

נִדְרָשׁ nidrash לְדוֹרְשֶׁיךָ ledorshecha ◆וְהִמָּצֵא vehimatze וְהִתְרַצֵּה vehitratze

לְעָם le'am עלם דּוֹפְקֵי dofkei דַּלְתֶיךָ delatecha◆ בְּהַזְכִּירָם behazkiram,

זְכוּת zechut אַבְרָהָם Avraham וֹ"פ אל, רי"ו ול"ב נתיבות החכמה, רמ"וז (אברים), עסמ"ב וט"ז

וְצִדְקַת vetzidkat כָּל kol ילי וַחֲסִידֶיךָ chasidecha◆ אותיות פשוטות

שְׁעֵה she'e נִיבָם nivam בְּהִתְקָרְבָם behitkarvam, בְּלוּלְבָם belulavam

לְשׁוֹחֲרֶךָ leshacharecha◆ זָכְרֵנוּ zochrenu יְהֹוָה Adonai

בִּרְצוֹן birtzon מהש"ע עָ"ה, ע"ב בְּרִבּוּעַ וְקָסֹ"א ע"ה, אל שדי ע"ה, עָמֶּךָ amecha:

תּוֹדִיעֵנִי todi'eni אֹרַח orach חַיִּים chayim אהיה אהיה יהוה, בינה ע"ה

שֹׂבַע sova שְׂמָחוֹת semachot אֶת et פָּנֶיךָ panecha ס"ג מ"ה ב"ן

נְעִמוֹת ne'imot בִּימִינְךָ bimincha נֶצַח netzach:

אָנָּא ana בֵּ"ן לכב בְּכֹחַ becho'ach◆ גְּדוּלַת gedulat יְמִינְךָ yeminecha◆

תַּתִּיר tatir צְרוּרָה tzerura:

אבג יתץ

HOSHA'ANOT (CIRCLING) FOR HOSHA'ANA RABBAH

THE SECOND HAKAFAH (CIRCLING)—ISAAC—GEVURAH

The speech of the *Hakafah* connects to *Binah* (the Surrounding of *Ima*) אל יוד הי ואו הי – ייא"י דס"ג.

The action of the *Hakafah* connects to Mercies of *Da'at* אל הי ויו יוד הי ואו יוד הא ואו יוד (ג' יודין ע"ה).

And the man that circles (אדם=45) connects to the Six Edges of *Zeir Anpin*:

אל יוד הא ואו הא (45=מ"ה) (קנ"א קנ"א קנ"א היוצאים מג' אלפין דמ"ה).

Meditate to connect to energy of protection (מגן =93) through the three Names אל (=31).

אֶרְחַץ erchatz בְּנִקָּיוֹן benikayon כַּפָּי kapai וַאֲסֹבְבָה va'asoveva אֶת et

מִזְבַּחֲךָ mizbachacha נגד, זז, אל יהוה יְהֹוָ֒ואַדֹנָיאהדונהי Adonai: לַשְׁמִעַ lashmi'a

בְּקוֹל bekol תּוֹדָה toda וּלְסַפֵּר ulsaper כָּל kol יל נִפְלְאוֹתֶיךָ nifle'otecha:

הוֹשַׁעְנָא hosha'ana • הוֹשַׁעְנָא hosha'ana:

לְמַעֲנָךְ lema'anach יל-ה Elohenu אֱלֹהֵינוּ lema'anach לְמַעֲנָךְ: בּוֹרְאֵנוּ bor'enu:

לְמַעֲנָךְ lema'anach גּוֹאֲלֵנוּ go'alenu: לְמַעֲנָךְ lema'anach דּוֹרְשֵׁנוּ dorshenu:

לְמַעֲנָךְ lema'anach אַדִּיר adir הר אַדִּירִים adirim הר: לְמַעֲנָךְ lema'anach

בּוֹרֵא bore רוּחַ ru'ach וְיוֹצֵר veyotzer הָרִים harim: לְמַעֲנָךְ lema'anach

גָּדוֹל gedol להו, ועם ד' אותיות מובה, יזל, אום הָעֵצָה haetza • מַשְׁפִּיל mashpil

וּמֵרִים umerim: לְמַעֲנָךְ lema'anach דּוֹבֵר dover צֶדֶק tzedek מַגִּיד magid

מֵישָׁרִים mesharim: לְמַעֲנָךְ lema'anach הַיּוֹדֵעַ hayode'a וָעֵד va'ed

אִם im יוהך, מ"א אותיות דפשוט, דמילוי ודמילוי דמילוי דאהיה ע"ה יִסָּתֵר yisater ב"פ מצר

אִישׁ ish be'echad בָּמִסְתָּרִים bamistarim: לְמַעֲנָךְ lema'anach וְהוּא vehu

בְּאֶחָד be'echad אהבה, דאגה וּמִי umi יל יְשִׁיבֶנּוּ yeshivenu: אֲמָרִים amarim:

THE SECOND HAKAFAH (CIRCLING)—ISAAC—GEVURAH

*"I shall wash my hands in purity and I shall circle around Your altar, Lord.
To proclaim in a voice of thankfulness, and to relate all Your wonders." (Psalms 26:6-7)
Please save now. Please save now.*

For Your sake, our God. For Your sake, our Creator. For Your sake, our Redeemer. For Your sake, our Seeker. For Your sake, the Mightiest of the mighty. For Your sake, Creator of the wind and Former of the mountains. For Your sake, Great One of counsel, Who humbles and uplifts. For Your sake, Speaker of righteousness, Teacher of upright principles. For Your sake, He Who knows and is witness, if a man would conceal himself in hidden places. For Your sake, He Who is One, and who can possibly respond to Him.

לְמַעַנְךָ lema'anach זָךְ zach יִיִ וְנָקִי venaki עֹ"ה קס"א וּמִתְבָּרֵר umitbarer עִם im

בָּרִים barim :לְמַעַנְךָ lema'anach וְחוֹפֵשׂ chofes בְּצָפוּן matzpun◆

וְחוֹקֵר vechoker כָּל kol יְלִי וְחַדָרִים chadarim: לְמַעַנְךָ lema'anach

טִפֶּחָה tipecha יְמִינוֹ yemino שָׁמַיִם shamayim יְפּ טֹל, יְפּ כוֹזוֹ◆ וְעָשָׂה ve'asa

מְאוֹרִים me'orim: לְמַעַנְךָ lema'anach יָסַד yasad אֶרֶץ eretz◆

בַּצֻרוֹת batzurot בִּקַע bike'a יְאוֹרִים ye'orim: לְמַעַנְךָ lema'anach כַּבִּיר kabir

כֹּחַ ko'ach◆ מְכֻבָּד mechubad בָּאוּרִים ba'urim: לְמַעַנְךָ lema'anach

לֹא lo יִתַּמּוּ yitamu שְׁנוֹתָיו shenotav לְדוֹר ledor דוֹרִים dorim:

הוֹשַׁעְנָא hosha'ana◆ הוֹשַׁעְנָא hosha'ana:

אָנָּא ana בֶּ"ן, לכב echad אֶחָד אהבה, דאגה (מילוי דס"ג) El אֵל ייא"י וּמְבַיֵּשׁ umvayesh

אוֹמְרִים omrim שְׁנַיִם shenayim◆ בְּחָצִי bachatzi הַשֵּׁם hashem בָּרָא bara קֹנ"א

עוֹלָמוֹת olamot בֶּ"ן, יהוה אלהים יהוה אדני, מילוי קס"א וס"ג, מ"ה ברבוע וע"ב עֹ"ה

בְּאוֹתִיוֹת be'otiyot שְׁנַיִם shenayim◆ יָצַר yatzar הַכֹּל hakol יְלִי בַּעֲבוּר ba'avur

אָדָם Adam מ"ה◆ וְעֶזְרוֹ ve'ezro שְׁנַיִם shenayim◆ הוֹשִׁיעֵנוּ hoshi'enu

בְּהַקָּפַת behakafat פְּעָמִים pe'amim שְׁנַיִם shenayim: אָנָּא ana בֶּ"ן, לכב

זְכֹר zechor עֹ"ב קס"א, יְהִי אוֹר עֹ"ה אָב av בָּנָה bana בְּבֵית bevet בֶּ"פ ראה

אֵל El ייא"י (מילוי דס"ג) מִזְבְּחוֹת mizbechot שְׁנַיִם shenayim◆ בְּנִסָּיוֹן benisayon

הָלַךְ halach מי"ה עִם im נְעָרִים ne'arim שְׁנַיִם shenayim◆ וּקְרָאתוֹ ukrato בֵן min

הַשָּׁמַיִם hashamayim יְפּ טֹל, יְפּ כוֹזוֹ ; ר"ת מ"ה פְּעָמִים pe'amim שְׁנַיִם shenayim◆

הוֹשִׁיעֵנוּ hoshi'enu בְּהַקָּפַת behakafat פְּעָמִים pe'amim שְׁנַיִם shenayim:

For Your sake, Pure and Immaculate One, Who acts with integrity with those who are faithful. For Your sake, Searcher of the hidden and Prober of all chambers. For Your sake, He Whose right palm created the Heavens, and Who made the luminaries. For Your sake, He Who founded the earth; He Who is powerful with might, glorified by those residing in the valleys. For Your sake, He Whose years will not end for endless generations.
Please save now. Please save now.
Please God, Who is One, Who shames those who say Two,
with half of the Name did He create words; with letters that were two, He formed everything for the sake of man and his helpmate, two, save us at the second circling. Please remember the patriarch (Abraham) who built in Bel El two altars. for the Test, he traveled with young men who were two, and You called to him from the Heavens, totaling two times, save us at the second circling.

הַכְּמִיר hichmir בֵּן ben זְכוֹר zechor ע״ב קס״א, יהי אור ע״ה לכב בֵּ״ן, ana אָנָּא

שְׁנַיִם shenayim בַּאֲמִירוֹת ba'amirot אָב av רַחֲמֵי rachamei

שְׁנַיִם shenayim וּלְאֻמִּים ulumim שְׁנַיִם shenayim גּוֹיִם goyim חֲנַנְתּוֹ chananto

גְּבִיר gevir הֱוֵה heve (למתק ז׳ מלכים שמותו) הַבְּרָכָה, עסמ״ב vayvarech וַיְבָרֶךְ

בְּהַקָּפַת behakafat הוֹשִׁיעֵנוּ hoshi'enu ♦shenayim שְׁנַיִם pe'amim פְּעָמִים

ע״ב קס״א, יהי אור זְכוֹר zechor לכב בֵּ״ן, ana אָנָּא :shenayim שְׁנַיִם pe'amim פְּעָמִים

♦shenayim שְׁנַיִם פִּי pi וְנָחַל venachal צָעִיר tzair יהה haya הָיָה ע״ה

אוֹתִיּוֹת וד׳ הֱוִיוֹת י׳ haYarden הַיַּרְדֵּן et אֶת bemaklo בְּמַקְלוֹ avar עָבַר

♦shenayim שְׁנַיִם lemachanot לִמְחָנוֹת יהוה יהה vehaya וְהָיָה

:shenayim שְׁנַיִם pe'amim פְּעָמִים behakafat בְּהַקָּפַת hoshi'enu הוֹשִׁיעֵנוּ

yedei יְדֵי al עַל torah תּוֹרָה hamashmi'enu הַמַּשְׁמִיעֵנוּ לכב בֵּ״ן, ana אָנָּא

aseret עֲשֶׂרֶת hamanchilenu הַמַּנְחִילֵנוּ ♦shenayim שְׁנַיִם ro'im רוֹעִים

♦shenayim שְׁנַיִם luchot לֻחוֹת al עַל ראה devarim דְּבָרִים

♦shenayim שְׁנַיִם edim עֵדִים banu בָּנוּ ume'id וּמֵעִיד hama'azin הַמַּאֲזִין

:shenayim שְׁנַיִם pe'amim פְּעָמִים behakafat בְּהַקָּפַת hoshi'enu הוֹשִׁיעֵנוּ

:hosha'ana הוֹשַׁעְנָא ♦hosha'ana הוֹשַׁעְנָא

leha'alot לְהַעֲלוֹת ne'ekad נֶעֱקַד, asher אֲשֶׁר nifkad נִפְקַד, berit בְּרִית

vegam וְגַם ne'esar נֶאֱסַר, kese כְּשֶׂה מ״ה בֵ״ן ♦ lefanecha לְפָנֶיךָ סֵ״ג

נִמְסַר nimsar, asot עֲשׂוֹת hatov הַטּוֹב והו be'enecha בְּעֵינֶיךָ ע״ה קס״א ; ריבוע מ״ה ♦

Please remember the son (Isaac) who aroused the compassion of his father through sayings that were two,
You granted him nations that were two and kingdoms that were two; and he blessed, "Be a lord," totaling
two times, save us at the second circling. Please remember the one (Jacob) who was younger yet inherited the
portion of two; he prepared savory dishes of kids that were two; he crossed the Jordan with his staff and
became camps totaling two; save us at the second circling. Please, He Who proclaimed to us the Torah
through shepherds who were two; Who has bequeathed to us ten pronouncements upon Tablets that were two;
Who summons to listen and calls for testimony for us witnesses who are two; save us at the second circling.
Please save now. Please save now.
The covenant of the remembered one, who was bound to bring up before You,
like a sheep was he tied and was also surrendered to do that which was favorable in Your eyes.

retze רְצֵה, giz'o גִּזְעוֹ, vechon וְחוֹן, zar'o זַרְעוֹ, be'et בְּעֵת, bo'am בּוֹאָם

lefanecha לְפָנֶיךָ, ve'im וְאִם, chovam וְחוֹבָם, ana עֲנֵה, vam בָם,

aseh עֲשֵׂה, na נָא, lema'an לְמַעַן, shemecha שְׁמֶךָ, zochrenu זָכְרֵנוּ

Adonai יְהֹוָה, birtzon בִּרְצוֹן

amecha עַמֶּךָ, zechut זְכוּת, Yitzchak יִצְחָק, bashachak בַּשַׁחַק,

chatum וְחָתוּם, bemidat בְּמִדַּת, haGevurah הַגְּבוּרָה, tizkor תִּזְכֹּר

Eli אֵלִי, Tzur צוּר, go'ali גּוֹאֲלִי, le'am לְעַם,

sho'el שׁוֹאֵל, mimach מִמְּךָ, ezra עֶזְרָה, akedato עֲקֵדָתוֹ

vetzidkato וְצִדְקָתוֹ, meshoch מְשׁוֹךְ, le'am לְעַם, bishmach בִּשְׁמֶךָ,

nikra נִקְרָא, chotmem וְחָתְמֵם, letova לְטוֹבָה, bindava בִּנְדָבָה,

El אֵל, ne'ezar נֶאְזָר, biGevurah בִּגְבוּרָה

minachalatcha מִנַּחֲלָתְךָ, usgulatcha וּסְגֻלָּתְךָ, lo לֹא, tichla תִכְלָא

rachamecha רַחֲמֶיךָ, zochrenu זָכְרֵנוּ, Adonai יְהֹוָה

amecha עַמֶּךָ, birtzon בִּרְצוֹן

todi'eni תּוֹדִיעֵנִי, orach אֹרַח, chayim וְחַיִּים

sova שֹׂבַע, semachot שְׂמָחוֹת, et אֶת, panecha פָּנֶיךָ

ne'imot נְעִמוֹת, bimincha בִּימִינְךָ, netzach נֶצַח

kabel קַבֵּל, rinat רִנַּת, amecha עַמֶּךָ, sagvenu שַׂגְּבֵנוּ

taharenu טַהֲרֵנוּ, nora נוֹרָא

קְרַע שָׂטָן

Accept favorably his stock
and be gracious to his seed, when they come before You, and if their sin testifies against you, then please do for the sake of Your Name. Remember us, Lord, when You favor Your people. The merit of Isaac, in the Heaven, who was sealed with the attribute of Gevurah; may you remember , my God, my Rock and my Redeemer, the people who ask You for help, his binding and his righteousness, extend to the nation that is called by Your Name; seal for good, benevolently, God, Who is girded with might. From Your heritage and Your treasure do not withhold Your mercy. Remember us, Lord, when You favor Your people.

*"You will show me the way of life, granting me the joy of your presence
and the pleasures of living with you forever." (Psalms 16:11)*

קְרַע שָׂטָן *Accept the singing of Your Nation. Strengthen and purify us, Awesome One.*

THE THIRD HAKAFAH (CIRCLING)—JACOB—TIFERET

The speech of the *Hakafah* connects to *Binah* (the Surrounding of *Ima*) יא"י דס"ג – יא"י ואו הי יוד אל.

The action of the *Hakafah* connects to Mercies of *Da'at* (נ' יודין ע"ה) הא יוד ואו הי הי ואו יוד ויו אל.

And the man that circles (אדם=45) connects to the Six Edges of *Zeir Anpin*:

אל יוד הא ואו הא (45=מ"ה) (קמ"ג קמ"ג קמ"ג היוצאים מג' אלפין דמ"ה).

Meditate to connect to energy of protection (מגן =93) through the three Names אל (=31).

את et וַאֲסֹבְבָה va'asoveva כַּפַּי kapai בְּנִקָּיוֹן benikayon אֶרְחַץ erchatz

מִזְבַּחֲךָ mizbachacha גנר, זך, אל יהוה יְהֹוָהאהדונהיאהדונהי Adonai לַשְׁמִעַ lashmi'a

בְּקוֹל bekol תּוֹדָה toda וּלְסַפֵּר ulsaper כָּל kol יל־ נִפְלְאוֹתֶיךָ nifle'otecha

הוֹשַׁעְנָא hosha'ana הוֹשַׁעְנָא hosha'ana

לְמַעַנְךָ lema'anach יְלהֹ Elohenu אֱלֹהֵינוּ lema'anach לְמַעַנְךָ lema'anach בּוֹרְאֵנוּ bor'enu

לְמַעַנְךָ lema'anach גּוֹאֲלֵנוּ go'alenu לְמַעַנְךָ lema'anach דּוֹרְשֵׁנוּ dorshenu

לְמַעַנְךָ lema'anach אַדִּיר adir הדי אַדִּירִים adirim הדי־ לְמַעַנְךָ lema'anach

בּוֹרֵא bore רוּחַ ruach וְיוֹצֵר veyotzer הָרִים harim לְמַעַנְךָ lema'anach

גָּדוֹל gedol לְהוו, ועם ד' אותיות מובה, יזל, אום הָעֵצָה ha'etza מַשְׁפִּיל mashpil

וּמֵרִים umerim לְמַעַנְךָ lema'anach דּוֹבֵר dover צֶדֶק tzedek מַגִּיד magid

מֵישָׁרִים mesharim לְמַעַנְךָ lema'anach הַיּוֹדֵעַ hayode'a וָעֵד va'ed

אִם im יוהך, מ"א אותיות דפשוט, דמילוי ודמילוי דמילוי דאהיה ע"ה יְסַתֵּר yisater ב"פ מצר

אִישׁ ish בַּמִּסְתָּרִים bamistarim לְמַעַנְךָ lema'anach וְהוּא vehu

בְּאֶחָד be'echad אהבה, ראגה, יל־ umi וּמִי yeshivenu יְשִׁיבֶנּוּ אֲמָרִים amarim

---

THE THIRD HAKAFAH (CIRCLING)—JACOB—TIFERET

"I shall wash my hands in purity and I shall circle around Your altar, Lord.
To proclaim in a voice of thankfulness, and to relate all Your wonders." (Psalms 26:6-7)
Please save now. Please save now.

For Your sake, our God. For Your sake, our Creator. For Your sake, our Redeemer. For Your sake, our Seeker. For Your sake, the Mightiest of the mighty. For Your sake, Creator of the wind and Former of the mountains. For Your sake, Great One of counsel, Who humbles and uplifts. For Your sake, Speaker of righteousness, Teacher of upright principles. For Your sake, He Who knows and is witness, if a man would conceal himself in hidden places. For Your sake, He Who is One, and who can possibly respond to Him.

לְמַעַנְךָ lema'anach — זָךְ zach — וְנַקִּי venaki [יוי עה"א קס"א] — וּמִתְבָּרֵר umitbarer — עִם im

בְּרִים :barim — לְמַעַנְךָ lema'anach — וְחוֹפֵשׂ chofes — בַּצְּפוּן matzpun◆

וְחוֹקֵר vechoker — כָּל kol [ילי] — וְחַדְרִים: chadarim — לְמַעַנְךָ lema'anach

טִפּוֹחַ tipecha — יְמִינוֹ yemino — שָׁמַיִם shamayim [יפ טל, יפ כוזו]◆ — וְעָשָׂה ve'asa◆

מְאוֹרִים: me'orim — לְמַעַנְךָ lema'anach — יָסַד yasad — אֶרֶץ eretz◆

בְּצוּרוֹת batzurot — כַּבִּיר kabir — לְמַעַנְךָ lema'anach — יְאוֹרִים: ye'orim — בִּקַע bike'a

כּוֹחַ ko'ach◆ — מְכֻבָּד mechubad — בָּאוּרִים: ba'urim — לְמַעַנְךָ lema'anach

לֹא lo — יִתַּמּוּ yitamu — שְׁנוֹתָיו shenotav — לְדוֹר ledor — דוֹרִים: dorim

הוֹשַׁעְנָא hosha'ana◆ — הוֹשַׁעְנָא: hosha'ana

אָנָּא ana [ב"ן, לכב] — הָאֵל haEl [לאה] — הַנִּקְדָּשׁ hanikdash — בִּקְדֻשּׁוֹת bikdushot

שְׁלֹשָׁה shelosha◆ — בָּרָא bara [קנ"א ב"ן, יהוה אלהים יהוה אדני, מילוי קס"א וס"ג, מ"ה ברבוע וע"ב ע"ה] — בְּמַעֲשֵׂה bema'ase

יוֹם yom [ב"ן, לכב] — בְּכָל bechol — בְּרֵאשִׁית vereshit — נגד, מזבוח, זן, אל יהוה

וּבַשְּׁבִיעִי uvashvi'i — וּבַשִּׁשִּׁי uvashishi — שְׁלֹשָׁה shelosha◆ — שְׁלֹשָׁה shelosha

בְּהַקָּפַת behakafat — הוֹשִׁיעֵנוּ hoshi'enu — שְׁלֹשָׁה shelosha◆ — שְׁלֹשָׁה shelosha

פְּעָמִים pe'amim — זְכוֹר zechor [ע"ב קס"א, יהי אור] — אָנָּא ana [ב"ן, לכב] — שְׁלֹשָׁה: shelosha — שְׁלֹשָׁה shelosha

שְׁלֹשָׁה shelosha◆ — מַלְאָכִים malachim — רָאָה ra'a [ראה] — אָב av [ע"ה]

שְׁלֹשָׁה shelosha◆ — סְאִים se'im — לְהַסְעִידָם lehas'idam — וַיְמַהֵר vaymaher

שְׁלֹשָׁה shelosha◆ — בְּרִית berit — בַּעֲלֵי ba'alei — אִתּוֹ ito — הָלְכוּ halchu

שְׁלֹשָׁה: shelosha — פְּעָמִים pe'amim — בְּהַקָּפַת behakafat — הוֹשִׁיעֵנוּ hoshi'enu

---

For Your sake, Pure and Immaculate One, Who acts with integrity with those who are faithful. For Your sake, Searcher of the hidden and Prober of all chambers. For Your sake, He Whose right palm created the Heavens, and Who made the luminaries. For Your sake, He Who founded the earth; He Who is powerful with might, glorified by those residing in the valleys. For Your sake, He Whose years will not end for endless generations.

Please save now. Please save now.

Please, God, Who is sanctified by three sanctifications;

Who brought into being at Creation three each day, and on the sixth and seventh, three, three, save us at the third circling. Please remember the patriarch (Abraham) who saw angels three, and he hurried to feed them three se'im, who was joined by treaty partners, three; save us at the third circling.

ana אָנָּא ב"ן, לכב ע"ב קס"א, יְהִי אוֹר יְהִי ע"ה zechor זְכוֹר ben בֶּן huchan הוּכַן

la'akeda לַעֲקֵדָה leyamim לְיָמִים גֹלך shelosha שְׁלֹשָׁה karat כָּרַת

berit בְּרִית im עִם am עָם melech מֶלֶךְ umere'ehu וּמֵרֵעֵהוּ vesar וְשַׂר tzeva'o צְבָאוֹ

shelosha שְׁלֹשָׁה bizchuto בִּזְכוּתוֹ nachalu נָחֲלוּ vanav בָּנָיו ketarim כְּתָרִים

shelosha שְׁלֹשָׁה hoshi'enu הוֹשִׁיעֵנוּ behakafat בְּהַקָּפַת pe'amim פְּעָמִים

shelosha שְׁלֹשָׁה ana אָנָּא ב"ן, לכב ע"ב קס"א, יְהִי אוֹר יְהִי ע"ה zechor זְכוֹר av אָב

chaza חָזָה sulam סֻלָּם be'olim בְּעוֹלִים veyordim וְיוֹרְדִים shelosha שְׁלֹשָׁה

ufitzel וּפִצֵּל bar'hatim בָּרְהָטִים maklot מַקְלוֹת shelosha שְׁלֹשָׁה

vayeshalach וַיְשַׁלַּח banav בָּנָיו letzo'an לְצֹעַן pe'amim פְּעָמִים shelosha שְׁלֹשָׁה

hoshi'enu הוֹשִׁיעֵנוּ behakafat בְּהַקָּפַת pe'amim פְּעָמִים shelosha שְׁלֹשָׁה

ana אָנָּא ב"ן, לכב hago'alenu הַגּוֹאֲלֵנוּ al עַל yedei יְדֵי achim אַחִים

shelosha שְׁלֹשָׁה hasam הַשָּׂם banu בָּנוּ ma'alot מַעֲלוֹת Kohanim כֹּהֲנִים

Leviyim לְוִיִּם veYisrael וְיִשְׂרָאֵל shelosha שְׁלֹשָׁה hamanchilenu הַמַּנְחִילֵנוּ

torah תּוֹרָה nevi'im נְבִיאִים uchtuvim וּכְתוּבִים shelosha שְׁלֹשָׁה

hoshi'enu הוֹשִׁיעֵנוּ behakafat בְּהַקָּפַת pe'amim פְּעָמִים shelosha שְׁלֹשָׁה

hosha'ana הוֹשַׁעְנָא hosha'ana הוֹשַׁעְנָא

limudach לִמּוּדָךְ vegam וְגַם yedidach יְדִידָךְ Yisrael יִשְׂרָאֵל lach לָךְ

mekora מְקוֹרָא asher אֲשֶׁר chalam וְחָלַם vehen וְהֵן sulam סֻלָּם

bamarom בַּמָּרוֹם lo לוֹ mora מוֹרָא El אֵל יא"י (מילוי דס"ג) echad אֶחָד

lecha לָךְ אהבה, דאגה pachad פַּחַד vayomer וַיֹּאמֶר ma מַה מ"ה nora נוֹרָא

Please remember the son (Isaac) who was prepared for the Binding after three days, he established a covenant with a king, his associates and his general, who were three; in his merit did his children inherit three crowns; save us at the third circling. Please remember the patriarch (Jacob) who beheld a ladder with ascending and descending, three, who peeled at the watering troughs sticks which were three, and who sent his children to Tzo'an on three occasions, save us at the third circling. Please, Who redeems us through siblings three; Who instituted among us levels: Kohanim, Levites and Israelites, three; Who has bequeathed to us Torah, Prophets and Writings, three; save us at the third circling. Please save now. Please save now.
Your pupil, and also Your beloved, whom You called by the name Israel, who dreamed, and behold a ladder in heights, causing him awe. One God, it is You that he feared saying: "How awe-inspiring [is this place],"

זְכוֹר zechor ע״ב קס״א, יהי אור ע״ה צִדְקוֹ tzidko, וְגַם vegam נַאֲקוֹ na'ako,

לִשְׁאֵרִית lish'erit נִשְׁאָרָה nish'ara♦ נַהֲלָאָה nahala'a אֲשֶׁר asher

נָשְׂאָה nas'a, זֶה ze כַּמֶּה kameh אִמָּךְ emecha♦ זָכְרֵנוּ zochrenu

יְהֹוָאדֹנָיאהדונהי Adonai בִּרְצוֹן birtzon מהש ע״ה, ע״ב בריבוע וקס״א ע״ה, אל שדי ע״ה

עַמָּךְ amecha: זְכוֹר zechor ע״ב קס״א, יהי אור ע״ה אֲחוּזוֹ achuz, וְגַם vegam

שָׁבוּץ shavutz, וְחָתוּם chatum בְּמִדַּת bemidat תִּפְאָרֶת Tiferet♦ מִדַּת midat

אֱמֶת emet אהיה פעמים אהיה, ז״פ ס״ג בֶּאֱמֶת be'emet, ז״פ ס״ג, ז״פ ס״ג

יְרֻשָׁה yerusha לוֹ lo וְכוֹתֶרֶת vechoteret♦ תִּפְאַרְתּוֹ tifarto בְּתֻמָּתוֹ betumato,

תָּמִיד tamid קס״א קנ״א קמ״ג בּוֹ bo נִקְשֶׁרֶת niksheret♦ וּדְמוּתוֹ udmuto,

וְצוּרָתוֹ vetzurato, וְזָקוּקָה chakuka ba'ateret♦ בַּעֲטֶרֶת hu הוּא

אִישׁ ish תָּם tam, בְּשִׁמְךָ bishmach נֶחְתָּם nechtam, שַׂמְתּוֹ samto,

עַל al כֵּס kes רַחֲמֶיךָ rachamecha♦ זָכְרֵנוּ zochrenu יְהֹוָאדֹנָיאהדונהי Adonai

בִּרְצוֹן birtzon מהש ע״ה, ע״ב בריבוע וקס״א ע״ה, אל שדי ע״ה עַמָּךְ amecha:

תּוֹדִיעֵנִי todi'eni אֹרַח orach וְחַיִּים chayim אהיה אהיה, יהוה בינה ע״ה

שֹׂבַע sova שְׂמָחוֹת semachot אֶת et פָּנֶיךָ panecha ס״ג מ״ה ב״ן

נְעִמוֹת ne'imot בִּימִינְךָ bimincha נֶצַח netzach:

נָא na גִּבּוֹר gibor♦ דּוֹרְשֵׁי dorshei יִחוּדְךָ yichudecha♦

כְּבָבַת kevavat שָׁמְרֵם shomrem:

נֶגֶד יכש

Remember his righteousness, as well as his cry, for the remaining remnant. Exhausted has She become She who has carried for so long Your fearsome exile. Remember us, Lord, when You favor Your people. Remember the one who grabbed hold as was also clinging, who was sealed with the attribute of Tiferet; the attribute of truth, truly is his heritage and crown. His splendor, in his perfection, is always bound to him; and his likeness and his image are engraved on the Tiara. He is a perfect man, who is sealed in Your Name, You have placed him on Your Throne of Mercy. Remember us, Lord, when You favor Your people.

*"You will show me the way of life, granting me the joy of your presence
and the pleasures of living with you forever." (Psalms 16:11)*

נֶגֶד יכש *Please, Mighty One, those who seek Your unity, guard them like the pupil of the eye.*

THE FOURTH HAKAFAH (CIRCLING)—MOSES—NETZACH

The speech of the *Hakafah* connects to *Binah* (the Surrounding of *Ima*) אל יוד הי ואו הי – יא"י דס"ג.

The action of the *Hakafah* connects to Mercies of *Da'at* אל יוד ויו הי יוד הי ואו הי יוד ואו הא (ג' יודין ע"ה).

And the man that circles (אדם=45) connects to the Six Edges of *Zeir Anpin*:

אל יוד הא ואו הא (45=ג"פ אלף הי יוד הא היוצאים מג' אלפין דמ"ה).

Meditate to connect to energy of protection (מגן =93) through the three Names אל (=31).

אֶרְחַץ erchatz בְּנִקָּיוֹן benikayon כַּפָּי kapai וַאֲסֹבְבָה va'asoveva אֶת et

מִזְבַּחֲךָ mizbachacha יְהֹוָהֵאלֹהֵינוּ Adonai: לִשְׁמִעַ lashmi'a

בְּקוֹל bekol תּוֹדָה toda וּלְסַפֵּר ulsaper כָּל kol נִפְלְאוֹתֶיךָ nifle'otecha:

הוֹשַׁעְנָא hosha'ana • הוֹשַׁעְנָא hosha'ana:

לְמַעַנְךָ lema'anach אֱלֹהֵינוּ Elohenu: לְמַעַנְךָ lema'anach בּוֹרְאֵנוּ bor'enu:

לְמַעַנְךָ lema'anach גּוֹאֲלֵנוּ go'alenu: לְמַעַנְךָ lema'anach דּוֹרְשֵׁנוּ dorshenu:

לְמַעַנְךָ lema'anach אַדִּיר adir אַדִּירִים adirim לְמַעַנְךָ lema'anach

בּוֹרֵא bore רוּחַ ru'ach וְיוֹצֵר veyotzer הָרִים harim: לְמַעַנְךָ lema'anach

גָּדוֹל gedol הָעֵצָה ha'etza • מַשְׁפִּיל mashpil

וּמֵרִים umerim: דּוֹבֵר dover צֶדֶק tzedek מַגִּיד magid

מֵישָׁרִים mesharim: לְמַעַנְךָ lema'anach הַיּוֹדֵעַ hayode'a וָעֵד va'ed

אִם im יִסָּתֵר yisater

אִישׁ ish בַּמִּסְתָּרִים bamistarim: לְמַעַנְךָ lema'anach וְהוּא vehu

בְּאֶחָד be'echad וּמִי umi יְשִׁיבֶנּוּ yeshivenu אֲמָרִים amarim:

THE FOURTH HAKAFAH (CIRCLING)—MOSES—NETZACH

"I shall wash my hands in purity and I shall circle around Your altar, Lord.
To proclaim in a voice of thankfulness, and to relate all Your wonders." (Psalms 26:6-7)
Please save now. Please save now.

For Your sake, our God. For Your sake, our Creator. For Your sake, our Redeemer. For Your sake, our Seeker. For Your sake, the Mightiest of the mighty. For Your sake, Creator of the wind and Former of the mountains. For Your sake, Great One of counsel, Who humbles and uplifts. For Your sake, Speaker of righteousness, Teacher of upright principles. For Your sake, He Who knows and is witness, if a man would conceal himself in hidden places. For Your sake, He Who is One, and who can possibly respond to Him.

לְמַעַנְךָ lema'anach זַךְ zach וְנַקִי venaki עה קסא וּמִתְבָּרֵר umitbarer עם im

בָּרִים barim ♦ לְמַעַנְךָ lema'anach וְחוֹפֵשׂ chofes מַצְפּוּן matzpun ♦

לְמַעַנְךָ lema'anach וְחֲדָרִים chadarim ♦ כָּל kol יל וְחוֹקֵר vechoker

וְעָשָׂה ve'asa ♦ שָׁמַיִם shamayim יל טל, יל כווי יְמִינוֹ yemino טִפְּחָה tipcha

אֶרֶץ eretz ♦ יָסַד yasad לְמַעַנְךָ lema'anach מְאוֹרִים me'orim ♦

כַּבִּיר kabir לְמַעַנְךָ lema'anach ♦ יְאוֹרִים ye'orim בָּקַע bike'a בַּצֻּרוֹת batzurot

לְמַעַנְךָ lema'anach ♦ בְּאוּרִים ba'urim מְכֻבָּד mechubad ♦ כֹּחַ ko'ach

דוֹרִים dorim ♦ לְדוֹר ledor שְׁנוֹתָיו shenotav יִתַּמּוּ yitamu לֹא lo

הוֹשַׁעְנָא hosha'ana ♦ הוֹשַׁעְנָא hosha'ana ♦

בִּיסוֹדוֹת bisodot עוֹלָמוֹ olamo הַבּוֹרֵא habore לכב בן אָנָּא ana

כִּסְאוֹ kis'o נוֹשְׂאֵי nos'ei הַנּוֹתֵן hanoten אבניתצ, וער, אהבת וזם ♦ אַרְבָּעָה arba'a

וְחַיּוֹת chayot אַרְבָּעָה arba'a ♦ הַמַּצִּיב hamatziv פִּנּוֹת pinot אַרְבָּעָה arba'a ♦

בַּחֲגִיגַת bachagigat הוֹשִׁיעֵנוּ hoshi'enu אַרְבָּעָה arba'a ♦ וּתְקוּפוֹת utkufot

זְכוֹר zechor לכב בן אָנָּא ana ♦ אַרְבָּעָה arba'a נלך יָמִים yamim

אס רו, בְּאוֹר be'or מִמִּזְרָח mimizrach הֵעִיר he'ir אָב av

וַיְּחַלֵּק vayechalek רָדַף radaf אַרְבָּעָה arba'a נלך לְיָמִים leyamim

בְּשַׂרְתּוֹ bisarto אַרְבָּעָה arba'a מְלָכִים melachim עַל al

אַרְבָּעָה arba'a ♦ לְדוֹרוֹת ledorot זַרְעוֹ zar'o לָשׁוּב lashuv

אַרְבָּעָה arba'a ♦ נלך יָמִים yamim בַּחֲגִיגַת bachagigat הוֹשִׁיעֵנוּ hoshi'enu

---

For Your sake, Pure and Immaculate One, Who acts with integrity with those who are faithful. For Your sake, Searcher of the hidden and Prober of all chambers. For Your sake, He Whose right palm created the Heavens, and Who made the luminaries. For Your sake, He Who founded the earth; He Who is powerful with might, glorified by those residing in the valleys. For Your sake, He Whose years will not end for endless generations.

Please save now. Please save now.

Please, He Who created His world with four elements,

Who appointed as bearers of His Throne four angels; Who established four corners, as well as four seasons, save us at the fourth circling. Please remember the patriarch (Abraham) who was roused from the with the light of day four; who pursued and was divided against kings that were four; You foretold him that his descendants would return after four generations; save us at the fourth circling.

ana אָנָּא בֵּן לכב   zechor זְכוֹר ע"ב קס"א, יהי אור ע"ה   ben בֶּן   hugash הֻגַּשׁ

la'akeda לַעֲקֵידָה   al עַל   karnot קַרְנוֹת   arba'a אַרְבָּעָה◆   chafar וְחָפַר

biFleshet בִּפְלֶשֶׁת   borot בּוֹרוֹת   arba'a אַרְבָּעָה◆   vayatek וַיַּעְתֵּק

lechevron לְחֶבְרוֹן   kiryat קִרְיַת   arba'a אַרְבָּעָה: hoshi'enu הוֹשִׁיעֵנוּ

bachagigat בַּחֲגִיגַת   yamim יָמִים נלך   arba'a אַרְבָּעָה: ana אָנָּא בֵּן לכב

zechor זְכוֹר ע"ב קס"א, יהי אור ע"ה   tam תָּם   ne'ezar נֶעֱזַר   be'imahot בָּאִמָּהוֹת

arba'a אַרְבָּעָה◆   mishfatim מִשְׁפָּטִים   lehinatzel לְהִנָּצֵל   chinen וְחֵן◆ arba'a אַרְבָּעָה◆

bidvarim בִּדְבָרִים   banav בָּנָיו   kilkalta כִּלְכַּלְתָּ   bitfilato בִּתְפִלָּתוֹ

yamim יָמִים נלך   bachagigat בַּחֲגִיגַת   hoshi'enu הוֹשִׁיעֵנוּ   arba'a אַרְבָּעָה:

bamidbar בַּמִּדְבָּר   hamolichenu הַמּוֹלִיכֵנוּ   ana אָנָּא בֵּן לכב   arba'a אַרְבָּעָה:

lemalot לְמַלֹּאת   tziva צִוָּה   arba'a אַרְבָּעָה◆   bidgalim בִּדְגָלִים

hamtzavenu הַמְצַוֵּנוּ   arba'a אַרְבָּעָה◆   turim טוּרִים   bachoshen בַּחֹשֶׁן

arba'a אַרְבָּעָה: beminim בְּמִינִים   bechag בֶּחָג   lehalelo לְהַלְלוֹ

arba'a אַרְבָּעָה: pe'amim פְּעָמִים   behakafat בַּהֲקָפַת   hoshi'enu הוֹשִׁיעֵנוּ

hosha'ana הוֹשַׁעְנָא: ◆hosha'ana הוֹשַׁעְנָא◆

al אַל ע"ה אלהים ד"פ, אל שדי, קס"א בריבוע ע"ב מהע, Moshe מֹשֶׁה   zechut זְכוּת

tinshe תִּנְשֶׁה,   chatum וְזֹתוּם   bemidat בְּמִדַת   haNetzach הַנֶּצַח◆

bizchuto בִּזְכוּתוֹ,   ve'anvato וְעַנְוָתוֹ,   oyvenu אוֹיְבֵינוּ   tenatze'ach תְּנַצֵּחַ◆

Please remember the son (Isaac) who
was brought near for the Binding upon four corners; who dug in the land of the Pelishitines four wells; and
who relocated to Hebron, city of four; save us at the fourth circling. Please remember the perfect one (Jacob)
who was assisted by four matriarchs; who pleaded to be saved from four tribulations; due to his prayer You
sustained his descendants with things totaling four; save us at the fourth circling. Please, He Who lead us in
the wilderness under four banners; He Who commanded that the breastplate be filled with four rows; He
Who has commanded us to praise Him on the Festival with four species; save us at the fourth circling.
Please save now. Please save now.
The merit of Moses, do not forget,
sealed with the attribute of Netzach; in his merit and his humility may You defeat our enemies.

וּבְהַר uvhar　הַמּוֹר haMor　שִׁיר shir　מִזְמוֹר mizmor,　נָשִׁיר nashir

וְכַלַמְנַצֵּחַ velamnatze'ach ◆ אֵל El יא״י (מילוי דס״ג)　נֶצַח netzach,　לָנֶצַח lanetzach

רוּם rachem　אברהם, ו׳פ אל׳, רי״י ול״ב נתיבות הוזכמה, רמ״ז (אברים), עסמ״ב וט״ז אותיות פעוטות

עַם am　יְהוָֹהַאהדֹנָהי Adonai　זָכְרֵנוּ zochrenu　◆ רוֹמִמְךָ romemecha

בִּרְצוֹן birtzon　עַמֶּךָ amecha מהש ע״ה, ע״ב בריבוע וקס״א ע״ה, אל שדי ע״ה　תּוֹרָה torah

תְּמִימָה temima סיני behar בְּהַר anav עָנָיו yarash יָרַשׁ, וּנְעִימָה unima

יוֹם yom arbaim אַרְבָּעִים, ayom אָיוֹם (מילוי דס״ג) אֵל el יא״י im עַם ◆ ה הויות, נמם.

עַמַד amad עָמַד sham שָׁם im עַם זן, אל יהוה　יְהוָֹהַאהדֹנָהי Adonai:

מְעוֹנַי me'onai ◆ אֵל el יא״י (מילוי דס״ג) אֱמֶת emet אהיה פעמים אהיה, ז״פ ס״ג תּוֹרַת torat

אֱמֶת emet אהיה פעמים אהיה, ז״פ ס״ג הִנְחִיל hinchil לְעַם le'am עלם

נֶאֱמָנַי ne'emanai ◆ צִדְקָתוֹ tzidkato, וְתוֹרָתוֹ vetorato,　זְכוֹר zechor ע״ב קס״א, יהי

נָא na מִשְּׁמֶיךָ mishamecha ◆ זָכְרֵנוּ zachrenu　יְהוָֹהַאהדֹנָהי Adonai אור ע״ה

בִּרְצוֹן birtzon מהש ע״ה, ע״ב בריבוע וקס״א ע״ה, אל שדי ע״ה　עַמֶּךָ amecha:

תּוֹדִיעֵנִי todi'eni אָרַח orach וְחַיִּים chayim אהיה אהיה יהוה, בינה ע״ה

שׂבַע sova　שְׂמָחוֹת semachot	אֶת et	פָּנֶיךָ panecha ס״ג מ״ה ב״ן

נְעִמוֹת ne'imot	בִּימִינְךָ bimincha	נֶצַח netzach:

בָּרְכֵם barchem	טַהֲרֵם taharem ◆	רַחֲמֵי rachamei ◆	צִדְקָתְךָ tzidkatecha ◆

תָּמִיד tamid	גָּמְלֵם gomlem:

בטר צתג

Upon Mount Moriah, a song, a psalm may we sing, and "to the conductor." Eternal God, forevermore show your compassion to the people who exalt You. Remember us, Lord, when You favor Your people. A Torah that is perfect and sweet did the humble one inherit at Mount Sinai; with the Awesome God for forty days did he remain there with the Lord; To receive the Torah, pure and clean from the Heavenly Abode. The true God, a true Torah did He bequeath to a faithful people. His righteousness and his Torah please remember from Your Heavens. Remember us, Lord, when you favor Your people.
"You will show me the way of life, granting me the joy of your presence
and the pleasures of living with you forever." (Psalms 16:11)
בטר צתג Bless them. Purify them. Your compassionate righteousness always grant them.

THE FIFTH HAKAFAH (CIRCLING)—AARON—HOD

The speech of the *Hakafah* connects to *Binah* (the Surrounding of *Ima*) אַל יוד הי ואו הי – יא"י דס"ג.

The action of the *Hakafah* connects to Mercies of *Da'at* אַל הי יוד ויו הי הי יוד ואו הא יוד ואו (ג' יודין ע"ה).

And the man that circles (אדם=45) connects to the Six Edges of *Zeir Anpin*:

אַל יוד הא ואו הא (45=מ"ה) (ג"פ אלף הה הא יוד הא היוצאים מג' אלפין דמ"ה).

Meditate to connect to energy of protection (מגן =93) through the three Names אל (=31).

אֶרְחַץ erchatz בְּנִקָּיוֹן benikayon כַּפַּי kapai וַאֲסֹבְבָה va'asoveva אֶת et

מִזְבַּחֲךָ mizbachacha נגד, זך, אל יהוה יְהֹוָה יאהדונהי:Adonai לַשְׁמִעַ lashmi'a

בְּקוֹל bekol תּוֹדָה toda וּלְסַפֵּר ulsaper כָּל kol יכי נִפְלְאוֹתֶיךָ:nifle'otecha

הוֹשַׁעְנָא hosha'ana ♦ הוֹשַׁעְנָא hosha'ana:

לְמַעַנְךָ lema'anach אֱלֹהֵינוּ Elohenu יהה: לְמַעַנְךָ lema'anach בּוֹרְאֵנוּ bor'enu:

לְמַעַנְךָ lema'anach גּוֹאֲלֵנוּ go'alenu: לְמַעַנְךָ lema'anach דּוֹרְשֵׁנוּ dorshenu:

לְמַעַנְךָ lema'anach אַדִּיר adir הרי אַדִּירִים adirim: לְמַעַנְךָ lema'anach

בּוֹרֵא bore רוּחַ ru'ach וְיוֹצֵר veyotzer הָרִים harim: לְמַעַנְךָ lema'anach

גְּדוֹל gedol להו, ועם ד' אותיות מבה, יזל, אום הָעֵצָה haetza ♦ מַשְׁפִּיל mashpil

וּמֵרִים umerim: לְמַעַנְךָ lema'anach דּוֹבֵר dover צֶדֶק tzedek מַגִּיד magid

מֵישָׁרִים mesharim: לְמַעַנְךָ lema'anach הַיּוֹדֵעַ hayode'a וָעֵד va'ed

אִם im יוהך, מ"א אותיות דפשוט, דמילוי ודמילוי דמילוי דאהיה ע"ה יְסָתֵר yisater ב"פ מצר

אִישׁ ish בַּמִּסְתָּרִים bamistarim: לְמַעַנְךָ lema'anach וְהוּא vehu

בְּאֶחָד be'echad אהבה, ראגה יכי וּמִי umi יִשִׁיבֶנּוּ yeshivenu אֲמָרִים amarim:

THE FIFTH HAKAFAH (CIRCLING)—AARON—HOD

"I shall wash my hands in purity and I shall circle around Your altar, Lord.
To proclaim in a voice of thankfulness, and to relate all Your wonders." (Psalms 26:6-7)
Please save now. Please save now.

For Your sake, our God. For Your sake, our Creator. For Your sake, our Redeemer. For Your sake, our Seeker. For Your sake, the Mightiest of the mighty. For Your sake, Creator of the wind and Former of the mountains. For Your sake, Great One of counsel, Who humbles and uplifts. For Your sake, Speaker of righteousness, Teacher of upright principles. For Your sake, He Who knows and is witness, if a man would conceal himself in hidden places. For Your sake, He Who is One, and who can possibly respond to Him.

עִם im וּמִתְבָּרֵר umitbarer וְנַקִי עֵ"ה קס"א venaki יְיָ zach זָךְ lema'anach לְמַעַנְךָ

בָּרִים barim לְמַעַנְךָ lema'anach וְחֹפֵשׂ chofes מַצְפּוּן matzpun

וְחוֹקֵר vechoker כָּל kol ילי וְחֲדָרִים chadarim לְמַעַנְךָ lema'anach

טִפְחָה tipcha יְמִינוֹ yemino שָׁמַיִם shamayim י"פ טל, י"פ כוזו ve'asa וְעָשָׂה

מְאוֹרִים me'orim לְמַעַנְךָ lema'anach יָסַד yasad אֶרֶץ eretz

בַּצֻּרוֹת batzurot בִּקַע bike'a יְאוֹרִים ye'orim לְמַעַנְךָ lema'anach כַּבִּיר kabir

מְכֻבָּד mechubad בָּאוּרִים ba'urim לְמַעַנְךָ lema'anach כּוֹחַ ko'ach

לֹא lo יִתַּמּוּ yitamu שְׁנוֹתָיו shenotav לְדוֹר ledor דּוֹרִים dorim

הוֹשַׁעְנָא hosha'ana הוֹשַׁעְנָא hosha'ana

אָנָא ana ב"ן לכב הַמְיַוֵּד hameyached לִכְבוֹדוֹ lichvodo שֵׁמוֹת shemot

וַחֲמִשָּׁה chamisha הַקוֹנֶה hakone בְּעוֹלָמוֹ be'olamo קִנְיָנִים kinyanim

וַחֲמִשָּׁה chamisha הַיּוֹצֵר hayotzer בִּבְרִיּוֹתָיו bivriyotav גִּבּוֹרִים giborim

וַחֲמִשָּׁה chamisha הוֹשִׁיעֵנוּ hoshi'enu בְּהַקָּפַת behakafat פְּעָמִים pe'amim

וַחֲמִשָּׁה chamisha אָנָא ana ב"ן לכב קס"א, עֵ"ב זְכוֹר zechor אָב av עֵ"ה אוֹר יְהִי

כָּרַת karat בְּרִית berit בִּבְתָרִים bivtarim וַחֲמִשָּׁה chamisha

וְהֵשִׁיב veheshiv רְכוּשׁ rechush לִמְלָכִים limlachim וַחֲמִשָּׁה chamisha

וְחָנַן vechanan עַל al הֲפִיכַת hafichat עָרִים arim וַחֲמִשָּׁה chamisha

הוֹשִׁיעֵנוּ hoshi'enu בְּהַקָּפַת behakafat פְּעָמִים pe'amim וַחֲמִשָּׁה chamisha

---

For Your sake, Pure and Immaculate One, Who acts with integrity with those who are faithful. For Your sake, Searcher of the hidden and Prober of all chambers. For Your sake, He Whose right palm created the Heavens, and Who made the luminaries. For Your sake, He Who founded the earth; He Who is powerful with might, glorified by those residing in the valleys. For Your sake, He Whose years will not end for endless generations. Please save now. Please save now.

Please, He Who has set aside for His glory five Names; Who owns in His world possessions live; Who formed among His creatures five mighty ones; save us at the fifth circling. Please remember the patriarch (Abraham) who established a covenant with halves from five, and who returned the booty of five kings, and who beseeched regarding the destruction of five cities; save us at the fifth circling.

אָנָּא ana בִּ"ן לכב זְכוֹר zechor ע"ב קס"א, יהי אור ע"ה הַנֶּעֱקַד hane'ekad בְּהַר behar

מוֹר mor שְׁעָרִים she'arim כתר וַחֲמִשָּׁה chamisha ◆ יָרַשׁ yarash מִדּוֹרוֹ mehoro

בְּרָכוֹת berachot וַחֲמִשָּׁה chamisha ◆ וְהִשְׁלִים vehishlim נֶפֶשׁ nefesh

נְקוּבָה nekuva בְּשֵׁמוֹת beshemot וַחֲמִשָּׁה chamisha : הוֹשִׁיעֵנוּ hoshi'enu

בְּהַקָּפַת behakafat פְּעָמִים pe'amim וַחֲמִשָּׁה chamisha : אָנָּא ana בִּ"ן לכב

זְכוֹר zechor ע"ב קס"א, יהי אור ע"ה תָּם tam נָעֲשׂוּ na'asu לוֹ lo נִסִּים nisim

וַחֲמִשָּׁה chamisha ◆ וַיַּצֵּג vayatzeg מִבָּנָיו mibanav אֻזִּים achim

וַחֲמִשָּׁה chamisha ◆ כָּפְרוֹ kafro עֵת shat לְנָזִיר lenazir הַמַּחֲלִיף hamachalif

וַחֲמִשָּׁה chamisha : הוֹשִׁיעֵנוּ hoshi'enu בְּהַקָּפַת behakafat פְּעָמִים pe'amim

וַחֲמִשָּׁה chamisha : אָנָּא ana בִּ"ן לכב הַמַּנְחִילֵנוּ hamanchilenu

וַחֲמִשָּׁה chamisha ◆ סְפָרִים sefarim הַמַּשְׁמִיעֵנוּ hamashmi'enu

וַחֲמִשָּׁה chamisha ◆ בְּקוֹלוֹת bekolot דִּבְּרוֹתָיו dibrotav הַכְּתוּבִים haketuvim

עַל al הַלֻּוזוֹת haluchot chamisha וַחֲמִשָּׁה chamisha וַחֲמִשָּׁה : chamisha

הוֹשִׁיעֵנוּ hoshi'enu בְּהַקָּפַת behakafat פְּעָמִים pe'amim וַחֲמִשָּׁה chamisha :

הוֹשַׁעְנָא hosha'ana ◆ הוֹשַׁעְנָא hosha'ana :

בִּזְכוּת bizchut אַהֲרֹן Aharon, רוֹן ron, יָרוֹן yaron, עַמָּךְ amach

בְּאוֹמְרָם be'omram הוֹשַׁעְנָא hosha'ana ◆ נֻוזְתָּם nechtam בִּכְבוֹד bechavod בוכו,

בְּמִצְנֶפֶת bemitznefet נָאֶה na'a, לְשַׁמֵּשׁ leshamesh בִּכְהֻנָּה bichehuna ◆

בִּגְדֵי bigdei פְּאֵר pe'er, לְפָאֵר lefa'er, שִׁמְךָ shimcha לָבַשׁ lavash

בֶּאֱמוּנָה be'emuna ◆ הוֹדוֹ hodo אהיה הַרְאֵה har'e לְעָם le'am עלם, נִכְאֶה nich'e,

---

Please remember the bound one (Isaac) on Mount Moriah with five gates, who inherited form his father five blessings, and whose perfected soul is described by five names; save us at the fifth circling. Please remember the perfect one (Jacob) form whom were performed five miracles, and who presented from his sons five brothers; he transmitted his gifts to the one set apart who granted give outfits; save us at the fifth circling. Please He Who bequeathed to us the Law, Five Books; Who proclaimed to us His commandments through five sounds, which were written upon the Tablets upon each five; save us at the fifth circling.
In the merit of Aaron let joyfully sing out, Your people, when they say "Hosha'ana."
Sealed by honor in a fine mitre [in order] to serve in the priesthood. Magnificent vestments, to glorify Your Name, did he faithfully wore; demonstrate his glory to a downtrodden people,

רָם ram — שׁוֹכֵן shochen — בִּמְעוֹנָה bime'ona — וּבִזְכוּתוֹ uvizchuto,

תְּפִלָתוֹ tefilato, — תּוֹשִׁיעַ toshia — לְזַעֲמֶיךָ liz'umecha (לְאֵלוּ שֶׁזָּעַמְתָּ עֲלֵיהֶם)

זָכְרֵנוּ zochrenu — יְהֹוָה/אֲדֹנָי Adonai בְּהֵשׁ ע"ה, ע"ב בְּרִבּוּעַ וְקָסָא ע"ה, birtzon בִּרְצוֹן

אֵל שַׁדַּי ע"ה עַמֶּךָ amecha: — בִּגְדֵי bigdei — קֹדֶשׁ kodesh, — לָקַח lakach

לְקַדֵּשׁ lekadesh, — לְשָׁרֵת lesharet — בָּם bam מ"ב — לִפְנִים lifnim — לִפְנֵי lifnai

וּלְבָשָׁם ulvasham, — בְּבוֹאוֹ bevo'o — שָׁם sham, — כְּקָדוֹשׁ kekadosh

כְּמַלְאָךְ kemal'ach — יְהֹוָה/אֲדֹנָי Adonai — בְּקָרְבְּנוֹתָיו bekorbenotav

וְעוֹלוֹתָיו ve'olotav, — הָיָה haya יה"ה — מְכַפֵּר mechaper — עַל al — עֲוֹנָי avonai

תְּפִלוֹתָיו tefilotav, — וּתְחִנוֹתָיו utchinotav, — זְכוֹר zechor ע"ב קס"א, יְהִי אוֹר ע"ה

הַיּוֹם hayom נָגֶד, מִזְבֵּחַ, זָן, אֵל יהוה — לְעָם le'am עֹלָם — אֱמוּנַי emunai,

וְתִתָּעֵם vetita'em, — וְתַרְגִּיעֵם vetargi'em, — בְּמִקְדָּשׁ bemikdash

הֲדוֹמֶךָ hadomecha. — זָכְרֵנוּ zochrenu — יְהֹוָה/אֲדֹנָי Adonai

בִּרְצוֹן birtzon מֶהֵשׁ ע"ה, ע"ב בְּרִבּוּעַ וְקָסָא ע"ה, אֵל שַׁדַּי ע"ה עַמֶּךָ amecha:

תּוֹדִיעֵנִי todi'eni — אֹרַח orach — חַיִּים chayim וְזִיל אֶהְיֶה אַהְיֶה יהוה, בִּינָה ע"ה

שֹׂבַע sova — שְׂמָחוֹת semachot — אֶת et — פָּנֶיךָ panecha ס"ג מ"ה ב"ן

נְעִמוֹת ne'imot — בִּימִינְךָ bimincha — נֶצַח netzach:

וְחָסִין chasin — קָדוֹשׁ kadosh — בְּרוֹב berov פ"פ אֶהְיֶה — טוּבְךָ tuvcha לאו

נַהֵל nahel — עֲדָתֶךָ adatecha:

וזקב טנע

Exalted One, Who dwells in the Abode. And due to his merit and his prayer, save those who are the objects of Your anger. Remember us, Lord, when You favor Your people. Holy vestments did he take to become sanctified, to serve in them in the Innermost Sanctuary, and he donned them upon his entering there, as one who is holy, as an angel of the Lord. Through his sacrifices and his burnt offerings he would atone for his sins; his prayers and his pleas remember today for a faithful people. And may You transfer them and calm them in the Sanctuary, Your Footstool. Remember us, Lord, when You favor Your people.

*"You will show me the way of life, granting me the joy of your presence
and the pleasures of living with you forever." (Psalms 16:11)*

וזקב טנע *Invincible and Mighty One, with the abundance of Your goodness, govern Your congregation.*

THE SIXTH HAKAFAH (CIRCLING)—JOSEPH—YESOD

The speech of the *Hakafah* connects to *Binah* (the Surrounding of *Ima*) אל יוד הי ואו הי – ייא"י דס"ג.

The action of the *Hakafah* connects to Mercies of *Da'at* אל ויו יוד הי ואו הי יוד הא יוד (ג' יודין ע"ה).

And the man that circles (אדם=45) connects to the Six Edges of *Zeir Anpin*:

אל יוד הא ואו הא (45=מ"ה) (ג"פ אלף הא יוד הי היוצאים מג' אלפין דמ"ה).

Meditate to connect to energy of protection (מגן=93) through the three Names אל (=31).

אֶרְחַץ erchatz בְּנִקָּיוֹן benikayon כַּפַּי kapai וַאֲסֹבְבָה va'asoveva אֶת et

מִזְבַּחֲךָ mizbachacha נגד, זז, אל יהוה יְהֹוָה Adonai: לִשְׁמֹעַ lashmi'a

בְּקוֹל bekol תּוֹדָה toda וּלְסַפֵּר ulsaper כָּל kol יני נִפְלְאוֹתֶיךָ nifle'otecha:

הוֹשַׁעְנָא hosha'ana ◆ הוֹשַׁעְנָא hosha'ana:

לְמַעַנְךָ lema'anach אֱלֹהֵינוּ Elohenu לְמַעַנְךָ lema'anach: בּוֹרְאֵנוּ bor'enu:

לְמַעַנְךָ lema'anach גֹּאֲלֵנוּ go'alenu: לְמַעַנְךָ lema'anach דּוֹרְשֵׁנוּ dorshenu:

לְמַעַנְךָ lema'anach אַדִּיר adir הֲרֵי adirim אַדִּירִים: לְמַעַנְךָ lema'anach

בּוֹרֵא bore רוּחַ ruach וְיוֹצֵר veyotzer הָרִים harim: לְמַעַנְךָ lema'anach

גְּדוֹל gedol הָעֵצָה ha'etza ◆ מַשְׁפִּיל mashpil

וּמֵרִים umerim: לְמַעַנְךָ lema'anach דּוֹבֵר dover צֶדֶק tzedek מַגִּיד magid

מֵישָׁרִים mesharim: לְמַעַנְךָ lema'anach הַיּוֹדֵעַ hayode'a וָעֵד va'ed

אִם im יִסָּתֵר yisater: לְמַעַנְךָ lema'anach בַּמִּסְתָּרִים bamistarim: אִישׁ ish

וְהוּא vehu: לְמַעַנְךָ lema'anach בַּמִּסְתָּרִים bamistarim: אִישׁ ish

בְּאֶחָד be'echad וּמִי umi יְשִׁיבֶנּוּ yeshivenu אֲמָרִים amarim:

THE SIXTH HAKAFAH (CIRCLING)—JOSEPH—YESOD

"I shall wash my hands in purity and I shall circle around Your altar, Lord.
To proclaim in a voice of thankfulness, and to relate all Your wonders." (Psalms 26:6-7)
Please save now. Please save now.

For Your sake, our God. For Your sake, our Creator. For Your sake, our Redeemer. For Your sake, our Seeker. For Your sake, the Mightiest of the mighty. For Your sake, Creator of the wind and Former of the mountains. For Your sake, Great One of counsel, Who humbles and uplifts. For Your sake, Speaker of righteousness, Teacher of upright principles. For Your sake, He Who knows and is witness, if a man would conceal himself in hidden places. For Your sake, He Who is One, and who can possibly respond to Him.

im עִם umitbarer וּמִתְבָּרֵר venaki עֲ"ה קס"א וְנָקִי יי zach זָךְ lema'anach לְמַעֲנָךְ

matzpun מַצְפּוּן chofes וְחוֹפֵשׂ lema'anach לְמַעֲנָךְ barim בָּרִים

lema'anach לְמַעֲנָךְ chadarim וְחַדָרִים kol יל כָּל vechoker וְחוֹקֵר

ve'asa וְעָשָׂה כוזו ש"פ טל, שׁ"פ shamayim שָׁמַיִם yemino יְמִינוֹ tipcha טִפְחָה

eretz אֶרֶץ yasad יָסַד lema'anach לְמַעֲנָךְ me'orim מְאוֹרִים

kabir כַּבִּיר lema'anach לְמַעֲנָךְ ye'orim יְאוֹרִים bike'a בִּקַּע batzurot בַּצּוּרוֹת

lema'anach לְמַעֲנָךְ ba'urim בָּאוּרִים mechubad מְכֻבָּד ko'ach כֹּחַ

dorim דּוֹרִים ledor לְדוֹר shenotav שְׁנוֹתָיו yitamu יִתַּמּוּ lo לֹא

hosha'ana הוֹשַׁעֲנָא hosha'ana הוֹשַׁעֲנָא

beyamim בְּיָמִים olamo עוֹלָמוֹ habore הַבּוֹרֵא בַּ"ן לכב ana אָנָּא

tzela'ot צְלָעוֹת shesh שֵׁשׁ ס"א habone הַבּוֹנֶה shisha שִׁשָּׁה

serafim שְׂרָפִים hayotzer הַיּוֹצֵר shisha שִׁשָּׁה litzdadim לִצְדָדִים

behakafat בְּהַקָּפַת hoshi'enu הוֹשִׁיעֵנוּ shisha שִׁשָּׁה bichnafayim בִּכְנָפַיִם

pe'amim פְּעָמִים zechor זְכוֹר עֲ"ב קס"א, יהי אור ע"ה ana אָנָּא בַּ"ן לכב shisha שִׁשָּׁה pe'amim פְּעָמִים

acharei אַחֲרֵי shisha שִׁשָּׁה to'evot תּוֹעֵבוֹת zanach זָנַח av אָב

nata נָטַע shisha שִׁשָּׁה banim בָּנִים lo לוֹ noldu נוֹלְדוּ zekunav זְקֻנָיו

eshel אֶשֶׁל uvorach וּבֹרַךְ beketz בְּקֵץ מנק shanim שָׁנִים shisha שִׁשָּׁה

hoshi'enu הוֹשִׁיעֵנוּ behakafat בְּהַקָּפַת pe'amim פְּעָמִים shisha שִׁשָּׁה

For Your sake, Pure and Immaculate One, Who acts with integrity with those who are faithful. For Your sake, Searcher of the hidden and Prober of all chambers. For Your sake, He Whose right palm created the Heavens, and Who made the luminaries. For Your sake, He Who founded the earth; He Who is powerful with might, glorified by those residing in the valleys. For Your sake, He Whose years will not end for endless generations.

Please save now. Please save now.

Please, He Who created His world in six days; Who built six sides in six directions; Who formed the Serafim with six wings; save us at the sixth circling. Please remember the patriarch (Abraham) who abandoned six abominations; after his old age there were born to him six sons; he planted an eshel tree and was blessed at the end of six years; save us at the sixth circling. Please remember the one (Isaac) bound in the place of six arrangements; You shielded him and You protected him from six difficulties; he dug pools of water for they who expounded upon them six levels; save us at the sixth circling.

אָנָּא *ana* בֵּ"ן לכב זְכוֹר *zechor* ע"ב קס"א, יהי אור ע"ה

הַנֶּעֱקַד *hane'ekad* בִּמְקוֹם *bimkom* מַעֲרָכוֹת *ma'arachot* שִׁשָׁה *shisha*◆

גּוֹנַנְתּוֹ *gonanto* וּמִלַּטְתּוֹ *umilateto* מִצָּרוֹת *mitzarot* שִׁשָׁה *shisha*◆ כָּרָה *kara*

מִקְוָאוֹת *mikva'ot* לְדוֹרְשֵׁי *ledorshei* בָּם *bam* מ"ב מַעֲלוֹת *ma'alot*

:שִׁשָׁה *shisha* הוֹשִׁיעֵנוּ *hoshi'enu* בְּהַקָּפַת *behakafat* פְּעָמִים *pe'amim*

:שִׁשָׁה *shisha* אָנָּא *ana* בֵּ"ן לכב זְכוֹר *zechor* ע"ב קס"א, יהי אור ע"ה תָּם *tam*

הוֹלִיד *holid* מִן *min* הַבְּכִירָה *habchira* שִׁשָׁה *shisha*◆ וְצִוָּה *vetziva*

קָחַת *kachat* מִנְחָה *mincha* מִבִּינִים *miminim* שִׁשָׁה *shisha*◆ וְהִגְבִּיר *vehigbir*

אָבִי *avi* שִׁשָׁה *shisha* הַמְבוֹרָכִים *hamvorachim* בְּשִׁשָׁה *beshisha*:

הוֹשִׁיעֵנוּ *hoshi'enu* בְּהַקָּפַת *behakafat* פְּעָמִים *pe'amim* שִׁשָׁה *shisha*:

אָנָּא *ana* בֵּ"ן לכב הַמְּחַבֵּר *hamechaber* לָאֵפוֹד *la'efod* שֵׁמוֹת *shemot* שִׁשָׁה *shisha*◆

הַמַּצִּיל *hamatzil* נְפָשׁוֹת *nefashot* בְּעָרֵי *be'arei* מִקְלָט *miklat* שִׁשָׁה *shisha*◆

הַמּוֹרִישֵׁנוּ *hamorishenu* וְזִכְבַת *chochmat* סְדָרִים *sedarim* שִׁשָׁה *shisha*:

הוֹשִׁיעֵנוּ *hoshi'enu* בְּהַקָּפַת *behakafat* פְּעָמִים *pe'amim* שִׁשָׁה *shisha*:

הוֹשַׁעֲנָא *hosha'ana*◆ הוֹשַׁעֲנָא *hosha'ana*:

זְכוּת *zechut* נִשְׁמַר *nishmar*, בְּרִית *berit* שָׁמַר *shamar*, בְּמִדַּת *bemidat*

הַיְסוֹד *haYesod* ההע וְחָתוּם *chatum*◆ לִמְלֹךְ *limloch* זָכָה *zacha*,

וּבְמַלְכוּתָה *uvimlucha*, לוֹ *lo* נִגְלָה *nigla* כֹּל *kol* יְלי סָתוּם *satum*◆

וּבִזְכוּתוֹ *uvizchuto*, לְאֻמָּתוֹ *le'umato*, גָּלָה *gale* קֵץ *ketz* מנק

הֶחָתוּם *hechatum*◆ וְתִרְדּוֹף *vetirdof*, וְגַם *vegam* תַּהֲדוֹף *tahadof*,

לִרְשָׁעִים *lirsha'im* יְסִיתוּם *yesitum*◆ זְכוּת *zechut* אָבוֹת *avot*,

רוֹכֵב *rochev* עֲרָבוֹת *aravot*, זְכוֹר *zechor* ע"ב קס"א, יהי אור ע"ה

הַיּוֹם *hayom* נגד, זז, מזבות, אל יהוה לְרוֹמְמֶךָ *leromemecha*◆

Please remember the perfect one (Jacob) who begot from the six eldest; and who commanded to bring a gift of six species; and gave might to he who fathered six; who are blessed with six; save us at the sixth circling. Please, He Who attached to the ephod the six Names; He Who saves lives through cities of refuge that were six; He Who bequeathed to us the wisdom of six orders; save us at the sixth circling. The merit of the one who was guarded, who guarded the covenant; with the attribute of Yesod was he sealed, his merited to reign, and in this kingdom to him was revealed all that is hidden. And in his merit, to his people revealed the sealed end; and may You pursue and also drive away the wicked who seduce them. The merit of the Fathers, You Who dwell in the Heavens, remember today for those who exalt You.

זָכְרֵנוּ zochrenu יְהֹוָה Adonai birtzon בִּרְצוֹן מהע ע״ה, ע״ב ברריבוע וקס״א ע״ה,

אל עדי ע״ה קנאה amecha עַמֶּךָ bizchut בִּזְכוּת Yosef יוֹסֵף ציון, ר״פ יהוה, קנאה

הֱיֵה heye יהה me'asef מְאַסֵף nachalatcha נַחֲלָתְךָ bevet בְּבֵית ב״פ ראה

קָדְשֶׁךָ kodshecha urtze וּרְצֵה El אֵל ייא״י (מילוי דס״ג) וָוֹ chai,

בְּנִיחוֹחַי benichochai tefilat תְּפִלַּת am עַם mekudashecha מִקְדָּשֶׁךָ

וּבְרִיתוֹ uvrito, וּזְכוּתוֹ uzchuto, זְכוֹר zechor ע״ב קס״א, יהי אור ע״ה le'am לְעַם עלם

מִגְּרָשֶׁךָ megorashecha chotmem וְחׇתְמֵם legila לְגִילָה vetzahala וְצׇהֳלָה,

וְקַבְּצֵם vekabtzem lemigrashecha לְמִגְרָשֶׁךָ hosha'ana הוֹשַׁעְנָא,

וְרַחֵם verachem אברהם, וז״פ אל, רי״ו ול״ב נתיבות החוכמה, רמ״וז (אברים), עסמ״ב וט״ז אותיות פשוטות

נָא na בִּזְכוּתוֹ bizchuto le'umecha לְאַמִּיךָ זָכְרֵנוּ zochrenu יְהֹוָה Adonai

birtzon בִּרְצוֹן מהע ע״ה, ע״ב ברריבוע וקס״א ע״ה, אל עדי ע״ה amecha עַמֶּךָ

זְכוּת zechut Pinchas פִּינְחָס hameyuchas הַמְּיוּחָס lemidat לְמִדַּת tzadik צַדִּיק

יְסוֹד yesod ההע olam עוֹלָם, livrit לִבְרִית kineh קִנֵּא, vayfalel וַיְפַלֵּל

עַם im קוֹנֶה kone, הַמֵּבִיא hamevi bemishpat בְּמִשְׁפָּט ע״ה ה״פ אלהים al עַל

כׇּל kol ; ילי עמם נֶעְלָם ne'elam vate'atzar וַתֵּעָצַר mishlachat מִשְׁלַוֹּת

צַר tzar, וְהוּא vehu נִתְבַּצַּר nitbatzar berum בְּרוּם olam עוֹלָם ר״ת ע״ב,

הֲגַם hagam רם (לא כולל אהיה). ♦ברום עולם = קס״א קנ״א קמ״ג וג״כ halom הֲלוֹם,

בְּרִית berit shalom שָׁלוֹם, chayim וְחַיִּים אהיה אהיה יהוה, בינה ע״ה

לְעֲדָתוֹ la'adato, karev קָרֵב ketz קֵץ מנק yeminecha יְמִינֶךָ

לַעֲדָתוֹ, ve'elom וְעֵלוֹם, lichhunat לְכׇהֳנַת olam עוֹלָם uvizchuto וּבִזְכוּתוֹ

Remember us, Lord, when You favor Your people.
In the merit of Joseph, may You gather Your heritage into Your Holy Sanctuary; and find favor, Living God, in my pleasing offerings, the prayers of a people that You sanctify. His covenant and his merit remember for Your exiled people; seal for joy and exultation and assemble them to Your expanse. Save please, be merciful, please, in his merit, to Your people. Remember us, Lord, when You favor Your people.
The merit of Pinchas,
of lineage to the attribute of the righteous one, foundation of the world, who was zealous for the covenant and who then prayed to the Creator, Who brings to justice for every hidden sin. And the mission of the aggressor was halted, and he was fortified in the heights of the universe, now, too, the covenant of peace, life and concealment, the priesthood forever. And in his merit, for his congregation, bring near the end of Your right hand.

זָכְרֵנוּ zochrenu   יְהֹוָה Adonai   בִּרְצוֹן birtzon   מהש׳ ע״ה,

בְּזָכוּת bizchut   עַמָּךְ amecha: ע״ב בריבוע וקס״א ע״ה, אל שדי ע״ה,   מִקַנֵּא mekane,

הֱיֵה heye   יהה one,   עוֹנֶה one,   לְשַׁוְעַת leshavat   מִקְדָּשֶׁיךָ mekudashecha◆

אַל El retze   רְצֵה retze   יא״י (מילוי דס״ג)   וְזֵי chai,   בְּנִיחוֹחַי benichochai,

וְזֶה vese   לְאִשֶּׁךָ le'ishecha◆   לָחְמִי lachmi   קָרְבְּנִי korbani   לְזִבְחִי חֵלֶף chelef

פְּזוּרָה pezura,   שַׁי shai   לַמּוֹרָא lamora,   יוֹבִילוּ yovilu   אֵל el   נְוֵה neve

קָדְשֶׁךָ kodshecha◆   וְחָתְמֵם chotmem   לְגִילָה legila,   וְצָהֳלָה vetzahala,

וְקַבְּצֵם vekabetzem   לְמִגְרָשֶׁיךָ lemigrashecha◆   הוֹשַׁעְנָא hosha'ana,

וְרַחֵם verachem   אברהם, וז״פ אל, רי״ו ול״ב נתיבות החכמה, רמ׳ו׳י (אברים), עסמ״ב וט״ו אותיות פשוטות

נָא na,   לְכָנָה lechana   אֲשֶׁר asher   נָטְעָה nata

יְמִינֶךָ yeminecha◆   זָכְרֵנוּ zochrenu   יְהֹוָה Adonai

בִּרְצוֹן birtzon   מהש׳ ע״ה, ע״ב בריבוע וקס״א ע״ה, אל שדי ע״ה,   עַמָּךְ amecha:

תּוֹדִיעֵנִי todi'eni   אֹרַח orach   וְזִיִים chayim   אהיה אהיה יהוה, בינה ע״ה

שֹׂבַע sova   שְׂמָחוֹת semachot   אֶת et   פָּנֶיךָ panecha   ס״ג מ״ה ב״ן

נְעִמוֹת ne'imot   בִּימִינְךָ bimincha   נֶצַח netzach:

יָחִיד yachid   גֵּאֶה ge'e◆   לְעַמָּךְ le'amcha   פְּנֵה pene   ע״ב ס״ג

זוֹכְרֵי zochrei   קְדוּשָׁתֶךָ kedusatecha:

יגל פזק

Remember us, Lord, when You favor Your people.

In the merit of the zealous one may You answer the cry of the people that You sanctifies; accept favorably, Living God, the pleasing offerings in place of my sacrifice the food of Your fire-offering. And the scattered sheep, a gift for the Awesome One, shall they bring up to Your Holy Sanctuary, seal for joy and exultation and assemble them to Your expanse. Save please and be merciful now, to the foundation that Your right hand has established. Remember us, Lord, when You favor Your people.

"You will show me the way of life, granting me the joy of your presence
and the pleasures of living with you forever." (Psalms 16:11)

יגל פזק *Sole and proud One, turn to Your people, those who remember Your sanctity.*

THE SEVENTH HAKAFAH (CIRCLING)—DAVID—MALCHUT

The speech of the *Hakafah* connects to *Binah* (the Surrounding of *Ima*) אל יוד הי ואו הי – ייא"י דס"ג.

The action of the *Hakafah* connects to Mercies of *Da'at*:

אל ג"פ יוד הה וו = קכ"ו = א אד אדנ אדנ"י (*Keter* for *Nukva*).

And the man that circles (אדם=45) connects to the Six Edges of *Zeir Anpin*:

אל יוד הא ואו הא (45=מ"ה) (קנ"א קנ"א קנ"א היוצאים מג' אלפין דמ"ה).

Meditate to connect to energy of protection (מגן =93) through the three Names אל (=31).

אֶרְחַץ erchatz בְּנִקָּיוֹן benikayon כַּפָּי kapai וַאֲסֹבְבָה va'asoveva אֶת et

מִזְבַּחֲךָ mizbachacha נגד, ז"ן, אל יהוה יְהֹוָ(אדניאהדונהי) Adonai לַשְׁמִעַ lashmi'a

בְּקוֹל bekol תּוֹדָה toda וּלְסַפֵּר ulsaper כָּל kol יל נִפְלְאוֹתֶיךָ nifle'otecha

הוֹשַׁעֲנָא hosha'ana • הוֹשַׁעֲנָא hosha'ana

לְמַעֲנָךְ lema'anach אֱלֹהֵינוּ Elohenu ילה לְמַעֲנָךְ lema'anach בּוֹרְאֵנוּ bor'enu

לְמַעֲנָךְ lema'anach גּוֹאֲלֵנוּ go'alenu לְמַעֲנָךְ lema'anach דּוֹרְשֵׁנוּ dorshenu

לְמַעֲנָךְ lema'anach אַדִּיר adir הרי אַדִּירִים adirim הרי לְמַעֲנָךְ lema'anach

בּוֹרֵא bore רוּחַ ru'ach וְיוֹצֵר veyotzer הָרִים harim לְמַעֲנָךְ lema'anach

גָּדוֹל gedol להוו, ועם ד' אותיות מבה, יזל, אום הָעֵצָה ha'etza • מַשְׁפִּיל mashpil

וּמֵרִים umerim לְמַעֲנָךְ lema'anach דּוֹבֵר dover צֶדֶק tzedek מַגִּיד magid

מֵישָׁרִים mesharim לְמַעֲנָךְ lema'anach הַיּוֹדֵעַ hayode'a וָעֵד va'ed

אִם im יוהך, מ"א אותיות דפשוט, דמילוי ודמילוי דמילוי דאהיה ע"ה יְסַתֵּר yisater ב"פ מצר

אִישׁ ish בַּמִּסְתָּרִים bamistarim לְמַעֲנָךְ lema'anach וְהוּא vehu

בְּאֶחָד be'echad אהבה, דאגה יל וּמִי umi אֲמָרִים amarim יְשִׁיבֵנוּ yeshivenu אֲמָרִים amarim

---

THE SEVENTH HAKAFAH (CIRCLING)—DAVID—MALCHUT

"I shall wash my hands in purity and I shall circle around Your altar, Lord. To proclaim in a voice of thankfulness, and to relate all Your wonders." (Psalms 26:6-7)

Please save now. Please save now.

For Your sake, our God. For Your sake, our Creator. For Your sake, our Redeemer. For Your sake, our Seeker. For Your sake, the Mightiest of the mighty. For Your sake, Creator of the wind and Former of the mountains. For Your sake, Great One of counsel, Who humbles and uplifts. For Your sake, Speaker of righteousness, Teacher of upright principles. For Your sake, He Who knows and is witness, if a man would conceal himself in hidden places. For Your sake, He Who is One, and who can possibly respond to Him.

לְמַעֲנָךְ lema'anach — זָךְ zach — וְנָקִי venaki יײ — עײה קסײא וּמִתְבָּרֵר umitbarer — עִם im

בָּרִים barim: — לְמַעֲנָךְ lema'anach — וְחוֹפֵשׂ chofes — מִצָּפוּן matzpun◆

וְחוֹקֵר vechoker — כָּל kol ילי — וְזְדָרִים chadarim: — לְמַעֲנָךְ lema'anach

טִפְּחָה tipecha — יְמִינוּ yemino — שָׁמַיִם shamayim יײפ טל, יײפ כוזו — וְעָשָׂה ve'asa◆

מְאוֹרִים me'orim: — לְמַעֲנָךְ lema'anach — יָסַד yasad — אֶרֶץ eretz◆

בָּצוּרוֹת batzurot — בִּקַע bike'a — יְאוֹרִים ye'orim: — לְמַעֲנָךְ lema'anach — כַּבִּיר kabir

כּוֹן ko'ach◆ — מְכֻבָּד mechubad — בָּאוּרִים ba'urim: — לְמַעֲנָךְ lema'anach

לֹא lo — יִתַּמּוּ yitamu — שְׁנוֹתָיו shenotav — לְדוֹר ledor — דוֹרִים dorim:

הוֹשַׁעֲנָא hosha'ana◆ — הוֹשַׁעֲנָא hosha'ana:

אָנָּא ana בײן, לכב ריבוע דסײג וײ אותיות — הַמַּקְדִּים hamakdim — לְעוֹלָם la'olam

דְּבָרִים devarim ראה — שִׁבְעָה shiv'a◆ — הַסּוֹדֵר hasoder — בְּרֵאשִׁית bereshit

לְיָמִים leyamim גלך — הַנֹּטֶה hanote — שָׁמַיִם shamayim יײפ טל, יײפ כוזו — שִׁבְעָה shiv'a◆

שִׁבְעָה shiv'a◆ — וְרוֹקַע veroka — אֲרָצוֹת aratzot — שִׁבְעָה shiv'a◆

הוֹשִׁיעֵנוּ hoshi'enu — בַּחֲגִיגַת bachagigat — יָמִים yamim גלך — שִׁבְעָה shiv'a

וּבְהַקָּפַת uvhakafat — פְּעָמִים pe'amim — שִׁבְעָה shiv'a: — אָנָּא ana בײן, לכב

זְכוֹר zechor עײב קסײא, יהי אור עײה — אָב av — הַבְטַחְתּוֹ hivtachto

לָרֶשֶׁת lareshet — אַרְצוֹת artzot — עֲמָמִים amamim — שִׁבְעָה shiv'a◆

For Your sake, Pure and Immaculate One, Who acts with integrity with those who are faithful. For Your sake, Searcher of the hidden and Prober of all chambers. For Your sake, He Whose right palm created the Heavens, and Who made the luminaries. For Your sake, He Who founded the earth; He Who is powerful with might, glorified by those residing in the valleys. For Your sake, He Whose years will not end for endless generations.

Please save now. Please save now.

Please, He Who preceded the world

by seven things, Who set up Creation in seven days; Who stretched out seven Heavens and Who spread out seven continents, save us on the celebration of seven days and at the seventh circling. Please remember the patriarch (Abraham) to whom You promised he would inherit the lands of seven nations;

(מצוות) תרי"ג = במילוי lechochma לְוֹזִכְמָה ראה ב"פ bayit בֵּית bana בָּנָה

berit בְּרִית karat כָּרַת shiv'a ◦ שִׁבְעָה amudeha עַמוּדֶיהָ vechatzav וְוֹצֵב

hoshi'enu הוֹשִׁיעֵנוּ shiv'a ◦ שִׁבְעָה bichvasot בִּכְבָשׂוֹת lenagid לְנַגִּיד

uvhakafat וּבַהַקָּפַת shiv'a נלך שִׁבְעָה yamim יָמִים bachagigat בַּוֹזֲגִיגַת

pe'amim פְּעָמִים shiv'a שִׁבְעָה ana אָנָּא: ב"ן, לכב zechor זְכוֹר ע"ב קס"א, יהי אור ע"ה

shiv'a ◦ שִׁבְעָה yamim נלך יָמִים leketz מנק לְקֵץ bisarto בִּשַּׂרְתּוֹ yachid יְוֹזִיד

shiv'a ◦ שִׁבְעָה leharim לֶהָרִים shevi'i שְׁבִיעִי har הַר al עַל huala הוּעֲלָה

samach שָׂמַוֹז עם ה' אותיות = ב"פ קס"א vayikra וַיִּקְרָא mayim מִים bemotz'o בְּמֹצְאוֹ

bachagigat בַּוֹזֲגִיגַת hoshi'enu הוֹשִׁיעֵנוּ shiv'a ◦ שִׁבְעָה ota אוֹתָהּ

pe'amim פְּעָמִים uvhakafat וּבַהַקָּפַת shiv'a שִׁבְעָה נלך yamim יָמִים

tam תָּם zechor זְכוֹר ב"ן, לכב ana אָנָּא: shiv'a שִׁבְעָה

shiv'a ◦ שִׁבְעָה pe'amim פְּעָמִים artza אַרְצָה hamishtachave הַמִּשְׁתַּוֹזֲוֶה

tzadik צַדִּיק yipol יִפּוֹל sheva שֶׁבַע shem שֵׁם al עַל

bishnei בִּשְׁנֵי tzerafto צְרַפְתּוֹ shiv'a ◦ שִׁבְעָה vakam וְקָם

shiv'a ◦ שִׁבְעָה vera'av וְרֶעָב shiv'a שִׁבְעָה sava שָׂבָע

shiv'a נלך שִׁבְעָה yamim יָמִים bachagigat בַּוֹזֲגִיגַת hoshi'enu הוֹשִׁיעֵנוּ

ana אָנָּא: ב"ן, לכב shiv'a שִׁבְעָה pe'amim פְּעָמִים uvhakafat וּבַהַקָּפַת

shiv'a ◦ שִׁבְעָה leyamim נלך לְיָמִים Shabbat שַׁבָּת hamanchilenu הַמַּנְוֹזִילֵנוּ

shiv'a ◦ שִׁבְעָה leshanim לְשָׁנִים hashemita הַשְּׁמִטָּה ushnat וּשְׁנַת

shiv'a ◦ שִׁבְעָה shavu'im שָׁבוּעִים leketz מנק לְקֵץ hayovel הַיּוֹבֵל ushnat וּשְׁנַת

---

who built a house of wisdom and hewed its seven pillars, and who established a covenant with the ruler by means of seven sheep, save us on the celebration of seven days and at the seventh circling. Please remember the one (Isaac) to whom You gave tiding at the end of seven days; he was brought up on the seventh mountain of seven mountains; he rejoiced when he discovered water and he called it Shiva, save us on the celebration of seven days and at the seventh circling. Please remember the perfect one (Jacob) who prostrated himself to the ground seven times; based on the verse: "the righteous one who will fall seven times and arise seven," (Proverbs 24:16); You purified him during the seven years of plenty and of seven hunger, save us on the celebration of seven days and at the seventh circling. Please, He Who has bequeathed to us the Sabbath, at seven days; and the Sabbatical year, at seven years; and the Jubilee year at the end of seven Sabbaticals,

hoshi'enu הוֹשִׁיעֵנוּ bachagigat בַּחֲגִיגַת yamim יָמִים גלך shiv'a שִׁבְעָה

uvhakafat וּבְהַקָּפַת pe'amim פְּעָמִים shiv'a שִׁבְעָה: ana אָנָּא ב"ן, לכב

hachokek הַחוֹקֵק zeman זְמַן cherutenu וְחֵרוּתֵנוּ yamim יָמִים גלך

vechag וְחַג habikurim הַבִּכּוּרִים leshavuim לְשָׁבוּעִים shiv'a שִׁבְעָה♦

velulav וְלוּלָב וחג, בינה, ע"ה, אהיה יהוה shiv'a שִׁבְעָה♦

vesuka וְסוּכָה סאל (יאהדונהי) venisuch וְנִסּוּךְ hamayim הַמַּיִם vechag וְחַג

hoshi'enu הוֹשִׁיעֵנוּ bachagigat בַּחֲגִיגַת yamim יָמִים גלך shiv'a שִׁבְעָה♦

uvhakafat וּבְהַקָּפַת pe'amim פְּעָמִים shiv'a שִׁבְעָה♦ shiv'a שִׁבְעָה:

zechor זְכוֹר segen סֶגֶן ע"ב קס"א, יהי אור ע"ה asher אֲשֶׁר nigen נִגֵּן alei עֲלֵי

asor עָשׂוֹר vegam וְגַם nevel נֶבֶל♦ beshirotav בְּשִׁירוֹתָיו

uzmirotav וּזְמִירוֹתָיו yehodun יְהוֹדוּן lach לָךְ bechol בְּכָל לכב tevel תֵּבֵל ב"פ

nimshach נִמְשַׁח lach לָךְ venegdach וְנֶגְדָּךְ זָן, מזבח, אל יהוה shach שָׁח♦ ר"ו

neso נְשׂוֹא lach לָךְ ol עוֹל vegam וְגַם sevel סֵבֶל♦ pede פְּדֵה neche'a נְכֵאָה♦ נשוא

mekora'a מְקוֹרָאָה♦ lecha לָךְ nachala נַחֲלָה vegam וְגַם chevel וְחֶבֶל♦

lehoshi'ah לְהוֹשִׁיעָה יהוה ש"ע נהורין lehargi'ah לְהַרְגִּיעָה♦ tigale תִּגָּלֶה

mimeromecha מִמְּרוֹמֶךָ♦ zochrenu זָכְרֵנוּ Adonai יְהֹוָה(אֲדֹנָי)אהדונהי birtzon בִּרְצוֹן

amecha עַמֶּךָ: מהע ע"ה, ע"ב בריבוע וקס"א ע"ה, אל שדי ע"ה bizchut בִּזְכוּת David דָּוִד,

ish אִישׁ yedid יְדִיד nechtam נֶחְתָּם bechter בְּכֶתֶר malchutecha מַלְכוּתְךָ♦

terachem תְּרַחֵם ג"פ רי"ו ; אברהם, וז"פ אל, רי"ו ול"ב נתיבות החכמה, רמ"ח (אברים), עסמ"ב וט"ז

vegam וְגַם tenachem תְּנַחֵם amecha עַמְּךָ venachalatecha וְנַחֲלָתְךָ♦ אותיות פשוטות

---

save us on the celebration of seven days and at the seventh circling. Please, He Who has enacted the time of our freedom seven days; and the Festival of the First Fruits after seven weeks; and the Lulav, and the Festival and the Sukkah, and the seven libations of water, save us on the celebration of seven days and at the seventh circling. Recall the monarch (King David) who played music upon the ten-stringed harp and also the lyre; with his songs and melodies they will praise You throughout the world. For You was he anointed and before You did he bow, carrying Your yoke as well as burden, redeem the downtrodden one that is referred to as Your heritage and also lot. To deliver her and to calm her, may You be revealed for Your heights. Remember us, Lord, when You favor Your people. In the merit of David, a man beloved, sealed with the crown of Your Kingdom, may you have mercy and also console Your people and Your heritage.

בִּזְכוּתוֹ bizchuto ,הַרְאֵה har'e ,לְעָם le'am עלם, נִכְאֶה nich'e ,בִּנְיַן binyan

,אָבוֹת avot וּזְכוּת uzchut ,וּנְוָתֶךָ unvatecha ◆ ראה ב״פ בֵּיתֶךָ betcha

נָא na ע״ה, יְהִי אוֹר קס״א, ע״ב זְכוֹר zechor ,מֵעֲרָבוֹת me'aravot

בִּזְכוּת bizchut ,וְנַשְׂאֵם venase'em ,וְנַטְלֵם venatelem ◆ la'adatecha לַעֲדָתֶךָ

אֲדֹנָי Adonai יְהֹוָה(אלהים יאהדונהי) zochrenu זָכְרֵנוּ ◆ temimecha תְּמִימֶיךָ shiv'a שִׁבְעָה

:amecha עַמֶּךָ ע״ה שדי אל ע״ה, וקס״א בריבוע ע״ב ע״ה, מהע birtzon בִּרְצוֹן

ילה Elohenu אֱלֹהֵינוּ ,אדני אהיה אלהים, לָנוּ lanu ע״ה אוֹר יְהִי קס״א, ע״ב zechor זְכוֹר

◆ umigiz'o וּמִגִּזְעוֹ ◆ Yishai יִשַׁי beno בְּנוֹ David דָּוִד zechut זְכוּת

◆ megorashai מְגוֹרָשַׁי et אֶת lekabetz לְקַבֵּץ ,choter חֹטֶר tetzav תְּצַו וְחֹטֶר

ve'et וְאֶת banai בָּנַי ve'et וְאֶת ,nidcho נִדְחוֹ esof אֱסוֹף ,uvizchuto וּבִזְכוּתוֹ

vedivrei וְדִבְרֵי ,bemalchutecha בְּמַלְכוּתֶךָ venagila וְנָגִילָה ◆ nashai נָשַׁי

Adonai אֲדֹנָי יְהֹוָה(אלהים יאהדונהי) zochrenu זָכְרֵנוּ ◆ nifle'otecha נִפְלְאֹתֶיךָ

:amecha עַמֶּךָ ע״ה שדי אל ע״ה, וקס״א בריבוע ע״ב ע״ה, מהע birtzon בִּרְצוֹן

ע״ה בינה יהוה, אהיה אהיה chayim וְחַיִּים orach אֹרַח todi'eni תּוֹדִיעֵנִי

ב״ן מ״ה ס״ג panecha פָּנֶיךָ et אֶת semachot שְׂמָחוֹת sova שֹׂבַע

:netzach נֶצַח bimincha בִּימִינְךָ ne'imot נְעִמוֹת

◆ tza'akatenu צַעֲקָתֵנוּ ushma וּשְׁמַע ◆ kabel קַבֵּל shavatenu שַׁוְעָתֵנוּ

:ta'alumot תַּעֲלוּמוֹת yode'a יוֹדֵעַ

שֹׂקוּ צִ״ת

In his merit show to a downtrodden people the rebuilding of Your House and Your dwelling place;
and the merit of the Fathers from the Heavens, please remember for Your congregation. Take them and carry
them in the merit of Your seven perfect ones. Remember us, Lord, when You favor Your people. Remember
for us, our God, the merit of David son of Yishai; and from his stock, command his bud to gather my
banished ones. And in his merit, gather his dispersion, and my children and my women; and let us rejoice
in Your kingdom and on account of Your wonders. Remember us, Lord, when You favor Your people.

"You will show me the way of life, granting me the joy of your presence
and the pleasures of living with you forever." (Psalms 16:11)

שֹׂקוּ צִ״ת *Accept our cry and hear our wail, You that knows all that is hidden.*

הוֹשַׁעְנָא hosha'ana • hosha'ana הוֹשַׁעְנָא:

אָנָּא ana בְּ"ן לכב הוֹשִׁיעָה hoshi'a יהוה ש"ע נהורין נָא na: (X2)

אָנָּא ana בְּ"ן לכב יַשֵׁר yasher עַם am בָּא ba • בְּהוֹשַׁעְנָא beHosha'ana

רַבָּא Raba קְנָ"א בְּ"ן, יהוה אלהים יהוה אדני, מילוי קס"א וס"ג, מ"ה ברבוע וע"ב ע"ה•

לְסַלְסְלָךְ lesalselach בְּוֹזְבָה bechiba • אֵל El יא"י (מילוי דס"ג) בְּוֹשִׁיעִי moshi'i:

וְוֹזִיעַ vechish נָא na פִּדְיוֹם pidyom • אֵל El יא"י (מילוי דס"ג) נוֹרָא nora

וְאָיוֹם ve'ayom • וּבִירוּשָׁלַיִם uvirushalayim כְּהַיּוֹם kehayom נגד, מזבוז, זן, אל יהוה•

נְהַלְלָךְ nehalelach בְּיוֹם beyom נגד, מזבוז, זן, אל יהוה • שְׁבִיעִי shevi'i•

הוֹשִׁיעָה hoshi'a יהוה ש"ע נהורין נָא na:

אָנָּא ana בְּ"ן לכב הוֹשִׁיעָה hoshi'a יהוה ש"ע נהורין נָא na: (X2)

אָנָּא ana בְּ"ן לכב סוּזֶה seche נָא na כָּלִיל kalil • מַמְלְכוֹת mamlechot

הָאֱלִיל ha'elil • וְאָרוֹן ve'aron עֲלֵי alei וְזְלִיל chalil • בְּוֹזֹג bechag

עַעֲשׁוּעִי sha'ashu'i • פְּדוּתִי peduti רָאָה ra'a ראה • וְגַם vegam גָּאֹה ga'o

גָּאֹה ga'a • וּבִירוּשָׁלַיִם uvirushalayim לְשָׁנָה leshana הַבָּאָה haba'a•

נְהַלְלָךְ nehalelach בְּיוֹם beyom נגד, מזבוז, זן, אל יהוה • שְׁבִיעִי shevi'i•

הוֹשִׁיעָה hoshi'a יהוה ש"ע נהורין נָא na:

אָנָּא ana בְּ"ן לכב הוֹשִׁיעָה hoshi'a יהוה ש"ע נהורין נָא na: (X2)

אָנָּא ana בְּ"ן לכב בְּנֵה bene שַׁעַר sha'ar הַשִּׁיר hashir • וְשָׁם vesham

לְךָ lecha אַשִּׁיר ashir • וְגַם vegam שַׁי shai לָךְ lecha שַׁי shai • אַתְשִׁיר atshir•

אֵל El יא"י (מילוי דס"ג) מַרְגוֹעִי margo'i • בְּקַבְּצְךָ bekabetzcha נָאֲנָקִים ne'enakim•

Save please. Save please.
Please bring salvation now. (X2)
Please set straight people that come on Hoshana Raba,
to exalt You out of love, God, my savior; please hurry redemption, awesome and fearsome God, and even
today in Jerusalem let us praise You on the seventh day. Please save now. Please bring salvation now. (X2)
Please, please totally remove the kingdoms of the gods and I shall sing out, accompanied by the flute
on the festival of my delight; He saw my redemption and He was exalted over the exalted, in Jerusalem
next year; let us praise You on the seventh day. Please save now. Please bring salvation now. (X2)
Please rebuild the gate of the song and there I shall sing
and also shall I present You with a gift, God of my serenity; when You gather those who are groaning

מִמֶּרְחַקִּים mimerchakim◆ וְסֻכָּתְךָ vesukatcha תָּקִים takim◆

נְהַלֶּלָךְ nehalelach בְּיוֹם beyom נֶגֶד, מִזְבֵּחַ, זָן, אֵל יהוה שְׁבִיעִי shevi'i◆

הוֹשִׁיעָה hoshi'a יהוה ע"ע נהורין נָא na:

אָנָּא ana בְּ"ן לכב הוֹשִׁיעָה hoshi'a יהוה ע"ע נהורין נָא na: (X2)

אָנָּא ana בְּ"ן לכב רְצֵה retze נָא na◆ וְקוֹמֵם vekomem◆ הַר har

הַשָּׁמֵם hashamem◆ וּמִגְדָּלְךָ umigdalcha תְּרוֹמֵם teromem◆ וְגַלֵּה vegaleh

קֵץ ketz מנק יִשְׁעִי yish'i◆ רוֹמְמוּתְךָ romemutcha הַרְאֵה har'e לְעַם le'am עלם

הַנִּכְאֶה hanich'e◆ וּמוּלְךָ umulcha יֵרָאֶה yera'e רי"ו ראה◆ נְהַלֶּלָךְ nehalelach

בְּיוֹם beyom נֶגֶד, מִזְבֵּחַ, זָן, אֵל יהוה שְׁבִיעִי shevi'i◆ הוֹשִׁיעָה hoshi'a יהוה ע"ע נהורין נָא na:

אָנָּא ana בְּ"ן לכב הוֹשִׁיעָה hoshi'a יהוה ע"ע נהורין נָא na: (X2)

אָנָּא ana בְּ"ן לכב יְדִידִים yedidim בְּטוּבְךָ betuvcha לאו רַוֵּה raveh◆

וְהוֹדְךָ vehodcha עָלָיו alav תְּשַׁוֶּה teshave◆ וְטוּבְךָ vetuvcha לאו אֲוַזֶּה achave◆

בְּתוֹךְ betoch עַם am צִיּוֹן Tziyon יוֹסֵף, ר"פ יהוה, קִנְאָה◆ נוֹשַׁעִי nosha'i◆ מַלֵּא maleh◆

מֵעַם me'am אֵלֶּה ele◆ וְשָׁם vesham לָךְ lecha נְוַזֶּה nechale◆

נְהַלֶּלָךְ nehalelach בְּיוֹם beyom נֶגֶד, מִזְבֵּחַ, זָן, אֵל יהוה שְׁבִיעִי shevi'i◆

הוֹשִׁיעָה hoshi'a יהוה ע"ע נהורין נָא na:

אָנָּא ana בְּ"ן לכב הוֹשִׁיעָה hoshi'a יהוה ע"ע נהורין נָא na: (X2)

אָנָּא ana בְּ"ן לכב וְזִילְךָ chelcha הַנְחֵל hanchel◆

וְזוֹמוֹת chomot קס"א קנ"א קמ"ג וּמב◆ וָזִיל vachel וְקָמִים vekamim גּוֹזֵל gachel◆

וְהַצְמַח vehatzmach אהיה יהוה יהוה אדני יִשְׁעִי yish'i◆ קְהָלִי kehali כּוֹנֵן konen כוכ

---

from remote lands and reestablish Your Sukkah; let us praise You on the seventh day.
Please save now. Please bring salvation now. (X2)
Please, find favor and reestablish the desolate mountain, and raise up Your fortress, and reveal the end,
my redemption; show Your exaltedness to the downtrodden people, and before You shall appear;
let us praise You on the seventh day. Please save now. Please bring salvation now. (X2)
Please, satiate the beloved ones in Your goodness, and cover them with Your glory, and I shall
relate Your goodness among the delivered people; fill Zion with this people, and there shall we pray
to You; let us praise You on the seventh day. Please save now. Please bring salvation now. (X2)
Please bequeath to Your multitude the wall and the embankment;
consume those who rise up, and sprout forth my deliverance; establish my congregation,

וְטוּבְךָ vetuvcha | לֹאִי | אֲשַׁנֵּן ashanen | וּלְשִׁמְךָ ulshimcha | אֲרַנֵּן aranen

נְהַלֶּלְךָ nehalelach | בַּיּוֹם beyom | נגד, מזבח, וז, אל יהוה | שְׁבִיעִי shevi'i

הוֹשִׁיעָה hoshi'a | יהוה ש"ע נהורין | נָא na

אָנָּא ana | בּ"ן לכב | הוֹשִׁיעָה hoshi'a | יהוה ש"ע נהורין | נָא na (X2)

אָנִי Ani | וָהוּ Vahu | אני | וְהוֹ | הוֹשִׁיעָה hoshi'a | יהוה ש"ע נהורין | נָא na (X2)

כְּהוֹשַׁעְתָּ kehoshata | יְדִידִים yedidim | מִכַּף mikaf | מַעֲבִידִים ma'avidim

וַתִּמְחַץ vatimchatz | לוּדִים ludim | אָצִים atzim | לְהַכְנִיעִי lehachni'i

אֲלוּבֵי aluvei | עוֹלֵב olev | לכב הַמְהַלְלִים hamehalelim | בְּכָל bechol | לכב לֵב lev

בְּאֶתְרוֹג be'etrog | ירח הַדּוֹמֶה hadomeh | כַּלֵּב lalev | נְהַלֶּלְךָ nehalelach

בַּיּוֹם beyom | נגד, מזבח, וז, אל יהוה | שְׁבִיעִי shevi'i | כֵּן ken | הוֹשַׁעְנָא hosha'ana

אָנִי Ani | וָהוּ Vahu | וְהוֹ | הוֹשִׁיעָה hoshi'a | יהוה ש"ע נהורין | נָא na (X2)

כְּהוֹשַׁעְתָּ kehoshata | וַתַּעֲזוֹר vata'azor | אָנוּשֵׁי anushei | מָזוֹר mazor

וַתְּאַזּוֹר vate'ezor | אֵזוֹר ezor | לִשְׁפֹּט lishpot | מַרְשִׁיעִי marshi'i

יֶתֶר yeter | פְּזוּרָה pezura | סוֹבְבֵי sovevei | תּוֹרָה torah | בְּלוּלָב belulav | וחיים,

נְהַלֶּלְךָ nehalelach | לַשִּׁדְרָה lashidra | הַדּוֹמֶה hadomeh | בינה ע"ה, אהיה אהיה יהוה | כֵּן ken

בַּיּוֹם beyom | נגד, מזבח, וז, אל יהוה | שְׁבִיעִי shevi'i | כֵּן ken | הוֹשַׁעְנָא hosha'ana

אָנִי Ani | וָהוּ Vahu | וְהוֹ | הוֹשִׁיעָה hoshi'a | יהוה ש"ע נהורין | נָא na (X2)

כְּהוֹשַׁעְתָּ kehoshata | סְגוּרֵי segurei | צָנוּק tzinok | נוֹאֲקִים no'akim | אָנוּק anok

וַתַּעֲנִיק vata'anik | עָנוּק anok | וְהִשְׁקַעְתָּ vehishk'ata | מַשְׁקִיעִי mashki'i

---

and I will constantly speak of Your goodness, and to Your Name shall I sing out;
let us praise You on the seventh day. Please save now. Please bring salvation now. (X2)
Ani Vahu (of the 72 Names of God) please bring salvation now. (X2)
Just as You saved the beloved ones from the hand of the enslavers and You struck the Ludim
who were driven to subjugate me; those humiliated by the scoffer who praise with all their heart,
with an etrog that resembles the heart; let us praise You on the seventh day. So save please now.
Ani Vahu (of the 72 Names of God) please bring salvation now. (X2)
Just as You saved and came to the aid of the afflicted
at loss for a remedy, and You girded to judge my persecutors; the remnants of the scattered, who circle
the Torah with a Lulav that resembles the spine; let us praise You on the seventh day. So save please now.
Ani Vahu (of the 72 Names of God) please bring salvation now. (X2)
Just as You saved those locked in confinement, who cried out in anguish,
and You bestowed gifts, and You drowned those who would drown me,

סוֹבְבִים sovevim ♦bemachanayim בְּמַחֲנֵיִם ♦bemazal בְּמַזָּל ♦moznayim מֹאזְנַיִם

בַּהֲדַס bahadas וזיים ע"ה hadomeh הַדּוֹמֶה laenayim לָעֵינַיִם ♦ ריבוע מ"ה♦

נְהַלֶלְךָ nehalelach beyom בְּיוֹם נגד, מזבוז, זז, אל יהוה ♦shevi'i שְׁבִיעִי

כֵן ken הוֹשַׁעְנָא hosha'ana:

אֲנִי Ani וְהוּ Vahu יהוה ש"ע נהורין hoshi'a הוֹשִׁיעָה נָא na: (X2)

כְּהוֹשַׁעְתָּ kehoshata peduyei פְּדוּיֵי am עַם ze זֶה ♦beyad בְּיַד וְזֹחֶה choze

וּמֹזֶה umazeh♦ vatashet וַתָּשֶׁת נְמִבְזֶה nemivze♦ choshek וְזֹושֵׁק לְהַטְבִּיעִי lehatbi'i♦

פּוֹתְחֵי potchei דְּלָתַיִם delatayim♦ letzaltzel לְצַלְצֵל בִּמְצִלְתַּיִם bimtziltayim♦

בַּעֲרָבָה ba'arava וזרע hadoma הַדּוֹמֶה לִשְׂפָתַיִם lisfatayim♦ נְהַלֶלְךָ nehalelach

בְּיוֹם beyom נגד, מזבוז, זז, אל יהוה ♦shevi'i שְׁבִיעִי♦ כֵן ken הוֹשַׁעְנָא hosha'ana:

אֲנִי Ani וְהוּ Vahu יהוה ש"ע נהורין hoshi'a הוֹשִׁיעָה נָא na: (X2)

אָנָּא ana בּ'ן לכב El אֵל (מילוי דס"ג) נָא na

הוֹשַׁעְנָא hosha'ana וְהוֹשִׁיעָה vehoshi'a יהוה ש"ע נהורין נָא na (X2)

אֵל El (מילוי דס"ג) נָא na otzarcha אוֹצָרְךָ hatov הַטּוֹב וְהוּ tiftach תִּפְתָּחוֹ

מִזְּבוּלָה mizvulah♦ veha'aretz וְהָאָרֶץ אלהים דההן ע"ה titen תִּתֵּן ב"פ כהת

יְבוּלָה yevulah♦ hosha'ana הוֹשַׁעְנָא vehoshi'a וְהוֹשִׁיעָה יהוה ש"ע נהורין נָא na:

אֵל El (מילוי דס"ג) נָא na nitfei נִטְפֵי nedavot נְדָבוֹת yeravu יְרַוּוּ

דִּשְׁאֵי dishei chatzir וְצִיר♦ vehisig וְהִשִּׂיג lachem לָכֶם dayish דַּיִשׁ et אֶת

בָּצִיר batzir♦ hosha'ana הוֹשַׁעְנָא vehoshi'a וְהוֹשִׁיעָה יהוה ש"ע נהורין נָא na:

---

those circling in groups during the constellation of the Balance with a hadas that resembles the eyes;
let us praise You on the seventh day. So save please now.
Ani Vahu (of the 72 Names of God) please bring salvation now. (X2)
Just as You saved those redeemed of this nation, through the prophet [that was asked] what is
[in your hand]. And You put to shame those who wanted to drown me; those who open the doors to play
the cymbals, with an Aravah that resembles the lips; let us praise You on the seventh day. So save please.
Ani Vahu (of the 72 Names of God) please bring salvation now. (X2)
Please God, please save now and bring salvation now. (X2)
God, please, open Your good repository from its Abode, so that the earth may give forth its produce.
Save now and bring salvation now.
God, please may the benevolent droplets quench the thirst of the grass and hay so that the threshing will last
for you until the harvest. Save now and bring salvation now.

אֵל El יא"י (מילוי דס"ג) נָא na יְבוּל yevul הָאָרֶץ ha'aretz אלהים דההן ע"ה

לְבָרֵךְ levarech הֵעָתֵר he'ater ♦ אָכוֹל achol וְשָׂבוֹעַ vesavo'a וְהוֹתֵר vehoter ♦

הוֹשַׁעְנָא hosha'ana וְהוֹשִׁיעָה vehoshi'a יהוה ע"ע נהורין נָא na ✦

אֵל El יא"י (מילוי דס"ג) נָא na יוֹם yom נגד, מזבח, זן, אל יהוה זֶה ze וְזֹאתוֹם chatom

נָא na וְזוֹתְמֵת use'ora וְשִׂעוֹרָה chita וְזטָה uvarech וּבָרֵךְ אכא ♦ chotemet

וְכְסֶמֶת vechusemet ♦ הוֹשַׁעְנָא hosha'ana וְהוֹשִׁיעָה vehoshi'a יהוה ע"ע נהורין נָא na ✦

אֵל El יא"י (מילוי דס"ג) נָא na וְגֶשֶׁם vegeshem נְדָבוֹת nedavot תְּחוֹלֵל techolel

רוּחַ ruach צָפוֹן tzafon ♦ uvarech וּבָרֵךְ שִׁבּוֹלֶת shibolet שׁוּעָל shu'al

וְשִׁיפוֹן veshifon ♦ הוֹשַׁעְנָא hosha'ana וְהוֹשִׁיעָה vehoshi'a יהוה ע"ע נהורין נָא na ✦

אֵל El יא"י (מילוי דס"ג) נָא na סַפֵּק sapek סְפָק sefek בְּכָל bechol לכב

וְזֹדֶשׁ chodesh י"ב הויות וְחֹדֶשׁ vechodesh י"ב הויות ♦ uvarech וּבָרֵךְ

אֹרֶז orez וְדוֹחַן vedochan uful וּפוֹל ♦ וְעֶדֶשׁ ve'edesh

הוֹשַׁעְנָא hosha'ana וְהוֹשִׁיעָה vehoshi'a יהוה ע"ע נהורין נָא na ✦

אֵל El יא"י (מילוי דס"ג) נָא na פָּצֵה petze שָׁנָה shana זוֹ zo מִשָּׁמִיר mishamir

וְשָׁיִת vashayit ♦ uvarech וּבָרֵךְ עֵץ etz שֶׁמֶן shemen זַיִת vezayit ♦

הוֹשַׁעְנָא hosha'ana וְהוֹשִׁיעָה vehoshi'a יהוה ע"ע נהורין נָא na ✦

אֵל El יא"י (מילוי דס"ג) נָא na בְּמָטָר bematar רַוֵּה rave וְזַרְבוֹנִי charbonei

יְשִׁימוֹן yeshimon ♦ uvarech וּבָרֵךְ גֶּפֶן gefen וּתְאֵנָה utena וְרִמּוֹן verimon ♦

הוֹשַׁעְנָא hosha'ana וְהוֹשִׁיעָה vehoshi'a יהוה ע"ע נהורין נָא na ✦

God, please consent to bless the produce of the land, to eat, be satiated and to leave over.
Save now and bring salvation now.
God, please seal this day, please a seal; and bless the wheat, the barley, and the spelt.
Save now and bring salvation now.
God, please let the northerly wind initiate the benevolent rain and bless the oats and the rye.
Save now and bring salvation now.
God, please provide sufficiently each and every month; and bless the rice, the millet, the beans, and the lentils.
Save now and bring salvation now.
God, please extricate this year, from the briars and thorns; and bless the oil trees and olives.
Save now and bring salvation now.
God, please quench with rain the dry wilderness; and bless the grapes, the figs, and the pomegranate.
Save now and bring salvation now.

אֵל El יא"י (מילוי דס"ג) נָא na רוֹמֵם romem עֲצֶרֶת atzeret עוֹלְלֵי olelei

טְפוּחִים tipuchim◆ וּבָרֵךְ uvarech אֱגוֹז egoz וְתָמָר vetamar

נָא na: וְהוֹשִׁיעָה vehoshi'a יהוה ש"ע נהורין הוֹשַׁעֲנָא hosha'ana וְתַפּוּחִים vetapuchim◆

אֵל El יא"י (מילוי דס"ג) נָא na יָדְךָ yadcha הַרְוֵז harchev וְרַבֶּה verabe

וְזֵיזֵי chazizei מֵעוֹנִים me'onim◆ וּבָרֵךְ uvarech בָּטְנִים botnim וּשְׁקֵדִים ushkedim

נָא na: וְהוֹשִׁיעָה vehoshi'a יהוה ש"ע נהורין הוֹשַׁעֲנָא hosha'ana וְעַרְמוֹנִים ve'armonim◆

בַּל bal מֵעַמְּךָ me'amcha צִדְקְךָ tzidkecha נָא na יא"י (מילוי דס"ג) אֵל El

וּכְרוּסְטְמֵל ukrustemal וְחָרוּב charuv וּבָרֵךְ uvarech יִפָּסֵק yipasek◆

נָא na: וְהוֹשִׁיעָה vehoshi'a יהוה ש"ע נהורין הוֹשַׁעֲנָא hosha'ana וַאֲפַרְסֵק va'afarsek◆

קְהִלָּה kehila וְזַכֵּךְ chaletz נָא na (דס"ג) (מילוי) יא"י El

וּבָרֵךְ uvarech תַּעֲרוֹג ta'arog◆ סְבִיבֶיךָ sevivecha אֲשֶׁר asher הָתוּת hatut

ירת◆ וְהָאֶתְרוֹג vehaetrog וְהָאֱגוֹז vehaegoz

נָא na: נהורין ש"ע יהוה וְהוֹשִׁיעָה vehoshi'a הוֹשַׁעֲנָא hosha'ana

אֵל El בִּמְטְרוֹת bemitrot שְׂבַע sava נָא na קְרָא kera נָא na

רְקִיעִים reki'im◆ וּבָרֵךְ uvarech כָּל kol ילי מִינֵי minei יְרָקוֹת yerakot

נָא na: וְהוֹשִׁיעָה vehoshia יהוה ש"ע נהורין הוֹשַׁעֲנָא hosha'ana וּזְרָעִים uzraim◆

אָנָּא ana בֵּ"ן לכב אֵל El יא"י (מילוי דס"ג) נָא na

(X2) נָא na: וְהוֹשִׁיעָה vehoshi'a יהוה ש"ע נהורין הוֹשַׁעֲנָא hosha'ana

---

God, please raise up the imprisoned young children; and bless the walnuts, the dates, and the apples.
Save now and bring salvation now.
God, please be magnanimous and make plentiful the Heavenly clouds;
and bless the pistachio nuts, the almonds and the chestnuts.
Save now and bring salvation now.
God, please, Your righteousness never cease from Your people;
and bless the carobs, the Crustumenian pears, and the peaches.
Save now and bring salvation now.
God, please deliver the congregation that longs to be near You;
and bless the berries, the walnuts and the citrons.
Save now and bring salvation now.
God, please proclaim plentitude with the rains of the skies; and bless all kinds of vegetables and grains.
Save now and bring salvation now.
Please God, please save now and bring salvation now. (X2)

עַל al   זֶה ze   אֶל יהוה זָן, מִזְבּוֹז, נֶגֶד,   יוֹם yom   נָא na   (מילוי דס"ג) ייא"י   אֵל El

קֵץ ketz   מִנֶּך mikaf   שְׂשׂוּעָה shesu'a   וְזֹכֵץ vechaletz   תַּפְסִיעַ tafsi'a •

מַשְׂשִׂיעַ mashsi'a •   גֶּפֶן gefen   מִמִּצְרַיִם miMitzrayim   מִצֵּר miMitzr   תַּסִּיעַ tasi'a •

הוֹשַׁעֲנָא hosha'ana   וְהַצְלִיחָה vehatzlicha   נָא na •

אֵל El   ייא"י (מילוי דס"ג)   נָא na   וּמִנּוֹף umiNof   נֶהָלְתָּ nehalta   גִּזְעֶיהָ giz'eha •

וַתַּפְרִיחַ vatafri'ach   זְמוֹרֵי zemorei   זְרוּעֶיהָ zeru'eha •   תְּגָרֵשׁ tegaresh   גּוֹיִם goyim

וַתִּטָּעֶהָ vatita'eha :   הוֹשַׁעֲנָא hosha'ana   וְהַצְלִיחָה vehatzlicha   נָא na •

אֵל El   ייא"י (מילוי דס"ג)   נָא na   סְמָדְרֶיהָ semadareha   הֵנִיצוֹת henitzota

בְּמֶרֶץ bemeretz •   וּפִנִּיתָ ufinita   לְפָנֶיהָ lefaneha   שִׁבְעָה shiva   גּוֹיִם goyim

בְּאֶרֶץ be'eretz •   וַתַּשְׁרֵשׁ vatashresh   שָׁרָשֶׁיהָ shorasheha   וַתְּמַלֵּא vatemale

אֶרֶץ aretz :   הוֹשַׁעֲנָא hosha'ana   וְהַצְלִיחָה vehatzlicha   נָא na •

אֵל El   ייא"י (מילוי דס"ג)   נָא na   פֵּארוֹת pe'erot   הִפְרַוַזְתָּ hifrachta

פְּרִים piryam •   וּבְטוֹב uvatov   והו   הִשְׂבַּעְתָּ hisbata   עֶדְיָם edyam •

תְּשַׁלַּוֹוּ teshalach   קְצִירָהּ ketzireha   עַד ad   יָם yam   ילי •

הוֹשַׁעֲנָא hosha'ana   וְהַצְלִיחָה vehatzlicha   נָא na •

אֵל El   ייא"י (מילוי דס"ג)   נָא na   הֲלֹא halo   אַתָּה Ata   נְטַעְתָּהּ neta'ata

וַתִּצְּרֶיהָ vatitzereha •   וּמֵאָז ume'az   ומב   נְצַרְתָּהּ netzarta

וְתִשְׁמְרֶהָ vatishmereha •   לָמָּה lama   פָּרַצְתָּ paratzta   גְּדֵרֶיהָ gedereha •

הוֹשַׁעֲנָא hosha'ana   וְהַצְלִיחָה vehatzlicha   נָא na •

God, please on this day may You leap toward the Redemption, and rescue those torn asunder from the fangs of the destroyer; You, Who brought out a vine from Egypt. Save now and bring success now.
God, please, from Nof did You lead its stock and You caused its sown buds to bloom; You expelled nations and You planted it. Save now and bring success now.
God, please, You caused her blossoms to quickly bloom, and You cleared before her the seven nations by humbling them; You rooted her roots and You filled the land. Save now and bring success now.
God, please, You blosom the branches with fruit, and in goodness did You satiate their mouths; and You spread its harvest to the sea. Save now and bring success now.
God, please it is not You Who has implanted her and guarded her, and always have you guarded and watched her; why, have You breached her fences? Save now and bring success now.

עֲזוּזוֹת ezuzot · רַב rav · קָדוֹשׁ kadosh · נָא na · (מילוי דס"ג) יא"י · אֵל El

מנק וּפְקֹד ufkod · lachazot כוֹזֹזוֹת יפ טל, יפ כזו · mishamayim מִשָּׁמַיִם · habet הַבֶּט

נָא na: · vehatzlicha וְהַצְלִיחָה · hosha'ana הוֹשַׁעְנָא · zot זֹאת · gefen גֶּפֶן

la'amusei לַעֲמוּסֵי · galeh גַּלֵּה לאו · tuvcha טוּבְךָ · na נָא · (מילוי דס"ג) יא"י · אֵל El

dat דָּת · nochalei נוֹחֲלֵי לאו · tuvcha טוּבְךָ · yisbe'u יִשְׂבְּעוּ · me'ayim מֵעַיִם

yish'avun יִשְׁאֲבוּן · hayeshu'a הַיְשׁוּעָה · umima'ayenei וּמִמַּעְיְנֵי · yomayim יוֹמַיִם

נָא na: · vehatzlicha וְהַצְלִיחָה · hosha'ana הוֹשַׁעְנָא · mayim מַיִם

נָא na · (מילוי דס"ג) יא"י El אֵל לכב בן · ana אָנָּא

(X2) Ata: אַתָּה · avinu אָבִינוּ נָא na · veharvicha וְהַרְוִיחָה · hosha'ana הוֹשַׁעְנָא

amutz אָמוּץ · av אָב · lema'an לְמַעַן · נָא na · (מילוי דס"ג) יא"י · El אֵל

betzilcha בְּצִלְךָ · mayim מַיִם · al עַל · alila עֲלִילָה · mimotze'ei מִמּוֹצָאֵי

mayim מַיִם · mishtifat מִשְׁטִיפַת · vehitzalto וְהִצַּלְתּוֹ · gonanto גּוֹנַנְתּוֹ

mabul מַבּוּל · lehavi לְהָבִיא · shelo שֶׁלֹא · nishbata נִשְׁבַּעְתָּ · biglalo בִּגְלָלוֹ

mayim מַיִם · timna תִּמְנַע · lo לֹא · ba'avuro בַּעֲבוּרוֹ · mayim מַיִם

נָא na: · veharvicha וְהַרְוִיחָה · hosha'ana הוֹשַׁעְנָא

av אָב · lema'an לְמַעַן · נָא na · (דס"ג) (מילוי) יא"י · El אֵל

mayim מַיִם · me'at מְעַט · נָא na · וזם · yukach יֻקַּח · na'am נָאָם · bogdim בּוֹגְדִים

acharecha אַחֲרֶיךָ · himshich הִמְשִׁיךְ · bogdim בּוֹגְדִים

mayim מַיִם · besha'olo בְּשָׁעֳלוֹ · moded מוֹדֵד · (מילוי דס"ג) יא"י · El אֵל

God, please, Holy One of great might, look down from the Heaven and see;
and remember this vineyard. Save now and bring success now.
God, please, reveal Your goodness to those carried in the womb,
may they be satiated with Your goodness, they who inherited the law of two thousand years,
and from the wellsprings of salvation may they draw water. Save now and bring success now.
Please, God please, save now and bring prosperity now. For You are our Father. (X2)
God, please, for the sake of the father who was strengthened over those who spread a libel regarding water;
under Your protective shade did You shield him and You did rescue him from a flood of water;
and on account of him You swore to not bring a flood of water, for his sake, do not withhold water.
Save now and bring prosperity now.
God, please, for the sake of the patriarch who said: "Let a bit of water be taken," (Gensis 18:4);
who drew the traitors for follow You, God, Who measures the waters with His fist,

בְּתֵק bitek　זָרִים zarim　עוֹבְדֵי ovdei　אֵשׁ esh　וּמַיִם umayim♦

בַּעֲבוּרוֹ ba'avuro　לֹא lo　תִּמְנַע timna　מַיִם mayim♦

הוֹשַׁעְנָא hosha'ana　וְהַרְוִיוָה veharvicha　נָא na:

אֵל El　יָיָ (מילוי דס"ג)　נָא na　לְמַעַן lema'an　בֵּן ben　הַנֶּעֱקַד hane'ekad

וְחָפַר vechafar　בְּאֵר be'er　קנ"א ב"ן, יהוה אלהים יהוה אדני, מילוי קס"א וס"ג, מ"ה ברבוע וע"ב ע"ה

מַיִם mayim♦　גָּר gar　בִּגְרָר bigrar　וְרָבוּ veravu　עַל al　הַמַּיִם hamayim♦

בְּשַׂרוּהוּ bisruhu　עֲבָדָיו avadav　מָצָאנוּ matzanu　מַיִם mayim♦

בַּעֲבוּרוֹ ba'avuro　לֹא lo　תִּמְנַע timna　מַיִם mayim♦

הוֹשַׁעְנָא hosha'ana　וְהַרְוִיוָה veharvicha　נָא na:

אֵל El　יָיָ (מילוי דס"ג)　נָא na　לְמַעַן lema'an　תָם tam　גַּל gal　אֶבֶן even

מֵעַל me'al　עלם בְּאֵר be'er　קנ"א ב"ן, יהוה אלהים יהוה אדני, מילוי קס"א וס"ג, מ"ה ברבוע וע"ב ע"ה

מַיִם mayim♦　דָּלָה dala　וְהִשְׁקָה vehishka　צֹאן tzon　לָבָן lavan　מַיִם mayim♦

וְהִצִּיג vehitzig　מַקְלוֹת maklot　בְּשִׁקָתוֹת beshikatot　הַמַּיִם hamayim♦

בַּעֲבוּרוֹ ba'avuro　לֹא lo　תִּמְנַע timna　מַיִם mayim♦

הוֹשַׁעְנָא hosha'ana　וְהַרְוִיוָה veharvicha　נָא na:

אֵל El　יָיָ (מילוי דס"ג)　נָא na　לְמַעַן lema'an　דָּגוּל dagul　מָשׁוּי mashuy

מִמַּיִם mimayim♦　הֶעֱבִיר he'evir　וְזִבְלְךָ chevlach　בְּתוֹךְ betoch　גַּלֵּי galei

מַיִם mayim♦　פָּתַח patach　צוּר tzur　אלהים דהין ע"ה וַיָּזוּבוּ vayazuvu　מַיִם mayim♦

בַּעֲבוּרוֹ ba'avuro　לֹא lo　תִּמְנַע timna　מַיִם mayim♦

הוֹשַׁעְנָא hosha'ana　וְהַרְוִיוָה veharvicha　נָא na:

Who split apart strangers worshippers of fire and water; for his sake, do not withhold water.
Save now and bring prosperity now.
God, please for the sake of the son who was bound, who dug wells of water; who lived in Gerar,
they quarreled over water; whose servants informed him: "We have discovered water," (Genesis 20:32);
for his sake, do not withhold water. Save now and bring prosperity now.
God, please for the sake of the perfected one, who rolled a stone from atop a well of water;
who drew and gave to drink water to Laban's sheep; and who set up wands at the water troughs;
for his sake do not withhold water. Save please and bring prosperity now.
God, please for the pre-eminent one who was pulled from the water;
who caused Your lot to pass through waves of water, who opened a rock and the waters flowed;
for his sake do not withhold water. Save please and bring prosperity now.

אָנָּא ana ב"ן לכב אֵל El יא"י (מילוי דס"ג) נָא na.

רְפָא refa נָא na. סְלַח selach יהוה ע"ב סָלוֹן נָא na.

הוֹשַׁעְנָא hosha'ana וְהוֹשִׁיעָה vehoshi'a יהוה ש"ע נהורין נָא na.

אָבִינוּ avinu אַתָּה Ata: (X2)

לְמַעַן lema'an אָב av נִפְקַד nifkad וַיִּבָּוֹן vayibachen. כְּכְלוֹת kichlot

דוֹר dor צוֹחֵן tzochen. וְנֹוֹן veNo'ach מָצָא matza חֵן chen מווי. בַּעֲבוּרוֹ ba'avuro

תַּלְבִּישׁ talbish תְּהִלָה tehila ע"ה אמת. לְעוֹרְכֵי le'orchei לָךְ lecha תְּפִלָה tefila

הוֹשַׁעְנָא hosha'ana וְהוֹשִׁיעָה vehoshi'a יהוה ש"ע נהורין נָא na: א"ת ב"ש אוכצ.

לְמַעַן lema'an נָאֱמָן ne'eman אַמִּיץ amitz בְּלִי beli וְׁשֵׁל cheshel.

וְנִצַּל venitzal מִכְׁשֵׁל mikeshel וַיִּטַּע vayita אֵׁשֶׁל eshel. בַּעֲבוּרוֹ ba'avuro

הַיּוֹם hayom נגד, מזבח, זן, אל יהוה גּוֹמְרֵי gomrei לָךְ lecha. תַּכְלֵל tachlel

הַלֵּל halel ללה. הוֹשַׁעְנָא hosha'ana וְהוֹשִׁיעָה vehoshi'a יהוה ש"ע נהורין נָא na:

לְמַעַן lema'an יָוִד yachid יהוה ריבוע יהוה מִקּוֹרָאִי mekorai. בֵּרְכוֹ bercho

רִיבוע מ"ה אֵל El יא"י (מילוי דס"ג) קֹנ"א ב"ן, יהוה אלהים יהוה אדני, בִּבְּאֵר biver רֹאִי ro'i.

מילוי קס"א וס"ג, מ"ה ברבוע וע"ב ע"ה לַחַי lachai רֹאִי ro'i. בַּעֲבוּרוֹ ba'avuro

הַיּוֹם hayom נגד, מזבח, זן, אל יהוה יוֹסְפֵי yosfei לָךְ lecha. יוּכְסַף yuchsaf

מוּסָף musaf יוסף. הוֹשַׁעְנָא hosha'ana וְהוֹשִׁיעָה vehoshi'a יהוה ש"ע נהורין נָא na:

לְמַעַן lema'an יָׁשֵׁן yashan בְּטַבּוּר betabur עוֹלָם olam. וְסוֹד vesod מיכ, י"פ האא

נֶעְלָם nelam וְׁזָלָם chalam. וַיַּחֲלֹם vayachalom וְהִנֵּה vehine סֻלָּם sulam.

בַּעֲבוּרוֹ ba'avuro תְּבָרֵךְ tevarech רֹבַע rova. סוֹבְבֵי sovevei שֶׁבַע sheva.

Please, God please, heal now, forgive now, save now and bring salvation now. For You are our Father. (X2)
For the sake of the father (No'ach), commanded and tested when a reeking generation perished,
"Noah found favor," (Genesis 6:8); for his sake, enwrap in praise those who arrange prayers to You.
Save now and bring salvation now.
For the sake of the loyal one (Abraham), courageous without weakness; who was saved from stumbling,
and who planted an eshel, for his sake, crown today those who complete the Halel to You.
Save now and bring salvation now.
For the sake of the one (Isaac) that was called single, God, the all-seeing blessed him at the well of Lachai Ro'i,
for his sake may today be cherished, those how add to You the Musaf. Save now and bring salvation now.
For the sake of the one (Jacob) who slept at the hub of the world, who dreamed of a hidden secret: "and he
dreamed, and behold, a ladder" (Genesis 28:12); for his sake, bless his stock who rotating seven [circles.]

hosha'ana הוֹשַׁעְנָא   vehoshi'a וְהוֹשִׁיעָה יהוה ע"פ נהורין   נָא na:

lema'an לְמַעַן   vatik וָתִיק   karan קֶרֶן   or עוֹר   panav פָּנָיו◆

ve'or וְאוֹר רו, א"ס   enav עֵינָיו ריבוע מ"ה   vehaish וְהָאִישׁ   Moshe מֹשֶׁה מהע,

ba'avuro בַּעֲבוּרוֹ ע"ב ברבוע קס"א, אל שדי, ד"פ אלהים ע"ה   anav עָנָיו◆   me'od מְאֹד

tevarech תְּבָרֵךְ   shana שָׁנָה◆   letzo'akei לְצוֹעֲקֵי   hosha'ana הוֹשַׁעְנָא◆

hosha'ana הוֹשַׁעְנָא   vehoshi'a וְהוֹשִׁיעָה יהוה ע"פ נהורין   נָא na:

lema'an לְמַעַן   po'alei פּוֹעֲלֵי   ra רַע   halam הָלַם◆   veshalom וְשָׁלוֹם   lo לוֹ

hushlam הֻשְׁלַם◆   berit בְּרִית   kehunat כְּהֻנַּת   olam עוֹלָם◆   ba'avuro בַּעֲבוּרוֹ

ge'on גְּאוֹן◆   aritz עָרִיץ   techaser תְּוֹחַסֵּר◆   vetashmia וְתַשְׁמִיעַ   mevaser מְבַשֵּׂר◆

hosha'ana הוֹשַׁעְנָא   vehoshi'a וְהוֹשִׁיעָה יהוה ע"פ נהורין   נָא na:

hoshi'enu הוֹשִׁיעֵנוּ ריבוע מ"ה   moshi'enu מוֹשִׁיעֵנוּ◆   ki כִּי   lecha לְךָ   enenu עֵינֵינוּ◆

ulcha וּלְךָ   lishu'atenu לִישׁוּעָתֵנוּ: (X2)

yoshev יוֹשֵׁב   kedem קֶדֶם   ayom אָיוֹם   venora וְנוֹרָא◆

yom יוֹם נגד, מזבח, זן, אל יהוה   ze זֶה   te'ametz תְּאַמֵּץ   sovevei סוֹבְבֵי

torah תּוֹרָה◆   veshana וְשָׁנָה   zo זוֹ   tehe תְּהֵא   shenat שְׁנַת   ora אוֹרָה:

ki כִּי   lecha לְךָ   enenu עֵינֵינוּ ריבוע מ"ה◆   ulcha וּלְךָ   lishu'atenu לִישׁוּעָתֵנוּ:

venofef וְנוֹפֵף   korecha קוֹרְאֶיךָ   beruach בְּרוּחַ   nemocha נְמוּכָה◆

sovevim סוֹבְבִים   shiv'a שִׁבְעָה   hayom הַיּוֹם נגד, מזבח, זן, אל יהוה

nesucha נְסוּכָה◆   veshana וְשָׁנָה   zo זוֹ   tehe תְּהֵא   shenat שְׁנַת   beracha בְּרָכָה:

ki כִּי   lecha לְךָ   enenu עֵינֵינוּ ריבוע מ"ה◆   ulcha וּלְךָ   lishu'atenu לִישׁוּעָתֵנוּ:

Save now and bring salvation now.

For the sake of the distinguished one (Moses), the skin of his face radiated luminescence as well as the light of his eyes, and the man Moses was very humble; for his sake, bless the year for those who shout "Hoshana."

Save now and bring salvation now.

For the sake of the one who (Pinchas) struck evildoers, and peace was given to him, a covenant of eternal priesthood, for his sake, diminish the arrogance of the wicked, and sound the herald of good tidings.

Save now and bring salvation now.

Save us, our Savior, for our eyes are upon You; So come and save us. (X2)

He Who dwells in the Heavens, frightful and awesome, on this day may You give strength to those circling the Torah; and let this year be a year of Light. For our eyes are upon You; So come and save us.

Uplift those who call to You with humility, who circle seven times today the princely Torah; and let this year be a year of blessing. For our eyes are upon You; So come and save us.

sagev שַׂגֵּב shana שָׁנָה zo זו mikol מִכֹּל •machala מַחֲלָה

veshita וְשִׂיתָהּ geshuma גְּשׁוּמָה deshuna דְּשׁוּנָה •utlula וּטְלוּלָה

veshana וְשָׁנָה zo זו tehe תְּהֵא shenat שְׁנַת •gila גִּילָה

ki כִּי לְךָ lecha עֵינֵינוּ enenu רְבוּעַ מ"ה. ulcha וּלְכָה lishu'atenu לִישׁוּעָתֵנוּ:

petachecha פְּתָחֶךָ harchev הַרְחֵב le'om לְאֹם yafa יָפָה ketirtza כְּתִרְצָה•

mitchanenet מִתְחַנֶּנֶת lefanecha לְפָנֶיךָ ס"ג מ"ה ב"ן behegyon בְּהֶגְיוֹן

•melitza מְלִיצָה veshana וְשָׁנָה zo זו tehe תְּהֵא shenat שְׁנַת ditza דִּיצָה:

ki כִּי לְךָ lecha עֵינֵינוּ enenu רְבוּעַ מ"ה. ulcha וּלְכָה lishu'atenu לִישׁוּעָתֵנוּ:

nosha נוֹשַׁע am עַם lemosha'ot לְמוֹשָׁעוֹת יא"י (מילוי דס"ג) לאה; haEl הָאֵל

bechasdecha בְּחַסְדְּךָ hosha'ana הוֹשַׁעְנָא •badonai בַּיהֹוָ-אדנ-י-אהדונה-י

meyachalim מְיַחֲלִים ladonai לַיהֹוָ-אדנ-י-אהדונה-י• ki כִּי lishu'atcha לִישׁוּעָתְךָ

kivinu קִוִּינוּ Adonai יְהֹוָ-אדנ-י-אהדונה-י• adam אָדָם מ"ה uvhema וּבְהֵמָה ב"ן, לכב lishu'atcha לִישׁוּעָתְךָ

toshi'a תּוֹשִׁיעַ Adonai יְהֹוָ-אדנ-י-אהדונה-י: ki כִּי lishu'atcha לִישׁוּעָתְךָ

kivinu קִוִּינוּ Adonai יְהֹוָ-אדנ-י-אהדונה-י: tiftach תִּפְתַּח eretz אֶרֶץ veyifru וְיִפְרוּ

•yesha יֶשַׁע le'am לְעָם עלם asher אֲשֶׁר bechipuram בְּכִפּוּרָם

peditam פְּדִיתָם •mipesha מִפֶּשַׁע ta'avat תַּאֲוַת anavim עֲנָוִים

shamata שָׁמַעְתָּ Adonai יְהֹוָ-אדנ-י-אהדונה-י• ki כִּי lishu'atcha לִישׁוּעָתְךָ

kivinu קִוִּינוּ Adonai יְהֹוָ-אדנ-י-אהדונה-י: mipeleg מִפֶּלֶג male מָלֵא rave רַוֵּה

•le'umecha לְאַמֶּךָ keyom כְּיוֹם נגד, מזבוז, זך, אל יהוה asher אֲשֶׁר yatzata יָצָאתָ

leyesha לְיֵשַׁע amecha עַמֶּךָ• yom יוֹם נגד, מזבוז, זך, אל יהוה asher אֲשֶׁר

ne'emar נֶאֱמַר bo בּוֹ vayosha וַיּוֹשַׁע Adonai יְהֹוָ-אדנ-י-אהדונה-י:

Fortify this year against all illness, and make it rainy, fertile and dewy;
and let this year be a year of rejoicing. For our eyes are upon You; So come and save us.
Open Your doors wide to a nation that is beautiful when her deeds are pleasing; who beseeches You with
proper expression; and let this year be a year of delight. For our eyes are upon You; So come and save us.
God, Who brings salvations to a people saved by the Lord; please save in Your kindness those who place their
hope in the Lord. For it is toward Your salvation that we hope, Lord; man and beast do You save, Lord. For it
is toward Your salvation that we hope, Lord. May You open the earth and let it be fruitful with deliverance for
the people, who with their forgiveness, You have redeemed from sin the desire of the humble You have heard,
Lord. For it is toward Your salvation that we hope, Lord. From a filled stream satiate Your people, as on the
day that You went out to save Your nation, the day about which is stated: "And the Lord saved." (Exodus 14:30)

יהה heye הָיָה Adonai : יְהֹוָה kivinu קִוִּינוּ lishu'atcha לִישׁוּעָתְךָ ki כִּי

batzar בַּצָּר one עוֹנֶה tzur צוּר lishu'a לִישׁוּעָה na נָא

re'e רְאֵה tiktzar תִּקְצַר lo לֹא yadcha יָדְךָ ki כִּי karev קָרֵב peduti פְּדוּתִי

ki כִּי Adonai : יְהֹוָה yeshu'atcha יְשׁוּעָתְךָ ta'avti תָּאַבְתִּי ki כִּי

hoshi'a הוֹשִׁיעָה Adonai : יְהֹוָה kivinu קִוִּינוּ lishu'atcha לִישׁוּעָתְךָ

mibet מִבֵּית tzo'ek צוֹעֵק asir אָסִיר

ose עוֹשֶׂה kele כֶּלֶא Tzur צוּר himatze הַמֵּצֵא leshav'i לְשַׁוְעִי

atzei עֲצֵי yisbe'u יִשְׂבְּעוּ maleh מָלֵא peleg פֶּלֶג petach פְּתוּחַ fele פֶּלֶא

kivinu קִוִּינוּ lishu'atcha לִישׁוּעָתְךָ ki כִּי Adonai : יְהֹוָה

shema שְׁמַע oznecha אָזְנְךָ hateh הַטֵּה Adonai : יְהֹוָה

hateruchot הַטְּרוּחוֹת nefashot נְפָשׁוֹת na נָא vehosha וְהוֹשַׁע na נָא

tabana תַּבַּעְנָה siftotam שִׂפְתוֹתָם techina תְּחִנָּה bema'arichei בְּמַאֲרִיכֵי

lishu'atcha לִישׁוּעָתְךָ ki כִּי ladonai : לַיהֹוָה yeshu'ata יְשׁוּעָתָה

shav'at שַׁוְעַת retze רְצֵה Adonai : יְהֹוָה kivinu קִוִּינוּ

meyachalim מְיַחֲלִים yeshu'atcha יְשׁוּעָתְךָ amelim אֲמֵלִים

geshamim גְּשָׁמִים notlim נוֹטְלִים sho'alim שׁוֹאֲלִים beyom בְּיוֹם umzonam וּמְזוֹנָם

vechish וְחִישׁ mizevulim מִזְּבוּלִים tazil תַּזִּיל utlalim וּטְלָלִים lulav לוּלָב

Adonai : יְהֹוָה ufduyei וּפְדוּיֵי ge'ulim גְּאוּלִים yelchu יֵלְכוּ

Adonai : יְהֹוָה kivinu קִוִּינוּ lishu'atcha לִישׁוּעָתְךָ ki כִּי

"For it is toward Your salvation that we hope, Lord." (Genesis 49:18)

Please be a salvation, Rock, Who answers at distress. Bring my redemption near for Your hand is not limited; see how I long for Your salvation, Lord. For it is toward Your salvation that we hope, Lord. Save the imprisoned one who shouts out from his prison; to my cry be available, Rock, Who performs wonders open an overflowing stream, so that the trees of the Lord become satiated. For it is toward Your salvation that we hope, Lord. Bend your ear, please hear and please save, the souls that are burdened with lengthy supplication; their lips express the salvation from God. For it is toward Your salvation that we hope, Lord. Accept favorably the cry of those cut off, who long for Your salvation, and ask for their sustenance on the day that they take the Lulav. The rains and dew may You cause to flow from the Heavens, and may they go speedily as liberated and as those redeemed by the Lord. For it is toward Your salvation that we hope, Lord.

קוֹל kol מְבַשֵׂר mevaser מְבַשֵׂר mevaser וְאוֹמֵר ve'omer (X7)

יָפֵה yefe נוֹף nof אֲנוֹפֵף anofef בְּחֶזְיוֹן bechezyon תְּעוּדָה te'uda

יִשְׂמַח yismach הַר har צִיּוֹן Tziyon יוסף, ר"פ יהוה, קנאה, משיחו תָּגֵלְנָה tagelna

בְּנוֹת benot יְהוּדָה Yehuda מְבַשֵׂר mevaser מְבַשֵׂר mevaser וְאוֹמֵר ve'omer

וָוֵי vavei נוּךְ navech אַפְּסֵג afaseg וְאַרְחִיב ve'archiv גְּבוּלֵךְ gevulech

כִּי ki יְהוָֹה Adonai יִהְיֶה yihye יי lach כָּךְ

לְאוֹר le'or רו, א"ס עוֹלָם olam וְשָׁלְמוּ veshalmu יְמֵי yemei אֶבְלֵךְ evlech

מְבַשֵׂר mevaser מְבַשֵׂר mevaser וְאוֹמֵר ve'omer

סֹבוּ sobu צִיּוֹן Tziyon יוסף, ר"פ יהוה, קנאה וְהַקִּיפוּהָ vehakifuha

סִפְרוּ sifru מִגְדָּלֶיהָ migdaleha שִׂישׂוּ sisu אַתָּה itah

מָשׂוֹשׂ masos כָּל kol יל הַמִּתְאַבְּלִים hamit'abelim עָלֶיהָ aleha פהל"ב

מְבַשֵׂר mevasher מְבַשֵׂר mevasher וְאוֹמֵר ve'omer

פֶּתַע peta אַשְׁלִיךְ ashlich עַל al אֱדוֹם edom נַעֲלַים na'alayim

פִּצְחוּ pitzchu רַנְּנוּ ranenu יַוְזְדָּיו yachdav וְזָרְבוֹת charvot

יְרוּשָׁלַים Yerushalayim מְבַשֵׂר mevasher מְבַשֵׂר mevasher וְאוֹמֵר ve'omer

קֵץ ketz מנ"ך יְשׁוּעָתִי yeshu'ati וְזַשְׁתִּי chashti מִבִּעוֹן mimon

שַׁוֹתַק shachak קֵרַבְתִּי keravti צִדְקָתִי tzidkati לֹא lo תִּרְוזָק tirchak

מְבַשֵׂר mevaser מְבַשֵׂר mevaser וְאוֹמֵר ve'omer

A voice heralds, heralds and proclaims. (X7)
The most beautiful of scenes shall I raise up through a prophetic vision;
let Mount Zion rejoice, let the daughters of Judah delight. It heralds, heralds and proclaims.
The pillars of Your Dwelling shall I raise up and I shall broaden your boundary; for the Lord will be for
you an everlasting Light and your days of mourning will end. It heralds, heralds and proclaims.
Circle Zion and walk around her, count her towers;
celebrate a rejoicing with her, all who have been mourning over her. It heralds, heralds and proclaims.
Suddenly shall I throw locks upon Edom, break into song;
sing in unison you ruins of Jerusalem. It heralds, heralds and proclaims.
The culmination of My salvation have I hurried from the Heavenly Abode;
I have brought My righteousness nearer so do not be distant. It heralds, heralds and proclaims.

הִתְעוֹרְרִי hit'oreri   מִמִּזְרָח mimizrach   וּבֹאִי uvo'i   מִמַּעֲרָב mima'arav ◆

הַר har   צִיּוֹן Tziyon   יַרְכְּתֵי yarketei   צָפוֹן tzafon   קִרְיַת kiryat

מֶלֶךְ melech   רָב rav: מְבַשֵּׂר mevaser   מְבַשֵּׂר mevaser   וְאוֹמֵר ve'omer:

קוֹל kol   מְבַשֵּׂר mevaser   מְבַשֵּׂר mevaser   וְאוֹמֵר ve'omer: (X2)

כַּכָּתוּב kakatuv: מַה ma   נָּאווּ navu   עַל al   הֶהָרִים heharim

רַגְלֵי raglei   מְבַשֵּׂר mevaser   מַשְׁמִיעַ mashmi'a   שָׁלוֹם shalom

מְבַשֵּׂר mevasher   טוֹב tov   מַשְׁמִיעַ mashmia   יְשׁוּעָה yeshu'a   אֹמֵר omer

לְצִיּוֹן leTziyon   מָלַךְ malach   אֱלֹהָיִךְ Elohayich:

וְנֶאֱמַר vene'emar: קוֹל kol   צֹפַיִךְ tzofayich   נָשְׂאוּ nas'u   קוֹל kol

יַחְדָּו yachdav   יְרַנֵּנוּ yeranenu   כִּי ki   עַיִן ayin   בְּעַיִן be'ayin

יִרְאוּ yir'u   בְּשׁוּב beshuv   יְהֹוָה Adonai   צִיּוֹן Tziyon:

וְנֶאֱמַר vene'emar: פִּצְחוּ pitzchu   רַנֵּנוּ ranenu   יַחְדָּו yachdav

חׇרְבוֹת chorvot   יְרוּשָׁלָיִם Yerushalayim   כִּי ki   נִחַם nicham

יְהֹוָה Adonai   עַמּוֹ amo   גָּאַל ga'al   יְרוּשָׁלָיִם Yerushalayim:

וְנֶאֱמַר vene'emar: כִּי ki   נִחַם nicham   יְהֹוָה Adonai

צִיּוֹן Tziyon   נִחַם nicham   כׇּל kol   וְחׇרְבֹתֶיהָ chorvoteha

וַיָּשֶׂם vayasem   מִדְבָּרָהּ midbarah   כְּעֵדֶן ke'eden   וְעַרְבָתָהּ ve'arvatah

כְּגַן kegan   יְהֹוָה Adonai   שָׂשׂוֹן sason   וְשִׂמְחָה vesimcha

יִמָּצֵא yimatze   בָהּ va   תּוֹדָה toda   וְקוֹל vekol   זִמְרָה zimra:

---

*Awaken from the east; come from the west Mount Zion at the northern side, the city of a great king.
It heralds, heralds and proclaims.
A voice heralds, heralds and proclaims. (X2)
As is written: "How beautiful upon the mountains are the feet of he who heralds, who announces peace, who heralds goodness, who announces deliverance, he shall say to Zion: 'Your God has reigned.'" (Isaiah 52:7)
And as is stated: "Hear, the watchmen! They lift up the voice, together do they sing; for they shall see, eye to eye, the Lord returning to Zion." (Isaiah 52:8) And as is stated: "Break forth into joy, sing together, waste places of Jerusalem; for the Lord had comforted His people, He had redeemed Jerusalem." (Isaiah 52:8) And as is stated: "For the Lord has consoled Zion, He has consoled all her ruins, and He has converted her wilderness into Eden, and her desolate area into a garden of the Lord. Joy and gladness prevail in her, thanksgiving and the sound of music." (Isaiah 51:3)*

וְנֶאֱמַר vene'emar : רָנּוּ ranu שָׁמַיִם shamayim י"פ טל, י"פ כו' וְגִילִי vegili

אֶרֶץ aretz (כתיב: יפצחו) ufitzchu הָרִים harim רִנָּה rina כִּי ki

נוֹחַם nicham יְהֹוָה Adonai עַמּוֹ amo וַעֲנִיָּו va'aniyav יְרַחֵם yerachem

אברהם, וז"פ אל, רי"ו ול"ב נתיבות החוכמה, רמ"ח (אברים), עסמ"ב וט"ז אותיות פשוטות:

וְנֶאֱמַר vene'emar : וְהָלְכוּ vehalchu עַמִּים amim רַבִּים rabim וְאָמְרוּ ve'amru

לְכוּ lechu וְנַעֲלֶה vena'ale אֶל el הַר har אֶל el יְהֹוָה Adonai אֶל el

בֵּית bet יַעֲקֹב Ya'akov אֱלֹהֵי Elohei דמב, מילוי ע"ב ; יכה ב"פ ראה

וְיוֹרֵנוּ veyorenu מִדְּרָכָיו midrachav וְנֵלְכָה venelcha בְּאֹרְחֹתָיו be'orchotav•

כִּי ki מִצִּיּוֹן miTziyon תֵּצֵא tetze תּוֹרָה torah וּדְבַר udvar ראה

וְנֶאֱמַר vene'emar : מִירוּשָׁלָיִם mirushalayim יְהֹוָה Adonai

וּפְדוּיֵי ufduyei יְהֹוָה Adonai יְשֻׁבוּן yeshuvun וּבָאוּ uvau

צִיּוֹן Tziyon בְּרִנָּה berina וְשִׂמְחַת vesimchat עוֹלָם olam

עַל al רֹאשָׁם rosham שָׂשׂוֹן sason וְשִׂמְחָה vesimcha יַשִּׂיגוּ yasigu

וְנָסוּ venasu יָגוֹן yagon וַאֲנָחָה va'anacha : וְנֶאֱמַר vene'emar : וָשָׂף chasaf

יְהֹוָה Adonai אֶת et זְרוֹעַ zero'a קָדְשׁוֹ kodsho לְעֵינֵי le'enei

כָּל kol הַגּוֹיִם hagoyim וְרָאוּ vera'u כָּל kol אַפְסֵי afsei אָרֶץ aretz

אֶת et יְשׁוּעַת yeshu'at אֱלֹהֵינוּ Elohenu וְנֶאֱמַר vene'emar :

And it is stated: "Let the Heavens sing out and let the Earth rejoice, and let the mountains break into song, for the Lord has consoled His people, and has taken pity on its poor." (Isaiah 49:13) And as is stated: "And many nations will go and say: 'Come let us go up to the mountain of the Lord, to the House of the God of Jacob; and He shall teach us of His ways, and we shall walk in His paths, for from Zion does the Torah go forth and the word of the Lord, from Jerusalem." (Isaiah 2:3) And as it is stated: "And the redeemed of the Lord shall return, and they shall come to Zion with joyous song, and the happiness they always had shall be upon their heads; they shall attain joy and happiness, and sorrow and sighing shall flee." (Isaiah 35:10) And as is stated: "The Lord has revealed His Holy arm before the eyes of all the nations; all ends of the world have seen the salvation of our God." (Isaiah 52:10) As is stated:

וְיִהְיוּ veyih'yu אל (יא"ל) דְּבָרַי devarai ראה אֵלֶּה ele אֲשֶׁר asher

הִתְחַנַּנְתִּי hitchananti לִפְנֵי lifnei יְהֹוָ֑ה Adonai קְרֹבִים kerovim

אֶל el יְהֹוָ֑ה Adonai אֱלֹהֵינוּ Elohenu ילה יוֹמָם yomam

וְלַיְלָה valayla מלה לַעֲשׂוֹת la'asot מִשְׁפַּט mishpat עה הפ אלהים עבְדּוֹ avdo

וּמִשְׁפַּט umishpat עה הפ אלהים עַמּוֹ amo יִשְׂרָאֵל Yisrael דְּבַר devar ראה

יוֹם yom נגד, מזבח, ז, אל יהוה בְּיוֹמוֹ beyomo: לְמַעַן lema'an דַּעַת da'at כָּל kol ילי

עַמֵּי amei הָאָרֶץ ha'aretz אלהים דההין עה כִּי ki יְהֹוָ֑ה Adonai הוּא hu

הָאֱלֹהִים haElohim ילה ; ר"ת יהה ; יהוה הוא האלהים = ענו עג"כ אֵין en עוֹד od:

Let the words of mine that I have pleaded before the Lord, be near the Lord, our God, day and night, to provide for the needs of His servant and the needs of His people, Israel, each thing on the day, so that all the nations of the world may know that it is the Lord who is God, there is no other." (I Kings 8:59-60)

THE ORDER OF THE BEATING OF THE WILLOW BRANCHES

The physical action of beating the willow branches upon the ground ignites spiritual forces that bury judgments and negativity into the ground. As the willow branch rises, purified sparks of Light are elevated, setting our souls aflame with the protective energy of The Creator. We beat the five willow branches five times, corresponding to the five final letters of the alphabet ךםןףץ, which represent the spiritual DNA code pertaining to Judgment.

On *Hosha'ana Rabbah* one should take five brnaches of willow and hold them together in his hand and say:

leshem לְשֵׁם   yichud יוֹזוּד   kudesha קוּדְשָׁא   berich בְּרִיךְ

hu הוּא   ushchinte וּשְׁכִינְתֵיה   (יאהדונהי)   bidchilu בִּדְחִילוּ

urchimu וּרְחִימוּ (יאהדויהה)   urchimu וּרְחִימוּ, udchilu וּדְחִילוּ (איההיוהה),

leyachda לְיַחֲדָא   shem שֵׁם   yud יוּ"ד   kei קֵי   bevav בְּוָא"ו   kei קֵי

beyichuda בְּיִחוּדָא   shelim שְׁלִים (יהוה)   beshem בְּשֵׁם   kol כָּל יִלִי

Yisrael יִשְׂרָאֵל, hineh הִנֵּה   anachnu אֲנַחְנוּ   vaim בָּאִים   lekayem לְקַיֵּם

mitzvat מִצְוַת   arava עֲרָבָה זרע.   minhag מִנְהַג   nevi'im נְבִיאִים

harishonim הָרִאשׁוֹנִים.   asher אֲשֶׁר   shorsham שָׁרְשָׁם   patu'ach פָּתוּוַ

al עַל   arvei עַרְבֵי   nachal נַוזַל.   letaken לְתַקֵּן   et אֶת   shorsha שָׁרְשָׁה ללה

bemakom בְּמָקוֹם   elyon עֶלְיוֹן.   vihi וִיהִי   no'am נֹעַם   Adonai אֲדֹנָי ללה

Elohenu אֱלֹהֵינוּ ילה   alenu עָלֵינוּ   uma'ase וּמַעֲשֵׂה   yadenu יָדֵינוּ

konena כּוֹנְנָה   alenu עָלֵינוּ   uma'ase וּמַעֲשֵׂה   yadenu יָדֵינוּ   konenehu כּוֹנְנֵהוּ:

vihi וִיהִי   ratzon רָצוֹן מהש ע"ה בריבוע וקס"א ע"ב, ע"ה, אל שדי ע"ה

milfanecha מִלְפָנֶיךָ ס"ג מ"ה בּן יְהֹוָאדִניֹאהדונהי Adonai   Elohenu אֱלֹהֵינוּ ילה

velohei וֵאלֹהֵי דמב, מילוי ע"ב ; ילה avotenu אֲבוֹתֵינוּ, El אֵל יא"י (מילוי דס"ג)

elyon עֶלְיוֹן, rochev רוֹכֵב   ba'aravot בְּעֲרָבוֹת, habocher הַבּוֹוזֵר

binvi'im בִּנְבִיאִים tovim טוֹבִים   uvminhagam וּבְמִנְהָגָם   hatovim הַטּוֹבִים.

THE ORDER OF THE BEATING OF THE WILLOW BRANCHES

For the sake of the unification of the Holy Blessed One and His Shechinah, with fear and love and with love and fear, in order to unify The Name Yud-Kei and Vav-Kei in perfect unity, and in the name of Israel, we have hereby come to fulfill the precept of the [beating of the] Aravah, a custom ordained by the early prophets, whose source emanates from brook willows to correct its root in the Supernal Place. "And may the pleasantness of the Lord, our God, be upon us and may He establish the work of our hands for us and may the work of our hands establish Him." (Psalms 90:17)
May it be pleasing before You, Lord, our God, and God of our forefathers,
Supreme God, Who rides in the highest Heavens, Who chooses good prophets and their good customs,

shetetzaref שֶׁתְּצָרֵף machshavtenu מַחֲשַׁבְתֵּנוּ bachavatat בַּחֲבָטַת

chamisha וַחֲמִשָּׁה badei בַּדֵי arava עֲרָבָה זרע ke'ilu כְּאִלוּ kivanu כִּוַּנּוּ

bechol בְּכָל לכב hakavanot הַכַּוָּנוֹת ketiknan כְּתִקְנָן♦ uvchen וּבְכֵן ע"ב, ריבוע יהוה

al עַל yedei יְדֵי chavatat וַחֲבָטַת chamisha וַחֲמִשָּׁה badei בַּדֵי arava עֲרָבָה זרע

pe'amim פְּעָמִים neged נֶגֶד מזבח, ז', אל יהוה bakarka בַּקַּרְקַע chamesh וְחָמֵשׁ

otiyot אוֹתִיּוֹת mantzepach מנצפ"ך gevurot גְּבוּרוֹת Adonai אֲדֹנָי ללה

Elohim אֱלֹהִים אהיה אדני ; ילה. ana אָנָא ב"ן becho'ach בְּכֹחַ לכב, segulat סְגֻלַּת

mitzvat מִצְוַת arava עֲרָבָה זרע zo זוֹ bemetek בְּמֶתֶק sefatayim שְׂפָתַיִם

tosif תּוֹסִיף lekach לְקַח shechinat שְׁכִינַת uzenu עֻזֵּנוּ chamesh וְחָמֵשׁ

gevurot גְּבוּרוֹת memutakot מְמֻתָּקוֹת bemetek בְּמֶתֶק ha'or הָאוֹר רז, א"ס,

tal טַל יוד הא ואו, הא יוד orot אוֹרֹת כוזו talecha טַלֶּךָ shem שֵׁם Yud יוֹד

Hei הֵא Vav וָו ha'ole הָעוֹלֶה tal ט"ל vechakala וְכַכַּלָּה מלה

ta'ade תַּעְדֶּה cheleha כֵּלֶיהָ lehityached לְהִתְיַחֵד im עִם doda דּוֹדָהּ

be'ahava בְּאַהֲבָה אוזד, דאגה ve'achava וְאַחֲוָה vere'ut וְרֵעוּת♦

uzru'eha וּזְרוּעֶיהָ tatzmi'ach תַּצְמִיחַ♦ zera זֶרַע ערבה kodesh קֹדֶשׁ

matzavta מַצָּבְתָּהּ le'ezrat לְעֶזְרַת מיכאל מלכיאל עוניאל מיכאל יְהֹוֹ אֲדֹנָ"יאהדונהי Adonai

bagiborim בַּגִּבּוֹרִים vetocha וְתוֹכָהּ ratzuf רָצוּף ahava אַהֲבָה אוזד, דאגה♦

bisfatayim בִּשְׂפָתַיִם yishak יִשַּׁק neshikin נְשִׁיקִין dirchimu דִּרְחִימוּ♦

Initials of the Names: אדני מנצפך (Gevurot—Judgments).

avo אָבוֹא bigvurot בִּגְבֻרוֹת Adonai אֲדֹנָי ללה Elohim יְהֹוִה אהיה azkir אַזְכִּיר

tzidkat'cha צִדְקָתְךָ levadecha לְבַדֶּךָ: dor דּוֹר ledor לְדוֹר

yeshabach יְשַׁבַּח:יוו ma'asecha מַעֲשֶׂיךָ ugvurotecha וּגְבוּרֹתֶיךָ yagidu יַגִּידוּ:

---

that You join our intention in the beating of the five willow branches as if we had intended all the intentions correctly. And thus, through the beating of the five willow branches, five times on the ground, corresponding to the five final letters, might of the Lord, God. Please, with the power of the spiritual benefit of this precept of Aravah, with sweetness of the light, a dew of lights is Your dew, the Name Yud, Kei, Vav, which totals thirty-nine. And as a bride, may she don her raiments, to be unified with her beloved in love and brotherhood and friendship. And may You cause her sowings to grow, a holy seed is her planting, to the aid of the Lord among the mighty, her inside paved with love; He shall kiss with lips, kisses of love.

א *I shall come with the powers of the Lord, God; I shall relate Your righteousness alone.*

ד *Generation to generation shall extol Your deeds, and relate Your mighty acts.*

ילה Elohim אֱלֹהִים · ir עִיר · yesamchu יְשַׂמְּחוּ · pelagav פְּלָגָיו · nahar נָהָר

mibnei מִבְּנֵי · yafyafita יָפְיָפִיתָ · elyon עֶלְיוֹן: · mishkenei מִשְׁכְּנֵי · kedosh קֹדֶשׁ

ken כֵּן · al עַל · besiftotecha בְּשְׂפְתוֹתֶיךָ · chen וָחֵן · hutzak הוּצַק · adam אָדָם

mi בִּי: · le'olam לְעוֹלָם · Elohim אֱלֹהִים ילה · berachecha בֵּרַכְךָ

kol כָּל · yashmia יַשְׁמִיעַ · Adonai יְהֹוָה · gevurot גְּבוּרוֹת · yemalel יְמַלֵּל

ir עִיר · bach בָּךְ · medubar מְדֻבָּר · nichbadot נִכְבָּדוֹת · tehilato תְּהִלָּתוֹ:

lelohim לֵאלֹהִים · nafshi נַפְשִׁי · tzam'a צָמְאָה · sela סֶלָה · haElohim הָאֱלֹהִים

penei פְּנֵי · ve'era'e וְאֵרָאֶה · avo אָבוֹא · matai מָתַי · chai וָי · leEl לְאֵל

ha'aretz הָאָרֶץ · pakadta פָּקַדְתָּ: · Elohim אֱלֹהִים

peleg פֶּלֶג · tashrena תַּעְשְׁרֶנָּה · rabat רַבַּת · vatshokekeha וַתְּשֹׁקְקֶהָ

ki כִּי · deganam דְּגָנָם · tachin תָּכִין · mayim מַיִם · maleh מָלֵא · Elohim אֱלֹהִים

olam עוֹלָם · Elohim אֱלֹהִים · kis'acha כִּסְאַךָ: · techineha תְּכִינֶהָ · chen כֵּן

malchutecha מַלְכוּתֶךָ: · shevet שֵׁבֶט · mishor מִישׁוֹר · shevet שֵׁבֶט · va'ed וָעֶד

avadecha עֲבָדֶיךָ · anachnu אֲנַחְנוּ · velanu וְלָנוּ

tashpi'a תַּשְׁפִּיעַ · lefanecha לְפָנֶיךָ · hamitpalelim הַמִּתְפַּלְּלִים

hachayim הַחַיִּים · or אוֹר · mishem מִשֵּׁם · lanu לָנוּ

veseva וְשֵׂיבָה · zikna זִקְנָה · ad עַד · vegam וְגַם

agid אַגִּיד · ad עַד · ta'azveni תַּעַזְבֵנִי · al אַל · Elohim אֱלֹהִים

gevuratecha גְּבוּרָתֶךָ: · yavo יָבוֹא · lechol לְכָל · ledor לְדוֹר · zero'acha זְרוֹעֶךָ

ג *The river, its streams will gladden the city of God, the Holy of the dwelling place of the Supreme One.*

י *You are more beautiful than people, charm has been poured upon Your lips,*
therefore God has blessed you ever more.

מב *Who can speak of the power of the Lord; proclaim all His praise.*

ג *Honorable matters are discussed in you, city of God, Selah.*

צ *My soul thirsts for God, for the living God; when will I come and appear before God.*

פ *You remember the earth and You water it, streams God filled with water;*
You prepare their grain for thus do You prepare it.

כ *Your Throne, God, is forever, a staff of justice is the staff of Your kingdom.*
And to us, Your servants, who pray before You, may You cause to flow to us from the Name
of the Light of Life. Also until old age and elderliness, God, do not forsake me;
until I relate Your power to generation; to all who may come, Your might.

וְתַאֲרִיךְ veta'arich — יָמֵינוּ yamenu — בְּטוֹב וְהוּ batov — וּשְׁנוֹתֵינוּ ushnotenu

בָּנְעִימִים bane'imim — דְּשֵׁנִים deshenim — וְרַעֲנַנִּים vera'ananim◆ — וְתֶן veten

לָנוּ lanu אלהים, אהיה אדני, אהיה אהיה יהוה, בינה ע"ה — וְחַיִּים chayim אהיה אהיה יהוה, בינה ע"ה — אֲרוּכִים arukim,

וְחַיִּים chayim אהיה אהיה יהוה, בינה ע"ה — שֶׁל shel — שָׁלוֹם shalom, — וְחַיִּים chayim

אהיה אהיה יהוה, בינה ע"ה — וְחַיִּים chayim אכא, — טוֹבָה tova — שֶׁל shel — וְחַיִּים chayim בינה ע"ה אהיה אהיה יהוה, בינה ע"ה

שֶׁל shel — בְּרָכָה beracha, — וְחַיִּים chayim אהיה אהיה יהוה, בינה ע"ה — שֶׁל shel

פַּרְנָסָה parnasa — טוֹבָה tova אכא, — וְחַיִּים chayim אהיה אהיה יהוה, בינה ע"ה — שֶׁל shel

וְחִלּוּץ chilutz — עֲצָמוֹת atzamot, — וְחַיִּים chayim אהיה אהיה יהוה, בינה ע"ה — שֶׁיֵּשׁ sheyesh

בָּהֶם bahem — יִרְאַת yir'at — וְחֵטְא chet'a, — וְחַיִּים chayim אהיה אהיה יהוה, בינה ע"ה

שֶׁאֵין she'en — בָּהֶם bahem — בּוּשָׁה busha — וּכְלִימָה uchlima,

וְחַיִּים chayim אהיה אהיה יהוה, בינה ע"ה — שֶׁל shel — עֹשֶׁר osher — וְכָבוֹד vechavod,

וְחַיִּים chayim אהיה אהיה יהוה, בינה ע"ה — שֶׁתְּהֵא shethe — בָּנוּ banu — אַהֲבַת ahavat

תּוֹרָה torah — וְיִרְאַת veyir'at — שָׁמַיִם shamayim — ל"פ טל, ל"פ כוזו,

וְחַיִּים chayim אהיה אהיה יהוה, בינה ע"ה — שֶׁתְּמַלֵּא shetemale — כָּל kol ילי,

מִשְׁאֲלוֹת mish'alot — לִבֵּנוּ libenu — לְטוֹבָה letova אכא — לַעֲבוֹדָתֶךָ la'avodatecha

(Eleven times the word וְחַיִּים—*chayim*—life, corresponding to the letters *Hei* ה and *Vav* ו)

וְאוֹצָרְךָ ve'otzarcha — הַטּוֹב hatov — תִּפְתַּח tiftach — לְהַשְׂבִּיעַ lehasbi'a

נֶפֶשׁ nefesh — שׁוֹקֵקָה shokeka◆ — וְרַוֵּה veraveh — פְּנֵי penei וחכמה בינה

תֵּבֵל tevel ל"פ ב"י — וְשַׂבַּע vesaba רל"י — אֶת et — הָעוֹלָם ha'olam

כֻּלוֹ kulo — מִטּוּבֶךָ mituvach לאו◆ — וּמַלֵּא umaleh — יָדֵינוּ yadenu

מִבִּרְכוֹתֶיךָ mibirchotecha — וּמֵעֹשֶׁר ume'osher — מַתְּנוֹת matnot — יָדֶיךָ yadecha◆

וְקַיֵּם vekayem — בָּנוּ banu — מִקְרָא mikra — שֶׁכָּתוּב shekatuv:

May You lengthen our days in goodness, and our years in pleasantness, fulfilled and vigorous. And grant us long life, a life of peace, a life of goodness, a life of blessing, a life of good livelihood, a life of physical strength, a life in which there is fear of sin, a life in which there is no shame or humiliation, a life of wealth and honor, a life in which there is within us love of Torah and fear of Heaven, a life in which You fulfill all our heart's requests for good to Your service. And Your good treasury may You open to satiate the thirsty soul; and quench the thirst of the face of the earth, and satiate the entire world from Your bounty. Fill our hands from Your blessings and form the wealth of Your gifts and fulfill for us the verse that is written:

otzaro אוֹצָרוֹ et אֶת־ ר״ת ייל lecha לְךָ Adonai יְהֹוָאדֹנָיאהדונהי yiftach יִפְתַּח

hatov הַטּוֹב והו ; ר״ת האא et אֶת־ hashamayim הַשָּׁמַיִם י״פ טל, י״פ כוזו

ulvarech וּלְבָרֵךְ be'ito בְּעִתּוֹ artzecha אַרְצֶךָ metar מְטַר־ latet לָתֵת

ufokdenu וּפָקְדֵנוּ ◆yadecha יָדֶךָ ma'ase מַעֲשֵׂה ילי kol כָּל־ et אֶת

et אֶת orera עוֹרְרָה ◆verachamim וְרַחֲמִים yeshu'a יְשׁוּעָה bifkudat בִּפְקֻדַּת

◆galuyotenu גָּלֻיּוֹתֵינוּ ◆lanu קָנוּ lishu'ata לִישׁוּעָתָה ulcha וּלְכָה gevuratecha גְּבוּרָתֶךָ vesa וְשָׂא

kanfot כַּנְפוֹת me'arba מֵאַרְבַּע yachad יַחַד vekabetzenu וְקַבְּצֵנוּ nes נֵס lekabetz לְקַבֵּץ אדני מ״ה

kol כָּל־ ha'aretz הָאָרֶץ אלהים דההין ע״ה ◆vehaya וְהָיָה יהוה ; יהוה ילי

Adonai יְהֹוָאדֹנָיאהדונהי al עַל־ lemelech לְמֶלֶךְ kol כָּל־ ילי ; עמם

ha'aretz הָאָרֶץ אלהים דההין ע״ה bayom בַּיּוֹם ע״ה נגד, מזבח, זן, אל יהוה

hahu הַהוּא yihye יִהְיֶה יי Adonai יְהֹוָאדֹנָיאהדונהי echad אֶחָד ע״ה אהבה, דאגה

ushmo וּשְׁמוֹ מהש ע״ה, ע״ב בריבוע וקס״א ע״ה, אל שדי ע״ה echad אֶחָד ע״ה אהבה, דאגה:

ana אָנָּא ב״ן, לכב יְהֹוָאדֹנָיאהדונהי Adonai lema'an לְמַעַן mitzvat מִצְוַת

ha'arava הָעֲרָבָה זרע hazot הַזֹּאת shehi שֶׁהִיא minhag מִנְהַג

nevi'im נְבִיאִים, asher אֲשֶׁר ole עוֹלֶה mispara מִסְפָּרָהּ orach אֹרַח

chayim חַיִּים אהיה אהיה יהוה, בינה ע״ה todi'eni תּוֹדִיעֵנִי◆ orach אֹרַח

chayim חַיִּים אהיה אהיה יהוה, בינה ע״ה sova שֹׂבַע semachot שְׂמָחוֹת et אֶת

panecha פָּנֶיךָ ס״ג מ״ה ב״ן ne'imot נְעִימוֹת bimincha בִּימִינְךָ netzach נֶצַח◆

"May the Lord open for you His good treasury, the Heaven, to give you rain to your land in its time and to bless your every handiwork. And may you lend many nations but you shall not borrow." (Deuteronomy 28:12) Evoke for us a remembrance of salvation and compassion. Awaken Your might and come to deliver us, and gather us speedily from all four corners of the Earth to our Land. "The Lord shall be King over the whole world and, on that day, the Lord shall be One and His Name One." (Zechariah 14:9) Please, Lord, in the merit of this precept of the wilow, which is a custom of the prophets, whose numerical value is "path of life," (=277) ""You will show me the way of life, granting me the joy of your presence and the pleasures of living with you forever." (Psalms 16:11)

mitzvat מִצְוַת lema'an לְמַעַן Adonai יְהוֹ..אדני..אהדונהי ב״ן, לכב ana אָנָּא

ezer עֵזֶר mispara מִסְפָּרָהּ ole עוֹלֶה asher אֲשֶׁר זרע ha'arava הָעֲרָבָה

ezer עֵזֶר berachamecha בְּרַחֲמֶיךָ ta'ase תַּעֲשֶׂה zera זֶרַע umispar וּמִסְפַּר

zera זֶרַע zar'i זַרְעִי kol כָּל יל׳ (ויא״י) אל veyih'yu וְיִהְיוּ seli שֶׁלִּי lazera לַזֶּרַע

zar'i זַרְעִי et אֶת utvarech וּתְבָרֵךְ Adonai יְהוֹ..אדני..אהדונהי berach בֵּרַךְ

Aharon אַהֲרֹן et אֶת tzivita צִוִּיתָ asher אֲשֶׁר baberachot בְּבֵרְכוֹת

et אֶת levarech לְבָרֵךְ banav בָּנָיו ve'et וְאֶת kohanecha כֹּהֲנֶךָ

kakatuv כַּכָּתוּב: אור דאגה be'ahava בְּאַהֲבָה Yisrael יִשְׂרָאֵל amcha עַמְּךָ

The initials of the three verses gives us the Holy Name: יהו.
In this section, there are 15 words, which are equal to the numerical value of the Holy Name: ההה.

(Right – Chesed)

veyishmerecha וְיִשְׁמְרֶךָ Adonai יְהוֹ..אדני..אהדונהי yevarechecha יְבָרֶכְךָ

ר״ת = יהוה ; וס״ת = מ״ה:

(Left – Gevurah)

panav פָּנָיו | Adonai יְהוֹ..אדני..אהדונהי ויו ז״ן ויו כף ya'er יָאֵר

בפסוק: אותיות יהה ; מגד vichuneka וִיחֻנֶּךָּ elecha אֵלֶיךָ

(Central – Tiferet)

elecha אֵלֶיךָ panav פָּנָיו | Adonai יְהוֹ..אדני..אהדונהי yisa יִשָּׂא

בפסוק: תיבות האא shalom שָׁלוֹם lecha לְךָ veyasem וְיָשֵׂם

(Malchut)

Yisrael יִשְׂרָאֵל benei בְּנֵי al עַל־ shemi שְׁמִי et אֶת־ vesamu וְשָׂמוּ

avarchem אֲבָרְכֵם: va'ani וַאֲנִי

Please, Lord, in the merit of this precept of the willow, whose numerical value is "assistance," (=207) and the numerical value of "seed," in Your compassion may You act helpfully on behalf of my offspring, and may all my offspring be "offspring blessed by the Lord." And may You bless my offspring with the blessings that You commanded Aaron, Your Priest, and his sons, to bless Your people, Israel, with love. As it is written: "May the Lord bless you and protect you. May the Lord enlighten His countenance for you and give you grace. May the Lord lift His countenance towards you and give you peace. And they shall place My Name upon the Children of Israel and I shall bless them." (Numbers 6:22-27)

אָנָּא ana — ב"ן, לכב — יְהֹוָ Adonai — לְמַעַן lema'an — עֲשָׂרָה asara

שְׁמוֹתֶיךָ shemotecha — הַקְּדוֹשִׁים hakedoshim — עִם im — בְּמִסְפַּר mispar — טוֹב tov — והו

שֶׁעוֹלֶה she'ole — מִסְפָּרָם misparam — כְּמִסְפַּר kemispar — עֲרָבָה arava — זרע,

תַּעֲלֶה ta'ale — לְרָצוֹן leratzon — מהטי ע"ה, ע"ב בריבוע וקס"א ע"ה, אל עדוי ע"ה

לְפָנֶיךָ lefanecha — מִצְוַת mitzvat — וְזַבְטַת chavatat — הָעֲרָבָה ha'arava — זרע

הַזֹּאת hazot — אֲשֶׁר asher — אֲנִי ani — אני — מוּכָן muchan — לַחְבֹּט lachbot

עַל al — הַקַּרְקַע hakarka — חָמֵשׁ chamesh — פְּעָמִים pe'amim — וּתְכַפֵּר utchaper

לָנוּ lanu — אלהים, אהיה אדני — עַל al — מַה ma — מ"ה — שֶׁחָטָאנוּ shechatanu

בְּפִינוּ befinu — וּבִשְׂפָתֵינוּ uvisfatenu — בְּכָל bechol — ילי — דִּבּוּר dibur

אָסוּר asur, — כִּי ki — עֲרָבָה arava זרע — דּוֹמֶה doma — לַשְּׂפָתַיִם lasfatayim ◆

אָנָּא ana — ב"ן, לכב — יְהֹוָ Adonai — לְמַעַן lema'an — מִצְוַת mitzvat

וְזַבְטַת chavatat — הָעֲרָבָה ha'arava זרע — הַזֹּאת hazot — וְחָמֵשׁ chamesh

פְּעָמִים pe'amim — עַל al — הַקַּרְקַע hakarka — תְּרַחֵם terachem — ג"פ רי"ו ;

עָלֵינוּ alenu — אברהם, וז"פ אל, רי"ו ול"ב נתיבות החכמה, רמו"ז (אברים), עסמ"ב וט"ו אותיות פשוטות

שֶׁלֹּא shelo — יִשְׁלֹט yishlot — עָלֵינוּ alenu — שׁוּם shum — מְקַטְרֵג mekatreg

וּמַשְׂטִין umastin, — וְלֹא velo — יִשְׁלֹט yishlot — בָּנוּ banu — שׁוּם shum

לָשׁוֹן lashon — הָרַע hara — וְעֵצָה ve'etza — רָעָה ra'a, — וְלֹא velo — יַעֲשֶׂה ya'ase

בָּנוּ banu — שׁוּם shum — רֹשֶׁם roshem — בֵּין ben — לְמַעְלָה lemala

בֵּין ben — לְמַטָּה lemato'a ◆ — וּתְקַיֵּם utkayem — בָּנוּ banu — מִקְרָא mikra

שֶׁכָּתוּב shekatuv — עַל al — יְדֵי yedei — יְשַׁעְיָה Yeshaya — נְבִיאֶךָ nevi'echa:

Please, Lord, in the merit of Your ten Holy Names (=260) with the numerical equivalent of "good" (=17), which totals in number, the numerical value of "Aravah" (=207), may there ascend favorably before You the precept of beating the willow, which I am prepared to beat on the ground five times. And may You forgive us for that which we have sinned with our mouths and with our lips, with all forbidden speech, for the willow is similar to lips. Please, Lord, in the merit of this precept of beating the wilow five times on the ground, may You take pity on us that there not rule over us any accuser or prosecutor; and may there not rule over us any slander or evil scheme, and may they have no effect upon us neither above nor below. And may you fulfill for us the verse that was written by Isaiah Your prophet:

kol כָּל כ״י   keli כְּלִי כ״י   yutzar יוּצַר   alayich עָלַיִךְ   lo לֹא   yitzlach יִצְלָ֣ח

vechol וְכָל יל״י   lashon לָשׁוֹן   takum תָּקוּם   כ״א   יהוה   itach אִתָּךְ

lamishpat לַמִּשְׁפָּט ע״ה ה״פ אלהים   tarshi'i תַּרְשִׁיעִי   zot זֹאת   nachalat נַחֲלַת

avdei עַבְדֵי   Adonai יְהוָֹאדנ״יאהדונהי   vetzidkatam וְצִדְקָתָם   me'iti מֵאִתִּי

ne'um נְאֻם Adonai יְהוָֹאדנ״יאהדונהי:

vehineh וְהִנֵּה anachnu אֲנַ֫חְנוּ amcha עַמְּךָ ve'anchalatecha וְנַחֲלָתֶךָ benei בְּנֵי

beritecha בְּרִיתֶךָ, benei בְּנֵי Avraham אַבְרָהָם ח״פ אל, רי״ו ול״ב נתיבות החוכמה, רמ״ח

(אברים), עסמ״ב וט״ו אותיות פשוטות   zera זֶ֫רַע ohavecha אוֹהַבְךָ, Yitzchak יִצְחָק ד״פ ב״ן

bincha בִּנְךָ Ya'akov יַעֲקֹב   היות, אידהנויה   adat עֲדַת akedecha עֲקֵדֶךָ,

uvotchim וּבוֹטְחִ֫ים lishu'atcha לִישׁוּעָתֶךָ metzapim מְצַפִּים vechorecha וּבְחֹרֶךָ,

al עַל tzidkotecha צִדְקוֹתֶיךָ ki כִּי ken כֵּן chen חֵן darkecha דַּרְכְּךָ la'asot לַעֲשׂוֹת

chesed חֶ֫סֶד ע״ב, ריבוע יהוה chinam וְחִנָּם tamid תָּמִיד ע״ה קס״א קנ״א קמ״ג◆

chanenu חָנֵּ֫נוּ Adonai יְהוָֹאדנ״יאהדונהי, chanenu וְחָנֵּ֫נוּ uvishuatcha וּבִישׁוּעָתֶךָ,

malknev מַלְכֵּ֫נוּ tarum תָּרוּם vetagbiha וְתַגְבִּיהַּ karnenu קַרְנֵ֫נוּ,

umaher וּמַהֵר chusha וְחֻ֫שָׁה le'ezratenu לְעֶזְרָתֵ֫נוּ, vechol וְכָל יל״י

hakamim הַקָּמִים alenu עָלֵ֫ינוּ lera'a לְרָעָה רהע mehera מְהֵרָה hafer הָפֵר

atzatam עֲצָתָם vekalkel וְקַלְקֵל machshevotam מַחְשְׁבוֹתָם◆ tipol תִּפֹּל

alehem עֲלֵיהֶם emata אֵימָ֫תָה vafachad וָפַ֫חַד ר״ת תעאו שם קדוש bigdol בִּגְדֹל

zero'acha זְרוֹעֲךָ yidemu יִדְּמוּ ka'aven כָּאָ֫בֶן ר״ת = טל, כוזו, יוד הא ואו:

יְהְיוּ [yih'yu] אל [al] (יא"י) כְּמֹץ [kemotz] לִפְנֵי [lifnei] רוּחַ [ru'ach] וּמַלְאַךְ [umalach]

יְהֹוָה [Adonai] דּוֹחֶה [doche]: וְקַיֶּם [vekayem] לָנוּ [lanu] אלהים, אהיה אדני

אֶת [et] בְּחַסְדֶּךָ [bechasdecha] אֱלֹהֵינוּ [Elohenu] ילה יְהֹוָה [Adonai]

אֲשֶׁר [asher] הִבְטַחְתָּנוּ [hivtachtanu] עַל [al] יְדֵי [yedei] יְשַׁעְיָה [Yeshaya]

עִמְּךָ [imecha] כִּי [ki] תִּירָא [tira] אַל [al] כָּאָמוּר [ka'amur] נְבִיאֶךָ [nevi'echa]

אֱלֹהֶיךָ [Elohecha] ילה אֲנִי [ani] כִּי [ki] תִּשְׁתָּע [tishta] אַל [al] אני [ani]

תְּמַכְתִּיךָ [temachticha] אַף [af] עֲזַרְתִּיךָ [azarticha] אַף [af] אִמַּצְתִּיךָ [imatzticha]

כֹּל [kol] ילי וְיִכָּלְמוּ [veyikalmu] יֵבֹשׁוּ [yevoshu] הֵן [hen] צִדְקִי [tzidki] בִּימִין [bimin]

כְּאַיִן [che'ayin] (יא"י) אל [al] יִהְיוּ [yih'yu] בָּךְ [bach] הַנֶּחֱרִים [hanecherim]

וְלֹא [velo] תְבַקְשֵׁם [tevakshem] רִיבֶךָ [rivecha]: אַנְשֵׁי [anshei] וְיֹאבְדוּ [veyovdu]

(יא"י) אל [al] יִהְיוּ [yih'yu] מַצֻּתֶךָ [matzutecha] אַנְשֵׁי [anshei] תִּמְצָאֵם [timtzaem]

כִּי [ki] מִלְחַמְתֶּךָ [milchamtecha]: אַנְשֵׁי [anshei] וּכְאֶפֶס [uchefes] כְּאַיִן [che'ayin]

מַחֲזִיק [machazik] מְוֹזִיק אֱלֹהֶיךָ [Elohecha] ילה יְהֹוָה [Adonai] אני [ani]

אֲנִי [ani] אני תִּירָא [tira] אַל [al] לְךָ [lecha] הָאֹמֵר [ha'omer] יְמִינֶךָ [yeminecha]

עֲזַרְתִּיךָ [azarticha]: אַל [al] תִּירְאִי [tiri] תוֹלַעַת [tola'at] יַעֲקֹב [Ya'akov] הויות,

עֲזַרְתִּיךָ [azarticha] אֲנִי [ani] יִשְׂרָאֵל [Yisrael] מְתֵי [metei] אהדנויה ידהונהי

קְדוֹשׁ [kedosh] וְגֹאֲלֵךְ [vego'alech] יְהֹוָה [Adonai] נְאֻם [ne'um]

חָרוּץ [charutz] וְזֹרֶג [lemorag] לְמוֹרַג [samtich] שַׂמְתִּיךְ [hineh] הִנֵּה [Yisrael]: יִשְׂרָאֵל

תָּדוּשׁ [tadush] פִּיפִיּוֹת [pifiyot] בַּעַל [ba'al] י"ב הויות, קס"א קנ"א [chadash] חָדָשׁ וְדִּישׁ [vadish]

תָּשִׂים [tasim]: כְּמֹץ [kamotz] וּגְבָעוֹת [ugva'ot] וְתָדֹק [vetadok] הָרִים [harim]

May they be like chaff before the wind, with the angel of the Lord pushing. And fulfill for us, the Lord, our God, in Your kindness, that which You promised us through Isaiah, Your prophet, as is stated: "Do not fear for I am with you, do not stray for I am Your God; I have strengthened you and I have assisted you, I have also supported you with My righteous right hand. Behold they will be ashamed and humiliated, all who are angry with you; they wil be as naught, and there will perish the men who quarrel with you. You will seek them but you will not find them, these people who feuded with you; they will be as naught and nonexistent, these people who battled you. For I am the Lord, your God, Who grasps you right hand; He Who says to you: 'Do not fear, I have assisted you; do not be fearful worm, Jacob, the people of Israel, I have helped you,' so says the Lord, and your Redeemer, the Holy One of Israel. Behold I have made you as a new sharp threshing implement with edges; you will thresh mountains and you will grind, and the hills you shall render as chaff.

וּסְעָרָה use'ara   תִּשָּׂאֵם tisa'em   וְרוּחַ veru'ach   תִּזְרֵם tizrem

תָּגִיל tagil   וְאַתָּה ve'ata   אוֹתָם otam   תָּפִיץ tafitz

בַּיהֹוָ֖ה badonai   בִּקְדוֹשׁ bikdosh   יִשְׂרָאֵל Yisrael   תִּתְהַלָּל tit'halal:

While beating the willows five times on the ground one should say:

וְזָבִיט chavit   וְזָבִיט chavit   וְלֹא vela   בְּרִיךְ barich:

While beating the willows on the ground one should meditate to lower the Five *Gevurot* in *Yesod* of *Nukva* and to sweeten them. While raising the willows, one should meditate to elevate the Five *Gevurot* in the secret of the *Neshikin* (kisses—the Upper Unificiation) for the Unificiation on *Simchat Torah*.

One also should meditate as follow:

First beating (first Judgment): גבורה א' סן זְּפְר יוד הא ואו

Second beating (second Judgment): גבורה ב' סן זְּפְר יוד הא ואו

Third beating (third Judgment): גבורה ג' סן זְּפְר יוד הא ואו

Fourth beating (fourth Judgment): גבורה ד' סן זְּפְר יוד הא ואו

Fifth beating (fifth Judgment): גבורה ה' סן זְּפְר יוד הא ואו

Then one should say "*Nishmat kol chai*" on pages 306-312 (until the words "*Ata El*").
And then say:

אֲנַחְנוּ anachnu   מְקַבְּלִים mekabelim   עָלֵינוּ alenu,   בְּלִי beli   נֶדֶר neder,

כִּי ki   לְשָׁנָה leshana   הַבָּאָה haba'a   בָּעֵת ba'et   וּבְעוֹנָה uva'ona   הַזֹּאת hazot,

נֹאמַר nomar: נִשְׁמַת nishmat   כָּל kol   חַי chai:

You shall winnow them and the wind will carry them off, and a storm will scatter them; and you will rejoice in the Lord, in the Holy One of Israel will you be praised." (Isaiah 40:10-16)

Beat, beat, but do not recite a blessing.

We accept upon ourselves, without making a vow that next year at this time and season we will say: "The soul of every living thing…"

KADDISH TITKABAL

יִתְגַּדַּל yitgadal וְיִתְקַדַּשׁ veyitkadash שדי ומילוי שדי ; י"א אותיות כמנין ו"ה

שְׁמֵהּ shemei (שם י"ה דע"ב) רַבָּא raba קנ"א ב"ן, יהוה אלהים יהוה אדני,

אָמֵן amen מילוי קס"א וס"ג, מ"ה ברבוע וע"ב ע"ה ; ר"ת = ו"פ אלהים ; ס"ת = ג"פ יב"ק אידהנויה.

בְּעָלְמָא be'alma דִּי di בְּרָא vera כִרְעוּתֵיהּ chir'utei

וְיַמְלִיךְ veyamlich מַלְכוּתֵיהּ mal'chutei וְיַצְמַח veyatzmach

פּוּרְקָנֵיהּ purkanei וִיקָרֵב vikarev מְשִׁיחֵיהּ meshichei אָמֵן amen אידהנויה.

בְּחַיֵּיכוֹן bechayechon וּבְיוֹמֵיכוֹן uvyomechon וּבְחַיֵּי uvchayei

דְכָל dechol בֵּית bet ילי יִשְׂרָאֵל Yisrael ב"פ ראה בַּעֲגָלָא ba'agala

וּבִזְמַן uvizman קָרִיב kariv וְאִמְרוּ ve'imru אָמֵן amen אָמֵן amen אידהנויה.

The congregation and the chazan say the following:

Twenty eight words (until be'alma) and twenty eight letters (until almaya)

יְהֵא yehe שְׁמֵהּ shemei (שם י"ה דס"ג) רַבָּא raba קנ"א ב"ן,

מְבָרַךְ mevarach ע"ה וע"ב ברבוע מ"ה וס"ג, קס"א מילוי, אדני, יהוה אלהים יהוה

לְעָלַם le'alam לְעָלְמֵי le'almei עָלְמַיָּא almaya יִתְבָּרַךְ yitbarach

Seven words with six letters each (שם בן מ"ב) – and seven times the letter Vav (שם בן מ"ב)

וְיִשְׁתַּבַּח veyishtabach י"פ ע"ב יהוה אל אבג יתץ.

וְיִתְפָּאַר veyitpa'ar הי גו יה קרע שטן וְיִתְרֹמַם veyitromam וה כוזו נגד יכש.

וְיִתְנַשֵּׂא veyitnase במוכסז בטר צתג וְיִתְהַדָּר veyit'hadar כוזו יה וזקב טנע.

וְיִתְעַלֶּה veyit'ale וה יוד ה יגל פזק וְיִתְהַלָּל veyit'halal א ואו הא שקו צית.

שְׁמֵהּ shemei (שם י"ה דמ"ה) דְּקוּדְשָׁא dekudsha בְּרִיךְ verich הוּא hu

אָמֵן amen אידהנויה.

KADDISH TITKABAL
May His great Name be more exalted and sanctified. (Amen)
In the world that He created according to His will, and may His kingdom reign. And may He cause His
redemption to sprout and may He bring the Mashiach closer. (Amen) In your lifetimes and in your days and
in the lifetime of all the House of Israel, speedily and in the near future, and you shall say, Amen. (Amen)
May His great Name be blessed forever and for all eternity. Blessed and lauded, and glorified, and exalted,
and extolled, and honored, and uplifted, and praised be the Name of the Holy Blessed One (Amen)

לְעֵלָּא le'ela מִן min כָּל kol ילי בִּרְכָתָא birchata ◆ שִׁירָתָא shirata ◆

תֻּשְׁבְּחָתָא tishbechata וְנֶחָמָתָא venechamata ◆ דַּאֲמִירָן da'amiran

בְּעָלְמָא be'alma וְאִמְרוּ ve'imru אָמֵן amen : אָמֵן amen אידהנויה.

תִּתְקַבַּל titkabal צְלוֹתָנָא tzelotana וּבָעוּתָנָא uva'utana

עִם im צְלוֹתְהוֹן tzelotehon וּבָעוּתְהוֹן uva'utehon דְּכָל dechol ילי

בֵּית bet ב״פ ראה Yisrael יִשְׂרָאֵל קֳדָם kadam אֲבוּנָא avuna

דְּבִשְׁמַיָּא devishmaya וְאִמְרוּ ve'imru אָמֵן amen : אָמֵן amen אידהנויה.

יְהֵא yehe שְׁלָמָא shelama רַבָּא raba קנ״א ב״ן, יהוה אלהים יהוה אדני, מילוי קס״א וס״ג,

מִן min שְׁמַיָּא shemaya אהיה אהיה יהוה, בינה ע״ה ◆ וְחַיִּים chayim מ״ה ברבוע וע״ב ע״ה shemaya ◆

וְשָׂבָע vesava וִישׁוּעָה vishu'a וְנֶחָמָה venechama וְשֵׁיזָבָא veshezava

וּרְפוּאָה urfu'a וּגְאֻלָּה ug'ula וּסְלִיחָה uslicha וְכַפָּרָה vechapara

וְרֶיוַח verevach וְהַצָּלָה vehatzala ◆ לָנוּ lanu אלהים, אהיה אדני יה אדני וּלְכָל ulchol

עַמּוֹ amo יִשְׂרָאֵל Yisrael וְאִמְרוּ ve'imru אָמֵן amen : אָמֵן amen אידהנויה.

Take three steps backwards and say:

עוֹשֶׂה ose שָׁלוֹם shalom

בִּמְרוֹמָיו bimromav ע״ב, ריבוע יהוה ◆ הוּא hu בְּרַחֲמָיו berachamav

יַעֲשֶׂה ya'ase שָׁלוֹם shalom עָלֵינוּ alenu ר״ת ע״ע נהרין ◆

וְעַל ve'al כָּל kol ילי ; עמם עַמּוֹ amo יִשְׂרָאֵל Yisrael וְאִמְרוּ ve'imru אָמֵן amen :

אָמֵן amen אידהנויה. ◆

Above all blessings, songs, praises, and words of consolation that may be said in the world, and you shall say, Amen. (Amen) May our prayers and pleas be accepted, together with the prayers and pleas of the entire House of Israel, before our Father in Heaven, and you say, Amen. (Amen) May there be abundant peace from Heaven; Life, contentment, salvation, consolation, deliverance, healing, redemption, pardon, atonement, comfort, and relief. For us and for His entire nation, Israel, and you shall say, Amen. (Amen) He, Who makes peace in His High Places, He, in His compassion, shall make peace upon us And upon His entire nation, Israel, and you shall say, Amen. (Amen)

Before we open the Ark we say:
On Shabbat we start here:

hu **הוּא** Adonai יְהֹוָאדֹנָיאהדונהי ki כִּי lada'at לָדַעַת hor'eta הָרְאֵתָ Ata אַתָּה

od עוֹד en אֵין haElohim הָאֱלֹהִים אהיה אדני ; ילה ; ה׳ הוא האלקים = עֵנוּ עג״כ ; ר״ת יהה

milvado מִלְבַדּוֹ אהיה אדני ; ילה kamocha כָּמוֹךָ en אֵין מ״ב: vaElohim בָאֱלֹהִים

kema'asecha כְּמַעֲשֶׂיךָ: ve'en וְאֵין ללה Adonai אֲדֹנָי

When the Holiday falls on weekdays we start here:

yehi יְהִי יְהֹוָאדֹנָיאהדונהי imanu עִמָּנוּ ילה Elohenu אֱלֹהֵינוּ Adonai יְהֹוָאדֹנָיאהדונהי ריבוע ס״ג, קס״א

al אַל אותיות ור׳ ע״ה avotenu אֲבוֹתֵינוּ יהה im עִם haya הָיָה ka'asher כַּאֲשֶׁר

hoshi'a הוֹשִׁיעָה יהוה ושי״ע נהורין yiteshenu יִטְּשֵׁנוּ: ve'al וְאַל ya'azvenu יַעַזְבֵנוּ

et אֶת amecha עַמֶּךָ ס״ת כהת, משיוה בן דוד ע״ה uvarech וּבָרֵךְ ע״ה et אֶת

ha'olam הָעוֹלָם: ad עַד venas'em וְנַשְּׂאֵם ur'em וּרְעֵם nachalatecha נַחֲלָתֶךָ

Moshe מֹשֶׁה מהש, vayomer וַיֹּאמֶר ha'aron הָאָרֹן binso'a בִּנְסֹעַ vay'hi וַיְהִי

Adonai יְהֹוָאדֹנָיאהדונהי | kuma קוּמָה קס״א (מקוה) ד״פ אלהים ע״ה אל שדי, אל ברבוע קס״א, ע״ב

mesanecha מְשַׂנְאֶיךָ veyanusu וְיָנֻסוּ oyvecha אֹיְבֶיךָ veyafutzu וְיָפֻצוּ

Adonai יְהֹוָאדֹנָיאהדונהי mipanecha מִפָּנֶיךָ: קס״א ס״ג מ״ה ב״ן kuma קוּמָה (מקוה) קס״א מִפָּנֶיךָ

uzecha עֻזֶּךָ: va'aron וַאֲרוֹן Ata אַתָּה limnuchatecha לִמְנוּחָתֶךָ

vachasidecha וַחֲסִידֶיךָ tzedek צֶדֶק yilbeshu יִלְבְּשׁוּ kohanecha כֹּהֲנֶיךָ

meshichecha מְשִׁיחֶךָ: al אַל tashev תָּשֵׁב penei פְּנֵי חכמה בינה yeranenu יְרַנֵּנוּ: ba'avur בַּעֲבוּר David דָּוִד avdecha עַבְדֶּךָ פוי, אל אדני

"You have shown to be known that the Lord is your God and there is none beside Him." (Deuteronomy 4:35) "There is none like You among the deities Lord and there is nothing like Your works." (Psalms 86:8) "May the Lord, our God, be with us as He was with our forefathers. May He not abandon or forsake us." (1 Kings 8:57) "Save Your people and bless Your heritage. Lead them and uplift them forever." (Psalms 28:9) When the Ark traveled forward, Moses would say: Arise, Lord. Let Your enemies be scattered and let those who hate You flee before You." (Numbers 10:35) "Arise Lord to Your resting place, You and the Ark of Your strength. Your priests don justice and your pious once shall sing. For the sake of David, Your servant, do not turn Your countenance away from Your anointed one." (Psalms 132:8-10)

OPENING OF THE ARK

Drawing the Light of *Chochmah*.
Rabbi Shimon bar Yochai says: "While the Ark is open, we should prepare ourselves with awe. Everyone should arouse an inner sense of wonder, as if we are actually standing on Mount Sinai, trembling as we behold the overwhelming expression of Light. Silent we stand, focused solely on the opportunity of hearing each sacred word of the scroll. When we take out the Torah in public to read, all the Gates of Mercy in Heaven are open, and we awaken a love from above."

Moshe מֹשֶׁה   vayomer וַיֹּאמֶר   ha'aron הָאָרֹן   binso'a בִּנְסֹעַ   vayhi וַיְהִי

kuma קוּמָה (קנ"א מקוה) | ע"ה אלהים ד"פ עו"די, אל וקס"א, בריבוע ע"ב מהש,

veyanusu וְיָנֻסוּ   oyvecha אֹיְבֶיךָ   veyafutzu וְיָפֻצוּ   Adonai יְהֹוָ

mesan'echa מְשַׂנְאֶיךָ   mipanecha מִפָּנֶיךָ   ס"ג מ"ה בו: ki כִּי

miTziyon מִצִּיּוֹן   tetze תֵצֵא   torah תּוֹרָה   udvar וּדְבַר

baruch בָּרוּךְ   shenatan שֶׁנָּתַן   Adonai יְהֹוָ   mirushalaim מִירוּשָׁלָֽםִ:

torah תּוֹרָה   le'amo לְעַמּוֹ   Yisrael יִשְׂרָאֵל   bikdushato בִּקְדֻשָּׁתוֹ.

THE THIRTEEN ATTRIBUTES

The 13 Attributes are 13 virtues or properties that reflect 13 aspects of our relationship with the Creator. These 13 Attributes are how we interact with God in our daily lives, whether we know it or not. They work like a mirror.

When we look into a mirror and smile, the image smiles back. When we look into a mirror and curse, the image curses back. If we perform a negative action in our world, the mirror reflects negative energy at us. There are 13 Attributes that have these reflecting properties within us. As we attempt to transform our reactive nature into proactive, this direct feedback guides and corrects us.

The number 13 also represents one above the 12 signs of the zodiac. The 12 signs control our find instinctive, reactive nature. The number 13 gives us control over the 12 signs, which, in essence, gives us control over our behavior.

OPENING OF THE ARK

"When the Ark traveled forward, Moses would say: Arise, Lord. Let Your enemies be scattered and let those who hate You flee before You." (Numbers 10:35) *"Because out of Zion shall the Torah emerge, and the Word of the Lord from Jerusalem."* (Isaiah 2:3) *Blessed is He Who gave the Torah to His Nation, Israel, due to His Holiness.*

On *Shabbat* or on *Chol Ham'oed* we skip the 13 Attributes and continue with *"Berich Shemei."*

We recite the verse three times:

יְהֹוָ‌ה‌ אֲדֹנָי‌אהדונהי‌ | יְהֹוָ‌ה‌ אֲדֹנָי‌אהדונהי‌ Adonai | Adonai

(1 אֵל el יאא"י מילוי דס"ג (Keter) 2) רַחוּם rachum (Chochmah) 3) וְחַנּוּן vechanun

(4 אֶרֶךְ erech (5 אַפַּיִם apayim (6 וְרַב verav ע"ב, ריבוע יהוה chesed וְחֶסֶד

(7 וֶאֱמֶת ve'emet אהיה פעמים אהיה, ז"פ ס"ג: 8) נֹצֵר notzer ע"ב, ריבוע יהוה chesed וְחֶסֶד

(9 לָאֲלָפִים la'alafim ר"ת שם נוזל שם (10 נֹשֵׂא nose עָוֹן avon (11 וָפֶשַׁע vafesha

(12 וְחַטָּאָה vechata'a (13 וְנַקֵּה venake קס"א (אלף הי יוד הי)

וע"י שם זה יכוין לברר ולנקות את נצוצי הקדושה שנפלו עם הקיטרוגים, להעלותם לשורשם:

THE PRAYER FROM THE ARI (THE PERSONAL WISH)

It is through the merit of Kabbalist Rav Isaac Luria (the Ari), that we have an opportunity to make a personal wish on the Holiday to effect change for the entire year. All too often, we ask for what we want instead of asking for what we really need to help us grow spiritually. Only through growth and inner transformation can we achieve lasting fulfillment as opposed to instant and momentary gratification.

רִבּוֹנוֹ ribono שֶׁל shel עוֹלָם olam, מַלֵּא male מִשְׁאֲלוֹתַי mishalotai

לְטוֹבָה letova אַבָּא, וְהָפֵק vehafek רְצוֹנִי retzoni, וְתֶן veten שְׁאֵלָתִי she'elati

וּמְחֹל umchol כָּל kol יְלִי עֲוֹנוֹתַי avonotai וְעֲוֹנוֹת va'avonot

בְּנֵי benei בֵּיתִי beti מְחִילָה mechila בְּחֶסֶד bechesed ע"ב, ריבוע יהוה,

מְחִילָה mechila בְּרַחֲמִים berachamim מצפץ, אלהים דיודין, י"פ יי"י

וְטַהֲרֵנִי vetahareni מֵהַפְּשָׁעִים mehapsha'im וְהַחֲטָאִים vehachata'im.

וְזָכְרֵנִי vezochreni בְּרָצוֹן beratzon מהש' ע"ה, ע"ב בריבוע וקס"א ע"ה, אל שדי ע"ה

טוֹב tov והו מִלְפָנֶיךָ milfanecha ס"ג מ"ה ב"ן

וּפָקְדֵנִי ufokdeni בִּפְקֻדַת bifkudat יְשׁוּעָה yeshu'a וְרַחֲמִים verachamim,

---

THE THIRTEEN ATTRIBUTES

"Lord, Lord, (1) God (Keter) (2) Compassionate (Chochmah) (3) Gracious (4) Greatly (5) Patient (6) Abounding with kindness (7) and truth (8) He keeps kindness (9) for the thousands (10) He bears iniquities (11) and sin (12) and transgression (13) and cleanses." (Exodus 34:6-7)

THE PRAYER FROM THE ARI (THE PERSONAL WISH)

Master of the world,

fulfill my requests favorably and bring out my desire and give me my request and forgive all my sins and the sins of the members of my household and forgiveness through favor, a forgiveness through mercy. Purify me from sins and crimes. And remember me favorably before You and visit me with redemption and mercy.

וְזָכְרֵנִי vezochreni לְוַיִּים lechayim אהיה אהיה, יהוה, בינה ע"ה טוֹבִים tovim

וְאֲרוּכִים ve'arukim, וּפַרְנָסָה ufarnasa טוֹבָה tova אכא וְכַלְכָּלָה vechalkala,

וְלֶחֶם velechem ג"פ יהוה לֶאֱכוֹל le'echol וּבֶגֶד uveged לִלְבּוֹשׁ lilbosh,

וְעוֹשֶׁר ve'osher וְכָבוֹד vechavod וְאֲרִיכוּת ve'arichut יָמִים yamim גכך

בְּתוֹרָתֶךָ betoratecha וּבְמִצְוֹתֶיךָ vevemitzotecha, וְהָפֵק vehafek תַּעֲלָה te'ala

וּרְפוּאָה urfu'a לְכָל lechol יה אדני lechol מַכְאוֹבֵי mach'ovei לִבֵּנוּ libenu,

וּתְבָרֵךְ utvarech מַעֲשֵׂי ma'asei יָדֵינוּ yadenu, וּגְזוֹר ugzor עָלֵינוּ alenu

גְּזֵרוֹת gezerot טוֹבוֹת tovot וּבַטֵּל uvatel מֵעָלֵינוּ me'alenu כָּל kol ילי

גְּזֵרוֹת gezerot קָשׁוֹת kashot וְרָעוֹת veraot. אָמֵן amen יאהדונהי כֵּן ken יְהִי yehi

רָצוֹן ratzon מהע ע"ה, ע"ב בריבוע וקס"א ע"ה, אל שדי ע"א (ייא"י מילוי דס"ג) אל יִהְיוּ yihyu

לְרָצוֹן leratzon מהע ע"ה, ע"ב בריבוע וקס"א ע"ה, אל שדי ע"א אֲמְרֵי imrei

פִי fi ר"ת אָלֶף = אלף למד דלת יוד ע"ה, שין למד דלת ע"ה וְהֶגְיוֹן vehegyon לִבִּי libi

לְפָנֶיךָ lefanecha ס"ג מ"ה ב"ן יְהֹוָאדֹנָייאהדונהי Adonai צוּרִי tzuri וְגֹאֲלִי vego'ali:

BERICH SHEMEI

This section is taken directly from the *Zohar* and appears in its original Aramaic. The *Berich Shemei* works like a time machine that literally transports our soul to Mount Sinai, when Moses received the tablets. By revisiting the exact time and place of the revelation, we are able to draw down aspects of the original Light through the reading of the Torah. The *Berich Shemei* contains 130 words. Adam was separated from his wife, Eve, for 130 years during which time he sinned. Each word in the prayer helps to correct one of those years. Each of us was included in the soul of Adam. We are Adam. Adam is merely the code name of the unified soul that includes every human being who has and will ever walk this planet.

בְּרִיךְ berich שְׁמֵיהּ shemei דְּמָארֵי demarei עָלְמָא alma

בְּרִיךְ berich כִּתְרָךְ kitrach וְאַתְרָךְ ve'atrach. יְהֵא yehe

רְעוּתָךְ re'utach עִם im עַמָּךְ amach יִשְׂרָאֵל Yisrael לְעָלַם le'alam.

Remember me for a good and long life and with good sustenance and with earnings and with bread to eat and with clothes to wear and with wealth, honor, and long days in the study of Your Torah and in fulfilling Your commandments. Send cure and healing to all the pains of our hearts and bless our handiwork, Amen, may it so be Your will. Sentence us with good verdicts and cancel for us all evil and hard verdicts. "And may the words of my mouth and the thoughts of my heart be favorable to You, Lord, my Rock and my Redeemer." (Psalms 19:15)

BERICH SHEMEI

Blessed is the Name of the Master of the World.
Blessed are Your Crown and Your Location. May Your desire be with Your Nation, Israel, forever.

וּפוּרְקַן ufurkan יְמִינָךְ yeminach אַחֲזֵי achzei לְעַמָּךְ le'amach

בְּבֵית bevet ב"פ ראה מִקְדָּשָׁךְ mikdashach לְאַמְטוּיֵי le'amtuye לָנָא lana

מִטּוּב mituv נְהוֹרָךְ nehorach וּלְקַבֵּל ulkabel צְלוֹתָנָא tzelotana

בְּרַחֲמִין berachamin יְהֵא yehe רַעֲוָא ra'ava קֳדָמָךְ kodamach

דְּתוֹרִיךְ detorich לַן lan חַיִּין chayin בְּטִיבוּ betivu וְלֶהֱוֵי velehevei אֲנָא ana ב"ן

עַבְדָּךְ avdach פוי, אל אדני פְּקִידָא pekida בְּגוֹ bego צַדִּיקַיָּא tzadikaya

לְמִרְחַם lemircham אברהם, ח"פ אל, רי"ו ול"ב נתיבות החכמה, רמ"ז (אברים), עסמ"ב וט"ז אותיות

עֲלַי alai ילי וּלְמִנְטַר ulmintar יָתִי yati וְיַת veyat כָּל kal ילי

דִּילִי dili וְדִי vedi לְעַמָּךְ le'amach יִשְׂרָאֵל Yisrael אַנְתְּ ant הוּא hu

זָן zan נגד, מזבח, אל יהוה לְכֹלָּא lechola וּמְפַרְנֵס umfarnes לְכֹלָּא lechola

אַנְתְּ ant הוּא hu שַׁלִּיט shalit עַל al כֹּלָּא kola אַנְתְּ ant הוּא hu

דְּשַׁלִּיט deshalit עַל al מַלְכַיָּא malchaya וּמַלְכוּתָא umalchuta דִּילָךְ dilach

אֲנָא ana ב"ן הִיא hee עַבְדָּא avda דְּקֻדְשָׁא dekudsha בְּרִיךְ berich

הוּא hu דְּסָגִידְנָא desagidna קַמֵּהּ kame וּמִן umin קַמֵּי kame דִּיקַר dikar

אוֹרַיְתֵהּ orayte בְּכָל bechol ב"ן, לכב עִדָּן idan וְעִדָּן ve'idan

לָא la עַל al אֱנָשׁ enash רָחִיצְנָא rachitzna וְלָא vela עַל al בַּר bar

אֱלָהִין elahin ילה סָמִיכְנָא samichna אֶלָא ela בֶּאֱלָהָא be'elaha

דִּשְׁמַיָּא dishmaya דְּהוּא dehu אֱלָהָא elaha קְשׁוֹט keshot

וְאוֹרַיְתֵהּ ve'orayte קְשׁוֹט keshot וּנְבִיאוֹהִי unvi'ohi קְשׁוֹט keshot

וּמַסְגֵּא umasgei לְמֶעְבַּד lemebad טָבְוָן tavevan וּקְשׁוֹט ukshot

---

The redemption of Your Right may You show to Your Nation in Your Temple. May You fill us with the best of Your enlightenment, and may You receive our prayers with mercy. May it be pleasing before You to lengthen our lives with good. And I, Your servant, shall be remembered together with the righteous ones. Have mercy on me and protect me, and all that I have, and all that belongs to Your Nation, Israel. You are the One Who nourishes all and provides all with their livelihood. You are the One Who controls everything. You have control over kings, and their kingdoms are Yours. I am the servant of the Holy Blessed One, as I prostrate myself before Him and before the glory of His Torah, at each and every moment. I put not my trust in any man, and I have no faith in the sons of the gods. My trust and faith are only in the God in Heaven, Who is the true God; His Torah is true; His prophets are true; and He abundantly performs compassion and truth.

bei בֵּיהּ ana אֲנָא ב"ן rachitz רָחִיץ velishme וְלִשְׁמֵהּ yakira יַקִּירָא

kadisha קַדִּישָׁא ana אֲנָא ב"ן emar אֵמַר tushbechan תֻּשְׁבְּחָן• yehe יְהֵא

ra'ava רַעֲוָא kodamach קָדָמָךְ detiftach דְּתִפְתַּח liba'i לִבָּאִי

be'oraytach בְּאוֹרַיְתָךְ• vetihav (וְתִיהַב) li לִי benin בְּנִין dichrin דִּכְרִין

de'avdin דְּעָבְדִין re'utach רְעוּתָךְ (•) vetashlim וְתַשְׁלִים mish'alin מִשְׁאֲלִין

deliba'i דְּלִבָּאִי veliba וְלִבָּא dechol דְּכָל־ ילי amach עַמָּךְ Yisrael יִשְׂרָאֵל

letav לְטַב ulchayin וּלְחַיִּין velishlam וְלִשְׁלָם amen אָמֵן יאהדונהי

TAKING OUT THE TORAH FROM THE ARK

The *Torah* is taken out to give us all a chance to make a personal connection with it, either by kissing or touching it. Sometimes, people rush to make their connection, pushing, crowding, and shoving others aside as they try to touch the scroll. Spiritually, these actions reflect energy opposite to that of the *Torah*. The *Torah* connection is not just physical. Connections to the *Torah* are made by way of a spiritual state of mind, which includes tolerance and care for others. One cannot be in the right spiritual frame of mind if he is rude to another individual.

baruch בְּרוּךְ hamakom הַמָּקוֹם shenatan שֶׁנָּתַן torah תּוֹרָה le'amo לְעַמּוֹ

Yisrael יִשְׂרָאֵל baruch בְּרוּךְ hu הוּא: ashrei אַשְׁרֵי ha'am הָעָם

ashrei אַשְׁרֵי lo לוֹ ע"ה אלהים ד"פ שדי, אל קס"א, בריבוע ע"ב מהע, משה, shekacha שֶׁכָּכָה

ha'am הָעָם ר"ת לאה sheAdonai שֶׁיְהֹוָה אדני אהדונהי Elohav אֱלֹהָיו ילה:

Before the Torah is carried to the bimah (podium), the chazan says:

gadelu גַּדְּלוּ ladonai לַיהֹוָה אדני אהדונהי iti אִתִּי uneromema וּנְרוֹמְמָה

shemo שְׁמוֹ מהע ע"ה, ע"ב בריבוע וקס"א ע"ה, אל שדי ע"ה yachdav יַחְדָּו:

In Him, I trust and I say praises
to His Holy and precious Name. May it be pleasing before You that You shall open my heart with Your
Torah (and that You may give me male sons, who shall fulfill Your desire). And may You fulfill the
requests of my heart and the heart of Your entire Nation, Israel, for good, for life, and for peace. Amen.

TAKING OUT THE TORAH FROM THE ARK

Blessed is the Providence Who had given the Torah to His nation, Israel,
Blessed is He. "Joyfull is the nationthat this is so for them, joyfull is the nation that the Lord is their God."
(Psalms 144:15) "Proclaim the Lord's greatness with me and let us exalt His Name together." (Psalms 34:4)

Then the congregation says the following while the Torah is carried to the bimah:

רי״ו vehagevura וְהַגְּבוּרָה hagedula הַגְּדֻלָּה Adonai יְ־הֹוָ־ה lecha לְךָ

ki כִּי ההה vehahod וְהַהוֹד vehanetzach וְהַנֵּצַח vehatiferet וְהַתִּפְאֶרֶת

lecha לְךָ uva'aretz וּבָאָרֶץ י״פ טל, י״פ כוו bashamayim בַּשָּׁמַיִם ילי chol כֹל

vehamitnase וְהַמִּתְנַשֵּׂא hamamlacha הַמַּמְלָכָה Adonai יְ־הֹוָ־ה

romemu רוֹמְמוּ ע״ה ריבוע אלהים ואלהים דיודין יה אדני lerosh לְרֹאשׁ lechol לְכָל

vehishtachavu וְהִשְׁתַּחֲווּ Elohenu אֱלֹהֵינוּ ילה Adonai יְ־הֹוָ־ה

romemu רוֹמְמוּ hu הוּא kadosh קָדוֹשׁ raglav רַגְלָיו lahadom לַהֲדֹם

lehar לְהַר vehishtachavu וְהִשְׁתַּחֲווּ ילה Elohenu אֱלֹהֵינוּ Adonai יְ־הֹוָ־ה

Elohenu אֱלֹהֵינוּ ילה Adonai יְ־הֹוָ־ה kadosh קָדוֹשׁ ki כִּי kodsho קָדְשׁוֹ

Some add this section:

biltecha בִּלְתֶּךָ en אֵין ki כִּי kadonai כַּיְ־הֹוָ־ה kadosh קָדוֹשׁ en אֵין

mi מִי ki כִּי ילה kelohenu כֵּאלֹהֵינוּ ע״ה אלהים דההן tzur צוּר ve'en וְאֵין ילי

tzur צוּר umi וּמִי ילי Adonai יְ־הֹוָ־ה mibal'adei מִבַּלְעֲדֵי מ״ב Eloha אֱלוֹהַּ

lanu לָנוּ tziva צִוָּה torah תּוֹרָה ילה Elohenu אֱלֹהֵינוּ zulati זוּלָתִי ע״ה אלהים דההן

ע״ה אלהים ד״פ אל עדיי, וקס״א, ע״ב בריבוע מהע, Moshe מֹשֶׁה אדני אהיה אלהים,

kehilat קְהִלַּת Yaakov יַעֲקֹב ו היות, יאהדונהי איהדנויה morasha מוֹרָשָׁה

hee הִיא ע״ה בינה יהוה, אהיה אהיה chayim וְחַיִּים etz עֵץ

me'ushar מְאֻשָּׁר vetomcheha וְתֹמְכֶיהָ ba בָּהּ ר״ת לההו lamachazikim לַמַּחֲזִיקִים

vechol וְכֹל no'am נֹעַם darchei דַּרְכֵי deracheha דְּרָכֶיהָ ילי

rav רָב shalom שָׁלוֹם shalom שָׁלוֹם netivoteha נְתִיבוֹתֶיהָ

michshol מִכְשׁוֹל lamo לָמוֹ ve'en וְאֵין toratecha תּוֹרָתֶךָ le'ohavei לְאֹהֲבֵי

"Yours, Lord, is the greatness, the strength, the splendor, the triumph, and the glory, and everything in the Heavens and the Earth. Yours, Lord, is the Kingdom and the sovereignty over every leader." (I Chronicles 29:11) "Exalt the Lord, our God, and prostrate yourselves at His footstool, is Holy. Exalt the Lord, our God, and prostrate yourselves at His Holy Mountain because the Lord, our God, is Holy." (Psalms 99:9)

"There is none as Holy as the Lord, because there is none other beside You. There is no Rock like our God." (I Samuel 2:2) "For Who is God beside the Lord? Who is a Rock, other than our God?" (Psalms 18:32) "The Torah that Moses commanded us with is a heritage for the congregation of Jacob." (Deuteronomy 33:4) "It is a tree of life to those who hold on to it, and those who support it are happy." (Proverb 3:18) "Its ways are the way of pleasantness and all its paths lead to peace." (Proverbs 3:17) "Abundance of peace for those who love Your Torah and for them there is no obstacle." (Psalms 119:165)

Adonai יְהֹוָ(אדניאהדונהי)וָה יִתֵּן yiten לְעַמּוֹ le'amo עֹז oz יְהֹוָ(אדניאהדונהי)וָה Adonai

יְבָרֵךְ yevarech ע"ב ס"ג מ"ה ב"ן, הברכה (לבמתק את ז' המלכים שמתו) אֶת־ et עַמּוֹ amo

בְּשָׁלוֹם vashalom ר"ת ע"ב, ריבוע יהוה: כִּי ki שֵׁם shem יְהֹוָ(אדניאהדונהי)וָה Adonai

אֶקְרָא ekra הָבוּ havu אזוֹר, אהבה, דאגה גֹּדֶל godel לֵאלֹהֵינוּ lelohenu ילה:

הַכֹּל hakol ילי tenu תְּנוּ tenu עֹז oz לֵאלֹהִים lelohim אהיה אדני ; ילה

וּתְנוּ utnu כָּבוֹד chavod לַתּוֹרָה latorah:

RAISING THE TORAH

After the scroll is placed on the *bimah* (the podium), a person is called up to raise the Torah for the congregation to see the specific section we will be reading from the Torah Scroll. As we raise the Torah, we meditate to also raise our level of consciousness. We should look at the parchment to try to see the first letter of that week's reading. We should also attempt to find the first letter of our Hebrew name within the text. You can use the *Talit* to help yourself focus (if you don't have a *Talit* you can use your finger).

וְזֹאת vezot הַתּוֹרָה hatorah אֲשֶׁר asher שָׂם sam מֹשֶׁה Moshe

לִפְנֵי lifnei בְּנֵי benei מהעו, ע"ב בריבוע וקס"א, אל שדי, ד"פ אלהים ע"ה יִשְׂרָאֵל Yisrael:

עֵדִי Shadai אל שדי = משה, מהעו, ע"ב בריבוע וקס"א, ד"פ אלהים ע"ה (מילוי דס"ג) ייא"י אֵל El

אֱמֶת emet אהיה פעמים אהיה, ז"פ ס"ג וּמֹשֶׁה uMoshe מהעו, ע"ב בריבוע וקס"א, אל שדי,

וְתוֹרָתוֹ vetorato ז"פ ס"ג אהיה פעמים אהיה ע"ה אֱמֶת emet ד"פ אלהים ע"ה

אֱמֶת emet אהיה פעמים אהיה, ז"פ ס"ג: תּוֹרָה torah צִוָּה tziva

מֹשֶׁה Moshe מהעו, ע"ב בריבוע וקס"א, אל שדי, ד"פ אלהים ע"ה אהיה אדני, אהיה אלהים לָנוּ lanu

מוֹרָשָׁה morasha קְהִלַּת kehilat יַעֲקֹב Yaakov ו' הויות, יאהדונהי: איהדונהי

הָאֵל haEl ייא"י (מילוי דס"ג) תָּמִים tamim דַּרְכּוֹ darko אִמְרַת imrat

צְרוּפָה tzerufa מָגֵן magen ג"פ אל (ייא"י מילוי דס"ג) יְהֹוָ(אדניאהדונהי)וָה Adonai

הוּא hu ר"ת מיכאל גבריאל נוריאל יה אדני לְכֹל lechol הַחוֹסִים hachosim בּוֹ bo:

"The Lord give might to his people, The Lord will bless his nation with peace." *(Psalms 29:11)*
"When I call out the Name of the Lord, proclaim greatness to our God." *(Duteronomy 32:3)*
"All should attribute power to God." *(Psalms 68:35)* And give honor to the Torah.

RAISING THE TORAH

"*And this is the Torah that Moses placed before the children of Israel.*" *(Deuteronomy 4:44)*
God is true and Moses is true and His Torah is true. "*The Torah, which Moses commanded us with, is a heritage for the Congregation of Jacob.*" *(Deuteronomy 33:4)* "*God, His ways are perfect. Lord's statement is pure. He is the Shield for all who take refuge in Him*" *(II Samuel 22:31)*

The *Torah* reading for the first day of *Sukkot* can be found on page 732.

The *Torah* reading for *Chol Hamo'ed* can be found on pages 743-745.

The *Torah* reading for *Shabbat Chol Hamo'ed* can be found on page 738.

The *Torah* reading for *Simchat Torah* can be found on page 746.

The *chazan* says:

et אֶת מ"ה יהוה ריבוע יהוה ריבוע יהוה barchu בָּרְכוּ Aharon אַהֲרֹן ב"פ ראה בית bet בֵּית

מלה׃ vechahen וְכֹהֵן kerav קְרַב מלה kohen כֹּהֵן, hamevorach הַמְבֹרָךְ Hashem ה'

The one who goes up to the *Torah (the "ole")* holds the Scroll with both his hands, and says:

imachem עִמָּכֶם Adonai יְהֹוָאדֹנִייאהדונהי

The congregation replies:

Hashem ה' yevarchecha יְבָרֶכְךָ

The *ole* continues:

(ויכוין "ברכו את ה' המבורך" – מ"ב ור"ך עֹהם שמאל וימין):

et אֶת מ"ה ריבוע יהוה יהוה ריבוע יהוה barchu בָּרְכוּ rabanan רַבָּנָן

ע"ה׃ הבת בן דוד ע"ה, משיח ס"ת כהת, hamevorach הַמְבֹרָךְ Adonai יְהֹוָאדֹנִייאהדונהי

The congregation then replies:

Neshamah		Ruach		Nefesh
hamevorach הַמְבוֹרָךְ		Adonai יְהֹוָאדֹנִייאהדונהי		baruch בָּרוּךְ
Yechidah				Chayah
va'ed וָעֶד׃	דס"ג	אותיות	ס"ג ו"י	ריבוע	le'olam לְעוֹלָם

The *ole* repeats this line after the congregation:

Neshamah		Ruach		Nefesh
hamevorach הַמְבוֹרָךְ		Adonai יְהֹוָאדֹנִייאהדונהי		baruch בָּרוּךְ
Yechidah				Chayah
va'ed וָעֶד׃	דס"ג	אותיות	ס"ג ו"י	ריבוע	le'olam לְעוֹלָם

THE READING

(The House of Aaron; bless the Lord, the Blessed One. Kohen, come close and stand and do your priestly duty.)
May the Lord be with you. May the Lord bless you.
Masters, Bless the Lord, the Blessed One.
Blessed is the Lord, the Blessed One, forever and for eternity.

And then says the following blessing:

בָּרוּךְ baruch אַתָּה Ata יְהֹוָה Adonai אֱלֹהֵינוּ Elohenu ילה

מֶלֶךְ melech הָעוֹלָם ha'olam אֲשֶׁר asher בָּחַר bachar- בָּנוּ banu

מִכָּל- mikol הָעַמִּים ha'amim וְנָתַן venatan לָנוּ lanu אלהים, אהיה אדני

אֶת et תּוֹרָתוֹ torato◆ בָּרוּךְ baruch אַתָּה Ata יְהֹוָה Adonai

נוֹתֵן noten אבג יתץ, ועיר הַתּוֹרָה hatorah◆

After the reading, the *ole* says the following blessing:

בָּרוּךְ baruch אַתָּה Ata יְהֹוָה Adonai אֱלֹהֵינוּ Elohenu ילה

מֶלֶךְ melech הָעוֹלָם ha'olam אֲשֶׁר asher נָתַן natan לָנוּ lanu אלהים, אהיה אדני

אֶת et תּוֹרָתוֹ torato תּוֹרַת torat- אֱמֶת emet אהיה פעמים אהיה, ז"פ ס"ג

וְחַיֵּי vechayei עוֹלָם olam נָטַע nata בְּתוֹכֵנוּ betochenu◆ בָּרוּךְ baruch

אַתָּה Ata יְהֹוָה Adonai נוֹתֵן noten אבג יתץ, ועיר הַתּוֹרָה hatorah◆

BLESSING OF HaGOMEL

אוֹדֶה ode יְהֹוָה Adonai בְּכָל- bechol ב"ן, לכב levav לֵבב בוכו

בְּסוֹד besod מיכ, י"פ האא יְשָׁרִים yesharim וְעֵדָה ve'eda סיט:

בָּרוּךְ baruch אַתָּה Ata יְהֹוָה Adonai אֱלֹהֵינוּ Elohenu ילה

מֶלֶךְ melech הָעוֹלָם ha'olam הַגּוֹמֵל hagomel לְחַיָּבִים lechayavim

טוֹבוֹת tovot, שֶׁגְּמָלַנִי shegemalani כָּל kol ילי טוֹב tuv והו◆

The congregation answers: אָמֵן amen יאהדונהי *And then the congregation recites:*

הָאֵל haEl לאה ; יא"י (מילוי דס"ג) שֶׁגְּמָלַךְ shegemalach כָּל kol ילי טוֹב tuv והו◆

הוּא hu יִגְמָלְךָ yigmolcha כָּל kol ילי טוֹב tuv והו סֶלָה sela◆

The person who says "Hagomel" recites silently:

אָמֵן amen יאהדונהי כֵּן ken יְהִי yehi רָצוֹן ratzon מהטע ע"ה, ע"ב בריבוע וקס"א וקס"א ע"ה, אל עדוי ע"ה◆

Blessed are You, Lord, our God, the King of the World,
Who chose us from among the nations and gave us His Torah. Blessed are You, Lord, Who gives the Torah.
Blessed are You, Lord, our God, King of the World, Who gave us His Torah,
the Torah of truth, and implanted within us eternal life. Blessed are You, Lord, Who gives the Torah.
BLESSING OF HaGOMEL
"I give thanks to the Lord whole heartedly, in the concealment of the upright and congregation." (Psalms 111:1)
Blessed are You, Lord, our God, King of the World, Who gives goodness to the guilty, Who bestows upon me
all that is good. The God, Who bestows upon you all the best, he will bestow upon you all the best, Selah.
Amen, so shall it be desired.

HALF KADDISH

יִתְגַּדַּל yitgadal וְיִתְקַדַּשׁ veyitkadash עוֹדִי וּמִילּוּי עוֹדִי ; י"א אוֹתִיּוֹת כְּמִנְיַן ו"ה

שְׁמֵהּ shemei (שֵׁם י"ה דע"ב) רַבָּא raba קנ"א ב"ן, יהוה אלהים יהוה אדני,

אָמֵן amen אִידְהֲנוּיֵהּ. מִילּוּי קס"א וס"ג, מ"ה בְּרִבּוּעַ וע"ב ע"ה ; ר"ת = ו"פ אלהים ; ס"ת = ג"פ יב"ק:

בְּעָלְמָא be'alma דִּי di בְּרָא vera כִרְעוּתֵיהּ kir'utei.

וְיַמְלִיךְ veyamlich מַלְכוּתֵיהּ mal'chutei. וְיַצְמַח veyatzmach

פּוּרְקָנֵיהּ purkanei. וִיקָרֵב vikarev מְשִׁיחֵיהּ meshichei: אָמֵן amen אִידְהֲנוּיֵהּ.

בְּחַיֵּיכוֹן bechayechon וּבְיוֹמֵיכוֹן uvyomechon וּבְחַיֵּי uvchayei

דְכָל dechol בֵּית bet ב"פ ראה יִשְׂרָאֵל Yisrael בַּעֲגָלָא ba'agala

וּבִזְמַן uvizman קָרִיב kariv וְאִמְרוּ ve'imru אָמֵן amen: אָמֵן amen אִידְהֲנוּיֵהּ.

The congregation and the *chazan* say the following:

Twenty eight words (until *be'alma*) and twenty eight letters (until *almaya*)

יְהֵא yehe שְׁמֵהּ shemei (שֵׁם י"ה דס"ג) רַבָּא raba קנ"א ב"ן,

מְבָרַךְ mevarach, יהוה אלהים אדני, מִילּוּי קס"א וס"ג, מ"ה בְּרִבּוּעַ וע"ב ע"ה

לְעָלַם le'alam לְעָלְמֵי le'almei עָלְמַיָּא almaya. יִתְבָּרַךְ yitbarach.

Seven words with six letters each (שֵׁם בָּ"ן מ"ב) and also seven times the letter *Vav* (שֵׁם בָּ"ן מ"ב).

וְיִשְׁתַּבַּח veyishtabach י"פ ע"ב יהוה אל אבג יתץ.

וְיִתְפָּאַר veyitpa'ar הי גו יה קרע שטן. וְיִתְרוֹמַם veyitromam וה כוזו נגד יכש.

וְיִתְנַשֵּׂא veyitnase במוכסז בטר צתג. וְיִתְהַדָּר veyit'hadar כוזו יה וזקב טנע.

וְיִתְעַלֶּה veyit'ale וה יוד ה יגל פזק. וְיִתְהַלָּל veyit'halal א ואו הא שקו צית.

שְׁמֵהּ shemei (שֵׁם י"ה דמ"ה) דְקֻדְשָׁא dekudsha בְּרִיךְ verich הוּא hu:

אָמֵן amen אִידְהֲנוּיֵהּ.

HALF KADDISH

May His great Name be more exalted and sanctified. (Amen) In the world that He created according to His will, and may His kingdom reign. And may He cause His redemption to sprout and may He bring the Mashiach closer. (Amen) In your lifetimes and in your days and in the lifetime of all the House of Israel, speedily and in the near future, and you should say, Amen. (Amen) May His great Name be blessed forever and for all eternity blessed and lauded, and glorified and exalted, And extolled and honored, and uplifted and praised, be the Name of the Holy Blessed One. (Amen)

לְעֵלָּא le'ela מִן min כָּל kol יכל ◆birchata בִּרְכָתָא ◆shirata שִׁירָתָא

תִּשְׁבְּחָתָא tishbechata וְנֶחָמָתָא ◆venechamata דַּאֲמִירָן da'amiran

בְּעָלְמָא be'alma וְאִמְרוּ ve'imru אָמֵן amen ◆ אָמֵן amen אִידהנויה.

On *Chol Hamo'ed* (not on *Shabbat*) continue on pg. 663.

BLESSING OF THE HAFTARAH

The *Maftir* (the *ole* for *Maftir*) recite this blessing before the reading of the *Haftarah*. It is recommended to read the *Haftarah* individually (along with the reader), as it is not a full connection to hear it only by the reader.

There is a level far higher than Divine Inspiration, called Prophecy. Many great people throughout history have received Divine Inspiration. This refers to the acquiring of knowledge or hidden secrets of life that would normally be beyond the accessibility of the average person. Further, the receiver of this knowledge understands it perfectly, without inaccuracy. In prophecy, a person attains a complete bond and attachment to the Creator. Kabbalist Rav Moshe Chaim Luzzatto explains that even prophecy must come through an intermediary, which acts as a lens through which one sees the vision. Attaining this level is a gradual, step-by-step process of elevation. The words in this blessing prepare us, the Vessel, for a powerful connection to the wisdom of the prophets in the *Haftarah*, the reading after the Torah. Making this connection helps us become prophets.

בָּרוּךְ baruch אַתָּה Ata יְהוָֹאדֹנָיאהדונהי Adonai אֱלֹהֵינוּ Elohenu יכה

מֶלֶךְ melech הָעוֹלָם ha'olam אֲשֶׁר asher בּוֹחֵר bachar

בִּנְבִיאִים binvi'im טוֹבִים tovim וְרָצָה veratza בְּדִבְרֵיהֶם vedivrehem

הַנֶּאֱמָרִים hane'emarim בָּאֱמֶת be'emet אהיה פעמים אהיה, ז"פ ס"ג◆

בָּרוּךְ baruch אַתָּה Ata יְהוָֹאדֹנָיאהדונהי Adonai הַבּוֹחֵר habocher

בַּתּוֹרָה batorah וּבְמֹשֶׁה uvMoshe מהש, ע"ב בריבוע קס"א, אל שדי, ד"פ אלהים ע"ה

עַבְדוֹ avdo וּבְיִשְׂרָאֵל uvYisrael עַמּוֹ amo וּבִנְבִיאֵי uvinvi'ei

הָאֱמֶת ha'emet אהיה פעמים אהיה, ז"פ ס"ה וְהַצֶּדֶק vehatzedek◆

Above all blessings, songs, praises,
and words of consolation that may be said in the world, and you shall say, Amen. (Amen)

BLESSING OF THE HAFTARAH

Blessed are You, Lord, our God, the King of the world, Who had chosen good prophets and
Who was pleased with their words that were uttered with truth. Blessed are You, Lord, who chose
the Torah and Moses, His servant, and Israel, His Nation, and the prophets of truth and righteousness.

BLESSING AFTER THE HAFTARAH

The reader says these blessings after the reading of the Haftarah:

אֱלֹהֵינוּ Elohenu יְהֹוָה Adonai אַתָּה Ata בָּרוּךְ baruch

כָּל kol צוּר tzur הָעוֹלָם ha'olam מֶלֶךְ melech

הַדּוֹרוֹת hadorot בְּכָל bechol צַדִּיק tzadik הָעוֹלָמִים ha'olamim

הָאוֹמֵר ha'omer הַנֶּאֱמָן hane'eman הָאֵל haEl

כָּל chol כִּי ki וּמְקַיֵּם umkayem הַמְדַבֵּר hamedaber וְעֹשֶׂה ve'ose

וְצֶדֶק vatzedek אֱמֶת emet דְּבָרָיו devarav

אֱלֹהֵינוּ Elohenu יְהֹוָה Adonai הוּא hu אַתָּה Ata נֶאֱמָן ne'eman

אֶחָד echad וְדָבָר vedavar דְּבָרֶיךָ devarecha וְנֶאֱמָנִים vene'emanim

יָשׁוּב yashuv לֹא lo אָחוֹר achor מִדְּבָרֶיךָ midevarecha

נֶאֱמָן ne'eman מֶלֶךְ melech אֵל El כִּי ki רֵיקָם rekam

יְהֹוָה Adonai אַתָּה Ata בָּרוּךְ baruch ◆ אַתָּה Ata וְרַחֲמָן verachaman

הָאֵל haEl הַנֶּאֱמָן hane'eman בְּכָל bechol דְּבָרָיו devarav

רַחֵם rachem

וְזֵייּנוּ chayenu בֵּית bet הִיא hee כִּי ki צִיּוֹן Tziyon עַל al

בִּמְהֵרָה bimhera תּוֹשִׁיעַ toshi'a נֶפֶשׁ nefesh וְלַעֲלוּבַת vela'aluvat

יְהֹוָה Adonai אַתָּה Ata בָּרוּךְ baruch ◆ בְיָמֵינוּ beyamenu

בְּבָנֶיהָ bevaneha צִיּוֹן Tziyon מְשַׂמֵּחַ mesame'ach

BLESSING AFTER THE HAFTARAH

Blessed are You, Lord, our God, King of the world, rock of all eternities, righteous in all generations. The trustworthy God Who says and does, Who speaks and fulfills, for all of His words are true and just. Trustworthy are You, Lord, our God, and trustworthy are Your words, and not one of Your words is turned back to its origin unfulfilled, for You, God, are a trustworthy and a compassionate King. Blessed are You, Lord, the God Who is trustworthy in all His words. Have mercy on Zion, for it is the house of our livelihood, and to the one whose spirit is humiliated bring salvation speedily in our days. Blessed are You, Lord, Who gladdens Zion with her sons.

שַׂמְּחֵנוּ samchenu | יהוה אדני ואדני Adonai | אֱלֹהֵינוּ Elohenu | יל״ה

בְּאֵלִיָּהוּ beEliyahu | לכב hanavi הַנָּבִיא | עַבְדֶּךָ avdecha | פוי, אל אדני

וּבְמַלְכוּת uvmalchut | bet בֵּית ב״פ ראה | דָּוִד David | מְשִׁיחֶךָ meshichecha,

בִּמְהֵרָה bimhera | יָבֹא yavo | וְיָגֵל veyagel | לבהו | לִבֵּנוּ libenu,

עַל al | כִּסְאוֹ kis'o | לֹא lo | יֵשֵׁב yeshev | זָר zar | וְלֹא velo

יִנְחֲלוּ yinchalu | עוֹד od | אֲחֵרִים acherim | אֶת et | כְּבוֹדוֹ kevodo,

כִּי ki | בְשֵׁם veshem | קָדְשְׁךָ kodshecha | נִשְׁבַּעְתָּ nishbata | לוֹ lo,

שֶׁלֹּא shelo | יִכְבֶּה yichbe | נֵרוֹ nero | לְעוֹלָם le'olam | ריבוע ס״ג י׳ אותיות דס״ג

וָעֶד va'ed. | בָּרוּךְ baruch | אַתָּה Ata | יהוה אדני ואדני Adonai

מָגֵן magen ג״פ אל (ייא״י מילוי דס״ג) ; ר״ת מיכאל גבריאל נוריאל | דָּוִד David.

עַל al | הַתּוֹרָה hatorah | וְעַל ve'al | הָעֲבוֹדָה ha'avoda

וְעַל ve'al | הַנְּבִיאִים hanevi'im | וְעַל ve'al | יוֹם yom ע״ה נגד, מזבח, זן, אל יהוה

(**on Shabbat add:** הַשַּׁבָּת haShabbat | הַזֶּה hazeh והו | וְעַל ve'al | יוֹם yom ע״ה נגד, מזבח, זן, אל יהוה:)

(**On Sukkot say:** וזג chag | הַסֻּכּוֹת haSukkot | הַזֶּה hazeh).

(**On Simchat Torah say:** שְׁמִינִי shemini | וזג chag | עֲצֶרֶת atzeret | הַזֶּה hazeh).

וְעַל ve'al | יוֹם yom ע״ה נגד, מזבח, זן, אל יהוה | טוֹב tov והו | מִקְרָא mikra

קֹדֶשׁ kodesh | הַזֶּה haze והו | שֶׁנָּתַתָּ shenatata | לָנוּ lanu אלהים, אהיה אדני

Adonai יהוה אדני ואדני | אֱלֹהֵינוּ Elohenu יל״ה (**on Shabbat add:** לִקְדֻשָּׁה likdusha

(velimnucha וְלִמְנוּחָה | לִכְבוֹד lechavod | וּלְתִפְאָרֶת ultifaret.

Gladden us, Lord, our God, through Eliyahu the prophet, Your servant, and with the Kingdom of the House of David, Your anointed, may he come speedily and cause our hearts to exult. On his throne let no stranger sit, nor let others inherit his honor anymore, For by Your Holy Name, You swore to him that his candlelight will never be extinguished for eternity. Blessed are You, Lord, the Shield of David.
For the Torah and for the Prophets and for this day
*(**On Shabbat:** of Sabbath and on this day)*
*(**on Sukkot:** of Sukkot) (**on Simchat Torah:** of Shmini the Holiday of Atzeret)*
and on this good day of Holy Convocation that You, Lord our God, had given us
*(**On Shabbat:** for holiness and contentment,) for honor and for splendor.*

anachnu אֲנַחְנוּ יכה Elohenu אֱלֹהֵינוּ Adonai יְהֹוָה/אֲדֹנָי יכי hakol הַכֹּל al עַל

lach לָךְ כל יום לאמרם דוד עתיקן ברכות מאה כנגד modim מוֹדִים

befi בְּפִי shimcha שִׁמְךָ yitbarach יִתְבָּרַךְ otach אוֹתָךְ umvarchim וּמְבָרְכִים

kol כָּל וָיֹ"י יכי chai חַי תמיד תָּמִיד

le'olam לְעוֹלָם ריבוע ס"ג וי אותיות דס"ג ◆va'ed וָעֶד

baruch בָּרוּךְ Ata אַתָּה Adonai יְהֹוָה/אֲדֹנָי mekadesh מְקַדֵּשׁ

(on Shabbat add: haShabbat הַשַּׁבָּת ve וְ) Yisrael יִשְׂרָאֵל vehazemanim וְהַזְּמַנִּים:

"Amen" is said by the one who said the blessing together with the congregation:

◆amen אָמֵן יאהדונהי

For *Simchat Torah:*

YIZKOR - PRAYER FOR THE DECEASED

A few special times during the year, we have the opportunity to help elevate the souls of loved ones who have left us. *Yom Kippur* is one of those times. We can take the Light that we are receiving and use it to help a loved one's soul ascend higher and more easily into the Upper Worlds. There is also a metaphysical void left in our life when a loved one passes on. Part of the Light that they automatically share with us is now missing. *Yizkor* helps to fill this void with their spiritual energy by making contact with the soul in the Upper World.

The Ari use to recite the short version of *Yizkor*. He explained that the words of the long version don't necessarily assist to in the elevation of the soul, but can sometimes disturb its process of elevation.

hamerachem הַמְרַחֵם אברהם, וז"פ אל, רי"ו ול"ב נתיבות החכמה, רמ"ח (אברים), עסמ"ב וט"ו אותיות

kol כָּל יכי al עַל beriyotav בְּרִיּוֹתָיו עמם; hu הוּא yachus יָחוּס פשוטות

veyachamol וְיַחֲמוֹל virachem וִירַחֵם אברהם, וז"פ אל, רי"ו ול"ב נתיבות החכמה, רמ"ח (אברים),

al עַל nefesh נֶפֶשׁ ru'ach רוּחַ uneshamah וּנְשָׁמָה עסמ"ב וט"ו אותיות פשוטות

shel שֶׁל (the deceased's name and their father's name) ru'ach רוּחַ Adonai יְהֹוָה/אֲדֹנָי

tenichenu תְּנִיחֵנוּ (for woman: tenichena תְּנִיחֶנָה) beGan בְּגַן (Eden עֶדֶן: רוח ה' = י"פ יהו) Eden:

For all of this we are grateful to You,
Lord our God, and bless we You. May Your Name be blessed by the mouth of all the living always
and for all eternity. And Your word, our King, is true and exists forever. Blessed are You Lord,
*King over the whole earth who sanctifies (**On Shabbat:** the Sabbath and) Israel and the Times. Amen.*

YIZKOR - PRAYER FOR THE DECEASED
May the One Who is merciful to all that
He had created take pity and spare and be merciful on the Nefesh, Ruach and Neshamah of (name),
the son/daughter of (the father's name). May the Spirit of God place him/her in the Garden of Eden.

TIKKUN HAGESHEM

The Prayer of the Rain - Twice a year, we have the opportunity to make connections to the waters of our planet, specifically, the dew and the rain. During *Sukkot*, our blessings are directed towards rainwater to ensure the appropriate measure of moisture for our planet. Balancing the inflow of rain is vital if we are to avoid an over abundance—flooding, or a deficiency—drought. Water represents the concept of sharing. But water can also represent destruction: Water in the lungs can end a human life, and flooding can destroy an entire community. The mystical words of this prayer endow water with the force of positivity so that it brings forth life, longevity, and renewal.

On *Simchat Torah* we say:

madkar מַדְכַּר   avdechon עַבְדְּכוֹן   kodamchon קָדָמְכוֹן   de'avar דְּעָבַר◆

zeman זְמַן   hatal הַטַּל   יוד הא ואו, כוו uva וּבָא   zeman זְמַן   hageshem הַגֶּשֶׁם

velo וְלֹא   lechayim לְחַיִּים◆   ע"ה (י"פ אל ול"ב נתיבות החכמה) אהיה אהיה יהוה, בינה ע"ה עובל

lemavet לְמָוֶת   velo וְלֹא   lesava לְשָׂבַע   lera'av לְרָעָב◆   livracha לִבְרָכָה

velo וְלֹא   liklala לִקְלָלָה◆   leshalom לְשָׁלוֹם   velo וְלֹא   lemilchama לְמִלְחָמָה◆

beseter בְּסֵתֶר   yoshev יוֹשֵׁב   le'avdut לְעַבְדוּת◆   velo וְלֹא   lecherut לְחֵרוּת

be'itam בְּעִתָּם: geshamenu גְּשָׁמֵינוּ   torid תּוֹרִיד   elyon עֶלְיוֹן   מצר ב"פ

mizvulav מִזְּבוּלָיו◆   yorid יוֹרִיד   revivim רְבִיבִים   shifat שִׁפְעַת

yevulav יְבוּלָיו◆   peri פְּרִי   velatet וְלָתֵת   zera זֶרַע   lehachayot לְהַחֲיוֹת

eglav אֲגָלָיו◆   im עִם   yorid יוֹרִיד   umalkosh וּמַלְקוֹשׁ◆   yore יוֹרֶה   matar מָטָר

etz עֵץ   peri פְּרִי   ילי kol כָּל   veshamen וְשָׁמֵן◆   dashen דָּשֵׁן   heyot הֱיוֹת

terem טֶרֶם   ofer עוֹפֶר◆   ushlach וּשְׁלַח   chish וְיִישׁ   ve'alav וְעָלָיו◆

yizkor יִזְכּוֹר   zachor זְכוֹר   ע"ב קס"א, יהי אור ע"ה   tzelalav צְלָלָיו◆   yenusun יְנוּסוּן

naul נָעוּל◆   gan גַּן   komem קוֹמֵם   ashelav אֲשֵׁלָיו◆   note'a נוֹטֵעַ   li לִי◆

TIKKUN HAGESHEM

Your servant declares before You

that the season of dew has passed and the season of rain has arrived, for life and not for death, for plenty and not for famine, for blessing and not for curse, for peace and not for war, for freedom and not for servitude. Who dwells in concealment on high, causes our rains to fall in their time. An abundance of rains may He cause to descend from His Heavenly residences, to keep offspring alive and to give forth the produce of His crops. The early rain and the late rain may He cause to descend in droplets, so that fat and plump will be all the fruits of the tree and its leaves. Hasten to send the "young buck" before its shadows shall disperse; may He remember for me the one who would plant his trees. Set upright the locked garden,

וּפַרְדֵּס ufardes רִמּוֹן rimon שְׁתִילָיו shetilav קִרְיַת kiryat וְנָה chana

דָּוִד David וּמִגְדָּל umigdal עֹז oz וַחֲיָלָיו chayalav שׁוֹבֵב shovev

לְצַוַּאר letzavar הַשֵּׁן hashen מְלוֹאֵי meluei הוֹד hod ההה כְּלִילָיו kelilav

בָּנוּי banuy לְתַלְפִּיּוֹת letalpiyot וְנָהֲרוּ venaharu כֹּל kol יֹלי

הַגּוֹיִם hagoyim אֵלָיו elav אֶלֶף elef המספר אלף = אלף למד דלת שׁין יוד

הַמָּגֵן hamagen ר"ת מיכאל גבריאל נוריאל תָּלוּי taluy עָלָיו alav: מְכַסֶּה mechase

שָׁמַיִם shamayim יֹ"פ טל, יֹ"פ כוזו בֶּעָבִים be'avim וּמַלְבִּישֵׁם umalbishem

וּמְחַלִיף umachalif זְמַנִּים zemanim עֲלֵי alei וְזוֹק chok וְרֶשֶׁם vareshem

אוֹצָרְךָ otzarcha הַטּוֹב hatov והו פָּתוּחַ petach נָא na לְהַחֲיוֹת lehachayot

בּוֹ bo כֹּל kol יֹלי נְפוּוּזִי nefuchei נָשָׁם neshem בֵּשִׁיב mashiv הָרוּוַ haruach

וּמוֹרִיד umorid הַגֶּשֶׁם hageshem עֹביל (י"פ אל ול"ב נתיבות החכמה) ר"ת מ"ה ע"ה:

אֵלֶיךָ elecha אלהים ההין יְשַׂבְּרוּ yesaberu מִקְצוֹת miktzot הָאָרֶץ ha'aretz

עַ"ה וְעַד ve'ad קְצוֹת ketzot אָדָם adam מ"ה וּבְהֵמָה uvhema ב"ן, לכב

וְכֹל vechol יֹלי יְצוּרֵי yetzurei אֲרָצוֹת aratzot בֵּשִׁיב mashiv הָרוּוַ haruach

עַל al מַיִם mayim וְשׁלֵחַ veshole'ach קְצוּצוֹת ketzutzot לְעִתּוֹת le'itot מ"ה

פְּנֵי penei וחכמה בינה וְזוּצוֹת chutzot: אוֹצָרְךָ otzarcha הַטּוֹב hatov והו

פָּתוּחַ petach נָא na לְהַחֲיוֹת lehachayot בּוֹ bo כֹּל kol יֹלי

נְפוּוּזִי nefuchei נָשָׁם neshem בֵּשִׁיב mashiv הָרוּוַ haruach ר"ת מ"ה

וּמוֹרִיד umorid הַגֶּשֶׁם hageshem עֹביל (י"פ אל ול"ב נתיבות החכמה) ע"ה:

---

and the pomegranate orchard—its saplings, the town in which David dwelled and the tower of strength of his troops. Return to the nape of ivory those filled with the splendor of its crowns. It is built for teaching, and all nations will flock to it; the shield of a thousand hanging upon it. Who covers the Heavens with clouds, and clothes them, and Who varies the times according to statute and order, please open Your good treasury to enliven through it all into whom breath has blown. Who causes wind to blow and rain to fall.

To You they look hopefully

from one end of the Earth to the other, man and beast and all creators of the lands, Who causes the wind to blow at designated times and send forth water through the thoroughfares. Please open Your good treasury to enliven through it all into whom breath has been blown. Who causes wind to blow and rain to fall.

צִמָּאוֹן tzima'on וְשָׂרָב vesharav וְכֹל vechol יל״י וְחָרְבוֹת charvot קָטוֹב katov.

תְּשַׁלַּח teshalach רוּחֲךָ ruchacha. וְיִהְיוּ veyih'yu יא״י (במילוי דס״ג) כְּגַן kegan

רָטוֹב ratov. אָדָם adam מ״ה לכב וּבְהֵמָה uvhema ב״ן, אֲשֶׁר asher הֶחֱשׁוּ hecheshu

מִטּוֹב mitov והו תִּפְתַּח tiftach יָדְךָ yadcha יִשְׂבְּעוּן yisbe'un טוֹב tov והו:

אוֹצָרְךָ otzarcha הַטּוֹב hatov והו פָּתוֹחַ petach נָא na. לְהַחֲיוֹת lehachayot

בּוֹ bo כֹּל kol יל״י נְפוּחֵי nefuchei נְשָׁם neshem. מֵשִׁיב mashiv הָרוּחַ haruach

וּמוֹרִיד umorid הַגֶּשֶׁם hageshem שׁבּיל (י״פ אל ול״ב נתיבות הוֹכמה) ע״ה: ר״ת מ״ה

תַּלְמֵי talmei צִיָּה tziya אֲשֶׁר asher נוֹתָרָה notra עֲרוּמָה aruma.

מִתְּנוּבַת mitnuvat דֶּשֶׁא deshe וְחָצִיר chatzir וְקָמָה vekama.

תַּפְרִיחַ tafriach נִצָּנֶיהָ nitzaneha וְתַלְבִּישֶׁהָ vetalbisha רִקְמָה rikma.

וּתְחַדֵּשׁ utchadesh י״ב הויות, קס״א קנ״א פְּנֵי penei וזכמה בינה אֲדָמָה adama:

אוֹצָרְךָ otzarcha הַטּוֹב hatov והו פָּתוֹחַ petach נָא na. לְהַחֲיוֹת lehachayot

בּוֹ bo כֹּל kol יל״י נְפוּחֵי nefuchei נְשָׁם neshem. מֵשִׁיב mashiv הָרוּחַ haruach

וּמוֹרִיד umorid הַגֶּשֶׁם hageshem שׁבּיל (י״פ אל ול״ב נתיבות הוֹכמה) ע״ה: ר״ת מ״ה

אָב av רַחֲמָן rachaman. נוֹשֵׂא nose וְזוֹבַת chovat לֵב lev עָקוֹשׁ akosh.

פְּדֵה pede נֶפֶשׁ nefesh תּוֹרֶךָ torecha מִיָּד miyad יָקוֹשׁ yakosh.

הַשְׁלִימָה hashlima נָא na דְּבָרֶיךָ devarecha. וְאִם ve'im יוהר, מ״א אותיות אהיה

בָּנוּ banu אֵין en מִילוי וּמילוי דמילוי מִתְקוֹשֵׁשׁ mitkoshesh וְקוֹשׁ vakosh.

וְנָתַתִּי venatati מְטַר metar אַרְצְכֶם artzechem בְּעִתּוֹ be'ito יוֹרֶה yore

וּמַלְקוֹשׁ umalkosh: אוֹצָרְךָ otzarcha הַטּוֹב hatov והו פָּתוֹחַ petach נָא na.

Thirst and torridity

and all destructive aridity may You send forth Your wind, and may they become as moistened garden. Man and beast that have been depleted of good, may You open Your hand, may You open Your good treasure to enliven through it all into whom breath has been blown. Who causes the wind to blow and the rain to fall.

The furrows of the thirsty that have been left

barren of produce of vegetation, grass and stalks, may You cause its blossoms to sprout, and may You clothe it in embroidered garments and may You renew the face of the Earth. Please open Your good treasury to enliven through it all into whom breath is blown, Who causes the wind to blow and the rain to fall. Merciful Father, Who forgives the iniquity of the corrupt heart; redeem the soul of Your dove from the grip of the trap. Please fulfill Your words, though there may not be amongst us scrupulous individuals, "I shall send rain upon your land in its proper time, both early rain and late rain." Please open Your good treasury

לְהַחֲיוֹת lehachayot בּוֹ bo כָּל kol ילי נְפוּחֵי nefuchei נְשֶׁם neshem◆

מֵשִׁיב mashiv הָרוּחַ haruach ר"ת מ"ה וּמוֹרִיד umorid הַגֶּשֶׁם hageshem

עביל (י"פ אל ול"ב נתיבות הוזכמה) ע"ה:

לְשׁוֹנִי leshoni כּוֹנַנְתָּ chonanta, אֱלֹהַי Elohai מילוי דע"ב, דמב ; ילי

וַתִּבְחַר vativchar◆ בְּשִׁירִים beshirim שֶׂשַׂמְתָּ shesamta, בְּפִי befi טוֹב tov והו

מִמִּסְחָר mimischar◆ וְנֶגְדָּךְ venegdach מזבוז, זן, אל יהוה כּוֹנַנְתָּ konanta,

מִמִּשְׁעוֹר mimishchar◆ וְלִי veli גָּרוֹן garon תַּתָּה tata,

נִחַר nichar◆ לֹא lo בְּקָרְאִי bekor'i וְיִצְרִי veyitzri הִלְבַּנְתָּ hilbanta,

צַוּוֹר tzachar◆ מצר צֶמֶר tzemer כְּמוֹ kemo וְלָכֵן velachen לֹא lo שָׁתָה shata,

סוֹחֲרוֹר secharchar◆ בִּי vi לְבָבִי levavi הֱיֵה heye יהה סִתְרִי sitri ב"פ מצר

וּכְמוֹר uchmachar◆ כְּאֶתְמוֹל ke'etmol עָתָה ata, מָגִנִּי magini אַתָּה Ata,

תָּאוֹר te'achar◆ אַל al אֱלֹהַי Elohai יִשְׂבְּעוּן yisbe'un יְדִידֶיךָ yedidecha

מֵאוֹצְרוֹת me'otzrot שָׁמַיִם shamayim י"פ טל, י"פ כווו ◆ וְשָׂבַע vesaba

אֲדָמָה adama לֹא lo שָׂבְעָה sav'a מַיִם mayim◆ פְּדוּת pedut תִּשְׁלַח tishlach

לְשׁוֹיִים lishchuyim פַּעֲמַיִם pa'amayim◆ יְחַיֵּנוּ yechayenu מִיּוֹמַיִם miyomayim:

אֱלֹהֵינוּ Elohenu ילה וֵאלֹהֵי velohei לכב ; מילוי דע"ב = דמב ; ילי אֲבוֹתֵינוּ avotenu

בְּגִשְׁמֵי begishmei אוֹרָה ora תָּאִיר ta'ir אֲדָמָה adama:

בְּגִשְׁמֵי begishmei בְּרָכָה beracha תְּבָרֵךְ tevarech אֲדָמָה adama:

בְּגִשְׁמֵי begishmei גִּילָה gila תָּגִיל tagil אֲדָמָה adama:

---

to enliven through it all into whom breath has been blown. Who causes the wind to blow and the rain to fall. My verbal skills You have established, my God, and You have selected among the songs that You placed in my mouth better than merchandise. Toward You, You have set my strides since the dawn. The voice that You gave me in my calling has never faltered. My inclination You have cleansed as bleached-white wool. Thus did You not set my heart within me whirling. Be my protective refuge now as yesterday and tomorrow; my shield You are. My God, do not delay. May your beloved ones be satiated from the Heavenly treasures and satiate the land that has not been sated with water. May you send redemption to those twice downtrodden, "May He strengthens us from the two days."

Our God, God of our forefathers, with rains of light may You illuminate the Earth; with rains of blessings may You bless the earth; with rains of gladness may You gladden the Earth;

בְּגִשְׁמֵי begishmei דִיצָה ditza תַּדְשֵׁן tedasen אֲדָמָה adama:

בְּגִשְׁמֵי begishmei הוֹד hod ההה תַּהֲדָר tehader אֲדָמָה adama:

בְּגִשְׁמֵי begishmei וְעַד va'ad טוֹב tov והו תְּוַעֵד tevaed אֲדָמָה adama:

בְּגִשְׁמֵי begishmei זִמְרָה zimra תְּזַמֵּר tezamer אֲדָמָה adama:

בְּגִשְׁמֵי begishmei וְֹחַיִּים chayim אהיה אהיה יהוה, בינה ע"ה

תְּחַיֶּה techaye אֲדָמָה adama:

בְּגִשְׁמֵי begishmei טוֹבָה tova אכא תֵּיטִיב tetiv אֲדָמָה adama:

בְּגִשְׁמֵי begishmei יְשׁוּעָה yeshua תּוֹשִׁיעַ toshia אֲדָמָה adama:

בְּגִשְׁמֵי begishmei כַּלְכָּלָה chalkala תְּכַלְכֵּל techalkel אֲדָמָה adama:

כְּמוֹ kemo שֶׁאַתָּה she'ata הוּא hu יְהֹוָ(אדני ואלהים ואדני) Adonai אֱלֹהֵינוּ Elohenu ילה

רַב rav לְהוֹשִׁיעַ lehoshia מַשִּׁיב mashiv הָרוּחַ haru'ach ר"ת מ"ה וּמוֹרִיד umorid

הַגֶּשֶׁם hageshem שׁוֹבִיל ע"ה (י"פ אל ול"ב נתיבות החוכמה ע"ה) לִבְרָכָה livracha: אָנָּא ana

הוֹרִידֵם horidem לְאוֹרָה le'ora, לִבְרָכָה livracha, לְגִילָה legila,

לְדִיצָה leditza, לְהוֹד lehod ההה, לְוַעַד leva'ad טוֹב tov והו, לְזִמְרָה lezimra,

לְחַיִּים lechayim אהיה אהיה יהוה, בינה ע"ה טוֹבִים tovim, לְטוֹבָה letova אכא,

לִישׁוּעָה lishua, לְכַלְכָּלָה lechalkala, כְּמוֹ kemo שֶׁאַתָּה she'ata

הוּא hu יְהֹוָ(אדני ואלהים ואדני) Adonai אֱלֹהֵינוּ Elohenu ילה רַב rav

לְהוֹשִׁיעַ lehoshi'a מַשִּׁיב mashiv, הָרוּחַ haru'ach ר"ת מ"ה וּמוֹרִיד umorid

הַגֶּשֶׁם hageshem שׁוֹבִיל ע"ה (י"פ אל ול"ב נתיבות החוכמה ע"ה) לִבְרָכָה livracha:

---

with rains of jubilation, may You enrich the Earth; with rains of splendor, may You embellish the Earth; with rains of goodly gathering may You prime the Earth; with rains of melody may You harmonize the Earth; with rains of life may You revitalize the Earth; with rains of goodness may You better the Earth; with rains of salvation may You save the Earth; with rains of sustenance may You sustain the Earth. Please cause them to fall for light, for blessing, for gladness, for jubilation, for splendor, for goodly gathering, for melody, for good life, for goodness, for salvation, for livelihood, and for sustenance; in the same fashion that You, Lord , our God, every noticeably capable of saving, cause the wind to blow and the rain to fall for blessing.

THE ASHREI

Twenty-one of the twenty-two letters of the Aramaic alphabet are encoded in the *Ashrei* in their correct order from *Alef* to *Tav*. King David, the author, left out the Aramaic letter *Nun* from this prayer, because *Nun* is the first letter in the Aramaic word *nefilah*, which means "falling." Falling refers to a spiritual decline, as in falling into the *klipa*. Feelings of doubt, depression, worry, and uncertainty are consequences of spiritual falling. Because the Aramaic letters are the actual instruments of Creation, this prayer helps to inject order and the power of Creation into our lives, without the energy of falling.

In this Psalm there are ten times the Name: יהוה for the Ten *Sefirot*. This Psalm is written according to the order of the *Alef Bet*, but the letter *Nun* is omitted to prevent falling.

ראה ב"פ vetecha בֵּיתֶךָ yoshvei יוֹשְׁבֵי (הכתר סוד) ashrei אַשְׁרֵי

ha'am הָעָם ashrei אַשְׁרֵי ‏:sela סֶלָה yehalelucha יְהַלְלוּךָ od עוֹד

lo לֹא מהע, משה, ע"ב בריבוע וקס"א, אל שדי, ד"פ אלהים ע"ה shekacha שֶׁכָּכָה

(*Keter*) she'Adonai עיהואדניהואהדונהי ר"ת לאה ha'am הָעָם ashrei אַשְׁרֵי

leDavid לְדָוִד יהלה, אהיה פעמים אהיה, ז"פ ס"ג ע"ה אמת, tehila תְּהִלָּה‏: יהל Elohav אֱלוֹהָיו

va'avarcha וַאֲבָרְכָה hamelech הַמֶּלֶךְ Elohai אֱלוֹהַי aromimcha אֲרוֹמִמְךָ

‏:va'ed וָעֶד אותיות דס"ג וי' ריבוע דס"ג le'olam לְעוֹלָם shimcha שִׁמְךָ

יהוה אל זן מזבח, נגד, ע"ה yom יוֹם לכב ב"פ, bechol בְּכָל

shimcha שִׁמְךָ יהוה מ"ה va'ahalela וַאֲהַלְלָה avarcheka אֲבָרְכֶךָ

‏:va'ed וָעֶד דס"ג אותיות וי' דס"ג ריבוע le'olam לְעוֹלָם

אום יזל, מבה, = אותיות ד' עם ; להו gadol גָּדוֹל

כלה אדני, umhulal וּמְהֻלָּל (*Chochmah*) Adonai יהואדניהואהדונהי

‏:cheker וְחֵקֶר en אֵין יהו veligdulato וְלִגְדֻלָּתוֹ me'od מְאֹד

THE ASHREI

"Joyful are those who dwell in You·House, they shall praise You, Selah." (Psalms 84:5)
"Joyful is the nation that this is theirs and joyful the nation that the Lord is their God." (Psalms 144:15)
"A praise of David.

א   I shall exalt You, my God, the King, and I shall bless Your Name forever and for eternity.

ב   I shall bless You every day and I shall praise Your Name forever and for eternity.

ג   The Lord is great and exceedingly praised. His greatness is unfathomable.

ר"ת דלים   ma'asecha מַעֲשֶׂיךָ   yeshabach יְשַׁבַּח   ledor לְדוֹר   dor דּוֹר

(=אכא) וה' אותיות סופיות בזֹזֶךְ: ugvurotecha וּגְבוּרֹתֶיךָ   yagidu יַגִּידוּ   ייז, כ"ב אותיות פשוטות

vedivrei וְדִבְרֵי   hodecha הוֹדֶךָ   kevod כְּבוֹד   hadar הֲדַר

אדֹנָי   אהיה   אלהים,   ר"ת   nifle'otecha נִפְלְאֹתֶיךָ

פֹ"ז: טהור כתם (בסוד   =   פ"ז   הפסוק   ר"ת   asicha אָשִׂיחָה

ugdulatcha וּגְדֻלָּתְךָ   yomeru יֹאמֵרוּ   nor'otecha נוֹרְאֹתֶיךָ   ve'ezuz וֶעֱזוּז

(מילוי דס"ג):   ס"ת = יא"י   ע"ב, ריבוע יהוה   ר"ת =   asaprena אֲסַפְּרֶנָּה   ס"ת (כתיב: וּגְדֻלּוֹתֶיךָ)

yabi'u יַבִּיעוּ   לאו   tuvcha טוּבְךָ   rav רַב־   zecher זֵכֶר

ר"י יהוה: ר"ת הפסוק =   ס"ת = ב"ן, יבם, לכב ;   yeranenu יְרַנֵּנוּ   vetzidkatcha וְצִדְקָתְךָ

(Binah)   Adonai יְהוָֹאדֹנָייֶאֱהֹוִה   verachum וְרַחוּם   chanun חַנּוּן

apayim אַפַּיִם   ר"ת   ס"ג = ב"ן   ס"ת =   = עשֹל   erech אֶרֶךְ   חנון ורחום יהוה = יהוה

ריבוע יהוה: chased וָחֶסֶד   ע"ב,   (כתיב: וְגָדוֹל)   ugdal וּגְדָל

al עַל־   verachamav וְרַחֲמָיו   (מילוי דס"ג)   ס"ת   ל"ף   ; אדֹנָי   יה

kol כָּל־   ילי ; עמם ;   ר"ת ריבוע ב"ן ע"ה   ma'asav מַעֲשָׂיו   ס"ת ע"ב, ריבוע יהוה:

ד   *One generation and the next shall praise Your deeds and tell of Your might.*
ה   *The brilliance of Your splendid glory and the wonders of Your acts, I shall speak of.*
ו   *They shall speak of the might of Your awesome acts and I shall tell of Your greatness.*
ז   *They shall express the remembrance of Your abundant goodness, and Your righteousness they shall joyfully proclaim.* ח *The Lord is merciful and compassionate, slow to anger and great in kindness.*
ט   *The Lord is good to all, His compassion extends over all His acts.*

יוֹדוּךָ yoducha (Gevurah) Adonai יְהוֹוָאדֹנָיאהדונהי kol כָּל ילי בְּמַעֲשֶׂיךָ ma'asecha

וַחֲסִידֶיךָ vachasidecha ר"ת אלהים, אהיה אדני יְבָרְכוּכָה yevarchucha ס"ת = מ"ה:

כְּבוֹד kevod מַלְכוּתְךָ malchutcha יֹאמֵרוּ yomeru וּגְבוּרָתְךָ ugvuratcha

יְדַבֵּרוּ yedaberu ר"ת הפסוק = אלהים, אהיה אדני ; ס"ת = ב"ן, יבמ, לכב:

לְהוֹדִיעַ lehodi'a לִבְנֵי livnei הָאָדָם ha'adam ר"ת אדני ללה, ארני

גְּבוּרֹתָיו gevurotav וּכְבוֹד uchvod הֲדַר hadar

מַלְכוּתוֹ malchuto ר"ת מ"ה וס"ת = רי"ו ; ר"ת הפסוק ע"ה = ק"כ צירופי אלהים:

מַלְכוּתְךָ malchutcha מַלְכוּת malchut כָּל kol ילי עֹלָמִים olamim

וּמֶמְשַׁלְתְּךָ umemshaltecha בְּכָל bechol ב"ן, לכב דּוֹר dor וָדֹר vador רי"ו:

(Tiferet) Adonai יְהוֹוָאדֹנָיאהדונהי אדני ריבוע somech סוֹמֵךְ

לְכָל lechol יה אדני ; סומך אדני לכל ר"ת סאל, אמן (יאהדונהי) הַנֹּפְלִים hanoflim

וְזוֹקֵף vezokef לְכָל lechol יה אדני הַכְּפוּפִים hakefufim גמב:

עֵינֵי enei ריבוע דמ"ה chol כֹּל ילי אֵלֶיךָ elecha יְשַׂבֵּרוּ yesaberu וְאַתָּה veAta

נוֹתֵן noten אבגיתצ, ושר לָהֶם lahem אֶת et אָכְלָם ochlam בְּעִתּוֹ be'ito:

י   *All that You have made shall thank You, Lord, and Your pious ones shall bless You.*

כ   *They shall speak of the glory of Your Kingdom and talk of Your mighty deeds.*

ל   *His mighty deeds He makes known to man and the glory of His splendid Kingdom.*

מ   *Yours is the Kingdom of all worlds and Your reign extends to each and every generation.*

ס   *The Lord supports all those who fell and holds upright all those who are bent over.*

ע   *The eyes of all look hopefully towards You, and You give them their food at its proper time.*

POTE'ACH ET YADECHA

We connect to the letters *Pei, Alef,* and *Yud* by opening our hands and holding our palms skyward. Our consciousness is focused on receiving sustenance and financial prosperity from the Light through our actions of personal tithing and sharing, our Desire to Receive for the Sake of Sharing. In doing so, we also acknowledge that the sustenance we receive comes from a higher source and is not of our own doing. According to the sages, if we do not meditate on this idea at this juncture, we must repeat the prayer.

פתוו (שע"ו נהורין למ"ה ולס"ה)

יוד הי ויו הי יוד הי ויו הי (וו' וזיורתי)   פותוו את ידרך ר"ת פאי

אלף למד אלף למד (ע"ע)   גימ' יאהדונהי זו"ן

יוד הא ואו הא (כל"א)   וחכמה דו"א ו"ק

אדני (ולנוקבא)   יסוד דנוק'

פּוֹתֵחַ pote'ach אֶת et יָדֶךָ yadecha ר"ת פאי וס"ת וחתך עם ג' אותיות = דִיקָרנֹוסָא

ובאתב"ש הוא סאל, פאי, אמן, יאהדונהי ; ועוד יכוין עם וחתך בשילוב יהוה – יֹוֹזֹהֹתֹוֹכֹהֹ

Drawing abundance and sustenance from *Chochmah* of *Zeir Anpin*

יוד הי ויו הי יוד הי ויו דלת הי יוד הי ויו יוד הי ויו הי יוד

וחתך סאל יאהדונהי

וּמַשְׂבִּיעַ umasbi'a וחתך עם ג' אותיות = דִיקָרנֹוסָא

ובא"ת ב"ש הוא סאל, אמן, יאהדונהי ; ועוד יכוין עם וחתך בשילוב יהוה – יֹוֹזֹהֹתֹוֹכֹהֹ

Drawing abundance and sustenance from *Chochmah* of *Zeir Anpin*

יוד הי ויו הי יוד הי ויו דלת הי יוד הי ויו יוד הי ויו הי יוד

לְכָל lechol יה אדני (להבמעיר מווזין ד–יה אל הנוקבא שהיא אדני)

וְחֵי chai כל וזי = אהיה אהיה יהוה, בינה ע"ה, וזיים

רָצוֹן ratzon מהשע ע"ה, ע"ב ברביוע וקס"א ע"ה, אל שדי ע"ה

ר"ת רוזל שהיא המלכות הצריכה לשפע

יוד יוד הי יוד הי ויו הי יוד הי ויו הי יוד יסוד דאבא

אלף הי יוד הי יסוד דאימא

להבמתיק רוזל וב' דמעין שֹך פר

Also meditate to draw abundance and sustenance and blessing to all the worlds from the *ratzon* mentioned above. You should meditate and focus on this verse because it is the essence of prosperity, and that God is intervening and sustaining and supporting all of Creation.

POTE'ACH ET YADECHA

פ   *Open*   *Your*   *Hands*   *and*   *satisfy*   *every*   *living*   *thing*   *with*   *desire.*

צַדִּיק tzadik יְהֹוָואֲדֹנָיאהדונהי Adonai (Yesod) בְּכֹל bechol ב"ן, לכב

דְּרָכָיו derachav וְחָסִיד vechasid בְּכֹל bechol ב"ן, לכב מַעֲשָׂיו ma'asav יֻבּמ, ב"ן

קָרוֹב karov יְהֹוָואֲדֹנָיאהדונהי Adonai (Malchut) לְכֹל lechol יה אֲדֹנָי

אֲשֶׁר asher אֲדֹנָי יה לְכֹל lechol קֹרְאָיו kor'av

יִקְרָאֻהוּ yikra'uhu בֶאֱמֶת ve'emet אהיה פעמים אהיה, ז"פ ס"ג

רָצוֹן retzon מהשע ע"ה, ע"ב בריבוע וקס"א ע"ה, אל שדי ע"ה יְרֵאָיו yere'av יַעֲשֶׂה ya'ase

וְאֶת־ ve'et ר"ת רי"י עוֲעָתָם shav'atam יִשְׁמַע yishma וְיוֹשִׁיעֵם veyoshi'em

שׁוֹמֵר shomer כ"א הויות שבתפילין יְהֹוָואֲדֹנָיאהדונהי Adonai (Netzach)

אֶת־ et כֹּל kol ילי אֹהֲבָיו ohavav ר"ת אכא

וְאֶת ve'et כָּל kol ילי הָרְשָׁעִים haresha'im יַשְׁמִיד yashmid

תְּהִלַּת tehilat יְהֹוָואֲדֹנָיאהדונהי Adonai (Hod) יְדַבֶּר yedaber ראה פִּי pi

וִיבָרֵך vivarech ע"ב ס"ג מ"ה ב"ן, הברכה (למתק את ז' המלכים שמתו) כָּל kol ילי

בָּשָׂר basar עָם shem שֵׁם kodsho קָדְשׁוֹ לְעוֹלָם le'olam ריבוע ס"ג וי' אותיות דס"ג

וָעֶד va'ed וַאֲנַחְנוּ va'anachnu נְבָרֵך nevarech יָהּ Yah מֵעַתָּה me'ata

וְעַד ve'ad עוֹלָם olam הַלְלוּיָהּ haleluya אלהים, אהיה אדני ; ללה:

RETURNING THE TORAH TO THE ARK

Before we return the Torah back to the Ark we recite the following verse twice:

יִמְלֹך yimloch יְהֹוָואֲדֹנָיאהדונהי Adonai | לְעוֹלָם le'olam ריבוע ס"ג י' אותיות דס"ג

אֱלֹהַיִך Elohayich ילה צִיּוֹן Tziyon יוסף, ו' הויות, קנאה לְדֹר ledor

וָדֹר vador רי"ו ; ר"ת אצלו (רמז שמלכות אצל ז"א) הַלְלוּיָהּ haleluya אלהים = אהיה אדני ; ללה:

צ   The Lord is righteous in all His ways and virtuous in all His deeds.
ק   The Lord is close to all who call Him, only to those who call Him truthfully.
ר   He shall fulfill the will of those who fear Him; He hears their wailing and saves them.
ש   The Lord protects all who love Him and He destroys the wicked.
ת   My lips utter the praise of the Lord and all flesh shall bless His Holy Name, forever and for eternity."
(Psalms 145) "And we shall bless the Lord forever and for eternity. Praise the Lord!" (Psalms 115:18)

RETURNING THE TORAH TO THE ARK

"The Lord will reign forever, your God, Zion, for each and every generation, Praise the Lord!" (Psalms 146:10)

mizmor מִזְמוֹר leDavid לְדָוִד havu הָבוּ אוֹז, אהבה, דאגה

ladonai לַיהֹוָהאדנייאהדונהי benei בְּנֵי ר"ת הבל elim אֵלִים הבו יהוה בני אלים = יעקב

havu הָבוּ kavod כָּבוֹד ladonai לַיהֹוָהאדנייאהדונהי דאגה, אהבה, אוֹז, וָעֹז va'oz׃

havu הָבוּ ladonai לַיהֹוָהאדנייאהדונהי דאגה, אהבה, אוֹז, kevod כְּבוֹד shemo שְׁמוֹ

מזהל ע"ה, ע"ב ברביעי וקס"א ע"ה, אל עדוי ע"ה ; הבו יהוה כבוד שמו = אדם דוד משיחו

hishtachavu הִשְׁתַּחֲווּ ladonai לַיהֹוָהאדנייאהדונהי behadrat בְּהַדְרַת ר"ת הבל

kodesh קֹדֶשׁ (שביום שבת צריך ללמוד קבלה) ר"ת למפרע קבלה kol קוֹל׃

Adonai יְהֹוָהאדנייאהדונהי al עַל־ hamayim הַמָּיִם ר"ת = אלף למד (וחסד – ואל עני רמוז

El אֵל־ יא"י (מילוי דס"ג) hakavod הַכָּבוֹד לאו hir'im הִרְעִים ה"פ אדני במילה בהמשך)׃

(להמתיק שכ"ה דינים) Adonai יְהֹוָהאדנייאהדונהי al עַל־ mayim מַיִם rabim רַבִּים

ר"ת הרעים (שכ"ה דינים – ועני השכינה דינים נמתקים ע"י עני שומות א"ל הרמוזים לעיל)׃

kol קוֹל־ Adonai יְהֹוָהאדנייאהדונהי bako'ach בַּכֹּחַ ר"ת יב"ק, אלהים יהוה, אהיה אדני יהוה

kol קוֹל־ Adonai יְהֹוָהאדנייאהדונהי behadar בֶּהָדָר ר"ת יב"ק, אלהים יהוה, אהיה אדני יהוה׃

kol קוֹל Adonai יְהֹוָהאדנייאהדונהי shover שֹׁבֵר arazim אֲרָזִים vayshaber וַיְשַׁבֵּר

Adonai יְהֹוָהאדנייאהדונהי et אֶת־ arzei אַרְזֵי haLevanon הַלְּבָנוֹן ר"ת האא׃

vayarkidem וַיַּרְקִידֵם kemo כְּמוֹ egel עֵגֶל Levanon לְבָנוֹן

veSiryon וְשִׂרְיֹן kemo כְּמוֹ ven בֶן re'emim רְאֵמִים׃ kol קוֹל־

Adonai יְהֹוָהאדנייאהדונהי chotzev חֹצֵב ס"ת הב"ל lahavot לַהֲבוֹת esh אֵשׁ׃

kol קוֹל Adonai יְהֹוָהאדנייאהדונהי יודווואדנייאהדונהי yachil יָחִיל ס"ת ללה, אדני midbar מִדְבָּר

yachil יָחִיל Adonai יְהֹוָהאדנייאהדונהי midbar מִדְבָּר kadesh קָדֵשׁ ר"ת = קון׃

---

*A Psalm of David: Render to the Lord, you sons of the powerful ones, render to the Lord
honor and might. Render to the Lord honor worthy of His Name, prostrate yourselves before the Lord
in the glory of His Holiness. The Voice of the Lord is upon the waters, The God of glory had thundered,
Lord is upon vast waters. The Voice of the Lord is powerful. The Voice of the Lord is majesty.
The Voice of the Lord breaks cedars, the Lord breaks the cedars of Lebanon. He makes them dance
around like a calf, Lebanon and Sirion like a wild young ox. The Voice of the Lord cleaves the flames
of fire. The Voice of the Lord convulses the wilderness; the Lord convulses the wilderness of Kadesh.*

קוֹל kol יְהֹוָ‎ Adonai יְחוֹלֵל yecholel אַיָּלוֹת ayalot

וַיֶּחֱשֹׂף vayechesof יְעָרוֹת ye'arot וּבְהֵיכָלוֹ uvhechalo כֻּלוֹ kulo אֹמֵר omer

כָּבוֹד kavod: יְהֹוָה Adonai לַמַּבּוּל lamabul יָשָׁב yashav

מֶלֶךְ melech יְהֹוָה Adonai וַיֵּשֶׁב vayeshev הבל וס"ת ילו ר"ת

עֹז oz יְהֹוָה Adonai לְעוֹלָם le'olam אותיות י' ס"ג ריבוע דס"ג:

יְבָרֵךְ yevarech יְהֹוָה Adonai יִתֵּן yiten לְעַמּוֹ le'amo הברכה עסמ"ב,

אֶת et עַמּוֹ amo בַשָׁלוֹם vashalom ר"ת ע"ב, ריבוע יהו: (למתק את ז' המלכים עמתו)

שׁוּבָה shuva לִמְעוֹנָךְ limonach וּשְׁכוֹן ushchon בְּבֵית bevet הוזע ב"פ ראה

מֵאֲוַיֶךְ ma'avayach ♦ כִּי ki כָּל chol פֶּה pe מילה ע"ה, אלהים, אהיה אדני ילי

וְכָל vechol לָשׁוֹן lashon יִתְּנוּ yitenu הוֹד hod וְהָדָר vehadar ילי ההה

לְמַלְכוּתֶךְ lemalchutach: וּבְנֻחֹה uvnucho יֹאמַר yomar שׁוּבָה shuva הוזע

יְהֹוָה Adonai רִבְבוֹת rivevot אַלְפֵי alfei יִשְׂרָאֵל Yisrael:

הֲשִׁיבֵנוּ hashivenu יְהֹוָה Adonai | אֵלֶיךְ elecha וְנָשׁוּבָה venashuva

חַדֵּשׁ chadesh ק"ס הויות, קס"א קנ"א י"ב וְנָשׁוּב (כתיב: יָמֵינוּ yamenu כְּקֶדֶם kekedem:

HALF KADDISH

יִתְגַּדַּל yitgadal ; י"א אותיות כמנין ו"ה עדי ומילוי עדי וְיִתְקַדַּשׁ veyitkadash

שְׁמֵיהּ shemei (שם י"ה דע"ב) רַבָּא raba קנ"א ב"ן, יהוה אלהים יהוה אדני,

אָמֵן amen אידהנויה: מילוי קס"א וס"ג, מ"ה ברבוע וע"ב ע"ה ; ר"ת = ו"פ אלהים ; ס"ת = ג"פ יב"ק:

The Voice of the Lord frightens the hinds and strips the forests bare, and in His Temple all proclaim His Glory. The Lord sat at the deluge, and the Lord sits as King forever. The Lord gives might to His people. The Lord will bless His people with peace." (Psalms 29) "Return to Your dwelling Place and reside in Your desirable House because every mouth and every tongue proclaim the majesty and the splendor of Your reign. And when It rested, he would say: Return, Lord, to the myriad thousands of Israel." (Numbers 10:36) "Bring us back to You, Lord, and we shall return, renew our days as of old." (Lamentations 5:21)

HALF KADDISH

May His great Name be more exalted and sanctified. (Amen)

בְּעָלְמָא be'alma   דִּי di   בְרָא vera   כִרְעוּתֵיהּ kir'utei◆

וְיַמְלִיךְ veyamlich   מַלְכוּתֵיהּ mal'chutei◆   וְיַצְמַח veyatzmach

פּוּרְקָנֵיהּ purkanei◆   וִיקָרֵב vikarev   מְשִׁיחֵיהּ meshichei: אָמֵן amen אידהנויה.

בְּחַיֵּיכוֹן bechayechon   וּבְיוֹמֵיכוֹן uvyomechon   וּבְחַיֵּי uvchayei

דְכָל dechol   ילי   בֵּית bet   ב"פ ראה   יִשְׂרָאֵל Yisrael   בַּעֲגָלָא ba'agala

וּבִזְמַן uvizman   קָרִיב kariv   וְאָמְרוּ ve'imru   אָמֵן amen: אָמֵן amen אידהנויה.

The congregation and the *chazan* say the following:

Twenty eight words (until *be'alma*) and twenty eight letters (until *almaya*)

יְהֵא yehe   שְׁמֵיהּ shemei   (שם י"ה דס"ג)   רַבָּא raba   קנ"א ב"ז,

מְבָרַךְ mevarach,   יהוה אלהים יהוה אדני, מילוי קס"א וס"ג, מ"ה ברבוע וע"ב ע"ה

לְעָלַם le'alam   לְעָלְמֵי le'almei   עָלְמַיָּא almaya◆   יִתְבָּרַךְ yitbarach◆

Seven words with six letters each (שם בן מ"ב) and seven times the letter *Vav* (שם בן מ"ב)

וְיִשְׁתַּבַּח veyishtabach   י"פ ע"ב יהוה אל אבג יתץ◆

וְיִתְפָּאַר veyitpa'ar   הי גו יה קרע שטן◆   וְיִתְרֹמַם veyitromam   וה כוזו נגד יכש◆

וְיִתְנַשֵּׂא veyitnase   במוכסז בטר צתג◆   וְיִתְהַדָּר veyit'hadar   כוזו יה וזקב טנע◆

וְיִתְעַלֶּה veyit'ale   וה יוד ה יגל פזק◆   וְיִתְהַלָּל veyit'halal   א ואו הא שקו צית◆

שְׁמֵיהּ shemei   (שם י"ה דמ"ה)   דְּקוּדְשָׁא dekudsha   בְּרִיךְ verich   הוּא hu:

אָמֵן amen אידהנויה.◆

לְעֵלָּא le'ela   מִן min   כָּל kol   ילי   בִּרְכָתָא birchata◆   שִׁירָתָא shirata◆

תֻּשְׁבְּחָתָא tishbechata   וְנֶחָמָתָא venechamata◆   דַּאֲמִירָן da'amiran

בְּעָלְמָא be'alma   וְאָמְרוּ ve'imru   אָמֵן amen: אָמֵן amen אידהנויה.

In the world that He created according to His will, and may His kingdom reign. And may He cause His redemption to sprout and may He bring the Mashiach closer. (Amen) In your lifetimes and in your days and in the lifetime of all the House of Israel, speedily and in the near future, and you should say, Amen. (Amen) May His great Name be blessed forever and for all eternity blessed and lauded, and glorified and exalted, and extolled and honored, and uplifted and praised, be the Name of the Holy Blessed One. (Amen) Above all blessings, songs, praises, and words of consolation that may be said in the world, and you shall say,

Amen. (Amen)

MUSAF OF SUKKOT AND SIMCHAT TORAH

yagid יַגִּיד ufi וּפִי tiftach תִּפְתָּח sefatai שְׂפָתַי (pause here) כלה Adonai אֲדֹנָי

ס"ת = בוכו: tehilatecha תְּהִלָּתֶךָ (כ"ב אותיות פשוטות [=אכא] וה' אותיות סופיות מנצפ"ך) יוד

THE FIRST BLESSING - INVOKES THE SHIELD OF ABRAHAM.

Abraham is the channel of the Right Column energy of positivity, sharing, and mercy. Sharing actions can protect us from all forms of negativity.

Chesed that becomes *Chochmah*

In this section there are 42 words, the secret of the 42-Letter Name of God and therefore it begins with the letter *Bet* (2) and ends with the letter *Mem* (40).

Bend your knees at "*baruch*," bow at "*Ata*" and straighten up at "*Adonai*."

המלכות לה' (אותיות הא"ב המסמלות את השפע המגיע) א–ת Ata אַתָּה baruch בָּרוּךְ

ילה Elohenu אֱלֹהֵינוּ (יא) Adonai יְהוָֹה אדני יאהדונהי

avotenu אֲבוֹתֵינוּ ילה ; דמב ע"ב, מילוי ; לכב velohei וֵאלֹהֵי

אותיות פשוטות וט"ו עסמ"ב (אברים), רמ"ח נתיבות החוכמה, ול"ב רי"ו אל, וו"פ (*Chochmah*) Avraham אַבְרָהָם ילה ; דמב ע"ב, מילוי Elohei אֱלֹהֵי

ד"פ ב"ן (*Binah*) Yitzchak יִצְחָק ילה ; דמב ע"ב, מילוי Elohei אֱלֹהֵי

אהדונהי יאהדונהי הויות, ו (*Da'at*) Yaakov יַעֲקֹב ילה ; דמב ע"ב, מילוי לכב velohei וֵאלֹהֵי

MUSAF OF SUKKOT AND SIMCHAT TORAH
THE AMIDAH
"My Lord, open my lips, and my mouth shall relate Your praise." (Psalms 51:17)
THE FIRST BLESSING
Blessed are You, Lord,
our God and God of our forefathers:the God of Abraham, the God of Isaac, and the God of Jacob.

haEl **הָאֵל** ; יא"י (מילוי דס"ג) hagadol **הַגָּדוֹל** הָאֵל הַגָּדוֹל = סיט ; גָדוֹל = להוֹ לאה

vehanora **וְהַנּוֹרָא** ר"ת ההה hagibor **הַגִּבּוֹר** אום, יזל, = מבה אותיות ד' עם

elyon **עֶלְיוֹן** יהוה ריבוע ע"ב, ר"ת ; (מילוי דס"ג) יא"י El **אֵל**

hakol **הַכֹּל** יכי kone **קוֹנֵה** tovim **טוֹבִים** chasadim **חֲסָדִים** gomel **גּוֹמֵל**

umevi **וּמֵבִיא** avot **אָבוֹת** chasdei **וְחַסְדֵּי** vezocher **וְזוֹכֵר**

lema'an **לְמַעַן** venehem **בְּנֵיהֶם** livnei **לִבְנֵי** go'el **גּוֹאֵל**

shemo **שְׁמוֹ** מהש ע"ה, ע"ב בריבוע וקס"א ע"ה, אל שדי ע"ה be'ahava **בְּאַהֲבָה** אזד, דאגה:

When saying the word "be'ahava" you should meditate to devote your soul to sanctify the Holy Name and accept upon yourself the four forms of death.

umagen **וּמָגֵן** umoshi'a **וּמוֹשִׁיעַ** ozer **עוֹזֵר** melech **מֶלֶךְ**

ג"פ אל (יא"י מילוי דס"ג) ; ר"ת ביכאל גבריאל נוריאל:

Bend your knees at "baruch," bow at "Ata" and straighten up at "Adonai."

אהיה יהו אלף הי יוד הי :(on Shabbat) **יְהֹוָה**

(הד) Adonai **יְהֹוָה**(יֶהֱוִה)אדֹנִיꞏiאהדונהי Ata **אַתָּה** baruch **בָּרוּךְ**

Avraham **אַבְרָהָם** ; ר"ת ביכאל גבריאל נוריאל ג"פ אל (יא"י מילוי דס"ג) magen **מָגֵן**

וח"פ אל, רי"ו ול"ב נתיבות הוחכמה, רמ"וז (אברים), עסמ"ב וט"ו אותיות פשוטות:

The great, mighty and Awesome God.
The Supernal God, Who bestows beneficial kindness and creates everything. Who recalls the kindness of the forefathers and brings a Redeemer to their descendants for the sake of His Name, lovingly. King, Helper, Savior and Shield. Blessed are You, Lord, the shield of Abraham.

THE SECOND BLESSING

THE ENERGY OF ISAAC IGNITES THE POWER FOR THE RESURRECTION OF THE DEAD.

Whereas Abraham represents the power of sharing, Isaac represents the Left Column energy of judgment. Judgment shortens the *tikkun* process and paves the way for our eventual resurrection.

Gevurah that becomes *Binah*.

In this section there are 49 words corresponding to the 49 gates of the Pure System in *Binah*.

ללה Adonai אֲדֹנָי רִיבוע ס״ג ו״י אותיות דס״ג le'olam לְעוֹלָם gibor גִּבּוֹר Ata אַתָּה

(ר״ת אַגְלָא והוא שם גדול ואמיץ, ובו היה יהודה מתגבר על אויביו. ע״ה אלד, בוכו).

lehoshi'a לְהוֹשִׁיעַ rav רַב Ata אַתָּה metim מֵתִים ס״ג mechaye מְחַיֵּה

Only on Simchat Torah:

מ״ה ר״ת haru'ach הָרוּחַ mashiv מַשִּׁיב

hageshem הַגֶּשֶׁם umorid וּמוֹרִיד

ע״ה:[ובטיל ו״י אל ול״ב נתיבות הוכמה] ע״ה:

If you mistakenly say "morid hatal," and realize this before the end of the blessing "baruch Ata Adonai," you should return to the beginning of the blessing "Ata gibor" and continue as usual. But if you only realize this after the end of the blessing, you should continue and not go back.

During Sukkot:

hatal הַטָּל morid מוֹרִיד

יוד הא ואו, כזזו, מספר אותיות דמילואי עסמ״ב ;
ר״ת מ״ה (יוד הא ואו הא):

If you mistakenly say "Mashiv haru'ach," and realize this before the end of the blessing "baruch Ata Adonai," you should return to the beginning of the blessing "Ata gibor" and continue as usual. But if you only realize this after the end of the blessing, you should start the Amidah from the beginning.

bechesed בְּחֶסֶד ע״ה בינה, יהוה אהיה אהיה chayim וְחַיִּים mechalkel מְכַלְכֵּל

berachamim בְּרַחֲמִים metim מֵתִים ס״ג mechaye מְחַיֵּה ע״ב, ריבוע יהוה,

somech סוֹמֵךְ (טלא דעתיק) rabim רַבִּים י״פ ייי, אלהים דההין, מצפ״ץ (בַמוכסז)

cholim חוֹלִים verofe וְרוֹפֵא (זו״ן) noflim נוֹפְלִים כוק, ריבוע אדני (אכדטם)

umekayem וּמְקַיֵּם asurim אֲסוּרִים umatir וּמַתִּיר מ״ה וד׳ אותיות. וזולה = מ״ה

chamocha כָּמוֹךָ ילי mi מִי afar עָפָר lishenei לִישֵׁנֵי emunato אֱמוּנָתוֹ

gevurot גְּבוּרוֹת ba'al בַּעַל (you should enunciate the letter *Ayin* in the word "ba'al")

memit מֵמִית melech מֶלֶךְ lach לָךְ dome דּוֹמֶה ילי umi וּמִי

yeshu'a יְשׁוּעָה umatzmi'ach וּמַצְמִיחַ (יוד הי ואו הי) ס״ג umchaye וּמְחַיֵּה

THE SECOND BLESSING

You are mighty forever, Lord. You resurrect the dead and are very capable of redeeming.

Only on Simchat Torah:
Who causes wind to blow and rain to fall.

During Sukkot:
Who causes dew to fall.

You sustain life with kindness and resurrect the dead with great compassion. You support those who have fallen, heal the sick, release the imprisoned, and fulfill Your faithful words to those who are asleep in the dust. Who is like You, Master of might, and Who can compare to You, King, Who causes death, Who gives life, and Who sprouts salvation?

וְנֶאֱמָן vene'eman   אַתָּה Ata   לְהַחֲיוֹת lehachayot   מֵתִים metim:

(יְהֹוָה on Shabbat:) אהיה יהו אלף הי יוד הי

בָּרוּךְ baruch   אַתָּה Ata   יְהֹוָאדֹנָי(יֱהֹוִה)(אֲדֹנָי)אהדונהי Adonai

מְחַיֶּה mechaye   ס"ג (יוד הי ואו הי)   הַמֵּתִים hametim   ר"ת מ"ה וס"ת מ"ה:

THE KEDUSHA OF KETER
The congregation recites this prayer together.

Keter is the highest level in the spiritual atmosphere. As we reach this high point in our connections, we stand with both legs together. It is also one of the most powerful prayers to help us connect to the seed level of life before there was any differentiation between the cells of the body. Our meditations during this time increase the production of stem cells in our body. Lifting a heavy chest filled with vast treasures is impossible if you use just a single string: The string will snap because it is too weak. However, if we unite and combine numerous strings, we will eventually build a rope. A rope can easily lift the treasure chest. By combining and uniting the congregation's prayers, we become a united force, capable of pulling down the most valuable spiritual treasures. Furthermore, this unity helps people who are not well-versed or knowledgeable in the connections. By uniting and meditating as one soul, we all receive the benefit because of the powerof unity, regardless of our knowledge and understanding. This prayer occurs in between the second and third blessings. It signifies the Central Column that unites the Left and Right Columns.

In this prayer the angels speak to each other, saying: "*Kadosh, Kadosh, Kadosh*" ("Holy, Holy, Holy"). When we recite these three words, we stand with our feet stand together as one. With each utterance of *Kadosh*, we jump a little higher in the air. Jumping is an act of restriction and it defies the force of gravity. Spiritually, gravity has the energy of the Desire to Receive for the Self Alone. It is the reactive force of our planet, always pulling everything toward itself.

The Secret of the *Kedusha* from the Ramchel:

We (humans) say *Kedusha* (Holiness) only from the power of the holiness of the angels. Because our way of making the Unification is to recite the "Shema" and the angles do so by the *Kedusha*. But even the correction of the angels is done by us. Because the angels' holiness originated from Abba and Ima they are protected from the negativity, as Abba and Ima do not allow the negativity to come closer, even to the external aspect of the angels.

For us, the negativity can grab hold onto the external aspect, which is the body. All of this is for now, during the *tikkun* process. But at the end of the *tikkun* process, even the body will be corrected and holy, so even the angels will draw their *Kedusha* from us. So for now, we say the *Kedusha* from the power of the angels, as we don't have the power to do it ourselves and we need to take it from the correction of the angels and by that we receive a small illumination, even for the body. This illumination is not strong enough to remove the negative forces totally but can only receive the holiness that is available now. So one should meditate, for the congregation prayer, to be as *Malchut* (you), which is now uniting with *Chesed*, *Gevurah* and *Tiferet* (the congregation). So then the awakening will rise up to *Arich Anpin* to draw the abundance of holiness to *Malchut* and from *Her* to us.

Saying the *Kedusha* (holiness) we meditate to bring the holiness of the Creator among us. As it says: "*Venikdashti betoch Benei Israel*" (God is hallowed among the children of Israel).

And You are faithful to resurrecting the dead. Blessed are You, Lord, Who resurrects the dead.

lecha כָּךְ yitnu יִתְּנוּ גאל ובאתב"ש ועד לעולם ימלוך ה' מלך ה' מלך ה' keter כֶּתֶר

mal'achim מַלְאָכִים (Zeir and Nukva) יְלה Elohenu אֱלֹהֵינוּ Adonai יְהֹוָהּ

Yisrael יִשְׂרָאֵל amecha עַמְּךָ im עִם (Abba and Ima) ma'la בְּמַעְלָה hamonei הֲמוֹנֵי

kulam כֻּלָּם yachad יַחַד .(by the Righteous) mata מַטָּה kevutzei קְבוּצֵי

ראה kadavar כַּדָּבָר yeshaleshu יְשַׁלֵּשׁוּ lecha לְךָ kedusha קְדֻשָּׁה

vekara וְקָרָא nevi'ach נְבִיאָךְ yad יַד al עַל ha'amur הָאָמוּר

:ve'amar וְאָמַר דרוזל פרקין אל י"ב מאירין דיעקב פרקין י"ב ze זֶה el אֶל ze זֶה

Meditate to elevate Malchut to Chesed, Gevurah, Tiferet of Supernal Ima.

kadosh קָדוֹשׁ (Tiferet) kadosh קָדוֹשׁ (Gevurah) | kadosh קָדוֹשׁ (Chesed)

יולי chol כֹּל melo מְלֹא שכינה פני Tzeva'ot צְבָאוֹת Adonai יְהֹוָהּ

:kevodo כְּבוֹדוֹ אלהים דההין ע"ה ha'aretz הָאָרֶץ

sho'alim שׁוֹאֲלִים umshartav וּמְשָׁרְתָיו olam עוֹלָם male מָלֵא kevodo כְּבוֹדוֹ

On *Shabbat*: Meditate to receive the extra soul called: *Neshamah* from the aspect of the day of *Shabbat*.

Binah	Chochmah	Da'at
Ima	Abba	Thirteenth *Mazal* (וּנְקָה)
ayeh ה	י	א

kevodo כְּבוֹדוֹ mekom מְקוֹם

Malchut (which is called ו כבוד — the honor of *Zeir Anpin*)

is in *Chochmah, Binah, Da'at* (also known as איה — *Ayeh*, as mention above).

לְהַעֲרִיצוֹ leha'aritzo איה מקום כבודו להעריצו ר"ת = אמן (יאהדונהי)

:ve'omrim וְאוֹמְרִים meshabechim מְשַׁבְּחִים le'umatam לְעֻמָּתָם

(או"א) בָּרוּךְ baruch כְּבוֹד kevod יְהֹוָהּ Adonai ; כבוד ה' = יוד הי ואו הה

:mimekomo מִמְּקוֹמוֹ עסמ"ב, הברכה (לבמתק את ז' המלכים שמתו) ; ר"ת ע"ב, ריבוע יהוה ; ר"ת מיכ:

KEDUSHA OF KETER

A crown they will give to You, Lord,

our God, the angels of the multitudes above, together with Your nation, Israel, who are assembled below. Together they will all recite the holiness three times, as the word spoken by Your prophet: "And each calls the other and says: Holy, Holy, Holy is the Lord of Hosts; the whole earth is filled with His glory." (*Isaiah 6:3*) His glory fills the world and His servants ask: Where is the place of His glory to adore Him? Facing one another, they praise and say: "Blessed is the glory of the Lord from His place." (*Ezekiel 3:12*) yifen יִפֶן hu הוּא (למתק את ז' המלכים שמתו) הברכה עסמ"ב, mimekomo מִמְּקוֹמוֹ

berachamav בְּרַחֲמָיו le'amo לְעַמּוֹ hameyachadim הַמְיַחֲדִים shemo שְׁמוֹ מהש' ע"ה,

erev עֶרֶב ע"ה, אל שדי ע"ה, אל"ב בריבוע וקס"א ע"ה, vavoker וָבֹקֶר bechol בְּכָל ב"ן, לכב

yom יוֹם ע"ה נגד, מזבוו, ז, אל יהוה ע"ה קס"א קס"א קנ"א קמ"ג tamid תָּמִיד

omrim אוֹמְרִים pa'amayim פַּעֲמַיִם be'ahava בְּאַהֲבָה אוזר, דאנה:

> **Meditate**, to devote your soul for the sanctification of the Holy Name, as well as to elevate your *Neshamah of Neshamah*, by the Name ע"ב, to become *Mayin Duchrin* to *Zeir Anpin* and to elevate your *Neshamah*, by the Name ס"ג, to become *Mayin Mayin* to so They can be unified in *Ima* (on *Shabbat*: *Zeir Anpin* in *Abba* and *Nukva* in *Ima*) in the secret of the Complete Unification.

shema שְׁמַע ע' רבתי Yisrael יִשְׂרָאֵל Adonai יְהֹוָ‑אדני‑אהדונהי Elohenu אֱלֹהֵינוּ ילה

Adonai יְהֹוָ‑אדני‑אהדונהי | echad אֶחָ‑ד ד' רבתי ; אהבה, דאנה:

hu הוּא Elohenu אֱלֹהֵינוּ ילה. avinu אָבִינוּ hu הוּא. malkenu מַלְכֵּנוּ.

hu הוּא moshi'enu מוֹשִׁיעֵנוּ. hu הוּא yoshi'enu יוֹשִׁיעֵנוּ veyigalenu וְיִגְאָלֵנוּ.

shenit שֵׁנִית. veyashmi'enu וְיַשְׁמִיעֵנוּ berachamav בְּרַחֲמָיו le'enei לְעֵינֵי ריבוע מ"ה

kol כָּל chai וָזִי ילי = כל וזי אהיה אהיה יהוה, בינה ע"ה, וזיים lemor לֵאמֹר.

hen הֵן ga'alti גָּאַלְתִּי et'chem אֶתְכֶם acharit אַחֲרִית kereshit כְּרֵאשִׁית ילה.

lih'yot לִהְיוֹת lachem לָכֶם lelohim לֵאלֹהִים אהיה אדני ; ילה.

ani אֲנִי Adonai יְהֹוָ‑אדני‑אהדונהי Elohechem אֱלֹהֵיכֶם ילה:

uvdivrei וּבְדִבְרֵי kodshach קָדְשְׁךָ katuv כָּתוּב lemor לֵאמֹר:

(זו"ן) יִמְלֹךְ yimloch קדוש ברוך ימלך ר"ת יב"ק, אלהים יהוה, אהיה אדני יהוה

Tziyon צִיּוֹן ledor לְדֹר vador וָדֹר Adonai יְהֹוָ‑אדני‑אהדונהי le'olam לְעוֹלָם ריבוע ס"ג ו' אותיות דס"ג Elohayich אֱלֹהַיִךְ ילה

Tziyon צִיּוֹן יוסף, ו' הויות, קנאה רי"ו ; ר"ת אצלו (מלכות אצל ז"א – ו)

haleluya הַלְלוּיָהּ אלהים, אהיה אדני ; ללה:

From His place, may He turn with compassion to His nation, who, evening and morning, twice each day, proclaims with constancy the Oneness of His Name, saying with love: "Hear Israel, the Lord is our God, the Lord is One." (Deuteronomy 6:4) He is our God. He is our Father. He is our King. He is our Savior. He will save and redeem us again and will let us hear, through His compassion to the eyes of all the living, and will say: Behold I have redeemed you in later times as I have in earlier times, in order to be a God for you. I am the Lord, your God. And in Your holy writings, the following is written: "The Lord will reign forever, your God, Zion, from one generation to the other, praise the Lord!" (Psalms 146:10)

THE THIRD BLESSING

This blessing connects us to Jacob, the Central Column and the power of restriction. Jacob is our channel for connecting mercy with judgment. By restricting our reactive behavior, we are blocking our Desire to Receive for the Self Alone. Jacob also gives us the power to balance our acts of mercy and judgment toward other people in our lives.

Tiferet that becomes *Da'at* (14 words).

אָתָּה Ata קָדוֹשׁ kadosh וְשִׁמְךָ veshimcha קָדוֹשׁ kadosh ר"ת = אור, רז, אין סוף.

וּקְדוֹשִׁים ukdoshim בְּכָל־ bechol יוֹם yom ב"ן, לכב ע"ה נגד, מזבוח, זן, אל יהוה

יְהַלְלוּךָ yehalelucha סֶלָה sela:

(on Shabbat: מוצפצ) אהיה יהו אלף הא יוד הא

בָּרוּךְ baruch אָתָּה Ata יְהֹוָה(יֱהֹוִה)(יֱהֹוִה)יאהדונהי Adonai

הָאֵל haEl הַקָּדוֹשׁ hakadosh לאה ; יא"י (מילוי דס"ג) י"פ מ"ה (יוד הא ואו הא):

Meditate here on the Name: יאהדונהי, as it can help to remove anger.

THE MIDDLE BLESSING

The middle blessing connects us to the true power of *Sukkot* and *Simchat Torah*. *Sukkot* and *Simchat Torah* are the seed of the entire year for Mercy and Happiness. Just as an apple seed begets an apple tree, a negative seed begets a negative year. Likewise, a positive seed generates a positive year. *Sukkot* and *Simchat Torah* are our opportunity to choose the seed we wish to plant for our coming year. The power of the letters in this Fourth Blessing is in their ability to automatically choose the correct seed we need and not necessarily the seed we want.

אָתָּה Ata בְּחַרְתָּנוּ vechartanu מִכָּל mikol יְלי הָעַמִּים ha'amim

אָהַבְתָּ ahavta אוֹתָנוּ otanu וְרָצִיתָ veratzita בָּנוּ banu

וְרוֹמַמְתָּנוּ veromamtanu מִכָּל mikol יְלי הַלְּשׁוֹנוֹת haleshonot

וְקִדַּשְׁתָּנוּ vekidashtanu בְּמִצְוֹתֶיךָ bemitzvotecha וְקֵרַבְתָּנוּ vekeravtanu

מַלְכֵּנוּ malkenu לַעֲבוֹדָתֶךָ la'avodatecha וְשִׁמְךָ veshimcha הַגָּדוֹל hagadol

וְהַקָּדוֹשׁ vehakadosh עָלֵינוּ alenu קָרָאתָ karata: לחו ; ועם ד' אותיות = מבה, יזל, אום

THE THIRD BLESSING
You are Holy, and Your Name is Holy
and the Holy Ones praise You every day, Selah. Blessed are You, Lord, the Holy God.
THE MIDDLE BLESSING
You have chosen us from among all the nations. You have loved us and have found favor in us.
You have exalted us above all the tongues and You have sanctified us with Your commandments.
You draw us close, our King, to Your service and proclaimed Your great and Holy Name upon us.

וַתִּתֶּן vatiten בְּיַּ כֵהַת לָנוּ lanu אלהים, אהיה אדני יְהֹוָה ואדֹנָי אהדונהי Adonai

אֱלֹהֵינוּ Elohenu ילה בְּאַהֲבָה be'ahava אוֹזר, דאגה, (On Shabbat add:)

שַׁבָּתוֹת shabbatot ו) לִמְנוּחָה limnucha מוֹעֲדִים mo'adim לְשִׂמְחָה lesimcha◆

וְחַגִּים chagim וּזְמַנִּים uzmanim לְשָׂשׂוֹן lesason◆ אֵת et

יוֹם yom עַ"ה נגד, מזבוח, זן, אל יהוה הַשַּׁבָּת haShabbat (On Shabbat add:) הַזֶּה hazeh והו◆

וְאֵת ve'et יוֹם yom עַ"ה נגד, מזבוח, זן, אל יהוה)

(On Sukkot say: וְחַג chag הַסֻּכּוֹת haSukkot הַזֶּה hazeh◆

(On Simchat Torah say: שְׁמִינִי shemini וְחַג chag עֲצֶרֶת atzeret הַזֶּה hazeh◆

אֵת et יוֹם yom עַ"ה נגד, מזבוח, זן, אל יהוה (On Chol Hamo'ed we skip the word "tov") טוֹב tov והו)

מִקְרָא mikra קֹדֶשׁ kodesh הַזֶּה hazeh והו◆ זְמַן zeman שִׂמְחָתֵנוּ simchatenu◆

בְּאַהֲבָה be'ahava אוֹזר, דאגה, מִקְרָא mikra קֹדֶשׁ kodesh◆

זֵכֶר zecher לִיצִיאַת litzi'at מִצְרָיִם Mitzrayim מצר◆

אֱלֹהֵינוּ Elohenu ילה וֵאלֹהֵי velohei לכב; מילוי עַ"ב, דמב; ילה אֲבוֹתֵינוּ avotenu

מִפְּנֵי mipnei וַחֲטָאֵינוּ chataenu גָּלִינוּ galinu מֵאַרְצֵנוּ me'artzenu◆

וְנִתְרַחַקְנוּ venitrachaknu מֵעַל me'al עלם אַדְמָתֵנוּ admatenu◆ וְאֵין ve'en

אֲנַחְנוּ anachnu יְכוֹלִים yecholim לַעֲלוֹת la'alot וְלֵרָאוֹת veleraot

וּלְהִשְׁתַּחֲווֹת ulhishtachavot לְפָנֶיךָ lefanecha סַ"ג מַ"ה בַּ"ן בְּבֵית bevet בַּ"פ ראה

בִּוְזִירָתְךָ bechiratach בִּנְוֵה binveh הַדָּרַךְ hadarach בַּ"פ יבַ"ק, קסַ"א סַ"ג

בַּבַּיִת babayit הַגָּדוֹל hagadol בַּ"פ ראה לַהוֹו; עם דַ' אותיות = מובה, יזל, אום

וְהַקָּדוֹשׁ vehakadosh שֶׁנִּקְרָא shenikra שִׁמְךָ shimcha עָלָיו alav מִפְּנֵי mipnei

הַיָּד hayad והו שֶׁנִּשְׁתַּלְּחָה shenishtalecha בְּמִקְדָּשֶׁךָ bemikdashach:

And may You give us, Lord, our God, with love (**on Shabbat add:** *Sabbath for rest and*) *holidays for happiness, festivals and time of joy, this day* (**on Shabbat add:** *of Sabbath and this day*) (**on Sukkot:** *of Sukkot*) (**on Simchat Torah:** *of Shmini the Holiday of Atzeret*) *and this good day of Holy Convocation; The time of our happiness. with love, a Holy Convocation, a remembrance of the exit from Egypt. Our God and the God of our fathers, because of our sins we are in exile from our land. We are far from our land. And we cannot come to pilgrim, be seen and bow before You, in Your house of choice. Your House of Glory, the big and Holy House called after Your Name, because of the hand that ruined Your Temple.*

YHI RATZON

This prayer connects to the desire to see the Holy Temple rebuilt. Even though, according to Kabbalah, the temple still exists on a spiritual level, the physical structure is missing, leaving our world incomplete. This prayer helps set in motion and accelerate the eventual construction of the physical temple.

Adonai יְהֹוָֹה milfanecha מִלְּפָנֶיךָ ratzon רָצוֹן yehi יְהִי

•avotenu אֲבוֹתֵינוּ velohei וֵאלֹהֵי Elohenu אֱלֹהֵינוּ

;utrachem וּתְרַחֵם shetashuv שֶׁתָּשׁוּב •rachaman רַחֲמָן melech מֶלֶךְ

•alenu עָלֵינוּ

•harabim הָרַבִּים berachamecha בְּרַחֲמֶיךָ mikdash'cha מִקְדָּשְׁךָ ve'al וְעַל

•kevodo כְּבוֹדוֹ utgadel וּתְגַדֵּל •mehera מְהֵרָה vetivnehu וְתִבְנֵהוּ

kevod כְּבוֹד galeh גַּלֵּה Elohenu אֱלֹהֵינוּ •malkenu מַלְכֵּנוּ •avinu אָבִינוּ

vehofa וְהוֹפַע •mehera מְהֵרָה alenu עָלֵינוּ malchutcha מַלְכוּתְךָ

kol כָּל le'enei לְעֵינֵי alenu עָלֵינוּ vehinase וְהִנָּשֵׂא

pezurenu פְּזוּרֵינוּ vekarev וְקָרֵב chai חַי

kanes כַּנֵּס unfutzotenu וּנְפוּצוֹתֵינוּ •hagoyim הַגּוֹיִם miben מִבֵּין

Adonai יְהֹוָֹה vahavi'enu וַהֲבִיאֵנוּ •aretz אֶרֶץ miyarketei מִיַּרְכְּתֵי

•berina בְּרִנָּה irach עִירָךְ leTziyon לְצִיּוֹן Elohenu אֱלֹהֵינוּ

mikdash'cha מִקְדָּשֶׁךָ ir עִיר velirushalayim וְלִירוּשָׁלַיִם

•olam עוֹלָם besimchat בְּשִׂמְחַת ana אָנָּא Elohenu אֱלֹהֵינוּ

korbenot קָרְבְּנוֹת et אֶת lefanecha לְפָנֶיךָ na'ase נַעֲשֶׂה vesham וְשָׁם

umusafim וּמוּסָפִים •kesidram כְּסִדְרָם temidim תְּמִידִים •chovotenu וְחוֹבוֹתֵינוּ

(musaf מוּסַף et אֶת :On weekdays we say) •kehilchatam כְּהִלְכָתָם

May it be Your will, Lord, our God, God of our forefathers, compassionate King, that You again have mercy upon us and upon Your Sanctuary, in Your abundant compassion, and may You rebuild it speedily and make great its glory. Our Father, our King, our God, Reveal the glory of Your Kingdom over us speedily and appear and be exalted over us, before the eyes of all the living. Draw near our scattered from among the nations, and gather our dispersed from the ends of the earth. And bring us, Lord, our God, to Zion, Your city, with joyous song, and to Jerusalem, city of Your Sanctuary, in everlasting joy. Please, our God, and there we shall perform before You our obligatory sacrifices: The daily-offerings in their proper order and the Musaf-offerings according to their prescribed laws. The Musaf-offerings

(On *Shabbat* we say: אֶת et יוֹם yom מוּסְפֵי musfei ע״ה נגד, מזבוז, זז, אל יהוה

הַשַׁבָּת haShabbat הֲזֶה hazeh hazeh והו. וְאֶת ve'et יוֹם yom ע״ה נגד, מזבוז, זז, אל יהוה

(On *Sukkot* say: וְזֹג chag הַסֻכּוֹת haSukkot הֲזֶה hazeh)◆

(On *Simchat Torah* say: שְׁמִינִי shemini וְזֹג chag עֲצֶרֶת atzeret הֲזֶה hazeh)◆

(On *Chol Hamo'ed* we skip the word "tov") טוֹב tov והו :אֶת et יוֹם yom ע״ה נגד, מזבוז, זז, אל יהוה

מִקְרָא mikra קֹדֶשׁ kodesh הֲזֶה hazeh והו. נַעֲשֶׂה na'ase

וְנַקְרִיב venakriv לְפָנֶיךָ lefanecha ס״ג מ״ה ב״ן בְּאַהֲבָה be'ahava אוזר, דאגה

כְּמִצְוַת kemitzvat רְצוֹנָךְ retzonach כְּמוֹ kemo שֶׁכָּתַבְתָּ shekatavta

עָלֵינוּ alenu בְּתוֹרָתָךְ betoratach עַל al יְדֵי yedei

מֹשֶׁה Moshe מהעד, ע״ב בריבוע וקס״א, אל עדי, ד״פ אלהים ע״ה עַבְדָּךְ avdecha פוי, אל יהוה:

אֱלֹהֵינוּ Elohenu ילה וֵאלֹהֵי velohei לכבב; מילוי ע״ב ,דמב; ילה אֲבוֹתֵינוּ avotenu,

מֶלֶךְ melech רַחֲמָן rachaman רַחֵם rachem אברהם, וח״פ אל, רי״ו ול״ב נתיבות החוכמה, רמ״וז

(איברים), עסמ״ב וט״ז אותיות פשוטות עָלֵינוּ alenu◆ טוֹב tov והו וּמֵטִיב umetiv

הִדְרֵשׁ hidaresh לָנוּ lanu אלהים, אדני אהיה, החוֹש שׁוּבָה shuva עָלֵינוּ alenu

בַּהֲמוֹן bahamon רַחֲמֶיךָ rachamecha◆ אֲבוֹת avot שֶׁעָשׂוּ she'asu

רְצוֹנֶךָ retzonecha◆ בְּנֵה bene בֵּיתְךָ vetcha ב״פ ראה כְּבַתְּחִלָה kevatechila◆

כּוֹנֵן konen כוק בֵּית bet ב״פ ראה מִקְדָּשְׁךָ mikdashcha עַל al מְכוֹנוֹ mechono◆

הַרְאֵנוּ harenu בְּבִנְיָנוֹ bevinyano◆ שַׂמְּחֵנוּ samchenu בְּתִקּוּנוֹ betikuno◆

וְהָשֵׁב vehashev שְׁכִינָתְךָ shechinatcha לְתוֹכוֹ letocho, וְהָשֵׁב vehashev

כֹּהֲנִים Kohanim לַעֲבוֹדָתָם la'avodatam, וּלְוִיִם uLviyim לְדוּכָנָם leduchanam

---

(on Shabbat we say: *Musaf-offerings of this day of Sabbath and of)* this day
(on Sukkot: *of Sukkot*) (on Simchat Torah: *of Shmini the Holiday of Atzeret*)
The (**On Chol Hamo'ed** we skip the word: *good*) day of Holy Convocation.
*we shall prepare and offer before You, with love, according to the commandment
of Your will, as You wrote for us in Your Torah, through Moses, Your servant.*
Our God and the God of our fathers, Compassionate King, have mercy upon us. Good and Kind, seek us.
Return to us with Your mass compassion. Because of Your fathers who obeyed Your will. Build Your house
as before. And bring back the Tamale to its place. Show us its rebuilding. Let us be happy with its
restoration. Bring Your Shechinah, and bring back the Kohanim to their works, the Lveites to their stand,

יִשְׂרָאֵל Yisrael — וְהָשֵׁב vehashev — וּלְזַמְרָם ulzimram — לְשִׁירָם leshiram

וְנֵרָאֶה venerae — נַעֲלֶה na'ale — וְשָׁם vesham — לִנְוֵיהֶם linvehem

בְּשָׁלֹשׁ beshalosh — לְפָנֶיךָ lefanecha — וְנִשְׁתַּחֲוֶה venishtachave

וְשָׁנָה veshana — שָׁנָה shana — בְּכָל bechol — רְגָלֵינוּ regalenu — פַּעֲמֵי pe'amei

פְּעָמִים pe'amim — שָׁלוֹשׁ shalosh — בַּתּוֹרָה batora — כַּכָּתוּב kakatuv

אֶת et — זְכוּרְךָ zechurcha — כָּל chol — יֵרָאֶה yera'e — בַּשָּׁנָה bashana

אֱלֹהֶיךָ Elohecha — יְהוָה Adonai — פְּנֵי penei

בַּמָּקוֹם bamakom — אֲשֶׁר asher — יִבְחָר yivchar — בְּחַג bechag — הַמַּצּוֹת hamatzot

וּבְחַג uvchag — הַשָּׁבוּעוֹת hashavu'ot — וּבְחַג uvchag — הַסֻּכּוֹת hasukot — וְלֹא velo

יֵרָאֶה yera'e — אֶת et — פְּנֵי penei — יְהוָה Adonai — רֵיקָם rekam:

אִישׁ ish — כְּמַתְּנַת kematnat — יָדוֹ yado — כְּבִרְכַּת kevirkat

יְהוָה Adonai — אֱלֹהֶיךָ Elohecha — אֲשֶׁר asher — נָתַן natan — לָךְ lach:

וְהֹשִׁיעֵנוּ vehasi'enu — יְהוָה Adonai — אֱלֹהֵינוּ Elohenu

אֶת et — בִּרְכַּת birkat — מוֹעֲדֶיךָ mo'adecha — לְחַיִּים lechayim

בְּשִׂמְחָה besimcha — וּבְשָׁלוֹם uvshalom — כַּאֲשֶׁר ka'asher — רָצִיתָ ratzita

וְאָמַרְתָּ ve'amarta — לְבָרְכֵנוּ levarchenu — כֵּן ken — תְּבָרְכֵנוּ tevarchenu

סֶלָה selah:

MEKADESH ISRAEL AND VEHAZEMANIM (THE TIMES)

On Shabbat add:) אֱלֹהֵינוּ Elohenu — וֵאלֹהֵי velohei

(אֲבוֹתֵינוּ avotenu — רְצֵה retze — נָא na — בִּמְנוּחָתֵינוּ vimnuchatenu

---

their singing and chanting. Bring Israel back to their dwelling place. There we shall come to bow before You, each year, during the three pilgrimage. As stated in the Torah: "Three times a year all your remembrance shall see the face of the Lord, your God, at the place of His choice on the holiday of the Matzot, on the holiday of Shavuot and the holiday of Sukkot, and no one should see the face of the Lord empty handed. Each person with his present as blessed by what the Lord, your God, gave you." (Deuteronomy 16:16-17)

And give us, Lord, our God Your blessing of Your holidays for happy and peaceful life.

As You desired and said to bless us. So You shall bless us Selah.

MEKADESH ISRAEL AND VEHAZEMANIM (THE TIMES)

(on Shabbat: *Our God and the God of our forefathers, please desire our rest.*)

kadeshenu קַדְּשֵׁנוּ ◆vemitzvotecha בְּמִצְוֹתֶיךָ ten תֵּן chelkenu וְתֵן חֶלְקֵנוּ

◆vetoratach בְּתוֹרָתֶךָ sabe'enu שַׂבְּעֵנוּ mituvach מִטּוּבֶךָ לאו◆

same'ach שַׂמֵּחַ nafshenu נַפְשֵׁנוּ ◆bishu'atach בִּישׁוּעָתֶךָ

vetaher וְטַהֵר libenu לִבֵּנוּ le'ovdecha לְעָבְדְּךָ פוי, אל יהוה ve'emet בֶּאֱמֶת

vehanchilenu וְהַנְחִילֵנוּ יְהֹוָה (אדני/אהיה/אדנוני) Adonai

Elohenu אֱלֹהֵינוּ ילה (add *Shabbat* On: הלה be'ahava בְּאַהֲבָה: אוזר, דאגה

uvratzon וּבְרָצוֹן מהש ע"ה, ע"ב בריבוע וקס"א ע"ה, אל שדי) vesimcha בְּשִׂמְחָה

uvsason וּבְשָׂשׂוֹן (add *Shabbat* On: שַׁבָּתוֹת shabatot וּ) מוֹעֲדֵי mo'adei

◆kodshecha קָדְשֶׁךָ veyismechu וְיִשְׂמְחוּ, vecha בְךָ kol כָּל ילי יִשְׂרָאֵל Yisrael

mekadshei מְקַדְּשֵׁי ◆shemecha שְׁמֶךָ baruch בָּרוּךְ Ata אַתָּה

Adonai יְהֹוָה (אדני/אהיה/אדנוני)

(on *Shabbat*: יה אדני) אהיה יהו אלף הה יוד הה

mekadesh מְקַדֵּשׁ (On *Shabbat* add: הַשַּׁבָּת hashabat וְ ve) יִשְׂרָאֵל Yisrael

vehazemanim וְהַזְּמַנִּים׃

THE FINAL THREE BLESSINGS

Through the merit of Moses, Aaron and Joseph, who are our channels for the final three blessings, we are able to bring down all the spiritual energy that we aroused with our prayers and blessings.

THE FIFTH BLESSING

During this blessing, referring to Moses, we should always meditate to try to know exactly what God wants from us in our life, as signified by the phrase, "Let it be the will of God." We ask God to guide us toward the work we came to Earth to do. The Creator cannot just accept the work that we want to do; we must carry out the work we were destined to do.

---

*Sanctify us with Your commandments and place our lot in Your Torah and satiate us from Your goodness and gladden our spirits with Your salvation. and purify our heart so as to serve You truly. And grant us, Lord, our God, (on **Shabbat**: with love and favor,) with happiness and joy (on **Shabbat**: Sabbaths and) the Holidays, and all Israel, who sanctify Your Name will be joyful with You. Blessed are You, Lord, who sanctifies (on **Shabbat**: the Sabbath) and Israel and the Times.*

Netzach

Meditate for the Supernal Desire (*Keter*) that is called *Metzach HaRatzon* (Forehead of the Desire).

רְצֵה retze אלף למד הה יוד מם

Meditate here to transform misfortune and tragedy (צרה) into desire and acceptance (רצה).

Yisrael יִשְׂרָאֵל be'amecha בְּעַמְּךָ ילה Elohenu אֱלֹהֵינוּ Adonai יהוּואדניאהדונהי

velitfilatam וְלִתְפִלָּתָם she'e שְׁעֵה vehashev וְהָשֵׁב ha'avoda הָעֲבוֹדָה

lidvir לִדְבִיר רי״ו betecha בֵּיתֶךָ ב״פ ראה. ve'ishei וְאִשֵּׁי Yisrael יִשְׂרָאֵל

utfilatam וּתְפִלָּתָם mehera מְהֵרָה be'ahava בְּאַהֲבָה אוזר, דאגה

tekabel תְּקַבֵּל מהש׳ ע״ה, ע״ב בריבוע וקס״א ע״ה, אל שדי ע״ה◆ beratzon בְּרָצוֹן

ut'hi וּתְהִי מהש׳ ע״ה, ע״ב בריבוע וקס״א ע״ה, אל שדי ע״ה leratzon לְרָצוֹן

tamid תָּמִיד ע״ה קס״א קנ״א קמ״ג avodat עֲבוֹדַת Yisrael יִשְׂרָאֵל amecha עַמֶּךָ:

veAta וְאַתָּה verachamecha בְּרַחֲמֶיךָ harabim הָרַבִּים◆

tachpotz תַּחְפֹּץ banu בָּנוּ vetirtzenu וְתִרְצֵנוּ

vetechezena וְתֶחֱזֶינָה enenu עֵינֵינוּ ריבוע מ״ה beshuvcha בְּשׁוּבְךָ

leTziyon לְצִיּוֹן יוסף, ו׳ הויות, קנאה מצפצ, אלהים דיודין, י״פ יי״י berachamim בְּרַחֲמִים:

baruch בָּרוּךְ Ata אַתָּה

(on Shabbat: אל) אהיה יהו אלף למד הי יוד מם

Adonai יהוּואדניאהדונהי

hamachazir הַמַּחֲזִיר shechinato שְׁכִינָתוֹ leTziyon לְצִיּוֹן שוסף, ו׳ הויות, קנאה:

THE FINAL THREE BLESSINGS
THE FIFTH BLESSING

Find favor, Lord, our God, in Your people, Israel, and turn to their prayer. Restore the service to the Inner Sanctuary of Your Temple. Accept the offerings of Israel and their prayer with favor, speedily, and with love. May it always be favorable to You, the service of Israel Your nation.

And You in Your great compassion take delight in us and be pleased with us. May our eyes witness Your return to Zion with compassion. Blessed are You, Lord, Who returns His Shechinah to Zion.

THE SIXTH BLESSING

This blessing is our thank you. Kabbalistically, the biggest 'thank you' we can give the Creator is to do exactly what we are supposed to do in terms of our spiritual work.

Hod

Bow your entire body at "*modim*" and straighten up at "*Adonai.*"

lach לָךְ anachnu אֲנַחְנוּ מאה ברכות עתיקן דוד לאמרם כל יום modim מוֹדִים

יכה Elohenu אֱלֹהֵינוּ (ו‌נ) Adonai יְהֹוָה hu הוּא sheAta שָׁאַתָּה

le'olam לְעוֹלָם avotenu אֲבוֹתֵינוּ יכה ; דמב , ע"ב, מילוי ; לכב velohei וֵאלֹהֵי

ע"ה דההון אלהים צוּר tzur tzurenu צוּרֵנוּ ◆va'ed וָעֶד דס"ג אותיות ו"י ס"ג ריבוע

בוריאל גבריאל מיכאל ר"ת ; (דס"ג מילוי יא"י) אל ג"פ umagen וּמָגֵן chayenu חַיֵּינוּ

node נוֹדֶה רי"ו vador וָדֹר ledor לְדֹר ◆hu הוּא Ata אַתָּה yish'enu יִשְׁעֵנוּ

chayenu וַחַיֵּינוּ al עַל ◆tehilatecha תְּהִלָּתֶךָ unsaper וּנְסַפֵּר lecha לָךְ

nishmotenu נִשְׁמוֹתֵינוּ ve'al וְעַל ◆beyadecha בְּיָדֶךָ hamesurim הַמְּסוּרִים

shebechol שֶׁבְּכָל nisecha נִסֶּיךָ ve'al וְעַל ◆lach לָךְ hapekudot הַפְּקוּדוֹת

אותיות וד' ע"ה קס"א אל יהוה זן, מזבוח, נגד, ע"ה ס"ג ריבוע imanu עִמָּנוּ yom יוֹם לכב ,ב"ן

shebechol שֶׁבְּכָל vetovotecha וְטוֹבוֹתֶיךָ nifle'otecha נִפְלְאוֹתֶיךָ ve'al וְעַל

hatov הַטּוֹב ◆vetzahorayim וְצָהֳרָיִם vavoker וָבֹקֶר erev עֶרֶב ◆et עֵת לכב ,ב"ן

lo לֹא ki כִּי הו rachamecha רַחֲמֶיךָ chalu כָלוּ lo לֹא ki כִּי hamerachem הַמְרַחֵם

lo לֹא ki כִּי פשוטות אותיות וט"ז עסמ"ב (אברים), רמ"ח החוכמה, נתיבות ול"ב רי"ו אל, וז"פ אברהם,

:lach לָךְ kivinu קִוִּינוּ me'olam מֵעוֹלָם ki כִּי chasadecha חֲסָדֶיךָ tamu תַמּוּ

THE SIXTH BLESSING

We give thanks to You, for it is You, Lord, Who is our God and the God of our forefathers, forever and for all eternity. You are our Rock, the Rock of our lives, and the shield of our salvation. From one generation to another, we shall give thanks to You and we shall tell of Your praise. For our lives that are entrusted in Your hands, for our souls that are in Your care, for Your miracles that are with us every day, and for Your wonders and Your favors that are with us at all times: evening, morning and afternoon. You are the good One, for Your compassion has never ceased. You are the compassionate One, for Your kindness has never ended, for we have always placed our hope in You.

MODIM DERABANAN

This prayer is recited by the congregation in the repetition when the *chazan* says "*modim*."

In this section there are 44 words which is the same numerical value as the Name:

ריבוע אהיה (א אה אהי אהיה).

מאה ברכות עתיקן דוד לאמרם כל יום	anachnu אֲנַחְנוּ	lach לָךְ			מוֹדִים modim
יל:ה Elohenu אֱלֹהֵינוּ	Adonai יְהֹוָֹאֲדֹנָֹיאהדונהי	hu הוּא	sheAta שָׁאַתָּה
avotenu אֲבוֹתֵינוּ	יל:ה ; דמב ע״ב, מילוי ; לכב	velohei וֵאלֹהֵי
basar בָּשָׂר יל chol כָּל יל:ה ; דמב ע״ב, מילוי	Elohei אֱלֹהֵי	yotzrenu יוֹצְרֵנוּ
vehoda'ot וְהוֹדָאוֹת	berachot בְּרָכוֹת	bereshit בְּרֵאשִׁית	yotzer יוֹצֵר
אום, יזל, מבה = אותיות ד׳ עם ; להו hagadol הַגָּדוֹל	leshimcha לְשִׁמְךָ
al עַל vehakadosh וְהַקָּדוֹשׁ shehecheyitanu שֶׁהֶחֱיִיתָנוּ vekiyamtanu וְקִיַּמְתָּנוּ
vete'esof וְתֶאֱסוֹף utchonenu וּתְחָנֵּנוּ techayenu תְּחַיֵּינוּ ken כֵּן
lishmor לִשְׁמוֹר kodshecha קָדְשֶׁךָ lechatzrot לְחַצְרוֹת galuyoteinu גָּלֻיּוֹתֵינוּ
ul'ovdecha וּלְעָבְדְּךָ retzoncha רְצוֹנֶךָ vela'asot וְלַעֲשׂוֹת chukecha חֻקֶּיךָ
she'anachnu שֶׁאֲנַחְנוּ al עַל shalem שָׁלֵם בוכו belevav בְּלֵבָב פוי, אל אדני
hahoda'ot הַהוֹדָאוֹת (מילוי דס״ג) El אֵל יא״י baruch בָּרוּךְ lach לָךְ modim מוֹדִים

ve'al וְעַל kulam כֻּלָּם yitbarach יִתְבָּרַךְ veyitromam וְיִתְרוֹמַם

veyitnase וְיִתְנַשֵּׂא tamid תָּמִיד ע״ה קס״א קנ״א קס״א קסה קנ״ג קמ״ג shimcha שִׁמְךָ

malkenu מַלְכֵּנוּ le'olam לְעוֹלָם ריבוע ס״ג וי׳ אותיות דס״ג va'ed וָעֶד

vechol וְכָל־ hachayim הַחַיִּים אהיה אהיה יהוה, בינה ע״ה, ריבוע יל׳ הֹוֹדַזֹּיֹיֹךָ yoducha יוֹדוּךָ sela סֶּלָה:

vihalelu וִיהַלְלוּ vivarchu וִיבָרְכוּ יהוה ריבוע יהוה ריבוע יהוה מ״ה

et אֵת־ shimcha שִׁמְךָ hagadol הַגָּדוֹל להו ; עם ד׳ אותיות = מבה, יזל, אום

MODIM DERABANAN

We give thanks to You, for it is You

Who is our God and God of our forefathers, the God of all flesh, our Maker and the Former of all Creation. Blessings and thanks to Your great and Holy Name for giving us life and for preserving us. So may You continue to give us life, be gracious to us, and gather our exiles to the courtyards of Your Sanctuary, so that we may keep Your laws, fulfill Your will, and serve You wholeheartedly. For this, we thank You. Bless the God of thanksgiving.

And for all those things, may Your Name be always blessed, exalted and extolled, our King, forever and ever, and all the living shall thank You, Selah. And they shall praise and bless Your great Name,

אהיה פעמים אהיה, ז"פ ס"ג ריבוע ס"ג ו"י אותיות דס"ג le'olam **לְעוֹלָם** be'emet **בֶּאֱמֶת**

וְהוּ tov **טוֹב** ki **כִּי** ; ki tov = יהוה, אהיה, אום, מבה, יול

yeshu'atenu **יְשׁוּעָתֵנוּ** (דס"ג) (מילוי) ייא"י ; לאה haEl **הָאֵל**

וְעֶזְרָתֵנוּ ve'ezratenu **סֶלָה** sela• הָאֵל haEl ; ייא"י (מילוי דס"ג) לאה (מילוי דס"ג) **הַטּוֹב** hatov וְהוּ

Bend your knees at "baruch," bow at "Ata" and straighten up at "Adonai."

(on Shabbat: אֱלֹהִים: מם יוד הה למד אלף יהו אהיה)

וְהוּ hatov **הַטּוֹב** (הי) Adonai **יְהֹוָֹאַדֹנָֹיֹאֱלֹהִיֹםֹ** Ata **אַתָּה** baruch **בָּרוּךְ**

שִׁמְךָ shimcha וּלְךָ ulcha **נָאֶה** na'e **לְהוֹדוֹת** lehodot ס"ת כהת, משיח בן דוד ע"ה:

For the blessing of the *Kohanim* see page 355.

THE FINAL BLESSING

We are emanating the energy of peace to the entire world. We also make it our intent to use our mouths only for good. Kabbalistically, the power of words and speech is unimaginable. We hope to use that power wisely, which is perhaps one of the most difficult tasks we have to carry out.

Yesod

sim **שִׂים** שִׂ"ים shalom **שָׁלוֹם**

ע"ה בינה יהוה, אהיה אהיה chayim **וְחַיִּים** uvracha **וּבְרָכָה** אכא tova **טוֹבָה**

יהוה ריבוע, ע"ב, vachesed **וָחֶסֶד** מוזי בריבוע, דמ"ה מילוי chen **וְחֵן**

alenu **עָלֵינוּ** verachamim **וְרַחֲמִים** אלהים ריבוע ע"ה tzedaka **צְדָקָה**

amecha **עַמֶּךָ** Yisrael **יִשְׂרָאֵל** עמם ; ילי kol **כָּל** ve'al **וְעַל**

דאגה אהבה, ke'echad **כְּאֶחָד** kulanu **כֻּלָּנוּ** avinu **אָבִינוּ** uvarchenu **וּבָרְכֵנוּ**

א"ס רו, א"ס ve'or **בְּאוֹר** ki **כִּי** ב"ן מ"ה ס"ג panecha **פָּנֶיךָ** ס"ג א"ס רו, be'or **בְּאוֹר**

Adonai **יְהֹוָֹאַדֹנָֹיֹ** אדני אהיה אלהים, lanu **לָּנוּ** natata **נָתַתָּ** ב"ן מ"ה ס"ג panecha **פָּנֶיךָ**

ע"ה בינה אהיה אהיה יהוה, vechayim **וְחַיִּים** torah **תוֹרָה** ילה Elohenu **אֱלֹהֵינוּ**

---

sincerely and forever, for It is good, the God of our salvation and our help, Selah, the good God. Blessed are You, Lord, whose Name is good and to You it is befitting to give thanks.

THE FINAL BLESSING

Place peace, goodness, blessing, life, grace, kindness, righteousness, and mercy upon us and upon all of Israel, Your people. Bless us all as one, our Father, with the Light of Your countenance, because it is with the Light of Your countenance that You, Lord, our God, have given us Torah and life,

אַהֲבָה ahava, אוזר, דאגה, וָוזֶסֶד vachesed, ע"ב, רִיבּוּע, יהוה.

צְדָקָה tzedaka, ע"ה ריבוע אלהים, וְרַחֲמִים verachamim, בְּרָכָה beracha

וְשָׁלוֹם veshalom, וְטוֹב vetov, יהו, בְּעֵינֶיךָ be'enecha, ע"ה קס"א ; ריבוע מ"ה

לְבָרְכֵנוּ levarchenu, וּלְבָרֵךְ ulvarech, אֶת et, כָּל kol, יכי, עַמְּךָ amecha

יִשְׂרָאֵל Yisrael, בְּרוֹב berov, י"פ, אהיה, עֹז oz, וְשָׁלוֹם veshalom:

בָּרוּךְ baruch אַתָּה Ata

(on Shabbat מצפצ: אהיה יהו אלף למד הה יוד מם)

Adonai יאהדונהיואדנייהוה

הַמְבָרֵךְ hamevarech, אֶת et, עַמּוֹ amo, יִשְׂרָאֵל Yisrael

ר"ת = אלהים (אילההוידם) = יב"ק, בַּשָּׁלוֹם bashalom, אָמֵן amen, יאהדונהי.

YIH'YU LERATZON

There are 42 letters in the verse in the secret of *Ana Beko'ach*.

יִהְיוּ yih'yu, אל (יא"י מילוי דס"ג), לְרָצוֹן leratzon, מהע ע"ה, ע"ב ברבוע וקס"א ע"ה, אל שדי ע"ה

אִמְרֵי imrei, פִי fi, ר"ת אֶלֶף = אלף למד דלת שין יוד ע"ה, וְהֶגְיוֹן vehegyon, libi לִבִּי

לְפָנֶיךָ lefanecha, ס"ג מ"ה ב"ן, יאהדונהיואדנייהוה Adonai, צוּרִי tzuri, וְגֹאֲלִי vego'ali:

ELOHAI NETZOR

אֱלֹהַי Elohai, מילוי ע"ב, דמב ; ילה, נְצוֹר netzor, לְשׁוֹנִי leshoni, מֵרָע mera.

וְשִׂפְתוֹתַי vesiftotai, מִדַּבֵּר midaber, ראה, מִרְמָה mirma, וְלִמְקַלְלַי velimkalelai.

נַפְשִׁי nafshi, תִדּוֹם tidom, וְנַפְשִׁי venafshi, כֶּעָפָר ke'afar

לַכֹּל lakol, יה אדני, תִהְיֶה tihye, פְּתַח petach, לִבִּי libi, בְּתוֹרָתֶךָ betoratecha.

---

love and kindness, righteousness and mercy, blessing and peace. May it be good in Your eyes to bless us and to bless Your entire nation, Israel, with abundant power and with peace. Blessed are You, Lord Who blesses His nation, Israel, with peace, Amen.

YIH'YU LERATZON
"May the utterances of my mouth and the thoughts of my heart find favor before You, Lord, my Rock and my Redeemer." (Psalms 19:15)

ELOHAI NETZOR
My God, guard my tongue from evil and my lips from speaking deceit. To those who curse me, let my spirit remain silent, and let my spirit be as dust for everyone. Open my heart in Your Torah

וְאַחֲרֵי ve'acharei   מִצְוֹתֶיךָ mitzvotecha   תִּרְדּוֹף tirdof   נַפְשִׁי nafshi♦

וְכָל־ vechol   יּלּי הַקָּמִים hakamim   עָלַי alai   לְרָעָה lera'a רהע♦   מְהֵרָה mehera

הָפֵר hafer   עֲצָתָם atzatam   וְקַלְקֵל vekalkel   מַחְשְׁבוֹתָם machshevotam♦

עֲשֵׂה ase   לְמַעַן lema'an   שְׁמֶךָ shemach♦   עֲשֵׂה ase   לְמַעַן lema'an

יְמִינֶךָ yeminach♦   עֲשֵׂה ase   לְמַעַן lema'an   תּוֹרָתֶךָ toratach♦   עֲשֵׂה ase

לְמַעַן lema'an   קְדֻשָּׁתֶךָ kedushatach♦   ר"ת הפסוק = מ"ה יהוה lema'an לְמַעַן

יְחַלְּצוּן yechaltzun   יְדִידֶיךָ yedidecha   ר"ת ילי יהוה ו ט"ע נהורין hoshi'a הוֹשִׁיעָה

יְמִינְךָ yemincha   va'aneni וַעֲנֵנִי   (כתיב: ועננו) ר"ת אל (ייא"י מילוי דס"ג)♦

Before we recite the next verse *"Yih'yu leratzon"* we have an opportunity to strengthen our connection to our soul using our name. Each person has a verse in the *Torah* that connects to their name. Either their name is in the verse, or the first and last letters of the name correspond to the first or last letters of a verse. For example, the name Yehuda begins with a *Yud* and ends with a *Hei*. Before we end the *Amidah*, we state that our name will always be remembered when our soul leaves this world.

YIH'YU LERATZON (THE SECOND)

There are 42 letters in the verse in the secret of *Ana Beko'ach*.

יְהְיוּ yih'yu אל (ייא"י מילוי דס"ג)   leratzon לְרָצוֹן מהטע ע"ה, ע"ב בריבוע וקס"א ע"ה, אל עדוי ע"ה

אִמְרֵי imrei   פִי fi ר"ת אלף = אלף למד עין דלת יוד ע"ה   וְהֶגְיוֹן vehegyon   לִבִּי libi

לְפָנֶיךָ lefanecha ס"ג מ"ה בן   יְהֹוָ֗ואהדונהי Adonai   צוּרִי tzuri   וְגֹאֲלִי vego'ali♦

---

and let my heart pursue Your commandments. All those who rise against me to do me harm, speedily nullify their plans and disturb their thoughts. Do so for the sake of Your Name. Do so for the sake of Your right. Do so for the sake of Your Torah. Do so for the sake of Your Holiness, "So that Your loved ones may be saved. Redeem Your right and answer me." (Psalms 60:7).

YIH'YU LERATZON (THE SECOND)

"May the utterances of my mouth
and the thoughts of my heart find favor before You, Lord, my Rock and my Redeemer." (Psalms 19:15)

OSE SHALOM

You take three steps backward;

shalom שָׁלוֹם ose עֹשֶׂה

Left
You turn to the left and say:

bimromav בִּמְרוֹמָיו ר"ת ע"ב, ריבוע יהוה

ya'ase יַעֲשֶׂה verachamav בְרַחֲמָיו hu הוּא

Right
You turn to the right and say:

alenu עָלֵינוּ ר"ת ע"ב נהורין shalom שָׁלוֹם

Yisrael יִשְׂרָאֵל amo עַמּוֹ ; עמם יל"י kol כָּל־ ve'al וְעַל

Center
You face the center and say:

amen אָמֵן יאהדונהי ve'imru וְאִמְרוּ

---

ratzon רָצוֹן yehi יְהִי מהשע ע"ה, ע"ב בריבוע וקס"א ע"ה, אל שדי ע"ה

Elohenu אֱלֹהֵינוּ ילה Adonai יהוה אדני יאהדונהי יְהֹוָה ס"ג מ"ה ב"ן milfanecha מִלְּפָנֶיךָ

shetivne שֶׁתִּבְנֶה, avotenu אֲבוֹתֵינוּ ילה ; מילוי ע"ב, דמב velohei וֵאלֹהֵי לכב

veyamenu בְיָמֵינוּ bimhera בִּמְהֵרָה hamikdash הַמִּקְדָּשׁ ראה ב"פ bet בֵּית

chukei וְחֻקֵי la'asot לַעֲשׂוֹת betoratach בְּתוֹרָתֶךָ chelkenu וְזַלְקֵנוּ veten וְתֵן

shalem שָׁלֵם בוכו belevav בְּלֵבָב פוי, אל אדני ul'ovdach וּלְעָבְדְּךָ retzonach רְצוֹנֶךָ

You take three steps forward.

OSE SHALOM

He, Who makes peace in His High Places, He, in His compassion,
shall make peace upon us. And upon His entire nation, Israel, and you should say, Amen.

May it be pleasing before You, Lord,
our God, and the God of our forefathers, that You shall rebuild the Temple speedily, in our days, and place
our lot in Your Torah, so that we may fulfill the laws of Your desire and serve You wholeheartedly.

KADDISH TITKABAL

יִתְגַּדַּל yitgadal וְיִתְקַדֵּשׁ veyitkadash שׁדִי וּמִלוּי שׁדִי ; י"א אותיות כמנין ו"ה

שְׁמֵיהּ shemei רַבָּא raba (שם י"ה דע"ב) קנ"א ב"ן, יהוה אלהים יהוה אדני,

אָמֵן amen מילוי קס"א וס"ג, מ"ה ברבוע וע"ב ע"ה ; ר"ת = ו"פ אלהים ; ס"ת = ג"פ יב"ק אידהנויה.

בְּעָלְמָא be'alma דִּי di בְּרָא vera כִרְעוּתֵיהּ chir'utei

וְיַמְלִיךְ veyamlich מַלְכוּתֵיהּ mal'chutei וְיַצְמַח veyatzmach

פּוּרְקָנֵיהּ purkanei וִיקָרֵב vikarev מְשִׁיחֵיהּ meshichei אָמֵן amen אידהנויה.

בְּחַיֵּיכוֹן bechayechon וּבְיוֹמֵיכוֹן uvyomechon וּבְחַיֵּי uvchayei

דְכָל dechol ילי בֵּית bet ב"פ ראה יִשְׂרָאֵל Yisrael בַּעֲגָלָא ba'agala

וּבִזְמַן uvizman קָרִיב kariv וְאִמְרוּ ve'imru אָמֵן amen אָמֵן amen אידהנויה.

The congregation and the chazan say the following:
Twenty eight words (until be'alma) and twenty eight letters (until almaya)

יְהֵא yehe שְׁמֵיהּ shemei (שם י"ה דס"ג) רַבָּא raba קנ"א ב"ן,

מְבָרַךְ mevarach יהוה אלהים יהוה אדני, מילוי קס"א וס"ג, מ"ה ברבוע וע"ב ע"ה,

לְעָלַם le'alam לְעָלְמֵי le'almei עָלְמַיָּא almaya יִתְבָּרַךְ yitbarach

Seven words with six letters each (שם בן מ"ב) and seven times the letter *Vav* (שם בן מ"ב).

וְיִשְׁתַּבַּח veyishtabach י"פ ע"ב יהוה אל אבג יתצ.

וְיִתְפָּאַר veyitpa'ar הי גו יה קרע שׂטן וְיִתְרוֹמַם veyitromam וה כוזו נגד יכש.

וְיִתְנַשֵּׂא veyitnase במוכסז בטר צתג וְיִתְהַדָּר veyit'hadar כוזו יה וזקב טנע.

וְיִתְעַלֶּה veyit'ale וה יוד ה יגל פזק וְיִתְהַלָּל veyit'halal א ואו הא שקו צית.

שְׁמֵיהּ shemei (שם י"ה) דְּקוּדְשָׁא dekudsha בְּרִיךְ verich הוּא hu

אָמֵן amen אידהנויה.

KADDISH TITKABAL

May His great Name be more exalted and sanctified. (Amen) In the world that He created according to His will, and may His kingdom reign. And may He cause His redemption to sprout and may He bring the Mashiach closer. (Amen) In your lifetimes and in your days and in the lifetime of all the House of Israel, speedily and in the near future, and you shall say, Amen. (Amen) May His great Name be blessed forever and for all eternity. Blessed and lauded, and glorified, and exalted, and extolled, and honored, and uplifted, and praised be the Name of the Holy Blessed One (Amen)

◆shirata שִׁירָתָא ◆birchata בִּרְכָתָא ילי kol כָּל min מִן le'ela לְעֵלָּא

da'amiran דַּאֲמִירָן ◆venechamata וְנֶחָמָתָא tishbechata תֻּשְׁבְּחָתָא

אמן אידהנויה. amen אָמֵן ∴amen אָמֵן ve'imru וְאִמְרוּ be'alma בְּעָלְמָא

uva'utana וּבָעוּתַנָא tzelotana צְלוֹתַנָא titkabal תִּתְקַבֵּל

ילי dechol דְּכָל uva'utehon וּבָעוּתְהוֹן tzelotehon צְלוֹתְהוֹן im עִם

avuna אֲבוּנָא kadam קֳדָם Yisrael יִשְׂרָאֵל ב״פ ראה bet בֵּית

◆amen אידהנויה amen אָמֵן ∴amen אָמֵן ve'imru וְאִמְרוּ devishmaya דְּבִשְׁמַיָּא

יְהֵא yehe שְׁלָמָא shelama רַבָּא raba קָנ״א ב״ק, יהוה אלהים יהוה אדני, מילוי קס״א וס״ג,

מ״ה ברבוע וע״ב ע״ה chayim וְחַיִּים ◆shemaya שְׁמַיָּא min מִן אהיה אהיה יהוה, בינה ע״ה

veshezava וְשֵׁיזָבָא venechama וְנֶחָמָה vishu'a וִישׁוּעָה vesava וְשָׂבָע

vechapara וְכַפָּרָה uslicha וּסְלִיחָה ug'ula וּגְאֻלָּה urfu'a וּרְפוּאָה

verevach וְרֵיוַח ◆vehatzala וְהַצָּלָה lanu לָנוּ אלהים, אהיה אדני ulchol וּלְכָל יה אדני

אמן אידהנויה amen אָמֵן ∴amen אָמֵן ve'imru וְאִמְרוּ Yisrael יִשְׂרָאֵל amo עַמּוֹ

Take three steps backwards and say:

ose עוֹשֶׂה shalom שָׁלוֹם

berachamav בְּרַחֲמָיו hu הוּא ◆יהוה, ריבוע ע״ב, bimromav בִּמְרוֹמָיו

◆נהורין ש״ע ר״ת alenu עָלֵינוּ shalom שָׁלוֹם ya'ase יַעֲשֶׂה

∴amen אָמֵן ve'imru וְאִמְרוּ Yisrael יִשְׂרָאֵל amo עַמּוֹ ילי ; עמם kol כָּל ve'al וְעַל

◆אידהנויה amen אָמֵן

Above all blessings, songs, praises, and words of consolation that may be said in the world, and you shall say, Amen. (Amen) May our prayers and pleas be accepted, together with the prayers and pleas of the entire House of Israel, before our Father in Heaven, and you say, Amen. (Amen) May there be abundant peace from Heaven; Life, contentment, salvation, consolation, deliverance, healing, redemption, pardon, atonement, comfort, and relief. For us and for His entire nation, Israel, and you shall say, Amen. (Amen) He, Who makes peace in His High Places, He, in His compassion, shall make peace upon us And upon His entire nation, Israel, and you shall say, Amen. (Amen)

KAVEH

We now connect to the World of Action, *Asiyah*. Something remarkable happens during the Kaveh. Having finished all our morning spiritual connections, we would like to now retain all this energy we have worked so hard for by sealing and securing it up. *Kaveh* takes us back up through the Upper Words of Action (*Asiyah*), Formation (*Yetzirah*), Creation (*Beriah*) and Emanation (*Atzilut*) to a realm known as *Arich Anpin* (Long Face). From this realm we still elevate higher, passed the realms of *Atik* (Ancient),and *Adam Kadmon* (Primordial Man) until we enter into the realm of the Light of the Endless Word. This journey retraces our steps through the Upper Words ensuring that we leave no openings behind for negativity to enter.

At this point, the Satan wants to prevent us from closing these openings, so he bombards us with a feeling of impatience that the prayers will be over soon. His goal is to lower our guard and weaken our concentration during this final stage so that we leave an opening for him to enter and sabotage our efforts and taint our Light with negative energy.

פהל	chazak וַחֲזַק	Adonai יְהֹוָ֯אדניאהדונהי	el אֶל	kaveh קַוֵּה		
vekave וְקַוֵּה	libecha לִבֶּךָ	veya'ametz וְיַאֲמֵץ		el אֶל	Adonai יְהֹוָ֯אדניאהדונהי:	
biltecha בִּלְתֶּךָ	en אֵין	ki כִּי	kadonai כַּיהֹוָ֯אדניאהדונהי	kadosh קָדוֹשׁ	en אֵין	
ki כִּי	ילה: kelohenu כֵּאלֹהֵינוּ	אלהים דההין ע"ה	tzur צוּר	ve'en וְאֵין		
Adonai יְהֹוָ֯אדניאהדונהי	mibal'adei מִבַּלְעֲדֵי	שם בן מ"ב Eloha אֱלוֹהַּ ילי	mi מִי			
Elohenu אֱלֹהֵינוּ:ילה	zulati זוּלָתִי	אלהים דההין ע"ה tzur צוּר ילי	umi וּמִי			

Connection to *Olam Asiyah* (Action).

גוקבא.	ילה הה	kelohenu כֵּאלֹהֵינוּ	הה	en אֵין
ז"א.	וו	kadonenu כַּאדוֹנֵנוּ	וו	en אֵין
אמא.		kemalkenu כְּמַלְכֵּנוּ	הה	en אֵין
אבא:		kemoshi'enu כְּמוֹשִׁיעֵנוּ	יוד	en אֵין

KAVEH

"Place hope in the Lord. Make your heart strong and courageous, and place your hope in the Lord." (Psalms 27:14). *"There is none as Holy as the Lord, for there is none besides You and there is no Rock to compare with our God."* (I Samuel 2:2) *"For who is God besides the Lord, and who is a Rock besides our God?"* (Psalms 18:32)*

There is none like our God.

There is none like our Master. There is none like our King. There is none like our Redeemer.

Connection to *Olam Yetzirah* (Formation).

נוקבא.	ילה	chelohenu	כֵּאלֹהֵינוּ	הא	מִי ילי mi
ז"א.		chadonenu	כַּאדוֹנֵנוּ	ואו	מִי ילי mi
אמא.		chemalkenu	כְּמַלְכֵּנוּ	הא	מִי ילי mi
אבא:		chemoshi'enu	כְּמוֹשִׁיעֵנוּ	יוד	מִי ילי mi

Connection to *Olam Beriah* (Creation).

אין, מי, נודה ר"ת אמן = יאהדונהי – וזיבור ז"א ומלכות.

נוקבא.	ילה	lelohenu	לֵאלֹהֵינוּ	הי	נוֹדֶה node
ז"א.		ladonenu	לַאדוֹנֵנוּ	ואו	נוֹדֶה node
אמא.		lemalkenu	לְמַלְכֵּנוּ	הי	נוֹדֶה node
אבא:		lemoshi'enu	לְמוֹשִׁיעֵנוּ	יוד	נוֹדֶה node

Connection to *Olam Atzilut* (Emanation).

נוקבא.	ילה	Elohenu	אֱלֹהֵינוּ	הי	בָּרוּךְ baruch
ז"א.		adonenu	אֲדוֹנֵנוּ	ויי	בָּרוּךְ baruch
אמא.		malkenu	מַלְכֵּנוּ	הי	בָּרוּךְ baruch
אבא:		moshi'enu	מוֹשִׁיעֵנוּ	יוד	בָּרוּךְ baruch

Connection to the Worlds above *Atzilut*,
Connection to *Keter* of *Arich Anpin* (Long Face).

ילה. Elohenu אֱלֹהֵינוּ hu הוּא Ata אַתָּה

Connection to the head of *Atik* (Ancient).

adonenu אֲדוֹנֵנוּ hu הוּא Ata אַתָּה

Connection to *Adam Kadmon* (Primordial Man).

malkenu מַלְכֵּנוּ hu הוּא Ata אַתָּה

Connection to the Endless Light, which is enclosed by *Adam Kadmon*.

moshi'enu מוֹשִׁיעֵנוּ hu הוּא Ata אַתָּה

Who is like our God? Who is like our Master? Who is like our King? Who is like our Redeemer?
We shall give thanks to our God, we shall give thanks to our Master, we shall give thanks to our King,
we shall give thanks to our Redeemer. Blessed is our God. Blessed is our Master. Blessed is our King.
Blessed is our Redeemer. You are our God. You are our Master. You are our King. You are our Redeemer.

Ata אַתָּה *Keneset Yisrael* (Congregation of *Yisrael*) תּוֹשִׁיעֵנוּ toshi'enu

אַתָּה Ata תָקוּם takum כ"א הויות שבהתפילין terachem תְּרַחֵם ג"פ רי"ו ; אברהם, וז"פ אל,

רי"ו ול"ב נתיבות החכמה, רמ"ח (אברים), עסמ"ב וט"ז אותיות פשוטות Tziyon צִיּוֹן יוסף, ו' הויות, קנאה

ki כִּי et עֵת et וֹ ki כִּי lechenena לְחֶנְנָהּ ki כִּי va בָא va בָא mo'ed מוֹעֵד:

(Some say "The *Ketoret* portion", on pg. 214-220 here)

TANA DEVEI ELIYAHU

It is said that people who learn the Torah bring peace. Because each Hebrew letter is imbued with mystical forces, reciting words that speak about bringing peace arouses the energy of peace within the world. The Hebrew word *Shalom* inspires feelings of peace and harmony within us. If we cannot develop peace within ourselves we cannot share peace with others, for one cannot share what he doesn't have. To conclude this connection we say that God will bless us with peace.

tana תָּנָא devei דְּבֵי Eliyahu אֵלִיָּהוּ לכבב: kol כָּל יני hashone הַשׁוֹנֶה

halachot הֲלָכוֹת bechol בְּכָל ב"ק, לכב yom יוֹם ע"ה נגד, מזבח, זך, אל יהוה

muvtach מוּבְטָח lo לוֹ shehu שֶׁהוּא ben בֶּן ha'olam הָעוֹלָם

haba הַבָּא shene'emar שֶׁנֶּאֱמַר: halichot הֲלִיכוֹת olam עוֹלָם lo לוֹ.

al אַל tikrei תִּקְרֵי halichot הֲלִיכוֹת ela אֶלָּא halachot הֲלָכוֹת:

amar אָמַר Ribi רְבִּי Elazar אֶלְעָזָר amar אָמַר Ribi רְבִּי Chanina חֲנִינָא:

talmidei תַּלְמִידֵי chachamim וַחֲכָמִים marbim מַרְבִּים shalom שָׁלוֹם

ba'olam בָּעוֹלָם. shene'emar שֶׁנֶּאֱמַר: vechol וְכָל יני banayich בָּנַיִךְ

limudei לְמוּדֵי Adonai יְהֹוָהֱאֱלֹהִיםֱאֲדֹנָי verav וְרַב shelom שְׁלוֹם banayich בָּנָיִךְ:

al אַל tikrei תִּקְרֵי banayich בָּנַיִךְ ela אֶלָּא bonayich בּוֹנַיִךְ: yehi יְהִי

shalom שָׁלוֹם bechelech בְּחֵילֵךְ shalva שַׁלְוָה be'armenotayich בְּאַרְמְנוֹתָיִךְ:

You shall redeem us. You shall rise
and be merciful to Zion, for the time for favor has come and it is the appointed time. (Psalms 102:14)

TANA DEVEI ELIYAHU

"It was taught in the learning House of Eliyahu that one who studies law rulings, every day, is assured to be present in the World to Come." (Megillah 28b) It was said: "The ways of the world are His." (Chavakuk 3:6) Do not read it as "ways" but as "law rulings." Rabbi Elazar said that Rabbi Chanina had said that learned scholars increase the peace in the world. (Brachot 64a; Yvamot 122b; Kritut 28b; Tamid 32b) As it is said: "And all your children are the students of God." (Isaiah 54:13) Do not read it as "your children" but as "your builders." May there be peace in your chambers and serenity in your palaces.

לְמַעַן lema'an   אַחַי achai   וְרֵעָי vere'ai   אֲדַבְּרָה־ adabra   נָא na

שָׁלוֹם shalom   בָּךְ bach: לְמַעַן lema'an   בֵּית־ bet   ב״פ   ראה

יְהֹוָה Adonai   אֱלֹהֵינוּ Elohenu   ילה   אֲבַקְשָׁה avaksha

טוֹב tov והו   לָךְ lach: וּרְאֵה ure'e   ראה   בָנִים vanim   לְבָנֶיךָ levanecha

שָׁלוֹם shalom   עַל־ al   יִשְׂרָאֵל Yisrael: שָׁלוֹם shalom   רָב rav

לְאֹהֲבֵי le'ohavei   תוֹרָתֶךָ toratecha   וְאֵין ve'en   לָמוֹ lamo   מִכְשׁוֹל michshol:

יְהֹוָה Adonai   עֹז oz   לְעַמּוֹ le'amo   יִתֵּן yiten   יְהֹוָה Adonai

יְבָרֵךְ yevarech   ע״ב   ס״ג   מ״ה   ב״ן, (למתק   הברכה   ב״ן   מ״ה   את   ז׳   המלכים   שמותו)

אֶת־ et   עַמּוֹ amo   בַשָּׁלוֹם vashalom   ר״ת   ע״ב,   ריבוע   יהוה:

KADDISH AL YISRAEL

This *Kaddish* helps elevate all souls in the secret of the Resurrection of Death. According to the Ari, if a person has lost a parent he should say this *Kaddish* through the whole first year, even on *Shabbat* and Holidays. Because, besides the fact that the *Kaddish* helps a soul to be saved from the spiritual cleansing of *Gehenom*, this *Kaddish* also helps to elevate a soul from one spiritual level to the one above and to enter to the Garden of Eden.

יִתְגַּדַּל yitgadal   וְיִתְקַדַּשׁ veyitkadash   שׁדי ומילוי שׁדי ; י״א אותיות כמנין ו״ה   ר״ה

שְׁמֵיהּ shemei   רַבָּא raba   (שׁם י״ה דע״ב)   קנ״א ב״ן, יהוה אלהים יהוה ארני,

בְּעָלְמָא be'alma   דִּי di   בְּרָא vera   כִרְעוּתֵיהּ chir'utei◆   מילוי קס״א וס״ג, מ״ה ברבוע וע״ב ע״ה ; ר״ת = ו״פ אלהים ; ס״ת = ג״פ יב״ק׃ אָמֵן amen אידהנויה.◆

וְיַמְלִיךְ veyamlich   מַלְכוּתֵיהּ malchutei◆   וְיַצְמַח veyatzmach

פּוּרְקָנֵיהּ purkanei◆   וִיקָרֵב vikarev   מְשִׁיחֵיהּ meshichei: אָמֵן amen אידהנויה.◆

"For the sake of my brothers and my friends, I shall seek peace concerning you. For the sake of the House of the Lord, our God, I shall seek well for you." *(Psalms 122:7-9)* "May you witness children for your children and peace for Israel." *(Psalms 128:6)* "There is abundance of peace for those who love Your Torah and for them, there is no obstacle." *(Psalms 128:6)* "May the Lord give strength to His people may the Lord bless His nation with peace." *(Psalms 29:11)*

KADDISH AL YISRAEL

May His great Name be more exalted and sanctified. (Amen)
In the world that He created according to His will, and may His Kingdom reign.
And may He cause His redemption to sprout and may He bring the Mashiach closer. (Amen)

bechayechon בְּחַיֵּיכוֹן   uvyomechon וּבְיוֹמֵיכוֹן   uvchayei וּבְחַיֵּי

dechol דְכָל   ילי bet בֵּית ב"פ ראה   Yisrael יִשְׂרָאֵל   ba'agala בַּעֲגָלָא

uvizman וּבִזְמַן   kariv קָרִיב   ve'imru וְאִמְרוּ   amen אָמֵן: amen אָמֵן אידהנויה◆

The congregation and the chazan say the following:

Twenty eight words (until be'alma) and twenty eight letters (until almaya)

yehe יְהֵא   shemei שְׁמֵהּ (שם י"ה דס"ג)   raba רַבָּא   קנ"א ב"ן,

mevarach מְבָרֵךְ,   יהוה אלהים יהוה אדני, מילוי קס"א וס"ג, מ"ה ברבוע וע"ב ע"ה

le'alam לְעָלַם   le'almei לְעָלְמֵי   almaya עָלְמַיָּא◆   yitbarach יִתְבָּרֵךְ◆

Seven words with six letters each (שם בן מ"ב) and seven times the letter Vav (שם בן מ"ב)

veyishtabach וְיִשְׁתַּבַּח י"פ ע"ב יהוה אל אבג יתץ◆

veyitpa'ar וְיִתְפָּאַר הי גו יה קרע שטן◆   veyitromam וְיִתְרֹמַם וה כוזו נגד יכש◆

veyitnase וְיִתְנַשֵּׂא במוכסז בטר צתג◆   veyit'hadar וְיִתְהַדָּר כוזו יה וזקב טנע◆

veyit'ale וְיִתְעַלֶּה וה יוד ה יגל פזק◆   veyit'halal וְיִתְהַלָּל א ואו הא שקו צית◆

shemei שְׁמֵהּ (שם י"ה)   dekudsha דְּקֻדְשָׁא   verich בְּרִיךְ   hu הוּא:

amen אָמֵן אידהנויה◆

le'ela לְעֵלָּא   min מִן   kol כָּל ילי   birchata בִּרְכָתָא◆   shirata שִׁירָתָא◆

tishbechata תֻּשְׁבְּחָתָא   venechamata וְנֶחָמָתָא◆   da'amiran דַּאֲמִירָן

be'alma בְּעָלְמָא   ve'imru וְאִמְרוּ   amen אָמֵן: amen אָמֵן אידהנויה◆

In your lifetimes and in your days and in the lifetime of all the House of Israel, speedily and in the near future, and you shall say, Amen. (Amen) May His great Name be blessed forever and for all eternity. Blessed and lauded, and glorified, and exalted, and extolled, and honored, and uplifted, and praised be the Name of the Holy Blessed One. (Amen) Above all blessings, songs, praises, and words of consolation that may be said in the world, and you shall say, Amen. (Amen)

al עַל Yisrael יִשְׂרָאֵל ve'al וְעַל rabanan רַבָּנָן ve'al וְעַל

talmidehon תַּלְמִידֵיהוֹן ve'al וְעַל kol כָּל ; עמם ילי talmidei תַּלְמִידֵי

talmidehon תַּלְמִידֵיהוֹן♦ de'askin דְּעָסְקִין be'oraita בְּאוֹרַיְתָא

kadishta קַדִּישְׁתָּא♦ di דִי ve'atra בְּאַתְרָא haden הָדֵין vedi וְדִי

vechol בְּכָל ב״ן, לכב ב״ז, atar אֲתַר ve'atar♦ וְאַתָר yehe יְהֵא

lana לָנָא ul'hon וּלְהוֹן ul'chon וּלְכוֹן china וְחִנָּא vechisda וְחִסְדָּא

verachamei♦ וְרַחֲמֵי min מִן kadam קֳדָם marei מָארֵי shemaya שְׁמַיָּא

ve'ara וְאַרְעָא ve'imru וְאִמְרוּ amen אָמֵן♦ amen אָמֵן אידהנויה.

yehe יְהֵא shelama שְׁלָמָא raba רַבָּא קנ״א ב״ן, יהוה אלהים יהוה אדני, מילוי קס״א וס״ג,

chayim וְחַיִּים♦ shemaya שְׁמַיָּא min מִן מ״ה ברבוע וע״ב ע״ה אהיה אהיה יהוה, בינה ע״ה

vesava וְשָׂבָע vishu'a וִישׁוּעָה venechama וְנֶחָמָה veshezava וְשֵׁיזָבָא

urefu'a וּרְפוּאָה uge'ula וּגְאֻלָּה uslicha וּסְלִיחָה vechapara וְכַפָּרָה

verevach וְרֶיוַח ulchol וּלְכָל יה אדני lanu לָנוּ אלהים, אהיה אדני יה אדני vehatzala♦ וְהַצָּלָה

amo עַמּוֹ Yisrael יִשְׂרָאֵל ve'imru וְאִמְרוּ amen אָמֵן♦ amen אָמֵן אידהנויה.

Take three steps backwards and say:

ose עוֹשֶׂה shalom שָׁלוֹם bimromav בִּמְרוֹמָיו ע״ב, ריבוע יהוה♦ hu הוּא

berachamav בְּרַחֲמָיו ya'ase יַעֲשֶׂה shalom שָׁלוֹם alenu עָלֵינוּ ר״ת ש״ע נהורין♦

ve'al וְעַל kol כָּל ; עמם ילי amo עַמּוֹ Yisrael יִשְׂרָאֵל ve'imru וְאִמְרוּ amen אָמֵן

amen אָמֵן אידהנויה♦

Upon Israel, His Sages, Their disciples, and all the students of their disciples who occupy themselves with the Holy Torah, in this place and in each and every location, may there be for us, for them, and for all, grace, kindness, and compassion from the Master of the Heavens and earth, and you shall say Amen. (Amen) May there be abundant peace from Heaven, life, contentment, salvation, consolation, deliverance, healing, redemption, pardon, atonement, comfort, and relief for us and for His entire Nation, Israel, and you shall say, Amen. (Amen) He, Who makes peace in His High Places, with His compassion He shall make peace for us And for His entire Nation, Israel. And you shall say, Amen. (Amen)

BARCHU

The *chazan* (or a person who said the *Kaddish Al Yisrael*) says:

et אֶת מ"ה רִיבוּע יְהוה רִיבוּע יְהוה barchu בָּרְכוּ rabanan רַבָּנָן׃

יְהֹוָאַדְנִיאַהדוּנָהִי Adonai הַמְבוֹרָךְ hamevorach ס"ת כהת, משיחו בן דוד ע"ה׃

First the congregation replies with the following and then the *chazan* (or a person who said the *Kaddish Al Yisrael*) repeats it:

Neshamah	Ruach	Nefesh
hamevorach הַמְבוֹרָךְ	Adonai יְהֹוָאַדְנִיאַהדוּנָהִי	baruch בָּרוּךְ

Yechidah					Chayah
va'ed וָעֶד׃	דס"ג אותיות ו"י	ס"ג רִיבוּע	le'olam לְעוֹלָם		

ALENU

Alenu is a cosmic sealing agent. It cements and secures all of our prayers, protecting them from any negative forces such as the *klipot*. All prayers prior to *Alenu* drew down what the kabbalists call Inner Light. *Alenu*, however, attracts Surrounding Light, which envelops our prayers with a protective force-field to block out the *klipot*.

Drawing Surrounding Light to *Atzilut*.

ועור יתן, אבג = לעשבחו עלינו leshabe'ach לְעָבֵּחַ דס"ג רִיבוּע alenu עָלֵינוּ

אדני לכלה, ר"ת hakol הַכֹּל ע"ה ס"ג ס"ת ; אני la'adon לַאֲדוֹן

Drawing Surrounding Light to *Beriah*.

ר"ת גלב (בא"ך ב"י יג"ל) bereshit בְּרֵאשִׁית leyotzer לְיוֹצֵר gedula גְּדֻלָּה latet לָתֵת

Drawing Surrounding Light to *Yetzirah*.

ha'aratzot הָאֲרָצוֹת kegoyei כְּגוֹיֵי asanu עָשָׂנוּ shelo שֶׁלֹּא

Drawing Surrounding Light to *Asiyah*.

ha'adama הָאֲדָמָה kemishpechot כְּמִשְׁפְּחוֹת samanu שָׂמָנוּ velo וְלֹא

BARCHU
Masters: Bless the Lord, the Blessed One.
Blessed be the Lord, the Blessed One, forever and for eternity.

ALENU
It is incumbent upon us to give praise to the Master of all and to attribute greatness to the Molder of Creation, for He did not make us like the nations of the lands. He did not place us like the families of the Earth

shelo שֶׁלֹּא   sam שָׂם   chelkenu וְחֶלְקֵנוּ   kahem כָּהֶם   vegoralenu וְגוֹרָלֵנוּ

kechol כְּכָל   hamonam הֲמוֹנָם   shehem שֶׁהֵם   mishtachavim מִשְׁתַּחֲוִים

lahevel לְהֶבֶל   varik וָרִיק   umitpalelim וּמִתְפַּלְלִים   el אֶל   el אֵל

lo לֹא   Yoshi'a יוֹשִׁיעַ

(pause here, and bow your entire body when you say "va'anachnu mishtachavim")

va'anachnu וַאֲנַחְנוּ   mishtachavim מִשְׁתַּחֲוִים   lifnei לִפְנֵי   melech מֶלֶךְ

malchei מַלְכֵי   hamelachim הַמְּלָכִים   hakadosh הַקָּדוֹשׁ   baruch בָּרוּךְ

hu הוּא   shehu שֶׁהוּא   note נוֹטֶה   shamayim שָׁמַיִם

veyosed וְיוֹסֵד   aretz אֶרֶץ   umoshav וּמוֹשַׁב

yekaro יְקָרוֹ   bashamayim בַּשָּׁמַיִם   mima'al מִמַּעַל

ush'chinat וּשְׁכִינַת   uzo עֻזּוֹ   begovhei בְּגָבְהֵי   meromim מְרוֹמִים

hu הוּא   Elohenu אֱלֹהֵינוּ   ve'en וְאֵין   od עוֹד   acher אַחֵר

emet אֱמֶת   malkenu מַלְכֵּנוּ   ve'efes וְאֶפֶס

zulato זוּלָתוֹ   kakatuv כַּכָּתוּב   batorah בַּתּוֹרָה: veyadata וְיָדַעְתָּ

hayom הַיּוֹם   vahashevota וַהֲשֵׁבֹתָ   el אֶל

levavecha לְבָבֶךָ   ki כִּי   Adonai יְהֹוָה   hu הוּא

haElohim הָאֱלֹהִים

bashamayim בַּשָּׁמַיִם   mima'al מִמַּעַל

ve'al וְעַל   ha'aretz הָאָרֶץ

mitachat מִתָּחַת   en אֵין   od עוֹד:

He did not make our lot like theirs and our destiny like that of their multitudes, for they prostrate themselves to futility and emptiness and they pray to a deity that does not help. But we prostrate ourselves before the King of all Kings, the Holy Blessed One. It is He Who spreads the Heavens and establishes the Earth. The Seat of His glory is in the Heaven above and the Divine Presence of His power is in the Highest of Heights. He is our God and there is no other. Our King is true and there is none beside Him. As it is written in the Torah: "And you shall know today and you shall take it to your heart that it is the Lord Who is God in the Heavens above and upon the Earth below, and there is none other." (Deuteronomy 4:39)

עַל כֵּן נְקַוֶּה לְּךָ יְהֹוָה אֱלֹהֵינוּ
al ken nekave lach Adonai Elohenu

לִרְאוֹת מְהֵרָה בְּתִפְאֶרֶת עֻזֶּךָ
lir'ot mehera betiferet uzach

לְהַעֲבִיר גִּלּוּלִים מִן הָאָרֶץ
leha'avir gilulim min ha'aretz

וְהָאֱלִילִים כָּרוֹת יִכָּרֵתוּן לְתַקֵּן
veha'elilim karot yikaretun letaken

עוֹלָם בְּמַלְכוּת שַׁדַּי וְכָל בְּנֵי
olam bemalchut Shadai vechol benei

בָשָׂר יִקְרְאוּ בִשְׁמֶךָ לְהַפְנוֹת אֵלֶיךָ
vasar yikre'u vishmecha lehafnot elecha

כָּל רִשְׁעֵי אָרֶץ יַכִּירוּ וְיֵדְעוּ כָּל
kol rish'ei aretz yakiru veyed'u kol

יוֹשְׁבֵי תֵבֵל כִּי לְךָ תִּכְרַע כָּל
yoshvei tevel ki lecha tichra kol

בֶּרֶךְ תִּשָּׁבַע כָּל לָשׁוֹן לְפָנֶיךָ
berech tishava kol lashon lefanecha

יְהֹוָה אֱלֹהֵינוּ יִכְרְעוּ וְיִפֹּלוּ
Adonai Elohenu yichre'u veyipolu

וְלִכְבוֹד שִׁמְךָ יְקָר יִתֵּנוּ וִיקַבְּלוּ
velichvod shimcha yekar yitenu vikabelu

כֻלָּם אֶת עוֹל מַלְכוּתֶךָ וְתִמְלֹךְ
chulam et ol malchutecha vetimloch

עֲלֵיהֶם מְהֵרָה לְעוֹלָם וָעֶד
alehem mehera le'olam va'ed

כִּי הַמַּלְכוּת שֶׁלְּךָ הִיא וּלְעוֹלְמֵי
ki hamalchut shelcha hee ul'olmei

עַד תִּמְלֹךְ בְּכָבוֹד כַּכָּתוּב
ad timloch bechavod kakatuv

בְּתוֹרָתֶךָ יְהֹוָה יִמְלֹךְ לְעֹלָם
betoratach Adonai yimloch le'olam

וָעֶד וְנֶאֱמַר וְהָיָה
va'ed vene'emar vehaya

יְהֹוָה לְמֶלֶךְ עַל כָּל
Adonai lemelech al kol

הָאָרֶץ בַּיּוֹם הַהוּא
ha'aretz bayom hahu

יִהְיֶה יְהֹוָה אֶחָד וּשְׁמוֹ
yih'ye Adonai echad ushmo

אֶחָד
echad

Consequently, we place our hope in You, Lord, our God, that we shall speedily see the glory of Your might, when You remove the idols from the Earth and the deities shall be completely destroyed to correct the world with the kingdom of the Almighty. And all mankind shall then call out Your Name and You shall turn back to Yourself all the wicked ones of the Earth. Then all the inhabitants of the world shall recognize and know that, for You, every knee bends and every tongue vows. Before You, Lord, our God, they shall kneel and fall and shall give honor to Your glorious Name. And they shall all accept the yoke of Your Kingdom and You shall reign over them, forever and ever. Because the kingdom is Yours. And forever and for eternity, You shall reign gloriously. As it is written in the Torah: "The Lord shall reign forever and ever," (Exodus 15:18) and it is also stated: "The Lord shall be King over the whole world and, on that day, the Lord shall be One and His Name One." (Zechariah 14:9)

VAYOMER

There is a specific angel that carries each prayer we make to the Upper Worlds. By reciting this additional prayer after *Alenu* we ensure that our prayers elevate into the Upper Worlds. There are four Yuds יייי within the verse "I am your God, your healer," which, according to the Ari, ignite the power of healing.

וַיֹּאמֶר vayomer אִם־ im יוהך, מ"א אותיות דפשוט, דמילוי ודמילוי דמילוי דמילוי דמילוי ע"ה

שָׁמוֹעַ shamo'a תִּשְׁמַע tishma לְקוֹל lekol | יְהוָֹה Adonai

אֱלֹהֶיךָ Elohecha וְהַיָּשָׁר vehayashar בְּעֵינָיו be'enav רביע מ"ה

תַּעֲשֶׂה ta'ase וְהַאֲזַנְתָּ veha'azanta לְמִצְוֹתָיו lemitzvotav וְשָׁמַרְתָּ veshamarta

כָּל־ kol חֻקָּיו chukav כָּל־ kol הַמַּחֲלָה hamachala

אֲשֶׁר־ asher שַׂמְתִּי samti בְמִצְרַיִם veMitzrayim לֹא־ lo אָשִׂים asim

אָלֶיךָ alecha כִּי ki אֲנִי ani יְהוָֹה Adonai

Corresponds to the four *Yuds* in the Holy Name: ע"ב (יוד הי ויו הי)

רֹפְאֶךָ rofecha ר"ת איר׃

עֵץ־ etz וְחַיִּים chayim אהיה אהיה יהוה, בינה ע"ה הִיא hee

לַמַּחֲזִיקִים lamachazikim ר"ת להוו בָּהּ ba וְתֹמְכֶיהָ vetomcheha

מְאֻשָּׁר me'ushar דְּרָכֶיהָ deracheha דַרְכֵי־ darchei נֹעַם no'am וְכָל־ vechol

נְתִיבוֹתֶיהָ netivoteha שָׁלוֹם shalom מִגְדַּל־ migdal עֹז oz שֵׁם shem

יְהוָֹה Adonai בֹּו bo יָרוּץ yarutz צַדִּיק tzadik וְנִשְׂגָּב׃ venisgav

מובע	עוי	מיץ
גרג	ווה	יצד
דצב	זדו	היי
לקה	עווה	ונק

כִּי ki בִי vi מ"ב יִרְבּוּ yirbu יָמֶיךָ yamecha וְיוֹסִיפוּ veyosifu לְךָ lecha

שְׁנוֹת shenot חַיִּים chayim אהיה אהיה יהוה, בינה ע"ה׃

VAYOMER

"And God said: If you shall listen to the voice of the Lord, your God, and do that which is upright in His eyes, and if you carefully heed His commandments and keep all His statutes, then all the illnesses that I had set upon Egypt, I shall not set upon you, for I am the Lord, your healer." (Exodus 15:26)
"It is a Tree of Life for those who hold on to it, and those who support it are joyful." (Proverbs 3:18)
"Its ways are ways of pleasantness and all its pathways are of peace." (Proverbs 3:17) "The Name of the Lord is a tower of strength. In it, a righteous person runs and is strengthened." (Proverbs 18:10)
"For through Me, your days shall be increased, and years of life shall be added to you." (Proverbs 9:11)

YEHI RATZON

The following connection helps us to make sure our prayers are accepted.
It also helps us to remove jealousy and envy from within.

milefanecha מִלְּפָנֶיךָ ratzon רָצוֹן yehi יְהִי

Elohai אֱלֹהַי Adonai יְהֹוָה velohei וֵאלֹהֵי

bidvar בִּדְבַר nikashel נִכָּשֵׁל shelo שֶׁלֹּא avotai אֲבוֹתַי

tahor טָהוֹר tame טָמֵא al עַל nomar נֹאמַר velo וְלֹא halacha הֲלָכָה

isur אִיסוּר al עַל velo וְלֹא tame טָמֵא tahor טָהוֹר al עַל velo וְלֹא

yikashlu יִכָּשְׁלוּ velo וְלֹא isur אִיסוּר mutar מוּתָּר al עַל velo וְלֹא mutar מוּתָּר

ani אֲנִי ve'esmach וְאֶשְׂמַח halacha הֲלָכָה bidvar בִּדְבַר chaverai וַחֲבֵרַי

veyismechu וְיִשְׂמְחוּ vo בּוֹ ani אֲנִי ekashel אֶכָּשֵׁל velo וְלֹא bahem בָּהֶם

chochmah וְחָכְמָה yiten יִתֵּן Adonai יְהֹוָה ki כִּי bi בִּי hem הֵם

gal גַּל utvuna וּתְבוּנָה da'at דַּעַת mipiv מִפִּיו

mitoratecha מִתּוֹרָתֶךָ nifla'ot נִפְלָאוֹת ve'abita וְאַבִּיטָה enai עֵינַי

There is an additional connection that helps us keep the Light in our consciousness the entire day. Before we close our prayer book and leave we recite this prayer to keep the angels with us all day.

lema'an לְמַעַן vetzidkatecha בְּצִדְקָתֶךָ necheni נְחֵנִי Adonai

darkecha דַּרְכֶּךָ lefanai לְפָנַי (כתיב: הוֹשֵׁר) hayshar הַיְשַׁר shorerai שׁוֹרְרָי

ledarko לְדַרְכּוֹ halach הָלַךְ veYaakov וְיַעֲקֹב

Elohim אֱלֹהִים mal'achei מַלְאֲכֵי vo בּוֹ vayifge'u וַיִּפְגְּעוּ

ka'asher כַּאֲשֶׁר Yaakov יַעֲקֹב vayomer וַיֹּאמֶר

vayikra וַיִּקְרָא ze זֶה Elohim אֱלֹהִים machane מַחֲנֶה ra'am רָאָם

Machanayim מַחֲנָיִם hahu הַהוּא hamakom הַמָּקוֹם shem שֵׁם

YEHI RATZON

May it be Your will,

Lord, my God and God of my forefathers, that we may not err in a matter of Halachah, and that we may not call impure pure or pure impure, or that we may not call forbidden permitted or permitted forbidden. That my colleagues may not err in a matter of Halachah and that I may rejoice in them, and that no offence may occur through me, and that my colleagues may rejoice in me. Because from his mouth Lord gives wisdom and understanding "open my eyes, so that I will see wonders from your Torah" (Psalms 119:18) "Lord, instruct me with Your righteousness, and against my foes lead me in Your ways." (Psalms 5:9) "And Jacob went on his way, and the angels of God met him. And Jacob, when he saw them, said: This is the camp of God. And he called that place Machanayim." (Genesis 32:2-3)

KIDDUSH FOR SUKKOT AND SIMCHAT TORAH DAY

All our prayers have been arousing spiritual energy from the Upper Worlds. But now we need to manifest and express this energy in our physical world so we can utilize it in a practical manner. The drinking of the wine is one of our methods for expressing this energy.

On *Shabbat* we add:

וְשָׁמְרוּ veshamru בְנֵי־ venei יִשְׂרָאֵל yisrael אֶת־ et הַשַּׁבָּת hashabat ר"ת ביאה
לַעֲשׂוֹת la'asot אֶת־ et הַשַּׁבָּת hashabat לְדֹרֹתָם ledorotam ר"ת אהל (זו אשתו, למשוך
נשמה קדושה ולא מסט"א) בְּרִית berit עוֹלָם olam: בֵּינִי beni וּבֵין uven בְּנֵי benei
יִשְׂרָאֵל yisrael אוֹת ot הִוא hi ר"ת ביאה לְעֹלָם le'olam ריבוע דס"ג וי' אותיות דס"ג כִּי־ ki
שֵׁשֶׁת sheshet יָמִים yamim נלך עָשָׂה asa יְהֹוָה אהדונהי Adonai אֶת־ et
הַשָּׁמַיִם hashamayim י"פ טל, י"פ כוזו וְאֶת־ ve'et הָאָרֶץ ha'aretz אלהים דההין ע"ה
וּבַיּוֹם uvayom ע"ה נגד, מזבח, זן, אל יהוה הַשְּׁבִיעִי hashevi'i שָׁבַת shavat
וַיִּנָּפַשׁ vayinafash:

אֵלֶּה ele מוֹעֲדֵי moadei יְהֹוָה אהדונהי Adonai מִקְרָאֵי mikra'ei קֹדֶשׁ kodesh
אֲשֶׁר־ asher תִּקְרְאוּ tikre'u אֹתָם otam בְּמוֹעֲדָם bemo'adam:
וַיְדַבֵּר vaydaber ראה מֹשֶׁה Moshe מהש, ע"ב בריבוע וקס"א, אל שדי, ד"פ אלהים ע"ה
אֶת־ et מֹעֲדֵי mo'adei יְהֹוָה אהדונהי Adonai אֶל־ el בְּנֵי benei יִשְׂרָאֵל Yisrael:

On *Shabbat* we add:

עַל al כֵּן ken בֵּרַךְ berach יְהֹוָה אהדונהי Adonai אֶת et
יוֹם yom ע"ה נגד, מזבח, זן, אל יהוה הַשַּׁבָּת hashabat וַיְקַדְּשֵׁהוּ vaykadshehu:

סַבְרִי savri מָרָנָן maranan (we answer: לְחַיִּים lechayim)
בָּרוּךְ baruch אַתָּה Ata יְהֹוָה אהדונהי Adonai אֱלֹהֵינוּ Elohenu מֶלֶךְ melech
הָעוֹלָם ha'olam בּוֹרֵא bore פְּרִי peri הַגָּפֶן hagefen:

KIDDUSH FOR SUKKOT AND SIMCHAT TORAH DAY

"And the children of Israel shall keep the Sabbath, to make the Sabbath an eternal covenant for all their generations. Between Me and the children of Israel, It is an eternal sign that in six days did the Lord make the Heavens and the Earth and on the Seventh Day, He was refreshed. For that reason, the Lord blessed the Sabbath day and made it Holy." (Exodus 31:17)

Those are the holiday of the Lord, Holy Covenant you shall call them, in their time.
And Moses spoke the Holidays of the Lord to the children of Israel

So the Lord blessed the day of Sabbath and made it Holy.

With your permission, my masters. (And answer: *To life!*)
Blessed are You, Lord, Our God, King of the universe, Who creates the fruit of the vine.

MINCHAH OF SUKKOT AND SIMCHAT TORAH

The numerical value of the word *Minchah* (103) is also the number of sub-worlds (within the five major worlds), controlled by the Left Column energy of judgment. The purpose of the *Minchah* prayer is not simply to make a connection to the Light of the Creator, it is to quiet the energy of judgment in the world.

Isaac the Patriarch is our channel to overcome judgment. Isaac came to this world to create a path that would lead us to sweetening the judgment in our lives.

LeShem Yichud

hu הוּא berich בְּרִיךְ kudesha קוּדְשָׁא yichud יְוזוד leshem לְשֵׁם

ur'chimu וּרְוזִימוּ bid'chilu בִּדְוזִילוּ (יאהדונהי) ush'chintei וּשְׁכִינְתֵּיהּ

leyachda לְיַוזְדָא (איההיוהה) ud'chilu וּדְוזִילוּ ur'chimu וּרְוזִימוּ (יאההויהה)

beyichuda בְּיִוזוּדָא kei קֵי bevav בּוַא"ו kei קֵי yud יו"ד shem שֵׁם

hine הִנֵּה, Yisrael יִשְׂרָאֵל kol כָּל beshem בְּשֵׁם (יהוה) shelim שְׁלִים

mincha מִנְוזָה tefilat תְּפִלַת lehitpalel לְהִתְפַּלֵל ba'im בָּאִים anachnu אֲנַוזְנוּ

(ve וְ kodesh קוֹדֶשׁ Shabbat שַׁבָּת on *Shabbat* add:) shel שֶׁל ע"ה בן ב"פ

(on *Sukkot* say: סֻכּוֹת Sukkot) (on *Simchat-Torah* say: שְׁמִינִי Shemini עֲצֶרֶת Atzeret).

alav עָלָיו avinu אָבִינוּ בן ד"פ Yitzchak יִצְוזָק shetiken שֶׁתִּקֵן

hamitzvot הַמִּצְוֹת כ kol כָּל im עִם hashalom הַשָּׁלוֹם

shorsha שׁוֹרְשָׁהּ et אֶת letaken לְתַקֵּן ba בָּהּ hakelulot הַכְּלוּלוֹת

ru'ach רוּוזַ nachat נַוזַת la'asot לַעֲשׂוֹת elyon עֶלְיוֹן bemakom בְּמָקוֹם

מהע ע"ה, ע"ב בריבוע וקס"א ע"ה, retzon רְצוֹן vela'asot וְלַעֲשׂוֹת leyotzrenu לְיוֹצְרֵנוּ

ללה Adonai אֲדֹנָי no'am נֹעַם vihi וִיהִי bor'enu בּוֹרְאֵינוּ אל שדי ע"ה

yadenu יָדֵינוּ uma'ase וּמַעֲשֵׂה alenu עָלֵינוּ ילה Elohenu אֱלֹהֵינוּ

konehu כּוֹנְנֵהוּ yadenu יָדֵינוּ uma'ase וּמַעֲשֵׂה alenu עָלֵינוּ konena כּוֹנְנָה

MINCHAH OF SUKKOT AND SIMCHAT TORAH - LESHEM YICHUD

For the sake of the unification

of The Holy Blessed One and His Shechinah, with fear and love and with love and fear, in order to unify The Name Yud-Kei and Vav-Kei in perfect unity, and in the name of Israel, we have hereby come to recite the prayer of Minchah for (on Shabbat add: the Holy Sabbath and) (on Sukkot: Sukkot) (on Simchat Torah: Shmini Atzeret), established by Isaac, our forefather, may peace be upon him, with all its commandments, to correct its root in the Supernal Place, to bring satisfaction to our Maker, and to fulfill the wish of our Creator. "And may the pleasantness of Lord, our God, be upon us and may He establishes the work of our hands for us and may the work of our hands establish Him." (Psalms 90:17)

THE SACRIFICES – KORBANOT - THE TAMID - (DAILY) OFFERING

Moshe מֹשֶׁה el אֶל־ Adonai יְהֹוָֹאדֹנִי־אהדונהי ראה vaydaber וַיְדַבֵּר

benei בְּנֵי et אֶת־ מהע, ע"ב ברביע וקס"א, פוי, אל אדני tzav צַו lemor לֵאמֹר

korbani קָרְבָּנִי et אֶת־ alehem אֲלֵהֶם ve'amarta וְאָמַרְתָּ Yisrael יִשְׂרָאֵל

tishmeru תִּשְׁמְרוּ nichochi נִיחֹחִי re'ach רֵיחַ le'ishai לְאִשַּׁי lachmi לַחְמִי

lahem לָהֶם ve'amarta וְאָמַרְתָּ :bemo'ado בְּמוֹעֲדוֹ li לִי lehakriv לְהַקְרִיב

ladonai לַיהֹוָֹאדֹנִי־אהדונהי takrivu תַּקְרִיבוּ asher אֲשֶׁר ha'ishe הָאִשֶּׁה ze זֶה

shenayim שְׁנַיִם temimim תְּמִימִם shana שָׁנָה benei בְּנֵי kevasim כְּבָשִׂים

:layom לַיּוֹם ע"ה נגד, מזבוח, ז, אל יהוה tamid תָּמִיד ע"ה קס"א קנ"א קמ"ג ola עֹלָה ר"ת עשל

vaboker בַּבֹּקֶר ta'ase תַּעֲשֶׂה אהבה, דאגה echad אֶחָד hakeves הַכֶּבֶשׂ et אֶת־

ben בֵּן ta'ase תַּעֲשֶׂה hasheni הַשֵּׁנִי hakeves הַכֶּבֶשׂ ve'et וְאֵת

solet סֹלֶת ha'efa הָאֵיפָה va'asirit וַעֲשִׂירִת :ha'arbayim הָעַרְבָּיִם

beshemen בְּשֶׁמֶן belula בְּלוּלָה ב"ן ב"פ ע"ה lemincha לְמִנְחָה

katit כָּתִית revi'it רְבִיעִת :hahin הַהִין olat עֹלַת ושר, אבגיתץ

ha'asuya הָעֲשֻׂיָה קמ"ג קנ"א קס"א קס"א ע"ה tamid תָּמִיד

behar בְּהַר Sinai סִינַי נמם, ה הויות (ה גבורות) lere'ach לְרֵיחַ nicho'ach נִיחֹחַ

ishe אִשֶּׁה ladonai לַיהֹוָֹאדֹנִי־אהדונהי: venisko וְנִסְכּוֹ revi'it רְבִיעִת

hahin הַהִין lakeves לַכֶּבֶשׂ ha'echad הָאֶחָד אהבה, דאגה bakodesh בַּקֹּדֶשׁ

hasech הַסֵּךְ nesech נֶסֶךְ shechar שֵׁכָר ב"ן י"פ לַיהֹוָֹאדֹנִי־אהדונהי:

THE SACRIFICES – KORBANOT - THE TAMID – (DAILY) OFFERING

"And the Lord spoke to Moses and said: Command the children of Israel and say to them, My offering, the bread of My fire-offering, My pleasing fragrance, you shall take care to sacrifice to Me at its specified time. And you shall say to them: This is the fire-offering that you shall sacrifice to God, perfect one-year-old sheep, two per day, as a regular daily offering; one sheep you shall do in the morning and the second sheep you shall do in the late afternoon. And one tenth of ephah of fine flour, for a meal-offering, mixed with one quarter of a hin of pressed oil. This is a regular burnt-offering that is made at Mount Sinai as a pleasing fragrance and as a fire-offering before the Lord. Its libation is one quarter of a hin for the one sheep in the Sanctuary, pour a libation of old wine before the Lord.

ben בֵּין   ta'ase תַּעֲשֶׂה   hasheni הַשֵּׁנִי   hakeves הַכֶּבֶשׂ   ve'et וְאֶת

uchnisko וּכְנִסְכּוֹ   haboker הַבֹּקֶר   keminchat כְּמִנְחַת   ha'arbayim הָעַרְבָּיִם

(elevation to *Beriah*)   re'ach רֵיחַ   (elevation to *Yetzirah*)   ishe אִשֵּׁה   ta'ase תַּעֲשֶׂה

✥(elevation to the Endless World) ladonai לַיהֹוָהאדניה (elevation to *Atzilut*) nicho'ach נִיחוֹחַ

THE INCENSE

These verses from the *Torah* and the *Talmud* speak about the 11 herbs and spices that were used in the Temple. These herbs and spices were used for one purpose: to help us remove the force of death from every area of our lives. This is one of the few prayers whose sole goal is the eradication of death. The *Zohar* teaches us that whoever has judgment pursuing him needs to connect to this incense. The 11 herbs and spices connect to 11 Lights that sustain the *klipot* (shells of negativity). When we uproot the 11 Lights from the *klipot* through the power of the incense, the *klipot* lose their life-force and die. In addition to bringing the 11 spices to the Temple, the people brought resin, wine, and other items with metaphysical properties to help battle the Angel of Death.

It says in the *Zohar*: "Come and see, whoever is pursued by judgment is in need of incense and must repent before his master, for incense helps judgment to disappear from him." The 11 herbs and spices correspond to the 11 Holy Illuminations that revive the *klipa*. By elevating them, the *klipa* will die. Through these 11 herbs, the *klipot* are pushed away and the energy-point that was giving them life is removed. And since the Pure Side and its livelihood disappear, the *klipot* is left with no life. Thus the secret of the incense is that it cleanses the force of plague and cancels it. The incense kills the Angel of Death and takes away his power to kill.

יכה   Elohenu אֱלֹהֵינוּ   Adonai יְהֹוָהאדניהאהדונהי   hu הוּא   Ata אַתָּה

ב"ן   מ"ה   ס"ג   lefanecha לְפָנֶיךָ   avotenu אֲבוֹתֵינוּ   shehiktiru שֶׁהִקְטִירוּ

(י"א הסממנים)   י"א   (הנבררים מהקליפות ע"י)   אדני   פעמים   י"א   ketoret קְטֹרֶת   et אֶת

ע"ה קנ"א, אדנ"י אלהים   hasamim הַסַּמִּים   (מצוות)   תרי"ג = ד' באתב"ש הק'   קטרת

kayam קָיָם   hamikdash הַמִּקְדָּשׁ   ראה ב"פ   shebet שֶׁבֵּית   bizman בִּזְמַן

מהע׳,   Moshe מֹשֶׁה   yad יַד   al עַל   otam אוֹתָם   tzivita צִוִּיתָ   ka'asher כַּאֲשֶׁר

✥betoratach בְּתוֹרָתֶךָ   kakatuv כַּכָּתוּב   nevia'ch נְבִיאָךְ   אל עדי וקס"א, ע"ב ברבוע

The second sheep you shall do in the afternoon like the meal-offering of the morning; its libation you shall do as a fire-offering of a fragrance which is pleasing to the Lord." (Numbers 28:1-8)

THE INCENSE

It is You, Lord, our God, before whom our forefathers burned the incense spices, during the time when the Temple existed, as You had commanded them through Moses, Your Prophet, and as it is written in Your Torah:

THE PORTION OF THE INCENSE

To raise the Sefirot from all of Nogah of Atzilut, Beriah, Yetzirah and Asiyah.

Moshe מֹשֶׁה el אֶל־ Adonai יְהֹוָה אֲדֹנָי אֲהֹדֹנָי vayomer וַיֹּאמֶר

(Tiferet, Netzach) samim סַמִּים lecha לְךָ kach קַח־ מוהע׳, ע״ב בריבוע וקס״א, אל שדי

vechelbena וְחֶלְבְּנָה (Yesod) ushchelet וּשְׁחֵלֶת (Hod) | nataf נָטָף ע״ה קנ״א, אדני אלהים

(Keter, Chochmah, Binah, Chesed, Gevurah) samim סַמִּים אל אדני פוי, ע״ה (Malchut)

bevad בְּבַד bad בַּד (Surrounding Light) zaka זַכָּה ulvona וּלְבֹנָה ע״ה קנ״א, אדני אלהים

יִהְיֶה יי ketoret קְטֹרֶת ota אֹתָהּ ve'asita וְעָשִׂיתָ yih'ye יִהְיֶה (הגבררים) י״א פעמים אדני

ma'ase מַעֲשֵׂה rokach רֹקַח (מצוות) קְטֹרֶת – הַק׳ בְּאתבַּ״ע ד׳ = תרי״ג מהקליפות ע״י י״א הסממנים;

kodesh קֹדֶשׁ tahor טָהוֹר memulach מְמֻלָּח roke'ach רֹקֵחַ שדי י״פ אכא ס״ת רוזו בכוחו לגרש החיצונים ויועיל לזכירה:

mimena מִמֶּנָּה veshachakta וְשָׁחַקְתָּ ha'edut הָעֵדֻת lifnei לִפְנֵי mimena מִמֶּנָּה venatata וְנָתַתָּה hadek הָדֵק

shama שָׁמָּה lecha לְךָ iva'ed אִוָּעֵד asher אֲשֶׁר mo'ed מוֹעֵד be'ohel בְּאֹהֶל

vene'emar וְנֶאֱמַר lachem לָכֶם tihye תִּהְיֶה kadashim קָדָשִׁים kodesh קֹדֶשׁ

vehiktir וְהִקְטִיר ketoret קְטֹרֶת Aharon אַהֲרֹן alav עָלָיו (הגבררים) י״א פעמים אדני

samim סַמִּים (הגבררים מהקליפות ע״י י״א הסממנים ; קְטֹרֶת – הַק׳ בְּאתבַּ״ע ד׳ = תרי״ג (מצוות)

behetivo בְּהֵיטִיבוֹ baboker בַּבֹּקֶר baboker בַּבֹּקֶר ע״ה קנ״א, אדני אלהים

uveha'alot וּבְהַעֲלֹת yaktirena יַקְטִירֶנָּה hanerot הַנֵּרֹת et אֶת־

ha'arbayim הָעַרְבַּיִם ben בֵּין hanerot הַנֵּרֹת et אֶת־ Aharon אַהֲרֹן

tamid תָּמִיד (הגבררים מהקליפות ע״י י״א הסממנים ; קְטֹרֶת – הַק׳ בְּאתבַּ״ע ד׳ = תרי״ג (מצוות) yaktirena יַקְטִירֶנָּה ketoret קְטֹרֶת ר״ת אהבה, דאגה, אוזר

ledorotechem לְדֹרֹתֵיכֶם Adonai יְהֹוָה אֲדֹנָי אֲהֹדֹנָי lifnei לִפְנֵי ע״ה קס״א קנ״א קמ״ג

THE PORTION OF THE INCENSE

"And the Lord said to Moses: Take for yourself spices, balsam sap, onycha, galbanum, and pure frankincense, each of equal weight. You shall prepare it as an incense compound: the work of a spice-mixer, well-blended, pure, and holy. You shall grind some of it fine and place it before the Testimony in the Tabernacle of Meeting, in which I shall meet with you. It shall be the Holy of Holies unto you." (Exodus 30:34-36) And God also said: "Aaron shall burn upon the Altar incense spices early each morning when he prepares the candles. And when Aaron raises the candles at sundown, he shall burn the incense spices as a continual incense-offering before God throughout all your generations." (Exodus 30:7-8)

THE WORKINGS OF THE INCENSE

The filling of the incense has two purposes: First, to remove the *klipot* in order to stop them from going up along with the elevation of the Worlds, and second, to draw Light to *Asiyah*. So meditate to raise the sparks of Light from all of the *Nogah* of *Azilut*, *Beriah*, *Yetzirah* and *Asiyah*.

Count the incense using your right hand, one by one, and don't skip even one, as it is said: "If one omits one of all the ingredients, he is liable to receive the penalty of death." And therefore, you should be careful not to skip any of them, because reciting this paragraph is a substitute for the actual burning of the incense.

אֲדֹנָי י"א פְּעָמִים haketoret הַקְּטֹרֶת pitum פִּטּוּם rabanan רַבָּנָן tanu תָּנוּ

(הַנִּבְרָרִים מֵהַקְּלִיפוֹת עַ"י י"א הַסַּמְמָנִים) קְטֹרֶת – הַקְּ בְּאתב"ע' ד' = תרי"ג (מִצְווֹת);

פִּטּוּם הַקְּטֹרֶת = יְהֹוָה יְהֹוָה יָה מוֹצְפָץ אֲדֹנָי יָה אֵל אֱלֹהִים מוֹצְפָץ (ו' מְרֻגְלָאִין דְשַׁבָּת)፡

דְיוּדִין אֱלֹהִים ע, = הַמִּסְפָּר me'ot מֵאוֹת shelosh שְׁלֹשׁ ketzad כֵּיצַד

hayu הָיוּ manim מָנִים ushmona וּשְׁמוֹנָה (י"ן) = מִלּוּי הע' הַמִּסְפָּר veshishim וְשִׁשִּׁים וְשִׁשִּׁים

veshishim וְשִׁשִּׁים me'ot מֵאוֹת ע, = הַמִּסְפָּר = אֱלֹהִים דְיוּדִין shelosh שְׁלֹשׁ va וָ בָּהּ

yemot יְמוֹת keminyan כְּמִנְיַן vachamisha וַחֲמִשָּׁה (י"ן) = מִלּוּי הע' הַמִּסְפָּר

לכ"ב ב"ן, bechol בְּכָל אֶל אֲדֹנָי פ"י, ע"ה mane מָנֶה hachama הַחַמָּה הַוֹחַמָּה

baboker בַּבֹּקֶר machatzito מַוֹחֲצִיתוֹ אֶל יהוה ז, מִזְבֵּחַ, נֵגֶר ע"ה yom יוֹם

manim מָנִים ushlosha וּשְׁלֹשָׁה ba'erev בָּעֶרֶב umachatzito וּמַוֹחֲצִיתוֹ

מִלָּה kohen כֹּהֵן machnis מַכְנִיס shemehem שְׁמֵהֶם קְמ"ג קנ"א וקמ"ג קס"א, yeterim יְתֵרִים

mehem מֵהֶם venotel וְנוֹטֵל אֵשׁ, יזל, מַכָּה = אוֹתִיּוֹת עִם ד' ; לָהוּ gadol גָּדוֹל

hakipurim הַכִּפּוּרִים אֶל יהוה ז, מִזְבֵּחַ, נֵגֶר ע"ה beyom בְּיוֹם chofnav וֹזְפָּנָיו melo מְלֹא

be'erev בָּעֶרֶב lamachteshet לַמַּכְתֶּשֶׁת machaziran מַוֹחֲזִירָן

lekayem לְקַיֵּם kedei כְּדֵי hakipurim הַכִּפּוּרִים אֶל יהוה ז, מִזְבֵּחַ, נֵגֶר ע"ה yom יוֹם

דָאָה אַהֲבָה, ve'achad וְאֶוֹחָד hadaka הַדַּקָּה min מִן daka דַּקָּה mitzvat מִצְווֹת

hen הֵן ve'elu וְאֵלּוּ va בָּהּ hayu הָיוּ samanim סַמָּנִים asar עֲשָׂר

THE WORKINGS OF THE INCENSE

Our Sages have taught: How was the compounding of the incense done? Three hundred and sixty-eight portions were contained therein. These corresponded to the number of days in the solar year, one portion for each day: Half of it in the morning and half at sundown. As for the remaining three portions, the High Priest, on Yom Kippur, filled both his hands with them. On the Eve of Yom Kippur, he would take them back to the mortar to fulfill the requirement that they should be very finely ground. Each portion contained eleven spices:

(1 הַצֳּרִי haTzori (Keter) מצפצ, אלהים דיודין, י"פ יי"י (2 ◆ וְהַצִּפּׂרֶן vehaTziporen (Yesod)

יהוה, אדני אהיה שדי ◆ (3 ◆ וְהַחֶלְבְּנָה vehaChelbena (Malchut) ע"ה פוי, אל אדני ◆

(4 וְהַלְּבׂנָה vehaLevona (Surrounding Light – שהוא אור לבן והוא יוזהי הנקרא אדון יוזיד)

מִשְׁקָל mishkal שִׁבְעִים shiv'im שִׁבְעִים shiv'im מָנֶה mane ע"ה פוי, אל אדני ◆

(5 מׂור Mor (Chesed) ◆ וּקְצִיעָה uKtzi'ah רהע (Gevurah – "כי מצפון תפתח הרעה",

◆ (Tiferet) Nerd נֵרְדְּ veShibolet וְשִׁבׂלֶת (7 ◆ צפון ◆ רוח סוד והגבורה

(8 וְכַרְכׂם veCharkom (Netzach) בֹן֯וֹחֶ֯ר, סנדלפון, ערי ◆ מִשְׁקָל mishkal עָשָׂה shisha

עָשָׂר asar עָשָׂה shisha עָשָׂר asar מָנֶה mane ע"ה פוי, אל אדני ◆ (9 קׂשְׂטְ Kosht

(Chochmah) שְׁנַיִם sheneim עָשָׂר asar. ◆ (10 קִלּוּפָה Kilufa (Binah) שְׁלׂשָׁה shelosha◆

(11 קִנָּמׂון Kinamon (Hod) ר"ת ג"פ ק' (בסוד קדוש קדוש קדוש קדוש) תִּשְׁעָה tish'ah ◆

בׂורִית borit כַּרְשִׁינָא karshina תִּשְׁעָה tish'ah קַבִּין kabin ◆ יֵין yen מיכ, י"פ האא

קַפְרִיסִין Kafrisin סְאִין se'in תְּלַת telat וְקַבִּין vekabin תְּלָתָא telata אהיה קבין

וְאִם ve'im יוהך, מ"א אותיות דפשוט, דמילוי ודמילוי דמילוי דאהיה ע"ה לׂא lo מָצָא matza

יֵין yen מיכ, י"פ האא קַפְרִיסִין Kafrisin מֵבִיא mevi וְחֻמַר chamar וְזֵיור chivar

עָתִּיק atik◆ מַעֲלֶה ma'ale רׂובַע rova◆ סְדׂומִית Sedomit מִלּׂוח melach רׂבַע Sedomit

עָשָׁן ashan כָּל kol יְלִי שֶׁהוּא shehu◆ רִבִּי Ribi נָתָן Natan הַבַּבְלִי haBavli

אׂומֵר omer: אַף af מִכְבַּת mikipat הַיַּרְדֵּן haYarden י' הויות וד' אותיות כָּל kol יְלי

שֶׁהִיא shehi◆ אִם im יוהך, מ"א אותיות דפשוט, דמילוי ודמילוי דמילוי דאהיה ע"ה נָתַן natan

בָּה ba דְּבַשׁ devash עור (דשופר) וי"ד (האוחז) = ע"ך דינין הגדלות פְּסָלָהּ pesala◆

וְאִם ve'im יוהך, מ"א אותיות דפשוט, דמילוי ודמילוי דמילוי דאהיה ע"ה וְזׂסֵר chiser

אׂחַת achat מִכָּל mikol יְלי סַמְמָנֶיהָ samemaneha וְזֵיֵּיב chayav מִיתָה mita:

---

1) Balsam. 2) Onycha. 3) Galbanum. 4) Frankincense; the weight of seventy portions each. 5) Myrrh. 6) Cassia. 7) Spikenard. 8) And Saffron; the weight of sixteen portions each. 9) Twelve portions of Costus. 10) Three of aromatic Bark 11) Nine of Cinnamon. Further, nine kavs of Lye of Carsina. And three kavs and three se'ehs of Cyprus wine. And if one should not find any Cyprus wine, he should bring an old white wine. And a quarter of the salt of Sodom. And a small measure of a smoke raising herb. Rabbi Natan, the Babylonian, advised also, a small amount of Jordan resin. If he added to it honey, he would make it defective. If he omits even one of all its herbs, he would be liable to death.

רַבָּן Raban שִׁמְעוֹן Shimon בֶּן ben גַּמְלִיאֵל Gamli'el אוֹמֵר omer:

הַצֳּרִי haTzori אֵינוֹ eno אֶלָּא ela שְׂרָף seraf

הַנּוֹטֵף hanotef מֵעֲצֵי me'atzei הַקְּטָף haketaf ◆

כַּרְשִׁינָא karshina לָמָה lema הִיא hee בָאָה va'a ◆ כְּדֵי kedei

לְשַׁפּוֹת leshapot בָּה ba אֶת et הַצִּפּוֹרֶן haTziporen

כְּדֵי kedei שֶׁתְּהֵא shetehe נָאָה na'a ◆ יַיִן yen

קַפְרִיסִין Kafrisin לָמָה lema הוּא hu בָא va ◆ כְּדֵי kedei

לִשְׁרוֹת lishrot בּוֹ bo אֶת et הַצִּפּוֹרֶן haTziporen

כְּדֵי kedei שֶׁתְּהֵא shetehe עַזָּה aza ◆ וַהֲלֹא vahalo מֵי mei רַגְלַיִם raglayim

יָפִין yafin לָהּ la אֶלָּא ela שֶׁאֵין she'en מַכְנִיסִין machnisin מֵי mei

רַגְלַיִם raglayim בַּמִּקְדָּשׁ bamikdash מִפְּנֵי mipenei הַכָּבוֹד hakavod ◆

תַּנְיָא tanya ◆ רִבִּי Ribi נָתָן Natan אוֹמֵר omer: כְּשֶׁהוּא keshehu

שׁוֹחֵק shochek אוֹמֵר omer הָדֵק hadek ◆ הֵיטֵב hetev ◆ הֵיטֵב hetev

הָדֵק hadek ◆ מִפְּנֵי mipenei שֶׁהַקּוֹל shehakol יָפֶה yafe לַבְּשָׂמִים labesamim ◆

פִּטְּמָהּ pitema לַחֲצָאִין lachatza'in כְּשֵׁרָה keshera ◆ לְשָׁלִישׁ leshalish

וְלִרְבִיעַ ulravi'a לֹא lo שָׁמַעְנוּ shamanu ◆ אָמַר amar רִבִּי Ribi

יְהוּדָה Yehuda: זֶה ze הַכְּלָל hakelal ◆ אִם im

כְּמִדָּתָהּ kemidata כְּשֵׁרָה keshera לַחֲצָאִין lachatza'in ◆

וְאִם ve'im וְחִסֵּר chiser

אַחַת achat מִכָּל mikol סַמְמָנֶיהָ samemaneha וְחַיָּב chayav מִיתָה mita:

Rabban Shimon ben Gamliel says: The balsam was a sap that only seeped from the balsam trees. For what purpose was the lye of Carsina added? In order to rub the Onycha with it to make it pleasant looking. For what purpose was the Cyprus wine added? In order to steep in it the Onycha. Urine is more appropriate for this, but urine is not brought into the Temple out of respect. It was taught that Rabbi Natan said: When he ground, he said: 'Grind it fine, grind it fine.' This is because voice is beneficial to the spices. If he compounds half the amount it is still valid, yet regarding a third or a quarter, we have no information. Rabbi Yehuda said: This is the general rule: If it is in its correct proportions, then half is valid. Yet if he omits one of all its spices, he is liable to death.

tanei תְּנֵי Var בַּר Kapara קַפָּרָא׃ achat אַחַת leshishim לְשִׁשִּׁים o אוֹ

leshiv'im לְשִׁבְעִים shana שָׁנָה hayta הָיְתָה va'a בָּאָה shel שֶׁל

shirayim שִׁירַיִם lachatza'in לַוְצָאִין ve'od וְעוֹד tanei תְּנֵי Var בַּר

Kapara קַפָּרָא׃ ilu אִלּוּ haya הָיָה יהה noten נוֹתֵן אבגיתץ, ושר ba בָּהּ

עו (דעתו) ו"ד (האוזן) = ע"ך דינין דגדלות devash דְּבַשׁ shel שֶׁל kortov קָרְטוֹב

en אֵין adam אָדָם מ"ה yachol יָכוֹל la'amod לַעֲמוֹד mipenei מִפְּנֵי

recha רֵיחוֹ velama וְלָמָה en אֵין me'arvin מְעָרְבִין ba בָּהּ devash דְּבַשׁ

עו (דעתו) ו"ד (האוזן) = ע"ך דינין דגדלות mipenei מִפְּנֵי shehatorah שֶׁהַתּוֹרָה

amra אָמְרָה ki כִּי chol כָּל ילי se'or שְׂאֹר ג' מווזן דאלהים דקטנות

devash דְּבַשׁ ילי vechol וְכָל א' = כללות שם אלהים ; ר' = ריבוע אלהים ; (ע' = אלהים דיודין

mimenu מִמֶּנּוּ taktiru תַּקְטִירוּ lo לֹא עו (דעתו) ו"ד (האוזן) = ע"ך דינין דגדלות

ishe אִשֶּׁה לַיהֹוָאֲדֹנָי ladonai׃ עוכן הם בוזינת דינין דקטנות ורגדלות לכן נאסרה הקרבתן

Right

Adonai יְהֹוָאֲדֹנָי Tzeva'ot צְבָאוֹת פני שכינה imanu עִמָּנוּ

misgav מִשְׂגָּב מושה, מהע, ע"ב בריבוע וקס"א, אל עֹדי, ריבוע דס"ג, קס"א, ע"ב ע"ה ור' אותיות

lanu לָנוּ אלהים, אהיה ארני אלהים, Elohei אֱלֹהֵי מילוי ע"ב, דמב ; ילה ד"פ אלהים ע"ה

Yaakov יַעֲקֹב י הויות, יאהרונהי, אירהנויה סֶלָה sela׃

Left

Adonai יְהֹוָאֲדֹנָי Tzeva'ot צְבָאוֹת פני שכינה ashrei אַשְׁרֵי

adam אָדָם מ"ה ; יהוה ; צבאות אשרי אדם = תפארת bote'ach בֹּטֵחַ

bach בָּךְ אדם בוטוו בך ; אמן = (יאהרונהי) ע"ה ; בוטוו בך = מילוי ע"ב ע"ה׃

Bar Kappara taught that once every sixty or seventy years the leftovers would accumulate to half the measure. Bar Kappara also taught that if one would add to it a Kortov (liquid messurment) of honey, no man would withstand its smell. Why is honey not mixed with it? Because the Torah had stipulated: Because any leaven or honey, you must not burn any of it as burnt-offering to the Lord. (Kritut 6; Yerushalmi, Yoma: ch.4)
(Right) *"The Lord of Hosts is with us, our strength is the God of Jacob, Selah."* (Psalms 46:12)
(Left) *"The Lord of Hosts, joyful is one who trusts in You."* (Psalms 84:13)

Central

לְהֹוָ֫אֱדֹנָיֵאהֹדֹנָהי ר"ת יהה hamelech הַמֶּלֶךְ ר"ע נְהוֹרִין ויש"ע יהוה hoshi'a הוֹשִׁ֫יעָה Adonai אֲדֹנָיֵאהֹדֹנָהי

לַעֲנֵ֫נוּ ya'anenu בַיֹּום beyom veyom ע"ה נגד, מזבח, זן, אל יהוה

קָרְאֵ֫נוּ kor'enu ר"ת יב"ק, אלהים יהוה, אהיה אדני יהוה ; ס"ת = ב"ן ועם כף דהמלך = ע"ב:

וְעָרְבָה ve'arva לַיֹהֹוָ֫אֱדֹנָיֵאהֹדֹנָהי ladonai

מִנְחַ֫ת minchat יְהוּדָה Yehuda וִירוּשָׁלָ֫ם virushalaim

כִּימֵ֫י kimei עוֹלָם olam וּכְשָׁנִ֫ים uch'shanim קַדְמֹנִיּֽוֹת kadmoniyot:

ANA BEKO'ACH (an explanation about the *Ana Beko'ach* can be found on pages 222-224)

The *Ana Beko'ach* is perhaps the most powerful prayer in the entire universe. Second-century Kabbalist Rav Nachunya ben HaKana was the first sage to reveal this combination of 42 letters, which encompass the power of Creation.

Chesed, Sunday *(Alef Bet Gimel Yud Tav Tzadik)* אבג יתץ

לְיְמִינֶ֫ךָ yeminecha◆   גְּדֻלַּת gedulat   בְּכֹ֫וחַ beko'ach◆   אָנָּא ana

תַּתִּיר tatir   צְרוּרָה tzerura:

Gevurah, Monday *(Kuf Resh Ayin Sin Tet Nun)* קרע שטן

שַׂגְּבֵ֫נוּ sagevenu◆   עַמְּךָ amecha   רִנַּת rinat◆   קַבֵּל kabel

נוֹרָא nora: טַהֲרֵ֫נוּ taharenu

Tiferet, Tuesday *(Nun Gimel Dalet Yud Kaf Shin)* נגד יכש

יְחוּדֶ֫ךָ yichudecha◆   דּוֹרְשֵׁי dorshei   גִּבּוֹר gibor◆   נָא na

שָׁמְרֵם shomrem: כְּבָבַת kevavat

(Central) *"Lord save us. The King shall answer us the day we call." (Psalms 20:10) "May the Lord find the offering of Yehuda and Jerusalem pleasing as He had always done and as in the years of old." (Malachi 3:4)*

ANA BEKO'ACH

Chesed, Sunday אבג יתץ

We beseech You, with the power of Your great right, undo this entanglement.

Gevurah, Monday קרע שטן

Accept the singing of Your Nation. Strengthen and purify us, Awesome One.

Tiferet, Tuesday נגד יכש

Please, Mighty One, those who seek Your unity, guard them like the pupil of the eye.

Netzach, Wednesday *(Bet Tet Resh Tzadik Tav Gimel)* בטר צתג

בָּרְכֵם barchem   טַהֲרֵם taharem◆   רַחֲמֵי rachamei   צִדְקָתְךָ tzidkatecha◆

תָּמִיד tamid   גָּמְלֵם gomlem◆

Hod, Thursday *(Chet Kuf Bet Tet Nun Ayin)* וזקב טנע

וְזִסִין chasin   קָדוֹשׁ kadosh◆   בְּרוֹב berov   טוּבְךָ tuvcha◆

נַהֵל nahel   עֲדָתְךָ adatecha◆

Yesod, Friday *(Yud Gimel Lamed Pei Zayin Kuf)* יגל פזק

יָחִיד yachid   גֵּאֶה ge'e◆   לְעַמְּךָ le'amecha   פְּנֵה pene◆

זוֹכְרֵי zochrei   קְדוּשָׁתֶךָ kedushatecha◆

Malchut, Saturday *(Shin Kuf Vav Tzadik Yud Tav)* שקו צית

שַׁוְעָתֵנוּ shav'atenu   קַבֵּל kabel◆   וּשְׁמַע ushma   צַעֲקָתֵנוּ tza'akatenu◆

יוֹדֵעַ yode'a   תַּעֲלוּמוֹת ta'alumot◆

BARUCH SHEM KEVOD

(Whisper) : יוזו אותיות   בָּרוּךְ baruch   שֵׁם shem   כְּבוֹד kevod   מַלְכוּתוֹ malchuto

לְעוֹלָם le'olam   ריבוע ס"ג וי' אותיות דס"ג   וָעֶד va'ed◆

Netzach, Wednesday בטר צתג
Bless them. Purify them. Your compassionate righteousness always grant them.

Hod, Thursday וזקב טנע
Invincible and Mighty One, with the abundance of Your goodness, govern Your congregation.

Yesod, Friday יגל פזק
Sole and proud One, turn to Your people, those who remember Your sanctity.

Malchut, Saturday שקו צית
Accept our cry and hear our wail, You that knows all that is hidden.

BARUCH SHEM KEVOD
"Blessed is the Name of Glory. His Kingdom is forever and for eternity." (Pesachim 56a)

THE ASHREI

Twenty-one of the twenty-two letters of the Aramaic alphabet are encoded in the *Ashrei* in their correct order from *Alef* to *Tav*. King David, the author, left out the Aramaic letter *Nun* from this prayer, because *Nun* is the first letter in the Aramaic word *nefilah*, which means "falling." Falling refers to a spiritual decline, as in falling into the *klipa*. Feelings of doubt, depression, worry, and uncertainty are consequences of spiritual falling. Because the Aramaic letters are the actual instruments of Creation, this prayer helps to inject order and the power of Creation into our lives, without the energy of falling.

In this Psalm there are ten times the Name: יהוה for the Ten *Sefirot*. This Psalm is written according to the order of the *Alef Bet*, but the letter *Nun* is omitted to prevent falling.

ראה ב"פ | vetecha בֵּיתֶ֑ךָ | yoshvei יוֹשְׁבֵ֣י | (סוד הכתר) | ashrei אַ֭שְׁרֵי

lo לֹ֥ו | מ"א ע"ה אלהים ד"פ שדי, אל וקס"א, ע"ב בריבוע משה, מ"ה, | shekacha שֶׁכָּ֣כָה | ha'am הָעָ֔ם | ashrei אַשְׁרֵ֥י | :sela סֶֽלָה | yehalelucha יְֽהַלְל֥וּךָ | od ע֣וֹד

(Keter) | she'Adonai שֶׁיֲהֹוָ֣אדניאהדונהי | ר"ת לאה | ha'am הָעָ֔ם | ashrei אַשְׁרֵ֣י

leDavid לְדָ֫וִ֥ד | ע"ה אמת, אהיה פעמים אהיה, ז"פ ס"ג יכה: | tehila תְּהִלָּ֗ה | Elohav אֱלֹהָֽיו

va'avarcha וַאֲבָרְכָ֥ה | hamelech הַמֶּ֑לֶךְ | Elohai אֱלוֹהַ֣י | aromimcha אֲרוֹמִמְךָ֣

:va'ed וָעֶֽד | דס"ג אותיות וי' ריבוע דס"ג | le'olam לְעוֹלָ֥ם | shimcha שִׁ֝מְךָ֗

יהוה אל זן מזבוח, נגד, ע"ה לכב ב"ן, | yom י֭וֹם | bechol בְּכָל־

:va'ed וָעֶֽד | דס"ג אותיות וי' ריבוע דס"ג | le'olam לְעוֹלָ֥ם | avarcheka אֲבָרֲכֶ֑ךָּ | va'ahalela וַאֲהַלְלָ֥ה | יהוה מ"ה | shimcha שִׁ֝מְךָ֗

אום יזל, ללה, מזבה, = אותיות ד' עם ; להו | gadol גָּ֘ד֤וֹל

ללה ארני, | umhulal וּמְהֻלָּ֣ל | (Chochmah) | Adonai יֲהֹוָ֣אדניאהדונהי

:cheker וְ֝לִגְדֻלָּת֗וֹ | en אֵ֣ין | יהו | veligdulato וְלִגְדֻלָּת֗וֹ | me'od מְאֹ֑ד

THE ASHREI

"Joyful are those who dwell in Your House, they shall praise You, Selah." (Psalms 84:5) "Joyful is the nation that this is theirs and joyful the nation that the Lord is their God." (Psalms 145:15) "A praise of David:

א   *I shall exalt You, my God, the King, and I shall bless Your Name forever and for eternity.*

ב   *I shall bless You every day and I shall praise Your Name forever and for eternity.*

ג   *The Lord is great and exceedingly praised. His greatness is unfathomable.*

ר"ת דלים   מַעֲשֶׂיךָ ma'asecha   יְשַׁבַּח yeshabach   לְדוֹר ledor   דּוֹר dor

וּגְבוּרֹתֶיךָ ugvurotecha   יַגִּידוּ yagidu   יי, כ"ב אותיות פשוטות (=אכא) וה' אותיות סופיות מנצפ"ך׃

וְדִבְרֵי vedivrei   הוֹדֶךָ hodecha   כְּבוֹד kevod   הֲדַר hadar

אֲדֹנָי   אהיה   אלהים,   ר"ת   נִפְלְאֹתֶיךָ nifle'otecha

טהור כתם (בסוד פ"ז = הפסוק ר"ת asicha אָשִׂיחָה פֹז)׃

וּגְדֻלָּתְךָ ugdulatcha   וְגְדוּלָּתְךָ yomeru   יֹאמֵרוּ no'rotecha נוֹרְאֹתֶיךָ   ve'ezuz וֶעֱזוּז

(כתיב: וּגְדֻלוֹתֶיךָ) ר"ת = ע"ב, ריבוע יהוה ס"ת = יא"י (מילוי דס"ג)׃ asaperena אֲסַפְּרֶנָּה

זֵכֶר zecher   רַב־ rav   טוּבְךָ tuvcha   לאו   יַבִּיעוּ yabi'u

וְצִדְקָתְךָ vetzidkatcha   יְרַנֵּנוּ yeranenu   ס"ת = ב"ן, יבמ, לכב ; ר"ת הפסוק = רי"ו יהוה׃

חַנּוּן chanun   וְרַחוּם verachum   יְהוֹוָהֹאֲדֹנָיֹאהֹדֹוֹנֹהֹיֹ Adonai   (Binah)

אֶרֶךְ erech   ס"ת = ס"ג ב"ן ; ס"ת = עאל = חנון ורחום יהוה   אַפַּיִם apayim ר"ת = יהוה

וְחֶסֶד chased   ע"ב, ריבוע יהוה   (כתיב: וּגְדוֹל)   וּגְדָל־ ugdal יהוה׃

טוֹב־ tov   והו   יְהוֹוָהֹאֲדֹנָיֹאהֹדֹוֹנֹהֹיֹ Adonai   (Chesed)   לַכֹּל lakol

עַל־ al   וְרַחֲמָיו verachamav   (מילוי דס"ג) ל"ז ; ס"ת ; אֲדֹנָי   יה

כָּל kol   ילי ; עמם ; ר"ת ריבוע ב"ן ע"ה ; ס"ת ע"ב, ריבוע יהוה׃ ma'asav מַעֲשָׂיו

ד   *One generation and the next shall praise Your deeds and tell of Your might.*

ה   *The brilliance of Your splendid glory and the wonders of Your acts, I shall speak of.*

ו   *They shall speak of the might of Your awesome acts and I shall tell of Your greatness.*

ז   *They shall express the remembrance of Your abundant goodness, and Your righteousness they shall joyfully proclaim.* ח *The Lord is merciful and compassionate, slow to anger and great in kindness.*

ט   *The Lord is good to all, His compassion extends over all His acts.*

יוֹדוּךָ yoducha יְהוֹוָאהּדוֹנהי Adonai (Gevurah) כָּל יכ kol מַעֲשֶׂיךָ ma'asecha

וַחֲסִידֶיךָ vachasidecha לִבְרְכוּכָה ר"ת אלהים, אהיה אדני ס"ת = מ"ה: yevarchucha

כְּבוֹד kevod מַלְכוּתְךָ malchutcha יֹאמֵרוּ yomeru וּגְבוּרָתְךָ ugvuratcha

יְדַבֵּרוּ yedaberu ר"ת הפסוק = אלהים, אהיה אדני ; ס"ת = ב"ן, יבמ, לכב:

לְהוֹדִיעַ lehodi'a לִבְנֵי livnei הָאָדָם ha'adam ר"ת ללה, אדני

גְּבוּרֹתָיו gevurotav וּכְבוֹד uchvod הָדַר hadar

מַלְכוּתוֹ malchuto ר"ת מ"ה וס"ת = רי"ו ; ר"ת הפסוק ע"ה = ק"כ צירופי אלהים:

מַלְכוּתְךָ malchutcha מַלְכוּת malchut כָּל יכ kol עֹלָמִים olamim

וּמֶמְשַׁלְתְּךָ umemshaltecha בְּכָל ב"ן, לכב bechol דּוֹר dor וָדֹר vador רי"ו:

סוֹמֵךְ somech רִיבוּע רָדני Adonai יְהוֹוָאהּדוֹנהי (Tiferet)

לְכָל lechol הַנֹּפְלִים hanoflim יה אדני ; סומך אדני לכל ר"ת סאל, אמן (יאהדונהי)

וְזוֹקֵף vezokef לְכָל lechol יה אדני הַכְּפוּפִים hakefufim נומם:

עֵינֵי enei רִיבוּע דמ"ה כֹל יכ chol אֵלֶיךָ elecha יְשַׂבֵּרוּ yesaberu וְאַתָּה veAta

נוֹתֵן noten אבגיתצ, ושר לָהֶם lahem אֶת et אָכְלָם ochlam בְּעִתּוֹ be'ito:

י   *All that You have made shall thank You, Lord, and Your pious ones shall bless You.*

כ   *They shall speak of the glory of Your Kingdom and talk of Your mighty deeds.*

ל   *His mighty deeds He makes known to man and the glory of His splendid Kingdom.*

מ   *Yours is the Kingdom of all worlds and Your reign extends to each and every generation.*

ס   *The Lord supports all those who fell and holds upright all those who are bent over.*

ע   *The eyes of all look hopefully towards You, and You give them their food at its proper time.*

Pote'ach Et Yadecha

We connect to the letters *Pei, Alef,* and *Yud* by opening our hands and holding our palms skyward. Our consciousness is focused on receiving sustenance and financial prosperity from the Light through our actions of tithing and sharing, our Desire to Receive for the Sake of Sharing. In doing so, we also acknowledge that the sustenance we receive comes from a higher source and is not of our own doing. According to the sages, if we do not meditate on this idea at this juncture, we must repeat the prayer.

פתּוֹ (שֹע"וֹ נֹהוֹרִין לֹמ"ה וֹלֹס"ה)

יוֹד הִי וֹיו הִי יוֹד הִי וֹיו הִי (וֹז' וֹזיוורתי)	פּותֹחוֹ את ידֹך ר"ת פּאי
אלֹף לֹמֹד אלֹף לֹמֹד (ע"ע)	גֹימ' יאהֹדֹונֹהי זֹו"ן
יוֹד הֹא וֹאו הֹא (לֹו"א)	וֹחכֹמֹה דֹו"א ו"ק
אֹדֹני (וֹלֹנוֹקֹבא)	יֹסוֹד דֹנוֹק'

פּוֹתֵחַ pote'ach **אֶת** et **יָדֶךָ** yadecha ר"ת פאי וֹס"ת וֹזתֹך עֹם ג' אוֹתֹיוֹת = **דִּיקַרְנֹוֹסָא**

וֹבאתֹב"ע הוֹא סֹאל, פֹאי, אמֹן, יאהֹדֹונֹהי ; וֹעוֹד יֹכוֹין עֹם וֹזתֹך בֹעֹילוֹב יהוה – **יוֹזְהָתֹוֹכָה**

אלֹף לֹמֹד הִי יוֹד מֹם אלֹף לֹמֹד הִי יוֹד מֹם מֹווֹזֹין דֹפֹנֹים דֹאוֹזוֹר אלֹהִים אלֹהִים
לֹהֹבֹמֹעֹיֹך פ"וֹ אוֹרוֹת לֹכֹל מֹילוֹי דֹכֹל

אוֹזוֹר דֹפֹרֹצֹוֹפֹי נֹה"י וֹוֹגֹ"ת	וֹזתֹך	אוֹזוֹר דֹפֹרֹצֹוֹפֹי נֹה"י וֹוֹגֹ"ת
דֹיֹצֹירֹה דֹרוֹזֹל הֹנֹקֹראת לֹאה		דֹפֹרֹצֹוֹף וֹזֹג"ת דֹיֹצֹירֹה דֹו"א
לֹף מֹד י וֹד ם	סֹאל יאהֹדֹונֹהי	לֹף מֹד י וֹד ם
אלֹף לֹמֹד הִי יוֹד מֹם		אלֹף לֹמֹד הִי יוֹד מֹם

וּמַשְׂבִּיעַ umasbi'a וֹזתֹך עֹם ג' אוֹתֹיוֹת = **דִּיקַרְנֹוֹסָא**

וֹבא"ת ב"ע הוֹא סֹאל, אמֹן, יאהֹדֹונֹהי ; וֹעוֹד יֹכוֹין עֹם וֹזתֹך בֹעֹילוֹב יהוה – **יוֹזְהָתֹוֹכָה**

אלֹף לֹמֹד הִי יוֹד מֹם אלֹף לֹמֹד הִי יוֹד מֹם מֹווֹזֹין דֹפֹנֹים דֹאוֹזוֹר אלֹהִים אלֹהִים
לֹהֹבֹמֹעֹיֹך פ"וֹ אוֹרוֹת לֹכֹל מֹילוֹי דֹכֹל

וֹאוֹזוֹר דֹפֹרֹצֹוֹפֹי נֹה"י וֹוֹגֹ"ת	וֹזתֹך	אוֹזוֹר דֹפֹרֹצֹוֹפֹי נֹה"י וֹוֹגֹ"ת
דֹיֹצֹירֹה דֹרוֹזֹל הֹנֹקֹראת לֹאה		דֹפֹרֹצֹוֹף נֹה"י דֹיֹצֹירֹה דֹו"א
לֹף מֹד י וֹד ם		לֹף מֹד י וֹד ם
אלֹף לֹמֹד הִי יוֹד מֹם		אלֹף לֹמֹד הִי יוֹד מֹם

לְכָל lechol יֹה אֹדֹני (לֹהֹבֹמֹעֹיֹך מֹווֹזֹין דֹ-יֹה אֹל הֹנוֹקֹבא שֹהֹיא אֹדֹני)

וָֹזֹי chai כֹל וֹזֹי = אהֹיה אהֹיה יהוה, בֹינֹה ע"ה, וֹזיֹים

רָצֹוֹן ratzon מֹהֹשֹע ע"ה, ע"ב ברֹיבוֹע וֹקֹס"א ע"ה, אֹל שֹדֹי ע"ה ; ר"ת רוֹזֹל שֹהֹיא המֹלֹכוֹת הצֹרֹיכֹה לֹשֹפֹע

יוֹד יוֹד הִי יוֹד הִי וֹיו יוֹד הִי וֹיו הִי וֹיו הִי יֹסוֹד דֹאבא
אלֹף הִי יוֹד הִי יֹסוֹד דֹאימא
לֹהֹבֹמֹיֹק רוֹזֹל וֹב' דֹמֹעֹין **שֹך פֹר**

We should also meditate to draw abundance and sustenance and blessing to all the worlds from the *ratzon* mentioned above. We should meditate and focus on this verse because it is the essence of prosperity, and meditate that God is intervening and sustaining and supporting all of Creation.

Pote'ach Et Yadecha

| פ | *Open* | *Your* | *Hands* | *and* | *satisfy* | *every* | *living* | *thing* | *with* | *desire.* |

צַדִּיק tzadik יְהֹוָואדנייאהדונהי Adonai (Yesod) בְּכֹל bechol ב"ן, לכב

דְּרָכָיו derachav וְחָסִיד vechasid בְּכֹל bechol ב"ן, לכב מַעֲשָׂיו ma'asav יבמ, ב"ן:

קָרוֹב karov יְהֹוָואדנייאהדונהי Adonai (Malchut) לְכֹל lechol יה אדני

יִקְרָאֻהוּ yikra'uhu בֶאֱמֶת ve'emet אהיה פעמים אהיה, ז"פ ס"ג: לְכֹל lechol יה אדני אֲשֶׁר asher קֹרְאָיו kor'av

רְצוֹן retzon יְרֵאָיו yere'av מהש ע"ה, ע"ב בריבוע וקס"א ע"ה, אל שדי ע"ה יַעֲשֶׂה ya'ase

וְיוֹשִׁיעֵם veyoshi'em יִשְׁמַע yishma שַׁוְעָתָם shav'atam וְאֶת ve'et ר"ת ריי:

שׁוֹמֵר shomer כ"א הויות עובהתפילין יְהֹוָואדנייאהדונהי Adonai (Netzach)

אֶת et כָּל kol ילי אֹהֲבָיו ohavav ר"ת אכא

וְאֵת ve'et כָּל kol ילי הָרְשָׁעִים haresha'im יַשְׁמִיד yashmid:

תְּהִלַּת tehilat יְהֹוָואדנייאהדונהי Adonai (Hod) יְדַבֶּר yedaber ראה

פִּי pi וִיבָרֵךְ vivarech ע"ב ס"ג מ"ה ב"ן, (למתק את הברכה) כָּל kol ילי בָּשָׂר basar שֵׁם shem קָדְשׁוֹ kodsho (המלכים שמתו)

לְעוֹלָם le'olam ריבוע ס"ג וי' אותיות דס"ג וָעֶד va'ed:

וַאֲנַחְנוּ va'anachnu נְבָרֵךְ nevarech יָהּ Yah מֵעַתָּה me'ata

וְעַד ve'ad עוֹלָם olam הַלְלוּיָהּ haleluya אלהים, אהיה ; אדני ללה:

צ *The Lord is righteous in all His ways and virtuous in all His deeds.*

ק *The Lord is close to all who call Him, and only to those who call Him truthfully.*

ר *He shall fulfill the will of those who fear Him; He hears their wailing and saves them.*

ש *The Lord protects all who love Him and He destroys the wicked.*

ת *My lips utter the praise of the Lord and all flesh shall bless His Holy Name, forever and for eternity."*
(Psalms 145) "And we shall bless the Lord forever and for eternity. Praise the Lord!" (Psalms 115:18)

UVA LETZIYON

This prayer is our connection to redemption. The prayer starts, "And a redeemer should come to *Zion*." The redeemer is a reference to the *Mashiach*. Kabbalistically, the *Mashiach* is not a righteous person who will come and save us and bring about *world peace*. *Mashiach* is a state of spirituality and consciousness that every individual can achieve. No one is coming to save us and do the work for us. We must each achieve our own level of spiritual growth and fulfillment, our personal *Mashiach*, and when a critical mass of people have reached this state, the global *Mashiach* will appear for humanity.

וּבָא לְצִיּוֹן uva leTziyon יוֹסֵף, ו׳ הוִיות, קְנאה גֹּאֵל go'el וּלְשָׁבֵי ulshavei פֶּשַׁע fesha

בְּיַעֲקֹב beYaakov ו׳ הוִיות, יאהדונהי, יאהדונהי אידהנויה נָאם ne'um יֱהֹוָהיאהדונהיאהדונהי Adonai:

וַאֲנִי va'ani אני ; ר״ת גוף בניו (עיירדו לוחיצונים בעון הוצאת ז״ל, ויוזזרו לגוף אוצר הנשמות, ויבוא גואל)

זֹאת zot בְּרִיתִי beriti אוֹתָם otam אָמַר amar יֱהֹוָהיאהדונהיאהדונהי Adonai

רוּוזִי ruchi אֲשֶׁר asher עָלֶיךָ alecha וּדְבָרַי udvarai אֲשֶׁר asher

שַׂמְתִּי samti בְּפִיךָ beficha לֹא־ lo יָמוּשׁוּ yamushu מִפִּיךָ mipicha

וּמִפִּי umipi זַרְעֲךָ zar'acha וּמִפִּי umipi זֶרַע zera זַרְעֲךָ zar'acha

אָמַר amar יֱהֹוָהיאהדונהיאהדונהי Adonai מֵעַתָּה me'ata וְעַד־ ve'ad עוֹלָם olam:

וְאַתָּה veAta קָדוֹשׁ kadosh יוֹשֵׁב yoshev תְּהִלּוֹת tehilot יִשְׂרָאֵל Yisrael:

וְקָרָא vekara זֶה ze אֶל־ el זֶה ze י״ב פרקין דיעקב מאירין לי״ב פרקין דרחל וְאָמַר ve'amar:

> **On Shabbat** Meditate on the letters *Tav* ת and *Tzadik* צ from: אבגית״ץ, which helps spiritual remembering.

(*Tiferet*) kadosh קָדוֹשׁ   (*Gevurah*) kadosh קָדוֹשׁ   (*Chesed*) | kadosh קָדוֹשׁ

יֱהֹוָהיאהדונהיאהדונהי Adonai צְבָאוֹת Tzeva'ot פני שכינה מְלֹא melo

כָּל־ chol ילי הָאָרֶץ ha'aretz אלהים דההין ע״ה כְּבוֹדוֹ kevodo:

וּמְקַבְּלִין umkabelin דֵּין den מִן min דֵּין den וְאָמְרִין ve'amrin

קַדִּישׁ kadish ב״פ אור, ב״פ רו, ב״פ אס בִּשְׁמֵי bishmei א״ס מְרוֹמָא meroma

עִלָּאָה ila'a בֵּית bet ב״פ ראה שְׁכִינְתֵּהּ shechinte

UVA LETZIYON

"A redeemer shall come to Zion and to those who shall turn away from sin from amongst [the House of] Jacob, so says the Lord. And as for Me, this is My Covenant with them, says the Lord. My spirit, which is upon you, and My words, that I have put in your mouth, shall not depart from your mouths, the mouths of your children, or the mouths of your children's children, says the Lord, from now and forever." (Isaiah 59:20-21) *"And You are Holy and await the praises of Israel. And one called to the other and said: Holy, Holy, Holy is the Lord of Hosts, the whole earth is filled with His glory."* (Isaiah 6:3) *And they receive consent from one another and say: Holy in the Highest Heavens is the abode of His Shechinah.*

קַדִּישׁ kadish ב"פ א"ס, ב"פ רו, ב"פ אור, ב"פ עַל־ al אַרְעָא ara עוֹבַד ovad

קַדִּישׁ kadish ב"פ א"ס, ב"פ רו, ב"פ אור, ב"פ ◆gevurte גְּבוּרְתֵהּ le'alam לְעָלַם

צְבָאוֹת Tzeva'ot Adonai יְהֹוָֹאדנייאהדונהי almaya: עָלְמַיָּא ule'almei וּלְעָלְמֵי

יְקָרֵהּ yekare: ziv זִיו ar'a אַרְעָא yli chol כָּל malya מַלְיָא שכינה פני

קוֹל kol acharai אֲחֹרַי va'eshma וָאֶשְׁמַע ru'ach רוּחַ vatisa'eni וַתִּשָּׂאֵנִי

בָּרוּךְ baruch gadol גָּדוֹל לְהוּ ; עם ד' אותיות = מבה, יזל, אום ra'ash רַעַשׁ

בִּמְקוֹמוֹ mimekomo Adonai יְהֹוָֹאדנייאהדונהי כבוד יהוה = יוד הי ואו הה kevod כְּבוֹד

עסמ"ב, הברכה (למתק את ז' המלכים עמותו) ; ר"ת = ע"ב, ריבוע יהוה ; ר"ת מ"ה, י"פ האא:

קָל kal batrai בַּתְרַי ushma'it וּשְׁמָעִית ◆rucha רוּחָא untalatni וּנְטָלַתְנִי

וְאָמְרִין ve'amrin dim'shabechin דִּמְשַׁבְּחִין sagi שַׂגִּיא zi'a זִיעַ גנמ (ה) גבורות)

מֵאֲתַר me'atar dadonai דִּיהֹוָֹאדנייאהדונהי yekara יְקָרָא berich בְּרִיךְ

יִמְלֹךְ yimloch | Adonai יְהֹוָֹאדנייאהדונהי ◆shechinte שְׁכִינְתֵּהּ ב"פ ראה bet בֵּית

Adonai יְהֹוָֹאדנייאהדונהי va'ed: וָעֶד ר"ת ייל אותיות דס"ג ; le'olam לְעֹלָם

ule'almei וּלְעָלְמֵי le'alam לְעָלַם ka'im קָאִם malchute מַלְכוּתֵהּ

עָלְמַיָּא almaya: Adonai יְהֹוָֹאדנייאהדונהי Elohei אֱלֹהֵי מילוי ע"ב, דמב ; ילה

אַבְרְהָם Avraham וז"פ אל, רי"ו ול"ב נתיבות החכמה, רמ"ח (אברים), עסמ"ב וט"ז אותיות פשוטות

אֲבֹתֵינוּ avotenu veYisrael וְיִשְׂרָאֵל ב"ן ד"פ Yitzchak יִצְחָק

שָׁמְרָה shomrah zot זֹאת לְעֹלָם le'olam ריבוע ס"ג וי' אותיות דס"ג

לְיֵצֶר leyetzer mach'shevot מַחְשְׁבוֹת levav לְבַב בוכו

עַמֶּךָ amecha vehachen וְהָכֵן levavam לְבָבָם elecha: אֵלֶיךָ

Holy, upon the Earth, is the work of His valor. Holy, forever and for all eternity, is the Lord of Hosts, the entire Earth is filled with the splendor of His glory. "And a wind carried me and from behind me I heard a great thunderous voice giving praise: Blessed is the glory of the Lord from His abode." (Ezikiel 3:12) And saying: Blessed is the glory of the Lord from the place of residence of His Shechinah. "The Lord shall reign forever and ever" (Exodus 15:18) The Lord, His Kingdom is established forever and for eternity. "The Lord, God of Abraham, Isaac, and Israel - our forefathers - safeguard this forever for the sake of the thoughts in the hearts of Your Nation, and direct their hearts toward You!" (1 Chronicles 29:18)

וְהוּא vehu רַחוּם rachum יְכַפֵּר yechaper רח"ת רי"ו עָוֹן avon (Abba of the klipa)

וְלֹא velo יַשְׁחִית yashchit (Ima of the klipa) וְהִרְבָּה vehirba לְהָשִׁיב lehashiv

אַפּוֹ apo (Zeir of the klipa) וְלֹא velo יָעִיר ya'ir כָּל־ kol ילי וַחֲמָתוֹ chamato

:(Nukva of the klipa) כִּי ki אַתָּה Ata אֲדֹנָי Adonai ללה טוֹב tov והו

וְסַלָּח vesalach (Avraham) חֶסֶד chesed יהוה ע"ב, ריבוע יהוה וְרַב־ verav (Yitzchak)

לְכָל־ lechol לֶחֹל אדני יה kor'echa קֹרְאֶיךָ (Yaakov): צִדְקָתְךָ tzidkat'cha צֶדֶק tzedek

לְעוֹלָם le'olam ריבוע ס"ג ו' אותיות דס"ג וְתוֹרָתְךָ vetorat'cha אֱמֶת emet

אֱמֶת emet אהיה פעמים אהיה, ז"פ ס"ג: תִּתֵּן titen ב"פ כהת אֱמֶת emet אהיה פעמים אהיה, ז"פ ס"ג

לְיַעֲקֹב leYaakov הויות, יאהדונהי אידהנויה ' חֶסֶד chesed ע"ב, ריבוע יהוה

לְאַבְרָהָם leAvraham וז"פ אל, רי"ו ול"ב נתיבות החכמה, רמ"ח (אברים), עסמ"ב וט"ו אותיות פשוטות

אֲשֶׁר asher נִשְׁבַּעְתָּ nishbata לַאֲבֹתֵינוּ la'avotenu מִימֵי mimei kedem קָדֶם:

בָּרוּךְ baruch אֲדֹנָי Adonai ללה yom יוֹם yom ע"ה נגד, מזבוח, זן אל יהוה יוֹם yom

לָנוּ lanu ya'amos יַעֲמָס־ ר"ת ייי אלהים, זן אל יהוה ע"ה נגד, מזבוח; ר"ת ייל

הָאֵל haEl לאה; אל (ייא"י מילוי דס"ג); ר"ת ילה יְשׁוּעָתֵנוּ yeshu'atenu סֶלָה sela:

יְהֹוָאדניליאהדונהי Adonai צְבָאוֹת Tzeva'ot פני שכינה עָמָּנוּ imanu

מִשְׂגָּב misgav מהע, ע"ה ור' אותיות ע"ב בריבוע וקס"א, ע"ב ברבוע, אל עזדי, ד"פ אלהים ע"ה ריבוע ס"ג, קס"א

לָנוּ lanu אלהים, אהיה אדני, ע"ב, דמב; ילה אֱלֹהֵי Elohei מילוי ע"ב, יַעֲקֹב Yaakov

צְבָאוֹת Tzeva'ot יְהֹוָאדניליאהדונהי Adonai אידהנויה יאהדונהי, הויות ' סֶלָה sela: פני שכינה

אַשְׁרֵי ashrei אָדָם adam מ"ה; יהוה צבאות אשרי אדם = תפארת = בֹּטֵחַ bote'ach

בָּךְ bach בוטח בך אדם = בוטח בך (יאהדונהי) ע"ה; אמן = בוטח בך = מילוי ע"ב ע"ה:

"And He is merciful and forgives iniquities and shall not destroy, and He frequently thwarts His wrath and will never arouse all His anger." (Psalms 78:38) "Because You, Lord, are good and forgiving and abound in kindness to all who call to You." (Psalms 86:5) "Your righteousness is an everlasting justice, and Your Torah is true." (Psalms 119:142) "You give truth to Jacob and kindness to Abraham, as You have vowed to our forefathers since the earliest days." (Michah 7:20) "Blessed is the Lord, Who heaps burdens upon us each and every day, the God of our salvation. Selah." (Psalms 68:20) "The Lord of Hosts is with us; the God of Jacob is our strength. Selah." (Psalms 46:12) "Lord of Hosts, joyful is the man who trusts in You." (Psalms 84:13)

יְ֒ה֒וֹ֒ה֒יֽאֵֽדֽוֹנֽיֽ ר"ת יהה hamelech הַמֶּלֶךְ יהוה וס"ע נהורין hoshi'a הוֹשִׁיעָה יהוה וס"ע נהורין Adonai יהוה יאדונהי

יַעֲנֵנוּ kor'enu קָרְאֵנוּ ע"ה נגד, מזבוח, זז, אל יהוה veyom ע"ה נגד, מזבוח, זז, אל יהוה בְיוֹם־ ya'anenu

ר"ת יב"ק, אלהים יהוה, אהיה אדני יהוה וס"ת ב"ן ועם אות כ' דהמלך = ע"ב:

BARUCH ELOHENU

Reciting the next verse *"baruch Elohenu"* with genuine happiness and a trusting heart
will generate extra Light in our lives and our *tikkun* process will be much easier.
Meditate to *devote your soul to sanctify the Holy Name (Kedushat HaShem).*

lichvodo לִכְבוֹדוֹ shebera'anu שֶׁבְּרָאָנוּ ילה Elohenu אֱלֹהֵינוּ baruch בָּרוּךְ

(connecting to the right information) hato'im הַתּוֹעִים min בֵּן vehivdilanu וְהִבְדִּילָנוּ

venatan וְנָתַן lanu לָנוּ אלהים, אהיה אדני יהוה torat תּוֹרַת emet אֱמֶת אהיה פעמים אהיה, ז"פ ס"ג

vechayei וְחַיֵּי olam עוֹלָם nata נָטַע betochenu בְּתוֹכֵנוּ. hu הוּא yiftach יִפְתַּח

libenu לִבֵּנוּ betorato בְּתוֹרָתוֹ. veyasim וְיָשִׂים belibenu בְּלִבֵּנוּ ahavato אַהֲבָתוֹ

veyir'ato וְיִרְאָתוֹ la'asot לַעֲשׂוֹת retzono רְצוֹנוֹ ule'ovdo וּלְעָבְדוֹ

belevav בְּלֵבָב בוכו shalem שָׁלֵם. lo לֹא niga נִיגַע larik לָרִיק

(Meditate here to be protected from night emission, so that the spiritual effort will not go to
negativity [*Rik* and *Behala*]. Also meditate to have righteous children following the way of the Light)

velo וְלֹא מהט ע"ה ratzon רָצוֹן yehi יְהִי labehala לַבֶּהָלָה. neled נֵלֵד velo וְלֹא

Adonai יְהֹוָהיאדונהי ס"ג מ"ה ב"ן milfanecha מִלְּפָנֶיךָ ע"ב בריבוע וקס"א, אל שדי ע"ה

avotenu אֲבוֹתֵינוּ ילה; מילוי ע"ב, רמב velohei וֵאלֹהֵי ילה Elohenu אֱלֹהֵינוּ

umitzvotecha וּמִצְוֹתֶיךָ chukecha חֻקֶּיךָ shenishmor שֶׁנִּשְׁמוֹר

venirash וְנִירַשׁ venichye וְנִחְיֶה venizke וְנִזְכֶּה. haze הַזֶּה ba'olam בָּעוֹלָם

haba הַבָּא: ha'olam הָעוֹלָם lechayei לְחַיֵּי uvracha וּבְרָכָה tova טוֹבָה

"Lord, save us. The King shall answer us on the day when we call him." (Psalms 20:10)

BARUCH ELOHENU

*Blessed is our God, Who created us for the sake of His glory, Who separated us from those who have been led
astray, Who gave us the Torah of truth, and Who implanted within us eternal life. May He open our hearts
with His Torah, and place within our hearts love for Him and fear of Him, to fulfill His will and to serve
Him wholeheartedly. May we not toil in vain, and may we not give birth to panic. May it be Your will, Lord,
our God and God of our forefathers, that we should keep Your statutes and Your commandments in this
world, and may we merit, live, and attain goodness and blessing for the life in the World to Come.*

לְמַעַן lema'an | יְזַמֶּרְךָ yezamercha | כָבוֹד chavod | וְלֹא velo | יִדֹּם yidom

יְהֹוָה Adonai ר"ת = אלהים, אהיה אדני | אֱלֹהַי Elohai מילוי ע"ב, דמב ; ילה

לְעוֹלָם le'olam אותיות דס"ג | ס"ג ו"י רביע | אוֹדֶךָ odeka : יְהֹוָה Adonai

וָחֵפֶץ chafetz | לְמַעַן lema'an | צִדְקוֹ tzidko | יַגְדִיל yagdil | תּוֹרָה torah ר"ת ציצ

וְיֶאֱדִיר veya'adir ר"ת = אבניתץ, ועד | וְיִבְטְחוּ veyivtechu | בְךָ vecha | יוֹדְעֵי yod'ei

שְׁמֶךָ shemecha | כִּי ki ר"ת יכש | לֹא lo | עָזַבְתָּ azavta | דֹרְשֶׁיךָ dorshecha

יְהֹוָה Adonai ס"ת כהת, משיוו בן דוד ע"ה : יְהֹוָה Adonai

אֲדֹנֵינוּ adonenu | מָה ma מ"ה | אַדִיר adir הרי | שִׁמְךָ shimcha | בְּכָל bechol

הָאָרֶץ ha'aretz אלהים דההן ע"ה : וְחִזְקוּ chizku | וְיַאֲמֵץ veya'ametz ב"ן, לכב ; ומב

לְבַבְכֶם levavchem | כָּל kol ילי | הַמְיַחֲלִים hameyachalim | לַיהֹוָה ladonai :

HALF KADDISH

יִתְגַּדַּל yitgadal | וְיִתְקַדַּשׁ veyitkadash עדי ומילוי עדי ; י"א אותיות כמנין ו"ה

שְׁמֵיהּ shemei (שם י"ה דע"ב) raba רַבָּא קנ"א ב"ן, יהוה אלהים יהוה אדני,

אָמֵן amen אידהנויה : בְּרָא vera בְּעָלְמָא be'alma מילוי קס"א וס"ג, מ"ה ברבוע וע"ב ע"ה ; ר"ת = ו"פ אלהים ; ס"ת = ג"פ יב"ק : דִּי di

כִּרְעוּתֵיהּ kir'utei

וְיַמְלִיךְ veyamlich | מַלְכוּתֵיהּ mal'chutei | וְיַצְמַח veyatzmach

פּוּרְקָנֵיהּ purkanei | וִיקָרֵב vikarev | מְשִׁיחֵיהּ meshichei : אָמֵן amen אידהנויה

"So that glory should make melodies to You and not be silent, Lord, my God, I shall forever thank You." (Psalms 30:13) "Lord desires righteousness: He makes the Torah great and powerful." (Isaiah 42:21) "And they shall place their trust in You, all those who know Your Name, for You have not abandoned those who seek You, Lord." (Psalms 9:11) "Lord, our Master, how mighty is Your Name throughout the world." (Psalms 8:2) Be strong and your hearts be courageous, all you, who place your hope in the Lord.

HALF KADDISH

May His great Name be more exalted and sanctified. (Amen)
In the world that He created according to His will, and may His kingdom reign.
And may He cause His redemption to sprout and may He bring the Mashiach closer. (Amen)

בְּחַיֵּיכוֹן bechayechon   וּבְיוֹמֵיכוֹן uvyomechon   וּבְחַיֵּי uvchayei

דְכָל dechol   יל״י   בֵּית bet   ב״פ ראה ב״פ   יִשְׂרָאֵל Yisrael   בַּעֲגָלָא ba'agala

וּבִזְמַן uvizman   קָרִיב kariv   וְאָמְרוּ ve'imru   אָמֵן amen: אָמֵן amen אידהנויה.

The congregation and the chazan say the following:

Twenty eight words (until be'alma) and twenty eight letters (until almaya)

יְהֵא yehe   שְׁמֵיהּ shemei (שֵׁם י״ה דס״ג)   רַבָּא raba   קנ״א ב״ז,

מְבָרַךְ mevarach,   ע״ה מ״ה ברבוע וע״ב קס״א מ״ה, מילוי אדני, יהוה אלהים יהוה

לְעָלַם le'alam   לְעָלְמֵי le'almei   עָלְמַיָּא almaya◆   יִתְבָּרֵךְ yitbarach◆

Seven words with six letters each (שֵׁם בֶּן מ״ב) and seven times the letter Vav (שֵׁם בֶּן מ״ב).

וְיִשְׁתַּבַּח veyishtabach   י״פ ע״ב יהוה אל אבג יתץ ◆

וְיִתְפָּאַר veyitpa'ar   הי גו יה קרע שטן ◆   וְיִתְרוֹמַם veyitromam   וה כוזו נגד יכש◆

וְיִתְנַשֵּׂא veyitnase   במוכסז בטר צתג ◆   וְיִתְהַדָּר veyit'hadar   כוזו יה וזקב טנע◆

וְיִתְעַלֶּה veyit'ale   וה יוד ה יגל פזק ◆   וְיִתְהַלָּל veyit'halal   א ואו הא עקו צית◆

שְׁמֵיהּ shemei (שֵׁם י״ה דמ״ה)   דְקוּדְשָׁא dekudsha   בְּרִיךְ verich   הוּא hu:

אָמֵן amen אידהנויה ◆

לְעֵלָּא le'ela   מִן min   כָּל kol   יל״י   בִּרְכָתָא birchata◆   שִׁירָתָא shirata◆

תֻּשְׁבְּחָתָא tishbechata   וְנֶחֱמָתָא venechamata◆   דַּאֲמִירָן da'amiran

בְּעָלְמָא be'alma   וְאָמְרוּ ve'imru   אָמֵן amen: אָמֵן amen אידהנויה.

On Shabbat we continue with "*Va'ani Tefilati*" on page 573.

On weekdays we continue with the *Amidah* on page 582.

In your lifetimes and in your days and in the lifetime of all the House of Israel, speedily and in the near future, and you shall say, Amen. (Amen) May His great Name be blessed forever and for all eternity. Blessed and lauded, and glorified, and exalted, and extolled, and honored, and uplifted, and praised be the Name of the Holy Blessed One (Amen) Above all blessings, songs, praises, and words of consolation that may be said in the world, and you shall say, Amen. (Amen)

VA'ANI TEFILATI

Va'ani Tefilati helps to remove all the judgment that will confront us in the coming week. While we recite *Va'ani Tefilati*, our intent and objective should be to convert all judgments headed our way into acts of mercy.

This verse should be said while standing even if there is no Torah scroll presents.

The *chazan* should put on a *Talit* before starting *Va'ani Tefilati* because this time is called "*Et Ratzon*" (time of satisfaction and acceptance) as the Light of *Mitzcha Dera'ava* (the Forehead of the desire) is revealed. Meditate on the letter **י** from **עקוצית** as *Zeir Anpin* is being elevated to the 500 *nimin* (cords) of *Dikna* of *Arich Anpin* (during the rest of the week - *Zeir Anpin* receives this illumination from a long distance), and He encloses these 500 *nimin* (represented by the Name: **יוד הי ויו הי**).

וְאֲנִי va'ani אני תְפִלָּתִי tefilati לְךָ lecha יְהוָֹה וֹאדני ואהדינהי Adonai

יוד הי ויו הי

Meditate to draw to *Zeir Anpin* the illumination of the 500 *nimin* of *Arich Anpin*.

עֵת et י״פ יהוה וי״פ אהיה מהש ע״ה, ע״ב בריבוע וקס״א ע״ה, אל שדי ע״ה רָצוֹן ratzon

Meditate to draw illumination from *Chesed* of *Atik Yomin* to the *Yesod* of *Atik Yomin* (which is enclosed by the Forehead of *Arich Anpin*), and to lower all the above mentioned illuminations to *Tiferet* of *Dikna* of *Arich Anpin*, which is the eighth *Mazal* ("*notzer chesed*" - *notzer* has the same letters as *ratzon*-desire), as this is where *Zeir Anpin* is going up in *Minchah* of *Shabbat*. Now, meditate to draw all the above mentioned illuminations to the Three Upper *Sefirot* of *Zeir Anpin* (which are in the place of *Keter, Chochmah, Binah, Da'at* of Supernal *Abba* and *Ima*). So first meditate to split and reveal the Three Upper *Sefirot* of Supernal *Abba* and *Ima* and only then to split the essence of the Three Upper *Sefirot* of *Zeir Anpin*, and by doing so, *Netzach, Hod, Yesod* of *Abba* and *Ima* (which are inside *Chochmah, Binah, Da'at* of *Zeir Anpin*, and where *Chochmah, Binah, Da'at* of *Beriah* were elevated) are split. **Then the *Mochin*** that used to be covered by *Netzach, Hod, Yesod* of Supernal *Abba* and *Ima* and inside the Forhead of *Zeir Anpin*, **are revealed** and They are illuminated in *Chochmah, Binah, Da'at* of the essence of *Zeir Anpin*. All the above processes sweeten the judgment that is revealed in the Forehead of *Zeir Anpin* and make it like *Mitzcha Dera'ava* - the Forehead of *Atik Yomin*.

Five Gevurot (Judgments)

אֶהְיֶה יְהוָה	אֶהְיֶה יְהוָה	אֶהְיֶה יְהוָה
	אֶהְיֶה יְהוָה	
אֶהְיֶה יְהוָה	אֶהְיֶה יְהוָה	אֶהְיֶה יְהוָה

Five Chasadim (Mercies)

אֶהְיֶה יְהוָה	אֶהְיֶה יְהוָה	אֶהְיֶה יְהוָה
	אֶהְיֶה יְהוָה	
אֶהְיֶה יְהוָה	אֶהְיֶה יְהוָה	אֶהְיֶה יְהוָה

אֱלֹהִים Elohim אהיה אדני ; ילה בְרָב־ berov וַחַסְדֶּךָ chasdecha

עֲנֵנִי aneni בֶּאֱמֶת be'emet אהיה פעמים אהיה, ז״פ ס״ג יִשְׁעֶךָ yishecha:

VA'ANI TEFILATI

"As for me, may my prayer to You, Lord, be a time of desire.
God, with the abundance of Your kindness, answer me with the truth of Your salvation." *(Psalms 69:14)*

Second time:

tefilati תְפִלָּתִי‎ אני va'ani וַאֲנִי

To connect *Malchut* to *Zeir Anpin*

Adonai יְהֹוָה(ואדני יאהדונהי) lecha לְךָ

Even though *Malchut* is not ascending to *Dikna* of *Arich Anpin*, you should meditate to draw the above mentioned illumination (*Mitzcha Dera'ava*) to *Malchut*. So now, meditate to draw illumination from *Chesed* of *Atik Yomin* to the *Yesod* of *Atik Yomin* and then to the Forehead of *Arich Anpin* and together with the illumination of the eighth *Mazal* to *Chochmah* and *Binah* of *Yaakov* and *Rachel*. Doing so causes Their *Mochin* (the following Names below, equal to the word "*et*" - 470) and the soul of *Nukva* (the four letters of the Name: יְהֹוָה‎ as follow) to be revealed (all together – the *Mochin* [470] and the soul [4] – equal *Da'at* – 474). And these *Mochin* are illuminating in the Forehead of *Yaakov* and *Rachel* and are sweetening the judgment in Their Forehead by the illumination of the Forehead of *Atik Yomin* (*Mitzcha Dera'ava*).

עֵת et י"פ יהוה וי"פ אהיה רָצוֹן ratzon מהטע ע"ה, ע"ב בריבוע וקס"א וקס"א ע"ה, אל שדי ע"ה

יְהֹוָה

י יה יהו יהוה

י יה יהו יהוה

יוד יוד הא יוד הא ואו יוד הא ואו הא

יוד יוד הה יוד הה וו יוד הה וו הה

יוד הה וו הה

chasdecha וְחַסְדֶּךָ berov בְּרֹב‎ ; ילה אהיה אדני Elohim אֱלֹהִים

yishecha יִשְׁעֶךָ‎ ס"ג ד"פ ,אהיה פעמים אהיה be'emet בֶּאֱמֶת aneni עֲנֵנִי

Meditate that now, during *Minchah* of *Shabbat* (after the repetition of *Musaf*), *Zeir* and *Nukva* are ascending to *Keter* of Supernal *Abba* and *Ima*. And *Beriah* ascended and enclosed the space of the essence of *Zeir Anpin*, to draw great Light to *Beriah* so we can receive the illumination of the *Torah*.

VA'ANI TEFILATI
"As for me, may my prayer to You, Lord, be a time of desire.
God, with the abundance of Your kindness, answer me with the truth of Your salvation." (Psalms 69:14)

OPENING OF THE ARK

Drawing the Light of Chochmah.

Rabbi Shimon bar Yochai says: "While the Ark is open, we should prepare ourselves with awe. Everyone should arouse an inner sense of wonder, as if we are actually standing on Mount Sinai, trembling as we behold the overwhelming expression of Light. Silent we stand, focused solely on the opportunity of hearing each sacred word of the scroll. When we take out the Torah in public to read, all the Gates of Mercy in Heaven are open, and we awaken a love from Above."

Moshe מֹשֶׁה vayomer וַיֹּאמֶר ha'aron הָאָרֹן binso'a בִּנְסֹעַ vay'hi וַיְהִי

(מקוה) קֹנ"א kuma קוּמָה ע"ה אלהים ד"פ אל עֹדי, וקס"א בריבוע ע"ב מהע,

veyanusu וְיָנֻסוּ oyvecha אֹיְבֶיךָ veyafutzu וְיָפֻצוּ Adonai יְהֹוָאדנִיאהדונהי

ki כִּי בֹ"ן מ"ה ס"ג mipanecha מִפָּנֶיךָ mesan'echa מְשַׂנְאֶיךָ

ראה udvar וּדְבַר torah תוֹרָה tetze תֵּצֵא קנאה הויות, ר יוסף, miTziyon מִצִיּוֹן

shenatan שֶׁנָּתַן baruch בָּרוּךְ mirushalaim מִירוּשָׁלָיִם: Adonai יְהֹוָאדנִיאהדונהי

bikdushato בִּקְדֻשָׁתוֹ◆ Yisrael יִשְׂרָאֵל le'amo לְעַמּוֹ torah תוֹרָה

BERICH SHEMEI

This section is taken directly from the *Zohar* and appears in its original Aramaic. The *Berich Shemei* works like a time machine that literally transports our soul to Mount Sinai, when Moses received the tablets. By revisiting the exact time and place of the revelation, we are able to draw down aspects of the original Light through the reading of the Torah. The *Berich Shemei* contains 130 words. Adam was separated from his wife, Eve, for 130 years during which time he sinned. Each word in the prayer helps to correct one of those years. Each of us was included in the soul of Adam. We are Adam. Adam is merely the code name of the unified soul that includes every human being who has and will ever walk this planet.

berich בְּרִיךְ alma עָלְמָא demarei דְּמָארֵי shemei שְׁמֵיהּ berich בְּרִיךְ

im עִם re'utach רְעוּתָךְ yehe יְהֵא ve'atrach וְאַתְרָךְ◆ kitrach כִּתְרָךְ

yeminach יְמִינָךְ ufurkan וּפוּרְקָן le'alam לְעָלַם◆ Yisrael יִשְׂרָאֵל amach עַמָּךְ

mikdashach מִקְדָּשָׁךְ◆ ראה ב"פ bevet בְּבֵית le'amach לְעַמָּךְ achzei אַחֲזֵי

OPENING OF THE ARK

"When the Ark traveled forward, Moses would say: Arise, Lord. Let Your enemies be scattered and let those who hate You flee before You." (Numbers 10:35) "Because out of Zion shall the Torah emerge, and the Word of the Lord from Jerusalem." (Isaiah 2:3) Blessed is He Who gave the Torah to His Nation, Israel, due to His Holiness.

BERICH SHEMEI

Blessed is the Name of the Master of the world. Blessed are Your Crown and Your Location. May Your desire be with Your Nation, Israel, forever. The redemption of Your Right may You show to Your Nation in Your Temple.

le'amtuye לְאַמְטוּיֵי lana לָנָא mituv מִטּוּב nehorach נְהוֹרָךְ ◆ulkabel וּלְקַבֵּל

tzelotana צְלוֹתָנָא berachamin בְּרַחֲמִין◆ yehe יְהֵא ra'ava רַעֲוָא

kodamach קֳדָמָךְ detorich דְּתוֹרִיךְ lan לַן chayin וַיִּין betivu בְּטִיבוּ◆

velehevei וְלֶהֱוֵי ana אֲנָא avdach עַבְדָּךְ פוי, אל ארני pekida פְּקִידָא

bego בְּגוֹ tzadikaya צַדִּיקַיָּא◆ lemircham לְמִרְחַם אברהם, וז"פ אל, רי"ו ול"ב נתיבות

yati יָתִי ulmintar וּלְמִנְטַר alai עֲלַי סשוות אותיות פשוטות עסמ"ב וט"ז אותיות פשוטות הוכמה, רמ"ח (אברים),

veyat וְיַת kal כָּל dili דִּלִי vedi וְדִי le'amach לְעַמָּךְ Yisrael יִשְׂרָאֵל◆

ant אַנְתְּ hu הוּא zan זָן נזר, מזבוח, אל יהוה lechola לְכֹלָא umfarnes וּמְפַרְנֵס

lechola לְכֹלָא◆ ant אַנְתְּ hu הוּא shalit שַׁלִּיט al עַל kola כֹּלָא◆ ant אַנְתְּ

hu הוּא deshalit דְּשַׁלִּיט al עַל malchaya מַלְכַיָּא umalchuta וּמַלְכוּתָא

dilach דִּילָךְ hee הִיא◆ ana אֲנָא avda עַבְדָּא dekudsha דְּקוּדְשָׁא

berich בְּרִיךְ hu הוּא desagidna דְּסַגִּידְנָא kame קַמֵּהּ umin וּמִן kame קַמֵּהּ

dikar דִּיקָר orayte אוֹרַיְתֵהּ bechol בְּכֹל lכבל idan עִידָן ve'idan וְעִידָן◆

la לָא al עַל enash אֱנָשׁ rachitzna רָחִיצְנָא◆ vela וְלָא al עַל

bar בַּר elahin אֱלָהִין samichna סָמִיכְנָא◆ ela אֶלָּא be'elaha בֵּאלָהָא

dishmaya דְּשְׁמַיָּא◆ dehu דְּהוּא elaha אֱלָהָא keshot קְשׁוֹט◆

ve'orayte וְאוֹרַיְתֵהּ keshot קְשׁוֹט unvi'ohi וּנְבִיאוֹהִי keshot קְשׁוֹט◆

umasgei וּמַסְגֵּי lemebad לְמֶעֱבַּד tavevan טַבְוָן ukshot וּקְשׁוֹט◆

bei בֵּיהּ ana אֲנָא rachitz רָחִיץ velishme וְלִשְׁמֵהּ yakira יַקִּירָא

kadisha קַדִּישָׁא ana אֲנָא emar אֲמַר tushbechan תֻּשְׁבְּחָן◆

May You fill us with the best of Your enlightenment, and may You receive our prayers with mercy. May it be pleasing before You to lengthen our lives with good. And I, Your servant, shall be remembered together with the righteous ones. Have mercy on me and protect me, and all that I have, and all that belongs to Your Nation, Israel. You are the One Who nourishes all and provides all with their livelihood. You are the One Who controls everything. You have control over kings, and their kingdoms are Yours. I am the servant of the Holy Blessed One, as I prostrate myself before Him and before the glory of His Torah, at each and every moment. I put not my trust in any man, and I have no faith in the sons of the gods. My trust and faith are only in the God in Heaven, Who is the true God; His Torah is true; His prophets are true; and He abundantly performs compassion and truth. In Him, I trust and I say praises to His Holy and precious Name.

yehe יְהֵא ra'ava רַעֲוָא kodamach קֳדָמָךְ detiftach דְּתִפְתַּח liba'i לִבָּאִי

be'oraytach בְּאוֹרַיְתָךְ (vetihav וְתֵיהַב) li לִי benin בְּנִין dichrin דְּכְרִין

de'avdin דְּעָבְדִין (re'utach רְעוּתָךְ) vetashlim וְתַשְׁלִים mish'alin מִשְׁאֲלִין

deliba'i דְּלִבָּאִי veliba וְלִבָּא dechol דְּכָל־ amach עַמָּךְ Yisrael יִשְׂרָאֵל

letav לְטָב ulchayin וּלְחַיִּין velishlam וְלִשְׁלָם amen אָמֵן

TAKING OUT THE TORAH FROM THE ARK

The Torah is taken out to give us all a chance to make a personal connection with it, either by kissing or touching it. Sometimes, people rush to make their connection, pushing, crowding, and shoving others aside as they try to touch the scroll. Spiritually, these actions reflect energy opposite to that of the Torah. The Torah connection is not just physical. Connections to the *Torah* are made by way of a spiritual state of mind, which includes tolerance and care for others. One cannot be in the right spiritual frame of mind if he is rude to another individual.

Before the Torah is carried to the bimah (podium), the chazan says:

gadelu גַּדְּלוּ ladonai לַיהֹוָה iti אִתִּי uneromema וּנְרוֹמְמָה

shemo שְׁמוֹ yachdav יַחְדָּו

Then the congregation says the following while the Torah is carried to the bimah:

lecha לְךָ Adonai יְהֹוָה hagedula הַגְּדֻלָּה vehagevura וְהַגְּבוּרָה

vehatiferet וְהַתִּפְאֶרֶת vehanetzach וְהַנֵּצַח vehahod וְהַהוֹד ki כִּי

chol כֹל bashamayim בַּשָּׁמַיִם uva'aretz וּבָאָרֶץ lecha לְךָ

Adonai יְהֹוָה hamamlacha הַמַּמְלָכָה vehamitnase וְהַמִּתְנַשֵּׂא

lechol לְכֹל lerosh לְרֹאשׁ romemu רוֹמְמוּ

Adonai יְהֹוָה Elohenu אֱלֹהֵינוּ vehishtachavu וְהִשְׁתַּחֲווּ

lahadom לַהֲדֹם raglav רַגְלָיו kadosh קָדוֹשׁ hu הוּא romemu רוֹמְמוּ

Adonai יְהֹוָה Elohenu אֱלֹהֵינוּ vehishtachavu וְהִשְׁתַּחֲווּ lehar לְהַר

kodsho קָדְשׁוֹ ki כִּי kadosh קָדוֹשׁ Adonai יְהֹוָה Elohenu אֱלֹהֵינוּ

May it be pleasing before You that You shall open my heart with Your Torah (and that You may give me male sons, who shall fulfill Your desire). And may You fulfill the requests of my heart and the heart of Your entire Nation, Israel, for good, for life, and for peace. Amen.

TAKING OUT THE TORAH FROM THE ARK

"Proclaim the Lord's greatness with me and let us exalt His Name together." (Psalms 34:4) "Yours, Lord, is the greatness, the strength, the splendor, the triumph, and the glory, and everything in the Heavens and the earth. Yours, Lord, is the Kingdom and the sovereignty over every leader." (I Chronicles 29:11) "Exalt the Lord, our God, and prostrate yourselves at His Footstool, is Holy. Exalt the Lord, our God, and prostrate yourselves at His Holy Mountain because the Lord, our God, is Holy." (Psalms 99:9)

Some add this section:

biltecha בִּלְתֶּךָ en אֵין ki כִּי kadonai כַּיהֹוָאדֹנָיאהדונהי kadosh קָדוֹשׁ en אֵין

ילי mi מִי ki כִּי ילה: kelohenu כֵּאלֹהֵינוּ אלהים דההין ע"ה tzur צוּר ve'en וְאֵין

tzur צוּר ילי umi וּמִי Adonai יְהֹוָאדֹנָיאהדונהי mibal'adei מִבַּלְעֲדֵי מ"ב Eloha אֱלוֹהַּ

lanu לָנוּ tziva צִוָּה torah תּוֹרָה ילה: Elohenu אֱלֹהֵינוּ zulati זוּלָתִי אלהים דההין ע"ה

etz עֵץ: Yaakov יַעֲקֹב ו' הויות, יאהדונהי אידהנויה: kehilat קְהִלַּת morasha מוֹרָשָׁה

אלהים, אהיה אדני ע"ב בריבוע וקס"א, אל עדיי, ד"פ אלהים ע"ה Moshe מֹשֶׁה מהטע,

chayim וְחַיִּים אהיה אהיה יהוה, בינה ע"ה hee הִיא ר"ת לההו lamachazikim לַמַּחֲזִיקִים

ba בָּה vetomcheha וְתֹמְכֶיהָ me'ushar מְאֻשָּׁר: deracheha דְּרָכֶיהָ

darchei דַרְכֵי no'am נֹעַם vechol וְכָל־ ילי netivoteha נְתִיבוֹתֶיהָ shalom שָׁלוֹם:

shalom שָׁלוֹם rav רָב le'ohavei לְאֹהֲבֵי toratecha תוֹרָתֶךָ ve'en וְאֵין lamo לָמוֹ

michshol מִכְשׁוֹל: Adonai יְהֹוָאדֹנָיאהדונהי oz עֹז le'amo לְעַמּוֹ yiten יִתֵּן

(המלכים שמתו) יְהֹוָאדֹנָיאהדונהי Adonai yevarech יְבָרֵךְ (למתק את ז' הברכה עסמ"ב,

et אֶת־ amo עַמּוֹ vashalom בְשָׁלוֹם ר"ת ע"ב, ריבוע יהוה:

ki כִּי shem שֵׁם יְהֹוָאדֹנָיאהדונהי Adonai ekra אֶקְרָא havu הָבוּ אוזר, אהבה, דאגה

oz עֹז tenu תְּנוּ ילי hakol הַכֹּל ילה: lelohenu לֵאלֹהֵינוּ godel גֹּדֶל לֵאלֹהִים

latorah לַתּוֹרָה: chavod כָּבוֹד utnu וּתְנוּ ; ילה אהיה אדני lelohim

RAISING THE TORAH

After the scroll is placed on the *bimah* (the podium), a person is called up to raise the Torah for the congregation to see the specific section we will be reading from the Torah Scroll. As we raise the Torah, we meditate to also raise our level of consciousness. We should look at the parchment to try to see the first letter of that week's reading. We should also attempt to find the first letter of our Hebrew name within the text. You can use the *Talit* to help yourself focus (if you don't have a *Talit* you can use your finger).

"There is none as Holy as the Lord, because there is none other beside You. There is no Rock like our God." (1 Samuel 2:2) "For Who is God beside the Lord? Who is a Rock, other than our God?" (Psalms 18:32) "The Torah that Moses commanded us with is a heritage for the congregation of Jacob." (Deuteronomy 33:4) "It is a tree of life to those who hold on to it, and those who support it are happy." (Proverb 3:18) "Its ways are the way of pleasantness and all its paths lead to peace." (Proverbs 3:17) "Abundance of peace for those who love Your Torah and for them there is no obstacle." (Psalms 119:165) "The Lord give might to his people, The Lord will bless his nation with peace." (Psalms 29:11) "When I call out the Name of the Lord, proclaim greatness to our God." (Dutoronomy 32:3) "All should attribute power to God and give honor to the Torah." (Psalms 68:35)

Moshe מֹשֶׁה sam שָׂם asher אֲשֶׁר hatorah הַתּוֹרָה vezot וְזֹאת

Yisrael יִשְׂרָאֵל: benei בְּנֵי lifnei לִפְנֵי מהע, ע"ב בריבוע וקס"א, אל עדי, ד"פ אלהים ע"ה

אֵל El יא"י (מילוי דס"ג) עֲדַּי Shadai אל עדי = מֹשֶׁה, מהע, ע"ב בריבוע וקס"א, ד"פ אלהים ע"ה

אֱמֶת emet אהיה פעמים אהיה, ז"פ ס"ג וּמֹשֶׁה uMoshe מהע, ע"ב בריבוע וקס"א, אל עדי,

vetorato וְתוֹרָתוֹ ד"פ ס"ג אלהים ע"ה אֱמֶת emet אהיה פעמים אהיה, ז"פ ס"ג

אֱמֶת emet אהיה פעמים אהיה, ז"פ ס"ג:ג torah תּוֹרָה tziva צִוָּה

לָנוּ lanu אלהים, אהיה אדני אהיה, מהע, ע"ב בריבוע וקס"א, אל עדי, ד"פ אלהים ע"ה Moshe מֹשֶׁה

מוֹרָשָׁה morasha kehilat קְהִלַּת Yaakov יַעֲקֹב הויות, יאהדונהי אידהנויה:

haEl הָאֵל יא"י (מילוי דס"ג) tamim תָּמִים darko דַּרְכּוֹ imrat אִמְרַת

יְהוָֹ Adonai יאהדונהי אדני (יא"י מילוי דס"ג) tzerufa צְרוּפָה magen מָגֵן ג"פ אל

hu הוּא מיכאל גבריאל נוריאל ארדי lechol לְכֹל hachosim הַחוֹסִים bo בּוֹ:

THE READING

To maximize the power of the connection, we must think to share all the energy we're receiving with everyone else. We should become channels for sharing spiritual Light. If we think only about ourselves, it is like blowing a fuse. No current will flow, even though the plug is connected into the socket. When you are called up (the *ole*) to recite the blessing before the Torah reading, you must visually connect with the letters of the Torah to ignite the power of his words. A blessing is recited before and after each of the readings. The first blessing is equivalent to plugging a wire (our soul) into a wall socket (the Torah). The last blessing draws the spiritual current to us to bring the Light into our lives.

Meditation for the people that go to the *Torah* during *Minchah*

The above mentioned Three Upper *Sefirot* (*Chochmah, Binah, Da'at* of *Zeir Anpin*) are now revealing the illumination of Supernal *Abba* inside Them and this illumination (*Yesod* of *Abba*) is going out. The three people that go up to the *Torah* during *Minchah* are: The first corresponds to *Chochmah*, the second corresponds to *Binah* and the third corresponds to *Da'at* (and as the sixth *Aliya* of *Shabbat* morning *Torah* reading is more significant because it is the aspect of *Yesod*, you should try to get the third *Aliya* of *Minchah*, which corresponds to *Da'at*, and is also for the correction of the *Yesod*.)

We call three people to the Torah and we read the portion of "*Vezot haberacha*" on pages 746-747, from"*vezot*"until "*alfei menashe*". The blessings for the Torah can be found on pages 499-500.

RAISING THE TORAH

"And this is the Torah that Moses placed before the children of Israel." (Deuteronomy 4:44)
God is true and Moses is true and His Torah is true. "The Torah, which Moses commanded us with, is a heritage for the Congregation of Jacob." (Deuteronomy 33:4) "God, His ways are perfect.
Lord's statement is pure. He is the Shield for all who take refuge in Him" (II Samuel 22:31)

RETURNING THE TORAH TO THE ARK

Before the Torah is carried back to the ark, the *chazan* says:

nisgav נִשְׂגָּב ki כִּי Adonai יְהֹוָה shem שֵׁם et אֶת־ yehalelu יְהַלְלוּ

levado לְבַדּוֹ shemo שְׁמוֹ

Then the congregation says while carrrying the Torah back to the Ark:

veshamayim וְשָׁמָיִם eretz אֶרֶץ al עַל־ hodo הוֹדוֹ

Yisrael יִשְׂרָאֵל livnei לִבְנֵי chasidav וְלַחֲסִידָיו lechol לְכָל־ tehila תְּהִלָּה le'amo לְעַמּוֹ keren קֶרֶן vayarem וַיָּרֶם

haleluya הַלְלוּיָהּ kerovo קְרֹבוֹ am עַם־

Then the *chazan* says:

haElohim הָאֱלֹהִים hu הוּא Adonai יְהֹוָה

haElohim הָאֱלֹהִים hu הוּא Adonai יְהֹוָה

ve'al וְעַל־ mima'al מִמַּעַל bashamayim בַּשָּׁמַיִם

od עוֹד en אֵין mitachat מִתָּחַת ha'aretz הָאָרֶץ

en אֵין Adonai אֲדֹנָי vaElohim בֵּאלֹהִים kamocha כָּמוֹךָ

shuva שׁוּבָה yomar יֹאמַר uvnucho וּבְנֻחֹה kema'asecha כְּמַעֲשֶׂיךָ ve'en וְאֵין

Yisrael יִשְׂרָאֵל alfei אַלְפֵי rivevot רִבְבוֹת Adonai יְהֹוָה hashivenu הֲשִׁיבֵנוּ

venashuva וְנָשׁוּבָה elecha אֵלֶיךָ | Adonai יְהֹוָה

kekedem כְּקֶדֶם yamenu יָמֵינוּ chadesh וְחַדֵּשׁ

RETURNING THE TORAH TO THE ARK

"Praised be the Name of the Lord, His Name alone is exalted His glory on Heaven and Earth. He raised funds to his nation, praise to his Chassidim, people of Israel his close nation, praise the Lord." (Psalms 148:13-14) "The Lord is the God! The Lord is the God! In the Heavens above and on the Earth below, there is no other." (Deuteronomy 4:39) "There is none like You among the gods, Lord, and there is nothing like Your handiwork." (Psalms 86:8) "And when the Ark rested, Moses would say, Return, Lord, to the tens of thousands of Israel." (Numbers 10:36) "Bring us back, Lord, and we shall return. Renew our days as of old." (Lamentataion 5:21)

ר"ת הפסוק = נפעל רווח נעלמה וזיו יוזידה ע"ה

ס"ג מ"ב ב"ן lefanecha לְפָנֶיךָ י"א פעמים אדני ketoret קְטֹרֶת tefilati תְפִלָּתִי tikon תִּכּוֹן

hakshiva הַקְשִׁיבָה arev עָרֶב minchat מִנְחַת kapai כַּפַּי mas'at מַשְׂאַת

יכה ; דמ"ב ע"ב, מילוי לכב ; velohai וֵאלֹהַי malki מַלְכִּי shave'i שַׁוְעִי lekol לְקוֹל

etpalal אֶתְפַּלָּל elecha אֵלֶיךָ ki כִּי

HALF KADDISH

י"א אותיות כמנין ו"ה ; עדי ומילוי עדי veyitkadash וְיִתְקַדַּשׁ yitgadal יִתְגַּדַּל

קנ"א ב"ן, יהוה אלהים יהוה אדני, raba רַבָּא (שם י"ה דע"ב) shemei שְׁמֵהּ

אידהנויה amen אָמֵן ; ג"פ יב"ק = ו"פ אלהים ; ס"ת = ר"ת ברבוע וע"ב ע"ה ; מ"ה וס"ג, מילוי קס"א

kir'utei כִרְעוּתֵיה vera בְרָא di דִי be'alma בְּעָלְמָא

veyatzmach וְיַצְמַח malchutei מַלְכוּתֵיה veyamlich וְיַמְלִיךְ

אידהנויה amen אָמֵן meshichei מְשִׁיחֵיה vikarev וִיקָרֵב purkanei פּוּרְקָנֵיה

uvchayei וּבְחַיֵּי uvyomechon וּבְיוֹמֵיכוֹן bechayechon בְּחַיֵּיכוֹן

ba'agala בַּעֲגָלָא Yisrael יִשְׂרָאֵל ב"פ ראה bet בֵּית יל dechol דְכָל

אידהנויה amen אָמֵן amen אָמֵן ve'imru וְאִמְרוּ kariv קָרִיב uvizman וּבִזְמַן

The congregation and the *chazan* say the following:

Twenty eight words (until *be'alma*) and twenty eight letters (until *almaya*)

קנ"א ב"ן, raba רַבָּא (שם י"ה דס"ג) shemei שְׁמֵיה yehe יְהֵא

mevarach מְבָרַךְ יהוה אלהים יהוה אדני, מילוי קס"א מ"ה וס"ג, ברבוע וע"ב ע"ה

yitbarach יִתְבָּרַךְ almaya עָלְמַיָא le'almei לְעָלְמֵי le'alam לְעָלַם

"Let my prayer be set before You, as the incense offering; the lifting up of my hand, as the afternoon meal offering." (Psalms 141:2) "Listen to the sound of my outcry, my King, My God for it is to You I am praying." (Psalms 5:3)

HALF KADDISH

May His great Name be more exalted and sanctified. (Amen)
In the world that He created according to His will, and may His kingdom reign. And may He cause His redemption to sprout and may He bring the Mashiach closer. (Amen) In your lifetimes and in your days and in the lifetime of all the House of Israel, speedily and in the near future, and you should say, Amen. (Amen) May His great Name be blessed forever and for all eternity blessed

Seven words with six letters each (שם בן מ"ב) and seven times the letter *Vav* (שם בן מ"ב)

וְיִשְׁתַּבַּח veyishtabach י"פ ע"ב יהוה אל אבג יתץ

וְיִתְפָּאַר veyitpa'ar הי גו יה קרע שטן וְיִתְרֹמַם veyitromam וה כווו נגד יכש

וְיִתְנַשֵּׂא veyitnase במוכסו בטר צתג וְיִתְהַדָּר veyit'hadar כווו יה וזקב טנע

וְיִתְעַלֶּה veyit'ale וה יוד ה יגל פזק וְיִתְהַלָּל veyit'halal א ואו הא שקו צית

שְׁמֵיהּ shemei (שם י"ה דמ"ה) דְּקֻדְשָׁא dekudsha בְּרִיךְ verich הוּא hu

אָמֵן amen אידהנויה

לְעֵלָּא le'ela מִן min כָּל kol יל birchata בִּרְכָתָא shirata שִׁירָתָא

תֻּשְׁבְּחָתָא tishbechata וְנֶחָמָתָא venechamata דַּאֲמִירָן da'amiran

בְּעָלְמָא be'alma וְאִמְרוּ ve'imru אָמֵן amen אָמֵן amen אידהנויה

THE AMIDAH

When we begin the connection, we take three steps backward, signifying our leaving this physical world. Then we take three steps forward to begin the *Amidah*. The three steps are:

1. Stepping into the land of Israel – to enter the first spiritual circle.
2. Stepping into the city of Jerusalem – to enter the second spiritual circle.
3. Stepping inside the Holy of Holies – to enter the innermost circle.

Before we recite the first verse of the *Amidah*, we ask: "*God, open my lips and let my mouth speak,*" thereby asking the Light to speak for us so that we can receive what we need and not just what we want. All too often, what we want from life is not necessarily the desire of the soul, which is what we actually need to fulfill us. By asking the Light to speak through us, we ensure that our connection will bring us genuine fulfillment and opportunities for spiritual growth and change.

and lauded, and glorified and exalted, And extolled
and honored, and uplifted and praised, be the Name of the Holy Blessed One. (Amen) Above all blessings,
songs, praises, and words of consolation that may be said in the world, and you shall say, Amen. (Amen)

The Format of the Ascension in *Minchah* of *Shabbat*

In the silent *Amidah,* *Zeir Anpin* (which means *Yisrael* and *Leah*), elevates to *Netzach, Hod, Yesod* of *Dikna* in its three *tikkunim* (corrections -which are the thirteenth *tikkun*, twelfth *tikkun* and eleventh *tikkun*), which means that the five *Tzelamim* of *Netzach, Hod, Yesod* of *Dikna* (which is the letter צ of the *Tzelem*), expand in the five *Partzufim* of *Netzach, Hod, Yesod* of *Keter* of *Zeir Anpin* (and it is called *Nefesh, Ruach, Neshamah, Chayah, Yachidah* of *Nefesh* of *Yechidah*) **So now,** *Keter, Chochmah, Binah* of *Zeir Anpin* are elevated to *Netzach, Hod, Yesod* of *Dikna*, and *Chesed, Gevurah, Tiferet* of *Zeir Anpin* are elevated to *Keter, Chochmah, Binah* of Supernal *Abba* and *Ima* and *Netzach, Hod, Yesod* of *Zeir Anpin* are elevated to *Chesed, Gevurah, Tiferet* of Supernal *Abba* and *Ima*. And *Yaakov* and *Rachel* (which are standing in *Netzach, Hod, Yesod* of *Chochmah* of *Zeir Anpin*, which means *Netzach, Hod, Yesod* of Supernal *Abba* and *Ima*) are elevated to *Chesed, Gevurah, Tiferet* of *Chochmah* of *Zeir Anpin* (which means to *Chesed, Gevurah, Tiferet* of Supernal *Abba* and *Ima*, and where *Netzach, Hod, Yesod* of *Zeir Anpin* are elevated now in *Minchah*). And *Netzach, Hod, Yesod* of *Zeir Anpin* become *Mochin* for *Chochmah, Binah, Da'at* of *Yaakov* and *Rachel*.

In the repetition, *Zeir Anpin* (which means *Yisrael* and *Leah*), elevates to *Chesed, Gevurah, Tiferet* of *Dikna* in its three *tikkunim* (corrections -which are the tenth *tikkun*, ninth *tikkun* and eighth *tikkun*), which means that the five *Tzelamim* of *Chesed, Gevurah, Tiferet* of *Dikna* of *Arich Anpin* (which is the letter ל of the *Tzelem*), expand in the five *Partzufim* of *Chesed, Gevurah, Tiferet* of *Keter* of *Zeir Anpin* (and it is called *Nefesh, Ruach, Neshamah, Chayah, Yachidah* of *Ruach* of *Yechidah*) **So now,** *Keter, Chochmah, Binah* of *Zeir Anpin* are elevated to *Chesed, Gevurah, Tiferet* of *Dikna*, and *Chesed, Gevurah, Tiferet* of *Zeir Anpin* are elevated to *Netzach, Hod, Yesod* of *Dikna*, and *Netzach, Hod, Yesod* of *Zeir Anpin* are elevated to *Chochmah, Binah, Da'at* of Supernal *Abba* and *Ima*. And *Yaakov* and *Rachel* (which are standing in *Chesed, Gevurah, Tiferet* of *Chochmah* of *Zeir Anpin*, which means *Chesed, Gevurah, Tiferet* of Supernal *Abba* and *Ima*) are elevated to *Keter, Chochmah, Binah* of *Chochmah* of *Zeir Anpin* (which means to *Keter, Chochmah, Binah* of Supernal *Abba* and *Ima*, and where *Netzach, Hod, Yesod* of *Zeir Anpin* are elevated now in the repetition of *Minchah*). And *Netzach, Hod, Yesod* of *Zeir Anpin* become *Mochin* for *Chochmah, Binah, Da'at* of *Yaakov* and *Rachel*.

On *Shabbat Chol Hamo'ed* continue with the *Amidah* on page 716.

yagid יַגִּיד ufi וּפִי tiftach תִּפְתָּח sefatai שְׂפָתַי (pause here) לכה Adonai אֲדֹנָי

יי (כ"ב אותיות פשוטות [=אכא] וה' אותיות סופיות סֹזֹוֹרֹף) ס"ת = בוכו: tehilatecha תְּהִלָּתֶךָ

THE FIRST BLESSING - INVOKES THE SHIELD OF ABRAHAM.

Abraham is the channel of the Right Column energy of positivity, sharing, and Mercy. Sharing actions can protect us from all forms of negativity.

Chesed that becomes Chochmah

In this section there are 42 words, the secret of the 42-Letter Name of God and therefore it begins with the letter *Bet* (2) and ends with the letter *Mem* (40).

Bend your knees at "*baruch*," bow at "*Ata*" and straighten up at "*Adonai*."

א   ב

(אותיות הא"ב המסמלות את השפע המגיע) לה' המלכות א-ת Ata אַתָּה baruch בָּרוּךְ

Adonai יהוהיאדנייאהדונהי Elohenu אֱלֹהֵינוּ (י"א) ילה

velohei לכב ; מילוי ע"ב, דמב ; ילה avotenu אֲבוֹתֵינוּ

Elohei מילוי ע"ב, דמב ; ילה (Chochmah) Avraham אַבְרָהָם אֱלֹהֵי

אותיות פשוטות וט"ז (אברים) עסמ"ב רמ"ח, החכמה, נתיבות ול"ב רי"ו אל, וז"ף

Elohei מילוי ע"ב, דמב ; ילה (Binah) Yitzchak יִצְחָק אֱלֹהֵי ד"פ ב"ן

velohei לכב ; מילוי ע"ב, דמב ; ילה (Da'at) Yaakov יַעֲקֹב וֶאֱלֹהֵי ו' הויות, יאהדונהי אידהנויה

THE AMIDAH

"My Lord, open my lips, and my mouth shall relate Your praise." (Psalms 51:17)

THE FIRST BLESSING

Blessed are You, Lord,
our God and God of our forefathers: the God of Abraham, the God of Isaac, and the God of Jacob.

לאה ; יא"י (מילוי דס"ג) hagadol הַגָּדוֹל הָאֵל הַגָּדוֹל = סיט ; גָּדוֹל = להו haEl הָאֵל

עם ד' אותיות = מבה, יזל, אום ר"ת ההה hagibor הַגִּבּוֹר vehanora וְהַנּוֹרָא◆

יא"י (מילוי דס"ג) ; ר"ת ע"ב, ריבוע יהוה El אֵל elyon עֶלְיוֹן◆

יל hakol הַכֹּל kone קוֹנֵה tovim◆ טוֹבִים chasadim וַחֲסָדִים gomel גוֹמֵל

umevi וּמֵבִיא avot◆ אָבוֹת chasdei וְחַסְדֵּי vezocher וְזוֹכֵר

lema'an לְמַעַן venehem בְּנֵיהֶם livnei לִבְנֵי go'el גּוֹאֵל

שְׁמוֹ shemo מהש ע"ה, ע"ב בריבוע וקס"א ע"ה, אל שדי ע"ה be'ahava בְּאַהֲבָה אוזר, דאגה:

When saying the word "be'ahava" you should meditate to devote your soul to sanctify the Holy Name and accept upon yourself the four forms of death.

umagen וּמָגֵן umoshi'a וּמוֹשִׁיעַ ozer עוֹזֵר melech מֶלֶךְ

ג"פ אל (יא"י מילוי דס"ג) ; ר"ת מיכאל גבריאל גוריאל:

Bend your knees at "baruch," bow at "Ata" and straighten up at "Adonai."

(on Shabbat: יְהֹוָה) אהיה יהו אלף הי יוד הי

(הד) Adonai יְהֹוָה(יְהֹוִאדִיל)יאהדונהי Ata אַתָּה baruch בָּרוּךְ

Avraham אַבְרָהָם ג"פ אל (יא"י מילוי דס"ג) ; ר"ת מיכאל גבריאל גוריאל magen מָגֵן

וז"פ אל, רי"ו ול"ב נתיבות החכמה, רמ"ח (אברים), עסמ"ב וט"ז אותיות פשוטות:

The great, mighty and Awesome God.
The Supernal God, Who bestows beneficial kindness and creates everything.
Who recalls the kindness of the forefathers and brings a Redeemer to their descendants for the sake of His Name, lovingly. King, Helper, Savior and Shield. Blessed are You, Lord, the shield of Abraham.

THE SECOND BLESSING

THE ENERGY OF ISAAC IGNITES THE POWER FOR THE RESURRECTION OF THE DEAD.

Whereas Abraham represents the power of sharing, Isaac represents the Left Column energy of Judgment. Judgment shortens the *tikkun* process and paves the way for our eventual resurrection.

Gevurah that becomes *Binah*.

In this section there are 49 words corresponding to the 49 Gates of the Pure System in *Binah*.

ללה Adonai אֲדֹנָי ר"ג וי' אותיות דס"ג ריבוע ס"ג le'olam לְעוֹלָם gibor גִּבּוֹר Ata אַתָּה

(ר"ת אַגְלָא והוא שם גדול ואמיץ, ובו היה יהודה מתגבר על אויביו. ע"ה אלד, בוכו.)

lehoshi'a לְהוֹשִׁיעַ rav רַב Ata אַתָּה metim מֵתִים ס"ג mechaye מְחַיֵּה

Only on *Simchat Torah*:   **During *Sukkot*:**

haru'ach הָרוּחַ ר"ת מ"ה mashiv מַשִּׁיב   hatal הַטָּל   morid מוֹרִיד

hageshem הַגֶּשֶׁם umorid וּמוֹרִיד   יוד הא ואו, כוזו, מספר אותיות דמילואי עסמ"ב ;

עסביל [י"ש (= י"פ אל) ול"ב נתיבות החוכמה] ע"ה:

ר"ת מ"ה (יוד הא או הא):

If you mistakenly say "*morid hatal*," and realize this before the end of the blessing "*baruch Ata Adonai*," you should return to the beginning of the blessing "*Ata gibor*" and continue as usual. But if you only realize this after the end of the blessing, you should continue and not go back.

If you mistakenly say "*Mashiv haru'ach*," and realize this before the end of the blessing "*baruch Ata Adonai*," you should return to the beginning of the blessing "*Ata gibor*" and continue as usual. But if you only realize this after the end of the blessing, you should start the *Amidah* from the beginning.

bechesed בְּחֶסֶד מ"ה ע"ה בינה, אהיה יהוה, אהיה chayim וְחַיִּים mechalkel מְכַלְכֵּל

berachamim בְּרַחֲמִים metim מֵתִים ס"ג mechaye מְחַיֵּה יהוה. ריבוע ע"ב,

somech סוֹמֵךְ (טלא דעתיק). rabim רַבִּים י"פ יי' ההין, אלהים מצפצ, (במוכסז)

cholim וְחוֹלִים verofe וְרוֹפֵא (וו"ן). noflim נוֹפְלִים כוק, ריבוע אדני (אכדטם)

umekayem וּמְקַיֵּם asurim אֲסוּרִים umatir וּמַתִּיר אותיות. וד מ"ה = וזולה

chamocha כָּמוֹךָ ילי mi מִי afar עָפָר lishenei לִישֵׁנֵי emunato אֱמוּנָתוֹ

gevurot גְּבוּרוֹת ba'al בַּעַל (you should enunciate the letter *Ayin* in the word "*ba'al*")

memit מֵמִית melech מֶלֶךְ lach לָךְ dome דּוֹמֶה ילי umi וּמִי

yeshu'a יְשׁוּעָה umatzmi'ach וּמַצְמִיחַ (יוד הי ואו הי) ס"ג umchaye וּמְחַיֵּה

THE SECOND BLESSING

You are mighty forever, Lord. You resurrect the dead and are very capable of redeeming.

Only on *Simchat Torah*:   **During *Sukkot*:**

Who causes wind to blow and rain to fall.   *Who causes dew to fall.*

You sustain life with kindness and resurrect the dead with great compassion. You support those who have fallen, heal the sick, release the imprisoned, and fulfill Your faithful words to those who are asleep in the dust. Who is like You, Master of might, and Who can compare to You, King, Who causes death, Who gives life, and Who sprouts salvation?

vene'eman וְנֶאֱמָן Ata אַתָּה lehachayot לְהַחֲיוֹת מֵתִים metim:

(on Shabbat אֱלֹהֵ יְהוֹ אֶלֶף הִי יוֹד הִי) יֱהוָה:

baruch בָּרוּךְ Ata אַתָּה יֱהוָֹה(יֱהֹוִה)(יֱהוֹה)יאהדונהי Adonai

mechaye מְחַיֵּה ס"ג (יוֹד הִי וָאו הִי) הַמֵּתִים hametim ר"ת מ"ה וס"ת מו"ה:

NAKDISHACH – THE KEDUSHA

The congregation recites this prayer together.

Saying the *Kedusha* (Holiness) we meditate to bring the holiness of the Creator among us. As it says: *"Venikdashti betoch Benei Israel"* (God is hallowed among the children of Israel).

nakdishach נַקְדִּישָׁךְ וְנַעֲרִיצָךְ vena'aritzach.

keno'am כְּנֹעַם si'ach שִׂיחַ מיכ, י"פ האא sod סוֹד שַׂרְפֵי sarfei

kodesh קֹדֶשׁ hameshaleshim הַמְשַׁלְּשִׁים lecha לְךָ קְדֻשָּׁה kedusha.

vechen וְכֵן katuv כָּתוּב al עַל yad יָד nevi'ach נְבִיאָךְ. vekara וְקָרָא

ze זֶה el אֶל ze זֶה י"ב פרקין דיעקב מאירים לי"ב פרקין דרחל ve'amar וְאָמַר:

kadosh קָדוֹשׁ | kadosh קָדוֹשׁ kadosh קָדוֹשׁ (סוֹד ג' רישין דעתיקא קדישא)

Adonai יֱהוָֹהאהדונהי Tzeva'ot צְבָאוֹת פני שכינה melo מְלֹא chol כָּל יל: kevodo כְּבוֹדוֹ ע"ה דההן אלהים ha'aretz הָאָרֶץ

le'umatam לְעֻמָּתָם meshabechim מְשַׁבְּחִים ve'omrim וְאוֹמְרִים:

(או"א) בָּרוּךְ baruch kevod כְּבוֹד יֱהוָֹהאהדונהי Adonai ; כבוד ה' = יוד הי ואו הה

mimekomo מִמְּקוֹמוֹ עסמ"ב, הברכה (למתק את ז' המלכים שמתו) ;ר"ת ע"ב, ריבוע יהוה; ר"ת מיכ:

uvdivrei וּבְדִבְרֵי kodshach קָדְשָׁךְ katuv כָּתוּב lemor לֵאמֹר:

(זו"ן) יִמְלֹךְ yimloch קָדִישׁ בָּרוּךְ ר"ת יב"ק, אלהים יהוה, אהיה אדני יהוה

Adonai יֱהוָֹהאהדונהי le'olam לְעוֹלָם ריבוע ס"ג וי' אותיות דס"ג Elohayich אֱלֹהַיִךְ ילה:

Tziyon צִיּוֹן יוסף, ו' היוות, קנאה ledor לְדֹר vador וָדֹר רי"ו; ר"ת אצלו (מלכות אצל ז"א – ו)

haleluya הַלְלוּיָהּ אלהים, אהיה אדני ; ללה:

And You are faithful to resurrecting the dead. Blessed are You, Lord, Who resurrects the dead.

NAKDISHACH

We sanctify You and we revere You, according to the pleasant words of the counsel of the Holy Angels, who recite Holy before You three times, as it is written by Your Prophet: "And each called to the other and said: Holy, Holy, Holy, Is the Lord of Hosts, the entire world is filled with His glory." (Isaiah 6:3) Facing them they give praise and say: "Blessed is the glory of the Lord from His Place." (Ezekiel 3:12) And in Your Holy Words, it is written as follows: "The Lord, your God, shall reign forever, for each and for every generation. Zion, Praise the Lord!" (Psalms 146:10)

THE THIRD BLESSING

This blessing connects us to Jacob, the Central Column and the power of restriction. Jacob is our channel for connecting Mercy with Judgment. By restricting our reactive behavior, we are blocking our Desire to Receive for the Self Alone. Jacob also gives us the power to balance our acts of Mercy and Judgment toward other people in our lives.

Tiferet **that becomes** *Da'at* (14 words).

אֵין סוֹף ‏, רז ‏, ר"ת = אוֹר kadosh קָדוֹשׁ veshimcha וְשִׁמְךָ kadosh קָדוֹשׁ Ata אַתָּה

אֵל יְהֹוָה ‏, זָ ‏, מזבח ‏, נגד ‏, ע"ה yom יוֹם לכב ‏, ב"ן bechol בְּכָל ukdoshim וּקְדוֹשִׁים

sela סֶלָה yehalelucha יְהַלְלוּךָ

(*on Shabbat*) מצפצ: אהלה יהו אלף הא יוד הא

Adonai יאהדונהי(יְהֹוִה)(אֲדֹנָי)יְהֹוָה Ata אַתָּה baruch בָּרוּךְ

(יוֹד הא ואו הא) י"פ מ"ה hakadosh הַקָּדוֹשׁ (מילוי דס"ג) יי"א"י ‏; לאה haEl הָאֵל

Meditate here on the Name: **יאהדונהי**, as it can help to remove anger.

THE MIDDLE BLESSING

The middle blessing connects us to the true power of *Sukkot* and *Simchat Torah*. *Sukkot* and *Simchat Torah* are the seed of the entire year for Mercy and Happiness. Just as an apple seed begets an apple tree, a negative seed begets a negative year. Likewise, a positive seed generates a positive year. *Sukkot* and *Simchat Torah* are our opportunity to choose the seed we wish to plant for our coming year. The power of the letters in this Fourth Blessing is in their ability to automatically choose the correct seed we need and not necessarily the seed we want.

ha'amim הָעַמִּים יל"י mikol מִכָּל vechartanu בְחַרְתָּנוּ Ata אַתָּה

banu בָּנוּ veratzita וְרָצִיתָ otanu אוֹתָנוּ ahavta אָהַבְתָּ

haleshonot הַלְּשׁוֹנוֹת יל"י mikol מִכָּל veromamtanu וְרוֹמַמְתָּנוּ

vekeravtanu וְקֵרַבְתָּנוּ bemitzvotecha בְּמִצְוֹתֶיךָ vekidashtanu וְקִדַּשְׁתָּנוּ

hagadol הַגָּדוֹל veshimcha וְשִׁמְךָ la'avodatecha לַעֲבוֹדָתֶךָ malkenu מַלְכֵּנוּ

karata קָרָאתָ alenu עָלֵינוּ vehakadosh וְהַקָּדוֹשׁ אום ‏, יזל ‏, מבה = אותיות ד' ועם ‏; להו

THE THIRD BLESSING

You are Holy, and Your Name is Holy, and the Holy Ones praise You every day,
for you are God, the Holy King Selah. Blessed are You, Lord, the Holy God.

THE MIDDLE BLESSING

You have chosen us from among all the nations. You have loved us and have found favor in us.
You have exalted us above all the tongues and You have sanctified us with Your commandments.
You draw us close, our King, to Your service and proclaimed Your great and Holy Name upon us.

וַתִּתֶּן vatiten ב"פ כהת לָנוּ lanu אלהים, אהיה ארני יְהֹוָאדֹנָיאהדונהי Adonai

אֱלֹהֵינוּ Elohenu ילה be'ahava בְּאַהֲבָה אותר, דאגה

(ו u) לִמְנוּחָה limnucha :On Shabbat add) שַׁבָּתוֹת shabbatot

מוֹעֲדִים mo'adim לְשִׂמְחָה lesimcha• וְחַגִּים chagim וּזְמַנִּים uzmanim

לְשָׂשׂוֹן lesason• אֶת et יוֹם yom ע"ה נגד, מזבוז, זן, אל יהוה (:On Shabbat add

הַשַּׁבָּת haShabbat הַזֶּה hazeh והו• וְאֶת ve'et יוֹם yom ע"ה נגד, מזבוז, זן, אל יהוה)

(:On Sukkot say חַג chag הַסֻּכּוֹת haSukkot הַזֶּה hazeh•)

(:On Simchat Torah say שְׁמִינִי shemini וְחַג chag עֲצֶרֶת atzeret הַזֶּה hazeh•)

אֶת et יוֹם yom ע"ה נגד, מזבוז, זן, אל יהוה tov טוֹב mikra מִקְרָא והו kodesh קֹדֶשׁ

הַזֶּה hazeh והו• זְמַן zeman שִׂמְחָתֵנוּ simchatenu• בְּאַהֲבָה be'ahava אותר, דאגה

מִקְרָא mikra קֹדֶשׁ kodesh• זֵכֶר zecher לִיצִיאַת litzi'at מִצְרָיִם Mitzrayim מצר•

אֱלֹהֵינוּ elhenu ילה וֵאלֹהֵי vElohei לכב ; מילוי ע"ב, דמב ; ילה וַאֲבוֹתֵינוּ avotenu

יַעֲלֶה ya'ale וְיָבֹא yavo וְיַגִּיעַ veyagi'a וְיֵרָאֶה veyera'e רי"ו וְיֵרָצֶה veyeratze

וְיִשָּׁמַע veyishama וְיִפָּקֵד veyipaked וְיִזָּכֵר veyizacher ר"ת = מ"ב

זִכְרוֹנֵנוּ zichronenu וְזִכְרוֹן vezichron ע"ב קס"א וגש"ב אֲבוֹתֵינוּ avotenu•

זִכְרוֹן zichron ע"ב קס"א וגש"ב יְרוּשָׁלַיִם Yerushalayim עִירָךְ irach•

וְזִכְרוֹן vezichron ע"ב קס"א וגש"ב מָשִׁיחַ mashi'ach בֶּן ben דָּוִד David ע"ה כהת ;

וְזִכְרוֹן vezichron ע"ב קס"א וגש"ב אֲרֹנָי• פוי, אל ארני ע"ה עַבְדָּךְ avdach בן דוד = ארני ע"ה

כָּל kol ילי עַמְּךָ amecha בֵּית bet ב"פ ראה יִשְׂרָאֵל Yisra'el

לְפָנֶיךָ lefanecha ס"ג מ"ה בן לִפְלֵיטָה lifleta לְטוֹבָה letova אכא•

לְחֵן lechen מילוי דמ"ה בריבוע ; מוזי לְחֶסֶד lechesed ע"ב, ריבוע יהוה

And may You give us, Lord, our God, with love (**on Shabbat add:** *Sabbath for rest and*)
Holidays for happiness, Festivals and time of joy, this day (**on Shabbat add:** *of Sabbath and this day*)
(**on Sukkot:** *of Sukkot*) (**on Simchat Torah:** *of Shmini the Holiday of Atzeret*)
and this good day of Holy Convocation; The time of our happiness.
with love, a Holy Convocation, a remembrance of the exit from Egypt.
Our God and the God of our fathers, may it rise and come and arrive and appear and find favor and be heard
and be considered and be remembered, our remembrance and the remembrance of our fathers, the remembrance
of Jerusalem, Your city, and the remembrance of Mashiach Ben David, Your servant, and the remembrance
of Your entire Nation, the House of Israel, before You for deliverance, for good, for grace, kindness

tovim טוֹבִים בינה ע"ה יהוה אהיה אהיה lechayim לְחַיִּים ◆ulrachamim וּלְרַחֲמִים

יהוה אל אל זן, נגד, מזבוז, ע"ה beyom בְּיוֹם ◆ulshalom וּלְשָׁלוֹם

(**On Shabbat add:** הַשַּׁבָּת haShabbat הַזֶּה hazeh והו ◆ וּבְיוֹם uvyom ע"ה נגד, מזבוז, זן, אל יהוה)

(**On Sukkot say:** וְזֶה chag הַסֻּכּוֹת haSukkot הַזֶּה hazeh)◆

(**On Simchat Torah say:** שְׁמִינִי shemini וְזֶה chag עֲצֶרֶת atzeret הַזֶּה hazeh)◆

והו ע"ה נגד, מזבוז, זן, אל יהוה והו tov טוֹב beyom בְּיוֹם

mikra מִקְרָא kodesh קֹדֶשׁ hazeh הַזֶּה והו ◆

(אברים), רמ"ו הוכמה נתיבות ל"ב רי"ו אל, וז"פ אברהם, lerachem לְרַחֵם

◆ulhoshi'enu וּלְהוֹשִׁיעֵנוּ alenu עָלֵינוּ bo בּוֹ פשוטות אותיות וט"ז עסמ"ב

ילה Elohenu אֱלֹהֵינוּ Adonai יהואדניהאהדונהי (from Zeir Anpin) zochrenu זָכְרֵנוּ

vo בּוֹ (from Nukva) ufokdenu וּפָקְדֵנוּ ◆ אכא letova לְטוֹבָה bo בּוֹ

lechayim לְחַיִּים vo בּוֹ (from Da'at) vehoshi'enu וְהוֹשִׁיעֵנוּ ◆livracha לִבְרָכָה

yeshu'a יְשׁוּעָה ראה bidvar בִּדְבַר ◆tovim טוֹבִים ע"ה בינה יהוה, אהיה אהיה

vachamol וַחֲמוֹל vechanenu וְחָנֵּנוּ chus חוּס ◆verachamim וְרַחֲמִים

פשוטות אותיות וט"ז עסמ"ב (אברים), רמ"ו הוכמה נתיבות ל"ב רי"ו אל, וז"פ אברהם, verachem וְרַחֵם

◆alenu עָלֵינוּ ריבוע מ"ה enenu עֵינֵינוּ elecha אֵלֶיךָ ki כִּי vehoshi'enu וְהוֹשִׁיעֵנוּ

Ata אָתָּה verachum וְרַחוּם chanun וְחַנּוּן melech מֶלֶךְ El אל ייא" ki כִּי

ילה Elohenu אֱלֹהֵינוּ Adonai יהואדניהאהדונהי vehashsyenu וְהוֹשִׁיעֵנוּ◆

ע"ה בינה יהוה, אהיה אהיה lechayim לְחַיִּים mo'adecha מוֹעֲדֶיךָ birkat בִּרְכַּת et אֶת

ratzita רָצִיתָ ka'asher כַּאֲשֶׁר ◆uvshalom וּבְשָׁלוֹם besimcha בְּשִׂמְחָה

selah סֶלָה tevarchenu תְּבָרְכֵנוּ ken כֵּן ◆levarchenu לְבָרְכֵנוּ ve'amarta וְאָמַרְתָּ

---

and compassion, for a good life and for peace on this Day (**on Shabbat say:** *of Sabbath and on this Day*) (**on Sukkot:** *of Sukkot*) (**on Simchat Torah:** *of Shmini the Holiday of Atzeret*) *on this good Day of Holy Convocation, to take pity on us and to save us. Remember us, Lord, our God, on it for good and consider us, on it, for blessing and deliver us on it for a good life with the words of deliverance and mercy. Take pity and be gracious to us and have mercy and be compassionate with us and save us, for our eyes turn to You, because You are God, King Who is gracious and compassionate.*
And give us, Lord, our God Your blessing of Your holidays for happy and peaceful life.
As You desired and said to bless us. So You shall bless us Selah.

MEKADESH ISRAEL VEHAZEMANIM (THE TIMES)

ילה ; מילוי ע״ב, דמב ; ילה אֱלֹהֵינוּ Elohenu ילה וֵאלֹהֵי velohei לכב ; מילוי :On *Shabbat* add)

אֲבוֹתֵינוּ avotenu רְצֵה retze נָא na בִּמְנוּחָתֵנוּ (vimnuchatenu

קַדְּשֵׁנוּ kadshenu בְּמִצְוֹתֶיךָ vemitzvotecha◆ תֵן ten וְלְקֵנוּ chelkenu

בְּתוֹרָתֶךָ vetoratach◆ שַׂבְּעֵנוּ sabe'enu מִטוּבֶךָ mituvach לאו◆

בִּישׁוּעָתֶךָ bishu'atach◆ נַפְשֵׁנוּ nafshenu שַׂמֵּחַ same'ach

בֶּאֱמֶת ve'emet פוי, אל יהוה לְעָבְדְּךָ le'ovdecha לִבֵּנוּ libenu וְטַהֵר vetaher

Adonai יְהֹוָה vehanchilenu וְהַנְחִילֵנוּ ס״ג ד״פ◆ אהיה פעמים אהיה

אֱלֹהֵינוּ Elohenu ילה :On *Shabbat* add) בְּאַהֲבָה be'ahava אוזר, דאגה

בְּשִׂמְחָה vesimcha (אל עדי, רקס״א ע״ב ברבוע מהע ע״ה, uvratzon וּבְרָצוֹן

וּבְשָׂשׂוֹן uvsason :On *Shabbat* add) שַׁבָּתוֹת shabatot (ו מוֹעֲדֵי mo'adei

קָדְשֶׁךָ kodshecha, וְיִשְׂמְחוּ veyismechu בְךָ vecha כָּל kol ילי יִשְׂרָאֵל Yisrael

מְקַדְּשֵׁי mekadshei שְׁמֶךָ shemecha◆ בָּרוּךְ baruch אַתָּה Ata

יְהֹוָה Adonai

:on *Shabbat*) אהיה יהו אלף הה יוד הה הה יה אדני)

מְקַדֵּשׁ mekadesh :On *Shabbat* add) הַשַּׁבָּת hashabat (ו וְ ve) יִשְׂרָאֵל Yisrael

וְהַזְּמַנִּים vehazemanim:

THE FINAL THREE BLESSINGS
Through the merit of Moses, Aaron and Joseph, who are our channels for the final three blessings, we are able to bring down all the spiritual energy that we aroused with our prayers and blessings.

THE FIFTH BLESSING
During this blessing, referring to Moses, we should always meditate to try to know exactly what God wants from us in our life, as signified by the phrase, "Let it be the will of God." We ask God to guide us toward the work we came to Earth to do. The Creator cannot just accept the work that we want to do; we must carry out the work we were destined to do.

MEKADESH ISRAEL VEHAZEMANIM (THE TIMES)
(on Shabbat: *Our God and the God of our forefathers, please desire our rest.*)
Sanctify us with Your commandments and place our lot in Your Torah and satiate us from Your goodness and gladden our spirits with Your salvation. And purify our heart so as to serve You truly. And grant us, Lord, our God, (on Shabbat: with love and favor,) with happiness and joy (on Shabbat: Sabbaths and) the Holidays, and all Israel, who sanctify Your Name will be joyful with You. Blessed are You, Lord, who sanctifies (on Shabbat: the Sabbath) and Israel and the Times.

Netzach

Meditate for the Supernal Desire (*Keter*) that is called *metzach haratzon* (Forehead of the Desire).

רְצֵה retze אלף למד הה יוד מם

Meditate here to transform misfortune and tragedy (צרה) into desire and acceptance (רצה).

Adonai יהוֹ(אהדנהי‪אהדונהי‬) Elohenu אֱלֹהֵינוּ ילה be'amecha בְּעַמְּךָ Yisrael יִשְׂרָאֵל

velitfilatam וְלִתְפִלָּתָם she'e שְׁעֵה◆ vehashev וְהָשֵׁב ha'avoda הָעֲבוֹדָה

lidvir לִדְבִיר רי״ו betecha בֵּיתֶךָ ב״פ ראה◆ ve'ishei וְאִשֵּׁי Yisrael יִשְׂרָאֵל

utfilatam וּתְפִלָּתָם mehera מְהֵרָה be'ahava בְּאַהֲבָה אוזר, דאגה

tekabel תְּקַבֵּל beratzon בְּרָצוֹן מהש׳ ע״ה, ע״ב בריבוע וקס״א ע״ה, אל שדי ע״ה◆

ut'hi וּתְהִי leratzon לְרָצוֹן מהש׳ ע״ה, ע״ב בריבוע וקס״א ע״ה, אל שדי ע״ה

tamid תָּמִיד ע״ה קס״א קנ״א קמ״ג avodat עֲבוֹדַת Yisrael יִשְׂרָאֵל amecha עַמֶּךָ׃

veAta וְאַתָּה verachamecha בְּרַחֲמֶךָ harabim הָרַבִּים◆

tachpotz תַּחְפֹּץ banu בָּנוּ vetirtzenu וְתִרְצֵנוּ vetechezena וְתֶחֱזֶינָה

enenu עֵינֵינוּ ריבוע מ״ה beshuvcha בְּשׁוּבְךָ leTziyon לְצִיּוֹן יוסף, ו׳ הויות, קנאה

berachamim בְּרַחֲמִים מצפצ, אלהים דיודין, י״פ יי״י׃

(on *Shabbat* אל:) אהיה יהו אלף למד הי יוד מם

baruch בָּרוּךְ Ata אַתָּה יהוֹ(אהדנהי‪אהדונהי‬) Adonai

hamachazir הַמַּחֲזִיר shechinato שְׁכִינָתוֹ leTziyon לְצִיּוֹן יוסף, ו׳ הויות, קנאה׃

THE FINAL THREE BLESSINGS
THE FIFTH BLESSING

Find favor, Lord, our God,
in Your People, Israel, and turn to their prayer.

Restore the service to the inner sanctuary of Your Temple. Accept the offerings of Israel and their prayer with favor, speedily, and with love. May the service of Your People Israel always be favorable to You.

And You in Your great compassion take delight in us and are pleased with us. May our eyes witness Your return to Zion with compassion. Blessed are You, Lord, Who returns His Shechinah to Zion.

THE SIXTH BLESSING

This blessing is our thank you. Kabbalistically, the biggest "thank you" we can give the Creator is to do exactly what we are supposed to do in terms of our spiritual work.

Hod

Bow your entire body at "modim" and straighten up at "Adonai."

מוֹדִים modim מאה ברכות עתיקן דוד לאמרם כל יום anachnu אֲנַחְנוּ כך lach

שָׁאַתָּה sheAta הוּא hu יְהֹוָה Adonai (וג) אֱלֹהֵינוּ Elohenu ילה

וֵאלֹהֵי velohei לכב ; מילוי ע"ב, דמב ; ילה avotenu אֲבוֹתֵינוּ לְעוֹלָם le'olam

ריבוע ס"ג ו' אותיות דס"ג אלהים דההן ע"ה tzur צוּר tzurenu צוּרֵנוּ וָעֶד va'ed

וְחַיֵּינוּ chayenu וּמָגֵן umagen ג"פ אל (ייא"י מילוי דס"ג) ; ר"ת מיכאל גבריאל נוריאל

יִשְׁעֵנוּ yish'enu אַתָּה Ata הוּא hu לְדֹר ledor וָדֹר vador רי"ו node נוֹדֶה

לָךְ lecha וּנְסַפֵּר unsaper תְּהִלָּתֶךָ tehilatecha עַל al וְחַיֵּינוּ chayenu

נִשְׁמוֹתֵינוּ nishmotenu וְעַל ve'al בְּיָדֶךָ beyadecha הַמְּסוּרִים hamesurim

שֶׁבְּכָל shebechol נִסֶּיךָ nisecha וְעַל ve'al לָךְ lach הַפְּקוּדוֹת hapekudot

עִמָּנוּ imanu יוֹם yom ע"ה נגד, מזבוח, זז, אל יהוה ריבוע ס"ג, קס"א קס"א וד' אותיות

וְעַל ve'al נִפְלְאוֹתֶיךָ nifle'otecha וְטוֹבוֹתֶיךָ vetovotecha שֶׁבְּכָל shebechol

ב"ן, לכב hatov הַטּוֹב vetzahorayim וְצָהֳרָיִם vavoker וָבֹקֶר erev עֶרֶב עֵת et

הַמְרַחֵם hamerachem rachamecha רַחֲמֶיךָ chalu כָלוּ lo לֹא ki כִּי והו

lo לֹא ki כִּי אברהם, וז"פ אל, רי"ו ול"ב נתיבות החכמה, רמ"וז (אברים), עסמ"ב וט"ז אותיות פעוטות

תַּמּוּ tamu וְחַסָדֶיךָ chasadecha כִּי ki מֵעוֹלָם me'olam קִוִּינוּ kivinu כך lach:

THE SIXTH BLESSING

We give thanks to You, for it is You, Lord, Who is our God and God of our forefathers, forever and for all eternity. You are our Rock, the Rock of our lives, and the Shield of our salvation. From one generation to another, we shall give thanks to You and we shall tell of Your praise. For our lives that are entrusted in Your hands, for our souls that are in Your care, for Your miracles that are with us every day, and for Your wonders and Your favors that are with us at all times: evening, morning and afternoon. You are the good One, for Your compassion has never ceased. You are the compassionate One, for Your kindness has never ended, for we have always placed our hope in You.

MODIM DeRABANAN

This prayer is recited by the congregation in the repetition when the chazan says "modim."

In this section there are 44 words, which is the same numerical value as the Name: ריבוע אהיה (א אה אהי אהיה).

lach כָּךְ anachnu אֲנַוְזְנוּ מאה ברכות שתיקן דוד לאמרם כל יום modim מוֹדִים

Elohenu אֱלֹהֵינוּ ילה Adonai יְהוָֹה(אדנּי־אהדונּהי) hu הוּא sheAta שָׁאַתָּה

avotenu אֲבוֹתֵינוּ ילה ; דמב מילוי ע״ב, לכב ; velohei וֵאלֹהֵי

yotzrenu יוֹצְרֵנוּ ♦basar בָּשָׂר ילי chol כָּל ; ילה דמב מילוי ע״ב, Elohei אֱלֹהֵי

vehoda'ot וְהוֹדָאוֹת berachot בְּרָכוֹת ♦bereshit בְּרֵאשִׁית yotzer יוֹצֵר

לְשִׁמְךָ leshimcha הַגָּדוֹל hagadol ; להו עם ד׳ אותיות = מבה, יזל, אום

♦vekiyamtanu וְקִיַּמְתָּנוּ shehecheyitanu שֶׁהֶוֹיֶיתָנוּ al עַל vehakadosh וְהַקָּדוֹשׁ

vete'esof וְתֶאֱסוֹף ♦utchonenu וּתְוֹנֵנוּ techayenu תְּוֹזַיֵּינוּ ken כֵּן

lishmor לִשְׁמוֹר ♦kodshecha קָדְשֶׁךָ lechatzrot לְוֹצְרוֹת galuyoteinu גָּלֻיוֹתֵינוּ

ul'ovdecha וּלְעָבְדֶךָ ♦retzoncha רְצוֹנֶךָ vela'asot וְלַעֲשׂוֹת chukecha וֹזֻקֶּיךָ

she'anachnu שֶׁאֲנַוְזְנוּ al עַל ♦shalem שָׁלֵם בוכו belevav בְּלֵבָב פוי, אל אדני

:hahoda'ot הַהוֹדָאוֹת (מילוי דס״ג) El אֵל יא״י baruch בָּרוּךְ ♦lach לָךְ modim מוֹדִים

veyitromam וְיִתְרוֹמַם yitbarach יִתְבָּרַךְ kulam כֻּלָּם ve'al וְעַל

shimcha שִׁמְךָ קמ״ג קנ״א קס״א ע״ה tamid תָּמִיד veyitnase וְיִתְנַשֵּׂא

♦va'ed וָעֶד דס״ג אותיות וי׳ ס״ג ריבוע le'olam לְעוֹלָם malkenu מַלְכֵּנוּ

:sela סֶלָה yoducha יוֹדוּךָ אהיה אהיה יהוה ע״ה בינה, hachayim הַוֹזַיִּים ילי vechol וְכָל

מ״ה ריבוע יהוה יהוה ריבוע יהוה vivarchu וִיבָרְכוּ vihalelu וִיהַלְלוּ

את et שִׁמְךָ shimcha הַגָּדוֹל hagadol ; להו עם ד׳ אותיות = מבה, יזל, אום

MODIM DeRABANAN

We give thanks to You, for it is You Lord,

our God and God of our forefathers, the God of all flesh, our Maker and the Former of all Creation. Blessings and thanks to Your great and Holy Name for giving us life and for preserving us. So may You continue to give us life, be gracious to us, and gather our exiles to the courtyards of Your Sanctuary, so that we may keep Your laws, fulfill Your will, and serve You wholeheartedly. For this, we thank You. Bless the God of thanksgiving.

And for all those things, may Your Name be always blessed, exalted and extolled, our King, forever and ever, and all the living shall thank You, Selah. And they shall praise and bless Your Great Name,

בְּאֶמֶת be'emet אהיה פעמים אהיה, ז"פ ס"ג רִיבוֹעַ ס"ג ו' אותיות דס"ג le'olam לְעוֹלָם ס"ג

כִּי ki טוֹב tov והו ; כִּי טוֹב = יהוה אהיה, אום, מבה, יל"ל

הָאֵל haEl לאה ; יא"י (מילוי דס"ג) yeshu'atenu יְשׁוּעָתֵנוּ ve'ezratenu וְעֶזְרָתֵנוּ

סֶלָה sela. הָאֵל haEl לאה ; יא"י (מילוי דס"ג) hatov הַטּוֹב והו:

Bend your knees at "baruch," bow at "Ata" and straighten up at "Adonai."

(on Shabbat:) אהיה יהו אלף למד כמד הה יוד מם אלהים:

בָּרוּךְ baruch אַתָּה Ata יְהוָֹאדְנִיֵּאהדונהי Adonai (הִי) הַטּוֹב hatov והו

שִׁמְךָ shimcha וּלְךָ ulcha נָאֶה na'e ס"ת כהת, משיוו בן דוד ע"ה: לְהוֹדוֹת lehodot

THE FINAL BLESSING

We are emanating the energy of peace to the entire world. We also make it our intent to use our mouths only for good. Kabbalistically, the power of words and speech is unimaginable. We hope to use that power wisely, which is perhaps one of the most difficult tasks we have to carry out.

Yesod

שִׂים sim שָׁלוֹם shalom

טוֹבָה tova אכא וּבְרָכָה uvracha חַיִּים chayim אהיה אהיה יהוה, בינה ע"ה

וְחֵן chen מילוי דמ"ה, מוזי בריבוע, וָחֶסֶד vachesed ע"ב, ריבוע יהוה

צְדָקָה tzedaka ע"ה ריבוע אלהים וְרַחֲמִים verachamim עָלֵינוּ alenu וְעַל ve'al

כָּל kol ילי ; עמם Yisrael יִשְׂרָאֵל amecha עַמֶּךָ uvarchenu וּבָרְכֵנוּ

אָבִינוּ avinu כֻּלָּנוּ kulanu כְּאֶחָד ke'echad אהבה, דאגה be'or בְּאוֹר רו, א"ס

פָּנֶיךָ panecha ס"ג מ"ה ב"ן ve'or בְּאוֹר רו, א"ס כִּי ki פָּנֶיךָ panecha ס"ג מ"ה ב"ן

אֱלֹהֵינוּ Elohenu ילה תּוֹרָה torah וְחַיִּים vechayim אהיה אהיה יהוה, בינה ע"ה.

sincerely and forever, for It is good, the God of our salvation and our help, Selah, the good God. Blessed are You, Lord, whose Name is good, and to You it is befitting to give thanks.

THE FINAL BLESSING

Place peace, goodness, blessing, life, grace, kindness, righteousness, and mercy upon us and upon all of Israel, Your People. Bless us all as one, our Father, with the Light of Your Countenance, because it is with the Light of Your Countenance that You, Lord, our God, have given us Torah and life,

יהוה♦ ריבוע ע"ב, וָחֶסֶד vachesed דאגה אוזר, ahava אַהֲבָה

beracha בְּרָכָה ♦verachamim וְרַחֲמִים אלהים ריבוע ע"ה tzedaka צְדָקָה

בְּעֵינֶיךָ be'enecha והו vetov וְטוֹב ♦veshalom וְשָׁלוֹם ע"ה קס"א ; ריבוע מ"ה

amecha עַמְּךָ ילי kol כָּל et אֶת ulvarech וּלְבָרֵךְ levarchenu לְבָרְכֵנוּ

♣veshalom וְשָׁלוֹם oz עֹז אהיה י"פ berov בְּרוֹב Yisrael יִשְׂרָאֵל

Ata אַתָּה baruch בָּרוּךְ

(on Shabbat: מצפצ) אהיה יהו אלף למד הא יוד מם

Adonai יאהדונהיואהדונהיאהדונהי יוֹהֲווֹ

Yisrael יִשְׂרָאֵל amo עַמּוֹ et אֶת hamevarech הַמְבָרֵךְ

♦amen אָמֵן יאהדונהי ♦bashalom בַּשָּׁלוֹם (יב"ק) = (אילההויהם) אלהים = ר"ת

YIH'YU LERATZON

There are 42 letters in the verse in the secret of *Ana Beko'ach.*

יְהִיוּ yih'yu אל (יא"י מילוי דס"ג) לְרָצוֹן leratzon מהש ע"ה, ע"ב בריבוע וקס"א ע"ה, אל שדי ע"ה

libi לִבִּי vehegyon וְהֶגְיוֹן אלף למד עין דלת יוד ע"ה = ר"ת אלף fi פִּי imrei אִמְרֵי

♣vego'ali וְגֹאֲלִי tzuri צוּרִי Adonai יאהדונהיואהדונהי יְהֹוָה ס"ג מ"ה ב"ן lefanecha לְפָנֶיךָ

ELOHAI NETZOR

♦mera מֵרָע leshoni לְשׁוֹנִי netzor נְצוֹר יְלָה ; דמב, מילוי ע"ב Elohai אֱלֹהַי

velimkalelai וְלִמְקַלְלַי ♦mirma מִרְמָה ראה midaber מִדַּבֵּר vesiftotai וּשְׂפָתוֹתַי

ke'afar כֶּעָפָר venafshi וְנַפְשִׁי ♦tidom תִדֹּם nafshi נַפְשִׁי

♦betoratecha בְּתוֹרָתֶךָ libi לִבִּי petach פְּתַח ♦tih'ye תִהְיֶה יה אדני lakol לַכֹּל

---

love and kindness, righteousness and mercy, blessing and peace. May it be good in Your Eyes to bless us and to bless Your entire Nation, Israel, with abundant power and with peace. Blessed are You, Lord, Who blesses His Nation, Israel, with peace, Amen.

YIH'YU LERATZON

"May the utterances of my mouth
and the thoughts of my heart find favor before You, Lord, my Rock and my Redeemer." (Psalms 19:15)

ELOHAI NETZOR

My God, guard my tongue from evil and my lips from speaking deceit. To those who curse me, let my spirit remain silent, and let my spirit be as dust for everyone. Open my heart to Your Torah

וְאַחֲרֵי ve'acharei מִצְוֹתֶיךָ mitzvotecha תִּרְדּוֹף tirdof נַפְשִׁי nafshi◆

וְכָל vechol הַקָּמִים יֹלִי hakamim עָלַי alai לְרָעָה rhe'a◆ lera'a מְהֵרָה mehera

הָפֵר hafer עֲצָתָם atzatam וְקַלְקֵל vekalkel מַחְשְׁבוֹתָם machshevotam◆

עֲשֵׂה ase לְמַעַן lema'an שְׁמָךְ shemach◆ לְמַעַן lema'an עֲשֵׂה ase לְמַעַן lema'an

עֲשֵׂה ase yeminach◆ יְמִינָךְ ase עֲשֵׂה lema'an לְמַעַן toratach◆ תּוֹרָתָךְ ase עֲשֵׂה

לְמַעַן lema'an kedushatach◆ קְדֻשָׁתָךְ ר"ת הפסוק = מ"ה יהוה lema'an לְמַעַן

יֵחָלְצוּן yechaltzun יְדִידֶיךָ yedidecha ר"ת ילי הוֹשִׁיעָה hoshi'a יהוה וע"ע נהורין

יְמִינָךְ yemincha וַעֲנֵנִי va'aneni (כתיב: ועננו) ר"ת אל (ייא"י מילוי דס"ג:)◆

Before we recite the next verse *"Yih'yu leratzon"* we have an opportunity to strengthen our connection to our soul using our name. Each person has a verse in the *Torah* that connects to their name. Either their name is in the verse, or the first and last letters of the name correspond to the first or last letters of a verse. For example, the name Yehuda begins with a *Yud* and ends with a *Hei*. Before we end the *Amidah*, we state that our name will always be remembered when our soul leaves this world.

YIH'YU LERATZON (THE SECOND)

There are 42 letters in the verse in the secret of *Ana Beko'ach.*

יִהְיוּ yih'yu אל (ייא"י מילוי דס"ג) לְרָצוֹן leratzon מהטע ע"ה, ע"ב בריבוע וקס"א ע"ה, אל שדי ע"ה

אִמְרֵי imrei פִי fi ר"ת אֶלֶף = אלף למד עין דלת יוד ע"ה וְהֶגְיוֹן vehegyon לִבִּי libi

לְפָנֶיךָ lefanecha ס"ג מ"ה בן יְהֹוָה Adonai צוּרִי tzuri וְגֹאֲלִי vego'ali:

---

and let my heart pursue Your commandments. All those who rise against me to do me harm, speedily nullify their plans and disturb their thoughts. Do so for the sake of Your Name. Do so for the sake of Your Right. Do so for the sake of Your Torah. Do so for the sake of Your Holiness, "So that Your loved ones may be saved. Redeem Your right and answer me." (Psalms 60:7)

YIH'YU LERATZON (THE SECOND)

"May the utterances of my mouth and the thoughts of my heart find favor before You, Lord, my Rock and my Redeemer." (Psalms 19:15)

OSE SHALOM

You take three steps backward;

עוֹשֶׂה שָׁלוֹם ose shalom

Left
You turn to the left and say:

בִּמְרוֹמָיו bimromav ר"ת ע"ב, ריבוע יהוה

הוּא hu בְּרַחֲמָיו verachamav יַעֲשֶׂה ya'ase

Right
You turn to the right and say:

שָׁלוֹם shalom עָלֵינוּ alenu ר"ת ע"ע נהורין

Center
You face the center and say:

וְעַל ve'al כָּל־ kol יל' ; עמם עַמּוֹ amo יִשְׂרָאֵל Yisrael

וְאִמְרוּ ve'imru אָמֵן amen יאהדונהי:

יְהִי yehi רָצוֹן ratzon מהש ע"ה, ע"ב, בריבוע וקס"א ע"ה, אל שדי ע"ה

מִלְּפָנֶיךָ milfanecha ס"ג מ"ה ב"ן יְהֹוָה Adonai יאהדונהי Elohenu אֱלֹהֵינוּ ילה

וֵאלֹהֵי velohei ילה ; מילוי ע"ב, דמב ; avotenu אֲבוֹתֵינוּ לכב ; שֶׁתִּבְנֶה shetivne

בֵּית bet ב"פ ראה הַמִּקְדָּשׁ hamikdash בִּמְהֵרָה bimhera veyamenu בְיָמֵינוּ

וְתֵן veten וְזִקְנִי chelkenu חֶלְקֵנוּ betoratach בְּתוֹרָתֶךָ לַעֲשׂוֹת la'asot וְחֻקֵּי chukei

רְצוֹנֶךָ retzonach ul'ovdach וּלְעָבְדְּךָ פו', אל אדני belevav בְּלֵבָב בוכו שָׁלֵם shalem.

You take three steps forward.

OSE SHALOM

He, Who makes peace in His High Places, He, in His compassion, shall make peace upon us.
And upon His entire nation, Israel, and you shall say, Amen.

May it be pleasing before You,
Lord, our God and God of our forefathers, that You shall rebuild the Temple speedily, in our days, and
place our lot in Your Torah, so that we may fulfill the laws of Your desire and serve You wholeheartedly.

KADDISH TITKABAL

יִתְגַּדַּל yitgadal וְיִתְקַדַּשׁ veyitkadash עֲדֵי וּמִילוּי עֲדֵי ; י"א אוֹתִיּוֹת כְּמִנְיַן ו"ה

שְׁמֵהּ shemei (שֵׁם י"ה דע"ב) רַבָּא raba קנ"א ב"ן, יהוה אלהים יהוה אדני,

אָמֵן amen אידהנויה.   מילוי קס"א וס"ג, מ"ה ברבוע וע"ב ע"ה ; ר"ת = ו"פ אלהים ; ס"ת = ג"פ יב"ק:

בְּעָלְמָא be'alma דִּי di בְּרָא vera כִּרְעוּתֵיהּ kir'utei.

וְיַמְלִיךְ veyamlich מַלְכוּתֵיהּ malchutei.   וְיַצְמַח veyatzmach

פּוּרְקָנֵהּ purkanei.   וִיקָרֵב vikarev מְשִׁיחֵיהּ meshichei: אָמֵן amen אידהנויה.

בְּחַיֵּיכוֹן bechayechon וּבְיוֹמֵיכוֹן uvyomechon וּבְחַיֵּי uvchayei

דְּכָל dechol יל בֵּית bet ב"פ ראה יִשְׂרָאֵל Yisrael בַּעֲגָלָא ba'agala

וּבִזְמַן uvizman קָרִיב kariv וְאִמְרוּ ve'imru אָמֵן amen: אָמֵן amen אידהנויה.

The congregation and the *chazan* say the following:

Twenty eight words (until *be'alma*) and twenty eight letters (until *almaya*)

יְהֵא yehe שְׁמֵהּ shemei (שֵׁם י"ה דס"ג) רַבָּא raba קנ"א ב"ן,

מְבָרַךְ mevarach, ע"ב ע"ה ס"ג וס"ג, מילוי קס"א אדני, יהוה אלהים יהוה

לְעָלַם le'alam לְעָלְמֵי le'almei עָלְמַיָּא almaya.   יִתְבָּרַךְ yitbarach.

Seven words with six letters each (שֵׁם בֶּן מ"ב) and seven times the letter *Vav* (שֵׁם בֶּן מ"ב):

וְיִשְׁתַּבַּח veyishtabach י"פ ע"ב יהוה אל אבג יתץ.

וְיִתְפָּאַר veyitpa'ar הי גו יה קרע שטן.   וְיִתְרוֹמַם veyitromam וה כוזו נגד יכש.

וְיִתְנַשֵּׂא veyitnase במוכסז בטר צתג.   וְיִתְהַדָּר veyit'hadar כוזו יה וזקב טנע.

וְיִתְעַלֶּה veyit'ale וה יוד ה א ואו הא שקו צית.   וְיִתְהַלָּל veyit'halal א ואו הא יגל פזק.

שְׁמֵהּ shemei (שֵׁם י"ה דמ"ה) דְּקֻדְשָׁא dekudsha בְּרִיךְ verich הוּא hu:

אָמֵן amen אידהנויה.

KADDISH TITKABAL

May His great Name be more exalted and sanctified. (Amen)
In the world that He created according to His will, and may His Kingdom reign. And may He cause His redemption to sprout and may He bring the Mashiach closer. (Amen) In your lifetimes and in your days and in the lifetime of all the House of Israel, speedily and in the near future, and you shall say, Amen. (Amen) May His great Name be blessed forever and for all eternity. Blessed and lauded, and glorified, and exalted, and extolled, and honored, and uplifted, and praised be the Name of the Holy Blessed One. (Amen)

le'ela לְעֵלָּא min מִן kol כָּל יל birchata בִּרְכָתָא shirata שִׁירָתָא♦

tishbechata תֻּשְׁבְּחָתָא venechamata וְנֶחָמָתָא♦ da'amiran דַּאֲמִירָן

be'alma בְּעָלְמָא ve'imru וְאִמְרוּ amen אָמֵן: amen אָמֵן אידהנויה.

titkabal תִּתְקַבַּל tzelotana צְלוֹתָנָא uva'utana וּבָעוּתָנָא

im עִם tzelotehon צְלוֹתְהוֹן uva'utehon וּבָעוּתְהוֹן dechol דְּכָל יל

bet בֵּית ב"פ ראה Yisrael יִשְׂרָאֵל kadam קֳדָם avuna אֲבוּנָא

devishmaya דְּבִשְׁמַיָּא ve'imru וְאִמְרוּ amen אָמֵן: amen אָמֵן אידהנויה♦

yehe יְהֵא shelama שְׁלָמָא raba רַבָּא קנ"א ב"ן, יהוה אלהים יהוה אדני, מילוי קס"א וס"ג,

min מִן shemaya שְׁמַיָּא♦ chayim וְחַיִּים מ"ה ברבוע וע"ב ע"ה אהיה אהיה יהוה, בינה ע"ה

vesava וְשָׂבָע vishu'a וִישׁוּעָה venechama וְנֶחָמָה veshezava וְשֵׁיזָבָא

urfu'a וּרְפוּאָה ug'ula וּגְאֻלָּה uslicha וּסְלִיחָה vechapara וְכַפָּרָה

verevach וְרֵיוַח vehatzala וְהַצָּלָה♦ lanu לָנוּ אלהים, אהיה אדני ulchol וּלְכָל יה אדני

amo עַמּוֹ Yisrael יִשְׂרָאֵל ve'imru וְאִמְרוּ amen אָמֵן: amen אָמֵן אידהנויה.

Take three steps backwards and say:

ose עוֹשֶׂה shalom שָׁלוֹם

bimromav בִּמְרוֹמָיו ע"ב, ריבוע יהוה♦ hu הוּא berachamav בְּרַחֲמָיו

ya'ase יַעֲשֶׂה shalom שָׁלוֹם alenu עָלֵינוּ ר"ת ש"ע נהורין♦

ve'al וְעַל kol כָּל יל ; עמם amo עַמּוֹ Yisrael יִשְׂרָאֵל ve'imru וְאִמְרוּ amen אָמֵן:

amen אָמֵן אידהנויה♦

Above all blessings, songs, praises, and words of consolation that may be said in the world, and you shall say, Amen. (Amen) May our prayers and pleas be accepted, together with the prayers and pleas of the entire House of Israel, before our Father in Heaven, and you say, Amen. (Amen) May there be abundant peace from Heaven; Life, contentment, salvation, consolation, deliverance, healing, redemption, pardon, atonement, comfort, and relief. For us and for His entire nation, Israel, and you shall say, Amen. (Amen) He, Who makes peace in His High Places, He, in His compassion, shall make peace upon us And upon His entire nation, Israel, and you shall say, Amen. (Amen)

> When the Holiday falls on *Shabbat* we add the Psalm of "*Haleluyah*."
> On *Shabbat Chol Hamo'ed* we say "*Haleluyah*" instead of "*Shir Hama'a lot LeDavid.*"

HALELUYA

According to the *Alef Bet* (bringing order to our life).

הַלְלוּיָהּ haleluya אלהים, אהיה אדני ; ילה ; ללה ; אֹדֶה **ode** יְהֹוֶהאדניאהדונהי **Adonai**

בְּכָל־ bechol מיכ, י"פ האא בּוכו בְּסוֹד besod בּ"ן, לכב לֵבָב levav יְשָׁרִים yesharim

וְעֵדָה ve'eda סיט: גְּדֹלִים gedolim מַעֲשֵׂי ma'asei יְהֹוֶהאדניאהדונהי Adonai

הוֹד־ hod הההּ יְהֹ lechol לְכָל־ derushim דְּרוּשִׁים אדני לְחֶפְצֵיהֶם:cheftzehem

לְעַד la'ad ב"פ ב"ן זֵכֶר zecher עָשָׂה asa לְנִפְלְאֹתָיו lenifle'otav וְחַנּוּן chanun עָמֶדֶת omedet וְצִדְקָתוֹ vetzidkato פָּעֳלוֹ pa'olo וְהָדָר vehadar הוֹד־ hod

נָתַן natan טֶרֶף teref = עשֹל: חַנּוּן ורחום יהוה Adonai יְהֹוֶהאדניאהדונהי verachum וְרַחוּם verachum

לִירֵאָיו lire'av בְּרִיתוֹ:berito ריבוע דס"ג ו' אותיות דס"ג לְעוֹלָם le'olam יִזְכֹּר yizkor

כֹּחַ ko'ach מַעֲשָׂיו ma'asav הִגִּיד higid לְעַמּוֹ le'amo לָתֵת latet לָהֶם lahem

נַחֲלַת nachalat גּוֹיִם:goyim מַעֲשֵׂי ma'asei יָדָיו yadav

אֱמֶת emet אלהים ה"פ ע"ה אהיה, ז"פ ס"ג פעמים אהיה, וּמִשְׁפָּט umishpat

נֶאֱמָנִים ne'emanim כָּל־ kol ילי פִּקּוּדָיו pikudav מנק:semuchim סְמוּכִים

לְעַד la'ad ב"פ ב"ן לְעוֹלָם le'olam ריבוע דס"ג ו' אותיות דס"ג עֲשׂוּיִם asuyim

בֶּאֱמֶת be'emet אהיה פעמים אהיה, ז"פ ס"ג וְיָשָׁר:veyashar פְּדוּת pedut שָׁלַוֹ pedut שָׁלַח shalach

לְעַמּוֹ le'amo בְּרִיתוֹ berito אותיות דס"ג ו' דס"ג ריבוע לְעוֹלָם le'olam צִוָּה־ tziva

קָדוֹשׁ kadosh שְׁמוֹ shemo ע"ב ברויבוע קס"א ע"ה, אל שדי ע"ה, מהש ע"ה: וְנוֹרָא venora

---

HALELUYA
"Praise the Lord!

א *I will give thanks to the Lord with my whole heart,* ב *in the council of the upright, and in the congregation.* ג *The works of the Lord are great,* ד *sought out of all them that have delight therein.* ה *His work is glory and majesty;* ו *and His righteousness endures forever.* ז *He has made a memorial for His wonderful works;* ח *the Lord is gracious and full of compassion.* ט *He has given food to those that fear Him;* י *He will ever be mindful of His covenant.* כ *He has declared to His people the power of His works,* ל *in giving them the heritage of the nations.* מ *The works of His hands are truth and justice;* נ *all His precepts are sure.* ס *They are established for ever and ever,* ע *they are done in truth and uprightness.* פ *He has sent redemption unto His people;* צ *He has commanded His covenant for ever;* ק *Holy and awesome is His Name.*

yir'at יִרְאַת (מצוות) תרי"ג = במילוי chochmah וְזִכְמָה reshit רֵאשִׁית

אֲדֹנָי יָה lechol לְכָל־ והו tov טוֹב sechel שֵׂכֶל Adonai יְהֹוָאדִנִיאהדונִהי

ב"פ ב"ן: la'ad לְעַד omedet עֹמֶדֶת tehilato תְּהִלָתוֹ osehem עֹשֵׂיהֶם

SHIR HAMA'ALOT LEDAVID

These verses connect us to the ancient Holy Temple, the energy center and source of all spiritual Light for the whole world. Since its distruction, the Aramaic letters in this connection re-establish the lines of communication with the spiritual essence of the Temple, giving us the ability to capture this energy for our personal lives.

samachti שָׂמַחְתִּי leDavid לְדָוִד hama'alot הַמַּעֲלוֹת shir שִׁיר

נלך: nelech נֵלֵךְ Adonai יְהֹוָאדִנִיאהדונִהי ב"פ ראה bet בֵּית li לִי be'omrim בְּאֹמְרִים

bish'arayich בִּשְׁעָרָיִךְ ר"ת רהע raglenu רַגְלֵינוּ hayu הָיוּ omdot עֹמְדוֹת

habenuya הַבְּנוּיָה Yerushalayim יְרוּשָׁלַםִ Yerushalayim: יְרוּשָׁלָםִ

yachdav: יַחְדָּו la כֹּה shechubera שֶׁחֻבְּרָה עַרי סנדלפון, מזמזר, ke'ir כְּעִיר

edut עֵדוּת Yah יָה shivtei שִׁבְטֵי shevatim שְׁבָטִים alu עָלוּ shesham שֶׁשָּׁם

Adonai: יְהֹוָאדִנִיאהדונִהי leshem לְשֵׁם lehodot לְהֹדוֹת leYisrael לְיִשְׂרָאֵל

ע"ה ה"פ אלהים lemishpat לְמִשְׁפָּט chis'ot כִּסְאוֹת yashvu יָשְׁבוּ shama שָׁמָּה ki כִּי

shelom שְׁלוֹם sha'alu שַׁאֲלוּ David: דָוִד ראה ב"פ levet לְבֵית kis'ot כִּסְאוֹת

yehi יְהִי ohavayich: אֹהֲבָיִךְ yishlayu יִשְׁלָיוּ Yerushalayim יְרוּשָׁלָםִ

be'armenotayich: בְּאַרְמְנוֹתָיִךְ shalva שַׁלְוָה bechelech בְּחֵילֵךְ shalom שָׁלוֹם

shalom שָׁלוֹם na נָא adabera אֲדַבְּרָה vere'ai וְרֵעָי achai אַחַי lema'an לְמַעַן

Adonai יְהֹוָאדִנִיאהדונִהי ראה ב"פ bet בֵּית lema'an לְמַעַן bach: בָּךְ

lach: לָךְ והו tov טוֹב avaksha אֲבַקְשָׁה ילה Elohenu אֱלֹהֵינוּ

ר *The fear of the Lord is the beginning of wisdom;*
ש *a good understanding have all they that do thereafter;* ת *His praise endures for ever."* (Psalms 111)

SHIR HAMA'ALOT LEDAVID

"A Song of Ascents by David: I rejoiced when they said to me: Let us go to the House of the Lord. Our legs stood immobile within your gates, Jerusalem. The built-up Jerusalem is like a city that has been united together. and the hills like young lambs. What ails you sea that you flee? Jordan, which you turn backward? Mountains, which you skip like rams? Hills, like young lambs? Before the Lord tremble, Earth, before the God of Jacob, Who turns the rock into a lake of water, the flint into a flowing fountain." (Psalms 113)

KADDISH YEHE SHELAMA

יִתְגַּדַּל yitgadal וְיִתְקַדַּשׁ veyitkadash שׁדי ומילוי שׁדי ; י"א אותיות כמנין ו"ה

שְׁמֵיהּ shemei (שם י"ה דע"ב) רַבָּא raba קנ"א ב"ן, יהוה אלהים יהוה אדני,

מילוי קס"א וס"ג, מ"ה ברבוע וע"ב ע"ה ; ר"ת = ו"פ אלהים ; ס"ת = ג"פ יב"ק] אָמֵן amen אידהנויה.

בְּעָלְמָא be'alma דִּי di בְּרָא vera בִּרְעוּתֵיהּ kir'utei.

וְיַמְלִיךְ veyamlich מַלְכוּתֵיהּ malchutei. וְיַצְמַח veyatzmach

פּוּרְקָנֵיהּ purkanei. וִיקָרֵב vikarev מְשִׁיחֵיהּ meshichei: אָמֵן amen אידהנויה.

בְּחַיֵּיכוֹן bechayechon וּבְיוֹמֵיכוֹן uvyomechon וּבְחַיֵּי uvchayei

דְכָל dechol יל בֵּית bet ב"פ ראה יִשְׂרָאֵל Yisrael בַּעֲגָלָא ba'agala

וּבִזְמַן uvizman קָרִיב kariv וְאִמְרוּ ve'imru אָמֵן amen: אָמֵן amen אידהנויה.

The congregation and the *chazan* say the following:

Twenty eight words (until be'alma) and twenty eight letters (until almaya)

יְהֵא yehe שְׁמֵיהּ shemei (שם י"ה דס"ג) רַבָּא raba קנ"א ב"ן,

מְבָרַךְ mevarach, יהוה אלהים אדני, מילוי קס"א וס"ג, מ"ה ברבוע וע"ב ע"ה

לְעָלַם le'alam לְעָלְמֵי le'almei עָלְמַיָּא almaya. יִתְבָּרַךְ yitbarach.

Seven words with six letters each (שם בן מ"ב) and seven times the letter Vav (שם בן מ"ב):

וְיִשְׁתַּבַּח veyishtabach י"פ ע"ב יהוה אל אבג יתצ.

וְיִתְפָּאַר veyitpa'ar הי גו יה קרע שטן. וְיִתְרֹמַם veyitromam וה כוזו נגד יכש.

וְיִתְנַשֵּׂא veyitnase במוכסז בטר צתג. וְיִתְהַדָּר veyit'hadar כוזו יה וזקב טנע.

וְיִתְעַלֶּה veyit'ale וה יוד ה יגל פזק. וְיִתְהַלָּל veyit'halal א ואו הא שקו צית.

שְׁמֵיהּ shemei (שם י"ה דמ"ה) דְּקוּדְשָׁא dekudsha בְּרִיךְ verich הוּא hu:

אָמֵן amen אידהנויה.

KADDISH YEHE SHELAMA

May His great Name be more exalted and sanctified. (Amen)
In the world that He created according to His will, and may His kingdom reign. And may He cause His redemption to sprout and may He bring the Mashiach closer. (Amen) In your lifetimes and in your days and in the lifetime of all the House of Israel, speedily and in the near future, and you shall say, Amen. (Amen) May His great Name be blessed forever and for all eternity. Blessed and lauded, and glorified, and exalted, and extolled, and honored, and uplifted, and praised be the Name of the Holy Blessed One. (Amen)

shirata שִׁירָתָא ♦ birchata בִּרְכָתָא ילי kol כָּל min בֶּן le'ela לְעֵלָּא

da'amiran דַּאֲמִירָן ♦ venechamata וְנֶחֱמָתָא tishbechata תֻּשְׁבְּחָתָא

amen אידהנויה. amen אָמֵן: ve'imru וְאִמְרוּ be'alma בְּעָלְמָא

yehe יְהֵא shelama שְׁלָמָא raba רַבָּא קנ״א ב״ן, יהוה אלהים יהוה אדני, מילוי קס״א וס״ג,

chayim וְחַיִּים ♦ shemaya שְׁמַיָּא min בֶּן מ״ה ברבוע וע״ב ע״ה אהיה אהיה יהוה, בינה ע״ה

veshezava וְשֵׁיזָבָא venechama וְנֶחָמָה vishu'a וִישׁוּעָה vesava וְשָׂבַע

vechapara וְכַפָּרָה uslicha וּסְלִיחָה uge'ula וּגְאֻלָּה urefu'a וּרְפוּאָה

ulchol וּלְכָל lanu לָנוּ ♦ vehatzala וְהַצָּלָה verevach וְרֵיוַח אלהים, אהיה אדני יה אדני

amo עַמּוֹ Yisrael יִשְׂרָאֵל ve'imru וְאִמְרוּ amen אָמֵן: amen אָמֵן אידהנויה.

Take three steps backwards and say:

hu הוּא ♦ ע״ב, ריבוע יהוה. bimromav בִּמְרוֹמָיו shalom שָׁלוֹם ose עוֹשֶׂה

alenu עָלֵינוּ ר״ת ש״ע נהורין♦ shalom שָׁלוֹם ya'ase יַעֲשֶׂה berachamav בְּרַחֲמָיו

amen אָמֵן: ve'imru וְאִמְרוּ Yisrael יִשְׂרָאֵל amo עַמּוֹ עמם ילי kol כָּל ve'al וְעַל

amen אָמֵן אידהנויה.♦

ALENU

Drawing Surrounding Light in order to be protected from the *klipot* (negative side).

leshabe'ach לְשַׁבֵּחַ ריבוע דס״ג עלינו לשבח = אבג יתץ, ושר alenu עָלֵינוּ

hakol הַכֹּל ר״ת ללה, אדני אני ; ס״ת ס״ג ע״ה la'adon לַאֲדוֹן

bereshit בְּרֵאשִׁית ר״ת גלב (באר״ך ב״י יג״ל) leyotzer לְיוֹצֵר gedula גְּדֻלָּה latet לָתֵת

ha'aratzot הָאֲרָצוֹת kegoyei כְּגוֹיֵי asanu עָשָׂנוּ shelo שֶׁלֹּא

ha'adama הָאֲדָמָה kemishpechot כְּמִשְׁפְּחוֹת samanu שָׂמָנוּ velo וְלֹא

Above all blessings, songs, praises, and words of consolation that may be said in the world, and you shall say, Amen. (Amen) May there be abundant peace from Heaven, life, contentment, salvation, consolation, deliverance, healing, redemption, pardon, atonement, comfort, and relief. For us and for His entire nation, Israel, and you shall say, Amen. (Amen) He, Who makes peace in His High Places, with His compassion He shall make peace for us and for His entire nation, Israel. And you shall say, Amen. (Amen)

ALENU

It is incumbent upon us to give praise to the Master of all and to attribute greatness to the Molder of Creation, for He did not make us like the nations of the lands. He did not place us like the families of the Earth

שֶׁלֹּא shelo · שָׂם sam · חֶלְקֵנוּ chelkenu · כָּהֶם kahem · וְגוֹרָלֵנוּ vegoralenu

כְּכָל kechol · הֲמוֹנָם hamonam ◆ · שֶׁהֵם shehem · מִשְׁתַּחֲוִים mishtachavim

לַהֶבֶל lahevel · וָרִיק varik · וּמִתְפַּלְלִים umitpalelim · אֶל el · אֶל el

לֹא lo · יוֹשִׁיעַ Yoshi'a ◆ · (pause here, and bow your entire body when you say "va'anchnu mishtachavim")

וַאֲנַחְנוּ va'anachnu · מִשְׁתַּחֲוִים mishtachavim · לִפְנֵי lifnei · מֶלֶךְ melech

מַלְכֵי malchei · הַמְּלָכִים hamelachim · הַקָּדוֹשׁ hakadosh · בָּרוּךְ baruch

הוּא hu ◆ · שֶׁהוּא shehu · נוֹטֶה note · שָׁמַיִם shamayim

וּמוֹשַׁב umoshav · אֶרֶץ aretz ◆ · וְיוֹסֵד veyosed

יְקָרוֹ yekaro · בַּשָּׁמַיִם bashamayim · בְּמַּעַל mima'al ◆

וּשְׁכִינַת ush'chinat · עֻזּוֹ uzo · בְּגָבְהֵי begovhei · מְרוֹמִים meromim ◆

הוּא hu · אֱלֹהֵינוּ eloheinu · וְאֵין ve'ein · עוֹד od · אַחֵר acher ◆

אֱמֶת emet · מַלְכֵּנוּ malkenu · וְאֶפֶס ve'efes

זוּלָתוֹ zulato ◆ · כַּכָּתוּב kakatuv · בַּתוֹרָה batorah ◆ · וְיָדַעְתָּ veyadata

הַיּוֹם hayom · וַהֲשֵׁבֹתָ vahashevota · אֶל־ el

לְבָבֶךָ lvavecha · כִּי ki · יְהוָ֑ה Adonai · הוּא hu

הָאֱלֹהִים haElohim · בַּשָּׁמַיִם bashamayim · בְּמַּעַל mima'al

וְעַל־ ve'al · הָאָרֶץ ha'aretz · מִתָּחַת mitachat

עוֹד od · אֵין en · עוֹד od

He did not make our lot like theirs and our destiny like that of their multitudes, for they prostrate themselves to futility and emptiness and they pray to a deity that does not help. But we prostrate ourselves before the King of all Kings, the Holy Blessed One. It is He Who spreads the Heavens and establishes the earth. The Seat of His glory is in the Heaven above and the Divine Presence of His power is in the Highest of Heights. He is our God and there is no other. Our King is true and there is none beside Him. As it is written in the Torah: "And you shall know today and you shall take it to your heart that it is the Lord Who is God in the Heavens above and upon the Earth below, and there is none other". (Deuteronomy 4:39)

Elohenu אֱלֹהֵינוּ Adonai יְהֹוָה lach לְךָ nekave נְקַוֶּה ken כֵּן al עַל

יל״ה lir'ot לִרְאוֹת betiferet בְּתִפְאֶרֶת mehera מְהֵרָה uzach עֻזָּךְ ס״ת כהת, משיוז

בן דוד ע״ה ha'aretz הָאָרֶץ min מִן gilulim גִּלּוּלִים leha'avir לְהַעֲבִיר אלהים דההין

ע״ה letaken לְתַקֵּן yikaretun יִכָּרֵתוּן karot כָּרוֹת veha'elilim וְהָאֱלִילִים

olam עוֹלָם benei בְּנֵי יל״י vechol וְכָל Shadai שַׁדָּי bemalchut בְּמַלְכוּת

eleicha אֵלֶיךָ lehafnot לְהַפְנוֹת vishmecha בְשִׁמְךָ yikre'u יִקְרְאוּ vasar בָּשָׂר

kol כָּל יל״י veyed'u וְיֵדְעוּ yakiru יַכִּירוּ aretz אָרֶץ rish'ei רִשְׁעֵי יל״י kol כָּל יל״י

lefanecha לְפָנֶיךָ ס״ג מ״ה ב״ן berech בֶּרֶךְ tishava תִּשָּׁבַע kol כָּל יל״י lashon לָשׁוֹן

יהֹוָה veyipolu וְיִפֹּלוּ yichre'u יִכְרְעוּ יל״ה Elohenu אֱלֹהֵינוּ Adonai יְהֹוָה

vikabelu וִיקַבְּלוּ yitenu יִתְּנוּ yekar יְקָר shimcha שִׁמְךָ velichvod וְלִכְבוֹד

vetimloch וְתִמְלֹךְ malchutecha מַלְכוּתֶךָ ol עֹל et אֶת chulam כֻּלָּם

va'ed וָעֶד le'olam לְעוֹלָם mehera מְהֵרָה alehem עֲלֵיהֶם ריבוע ס״ג ו״י אותיות דס״ג

ul'olmei וּלְעוֹלְמֵי hee הִיא shelcha שֶׁלְּךָ hamalchut הַמַּלְכוּת ki כִּי

kakatuv כַּכָּתוּב bechavod בְּכָבוֹד timloch תִּמְלֹךְ ad עַד

le'olam לְעֹלָם yimloch יִמְלֹךְ | Adonai יְהֹוָה betoratach בְּתוֹרָתֶךְ

יהֹוָה vehaya וְהָיָה vene'emar וְנֶאֱמַר va'ed וָעֶד ריבוע ס״ג ו״י אותיות דס״ג ; ר״ת יל

ha'aretz הָאָרֶץ bayom בַּיּוֹם ע״ה lemelech לְמֶלֶךְ Adonai יְהֹוָה al עַל kol כָּל יל״י

echad אֶחָד Adonai יְהֹוָה yih'ye יִהְיֶה hahu הַהוּא

echad אֶחָד ushmo וּשְׁמוֹ

Consequently, we place our hope in You, Lord, our God, that we shall speedily see the glory of Your might, when You remove the idols from the earth and the deities shall be completely destroyed to correct the world with the kingdom of the Almighty. And all mankind shall then call out Your Name and You shall turn back to Yourself all the wicked ones of the Earth. Then all the inhabitants of the world shall recognize and know that, for You, every knee bends and every tongue vows. Before You, Lord, our God, they shall kneel and fall and shall give honor to Your glorious Name. And they shall all accept the yoke of Your Kingdom and You shall reign over them, forever and ever. Because the kingdom is Yours. And forever and for eternity, You shall reign gloriously. As it is written in the Torah: "The Lord shall reign forever and ever," (Exodus 15:18) and it is also stated: "The Lord shall be King over the whole world and, on that day, the Lord shall be One and His Name One." (Zechariah 14:9)

ARVIT OF MOTZA'EI SUKKOT AND SIMCHAT TORAH

In the evening prayer of *Arvit*, we connect to Jacob the Patriarch, who is the channel for Central Column energy. He helps us connect the two energies of Judgment and Mercy in a balanced way. It is said that the whole world was created only for Jacob, who embodies truth: "Give truth to Jacob" *(Michah 7:20)*. To activate the power of our prayer, and specifically the power of the prayer of *Arvit*, we must be truthful with others and, most importantly, with ourselves.

LESHEM YICHUD

hu הוּא   berich בְּרִיךְ   kudsha קוּדְשָׁא   yichud יִחוּד   leshem לְשֵׁם

ush'chintei וּשְׁכִינְתֵּיהּ (יאהדונהי)   bid'chilu בִּדְחִילוּ   ur'chimu וּרְחִימוּ

leyachda לְיַחֲדָא (איההויהה)   ud'chilu וּדְחִילוּ   ur'chimu וּרְחִימוּ (יאההויהה)

beyichuda בְּיִחוּדָא   kei קֵי   bevav בְּוָא"ו   kei קֵי   yud יו"ד   shem שֵׁם

Yisrael יִשְׂרָאֵל   kol כָּל   beshem בְּשֵׁם (יהוה)   shelim שְׁלִים

tefilat תְּפִלַּת   lehitpalel לְהִתְפַּלֵּל   ba'im בָּאִים   anachnu אֲנַחְנוּ   hine הִנֵּה

avinu אָבִינוּ   Yaakov יַעֲקֹב   shetiken שֶׁתִּקֵּן   arvit עַרְבִית

hamitzvot הַמִּצְוֹת   kol כָּל   im עִם   hashalom הַשָּׁלוֹם   alav עָלָיו

shorsha שׁוֹרְשָׁהּ   et אֶת   letaken לְתַקֵּן   ba בָּהּ   hakelulot הַכְּלוּלוֹת

ru'ach רוּחַ   nachat נַחַת   la'asot לַעֲשׂוֹת   elyon עֶלְיוֹן   bemakom בִּמְקוֹם

leyotzrenu לְיוֹצְרֵנוּ   vela'asot וְלַעֲשׂוֹת   retzon רְצוֹן

Adonai אֲדֹנָי   no'am נֹעַם   vihi וִיהִי   bor'enu בּוֹרְאֵנוּ

yadenu יָדֵינוּ   uma'ase וּמַעֲשֵׂה   alenu עָלֵינוּ   Elohenu אֱלֹהֵינוּ

konenehu כּוֹנְנֵהוּ   yadenu יָדֵינוּ   uma'ase וּמַעֲשֵׂה   alenu עָלֵינוּ   konena כּוֹנְנָה

ARVIT OF MOTZA'EI SUKKOT AND SIMCHAT TORAH - LESHEM YICHUD

For the sake of unification of The Holy Blessed One and His Shechinah, with fear and love and with love and fear, in order to unify The Name Yud-Kei and Vav-Kei in perfect unity, and in the name of Israel, we have hereby come to recite the prayer of Arvit, established by Jacob, our forefather, may peace be upon him, With all its commandments, to correct its root in the Supernal Place, to bring satisfaction to our Maker, and to fulfill the wish of our Creator. "And may the pleasantness of Lord, our God, be upon us and may He establish the work of our hands for us and may the work of our hands establish Him." (Psalms 90:17)

Right

יְהֹוָ֫ה Adonai צְבָאוֹת Tzeva'ot פְּנֵי שְׁכִינָה עִמָּנוּ imanu

רִבּוּעַ ס״ג, קס״א ע״ה ור׳ אוֹתִיּוֹת מוֹשֶׂה, מהע, רִבּוּעַ ע״ב וקס״א, אל שׁדי, מִשְׂגָּב misgav

ד״פ אלהים ע״ה לָנוּ lanu אלהים, אהיה אדני אֱלֹהֵי Elohei מִלּוּי ע״ב, דמב ; ילה

יַעֲקֹב Yaakov י׳ הַוָיוֹת, יאהדונהי אידהנויה סֶלָה sela:

Left

יְהֹוָ֫ה Adonai צְבָאוֹת Tzeva'ot פְּנֵי שְׁכִינָה אַשְׁרֵי ashrei

אָדָם adam מ״ה ; ה׳ צְבָאוֹת אַשְׁרֵי אָדָם = תִּפְאֶרֶת בֹּטֵחַ bote'ach

בָּךְ bach אָדָם בֹּטֵחַ בָּךְ = אמן (יאהדונהי) ע״ה ; בֹּטֵחַ בָּךְ = מִלּוּי ע״ב ע״ה:

Central

יְהֹוָ֫ה Adonai הוֹשִׁיעָה hoshi'a יהוה וש״ע נהורין הַמֶּלֶךְ hamelech ר״ת יהה

בַּיּוֹם veyom ע״ה נגד, מזבוח, זן, אל יהוה יַעֲנֵנוּ ya'anenu קְרָאֵנוּ kor'enu

ר״ת יב״ק, אלהים יהוה, אהיה אדני יהוה ; ס״ת = ב״ן ועם אות כ׳ דהמלך = ע״ב:

HALF KADDISH

יִתְגַּדַּל yitgadal וְיִתְקַדַּשׁ veyitkadash שׁדי ומלוי שׁדי ; י״א אוֹתִיּוֹת כמנין ו״ה

שְׁמֵהּ shemei רַבָּא raba (שׁם י״ה דע״ב) קנ״א ב״ן, יהוה אלהים יהוה אדני,

אָמֵן amen אידהנויה מִלּוּי קס״א וס״ג, מ״ה ברבוע וע״ב ע״ה ; ר״ת = ו״פ אלהים ; ס״ת = ג״פ יב״ק:

בְּעָלְמָא be'alma דִּי di בְּרָא vera כִּרְעוּתֵיהּ chir'utei

וְיַמְלִיךְ veyamlich מַלְכוּתֵיהּ mal'chutei וְיַצְמַח veyatzmach

פּוּרְקָנֵיהּ purkanei וִיקָרֵב vikarev מְשִׁיחֵיהּ meshichei: אָמֵן amen אידהנויה.

"The Lord of Hosts, joyful is one who trusts in You." (Psalms 84:13)
"The Lord of Hosts is with us. The God of Jacob is a refuge for us, Selah.
Lord redeem us. The King shall answer us on the day we call Him." (Psalms 20:10)
HALF KADDISH
May His great Name be more exalted and sanctified. (Amen)
In the world that He created according to His will, and may His Kingdom reign.
And may He cause His redemption to sprout and may He bring the Mashiach closer. (Amen)

uvchayei וּבְחַיֵּי uvyomechon וּבְיוֹמֵיכוֹן bechayechon בְּחַיֵּיכוֹן

ba'agala בַּעֲגָלָא Yisrael יִשְׂרָאֵל בֵּ"פ ראה bet בֵּית ילי dechol דְּכָל

uvizman וּבִזְמַן kariv קָרִיב ve'imru וְאִמְרוּ amen אָמֵן amen אָמֵן אידהנויה.

The congregation and the *chazan* say the following:

Twenty eight words (until *be'alma*) – meditate:

מילוי דמילוי דע"ב (יוד ויו דלת הי יוד ויו יוד הי יוד)

Twenty eight letters (until *almaya*) – meditate:

מילוי דמילוי דס"ג (יוד ויו דלת הי יוד ואו אלף ואו הי יוד)

yehe יְהֵא shemei שְׁמֵיהּ (שם י"ה דס"ג) raba רַבָּא קנ"א ב"ן,

mevarach מְבָרַךְ ע"ה ע"ב ברבוע מ"ה וס"ג, קס"א מילוי, אדני, יהוה אלהים יהוה

yitbarach יִתְבָּרַךְ almaya עָלְמַיָּא le'almei לְעָלְמֵי le'alam לְעָלַם

Seven words with six letters each (שם בן מ"ב) – meditate:

יהוה ← יוד הי ויו הי ← מילוי דמילוי דע"ב (יוד ויו דלת הי יוד ויו יוד הי יוד)

Also, seven times the letter *Vav* (שם בן מ"ב) – meditate:

יהוה ← יוד הי ואו הי ← מילוי דמילוי דס"ג (יוד ויו דלת הי יוד ואו אלף ואו הי יוד).

veyishtabach וְיִשְׁתַּבַּח י"פ ע"ב יהוה אל אבג יתץ.

veyitpa'ar וְיִתְפָּאַר הי נו יה קרע שטן. veyitromam וְיִתְרֹמַם וה כוזו נגד יכש.

veyitnase וְיִתְנַשֵּׂא במוכסז בטר צתג. veyit'hadar וְיִתְהַדָּר כוזו יה וזקב טנע.

veyit'ale וְיִתְעַלֶּה וה יוד ה יגל פזק. veyit'halal וְיִתְהַלָּל א ואו הא שקו צית.

shemei שְׁמֵיהּ (שם י"ה דמ"ה) dekudsha דְּקוּדְשָׁא verich בְּרִיךְ hu הוּא:

amen אָמֵן אידהנויה.

le'ela לְעֵלָּא min מִן kol כָּל ילי birchata בִּרְכָתָא shirata שִׁירָתָא

tishbechata תֻּשְׁבְּחָתָא venechamata וְנֶחָמָתָא da'amiran דַּאֲמִירָן

be'alma בְּעָלְמָא ve'imru וְאִמְרוּ amen אָמֵן amen אָמֵן אידהנויה.

In your lifetimes and in your days and in the lifetime of all the House of Israel, speedily and in the near future, and you should say, Amen. (Amen) May His great Name be blessed forever and for all eternity blessed and lauded, and glorified and exalted, and extolled and honored, and uplifted and praised be, the Name of the Holy Blessed One. (Amen) Above all blessings, songs, praises, and words of consolation that may be said in the world, and you shall say, Amen. (Amen)

VEHU RACHUM

"Vehu Rachum" contains thirteen words. The number thirteen denotes the Thirteen Attributes of Mercy, which, in this instance, we recite to cool down the fires of hell for all who reside there.

There are 13 words corresponding to the 13 Atributes of Mercy of *Arich Anpin*.

(Abba of the klipa) avon עָוֹן ר״ת רי״ו yechaper יְכַפֵּר rachum רַחוּם vehu וְהוּא

lehashiv לְהָשִׁיב vehirba וְהִרְבָּה *(Ima of the klipa)* yashchit יַשְׁחִית velo וְלֹא

chamato וַחֲמָתוֹ יכ׳ kol כָּל ya'ir יָעִיר velo וְלֹא *(Zeir of the klipa)* apo אַפּוֹ

נטורין וע״ע יהוה hoshi'a הוֹשִׁיעָה Adonai יְהֹוָה Adonai *(Nukva of the klipa)*

יהוה אל זן מזבוח, נגד, ע״ה veyom בַּיּוֹם ya'anenu יַעֲנֵנוּ ר״ת יהה hamelech הַמֶּלֶךְ

ע״בב kor'enu קָרְאֵנוּ ר״ת יב״ק, אלהים יהוה, אהיה אדני יהוה ; ס״ת ב״ן ועם כ׳ דהמלך = ע״בב

BARCHU

The *chazan* says:

Adonai יְהֹוָה et אֶת יהוה ריבוע יהוה ריבוע מ״ה barchu בָּרְכוּ

ע״ה בן דוד מ״ח, מ״ח ס״ת ע״ה hamevorach הַמְבֹרָךְ

First the congregation replies the following, and then the *chazan* repeats it:

Neshamah   *Ruach*   *Nefesh*

hamevorach הַמְבֹרָךְ Adonai יְהֹוָה baruch בָּרוּךְ

Yechidah   *Chayah*

va'ed וָעֶד ריבוע ס״ג וי׳ אותיות דס״ג le'olam לְעוֹלָם

VEHU RACHUM
And He is merciful,
forgives iniquity, and does not destroy; He frequently diverts His anger and does not arouse all His wrath."
(Psalms 70:38) *"Lord save us. The King shall answer on the day that we call Him." (Psalms 20:10)*
BARCHU
Bless the Lord, the Blessed One.
Blessed be the Lord, the Blessed One, forever and for eternity.

HaMa'ariv Aravim – First Chamber – Livnat Hasapir

In the time of *Arvit*, we have an opportunity to connect to four different "Chambers" in the House of the King - Chamber of Sapphire Stone (*Livnat Hasapir*), Chamber of Love (*Ahavah*), Chamber of Desire (*Ratzon*), and the Chamber of Holy of Holies (*Kodesh HaKodeshim*). Each Chamber connects us to another level in the spiritual plane. The blessing connecting us to the First Chamber, *Livnat Hasapir*, contains 53 words, which is also the numerical value of the word gan גן, meaning "garden," therefore connecting us to the Garden of Eden of our world.

Hechal Livnat Hasapir (the Chamber of Sapphire Stone) *of Nukva* in *Beriah*.

יכה Elohenu אֱלֹהֵינוּ Adonai יְהֹוָאדִנִיאהרונהי Ata אַתָּה baruch בָּרוּךְ

ma'ariv מַעֲרִיב bidvaro בִּדְבָרוֹ asher אֲשֶׁר ha'olam הָעוֹלָם melech מֶלֶךְ

(מצוות) תרי"ג = במילוי (Atzilut) bechochmah בְּחָכְמָה aravim עֲרָבִים

(Beriah) bitvuna בִּתְבוּנָה כתר she'arim שְׁעָרִים pote'ach פּוֹתֵחַ

et אֶת umachalif וּמַחֲלִיף (Yetzirah) itim עִתִּים meshane מְשַׁנֶּה

hakochavim הַכּוֹכָבִים et אֶת umsader וּמְסַדֵּר (Asiyah) hazemanim הַזְּמַנִּים

baraki'a בָּרָקִיעַ bemishmerotehem בְּמִשְׁמְרוֹתֵיהֶם (The Seven Planets)

golel גּוֹלֵל מלה valayla וְלַיְלָה yomam יוֹמָם bore בּוֹרֵא kirtzono כִּרְצוֹנוֹ

אוֹר or רו, אין סוף שך נצוצות של ו' המלכים choshech וְחֹשֶׁךְ mipenei מִפְּנֵי

וְחֹשֶׁךְ or אוֹר mipenei מִפְּנֵי המלכים של ו' נצוצות שך vechoshech רו, אין סוף

layla לַיְלָה umevi וּמֵבִיא ע"ה נגד, מזבוח, זן, אל יהוה yom יוֹם hama'avir הַמַּעֲבִיר

uven וּבֵין אל יהוה זן, מזבוח, נגד, ע"ה yom יוֹם ben בֵּין umavdil וּמַבְדִּיל מלה

shemo שְׁמוֹ פני שכינה Tzeva'ot צְבָאוֹת Adonai יְהֹוָאדִנִיאהרונהי מלה layla לַיְלָה

baruch בָּרוּךְ Adonai יְהֹוָאדִנִיאהרונהי ע"ה אל סודי ע"ה, ע"ב בריבוע וקס"א ע"ה, מהש ע"ה

aravim עֲרָבִים hama'ariv הַמַּעֲרִיב Adonai יְהֹוָאדִנִיאהרונהי Ata אַתָּה

HaMa'ariv Aravim – First Chamber – Livnat Hasapir

Blessed are You, Lord, our God, King of the universe,

Who brings with His words evenings with wisdom. He opens gates with understanding. He changes the seasons and varies the times and arranges the stars in their constellations in the sky, according to His will. He creates day and night and rolls Light away from before darkness, and darkness from before Light. He is the One Who causes the day to pass and brings on night and separates between day and night. Lord of Hosts, His Name is the Lord. Blessed are You, Lord, who brings on evenings.

AHAVAT OLAM – SECOND CHAMBER - LOVE

This blessing connects us to the Second Chamber, *Ahavah* (Love) and its purpose is to inspire us with a renewed love for others and for the world.

> *Hechal Ahavah* (the Chamber of Love) of *Nukva* in *Beriah*.
> The following paragraph has 50 words corresponding to the 50 Gates of *Binah*.

ahavat אַהֲבַת · olam עוֹלָם · bet בֵּית ב״פ רא״ה · Yisrael יִשְׂרָאֵל · amecha עַמְּךָ

♦ahavta אָהַבְתָּ · torah תּוֹרָה (Atzilut) · umitzvot וּמִצְוֹת (Beriah) · chukim וְחֻקִּים

(Yetzirah) umishpatim וּמִשְׁפָּטִים · (Asiyah) otanu אוֹתָנוּ · ♦limadeta לִמַּדְתָּ

al עַל · ken כֵּן · Adonai יְהֹוָה · Elohenu אֱלֹהֵינוּ יְלֹה

beshochvenu בְּשָׁכְבֵנוּ · uvkumenu וּבְקוּמֵנוּ · nasi'ach נָשִׂיחַ · bechukecha בְּחֻקֶּיךָ

venismach וְנִשְׂמַח · vena'aloz וְנַעֲלֹוז · bedivrei בְּדִבְרֵי · talmud תַּלְמוּד

toratecha תּוֹרָתֶךָ · umitzvotecha וּמִצְוֹתֶיךָ · vechukotecha וְחֻקּוֹתֶיךָ

le'olam לְעוֹלָם רִיבּוֹעַ דס״ג וי׳ אותיות דס״ג · va'ed♦ וָעֶד · ki כִּי · hem הֵם

chayenu וְחַיֵּינוּ · ve'orech וְאֹרֶךְ · yamenu יָמֵינוּ · uvahem וּבָהֶם · nehge נֶהְגֶּה

yomam יוֹמָם · valayla וְלַיְלָה מלה♦ · ve'ahavatcha וְאַהֲבָתְךָ · lo לֹא · tasur תָסוּר

mimenu מִמֶּנּוּ · le'olamim♦ לְעוֹלָמִים · baruch בָּרוּךְ · Ata אַתָּה

Adonai יְהֹוָה · ohev אוֹהֵב · et אֶת · amo עַמּוֹ · Yisrael יִשְׂרָאֵל:

THE SHEMA (to learn more about the *Shema* go to page 330)

The *Shema* is one of the most powerful tools to draw the energy of healing to our lives. The true power of the *Shema* is unleashed when we recite this prayer while meditating on others who need healing energy.

1) In order to receive the Light of the *Shema*, you have to accept upon yourself the precept of: "Love your neighbor as yourself," and see yourself united with all the souls that comprise the Original Adam.
2) You need to meditate to connect to the precept of the Reciting of *Shema* twice a day.
3) Before saying the *Shema* you should cover your eyes with your right hand (saying the words "*Shema Yisrael ... le'olam va'ed.*") And you should read the *Shema* with deep meditation, chanting it with the intonations. It is necessary to be careful with the pronunciation of all the letters.

AHAVAT OLAM – SECOND CHAMBER - LOVE

With eternal love, You have loved Your Nation, the House of Israel.
Torah, commandments, statutes, and laws, You have taught us. Therefore, Lord, our God, when we lie down and when we rise up, we shall discuss Your statutes and we shall rejoice and exult in the words of the teachings of Your Torah, Your commandments, and Your statutes, forever and ever. They are our lifetimes and the length of our days; with them we shall direct ourselves day and night. And Your love, You shall never remove from us. Blessed are You, Lord, Who loves His Nation, Israel.

First, meditate in general on the first *Yichud* of the four *Yichuds* of the Name: יהוה, and in particular to awaken the letter ה, and then to connect it with the letter ו. Then connect the letter י and the letter ה together in the following order: *Hei* (ה), *Hei-Vav* (ה"ו), then *Yud-Hei* (י"ה), which adds up to 31, the secret of יא"י of the Name ס"ג. It is good to meditate on this *Yichud* before reciting any *Shema* because it acts as a replacement for the times that you may have missed reading the *Shema*. This *Yichud* has the same ability to create a Supernal connection like the reading of the *Shema* - to raise *Zeir* and *Nukva* together for the *Zivug* of *Abba* and *Ima*.

Shema – שׁמַע

General Meditation: שׁמַ ע — to draw the energy from the Seven Lower *Sefirot* of *Ima* to the *Nukva*, which enables the *Nukva* to elevate the *Mayin Nukvin* (awakening from Below).

Particular Meditation: שׁמ = יהוה ּ שׂדי and five times the letters י and ד of ב"ן = ע [The letter *Hei* (ה) is formed by the letters *Dalet* (ד) and *Yud* (י), so in ב"ן we have four times the letter ה plus another time the letters י and ד from יוד of ב"ן.]. Also the three letters ו (18) - that are left from ב"ן, plus ב"ן itself (52) equals ע (70).

Yisrael – יִשְׂרָאֵל

General Meditation: שׂיר אל — to draw energy from *Chesed* and *Gevurah* of *Abba* to *Zeir Anpin*, to do his action in the secret of *Mayin Duchrin* (awakening from Above).

Particular Meditation: (the rearranged letters of the word *Yisrael*) – שׂר אלי

אלהים דיודין (אלף למד הי יוד מם) = ע',
רבוע אלהים (א אל אלה אלהי אלהים) = ר',
מ"א אותיות רבוע אלהים במילואו (אלף אלף למד אלף למד הי אלף למד הי יוד אלף למד הי יוד מם) = אל"י.
Also meditate to draw the Inner *Mochin* of *Abba* of *Katnut* into *Zeir Anpin*.

Adonai Elohenu Adonai - יהוה אלהינו יהוה

General Meditation: to draw energy to *Abba*, *Ima* and *Da'at* from *Arich Anpin*,

Particular Meditation: ע"ב (יוד הי ויו הי) קס"א (אלף הי יוד הי) ע"ב (יוד הי וי הי).

Echad – אֶחַד
(The secret of the complete *Yichud-Unification*)

The letters *Alef* א and *Chet* ח from *Echad* אחד are *Zeir Anpin* and the letter *Dalet* ד is *Nukva*. **You should meditate** to devote your soul for the sanctification of the Holy Name, thereby elevating your *Nefesh*, *Ruach*, *Neshamah* and *Neshamah* of *Neshamah* with *Zeir Anpin* and *Nukva* (using the Names: ע"ב and ס"ג) to *Abba* and *Ima* as the secret of *Mayin Nukvin*, and by that energy, *Abba* and *Ima* will be unified in the secret of the Name: יאהדונהי. **Also meditate** to draw out the Inner Six Edges of *Gadlut* of *Ima* into *Zeir Anpin*. The Drop, which is ע"ב, is drawn out from the external of *Arich Anpin*, and descends to *Yesod* of *Ima*, where it becomes: ע"ב ס"ג מ"ה ב"ן, and the four spelled out אהיה (אלף הי יוד הי, אלף הי יוד הי, אלף הה יוד הא, אלף הה יוד הה) become Her clothing. As a result, *Zeir Anpin* now has four spelled out יה"ו (יוד הי ויו, יוד הי ואו, יוד הא ואו, יוד הה וו), four spelled out אה"י (אלף הי יוד, אלף הי יוד, אלף הא יוד, אלף הה יוד) and the Inner Six Edges of *Gadlut* of *Ima*. **Also meditate** on the Name: אל"ף ה"י וי"ו ה"י, which is the entire *Mochin* in the secret of *Da'at*. **And also meditate** (according to the Ramchal) on the four spelled out *Alef* (אלף=111) of the Name: אהי"ה that is equal to the word *Midat* (444), making the *Keter* for Leah.

Baruch Shem - בָּרוּך שֵׁם כְּבוֹד מַלְכוּתוֹ לְעוֹלָם וָעֶד
Baruch Shem Kevod – Chochmah, Binah, Da'at of Leah;
Malchuto – Her *Keter*; **Le'olam** – the rest of Her *Partzuf*;
Va'ed – the four היה (4 times 20 equal to *Va'ed*=80) will make the *Keter* for Rachel .
And the four spelled out היה (הי יוד הי, הי ויו הי, הא יוד הי, הא יוד הה יוד הה) will make the rest of Her body.

Adonai יהוֹאדניהיאהדונהי ע׳ רבתי Yisrael יִשְׂרָאֵל shema שְׁמַע

echad אֶחָֽד ד׳ רבתי ; אהבה, דאגה׃ | Adonai יהוֹאדניהיאהדונהי ילה Elohenu אֱלֹהֵינוּ

malchuto מַלְכוּתוֹ, kevod כְּבוֹד shem שֵׁם baruch בָּרוּךְ יחו אותיו (: Whisper)

va'ed וָעֶֽד׃ אותיות דס״ג ו׳ ריבוע דס״ג le'olam לְעוֹלָם

Yud, Chochmah, head – 42 words corresponding to the Holy 42-Letter Name of God.

ב   א

et אֵת (ה׳ אהבת על מ״ע לקיים יכוין) ; סוף אין ב״פ רו, ב״פ אור, ב״פ ve'ahavta וְאָהַבְתָּ

יהוֹאדניהיאהדונהי Adonai Elohecha אֱלֹהֶיךָ ילה ; ס״ת כהת, משיוו בן דוד ע״ה

nafshecha נַפְשְׁךָ לכב ,ב״ן uvchol וּבְכָל levavcha לְבָבְךָ לכב ,ב״ן bechol בְּכָל

hadevarim הַדְּבָרִים vehayu וְהָיוּ me'odecha מְאֹדֶךָ לכב ,ב״ן uvchol וּבְכָל

hayom הַיּוֹם metzavecha מְצַוְּךָ anochi אָנֹכִי asher אֲשֶׁר ha'ele הָאֵלֶּה

veshinantam וְשִׁנַּנְתָּם levavecha לְבָבֶךָ al עַל (pause here) ע״ה גנד, מזבוה, זן, אל יהוה

beshivtecha בְּשִׁבְתְּךָ מ״ב bam בָּם vedibarta וְדִבַּרְתָּ levanecha לְבָנֶיךָ

vaderech בַדֶּרֶךְ uvlechtecha וּבְלֶכְתְּךָ ראה ב״פ bevetecha בְּבֵיתֶךָ

uvkumecha וּבְקוּמֶךָ׃ uvshochbecha וּבְשָׁכְבְּךָ קס״א ס״ג ,יב״ק ב״פ

yadecha יָדֶךָ al עַל le'ot לְאוֹת ukshartam וּקְשַׁרְתָּם

THE SHEMA

"Hear Israel, the Lord our God. The Lord is One." *(Deuteronomy 6:4)*
"Blessed is the glorious Name, His Kingdom is forever and for eternity." *(Pesachim 56a)*

"And you shall love the Lord, your God, with all your heart and with all your soul and with all that you possess. Let those words that I command you today be upon your heart. And you shall teach them to your children and you shall speak of them while you sit in your home and while you walk on your way and when you lie down and when you rise. You shall bind them as a sign upon your hand

וְהָיוּ vehayu   לְטֹטָפֹת letotafot   בֵּין ben   עֵינֶיךָ enecha

עַל־ al   וּכְתַבְתָּם uchtavtam   מ"ה: ריבוע   ;   קס"א   ע"ה

מְזֻזוֹת mezuzot   (זז מות) נית   בֵּיתֶךָ betecha   ב"פ ראה   וּבִשְׁעָרֶיךָ uvish'arecha:

VEHAYA IM SHAMO'A

Hei, Binah, arms and body — 72 words corresponding to the 72 Names of God.

וְהָיָה vehaya   יהוה ; יהה : יוה"ר, מ"א אותיות דפשוט, דמילוי ודמילוי דמילוי דמילוי דאהיה ע"ה   אִם־ im

שָׁמֹעַ shamo'a   תִּשְׁמְעוּ tishme'u   אֶל־ el   מִצְוֹתַי mitzvotai   אֲשֶׁר asher

אָנֹכִי anochi   מְצַוֶּה metzave   אֶתְכֶם etchem   הַיּוֹם hayom   ע"ה נגד, מזבוח, זן, אל יהוה

לְאַהֲבָה le'ahava   אוזר, דאגה   (pause here)   אֶת־ et   יְהֹוָה Adonai

אֱלֹהֵיכֶם Elohechem   (enunciate the letter *Ayin* in the word *"ul'ovdo"*)   וּלְעָבְדוֹ ul'ovdo

בְּכָל־ bechol   לְבַבְכֶם levavchem   וּבְכָל־ uvchol

נַפְשְׁכֶם nafshechem: וְנָתַתִּי venatati   מְטַר־ metar   אַרְצְכֶם artzechem

בְּעִתּוֹ be'ito   יוֹרֶה yore   וּמַלְקוֹשׁ umalkosh   וְאָסַפְתָּ ve'asafta   דְגָנֶךָ deganecha

וְתִירֹשְׁךָ vetiroshcha   וְיִצְהָרֶךָ veyitz'harecha: וְנָתַתִּי venatati   עֵשֶׂב esev

---

and they shall be as frontlets between your eyes.
And you shall write them upon the doorposts of your house and your gates." (Deuteronomy 6:5-9)

VEHAYA IM SHAMO'A

"And it shall come to be that if you shall listen to My commandments that I am commanding you with today to love the Lord, your God, and to serve Him with all your heart and with all your soul, then I shall send rain upon your land in its proper time, both early rain and late rain. You shall then gather your grain and your wine and your oil. And I shall give grass

מנד　　　　כוכ　　　　להוו　　　　יוזו

vesavata וְשָׂבָעְתָּ: ve'achalta וְאָכַלְתָּ livhemtecha לִבְהֶמְתֶּךָ besadcha בְּשָׂדְךָ

ההה　　　　ייי　　　　רהע　　　וזעם　　　　אני

levavchem לְבַבְכֶם yifte יִפְתֶּה pen פֶּן lachem לָכֶם hishamru הִשָּׁמְרוּ

סאל　　　　ילה　　　　ויל　　　　מיכ

acherim אֲחֵרִים elohim אֱלֹהִים va'avadetem וַעֲבַדְתֶּם vesartem וְסַרְתֶּם

עשׂל　　　　　　ערי

lahem לָהֶם: vehishtachavitem וְהִשְׁתַּחֲוִיתֶם (הקליפות) נגד (העומד) משׂה

הוזע　　　דני　　　והו　　　　מיה

bachem בָּכֶם Adonai יְהֹוָהּ af אַף (pause here) vechara וְחָרָה

מבה　　　ניח　　　גנא　　　עמם

velo וְלֹא יִ"פ טל, יִ"פ כוזו hashamayim הַשָּׁמַיִם et אֶת ve'atzar וְעָצַר

מצר　　　הרוז　　　ייל　　　פוי

titen תִתֵּן ב"פ כהת lo לֹא veha'adama וְהָאֲדָמָה matar מָטָר ייי yihye יִהְיֶה

דמב　　　מוזי　　　ענו　　　יהה　　ומב

me'al מֵעַל עלם mehera מְהֵרָה va'avadetem וַאֲבַדְתֶּם yevula יְבוּלָהּ et אֶת

וזבו　　　איע　　　　מנק

asher אֲשֶׁר hatova הַטֹּבָה ע"ה אלהים דההן ha'aretz הָאָרֶץ

היי　　　יבם　　　ראה

Vav, Zeir Anpin lachem לָכֶם: noten נֹתֵן אבג יתצ, ושׂר Adonai יְהֹוָה

מום

stomach — 50 words corresponding to the 50 Gates of *Binah* vesamtem וְשַׂמְתֶּם

א　　　ה　　　י　　　ה　　　א

levavchem לְבַבְכֶם al עַל ele אֵלֶּה ראה devarai דְּבָרַי et אֶת

א　　　ה　　　י　　　ה

otam אֹתָם ukshartem וּקְשַׁרְתֶּם nafshechem נַפְשְׁכֶם ve'al וְעַל

---

in your field for your cattle. And you shall eat and you shall be satiated. Be careful lest your heart be seduced and you may turn away and serve alien deities and prostrate yourself before them. And the wrath of the Lord shall be upon you and He shall stop the Heavens and there shall be no more rain and the earth shall not give forth its crop. And you shall quickly perish from the good land that the Lord has given you. And you shall place those words of Mine upon your heart and upon your soul and you shall bind them

לְאוֹת (le'ot) · ר"ת · לאו · עַל־ (al) · יֶדְכֶם (yedchem) · וְהָיוּ (vehayu)

לְטוֹטָפֹת (letotafot) · בֵּין (ben) · עֵינֵיכֶם (enechem) · רִיבוּע · מ"ה:

וְלִמַּדְתֶּם (velimadetem) · אֹתָם (otam) · אֶת־ (et) · בְּנֵיכֶם (benechem)

לְדַבֵּר (ledaber) · ראה · בָּם (bam) · שׂים · בֵן · מ"ב · בְּשִׁבְתְּךָ (beshivtecha)

בְּבֵיתֶךָ (bevetecha) · ב"פ ראה · וּבְלֶכְתְּךָ (uvlechtecha) · בַּדֶּרֶךְ (vaderech) · ב"פ יב"ק, ס"ג קס"א

וּבְשָׁכְבְּךָ (uvshochbecha) · וּבְקוּמֶךָ (uvkumecha): · וּכְתַבְתָּם (uchtavtam) · עַל־ (al)

מְזוּזוֹת (mezuzot) · בֵּיתֶךָ (betecha) · ב"פ ראה · וּבִשְׁעָרֶיךָ (uvish'arecha): · לְמַעַן (lema'an)

יִרְבּוּ (yirbu) · יְמֵיכֶם (yemechem) · ר"ת · ייל · וִימֵי (vimei) · בְּנֵיכֶם (venechem)

עַל (al) · הָאֲדָמָה (ha'adama) · אֲשֶׁר (asher) · (enunciate the letter *Ayin* in the word "nishba")

נִשְׁבַּע (nishba) · יכוין · לשבועות · המבול · יְהֹוָה (Adonai) אדנ"י אהדונ"הי

לַאֲבֹתֵיכֶם (la'avotechem) · לָתֵת (latet) · לָהֶם (lahem) · כִּימֵי (kimei)

הַשָּׁמַיִם (hashamayim) · טל י"פ, כוזו י"פ · עַל־ (al) · הָאָרֶץ (ha'aretz) · אלהים דההין ע"ה:

---

as a sign upon your hands and they shall be as frontlets between your eyes. And you shall teach them to your children and speak of them while you sit at home and while you walk on your way and when you lie down and when you rise. You shall write them upon the doorposts of your house and upon your gates. This is so that your days shall be numerous and so shall the days of your children upon the Earth that the Lord had sworn to your fathers to give them as the days of the Heavens upon the Earth." (Deuteronomy 11:13-21)

VAYOMER

Hei, Malchut, legs and reproductive organs,

72 words corresponding to the 72 Names of God in direct order (according to the Ramchal).

עֹאם Moshe מֹשֶׁה   סבט el אֶל   ייִי Adonai יְהֹוָה   ווו vayomer וַיֹּאמֶר

אוֹא el אֶל   ליה ראה daber דַּבֵּר   מבטע lemor לֵאמֹר

מהטע, ע״ב ברביוע וקס״א, אל שדי, ד״פ אלהים ע״ה

המע ve'asu וְעָשׂוּ   להו alehem אֲלֵהֶם   אגד ve'amarta וְאָמַרְתָּ   הוי Yisrael יִשְׂרָאֵל   כמת benei בְּנֵי

לוו vigdehem בִּגְדֵיהֶם   המם kanfei כַּנְפֵי   היי al עַל   מרה tzitzit צִיצִת   יצל lahem לָהֶם

נמך tzitzit צִיצִת   פגל al עַל   לוי venatnu וְנָתְנוּ   כבי ledorotam לְדֹרֹתָם

ווהו techelet תְּכֵלֶת   בּ״ן יּ״פ   מנה petil פְּתִיל   אלהים אדני קנ״א, ע״ה   יוזי hakanaf הַכָּנָף

רכי oto אֹתוֹ   שאה ur'item וּרְאִיתֶם   ירת letzitzit לְצִיצִת   השא lachem לָכֶם   יהה ; יהוה   ניה vehaya וְהָיָה

להוו Adonai יְהֹוָה   ייי mitzvot מִצְוֹת   ילי   והר kol כָּל   ליב et אֶת   אום uzchartem וּזְכַרְתֶּם

רהע acharei אַחֲרֵי   וזום taturu תָתוּרוּ   אני velo וְלֹא   מגד otam אֹתָם   כעק va'asitem וַעֲשִׂיתֶם

מכך enechem עֵינֵיכֶם   ריבוע ve'acharei וְאַחֲרֵי   מ״ה   השה   יוזו levavchem לְבַבְכֶם

You should meditate on the precept:
"not to follow negative sexual thoughts of the heart and the sights of the eyes for prostitution."

VAYOMER

"And the Lord spoke to Moses and said,
Speak to the children of Israel and say to them that they should make for themselves Tzitzit,
on the corners of their garments, throughout all their generations. And they must place upon the Tzitzit,
of each corner, a blue strand. And this shall be to you as a Tzitzit: you shall see it and remember
the commandments of the Lord and fulfill them. And you shall not stray after your hearts and your eyes,

lema'an לְמַעַן :acharehem אַחֲרֵיהֶם zonim זֹנִים atem אַתֶּם asher אֲשֶׁר

mitzvotai מִצְוֹתָי kol כָּל et אֶת va'asitem וַעֲשִׂיתֶם tizkeru תִּזְכְּרוּ

lelohechem לֵאלֹהֵיכֶם kedoshim קְדֹשִׁים vihyitem וִהְיִיתֶם

asher אֲשֶׁר Elohechem אֱלֹהֵיכֶם Adonai יְהֹוָה ani אֲנִי

Mitzrayim מִצְרַיִם me'eretz מֵאֶרֶץ etchem אֶתְכֶם hotzeti הוֹצֵאתִי

> You should meditate to remember the exodus from *Mitzrayim* (Egypt).

lihyot לִהְיוֹת lachem לָכֶם lelohim לֵאלֹהִים

ani אֲנִי Adonai יְהֹוָה Elohechem אֱלֹהֵיכֶם

Be careful to complete this paragraph together with the *chazan* and the congregation, and say the word *"emet"* out loud. The *chazan* should say the word *"emet"* in silence.

emet אֱמֶת אהיה פעמים אהיה, ז"פ ס"ג

The congregation should be silent, listen and hear the words *"Adonai Elohechem emet"* spoken by the *chazan*. If you did not complete the paragraph together with the *chazan* you should repeat the last three words on your own. With these three words the *Shema* is completed.

Adonai יְהֹוָה Elohechem אֱלֹהֵיכֶם

emet אֱמֶת אהיה פעמים אהיה, ז"פ ס"ג

---

after which you adulterate. This is so that you shall remember to fulfill all My commandments and thereby be holy before your God. I am the Lord, your God, Who brought you out of the land of Egypt to be your God. I, the Lord, your God, is true." (Numbers 15:37-41) the Lord, your God, is true!

VE'EMUNA – THIRD CHAMBER – RATZON

Ve'emuna connects us to the Third Chamber in the House of the King: *Ratzon*, or desire. Before we can connect to any form of spiritual energy, we need to feel a want or desire. Desire is the vessel that draws spiritual Light. A small desire draws a small amount of Light. A large desire draws a large amount.

Hechal Ratzon (the Chamber of Desire) of *Nukva* in *Beriah*.

עֲלֵינוּ ,alenu	וְקָיָם vekayam	וְקָיָם zot זֹאת ילי kol כָּל (בוניה לילה)	ve'emuna וֶאֱמוּנָה				
וְאֵין ve'en ילה	Elohenu אֱלֹהֵינוּ	Adonai יְהֹוָהאהדונהי	hu הוּא	ki כִּי			
עַמּוֹ amo.	Yisrael יִשְׂרָאֵל	va'anachnu וַאֲנַחְנוּ	zulato זוּלָתוֹ.				
הַגּוֹאֲלֵנוּ hago'alenu	melachim מְלָכִים.	miyad מִיַּד	hapodenu הַפּוֹדֵנוּ				
עָרִיצִים aritzim. ילי	kol כָּל	mikaf מִכַּף	malkenu מַלְכֵּנוּ				
לָנוּ lanu אלהים, אהיה אדני	hanifra הַנִּפְרָע (מילוי דס"ג) ; ייא"י לאה	haEl הָאֵל					
לְכֹל lechol יה אדני	gemul גְּמוּל	hameshalem הַמְשַׁלֵּם	mitzarenu מִצָּרֵינוּ.				
נַפְשֵׁנוּ nafshenu	hasam הַשָּׂם	nafshenu נַפְשֵׁנוּ:	oyvei אוֹיְבֵי				
לַמּוֹט lamot	נָתַן natan	וְלֹא־ velo אהיה אהיה יהוה, בינה ע"ה	bachayim בַּחַיִּים				
בָּמוֹת bamot	עַל al	hamadrichenu הַמַּדְרִיכֵנוּ	raglenu רַגְלֵנוּ.				
כָּל kol ילי ; עמם	עַל al	karnenu קַרְנֵנוּ	vayarem וַיָּרֶם	oyvenu אוֹיְבֵינוּ.			
הָעוֹשֶׂה ha'ose (מילוי דס"ג) ; ייא"י לאה	haEl הָאֵל	son'enu שׂוֹנְאֵינוּ.					
בְּפַרְעֹה beFar'o.	unkama וּנְקָמָה	nisim נִסִּים אדני אהיה אלהים,	lanu לָנוּ				
בְּנֵי benei	be'admat בְּאַדְמַת	uvmoftim וּבְמוֹפְתִים	be'otot בְּאוֹתוֹת				
כָּל kol ילי	ve'evrato בְּעֶבְרָתוֹ	hamake הַמַּכֶּה	Cham חָם.				
אֵת et	vayotzi וַיּוֹצֵא מצר־.	Mitzrayim מִצְרָיִם	bechorei בְּכוֹרֵי				
עוֹלָם olam.	lecherut לְחֵרוּת	mitocham מִתּוֹכָם	Yisrael יִשְׂרָאֵל	amo עַמּוֹ			

VE'EMUNA – THIRD CHAMBER - RATZON

And trustworthy. All this and He are set upon us because He is the Lord, our God, and there is none other. And we are Israel, His Nation. He redeems us from the hands of kings. He is our King, Who delivers us from the reach of tyrants; The God, Who avenges us against our enemies. He pays our mortal enemies their due. He Who keeps us alive and does not allow our feet to falter; He Who lets us walk upon the plains of our foes. He Who raises our worth over all our enemies. He is God, Who wrought for us retribution against Pharaoh, with signs and wonders, in the land of the children of Cham. He Who struck down with His anger at the first-born of Egypt, and brought out His Nation, Israel, from amongst them to everlasting freedom.

הַמַּעֲבִיר hama'avir בָּנָיו banav

בֵּין ben גִּזְרֵי gizrei יָם yam ילי סוּף Suf◆ וְאֶת ve'et רוֹדְפֵיהֶם rodfehem

וְאֶת ve'et שׂוֹנְאֵיהֶם son'ehem בִּתְהוֹמוֹת bitehomot טִבַּע tiba◆ רָאוּ ra'u

בָנִים vanim אֶת et גְּבוּרָתוֹ gevurato שִׁבְּחוּ shibechu וְהוֹדוּ vehodu אהיה

לִשְׁמוֹ lishmo מהטע ע"ה, ע"ב בריבוע וקס"א ע"ה, אל שדי ע"ה◆ וּמַלְכוּתוֹ umalchuto

בְּרָצוֹן beratzon מהטע ע"ה, ע"ב בריבוע וקס"א ע"ה, אל שדי ע"ה קִבְּלוּ kibelu

עֲלֵיהֶם alehem◆ מהטע, ע"ב בריבוע וקס"א ע"ה, אל שדי, ד"פ אלהים ע"ה מֹשֶׁה Moshe

וּבְנֵי uvnei יִשְׂרָאֵל Yisrael ר"ת ע"ה נגד, מזבוז, זן, אל יהוה לְךָ lecha עָנוּ anu

שִׁירָה shira בְּשִׂמְחָה besimcha רַבָּה raba וְאָמְרוּ ve'amru כֻלָּם chulam:

מִי mi ילי כָמֹכָה chamocha בָּאֵלִם ba'elim יְהֹוָה Adonai

מִי mi ילי כָּמֹכָה kamocha נֶאְדָּר nedar ר"ת ע"ב, ריבוע יהוה ; ס"ת מ"ה

בַּקֹּדֶשׁ bakodesh ר"ת יב"ק, אלהים יהוה, אהיה אדני יהוה נוֹרָא nora תְהִלֹּת tehilot

עֹשֵׂה ose פֶלֶא fele: מַלְכוּתְךָ malchutcha יְהֹוָה Adonai

אֱלֹהֵינוּ Elohenu ילה רָאוּ ra'u בָנֶיךָ vanecha עַל al הַיָּם hayam ילי

יוֹ֒חַד yachad כֻלָּם kulam הוֹדוּ hodu אהיה וְהִמְלִיכוּ vehimlichu

וְאָמְרוּ ve'amru: יְהֹוָה Adonai | יִמְלֹךְ yimloch לְעֹלָם le'olam

רביבוע ס"ג וי' אותיות דס"ג ; ר"ת ייל וָעֶד va'ed◆ וְנֶאֱמַר vene'emar: כִּי ki פָּדָה fada

יְהֹוָה Adonai אֶת et יַעֲקֹב Yaakov

וּגְאָלוֹ ug'alo מִיַּד miyad וֹזָק chazak פהל מִמֶּנּוּ mimenu: בָּרוּךְ baruch

אַתָּה Ata יְהֹוָה Adonai גָּאַל ga'al באתב"ש כתר יִשְׂרָאֵל Yisrael:

He Who caused His children to pass between the sections of the Sea of Reeds, while their pursuers and their enemies, He drowned in the depths. The children saw His might and they praised and gave thanks to His Name; they accepted His sovereignty over them willingly. Moses and the children of Israel raised their voices in song to Him, with great joy, and they all said, as one "Who is like You among the gods, Lord? Who is like You, awesome in holiness, tremendous in praise and Who works wonders?" (Exodus 15:11) Our children saw Your Kingdom, Lord, our God, upon the sea, and they all in unison gave thanks to You and accepted Your sovereignty and said: "The Lord shall reign forever and ever." (Exodus 15:18) And it is stated: "For the Lord has delivered Jacob and redeemed him from the hand of one that is stronger than he." (Jeremiah 31:10) Blessed are You, Lord, Who redeemed Israel.

HASHKIVENU – FOURTH CHAMBER – HOLY OF HOLIES

The Fourth Chamber is *Kodesh HaKodeshim,* the Holy of Holies, which is our link to the next level that we reach through the *Amidah.*

Hechal Kodesh HaKodashim (the Chamber of the Holy of Holies) of *Nukva* in *Beriah.*

לאה   ר"ת   leshalom לְשָׁלוֹם   avinu אָבִינוּ   hashkivenu הַשְׁכִּיבֵנוּ

אהיה אהיה יהוה, בינה ע"ה   lechayim לְחַיִּים   malkenu מַלְכֵּנוּ   veha'amidenu וְהַעֲמִידֵנוּ

alenu עָלֵינוּ   ufros וּפְרוֹשׂ   ulshalom וּלְשָׁלוֹם   tovim טוֹבִים

vetakenenu וְתַקְּנֵנוּ   shelomecha שְׁלוֹמֶךָ   (יאהדונהי) סוכה = סאל, אמן   sukat סֻכַּת

ס"ג מ"ה ב"ן   milfanecha מִלְּפָנֶיךָ   אכא   tova טוֹבָה   be'etza בְּעֵצָה   malkenu מַלְכֵּנוּ

shemecha שְׁמֶךָ   lema'an לְמַעַן   mehera מְהֵרָה   vehoshi'enu וְהוֹשִׁיעֵנוּ

makat מַכַּת   me'alenu מֵעָלֵינוּ   vehaser וְהָסֵר◆   ba'adenu בַּעֲדֵנוּ   vehagen וְהָגֵן

מ"ה עם ד' אותיות   choli וְחֹלִי = וזולה◆   cherev וְחֶרֶב◆   dever דֶּבֶר◆   oyev אוֹיֵב◆

◆veyagon וְיָגוֹן   ra'av רָעָב◆   רהע   ra'a רָעָה◆   דההון אלהים   tzara צָרָה

vehaser וְהָסֵר   shevor שְׁבוֹר   umagefa וּמַגֵּפָה◆   umashchit וּמַשְׁחִית◆

uvtzel וּבְצֵל◆   ume'acharenu וּמֵאַחֲרֵינוּ◆   milfanenu מִלְּפָנֵינוּ   hasatan הַשָּׂטָן

tzetenu צֵאתֵנוּ   ushmor וּשְׁמוֹר   tastirenu תַּסְתִּירֵנוּ◆   kenafecha כְּנָפֶיךָ

tovim טוֹבִים   בינה ע"ה, יהוה אהיה אהיה   lechayim לְחַיִּים   uvo'enu וּבוֹאֵנוּ

יא"י   El אֵל   ki כִּי   olam עוֹלָם: ve'ad וְעַד   me'ata מֵעַתָּה   ulshalom וּלְשָׁלוֹם

Ata אַתָּה   (מילוי דס"ג)   umatzilenu וּמַצִּילֵנוּ   כ"א הויות שובתפילין   shomrenu שׁוֹמְרֵנוּ

מלה◆   layla לַיְלָה   umipachad וּמִפַּחַד   ra רַע   ra'a רָאָה   davar דָּבָר יל   mikol מִכָּל

כ"א הויות שובתפילין   shomer שׁוֹמֵר   Adonai יְהֹוָה (אדניאהדונהיאלהים)   Ata אַתָּה   baruch בָּרוּךְ

יאהדונהי   amen אָמֵן◆   ב"פ ב"ן   la'ad לָעַד   Yisrael יִשְׂרָאֵל   amo עַמּוֹ   et אֶת

HASHKIVENU – FOURTH CHAMBER – HOLY OF HOLIES

Lay us down in peace, Father, and stand us up, our King, for good life and for peace. Spread over us Your protection of peace. Set us straight with good counsel from You and save us speedily for the sake of Your Name. And remove from us the blow of our enemy, pestilence, sword, illness, distress, evil, famine, sorrow, ruin, and plague. Destroy and remove Satan from before us and from behind us. Hide us in the shade of Your Wings and watch over our goings and our comings, for a good life and for peace, from now and until eternity. For You, God, are our Guardian and our Rescuer from all evil things and from the terror of the night. Blessed are You, Lord, Who guards His Nation, Israel, forever. Amen!

HALF KADDISH

יִתְגַּדַּל veyitkadash וְיִתְקַדֵּשׁ yitgadal   עֹדִי וּמִלּוּי עֹדִי ; י"א אוֹתִיּוֹת כְּמִנְיַן ו"ה

שְׁמֵיהּ shemei (שֵׁם י"ה דע"ב) raba רַבָּא   קָנ"א ב"ן, יְהֹוָה אֱלֹהִים יְהֹוָה אֲדֹנָי,

amen אָמֵן אידהנויה.   מִלּוּי קָס"א וס"ג, מ"ה בְּרִבּוּעַ וע"ב ע"ה ; ר"ת = ו"פ אֱלֹהִים ; ס"ת = ג"פ יב"ק.

be'alma בְּעָלְמָא   di דִּי   vera בְּרָא   chir'utei כִרְעוּתֵיהּ.

veyamlich וְיַמְלִיךְ   malchutei מַלְכוּתֵיהּ.   veyatzmach וְיַצְמַח

purkanei פּוּרְקָנֵיהּ.   vikarev וִיקָרֵב   meshichei מְשִׁיחֵיהּ:   amen אָמֵן אידהנויה.

bechayechon בְּחַיֵּיכוֹן   uvyomechon וּבְיוֹמֵיכוֹן   uvchayei וּבְחַיֵּי

dechol דְּכָל   bet בֵּית   Yisrael יִשְׂרָאֵל   ba'agala בַּעֲגָלָא

uvizman וּבִזְמַן   kariv קָרִיב   ve'imru וְאִמְרוּ   amen אָמֵן: amen אָמֵן אידהנויה.

The congregation and the chazan say the following:

Twenty eight words (until *be'alma*), meditate: (יוֹד וָיו דָלֶת הֵי יוֹד וָיו יוֹד וָיו הֵי יוֹד) מִלּוּי דְּמִילּוּי דע"ב
Twenty eight letters (until *almaya*), meditate: (יוֹד וָיו דָלֶת הֵי יוֹד וָיו יוֹד וָיו הֵי יוֹד) מִלּוּי דְּמִילּוּי דע"ב

yehe יְהֵא   shemei שְׁמֵיהּ (שֵׁם י"ה דס"ג) raba רַבָּא   קָנ"א ב"ן,

mevarach מְבָרַךְ,   יְהֹוָה אֱלֹהִים יְהֹוָה אֲדֹנָי, מִלּוּי קָס"א וס"ג, מ"ה בְּרִבּוּעַ וע"ב ע"ה

le'alam לְעָלַם   le'almei לְעָלְמֵי   almaya עָלְמַיָּא.   yitbarach יִתְבָּרַךְ.

HALF KADDISH

May His great Name be more exalted and sanctified. (Amen)
In the world that He created according to His will, and may His kingdom reign. And may He cause His redemption to sprout and may He bring the Mashiach closer. (Amen) In your lifetimes and in your days and in the lifetime of all the House of Israel, speedily and in the near future, and you should say, Amen. (Amen) May His great Name be blessed forever and for all eternity blessed

Seven words with six letters each (שם בן מ"ב) – meditate:

יהוה ← יוד הי ויו הי ← מילוי דמילוי דע"ב (יוד ויו דלת הי יוד ויו יוד ויו הי יוד)

Also, seven times the letter *Vav* (שם בן מ"ב) – meditate:

יהוה ← יוד הי ויו הי ← מילוי דמילוי דע"ב (יוד ויו דלת הי יוד ויו יוד ויו הי יוד).

veyishtabach יהוה אל אבג יתץ ← ע"ב י"פ וְיִשְׁתַּבַּח

veyitromam וה כוזו נגד יכש ← veyitpa'ar הי גו יה קרע שטן ← וְיִתְרַמֵם ◆ וְיִתְפָּאַר

veyit'hadar כוזו יה וזקב טנע ← veyitnase במוכסז בטר צתג ← וְיִתְהַדָּר ◆ וְיִתְנַשֵּׂא

veyit'ale וה יוד ה יגל פזק ← veyit'halal א ואו הא שקו צית ← וְיִתְהַלָּל ◆ וְיִתְעַלֶּה

hu הוּא verich בְּרִיךְ dekudsha דְּקוּדְשָׁא (שם י"ה דמ"ה) shemei שְׁמֵיהּ

amen אידהנויה ◆ אָמֵן

shirata שִׁירָתָא ◆ birchata בִּרְכָתָא ◆ kol כָּל ילי min מִן le'ela לְעֵלָּא

da'amiran דַּאֲמִירָן ◆ venechamata וְנֶחָמָתָא ◆ tishbechata תֻּשְׁבְּחָתָא

amen אידהנויה אָמֵן amen אָמֵן ve'imru וְאִמְרוּ be'alma בְּעָלְמָא

THE AMIDAH

When we begin the connection, we take three steps backward, signifying our leaving this physical world. Then we take three steps forward to begin the *Amidah*. The three steps are:

1. Stepping into the land of Israel – to enter the first spiritual circle.
2. Stepping into the city of Jerusalem – to enter the second spiritual circle.
3. Stepping inside the Holy of Holies – to enter the innermost circle.

Before we recite the first verse of the *Amidah*, we ask: "*God, open my lips and let my mouth speak*," thereby asking the Light to speak for us so that we can receive what we need and not just what we want. All too often, what we want from life is not necessarily the desire of the soul, which is what we actually need to fulfill us. By asking the Light to speak through us, we ensure that our connection will bring us genuine fulfillment and opportunities for spiritual growth and change.

---

and lauded, and glorified and exalted, And extolled and honored,
and uplifted and praised, be the Name of the Holy Blessed One. (Amen) Above all blessings,
songs, praises, and words of consolation that may be said in the world, and you shall say, Amen. (Amen)

yagid יַגִּיד ufi וּפִי tiftach תִּפְתָּח sefatai שְׂפָתַי (pause here) כלה Adonai אֲדֹנָי

י'ז (כ'ב אותיות פעוטות [=אכא] וה' אותיות סופיות סֹזֹזֹךֹ) tehilatecha תְּהִלָּתֶךָ ס'ת = בוכו:

THE FIRST BLESSING - INVOKES THE SHIELD OF ABRAHAM.

Abraham is the channel of the Right Column energy of positivity, sharing, and Mercy. Sharing actions can protect us from all forms of negativity.

Chesed that becomes Chochmah

In this section there are 42 words, the secret of the 42-Letter Name of God and therefore it begins with the letter *Bet* (2) and ends with the letter *Mem* (40).

Bend your knees at "baruch," bow at "Ata" and straighten up at "Adonai."

ב   א

(אותיות הא'ב המסמלות את השפע המגיע) לה' המלכות   א-ת   Ata אַתָּה baruch בָּרוּךְ

י

ילה   Elohenu אֱלֹהֵינוּ   (י'א)   Adonai יְהוָֹואדנייאהדונהי יְהֹוָה:

ת

◆avotenu אֲבוֹתֵינוּ   יְלֹה ; דמב, ע'ב, מילוי ; לכב velohei וֵאלֹהֵי

ק

(*Chochmah*) Avraham אַבְרָהָם   יְלֹה ; דמב, ע'ב, מילוי Elohei אֱלֹהֵי

וז'פ אל, רי'ו ול'ב נתיבות הוכמה, רמ'ח (אברים), עסמ'ב וט'ז אותיות פעוטות

שׂ   ע

ב'ן ד'פ (*Binah*) Yitzchak יִצְחֹק   יְלֹה ; דמב, ע'ב, מילוי Elohei אֱלֹהֵי

י   ט

היות אידהנייה היות, יאהדונהי ז' (*Da'at*) Yaakov יַעֲקֹב יְלֹה ; דמב, ע'ב מילוי ; לכב velohei וֵאלֹהֵי

THE AMIDAH

"My Lord, open my lips, and my mouth shall relate Your praise." (Psalms 51:17)

THE FIRST BLESSING

Blessed are You, Lord,
our God and God of our forefathers: the God of Abraham, the God of Isaac, and the God of Jacob.

haEl הָאֵל ; יא"י (מילוי דס"ג) לאה ; hagadol הַגָּדוֹל הָאֵל הַגָּדוֹל = סיט ; גדול = להוו

hagibor הַגִּבּוֹר ר"ת ההה vehanora וְהַנּוֹרָא עם ד' אותיות = מובה, יזל, אום

El אֵל יא"י (מילוי) דס"ג ; ר"ת ע"ב, ריבוע יהוה elyon עֶלְיוֹן

gomel גּוֹמֵל וְחַסְדֵי chasadim טוֹבִים tovim קוֹנֵה kone הַכֹּל hakol ילי

vezocher וְזוֹכֵר וְחַסְדֵי chasdei אָבוֹת avot וּמֵבִיא umevi

go'el גּוֹאֵל לִבְנֵי livnei בְּנֵיהֶם venehem לְמַעַן lema'an

שְׁמוֹ shemo אוֹזֶד, דאּ:ה be'ahava בְּאַהֲבָה מהשׁע ע"ה, ע"ב בריבוע וקס"א ע"ה, אל שׁדי ע"ה

When saying the word *"be'ahava"* you should meditate to devote your soul to sanctify the Holy Name and accept upon yourself the four forms of death.

melech מֶלֶךְ ozer עוֹזֵר umoshi'a וּמוֹשִׁיעַ umagen וּמָגֵן

ג"פ אל (יא"י מילוי דס"ג) ; ר"ת מיכאל גבריאל נוריאל:

Bend your knees at *"baruch,"* bow at *"Ata"* and straighten up at *"Adonai."*

baruch בָּרוּךְ Ata אַתָּה יְהֹוָה Adonai (הד)

magen מָגֵן ג"פ אל (יא"י מילוי דס"ג) ; ר"ת מיכאל גבריאל נוריאל Avraham אַבְרָהָם

וז"פ אל, רי"ו ול"ב נתיבות הוחכמה, רמ"ח (אברים), עסמ"ב וט"ז אותיות פשוטות:

The great, mighty and Awesome God.
The Supernal God, Who bestows beneficial kindness and creates everything. Who recalls the kindness of the forefathers and brings a Redeemer to their descendants for the sake of His Name, lovingly. King, Helper, Savior and Shield. Blessed are You, Lord, the shield of Abraham.

THE SECOND BLESSING

THE ENERGY OF ISAAC IGNITES THE POWER FOR THE RESURRECTION OF THE DEAD.

Whereas Abraham represents the power of sharing, Isaac represents the Left Column energy of Judgment. Judgment shortens the *tikkun* process and paves the way for our eventual resurrection.

Gevurah that becomes *Binah*.

In this section there are 49 words corresponding to the 49 Gates of the Pure System in *Binah*.

ללה Adonai אֲדֹנָי ס"ג וי' אותיות דס"ג le'olam לְעוֹלָם gibor גִּבּוֹר Ata אַתָּה

(ר"ת אַגְלָא והוא שם גדול ואמיץ, ובו היה יהודה מתגבר על אויביו. ע"ה אלד, בוכו).

◆lehoshi'a לְהוֹשִׁיעַ rav רַב ◆Ata אַתָּה metim מֵתִים ס"ג mechaye מְחַיֵּה

Only on *Motza'ei Simchat Torah*:	During *Sukkot*:
ר"ת מ"ה haru'ach הָרוּחַ mashiv מַשִּׁיב	hatal הַטָּל morid מוֹרִיד
hageshem הַגֶּשֶׁם umorid וּמוֹרִיד	יוד הא ואו, כווו, מספר אותיות דמילואי עסמ"ב ;
עוֹבִיל [י"ע (= י"פ אל) ול"ב נתיבות החזכמה] ע"ה:	ר"ת מ"ה (יוד הא ואו הא):
If you mistakenly say "*morid hatal*," and realize this before the end of the blessing "*baruch Ata Adonai*," you should return to the beginning of the blessing "*Ata gibor*" and continue as usual. But if you only realize this after the end of the blessing, you should continue and not go back.	If you mistakenly say "*Mashiv haru'ach*," and realize this before the end of the blessing "*baruch Ata Adonai*," you should return to the beginning of the blessing "*Ata gibor*" and continue as usual. But if you only realize this after the end of the blessing, you should start the *Amidah* from the beginning.

bechesed בְּחֶסֶד ר"ת בינה ע"ה אהיה יהוה, אהיה אהיה chayim חַיִּים mechalkel מְכַלְכֵּל

berachamim בְּרַחֲמִים metim מֵתִים ס"ג mechaye מְחַיֵּה יהוה. ע"ב, ריבוע

somech סוֹמֵךְ (טלא דעתיק). rabim רַבִּים י"פ יי אלהים ההון, מצפצ (במוכסז)

cholim חוֹלִים verofe וְרוֹפֵא (זו"ן) ◆ noflim נוֹפְלִים אדני ריבוע כוק, (אכדטם)

umekayem וּמְקַיֵּם ◆asurim אֲסוּרִים umatir וּמַתִּיר ◆ אותיות. וד' מ"ה = וחולה

chamocha כָּמוֹךָ ילי mi מִי ◆afar עָפָר lishenei לִישֵׁנֵי emunato אֱמוּנָתוֹ

gevurot גְּבוּרוֹת ba'al בַּעַל (you should enunciate the letter *Ayin* in the word *"ba'al"*)

memit מֵמִית melech מֶלֶךְ ◆lach לָךְ dome דוֹמֶה ילי umi וּמִי

◆yeshu'a יְשׁוּעָה umatzmi'ach וּמַצְמִיחַ (יוד הי ואו הי) ס"ג umchaye וּמְחַיֶּה

THE SECOND BLESSING

You are mighty forever, Lord. You resurrect the dead and are very capable of redeeming.

Only on *Motza'ei Simchat Torah*:	During *Sukkot*:
Who causes wind to blow and rain to fall.	*Who causes dew to fall.*

You sustain life with kindness and resurrect the dead with great compassion. You support those who have fallen, heal the sick, release the imprisoned, and fulfill Your faithful words to those who are asleep in the dust. Who is like You, Master of might, and Who can compare to You, King, Who causes death, Who gives life, and Who sprouts salvation?

וְנֶאֱמָן vene'eman   אַתָּה Ata   לְהַחֲיוֹת lehachayot   מֵתִים metim:

בָּרוּךְ baruch   אַתָּה Ata   יְ־הֹוָ־ה(יֱ־הֹוִ־ה)יאהדונהי Adonai

מְחַיֵּה mechaye   ס"ג (יוד הי ואו הי)   הַמֵּתִים hametim   ר"ת מ"ה וס"ת מ"ה:

THE THIRD BLESSING

This blessing connects us to Jacob, the Central Column and the power of restriction. Jacob is our channel for connecting mercy with judgment. By restricting our reactive behavior, we are blocking our Desire to Receive for the Self Alone. Jacob also gives us the power to balance our acts of mercy and judgment toward other people in our lives.

Tiferet that becomes *Da'at* (14 words).

אַתָּה Ata   קָדוֹשׁ kadosh   וְשִׁמְךָ veshimcha   קָדוֹשׁ kadosh ר"ת = אור, רז, אין סוף∙

וּקְדוֹשִׁים ukdoshim   בְּכָל־ bechol ב"ן, לכב   יוֹם yom ע"ה נגד, מזבוח, ח, אל יהוה

יְהַלְלוּךָ yehalelucha   סֶלָה sela:

בָּרוּךְ baruch   אַתָּה Ata   יְ־הֹוָ־ה(יֱ־הֹוִ־ה)יאהדונהי Adonai

הָאֵל haEl לאה ; יא"י (מילוי דס"ג)   הַקָּדוֹשׁ hakadosh י"פ מ"ה (יוד הא ואו הא):

Meditate here on the Name: יאהדונהי, as it can help to remove anger.

THIRTEEN MIDDLE BLESSINGS

There are thirteen blessings in the middle of the *Amidah* that connect us to the Thirteen Attributes.

THE FIRST (FOURTH) BLESSING

This blessing helps us transform information into knowledge by helping us internalize everything that we learn.

Chochmah

In this blessing there are 17 words, the same numerical value as the word *tov* (good) in the secret of *Etz HaDa'at Tov vaRa*, (Tree of Knowledge Good and Evil), where we connect only to the *Tov*.

אַתָּה Ata   חוֹנֵן chonen   לְאָדָם le'adam   מ"ה   דַּעַת da'at∙

וּמְלַמֵּד umlamed   לֶאֱנוֹשׁ le'enosh   בִּינָה bina ע"ה   אהיה אהיה יהוה   חיים∙

And You are faithful to resurrecting the dead. Blessed are You, Lord, Who resurrects the dead.

THE THIRD BLESSING

You are Holy, and Your Name is Holy, and the Holy Ones praise You every day, for you are God, the Holy King Selah. Blessed are You, Lord, the Holy God.

THIRTEEN MIDDLE BLESSINGS - THE FIRST (FOURTH) BLESSING

You graciously grant knowledge to man and understanding to humanity.

On *Motza'ei Shabbat* **(Saturday night)** and on *Motza'ei Chag* we add the following:

ATA CHONANTANU

This connection helps us differentiate good from evil during the week. All too often we attract the wrong people and embrace the wrong opportunities in our life. This connection gives us the sixth sense to perceive the long-term consequences.

יכה Elohenu אֱלֹהֵינוּ Adonai יְהֹוָהאֵהדונהי chonantanu וֹזוֹנַנְתָּנוּ Ata אַתָּה

lehavdil לְהַבְדִּיל amarta אָמַרְתָּ Ata אַתָּה ,vehaskel וְהַשְׂכֵּל mada מַדַּע

א״ס רז, or אוֹר uven וּבֵין lechol לְכֹל kodesh קֹדֶשׁ ben בֵּין

,la'amim לְעַמִּים Yisrael יִשְׂרָאֵל uven וּבֵין lechoshech לְחֹשֶׁךְ

lesheshet לְשֵׁשֶׁת hashevi'i הַשְּׁבִיעִי ע״ה נגד, מזבוח, זן, אל יהוה yom יוֹם uven וּבֵין

yemei יְמֵי hama'ase הַמַּעֲשֶׂה. keshem כְּשֵׁם shehivdaltanu שֶׁהִבְדַּלְתָּנוּ

me'amei מֵעַמֵּי Elohenu אֱלֹהֵינוּ יכה Adonai יְהֹוָהאֵהדונהי

,ha'adama הָאֲדָמָה umimishpechot וּמִמִּשְׁפְּחוֹת ha'aratzot הָאֲרָצוֹת

ra רַע misatan מִשָּׂטָן vehatzilenu וְהַצִּילֵנוּ pedenu פְּדֵנוּ kach כָּךְ

kashot קָשׁוֹת gezerot גְּזֵרוֹת umikol וּמִכָּל ra רַע umipega וּמִפֶּגַע

:ba'olam בָּעוֹלָם lavo לָבֹא hamitrageshot הַמִּתְרַגְּשׁוֹת vera'ot וְרָעוֹת

(מצוות) תרי״ג = במילוי chochmah וְחָכְמָה me'itecha מֵאִתְּךָ vechonenu וְחָנֵנוּ

:וחבו ר״ת vada'at וְדַעַת ווזיים ,יהוה אהיה אהיה ע״ה binah בִּינָה

:hada'at הַדַּעַת chonen חוֹנֵן Adonai יְהֹוָהאֵהדונהי Ata אַתָּה baruch בָּרוּךְ

ATA CHONANTANU

You have graciously granted us, Lord our God, knowledge and intelegence. You commanded us to separate between the Holy and non-holy, between Light and darkness, between Israel and the nations and between the seventh day and the six days of Creation. Just as You separated us, Lord our God, from the nations of the lands and from the families of earth, so may You redeem us and rescue us from any evil adversary, from any mishap, and from all types of harsh and evil decrees which enthusiastically come to the world.

Graciously grant us, from Yourself,
wisdom, understanding and knowledge. Blessed are You, Lord, Who graciously grants knowledge.

THE SECOND (FIFTH) BLESSING

This blessing keeps us in the Light. Everyone at one time or another succumbs to the doubt and uncertainty that the Satan constantly implants in us. If we make the unfortunate mistake of stepping back and falling away from the Light, we do not want the Creator to mirror our actions and step away from us. Instead, we want Him to catch us. In the box below there are certain lines that we can recite and meditate on for others who may be stepping back. The war against the Satan is the oldest war known to man. And the only way to defeat the Satan is to unite, share, help and pray for each other.

Binah

In this blessing there are 15 words, as the powerful action of *Teshuva* (repentance) raises 15 levels on the way to *Kise Hakavod* (the Throne of Honor). It goes through seven *Reki'im* (firmaments), seven *Avirim* (air), and another firmament on top of the Holy Animals (together this adds up to 15). Also, there are 15 words in the two main verses of Isaiah the Prophet and King David that speak of *Teshuva* (Isaiah 55:7; Psalms 32:5). The number 15 is also the secret of the Name: יה.

הֲשִׁיבֵנוּ hashivenu אָבִינוּ avinu לְתוֹרָתֶךָ letoratecha (וֹסֵד טוֹבָה - יְהוָֹאֲדֹנָיֵאהדונֹהי)

וְקָרְבֵנוּ vekarvenu מַלְכֵּנוּ malkenu לַעֲבוֹדָתֶךָ la'avodatecha

וְהַחֲזִירֵנוּ vehachazirenu בִּתְשׁוּבָה bitshuva שְׁלֵמָה shelema

לְפָנֶיךָ lefanecha ס"ג מ"ה ב"ן

If you want to pray for another and help them in their spiritual process say:

יְהִי yehi רָצוֹן ratzon מהטי ע"ה, ע"ב בריבוע וקס"א ע"ה, אל שדי ע"ה
מִלְפָנֶיךָ milfanecha ס"ג מ"ה ב"ן יְהוָֹאֲדֹנָיֵאהדונֹהי Adonai אֱלֹהַי Elohai מילוי ע"ב, דמב;ילה
וֵאלֹהֵי velohei לכב ; מילוי ע"ב, דמב ; ילה אֲבוֹתַי avotai עָתוֹחְתוּר shetachtor
וְחֲתִירָה chatira מִתַּחַת mitachat כִּסֵּא kise כְּבוֹדֶךָ kevodecha וּתְקַבֵּל utkabel
בִּתְשׁוּבָה bitshuva אֶת et (the person's name and his/her father's name) כִּי ki יְמִינְךָ yemincha
יְהוָֹאֲדֹנָיֵאהדונֹהי Adonai פְּשׁוּטָה peshuta לְקַבֵּל lekabel שָׁבִים shavim

---

בָּרוּךְ baruch אַתָּה Ata יְהוָֹאֲדֹנָיֵאהדונֹהי Adonai

הָרוֹצֶה harotze בִּתְשׁוּבָה bitshuva

THE SECOND (FIFTH) BLESSING

Bring us back, our Father, to Your Torah,
and bring us close, our King, to Your service, and cause us to return with perfect repentance before You.

May it be pleasing before You, Lord, my God and God of my forefathers, that You shall dig deep beneath the Throne of Your glory and accept as repentant (the person's name and his/her father' name) because Your Right Hand, Lord, extends outwards to receive those who repent.

Blessed are You, Lord, Who desires repentance.

THE THIRD (SIXTH) BLESSING

This blessing helps us achieve true forgiveness. We have the power to cleanse ourselves of our negative behavior and hurtful actions toward others through forgiveness. This blessing does not mean we plead for forgiveness and our slate is wiped clean. Forgiveness refers to the methodologies for washing away the residue that comes from our iniquities. There are two ways to wash away the residue: physical and spiritual. We collect physical residue when we are in denial of our misdeeds and the laws of cause and effect. We cleanse ourselves when we experience any kind of pain, whether it is financial, emotional, or physical. If we choose to cleanse spiritually, we forgo the physical cleansing. We do so by arousing the pain in ourselves that we caused to others. We feel the other person; and with a truthful heart, recite this prayer experiencing the hurt and heartache we inflicted on others. This form of spiritual cleansing prevents us from having to cleanse physically.

Chesed

In this blessing there are 21 words which is the numerical value of the Holy Name: אהיה.

(יאהדונהי) אמן סאל, ר"ת avinu אָבִינוּ אדני אהיה אלהים, lanu לָנוּ ע"ב יהוה selach סְלַח

= ע"ה לנו מוזול ; אדני אהיה אלהים, lanu לָנוּ mechol מְחוֹל ◆chatanu וְטָאנוּ ki כִּי

(מילוי דס"ג) יא"י אותיות וו' קס"א El אֵל ki כִּי ◆fashanu פָשָׁעֵנוּ ki כִּי malkenu מַלְכֵּנוּ

Ata אַתָּה baruch בָּרוּךְ ∶Ata אַתָּה ע"ב יהוה vesalach וְסָלַח והו tov טוֹב

∶lislo'ach לִסְלוֹחַ hamarbe הַמַּרְבֶּה chanun וְחַנּוּן Adonai יְהֹוִהאדניאהדונהי

THE FOURTH (SEVENTH) BLESSING

This blessing helps us achieve redemption after we are spiritually cleansed.

Gevurah

(כנגד הגבורה) באשה, אברים) רג"ב ר"ת ve'onyenu בְעָנְיֵנוּ na נָא ראה re'e רְאֵה

lega'olenu לְגָאֳלֵנוּ umaher וּמַהֵר ◆rivenu רִיבֵנוּ veriva וְרִיבָה

shemecha שְׁמֶךָ lema'an לְמַעַן shelema שְׁלֵמָה מ"ה ge'ula גְאֻלָה

∶Ata אַתָּה פהל chazak וְחֹזֵק go'el גּוֹאֵל (מילוי דס"ג) יא"י El אֵל ki כִּי

∶Yisrael יִשְׂרָאֵל go'el גּוֹאֵל Adonai יְהֹוִהאדניאהדונהי Ata אַתָּה baruch בָּרוּךְ

THE FIFTH (EIGHTH) BLESSING

This blessing gives us the power to heal every part of our body. All healing originates from the Light of the Creator. Accepting and understanding this truth opens us to receive this Light. We should also think of sharing this healing energy with others.

THE THIRD (SIXTH) BLESSING

Forgive us, our Father, for we have transgressed. Pardon us, our King, for we have sinned, because You are a good and forgiving God. Blessed are You, Lord, Who is gracious and forgives magnanimously.

THE FOURTH (SEVENTH) BLESSING

Behold our poverty and take up our fight; hurry to redeem us with a complete redemption for the sake of Your Name, because You are a powerful and a redeeming God. Blessed are You, Lord, Who redeems Israel.

Tiferet

ר"ת   רי"ו   venerafe וְנֵרָפֵא   Adonai יְהֹוָה   refa'enu רְפָאֵנוּ

tehilatenu תְהִלָּתֵנוּ   ki כִּי   venivashe'a וְנִוָּשֵׁעָה   hoshi'enu הוֹשִׁיעֵנוּ

umarpe וּמַרְפֵּא   arucha אֲרוּכָה   veha'ale וְהַעֲלֵה   ר"ת = ב"פ רי"ו.   Ata אַתָּה

אדני   יה   ulchol וּלְכָל   tachalu'enu תַחֲלוּאֵינוּ   אדני   יה   lechol לְכָל

אדני   יה   ulchol וּלְכָל   makotenu מַכּוֹתֵינוּ   mach'ovenu מַכְאוֹבֵינוּ

To pray for healing for yourself and/or others add the following, in the parentheses below, insert the names:

ע"ה   אל   עַדִי   ע"ה מהע"א וקס"א   ע"ב,   ברבוע   ע"ה,   מהע ע"ה,   ratzon רָצוֹן   yehi יְהִי

יולה ; דמב ע"ב, מילוי   Elohai אֱלֹהַי   Adonai יְהֹוָה   ס"ג מ"ה ב"ן   milfanecha מִלְּפָנֶיךָ

shetirpa'eni שֶׁתִּרְפָּאֵנִי   avotai אֲבוֹתַי   יולה ; דמב ע"ב, מילוי ; לכב   velohei וֵאלֹהֵי

((insert their mother's name) (bat בַּת :Women) ben בֶּן (insert the person's name) vetirpa וְתִרְפָּא)

hanefesh הַנֶּפֶשׁ   refu'at רְפוּאַת   shelema שְׁלֵמָה   refu'a רְפוּאָה

פהל   chazak וְחָזָק   she'ehye שֶׁאֶהְיֶה   kedei כְּדֵי   haguf הַגּוּף,   urfu'at וּרְפוּאַת

ve'amitz וְאָמִיץ,   bivri'ut בִּבְרִיאוּת   (פהל)   chazaka וְחָזְקָה   :Women)

ve'arba'im וְאַרְבָּעִים   bematayim בְּמָאתַיִם,   ko'ach כֹּחַ   (ve'amitzat וְאָמִיצַת   :Women)

ushmona וּשְׁמוֹנָה   רמ"ח (אברים), אברהם, ח"פ אל, רי"ו ול"ב נתיבות החוכמה, עסמ"ב וט"ו אותיות

(ushnayim וּשְׁנַיִם   vechamishim וַחֲמִשִׁים   bematayim בְּמָאתַיִם   :Women)   פשוטות

דיודין   אלהים = ע'   המספר = מאות   me'ot מֵאוֹת   ushlosh וּשְׁלֹשׁ   evarim אֵבָרִים

shel שֶׁל   gidim גִּידִים   vachamisha וַחֲמִשָּׁה   (יך) וְחֲמִשָּׁה = מילוי העו'   המספר = veshishim וְשִׁשִׁים   וְשִׁשִׁים

hakedosha הַקְּדוֹשָׁה.   toratcha תוֹרָתְךָ   lekiyum לְקִיּוּם,   vegufi וְגוּפִי   nishmati נִשְׁמָתִי

---

vene'eman וְנֶאֱמָן   rachaman רַחֲמָן   rofe רוֹפֵא   (מילוי דס"ג)   El אֵל   ki כִּי   יא"י

rofe רוֹפֵא   Adonai יְהֹוָה   Ata אַתָּה   baruch בָּרוּךְ   Ata: אַתָּה

Yisrael יִשְׂרָאֵל   amo עַמּוֹ   וד' אותיות (יוד הא ואו הא)   וזלה = מ"ה   cholei חוֹלֵי   ve'zulti וְזוּלִי

ר"ת רפ"ו (להעלות הניצוצות שנפלו לקליפה דמשם באים התזלואים):

THE FIFTH (EIGHTH) BLESSING

Heal us, Lord, and we shall heal. Save us and we shall be saved.
For You are our praise. Bring cure and healing to all our ailments, to all our pains, and to all our wounds.

May it be pleasing before You, Lord, my God and God of my forefathers, that You would heal me (and the person's name and their mother's name) completely with healing of the spirit and healing of the body, so that I shall be strong in health and vigorous in my strength in all 248 (a woman says: 252) organs and 365 sinews of my soul and my body, so that I shall be able to keep Your Holy Torah.

Because You are a healing,
compassionate, and trustworthy God, blessed are You, Lord, Who heals the sick of His People, Israel.

THE SIXTH (NINTH) BLESSING

This blessing draws sustenance and prosperity for the entire globe and provides us with personal sustenance. We would like all of our years to be filled with dew and rain, the sustaining lifeblood of our world.

Netzach

On *Chol Hamo'ed Sukkot* the following is said:

If you mistakenly say "barech alenu" instead of "barchenu", and realize this before the end of the *Amidah* ("yihyu leratzon" – the second one), then you should return and say "barchenu" and continue as usual. If you realize this later, you should start the *Amidah* from the beginning.

bechol בְּכָל־ ילה Elohenu אֱלֹהֵינוּ Adonai יְהֹוָה barchenu בָּרְכֵנוּ

shenatenu שְׁנָתֵנוּ uvarech וּבָרֵךְ •yadenu יָדֵינוּ ma'asei מַעֲשֵׂי

betalelei בְּטַלְלֵי ratzon רָצוֹן

utehi וּתְהִי undava וּנְדָבָה beracha בְּרָכָה

vesava וְשָׂבַע chayim וְחַיִּים acharita אַחֲרִיתָהּ

•livracha לִבְרָכָה hatovot הַטּוֹבוֹת kashanim כַּשָּׁנִים veshalom וְשָׁלוֹם

If you want to pray for sustenance you can add:

milfanecha מִלְּפָנֶיךָ ratzon רָצוֹן yehi יְהִי

velohei וֵאלֹהֵי Elohenu אֱלֹהֵינוּ Adonai יְהֹוָה

li לִי shetiten שֶׁתִּתֵּן avotenu אֲבוֹתֵינוּ

hayom הַיּוֹם shulchani שׁוּלְחָנִי al עַל hasemuchim הַסְּמוּכִים ulchol וּלְכָל

velo וְלֹא bechavod בְּכָבוֹד umzonotehem וּמְזוֹנוֹתֵיהֶם mezonotai מְזוֹנוֹתַי yom יוֹם uvchol וּבְכָל

bizchut בִּזְכוּת be'isur בְּאִיסּוּר velo וְלֹא beheter בְּהֶיתֵּר bevizui בְּבִזּוּי

hagadol הַגָּדוֹל shimcha שִׁמְךָ

Do not pronounce this name): דִּיקַרְנוֹסָא

THE SIXTH (NINTH) BLESSING

On *Chol Hamo'ed Sukkot* the following is said:

Bless us, Lord, our God, in all our endeavors, and bless our years with the dews of good will, blessing, and benevolence. May its conclusion be life, contentment, and peace, as with other years for blessing.

May it be pleasing before You, Lord, my God and God of my forefathers, that You would provide for me and for my household, today and everyday, mine and their nourishment, with dignity and not with shame, in a permissible but not a forbidden manner, by virtue of Your great Name

lachem לָכֶם vaharikoti וַהֲרִיקֹתִי mipasuk מִפָּסוּק: hayotze הַיּוֹצֵא

nesa נְסָה umipasuk וּמִפָּסוּק: dai דַּי beli בְּלִי ad עַד beracha בְּרָכָה

Adonai יְהֹוָה or אוֹר or panecha פָּנֶיךָ alenu עָלֵינוּ

basar בְּשָׂר matnot מַתְּנוֹת lidei לִידֵי tatzrichenu תַּצְרִיכֵנוּ ve'al וְאַל

vadam וְדָם ki כִּי im אִם chinam וְחִנָּם matnat מַתְּנַת ume'otzar וּמֵאוֹצַר hamele'a הַמְּלֵאָה miyadcha מִיָּדְךָ

techalkelni תְּכַלְכְּלֵנִי vetashpi'eni וְתַשְׂפִּיעֵנִי amen אָמֵן sela סֶלָה.

ki כִּי El אֵל tov טוֹב umetiv וּמֵטִיב

Ata אַתָּה umvarech וּמְבָרֵךְ hashanim הַשָּׁנִים: baruch בָּרוּךְ

Ata אַתָּה Adonai יְהֹוָה mevarech מְבָרֵךְ hashanim הַשָּׁנִים:

On *Motza'ei Simchat Torah* the following is said:

If you mistakenly say "*barchenu*" instead of "*barech alenu*", and realize this before the end of the blessing "*baruch Ata Adonai*," you should return to say "*barech alenu*" and continue as usual. If you only realize this after, you should say "*Veten tal umatar livracha*" in "*shome'a tefila*." If you only relize this after you have already started "*retze*" you should start the *Amidah* from the beginning

barech בָּרֵךְ alenu עָלֵינוּ Adonai יְהֹוָה Elohenu אֱלֹהֵינוּ

et אֶת hashana הַשָּׁנָה hazot הַזֹּאת. ve'et וְאֶת kol כָּל

minei מִינֵי tevu'ata תְּבוּאָתָהּ letova לְטוֹבָה. veten וְתֵן

tal טַל umatar וּמָטָר livracha לִבְרָכָה al עַל kol כָּל

penei פְּנֵי verave וְרַוֵּה ha'adama הָאֲדָמָה. penei פְּנֵי

tevel תֵּבֵל vesaba וְשַׂבַּע et אֶת ha'olam הָעוֹלָם

kulo כֻּלּוֹ mituvach מִטּוּבָךְ. umale וּמַלֵּא yadenu יָדֵינוּ

mibirchotecha מִבִּרְכוֹתֶיךָ ume'osher וּמֵעֹשֶׁר mat'not מַתְּנוֹת yadecha יָדֶיךָ.

---

that comes from the verse: "pour down for you blessing until there be no room to suffice for it" (Malachi 3:10) and from the verse: "Raise up over us the light of Your countenance, Lord" (Psalms 4:7), and we will not require the gifts of flesh and blood, but only from your hand which is full, and from the treasure of the free gift you shall support and nurish me. Amen. Sela.

for You are a good
and a beneficent God and You bless the years. Blessed are You, Lord, Who blesses the years.

On *Motza'ei Simchat Torah* the following is said:

Bless us, Lord, our God, this year and all its kinds of crops for good. And give dew and rain for blessing over the entire face of the Earth. Quench the thirst of the face of the Earth and satiate the entire world from Your bounty. Fill our hands with Your blessings and from the wealth of gifts of Your Hands.

If you want to pray for sustenance you can add:

יְהִי yehi רָצוֹן ratzon מהע ע"ה, ע"ב ברביוע וקס"א ע"ה, אל שדי ע"ה מִלְּפָנֶיךָ milfanecha

ס"ג מ"ה ב"ן יְהֹוָ֨ה Adonai אַדנֹהי Elohenu יְהֹה ילה אֱלֹהֵינוּ Elohenu וֵאלֹהֵי velohei

לכב ; מילוי ע"ב, דמב ; ילה אֲבוֹתֵינוּ avotenu שֶׁתִּתֵּן shetiten ב"פ כהת לִי li

(וְכֵן) vechen לְ (insert the person's name) בֵּן ben (Women: בַּת bat) (insert their father's name)

וּלְכָל ulchol יה ארני הַסְּמוּכִים hasmuchim עַל al שׁוּלְחָנִי shulchani הַיּוֹם hayom

ע"ה נגד, מזבוה, זן, אל יהוה וּבְכָל uvchol ב"ן, ע"ה נגד, מזבוה, זן, אל יהוה יוֹם yom לכב ב"ן, לכב וּבְכָל

מְזוֹנוֹתַי mezonotai וּמְזוֹנוֹתֵיהֶם umzonotehem בְּכָבוֹד bechavod בוכו וְלֹא velo

בְּזכּוּת bizchut בְּאִיסוּר be'isur וְלֹא velo בְּהֶיתֵּר beheter בְבִזּוּי bevizuy

שִׁמְךָ shimcha הַגָּדוֹל hagadol להוֹ ; עם ד' אותיות = מבה, יזל, אום

(Do not pronounce this name) דְּיִקְרָנוֹסָא וזהך עם ג' אותיות – ובאתב"ש סאל, אמן, יאהדונהי)

הַיּוֹצֵא hayotze מִפָּסוּק mipasuk וַהֲרִיקֹתִי vaharikoti לָכֶם lachem

בְּרָכָה beracha עַד ad בְּלִי beli דַּי dai וּמִפָּסוּק umipasuk נָסָה nesa

עָלֵינוּ alenu אוֹר or רו, אין סוף פָּנֶיךָ panecha ס"ג מ"ה ב"ן יְהֹוָ֨ה Adonai

וְאַל ve'al תַּצְרִיכֵנוּ tatzrichenu לִידֵי lidei מַתְּנוֹת matnot בָּשָׂר basar

וָדָם vadam כִּי ki אִם im יוֹהך, מ"א אותיות אהיה בפשוטו ומילואו ומילוי דמילואו ע"ה

מִיָּדְךָ miyadcha הַמְּלֵאָה hamele'a וּמֵאוֹצַר ume'otzar מַתְּנַת matnat וְגַם vegam chinam

תְּכַלְכְּלֵנִי techalkelni וְתַשְׂפִּיעֵנִי vetashpi'eni אָמֵן amen יאהדונהי סֶלָה sela.

שָׁמְרָה shomra וְהַצִּילָה vehatzila זוֹ zo שָׁנָה shana מִכָּל mikol ילי

דְּבָר davar רָעה ra רַע וּמִכָּל umikol ילי מִינֵי minei מַשְׁחִית mashchit

וּמִכָּל umikol ילי מִינֵי minei פּוּרְעָנֻות pura'nut וַעֲשֵׂה va'ase לָה la

תִּקְוָה tikva טוֹבָה tova אכא וְאַחֲרִית ve'acharit שָׁלוֹם shalom חוּס chus

---

May it be pleasing before You, Lord, my God and God of my forefathers, that You would provide for me and for my household, today and everyday, mine and their nourishment, with dignity and not with shame, in a permissible but not a forbidden manner, by virtue of your great name that comes from the verse: "pour down for you blessing until there be no room to suffice for it" (Malachi 3:10) and from the verse: "Raise up over us the light of Your countenance, Lord" (Psalm 4:7), and we will not require the gifts of flesh and blood, but only from your hand which is full, from the treasure of the free gift you shall support and nurish me. Amen. Sela.

Protect and save this year from all evil and from all manner of destruction and from all manner of tribulation. Make for it a good hope and a peaceful ending. Take pity

וְרַחֵם verachem   אברהם, ח"פ אל, רי"ו ול"ב נתיבות החוכמה, רמ"ח (אברים), עסמ"ב וט"ו אותיות פשוטות

עָלֶיהָ aleha   פהל ve'al וְעַל   kol כָּל־   ילי ; עמם tevu'ata תְּבוּאָתָה

וּפֵירוֹתֶיהָ uferoteha   uvarcha וּבָרְכָה   begishmei בְּגִשְׁמֵי

רָצוֹן ratzon   מהש ע"ה, ע"ב, בריבוע וקס"א ע"ה, אל שדי ע"ה

בְּרָכָה beracha   וּנְדָבָה undava   בינה (וע"ה) אהיה אהיה יהוה, וזיים)

וּתְהִי utehi   אַחֲרִיתָה acharita   וְחַיִּים chayim   אהיה אהיה יהוה, בינה ע"ה

וְשָׂבָע vesava   וְשָׁלוֹם veshalom   כַּשָּׁנִים kashanim   הַטּוֹבוֹת hatovot

לִבְרָכָה livracha   כִּי ki   אֵל El   ייא"י (מילוי דס"ג) טוֹב tov   וּמֵטִיב umetiv   והו

אַתָּה Ata   וּמְבָרֵךְ umvarech   הַשָּׁנִים ∷hashanim   בָּרוּךְ baruch

אַתָּה Ata   יְהֹוָה Adonai   מְבָרֵךְ mevarech   הַשָּׁנִים ∷hashanim

THE SEVENTH (TENTH) BLESSING

This blessing gives us the power to positively influence all of humanity. Kabbalah teaches that each individual affects the whole. We affect the world, and the rest of the world affects us, even though we cannot perceive this relationship with our five senses. We call this relationship quantum consciousness.

Hod

תְּקַע teka   ב"פ מזְזֵּךְ וי' אותיות   בְּשׁוֹפָר beshofar   גָּדוֹל gadol   להו ; עם ד' אותיות =

לְקַבֵּץ lekabetz   מבה, יזל, אום מ"ה אדני נֵס nes   וְשָׂא vesa   לְחֵרוּתֵנוּ lecherutenu

מֵאַרְבַּע me'arba   יַחַד yachad   וְקַבְּצֵנוּ vekabetzenu   גָּלֻיּוֹתֵנוּ galuyotenu

כַּנְפוֹת kanfot   וּבּו (בסגולתו להוציא ניצוצות מן הקליפות) ויכוין וַזָּבוֹן עם נקודותיו = ע"ב, ריבוע יהוה

הָאָרֶץ ha'aretz   אלהים דההין ע"ה ; ר"ת = אדני לְאַרְצֵנוּ le'artzenu∷

> The following is recited throughout the entire year:
> The following meditation helps us to release and redeem all the remaining sparks of Light we have lost through our irresponsible actions (especially sexual misconduct):

and have mercy upon it and upon all its crops and fruits; bless it with rains of goodwill, blessing, and benevolence. And may its end be life, contentment, and peace, for You are a good and a beneficent God and You bless the years. Blessed are You, Lord, Who blesses the years.

THE SEVENTH (TENTH) BLESSING
Blow a great Shofar for our freedom and
raise a banner to gather our exiles, and gather us speedily from all four corners of the Earth to our Land.

milfanecha מִלְפָנֶיךָ מהש׳ ע״ה, ע״ב בריבוע וקס״א ע״ה, אל שדי ע״ה ratzon רָצוֹן yehi יְהִי

ס״ג מ״ה ב״ן יְהֹוָאֲדֹנָהִיאֱהֹדֹנָהִי מילוי ע״ב, דמב ; ילה Elohai אֱלֹהַי Adonai אֲדֹנָי

tipa טִיפָּה ילי shekol שֶׁכָּל avotai אֲבוֹתַי ; ילה ; דמב לכב ; מילוי ע״ב, דמב ; ילה velohei וֵאלֹהֵי

levatala לְבַטָלָה mimeni מִמֶנִּי sheyatza שֶׁיָצָא keri קְרִי shel שֶׁל vetipa וְטִיפָּה

shelo שֶׁלֹּא uvifrat וּבְפְרָט bichlal בִּכְלָל Yisrael יִשְׂרָאֵל ילי umikol וּמִכָּל

beratzon בְּרָצוֹן ben בֵּין be'ones בְּאוֹנֶס ben בֵּין mitzva מִצְוָה bimkom בִּמְקוֹם

ben בֵּין beshogeg בְּשׁוֹגֵג ben בֵּין מהש׳ ע״ה, ע״ב בריבוע וקס״א ע״ה, אל שדי ע״ה

bema'ase בְּמַעֲשֶׂה, uven וּבֵין behirhur בְּהִרְהוּר ben בֵּין bemezid בְּמֵזִיד,

acher אַחֵר begilgul בְּגִלְגּוּל ben בֵּין ze זֶה begilgul בְּגִלְגּוּל ben בֵּין

hakelipot הַקְּלִיפּוֹת shetaki שֶׁתָּקִיא, bakelipot בַּקְּלִיפּוֹת venivla וְנִבְלַע

bizechut בְּזְכוּת ba בָּה shenivle'u שֶׁנִּבְלְעוּ keri קְרִי hanitzotzot הַנִּיצוֹצוֹת

hayotze הַיוֹצֵא להו ; עם ד׳ אותיות = מבה, יזל, אום shimcha שִׁמְךָ hagadol הַגָּדוֹל

מפסוק ר״ת חזו ו־ילי vayki'enu וַיְקִאֶנּוּ bala בָּלַע ומב chayil וַיִל :mipasuk מִפָּסוּק

uvizchut וּבְזְכוּת ; ס״ת וזל וּבְזְכוּת ; ס״ת וזל (מילוי דס״ג) יא״י El אֵל yorishenu יֹרִשֶׁנּוּ mibitno מִבִּטְנוֹ

kedusha קְדוּשָׁה limkom לִמְקוֹם shetachazirem שֶׁתַּחֲזִירֵם shimcha שִׁמְךָ hagadol הַגָּדוֹל להו ; עם ד׳ אותיות = מבה, יזל, אום יוֹזֶהֱבֹוָה

.ase עֲשֵׂה מ״ה ; ריבוע ע״ה ; קס״א be'enecha בְּעֵינֶיךָ והו vehatov וְהַטוֹב

You should meditate to correct the thought that caused the loss of the sparks of Light. Also meditate on the Names that control our thoughts for each of the six days of the week as follow:

Sunday	יְהֹוָה	וְשֵׁם: דְּמַרְגְּלָא אֲהִיָה מֶן א טֹפְטֹפִיָּה וַאו זִין וַאו כַּף צָבָא עַל					.Beriah
Monday	יְהֹוָה	וְשֵׁם: דְּמַרְגְּלָא אֲהִיָה מֶן ה טֹפְטֹפִיָּה וַאו זִין וַאו כַּף מִגֵּן עַל					.Yetzirah
Tuesday	מִצְפָּץ	וְשֵׁם: דְּמַרְגְּלָא אֲהִיָה מֶן י טֹפְטֹפִיָּה וַאו זִין וַאו כַּף פּוֹדֵר צֹה					.Asiyah
Wednesday	אֵל	וְשֵׁם: דְּמַרְגְּלָא יְהוֹ מֶן י טֹפְטֹפִיָּה וַאו זִין וַאו כַּף פּוֹדֵר צֹה					.Asiyah
Thursday	אֱלֹהִים	וְשֵׁם: דְּמַרְגְּלָא יְהוֹ מֶן ה טֹפְטֹפִיָּה וַאו זִין וַאו כַּף מִגֵּן עַל					.Yetzirah
Friday	מִצְפָּץ	וְשֵׁם: דְּמַרְגְּלָא יְהוֹ מֶן ו טֹפְטֹפִיָּה וַאו זִין וַאו כַּף צָבָא עַל					.Beriah

Each of these Names (עַל צָבָא, כַּף וַאו זִין וַאו, טֹפְטֹפִיָּה), adds up to 193, which is the same numerical value as the word zokef (raise). These Names raise the Holy Spark from the Chitzoniyim. Also, when you say the words "mekabetz nidchei" (in the continuation of the blessing), which adds up to 304 — the same numerical value of Shin, Dalet (demon), you should meditate to collect all the lost sparks and cancel out the power of the negative forces.

May it be pleasing before You, Lord, my God and God of my forefathers, that every drop and drop of keri that came out of me for vain, and from all of Israel in general, and especially not as a cause of precept, if it was coerced or willfully, with intention or without, by passing thought or by an action, in this lifetime or in previous, and it was swallowed by the klipa, that the klipa will vomit all the sparks of keri that was swollen by it, by virtue of your great name that comes from the verse: "He swallowed up wealth and vomited it out, and from his belly God will cast it." (Job 20:15), and by the virtue of Your great Name you will return them to the Holy Place, and do what is good in Your eyes.

בְּרוּךְ baruch אַתָּה Ata יְהֹוָואדנייאהדונהי Adonai ; יכוין חובי בעילוב יהוה כזה: יְוֹזֶהְבֹּוֹזֶה

מְקַבֵּץ mekabetz ע"ב ס"ג מ"ה ב"ן, הברכה (למתק את ז' המלכים עמתו)

נִדְחֵי nidchei ע"ב, ריבוע יהוה amo עַמּוֹ וחבי יִשְׂרָאֵל Yisrael:

THE EIGHTH (ELEVENTH) BLESSING

This blessing helps us to balance Judgment with Mercy. As Mercy is time, we can use it to change ourselves before Judgment occurs.

Yesod

הָשִׁיבָה hashiva שׁוֹפְטֵינוּ shoftenu כְּבָרִאשׁוֹנָה kevarishona◆

וְיוֹעֲצֵינוּ veyo'atzenu כְּבַתְּחִלָּה kevatechila ר"ת שכ"ה (דינים זכרים עב'סוד) ויהוה (הממתקם)◆

וְהָסֵר vehaser מִמֶּנּוּ mimenu יָגוֹן yagon (סמאל) וַאֲנָחָה va'anacha (לילית)◆

וּמְלוֹךְ umloch עָלֵינוּ aleinu מְהֵרָה mehera אַתָּה Ata

יְהֹוָואדנייאהדונהי Adonai לְבַדְּךָ levadcha◆ בְּחֶסֶד bechesed ע"ב, ריבוע יהוה

וּבְרַחֲמִים uvrachamim מצפצ, אלהים דיודין, י"פ יי' ; להמתיק ברוזמים דיני צדק ומעפט

בְּצֶדֶק betzedek וּבְמִשְׁפָּט uvmishpat ע"ה = ה"פ אלהים: בָּרוּךְ baruch אַתָּה Ata

יְהֹוָוַואדנייאהדונהי Adonai מֶלֶךְ melech אוֹהֵב ohev ממתיק דיני

צְדָקָה tzedaka ע"ה ריבוע אלהים וּמִשְׁפָּט umishpat ע"ה ה"פ אלהים:

THE NINTH (TWELFTH) BLESSING

This blessing helps us remove all forms of negativity, whether it comes from people, situations or even the negative energy of the Angel of Death [[(**do not pronounce these names**) *Sa-ma-el* (male aspect) and *Li-li-th* (female aspect), which are encoded here], by using the Holy Name: *Shadai* שׁדי, which is encoded mathematically into the last four words of this blessing and also appears inside a *Mezuzah* for the same purpose.

Blessed are You, Lord, Who gathers the displaced of His Nation, Israel.

THE EIGHTH (ELEVENTH) BLESSING

Restore our judges, as at first, and our mentors, as in the beginning. Remove from us sorrow and moaning. Reign over us soon, You alone, Lord, with kindness and compassion, with righteousness and justice. Blessed are You, Lord, the King Who loves righteousness and justice.

Keter

tikva תִּקְוָה tehi תְּהִי al אַל velamalshinim וְלַמַּלְשִׁינִים laminim לַמִּינִים

וְכָל־ יל׳ הַזֵּדִים hazedim כְּרֶגַע kerega ג״פ אלהים עם ט״ו אותיות פשוטות vechol

(סמאל) oyvecha אוֹיְבֶיךָ יל׳ vechol וְכָל־ ◆yovedu יֹאבֵדוּ

◆yikaretu יִכָּרֵתוּ mehera מְהֵרָה (לילית) son'echa שׂוֹנְאֶיךָ יל׳ vechol וְכָל־

te'aker תְּעַקֵּר mehera מְהֵרָה harish'a הָרִשְׁעָה umalchut וּמַלְכוּת

bimhera בִּמְהֵרָה vetachni'em וְתַכְנִיעֵם utchalem וּתְכַלֵּם utshaber וּתְשַׁבֵּר

Adonai יְהֹוָה(יְהֹוָהאהי)יאהדונהי Ata אַתָּה baruch בָּרוּךְ veyamenu בְּיָמֵינוּ

שׁוֹבֵר shover אוֹיְבִים oyvim וּמַכְנִיעַ umachni'a זֵדִים zedim ר״ת = עדי׃

THE TENTH (THIRTEENTH) BLESSING

This blessing surrounds us with total positivity to help us always be at the right place at the right time. It also helps attract only positive people into our lives.

Yesod

hachasidim הַחֲסִידִים ve'al וְעַל עולם יסוד צדיק hatzadikim הַצַּדִּיקִים al עַל

◆Yisrael יִשְׂרָאֵל ראה ב״פ bet בֵּית amecha עַמְּךָ she'erit שְׁאֵרִית ve'al וְעַל

◆sofrehem סוֹפְרֵיהֶם ראה ב״פ bet בֵּית peletat פְּלֵיטַת ve'al וְעַל

yehemu יֶהֱמוּ ◆ve'alenu וְעָלֵינוּ hatzedek הַצֶּדֶק gerei גֵּרֵי ve'al וְעַל

יל׳ Elohenu אֱלֹהֵינוּ Adonai יְהֹוָה(אהדי)יאהדונהי rachamecha רַחֲמֶיךָ na נָא

ארני יה lechol לְכָל־ והי tov טוֹב ב״ן י״פ sachar שָׂכָר veten וְתֵן

הַבּוֹטְחִים habotchim בְּשִׁמְךָ beshimcha בֶּאֱמֶת be'emet אהיה פעמים אהיה, ז״פ ס״ג◆

THE NINTH (TWELFTH) BLESSING

For the heretics and for the slanderers, let there be no hope.

Let all the wicked perish in an instant. And may all Your foes and all Your haters be speedily cut down. And as for the evil government, may You quickly uproot and smash it, and may You destroy and humble it, speedily in our days. Blessed are You, Lord, Who smashes foes and humbles the wicked.

THE TENTH (THIRTEENTH) BLESSING

On the righteous, on the pious, on the remnants of the House of Israel, on the remnants of their writers' academies, on the righteous converts, and on us, may Your compassion be stirred, Lord, our God. And give good reward to all those who truly trust in Your Name.

וְשִׂים vesim וְחֶלְקֵנוּ chelkenu עִמָּהֶם imahem וּלְעוֹלָם ul'olam ריבוע ס"ג ו' אותיות דס"ג

לֹא lo נֵבוֹשׁ nevosh כִּי ki בָּךְ vecha בָּטַחְנוּ batachnu♦

וְעַל ve'al וְחַסְדְּךָ chasdecha הַגָּדוֹל hagadol להו ; עם ד' אותיות = מבה, יזל, אום

בֶּאֱמֶת be'emet אהיה פעמים אהיה, ז"פ ס"ג נִשְׁעָנֵנוּ nish'anenu♦

בָּרוּךְ baruch אַתָּה Ata יְהוָֹואדֹנָיאהדֹונֹהי Adonai מִשְׁעָן mish'an

וּמִבְטַח umivtach לַצַּדִּיקִים latzadikim ר"ת יומל (כל מי שעשמול נקרא צדיק)♦

THE ELEVENTH (FOURTEENTH) BLESSING

This blessing connects us to the power of Jerusalem, to the building of the Temple, and to the preparation for the *Mashiach*.

Hod

תִּשְׁכּוֹן tishkon בְּתוֹךְ betoch יְרוּשָׁלַיִם Yerushalayim עִירְךָ ircha

כַּאֲשֶׁר ka'asher דִּבַּרְתָּ dibarta ראה וְכִסֵּא vechise דָּוִד David

עַבְדְּךָ avdecha פוי, אל אדני מְהֵרָה mehera בְּתוֹכָהּ vetocha תָּכִין tachin

Meditate here that *Mashiach Ben Yosef* shall not be killed by the wicked *Armilos* **(Do not pronounce)**.

וּבְנֵה uvne אוֹתָהּ ota בִּנְיַן binyan עוֹלָם olam בִּמְהֵרָה bimhera

בְּיָמֵינוּ veyamenu♦ בָּרוּךְ baruch אַתָּה Ata יְהוָֹואדֹנָיאהדֹונֹהי Adonai

בּוֹנֵה bone ס"ג יְרוּשָׁלָיִם Yerushalayim♦

THE TWELFTH (FIFTEENTH) BLESSING

This blessing helps us achieve a personal state of *Mashiach* by transforming our reactive nature into becoming proactive. Just as there is a global *Mashiach*, each person has a personal *Mashiach* within. When enough people achieve their transformation, the way will be paved for the appearance of the global *Mashiach*.

---

and place our lot with them. And may we never be embarrassed, for it is in You that we place our trust; it is upon Your great compassion that we truly rely. Blessed are You, Lord, the support and security of the righteous.

THE ELEVENTH (FOURTEENTH) BLESSING

May You dwell in Jerusalem, Your City,
as You have promised. And may You establish the throne of David, Your servant, speedily within it and build it as an eternal structure, speedily in our days Blessed are You, Lord, Who builds Jerusalem.

Netzach

This blessing contains 20 words, which is the same number of words in *"Ki nicham Adonai Tziyon nicham kol chorvoteha..." (Isaiah 51:3)*, a verse that speaks about the Final Redemption.

אֶת et צֶמַח tzemach יהוה אהוה יהוה אהיה יהוה ארני דָּוִד David

עַבְדְּךָ avdecha פוי, אל ארני מְהֵרָה mehera תַצְמִיחַ tatzmia'ch וְקַרְנוֹ vekarno

תָרוּם tarum בִּישׁוּעָתֶךָ bishu'atecha◆ כִּי ki לִישׁוּעָתְךָ lishu'atcha

קִוִּינוּ kivinu כָּל kol יְלי הַיּוֹם hayom ע"ה נגד, מזבוז, זן, אל יהוה

You should meditate and ask here for the Final Redemption to occur right away.

בָּרוּךְ baruch אַתָּה Ata יְהֹוָ אדני אהדונהי Adonai

מַצְמִיחַ matzmi'ach קֶרֶן keren יְשׁוּעָה yeshu'a✦

THE THIRTEENTH (SIXTEENTH) BLESSING

This blessing is the most important of all blessings, because here we acknowledge all of our reactive behavior. We make reference to our wrongful actions in general, and we also specify a particular incident. The section inside the box provides us with an opportunity to ask the Light for personal sustenance. The Ari states that throughout this prayer, even on fast days, we have a personal angel accompanying us. If we meditate upon this angel, all our prayers must be answered. The Thirteenth Blessing is one above the twelve zodiac signs, and it raises us above the influence of the stars and planets.

Tiferet

שְׁמַע shema קוֹלֵנוּ kolenu יְהֹוָ אדני אהדונהי Adonai (יוד הה וו הה)

אֱלֹהֵינוּ Elohenu ילה (אבג יתץ)◆ אָב av הָרַחֲמָן harachaman רַחֵם rachem

עָלֵינוּ alenu אברהם, וז"פ אל, רי"ו ול"ב נתיבות החוכמה, רמ"וז (אברים), עסמ"ב וט"ז אותיות פשוטות

(קרע שטן)◆ וְקַבֵּל vekabel בְּרַחֲמִים berachamim מצפצ, אלהים דיודין, י"פ יי

וּבְרָצוֹן uvratzon מהש ע"ה, ע"ב בריבוע וקס"א ע"ה, אל שדי ע"ה אֶת et

תְּפִלָּתֵנוּ tefilatenu (נגד יכש)◆ כִּי ki אֵל El יא"י (מילוי) (דס"ג)

שׁוֹמֵעַ shome'a תְּפִלּוֹת tefilot וְתַחֲנוּנִים vetachanunim אַתָּה Ata (בטר צתג)◆

THE TWELFTH (FIFTEENTH) BLESSING

The offspring of David, Your servant, may You speedily cause to sprout.
And may You raise their worth with Your salvation, because it is for Your salvation that we have hoped all day long. Blessed are You, Lord, Who sprouts out the worth of the salvation.

THE THIRTEENTH (SIXTEENTH) BLESSING

Hear our voice, Lord, our God. Merciful Father, have mercy over us.
Accept our prayer with compassion and favor, because You are God, Who hears prayers and supplications.

It is good for you to be aware, acknowledge and confess your prior negative actions and to ask for your livelihood here:

ribono רבּוֹנוֹ shel שֶׁל olam עוֹלָם, chatati וְחָטָאתִי aviti עָוִיתִי

ufashati וּפָשַׁעְתִּי lefanecha לְפָנֶיךָ ס"ג מ"ה ב"ן yehi יְהִי ratzon רָצוֹן מהש"ע ע"ה,

shetimchol שֶׁתִּמְחוֹל ע"ב בריבוע וקס"א ע"ה, אל שדי ע"ה, ב"ן מ"ה ס"ג milfanecha מִלְפָנֶיךָ

vetislach וְתִסְלַח li לִי utchaper וּתְכַפֵּר al עַל ע"ב יהוה kol כָּל יל ילי ; עמם

ma מַה מ"ה shechatati שֶׁחָטָאתִי veshe'aviti וְשֶׁעָוִיתִי veshepashati וְשֶׁפָּשַׁעְתִּי

lefanecha לְפָנֶיךָ ס"ג מ"ה ב"ן miyom מִיוֹם ע"ה נגד, מזבוח, זן, אל יהוה

shenivreti שֶׁנִבְרֵאתִי ad עַד hayom הַיוֹם ע"ה נגד, מזבוח, זן, אל יהוה והו haze הַזֶה

uvifrat וּבִפְרָט (mention here a specific negative action or behavior you have and ask for forgivness)

vihi וִיהִי ratzon רָצוֹן מהש"ע ע"ה, ע"ב בריבוע וקס"א ע"ה, אל שדי ע"ה

milfanecha מִלְפָנֶיךָ ס"ג מ"ה ב"ן Adonai יְהֹוָאדֹנָהִ־אֲהֹדֹנָהי Elohenu אֱלֹהֵינוּ ילה

velohei וֵאלֹהֵי ילה ; מילוי ע"ב, דמב avotenu אֲבוֹתֵינוּ לכב ; shetazmin שֶׁתַּזְמִין

parnasatenu פַּרְנָסָתֵנוּ umzonotenu וּמְזוֹנוֹתֵינוּ li לִי ulchol וּלְכָל יה אדני

anshei אַנְשֵׁי veti בֵיתִי hayom הַיוֹם ע"ה נגד, מזבוח, זן, אל יהוה ב"פ ראה

uvchol וּבְכָל ב"ן, לכב yom יוֹם ע"ה נגד, מזבוח, זן, אל יהוה

vayom וָיוֹם ע"ה נגד, מזבוח, זן, אל יהוה berevach בְּרֶיוַח velo וְלֹא

vetzimtzum וְצִמְצוּם, bechavod בְּכָבוֹד בוכו velo וְלֹא bevizui בְּבִזּוּי,

benachat בְּנַחַת velo וְלֹא vetza'ar בְּצַעַר, velo וְלֹא etztarech אֶצְטָרֵךְ

lematenot לְמַתְנוֹת basar בָּשָׂר vadam וְדָם velo וְלֹא lehalva'atam לְהַלְוָאָתָם,

ela אֶלֹא miyadcha מִיָדְךָ harchava הָרְחָבָה vehapetucha וְהַפְּתוּחָה

vehamele'a וְהַמְּלֵאָה uvizchut וּבִזְכוּת shimcha שִׁמְךָ hagadol הַגָדוֹל

(Do not pronounce this Name): דִיקַרְנוֹסָא וחזר עם ג' אותיות אום, יזל = מבה = אותיות ד' עם ; להו

al עַל hamemune הַמְמוּנֶה (יאהדונהי ,אל = ס אל, אמן, ובאתב"ע – haparnasa הַפַּרְנָסָה:

Master of the World!
I have transgressed. I have committed iniquity and I have sinned before You. May it be Your will that You would pardon, forgive and excuse all my transgressions, and all the iniquities that I have committed, and all the sins that I have sinned before You, ever since the day I was created and until this day (and especially…). May it be pleasing before You, Lord, our God and God of my forefathers, that You would provide for my livelihood and sustenance, and that of my household, today and each and every day, with abundance and not with meagerness; with dignity and not with shame; with comfort and not with suffering; and that I may not require the gifts of flesh and blood, nor their loans, but only from Your Hand, which is generous, open, and full, and by virtue of Your great Name, which is responsible for livelihood.

malkenu מַלְכֵּנוּ ב"ן מ"ה ס"ג umilfanecha וּמִלְפָנֶיךָ

(וזקב טנע) te'shivenu תְּשִׁיבֵנוּ al אַל rekam רֵיקָם

tefilatenu תְּפִלָּתֵנוּ: ushma וּשְׁמַע va'anenu וַעֲנֵנוּ chonenu וְחָנֵּנוּ

pe פֶּה ילי kol כָּל tefilat תְּפִלַּת shome'a שׁוֹמֵעַ Ata אַתָּה ki כִּי

(פה דו"א) מילה ; וע"ה אלהים, אהיה אדני (יגל פוק)

Adonai (יְהוָֹה)יאהדונהי יְהֹוָֹה Ata אַתָּה baruch בָּרוּךְ

You should meditate here on the Holy Name: אראריתא"א

Rav Chaim Vital says: "I have found in the books of the kabbalists that person's prayer, who meditates on this Name in the blessing *shome'a tefila*, will never go unanswered."

שׁוֹמֵעַ תְּפִלָּה (שׁקוֹ צית) אתב"ש אוכצ, ב"ן ארני וניקודה ע"ה = יוד הי וו הה: tefila shome'a

THE FINAL THREE BLESSINGS

Through the merit of Moses, Aaron and Joseph, who are our channels for the final three blessings, we are able to bring down all the spiritual energy that we aroused with our prayers and blessings.

THE SEVENTEENTH BLESSING

During this blessing, referring to Moses, we should always meditate to try to know exactly what God wants from us in our life, as signified by the phrase, "Let it be the will of God." We ask God to guide us toward the work we came to Earth to do. The Creator cannot just accept the work that we want to do; we must carry out the work we were destined to do.

Netzach

You have made requests (of daily needs) to God. Now, after asking for your needs to be met, you should praise the Creator in the last three blessings. This is like a person who has received what he needs from his Master and departs from Him. You should say *"retze"* and meditate for the Supernal Desire (*Keter*) that is called *metzach haratzon* (the Forehead of the Desire).

רְצֵה retze אלף למד הה יוד מם

Meditate here to transform misfortune and tragedy (צרה) into desire and acceptance (רצה).

יְהֹוָֹה אהדהייאהדונהי Adonai אֱלֹהֵינוּ Elohenu ילה בְּעַמְּךָ be'amecha יִשְׂרָאֵל Yisrael

וְלִתְפִלָּתָם velitfilatam שְׁעֵה she'e וְהָשֵׁב vehashev הָעֲבוֹדָה ha'avoda

---

And from before You,
our King, do not turn us away empty-handed but be gracious, answer us, and hear our prayer.
Because You hear the prayer of every mouth. Blessed are You, Lord, Who hears prayers.

THE FINAL THREE BLESSINGS - THE SEVENTEENTH BLESSING

Find favor, Lord, our God, in Your People, Israel, and turn to their prayer. Restore the service

Yisrael יִשְׂרָאֵל ve'ishei וְאִשֵּׁי ∙ ב"פ ראה. betecha בֵּיתֶךָ רי"ו lidvir לִדְבִיר

דאגה אוזר, be'ahava בְּאַהֲבָה mehera מְהֵרָה utfilatam וּתְפִלָּתָם

∙ע"ה עדי אל ,ע"ה וקס"א ע"ב בר יבוע ,ע"ה ע"ב מהש beratzon בְּרָצוֹן tekabel תְּקַבֵּל

ע"ה עדי אל ,ע"ה וקס"א ע"ב ברי בוע ,ע"ה ע"ב מהש leratzon לְרָצוֹן ut'hi וּתְהִי

amecha עַמְּךָ Yisrael יִשְׂרָאֵל avodat עֲבוֹדַת קמ"ג קנ"א קס"א ע"ה tamid תָּמִיד

On *Chol Hamo'ed Sukkot* we add:

During Sukkot there is an extra surge of spiritual energy in our midst. These additional blessings are our antenna for drawing this extra power into our lives.

If you mistakenly forgot to say "*ya'ale veyavo*," and realize this before the end of the blessing "*baruch Ata Adonai*," you should return to say "*ya'ale veyavo*" and continue as usual. If you realize this after the end of the blessing "*hamachazir shechinato leTziyon*" but before you start the next blessing "*modim*" you should say "*ya'ale veyavo*" there and continue as usual. If you only realize this after you have started the next blessing "*modim*" but before the second "*yih'yu leratzon*" (on pg. 649) you should return to "*retze*" (pg. 643) and continue from there. If you realize this after (the second "*yih'yu leratzon*") you should start the *Amidah* from the beginning.

avotenu אֲבוֹתֵינוּ ילה ; דמב ,ע"ב מילוי ; לכב velohei וֵאלֹהֵי ילה Elohenu אֱלֹהֵינוּ

veyeratze וְיֵרָצֶה רי"ו veyera'e וְיֵרָאֶה veyagi'a וְיַגִּיעַ veyavo וְיָבֹא ya'ale יַעֲלֶה

(ו פ"ז) ר"ת מ"ב ר"ת veyizacher וְיִזָּכֵר veyipaked וְיִפָּקֵד veyishama וְיִשָּׁמַע

∙avotenu אֲבוֹתֵינוּ ונ"ע ב קס"א ע"ב vezichron וְזִכְרוֹן zichronenu זִכְרוֹנֵנוּ

∙irach עִירָךְ Yerushalayim יְרוּשָׁלַיִם ונ"ב קס"א ע"ב zichron זִכְרוֹן

David דָּוִד ben בֶּן mashi'ach מְשִׁיחַ ונ"ע"ב קס"א ע"ב vezichron וְזִכְרוֹן

ונ"ע"ב קס"א ע"ב vezichron וְזִכְרוֹן ∙ אל אדני ,פוי avdach עַבְדְּךָ ע"ה כהת = אדני ע"ה ; בן דוד ; ע"ה כהת

Yisrael יִשְׂרָאֵל ב"פ ראה bet בֵּית amecha עַמְּךָ יֹלי kol כָּל

∙אכא letova לְטוֹבָה ב"ן lifleta לִפְלֵיטָה מ"ה ב"ן ס"ג lefanecha לְפָנֶיךָ

יהוה ריבוע lechesed לְחֶסֶד מוזי ברי בוע ,דמ"ה מילוי lechen לְחֵן

ע"ה בינה יהוה אהיה אהיה lechayim לְחַיִּים ∙ulrachamim וּלְרַחֲמִים

∙יהוה אל ,ז מזבוח ,נגד ע"ה beyom בְּיוֹם ∙ulshalom וּלְשָׁלוֹם tovim טוֹבִים

---

to the inner sanctuary of Your Temple. Accept the offerings of Israel and their prayer with favor, speedily, and with love. May the service of Your People Israel always be favorable to You.

On *Chol Hamo'ed Sukkot* we add:

Our God and God of our forefathers,

may it rise, come, arrive, appear, find favor, be heard, be considered, and be remembered, our remembrance and the remembrance of our forefathers: the remembrance of Jerusalem, Your City, and the remembrance of Mashiach, Son of David, Your servant, and the remembrance of Your entire Nation, the House of Israel, before You for deliverance, for good, for grace, kindness, and compassion, for a good life, and for peace on the day of:

וְחַג chag הַסֻּכּוֹת haSukkot הַזֶּה hazeh והו

בְּיוֹם beyom ע"ה נגד, מזבוח, זז, אל יהוה מִקְרָא mikra קֹדֶשׁ kodesh הַזֶּה haze והו.

לְרַחֵם lerachem אברהם, וו"פ אל, רי"ו ול"ב נתיבות הַוֹחכמה, רמ"ז (אברים),

עסמ"ב וט"ז אותיות פשוטות בּוֹ bo עָלֵינוּ alenu וּלְהוֹשִׁיעֵנוּ ulhoshi'enu.

זָכְרֵנוּ zochrenu יְהֹוָאדֹנָי Adonai אֱלֹהֵינוּ Elohenu ילה בּוֹ bo

לְטוֹבָה letova אכא. וּפָקְדֵנוּ ufokdenu vo בּוֹ לִבְרָכָה livracha.

וְהוֹשִׁיעֵנוּ vehoshi'enu בּוֹ vo לְחַיִּים lechayim אהיה יהוה, אהיה בינה ע"ה

טוֹבִים tovim. בִּדְבַר bidvar ראה יְשׁוּעָה yeshu'a yeshu'a וְרַחֲמִים verachamim.

חוּס chus וְחָנֵּנוּ vechonenu וַחֲמוֹל vachamol וְרַחֵם verachem אברהם, וו"פ אל,

רי"ו ול"ב נתיבות הַוֹחכמה, רמ"ז (אברים), עסמ"ב וט"ז אותיות פשוטות עָלֵינוּ alenu.

וְהוֹשִׁיעֵנוּ vehoshi'enu כִּי ki אֵלֶיךָ elecha עֵינֵינוּ enenu רביע מ"ה. כִּי ki

אֵל El יא"י (מילוי דס"ג) מֶלֶךְ melech וְחַנּוּן chanun וְרַחוּם verachum אָתָּה Ata:

וְאַתָּה veAta בְּרַחֲמֶךָ verachamecha הָרַבִּים harabim. תַּחְפּוֹץ tachpotz

בָּנוּ banu וְתִרְצֵנוּ vetirtzenu וְתֶחֱזֶינָה vetechezena עֵינֵינוּ enenu רביע מ"ה

בְּשׁוּבְךָ beshuvcha לְצִיּוֹן leTziyon יוסף, ו' הויות, קנאה בְּרַחֲמִים berachamim.

בָּרוּךְ baruch ייי יפ ייי Ata אַתָּה יְהֹוָאדֹנָי Adonai מצפצ, אלהים דיודין,

הַמַּחֲזִיר hamachazir שְׁכִינָתוֹ shechinato לְצִיּוֹן leTziyon יוסף, ו' הויות, קנאה:

This festival of Sukkot, on this Holy Day of Convocation.
To take pity on us and to save us.
Remember us, Lord, our God, on this day, for good; consider us on it for blessing; and deliver us on it for a good life, with the words of deliverance and mercy. Take pity and be gracious to us, have mercy and be compassionate with us, and save us, for our eyes turn to You, because You are God, the King Who is gracious and compassionate.

And You in Your great compassion take delight in us and are pleased with us. May our eyes witness Your return to Zion with compassion. Blessed are You, Lord, Who returns His Shechinah to Zion.

THE EIGHTEENTH BLESSING

This blessing is our thank you. Kabbalistically, the biggest "thank you" we can give the Creator is to do exactly what we are supposed to do in terms of our spiritual work.

Hod

Bow your entire body at "*modim*" and straighten up at "*Adonai*."

מוֹדִים modim מאה ברכות שתיקן דוד לאמרם כל יום אֲנַ֫חְנוּ anachnu לָךְ lach

שֶׁאַתָּה sheAta הוּא hu יְהֹוָהאהדונהיאדני Adonai (וֹ) אֱלֹהֵ֫ינוּ Elohenu ילה

וֵאלֹהֵי velohei לכב ; מילוי ע"ב, דמב ; ילה אֲבוֹתֵ֫ינוּ avotenu לְעוֹלָם le'olam

צוּרֵ֫נוּ tzurenu צוּר tzur אותיות דס"ג ו' ס"ג ריבוע וְעֵד va'ed עה דההן אלהים ע"ה

וּמָגֵן umagen ר"ת מיכאל גבריאל נוריאל ; ג"פ אל (ייא"י מילוי דס"ג) חַיֵּ֫ינוּ chayenu

אַתָּה Ata הוּא hu ledor לְדֹר vador וָדֹר ר"יו node נוֹדֶה yish'enu יִשְׁעֵ֫נוּ

לְךָ lecha unsaper וּנְסַפֵּר tehilatecha תְּהִלָּתֶ֫ךָ al עַל chayenu וְחַיֵּ֫ינוּ

hamesurim הַמְּסוּרִים beyadecha בְּיָדֶ֫ךָ ve'al וְעַל nishmotenu נִשְׁמוֹתֵ֫ינוּ

hapekudot הַפְּקוּדוֹת lach לָךְ ve'al וְעַל nisecha נִסֶּ֫יךָ shebechol שֶׁבְּכָל

imanu עִמָּ֫נוּ ריבוע ס"ג, אל יהוה זן, מזבוֹז נגד, ע"ה yom יוֹם לכב, ב"ן

ve'al וְעַל nifle'otecha נִפְלְאוֹתֶ֫יךָ vetovotecha וְטוֹבוֹתֶ֫יךָ shebechol שֶׁבְּכָל

erev עֶרֶב et עֵת לכב, ב"ן vavoker וָבֹקֶר vetzahorayim וְצָהֳרָ֫יִם hatov הַטּוֹב

ki כִּי lo לֹא chalu כָלוּ rachamecha רַחֲמֶ֫יךָ hamerachem הַמְרַחֵם וֹהו

lo לֹא ki כִּי אברהם, וֹ"פ אל, רי"ו ול"ב נתיבות הוֹזכמה, רמ"וֹ (אברים), עסמ"ב וֹט"ו אותיות פשוטות

tamu תַּמּוּ chasadecha וַחֲסָדֶ֫יךָ ki כִּי me'olam מֵעוֹלָם kivinu קִוִּ֫ינוּ lach לָךְ:

THE EIGHTEENTH BLESSING

We give thanks to You, for it is You, Lord, Who is our God and God of our forefathers, forever and for all eternity. You are our Rock, the Rock of our lives, and the Shield of our salvation. From one generation to another, we shall give thanks to You and we shall tell of Your praise. For our lives that are entrusted in Your hands, for our souls that are in Your care, for Your miracles that are with us every day, and for Your wonders and Your favors that are with us at all times: evening, morning and afternoon. You are the good One, for Your compassion has never ceased. You are the compassionate One, for Your kindness has never ended, for we have always placed our hope in You.

veyitromam וְיִתְרוֹמַם yitbarach יִתְבָּרַךְ kulam כֻּלָּם ve'al וְעַל

shimcha שִׁמְךָ קמ״ג קנ״א קס״א קס״א ע״ה tamid תָּמִיד veyitnase וְיִתְנַשֵּׂא

va'ed וְעֶד אותיות דס״ג ס״ג וי׳ ריבוע le'olam לְעוֹלָם malkenu מַלְכֵּנוּ

sela סֶלָה yoducha יוֹדוּךָ אהיה אהיה יהוה, בינה ע״ה hachayim הַחַיִּים יל׳ vechol וְכָל

et אֶת מ״ה ריבוע יהוה vivarchu וִיבָרְכוּ יהוה vihalelu וִיהַלְלוּ

be'emet בֶּאֱמֶת יזל, אום עם ד׳ אותיות = מבה, לַהוּ ; hagadol הַגָּדוֹל shimcha שִׁמְךָ

tov טוֹב ki כִּי אותיות דס״ג וי׳ ס״ג ריבוע ז״פ ס״ג, אהיה פעמים אהיה. le'olam לְעוֹלָם והו ;

yeshu'atenu יְשׁוּעָתֵנוּ (מילוי דס״ג) יא״י ; לאה haEl הָאֵל יזל, מבה, אום, אהיה, יהוה = טוֹב כי

hatov הַטּוֹב (מילוי דס״ג) יא״י ; לאה haEl הָאֵל sela סֶלָה ve'ezratenu וְעֶזְרָתֵנוּ והו :

Bend your knees at "baruch," bow at "Ata" and straighten up at "Adonai."

hatov הַטּוֹב (הי) Adonai יְהֹוָאדֹנָי Ata אַתָּה baruch בָּרוּךְ והו

shimcha שִׁמְךָ na'e נָאֶה ulcha וּלְךָ lehodot לְהוֹדוֹת ס״ת כהת, משיוו בן דוד ע״ה :

THE FINAL BLESSING

We are emanating the energy of peace to the entire world. We also make it our intent to use our mouths only for good. Kabbalistically, the power of words and speech is unimaginable. We hope to use that power wisely, which is perhaps one of the most difficult tasks we have to carry out.

Yesod

shalom שָׁלוֹם sim שִׂים

tova טוֹבָה אבא uvracha וּבְרָכָה chayim וְחַיִּים אהיה אהיה יהוה, בינה ע״ה

chen וְחֵן מילוי דמ״ה ברבוע, מוזי vachesed וָחֶסֶד ע״ב, ריבוע יהוה

tzedaka צְדָקָה ע״ה ריבוע אלהים verachamim וְרַחֲמִים alenu עָלֵינוּ

ve'al וְעַל kol כָּל ילי ; עמם Yisrael יִשְׂרָאֵל amecha עַמֶּךָ

And for all those things, may Your Name be always blessed, exalted and extolled, our King, forever and ever, and all the living shall thank You, Selah. And they shall praise and bless Your Great Name, sincerely and forever, for It is good, the God of our salvation and our help, Selah, the good God. Blessed are You, Lord, whose Name is good, and to You it is befitting to give thanks.

THE FINAL BLESSING
Place peace, goodness,
blessing, life, grace, kindness, righteousness, and mercy upon us and upon all of Israel, Your People.

וּבָרְכֵנוּ uvarchenu אָבִינוּ avinu כֻּלָּנוּ kulanu כְּאֶחָד ke'echad אהבה, דאגה

בְּאוֹר be'or רו, א"ס, א"ס רו, א"ס ki כִּי בְּ"ן מ"ה ס"ג panecha פָּנֶיךָ be'or בְּאוֹר ve'or

פָּנֶיךָ panecha ס"ג מ"ה בְּ"ן natata נָתַתָּ lanu לָנוּ אלהים, אהיה אדני

יְהֹוָה Adonai אֱלֹהֵינוּ Elohenu ילה torah תּוֹרָה vechayim וְחַיִּים

אַהֲבָה ahava אוזר, דאגה, בינה ע"ה vachesed וָחֶסֶד ע"ב, ריבוע יהוה

צְדָקָה tzedaka ע"ה ריבוע אלהים verachamim וְרַחֲמִים beracha בְּרָכָה

וְשָׁלוֹם veshalom vetov וְטוֹב והו be'enecha בְּעֵינֶיךָ ע"ה קס"א ; ריבוע מ"ה

לְבָרְכֵנוּ levarchenu וּלְבָרֵךְ ulvarech אֶת et כָּל kol עַמְּךָ ילי amecha

יִשְׂרָאֵל Yisrael בְּרוֹב berov י"פ אהיה oz עֹז וְשָׁלוֹם veshalom

בָּרוּךְ baruch אַתָּה Ata יֹהֹוָה Adonai

הַמְבָרֵךְ hamevarech אֶת et עַמּוֹ amo יִשְׂרָאֵל Yisrael

ר"ת = אלהים (אילההויהם) = יב"ק בְּשָׁלוֹם bashalom אָמֵן amen

YIH'YU LERATZON

There are 42 letters in the verse in the secret of *Ana Beko'ach*.

יְהִיוּ yih'yu לְרָצוֹן leratzon מהע ע"ה, ע"ב בריבוע וקס"א ע"ה, אל עדי ע"ה

אִמְרֵי imrei פִי fi ר"ת אֶלֶף = אלף למבד עין דלת יוד ע"ה וְהֶגְיוֹן vehegyon לִבִּי libi

לְפָנֶיךָ lefanecha ס"ג מ"ה בְּ"ן יְהֹוָה Adonai צוּרִי tzuri וְגֹאֲלִי vego'ali

---

Bless us all as one, our Father, with the Light of Your Countenance, because it is with the Light of Your Countenance that You, Lord, our God, have given us Torah and life, love and kindness, righteousness and mercy, blessing and peace. May it be good in Your Eyes to bless us and to bless Your entire Nation, Israel, with abundant power and with peace. Blessed are You, Lord, Who blesses His Nation, Israel, with peace, Amen.

YIH'YU LERATZON

*"May the utterances of my mouth
and the thoughts of my heart find favor before You, Lord, my Rock and my Redeemer." (Psalms 19:15)*

ELOHAI NETZOR

אֱלֹהַי Elohai מילוי ע"ב, דמב ; ילה netzor נְצֹר leshoni לְשׁוֹנִי mera מֵרָע◆

וְשִׂפְתוֹתַי vesiftotai מְדַבֵּר midaber ראה מִרְמָה mirma◆ וְלִמְקַלְלַי velimkalelai◆

נַפְשִׁי nafshi תִדֹּם tidom◆ וְנַפְשִׁי venafshi כֶּעָפָר ke'afar

לַכֹּל lakol יה אדני תִהְיֶה tih'ye◆ פָּתַח petach לִבִּי libi בְּתוֹרָתֶךָ betoratecha◆

וְאַחֲרֵי ve'acharei מִצְוֹתֶיךָ mitzvotecha תִּרְדּוֹף tirdof נַפְשִׁי nafshi◆

וְכָל vechol הַקָּמִים hakamim עָלַי alai לְרָעָה lera'a רהע◆ מְהֵרָה mehera

הָפֵר hafer עֲצָתָם atzatam וְקַלְקֵל vekalkel מַחְשְׁבוֹתָם machshevotam◆

עֲשֵׂה ase לְמַעַן lema'an שְׁמֶךָ shemach◆ עֲשֵׂה ase לְמַעַן lema'an

יְמִינֶךָ yeminach◆ עֲשֵׂה ase לְמַעַן lema'an תּוֹרָתֶךָ toratach◆ עֲשֵׂה ase

לְמַעַן lema'an קְדוּשָׁתֶךָ kedushatach◆ ר"ת הפסוק = מ"ה יהוה

יֵחָלְצוּן yechaltzun יְדִידֶיךָ yedidecha ר"ת יהוה הוֹשִׁיעָה hoshi'a

יְמִינֶךָ yemincha וַעֲנֵנִי va'aneni (כתיב: וְעֵנֵנִי)

Before we recite the next verse *"Yih'yu leratzon"* we have an opportunity to strengthen our connection to our soul using our name. Each person has a verse in the Torah that connects to their name. Either their name is in the verse, or the first and last letters of the name correspond to the first or last letters of a verse.

YIH'YU LERATZON (THE SECOND)
There are 42 letters in the verse in the secret of *Ana Beko'ach*.

יִהְיוּ yih'yu לְרָצוֹן leratzon

אִמְרֵי imrei פִי fi וְהֶגְיוֹן vehegyon לִבִּי libi

לְפָנֶיךָ lefanecha Adonai צוּרִי tzuri וְגֹאֲלִי vego'ali

ELOHAI NETZOR

My God, guard my tongue from evil and my lips from speaking deceit. To those who curse me, let my spirit remain silent, and let my spirit be as dust for everyone. Open my heart to Your Torah and let my heart pursue Your commandments. All those who rise against me to do me harm, speedily nullify their plans and disturb their thoughts. Do so for the sake of Your Name. Do so for the sake of Your Right. Do so for the sake of Your Torah. Do so for the sake of Your Holiness, "So that Your loved ones may be saved. Redeem Your right and answer me." (Psalms 60:7)

YIH'YU LERATZON (THE SECOND)
"May the utterances of my mouth and the thoughts of my heart find favor before You, Lord, my Rock and my Redeemer." (Psalms 19:15)

OSE SHALOM

You take three steps backward;

שָׁלוֹם shalom   עוֹשֶׂה ose

Left
You turn to the left and say:

בִּמְרוֹמָיו bimromav

הוּא hu   בִּרְוַחֲמָיו verachamav   יַעֲשֶׂה ya'ase

Right
You turn to the right and say:

שָׁלוֹם shalom   עָלֵינוּ alenu

וְעַל ve'al   כָּל kol   עַמּוֹ amo   יִשְׂרָאֵל Yisrael

Center
You face the center and say:

וְאִמְרוּ ve'imru   אָמֵן amen

יְהִי yehi   רָצוֹן ratzon   מִלְפָנֶיךָ milfanecha

אֱלֹהֵינוּ Elohenu   יְהֹוָה Adonai

שֶׁתִּבְנֶה shetivne   אֲבוֹתֵינוּ avotenu,   וֵאלֹהֵי velohei

בְיָמֵינוּ veyamenu   בִּמְהֵרָה bimhera   הַמִּקְדָּשׁ hamikdash   בֵּית bet

וְחֻקֵּי chukei   לַעֲשׂוֹת la'asot   בְּתוֹרָתָךְ betoratach   חֶלְקֵנוּ chelkenu   וְתֵן veten

שָׁלֵם shalem   בְּלֵבָב belevav   וּלְעָבְדָךְ ul'ovdach   רְצוֹנָךְ retzonach

You take three steps forward.

OSE SHALOM

He, Who makes peace in His High Places, He, in His compassion, shall make peace upon us.
And upon His entire nation, Israel, and you shall say, Amen.

May it be pleasing before You,
Lord, our God and God of our forefathers, that You shall rebuild the Temple speedily, in our days, and place our lot in Your Torah, so that we may fulfill the laws of Your desire and serve You wholeheartedly.

KADDISH TITKABAL

יִתְגַּדַּל veyitkadash וְיִתְקַדַּשׁ yitgadal ; שׁדי ומילוי שׁדי ; י"א אותיות כמנין ו"ה

שְׁמֵהּ shemei (שׁם י"ה דע"ב) רַבָּא raba קנ"א ב"ן, יהוה אלהים יהוה ארני,

מילוי קס"א וס"ג, מ"ה ברבוע וע"ב ע"ה ; ר"ת = ו"פ אלהים ; ס"ת = ג"פ יב"ק אָמֵן amen אידהנויה.

בְּעָלְמָא be'alma דִּי di בְּרָא vera כִרְעוּתֵהּ chir'utei.

וְיַמְלִיךְ veyamlich מַלְכוּתֵהּ malchutei. וְיַצְמַח veyatzmach

פּוּרְקָנֵהּ purkanei. וִיקָרֵב vikarev מְשִׁיחֵהּ meshichei: אָמֵן amen אידהנויה.

בְּחַיֵּיכוֹן bechayechon וּבְיוֹמֵיכוֹן uvyomechon וּבְחַיֵּי uvchayei

דְכָל dechol בֵּית bet ילו רַאה ב"פ יִשְׂרָאֵל Yisrael בַּעֲגָלָא ba'agala

וּבִזְמַן uvizman קָרִיב kariv וְאִמְרוּ ve'imru אָמֵן amen: אָמֵן amen אידהנויה.

The congregation and the *chazan* say the following:

מילוי דמילוי דע"ב (יוד ויו דלת הי יוד ויו יוד ויו הי יוד)
Twenty eight words (until *be'alma*), meditate:
מילוי דמילוי דע"ב (יוד ויו דלת הי יוד ויו יוד ויו הי יוד)
Twenty eight letters (until *almaya*), meditate:

יְהֵא yehe שְׁמֵהּ shemei (שׁם י"ה דס"ג) רַבָּא raba קנ"א ב"ן,

יהוה אלהים ארני, מילוי קס"א וס"ג, מ"ה ברבוע וע"ב ע"ה מְבָרַךְ mevarach,

לְעָלַם le'alam לְעָלְמֵי le'almei עָלְמַיָּא almaya. יִתְבָּרַךְ yitbarach

Seven words with six letters each (שׁם בן מ"ב) – meditate:
יהוה + יוד הי ויו הי + מילוי דמילוי דע"ב (יוד ויו דלת הי יוד ויו יוד ויו הי יוד)
Also, seven times the letter *Vav* (שׁם בן מ"ב) – meditate:
יהוה + יוד הי ויו הי + מילוי דמילוי דע"ב (יוד ויו דלת הי יוד ויו יוד ויו הי יוד).

וְיִשְׁתַּבַּח veyishtabach י"פ ע"ב יהוה אל אבג יתץ.

וְיִתְפָּאַר veyitpa'ar הי נו יה קרע שׂטן. וְיִתְרֹמַם veyitromam וה כוזו נגד יכש.

וְיִתְנַשֵּׂא veyitnase במוכסז בטר צתג. וְיִתְהַדָּר veyit'hadar כוזו יה וזקב טנע.

וְיִתְעַלֶּה veyit'ale וה יוד ה יגל פזק. וְיִתְהַלָּל veyit'halal א ואו הא שׂקו צית.

שְׁמֵהּ shemei (שׁם י"ה דמ"ה) דְּקוּדְשָׁא dekudsha בְּרִיךְ verich הוּא hu:

אָמֵן amen אידהנויה.

KADDISH TITKABAL

May His great Name be more exalted and sanctified. (Amen) In the world that He created according to His will, and may His Kingdom reign. And may He cause His redemption to sprout and may He bring the Mashiach closer. (Amen) In your lifetimes and in your days and in the lifetime of all the House of Israel, speedily and in the near future, and you shall say, Amen. (Amen) May His great Name be blessed forever and for all eternity. Blessed and lauded, and glorified, and exalted, and extolled, and honored, and uplifted, and praised be the Name of the Holy Blessed One. (Amen)

לְעֵלָּא le'ela   מִן min   כָּל kol יכי   בִּרְכָתָא birchata   שִׁירָתָא shirata

תֻּשְׁבְּחָתָא tishbechata   וְנֶחָמָתָא venechamata   דַּאֲמִירָן da'amiran

בְּעָלְמָא be'alma   וְאִמְרוּ ve'imru   אָמֵן amen   אָמֵן amen אידהנויה.

תִּתְקַבַּל titkabal   צְלוֹתָנָא tzelotana   וּבָעוּתָנָא uva'utana

עִם im   צְלוֹתְהוֹן tzelotehon   וּבָעוּתְהוֹן uva'utehon   דְּכָל dechol יכי

בֵּית bet ב"פ ראה   יִשְׂרָאֵל Yisrael   קֳדָם kadam   אֲבוּנָא avuna

דְּבִשְׁמַיָּא devishmaya   וְאִמְרוּ ve'imru   אָמֵן amen   אָמֵן amen אידהנויה.

יְהֵא yehe   שְׁלָמָא shelama   רַבָּא raba קנ"א ב"ן, יהוה אלהים יהוה אדני, מילוי קס"א וס"ג,

מִן min   שְׁמַיָּא shemaya מ"ה ברבוע וע"ב ע"ה אהיה אהיה יהוה, בינה ע"ה   וְחַיִּים chayim

וְשָׂבָע vesava   וִישׁוּעָה vishu'a   וְנֶחָמָה venechama   וְשֵׁיזָבָא veshezava

וּרְפוּאָה urfu'a   וּגְאֻלָּה ug'ula   וּסְלִיחָה uslicha   וְכַפָּרָה vechapara

וְרֶיוַח verevach   וְהַצָּלָה vehatzala   לָנוּ lanu אלהים, אהיה אדני   וּלְכָל ulchol יה אדני

עַמּוֹ amo   יִשְׂרָאֵל Yisrael   וְאִמְרוּ ve'imru   אָמֵן amen   אָמֵן amen אידהנויה.

Take three steps backwards and say:

עוֹשֶׂה ose   שָׁלוֹם shalom

בִּמְרוֹמָיו bimromav ע"ב, ריבוע יהוה.   הוּא hu   בְּרַחֲמָיו berachamav

יַעֲשֶׂה ya'ase   שָׁלוֹם shalom   עָלֵינוּ alenu ר"ת ש"ע נהורין

וְעַל ve'al   כָּל kol יכי ; עמם   עַמּוֹ amo   יִשְׂרָאֵל Yisrael   וְאִמְרוּ ve'imru   אָמֵן amen

אָמֵן amen אידהנויה.

Above all blessings, songs, praises, and words of consolation that may be said in the world, and you shall say, Amen. (Amen) May our prayers and pleas be accepted, together with the prayers and pleas of the entire House of Israel, before our Father in Heaven, and you say, Amen. (Amen) May there be abundant peace from Heaven; Life, contentment, salvation, consolation, deliverance, healing, redemption, pardon, atonement, comfort, and relief. For us and for His entire nation, Israel, and you shall say, Amen. (Amen) He, Who makes peace in His High Places, He, in His compassion, shall make peace upon us And upon His entire nation, Israel, and you shall say, Amen. (Amen)

SHIR LAMA'ALOT

מ"ה ריבוע | enai עֵינַי | esa אֶשָּׂא | lama'alot לַמַּעֲלוֹת | shir שִׁיר

ezri עֶזְרִי | yavo יָבֹא | me'ayin מֵאַיִן | heharim הֶהָרִים | el אֶל־

shamayim שָׁמָיִם | ose עֹשֵׂה | Adonai יְהֹוָה | me'im מֵעִם | ezri עֶזְרִי

י"פ טל, י"פ כוזו | raglecha רַגְלֶךָ | lamot לַמּוֹט | yiten יִתֵּן | al אַל־ | va'aretz וָאָרֶץ

yanum יָנוּם | lo לֹא־ | hine הִנֵּה | shomrecha שֹׁמְרֶךָ | yanum יָנוּם | al אַל־

כ"א ההויות שבתפילין | shomer שׁוֹמֵר | דא"א | ע"ע נהורין | yishan יִישָׁן | velo וְלֹא

shomrecha שֹׁמְרֶךָ | Adonai יְהֹוָה | Yisrael יִשְׂרָאֵל׃

היי | yeminecha יְמִינֶךָ | yad יַד | al עַל־ | tzilecha צִלְּךָ | Adonai יְהֹוָה

ילה ר"ת | yakeka יַכֶּכָּה | lo לֹא־ | hashemesh הַשֶּׁמֶשׁ | yomam יוֹמָם

Adonai יְהֹוָה | מלה׃ | balayla בַּלָּיְלָה | veyare'ach וְיָרֵחַ

yishmor יִשְׁמֹר | ra רָע | ילי | mikol מִכָּל־ | yishmorcha יִשְׁמָרְךָ

yishmor יִשְׁמֹר | Adonai יְהֹוָה | מי"כ׃ | nafshecha נַפְשֶׁךָ | et אֶת־

והב׃ | olam עוֹלָם | ve'ad וְעַד־ | me'ata מֵעַתָּה | uvo'echa וּבוֹאֶךָ | tzetcha צֵאתְךָ

KADDISH YEHE SHELAMA

שדי ומילוי שדי ; י"א אותיות כמנין ו"ה | veyitkadash וְיִתְקַדַּשׁ | yitgadal יִתְגַּדַל

קנ"א ב"ן, יהוה אלהים יהוה אדני, | (שם י"ה דע"ב) | raba רַבָּא | shemei שְׁמֵיהּ

מילוי קס"א וס"ג, מ"ה ברבוע וע"ב ע"ה ; ר"ת = ו"פ אלהים ; ס"ת = ג"פ יב"ק | amen אָמֵן אידהנויה♦

chir'utei כִרְעוּתֵיהּ | vera בְּרָא | di דִי | be'alma בְּעָלְמָא

veyatzmach וְיַצְמַח | malchutei מַלְכוּתֵיהּ | veyamlich וְיַמְלִיךְ

amen אָמֵן אידהנויה♦ | meshichei מְשִׁיחֵיהּ | vikarev וִיקָרֵב | purkanei פּוּרְקָנֵיהּ♦

SHIR LAMA'ALOT

"*A Song of Ascents: I lift up my eyes to the mountains; from where will my help come? My help is from the Lord, Creator of the Heavens and the Earth. He will not allow your legs to falter. Your Guardian shall not sleep. Behold: the Guardian of Israel shall neither slumber nor sleep. The Lord is your Guardian. The Lord is your protective shade at your right hand. During the day, the sun shall not harm you, nor shall the moon, at night. The Lord shall protect you from all evil, He will guard your soul. He shall guard you when you leave and when you come, from now and for eternity.*" (Psalms 121)

KADDISH YEHE SHELAMA

May His great Name be more exalted and sanctified. (Amen)
In the world that He created according to His will, and may His kingdom reign.
And may He cause His redemption to sprout and may He bring the Mashiach closer. (Amen)

וּבְחַיֵּי uvchayei — וּבְיוֹמֵיכוֹן uvyomechon — בְּחַיֵּיכוֹן bechayechon

דְכָל dechol — יְלִי בֵּית bet — ב"פ ראה — יִשְׂרָאֵל Yisrael — בַּעֲגָלָא ba'agala

וּבִזְמַן uvizman — קָרִיב kariv — וְאִמְרוּ ve'imru — אָמֵן amen — אָמֵן אידהנויה amen

The congregation and the *chazan* say the following:

Twenty eight words (until *be'alma*), meditate:
מִילוּי דְמִילוּי דֶּס"ג (יוד ויו דלת הי ואו אלף ואו הי יוד)

Twenty eight letters (until *almaya*), meditate:
מִילוּי דְמִילוּי דְמַ"ה (יוד ואו דלת הא אלף ואו הי ואו הא אלף)

יְהֵא yehe — שְׁמֵיהּ shemei — (שם י"ה דס"ג) — רַבָּא raba — קנ"א ב"ן

יהוה אלהים יהוה אדני, מילוי קס"א, מ"ה ברבוע וע"ב ע"ה — מְבָרַךְ mevarach,

לְעָלַם le'alam — לְעָלְמֵי le'almei — לְעָלְמַיָּא le'almaya — יִתְבָּרַךְ yitbarach

Seven words with six letters each (שם בן מ"ב) – meditate:
יהוה + יוד הי ואו הי + מילוי דמילוי דס"ג (יוד ויו דלת הי ואו אלף ואו הי יוד) ;

Also, seven times the letter *Vav* (שם בן מ"ב) – meditate:
יהוה + יוד הא ואו הא + מילוי דמילוי דמ"ה (יוד ואו דלת הא אלף ואו הי ואו הא אלף).

וְיִשְׁתַּבַּח veyishtabach — י"פ ע"ב יהוה אל אבג יתץ

וְיִתְפָּאַר veyitpa'ar — הי גו יה קרע שטן veyitromam וְיִתְרוֹמַם — וה כוזו נגד יכש

וְיִתְנַשֵּׂא veyitnase — במוכסז בטר צתג veyit'hadar וְיִתְהַדָּר — כוזו יה וזקב טנע

וְיִתְעַלֶּה veyit'ale — וה יוד ה יגל פזק veyit'halal וְיִתְהַלָּל — א ואו הא שקו צית

שְׁמֵיהּ shemei — (שם י"ה דמ"ה) — דְקֻדְשָׁא dekudsha — בְּרִיךְ verich — הוּא hu

אָמֵן אידהנויה amen

לְעֵלָּא le'ela — מִן min — כָּל kol — יְלִי — בִּרְכָתָא birchata — שִׁירָתָא shirata

תִּשְׁבְּחָתָא tishbechata — וְנֶחָמָתָא venechamata — דַּאֲמִירָן da'amiran

בְּעָלְמָא be'alma — וְאִמְרוּ ve'imru — אָמֵן amen — אָמֵן אידהנויה amen

---

In your lifetimes and in your days and in the lifetime of all the House of Israel, speedily and in the near future, and you shall say, Amen. (Amen) May His great Name be blessed forever and for all eternity. Blessed and lauded, and glorified, and exalted, and extolled, and honored, and uplifted, and praised be the Name of the Holy Blessed One. (Amen) Above all blessings, songs, praises, and words of consolation that may be said in the world, and you shall say, Amen. (Amen)

יְהֵא yehe שְׁלָמָא shelama רַבָּא raba קנ"א ב"ך, יהוה אלהים יהוה אדני, מילוי קס"א וס"ג,

מ"ה ברבוע וע"ב ע"ה chayim וְחַיִּים shemaya שְׁמַיָּא min מִן aהיה אהיה יהוה, בינה ע"ה

veshezava וְשֵׁיזָבָא venechama וְנֶחָמָה vishu'a וִישׁוּעָה vesava וְשָׂבַע

urefu'a וּרְפוּאָה uge'ula וּגְאֻלָּה uslicha וּסְלִיחָה vechapara וְכַפָּרָה

ulchol וּלְכָל יה אדני verevach וְרֶיוַח vehatzala וְהַצָּלָה lanu לָנוּ אלהים, אהיה אדני

amo עַמּוֹ Yisrael יִשְׂרָאֵל ve'imru וְאִמְרוּ amen אָמֵן amen אָמֵן אידהנויה.

Take three steps backwards and say:

ose עוֹשֶׂה shalom שָׁלוֹם bimromav בִּמְרוֹמָיו ע"ב, ריבוע יהוה. hu הוּא

berachamav בְּרַחֲמָיו ר"ת ש"ע נהורין. ya'ase יַעֲשֶׂה shalom שָׁלוֹם alenu עָלֵינוּ

ve'al וְעַל kol כָּל ילי ; עמם amo עַמּוֹ Yisrael יִשְׂרָאֵל ve'imru וְאִמְרוּ amen אָמֵן:

amen אָמֵן אידהנויה.

BARCHU

The chazan (or a person who said the Kaddish Yehe Shelama) says:

rabanan רַבָּנָן: barchu בָּרְכוּ יהוה ריבוע יהוה מ"ה et אֶת

Adonai יֱהֹוָׂאדֹנָׂיאהֹדֹנָׂי ס"ת כהת, משייזו בן דוד ע"ה: hamevorach הַמְבוֹרָךְ

First the congregation replies with the following,
and then the chazan (or a person who said the "Kaddish Yehe Shelama") repeats it:

Neshamah *Ruach* *Nefesh*

baruch בָּרוּךְ Adonai יֱהֹוָׂאדֹנָׂיאהֹדֹנָׂי hamevorach הַמְבוֹרָךְ

Yechidah *Chayah*

le'olam לְעוֹלָם ריבוע ס"ג וי' אותיות דס"ג va'ed וָעֶד:

May there be abundant peace from Heaven, life, contentment, salvation, consolation, deliverance, healing, redemption, pardon, atonement, comfort, and relief. For us and for His entire nation, Israel, and you shall say, Amen. (Amen) He, Who makes peace in His High Places, with His compassion He shall make peace for us and for His entire nation, Israel. And you shall say, Amen. (Amen)

BARCHU

Masters: Bless the Lord, the Blessed One.
Blessed be the Lord, the Blessed One, forever and for eternity.

ALENU

Alenu is a cosmic sealing agent. It cements and secures all of our prayers, protecting them from any negative forces such as the *klipot*. All prayers prior to *Alenu* drew down what the kabbalists call Inner Light. *Alenu*, however, attracts Surrounding Light, which envelops our prayers with a protective force-field to block out the *klipot*.

Drawing Surrounding Light in order to be protected from the *klipot* (negative side).

עָלֵינוּ alenu   רִבּוּעַ דס"ג   לְשַׁבֵּחַ leshabe'ach   עָלֵינוּ לְשַׂבּוֹ = אבג יתץ, ועור

לַאֲדוֹן la'adon   אֲנִי ;   ס"ת ס"ג ע"ה   הַכֹּל hakol   ר"ת כלכה, אדני

לָתֵת latet   גְּדֻלָּה gedula   לְיוֹצֵר leyotzer   בְּרֵאשִׁית bereshit   ר"ת גלב (כאי"ך ב"י יג"ל)

שֶׁלֹּא shelo   עָשָׂנוּ asanu   כְּגוֹיֵי kegoyei   הָאֲרָצוֹת ha'aratzot

וְלֹא velo   שָׂמָנוּ samanu   כְּמִשְׁפְּחוֹת kemishpechot   הָאֲדָמָה ha'adama

שֶׁלֹּא shelo   שָׂם sam   וְחֶלְקֵנוּ chelkenu   כָּהֶם kahem   וְגוֹרָלֵנוּ vegoralenu

כְּכָל kechol   הֲמוֹנָם hamonam   שֶׁהֵם shehem   מִשְׁתַּחֲוִים mishtachavim

לַהֶבֶל lahevel   וָרִיק varik   וּמִתְפַּלְלִים umitpalelim   אֶל el   אֵל el   לֹא lo

(pause here, and bow your entire body when you say "*va'anachnu mishtachavim*")   יוֹשִׁיעַ Yoshi'a

וַאֲנַחְנוּ va'anachnu   מִשְׁתַּחֲוִים mishtachavim   לִפְנֵי lifnei   מֶלֶךְ melech

מַלְכֵי malchei   הַמְּלָכִים hamelachim   הַקָּדוֹשׁ hakadosh   בָּרוּךְ baruch

הוּא hu   שֶׁהוּא shehu   נוֹטֶה note   שָׁמַיִם shamayim   י"פ טל, י"פ כוזו ; ר"ת = י"פ אדני

וְיוֹסֵד veyosed   אֶרֶץ aretz   וּמוֹשַׁב umoshav   עובי ספירות של נוקבא דז"א

יְקָרוֹ yekaro   בַּשָּׁמַיִם bashamayim   י"פ טל, י"פ כוזו   מִמַּעַל mima'al   עלם

וּשְׁכִינַת ush'chinat   עֻזּוֹ uzo   בְּגָבְהֵי begovhei   מְרוֹמִים meromim

הוּא hu   אֱלֹהֵינוּ Elohenu   ילה   וְאֵין ve'en   עוֹד od   אַחֵר acher

---

ALENU

It is incumbent upon us to give praise to the Master of all and to attribute greatness to the Molder of Creation, for He did not make us like the nations of the lands. He did not place us like the families of the Earth He did not make our lot like theirs and our destiny like that of their multitudes, for they prostrate themselves to futility and emptiness and they pray to a deity that does not help. But we prostrate ourselves before the King of all Kings, the Holy Blessed One. It is He Who spreads the Heavens and establishes the Earth. The Seat of His glory is in the Heaven above and the Divine Presence of His power is in the Highest of Heights. He is our God and there is no other.

וְאֶפֶס ve'efes מַלְכֵּנוּ malkenu ... אֱמֶת emet

וְיָדַעְתָּ veyadata בַּתּוֹרָה: batorah כַּכָּתוּב kakatuv ... זוּלָתוֹ zulato

אֶל el וַהֲשֵׁבֹתָ vahashevota ... הַיּוֹם hayom

הוּא hu יְהֹוָה Adonai כִּי ki ... לְבָבֶךָ levavecha

הָאֱלֹהִים haElohim

בַּשָּׁמַיִם bashamayim ... מִמַּעַל mima'al

הָאָרֶץ ha'aretz וְעַל ve'al ... מִתָּחַת mitachat

עוֹד od: אֵין en ... מֵתַּחַת

עַל al כֵּן ken נְקַוֶּה nekave לָךְ lach ... יְהֹוָה Adonai

אֱלֹהֵינוּ Elohenu ... לִרְאוֹת lir'ot מְהֵרָה mehera בְּתִפְאֶרֶת betiferet

עֻזֶּךָ uzach ... לְהַעֲבִיר leha'avir גִּלּוּלִים gilulim מִן min

הָאָרֶץ ha'aretz ... וְהָאֱלִילִים veha'elilim כָּרוֹת karot

יִכָּרֵתוּן yikaretun לְתַקֵּן letaken עוֹלָם olam בְּמַלְכוּת bemalchut

שַׁדַּי Shadai וְכָל vechol בְּנֵי benei בָשָׂר vasar יִקְרְאוּ yikre'u

בִשְׁמֶךָ vishmecha לְהַפְנוֹת lehafnot אֵלֶיךָ elecha כָּל kol רִשְׁעֵי rish'ei

אָרֶץ aretz יַכִּירוּ yakiru וְיֵדְעוּ veyed'u כָּל kol יוֹשְׁבֵי yoshvei

תֵבֵל tevel כִּי ki לְךָ lecha תִּכְרַע tichra כָּל kol בֶּרֶךְ berech

תִּשָּׁבַע tishava כָּל kol לָשׁוֹן lashon לְפָנֶיךָ lefanecha

---

Our King is true and there is none beside Him. As it is written in the Torah: "And you shall know today and you shall take it to your heart that it is the Lord Who is God in the Heavens above and upon the Earth below, and there is none other". (Deuteronomy 4:39) Consequently, we place our hope in You, Lord, our God, that we shall speedily see the glory of Your might, when You remove the idols from the Earth and the deities shall be completely destroyed to correct the world with the kingdom of the Almighty. And all mankind shall then call out Your Name and You shall turn back to Yourself all the wicked ones of the Earth. Then all the inhabitants of the world shall recognize and know that, for You, every knee bends and every tongue vows. Before You, veyipolu וְיִפֹּלוּ yichre'u יִכְרְעוּ ילה Elohenu אֱלֹהֵינוּ Adonai יְהֹוָ֒

vikabelu וִיקַבְּלוּ ◆yitenu יִתֵּנוּ yekar יְקָר shimcha שִׁמְךָ velichvod וְלִכְבוֹד

vetimloch וְתִמְלוֹךְ ◆malchutecha מַלְכוּתֶךָ ol עֹל et אֶת chulam כֻלָּם

◆va'ed וָעֶד le'olam לְעוֹלָם mehera מְהֵרָה alehem עֲלֵיהֶם

ul'olmei וּלְעוֹלְמֵי ◆hee הִיא shelcha שֶׁלְּךָ hamalchut הַמַּלְכוּת ki כִּי

kakatuv כַּכָּתוּב בוכו◆ bechavod בְּכָבוֹד timloch תִּמְלוֹךְ ad עַד

le'olam לְעֹלָם yimloch יִמְלֹךְ | Adonai יְהֹוָ֒ ׃betoratach בְּתוֹרָתֶךָ

וְהָיָה vehaya ◆vene'emar וְנֶאֱמַר ◆va'ed וָעֶד

kol כָּל al עַל lemelech לְמֶלֶךְ Adonai יְהֹוָ֒

hahu הַהוּא bayom בַּיּוֹם ha'aretz הָאָרֶץ

ushmo וּשְׁמוֹ yihye יִהְיֶה Adonai יְהֹוָ֒ echad אֶחָד

echad אֶחָד

If you prayed alone recite the following before you start Arvit and before "Alenu" instead of "Barchu":

omedet עוֹמֶדֶת achat אַוַת chaya וְזִיהָ Akiva עֲקִיבָא Rabi רַבִּי amar אָמַר

al עַל vechakuk וְחָקוּק Yisrael יִשְׂרָאֵל ushma וּשְׁמָה baraki'a בָּרָקִיעַ

be'emtza בְּאֶמְצַע omedet עוֹמֶדֶת ◆Yisrael יִשְׂרָאֵל mitzcha מִצְחָהּ

et אֶת barchu בָּרְכוּ ve'omeret וְאוֹמֶרֶת haraki'a הָרָקִיעַ

vechol וְכֹל hamevorach הַמְבוֹרָךְ Adonai יְהֹוָ֒

Adonai יְהֹוָ֒ baruch בָּרוּךְ ׃onim עוֹנִים mala מַעְלָה gedudei גְּדוּדֵי

◆va'ed וָעֶד le'olam לְעוֹלָם hamevorach הַמְבוֹרָךְ

Lord, our God, they shall kneel and fall and shall give honor to Your glorious Name. And they shall all accept the yoke of Your Kingdom and You shall reign over them, forever and ever. Because the kingdom is Yours. And forever and for eternity, You shall reign gloriously. As it is written in the Torah: "The Lord shall reign forever and ever," (Exodus 15:18) and it is also stated: "The Lord shall be King over the whole world and, on that day, the Lord shall be One and His Name One." (Zechariah 14:9)

Rabbi Akiva said: Standing in Heaven, there is one animal named Israel, and Israel is engraved on her forehead, and she is standing in mid-Heaven saying: Bless the Lord, the Blessed One, and all of Heaven's armies are answering: Blessed be the Lord, the Blessed One, forever and for eternity.

HAVDALAH

To complete and close out the *Shabbat* or the Holiday, we do *Havdalah,* which literally meaning "separation." Many times, the people we think are our friends are actually our enemies, and the people we think are our enemies are actually our friends. If we share personal and intimate information about ourselves with our so-called friends, should they ever become our enemies, they will become the most dangerous kind of enemy we can possibly have. Therefore, knowing how to differentiate between good and evil is vital if we are to achieve a sense of peace and serenity in our life. Participating in *Havdalah* helps us gain a deeper understanding, insight, and greater awareness about what is good and bad for our personal life.

Some start here:

אָנָּא ana ב"ן יְהֹוָאהדונהי Adonai הוֹשִׁיעָה hoshi'a יהוה וע"ע נהורין אָנָּא na׃

אָנָּא ana ב"ן יְהֹוָאהדונהי Adonai הוֹשִׁיעָה hoshi'a יהוה וע"ע נהורין אָנָּא na׃

אָנָּא ana ב"ן יְהֹוָאהדונהי Adonai הַצְלִיחָה hatzlicha אָנָּא na׃

אָנָּא ana ב"ן יְהֹוָאהדונהי Adonai הַצְלִיחָה hatzlicha אָנָּא na׃

הַצְלִיחֵנוּ hatzlichenu • הַצְלִיח hatzli'ach דְּרָכֵינוּ derachenu • הַצְלִיחוֹ hatzli'ach

לְמוּדֵינוּ limudenu • וּשְׁלַח ushlach בְּרָכָה beracha רְוָחָה revacha

וְהַצְלָחָה vehatzlacha בְּכָל bechol ב"ן, לכב מַעֲשֵׂה ma'ase יָדֵינוּ yadenu,

כְּדִכְתִיב kedichtiv: יִשָּׂא yisa בְּרָכָה veracha מֵאֵת me'et ר"ת יבמ, ב"ן

מֵאֱלֹהֵי melohei ; יהה אלהים ריבוע ע"ה וּצְדָקָה utzdaka Adonai יְהֹוָאהדונהי

לַיְהוּדִים layehudim מלה: יהוה ס"ת ; ע"ה שכינה ; דמב ; ילה יִשְׁעוֹ yish'o

הָיְתָה hayta אוֹרָה ora וְשִׂמְחָה vesimcha וְשָׂשֹׂן vesason וִיקָר vikar,

וּכְתִיב uchtiv: וַיְהִי vayhi דָוִד David לְכָל lechol יה אדני דרְכָו derachav

מַשְׂכִּיל maskil וַיְהֹוָאהדונהי vadonai עִמּוֹ imo: כֵּן ken יִהְיֶה yihye יייי

עִמָּנוּ imanu ריבוע ס"ג, קס"א ע"ה ע"ה קס"א וד' אותיות תָּמִיד tamid ע"ה קס"א קנ"א קמ"ג׃

Continue *"kos yeshu'ot esa..."* on the next page.

Meditation for spiritual memory (before saying *Havdalah*):

משבענא עליך פורה שר של שכוחה שתחסיר לב טפש ממני ותשליכהו על טורי רומיא ארמימ"ס רמימ"ס מימ"ס ימ"ס מ"ס ס.

וְנֹחַ veNo'ach מָצָא matza וֵֹן chen מילוי ריבוע מ"ה, מזוי בְּעֵינֵי be'enei מ"ה ריבוע יְהֹוָאהדונהי Adonai׃

HAVDALAH

"Please, Lord, save us. Please, Lord, save us. Please, Lord, give us success. Please, Lord, give us success." (Psalms 118:25) Give us success, make our ways successful, make our studies successful, and send blessing and tranquillity to all the work of our hands, as it was written: "He shall receive blessing from Lord and righteousness from the God of his salvation." (Psalms 24:5) "And to the Jews it was Light and gladness and joy and honor." (Esther 8:16) And it was also written: "And David was successful in all his ways and the Lord is with him. May He so be with us always." (1 Samuel 18:14)

We shouldn't add water to the Havdalah wine.

הִנֵּה hineh אֵל el (מילוי) (דס"ג) יא"י יְשׁוּעָתִי yeshu'ati אֶבְטַח evtach

וְלֹא velo אֶפְחָד efchad כִּי ki עָזִּי ozi אלהים ע"ה, אהיה אדני ע"ה וְזִמְרָת vezimrat

יָהּ Yah יְהֹוָה Adonai וַיְהִי vayehi לִי li לִישׁוּעָה lishu'a:

וּשְׁאַבְתֶּם ush'avtem מַיִם mayim בְּשָׂשׂוֹן besason מִמַּעַיְנֵי mima'aynei

הַיְשׁוּעָה haycshu'a: לַיהֹוָה ladonai הַיְשׁוּעָה hayeshu'a עַל al

עַמְּךָ amecha בִרְכָתֶךָ virchatecha סֶּלָה sela: יְהֹוָה Adonai

צְבָאוֹת Tzeva'ot פני שכינה ריבוע ס"ג, קס"א ע"ה ו"ד אותיות עִמָּנוּ imanu

מִשְׂגָּב misgav לָנוּ lanu אלהים, אהיה אדני

אֱלֹהֵי Elohei יַעֲקֹב Yaakov סֶלָה sela:

יְהֹוָה Adonai צְבָאוֹת Tzeva'ot אַשְׁרֵי ashrei אָדָם adam

בֹּטֵחַ bote'ach בָּךְ bach

יְהֹוָה Adonai הוֹשִׁיעָה hoshi'a

הַמֶּלֶךְ hamelech יַעֲנֵנוּ ya'anenu בְיוֹם veyom

קָרְאֵנוּ kor'enu

לַיְּהוּדִים layehudim הָיְתָה hay'ta אוֹרָה ora וְשִׂמְחָה vesimcha

וְשָׂשׂן vesason וִיקָר vikar: כֵּן ken תִּהְיֶה tihye לָנוּ lanu אלהים, אהיה אדני

כּוֹס kos אלהים, אהיה אדני

יְשׁוּעוֹת yeshu'ot אֶשָּׂא esa וּבְשֵׁם uvshem יְהֹוָה Adonai אֶקְרָא ekra:

"Behold God is my salvation, I will trust and not be afraid. Indeed, the Lord is my strength and my song and He has become my salvation. You shall draw water with joy from the wells of salvation." (Isaiah 12:2-3) "Salvation belongs to the Lord, may Your blessings be upon Your people, Selah." (Psalms 3:9) "The Lord of Hosts is with us, the God of Jacob is a refuge for us, Selah." (Psalms 84:13) "Lord of Hosts, happy is the man who trusts in You. Lord, save us; may the King answer us on the day we call." (Psalms 20:10) "The Judeans had radiance and happiness, joy and honor." (Esther 8:16) "So may it be for us. I will raise the cup of salvations and invoke the Name of the Lord." (Psalms 116:13)

savri סָבְרִי בִּירְנָן maranan

(and the others reply :) לְחַיִּים lechayim אהיה אהיה יהוה, בינה ע"ה

BORE PERI HAGEFEN

בָּרוּךְ baruch אַתָּה Ata יְהֹוָואדניאהדונהי Adonai (יוד הי ויו הי) יְהֹוָה Adonai אֱלֹהֵינוּ Elohenu

יל: מֶלֶךְ melech הָעוֹלָם ha'olam בּוֹרֵא bore פְּרִי peri הַגָּפֶן hagefen:

On Saturday night (*Motza'ei Shabbat*) we add the blessings over the *Besamim* and over the fire:

BORE ATZEI BESAMIM

Havdalah includes smelling the fragrance of the myrtle branch (if we don't have a myrtle branch we can use another source of natural fragrance) to fill the void created by the departure of the extra soul that was present within us throughout the *Shabbat*.

You should take one bundle of the three myrtles (the one that you used on *Shabbat*) and meditate that they correspond to *Nefesh, Ruach* and *Neshamah* in order to save the energy of the additional soul (from all three aspects) of *Shabbat* and that's done right now by these three myrtles and the action of smelling them. Hold the myrtles in your right hand and when you smell them inhale their fragrance deeply into your nostrils three times (corresponding to *Nefesh, Ruach* and *Neshamah*). Also meditate on the four words as follow (without pronouncing it):

רֵיחַ נִיחוֹחַ אֶשֶׂה לַיהֹוָואדניאהדונהי:

בָּרוּךְ baruch אַתָּה Ata יְהֹוָואדניאהדונהי Adonai (יוד הי ואו הי)

אֱלֹהֵינוּ Elohenu יל: מֶלֶךְ melech הָעוֹלָם ha'olam בּוֹרֵא bore

עֲצֵי atzei (עִשְׂבֵי isbei) (מִינֵי minei) בְּשָׂמִים vesamim:

BORE ME'OREI HAESH

We then make our right hand into a fist, hiding the thumb under the four fingers and look at the *Havdalah* candle's reflection in the nails of our four fingers. The ancient Kabbalists teach us that the body of Adam was actually made of this enamel. As *Shabbat* concludes, negative forces and entities immediately swarm around us like hungry predators trying to rob us of our Light. The first place they strike are the fingers, specifically the fingernails. The candlelight reflected in our nails wipes them all out.

With your permission, my masters. (and the others reply) *for life!*

BORE PERI HAGEFEN

Blessed are You, Lord, our God, the King of the world, Who creates the fruit of the vine.

BORE ATZEI BESAMIM

Blessed are You, Lord,
our God, the King of the world, Who creates the plants (spices) (varieties) of fragrance.

We use a special candle made of wax that is lit like a torch for the connection with this blessing. You should fold the top of the right hand fingers into your right palm and the thumb is covered underneath. And the fingers should be folded tightly towards your face and towards the candle. You should hold the right hand and the fingers up by bending your elbow and face of the fingers towards your face and then you should fold the tops of the fingers into the palm and you should straighten the back of your fingers up against the candle. Indeed your fingers should be folded down on top of the thumb as it is mentioned and you should look only at reflection of the Light that comes back from your fingernails and not at the rest of your fingers. And the reason is because in the four fingers there are 2500 outside forces that suck energy from the fingers and this is why we show it in front of the flame of the candle (that represents the *Shechinah*) to subdue them. And we bless "*bore me'orei ha'esh*" because we want to connect to their creator and not to them.

(הא ואו הא יוד) Adonai יְהֹוָה(אדני־אהדונהי) Ata אַתָּה baruch בָּרוּךְ

ha'olam הָעוֹלָם melech מֶלֶךְ ילה Elohenu אֱלֹהֵינוּ

bore בּוֹרֵא me'orei מְאוֹרֵי ha'esh הָאֵשׁ שאה׃

HAMAVDIL

The final blessing separates the good from evil, giving us the ability to distinguish between these two forces in every area of our life.

ילה Elohenu אֱלֹהֵינוּ Adonai יְהֹוָה(אדני־אהדונהי) Ata אַתָּה baruch בָּרוּךְ

kodesh קֹדֶשׁ ben בֵּין hamavdil הַמַּבְדִּיל ha'olam הָעוֹלָם melech מֶלֶךְ

lechoshech לַחֹשֶׁךְ or אוֹר uven וּבֵין lechol לְחוֹל

yom יוֹם uven וּבֵין la'amim לָעַמִּים Yisrael יִשְׂרָאֵל uven וּבֵין

yemei יְמֵי lesheshet לְשֵׁשֶׁת hashevi'i הַשְּׁבִיעִי

Adonai יְהֹוָה(אדני־אהדונהי) Ata אַתָּה baruch בָּרוּךְ hama'ase הַמַּעֲשֶׂה

hamavdil הַמַּבְדִּיל ben בֵּין kodesh קֹדֶשׁ lechol לְחוֹל (יוד הה וו הה) (קליפת נגה)׃

On *Sukkot* one should recite the blessing of "*Leshev BaSukkah*" on page 127 before seating and drinking from the wine.

After performing the *Havdalah* you should sit and drink "*revi'it*" (approximately three ounces of the wine) and then say the last blessing. If you cannot drink from the wine you should give this to somebody else that has the intention to complete his obligation to drink (instead of you) and this other person should say the last blessing. But if the other person didn't have the intention to complete his obligation to drink he should just bless "*bore pri hagefen*" and drink.

BORE ME'OREI HAESH
Blessed are You, Lord, our God, King of the world, Who creates the luminaries of fire.

HAMAVDIL
Blessed are You, Lord, our God, King of the world, Who separates between the Holy and the mundane and between Light and darkness, and between Israel and the other nations, and between the Seventh Day and the six days of action. Blessed are You, Lord, Who separates between the Holy and the mundane.

RETURNING THE TORAH TO THE ARK

Placing the Torah in the Ark is similar to depositing money in a bank. For example, anytime we want to draw out funds, we have a cash reserve waiting for us at our local bank. The Ark is our bank of Light. All the spiritual energy that we've generated is now on reserve waiting for us to draw upon it throughout our week.

Before the Torah is carried back to the Ark, the chazan says:

מ"ב levado לְבַדּוֹ מהע ע"ה, ע"ב בריבוע וקס"א ע"ה, אל שדי ע"ה shemo שְׁמוֹ

nisgav נִשְׂגָּב ki כִּי Adonai יְהֹוָהאדנילאהדונהי shem שֵׁם et אֶת־ yehalelu יְהַלְלוּ

Then the congregation says while carrrying the Torah back to the Ark:

י"פ טל, י"פ כוזו veshamayim וְשָׁמָיִם eretz אֶרֶץ al עַל־ אהיה hodo הוֹדוֹ

אהיה פעמים אהיה, tehila תְהִלָּה ע"ה אמת, אהיה פעמים אהיה, le'amo לְעַמוֹ keren קֶרֶן vayarem וַיָּרֶם

Yisrael יִשְׂרָאֵל livnei לִבְנֵי chasidav וְחֲסִידָיו יה אדני lechol לְכָל־ ז"פ ס"ג

; ללה: am עַם־ אלהים, אהיה אדני haleluya הַלְלוּיָה kerovo קְרֹבוֹ

Then the chazan says:

אהיה אדני ; ילה ; ר"ת יהה haElohim הָאֱלֹהִים hu הוּא Adonai יְהֹוָהאדנילאהדונהי

ועולה למנין ענו עם ג' כוללים: haElohim הָאֱלֹהִים hu הוּא Adonai יְהֹוָהאדנילאהדונהי

אהיה אדני ; ילה ; ר"ת יהה ועולה למנין ענו עם ג' כוללים: bashamayim בַּשָׁמַיִם י"פ טל, י"פ כוזו

mitachat מִתָּחַת ע"ה ההין דההין אלהים ha'aretz הָאָרֶץ ve'al וְעַל־ עלם mima'al מִמַּעַל

vaElohim בָאֱלֹהִים kamocha כָּמוֹךָ en אֵין־ od: עוֹד en אֵין

kema'asecha: כְּמַעֲשֶׂיךָ ve'en וְאֵין ללה Adonai אֲדֹנָי ; ילה אהיה אדני

Adonai יְהֹוָהאדנילאהדונהי הושע shuva שׁוּבָה yomar יֹאמַר uvnucho וּבְנֻחֹה

hashivenu הֲשִׁיבֵנוּ Yisrael: יִשְׂרָאֵל alfei אַלְפֵי rivevot רִבְבוֹת

(כתיב : וְנָשׁוּב) venashuva וְנָשׁוּבָה elecha אֵלֶיךָ | Adonai יְהֹוָהאדנילאהדונהי

kekedem: כְּקֶדֶם yamenu יָמֵינוּ קנ"א קנ"א, קס"א, הויות, י"ב chadesh וְחַדֵּשׁ

RETURNING THE TORAH TO THE ARK

"Praised be the Name of the Lord,
His Name alone is exalted His glory on Heaven and Earth. He raised funds to his nation, praise to his
Chassidim, people of Israel his close nation, praise the Lord." (Psalms 148:13-14) "The Lord is the God!
The Lord is the God! In the Heavens above and on the Earth below, there is no other." (Deuteronomy 4:39)
"There is none like You among the gods, Lord, and there is nothing like Your handiwork." (Psalms 86:8)
"And when the Ark rested, Moses would say, Return, Lord, to the tens of thousands of Israel."
(Numbers 10:36) "Bring us back, Lord, and we shall return. Renew our days as of old." (Lamentataion 5:21)

THE ASHREI

Twenty-one of the twenty-two letters of the Aramaic alphabet are encoded in the *Ashrei* in their correct order from *Alef* to *Tav*. King David, the author, left out the Aramaic letter *Nun* from this prayer, because *Nun* is the first letter in the Aramaic word *nefilah*, which means "falling." Falling refers to a spiritual decline, as in falling into the *klipa*. Feelings of doubt, depression, worry, and uncertainty are consequences of spiritual falling. Because the Aramaic letters are the actual instruments of Creation, this prayer helps to inject order and the power of Creation into our lives, without the energy of falling.

In this Psalm there are ten times the Name: יהוה for the Ten *Sefirot*. This Psalm is written according to the order of the *Alef Bet*, but the letter *Nun* is omitted to prevent falling.

אַשְׁרֵי ashrei (סוד הכתר) yoshvei יוֹשְׁבֵי vetecha בֵיתֶךָ ב"פ ראה

עוֹד od יְהַלְלוּךָ yehalelucha סֶלָה sela: אַשְׁרֵי ashrei הָעָם ha'am

שֶׁכָּכָה shekacha מהע, מ"ה, ע"ב בריבוע וקס"א, אל שדי, ד"פ אלהים ע"ה לוֹ lo

אַשְׁרֵי ashrei הָעָם ha'am ר"ת לאה שֶׁיְהוָֹה she'Adonai (*Keter*)

אֱלֹהָיו Elohav יְלה: תְהִלָּה tehila ע"ה אמת, אהיה פעמים אהיה, ז"פ ס"ג לְדָוִד leDavid

אֲרוֹמִמְךָ aromimcha אֱלוֹהַי Elohai הַמֶּלֶךְ hamelech וַאֲבָרְכָה va'avarcha

שִׁמְךָ shimcha לְעוֹלָם le'olam ריבוע דס"ג ו"י אותיות דס"ג וָעֶד :va'ed

בְּכָל bechol ב"ן, לכב ע"ה יום yom נגד, מזבוח, זן אל יהוה

אֲבָרְכֶךָּ avarcheka וַאֲהַלְלָה va'ahalela מ"ה יהוה שִׁמְךָ shimcha

לְעוֹלָם le'olam ריבוע דס"ג ו"י אותיות דס"ג וָעֶד :va'ed

גָּדוֹל gadol להוו ; עם ד' אותיות = מזבה, יזל, אום

יְהוָֹה Adonai (*Chochmah*) וּמְהֻלָּל umhulal אדני, לכה

מְאֹד me'od וְלִגְדֻלָּתוֹ veligdulato והו אֵין en חֵקֶר: cheker

---

THE ASHREI

"Joyful are those who dwell in Your House, they shall praise You, Selah." (Psalms 84:5)
"Joyful is the nation that this is theirs and joyful the nation that the Lord is their God." (Psalms 144:15)
"A praise of David.

א   *I shall exalt You, my God, the King, and I shall bless Your Name forever and for eternity.*
ב   *I shall bless You every day and I shall praise Your Name forever and for eternity.*
ג   *The Lord is great and exceedingly praised. His greatness is unfathomable.*

דּוֹר dor לְדוֹר ledor יְשַׁבַּח yeshabach מַעֲשֶׂיךָ ma'asecha ר"ת דלים

וְגְבוּרֹתֶיךָ ugvurotecha יַגִּידוּ yagidu יז, כ"ב אותיות פשוטות (=אכא) וה' אותיות סופיות מנצפך:

הֲדַר hadar כְּבוֹד kevod הוֹדֶךָ hodecha וְדִבְרֵי vedivrei

נִפְלְאוֹתֶיךָ nifle'otecha ר"ת אלהים, אהיה אדני

אֲשִׂיחָה asicha ר"ת הַפָּסוּק = פ"ז (בְּסוֹד כתם טהור פז):

וֶעֱזוּז ve'ezuz נוֹרְאֹתֶיךָ nor'otecha יֹאמֵרוּ yomeru וּגְדוּלָּתְךָ ugdulatcha

אֲסַפְּרֶנָּה asaprena ס"ת = ייא' (מילוי דס"ג): ר"ת = ע"ב, ריבוע יהוה (כתיב: וגדלותיך)

זֵכֶר zecher רַב rav טוּבְךָ tuvcha לאו יַבִּיעוּ yabi'u

וְצִדְקָתְךָ vetzidkatcha יְרַנֵּנוּ yeranenu ס"ת = ב"ן, יבמ, לכב ; ר"ת הַפָּסוּק = רי"ו יהוה:

חַנּוּן chanun וְרַחוּם verachum Adonai יְהוָֹ֥ה/אדני/יאהדונהי (Binah)

וּגְדָל ugdal (כתיב : וגדול) אֶרֶך erech ס"ת = ס"ג ב"ן אַפַּיִם apayim ר"ת = יהוה ; וחנון ורחום יהוה = עאל

וְחֶסֶד chased ע"ב, ריבוע יהוה:

טוֹב tov והו Adonai יְהוָֹ֥ה/אדני/יאהדונהי (Chesed) לַכֹּל lakol

עַל al וְרַחֲמָיו verachamav (מילוי דס"ג) כ"ז ס"ת ; יה אדני יה

כָּל kol ; עמם ; ר"ת ריבוע ב"ן ע"ה מַעֲשָׂיו ma'asav ס"ת ע"ה ע"ב, ריבוע יהוה:

ד One generation and the next shall praise Your deeds and tell of Your might.

ה The brilliance of Your splendid glory and the wonders of Your acts, I shall speak of.

ו They shall speak of the might of Your awesome acts and I shall tell of Your greatness.

ז They shall express the remembrance of Your abundant goodness, and Your righteousness they shall joyfully proclaim. ח The Lord is merciful and compassionate, slow to anger and great in kindness.

ט The Lord is good to all, His compassion extends over all His acts.

יוֹדוּךָ yoducha (Gevurah) Adonai לַיהֹוָה(אַדְנָיאהדונהי) kol כָּל־ יל׳ מַעֲשֶׂיךָ ma'asecha

וַחֲסִידֶיךָ vachasidecha ר״ת אלהים, אהיה אדני ס״ת = מ״ה: yevarchucha לְבָרְכוּכָה

כָּבוֹד kevod מַלְכוּתְךָ malchutcha יֹאמֵרוּ yomeru וּגְבוּרָתְךָ ugvuratcha

יְדַבֵּרוּ yedaberu ר״ת הפסוק = אלהים, אהיה אדני ; ס״ת = ב״ן, יבם, לכב:

לְהוֹדִיעַ lehodi'a לִבְנֵי livnei הָאָדָם ha'adam ר״ת ללה, אדני

גְּבוּרֹתָיו gevurotav וּכְבוֹד uchvod הֲדַר hadar

מַלְכוּתוֹ malchuto ר״ת מ״ה וס״ת = רי״ו ; ר״ת הפסוק ע״ה = ק״כ צירופי אלהים:

מַלְכוּתְךָ malchutcha מַלְכוּת malchut כָּל־ kol יל׳ עֹלָמִים olamim

וּמֶמְשַׁלְתְּךָ umemshaltecha בְּכָל־ bechol ב״ן, לכב דּוֹר dor וָדֹר vador רי״ו:

סוֹמֵךְ somech ריבוע אדני יְהֹוָה(אַדנָיאהדונהי) Adonai (Tiferet)

לְכָל־ lechol יה אדני ; סומך אדני לכל ר״ת סאל, אמן (יאהדונהי) הַנֹּפְלִים hanoflim

וְזוֹקֵף vezokef לְכָל־ lechol יה אדני הַכְּפוּפִים hakefufim גמם:

עֵינֵי enei ריבוע דמ״ה כֹל chol יל׳ אֵלֶיךָ elecha יְשַׂבֵּרוּ yesaberu וְאַתָּה veAta

נוֹתֵן noten אבגיתץ, ועוֹר לָהֶם lahem אֶת־ et אָכְלָם ochlam בְּעִתּוֹ be'ito:

י *All that You have made shall thank You, Lord, and Your pious ones shall bless You.*

כ *They shall speak of the glory of Your Kingdom and talk of Your mighty deeds.*

ל *His mighty deeds He makes known to man and the glory of His splendid Kingdom.*

מ *Yours is the Kingdom of all worlds and Your reign extends to each and every generation.*

ס *The Lord supports all those who fell and holds upright all those who are bent over.*

ע *The eyes of all look hopefully towards You, and You give them their food at its proper time.*

POTE'ACH ET YADECHA

We connect to the letters *Pei, Alef,* and *Yud* by opening our hands and holding our palms skyward. Our consciousness is focused on receiving sustenance and financial prosperity from the Light through our actions of personal tithing and sharing, our Desire to Receive for the Sake of Sharing. In doing so, we also acknowledge that the sustenance we receive comes from a higher source and is not of our own doing. According to the sages, if we do not meditate on this idea at this juncture, we must repeat the prayer.

פתוח (ע"ע"ח נהורין למ"ה ולס"ה)

פותוח את ידך ר"ת פאי	יוד הי ויו הי יוד הי ויו הי (ו' וזיוורתי)
גימ' יאהדונהי ז"ן	אלף למד אלף למד (ע"ב)
חוכמה דז"א ו"ק	יוד הא ואו הא (כ"ו"א)
יסוד דנוק'	אדני (ולנוקבא)

פּוֹתֵחַ pote'ach אֶת et יָדֶךָ yadecha ר"ת פאי וס"ת וחתך עם ג' אותיות = דִיקְרְנוֹסָא

ובאתב"ע הוא סאל, פאי, אמן, יאהדונהי ; ועוד יכוין עם וחתך בשילוב יהוה – יוֹזְהַתוּכָה

Drawing abundance and sustenance from *Chochmah* of *Zeir Anpin*

יוד הי ויו הי יוד הי ויו הי דלת הי יוד הי ויו הי יוד

וחתך סאל יאהדונהי

וּמַשְׂבִּיעַ umasbi'a וחתך עם ג' אותיות = דִיקְרְנוֹסָא

ובא"ת ב"ע הוא סאל, אמן, יאהדונהי ; ועוד יכוין עם וחתך בשילוב יהוה – יוֹזְהַתוּכָה

Drawing abundance and sustenance from *Chochmah* of *Zeir Anpin*

יוד הי ויו הי יוד הי ויו הי דלת הי יוד הי ויו הי יוד

לְכָל־ lechol יה אדני (להמשיך מווזין ד-יה אל הנוקבא שהיא אדני)

וְחַי chai כל וחי = אהיה אהיה יהוה, בינה ע"ה, וחיים

רָצוֹן ratzon מהשי ע"ה, ע"ב בריבוע וקס"א ע"ה, אל שדי ע"ה

ר"ת רווֹל שהיא המלכות הצריכה לעפעל

יוד יוד הי יוד הי ויו יוד הי ויו הי יוד הי ויו הי יסוד דאבא

אלף הי יוד הי יסוד דאימא

להמתיק רווֹל וב' דמעין שׂך פר

Also meditate to draw abundance and sustenance and blessing to all the worlds from the *ratzon* mentioned above. You should meditate and focus on this verse because it is the essence of prosperity, and that God is intervening and sustaining and supporting all of Creation.

POTE'ACH ET YADECHA

| פ | Open | Your | Hands | and | satisfy | every | living | thing | with | desire. |

לכב ,ב"ן bechol בְּכָל (Yesod) Adonai יְהוָוהיאהדונהי tzadik צַדִּיק

ma'asav מַעֲשָׂיו לכב ב"ן bechol בְּכָל vechasid וְחָסִיד derachav דְּרָכָיו יבמ, ב"ן

אדני יה lechol לְכָל (Malchut) Adonai יְהוָהאהדונהי karov קָרוֹב

asher אֲשֶׁר אדני יה lechol לְכָל kor'av קֹרְאָיו

ז"פ ס"ג אהיה, פעמים אהיה אהיה ve'emet בֶּאֱמֶת yikra'uhu יִקְרָאֻהוּ

ya'ase יַעֲשֶׂה yere'av יְרֵאָיו מהטע ע"ה, ע"ב בריבוע וקס"א ע"ה, אל שדי ע"ה retzon רְצוֹן

veyoshi'em וְיוֹשִׁיעֵם yishma יִשְׁמַע shav'atam שַׁוְעָתָם ve'et וְאֶת ר"ת ריי

(Netzach) Adonai יְהוָואהדונהי שובתפילין הויות כ"א shomer שׁוֹמֵר

אכא ר"ת ohavav אֹהֲבָיו ילי kol כָּל et אֶת

yashmid יַשְׁמִיד haresha'im הָרְשָׁעִים ילי kol כָּל ve'et וְאֶת

pi פִּי ראה yedaber יְדַבֵּר (Hod) Adonai יְהוָואהדונהי tehilat תְּהִלַּת

kol כָּל ילי (למתק את ז' המלכים שמתו) הברכה ע"ב ס"ג מ"ה ב"ן vivarech וִיבָרֵךְ

le'olam לְעוֹלָם kodsho קָדְשׁוֹ shem שֵׁם basar בָּשָׂר ריבוע ס"ג וי' אותיות דס"ג

me'ata מֵעַתָּה Yah יָהּ nevarech נְבָרֵךְ va'anachnu וַאֲנַחְנוּ va'ed וָעֶד

ve'ad וְעַד olam עוֹלָם haleluya הַלְלוּיָהּ אלהים, אהיה אדני ; ללה

UVA LETZIYON

This prayer is our connection to redemption. The prayer starts, "And a redeemer should come to *Zion*." The redeemer is a reference to the *Mashiach*. Kabbalistically, the *Mashiach* is not a righteous person who will come and save us and bring about *world peace*. *Mashiach* is a state of spirituality and consciousness that every individual can achieve. No one is coming to save us and do the work for us. We must each achieve our own level of spiritual growth and fulfillment, our personal *Mashiach*, and when a critical mass of people have reached this state, the global *Mashiach* will appear for humanity.

צ *The Lord is righteous in all His ways and virtuous in all His deeds.*
ק *The Lord is close to all who call Him, only to those who call Him truthfully.*
ר *He shall fulfill the will of those who fear Him; He hears their wailing and saves them.*
ש *The Lord protects all who love Him and He destroys the wicked.*
ת *My lips utter the praise of the Lord and all flesh shall bless His Holy Name, forever and for eternity."*
(Psalms 145) *"And we shall bless the Lord forever and for eternity. Praise the Lord!"* (Psalms 115:18)

fesha פֶּשַׁע ulshavei וּלְשָׁבֵי go'el גּוֹאֵל קנאה, ר הויות, יוסף leTziyon לְצִיּוֹן uva וּבָא

בְּיַעֲקֹב beYaakov ז הויות, יאהדונהי אידהנויה ne'um נְאֻם יהוה Adonai:

וַאֲנִי va'ani אני ; ר"ת גוף בניו (שירדו לוזיצונים בעוז הוצאת ז"ל, ויוזרו לגוף אוצר הנשמות, ויבא גואל)

זֹאת zot בְּרִיתִי beriti אוֹתָם otam אָמַר amar יהוה Adonai

רוּחִי ruchi אֲשֶׁר asher עָלֶיךָ alecha וּדְבָרַי udvarai אֲשֶׁר asher

שַׂמְתִּי samti בְּפִיךָ beficha לֹא lo יָמוּשׁוּ yamushu מִפִּיךָ mipicha

וּמִפִּי umipi זַרְעֲךָ zar'acha זֶרַע zera וּמִפִּי umipi זַרְעֲךָ zar'acha

אָמַר amar יהוה Adonai מֵעַתָּה me'ata וְעַד ve'ad עוֹלָם olam:

וְאַתָּה veAta קָדוֹשׁ kadosh יוֹשֵׁב yoshev תְּהִלּוֹת tehilot יִשְׂרָאֵל Yisrael:

וְקָרָא vekara זֶה ze אֶל el זֶה ze י"ב פרקין דיעקב מאירין לי"ב פרקין דרוזל

וְאָמַר ve'amar קָדוֹשׁ kadosh (Chesed) | קָדוֹשׁ kadosh (Gevurah)

קָדוֹשׁ kadosh (Tiferet) יהוה Adonai צְבָאוֹת Tzeva'ot פני שכינה

מְלֹא melo כָּל chol יְלוּ הָאָרֶץ ha'aretz אלהים דההן ע"ה כְּבוֹדוֹ kevodo:

וּמְקַבְּלִין umkabelin דֵּין den מִן min דֵּין den וְאָמְרִין ve'amrin◆

קַדִּישׁ kadish א"ס ב"פ אור, ב"פ רו, ב"פ ב"פ בִּשְׁמֵי bishmei

מְרוֹמָא meroma עִלָּאָה ila'a בֵּית bet ב"פ ראה שְׁכִינְתֵּהּ shechinte◆

קַדִּישׁ kadish ב"פ אור, ב"פ רו, ב"פ א"ס עַל al אַרְעָא ara עוֹבַד ovad

◆gevurte גְּבוּרְתֵּהּ קַדִּישׁ kadish ב"פ אור, ב"פ רו, ב"פ א"ס לְעָלַם le'alam

וּלְעָלְמֵי ule'almei עָלְמַיָּא almaya: יהוה Adonai צְבָאוֹת Tzeva'ot

מַלְיָא malya כָּל chol אַרְעָא ar'a יְלוּ זִיו ziv יְקָרֵהּ yekare: פני שכינה

UVA LETZIYON

"A redeemer shall come to Zion

and to those who shall turn away from sin from amongst [the House of] Jacob, so says the Lord. And as for Me, this is My Covenant with them, says the Lord. My spirit, which is upon you, and My words, that I have put in your mouth, shall not depart from your mouths, the mouths of your children, or the mouths of your children's children, says the Lord, from now and forever." (Isaiah 59:20-21) "And You are holy and await the praises of Israel. And one called to the other and said: Holy, Holy, Holy is the Lord of Hosts, the whole earth is filled with His glory." (Isaiah 6:3) And they receive consent from one another and say: Holy in the Highest Heavens is the abode of His Shechinah. Holy, upon the Earth, is the work of His valor. Holy, forever and for all eternity, is the Lord of Hosts, the entire Earth is filled with the splendor of His glory.

וַתִּשָּׂאֵנִי vatisa'eni   רוּחַ ru'ach   וָאֶשְׁמַע va'eshma   אַחֲרַי acharai   קוֹל kol

רַעַשׁ ra'ash   לְהוּ ; עִם ד' אוֹתִיוֹת = מבה, יוֹל, אום   גָּדוֹל gadol   בָּרוּךְ baruch

כָּבוֹד kevod   יְהֹוָאדֹנָיאהדונהי Adonai   כְּבוֹד יהוה = יוֹד הי ואו הה   בִּמְּקוֹמוֹ mimekomo

עסמ"ב, הברכה (למתק את ז' המלכים עמתו) ; ר"ת = ע"ב, ריבוע יהוה ; ר"ת מ"ב, י"פ האא:

וּנְטָלַתְנִי untalatni   רוּחָא rucha   וּשְׁמָעִית ushma'it   בָּתְרַי batrai   קָל kal

זִיעַ zi'a   שַׂגִּיא sagi   דִּמְשַׁבְּחִין dim'shabechin   וְאָמְרִין ve'amrin   גמם (ה' גבורות)

בְּרִיךְ berich   יְקָרָא yekara   דַּיהֹוָאדֹנָיאהדונהי dadonai   מֵאֲתַר me'atar

בֵּית bet   ב"פ ראה   שְׁכִינְתֵהּ shechinte   יְהֹוָאדֹנָיאהדונהי Adonai | יִמְלֹךְ yimloch

לְעֹלָם le'olam   ריבוע ס"ג ו"י אוֹתִיוֹת דס"ג ; ר"ת יל   וָעֶד va'ed: יְהֹוָאדֹנָיאהדונהי Adonai

מַלְכוּתֵהּ malchute   קָאֵם ka'im   לְעָלַם le'alam   וּלְעָלְמֵי ule'almei

עָלְמַיָּא almaya: יְהֹוָאדֹנָיאהדונהי Adonai   אֱלֹהֵי Elohei   מילוי ע"ב, דמב ; ילה

אַבְרָהָם Avraham   ו"פ אל, רי"ו ול"ב נתיבות החוכמה, רמ"ח (אברים), עסמ"ב וט"י אוֹתִיוֹת פשׁוּטוֹת

יִצְחָק Yitzchak   ר"פ   ב"ן   וְיִשְׂרָאֵל veYisrael   אֲבֹתֵינוּ avotenu

שָׁמְרָה־ shomrah   זֹאת zot   לְעוֹלָם le'olam   ריבוע ס"ג ו"י אוֹתִיוֹת דס"ג

לְיֵצֶר leyetzer   מַחְשְׁבוֹת mach'shevot   לְבַב levav   בוכו

עַמֶּךָ amecha   וְהָכֵן vehachen   לְבָבָם levavam   אֵלֶיךָ elecha:

וְהוּא vehu   רַחוּם rachum   יְכַפֵּר yechaper   ר"ת רי"ו   עָוֹן avon (*Abba* of the *klipa*)

וְלֹא velo   יַשְׁחִית yashchit (*Ima* of the *klipa*)   וְהִרְבָּה vehirba

לְהָשִׁיב lehashiv   אַפּוֹ apo (*Zeir* of the *klipa*)   וְלֹא־ velo

יָעִיר ya'ir   כָּל־ kol   ילי   וְחֲמָתוֹ chamato (*Nukva* of the *klipa*):

"And a wind carried me and from behind me I heard a great thunderous voice giving praise: Blessed is the glory of the Lord from His Abode." (Ezikiel 3:12) And saying: Blessed is the glory of the Lord from the place of residence of His Shechinah. "The Lord shall reign forever and ever" (Exodus 15:18) The Lord, His Kingdom is established forever and for eternity. "The Lord, God of Abraham, Isaac, and Israel - our forefathers - safeguard this forever for the sake of the thoughts in the hearts of Your Nation, and direct their hearts toward You!" (1 Chronicles 29:18) "And He is merciful and forgives iniquities and shall not destroy, and He frequently thwarts His wrath and will never arouse all His anger." (Psalms 78:38)

כִּי־ אַתָּה ki Ata אֲדֹנָי Adonai כלה טוֹב tov והו וְסָלָח vesalach יהוה ע"ב

וְרַב־ lechol לְכֹל־ ע"ב, ריבוע יהוה (Avraham) chesed וָחֶסֶד (Yitzchak) verav יה ארני

קֹרְאֶיךָ kor'echa ‫:‬(Yaakov) צִדְקָתְךָ tzidkat'cha צֶדֶק tzedek

לְעוֹלָם le'olam ריבוע ס"ג ו' אותיות דס"ג וְתוֹרָתְךָ vetorat'cha אֱמֶת emet

תִּתֵּן titen ב"פ כהת אֱמֶת emet אהיה פעמים אהיה, ז"פ ס"ג

לְיַעֲקֹב leYaakov ו' הויות, יאהדונהי אידהנויה וָחֶסֶד chesed ע"ב, ריבוע יהוה

לְאַבְרָהָם leAvraham ח"פ אל, רי"ו ול"ב נתיבות החכמה, רמ"ח (אברים), עסמ"ב וט"ז אותיות פשוטות

אֲשֶׁר־ asher נִשְׁבַּעְתָּ nishbata לַאֲבֹתֵינוּ la'avotenu מִימֵי mimei קֶדֶם kedem‫:‬ yom

בָּרוּךְ baruch אֲדֹנָי Adonai כלה yom ע"ה נגד, מזבוח, זן אל יהוה יוֹם yom

הָאֵל haEl לָאה ; אל (ייא"י מילוי דס"ג) ; ר"ת ייל ; ע"ה נגד, מזבוח, זן אל יהוה, אהיה אדני, לָנוּ lanu יַעֲמָס־ ya'amos ר"ת ייי

יְהֹוָ‍ַאֲדֹנָיאהדונהי imanu עָמָּנוּ פני שכינה צְבָאוֹת Tzeva'ot Adonai יְשׁוּעָתֵנוּ yeshu'atenu סֶלָה sela‫:‬

מִשְׂגָּב־ misgav מהטע, ע"ב בריבוע וקס"א, אל עדי, ד"פ אלהים ע"ה ריבוע ס"ג, קס"א ע"ה וד' אותיות

לָנוּ lanu אלהים, אהיה ארני מילוי ע"ב, דמב ; ילה אֱלֹהֵי Elohei יַעֲקֹב Yaakov

צְבָאוֹת Tzeva'ot אידהנויה יאהדונהי, הויות ז' יְהֹוָ‍ַאֲדֹנָיאהדונהי Adonai סֶלָה sela‫:‬ פני שכינה

אַשְׁרֵי ashrei אָדָם adam מ"ה ; יהוה צבאות אשרי אדם = תפארת בָּטֵחַ bote'ach

בָּךְ bach אדם בוטח בך = אמן (יאהדונהי) ע"ה ; בוטח בך = ע"ה בָּךְ bach מילוי ע"ב ע"ה ע"ב‫:‬

יְהֹוָ‍ַאֲדֹנָיאהדונהי Adonai hoshi'a הוֹשִׁיעָה יהוה וש"ע נהורין וש"ע נהורין ר"ת יהה hamelech הַמֶּלֶךְ

לְעֲנֵנוּ ya'anenu בְיוֹם־ veyom ע"ה נגד, מזבוח, זן, אל יהוה קָרְאֵנוּ kor'enu

ר"ת יב"ק, אלהים יהוה, אהיה ארני יהוה, וס"ת ב"ן ועם אות כ' דהמלך = ע"ב‫:‬

"Because You, Lord, are good and forgiving and abound in kindness to all who call to You." (Psalms 86:5) "Your righteousness is an everlasting justice, and Your Torah is true." (Psalms 119:142) "You give truth to Jacob and kindness to Abraham, as You have vowed to our forefathers since the earliest days." (Michah 7:20) "Blessed is the Lord, Who heaps burdens upon us each and every day, the God of our salvation. Selah." (Psalms 68:20) "The Lord of Hosts is with us; the God of Jacob is our strength. Selah." (Psalms 46:12) "Lord of Hosts, joyful is the man who trusts in You." (Psalms 84:13) "Lord, save us. The King shall answer us on the day when we call him." (Psalms 20:10)

BARUCH ELOHENU

Reciting the next verse *"baruch Elohenu"* with genuine happiness and a trusting heart will generate extra Light in our lives and our *tikkun* process will be much easier. Meditate to devote your soul to sanctify the Holy Name (*Kedushat HaShem*).

lichvodo לִכְבוֹדוֹ shebera'anu שֶׁבְּרָאָנוּ יִלה Elohenu אֱלֹהֵינוּ baruch בָּרוּךְ

(connecting to the right information) hato'im הַתּוֹעִים min מִן vehivdilanu וְהִבְדִּילָנוּ

ז"פ ס"ג אהיה פעמים אהיה emet אֱמֶת torat תּוֹרַת אלהים, אהיה אדני lanu לָנוּ venatan וְנָתַן

yiftach יִפְתַּח hu הוּא betochenu בְּתוֹכֵנוּ nata נָטַע olam עוֹלָם vechayei וְחַיֵּי וֹזיי

ahavato אַהֲבָתוֹ belibenu בְּלִבֵּנוּ veyasim וְיָשִׂים betorato בְּתוֹרָתוֹ libenu לִבֵּנוּ

ule'ovdo וּלְעָבְדוֹ retzono רְצוֹנוֹ la'asot לַעֲשׂוֹת veyir'ato וְיִרְאָתוֹ

larik לָרִיק niga נִיגַע lo לֹא shalem שָׁלֵם בוכו belevav בְּלֵבָב

(Meditate here to be protected from night emission, so that the spiritual effort will not go to negativity [*Rik* and *Behala*]. Also meditate to have righteous children following the way of the Light)

מהש ע"ה, ratzon רָצוֹן yehi יְהִי labehala לַבֶּהָלָה neled נֵלֵד velo וְלֹא

ע"ב בריבוע וקס"א ע"ה, אל שדי ע"ה, ס"ג מ"ה ב"ן Adonai יְהֹוָאדִ׳ילּיאהדונהי milfanecha מִלְּפָנֶיךָ

avotenu אֲבוֹתֵינוּ יִלה ; מילוי ע"ב, דמב velohei וֵאלֹהֵי לכב ; מילוי יִלה Elohenu אֱלֹהֵינוּ

umitzvotecha וּמִצְוֹתֶיךָ chukecha וְחֻקֶּיךָ shenishmor שֶׁנִּשְׁמוֹר

venirash וְנִירַשׁ venichye וְנִחְיֶה venizke וְנִזְכֶּה יהו haze הַזֶּה ba'olam בָּעוֹלָם

haba הַבָּא אכא ha'olam הָעוֹלָם lechayei לְחַיֵּי לוזיי uvracha וּבְרָכָה tova טוֹבָה

yidom יִדֹּם velo וְלֹא chavod כָּבוֹד yezamercha יְזַמֶּרְךָ lema'an לְמַעַן

יִלה ; מילוי ע"ב, דמב Elohai אֱלֹהַי אהיה אדני, אהיה = אלהים, ר"ת Adonai יְהֹוָאדִ׳ילּיאהדונהי

odeka אוֹדֶךָּ דס"ג אותיות וי ס"ג ריבוע le'olam לְעוֹלָם

BARUCH ELOHENU

Blessed is our God,

Who created us for the sake of His glory, Who separated us from those who have been led astray, Who gave us the Torah of truth, and Who implanted within us eternal life. May He open our hearts with His Torah, and place within our hearts love for Him and fear of Him, to fulfill His will and to serve Him wholeheartedly. May we not toil in vain, and may we not give birth to panic. May it be Your will, Lord, our God and God of our forefathers, that we should keep Your statutes and Your commandments in this world, and may we merit, live, and attain goodness and blessing for the life in the World to Come. "So that glory should make melodies to You and not be silent, Lord, my God, I shall forever thank You." (Psalms 30:13)

יְהֹוָאדֹנָיאהדונהי Adonai וְחָפֵץ chafetz לְמַעַן lema'an צִדְקוֹ tzidko יַגְדִּיל yagdil

תּוֹרָה torah ר"ת צ"ת veya'adir וְיַאְדִּיר ר"ת = אבגיתץ, ועו"ר veyivtechu וְיִבְטְחוּ

בְךָ vecha יוֹדְעֵי yod'ei שְׁמֶךָ shemecha כִּי ki ר"ת יכע לֹא lo עָזַבְתָּ azavta

דֹרְשֶׁיךָ dorshecha יְהֹוָאדֹנָיאהדונהי Adonai ס"ת כהת, משיוו בן דוד ע"ה:

יְהֹוָאדֹנָיאהדונהי Adonai אֲדֹנֵינוּ adonenu מָה־ ma מ"ה אַדִּיר adir הרי

שִׁמְךָ shimcha בְּכָל־ bechol ב"ן, לכב ; ומב הָאָרֶץ ha'aretz אלהים דההן ע"ה:

חִזְקוּ chizku וְיַאֲמֵץ veya'ametz לְבַבְכֶם levavchem

כֹּל kol ילי הַמְיַחֲלִים hameyachalim לַיְהֹוָאדֹנָיאהדונהי ladonai:

BET YAAKOV

In this prayer we are reminded that there is only one God and that we should not serve other gods. Today, other gods come in the form of addictions to money, career, or other people's perception of us, to name a few. When we allow the trapping of the material word to give sway over us, we are serving other gods. God's nature is proactive and sharing. When we live our lives in a proactive, sharing manner, we bring God's Light into our lives.

בֵּית bet ב"פ ראה Yaakov יַעֲקֹב ו' הויות, יאהדונהי אידהנויה

לְכוּ lechu וְנֵלְכָה venelcha בְּאוֹר be'or רו, אין סוף יְהֹוָאדֹנָיאהדונהי Adonai:

כִּי ki כָּל־ kol ילי הָעַמִּים ha'amim יֵלְכוּ yelchu אִישׁ ish בְּשֵׁם beshem

אֱלֹהָיו elohav ילה וַאֲנַחְנוּ va'anachnu נֵלֵךְ nelech גלך בְּשֵׁם־ beshem

יְהֹוָאדֹנָיאהדונהי Adonai אֱלֹהֵינוּ Elohenu ילה לְעוֹלָם le'olam ריבוע ס"ג ו' ואותיות דס"ג

וָעֶד va'ed: יְהִי yehi יְהֹוָאדֹנָיאהדונהי Adonai אֱלֹהֵינוּ Elohenu ילה עִמָּנוּ imanu

כַּאֲשֶׁר ka'asher היה אותיות ו"ד ע"ה קס"א, דס"ג, מילוי הָיָה haya יהה עִם־ im

אֲבוֹתֵינוּ avotenu אַל־ al יַעַזְבֵנוּ ya'azvenu וְאַל־ ve'al יִטְּשֵׁנוּ yiteshenu:

"Lord desires righteousness: He makes the Torah great and powerful." (Isaiah 42:21) *"And they shall place their trust in You, all those who know Your Name, for You have not abandoned those who seek You, Lord."* (Psalms 9:11) *"Lord, our Master, how mighty is Your Name throughout the world."* (Psalms 8:2) Be strong and your hearts be courageous, all you, who place your hope in the Lord.*

BET YAAKOV

"The House of Jacob come, let us walk by the Light of the Lord." (Isaiah 2:5) *"For all the nations shall each walk in the name of his god, but we shall walk in the Name of the Lord, our God, forever and ever."* (Michah 4:5) *"May the Lord, our God, be with us as He was with our forefathers. May He not abandon or forsake us,*

לְהַטּוֹת lehatot   לְבָבֵנוּ levavenu   אֵלָיו elav   לָלֶכֶת lalechet   בְּכָל bechol

וְחֻקָּיו vechukav   מִצְוֹתָיו mitzvotav   וְלִשְׁמֹר velishmor   דְּרָכָיו derachav

וּמִשְׁפָּטָיו umishpatav   אֲשֶׁר asher   צִוָּה tziva   אֶת et   אֲבוֹתֵינוּ avotenu

וְיִהְיוּ veyihyu   דְבָרַי devarai   אֵלֶּה ele   אֲשֶׁר asher

הִתְחַנַּנְתִּי hitchananti   לִפְנֵי lifnei   יְהֹוָה Adonai   קְרֹבִים kerovim

אֶל el   יְהֹוָה Adonai   אֱלֹהֵינוּ Elohenu   יוֹמָם yomam

וְלַיְלָה valayla   לַעֲשׂוֹת la'asot | מִשְׁפַּט mishpat

עַבְדּוֹ avdo   וּמִשְׁפַּט umishpat   עַמּוֹ amo   יִשְׂרָאֵל Yisrael

דְּבַר devar   יוֹם yom   בְּיוֹמוֹ beyomo

לְמַעַן lema'an   דַּעַת da'at   כָּל kol   עַמֵּי amei

הָאָרֶץ ha'aretz   כִּי ki   יְהֹוָה Adonai   הוּא hu

הָאֱלֹהִים haElohim   אֵין en   עוֹד od

SHIR HAMA'ALOT

The 57 words in this paragraph correspond to the numeric value of *Nun* נ, *Gimel* ג, *Dalet* ד, in the *Ana Becho'ach*, the 42-Letters Name of God. This number is also the value of the word *Zan* זן, which is the Aramaic word for sustenance. It is important to recite this prayer as a single unit without any distraction between words. The unity of the prayer is the spark that ignites the power of sustenance.

שִׁיר shir   הַמַּעֲלוֹת hama'alot   לְדָוִד leDavid   לוּלֵי lulei   יְהֹוָה Adonai

שֶׁהָיָה shehaya   לָנוּ lanu   יֹאמַר yomar   נָא na

יִשְׂרָאֵל Yisrael   לוּלֵי lulei   יְהֹוָה Adonai   שֶׁהָיָה shehaya

לָנוּ lanu   בְּקוּם bekum   עָלֵינוּ alenu   אָדָם adam

---

so we may bend our hearts to Him, walk in all His ways, keep His commandments, His statutes, and His laws, as He commanded our forefathers. Let those words, which I have pleaded before the Lord, be near the Lord, our God, day and night, to provide for the needs of His servant and the needs of His nation, Israel. All the nations of the earth shall know that the Lord is the God and there is none other." (I Kings 8:57-60)

SHIR HAMA'ALOT

"A Song of David: If it was not for the Lord, Who was there for us,
let Israel now say: If it was not for the Lord, Who was there for us when men rose against us,

bacharot בַּוְזָרוֹת bela'unu בְּלָעוּנוּ אהיה אהיה יהוה, בינה ע"ה chayim וְזַיִּים azai אֲזַי

apam (נוקבא דס"מ) azai אֲזַי הַמַּיִם hamayim שְׁטָפוּנוּ shetafunu אַפָּם :banu בָּנוּ

azai אֲזַי :nafshenu נַפְשֵׁנוּ al עַל avar עָבַר nachla נַוְזְלָה (לילית וכת דלהון)

:hazedonim הַזֵּידוֹנִים hamayim הַמַּיִם nafshenu נַפְשֵׁנוּ al עַל avar עָבַר

teref טֶרֶף netananu נְתָנָנוּ shelo שֶׁלֹּא Adonai יְהֹוָאדְנִיְאהדונהי baruch בָּרוּך

nimleta נִמְלְטָה ketzipor כְּצִפּוֹר nafshenu נַפְשֵׁנוּ :leshinehem לְשִׁנֵּיהֶם

nishbar נִשְׁבָּר hapach הַפַּח yokshim יוֹקְשִׁים mipach מִפַּח

beshem בְּשֵׁם ezrenu עֶזְרֵנוּ :nimlatnu נִמְלָטְנוּ va'anachnu וַאֲנַוְזְנוּ

:va'aretz וָאָרֶץ ימ טל, ימ כוזו, ימ shamayim שָׁמַיִם ose עֹשֵׂה Adonai יְהֹוָאדְנִיְאהדונהי

SHIR SHEL YOM

The next six Psalms connect us to the six days of the week and to the six days of Creation. Each day we say the Psalm that corresponds to the unique expression of the spiritual Light of that day. Connecting to the original seed level of the six days of Creation gives us the power to alter our destiny.

SUNDAY - CHESED - ABRAHAM

Meditate that on Sunday, *Chesed* of *Atzilut* is illuminating יְהֹוָה

Also meditate on the Name: אבגיתץ which includes all the Names of *Ana Beko'ach*.

And on the Name: יְהֹוָה

(Tetragrammaton with the vowels of the initials of the verse: "בראשית ברא אלהים את")

אל יהוה ז', מזבוז, נגד, ע"ה yom יוֹם ז', אל יהוה מזבוז, נגד, ע"ה hayom הַיּוֹם

:kodesh קוֹדֶשׁ beShabbat בְּשַׁבָּת דאגה אהבה, echad אֶוָזד

---

then they would have swallowed us alive, when their anger raged against us. The waters would have flooded us, and the stream engulfed us. The evil waters would have engulfed us. Blessed is the Lord, Who did not allow us to be prey to their teeth. Our soul escaped like a bird from the snare of the trappers. The snare broke and we escaped. Our help is the Name of the Lord, Who forms the Heavens and the Earth." (Psalms 124)

SHIR SHEL YOM
SUNDAY - CHESED - ABRAHAM
Today is day one of the counting to the Holy Sabbath.

(pause) mizmor מִזְמוֹר leDavid לְדָוִד

umelo'a וּמְלוֹאָהּ ה"ע דההין אלהים אדני־אהדונהי ha'aretz הָאָרֶץ ladonai לַיהוָֹה

hu הוּא ki כִּי: va בָהּ ר"ו ב"פ veyoshvei וְיֹשְׁבֵי tevel תֵּבֵל

neharot נְהָרוֹת ve'al וְעַל־ yesada יְסָדָהּ נלך yamim יַמִּים al עַל

ya'ale יַעֲלֶה ילי mi מִי: קמ"ג = והכולל התיבה עם yechoneneha יְכוֹנְנֶהָ

yakum יָקוּם ילי umi וּמִי Adonai יְהוָֹה־אדני־אהדונהי ב"ן ר"ת יבמ, vehar בְּהַר־

bimkom בִּמְקוֹם kodsho קָדְשׁוֹ ר"ת יב"ק, אלהים יהוה, אהיה אדני יהוה ; ס"ת מום, אלהים:

neki נְקִי ע"ה קס"א, אדני אלהים (מזרע לבטלה) chapayim כַפַּיִם ע"ה קנ"א, אדני אלהים

uvar וּבַר־ יצוק, ד"פ ב"ן בוכו ; בר לבב = ע"ב ס"ג מ"ה ב"ן, levav לֵבָב

lashav לַשָׁוְא nasa נָשָׂא lo לֹא־ asher אֲשֶׁר הברכה (למתק את ז' המלכים שמותו)

lemirma לְמִרְמָה: nishba נִשְׁבַּע velo וְלֹא (כתיב: נפשו) nafshi נַפְשִׁי

Adonai יְהוָֹה־אדני־אהדונהי ב"ן ר"ת יבמ, me'et מֵאֵת veracha בְרָכָה yisa יִשָׂא

meElohei מֵאֱלֹהֵי ; יהה ריבוע אלהים מילוי ע"ה, דמב ; ילה utz'daka וּצְדָקָה

dorshav דֹּרְשָׁיו dor דּוֹר ze זֶה: יהוה ס"ת ; ע"ה שכינה yish'o יִשְׁעוֹ

fanecha פָנֶיךָ ס"ג מ"ה ב"ן mevakshei מְבַקְשֵׁי (כתיב: דרשו)

Yaakov יַעֲקֹב ז' הויות, יאהדונהי אידהנויה :sela סֶלָה se'u שְׂאוּ she'arim שְׁעָרִים כתר

rashechem רָאשֵׁיכֶם vehinase'u וְהִנָּשְׂאוּ ר' שהוא זעיר אנפין וה' שהיא מלכות - נשאו

pitchei פִּתְחֵי olam עוֹלָם melech מֶלֶך veyavo וְיָבוֹא hakavod הַכָּבוֹד לאו:

ze זֶה ילי mi מִי melech מֶלֶךְ ר"ת פ"ז = בסוד כתם טהור פז

izuz עִזּוּז hakavod הַכָּבוֹד לאו יְהוָֹה־אדני־אהדונהי Adonai ; כבוד יהוה = יוד הי ואו הה

milchama מִלְחָמָה: gibor גִּבּוֹר Adonai יְהוָֹה־אדני־אהדונהי vegibor וְגִבּוֹר

"*A Psalm to David: The Earth and all it contains belong to the Lord, as the habitation and all who dwell in it. He founded it upon the seas and established it upon the rivers. Who shall ascend the Mountain of the Lord and who shall stand in His Holy Place? He whose hands are clean, whose heart is pure, and who neither has sworn in vain by his soul nor vowed falsely. He shall receive a blessing from the Lord and charity from the God of his salvation. This is the generation of those who seek Him, who seek your countenance, Jacob, Selah! Raise up your hand gates, and become uplifted, you portals of the world, and let the glorious King in. Who is the glorious King? It is the Lord, Who is powerful and valiant. The Lord, Who is mighty in war.*"

se'u שְׂאוּ | she'arim שְׁעָרִים | כתר | rashechem רָאשֵׁיכֶם

use'u וּשְׂאוּ | ו' | עִילָאָה | שׁהוּא | ת"ת | נשׂא | pitchei פִּתְחֵי

olam עוֹלָם | veyavo וְיָבֹא | melech מֶלֶךְ | hakavod הַכָּבוֹד | לאו:

mi מִי | ילי | hu הוּא | ze זֶה | melech מֶלֶךְ | hakavod הַכָּבוֹד | לאו

Adonai יְהֹוָאדֹנָיאהדונהי | ; כבוד יהוה = יוד הי ואו הה | Tzevaot צְבָאוֹת | פני שכינה | שכינה

hu הוּא | melech מֶלֶךְ | hakavod הַכָּבוֹד | לאו | sela סֶלָה:

Continue with "*hoshi'enu*" on page 685.

MONDAY - GEVURAH - ISAAC

Meditate that on Monday, *Gevurah* of *Atzilut* is illuminating יְהֹוָה

Also meditate on the Name: קְרָעשְׂטָן and on the Name: יְהֹוָה

(Tetragrammaton with the vowels of the initials of the verse: "וַיֹּאמֶר אֱלֹהִים יְהִי רָקִיעַ")

In this Psalm there are 15 verses, which correspond to the Holy Name: י"ה

hayom הַיּוֹם ע"ה נגד, מזבח, זן, אל יהוה

yom יוֹם ע"ה נגד, מזבח, זן, אל יהוה | sheni שֵׁנִי | beShabbat בְּשַׁבָּת | kodesh קוֹדֶשׁ:

shir שִׁיר | mizmor מִזְמוֹר | livnei לִבְנֵי | Korach קֹרַח: | gadol גָּדוֹל | להו ;

Adonai יְהֹוָאדֹנָיאהדונהי | umhulal וּמְהֻלָּל ס"ת ללה, אדני | עם ד' אותיות = מזבה, יזל, אום

me'od מְאֹד | be'ir בְּעִיר בֹּוזֶכֶר, סנדלפון, ערי | Elohenu אֱלֹהֵינוּ ילה

har הַר | kodsho קָדְשׁוֹ: | yefe יְפֵה | nof נוֹף | mesos מְשׂוֹשׂ | kol כָּל ילי

ha'aretz הָאָרֶץ | אלהים דההין ע"ה | har הַר | Tziyon צִיּוֹן יוסף, ו' הויות, קנאה

yarketei יַרְכְּתֵי | tzafon צָפוֹן | kiryat קִרְיַת | melech מֶלֶךְ | rav רָב:

Elohim אֱלֹהִים אהיה אדני | ; ילה | be'armenoteha בְּאַרְמְנוֹתֶיהָ | noda נוֹדַע

lemisgav לְמִשְׂגָּב מושה, מהט, ע"ב בריבוע וקס"א, אל שדי, ד"פ אלהים ע"ה: | ki כִּי

hine הִנֵּה | hamelachim הַמְּלָכִים | no'adu נוֹעֲדוּ | avru עָבְרוּ | yachdav יוֹזְדָּו:

Raise up your heads gates, and lift up your eternal portals and let the glorious King in. Who is the glorious King? It is the Lord of Hosts. He is the glorious King, Selah." (Psalms 24) [Save us]

MONDAY - GEVURAH - ISAAC

Today is the second day of the counting to the Holy Sabbath.
"A song and a Psalms of the sons of Korach:
The Lord is great and exceedingly praised in the city of our God, His Holy Mountain - a beautiful scene and a source of joy for the entire land, Mount Zion, at the northern side, the city of a great King. God is known in her palaces as powerful. Behold, the kings have gathered and set out together.

הֵמָּה hema רָאוּ rau כֵּן ken תָּמָהוּ tamahu נִבְהֲלוּ nivhalu נֶחְפָּזוּ nechpazu:

רְעָדָה re'ada אֲחָזָתַם achazatam שָׁם sham וְזִיל chil ומ"ב כַּיּוֹלֵדָה kayoleda:

בְּרוּחַ beru'ach קָדִים kadim תְּשַׁבֵּר teshaber אֳנִיּוֹת oniyot תַּרְשִׁישׁ Tarshish:

כַּאֲשֶׁר ka'asher שָׁמַעְנוּ shamanu כֵּן ken רָאִינוּ ra'inu

בְּעִיר be'ir צְבָאוֹת Tzeva'ot יְהֹוָה Adonai פני שכינה

בְּעִיר be'ir אֱלֹהֵינוּ Elohenu אֱלֹהִים Elohim אהיה אדני ; ילה

יְכוֹנְנֶהָ yechoneneha עַד ad עוֹלָם olam סֶלָה sela:

דִּמִּינוּ diminu אֱלֹהִים Elohim אהיה אדני ; ילה וְחַסְדֶּךָ chasdecha בְּקֶרֶב bekerev

הֵיכָלֶךָ hechalecha: כְּשִׁמְךָ keshimcha אֱלֹהִים Elohim אהיה אדני ; ילה

כֵּן ken תְּהִלָּתְךָ tehilatcha עַל־ al קַצְוֵי־ katzvei אֶרֶץ eretz צֶדֶק tzedek

מָלְאָה mal'a יְמִינֶךָ yeminecha: יִשְׂמַח yismach הַר־ har

צִיּוֹן Tziyon תָּגֵלְנָה tagelna בְּנוֹת benot יְהוּדָה Yehuda

לְמַעַן lema'an מִשְׁפָּטֶיךָ mishpatecha: סֹבּוּ sobu צִיּוֹן Tziyon

וְהַקִּיפוּהָ vehakifuha סִפְרוּ sifru מִגְדָּלֶיהָ migdaleha: שִׁיתוּ shitu

לִבְּכֶם libchem לְחֵילָה lechela פַּסְּגוּ pasegu אַרְמְנוֹתֶיהָ armenoteha

לְמַעַן lema'an תְּסַפְּרוּ tesaperu לְדוֹר ledor אַחֲרוֹן acharon:

כִּי ki זֶה ze אֱלֹהִים Elohim אהיה אדני ; ילה אֱלֹהֵינוּ Elohenu ילה

עוֹלָם olam וָעֶד va'ed הוּא hu יְנַהֲגֵנוּ yenahagenu עַל־ al מוּת mut:

Continue with "hoshi'enu" on page 685.

They saw and were astonished. They panicked and quickly fled. A tremble took hold of them; fright like that of a woman in labor. With an easterly wind, You smashed the ships of Tarshish. As we have heard, so we have seen in the city of the Lord of Hosts, in the city of our God. May God establish it forever, Selah! God, we had hoped for Your kindness in the midst of Your Sanctuary. As is Your Name, God, so is Your praise in all corners of the Earth. Righteousness fills Your right hand. Mount Zion shall rejoice and the daughters of Judah shall delight, for the sake of Your judgments. Surround Zion and walk around her. Count her towers. Set Your Heart to Her walls and raise her walls, so that You may relate to the next generation. For this is the Lord, our God, for all eternity He shall lead us forever." (Psalms 48) [Save us]

TUESDAY – TIFERET – JACOB

Meditate that on Tuesday, *Tiferet* of *Atzilut* is illuminating יְהֹוָה

Also meditate on the Name: נָגְדִיכַשׁ and on the Name: יְהֵוָה

(Tetragrammaton with the vowels of the initials of the verse: "וַיֹּאמֶר אֱלֹהִים יִקָּווּ הַמַּיִם")

ע"ה נגד, מזבוז, זן, אל יהוה hayom הַיּוֹם

kodesh קֹדֶשׁ beShabbat בְּשַׁבָּת shelishi שְׁלִישִׁי אל יהוה, זן, מזבוז, נגד ע"ה yom יוֹם

ילה ; אדני אהיה Elohim אֱלֹהִים leAsaf לְאָסָף mizmor מִזְמוֹר

bekerev בְּקֶרֶב (מילוי דס"ג) ייא"י El אֵל ba'adat בַּעֲדַת nitzav נִצָּב

matai מָתַי ad עַד yishpot יִשְׁפֹּט ; ילה אדני אהיה Elohim אֱלֹהִים

resha'im רְשָׁעִים בינה וחכמה ufnei וּפְנֵי avel עָוֶל tishpetu תִּשְׁפְּטוּ

יוסף veyatom וְיָתוֹם dal דָל shiftu שִׁפְטוּ sela סֶלָה tis'u תִּשְׂאוּ

dal דָל paltu פַּלֵּטוּ hatz'diku הַצְדִּיקוּ varash וָרָשׁ מ"ה ריבוע ani עָנִי

hatzilu הַצִּילוּ resha'im רְשָׁעִים miyad מִיַּד ve'evyon וְאֶבְיוֹן

bachashecha בַּחֲשֵׁכָה yavinu יָבִינוּ velo וְלֹא yad'u יֵדְעוּ lo לֹא

aretz אָרֶץ mosdei מוֹסְדֵי ילי kol כָּל yimotu יִמּוֹטוּ yit'halachu יִתְהַלָּכוּ

atem אַתֶּם ילה ; אדני אהיה Elohim אֱלֹהִים amarti אָמַרְתִּי אני ani אֲנִי

מ"ה ke'adam כְּאָדָם achen אָכֵן kulchem כֻּלְּכֶם elyon עֶלְיוֹן uvnei וּבְנֵי

hasarim הַשָּׂרִים דאגה אהבה, uche'achad וּכְאַחַד temutun תְּמוּתוּן

ילה ; אדני אהיה Elohim אֱלֹהִים (מקוה) קנ"א kuma קוּמָה tipolu תִּפֹּלוּ

ki כִּי ע"ה דההין אלהים ha'aretz הָאָרֶץ shofta שָׁפְטָה

hagoyim הַגּוֹיִם ב"ן, לכב bechol בְּכָל tinchal תִנְחַל Ata אַתָּה

Continue with "*hoshi'enu*" on page 685.

TUESDAY - TIFERET - JACOB

Today is the third day of the counting to the Holy Sabbath.
"A Psalms of Asaf:

God is present in the supernal assembly. Amidst judges, He judges. Until when shall you judge dishonestly and show favor to the wicked? Selah! Judge the destitute and the orphan. Rule in favor of the poor and the needy. Rescue the destitute and the wretched. Deliver them from the hands of the wicked, who do not know or understand that they walk in darkness; they cause the foundations of the Earth to collapse. I had said that you are like angels and are all sons of the Supernal, yet, you shall die like Adam and shall fall like one of the princes. Rise, God, and judge the world for You shall bequeath upon all the nations." (Psalms 82) [Save us]

WEDNESDAY - NETZACH - MOSES

Meditate that on Wednesday, *Netzach* of *Atzilut* is illuminating יְהֹוָה

Also meditate on the Name: בטרצתג and on the Name: יְהֹוָה

(Tetragrammaton with the vowels of the initials of the verse: "וַיֹּאמֶר אֱלֹהִים יְהִי מְאוֹרֹת")

הַיּוֹם hayom ע"ה נגד, מזבח, זן, אל יהוה

יוֹם yom ע"ה נגד, מזבח, זן, אל יהוה, זן ; revi'i רְבִיעִי beShabbat בְּשַׁבָּת kodesh קוֹדֶשׁ:

אֵל El יא"י (מילוי דס"ג) nekamot נְקָמוֹת Adonai יְהֹוָאדֹנָיאהדונהי ; ר"ת אני

אֵל El יא"י (מילוי דס"ג) nekamot נְקָמוֹת ר"ת = יב"ק, אלהים יהוה, אהיה אדני יהוה

הוֹפִיעַ hofi'a: hinase הִנָּשֵׂא shofet שֹׁפֵט ha'aretz הָאָרֶץ אלהים דההין ע"ה

הָשֵׁב hashev ר"ת = שדי ע"ה gemul גְּמוּל al עַל ge'im גֵּאִים: ad עַד

מָתַי matai ad עַד Adonai יְהֹוָאדֹנָיאהדונהי resha'im רְשָׁעִים matai מָתַי

רְשָׁעִים resha'im ya'alozu יַעֲלֹזוּ: ג"פ אב" yabi'u יַבִּיעוּ yedaberu יְדַבְּרוּ

עָתָק atak yit'amru יִתְאַמְּרוּ kol כָּל ילי po'alei פֹּעֲלֵי aven אָוֶן: amecha עַמְּךָ

יְהֹוָאדֹנָיאהדונהי Adonai yedake'u יְדַכְּאוּ venachalatcha וְנַחֲלָתְךָ ye'anu יְעַנּוּ:

אַלְמָנָה almana veger וְגֵר yaharogu יַהֲרֹגוּ vitomim וִיתוֹמִים yeratzechu יְרַצֵּחוּ:

וַיֹּאמְרוּ vayomru lo לֹא yir'e יִרְאֶה רי"י Yah יָהּ velo וְלֹא yavin יָבִין

אֱלֹהֵי Elohei מילוי ע"ב, דמב ; ילה Yaakov יַעֲקֹב ז' הויות, יאהדונהי אידהנויה: binu בִּינוּ

בֹּעֲרִים bo'arim ba'am בָּעָם uchsilim וּכְסִילִים matai מָתַי taskilu תַּשְׂכִּילוּ:

הֲנֹטַע hanota ozen אֹזֶן ואו הי יוד הה הה halo הֲלֹא yishma יִשְׁמָע

אִם im יוהך, מ"א אותיות דפשוט, דמילוי ודמילוי דמילוי דאהיה ע"ה yotzer יֹצֵר

עַיִן ayin ריבוע מ"ה halo הֲלֹא yabit יַבִּיט: hayoser הַיֹּסֵר goyim גּוֹיִם

הֲלֹא halo yochi'ach יוֹכִיחַ hamelamed הַמְלַמֵּד adam אָדָם מ"ה da'at דָּעַת:

WEDNESDAY - NETZACH - MOSES

Today is the fourth day of the counting to the Holy Sabbath.

'The God of retribution is the Lord. God of retribution, appear. Arise, You Judge of the Earth. Repay the arrogant their due. How long shall the wicked, Lord, how long shall the wicked rejoice? They express themselves and speak with arrogance. All the evil-doers are proud; Lord, they debase Your Nation and they torture Your Children. They kill widow and convert; they murder orphans. And they say: The Lord does not see, and the God of Jacob does not understand. You should understand, you imbeciles among the people, and you fools: when shall you become wise? Can the One Who implanted the ear, not hear? Can the One Who formed the eye, not behold? Shall the One Who punishes nations, not admonish? He Who teaches man knowledge.'

מ"ה adam אָדָם machshevot מַחְשְׁבוֹת yode'a יֹדֵעַ Adonai יְהֹוָה(אדנייאהדונהי)

hagever הַגֶּבֶר ashrei אַשְׁרֵי מילוי דס"ג: havel הָבֶל hema הֵמָּה ki כִּי

umitorat'cha וּמִתּוֹרָתְךָ Yah יָּהּ teyasrenu תְּיַסְּרֶנּוּ asher אֲשֶׁר

ad עַד ra רָע mimei מִימֵי lo לוֹ lehashkit לְהַשְׁקִיט telamedenu: תְּלַמְּדֶנּוּ

yitosh יִטֹּשׁ lo לֹא ki כִּי shachat: שָׁחַת larasha לָרָשָׁע yikare יִכָּרֶה

ya'azov: יַעֲזֹב lo לֹא venachalato וְנַחֲלָתוֹ amo עַמּוֹ Adonai יְהֹוָה(אדנייאהדונהי)

אלהים ה"פ ע"ה mishpat מִשְׁפָּט yashuv יָשׁוּב tzedek צֶדֶק ad עַד ki כִּי

ילי mi מִי lev: לֵב yishrei יִשְׁרֵי kol כָּל ve'acharav וְאַחֲרָיו

yityatzev יִתְיַצֵּב ילי mi מִי mere'im מְרֵעִים im עִם li לִי yakum יָקוּם

Adonai יְהֹוָה(אדנייאהדונהי) lulei לוּלֵי aven: אָוֶן po'alei פֹּעֲלֵי im עִם li לִי

nafshi: נַפְשִׁי duma דוּמָה shachna שָׁכְנָה kim'at כִּמְעַט li לִי ezrata עֶזְרָתָה

ר"ת = ב"ן יוהך, מ"א אותיות דפשוט, דמילוי ודמילוי דמילוי דאהיה ע"ה im אִם amarti אָמַרְתִּי

Adonai יְהֹוָה(אדנייאהדונהי) chasdecha וְחַסְדְּךָ ragli רַגְלִי mata מָטָה

עדי bekirbi בְּקִרְבִּי sar'apai שַׂרְעַפַּי י"פ אהיה berov בְּרֹב אגל"י yis'adeni יִסְעָדֵנִי

(זו מות): ר"ת נית nafshi נַפְשִׁי yesha'ashe'u יְשַׁעַשְׁעוּ tanchumecha תַּנְחוּמֶיךָ

yotzer יֹצֵר havot הַוּוֹת kise כִּסֵּא hayechovrecha הַיְחָבְרְךָ

al עַל yagodu יָגוֹדּוּ chok: וְחֹק alei עֲלֵי amal עָמָל

קס"א ע"ה naki נָקִי vedam וְדָם tzadik צַדִּיק nefesh נֶפֶשׁ

li לִי Adonai יְהֹוָה(אדנייאהדונהי) vayehi וַיְהִי yarshi'u: יַרְשִׁיעוּ

אלהים ד"פ אל עדי, וקס"א, בריבוע ע"ב, מהע, משה, lemisgav לְמִשְׂגָּב ע"ה

Lord knows the thoughts of man that they are in vain. Fortunate is the man whom You chastise, Lord, and from Your Torah, You teach him, so that he would be secure against bad times, until a deep abyss is dug for the wicked. The Lord does not forsake His Nation or abandon His Heritage, for until justice is done, the judgment shall last. Following Him are all who are upright at heart. Who shall rise for me against evil-doers? Who shall stand by me against the workers of iniquity? Was it not for the Lord Who had helped me, then my soul would have dwelt in Hell. If I said that my foot slipped, Your kindness, Lord, would support me. When many depressing thoughts were within me, Your consoling words would cheer my soul. Can a throne of evil be linked with You by one who fashions injustice into law? They gather against the life of the righteous, and they condemn innocent blood. But the Lord became my strength,

ילה ; רמב ע"ב, ; מילוי לכב (אליהו הַנָּבִיא) velohai וֵאלֹהַי

vayashev וַיֵּשֶׁב הרחו machsi מַחְסִי ע"ה דההין אלהים letzur לְצוּר

yatzmitem יַצְמִיתֵם uvra'atam וּבְרָעָתָם onam אוֹנָם et אֶת־ alehem עֲלֵיהֶם

יֿלה: Elohenu אֱלֹהֵינוּ Adonai יְהֹואדניואהדונהי yatzmitem יַצְמִיתֵם

Continue with *"hoshi'enu"* on page 685.

THURSDAY - HOD - AARON

Meditate that on Thursday, *Hod* of *Atzilut* is illuminating יְהֹוָה

Also meditate on the Name: וֹזְקְבְטֹנֵע and on the Name: יְהֹוָה

(Tetragrammaton with the vowels of the initials of the verse: "וַיֹּאמֶר אֱלֹהִים יִשְׁרְצוּ הַמַּיִם")

In this Psalm there are 126 words corresponding to the Holy Name: כוז = (א אד אדני אדני) ריבוע אדני

אֶל יהוה זֹ, מזבוח, נגר, ע"ה hayom הַיּוֹם

kodesh קוֹדֶשׁ beShabbat בְּשַׁבָּת chamishi וַחֲמִישִׁי אֶל יהוה זֹ, מזבוח, נגר ע"ה yom יוֹם

harninu הַרְנִינוּ leAsaf לְאָסָף hagitit הַגִּתִּית al עַל־ lamnatze'ach לַמְנַצֵּחַ

hari'u הָרִיעוּ אלהים דאלפין uzenu עוֹזֵּנוּ אדני ; יֿלה lelohim לֵאלֹהִים

ר"ת יֿלה ; איהדנויה יאהדונהי הויות, זֹ Yaakov יַעֲקֹב יֿלה ; רמב ע"ב, מילוי lelohei לֵאלֹהֵי

na'im נָעִים kinor כִּנּוֹר tof תֹּף utnu וּתְנוּ zimra זִמְרָה se'u שְׂאוּ

קנ"א קס"א הויות, י"ב vachodesh בַּחֹדֶשׁ tik'u תִּקְעוּ navel נָבֶל im עִם

chagenu וַגֵּנוּ leyom לְיוֹם אֶל יהוה זֹ, מזבוח, נגר ע"ה bakese בַּכֶּסֶה shofar שׁוֹפָר

אלהים ה"פ ע"ה mishpat מִשְׁפָּט hu הוּא leYisrael לְיִשְׂרָאֵל chok חֹק ki כִּי וֹזֵק

איהדנויה: יאהדונהי הויות, זֹ Yaakov יַעֲקֹב יֿלה ; רמב ע"ב, מילוי lelohei לֵאלֹהֵי

eretz אֶרֶץ al עַל־ betzeto בְּצֵאתוֹ samo שָׂמוֹ bihosef בִּיהוֹסֵף edut עֵדוּת

eshma אֶשְׁמָע yadati יָדַעְתִּי lo לֹא sefat שְׂפַת מצר Mitzrayim מִצְרָיִם

---

and my God was the Rock of my refuge. He shall turn their evil acts against them and shall strike them down with their wickedness. The Lord, our God, shall strike them down." (Psalms 94)[Save us]

THURSDAY - HOD - AARON
Today is the fifth day of the counting to the Holy Sabbath.
'To the Chief musician, set for the Gittit, by Asaf:
Sing with joy to the God of our strength. Hail loudly the God of Jacob. Take to singing and beat the drum, a pleasant harp together with the lyre. Blow the Shofar at the renewal of the month upon the concealment of the moon for our day of festival. Because it is a statute for Israel, a judgment day for the God of Jacob. Vestments were put on Joseph when he went out over the land for Egypt, where he heard a language that he never knew.

midud מִדּוּד kapav כַּפָּיו shichmo שִׁכְמוֹ misevel מִסֵּבֶל hasiroti הַסִירוֹתִי

karata קָרָאתָ (אלהים דההין) batzara בַּצָרָה ta'avorna תַּעֲבֹרְנָה:

ra'am רַעַם (ב"פ מצר) beseter בְּסֵתֶר e'encha אֶעֶנְךָ va'achaletzeka וָאֲחַלְּצֶךָ

sela סֶלָה meriva מְרִיבָה (עממ; יל') mei מֵי al עַל evchoncha אֶבְחָנְךָ:

Yisrael יִשְׂרָאֵל bach בָּךְ ve'a'ida וְאָעִידָה ami עַמִּי shema שְׁמַע

im אִם (יוהך, מ"א אותיות דפשוט, דמילוי ודמילוי דמילוי דאהיה ע"ה) tishma תִּשְׁמַע li לִי:

lo לֹא yihye יִהְיֶה (יי) vecha בְךָ el אֵל zar זָר (רוֹל = אל זר) (דקליפה)

anochi אָנֹכִי nechar נֵכָר: le'el לְאֵל tishtachave תִשְׁתַּחֲוֶה velo וְלֹא

hama'alcha הַמַּעַלְךָ (ילה) Elohecha אֱלֹהֶיךָ Adonai יְהֹוָה

picha פִּיךָ harchev הַרְחֶב (מצר) Mitzrayim מִצְרַיִם me'eretz מֵאֶרֶץ

lekoli לְקוֹלִי ami עַמִּי shama שָׁמַע velo וְלֹא: va'amal'ehu וַאֲמַלְאֵהוּ

va'ashalechehu וָאֲשַׁלְּחֵהוּ li לִי: ava אָבָה lo לֹא veYisrael וְיִשְׂרָאֵל

bemo'atzotehem בְּמוֹעֲצוֹתֵיהֶם: yelchu יֵלְכוּ libam לִבָּם bishrirut בִּשְׁרִירוּת

bidrachai בִּדְרָכַי Yisrael יִשְׂרָאֵל li לִי shome'a שֹׁמֵעַ ami עַמִּי lu לוּ

achni'a אַכְנִיעַ oyvehem אוֹיְבֵיהֶם kim'at כִּמְעַט: yehalechu יְהַלֵּכוּ

mesan'ei מְשַׂנְאַי: yadi יָדִי ashiv אָשִׁיב tzarehem צָרֵיהֶם ve'al וְעַל

itam עִתָּם vihi וִיהִי lo לוֹ yechachashu יְכַחֲשׁוּ Adonai יְהֹוָה

vaya'achilehu וַיַּאֲכִילֵהוּ (דס"ג אותיות וי' דס"ג ריבוע) le'olam לְעוֹלָם

umitzur וּמִצּוּר (אכא) chita חִטָּה mechelev מֵחֵלֶב (אלהים דההין) ע"ה

asbi'eka אַשְׂבִּיעֶךָ (ועם י"ד האווזז הרי ע"ך דינין דגדלות) devash דְּבַשׁ שו' דשופר:

Continue with "hoshi'enu" on page 685.

I removed the load from his shoulder; his hands I withdrew from the pots. In trouble you have called and I rescued you. I answer your secret call with thunder. I tested you at the waters of Merivah. Selah. My People listen and I shall warn you: Israel, if you would only listen to Me. There shall not be among you a foreign deity, nor should you bow to an alien god. I am the Lord, your God, Who brought you out of the land of Egypt. Open your mouth wide and I shall fill it. My People did not heed My words. Israel did not obey Me. I banished them to the folly of their hearts. They walked in their evil counsel. If My Nation would listen to Me, and Israel would walk in My ways, I would completely subdue their enemies and would turn My Hand against their oppressors. The haters of the Lord deny Him, but Israel's time shall be forever. I shall feed him from the best of the wheat and satiate you with honey drawn from rocks." (Psalms 81) [Save us]

FRIDAY - YESOD - JOSEPH

Meditate that on Friday, *Yesod* of *Atzilut* is illuminating יְהֹוִוּהוּ

Also meditate on the Name: יְהֹוָה and on the Name: יגלפּזק

(Tetragrammaton with the vowels of the initials of the verse: "וַיֹּאמֶר אֱלֹהִים תּוֹצֵא הָאָרֶץ")

In this Psalm there are 45 words, corresponding to the Holy Name: מ"ה (יוד הא ואו הא)

הַיּוֹם hayom ע"ה נגד, מזבח, ז, אל יהוה

יוֹם yom ע"ה נגד, מזבח, ז, אל יהוה הַשִּׁשִּׁי hashishi בְּשַׁבָּת beShabbat קֹדֶשׁ kodesh:

יְהֹוָ Adonai מָלָךְ malach גֵּאוּת ge'ut לָבֵשׁ lavesh לָבֵשׁ lavesh

יְהֹוָ Adonai עֹז oz הִתְאַזָּר hit'azar אַף־ af ר"ת = אלהים, אהיה אדני

תִּכּוֹן tikon תֵּבֵל tevel בַּל־ bal תִּמּוֹט timot: נָכוֹן nachon כִּסְאֲךָ kis'acha

מֵאָז me'az ומב מֵעוֹלָם me'olam אָתָּה Ata ר"ת הפסוק קנ"א, אדני אלהים:

נָשְׂאוּ nas'u נְהָרוֹת neharot יְהֹוָ Adonai נָשְׂאוּ nas'u ר"ת = קין

נְהָרוֹת neharot קוֹלָם kolam יִשְׂאוּ yis'u נְהָרוֹת neharot דָּכְיָם dochyam ר"ת דו"י:

מִקֹּלוֹת mikolot מַיִם mayim רַבִּים rabim אַדִּירִים adirim הרי

מִשְׁבְּרֵי־ mishberei יָם yam ; ר"ת אמי אַדִּיר adir הרי

בַּמָּרוֹם bamarom יְהֹוָ Adonai ; ר"ת אבי: עֵדֹתֶיךָ edotecha

נֶאֶמְנוּ ne'emnu מְאֹד me'od ר"ת = קין לְבֵיתְךָ levetcha ב"פ ראה

נָאֲוָה na'avah קֹדֶשׁ kodesh יְהֹוָ Adonai לְאֹרֶךְ le'orech

יָמִים yamim נלך ; ר"ת ילי ; אדני = יהוה לאורך ימים = ש"ע נהורין עם י"ג אותיות:

Continue with *"hoshi'enu"* on page 685.

FRIDAY - YESOD - JOSEPH
Today is the sixth day of the counting to the Holy Sabbath.
"The Lord reigns. He clothes Himself with pride.
The Lord clothes Himself and girds Himself with might. He also established the world firmly, so that it would not collapse. Your Throne has been established. Ever since that time, You have been forever. The rivers have lifted, Lord, the rivers have raised their voices. The rivers shall raise their powerful waves. More than the roaring of many waters and the powerful waves of the sea, You are mighty in the High Places, Lord. Your testimonies are extremely trustworthy. Your House is the Holy Sanctuary. The Lord shall be for the length of days." (Psalms 93) [Save us]

HOSHI'ENU

Receiving extra energy for the day

After reciting the daily Psalms, the following is said:

ילה ‏ Elohenu אֱלֹהֵינוּ ‏ Adonai יְהֹוָאהדונהי ‏ hoshi'enu הוֹשִׁיעֵנוּ

leshem לְשֵׁם ‏ lehodot לְהוֹדוֹת ‏ hagoyim הַגּוֹיִם ‏ min מִן ‏ vekabetzenu וְקַבְּצֵנוּ

bit'hilatecha בִּתְהִלָּתֶךָ ‏ lehishtabe'ach לְהִשְׁתַּבֵּחַ ‏ kodshecha קָדְשֶׁךָ

ילה ; דמב , ע"ב מילוי Elohei אֱלֹהֵי ‏ Adonai יְהֹוָאהדונהי ‏ baruch בָּרוּךְ

ha'olam הָעוֹלָם ‏ min מִן ‏ (מצוות) תרי"ג = ישראל אלהי יהוה ; אדני = ס"ת Yisrael יִשְׂרָאֵל

ha'am הָעָם ‏ ילי kol כָּל ‏ ve'amar וְאָמַר ‏ ha'olam הָעוֹלָם ‏ ve'ad וְעַד

ללה ; אדני , אהיה אלהים, haleluya הַלְלוּיָהּ ‏ יאהדונהי ‏ amen אָמֵן

קנאה , היות ו , יוסף miTziyon מִצִּיּוֹן ‏ Adonai יְהֹוָאהדונהי ‏ baruch בָּרוּךְ

ללה ; אדני אהיה אלהים, haleluya הַלְלוּיָהּ ‏ Yerushalayim יְרוּשָׁלָיִם ‏ shochen שֹׁכֵן

ילה ; אדני אהיה Elohim אֱלֹהִים ‏ Adonai יְהֹוָאהדונהי ‏ baruch בָּרוּךְ

nifla'ot נִפְלָאוֹת ‏ ose עֹשֵׂה ‏ Yisrael יִשְׂרָאֵל ‏ ילה ; דמב , ע"ב מילוי Elohei אֱלֹהֵי

le'olam לְעוֹלָם ‏ kevodo כְּבוֹדוֹ ‏ shem שֵׁם ‏ uvaruch וּבָרוּךְ ‏ מ"ב : levado לְבַדּוֹ

ילי kol כָּל ‏ et אֶת ‏ chevodo כְבוֹדוֹ ‏ veyimale וְיִמָּלֵא ‏ דס"ג אותיות ו"י ס"ג ריבוע

יאהדונהי ve'amen וְאָמֵן ‏ יאהדונהי amen אָמֵן ‏ דההין ע"ה אלהים ha'aretz הָאָרֶץ

Continue Half *Kaddish* on pages 517-518 and then *Musaf* from page 519 to page 550.

HOSHI'ENU

"Save us, Lord, our God, and gather us from among the nations to give thanks to Your Holy Name and to find ourselves glorified in Your praise. Blessed is the Lord, God of Israel, from this world to the Next World, and all the people shall say: Amen! Praise the Lord!" (Psalms 106:47-48) "Blessed is the Lord from Zion. He Who dwells in Jerusalem. Praise the Lord!" (Psalms 135:21) Blessed is the Lord, our God, God of Israel, Who alone does wonders. And blessed is the Name of His glory forever. And His glory shall fill the entire world. Amen and Amen.

THE AMIDAH OF ARVIT OF SHABBAT AND CHOL HAMO'ED

yagid יַגִּיד ufi וּפִי tiftach תִּפְתָּח sefatai שְׂפָתַי (pause here) כלה: Adonai אֲדֹנָי

יוֹ (כ"ב אותיות פשוטות [=אכא] וה' אותיות סופיות מנצפ"ך) ס"ת = בוכו: tehilatecha תְּהִלָּתֶךָ

THE FIRST BLESSING - INVOKES THE SHIELD OF ABRAHAM.

Abraham is the channel of the Right Column energy of positivity, sharing, and Mercy. Sharing actions can protect us from all forms of negativity.

Chesed that becomes *Chochmah*

In this section there are 42 words, the secret of the 42-Letter Name of God and therefore it begins with the letter *Bet* (2) and ends with the letter *Mem* (40).

Bend your knees at "*baruch*," bow at "*Ata*" and straighten up at "*Adonai*."

ב   א

המלכות לה' המגיע העושה את המסמלות הא"ב (אותיות א–ת) Ata אַתָּה baruch בָּרוּךְ

ג

יכה Elohenu אֱלֹהֵינוּ (יא) Adonai ואדני יאהדונהי יְהֹוָה

ת

avotenu אֲבוֹתֵינוּ ; יכה ; דמב ע"ב, מילוי ; לכב velohei וֵאלֹהֵי

ק

(Chochmah) Avraham אַבְרָהָם יכה ; דמב ע"ב, מילוי Elohei אֱלֹהֵי
אותיות פשוטות וט"ז עסמ"ב (אברים), רמ"ז הוזכמה, נתיבות ול"ב רי"ו אל, וז"פ

ש ע

ד"פ בן (Binah) Yitzchak יִצְחָק יכה ; דמב ע"ב, מילוי Elohei אֱלֹהֵי

ז ט

איהדונויה יאהדונהי הויות, ז' (Da'at) Yaakov יַעֲקֹב יכה ; דמב ע"ב, מילוי לכב velohei וֵאלֹהֵי

THE AMIDAH

"My Lord, open my lips, and my mouth shall relate Your praise." (Psalms 51:17)

THE FIRST BLESSING

Blessed are You, Lord,
our God and God of our forefathers: the God of Abraham, the God of Isaac, and the God of Jacob.

הָאֵל haEl ; יא"י (מילוי דס"ג) ; לאה ; האל הגדול = סיט ; גדול = להוו hagadol הַגָּדוֹל

וְהַנּוֹרָא vehanora ר"ת ההה hagibor הַגִּבּוֹר עם ד' אותיות = מבה, יזל, אום

אֵל El יא"י (מילוי דס"ג) ; ר"ת ע"ב, ריבוע יהוה עֶלְיוֹן elyon

גּוֹמֵל gomel וְחֲסָדִים chasadim טוֹבִים tovim קוֹנֶה kone הַכֹּל hakol ילי

וְזוֹכֵר vezocher חַסְדֵּי chasdei אָבוֹת avot וּמֵבִיא umevi

גּוֹאֵל go'el לִבְנֵי livnei בְּנֵיהֶם venehem לְמַעַן lema'an

שְׁמוֹ shemo מהשע ע"ה, ע"ב בריבוע וקס"א ע"ה, אל שדי ע"ה בְּאַהֲבָה be'ahava אוזד, דאה:

When saying the word "be'ahava" you should meditate to devote your soul to sanctify the Holy Name and accept upon yourself the four forms of death.

מֶלֶךְ melech עוֹזֵר ozer וּמוֹשִׁיעַ umoshi'a וּמָגֵן umagen

ג"פ אל (יא"י מילוי דס"ג) ; ר"ת מיכאל גבריאל נוריאל:

Bend your knees at "baruch," bow at "Ata" and straighten up at "Adonai."

אהיה יהו יְהֹוָה

בָּרוּךְ baruch אַתָּה Ata יְהֹוָה(יֱהֹוִה)יאהדונהי Adonai (הד)

מָגֵן magen אַבְרָהָם Avraham ג"פ אל (יא"י מילוי דס"ג) ; ר"ת מיכאל גבריאל נוריאל

וֹ"פ אל, רי"ו ול"ב נתיבות החוכמה, רמ"וז (אברים), עסמ"ב וט"ז אותיות פשוטות:

The great, mighty and Awesome God.

The Supernal God, Who bestows beneficial kindness and creates everything. Who recalls the kindness of the forefathers and brings a Redeemer to their descendants for the sake of His Name, lovingly. King, Helper, Savior and Shield. Blessed are You, Lord, the shield of Abraham.

THE SECOND BLESSING

THE ENERGY OF ISAAC IGNITES THE POWER FOR THE RESURRECTION OF THE DEAD.

Whereas Abraham represents the power of sharing, Isaac represents the Left Column energy of Judgment. Judgment shortens the *tikkun* process and paves the way for our eventual resurrection.

Gevurah that becomes *Binah.*

In this section there are 49 words corresponding to the 49 Gates of the Pure System in *Binah*.

ללה Adonai אֲדֹנָי רביעו ס"ג וי' אותיות דס"ג le'olam לְעוֹלָם gibor גִּבּוֹר Ata אַתָּה

(ר"ת אגלא והוא שם גדול ואמיץ, ובו היה יהודה מתגבר על אויביו. ע"ה אלד, בוכו). lehoshi'a לְהוֹשִׁיעַ rav רַב Ata אַתָּה metim מֵתִים ס"ג mechaye מְחַיֵּה

יוד הא ואו, כוזו, מספר אותיות דמילוּאי עסמ"ב ; ר"ת מ"ה: hatal הַטָּל morid מוֹרִיד

If you mistakenly say "Mashiv haru'ach," and realize this before the end of the blessing "baruch Ata Adonai," you should return to the beginning of the blessing "Ata gibor" and continue as usual. But if you only realize this after the end of the blessing, you should start the Amidah from the beginning.

bechesed בְּחֶסֶד אהיה אהיה יהוה, בינה ע"ה chayim וְחַיִּים mechalkel מְכַלְכֵּל

berachamim בְּרַחֲמִים מֵתִים metim ס"ג mechaye מְחַיֵּה יהוה. ע"ב, רביעו ס"ג

somech סוֹמֵךְ (טלא דעתיקא) rabim רַבִּים י"פ יי אלהים דההין, מצפצ, (במוכסו)

cholim חוֹלִים verofe וְרוֹפֵא (זו"ן) noflim נוֹפְלִים אדני רביעו כוכ, (אכדטם)

umekayem וּמְקַיֵּם asurim אֲסוּרִים umatir וּמַתִּיר אותיות, מ"ה וד' (וכולה =

chamocha כָּמוֹךָ ילי mi מִי afar עָפָר lishenei לִישֵׁנֵי emunato אֱמוּנָתוֹ

gevurot גְּבוּרוֹת ba'al בַּעַל (you should enunciate the letter *Ayin* in the word *"ba'al"*)

memit מֵמִית melech מֶלֶךְ lach לָךְ dome דּוֹמֶה ילי umi וּמִי

yeshu'a יְשׁוּעָה umatzmi'ach וּמַצְמִיחַ (יוד הי ואו הי) ס"ג umchaye וּמְחַיֶּה

metim מֵתִים lehachayot לְהַחֲיוֹת Ata אַתָּה vene'eman וְנֶאֱמָן

אהיה יהו יהוה

Adonai יְהֹוָאדֹנִי(יְהֹוִה)(אֲדֹנָי אהדונהי)יאהדונהי Ata אַתָּה baruch בָּרוּךְ

hametim הַמֵּתִים (יוד הי ואו הי) ס"ג mechaye מְחַיֶּה ר"ת מ"ה וס"ת מ"ה:

THE SECOND BLESSING

You are mighty forever, Lord. You resurrect the dead and are very capable of redeeming. Who causes dew to fall. You sustain life with kindness and resurrect the dead with great compassion. You support those who have fallen, heal the sick, release the imprisoned, and fulfill Your faithful words to those who are asleep in the dust. Who is like You, Master of might, and Who can compare to You, King, Who causes death, Who gives life, and Who sprouts salvation? And You are faithful to resurrecting the dead. Blessed are You, Lord, Who resurrects the dead.

THE THIRD BLESSING

This blessing connects us to Jacob, the Central Column and the power of restriction. Jacob is our channel for connecting Mercy with Judgment. By restricting our reactive behavior, we are blocking our Desire to Receive for the Self Alone. Jacob also gives us the power to balance our acts of Mercy and Judgment toward other people in our lives.

Tiferet **that becomes** *Da'at* (14 words).

אַתָּה Ata קָדוֹשׁ kadosh וְשִׁמְךָ veshimcha קָדוֹשׁ kadosh ר"ת = אור, רז, אין סוף

וּקְדוֹשִׁים ukdoshim בְּכָל bechol ב"ן, לכב יוֹם yom ע"ה נגד, מזבוח, זן, אל יהוה

יְהַלְלוּךָ yehalelucha סֶלָה sela

אהלה יהו מוצפצ

בָּרוּךְ baruch אַתָּה Ata יְהֹוָה(אדני)(יהֹואדהי)יאהדונהי Adonai

הָאֵל haEl הַקָּדוֹשׁ hakadosh (מילוי דס"ג) יא"י ; לאה י"פ מ"ה (יוד הא ואו הא):

Meditate here on the Name: יאהדונהי, as it can help to remove anger.

THE FOURTH BLESSING

In the fourth blessing – *Mekadesh haShabbat* (sanctifies the *Shabbat*), meditate to draw the *Mochin* of *Keter* to *Nukva* and this is the secret of the groom sanctifying (*Mekadesh*) the bride (*Shabbat*).

אַתָּה Ata קִדַּשְׁתָּ kidashta

אֶת et יוֹם yom ע"ה נגד, מזבוח, זן, אל יהוה הַשְּׁבִיעִי hashevi'i לִשְׁמֶךָ lishmecha

Meditate on the Holy Name: יוד הי ואו הי and then pause for few seconds.

תַּכְלִית tachlit מַעֲשֵׂה ma'ase שָׁמַיִם shamayim י"פ טל, י"פ כוזו וְאָרֶץ va'aretz

וּבֵרַכְתּוֹ uverachto מִכָּל mikol ילי הַיָּמִים hayamim נלך

וְקִדַּשְׁתּוֹ vekidashto מִכָּל mikol ילי הַזְּמַנִּים hazmanim וְכֵן vechen

כָּתוּב katuv בְּתוֹרָתֶךָ betoratach:

THE THIRD BLESSING

You are Holy, and Your Name is Holy, and the Holy Ones praise You every day,
for you are God, the Holy King Selah. Blessed are You, Lord, the Holy God.

THE FOURTH BLESSING

You have sanctified the seventh day
for Your Name's sake, as the conclusion of the creation of the Heavens and the Earth. And You have blessed it of all days, and You have sanctified it of all seasons, and it is also written in Your Torah:

VAY'CHULU

These verses from the Torah connect us to the very first *Shabbat* that occurred in the Garden of Eden. This *Shabbat* was the seed of the creation of our universe. By connecting ourselves to the original seed, we capture the force of Creation, bringing rejuvenation and renewal into our lives.

Meditate on the letter 'שׁ from the Name: שְׁקוּצִית

וַיְכֻלּוּ vay'chulu (י יה יהו יהוה) רִיבּוּעַ יהוה ,ע"ב hashamayim הַשָּׁמַיִם טֵל, י"פ כוזו י"פ

וְהָאָרֶץ veha'aretz אלהים דההין ע"ה ; ר"ת והו ; ילי vechol וְכָל־ tzeva'am צְבָאָם ס"ת צלב:

וַיְכַל vaychal אלהים Elohim אהיה אדני ; ילה bayom בַּיּוֹם נגד, מזבוז, זן, אל יהוה ע"ה

hashevi'i הַשְּׁבִיעִי melachto מְלַאכְתּוֹ asher אֲשֶׁר asa עָשָׂה

וַיִּשְׁבֹּת vayishbot bayom בַּיּוֹם נגד, מזבוז, זן, אל יהוה ע"ה hashevi'i הַשְּׁבִיעִי

מִכָּל־ mikol melachto מְלַאכְתּוֹ asher אֲשֶׁר asa עָשָׂה: וַיְבָרֶךְ vayvarech

אֱלֹהִים Elohim אהיה אדני ; ילה ; אֶת־ et (שמתו המלכים ז' את הברכה, למתק) עסמ"ב,

יוֹם yom נגד, מזבוז, זן, אל יהוה ע"ה hashevi'i הַשְּׁבִיעִי וַיְקַדֵּשׁ vaykadesh אֹתוֹ oto

כִּי ki vo בּוֹ shavat שָׁבַת mikol מִכָּל־ melachto מְלַאכְתּוֹ asher אֲשֶׁר

בָּרָא bara מ"ה ברבוע וע"ב ע"ה מילוי קס"א וס"ג, אדני, יהוה אלהים יהוה ,ב"ן קנ"א

אֱלֹהִים Elohim אהיה אדני ; ילה ; לַעֲשׂוֹת la'asot:

YISMECHU

"*Zecher Lema'ase Beresheet*" (Remembrance of the Work of Creation) – this verse is referring to the original *Shabbat* that occurred in the Garden of Eden. To activate the power of our *Shabbat*, we must realize that we are connecting to the primordial spiritual energy that was revealed during the first *Shabbat*. Both Einstein and Moses understood that time was an illusion. Time is like a revolving wheel. The same spoke of energy that occurred on the original *Shabbat* comes around again every week. Events do not pass by us like a one-way freight train. We move through the wheel of time, revisiting the same moments each year. The only things that change are the "set decorations" to give us the illusion of a new day, a new-year, and a new life.

Now the *Malchut* is called: וזק"ל (field) as the numerical value of the following combinations: יאהדונהי יאההויהה that are incorporated in Her now.
In "*yismechu*" there are 24 words, corresponding to the 24 *kishutei kala* (adornments of the Bride).

VAY'CHULU
"*And the Heavens and the Earth were completed and all their hosts.*
And God completed, on the seventh day, His work that He had done. And He abstained, on the seventh day, from all His work which He had done. And God blessed the seventh day and He sanctified it, for on it He had abstained from all His work which God had created to do." (Genesis 2:1-3)

yismechu יִשְׂמְחוּ vemalchutach בְּמַלְכוּתֶךָ shomrei שׁוֹמְרֵי כ״א הויות עכבתפילין

Shabbat שַׁבָּת vekor'ei וְקוֹרְאֵי oneg עֹנֶג am עַם mekadshei מְקַדְּשֵׁי

shevi'i שְׁבִיעִי kulam כֻּלָּם yisbe'u יִשְׂבְּעוּ veyit'angu וְיִתְעַנְּגוּ

mituvach מִטּוּבֶךָ vehashevi'i וְהַשְּׁבִיעִי ratzita רָצִיתָ bo בּוֹ

vekidashto וְקִדַּשְׁתּוֹ chemdat וְחֶמְדַּת yamim יָמִים נ״ך oto אוֹתוֹ karata קָרָאתָ

zecher זֵכֶר lema'ase לְמַעֲשֵׂה vereshit בְּרֵאשִׁית ר״ת מ״ב – עם בן מ״ב:

MEKADESH HASHABBAT

"Who sanctifies the Shabbat" - During the week, our battle with the negative forces in life is balanced fifty-fifty. On *Shabbat*, however, the playing field is tilted in our favor. We can therefore defeat the Satan on every *Shabbat*. For this reason, *Shabbat* is considered to be a gift. In the Game of Life, *Shabbat* is like our power play. We have an extra-man advantage.

Elohenu אֱלֹהֵינוּ ילה velohei וֵאלֹהֵי לכב ; מילוי דע״ב, דמב ; ילה

avotenu אֲבוֹתֵינוּ retze רְצֵה na נָא vimnuchatenu בִמְנוּחָתֵנוּ

kadeshenu קַדְּשֵׁנוּ bemitzvotecha בְּמִצְוֹתֶיךָ sim שִׂים chelkenu וְלְקֵנוּ

betoratach בְּתוֹרָתֶךָ sabe'enu שַׂבְּעֵנוּ mituvach מִטּוּבֶךָ same'ach שַׂמֵּחַ

nafshenu נַפְשֵׁנוּ bishu'atach בִּישׁוּעָתֶךָ vetaher וְטַהֵר libenu לִבֵּנוּ

le'ovdecha לְעָבְדְּךָ be'emet בֶּאֱמֶת פו׳, אל אדנ׳ אהיה פעמים אהיה, ז״פ ס״ג

vehanchilenu וְהַנְחִילֵנוּ Adonai יְהֹוָהאלהדונהיאהדונהי Elohenu אֱלֹהֵינוּ ילה

be'ahava בְּאַהֲבָה אוזר, דאגה uvratzon וּבְרָצוֹן מהש ע״ה, ע״ב בריבוע וקס״א ע״ה,

Shabbat שַׁבָּת ע״ה kodshecha קָדְשֶׁךָ veyanuchu וְיָנוּחוּ va בָהּ אל שדי ע״ה

The word *"va"* (בָהּ) is in a female form, because on the night of *Shabbat* the main elevation and ascent is for the *Nukva* (the female aspect), as *Zeir Anpin* (the male aspect) does not have ascent on the night of *Shabbat* (but His *Chesed*, *Gevurah*, *Tiferet* are expanded and are including His *Chochmah*, *Binah*, *Da'at*, and His *Chochmah*, *Binah*, *Da'at* are including the Surrounding *Mochin*).

YISMECHU

All those who observe the Sabbath and who call It a delight. The people who sanctify the seventh (day). They will all be satiated and delighted from Your goodness. And the seventh, You found favor in it and sanctified It. Most coveted of days, You have called it, a remembrance of the works of Creation.

MEKADESH HASHABBAT

Our God and the God of our forefathers, please desire our rest.
Sanctify us with Your commandments and grant us our share in Your Torah, satisfy us from Your goodness and gladden our souls with Your salvation, and purify our hearts to serve You sincerely. Lord, our God, with love and favor, grant us Your Holy Sabbath as a heritage, and may should rest in it

כָּל kol יְלֵי יִשְׂרָאֵל Yisrael מְקַדְשֵׁי mekadeshei שְׁמֶךָ shemecha•

אהיה יהו יה אדני

בָּרוּךְ baruch אַתָּה Ata יְהֹוָ֑ואדנילאיאהדונהי Adonai

> Meditate on the *Neshikin* (kisses - the Upper Unification),
> **from** the Ten *Sefirot* of *Chochomah* of *Keter* of the five *Partzufim* of *Netzach, Hod, Yesod* of *Chesed, Gevurah, Tiferet* of *Chochmah* of *Zeir Anpin* **to** the Ten *Sefirot* of *Chochomah* of *Keter* of the five *Partzufim* of *Netzach, Hod, Yesod* of *Chesed, Gevurah, Tiferet* of *Chochmah* of *Yaakov* and *Rachel*.

Chochmah	Da'at	Binah
א	י	ה
יהוה	יְהֹוָה מצפץ	יהוה
אֲהֲיָה	אהיה אהיה	אֲהֲיָה
יָהֹוָה	יְהֹוָה	יָהֹוָה

Meditate to draw illumination **to** *Keter* of *Yaakov* and *Rachel* (which They are now standing in *Netzach, Hod, Yesod* of *Zeir Anpin*) **from** the three *Mochin* (on the left) *Chochmah, Binah, Da'at* — of first *Gadlut* enclosed by *Netzach, Hod, Yesod* and *Chesed, Gevurah, Tiferet* of *Yisrael Saba* and *Tevunah* (which the *Mochin* are now in *Chochmah, Binah, Da'at* of *Zeir Anpin*).

Also draw *Malchut* of *Keter* of all five *Partzufim* of *Netzach, Hod, Yesod* of *Chesed, Gevurah, Tiferet* of *Binah* of the Internal of *Zeir Anpin* **to** *Keter* of all five *Partzufim* of *Netzach, Hod, Yesod* of *Chesed, Gevurah, Tiferet* of *Binah* of the Internal of *Yaakov* and *Rachel*. **Also draw** *Malchut* of *Keter* of all five *Partzufim* of *Chesed, Gevurah, Tiferet* of *Chesed, Gevurah, Tiferet* of *Binah* of the External of *Zeir Anpin* **to** *Keter* of five *Partzufim* of *Chesed, Gevurah, Tiferet* of *Chesed, Gevurah, Tiferet* of *Binah* of the External of *Yaakov* and *Rachel* (*Keter* of *Yaakov* and *Rachel* which stands in the Chest of *Zeir Anpin*):

אֲהֲיָה יְהֹוָה

(to the three Vessels of *Keter* of *Nukva*)

יוד הא ואו הה   יוד יוד הא יוד הא ואו יוד הא ואו הה   יוד הא ואו הה   יה יהו יהוה

מְקַדֵּשׁ mekadesh הַשַּׁבָּת haShabbat:

THE FINAL THREE BLESSINGS

Through the merit of Moses, Aaron and Joseph, who are our channels for the final three blessings, we are able to bring down all the spiritual energy that we aroused with our prayers and blessings.

THE FIFTH BLESSING

During this blessing, referring to Moses, we should always meditate to try to know exactly what God wants from us in our life, as signified by the phrase, "Let it be the will of God." We ask God to guide us toward the work we came to Earth to do. The Creator cannot just accept the work that we want to do; we must carry out the work we were destined to do.

Netzach

Meditate for the Supernal Desire (*Keter*) that is called *metzach haratzon* (Forehead of the Desire).

רְצֵה retze אלף למד הה יוד מם

Meditate here to transform misfortune and tragedy (צרה) into desire and acceptance (רצה).

יְהֹוָ֑ואדנילאיאהדונהי Adonai אֱלֹהֵינוּ Elohenu יְלֵה בְּעַמְּךָ be'amecha יִשְׂרָאֵל Yisrael

---

all of Israel, the sanctifiers of Your Name. Blessed are You, Lord, Who sanctifies the Sabbath.

THE FINAL THREE BLESSINGS - THE FIFTH BLESSING

Find favor, Lord, our God, in Your People, Israel,

וְלִתְפִלָּתָם velitfilatam שְׁעֵה she'e • וְהָשֵׁב vehashev הָעֲבוֹדָה ha'avoda

לִדְבִיר lidvir רי״י בֵּיתֶךָ betecha ב״פ ראה• וְאִשֵּׁי ve'ishei יִשְׂרָאֵל Yisrael

וּתְפִלָּתָם utfilatam מְהֵרָה mehera בְּאַהֲבָה be'ahava אוזר, דאגה

תְּקַבֵּל tekabel בְּרָצוֹן beratzon מהע ע״ה, ע״ב ברבוע וקס״א ע״ה, אל שדי ע״ה•

וּתְהִי ut'hi לְרָצוֹן leratzon מהע ע״ה, ע״ב ברבוע וקס״א ע״ה, אל שדי ע״ה

תָּמִיד tamid ע״ה קס״א קנ״א קמ״ג עֲבוֹדַת avodat יִשְׂרָאֵל Yisrael עַמֶּךָ amecha:

YA'ALE VEYAVO

During *Sukkot*, there is an extra surge of spiritual energy in our midst. "Ya'ale Veyavo" is our antenna for drawing this extra power into our lives.

If you mistakenly forgot to say "*ya'ale veyavo*," and realize this before the end of the blessing "*baruch Ata Adonai*," you should return to say "*ya'ale veyavo*" and continue as usual. If you realize this after the end of the blessing "*hamachazir shechinato leTziyon*" but before you start the next blessing "*modim*" you should say "*ya'ale veyavo*" there and continue as usual. If you only realize this after you have started the next blessing "*modim*" but before the second "*yih'yu leratzon*" (on pg. 698) you should return to "*retze*" (pg. 692) and continue from there. If you realize this after the second "*yih'yu leratzon*" you should start the *Amidah* from the beginning.

אֱלֹהֵינוּ Elohenu ילה וֵאלֹהֵי velohei ילה ; מילוי ע״ב, דמב ; ילה לכב וַאֲבוֹתֵינוּ avotenu

יַעֲלֶה ya'ale וְיָבֹא veyavo וְיַגִּיעַ veyagi'a וְיֵרָאֶה veyera'e רי״ו וְיֵרָצֶה veyeratze

וְיִשָּׁמַע veyishama וְיִפָּקֵד veyipaked וְיִזָּכֵר veyizacher ר״ת מ״ב (ז״פ ו׳)

זִכְרוֹנֵנוּ zichronenu וְזִכְרוֹן vezichron ע״ב קס״א וגש״ב אֲבוֹתֵינוּ avotenu•

זִכְרוֹן zichron ע״ב קס״א וגש״ב יְרוּשָׁלַיִם Yerushalayim עִירָךְ irach•

וְזִכְרוֹן vezichron ע״ב קס״א וגש״ב מָשִׁיחַ mashi'ach בֶּן ben דָּוִד David עָ״ה כהת ; בן

וְזִכְרוֹן vezichron ע״ב קס״א וגש״ב עַבְדָּךְ avdach פוי, אל אדני• כֹּל kol

עַמֶּךָ amecha בֵּית bet ב״פ ראה יִשְׂרָאֵל Yisrael לְפָנֶיךָ lefanecha ס״ג מ״ה בן

לִפְלֵיטָה lifleta לְטוֹבָה letova אכא• לְחֵן lechen מילוי דמ״ה ברבוע, מוזי

לְחֶסֶד lechesed ע״ב, ריבוע יהוה וּלְרַחֲמִים ulrachamim•

---

and turn to their prayer.
Restore the service to the Inner Sanctuary of Your Temple. Accept the offerings of Israel and their prayer with favor, speedily, and with love. May the service of Your People Israel always be favorable to You.

YA'ALE VEYAVO

Our God and God of our forefathers, may it rise, come, arrive, appear, find favor, be heard, be considered, and be remembered, our remembrance and the remembrance of our forefathers: The remembrance of Jerusalem, Your City, and the remembrance of Mashiach, Son of David, Your servant, and the remembrance of Your entire Nation, the House of Israel, before You for deliverance, for good, for grace,

וּלְעוֹלָם ulshalom • טוֹבִים tovim ע"ה, בִּינָה יהוה, אֶהְיֶה אֶהְיֶה lechayim לְחַיִּים

וְהוּ hazeh הַזֶּה haSukkot הַסֻּכּוֹת chag וְחַג אֶל יהוה: זֶן, מִזְבּוּוֹ, נֶגֶד ע"ה beyom בְּיוֹם

וְהוּ • hazeh הַזֶּה kodesh קֹדֶשׁ mikra מִקְרָא אֶל יהוה זֶן, מִזְבּוּוֹ, נֶגֶד ע"ה beyom בְּיוֹם

אוֹתִיּוֹת וט"ז עסמ"ב (אברים), רמ"ז הַחָכְמָה נְתִיבוֹת ול"ב רִי"ו אל, וח"פ אברהם, lerachem לְרַחֵם

zochrenu זָכְרֵנוּ • ulhoshi'enu וּלְהוֹשִׁיעֵנוּ alenu עָלֵינוּ bo בּוֹ פְּשׁוּטוֹת

אכא • letova לְטוֹבָה bo בּוֹ ילה Elohenu אֱלֹהֵינוּ Adonai אֲדֹנָיאהדונהי יְהוָה

vo בּוֹ vehoshi'enu וְהוֹשִׁיעֵנוּ • livracha לִבְרָכָה vo בּוֹ ufokdenu וּפָקְדֵנוּ

ראה bidvar בִּדְבַר • tovim טוֹבִים ע"ה בִּינָה יהוה, אֶהְיֶה אֶהְיֶה lechayim לְחַיִּים

vechonenu וְחָנֵּנוּ chus וְחוּס • verachamim וְרַחֲמִים yeshu'a יְשׁוּעָה

(אברים), רמ"ז הַחָכְמָה נְתִיבוֹת ול"ב רִי"ו אל, וח"פ אברהם, verachem וְרַחֵם vachamol וַחֲמוֹל

vehoshi'enu וְהוֹשִׁיעֵנוּ • alenu עָלֵינוּ פְּשׁוּטוֹת אוֹתִיּוֹת וט"ז עסמ"ב

(מילוי דס"ג) יא"י El אֵל ki כִּי • מ"ה רִיבוּע enenu עֵינֵינוּ elecha אֵלֶיךָ ki כִּי

Ata אַתָּה verachum וְרַחוּם chanun חַנּוּן melech מֶלֶךְ

• harabim הָרַבִּים verachamecha בְּרַחֲמֶךָ veAta וְאַתָּה

vetechezena וְתֶחֱזֶינָה vetirtzenu וְתִרְצֵנוּ banu בָּנוּ tachpotz תַּחְפֹּץ

קָנאה הֱיוֹת, ר יוֹסֵף, leTziyon לְצִיּוֹן beshuvcha בְּשׁוּבְךָ מ"ה רִיבוּע enenu עֵינֵינוּ

י"פ יי"י דיודין, אלהים מצפץ, berachamim בְּרַחֲמִים

אהיה יהו אל

Adonai יְהוָהאֲדֹנָיאהדונהי Ata אַתָּה baruch בָּרוּךְ

קָנאה הֱיוֹת, ר יוֹסֵף, leTziyon לְצִיּוֹן shechinato שְׁכִינָתוֹ hamachazir הַמַּחֲזִיר

---

kindness, and compassion, for a good life, and for peace on the day of: This festival of Sukkot, on this Holy Day of Convocation. To take pity on us and to save us. Remember us, Lord, our God, on this day, for good; consider us on it for blessing; and deliver us on it for a good life, with the words of deliverance and mercy. Take pity and be gracious to us, have mercy and be compassionate with us, and save us, for our eyes turn to You, because You are God, the King Who is gracious and compassionate. And You in Your great compassion take delight in us and are pleased with us. May our eyes witness Your return to Zion with compassion. Blessed are You, Lord, Who returns His Shechinah to Zion.

THE SIXTH BLESSING

This blessing is our thank you. Kabbalistically, the biggest "thank you" we can give the Creator is to do exactly what we are supposed to do in terms of our spiritual work.

Hod

Bow your entire body at "*modim*" and straighten up at "*Adonai*."

lach לָךְ anachnu אֲנַחְנוּ כל יום לאמרם דוד שתיקן ברכות מאה modim מוֹדִים

Elohenu אֱלֹהֵינוּ (ו"ג) Adonai יְהֹוָה hu הוּא sheAta שָׁאַתָּה

le'olam לְעוֹלָם avotenu אֲבוֹתֵינוּ velohei וֵאלֹהֵי

tzur צוּר tzurenu צוּרֵנוּ va'ed וָעֶד

umagen וּמָגֵן chayenu חַיֵּינוּ

node נוֹדֶה vador וָדֹר ledor לְדֹר hu הוּא Ata אַתָּה yish'enu יִשְׁעֵנוּ

chayenu וְחַיֵּינוּ al עַל tehilatecha תְּהִלָּתֶךָ unsaper וּנְסַפֵּר lecha לָךְ

nishmotenu נִשְׁמוֹתֵינוּ ve'al וְעַל beyadecha בְּיָדֶךָ hamesurim הַמְּסוּרִים

shebechol שֶׁבְּכָל nisecha נִסֶּיךָ ve'al וְעַל lach לָךְ hapekudot הַפְּקוּדוֹת

yom יוֹם imanu עִמָּנוּ

shebechol שֶׁבְּכָל vetovotecha וְטוֹבוֹתֶיךָ nifle'otecha נִפְלְאוֹתֶיךָ ve'al וְעַל

hatov הַטּוֹב vetzahorayim וְצָהֳרַיִם vavoker וָבֹקֶר erev עֶרֶב et עֵת

hamerachem הַמְרַחֵם rachamecha רַחֲמֶיךָ chalu כָלוּ lo לֹא ki כִּי

lo לֹא ki כִּי

lach לָךְ kivinu קִוִּינוּ me'olam מֵעוֹלָם ki כִּי chasadecha חֲסָדֶיךָ tamu תַמּוּ

THE SIXTH BLESSING

We give thanks to You, for it is You, Lord, Who is our God and God of our forefathers, forever and for all eternity. You are our Rock, the Rock of our lives, and the Shield of our salvation. From one generation to another, we shall give thanks to You and we shall tell of Your praise. For our lives that are entrusted in Your hands, for our souls that are in Your care, for Your miracles that are with us every day, and for Your wonders and Your favors that are with us at all times: evening, morning and afternoon. You are the good One, for Your compassion has never ceased. You are the compassionate One, for Your kindness has never ended, for we have always placed our hope in You.

ve'al וְעַל   kulam כָּלָם   yitbarach יִתְבָּרַךְ   veyitromam וְיִתְרוֹמָם

veyitnase וְיִתְנַשֵּׂא tamid תָּמִיד ע״ה קס״ה קס״א קנ״א קמ״ג shimcha שִׁמְךָ

malkenu מַלְכֵּנוּ le'olam לְעוֹלָם רִיבּוּעַ ס״ג ו״י אותיות דס״ג va'ed וָעֶד◆

vechol וְכָל־ hachayim הַחַיִּים יל׳ אהיה אהיה יהוה, בינה ע״ה yoducha יוֹדוּךָ sela סֶלָה:

et אֶת־ vivarchu וִיבָרְכוּ יהוה רִיבּוּעַ יהוה מ״ה vihalelu וִיהַלְלוּ

be'emet בֶּאֱמֶת hagadol הַגָּדוֹל לְהוּ ; עִם ד׳ אותיות = מבה, יכל, אום shimcha שִׁמְךָ

ki כִּי tov טוֹב רִיבּוּעַ ס״ג ו״י אותיות דס״ג ז״פ ס״ג אהיה פעמים אהיה le'olam לְעוֹלָם ; והו

yeshu'atenu יְשׁוּעָתֵנוּ haEl הָאֵל לאה ; יא״י (מילוי דס״ג) יכל, מבה, אום, אהיה = יהוה; כי טוב

ve'ezratenu וְעֶזְרָתֵנוּ sela סֶלָה haEl הָאֵל◆ לאה ; יא״י (מילוי דס״ג) hatov הַטּוֹב והו:

Bend your knees at "baruch," bow at "Ata" and straighten up at "Adonai."

אהיה יהו אלהים

baruch בָּרוּךְ Ata אַתָּה יְהֹוָהאדני Adonai (הי) hatov הַטּוֹב והו

shimcha שִׁמְךָ ulcha וּלְךָ na'e נָאֶה lehodot לְהוֹדוֹת ס״ת כהת, משיוו בן דוד ע״ה:

THE FINAL BLESSING

We are emanating the energy of peace to the entire world. We also make it our intent to use our mouths only for good. Kabbalistically, the power of words and speech is unimaginable. We hope to use that power wisely, which is perhaps one of the most difficult tasks we have to carry out.

Yesod

sim שִׂים shalom שָׁלוֹם

tova טוֹבָה uvracha וּבְרָכָה אכא chayim וְחַיִּים אהיה אהיה יהוה, בינה ע״ה

chen חֵן מילוי דמ״ה ברִיבּוּעַ, מוזי vachesed וָחֶסֶד ע״ב, רִיבּוּעַ יהוה

tzedaka צְדָקָה ע״ה רִיבּוּעַ אלהים verachamim וְרַחֲמִים alenu עָלֵינוּ

And for all those things, may Your Name be always blessed, exalted and extolled, our King, forever and ever, and all the living shall thank You, Selah. And they shall praise and bless Your Great Name, sincerely and forever, for It is good, the God of our salvation and our help, Selah, the good God. Blessed are You, Lord, whose Name is good, and to You it is befitting to give thanks.

THE FINAL BLESSING

Place peace, goodness, blessing, life, grace, kindness, righteousness, and mercy upon us

וְעַל ve'al — כָּל kol ; עמם ; ילי — יִשְׂרָאֵל Yisrael — עַמֶּךָ amecha — וּבָרְכֵנוּ uvarchenu

אָבִינוּ avinu — כְּאֶחָד ke'echad — אהבה, דאגה — כֻּלָּנוּ kulanu — בְּאוֹר be'or — רו, א"ס

פָּנֶיךָ panecha — ס"ג מ"ה ב"ן — כִּי ki — בְאוֹר ve'or — רו, א"ס — פָנֶיךָ panecha — ס"ג מ"ה ב"ן

נָתַתָּ natata — לָנוּ lanu — אלהים, אהיה ארני — יְהֹוָה Adonai

אֱלֹהֵינוּ Elohenu — ילה — תּוֹרָה torah — וְחַיִּים vechayim — אהיה אהיה יהוה, בינה ע"ה

אַהֲבָה ahava — אוזר, דאגה — וָחֶסֶד vachesed — ע"ב, ריבוע יהוה

צְדָקָה tzedaka — ע"ה ריבוע אלהים — וְרַחֲמִים verachamim — בְּרָכָה beracha

וְשָׁלוֹם veshalom — יהו — וְטוֹב vetov — בְּעֵינֶיךָ be'enecha — ע"ה קס"א ; ריבוע מ"ה

לְבָרְכֵנוּ levarchenu — וּלְבָרֵךְ ulvarech — אֶת et — כָּל kol — ילי — עַמְּךָ amecha

יִשְׂרָאֵל Yisrael — בְּרוֹב berov — י"פ — אהיה — עֹז oz — וְשָׁלוֹם veshalom

אהיה יהו מצפצ

בָּרוּךְ baruch — אַתָּה Ata — יֻוֹדֵהֵוָואֵהֵדֹוָנֵהֵיֵאֵהֲדֹונֵהֵי — יְהֹוָה Adonai

הַמְבָרֵךְ hamevarech — אֶת et — עַמּוֹ amo — יִשְׂרָאֵל Yisrael

ר"ת = אלהים (אילההויהם) = יב"ק — בְּשָׁלוֹם bashalom — אָמֵן amen — יאהדונהי

YIH'YU LERATZON

There are 42 letters in the verse in the secret of *Ana Beko'ach*.

יִהְיוּ yih'yu — אל (ייא"י מילוי דס"ג) מהש ע"ה, ע"ב בריבוע וקס"א ע"ה, אל עדי ע"ה — לְרָצוֹן leratzon

אִמְרֵי imrei — פִי fi — ר"ת אלף = אלף למד עיין יוד ע"ה — וְהֶגְיוֹן vehegyon — לִבִּי libi

לְפָנֶיךָ lefanecha — ס"ג מ"ה ב"ן — יְהֹוָה Adonai — צוּרִי tzuri — וְגֹאֲלִי vego'ali

---

and upon all of Israel, Your People. Bless us all as one, our Father, with the Light of Your Countenance, because it is with the Light of Your Countenance that You, Lord, our God, have given us Torah and life, love and kindness, righteousness and mercy, blessing and peace. May it be good in Your Eyes to bless us and to bless Your entire Nation, Israel, with abundant power and with peace. Blessed are You, Lord, Who blesses His Nation, Israel, with peace, Amen.

YIH'YU LERATZON

"May the utterances of my mouth and the thoughts of my heart find favor before You, Lord, my Rock and my Redeemer." (Psalms 19:15)

ELOHAI NETZOR

אֱלֹהַי Elohai מילוי ע"ב, דמב ; ילה netzor נְצֹור leshoni לְשׁוֹנִי mera מֵרָע◆

וְשִׂפְתוֹתַי vesiftotai midaber מִדַּבֵּר ראה mirma מִרְמָה◆ velimkalelai וְלִמְקַלְלַי

נַפְשִׁי nafshi tidom תִדֹּם◆ venafshi וְנַפְשִׁי ke'afar כֶּעָפָר

לַכֹּל lakol יה אדני תִהְיֶה tih'ye◆ patach פָּתַח petach לִבִּי libi betoratecha בְּתוֹרָתֶךָ◆

וְאַחֲרֵי ve'acharei mitzvotecha מִצְוֹתֶיךָ tirdof תִרְדּוֹף nafshi נַפְשִׁי◆

וְכָל־ vechol יל הַקָּמִים hakamim עָלַי alai לְרָעָה lera'a רהע◆ מְהֵרָה mehera

הָפֵר hafer עֲצָתָם atzatam וְקַלְקֵל vekalkel מַחְשְׁבוֹתָם machshevotam◆

עֲשֵׂה ase לְמַעַן lema'an שְׁמָךְ shemach◆ לְמַעַן lema'an עֲשֵׂה ase

עֲשֵׂה ase◆ yeminach יְמִינֶךָ◆ עֲשֵׂה ase לְמַעַן lema'an toratach תוֹרָתָךְ◆

לְמַעַן lema'an kedushatach קְדֻשָּׁתֶךָ◆ ר"ת הפסוק = מ"ה יהוה לְמַעַן lema'an

יְחַלְצוּן yechaltzun yedidecha יְדִידֶיךָ ר"ת ילי hoshi'a הוֹשִׁיעָה יהוה וש"ע נהורין

יְמִינֶךָ yemincha va'aneni וַעֲנֵנִי (כתיב : וְעֵנֵנוּ) ר"ת אל (ייא"י מילוי דס"ג)❖

Before we recite the next verse "*Yih'yu leratzon*" we have an opportunity to strengthen our connection to our soul using our name. Each person has a verse in the Torah that connects to their name. Either their name is in the verse, or the first and last letters of the name correspond to the first or last letters of a verse. For example, the name Yehuda begins with a *Yud* and ends with a *Hei*. Before we end the *Amidah*, we state that our name will always be remembered when our soul leaves this world.

YIH'YU LERATZON (THE SECOND)
There are 42 letters in the verse in the secret of *Ana Beko'ach*.

יִהְיוּ yih'yu אל (ייא"י מילוי דס"ג) leratzon לְרָצוֹן מהטע ע"ה, ע"ב ברבוע וקס"א וקס"א ע"ה, אל שדי ע"ה

אִמְרֵי imrei פִי fi ר"ת אֶלֶף = אלף למד מם שׂין דלת יוד ע"ה vehegyon וְהֶגְיוֹן libi לִבִּי

לְפָנֶיךָ lefanecha ס"ג מ"ה בן יְהֹוָ֒ה אדניאיאהדונהי Adonai tzuri צוּרִי vego'ali וְגֹאֲלִי❖

ELOHAI NETZOR

My God, guard my tongue from evil and my lips from speaking deceit. To those who curse me, let my spirit remain silent, and let my spirit be as dust for everyone. Open my heart to Your Torah and let my heart pursue Your commandments. All those who rise against me to do me harm, speedily nullify their plans and disturb their thoughts. Do so for the sake of Your Name. Do so for the sake of Your Right. Do so for the sake of Your Torah. Do so for the sake of Your Holiness, "So that Your loved ones may be saved. Redeem Your Right and answer me." (Psalms 60:7)

YIH'YU LERATZON (THE SECOND)
"May the utterances of my mouth and the thoughts of my heart find favor before You, Lord, my Rock and my Redeemer." (Psalms 19:15)

OSE SHALOM

You take three steps backward;

shalom שָׁלוֹם ose עוֹשֶׂה

Left
You turn to the left and say:

בִּמְרוֹמָיו bimromav ר"ת ע"ב, ריבוע יהוה

ya'ase יַעֲשֶׂה verachamav בְּרַחֲמָיו hu הוּא

Right
You turn to the right and say:

שָׁלוֹם ר"ת ש"ע נהורין alenu עָלֵינוּ shalom שָׁלוֹם

Center
You face the center and say:

Yisrael יִשְׂרָאֵל amo עַמּוֹ ; עמם יל kol כָּל ve'al וְעַל

amen אָמֵן יאהדונהי ve'imru וְאִמְרוּ

yehi יְהִי ratzon רָצוֹן מהש ע"ה, ע"ב בריבוע וקס"א ע"ב, מהש ע"ה אל שדי ע"ה

milfanecha מִלְפָנֶיךָ ס"ג מ"ה ב"ן יְהֹוָואדניל יאהדונהי ב"ן מ"ה Adonai יהוה Elohenu אֱלֹהֵינוּ ילה

shetivne שֶׁתִבְנֶה ,avotenu אֲבוֹתֵינוּ ילה ; מילוי ע"ב, דמב לכב velohei וֵאלֹהֵי

veyamenu בְיָמֵינוּ bimhera בִּמְהֵרָה hamikdash הַמִקְדָּש ע"ב ב"פ ראה bet בֵּית

chukei וְחֻקֵי la'asot לַעֲשׂוֹת betoratach בְתוֹרָתֶךָ chelkenu וְחֶלְקֵנוּ veten וְתֵן

shalem שָׁלֵם ביכו belevav בְּלֵבָב פוי, אל אדני ul'ovdach וּלְעָבְדֶּךָ retzonach רְצוֹנֶךָ

You take three steps forward.

Continue with *"Birkat Me'en Sheva"* on page 111 until page 123.

OSE SHALOM

He, Who makes peace in His High Places, He, in His compassion, shall make peace upon us.
And upon His entire nation, Israel, and you shall say, Amen.

May it be pleasing before You,
Lord, our God and God of our forefathers, that You shall rebuild the Temple speedily, in our days, and place our lot in Your Torah, so that we may fulfill the laws of Your desire and serve You wholeheartedly.

THE AMIDAH OF SHACHARIT OF SHABBAT AND CHOL HAMO'ED

yagid יַגִּיד ufi וּפִי tiftach תִּפְתָּח sefatai שְׂפָתַי (pause here) לכה Adonai אֲדֹנָי

יוז (כ"ב אותיות פשוטות [=אכא] וה' אותיות סופיות מנצפ"ך) ס"ת = בוכו: tehilatecha תְּהִלָּתֶךָ

THE FIRST BLESSING - INVOKES THE SHIELD OF ABRAHAM.

Abraham is the channel of the Right Column energy of positivity, sharing, and Mercy. Sharing actions can protect us from all forms of negativity.

Chesed that becomes *Chochmah*

In this section there are 42 words, the secret of the 42-Letter Name of God and therefore it begins with the letter *Bet* (2) and ends with the letter *Mem* (40).

Bend your knees at "*baruch*," bow at "*Ata*" and straighten up at "*Adonai*."

המלכות לה' המגיע העשפע את המסמלות האא"ב (אותיות האא"ב) א-ת Ata אַתָּה baruch בָּרוּךְ

יולה Elohenu אֱלֹהֵינוּ (י"א) Adonai אהדונהי אלהינו יְהֹוָה

•avotenu אֲבוֹתֵינוּ יולה ; דמב, ע"ב, מילוי ; לכב velohei וֵאלֹהֵי

(*Chochmah*) Avraham אַבְרָהָם יולה ; דמב, ע"ב, מילוי Elohei אֱלֹהֵי

פשוטות אותיות וט"ז עסמ"ב (אברים), רמ"ח, הוזכמה נתיבות ול"ב רי"ו אל, ו"פ

(*Binah*) Yitzchak יִצְחָק יולה ; דמב, ע"ב, מילוי Elohei אֱלֹהֵי ד"פ ב"ן

(*Da'at*) Yaakov יַעֲקֹב יולה ; דמב ע"ב מילוי ; לכב velohei וֵאלֹהֵי הויות, יאהדונהי אידהנויה ז'

THE AMIDAH OF SHACHARIT OF SHABBAT AND CHOL HAMO'ED

"My Lord, open my lips, and my mouth shall relate Your praise." (Psalms 51:17)

THE FIRST BLESSING

Blessed are You, Lord,

our God and God of our forefathers: the God of Abraham, the God of Isaac, and the God of Jacob.

haEl הָאֵל ; לאה (מילוי דס"ג) יא"י ; האל הגדול hagadol הַגָּדוֹל האל הגדול = סיט ; גדול = להו

vehanora וְהַנּוֹרָא רֹה ההה ר"ת hagibor הַגִּבּוֹר עם ד' אותיות = מבה, יזל, אום

elyon עֶלְיוֹן יהוה ריבוע ע"ב, ר"ת ; (מילוי דס"ג) יא"י El אֵל

hakol הַכֹּל kone קוֹנֶה tovim טוֹבִים chasadim וַחֲסָדִים gomel גּוֹמֵל

umevi וּמֵבִיא avot אָבוֹת chasdei וְחַסְדֵי vezocher וְזוֹכֵר

lema'an לְמַעַן venehem בְּנֵיהֶם livnei לִבְנֵי go'el גּוֹאֵל

shemo שְׁמוֹ מהטע ע"ה, ע"ב בריבוע וקס"א ע"ה, אל שדי ע"ה be'ahava בְּאַהֲבָה אוזר, דאגה:

When saying the word "be'ahava" you should meditate to devote your soul to sanctify the Holy Name and accept upon yourself the four forms of death.

umagen וּמָגֵן umoshi'a וּמוֹשִׁיעַ ozer עוֹזֵר melech מֶלֶךְ

ג"פ אל (יא"י מילוי דס"ג) ; ר"ת מיכאל גבריאל נוריאל:

Bend your knees at "baruch," bow at "Ata" and straighten up at "Adonai."

אהיה יהו יְהֹוָה

(הד) Adonai יַהֲדֹוָנַהֵי(יְהֹוַאֲדֹנָהֵי)יאהדונהי Ata אַתָּה baruch בָּרוּךְ

Avraham אַבְרָהָם ג"פ אל (יא"י מילוי דס"ג) ; ר"ת מיכאל גבריאל נוריאל magen מָגֵן

וז"פ אל, רי"ו ול"ב נתיבות הוזכמה, רמ"וז (אברים), עסמ"ב וט"ו אותיות פשוטות:

The great, mighty and Awesome God.

The Supernal God, Who bestows beneficial kindness and creates everything. Who recalls the kindness of the forefathers and brings a Redeemer to their descendants for the sake of His Name, lovingly. King, Helper, Savior and Shield. Blessed are You, Lord, the shield of Abraham.

THE SECOND BLESSING

THE ENERGY OF ISAAC IGNITES THE POWER FOR THE RESURRECTION OF THE DEAD.

Whereas Abraham represents the power of sharing, Isaac represents the Left Column energy of Judgment. Judgment shortens the *tikkun* process and paves the way for our eventual resurrection.

Gevurah that becomes *Binah*.

In this section there are 49 words corresponding to the 49 Gates of the Pure System in *Binah*.

ללה Adonai אֲדֹנָי ריבוע ס"ג וי' אותיות דס"ג le'olam לְעוֹלָם gibor גִּבּוֹר Ata אַתָּה

(ר"ת אֲגְלָא והוא שם גדול ואמיץ, ובו היה יהודה מתגבר על אויביו. ע"ה אלד', בוכו).

lehoshi'a לְהוֹשִׁיעַ rav רַב Ata אַתָּה metim מֵתִים ס"ג mechaye מְחַיֵּה

morid מוֹרִיד hatal הַטָּל יוד הא ואו, כוזו, מספר אותיות דמילואי עסמ"ב ; ר"ת מ"ה:

If you mistakenly say "Mashiv haru'ach," and realize this before the end of the blessing "baruch Ata Adonai," you should return to the beginning of the blessing "Ata gibor" and continue as usual. But if you only realize this after the end of the blessing, you should start the Amidah from the beginning.

bechesed בְּחֶסֶד ע"ה בינה אהיה יהוה, אהיה chayim וְחַיִּים mechalkel מְכַלְכֵּל

berachamim בְּרַחֲמִים metim מֵתִים ס"ג mechaye מְחַיֵּה יהוה. ע"ב, ריבוע

somech סוֹמֵךְ (טלא דעתיק) rabim רַבִּים י"פ ייי אלהים דההין, מצפצ (במוכסז)

cholim חוֹלִים verofe וְרוֹפֵא (זו"ן) noflim נוֹפְלִים כוק, ריבוע אדני (אכדטם)

umekayem וּמְקַיֵּם asurim אֲסוּרִים umatir וּמַתִּיר מ"ה יוד ד' אותיות. וזולה = מ"ה

chamocha כָּמוֹךְ mi מִי ילי afar עָפָר lishenei לִישֵׁנֵי emunato אֱמוּנָתוֹ

gevurot גְּבוּרוֹת ba'al בַּעַל (you should enunciate the letter *Ayin* in the word "*ba'al*")

memit מֵמִית melech מֶלֶךְ lach לָךְ dome דּוֹמֶה umi וּמִי ילי

yeshu'a יְשׁוּעָה umatzmi'ach וּמַצְמִיחַ (יוד הי ואו הי) ס"ג umchaye וּמְחַיֵּה

metim מֵתִים lehachayot לְהַחֲיוֹת Ata אַתָּה vene'eman וְנֶאֱמָן

אהיה יהו יהוה

Adonai יְהֹוָה(יְהֹוָאדֹנִי)(אהדונהי) Ata אַתָּה baruch בָּרוּךְ

hametim הַמֵּתִים (יוד הי ואו הי) ס"ג mechaye מְחַיֵּה ר"ת מ"ה וס"ת מ"ה:

THE SECOND BLESSING

You are mighty forever, Lord. You resurrect the dead and are very capable of redeeming. Who causes dew to fall. You sustain life with kindness and resurrect the dead with great compassion. You support those who have fallen, heal the sick, release the imprisoned, and fulfill Your faithful words to those who are asleep in the dust. Who is like You, Master of might, and Who can compare to You, King, Who causes death, Who gives life, and Who sprouts salvation? And You are faithful to resurrecting the dead. Blessed are You, Lord, Who resurrects the dead.

ز

NAKDISHACH

נַקְדִּישָׁךְ nakdishach וְנַעֲרִיצָךְ vena'aritzach •

שַׂרְפֵי sarfei האא י"פ מ"כ, סוד sod שִׂיחַ si'ach כְּנֹעַם keno'am

קֹדֶשׁ kodesh הַמְּשַׁלְּשִׁים hameshaleshim לְךָ lecha קְדֻשָּׁה kedusha •

וְכֵן vechen כָּתוּב katuv עַל al יַד yad נְבִיאָךְ nevi'ach • וְקָרָא vekara

זֶה ze אֶל el זֶה ze י"ב פרקין דיעקב מאירים לי"ב פרקין דרחל וְאָמַר ve'amar:

קָדוֹשׁ | kadosh קָדוֹשׁ kadosh קָדוֹשׁ kadosh (סוד ג' רישין דעתיקא קדישא)

יָיְ/אדני/אהדונהי Adonai צְבָאוֹת Tzeva'ot פני שכינה מְלֹא melo כָּל chol יל"י

הָאָרֶץ ha'aretz אלהים דההין ע"ה כְּבוֹדוֹ kevodo:

לְעֻמָּתָם le'umatam מְשַׁבְּחִים meshabechim וְאוֹמְרִים ve'omrim:

(או"א) בָּרוּךְ baruch כְּבוֹד kevod יָיְ/אדני/אהדונהי Adonai ; כבוד ה' = יוד הי ואו הה

מִמְּקוֹמוֹ mimekomo עסמ"ב, הברכה (למתק את ז' המלכים עמתו) ; ר"ת ע"ב, ריבוע יהוה ; ר"ת מיכ:

וּבְדִבְרֵי uvdivrei קָדְשָׁךְ kodshach כָּתוּב katuv לֵאמֹר lemor:

(וו"ן) יִמְלֹךְ yimloch קָדוֹשׁ בָּרוּךְ ר"ת ימלך יב"ק, אלהים יהוה, אהיה אדני יהוה

יָיְ/אדני/אהדונהי Adonai לְעוֹלָם le'olam ריבוע ס"ג ו' אותיות דס"ג אֱלֹהַיִךְ Elohayich יל"ה

צִיּוֹן Tziyon יוסף, ו' הויות, קנאה ; לְדֹר ledor וָדֹר vador רי"ו ; ר"ת אצלו (מלכות אצל ז"א - ו)

הַלְלוּיָהּ haleluya אלהים, אהיה אדני ; ללה:

THE THIRD BLESSING

This blessing connects us to Jacob, the Central Column and the power of restriction. Jacob is our channel for connecting Mercy with Judgment. By restricting our reactive behavior, we are blocking our Desire to Receive for the Self Alone. Jacob also gives us the power to balance our acts of Mercy and Judgment toward other people in our lives.

NAKDISHACH

We sanctify You and we revere You,
according to the pleasant words of the counsel of the Holy Angels, who recite Holy before You three times, as it is written by Your Prophet: "And each called to the other and said: Holy, Holy, Holy, Is the Lord of Hosts, the entire world is filled with His glory." (Isaiah 6:3) Facing them they give praise and say: "Blessed is the glory of the Lord from His Place." (Ezekiel 3:12) And in Your Holy Words, it is written as follows: "The Lord, your God, shall reign forever, for each and for every generation. Zion, Praise the Lord!" (Psalms 146:10)

Tiferet that becomes *Da'at* (14 words).

ר"ת = אור, רז, אין סוף. kadosh קָדוֹשׁ veshimcha וְשִׁמְךָ kadosh קָדוֹשׁ Ata אַתָּה

ב"ן, לכב ע"ה נגד, מזבוח, זן, אל יהוה yom יוֹם bechol בְּכֹל ukdoshim וּקְדוֹשִׁים

sela: סֶלָה yehalelucha יְהַלְלוּךָ

אהלה יהו מוצפץ

Adonai יְהֹוָה(אֲדֹנָי)(יְהֹוָה(אֲדֹנָי)(יְהֹוָה)אהדונהי Ata אַתָּה baruch בָּרוּךְ

הָאֵל haEl לאה ; ייא"י (מילוי דס"ג) הַקָּדוֹשׁ י"פ מ"ה (יוד הא ואו הא): hakadosh

Meditate here on the Name: **יאהדונהי**, as it can help to remove anger.

THE FOURTH BLESSING - YISMACH MOSHE

The fourth blessing is the middle blessing corresponding to *Malchut*, which is the middle between *Chesed*, *Gevurah*, *Tiferet* (the three partriarchs - the three first blessings) and between *Netzah*, *Hod*, *Yesod* (the three last blessings) as it is explained in *Tikunei Zohar*.

Meditate on the letter **ו** (*Vav*) from the Name: **עקוצי"ת**

מטיזו (ז"א) yismach יִשְׂמַח (א) מהטע, ע"ב בריבוע קס"א, אל שדי, ד"פ אלהים ע"ה Moshe מֹשֶׁה

ר"ת = ב"ן (שֹעֹנֶפֶל בחזלק משה והמתיקו בר"ת כי עֶבֶד נֶאֱמָן עם ג' תיבות = קמ"ג) bematenat בְּמַתְּנַת

(שֹעֹלה במקיפים דצלם דא"א ע"י וניתנו לו המווזין הֹנֹו' במתנה וירֹש המקֹום וֹנֹעֹשֹׂו חֹלקֹו) chelko וְחֶלְקוֹ

lo לוֹ karata קָרָאתָ (דֹעֹיל) קמ"ג ne'eman נֶאֱמָן eved עֶבֶד ki כִּי

ר"ת = ה' הויות (הֹווֹ הֹבָאים בראשֹ ז"א) (פֹירֹושֹׁ: בחזֹול ע"י עֶבֶד נֶאֱמָן שֹהֹוֹא מֹטֹטֹרֹוֹן הֹיֹה הֹזֹיֹווֹג
ר"ל בהתֹלֹבֹשֹעֹוֹת הֹיֹצֹירֹה, מֹשֹׂא"כ בֹשֹעֹבֹת שֹהֹזֹיֹוווֹג הֹוֹא בֹמֹקֹומֹו בֹאֹצֹילֹות שֹלֹא ע"י הֹעֹבֹד הֹנֹזֹכֹר).

natata נָתַתָּ berosho בְּרֹאשׁוֹ tiferet תִּפְאֶרֶת kelil כְּלִיל

; גֹגֹם Sinai סִינַי har הַר al עַל ס"ג מ"ה ב"ן lefanecha לְפָנֶיךָ be'amdo בְּעָמְדוֹ

ר"ת = קֹל"ה (הֹ"ג הֹבֹאֹן לֹנֹוקֹבֹא דֹעֹתֹה קֹלֹה); סֹינֹי – ס' – שֹמֹשֹה עֹמֹו בֹס' הֹמֹסֹכֹתֹות שֹעֹקֹיֹבֹל בֹהֹר סֹינֹי.

THE THIRD BLESSING
You are Holy, and Your Name is Holy, and the Holy Ones praise You every day,
for you are God, the Holy King Selah. Blessed are You, Lord, the Holy God.
THE FOURTH BLESSING - YISMACH MOSHE
Moses rejoiced in the gift of his portion for You have called Him a faithful servant.
A crown of splendor You had placed on his head when he stood before You on Mount Sinai.

beyado בְּיָדוֹ horid הוֹרִיד avanim אֲבָנִים luchot לוּחוֹת shenei שְׁנֵי

◆Shabbat שַׁבָּת shemirat שְׁמִירַת bahem בָּהֶם vechatuv וְכָתוּב

❖betoratach בְּתוֹרָתֶךְ katuv כָּתוּב vechen וְכֵן

VESHAMRU

We have the ability to join Heaven and Earth through the power of the *Alef, Hei, Vav, and Hei* אהוה. Our objective is to imbue our chaotic physical domain with the various spiritual attributes of Heaven.

Meditate to include the attribute of the night (*Shamor*) in the attribute of the day (*Zachor*).

haShabbat הַשַׁבָּת et אֶת- Yisrael יִשְׂרָאֵל venei בְנֵי- veshamru וְשָׁמְרוּ

ledorotam לְדֹרֹתָם haShabbat הַשַׁבָּת et אֶת- la'asot לַעֲשׂוֹת ר"ת ביאה

olam עוֹלָם berit בְּרִית (מסט"א ולא קְדוּשָׁה נְשָׁמָה לְמָשׁוֹר, אִשְׁתּוֹ (וּ) ר"ת אהל

hee הוּא ot אוֹת Yisrael יִשְׂרָאֵל benei בְּנֵי uven וּבֵין beni בֵּינִי ר"ת ביאה

yamim יָמִים sheshet שֵׁשֶׁת ki כִּי- le'olam לְעֹלָם י אוֹתִיוֹת דס"ג ריבוע דס"ג נלך

hashamayim הַשָׁמַיִם et אֶת- Adonai יְהֹוָה asa עָשָׂה י"פ טל, י"פ כוזו

uvayom וּבַיוֹם ha'aretz הָאָרֶץ ve'et וְאֶת- אלהים דההן ע"ה ע"ה נגד, מזבוח, זן, אל יהוה

hashevi'i הַשְׁבִיעִי shavat שָׁבַת vayinafash וַיִּנָפַשׁ

VELO NETATO

Shabbat is a powerful gift given to us for the purpose of cleansing ourselves from our wrongful actions throughout the week. Without *Shabbat*, we are forced to face the harsh consequences of our actions at some future date – the source of all the chaos that wreaks havoc in our lives. *Shabbat*, however, is a proactive way to cleanse ourselves. The repercussions and judgments hanging over our heads are dealt with in an extremely merciful manner. Additionally, *Shabbat* gradually removes the negative qualities in our character that cause us to perform hurtful actions in the first place.

He brought down two stone tablets in his hand,
on which was inscribed the observance of the Sabbath. And so it is written in Your Torah:

VESHAMRU

"And the children of Israel shall keep the Sabbath, to make the Shabbat an eternal covenant for all their generations. Between Me and the children of Israel, It is an eternal sign that in six days did the Lord make the Heavens and the Earth and on the Seventh Day, He was refreshed." (Exodus 31:16-17)

Shabbat is not given to everyone. We must truly merit it. It is for this reason that not everyone is observant or aware of the powerful opportunity this day offers. We must truly appreciate the opportunity to participate in *Shabbat*. However, this can be difficult because the cleansing power of *Shabbat* is sometimes heavy and draining. We can become impatient, tired, or restless as the body undergoes cleansing during the Torah reading and prayers. To compound this situation, Satan takes advantage of these bodily responses and bombards us with more negative thoughts. The way to defeat Satan and rise above the heaviness is simply to desire the *Shabbat* with all our heart and soul and appreciate all that it can do for us.

Adonai יְהֹוָהאדניאהדונהי   יוד נון דלת אלף למד מם אלף   netato נְתָתוֹ   velo וְלֹא

velo וְלֹא   ha'aratzot הָאֲרָצוֹת   legoyei לְגוֹיֵי   יכה   Elohenu אֱלֹהֵינוּ

elilim אֱלִילִים   le'ovdei לְעוֹבְדֵי   malkenu מַלְכֵּנוּ   hinchalto הִנְחַלְתּוֹ

arelim עֲרֵלִים   yishkenu יִשְׁכְּנוּ   lo לֹא   bimnuchato בִּמְנוּחָתוֹ   gam גַּם

netato נְתָתוֹ   Yisrael יִשְׂרָאֵל   le'amcha לְעַמְּךָ   ki כִּי

> Meditate to draw illumination and *Torah* to *Malchut* so She can get a new Name: אלף למד מם דלת אלף למד נון יוד (instead of the Name אֲדֹנָ"י אֵל She used to have), which has the same numerical value of the word נְתָתוֹ (*netato*).

be'ahava בְּאַהֲבָה   אוֹהֵב, דאגה, הויות, יאהדונהי אידהנויה   Yaakov יַעֲקֹב   lezera לְזֶרַע   כוֹרֵעַ, דאגה

asher אֲשֶׁר   bam בָּם מ"ב   bacharta בָּחַרְתָּ בּוֹרֵת

YISMECHU

yismechu יִשְׂמְחוּ   vemalchutach בְמַלְכוּתָךְ   shomrei שׁוֹמְרֵי   כ"א ההויות שבתפילין

Shabbat שַׁבָּת   vekorei וְקוֹרְאֵי   oneg עוֹנֶג   am עַם   mekadshei מְקַדְּשֵׁי

shevi'i שְׁבִיעִי   kulam כֻּלָּם   yisbe'u יִשְׂבְּעוּ   veyit'angu וְיִתְעַנְּגוּ

bo בּוֹ   ratzita רָצִיתָ   vehashevi'i וְהַשְּׁבִיעִי   לאו   mituvach מִטּוּבָךְ

oto אוֹתוֹ   נלך yamim יָמִים   chemdat וְחֶמְדַּת   vekidashto וְקִדַּשְׁתּוֹ

karata קָרָאתָ

VELO NETATO

You did not give It, Lord, our God, to the nations of the lands, nor did You make it the inheritance, our King, of the worshipers of graven idols. And in Its contentment, the uncircumcised shall not abide. For to Israel, Your nation, You have given it in love, to the seed of Jacob, whom You have chosen.

YISMECHU

They shall rejoice in Your Kingship, those who observe the Sabbath and call it a delight, the nation that sanctifies the Seventh. They will all be satisfied and delighted from Your goodness. And the Seventh, You found favor in It and sanctified It. The most coveted of days, You called It.

MEKADESH HASHABBAT

avotenu אֲבוֹתֵינוּ ילה ; מילוי דע״ב, דמ״ב ; לכב velohei וֵאלֹהֵי ילה Elohenu אֱלֹהֵינוּ

kadshenu קַדְּשֵׁנוּ ◆vimnuchatenu בִּמְנוּחָתֵנוּ na נָא retze רְצֵה

betoratach בְּתוֹרָתֶךָ chelkenu וְחֶלְקֵנוּ sim שִׂים bemitzvotecha בְּמִצְוֹתֶיךָ

nafshenu נַפְשֵׁנוּ same'ach שַׂמֵּחַ ◆לאו mituvach מִטּוּבֶךָ sabe'enu שַׂבְּעֵנוּ

le'ovdecha לְעָבְדֶּךָ libenu לִבֵּנוּ vetaher וְטַהֵר ◆bishu'atach בִּישׁוּעָתֶךָ

vehanchilenu וְהַנְחִילֵנוּ זף ס״ג, אהיה פעמים אהיה, אל אדני, פוי, be'emet בֶּאֱמֶת

דאגה אוזר, be'ahava בְּאַהֲבָה ילה Elohenu אֱלֹהֵינוּ אדני אהיה אהיה יהוה Adonai

ע״ה, שדי אל, ע״ה, ברביע קס״א, ע״ב, ע״ה, מהש uvratzon וּבְרָצוֹן

vo בּוֹ veyanuchu וְיָנוּחוּ ◆kodshecha קָדְשֶׁךָ Shabbat שַׁבַּת

◆shemecha שְׁמֶךָ mekadshei מְקַדְּשֵׁי Yisrael יִשְׂרָאֵל ילי kol כָּל

אהיה יהו יה אדני

Adonai יהוה אדני אהיה אהיה Ata אַתָּה baruch בָּרוּךְ

Meditate on the *Neshikin* (kisses - the upper unification),
from the Ten *Sefirot* of *Chochomah* of *Keter* of the five *Partzufim* of *Netzach, Hod, Yesod*
(in the repetition: *Chesed, Gevurah, Tiferet*) of *Chochmah* of *Zeir Anpin*
to the Ten *Sefirot* of *Chochomah* of *Keter* of the five *Partzufim* of *Netzach, Hod, Yesod*
(in the repetition: *Chesed, Gevurah, Tiferet*) of *Chochmah* of *Yaakov* and *Rachel*.

Chochmah	Da'at	Binah
א	י	ה
יהוה	מצפצ	יהוה
אהיה	אהיה	אהיה
יהוה	יהוה	יהוה

Meditate to draw illumination to *Keter* of *Yaakov* and *Rachel*
(who are now standing in *Netzach, Hod, Yesod* of *Zeir Anpin*)
from the three *Mochin* – *Chochmah, Binah, Da'at* – of Second *Gadlut*
enclosed by *Netzach, Hod, Yesod* **(in the repetition**:
Chesed, Gevurah, Tiferet) of Supernal *Abba* and *Ima*
(who are the *Mochin* are in *Chochmah, Binah, Da'at* of *Zeir Anpin*).

Also draw *Malchut* of *Keter* of all five *Partzufim* of *Netzach, Hod, Yesod* **(in the repetition**: *Chesed, Gevurah, Tiferet*) of *Chochmah* of the Internal of *Zeir Anpin* **to** *Keter* of all five *Partzufim* of *Netzach, Hod, Yesod* **(in the repetition**: *Chesed, Gevurah, Tiferet*) of *Chochmah* of the External and Internal of *Yaakov* and *Rachel* **to** *Keter* of *Yaakov* and *Rachel* who stands in the Chest of *Zeir Anpin*:

אהיה יהוה
(to the three Vessels of *Keter* of *Nukva*)

יה יהו יהוה יוד הא ואו הה יוד הא ואו יוד הא ואו הה יוד הא ואו הה

מְקַדֵּשׁ mekadesh הַשַּׁבָּת haShabbat:

MEKADESH HASHABBAT
Our God and God of our forefathers,
please desire our rest. Sanctify us with Your commandments and grant our share in Your Torah.
Satisfy us from Your goodness, gladden our souls with Your salvation, and purify our hearts to serve You
sincerely. Lord, our God, with love and favor, grant us Your Holy Sabbath as a heritage. And may all
of Israel, the sanctifiesof Your Name. Rest on It. Blessed are You, Lord, Who sanctifies the Sabbath.

THE FINAL THREE BLESSINGS

Through the merit of Moses, Aaron and Joseph, who are our channels for the final three blessings, we are able to bring down all the spiritual energy that we aroused with our prayers and blessings.

THE FIFTH BLESSING

During this blessing, referring to Moses, we should always meditate to try to know exactly what God wants from us in our life, as signified by the phrase, "Let it be the will of God." We ask God to guide us toward the work we came to Earth to do. The Creator cannot just accept the work that we want to do; we must carry out the work we were destined to do.

Netzach

Meditate for the Supernal Desire (*Keter*) that is called *metzach haratzon* (Forehead of the Desire).

רְצֵה retze אלף למד הה יוד מם

Meditate here to transform misfortune and tragedy (צרה) into desire and acceptance (רצה).

Adonai יְהֹוָואהדונהי   Elohenu אֱלֹהֵינוּ ילה   be'amecha בְּעַמְּךָ   Yisrael יִשְׂרָאֵל

velitfilatam וְלִתְפִלָּתָם   she'e שְׁעֵה◆   vehashev וְהָשֵׁב   ha'avoda הָעֲבוֹדָה

lidvir לִדְבִיר רי"ו   betecha בֵּיתֶךָ ב"פ ראה◆   ve'ishei וְאִשֵּׁי   Yisrael יִשְׂרָאֵל

utfilatam וּתְפִלָּתָם   mehera מְהֵרָה   be'ahava בְּאַהֲבָה   אוזר, דאגה

tekabel תְּקַבֵּל   beratzon בְּרָצוֹן מהש ע"ה, ע"ב בריבוע וקס"א ע"ה, אל שדי ע"ה◆

ut'hi וּתְהִי   leratzon לְרָצוֹן מהש ע"ה, ע"ב בריבוע וקס"א ע"ה, אל שדי ע"ה

tamid תָּמִיד ע"ה קס"א קנ"א קמ"ג   avodat עֲבוֹדַת   Yisrael יִשְׂרָאֵל   amecha עַמֶּךָ◆

YA'ALE VEYAVO

During *Sukkot*, there is an extra surge of spiritual energy in our midst. "Ya'ale Veyavo" is our antenna for drawing this extra power into our lives.

If you mistakenly forgot to say "*ya'ale veyavo*," and realize this before the end of the blessing "*baruch Ata Adonai*," you should return to say "*ya'ale veyavo*" and continue as usual. If you realize this after the end of the blessing "*hamachazir shechinato leTziyon*" but before you start the next blessing "*modim*" you should say "*ya'ale veyavo*" there and continue as usual. If you only realize this after you have started the next blessing "*modim*" but before the second "*yih'yu leratzon*" (on pg. 714) you should return to "*retze*" (pg. 708) and continue from there. If you realize this after the second "*yih'yu leratzon*" you should start the *Amidah* from the beginning.

THE FINAL THREE BLESSINGS - THE FIFTH BLESSING

Find favor, Lord, our God, in Your People, Israel, and turn to their prayer.
Restore the service to the inner sanctuary of Your Temple. Accept the offerings of Israel and their prayer with favor, speedily, and with love. May the service of Your People Israel always be favorable to You.

אֲבוֹתֵינוּ avotenu יֵלֹה ; דמב ,מילוי ע"ב ; לכב velohei וֵאלֹהֵי יֵלֹה Elohenu אֱלֹהֵינוּ

וְיֵרָצֶה veyeratze רֵי"וּ veyera'e וְיֵרָאֶה veyagi'a וְיַגִּיעַ veyavo וְיָבֹא ya'ale יַעֲלֶה

(ז"פ ו) ר"ת מ"ב veyizacher וְיִזָּכֵר veyipaked וְיִפָּקֵד veyishama וְיִשָּׁמַע

◆avotenu אֲבוֹתֵינוּ ונש"ב קס"א ע"ב vezichron וְזִכְרוֹן zichronenu זִכְרוֹנֵנוּ

◆irach עִירֶךְ Yerushalayim יְרוּשָׁלַיִם ונש"ב קס"א ע"ב zichron זִכְרוֹן

בן ; כהת ע"ה David דָּוִד ben בֶּן mashi'ach מְשִׁיחַ ונש"ב קס"א ע"ב vezichron וְזִכְרוֹן

דוד = אדני ע"ה kol כָּל avdach עַבְדָּךְ אל אדני ,פוי vezichron וְזִכְרוֹן ונש"ב קס"א ע"ב

יל עַמְּךָ amecha בֵּית bet ראה ב"פ Yisrael יִשְׂרָאֵל lefanecha לְפָנֶיךָ ס"ג מ"ה ב"ן

ברביע, מוזי דמ"ה מילוי lechen לְחֵן אכא◆ letova לְטוֹבָה lifleta לִפְלֵיטָה

◆ulrachamim וּלְרַחֲמִים יהוה ריבוע ע"ב, lechesed לְחֶסֶד

◆ulshalom וּלְשָׁלוֹם tovim טוֹבִים אהיה אהיה יהוה, בינה ע"ה, lechayim לְחַיִּים

והו hazeh הַזֶּה haSukkot הַסֻּכּוֹת chag חַג זג ע"ה נגד, מזבוז, זן, אל יהוה: beyom בְּיוֹם

◆והו hazeh הַזֶּה kodesh קֹדֶשׁ mikra מִקְרָא ע"ה נגד, מזבוז, זן, אל יהוה beyom בְּיוֹם

אברהם, וז"פ אל, רי"ו ול"ב נתיבות החוכמה, רמ"ח (אברים), עסמ"ב וט"ז אותיות lerachem לְרַחֵם

פשוטות zochrenu זָכְרֵנוּ ◆ulhoshi'enu וּלְהוֹשִׁיעֵנוּ alenu עָלֵינוּ bo בּוֹ

אכא◆ letova לְטוֹבָה bo בּוֹ יֵלֹה Elohenu אֱלֹהֵינוּ Adonai יְהֹוָהאדנייאהדונהי

vo בּוֹ vehoshi'enu וְהוֹשִׁיעֵנוּ ◆livracha לִבְרָכָה vo בּוֹ ufokdenu וּפָקְדֵנוּ

◆tovim טוֹבִים ע"ה בינה אהיה אהיה יהוה, lechayim לְחַיִּים

chus וֿוֿס ◆verachamim וְרַחֲמִים yeshu'a יְשׁוּעָה ראה bidvar בִּדְבַר

אל, וז"פ אברהם, verachem וְרַחֵם vachamol וֿוֿחֲמוֹל vechonenu וְחָנֵּנוּ

◆alenu עָלֵינוּ פשוטות אותיות וט"ז עסמ"ב (אברים), רמ"ח החוכמה, נתיבות ול"ב רי"ו

YA'ALE VEYAVO

Our God and God of our forefathers, may it rise, come, arrive, appear, find favor, be heard, be considered, and be remembered, our remembrance and the remembrance of our forefathers: the remembrance of Jerusalem, Your City, and the remembrance of Mashiach, Son of David, Your servant, and the remembrance of Your entire Nation, the House of Israel, before You for deliverance, for good, for grace, kindness, and compassion, for a good life, and for peace on the day of: This festival of Sukkot, on this Holy Day of Convocation To take pity on us and to save us. Remember us, Lord, our God, on this day, for good; consider us on it for blessing; and deliver us on it for a good life, with the words of deliverance and mercy. Take pity and be gracious to us, have mercy and be compassionate with us, ki כִּי ✦מ״ה ריבוע enenu עֵינֵינוּ elecha אֵלֶיךָ ki כִּי vehoshi'enu וְהוֹשִׁיעֵנוּ

Ata אַתָּה: verachum וְרַחוּם chanun וְחַנּוּן melech מֶלֶךְ (מילוי דס״ג) יי״א El אֵל

✦harabim הָרַבִּים verachamecha בְּרַחֲמֶיךָ veAta וְאַתָּה

vetechezena וְתֶחֱזֶינָה vetirtzenu וְתִרְצֵנוּ banu בָּנוּ tachpotz תַּחְפֹּץ

קנאה הויות, ו יוסף, leTziyon לְצִיּוֹן beshuvcha בְּשׁוּבְךָ מ״ה ריבוע enenu עֵינֵינוּ

יי״פ דיודין, אלהים מצפ״צ, berachamim בְּרַחֲמִים

אהיה יהו אל

Adonai יאהדונהיאהדונהייהוה Ata אַתָּה baruch בָּרוּךְ

קנאה: הויות, ו יוסף, leTziyon לְצִיּוֹן shechinato שְׁכִינָתוֹ hamachazir הַמַּחֲזִיר

THE SIXTH BLESSING

This blessing is our thank you. Kabbalistically, the biggest "thank you" we can give the Creator is to do exactly what we are supposed to do in terms of our spiritual work.

Hod

Bow your entire body at "*modim*" and straighten up at "*Adonai*."

lach לָךְ anachnu אֲנַחְנוּ יום כל לאמרם דוד שתיקן ברכות מאה modim מוֹדִים

ילה Elohenu אֱלֹהֵינוּ (ו״ג) Adonai יאהדונהיאהדונהייהוה hu הוּא sheAta שֶׁאַתָּה

le'olam לְעוֹלָם avotenu אֲבוֹתֵינוּ ילה ; דמ״ב ע״ב, מילוי ; velohei וֵאלֹהֵי

ע״ה ההון אלהים tzur צוּר tzurenu צוּרֵנוּ va'ed וָעֶד דס״ג אותיות וי ס״ג ריבוע

נוריאל גבריאל מיכאל בית ר״ת ; (דס״ג מילוי יי״א) אל ג״פ umagen וּמָגֵן chayenu וְחַיֵּינוּ

רי״ו vador וָדֹר ledor לְדֹר hu הוּא Ata אַתָּה yish'enu יִשְׁעֵנוּ

✦tehilatecha תְּהִלָּתֶךָ unsaper וּנְסַפֵּר lecha לְךָ node נוֹדֶה

✦beyadecha בְּיָדֶךָ hamesurim הַמְּסוּרִים chayenu וְחַיֵּינוּ al עַל

---

and save us, for our eyes turn to You, because You are God, the King Who is gracious and compassionate. And You in Your great compassion take delight in us and are pleased with us. May our eyes witness Your return to Zion with compassion. Blessed are You, Lord, Who returns His Shechinah to Zion.

THE SIXTH BLESSING

We give thanks to You,

for it is You, Lord, Who is our God and God of our forefathers, forever and for all eternity. You are our Rock, the Rock of our lives, and the Shield of our salvation. From one generation to another, we shall give thanks to You and we shall tell of Your praise. For our lives that are entrusted in Your hands,

ve'al וְעַל   nishmotenu נִשְׁמוֹתֵינוּ   hapekudot הַפְּקוּדוֹת   lach לָךְ◆   ve'al וְעַל◆

nisecha נִסֶּיךָ   shebechol שֶׁבְּכָל   yom יוֹם

imanu עִמָּנוּ   ve'al וְעַל◆   nifle'otecha נִפְלְאוֹתֶיךָ

vetovotecha וְטוֹבוֹתֶיךָ   shebechol שֶׁבְּכָל   et עֵת◆   erev עֶרֶב

vavoker וָבֹקֶר   vetzahorayim וְצָהֳרַיִם◆   hatov הַטּוֹב   ki כִּי   lo לֹא

rachamecha רַחֲמֶיךָ   hamerachem הַמְּרַחֵם◆   chalu כָלוּ

chasadecha חֲסָדֶיךָ   ki כִּי◆   tamu תַמּוּ   lo לֹא   ki כִּי

vehasecha וְסַדֶּיךָ◆   ki כִּי   me'olam מֵעוֹלָם   kivinu קִוִּינוּ   lach לָךְ׃

MODIM DERABANAN

This prayer is recited by the congregation in the repetition when the *chazan* says "*modim*."

In this section there are 44 words which, is the same numerical value as the Name: רִיבּוּעַ אהיה (א אה אהי אהיה).

modim מוֹדִים   anachnu אֲנַחְנוּ   lach לָךְ

sheAta שָׁאַתָּה   hu הוּא   Adonai יְהֹוָה   Elohenu אֱלֹהֵינוּ

velohei וֵאלֹהֵי   Elohei אֱלֹהֵי   avotenu אֲבוֹתֵינוּ

yotzer יוֹצֵר   bereshit בְּרֵאשִׁית◆   chol כָל   basar בָּשָׂר◆   yotzrenu יוֹצְרֵנוּ

yotzer יוֹצֵר   bereshit בְּרֵאשִׁית◆   berachot בְּרָכוֹת   vehoda'ot וְהוֹדָאוֹת

leshimcha לְשִׁמְךָ   hagadol הַגָּדוֹל◆   vehakadosh וְהַקָּדוֹשׁ

ken כֵּן   techayenu תְּחַיֵּינוּ   shehecheyitanu שֶׁהֶחֱיִיתָנוּ al עַל   vekiyamtanu וְקִיַּמְתָּנוּ◆

galuyoteinu גָּלֻיּוֹתֵינוּ   lechatzrot לְחַצְרוֹת   utchonenu וּתְחָנֵּנוּ◆   vete'esof וְתֶאֱסֹף

chukecha חֻקֶּיךָ   vela'asot וְלַעֲשׂוֹת   retzoncha רְצוֹנֶךָ◆   kodshecha קָדְשֶׁךָ◆   lishmor לִשְׁמוֹר   ul'ovdecha וּלְעָבְדְּךָ◆

modim מוֹדִים   lach לָךְ◆   baruch בָּרוּךְ   El אֵל   belevav בְּלֵבָב   shalem שָׁלֵם◆   al עַל   she'anachnu שֶׁאֲנַחְנוּ◆   hahoda'ot הַהוֹדָאוֹת׃

---

for our souls that are in Your care,

for Your miracles that are with us every day, and for Your wonders and Your favors that are with us at all times: evening, morning and afternoon. You are the good One, for Your compassion has never ceased. You are the compassionate One, for Your kindness has never ended, for we have always placed our hope in You.

MODIM DERABANAN

We give thanks to You, for it is You Lord,

our God and God of our forefathers, the God of all flesh, our Maker and the Former of all Creation. Blessings and thanks to Your great and Holy Name for giving us life and for preserving us. So may You continue to give us life, be gracious to us, and gather our exiles to the courtyards of Your Sanctuary, so that we may keep Your laws, fulfill Your will, and serve You wholeheartedly. For this, we thank You. Bless the God of thanksgiving.

וְעַל ve'al   כֻּלָּם kulam   יִתְבָּרַךְ yitbarach   וְיִתְרוֹמָם veyitromam

וְיִתְנַשֵּׂא veyitnase   תָּמִיד tamid   ע"ה קס"א קנ"א קמ"ג   שִׁמְךָ shimcha

מַלְכֵּנוּ malkenu   לְעוֹלָם le'olam   ריבוע ס"ג וי' אותיות דס"ג   וָעֶד va'ed

וְכָל vechol   הַחַיִּים hachayim ילי אהיה אהיה יהוה, בינה ע"ה   יוֹדוּךָ yoducha   סֶלָה sela

וִיהַלְלוּ vihalelu   וִיבָרְכוּ vivarchu יהוה יהוה ריבוע יהוה   אֶת־ et

שִׁמְךָ shimcha   הַגָּדוֹל hagadol להו ; עם ד' אותיות = מובה, יכל, אום   בֶּאֱמֶת be'emet

לְעוֹלָם le'olam ריבוע ס"ג וי' אותיות דס"ג, ז"פ ס"ג אהיה פעמים אהיה ;   כִּי ki   טוֹב tov והו ;

יְשׁוּעָתֵנוּ yeshu'atenu כי טוב = יהוה אהיה, אום, מובה, יכל, יא"י (מילוי דס"ג)   הָאֵל haEl לאה ; יא"י

וְעֶזְרָתֵנוּ ve'ezratenu לאה ; יא"י (מילוי דס"ג)   סֶלָה sela   הָאֵל haEl   הַטּוֹב hatov והו :

Bend your knees at "baruch," bow at "Ata" and straighten up at "Adonai."

אהיה יה אלהים

בָּרוּךְ baruch   אַתָּה Ata   יְהֹוָה (הי) יאההויהה אדוני Adonai   הַטּוֹב hatov והו

שִׁמְךָ shimcha   וּלְךָ ulcha   נָאֶה na'e   לְהוֹדוֹת lehodot ס"ת כהת, משיח בן דוד ע"ה :

For the blessing of the *Kohanim* go to page 355.

THE FINAL BLESSING

We are emanating the energy of peace to the entire world. We also make it our intent to use our mouths only for good. Kabbalistically, the power of words and speech is unimaginable. We hope to use that power wisely, which is perhaps one of the most difficult tasks we have to carry out.

Yesod

שָׂלוֹם shalom   שִׂים sim

טוֹבָה tova אכא   וּבְרָכָה uvracha   וְחַיִּים chayim אהיה אהיה יהוה, בינה ע"ה

וָחֵן chen מילוי דמ"ה   בריבוע, מוזי   וָחֶסֶד vachesed ע"ב, ריבוע יהוה

צְדָקָה tzedaka ע"ה ריבוע אלהים   וְרַחֲמִים verachamim   עָלֵינוּ alenu

---

And for all those things, may Your Name be always blessed, exalted and extolled, our King, forever and ever, and all the living shall thank You, Selah. And they shall praise and bless Your Great Name, sincerely and forever, for It is good, the God of our salvation and our help, Selah, the good God. Blessed are You, Lord, whose Name is good, and to You it is befitting to give thanks.

THE FINAL BLESSING

Place peace, goodness, blessing, life, grace, kindness, righteousness, and mercy upon us

וְעַל־ ve'al וּבָרְכֵנוּ uvarchenu עַמְּךָ amecha יִשְׂרָאֵל Yisrael כָּל־ kol

אָבִינוּ avinu כֻּלָּנוּ kulanu כְּאֶחָד ke'echad בָּאוֹר be'or

פָּנֶיךָ panecha כִּי ki בָּאוֹר ve'or פָּנֶיךָ panecha

נָתַתָּ natata לָנוּ lanu יְהֹוָה Adonai

אֱלֹהֵינוּ Elohenu תּוֹרָה torah וְחַיִּים vechayim

אַהֲבָה ahava וָחֶסֶד vachesed

צְדָקָה tzedaka וְרַחֲמִים verachamim בְּרָכָה beracha

וְשָׁלוֹם veshalom וְטוֹב vetov בְּעֵינֶיךָ be'enecha

לְבָרְכֵנוּ levarchenu וּלְבָרֵךְ ulvarech אֶת et כָּל־ kol עַמְּךָ amecha

יִשְׂרָאֵל Yisrael בְּרוֹב berov עֹז oz וְשָׁלוֹם veshalom

בָּרוּךְ baruch אַתָּה Ata יְהֹוָה Adonai

הַמְבָרֵךְ hamevarech אֶת et עַמּוֹ amo יִשְׂרָאֵל Yisrael

בַּשָּׁלוֹם bashalom אָמֵן amen

YIH'YU LERATZON

There are 42 letters in the verse in the secret of *Ana Beko'ach*.

יִהְיוּ yih'yu לְרָצוֹן leratzon

אִמְרֵי־ imrei פִי fi וְהֶגְיוֹן vehegyon לִבִּי libi

לְפָנֶיךָ lefanecha יְהֹוָה Adonai צוּרִי tzuri וְגֹאֲלִי vego'ali

---

and upon all of Israel, Your People. Bless us all as one, our Father, with the Light of Your Countenance, because it is with the Light of Your Countenance that You, Lord, our God, have given us Torah and life, love and kindness, righteousness and mercy, blessing and peace. May it be good in Your Eyes to bless us and to bless Your entire Nation, Israel, with abundant power and with peace. Blessed are You, Lord, Who blesses His Nation, Israel, with peace, Amen.

YIH'YU LERATZON

"May the utterances of my mouth and the thoughts of my heart find favor before You, Lord, my Rock and my Redeemer." (Psalms 19:15)

ELOHAI NETZOR

מֵרָע mera ◆ לְשׁוֹנִי leshoni נְצוֹר netzor ; ילה רמב ע"ב, מילוי אֱלֹהַי Elohai

וְלִמְקַלְלַי velimkalelai ◆ מִרְמָה mirma ◆ ראה מִדַּבֵּר midaber וְשִׂפְתוֹתַי vesiftotai

כֶּעָפָר ke'afar וְנַפְשִׁי venafshi ◆ תִדּוֹם tidom ◆ נַפְשִׁי nafshi

בְּתוֹרָתֶךָ betoratecha ◆ לִבִּי libi פְּתַח petach ◆ תִהְיֶה tih'ye ה אדני lakol לַכֹּל

נַפְשִׁי nafshi ◆ תִּרְדּוֹף tirdof מִצְוֹתֶיךָ mitzvotecha וְאַחֲרֵי ve'acharei ◆ וְאוֹזְרִי

מְהֵרָה mehera ◆ רהע לְרָעָה lera'a עָלַי alai הַקָּמִים hakamim ילי vechol וְכָל

מַחְשְׁבוֹתָם machshevotam ◆ וְקַלְקֵל vekalkel עֲצָתָם atzatam הָפֵר hafer

לְמַעַן lema'an עֲשֵׂה ase ◆ שְׁמֶךָ shemach לְמַעַן lema'an עֲשֵׂה ase

עֲשֵׂה ase ◆ תּוֹרָתֶךָ toratach לְמַעַן lema'an עֲשֵׂה ase ◆ יְמִינָךְ yeminach

לְמַעַן lema'an ר"ת הפסוק = מ"ה יהוה ◆ קְדֻשָּׁתֶךָ kedushatach לְמַעַן lema'an

יֵחָלְצוּן yechaltzun ◆ יְדִידֶיךָ yedidecha ר"ת ילי הוֹשִׁיעָה hoshi'a יהוה נהורין ◆ יִזְלְצוּן

יְמִינֶךָ yemincha va'aneni וַעֲנֵנִי (כתיב: וַעֲנֵנוּ) ר"ת אל (ייא"י מילוי דס"ג)

Before we recite the next verse "Yih'yu leratzon" we have an opportunity to strengthen our connection to our soul using our name. Each person has a verse in the Torah that connects to their name. Either their name is in the verse, or the first and last letters of the name correspond to the first or last letters of a verse. For example, the name Yehuda begins with a *Yud* and ends with a *Hei*. Before we end the *Amidah*, we state that our name will always be remembered when our soul leaves this world.

YIH'YU LERATZON (THE SECOND)
There are 42 letters in the verse in the secret of *Ana Beko'ach*.

יִהְיוּ yih'yu אל (ייא"י מילוי דס"ג) לְרָצוֹן leratzon מהטע ע"ה, ע"ב בריבוע וקס"א ע"ה, אל סודי ע"ה

לִבִּי libi וְהֶגְיוֹן vehegyon ר"ת אלף = אלף למד שין דלת יוד ע"ה פִּי fi imrei אִמְרֵי

וְגֹאֲלִי vego'ali צוּרִי tzuri Adonai יְהֹוָ×ואֲדֹנִיואֲהֹדֹנֶהֵי ס"ג מ"ה ב"ן lefanecha לְפָנֶיךָ

ELOHAI NETZOR
My God, guard my tongue from evil and my lips from speaking deceit. To those who curse me, let my spirit remain silent, and let my spirit be as dust for everyone. Open my heart to Your Torah and let my heart pursue Your commandments. All those who rise against me to do me harm, speedily nullify their plans and disturb their thoughts. Do so for the sake of Your Name. Do so for the sake of Your Right. Do so for the sake of Your Torah. Do so for the sake of Your Holiness, "So that Your loved ones may be saved. Redeem Your Right and answer me." (Psalms 60:7)

YIH'YU LERATZON (THE SECOND)
"May the utterances of my mouth and the thoughts of my heart find favor before You, Lord, my Rock and my Redeemer." (Psalms 19:15)

OSE SHALOM

You take three steps backward;

ose עוֹשֶׂה shalom שָׁלוֹם

Left
You turn to the left and say:

בִּמְרוֹמָיו bimromav ר"ת ע"ב, ריבוע יהוה

hu הוּא verachamav בְּרַחֲמָיו ya'ase יַעֲשֶׂה

Right
You turn to the right and say:

shalom שָׁלוֹם alenu עָלֵינוּ ר"ת ס"ג נהורין

kol כָּל־ ve'al וְעַל ; עמם amo עַמּוֹ יל Yisrael יִשְׂרָאֵל

Center
You face the center and say:

ve'imru וְאִמְרוּ amen אָמֵן יאהדונהי:

yehi יְהִי ratzon רָצוֹן מהש' ע"ה, ע"ב בריבוע וקס"א ע"ה, אל עודי ע"ה

milfanecha מִלְּפָנֶיךָ ס"ג מ"ה ב"ן יְהֹוָ‏אַדְנָ‏יאהדונהי Adonai אֲדֹנָי Elohenu אֱלֹהֵינוּ ילה

velohei וֵאלֹהֵי מילוי ע"ב, דמב ; ילה avotenu אֲבוֹתֵינוּ ,shetivne שֶׁתִּבְנֶה

bet בֵּית ב"פ ראה hamikdash הַמִּקְדָּשׁ bimhera בִּמְהֵרָה veyamenu בְיָמֵינוּ

veten וְתֵן chelkenu וְחֶלְקֵנוּ betoratach בְּתוֹרָתֶךָ la'asot לַעֲשׂוֹת chukei וְחֻקֵּי

retzonach רְצוֹנֶךָ ul'ovdach וּלְעָבְדֶךָ פוי, אל אדני belevav בְּלֵבָב בוכו shalem שָׁלֵם.

You take three steps forward.

Continue with the "*Halel*" on page 375.

OSE SHALOM

He, Who makes peace in His High Places, He, in His compassion, shall make peace upon us.
And upon His entire nation, Israel, and you shall say, Amen.

May it be pleasing before You,
Lord, our God and God of our forefathers, that You shall rebuild the Temple speedily, in our days, and place our lot in Your Torah, so that we may fulfill the laws of Your desire and serve You wholeheartedly.

THE AMIDAH OF MINCHAH OF SHABBAT AND CHOL HAMO'ED

yagid יַגִּיד ufi וּפִי tiftach תִּפְתָּח sefatai שְׂפָתַי (pause here) לל"ה Adonai אֲדֹנָי

יו" (כ"ב אותיות פעולות [=אבא] וה' אותיות סופיות סֹזֹזֹר) תְּהִלָּתֶךָ tehilatecha ס"ת = בוכו:

THE FIRST BLESSING - INVOKES THE SHIELD OF ABRAHAM.

Abraham is the channel of the Right Column energy of positivity, sharing, and Mercy. Sharing actions can protect us from all forms of negativity.

Chesed that becomes *Chochmah*

In this section there are 42 words, the secret of the 42-Letter Name of God and therefore it begins with the letter *Bet* (2) and ends with the letter *Mem* (40).

Bend your knees at "*baruch*," bow at "*Ata*" and straighten up at "*Adonai*."

ב   א

לל"ה (אותיות הא"ב המסמלות את העשפע המגיע) לה' המלכות א-ת Ata אַתָּה baruch בָּרוּךְ

ג

יל"ה   Elohenu אֱלֹהֵינוּ   (יא)   Adonai אדני יאהדונהי יְהֹוָה

ת

♦avotenu אֲבוֹתֵינוּ יל"ה ; דמב , ע"ב , מילוי ; לכב velohei וֵאלֹהֵי

ק

(Chochmah) Avraham אַבְרָהָם יל"ה ; דמב , ע"ב , מילוי Elohei אֱלֹהֵי

וז"פ אל, רי"ו ול"ב נתיבות הוזכמה, רמ"וז (אברים), עסמ"ב וט"ז אותיות פעוטות

ש   ע

ד"פ ב"ן (Binah) Yitzchak יִצְחָק יל"ה ; דמב , ע"ב , מילוי Elohei אֱלֹהֵי

ו   ט

י"ר הויות, יאהדונהי אידהנויה ו' (Da'at) Yaakov יַעֲקֹב יל"ה ; דמב , ע"ב מילוי ; לכב velohei וֵאלֹהֵי

THE AMIDAH OF MINCHAH OF SHABBAT AND CHOL HAMO'ED

"My Lord, open my lips, and my mouth shall relate Your praise." (Psalms 51:17)

THE FIRST BLESSING

Blessed are You, Lord,
our God and God of our forefathers: the God of Abraham, the God of Isaac, and the God of Jacob.

האל הַגָּדוֹל (יא"י (מילוי דס"ג) ; לאה haEl הָאֵל ; גדול = לההו

הַגָּדוֹל hagadol ; האל הגדול = סיט

וְהַנּוֹרָא vehanora הַגִּבּוֹר hagibor ר"ת הההה מובה, יזל, אום = מובה עם ד' אותיות

עֶלְיוֹן elyon אֵל El יא"י (מילוי דס"ג) ; ר"ת ע"ב, ריבוע יהוה יל

גּוֹמֵל gomel וְחֲסָדִים chasadim טוֹבִים tovim קוֹנֵה kone הַכֹּל hakol

וְזוֹכֵר vezocher חַסְדֵי chasdei אָבוֹת avot וּמֵבִיא umevi

גּוֹאֵל go'el לִבְנֵי livnei בְּנֵיהֶם venehem לְמַעַן lema'an

שְׁמוֹ shemo בְּאַהֲבָה be'ahava מוהש ע"ה, ע"ב בריבוע וקס"א ע"ה, אל שדי ע"ה אוזר, דאגה:

> When saying the word "be'ahava" you should meditate to devote your soul to sanctify the Holy Name and accept upon yourself the four forms of death.

מֶלֶךְ melech עוֹזֵר ozer וּמוֹשִׁיעַ umoshi'a וּמָגֵן umagen

ג"פ אל (יא"י מילוי דס"ג) ; ר"ת מיכאל גבריאל נוריאל:

Bend your knees at "baruch," bow at "Ata" and straighten up at "Adonai."

אהיה יהו יְהֹוָה

בָּרוּךְ baruch אַתָּה Ata יְהֹוָה (יַהַוַאהַדַנַה)(יַהַוַהַה)יאהדונהי Adonai (הד)

מָגֵן magen ג"פ אל (יא"י מילוי דס"ג) ; ר"ת מיכאל גבריאל נוריאל אַבְרָהָם Avraham

וז"פ אל, רי"ו ול"ב נתיבות החוכמה, רמ"ח (אברים), עסמ"ב וט"ז אותיות פעוטות:

The great, mighty and Awesome God.

The Supernal God, Who bestows beneficial kindness and creates everything. Who recalls the kindness of the forefathers and brings a Redeemer to their descendants for the sake of His Name, lovingly. King, Helper, Savior and Shield. Blessed are You, Lord, the shield of Abraham.

THE SECOND BLESSING

THE ENERGY OF ISAAC IGNITES THE POWER FOR THE RESURRECTION OF THE DEAD.

Whereas Abraham represents the power of sharing, Isaac represents the Left Column energy of Judgment. Judgment shortens the *tikkun* process and paves the way for our eventual resurrection.

Gevurah **that becomes** *Binah.*

In this section there are 49 words corresponding to the 49 Gates of the Pure System in *Binah.*

ללה Adonai אֲדֹנָי ר"ת אותיות דס"ג וי' אותיות le'olam לְעוֹלָם gibor גִּבּוֹר Ata אַתָּה

(ר"ת אֲגֶלָא והוא עם גָּדוֹל ואמיץ, ובו היה יהודה מתגבר על אויביו. ע"ה אלד, בוכו).

lehoshi'a לְהוֹשִׁיעַ rav רַב Ata אַתָּה metim מֵתִים ס"ג mechaye מְחַיֵּה

morid מוֹרִיד hatal הַטָּל יוד הא וא, כוזו, מספר אותיות דמילואי עסמ"ב ; ר"ת מ"הֹ:

If you mistakenly say "Mashiv haru'ach," and realize this before the end of the blessing "baruch Ata Adonai," you should return to the beginning of the blessing "Ata gibor" and continue as usual. But if you only realize this after the end of the blessing, you should start the Amidah from the beginning.

bechesed בְּחֶסֶד מ"ה ע"ה בינה, אהיה יהוה אהיה chayim וַיִּים mechalkel מְכַלְכֵּל

berachamim בְּרַחֲמִים metim מֵתִים ס"ג mechaye מְחַיֵּה יהוה. ע"ב, ריבוע

somech סוֹמֵךְ (טלא דעתיק) rabim רַבִּים י"פ יי אלהים דההין, (במוכסז) מצפצ, אלהים

cholim חוֹלִים verofe וְרוֹפֵא (ז"ו). noflim נוֹפְלִים אדני ריבוע כוק, (אכדטם)

umekayem וּמְקַיֵּם asurim אֲסוּרִים umatir וּמַתִּיר אותיות וד' מ"ה = וזולה.

chamocha כָּמוֹךָ ילי mi מִי afar עָפָר lishenei לִישֵׁנֵי emunato אֱמוּנָתוֹ

gevurot גְּבוּרוֹת ba'al בַּעַל (you should enunciate the letter *Ayin* in the word "ba'al")

memit מֵמִית melech מֶלֶךְ lach לָךְ dome דוֹמֶה ילי umi וּמִי

yeshu'a יְשׁוּעָה umatzmi'ach וּמַצְמִיחַ (יוד הי ואו הי) ס"ג umchaye וּמְחַיֵּה

metim מֵתִים lehachayot לְהַחֲיוֹת Ata אַתָּה vene'eman וְנֶאֱמָן

אהיה יהו יהוה

Adonai יְהֹוָה(יֱהֹוִה)(יֵאֲהֹדֹנֱהֹי)יאהדונהי Ata אַתָּה baruch בָּרוּךְ

hametim הַמֵּתִים (יוד הי ואו הי) ס"ג mechaye מְחַיֵּה ר"ת מ"ה וס"ת מ"הֹ:

THE SECOND BLESSING

You are mighty forever, Lord. You resurrect the dead and are very capable of redeeming. Who causes dew to fall. You sustain life with kindness and resurrect the dead with great compassion. You support those who have fallen, heal the sick, release the imprisoned, and fulfill Your faithful words to those who are asleep in the dust. Who is like You, Master of might, and Who can compare to You, King, Who causes death, Who gives life, and Who sprouts salvation? And You are faithful to resurrecting the dead. Blessed are You, Lord, Who resurrects the dead.

NAKDISHACH

vena'aritzach וְנַעֲרִיצָךְ nakdishach נַקְדִּישָׁךְ

sarfei שַׂרְפֵי האא י"פ מ"כ, sod סוֹד si'ach שִׂיחַ keno'am כְּנֹעַם

kedusha קְדֻשָּׁה lecha לָךְ hameshaleshim הַמְשַׁלְּשִׁים kodesh קֹדֶשׁ

vekara וְקָרָא nevi'ach נְבִיאָךְ yad יַד al עַל katuv כָּתוּב vechen וְכֵן

ve'amar וְאָמַר דרוזל לי"ב פרקין דיעקב מאירים י"ב ze זֶה el אֶל ze זֶה

Although Zeir Anpin elevates only as far as Tiferet of Dikna but not to Chochmah of Dikna:

Meditate to draw illumination from Chochmah of Dikna to Zeir Anpin | kadosh קָדוֹשׁ

Meditate to draw illumination from Tiferet of Dikna (8th Mazal) to Zeir Anpin kadosh קָדוֹשׁ

Meditate to draw illumination from Yesod of Dikna (13th Mazal) to Zeir Anpin kadosh קָדוֹשׁ

(סוד ג' רישין דעתיקא קדישא) פני שכינה tzeva'ot צְבָאוֹת Adonai יְהוָֹאדנִיאהדונהי

kevodo כְּבוֹדוֹ אלהים ע"ה דההין ילי ha'aretz הָאָרֶץ chol כָּל melo מְלֹא

ve'omrim וְאוֹמְרִים meshabechim מְשַׁבְּחִים le'umatam לְעֻמָּתָם

(או"א) baruch בָּרוּךְ kevod כְּבוֹד Adonai יְהוָֹאדנִיאהדונהי ; כבוד ה' = יוד הי ואו הה

mimekomo מִמְּקוֹמוֹ עסמ"ב, הברכה (לבמתק את ז' המלכים שמתו) ;ר"ת ע"ב, ריבוע יהוה ;ר"ת מיכ:

uvdivrei וּבְדִבְרֵי kodshach קָדְשָׁךְ katuv כָּתוּב lemor לֵאמֹר:

(זו"ן) yimloch יִמְלֹךְ קָדוֹשׁ בָּרוּךְ ר"ת יב"ק, אלהים יהוה, אהיה אדני יהוה

Elohayich אֱלֹהַיִךְ le'olam לְעוֹלָם ריבוע ס"ג וי' אותיות דס"ג Adonai יְהוָֹאדנִיאהדונהי ילה

Tziyon צִיּוֹן יוסף, ו' הויות, קנאה ; ר"ת אצלו (מלכות אצל ז"א - ו) ledor לְדֹר vador וָדֹר רי"ו;

haleluya הַלְלוּיָהּ אלהים, אהיה אדני ; ללה:

THE THIRD BLESSING

This blessing connects us to Jacob, the Central Column and the power of restriction. Jacob is our channel for connecting Mercy with Judgment. By restricting our reactive behavior, we are blocking our Desire to Receive for the Self Alone. Jacob also gives us the power to balance our acts of Mercy and Judgment toward other people in our lives.

NAKDISHACH

We sanctify You and we revere You,
according to the pleasant words of the counsel of the Holy Angels, who recite Holy before You three times,
as it is written by Your Prophet: "And each called to the other and said: Holy, Holy, Holy, Is the Lord of Hosts,
the entire world is filled with His glory." (Isaiah 6:3) Facing them they give praise and say:
"Blessed is the glory of the Lord from His Place." (Ezekiel 3:12) And in Your Holy Words, it is written as follows:
"The Lord, your God, shall reign forever, for each and for every generation. Zion, Praise the Lord!" (Psalms 146:10)

Tiferet that becomes *Da'at* (14 words).

אַתָּה Ata קָדוֹשׁ kadosh וְשִׁמְךָ veshimcha קָדוֹשׁ kadosh ר"ת = אור, רז, אין סוף♦

וּקְדוֹשִׁים ukdoshim בְּכָל־ bechol ב"ן, לכב יוֹם yom ע"ה נגד, מזבוח, זן, אל יהוה

יְהַלְלוּךָ yehalelucha סֶלָה sela:

אהלה יהו מצפצ

בָּרוּךְ baruch אַתָּה Ata יְהֹוֶה (יְהֹוִאַדְנִ"י)(יְהֹוֶאדְנִ"י)יאהדונהי Adonai

הָאֵל haEl הַקָדוֹשׁ hakadosh י"פ מ"ה (יוד הא ואו הא)♦ לאה ; ייא"י (מילוי דס"ג)

Meditate here on the Name: **יאהדונהי**, as it can help to remove anger.

THE FOURTH BLESSING - ATA ECHAD

The fourth blessing is the middle blessing corresponding to *Malchut*, which is the middle between *Chesed*, *Gevurah*, *Tiferet* (the three partriarchs - the three first blessings) and between *Netzah*, *Hod*, *Yesod* (the three last blessings) as it is explained in *Tikunei HaZohar*.

Meditate on the letter ת (*Tav*) from the Name: **שָׁקוּצִי"ת**.

אַתָּה Ata אֶוֹֽזֽד echad אהבה, דאגה

The letters *Alef* א and *Chet* ח are *Zeir Anpin* and the letter *Dalet* ד (4) is the four letters *Yud* י from the Name: **יוד הי ויו הי**, as *Zeir Anpin* ascends to the 500 *nimin* (chords) of *Arich Anpin*. Also, *Zeir Anpin* (represented by the word "*Ata*") receives from the Thirteen *Tikunnei Dikna* (represented by the word "*echad*" – equals 13). Also, *Abba* (also represented by the word "*Ata*") ascends with *Zeir Anpin* to the Thirteen *Tikunnei Dikna*, and They all become one (*echad*).

וְשִׁמְךָ veshimcha אֶוֹֽזֽד echad אהבה, דאגה.

Nukva (represented by the word "*shimcha*"), and although She (*Yaakov* and *Rachel*) does not ascend to Thirteen *Tikunnei Dikna*, She receives illumination from there. Also *Ima* (also represented by the word "*shimcha*") ascends with *Zeir Anpin* to the Thirteen *Tikunnei Dikna*, and They all become one.

וּמִי umi ילי che'amecha כְּעַמְּךָ keYisrael כְּיִשְׂרָאֵל

THE THIRD BLESSING
You are Holy, and Your Name is Holy, and the Holy Ones praise You every day,
for you are God, the Holy King Selah. Blessed are You, Lord, the Holy God.

THE FOURTH BLESSING - ATA ECHAD
You are One and Your Name is One, and there is none like Your People, Israel,

גּוֹי goy אֶוֹּד echad אהבה, דאגה

> Da'at ascends with *Abba* and *Ima* to the Thirteen *Tikunnei Dikna*.
> Three times the word "*echad*" equals 39 which is the same numerical value as the Holy Name: יוד הא ואו (also numerical value of ט"ל - dew), which is *Zeir Anpin*, that ascends with *Abba* and *Ima*.

בָּאָרֶץ ba'aretz

> *Yaakov* and *Rachel* (now stand in the place of *Abba*)
> become an accommodation to *Zeir Anpin* that was elevated to *Dikna* of *Arich Anpin*.

תִּפְאֶרֶת tiferet   גְּדֻלָּה gedula   וַעֲטֶרֶת va'ateret   יְשׁוּעָה yeshu'a

יוֹם yom ע"ה נגד, מזבח, ז, אל יהוה   מְנוּחָה menucha   וּקְדֻשָׁה ukdusha

לְעַמֶּךְ le'amecha   נָתַתָּ natata   אַבְרָהָם Avraham (Chesed)   וז"פ אל,

רי"ו ול"ב נתיבות החכמה, רמ"ח (אברים), עסמ"ב וט"ז אותיות פשוטות   יָגֵל yagel לְהוֹן

יִצְחָק Yitzchak (Gevurah) ד"פ ב"ן   יְרַנֵן yeranen

יַעֲקֹב Yaakov (Tiferet) ז' הויות, יאהדונהי אידהנויה

וּבָנָיו uvanav (Netzach, Hod, Yesod)

> Drawing Light from *Chochmah*, *Binah*, *Da'at* of *Zeir Anpin* (which was elevated to *Netzach*, *Hod*, *Yesod* of *Dikna*) to the Six Edegs (*Chesed*, *Gevurah*, *Tiferet*, *Netzach*, *Hod*, *Yesod*).

יָנוּחוּ yanuchu ר"ת = אל יהוה By ascending, *Nukva* receives a new Name: בוֹ vo

מְנוּחַת menuchat   אַהֲבָה ahava (Abba)   אוֹזד, דאגה

וּנְדָבָה undava (Ima) בינה, אהיה יהוה אהיה וע"ה וזיים.   מְנוּחַת menuchat

אֱמֶת emet אהיה פעמים אהיה, ז"פ ס"ג (Zeir Anpin) לכולם יש להם מנוחה שעולים לא"א)

וֶאֱמוּנָה ve'emuna (Nukva) שגם יש לה מנוחה שענמשך לה הארה מא"א)

---

one nation on Earth.
The splendor and greatness and the crown of salvation,
a Day of rest and Holiness, You had given to Your People. Abraham would rejoice, Isaac would exult, and Jacob and his children will rest on it; A rest of love and magnanimity; A rest of truth and of faith;

מְנוּחַת menuchat   שָׁלוֹם shalom   הַשְׁקֵט hashket   ר״ת משה = אל שדי

By ascending, *Zeir Anpin* gives His Name to *Nukva* and receives a new Name: **אל שדי**

שָׁאַתָּה sheAta   שְׁלֵמָה shelema   מְנוּחָה menucha   וָבֶטַח vavetach

הוּא hu   רוֹצֶה rotze   בָּה va   יַכִּירוּ yakiru   בָּנֶיךָ vanecha   *(Yisrael)*

וְיֵדְעוּ veyedu   כִּי ki   מֵאִתְּךָ me'itcha   *(Keter of Arich Anpin)*

הִיא hee   מְנוּחָתָם menuchatam   (כי משם נמשך הארה לישראל מא״א)

וְעַל ve'al   מְנוּחָתָם menuchatam   יַקְדִּישׁוּ yakdishu   אֶת et   שִׁמֶךָ shemecha:

Abba and *Ima* are elevated to *Arich Anpin* for the Supernal Unification. So for the Unificataion They need *Mayin Nukvin* from the unification of *Zeir* and *Nukva*. But because *Zeir Anpin* was elevated with Them, *Nukva* is left by Herself and She cannot create *Mayin Nukvin* without *Zeir*. So meditate: to devote your soul for the sanctification of the Holy Name, accept upon yourself the four forms of death, and to elevate your *Nefesh, Ruach, Neshamah, Chayah, Yechidah*, together with the *Partzufim* of *Netzach, Hod, Yesod* (**in the repetition:** *Chesed, Gevurah, Tiferet*) of *Yaakov* and *Rachel* to become as *Mayin Nukvin* to unify *Abba* and *Ima* (They are standing in *Dikna* of *Arich Anpin*). You should meditate that the Supernal Unification of *Abba* and *Ima* is in the general *Partzufim* of *Netzach, Hod, Yesod* (**in the repetition:** *Chesed, Gevurah, Tiferet*).

MEKADESH HASHABBAT

אֱלֹהֵינוּ Elohenu יכה   וֵאלֹהֵי velohei ; לכב   ; מילוי דע״ב, דמ״ב ; יכה יכה

אֲבוֹתֵינוּ avotenu   רְצֵה retze   נָא na   בִּמְנוּחָתֵנוּ vimnuchatenu

קַדְּשֵׁנוּ kadeshenu   בְּמִצְוֹתֶיךָ bemitzvotecha   שִׂים sim   וְחֶלְקֵנוּ chelkenu

בְּתוֹרָתֶךָ betoratach   שַׂבְּעֵנוּ sabe'enu   מִטּוּבֶךָ mituvach   לאו

A rest of peace and tranquility and security; A perfect rest in which You find favor. Your children will recognize and they shall know, that from You comes their rest and upon their rest, they shall sanctify Your Name.

MEKADESH HASHABBAT
Our God and God of our forefathers, please desire our rest.
Sanctify us with Your commandments and grant our share in Your Torah. Satisfy us from Your goodness,

שַׂמֵּחַ same'ach · נַפְשֵׁנוּ nafshenu · בִּישׁוּעָתֶךָ bishu'atach ◆ וְטַהֵר vetaher

לִבֵּנוּ libenu · לְעָבְדְּךָ le'avdecha · בֶּאֱמֶת be'emet (פוי, אל אדני אהיה פעמים אהיה, ז"פ ס"ג ◆)

וְהַנְחִילֵנוּ vehanchilenu · יְהֹוָ‎ה Adonai · אֱלֹהֵינוּ Elohenu (ילה)

בְּאַהֲבָה be'ahava · וּבְרָצוֹן uvratzon (אוזר, דאגה, מהטע ע"ה, ע"ב בריבוע קס"א ע"ה, אל שדי ע"ה,)

שַׁבַּת Shabbat · קָדְשֶׁךָ kodshecha ◆ וְיָנוּחוּ veyanuchu · בוֹ vo

כֹּל kol (ילי) · יִשְׂרָאֵל Yisrael · מְקַדְּשֵׁי mekadshei · שְׁמֶךָ shemecha ◆

אהיה יהו יה אדני

בָּרוּךְ baruch · אַתָּה Ata · יְהֹוָ‎ה Adonai

Meditate on the *Neshikin* (kisses - the upper unification),
from the Ten *Sefirot* of *Chochomah* of *Keter* of the five *Partzufim* of *Netzach, Hod, Yesod*
(in the repetition: *Chesed, Gevurah, Tiferet)* of *Keter* of *Zeir Anpin*
to the Ten *Sefirot* of *Chochomah* of *Keter* of the five *Partzufim* of *Netzach, Hod, Yesod*
(in the repetition: *Chesed, Gevurah, Tiferet)* of *Keter* of *Yaakov* and *Rachel*.

Chochmah	Da'at	Binah
א	י	ה
יהוה	מצפץ	יְהֹוָה
אהיה	אהיה	אֱהֵיֵ
יהוה	יהוה	יְהֹוָה

Meditate to draw Illumination to *Keter* of *Yaakov* and *Rachel* (which stand in *Netzach, Hod, Yesod* of *Zeir Anpin*, which its in *Chesed, Gevurah, Tiferet*
[in the repetition: *Chochmah, Binah, Da'at]* of *Abba* and *Ima*)
from the three *Mochin* – *Chochmah, Binah, Da'at* – enclosed by *Netzach, Hod, Yesod* **(in the repetition:** *Chesed, Gevurah, Tiferet)* of *Dikna* of *Arich Anpin* (Who are the *Mochin* are in *Chochmah, Binah, Da'at* of *Zeir Anpin* – through *Chesed, Gevurah, Tiferet* of *Zeir Anpin*).
Also draw *Malchut* of *Keter* of all the five *Partzufim* of *Netzach, Hod, Yesod* **(in the repetition:** *Chesed, Gevurah, Tiferet)* of *Keter* of Internal of *Zeir Anpin* **to** *Keter* of all the five *Partzufim* of *Netzach, Hod, Yesod* **(in the repetition:** *Chesed, Gevurah, Tiferet)* of *Keter* of External and Internal of *Yaakov* and *Rachel* **to** *Keter* of *Yaakov* and *Rachel* Who stands in the Chest of *Zeir Anpin*:

אהיה יהוה

(to the three Vessels of *Keter* of *Nukva*)

יוד הא ואו הה · יוד יוד הא יוד הא ואו יוד הא ואו הה · יה יהו יהוה

מְקַדֵּשׁ mekadesh · הַשַּׁבָּת haShabbat:

---

gladden our souls with Your salvation, and purify our hearts to serve You sincerely. Lord, our God, with love and favor, grant us Your Holy Sabbath as a heritage. And may all of Israel, the sanctifies of Your Name rest on It. Blessed are You, Lord, Who sanctifies the Sabbath.

THE FINAL THREE BLESSINGS

Through the merit of Moses, Aaron and Joseph, who are our channels for the final three blessings, we are able to bring down all the spiritual energy that we aroused with our prayers and blessings.

THE FIFTH BLESSING

During this blessing, referring to Moses, we should always meditate to try to know exactly what God wants from us in our life, as signified by the phrase, "Let it be the will of God." We ask God to guide us toward the work we came to Earth to do. The Creator cannot just accept the work that we want to do; we must carry out the work we were destined to do.

Netzach

Meditate for the Supernal Desire (*Keter*) that is called *metzach haratzon* (Forehead of the Desire).

רְצֵה retze אלף למד הה יוד מם

Meditate here to transform misfortune and tragedy (צרה) into desire and acceptance (רצה).

יְהֹוָה Adonai Elohenu אֱלֹהֵינוּ be'amecha בְּעַמְּךָ Yisrael יִשְׂרָאֵל

velitfilatam וְלִתְפִלָּתָם she'e שְׁעֵה vehashev וְהָשֵׁב ha'avoda הָעֲבוֹדָה

lidvir לִדְבִיר betecha בֵּיתֶךָ ve'ishei וְאִשֵּׁי Yisrael יִשְׂרָאֵל

utfilatam וּתְפִלָּתָם mehera מְהֵרָה be'ahava בְּאַהֲבָה

tekabel תְּקַבֵּל beratzon בְּרָצוֹן

ut'hi וּתְהִי leratzon לְרָצוֹן

tamid תָּמִיד avodat עֲבוֹדַת Yisrael יִשְׂרָאֵל amecha עַמֶּךָ

YA'ALE VEYAVO

During *Sukkot*, there is an extra surge of spiritual energy in our midst. "Ya'ale Veyavo" is our antenna for drawing this extra power into our lives.

If you mistakenly forgot to say "*ya'ale veyavo*," and realize this before the end of the blessing "*baruch Ata Adonai*," you should return to say "*ya'ale veyavo*" and continue as usual. If you realize this after the end of the blessing "*hamachazir shechinato leTziyon*" but before you start the next blessing "*modim*" you should say "*ya'ale veyavo*" there and continue as usual. If you only realize this after you have started the next blessing "*modim*" but before the second "*yih'yu leratzon*" (on pg. 730) you should return to "*retze*" (pg. 724) and continue from there. If you realize this after the second "*yih'yu leratzon*" you should start the *Amidah* from the beginning.

THE FINAL THREE BLESSINGS - THE FIFTH BLESSING

Find favor, Lord, our God, in Your People, Israel, and turn to their prayer.
Restore the service to the inner sanctuary of Your Temple. Accept the offerings of Israel and their prayer with favor, speedily, and with love. May the service of Your People Israel always be favorable to You.

אֱלֹהֵינוּ Elohenu ילה ; מילוי ע"ב, דמב ; ילה וֵאלֹהֵי velohei לכב ; מילוי ע"ב, דמב ; ילה אֲבוֹתֵינוּ avotenu

יַעֲלֶה ya'ale וְיָבֹא veyavo וְיַגִּיעַ veyagi'a רי"ו וְיֵרָאֶה veyera'e וְיֵרָצֶה veyeratze

וְיִשָּׁמַע veyishama וְיִפָּקֵד veyipaked וְיִזָּכֵר veyizacher ר"ת מ"ב (ז"פ ו)

זִכְרוֹנֵנוּ zichronenu וְזִכְרוֹן vezichron ע"ב קס"א ונ"ע"ב אֲבוֹתֵינוּ avotenu◆

זִכְרוֹן zichron ע"ב קס"א ונ"ע"ב יְרוּשָׁלַיִם Yerushalayim עִירָךְ irach◆

וְזִכְרוֹן vezichron ע"ב קס"א ונ"ע"ב מָשִׁיחַ mashi'ach בֶּן ben דָּוִד David ע"ה כהת ; בן

עַבְדָּךְ avdach פ"ו, אל אדני וְזִכְרוֹן vezichron ע"ב קס"א ונ"ע"ב כָּל kol דוד = אדני ע"ה ; ארני ע"ה

עַמְּךָ amecha ילו בֵּית bet Yisrael יִשְׂרָאֵל ב"פ ראה לְפָנֶיךָ lefanecha ס"ג מ"ה ב"ן

לִפְלֵיטָה lifleta לְטוֹבָה letova אכא◆ לְחֵן lechen מילוי דמ"ה בריבוע, מוזי

לְחֶסֶד lechesed ע"ב, ריבוע יהוה וּלְרַחֲמִים ulrachamim◆

לְחַיִּים lechayim אהיה אהיה יהוה, בינה ע"ה טוֹבִים tovim וּלְשָׁלוֹם ulshalom◆

בְּיוֹם beyom ע"ה נגד, מזבח, זן, אל יהוה: וְחַג chag הַסֻּכּוֹת haSukkot הַזֶּה haze והו

בְּיוֹם beyom ע"ה נגד, מזבח, זן, אל יהוה מִקְרָא mikra קֹדֶשׁ kodesh הַזֶּה haze והו◆

לְרַחֵם lerachem אברהם, וו"פ אל, רי"ו ול"ב נתיבות החוכמה, רמ"ז (אברים), עסמ"ב וט"ז אותיות פשוטות

בּוֹ bo עָלֵינוּ alenu וּלְהוֹשִׁיעֵנוּ ulhoshi'enu◆ זָכְרֵנוּ zochrenu

יְהֹוָאדֹנָיאהדונהי Adonai אֱלֹהֵינוּ Elohenu ילה בּוֹ bo לְטוֹבָה letova אכא◆

וּפָקְדֵנוּ ufokdenu בוֹ vo לִבְרָכָה livracha◆ וְהוֹשִׁיעֵנוּ vehoshi'enu בוֹ vo

לְחַיִּים lechayim אהיה אהיה יהוה, בינה ע"ה טוֹבִים tovim◆

בִּדְבַר bidvar ראה יְשׁוּעָה yeshu'a וְרַחֲמִים verachamim◆ וְחוּס chus

וְחָנֵּנוּ vechonenu וַחֲמֹל vachamol וְרַחֵם verachem אברהם, וו"פ אל,

עָלֵינוּ alenu◆ רי"ו ול"ב נתיבות החוכמה, רמ"ז (אברים), עסמ"ב וט"ז אותיות פשוטות

YA'ALE VEYAVO

Our God and God of our forefathers, may it rise, come, arrive, appear, find favor, be heard, be considered, and be remembered, our remembrance and the remembrance of our forefathers: the remembrance of Jerusalem, Your City, and the remembrance of Mashiach, Son of David, Your servant, and the remembrance of Your entire Nation, the House of Israel, before You for deliverance, for good, for grace, kindness, and compassion, for a good life, and for peace on the day of: This festival of Sukkot, on this Holy Day of Convocation; To take pity on us and to save us. Remember us, Lord, our God, on this day, for good; consider us on it for blessing; and deliver us on it for a good life, with the words of deliverance and mercy. Take pity and be gracious to us, have mercy and be compassionate with us,

וְהוֹשִׁיעֵנוּ ki כִּי מ"ה רֵבִיעַ עֵינֵינוּ enenu אֵלֶיךָ elecha כִּי ki וְהוֹשִׁיעֵנוּ vehoshi'enu

אֵל El יא"י (מילוי דס"ג) מֶלֶךְ melech וְחַנּוּן chanun וְרַחוּם verachum אַתָּה Ata:

וְאַתָּה veAta בְּרַחֲמֶךָ verachamecha הָרַבִּים harabim•

תַּחְפֹּץ tachpotz בָּנוּ banu וְתִרְצֵנוּ vetirtzenu וְתֶחֱזֶינָה vetechezena

עֵינֵינוּ enenu מ"ה רֵבִיעַ בְּשׁוּבְךָ beshuvcha לְצִיּוֹן leTziyon יוסף, ו' הויות, קנאה:

בְּרַחֲמִים berachamim מצפצ, אלהים דיודין, י"פ ייי:

אהיה יהו אל

בָּרוּךְ baruch אַתָּה Ata יְהוָ֑ה ואדני אהיה ואהדונהי Adonai

הַמַּחֲזִיר hamachazir שְׁכִינָתוֹ shechinato לְצִיּוֹן leTziyon יוסף, ו' הויות, קנאה:

THE SIXTH BLESSING

This blessing is our thank you. Kabbalistically, the biggest "thank you" we can give the Creator is to do exactly what we are supposed to do in terms of our spiritual work.

Hod

Bow your entire body at "modim" and straighten up at "Adonai."

מוֹדִים modim מאה ברכות עתיקן דוד לאמרם כל יום אֲנַחְנוּ anachnu לָךְ lach

שָׁאַתָּה sheAta הוּא hu יְהוָ֑ה ואדני אהיה ואהדונהי Adonai (וג) אֱלֹהֵינוּ Elohenu ילה

וֵאלֹהֵי velohei אֲבוֹתֵינוּ avotenu ילה ; מילוי ע"ב, דמב ; לכב מילוי ע"ב לֵעוֹלָם le'olam

צוּר tzur אלהים דההן ע"ה רֵבִיעַ ס"ג ו"י אותיות דס"ג צוּרֵנוּ tzurenu וָעֶד va'ed•

חַיֵּינוּ chayenu וּמָגֵן umagen (יא"י מילוי דס"ג) אל ג"פ ; ר"ת מיכאל גבריאל נוריאל וְיִשְׁעֵנוּ yish'enu רי"ו

אַתָּה Ata הוּא hu• לְדֹר ledor וָדֹר vador רי"ו

נוֹדֶה node לְךָ lecha וּנְסַפֵּר unsaper תְּהִלָּתֶךָ tehilatecha•

עַל al וְחַיֵּינוּ chayenu הַמְּסוּרִים hamesurim בְּיָדֶךָ beyadecha•

---

and save us, for our eyes turn to You, because You are God, the King Who is gracious and compassionate. And You in Your great compassion take delight in us and are pleased with us. May our eyes witness Your return to Zion with compassion. Blessed are You, Lord, Who returns His Shechinah to Zion.

THE SIXTH BLESSING

We give thanks to You,

for it is You, Lord, Who is our God and God of our forefathers, forever and for all eternity. You are our Rock, the Rock of our lives, and the Shield of our salvation. From one generation to another, we shall give thanks to You and we shall tell of Your praise. For our lives that are entrusted in Your hands,

וְעַל ve'al • כָּךְ lach • הַפְּקוּדוֹת hapekudot • נִשְׁמוֹתֵינוּ nishmotenu • וְעַל ve'al

נִסֶּיךָ nisecha • שֶׁבְּכָל shebechol • ב"ן, לכב יוֹם yom ע"ה נגד, מזבח, זן, אל יהוה

עִמָּנוּ imanu • ריבוע ס"ג, קס"א ע"ה וד' אותיות • וְעַל ve'al • נִפְלְאוֹתֶיךָ nifle'otecha

וְטוֹבוֹתֶיךָ vetovotecha • שֶׁבְּכָל shebechol • ב"ן, לכב עֵת et • עֶרֶב erev

וָבֹקֶר vavoker • וְצָהֳרָיִם vetzahorayim • הַטּוֹב hatov • כִּי ki • לֹא lo

כָּלוּ chalu • רַחֲמֶיךָ rachamecha • הַמְרַחֵם hamerachem • אברהם, וז"פ אל, רי"ו ול"ב

תַמּוּ tamu • כִּי ki • לֹא lo • חֲסָדֶיךָ chasadecha • מֵעוֹלָם me'olam • קִוִּינוּ kivinu • לָךְ lach:

MODIM DERABANAN

This prayer is recited by the congregation in the repetition when the *chazan* says *"modim."*

In this section there are 44 words, which is the same numerical value as the Name:
ריבוע אהיה (א אה אהי אהיה).

מוֹדִים modim • מאה ברכות עתקן דוד לאמרם כל יום • אֲנַחְנוּ anachnu • כָּךְ lach

שָׁאַתָּה sheAta • הוּא hu • יְהֹוָאֲדֹנָיֱהֹוִהֲדֹנָי Adonai • אֱלֹהֵנוּ Elohenu • ילה

וֵאלֹהֵי velohei • לכב ; ע"ב, דמב • אֲבוֹתֵינוּ avotenu

אֱלֹהֵי Elohei • כָּל chol ; יֵלֵי • בָּשָׂר basar • יוֹצְרֵנוּ yotzrenu

יוֹצֵר yotzer • בְּרֵאשִׁית bereshit • בְּרְכוֹת berachot • וְהוֹדָאוֹת vehoda'ot

לְשִׁמְךָ leshimcha • הַגָּדוֹל hagadol • ; לְהֶן • וְהַקָּדוֹשׁ vehakadosh • עַל al • שֶׁהֶחֱיִיתָנוּ shehecheyitanu • וְקִיַּמְתָּנוּ vekiyamtanu•

כֵּן ken • תְּחַיֵּנוּ techayenu • וּתְחָנֵּנוּ utchonenu• • וְתֶאֱסוֹף vete'esof

גָּלֻיּוֹתֵינוּ galuyotenu • לְחַצְרוֹת lechatzrot • קָדְשֶׁךָ kodshecha• • לִשְׁמֹר lishmor

חֻקֶּיךָ chukecha • וְלַעֲשׂוֹת vela'asot • רְצוֹנֶךָ retzoncha• • וּלְעָבְדְּךָ ul'ovdecha

בְּלֵבָב belevav • שָׁלֵם shalem• • עַל al • שֶׁאֲנַחְנוּ she'anachnu

מוֹדִים modim • לָךְ lach• • בָּרוּךְ baruch • אֵל El • הַהוֹדָאוֹת hahoda'ot:

---

for our souls that are in Your care,

for Your miracles that are with us every day, and for Your wonders and Your favors that are with us at all times: evening, morning and afternoon. You are the good One, for Your compassion has never ceased. You are the compassionate One, for Your kindness has never ended, for we have always placed our hope in You.

MODIM DERABANAN

We give thanks to You, for it is You Lord,

our God and God of our forefathers, the God of all flesh, our Maker and the Former of all Creation. Blessings and thanks to Your great and Holy Name for giving us life and for preserving us. So may You continue to give us life, be gracious to us, and gather our exiles to the courtyards of Your Sanctuary, so that we may keep Your laws, fulfill Your will, and serve You wholeheartedly. For this, we thank You. Bless the God of thanksgiving.

veyitromam וְיִתְרוֹמַם   yitbarach יִתְבָּרַךְ   kulam כֻּלָּם   ve'al וְעַל

shimcha שִׁמְךָ קמ"ג קנ"א קס"א קס"א ע"ה   tamid תָּמִיד   veyitnase וְיִתְנַשֵּׂא

•va'ed וָעֶד דס"ג אותיות וי'   le'olam לְעוֹלָם ריבוע ס"ג וי'   malkenu מַלְכֵּנוּ

:sela סֶלָה   yoducha יוֹדוּךָ בינה ע"ה אהיה אהיה יהוה,   hachayim הַחַיִּים יל'   vechol וְכָל־

et אֶת־ מ"ה   vihalelu וִיהַלְלוּ יהוה ריבוע יהוה   vivarchu וִיבָרְכוּ יהוה

be'emet בֶּאֱמֶת יכל, אום ד' אותיות = מבה; עם להו   hagadol הַגָּדוֹל   shimcha שִׁמְךָ

; והו tov טוֹב ki כִּי ו' אותיות דס"ג ס"ג ריבוע le'olam לְעוֹלָם אהיה פעמים אהיה, ז"פ ס"ג

yeshu'atenu יְשׁוּעָתֵנוּ מבה, אום, אהיה = יהוה = כי טוב   haEl הָאֵל לאה ; יא"י (מילוי דס"ג) יכל,

:והו hatov הַטּוֹב לאה ; יא"י (מילוי דס"ג) haEl הָאֵל •sela סֶלָה ve'ezratenu וְעֶזְרָתֵנוּ

Bend your knees at "baruch," bow at "Ata" and straighten up at "Adonai."

אהיה יהו אלהים

והו hatov הַטּוֹב (הי) Adonai יָהֹוָואֲדֹנָהִידֵאַי Ata אַתָּה baruch בָּרוּךְ

:שמיון בן דוד ע"ה lehodot לְהוֹדוֹת ס"ת כהת, משיון בן דוד ע"ה na'e נָאֶה ulcha וּלְךָ shimcha שִׁמְךָ

THE FINAL BLESSING

We are emanating the energy of peace to the entire world. We also make it our intent to use our mouths only for good. Kabbalistically, the power of words and speech is unimaginable. We hope to use that power wisely, which is perhaps one of the most difficult tasks we have to carry out.

Yesod

shalom שָׁלוֹם   sim שִׂים

tova טוֹבָה אבא   uvracha וּבְרָכָה   chayim וְחַיִּים בינה ע"ה אהיה אהיה יהוה,

chen חֵן מילוי   vachesed וָחֶסֶד ע"ב, ריבוע יהוה בריבוע, דמ"ה מילוי

tzedaka צְדָקָה ע"ה ריבוע אלהים   verachamim וְרַחֲמִים   alenu עָלֵינוּ

And for all those things, may Your Name be always blessed, exalted and extolled, our King, forever and ever, and all the living shall thank You, Selah. And they shall praise and bless Your Great Name, sincerely and forever, for It is good, the God of our salvation and our help, Selah, the good God. Blessed are You, Lord, whose Name is good, and to You it is befitting to give thanks.

THE FINAL BLESSING

Place peace, goodness, blessing, life, grace, kindness, righteousness, and mercy upon us

וְעַל־ ve'al כָּל־ kol ; עמם יﬠ Yisrael יִשְׂרָאֵל amecha עַמְּךָ uvarchenu וּבָרְכֵנוּ

אָבִינוּ avinu כֻּלָּנוּ kulanu כְּאֶחָד ke'echad אהבה, דאגה be'or בְּאוֹר רו, א"ס

פָּנֶיךָ panecha ס"ג מ"ה ב"ן ki כִּי ve'or בְּאוֹר רו, א"ס panecha פָּנֶיךָ ס"ג מ"ה ב"ן

נָתַתָּ natata לָנוּ lanu אלהים, אהיה אדני Adonai יָהֹיאהדונהי

אֱלֹהֵינוּ Elohenu ילה torah תּוֹרָה vechayim וְחַיִּים אהיה אהיה יהוה, בינה ע"ה ◆

אַהֲבָה ahava אוֹד, דאגה vachesed וָחֶסֶד ע"ב, ריבוע יהוה ◆

צְדָקָה tzedaka ע"ה ריבוע אלהים verachamim ◆ וְרַחֲמִים beracha בְּרָכָה

וְשָׁלוֹם veshalom ◆ vetov וְטוֹב והו be'enecha בְּעֵינֶיךָ ע"ה קס"א ; ריבוע מ"ה

לְבָרְכֵנוּ levarchenu ulvarech וּלְבָרֵךְ et אֶת־ kol כָּל־ ילי amecha עַמְּךָ

יִשְׂרָאֵל Yisrael berov בְּרוֹב־ י"פ אהיה oz עֹז veshalom וְשָׁלוֹם

אהיה יהו מצפצ

בָּרוּךְ baruch אַתָּה Ata יודוווהדניאהילויאהדונהי Adonai

הַמְבָרֵךְ hamevarech et אֶת amo עַמּוֹ Yisrael יִשְׂרָאֵל

ר"ת = אלהים (אילהויהם) = יב"ק bashalom ◆ בְּשָׁלוֹם amen אָמֵן יאהדונהי ◆

YIH'YU LERATZON
There are 42 letters in the verse in the secret of *Ana Beko'ach*.

יִהְיוּ yih'yu אל (ייא"י מילוי דס"ג) leratzon לְרָצוֹן מהטע ע"ה, ע"ב בריבוע וקס"א וקס"א ע"ה, אל שדי ע"ה

אִמְרֵי imrei fi פִי ר"ת אלף = אלף למד מם דלת יוד ע"ה vehegyon וְהֶגְיוֹן libi לִבִּי

לְפָנֶיךָ lefanecha ס"ג מ"ה ב"ן Adonai יָהֹיאהדונהי tzuri צוּרִי vego'ali וְגֹאֲלִי

---

and upon all of Israel, Your People. Bless us all as one, our Father, with the Light of Your Countenance, because it is with the Light of Your Countenance that You, Lord, our God, have given us Torah and life, love and kindness, righteousness and mercy, blessing and peace. May it be good in Your Eyes to bless us and to bless Your entire Nation, Israel, with abundant power and with peace. Blessed are You, Lord, Who blesses His Nation, Israel, with peace, Amen.

YIH'YU LERATZON
"May the utterances of my mouth and the thoughts of my heart find favor before You, Lord, my Rock and my Redeemer." (Psalms 19:15)

ELOHAI NETZOR

אֱלֹהַי Elohai מילוי ע"ב, דמצ ; ילה ; נְצוֹר netzor לְשׁוֹנִי leshoni מֵרָע mera◆

וְשִׂפְתוֹתַי vesiftotai מִדַּבֵּר midaber ראה מִרְמָה mirma◆ וְלִמְקַלְלַי velimkalelai

נַפְשִׁי nafshi תִדּוֹם tidom◆ וְנַפְשִׁי venafshi כֶּעָפָר ke'afar

לַכֹּל lakol יה אדני תִּהְיֶה tih'ye◆ פְּתַח petach לִבִּי libi בְּתוֹרָתֶךָ betoratecha◆

וְאַחֲרֵי ve'acharei מִצְוֹתֶיךָ mitzvotecha תִּרְדּוֹף tirdof נַפְשִׁי nafshi◆

וְכָל vechol יִלי הַקָּמִים hakamim עָלַי alai לְרָעָה lera'a רהע◆ מְהֵרָה mehera

הָפֵר hafer עֲצָתָם atzatam וְקַלְקֵל vekalkel מַחְשְׁבוֹתָם machshevotam◆

עֲשֵׂה ase לְמַעַן lema'an שְׁמֶךָ shemach◆ עֲשֵׂה ase לְמַעַן lema'an

יְמִינֶךָ yeminach◆ עֲשֵׂה ase לְמַעַן lema'an תּוֹרָתֶךָ toratach◆ עֲשֵׂה ase

לְמַעַן lema'an קְדֻשָּׁתֶךָ kedushatach◆ ר"ת הפסוק = מ"ה יהוה לְמַעַן lema'an

יֵחָלְצוּן yechaltzun יְדִידֶיךָ yedidecha ר"ת ילי יהוה הוֹשִׁיעָה hoshi'a יהוה וע"ע נהורין

יְמִינְךָ yemincha וַעֲנֵנִי va'aneni (כתיב : וְעֵנֵנוּ) ר"ת אל (ייא"י מילוי דס"ג) ♦

Before we recite the next verse *"Yih'yu leratzon"* we have an opportunity to strengthen our connection to our soul using our name. Each person has a verse in the *Torah* that connects to their name. Either their name is in the verse, or the first and last letters of the name correspond to the first or last letters of a verse. For example, the name Yehuda begins with a *Yud* and ends with a *Hei*. Before we end the *Amidah*, we state that our name will always be remembered when our soul leaves this world.

YIH'YU LERATZON (THE SECOND)

There are 42 letters in the verse in the secret of *Ana Beko'ach*.

יִהְיוּ yih'yu אל (ייא"י מילוי דס"ג) לְרָצוֹן leratzon מהש ע"ה, ע"ב בריבוע וקס"א ע"ה, אל שדי ע"ה

אִמְרֵי imrei פִי fi ר"ת אֶלֶף = אלף למד שין דלת יוד ע"ה וְהֶגְיוֹן vehegyon לִבִּי libi

לְפָנֶיךָ lefanecha ס"ג מ"ה ב"ן יְהֹוָאדֹנָיאהדונהי Adonai צוּרִי tzuri וְגֹאֲלִי vego'ali ♦

ELOHAI NETZOR

My God, guard my tongue from evil and my lips from speaking deceit. To those who curse me, let my spirit remain silent, and let my spirit be as dust for everyone. Open my heart to Your Torah and let my heart pursue Your commandments. All those who rise against me to do me harm, speedily nullify their plans and disturb their thoughts. Do so for the sake of Your Name. Do so for the sake of Your Right. Do so for the sake of Your Torah. Do so for the sake of Your Holiness, "So that Your loved ones may be saved. Redeem Your Right and answer me." (Psalms 60:7)

YIH'YU LERATZON (THE SECOND)

"May the utterances of my mouth and the thoughts of my heart find favor before You, Lord, my Rock and my Redeemer." (Psalms 19:15)

Ose Shalom

You take three steps backward;

Left
You turn to the left and say:

shalom שָׁלוֹם ose עֹשֶׂה

bimromav בִּמְרוֹמָיו ר"ת ע"ב, ריבוע יהוה

Right
You turn to the right and say:

ya'ase יַעֲשֶׂה verachamav בְּרַחֲמָיו hu הוּא

shalom שָׁלוֹם alenu עָלֵינוּ ר"ת ש"ע נהורין

Center
You face the center and say:

Yisrael יִשְׂרָאֵל amo עַמּוֹ עמם ; ילי kol כָּל ve'al וְעַל

ve'imru וְאִמְרוּ amen אָמֵן יאהדונהי:

yehi יְהִי ratzon רָצוֹן מהש ע"ה, ע"ב ע"ה, בריבוע וקס"א ע"ה אל שדי ע"ה

milfanecha מִלְפָנֶיךָ ס"ג מ"ה ב"ן יְהֹוָאֱלֹהֵינוּ Adonai אֲדֹנָי Elohenu אֱלֹהֵינוּ ילה

velohei וֵאלֹהֵי ילה ; דמב ע"ב, מילוי לכב ; avotenu אֲבוֹתֵינוּ, shetivne שֶׁתִּבְנֶה

bet בֵּית ב"פ ראה hamikdash הַמִּקְדָּשׁ bimhera בִּמְהֵרָה veyamenu בְיָמֵינוּ

veten וְתֵן chelkenu וְחֶלְקֵנוּ betoratach בְּתוֹרָתֶךָ la'asot לַעֲשׂוֹת chukei חֻקֵּי

retzonach רְצוֹנֶךָ ul'ovdach וּלְעָבְדְךָ פוי, אל אדני belevav בְּלֵבָב בוכו shalem שָׁלֵם

You take three steps forward.

Continue with "*Kaddish Titkabal*" on page 599.

Ose Shalom

He, Who makes peace in His High Places, He, in His compassion, shall make peace upon us. And upon His entire nation, Israel, and you shall say, Amen.

May it be pleasing before You, Lord, our God and God of our forefathers, that You shall rebuild the Temple speedily, in our days, and place our lot in Your Torah, so that we may fulfill the laws of Your desire and serve You wholeheartedly.

TORAH READING FOR THE FIRST DAY OF SUKKOT

וַיְדַבֵּ֣ר יְהֹוָ֖הֱלֹהִיאהדונהי אֶל־מֹשֶׁ֥ה לֵּאמֹֽר׃ שׁ֣וֹר אוֹ־כֶ֤שֶׂב אוֹ־עֵז֙ כִּ֣י יִוָּלֵ֔ד וְהָיָ֛ה

שִׁבְעַ֥ת יָמִ֖ים תַּ֣חַת אִמּ֑וֹ וּמִיּ֤וֹם הַשְּׁמִינִי֙ וָהָ֔לְאָה יֵרָצֶ֕ה לְקׇרְבַּ֥ן אִשֶּׁ֖ה

לַיהֹוָֽהֱלֹהִיאהדונהי׃ וְשׁ֖וֹר אוֹ־שֶׂ֑ה אֹת֣וֹ וְאֶת־בְּנ֗וֹ לֹ֥א תִשְׁחֲט֖וּ בְּי֥וֹם אֶחָֽד׃ וְכִֽי־

תִזְבְּח֧וּ זֶֽבַח־תּוֹדָ֛ה לַיהֹוָ֖הֱלֹהִיאהדונהי לִֽרְצֹנְכֶ֥ם תִּזְבָּֽחוּ׃ בַּיּ֤וֹם הַהוּא֙ יֵֽאָכֵ֔ל לֹֽא־

תוֹתִ֥ירוּ מִמֶּ֖נּוּ עַד־בֹּ֑קֶר אֲנִ֖י יְהֹוָֽהֱלֹהִיאהדונהי׃ וּשְׁמַרְתֶּם֙ מִצְוֺתַ֔י וַעֲשִׂיתֶ֖ם אֹתָ֑ם

אֲנִ֖י יְהֹוָֽהֱלֹהִיאהדונהי׃ וְלֹ֤א תְחַלְּלוּ֙ אֶת־שֵׁ֣ם קׇדְשִׁ֔י וְנִקְדַּשְׁתִּ֕י בְּת֖וֹךְ בְּנֵ֣י יִשְׂרָאֵ֑ל

אֲנִ֖י יְהֹוָ֖הֱלֹהִיאהדונהי מְקַדִּשְׁכֶֽם׃ הַמּוֹצִ֤יא אֶתְכֶם֙ מֵאֶ֣רֶץ מִצְרַ֔יִם לִהְי֥וֹת לָכֶ֖ם

לֵֽאלֹהִ֑ים אֲנִ֖י יְהֹוָֽהֱלֹהִיאהדונהי׃ *(Levi on Shabbat)* וַיְדַבֵּ֥ר יְהֹוָ֖הֱלֹהִיאהדונהי אֶל־מֹשֶׁ֥ה

לֵּאמֹֽר׃ דַּבֵּ֞ר אֶל־בְּנֵ֤י יִשְׂרָאֵל֙ וְאָמַרְתָּ֣ אֲלֵהֶ֔ם מוֹעֲדֵ֣י יְהֹוָ֖הֱלֹהִיאהדונהי

אֲשֶׁר־תִּקְרְא֥וּ אֹתָ֖ם מִקְרָאֵ֣י קֹ֑דֶשׁ אֵ֥לֶּה הֵ֖ם מוֹעֲדָֽי׃ שֵׁ֣שֶׁת יָמִים֮ תֵּעָשֶׂ֣ה

מְלָאכָה֒ וּבַיּ֣וֹם הַשְּׁבִיעִ֗י שַׁבַּ֤ת שַׁבָּתוֹן֙ מִקְרָא־קֹ֔דֶשׁ כׇּל־מְלָאכָ֖ה לֹ֣א תַעֲשׂ֑וּ

שַׁבָּ֥ת הִ֛וא לַיהֹוָ֖הֱלֹהִיאהדונהי בְּכֹ֖ל מוֹשְׁבֹֽתֵיכֶֽם׃ *(Third on Shabbat)* Levi

אֵ֚לֶּה מוֹעֲדֵ֣י יְהֹוָ֔הֱלֹהִיאהדונהי מִקְרָאֵ֖י קֹ֑דֶשׁ אֲשֶׁר־תִּקְרְא֥וּ אֹתָ֖ם בְּמוֹעֲדָֽם׃

בַּחֹ֣דֶשׁ הָרִאשׁ֗וֹן בְּאַרְבָּעָ֥ה עָשָׂ֛ר לַחֹ֖דֶשׁ בֵּ֣ין הָעַרְבָּ֑יִם פֶּ֖סַח לַיהֹוָֽהֱלֹהִיאהדונהי׃

וּבַחֲמִשָּׁ֨ה עָשָׂ֜ר י֤וֹם לַחֹ֨דֶשׁ֙ הַזֶּ֔ה חַ֥ג הַמַּצּ֖וֹת לַיהֹוָ֑הֱלֹהִיאהדונהי שִׁבְעַ֥ת יָמִ֖ים

מַצּ֥וֹת תֹּאכֵֽלוּ׃ בַּיּוֹם֙ הָרִאשׁ֔וֹן מִקְרָא־קֹ֖דֶשׁ יִהְיֶ֣ה לָכֶ֑ם כׇּל־מְלֶ֥אכֶת

עֲבֹדָ֖ה לֹ֥א תַעֲשֽׂוּ׃ וְהִקְרַבְתֶּ֥ם אִשֶּׁ֛ה לַיהֹוָ֖הֱלֹהִיאהדונהי שִׁבְעַ֣ת יָמִ֑ים בַּיּ֤וֹם

הַשְּׁבִיעִי֙ מִקְרָא־קֹ֔דֶשׁ כׇּל־מְלֶ֥אכֶת עֲבֹדָ֖ה לֹ֥א תַעֲשֽׂוּ׃ *(Fourth on Shabbat)*

TORAH READING FOR THE FIRST DAY OF SUKKOT

"And the Lord spoke to Moses saying: When a bullock, a sheep or a goat is born, it shall remain seven days with his mother, and from the eighth day and thenceforth it shall be favorably receives as an fire offering to the Lord. And an ox or sheep, you shall not kill it and its young both on the same day. And a sacrifice of thanksgiving offering to the Lord you shall offer it that it may be favorably receive of you. It shall be eaten on the same day, and you shall leave none of it until the morning, I am the Lord. And you shall keep my commandments and do them I am the Lord. You shall not profane My Holy Name and I will sanctify among the children of Israel, I am the Lord who sanctify you. Who took you out of Egypt to be your God, I am the Lord. **(LEVI ON SHABBAT)** *And the Lord spoke to Moses, saying: Speak to the children of Israel, and tell them, those are the holidays of the Lord that you shall call Holy Convocations, those are my holidays. Six days you shall work and on the seventh day is Sabbath of rest Holy Convocation, no work shall be done; it is Sabbath for the Lord in all your dwellings.* **LEVI (ISRAEL ON SHABBAT)** *Those are the holidays of the Lord, Holy Convocations which you proclaim in their seasons. On the first month on the fourteenth day of the month, towards evening is Pesach for the Lord. And on the fifteenth day for the same month is the Matzot (unleavened bread) holiday for the Lord, seven days you shall eat matzot. The first day will be a Holy Convocation, no work shall be done. And you shall offer fire offering to the Lord for seven days, and on the seventh day Holy Convocation no work shall be done.* **(FOURTH OF SABBATH)**

וַיְדַבֵּ֥ר יְהֹוָ֖האֲדֹנָי אֶל־מֹשֶׁ֥ה לֵּאמֹֽר: דַּבֵּ֞ר אֶל־בְּנֵ֤י יִשְׂרָאֵל֙ וְאָמַרְתָּ֣
אֲלֵהֶ֔ם כִּֽי־תָבֹ֣אוּ אֶל־הָאָ֗רֶץ אֲשֶׁ֤ר אֲנִי֙ נֹתֵ֣ן לָכֶ֔ם וּקְצַרְתֶּ֖ם אֶת־קְצִירָ֑הּ
וַהֲבֵאתֶ֥ם אֶת־עֹ֛מֶר רֵאשִׁ֥ית קְצִֽירְכֶ֖ם אֶל־הַכֹּהֵֽן: וְהֵנִ֧יף אֶת־הָעֹ֛מֶר לִפְנֵ֥י
יְהֹוָ֖האֲדֹנָי לִרְצֹֽנְכֶ֑ם מִֽמׇּחֳרַת֙ הַשַּׁבָּ֔ת יְנִיפֶ֖נּוּ הַכֹּהֵֽן: וַעֲשִׂיתֶ֕ם בְּי֥וֹם
הֲנִֽיפְכֶ֖ם אֶת־הָעֹ֑מֶר כֶּ֣בֶשׂ תָּמִ֧ים בֶּן־שְׁנָת֛וֹ לְעֹלָ֖ה לַֽיהֹוָֽהאֲדֹנָֽי:
וּמִנְחָת֩וֹ שְׁנֵ֨י עֶשְׂרֹנִ֜ים סֹ֣לֶת בְּלוּלָ֥ה בַשֶּׁ֛מֶן אִשֶּׁ֥ה לַֽיהֹוָ֖האֲדֹנָי רֵ֣יחַ נִיחֹ֑חַ
וְנִסְכֹּ֥ה יַ֖יִן רְבִיעִ֥ת הַהִֽין: וְלֶ֩חֶם֩ וְקָלִ֨י וְכַרְמֶ֜ל לֹ֣א תֹֽאכְל֗וּ עַד־עֶ֙צֶם֙
הַיּ֣וֹם הַזֶּ֔ה עַ֚ד הֲבִ֣יאֲכֶ֔ם אֶת־קׇרְבַּ֖ן אֱלֹֽהֵיכֶ֑ם חֻקַּ֤ת עוֹלָם֙ לְדֹרֹ֣תֵיכֶ֔ם
בְּכֹ֖ל מֹשְׁבֹֽתֵיכֶֽם: *(Fifth on Shabbat) Israel* וּסְפַרְתֶּ֤ם לָכֶם֙ מִמׇּחֳרַ֣ת הַשַּׁבָּ֔ת
מִיּוֹם֙ הֲבִ֣יאֲכֶ֔ם אֶת־עֹ֖מֶר הַתְּנוּפָ֑ה שֶׁ֥בַע שַׁבָּת֖וֹת תְּמִימֹ֥ת תִּהְיֶֽינָה:
עַ֣ד מִֽמׇּחֳרַ֤ת הַשַּׁבָּת֙ הַשְּׁבִיעִ֔ת תִּסְפְּר֖וּ חֲמִשִּׁ֣ים י֑וֹם וְהִקְרַבְתֶּ֛ם
מִנְחָ֥ה חֲדָשָׁ֖ה לַֽיהֹוָֽהאֲדֹנָֽי: מִמּֽוֹשְׁבֹ֨תֵיכֶ֜ם תָּבִ֣יאוּ ׀ לֶ֣חֶם תְּנוּפָ֗ה שְׁתַּ֛יִם
שְׁנֵ֣י עֶשְׂרֹנִ֗ים סֹ֣לֶת תִּהְיֶ֔ינָה חָמֵ֖ץ תֵּֽאָפֶ֑ינָה בִּכּוּרִ֖ים לַֽיהֹוָֽהאֲדֹנָֽי:
וְהִקְרַבְתֶּ֣ם עַל־הַלֶּ֗חֶם שִׁבְעַ֨ת כְּבָשִׂ֤ים תְּמִימִם֙ בְּנֵ֣י שָׁנָ֔ה וּפַ֧ר בֶּן־בָּקָ֛ר אֶחָ֖ד
וְאֵילִ֣ם שְׁנָ֑יִם יִהְי֤וּ עֹלָה֙ לַֽיהֹוָ֔ה וּמִנְחָתָם֙ וְנִסְכֵּיהֶ֔ם אִשֵּׁ֥ה רֵֽיחַ־נִיחֹ֖חַ
לַֽיהֹוָֽהאֲדֹנָֽי: וַעֲשִׂיתֶ֞ם שְׂעִיר־עִזִּ֥ים אֶחָ֖ד לְחַטָּ֑את וּשְׁנֵ֧י כְבָשִׂ֛ים בְּנֵ֥י שָׁנָ֖ה
לְזֶ֣בַח שְׁלָמִֽים: וְהֵנִ֣יף הַכֹּהֵ֣ן ׀ אֹתָ֡ם עַל֩ לֶ֨חֶם הַבִּכֻּרִ֤ים תְּנוּפָה֙
לִפְנֵ֣י יְהֹוָ֔האֲדֹנָי עַל־שְׁנֵ֖י כְּבָשִׂ֑ים קֹ֚דֶשׁ יִהְי֣וּ לַֽיהֹוָֽהאֲדֹנָֽי לַכֹּהֵֽן:

And the Lord spoke to Moses, saying: Speak to the children of Israel and tell them, when you come to the land I give you and you reap the harvest, and bring the Omer of your first harvest to the Kohen. And the Kohen will wave the Omer before the Lord so that it may be favorably received for you, morrow the Sabbath the Kohen will wave it. And on the day you wave the Omer you shall offer a male sheep without blemish of the first year for a burnt offering to the Lord. And the meet offering thereof shall be two tenth parts of fine flour mingled with oil, as fire offering for the Lord for a sweet savor with its drink offering of wine, the fourth part of a hin. And neither bread, nor parched corn nor green ears shall you eat until the self-same day, until you bring you God offering statute forever throughout your generations in all your dwellings. **Israel (Fifth on Sabbath)** *And you shall count for you, from the morrow of the Sabbath, from the day you brought the Omer of the wave offering, seven full Sabbaths. Until the morrow after the seventh Sabbath you shall count fifty days, and then you shall offer new meet-offering for the Lord. From your habitations you shall bring two wave-loaves of two tenth parts of fine flour shall they be, leavened shall they be baked; they are the first fruits for the Lord. And with the bread you shall offer seven sheep without blemish of the first year, and one young bullock, and two rams, they shall be for burnt offering to the Lord, with their meet-offering and their drink offerings, an offering made by fire, of a sweet savor to the the Lord. And you shall sacrifice one he-goat for a sin-offering and two sheep of the first year for a peace offering. And the Kohen will wave them together with the bread of the first fruits before the Lord, over the two sheep holy they shall be for the Lord for the Kohen.*

וּקְרָאתֶ֣ם בְּעֶ֗צֶם ׀ הַיּ֤וֹם הַזֶּה֙ מִקְרָא־קֹ֨דֶשׁ֙ יִהְיֶ֣ה לָכֶ֔ם כָּל־מְלֶ֣אכֶת עֲבֹדָ֔ה

לֹ֣א תַעֲשׂ֑וּ חֻקַּ֤ת עוֹלָם֙ בְּכָל־מוֹשְׁבֹ֣תֵיכֶ֔ם לְדֹרֹֽתֵיכֶֽם: וּֽבְקֻצְרְכֶ֞ם אֶת־קְצִ֣יר

אַרְצְכֶ֗ם לֹֽא־תְכַלֶּ֞ה פְּאַ֤ת שָֽׂדְךָ֙ בְּקֻצְרֶ֔ךָ וְלֶ֥קֶט קְצִֽירְךָ֖ לֹ֣א תְלַקֵּ֑ט לֶֽעָנִ֤י וְלַגֵּר֙

תַּעֲזֹ֣ב אֹתָ֔ם אֲנִ֖י יְהֹוָ֥ה(אהדנהי)אהדנהי אֱלֹהֵיכֶֽם: (Sixth on Shabbat) Fourth וַיְדַבֵּ֥ר

יְהֹוָה֙(אהדנהי)אהדנהי אֶל־מֹשֶׁ֥ה לֵּאמֹֽר: דַּבֵּ֞ר אֶל־בְּנֵ֤י יִשְׂרָאֵל֙ לֵאמֹ֔ר בַּחֹ֣דֶשׁ

הַשְּׁבִיעִ֜י בְּאֶחָ֣ד לַחֹ֗דֶשׁ יִהְיֶ֤ה לָכֶם֙ שַׁבָּת֔וֹן זִכְר֥וֹן תְּרוּעָ֖ה מִקְרָא־קֹֽדֶשׁ:

כָּל־מְלֶ֥אכֶת עֲבֹדָ֖ה לֹ֣א תַעֲשׂ֑וּ וְהִקְרַבְתֶּ֥ם אִשֶּׁ֖ה לַֽיהֹוָֽה(אהדנהי)אהדנהי: וַיְדַבֵּ֥ר

יְהֹוָה֙(אהדנהי)אהדנהי אֶל־מֹשֶׁ֥ה לֵּאמֹֽר: אַ֡ךְ בֶּעָשׂ֣וֹר לַחֹ֩דֶשׁ֩ הַשְּׁבִיעִ֨י הַזֶּ֜ה י֤וֹם

הַכִּפֻּרִים֙ ה֗וּא מִקְרָא־קֹ֨דֶשׁ֙ יִהְיֶ֣ה לָכֶ֔ם וְעִנִּיתֶ֖ם אֶת־נַפְשֹׁתֵיכֶ֑ם וְהִקְרַבְתֶּ֥ם

אִשֶּׁ֖ה לַֽיהֹוָֽה(אהדנהי)אהדנהי: וְכָל־מְלָאכָה֙ לֹ֣א תַעֲשׂ֔וּ בְּעֶ֖צֶם הַיּ֣וֹם הַזֶּ֑ה כִּ֣י י֤וֹם

כִּפֻּרִים֙ ה֔וּא לְכַפֵּ֣ר עֲלֵיכֶ֔ם לִפְנֵ֖י יְהֹוָ֥ה(אהדנהי)אהדנהי אֱלֹהֵיכֶֽם: כִּ֤י כָל־הַנֶּ֨פֶשׁ֙ אֲשֶׁ֣ר

לֹֽא־תְעֻנֶּ֔ה בְּעֶ֖צֶם הַיּ֣וֹם הַזֶּ֑ה וְנִכְרְתָ֖ה מֵֽעַמֶּֽיהָ: וְכָל־הַנֶּ֗פֶשׁ אֲשֶׁ֤ר תַּעֲשֶׂה֙

כָּל־מְלָאכָ֔ה בְּעֶ֖צֶם הַיּ֣וֹם הַזֶּ֑ה וְהַֽאֲבַדְתִּ֛י אֶת־הַנֶּ֥פֶשׁ הַהִ֖וא מִקֶּ֥רֶב עַמָּֽהּ:

כָּל־מְלָאכָ֖ה לֹ֣א תַעֲשׂ֑וּ חֻקַּ֤ת עוֹלָם֙ לְדֹרֹ֣תֵיכֶ֔ם בְּכֹ֖ל מֹֽשְׁבֹֽתֵיכֶֽם:

שַׁבַּ֨ת שַׁבָּת֥וֹן הוּא֙ לָכֶ֔ם וְעִנִּיתֶ֖ם אֶת־נַפְשֹֽׁתֵיכֶ֑ם בְּתִשְׁעָ֤ה לַחֹ֨דֶשׁ֙

בָּעֶ֔רֶב מֵעֶ֣רֶב עַד־עֶ֔רֶב תִּשְׁבְּת֖וּ שַׁבַּתְּכֶֽם: Fifth (Seventh on Shabbat)

וַיְדַבֵּ֥ר יְהֹוָה֙(אהדנהי)אהדנהי אֶל־מֹשֶׁ֥ה לֵּאמֹֽר: דַּבֵּ֞ר אֶל־בְּנֵ֤י יִשְׂרָאֵל֙ לֵאמֹ֔ר בַּחֲמִשָּׁה֩

עָשָׂ֨ר י֜וֹם לַחֹ֣דֶשׁ הַשְּׁבִיעִ֣י הַזֶּ֗ה חַ֧ג הַסֻּכּ֛וֹת שִׁבְעַ֥ת יָמִ֖ים לַֽיהֹוָֽה(אהדנהי)אהדנהי:

And you shall proclaim on this day that it is Holy Convocation to you, no work shall be done, it shall be a statute for ever in all your dwellings throughout your generations. And when you reap the harvest of your land, you shall not cut away all together the corners of the field and the gleaning of the harvest you shall not gather, for the poor and the stranger you shall leave them, I am the Lord Your God. **FOURTH (SIXTH ON SABBATH)** *And the Lord spoke to Moses, saying: Speak to the children of Israel and tell them on the seventh month, on the first day of the month a rest day shall be for you, of sounding the cornet, a Holy Convocation. No work shall be done and you shall make fire-offering for the Lord. And the Lord spoke to Moses, saying: But on the tenth day of this seventh month is the Day of Atonement, Holy Convocation is for you and you shall fast and offer a fire-offering for the Lord. No work shall be done on this same day for it is a Day of Atonement to atone you before the Lord Your God. For any one that fast not on this day shall be cut off from among the people. And any person that shall work on this same day, I will destroy him from among the people. No work shall be done; it is a statute for ever throughout your generation in all your dwellings. A Sabbath of rest it shall be for you, and you shall fast on the ninth day of the month in the evening, from evening to evening you shall celebrate your Sabbath.* **FIFTH (SEVENTH ON SABBATH)** *And the Lord spoke to Moses, saying: Speak to the children of Israel and tell them on the fifteen day of this seventh month is the holiday of Sukkot for the Lord for seven days.*

בַּיּוֹם הָרִאשׁוֹן מִקְרָא־קֹדֶשׁ כָּל־מְלֶאכֶת עֲבֹדָה לֹא תַעֲשׂוּ: שִׁבְעַת יָמִים
תַּקְרִיבוּ אִשֶּׁה לַיהוָֹה בַּיּוֹם הַשְּׁמִינִי מִקְרָא־קֹדֶשׁ יִהְיֶה לָכֶם
וְהִקְרַבְתֶּם אִשֶּׁה לַיהוָֹה עֲצֶרֶת הִוא כָּל־מְלֶאכֶת עֲבֹדָה לֹא תַעֲשׂוּ:
אֵלֶּה מוֹעֲדֵי יְהוָֹה אֲשֶׁר־תִּקְרְאוּ אֹתָם מִקְרָאֵי קֹדֶשׁ לְהַקְרִיב
אִשֶּׁה לַיהוָֹה עֹלָה וּמִנְחָה זֶבַח וּנְסָכִים דְּבַר־יוֹם בְּיוֹמוֹ: מִלְּבַד
שַׁבְּתֹת יְהוָֹה וּמִלְּבַד מַתְּנוֹתֵיכֶם וּמִלְּבַד כָּל־נִדְרֵיכֶם וּמִלְּבַד
כָּל־נִדְבֹתֵיכֶם אֲשֶׁר תִּתְּנוּ לַיהוָֹה: אַךְ בַּחֲמִשָּׁה עָשָׂר יוֹם לַחֹדֶשׁ
הַשְּׁבִיעִי בְּאָסְפְּכֶם אֶת־תְּבוּאַת הָאָרֶץ תָּחֹגּוּ אֶת־חַג־יְהוָֹה שִׁבְעַת
יָמִים בַּיּוֹם הָרִאשׁוֹן שַׁבָּתוֹן וּבַיּוֹם הַשְּׁמִינִי שַׁבָּתוֹן: וּלְקַחְתֶּם לָכֶם בַּיּוֹם
הָרִאשׁוֹן פְּרִי עֵץ הָדָר כַּפֹּת תְּמָרִים וַעֲנַף עֵץ־עָבֹת וְעַרְבֵי־ נָחַל וּשְׂמַחְתֶּם
לִפְנֵי יְהוָֹה אֱלֹהֵיכֶם שִׁבְעַת יָמִים: וְחַגֹּתֶם אֹתוֹ חַג לַיהוָֹה
שִׁבְעַת יָמִים בַּשָּׁנָה חֻקַּת עוֹלָם לְדֹרֹתֵיכֶם בַּחֹדֶשׁ הַשְּׁבִיעִי תָּחֹגּוּ אֹתוֹ:
בַּסֻּכֹּת תֵּשְׁבוּ שִׁבְעַת יָמִים כָּל־הָאֶזְרָח בְּיִשְׂרָאֵל יֵשְׁבוּ בַּסֻּכֹּת: לְמַעַן יֵדְעוּ
דֹרֹתֵיכֶם כִּי בַסֻּכּוֹת הוֹשַׁבְתִּי אֶת־בְּנֵי יִשְׂרָאֵל בְּהוֹצִיאִי אוֹתָם מֵאֶרֶץ
מִצְרַיִם אֲנִי יְהוָֹה אֱלֹהֵיכֶם: וַיְדַבֵּר מֹשֶׁה אֶת־מֹעֲדֵי יְהוָֹה
אֶל־בְּנֵי יִשְׂרָאֵל:

After the reading say Half *Kaddish* on pages 501-502, and then read the *Maftir* on page 736.

On the first day a Holy Convocation shall be no work shall be done. Seven day you shall sacrifice fire offerings for the Lord and on the eighth day Holy Convocation shall be for you, and you shall sacrifice fire offering for the Lord, it is solemn assembly no work shall be done. Those are the holidays of the Lord, which you proclaim to be holy convocations, to sacrifice fire offering to the Lord, burnt offering and meat offering, sacrifice, and drink offering, everything upon its day. Beside the Sabbaths of the Lord, and beside your gifts, and beside all your vows, and beside all your freewill offering, which you shall give the Lord. But on the fifteenth day of the seventh month, when you gather in the fruit of the land, you shall celebrate the holiday of the Lord for seven days, the first day shall be a day of rest and on the eighth day. And you shall take to yourself on the first day citrus fruits, branches of palm trees, and the boughs of the myrtle tree, and willows of the brook, and you shall rejoice before the Lord you God seven days. And you shall celebrate it for Lord for seven days in the year, it shall be a statute for ever throughout your generations, in the seventh month you shall celebrate it. In the Sukkah you shall dwell for seven day, all that is an Israel shall dwell in the Sukkah. So that all your generations may know, that I sat the children of Israel to in the Sukkah, when I brought them out of Egypt, I am the Lord Your God. And Moses spoke the holidays of the Lord to the children of Israel." (Leviticus 22:26-23:44)

MAFTIR FOR SUKKOT

וּבַחֲמִשָּׁה֩ עָשָׂ֨ר י֜וֹם לַחֹ֣דֶשׁ הַשְּׁבִיעִ֗י מִקְרָא־קֹ֨דֶשׁ֙ יִהְיֶ֣ה לָכֶ֔ם כָּל־מְלֶ֥אכֶת
עֲבֹדָ֖ה לֹ֣א תַעֲשׂ֑וּ וְחַגֹּתֶ֥ם חַ֛ג לַיהוָֹ֖ה אדני־אלהים שִׁבְעַ֥ת יָמִֽים: וְהִקְרַבְתֶּ֨ם עֹלָ֜ה
אִשֵּׁ֨ה רֵ֤יחַ נִיחֹ֙חַ֙ לַיהֹוָ֔ה אדני־אלהים פָּרִ֧ים בְּנֵֽי־בָקָ֛ר שְׁלֹשָׁ֥ה עָשָׂ֖ר אֵילִ֣ם שְׁנָ֑יִם
כְּבָשִׂ֧ים בְּנֵֽי־שָׁנָ֛ה אַרְבָּעָ֥ה עָשָׂ֖ר תְּמִימִ֥ם יִהְיֽוּ: וּמִנְחָתָ֗ם סֹ֤לֶת בְּלוּלָ֣ה בַשֶּׁ֔מֶן
שְׁלֹשָׁ֣ה עֶשְׂרֹנִ֗ים לַפָּ֤ר הָֽאֶחָד֙ לִשְׁלֹשָׁ֣ה עָשָׂ֣ר פָּרִ֔ים שְׁנֵ֤י עֶשְׂרֹנִים֙ לָאַ֣יִל
הָֽאֶחָ֔ד לִשְׁנֵ֖י הָֽאֵילִֽם: וְעִשָּׂר֤וֹן עִשָּׂרוֹן֙ לַכֶּ֣בֶשׂ הָֽאֶחָ֔ד לְאַרְבָּעָ֥ה עָשָׂ֖ר
כְּבָשִֽׂים: וּשְׂעִיר־עִזִּ֥ים אֶחָ֖ד חַטָּ֑את מִלְּבַד֙ עֹלַ֣ת הַתָּמִ֔יד מִנְחָתָ֖הּ וְנִסְכָּֽהּ:

Say the blessing before the *Haftarah* on page 502, and then read the *Haftarah* below.

HAFATRAH FOR THE FIRST DAY OF SUKKOT

הִנֵּ֥ה יֽוֹם־בָּ֖א לַיהוָֹ֑ה אדני־אלהים וְחֻלַּ֥ק שְׁלָלֵ֖ךְ בְּקִרְבֵּֽךְ: וְאָסַפְתִּ֨י אֶת־כָּל־הַגּוֹיִ֣ם |
אֶל־יְרֽוּשָׁלַ֘͏ִם֮ לַמִּלְחָמָה֒ וְנִלְכְּדָ֣ה הָעִ֗יר וְנָשַׁ֙סּוּ֙ הַבָּ֣תִּ֔ים וְהַנָּשִׁ֖ים תשכבנה
(כתיב: תשגלנה) וְיָצָ֞א חֲצִ֤י הָעִיר֙ בַּגּוֹלָ֔ה וְיֶ֣תֶר הָעָ֔ם לֹ֥א יִכָּרֵ֖ת מִן־הָעִֽיר: וְיָצָ֣א
יְהוָֹ֗ה אדני־אלהים וְנִלְחַ֛ם בַּגּוֹיִ֥ם הָהֵ֖ם כְּי֣וֹם הִלָּֽחֲמ֑וֹ בְּי֥וֹם קְרָֽב: וְעָֽמְד֣וּ רַגְלָ֣יו בַּיּֽוֹם־
הַה֞וּא עַל־הַ֣ר הַזֵּיתִ֗ים אֲשֶׁ֨ר עַל־פְּנֵ֤י יְרֽוּשָׁלַ֙͏ִם֙ מִקֶּ֔דֶם וְנִבְקַע֩ הַ֨ר הַזֵּיתִ֤ים
מֵחֶצְיוֹ֙ מִזְרָ֣חָה וָיָ֔מָּה גֵּ֖יא גְּדוֹלָ֣ה מְאֹ֑ד וּמָ֨שׁ חֲצִ֤י הָהָר֙ צָפ֔וֹנָה וְחֶצְיוֹ־נֶֽגְבָּה:
וְנַסְתֶּ֣ם גֵּֽיא־הָרַ֗י כִּֽי־יַגִּ֣יעַ גֵּֽי־הָרִים֮ אֶל־אָצַל֒ וְנַסְתֶּ֗ם כַּאֲשֶׁ֤ר נַסְתֶּם֙ מִפְּנֵ֣י
הָרַ֔עַשׁ בִּימֵ֖י עֻזִּיָּ֣ה מֶֽלֶךְ־יְהוּדָ֑ה וּבָא֙ יְהוָֹ֣ה אדני־אלהים אֱלֹהַ֔י כָּל־קְדֹשִׁ֖ים עִמָּֽךְ:

MAFTIR FOR SUKKOT

"And on the fifteenth day of the seventh month shall you have a Holy Convocation, no service work shall be done, and you shall celebrate the holiday for the Lord for seven days. And you shall bring as a burnt offering a sacrifice made by fire, for a sweet savor to the Lord, thirteen young bulls, two rams, fourteen sheep of the first year without a blemish. And their meal offering shall be of fine flour mingled with oil, three tenth parts for every bull of the thirteen bulls, two tenth parts for each ram of the two rams. And one tenth part for every sheep of the fourteen sheep; and one he-goat for a sin-offering, beside the continual burnt-offering, its meal-offering, and drink -offering." (Numbers 29:12-16)

HAFATRAH FOR THE FIRST DAY OF SUKKOT

"Behold, a day is coming for the Lord, your spoil shall be divided in your midst. I shall gather all the nations to Jerusalem to wage war, the city will be conquered, the home plundered and the women violated, half of the city will go into exile, and the rest of the people will not be cut off from the city. Then the Lord will go out to wage war against those nations as on the day He warred, the day of battle. And His feet will stand astride, on that day, on Mount Olives, which faces Jerusalem on the east, and the Mount of Olives will split at its center, eastward making a huge ravine; and half of the mountain moved northward and half southward. Then you will flee, for the ravine will extend to Atzal, and you will flee as you fled from the earthquake in the days of King Uz'ziah of Judea; and the Lord, my God will come with all the angels to you aid.

וְהָיָה בַיּוֹם הַהוּא לֹא־יִהְיֶה אוֹר יְקָרוֹת וְקִפָּאוֹן (כתיב: יקפאון): וְהָיָה יוֹם־אֶחָד
הוּא יִוָּדַע לַיהֹוָ֖ה אֱלֹהִים לֹא־יוֹם וְלֹא־לָיְלָה וְהָיָה לְעֵת־עֶרֶב יִהְיֶה־אוֹר:
וְהָיָה | בַּיּוֹם הַהוּא יֵצְאוּ מַיִם־חַיִּים מִירוּשָׁלַם וְחֶצְיָם אֶל־הַיָּם הַקַּדְמוֹנִי
וְחֶצְיָם אֶל־הַיָּם הָאַחֲרוֹן בַּקַּיִץ וּבַחֹרֶף יִהְיֶה: וְהָיָה יְהֹוָ֖ה לְמֶלֶךְ עַל־
כָּל־הָאָרֶץ בַּיּוֹם הַהוּא יִהְיֶה יְהֹוָ֖ה אֶחָד וּשְׁמוֹ אֶחָד: יִסּוֹב
כָּל־הָאָרֶץ כָּעֲרָבָה מִגֶּבַע לְרִמּוֹן נֶגֶב יְרוּשָׁלָ֑ם וְרָאֲמָה וְיָשְׁבָה תַחְתֶּיהָ
לְמִשַּׁעַר בִּנְיָמִן עַד־מְקוֹם שַׁעַר הָרִאשׁוֹן עַד־שַׁעַר הַפִּנִּים וּמִגְדַּל חֲנַנְאֵל
עַד יִקְבֵי הַמֶּלֶךְ: וְיָשְׁבוּ בָהּ וְחֵרֶם לֹא יִהְיֶה־עוֹד וְיָשְׁבָה יְרוּשָׁלַ֖ם לָבֶטַח:
וְזֹאת | תִּהְיֶה הַמַּגֵּפָה אֲשֶׁר יִגֹּף יְהֹוָ֖ה אֶת־כָּל־הָעַמִּים אֲשֶׁר צָבְאוּ
עַל־יְרוּשָׁלָ֑ם הָמֵק | בְּשָׂרוֹ וְהוּא עֹמֵד עַל־רַגְלָיו וְעֵינָיו תִּמַּקְנָה בְחֹרֵיהֶן
וּלְשׁוֹנוֹ תִּמַּק בְּפִיהֶם: וְהָיָה בַּיּוֹם הַהוּא תִּהְיֶה מְהוּמַת־יְהֹוָ֖ה רַבָּה
בָהֶם וְהֶחֱזִיקוּ אִישׁ יַד רֵעֵהוּ וְעָלְתָה יָדוֹ עַל־יַד רֵעֵהוּ: וְגַם־יְהוּדָה תִּלָּחֵם
בִּירוּשָׁלָ֑ם וְאֻסַּף חֵיל כָּל־הַגּוֹיִם סָבִיב זָהָב וָכֶסֶף וּבְגָדִים לָרֹב מְאֹד: וְכֵן
תִּהְיֶה מַגֵּפַת הַסּוּס הַפֶּרֶד הַגָּמָל וְהַחֲמוֹר וְכָל־הַבְּהֵמָה אֲשֶׁר יִהְיֶה בַּמַּחֲנוֹת
הָהֵמָּה כַּמַּגֵּפָה הַזֹּאת: וְהָיָה כָּל־הַנּוֹתָר מִכָּל־הַגּוֹיִם הַבָּאִים עַל־יְרוּשָׁלָ֑ם
וְעָלוּ מִדֵּי שָׁנָה בְשָׁנָה לְהִשְׁתַּחֲוֹת לְמֶלֶךְ יְהֹוָ֖ה צְבָאוֹת וְלָחֹג אֶת־חַג
הַסֻּכּוֹת: וְהָיָה אֲשֶׁר לֹא־יַעֲלֶה מֵאֵת מִשְׁפְּחוֹת הָאָרֶץ אֶל־יְרוּשָׁלַ֖ם
לְהִשְׁתַּחֲוֹת לְמֶלֶךְ יְהֹוָ֖ה צְבָאוֹת וְלֹא עֲלֵיהֶם יִהְיֶה הַגָּשֶׁם:

And it will happen on that day that there will be neither clear light nor heavy darkness. This day shall be known only to the Lord, nor day nor night, and toward evening there will be light. And on that day live water will flow from Jerusalem, half to the eastern sea and half to the last sea, in the summer and winter it shall continue. And on that day the Lord shall be king over all land, and on that day the Lord will be One and His Name be One. The entire earth will transformed to a plain, from the hill of Geva to Rimmon south of Jerusalem, the City will rise high, on its original site, from the Gate of Benjamin until the place of the First Gate to the Inner Gate, and from the Tower of Channanel to the royal wine cellar. They will dwell within her and there shall be no more excommunication, and Jerusalem shall dwell secure. This will be the plague with which the Lord will smite all the nations that rallied against Jerusalem. Their flash will rot while they still stand erect, and their eyes will rot in their sockets, and their tongue will rot in their mouths. And on that day the Lord confusion will be great upon them, they will hold one each other hand, and he will overpower his friend's hand. Even Judea will be forced to fight against Jerusalem, and all the army of all the nations will gathered around a great abundance of gold, silver and garments. Similar will be the plague in the horses, mules, camels, donkeys, and all the animals that will be in those camps, like the above plague. And all those who will be left from among all the nations that come upon Jerusalem, will ascend every year to prostrate themselves before the Lord, King of Hosts and to celebrate the holiday of Sukkot. And any of the families of the land that will not ascend to Jerusalem to prostrate to the Lord, King of Hosts, the rain will not fall upon them.

וְאִם־מִשְׁפַּ֣חַת מִצְרַ֧יִם לֹא־תַעֲלֶ֛ה וְלֹ֥א בָאָ֖ה וְלֹ֣א עֲלֵיהֶ֑ם תִּֽהְיֶ֣ה הַמַּגֵּפָ֗ה אֲשֶׁ֨ר יִגֹּ֤ף יְהֹוָֽאֲדֹנָֽי אֶת־הַגּוֹיִ֔ם אֲשֶׁ֣ר לֹ֥א יַֽעֲל֔וּ לָחֹ֖ג אֶת־חַ֥ג הַסֻּכּֽוֹת: זֹ֣את תִּֽהְיֶ֖ה חַטַּ֣את מִצְרָ֑יִם וְחַטַּאת֙ כָּל־הַגּוֹיִ֔ם אֲשֶׁ֣ר לֹ֣א יַֽעֲל֔וּ לָחֹ֖ג אֶת־חַ֥ג הַסֻּכּֽוֹת: בַּיּ֣וֹם הַה֗וּא יִֽהְיֶה֙ עַל־מְצִלּ֣וֹת הַסּ֔וּס קֹ֖דֶשׁ לַֽיהֹוָֽאֲדֹנָֽי וְהָיָ֤ה הַסִּירוֹת֙ בְּבֵ֣ית יְהֹוָֽאֲדֹנָֽי כַּמִּזְרָקִ֖ים לִפְנֵ֥י הַמִּזְבֵּֽחַ: וְהָיָ֡ה כָּל־סִ֣יר בִּירֽוּשָׁלַ֨͏ִם וּבִֽיהוּדָ֜ה קֹ֗דֶשׁ לַֽיהֹוָֽאֲדֹנָ֣י צְבָא֔וֹת וּבָ֨אוּ֙ כָּל־הַזֹּ֣בְחִ֔ים וְלָקְח֥וּ מֵהֶ֖ם וּבִשְּׁל֣וּ בָהֶ֑ם וְלֹא־יִהְיֶ֨ה כְנַֽעֲנִ֥י ע֛וֹד בְּבֵית־יְהֹוָֽאֲדֹנָ֥י צְבָא֖וֹת בַּיּ֥וֹם הַהֽוּא:

Say the blessing after the *Haftarah* on pages 503-504.

TORAH READING FOR SHABBAT CHOL HAMO'ED

וַיֹּ֨אמֶר מֹשֶׁ֜ה אֶל־יְהֹוָֽאֲדֹנָ֗י רְ֠אֵ֠ה אַתָּ֞ה אֹמֵ֤ר אֵלַי֙ הַ֚עַל אֶת־הָעָ֣ם הַזֶּ֔ה וְאַתָּה֙ לֹ֣א הֽוֹדַעְתַּ֔נִי אֵ֥ת אֲשֶׁר־תִּשְׁלַ֖ח עִמִּ֑י וְאַתָּ֣ה אָמַ֗רְתָּ יְדַעְתִּ֨יךָ֙ בְשֵׁ֔ם וְגַם־מָצָ֥אתָ חֵ֖ן בְּעֵינָֽי: וְעַתָּ֡ה אִם־נָא֩ מָצָ֨אתִי חֵ֜ן בְּעֵינֶ֗יךָ הֽוֹדִעֵ֤נִי נָא֙ אֶת־דְּרָכֶ֔ךָ וְאֵדָ֣עֲךָ֔ לְמַ֥עַן אֶמְצָא־חֵ֖ן בְּעֵינֶ֑יךָ וּרְאֵ֕ה כִּ֥י עַמְּךָ֖ הַגּ֥וֹי הַזֶּֽה: וַיֹּאמַ֑ר פָּנַ֥י יֵלֵ֖כוּ וַהֲנִחֹ֥תִי לָֽךְ: וַיֹּ֖אמֶר אֵלָ֑יו אִם־אֵ֤ין פָּנֶ֨יךָ֙ הֹֽלְכִ֔ים אַֽל־תַּעֲלֵ֖נוּ מִזֶּֽה: וּבַמֶּ֣ה ׀ יִוָּדַ֣ע אֵפ֗וֹא כִּֽי־מָצָ֨אתִי חֵ֤ן בְּעֵינֶ֨יךָ֙ אֲנִ֣י וְעַמֶּ֔ךָ הֲל֛וֹא בְּלֶכְתְּךָ֖ עִמָּ֑נוּ וְנִפְלֵ֣ינוּ אֲנִ֣י וְעַמְּךָ֗ מִכָּ֨ל־הָעָ֔ם אֲשֶׁ֖ר עַל־פְּנֵ֥י הָֽאֲדָמָֽה: *Levi*

And if the family of Egypt will not ascend and will not come they will suffer from the plague with which the Lord afflict the nations that did not ascended to celebrate the holiday of Sukkot. This will be the punishment of Egypt and the punishment of all the nations that will not ascend to celebrate the holiday of Sukkot. And on this day the bells on the horses will sanctify for Lord, and the cauldrons in the house of Lord will become as numerous basins before the Altar. And each cauldron in Jerusalem and Judea will be sanctified to Lord of Hosts, and all who bring offerings will come and take from them, cook in them, and there shall be no Canaanite in the house of the Lord of Hosts on that day." *(Zacariah 14:1-21)*

TORAH READING FOR SHABBAT CHOL HAMO'ED

"And Moses said to the Lord: 'Look, You say to me, 'take this people onward,' but You did not inform me whom You will send with me, and You had said: 'I have distinguished you with high repute and you have also found favor in My eyes.' And now, if I have indeed found favor in Your eyes, let me know Your ways, that I may know You, in order that I may find favor in Your eyes, but see to it that this nation remains Your people. He said, 'My Own Presence will go along and provide you rest.' He said to Him, 'If Your Presence does not go along, do not bring us onward from here. How, then will it be known that I have found favor in Your eyes, I and Your people, unless You accompany us, and thereby distinguish me and Your people from every people that is on the face of the earth?' LEVI

וַיֹּאמֶר יְהֹוָה אֶל־מֹשֶׁה גַּם אֶת־הַדָּבָר הַזֶּה אֲשֶׁר דִּבַּרְתָּ אֶעֱשֶׂה

כִּי־מָצָאתָ חֵן בְּעֵינַי וָאֵדָעֲךָ בְּשֵׁם: וַיֹּאמַר הַרְאֵנִי נָא אֶת־כְּבֹדֶךָ: וַיֹּאמֶר

אֲנִי אַעֲבִיר כָּל־טוּבִי עַל־פָּנֶיךָ וְקָרָאתִי בְשֵׁם יְהֹוָה לְפָנֶיךָ וְחַנֹּתִי

אֶת־אֲשֶׁר אָחֹן וְרִחַמְתִּי אֶת־אֲשֶׁר אֲרַחֵם: *Israel* וַיֹּאמֶר לֹא תוּכַל לִרְאֹת

אֶת־פָּנָי כִּי לֹא־יִרְאַנִי הָאָדָם וָחָי: וַיֹּאמֶר יְהֹוָה הִנֵּה מָקוֹם אִתִּי

וְנִצַּבְתָּ עַל־הַצּוּר: וְהָיָה בַּעֲבֹר כְּבֹדִי וְשַׂמְתִּיךָ בְּנִקְרַת הַצּוּר וְשַׂכֹּתִי כַפִּי

עָלֶיךָ עַד־עָבְרִי: וַהֲסִרֹתִי אֶת־כַּפִּי וְרָאִיתָ אֶת־אֲחֹרָי וּפָנַי לֹא יֵרָאוּ: *Fourth*

וַיֹּאמֶר יְהֹוָה אֶל־מֹשֶׁה פְּסָל־לְךָ שְׁנֵי־לֻחֹת אֲבָנִים כָּרִאשֹׁנִים

וְכָתַבְתִּי עַל־הַלֻּחֹת אֶת־הַדְּבָרִים אֲשֶׁר הָיוּ עַל־הַלֻּחֹת הָרִאשֹׁנִים אֲשֶׁר

שִׁבַּרְתָּ: וֶהְיֵה נָכוֹן לַבֹּקֶר וְעָלִיתָ בַבֹּקֶר אֶל־הַר סִינַי וְנִצַּבְתָּ לִי שָׁם עַל־

רֹאשׁ הָהָר: וְאִישׁ לֹא־יַעֲלֶה עִמָּךְ וְגַם־אִישׁ אַל־יֵרָא בְּכָל־הָהָר גַּם־הַצֹּאן

וְהַבָּקָר אַל־יִרְעוּ אֶל־מוּל הָהָר הַהוּא: *Fifth* וַיִּפְסֹל שְׁנֵי־לֻחֹת אֲבָנִים

כָּרִאשֹׁנִים וַיַּשְׁכֵּם מֹשֶׁה בַבֹּקֶר וַיַּעַל אֶל־הַר סִינַי כַּאֲשֶׁר צִוָּה יְהֹוָה

אֹתוֹ וַיִּקַּח בְּיָדוֹ שְׁנֵי לֻחֹת אֲבָנִים: וַיֵּרֶד יְהֹוָה בֶּעָנָן וַיִּתְיַצֵּב

עִמּוֹ שָׁם וַיִּקְרָא בְשֵׁם יְהֹוָה: וַיַּעֲבֹר יְהֹוָה | עַל־פָּנָיו

וַיִּקְרָא יְהֹוָה | יְהֹוָה אֵל רַחוּם וְחַנּוּן אֶרֶךְ אַפַּיִם וְרַב־חֶסֶד

וֶאֱמֶת: נֹצֵר חֶסֶד לָאֲלָפִים נֹשֵׂא עָוֹן וָפֶשַׁע וְחַטָּאָה וְנַקֵּה לֹא יְנַקֶּה

פֹּקֵד | עֲוֹן אָבוֹת עַל־בָּנִים וְעַל־בְּנֵי בָנִים עַל־שִׁלֵּשִׁים וְעַל־רִבֵּעִים:

---

*And the Lord said to Moses: 'I will even do this thing of which you have spoken, for you have found favor in My eyes, and I have distinguished you with high repute.' And He said: 'Show me now Your glory.' And He said: 'I will cause all of My goodness to pass before you, and I will call out with the Name of the Lord before you, I will be gracious when I wish to be gracious, and I will be merciful when I wish to show mercy.' **ISRAEL** And He said: 'You cannot see My face, for no human can see My face and live. And the Lord said: 'Behold there is a place near Me, you may stand on the rock. And when My glory passes by, I shall place you in a cleft of the rock, I shall shield you with My hand until I have passed. Then I shall remove My hand, and you will see My back, but My face will not be seen.' **FOURTH** And the Lord said to Moses, 'Carve yourself two stone tablets, like the first ones, and I will inscribe upon the tablets the words that were on the first tablets which you shattered. By prepared in the morning, climb up Mount Sinai in the morning and stand by Me on the mountain top. No man is to climb up with you not should anyone be seen on the entire mountain, even the sheep and cattle are not to braze facing that mounting.' **FIFTH** And he carved two stone tablets like the first ones. Moses arose in the morning and climbed up Mount Sinai as the Lord had commanded him, and he took the two stone tablets in his hand. The Lord descended in a cloud and stood with him there, and he called out with the Name of the Lord. And the Lord passed before him and proclaimed: 'Lord, Lord, God, Compassionate and Gracious, Slow to anger, and Abundant in Kindness for thousands of generations, Forgiver for iniquity, willful sin, and error, and who cleanse but does not cleanse completely, He recalls the sin of parents upon children and grandchildren, for the third and fourth generations.'*

וַיְמַהֵר מֹשֶׁה וַיִּקֹּד אַרְצָה וַיִּשְׁתָּחוּ: וַיֹּאמֶר אִם־נָא מָצָאתִי חֵן בְּעֵינֶיךָ אֲדֹנָי
יֵלֶךְ־נָא אֲדֹנָי בְּקִרְבֵּנוּ כִּי עַם־קְשֵׁה־עֹרֶף הוּא וְסָלַחְתָּ לַעֲוֺנֵנוּ וּלְחַטָּאתֵנוּ
וּנְחַלְתָּנוּ: וַיֹּאמֶר הִנֵּה אָנֹכִי כֹּרֵת בְּרִית נֶגֶד כָּל־עַמְּךָ אֶעֱשֶׂה נִפְלָאֹת אֲשֶׁר
לֹא־נִבְרְאוּ בְכָל־הָאָרֶץ וּבְכָל־הַגּוֹיִם וְרָאָה כָל־הָעָם אֲשֶׁר־אַתָּה בְקִרְבּוֹ
אֶת־מַעֲשֵׂה יְהֹוָה כִּי־נוֹרָא הוּא אֲשֶׁר אֲנִי עֹשֶׂה עִמָּךְ: *Sixth* שְׁמָר־
לְךָ אֵת אֲשֶׁר אָנֹכִי מְצַוְּךָ הַיּוֹם הִנְנִי גֹרֵשׁ מִפָּנֶיךָ אֶת־הָאֱמֹרִי וְהַכְּנַעֲנִי
וְהַחִתִּי וְהַפְּרִזִּי וְהַחִוִּי וְהַיְבוּסִי: הִשָּׁמֶר לְךָ פֶּן־תִּכְרֹת בְּרִית לְיוֹשֵׁב הָאָרֶץ
אֲשֶׁר אַתָּה בָּא עָלֶיהָ פֶּן־יִהְיֶה לְמוֹקֵשׁ בְּקִרְבֶּךָ: כִּי אֶת־מִזְבְּחֹתָם תִּתֹּצוּן
וְאֶת־מַצֵּבֹתָם תְּשַׁבֵּרוּן וְאֶת־אֲשֵׁרָיו תִּכְרֹתוּן: כִּי לֹא תִשְׁתַּחֲוֶה לְאֵל אַחֵר
כִּי יְהֹוָה קַנָּא שְׁמוֹ אֵל קַנָּא הוּא: פֶּן־תִּכְרֹת בְּרִית לְיוֹשֵׁב הָאָרֶץ
וְזָנוּ | אַחֲרֵי אֱלֹהֵיהֶם וְזָבְחוּ לֵאלֹהֵיהֶם וְקָרָא לְךָ וְאָכַלְתָּ מִזִּבְחוֹ: וְלָקַחְתָּ
מִבְּנֹתָיו לְבָנֶיךָ וְזָנוּ בְנֹתָיו אַחֲרֵי אֱלֹהֵיהֶן וְהִזְנוּ אֶת־בָּנֶיךָ אַחֲרֵי אֱלֹהֵיהֶן:
אֱלֹהֵי מַסֵּכָה לֹא תַעֲשֶׂה־לָּךְ: *Seventh* אֶת־חַג הַמַּצּוֹת תִּשְׁמֹר שִׁבְעַת יָמִים
תֹּאכַל מַצּוֹת אֲשֶׁר צִוִּיתִךָ לְמוֹעֵד חֹדֶשׁ הָאָבִיב כִּי בְּחֹדֶשׁ הָאָבִיב יָצָאתָ
מִמִּצְרָיִם: כָּל־פֶּטֶר רֶחֶם לִי וְכָל־מִקְנְךָ תִּזָּכָר פֶּטֶר שׁוֹר וָשֶׂה: וּפֶטֶר חֲמוֹר
תִּפְדֶּה בְשֶׂה וְאִם־לֹא תִפְדֶּה וַעֲרַפְתּוֹ כֹּל בְּכוֹר בָּנֶיךָ תִּפְדֶּה וְלֹא־יֵרָאוּ פָנַי
רֵיקָם: שֵׁשֶׁת יָמִים תַּעֲבֹד וּבַיּוֹם הַשְּׁבִיעִי תִּשְׁבֹּת בֶּחָרִישׁ וּבַקָּצִיר תִּשְׁבֹּת:

And Moses hastened to kneel upon the ground and prostrate himself. He said: 'If I have found favor in Your eyes, Lord, may the Lord go among us, for it is a stiff-necked people, so may Your forgive our iniquity and our sin, and make us Your heritage.' And he said: 'Behold I seal a covenant, before your entire nation I will make distinctions such as have never been created in the entire world and among all the nations, and the entire people among whom you are will see the work of the Lord, which is awesome, that I am about to do with you.' **SIXTH** *Be careful of what I command you today, behold I drive out before you the Emorite, the Canaanite, the Chittite, the Perizite, the Chivvite, and the Jevusite. Beware lest you seal a covenant with the inhabitants of the land to which you come, lest it be a snare among you. Rather you are to break apart their altars, smash their pillars and cut down their sacred trees. For you are not to prostrate yourselves to an alien god, for the very name of the Lord is 'Jealous One,' He is a jealous God. Lest you seal a covenant with the inhabitants of the land and you stray after their gods, sacrifice to their gods, and they invite you and you eat from their offering! And you select their daughters for your sons, and their daughter stray after their gods and entice your sons to stray after their gods! Do not make yourselves molten gods!* **SEVENTH** *You are to observe the holiday of Matzot, for seven days you are to eat Matzot as I commanded you, at the appointed time in the month of spring, for in the month of spring you went out of Egypt. Every first offspring of a womb is Mine, and all your flock that produces a male, the first offspring of cattle or sheep. The first offspring of a donkey you are to redeem with a lamb or kid, and if you do not redeem it, you are to cut the back of its neck, you are to redeem every firstborn of your son, they may not appear before Me empty-handed. Six days you are to work and on the seventh day you are to refrain from work, you are to refrain from plowing and harvest.*

וְחַג שֶׁבֻעֹת תַּעֲשֶׂה לְךָ בִּכּוּרֵי קְצִיר חִטִּים וְחַג הָאָסִיף תְּקוּפַת הַשָּׁנָה:
שָׁלֹשׁ פְּעָמִים בַּשָּׁנָה יֵרָאֶה כָּל־זְכוּרְךָ אֶת־פְּנֵי הָאָדֹן | יְהֹוָה אֱלֹהֵי
יִשְׂרָאֵל: כִּי־אוֹרִישׁ גּוֹיִם מִפָּנֶיךָ וְהִרְחַבְתִּי אֶת־גְּבֻלֶךָ וְלֹא־יַחְמֹד אִישׁ אֶת־
אַרְצְךָ בַּעֲלֹתְךָ לֵרָאוֹת אֶת־פְּנֵי יְהֹוָה אֱלֹהֶיךָ שָׁלֹשׁ פְּעָמִים בַּשָּׁנָה:
לֹא־תִשְׁחַט עַל־חָמֵץ דַּם־זִבְחִי וְלֹא־יָלִין לַבֹּקֶר זֶבַח חַג הַפָּסַח: רֵאשִׁית
בִּכּוּרֵי אַדְמָתְךָ תָּבִיא בֵּית יְהֹוָה אֱלֹהֶיךָ לֹא־תְבַשֵּׁל גְּדִי בַּחֲלֵב אִמּוֹ:

After the reading, say Half *Kaddish* on pages 501-502, read the *Maftir* according to the day on pages 743-744, and then say the blessing before the *Haftarah* on page 502.

HAFTARAH FOR SHABBAT CHOL HAMO'ED

וְהָיָה | בַּיּוֹם הַהוּא בְּיוֹם בּוֹא גוֹג עַל־אַדְמַת יִשְׂרָאֵל נְאֻם אֲדֹנָי
יְהֹוִה תַּעֲלֶה חֲמָתִי בְּאַפִּי: וּבְקִנְאָתִי בְאֵשׁ־עֶבְרָתִי דִבַּרְתִּי אִם־לֹא |
בַּיּוֹם הַהוּא יִהְיֶה רַעַשׁ גָּדוֹל עַל אַדְמַת יִשְׂרָאֵל: וְרָעֲשׁוּ מִפָּנַי דְּגֵי הַיָּם
וְעוֹף הַשָּׁמַיִם וְחַיַּת הַשָּׂדֶה וְכָל־הָרֶמֶשׂ הָרֹמֵשׂ עַל־הָאֲדָמָה וְכֹל הָאָדָם
אֲשֶׁר עַל־פְּנֵי הָאֲדָמָה וְנֶהֶרְסוּ הֶהָרִים וְנָפְלוּ הַמַּדְרֵגוֹת וְכָל־חוֹמָה לָאָרֶץ
תִּפּוֹל: וְקָרָאתִי עָלָיו לְכָל־הָרַי חֶרֶב נְאֻם אֲדֹנָי יְהֹוִה חֶרֶב אִישׁ
בְּאָחִיו תִּהְיֶה: וְנִשְׁפַּטְתִּי אִתּוֹ בְּדֶבֶר וּבְדָם וְגֶשֶׁם שׁוֹטֵף וְאַבְנֵי אֶלְגָּבִישׁ
אֵשׁ וְגָפְרִית אַמְטִיר עָלָיו וְעַל־אֲגַפָּיו וְעַל־עַמִּים רַבִּים אֲשֶׁר אִתּוֹ:

You are to mark the holiday of Shavuot with the first fruits of your wheat harvest, and the holiday of the Harvest at the year's change of seasons. Three times a year all your males are to appear before the Master, the Lord, God of Israel. For I shall banish nations before you and broaden your boundary, no man will covet your land when you go up to appear before the Lord, your God, three times a year. You may not slaughter My blood-offering while in possession of leavened food, nor may the offering of the Pesach holiday be left overnight until morning. The first of your land's early produce you are to bring to the Temple of the Lord, your God, do not cook a kid in its mother's milk." (Exodus 33:12-34:26)

HAFTARAH FOR SHABBAT CHOL HAMO'ED

"And it shall be on that day, the day Gog came on the soil of Israel, the words of my Lord, God, My raging anger shall flare up. For in My indignation and in My blazing worth I have spoken. I take on oath that on that day a great earthquake shall come upon the soil of Israel. And there shall quake before Me the fish of the sea, the birds of the sky, the beasts of the field, all creeping things that move on the ground, and every human being on the face of the earth. Mountains shall be overthrown, cliffs shall topple, and every wall shall topple to the ground. I will summon the sward against him to all My mountains, the word of the Lord, God. Every man's sward shall be against his brother. I will punish him with pestilence and with blood, torrential rain, hailstones, and sulfurous fire upon him and his cohorts, and the many people that are with him.

וְהִתְגַּדִּלְתִּי וְהִתְקַדִּשְׁתִּי וְנוֹדַעְתִּי לְעֵינֵי גּוֹיִם רַבִּים וְיָדְעוּ כִּי־אֲנִי
יְהֹוָ֖הֽ: וְאַתָּה בֶן־אָדָם הִנָּבֵא עַל־גּוֹג וְאָמַרְתָּ כֹּה אָמַר אֲדֹנָי
יְהֹוִ֖הֽ הִנְנִי אֵלֶיךָ גּוֹג נְשִׂיא רֹאשׁ מֶשֶׁךְ וְתֻבָל: וְשֹׁבַבְתִּיךָ
וְשִׁשֵּׁאתִיךָ וְהַעֲלִיתִיךָ מִיַּרְכְּתֵי צָפוֹן וַהֲבִאוֹתִךָ עַל־הָרֵי יִשְׂרָאֵל: וְהִכֵּיתִי
קַשְׁתְּךָ מִיַּד שְׂמֹאולֶךָ וְחִצֶּיךָ מִיַּד יְמִינְךָ אַפִּיל: עַל־הָרֵי יִשְׂרָאֵל תִּפּוֹל
אַתָּה וְכָל־אֲגַפֶּיךָ וְעַמִּים אֲשֶׁר אִתָּךְ לְעֵיט צִפּוֹר כָּל־כָּנָף וְחַיַּת הַשָּׂדֶה
נְתַתִּיךָ לְאָכְלָה: עַל־פְּנֵי הַשָּׂדֶה תִּפּוֹל כִּי אֲנִי דִבַּרְתִּי נְאֻם אֲדֹנָי
יְהֹוִ֖הֽ: וְשִׁלַּחְתִּי־אֵשׁ בְּמָגוֹג וּבְיֹשְׁבֵי הָאִיִּים לָבֶטַח וְיָדְעוּ כִּי־אֲנִי
יְהֹוָ֖הֽ: וְאֶת־שֵׁם קָדְשִׁי אוֹדִיעַ בְּתוֹךְ עַמִּי יִשְׂרָאֵל וְלֹא־אַחֵל
אֶת־שֵׁם־קָדְשִׁי עוֹד וְיָדְעוּ הַגּוֹיִם כִּי־אֲנִי יְהֹוָ֖הֽ קָדוֹשׁ בְּיִשְׂרָאֵל:
הִנֵּה בָאָה וְנִהְיָתָה נְאֻם אֲדֹנָי יְהֹוִ֖הֽ הוּא הַיּוֹם אֲשֶׁר דִּבַּרְתִּי:
וְיָצְאוּ יֹשְׁבֵי | עָרֵי יִשְׂרָאֵל וּבִעֲרוּ וְהִשִּׂיקוּ בְּנֶשֶׁק וּמָגֵן וְצִנָּה בְּקֶשֶׁת
וּבְחִצִּים וּבְמַקֵּל יָד וּבְרֹמַח וּבִעֲרוּ בָהֶם אֵשׁ שֶׁבַע שָׁנִים: וְלֹא־יִשְׂאוּ עֵצִים
מִן־הַשָּׂדֶה וְלֹא יַחְטְבוּ מִן־הַיְּעָרִים כִּי בַנֶּשֶׁק יְבַעֲרוּ־אֵשׁ וְשָׁלְלוּ
אֶת־שֹׁלְלֵיהֶם וּבָזְזוּ אֶת־בֹּזְזֵיהֶם נְאֻם אֲדֹנָי יְהֹוִ֖הֽ: וְהָיָה בַיּוֹם הַהוּא
אֶתֵּן לְגוֹג | מְקוֹם־שָׁם קֶבֶר בְּיִשְׂרָאֵל גֵּי הָעֹבְרִים קִדְמַת הַיָּם וְחֹסֶמֶת
הִיא אֶת־הָעֹבְרִים וְקָבְרוּ שָׁם אֶת־גּוֹג וְאֶת־כָּל־הֲמוֹנֹה וְקָרְאוּ גֵּיא
הֲמוֹן גּוֹג: וּקְבָרוּם בֵּית יִשְׂרָאֵל לְמַעַן טַהֵר אֶת־הָאָרֶץ שִׁבְעָה וְחֳדָשִׁים:

I will be exalted and sanctified, and I will become known in the eyes of many nations, and they shall know that I am Lord. And you, man, prophesy against God and say: So says the Lord, God, See I am against you, Gog, prince, leader of Meshech and Tuval. I shall lead you astray and seduce you, and I shall cause you to advance from the farthest north and bring you to the mountains of Israel. I will strike your bow from your left hand, and I will cast down your arrows from your right hand, You shall fall upon Israel's mountains, you and all your cohorts and the nations that are with you. I will present you as carrion for every winged bird and beast of the field. You will fall upon the open field, for I have spoken, the words of the Lord, God. And I will set fire against Magog and against those who dwell confidently in the islands, and they shall know that I am Lord. I will make known My holy Name among My people Israel, and I will never more desecrate My holy Name, and the nations shall know that I am Lord, the Holy One in Israel. Behold, it has come and happened, the words of the Lord, God, this is the day of which I have spoken. Then the inhabitants of Israel's cities will go out and make fires and feed them with weapons, shield and buckles, with bow and with arrows, with hand-club and spear, and shall fuel fire with them for seven years. They will not carry wood from the field, not cut it from the forests, for with weapons they shall feed the fires. They will despoil those who despoiled them and plunder those who plunder them, the words of the Lord, God. On that day I shall assign a burial site, for Gog, there in Israel, the valley of the travelers, and there they will bury Gog and all his horde, and call in the Valley of Gog's Horde. The family of Israel will bury them for seven months, in order to cleanse the Land.

וְקָבְרוּ כָל־עַם הָאָרֶץ וְהָיָה לָהֶם לְשֵׁם יוֹם הִכָּבְדִי נְאֻם אֲדֹנָי

יֱהֹוִה: וְאַנְשֵׁי תָמִיד יַבְדִּילוּ עֹבְרִים בָּאָרֶץ מְקַבְּרִים אֶת־הָעֹבְרִים

אֶת־הַנּוֹתָרִים עַל־פְּנֵי הָאָרֶץ לְטַהֲרָהּ מִקְצֵה שִׁבְעַת־חֳדָשִׁים יַחְקֹרוּ: וְעָבְרוּ

הָעֹבְרִים בָּאָרֶץ וְרָאָה עֶצֶם אָדָם וּבָנָה אֶצְלוֹ צִיּוּן עַד קָבְרוּ אֹתוֹ

הַמְקַבְּרִים אֶל־גֵּיא הֲמוֹן גּוֹג: וְגַם שֶׁם־עִיר הֲמוֹנָה וְטִהֲרוּ הָאָרֶץ:

Say the blessing after the *Haftarah* on pages 503-504.

THE TORAH READING FOR THE 16TH DAY OF TISHREI – 1ST OF CHOL HAMO'ED
Four people are called to go to the Torah on *Chol Hamo'ed*.

וּבַיּוֹם הַשֵּׁנִי פָּרִים בְּנֵי־בָקָר שְׁנֵים עָשָׂר אֵילִם שְׁנָיִם כְּבָשִׂים בְּנֵי־שָׁנָה

אַרְבָּעָה עָשָׂר תְּמִימִם: וּמִנְחָתָם וְנִסְכֵּיהֶם לַפָּרִים לָאֵילִם וְלַכְּבָשִׂים

בְּמִסְפָּרָם כַּמִּשְׁפָּט: וּשְׂעִיר־עִזִּים אֶחָד וְזֹאת מִלְּבַד עֹלַת הַתָּמִיד

וּמִנְחָתָהּ וְנִסְכֵּיהֶם:

On Chol Hamo'ed (not on *Shabbat*) say Half *Kaddish* on pages 501-502, then return the Torah to the ark on page 663, and then continue with *Shachrit* for *Chol Hamoe'd* on page 664.

THE TORAH READING FOR THE 17TH DAY OF TISHREI – 2ND OF CHOL HAMO'ED
Four people are called to go to the Torah on *Chol Hamo'ed*.
If *Shabbat Chol Hamo'ed* falls on the 17th day of *Tishrei* we read this section as the *Maftir*.

וּבַיּוֹם הַשְּׁלִישִׁי פָּרִים עַשְׁתֵּי־עָשָׂר אֵילִם שְׁנָיִם כְּבָשִׂים בְּנֵי־שָׁנָה אַרְבָּעָה

עָשָׂר תְּמִימִם: וּמִנְחָתָם וְנִסְכֵּיהֶם לַפָּרִים לָאֵילִם וְלַכְּבָשִׂים בְּמִסְפָּרָם

כַּמִּשְׁפָּט: וּשְׂעִיר וְזֹאת מִלְּבַד עֹלַת הַתָּמִיד וּמִנְחָתָהּ וְנִסְכָּהּ:

On Chol Hamo'ed say Half *Kaddish* on pages 501-502, then return the Torah to the ark on page 663, and then continue with *Shachrit* for *Chol Hamoe'd* on page 664. **On Shabbat Chol Hamo'ed** continue with the *Haftarah* on page 741.

All the people of the Land will bury, and it will cause them renown, the day I manifest My Glory, the words of the Lord, God. They will designate permanent officials passing through the land, burying, with passersby, those that remain upon the open field in order to cleanse it, after seven months, they are to seek out. As the passersby traverse the land and see a human bone, then they shall build a marker near it, until the buriers bury it in the Valley of Gog's Horde. There shall also be a city called Hamonah, thus will they cleanse the land." (Ezikiel 38:18-39:16)

THE TORAH READING FOR THE 16TH DAY OF TISHREI – 1ST OF CHOL HAMO'ED
"And on the second day, twelve young bulls, two rams, fourteen lambs within their first year, they are to be unblemished. And their meal-offerings and their libations for the bulls, the rams, and the lambs, in their proper numbers as required; and one he-goat for a sin-offering, aside from the continual elevation-offering, its meal-offering and their libations." (Numbers 29:17-19)

THE TORAH READING FOR THE 17TH DAY OF TISHREI – 2ND OF CHOL HAMO'ED
"And on the third day, eleven bulls, two rams, fourteen lambs within their first year, they are to be unblemished. And their meal-offerings and their libations for the bulls, the rams, and the lambs, in their proper numbers as required. And one he-goat for a sin-offering, aside from the continual elevation-offering and its meal-offering and its libation." (Numbers 29:20-22)

TORAH READING FOR SUKKOT

THE TORAH READING FOR THE 18TH DAY OF TISHREI – 3RD OF CHOL HAMO'ED
Four people are called to go to the Torah on *Chol Hamo'ed*.

וּבַיּ֣וֹם הָרְבִיעִ֗י פָּרִ֤ים עֲשָׂרָה֙ אֵילִ֣ם שְׁנָ֔יִם כְּבָשִׂ֧ים בְּנֵי־שָׁנָ֛ה אַרְבָּעָ֥ה עָשָׂ֖ר
תְּמִימִֽם: מִנְחָתָ֣ם וְנִסְכֵּיהֶ֡ם לַ֠פָּרִים לָאֵילִ֧ם וְלַכְּבָשִׂ֛ים בְּמִסְפָּרָ֖ם כַּמִּשְׁפָּֽט:
וּשְׂעִיר־עִזִּ֥ים אֶחָ֖ד מִלְּבַד֙ עֹלַ֣ת הַתָּמִ֔יד מִנְחָתָ֖הּ וְנִסְכָּֽהּ:

On Chol Hamo'ed (not on *Shabbat*) say *Kaddish* on pages 501-502, then return the Torah to the ark on page 663, and then continue with *Shachrit* for *Chol Hamoe'd* on page 664.

THE TORAH READING FOR THE 19TH DAY OF TISHREI – 4TH OF CHOL HAMO'ED
Four people are called to go to the Torah on *Chol Hamo'ed*.
If *Shabbat Chol Hamo'ed* falls on the 19th day of *Tishrei* we read this section as the *Maftir*.

וּבַיּ֣וֹם הַחֲמִישִׁ֗י פָּרִ֤ים תִּשְׁעָה֙ אֵילִ֣ם שְׁנָ֔יִם כְּבָשִׂ֧ים בְּנֵי־שָׁנָ֛ה אַרְבָּעָ֥ה עָשָׂ֖ר
תְּמִימִֽם: וּמִנְחָתָ֣ם וְנִסְכֵּיהֶ֡ם לַ֠פָּרִים לָאֵילִ֧ם וְלַכְּבָשִׂ֛ים בְּמִסְפָּרָ֖ם כַּמִּשְׁפָּֽט:
וּשְׂעִ֥יר אֶחָ֖ד מִלְּבַד֙ עֹלַ֣ת הַתָּמִ֔יד וּמִנְחָתָ֖הּ וְנִסְכָּֽהּ:

On Chol Hamo'ed say *Kaddish* on pages 501-502, then return the Torah to the ark on page 663, and then continue with *Shachrit* for *Chol Hamoe'd* on page 664. **On Shabbat Chol Hamo'ed** continue with the *Haftarah* on page 741.

THE TORAH READING FOR THE 20TH DAY OF TISHREI – 5TH OF CHOL HAMO'ED
Four people are called to go to the Torah on *Chol Hamo'ed*.
If *Shabbat Chol Hamo'ed* falls on the 20th day of *Tishrei* we read this section as the *Maftir*.

וּבַיּ֣וֹם הַשִּׁשִּׁ֗י פָּרִ֤ים שְׁמֹנָה֙ אֵילִ֣ם שְׁנָ֔יִם כְּבָשִׂ֧ים בְּנֵי־שָׁנָ֛ה אַרְבָּעָ֥ה עָשָׂ֖ר
תְּמִימִֽם: וּמִנְחָתָ֣ם וְנִסְכֵּיהֶ֡ם לַ֠פָּרִים לָאֵילִ֧ם וְלַכְּבָשִׂ֛ים בְּמִסְפָּרָ֖ם כַּמִּשְׁפָּֽט:
וּשְׂעִ֥יר אֶחָ֖ד מִלְּבַד֙ עֹלַ֣ת הַתָּמִ֔יד מִנְחָתָ֖הּ וְנִסְכֶּֽיהָ:

On Chol Hamo'ed say *Kaddish* on pages 501-502, then return the Torah to the ark on page 663, and then continue with *Shachrit* for *Chol Hamoe'd* on page 664. **On Shabbat Chol Hamo'ed** continue with the *Haftarah* on page 741.

THE TORAH READING FOR THE 18TH DAY OF TISHREI – 3RD OF CHOL HAMO'ED
"And on the fourth day, ten bulls, two rams, fourteen lambs within their first year, they are to be unblemished. And their meal-offerings and their libations for the bulls, the rams, and the lambs, in their proper numbers as required; and one he-goat for a sin-offering, aside from the continual elevation-offering, its meal-offering and its libation." (Numbers 29:23-25)

THE TORAH READING FOR THE 19TH DAY OF TISHREI – 4TH OF CHOL HAMO'ED
"And on the fifth day nine bulls, two rams, fourteen lambs within their first year, they are to be unblemished. And their meal-offerings and their libations for the bulls, the rams, and the lambs, in their proper numbers as required; and one he-goat for a sin-offering, aside from the continual elevation-offering, its meal-offering and its libation." (Numbers 29:26-28)

THE TORAH READING FOR THE 20TH DAY OF TISHREI – 5TH OF CHOL HAMO'ED
"And of the sixth day, eight bulls, tow rams, fourteen lambs within their first year, they are to be unblemished. And their meal-offerings and their libations for the bulls, the rams, and the lambs, in their proper numbers as required; and one he-goat for a sin-offering, aside from the continual elevation-offering, its meal-offering and its libations." (Numbers 29:29-31)

THE TORAH READING FOR HOSHA'ANAH RABBAH

Four people are called to go to the Torah on *Hosha'ana Rabbah*.

וּבַיּוֹם הַשְּׁבִיעִי פָּרִים שִׁבְעָה אֵילִם שְׁנַיִם כְּבָשִׂים בְּנֵי־שָׁנָה אַרְבָּעָה עָשָׂר תְּמִימִם: וּמִנְחָתָם וְנִסְכֵּיהֶם לַפָּרִים לָאֵילִם וְלַכְּבָשִׂים בְּמִסְפָּרָם כְּמִשְׁפָּטָם: וְשָׂעִיר חַטָּאת אֶחָד מִלְּבַד עֹלַת הַתָּמִיד מִנְחָתָהּ וְנִסְכָּהּ:

On *Hosha'ana Rabbah* say Half *Kaddish* on pages 501-502, then return the Torah to the ark on page 663, and then continue with *Shachrit* for *Chol Hamoe'd* on page 664.

THE TORAH READING FOR HOSHA'ANAH RABBAH

"And of the seventh day, seven bulls, tow rams, fourteen lambs within their first year, they are to be unblemished. And their meal-offerings and their libations for the bulls, the rams, and the lambs, in their proper numbers as required; and one he-goat for a sin-offering, aside from the continual elevation-offering, its meal-offering and its libation." (Numbers 29:29-31)

TORAH READING FOR SIMCHAT TORAH

וְזֹאת הַבְּרָכָה אֲשֶׁר בֵּרַךְ מֹשֶׁה אִישׁ הָאֱלֹהִים אֶת־בְּנֵי יִשְׂרָאֵל לִפְנֵי
מוֹתוֹ: וַיֹּאמַר יְהֹוָﬞהﬞﬞ מִסִּינַי בָּא וְזָרַח מִשֵּׂעִיר לָמוֹ הוֹפִיעַ מֵהַר פָּארָן
וְאָתָה מֵרִבְבֹת קֹדֶשׁ מִימִינוֹ אֵשׁ דָּת (כתיב: אשדת) לָמוֹ: אַף חֹבֵב עַמִּים
כָּל־קְדֹשָׁיו בְּיָדֶךָ וְהֵם תֻּכּוּ לְרַגְלֶךָ יִשָּׂא מִדַּבְּרֹתֶיךָ: תּוֹרָה צִוָּה־לָנוּ מֹשֶׁה
מוֹרָשָׁה קְהִלַּת יַעֲקֹב: וַיְהִי בִישֻׁרוּן מֶלֶךְ בְּהִתְאַסֵּף רָאשֵׁי עָם יַחַד שִׁבְטֵי
יִשְׂרָאֵל: יְחִי רְאוּבֵן וְאַל־יָמֹת וִיהִי מְתָיו מִסְפָּר: וְזֹאת לִיהוּדָה וַיֹּאמַר
שְׁמַע יְהֹוָﬞהﬞﬞ קוֹל יְהוּדָה וְאֶל־עַמּוֹ תְּבִיאֶנּוּ יָדָיו רָב לוֹ וְעֵזֶר מִצָּרָיו
תִּהְיֶה: Levi וּלְלֵוִי אָמַר תֻּמֶּיךָ וְאוּרֶיךָ לְאִישׁ חֲסִידֶךָ אֲשֶׁר נִסִּיתוֹ בְּמַסָּה
תְּרִיבֵהוּ עַל־מֵי מְרִיבָה: הָאֹמֵר לְאָבִיו וּלְאִמּוֹ לֹא רְאִיתִיו וְאֶת־אֶחָיו לֹא
הִכִּיר וְאֶת־בָּנָו לֹא יָדָע כִּי שָׁמְרוּ אִמְרָתֶךָ וּבְרִיתְךָ יִנְצֹרוּ: יוֹרוּ מִשְׁפָּטֶיךָ
לְיַעֲקֹב וְתוֹרָתְךָ לְיִשְׂרָאֵל יָשִׂימוּ קְטוֹרָה בְּאַפֶּךָ וְכָלִיל עַל־מִזְבְּחֶךָ: בָּרֵךְ
יְהֹוָﬞהﬞﬞ חֵילוֹ וּפֹעַל יָדָיו תִּרְצֶה מְחַץ מָתְנַיִם קָמָיו וּמְשַׂנְאָיו
מִן־יְקוּמוּן: לְבִנְיָמִן אָמַר יְדִיד יְהֹוָﬞהﬞﬞ יִשְׁכֹּן לָבֶטַח עָלָיו חֹפֵף עָלָיו
כָּל־הַיּוֹם וּבֵין כְּתֵפָיו שָׁכֵן: Israel וּלְיוֹסֵף אָמַר מְבֹרֶכֶת יְהֹוָﬞהﬞﬞ אַרְצוֹ
מִמֶּגֶד שָׁמַיִם מִטָּל וּמִתְּהוֹם רֹבֶצֶת תָּחַת: וּמִמֶּגֶד תְּבוּאֹת שָׁמֶשׁ
וּמִמֶּגֶד גֶּרֶשׁ יְרָחִים: וּמֵרֹאשׁ הַרְרֵי־קֶדֶם וּמִמֶּגֶד גִּבְעוֹת עוֹלָם:

TORAH READING FOR SIMCHAT TORAH

'This is the blessing that Moses, the man of God blessed upon the children of Israel, before his death. And he said: The Lord approached from Sinai, having shone forth to them from Se'ir, having appeared from Mount Paran, and then approached with some of the holy myriads, from His right hand He presented the fiery Torah to them. Indeed, You greatly loved the tribes, all His righteous ones were in Your hands, for they planted themselves at Your feet, accepting the burden of Your utterances: "The Torah which Moses charged us is the heritage of the Congregation of Jacob. He became King over Yeshurun when the leaders of the nation gathered, the tribes of Israel in unity." May Reuben live and not die, and may his population be counted among the others. And this he said to Judea: Hear, Lord, Judea's prayer and return him safely to his people, may his hands gain him triumph and may You remain a helper against his enemies.' **LEVI** *And to Levy he said: Your Tumim and your Urim devout one, whom You tested at Massah and whom You challenged at the waters of Meribah. The one who said of his father and mother, "I have not favored him," he disregarded his brothers and ignored his own children, for they have observed Your word, and preserved Your covenant. Thus it is they who are worthy to teach Your law to Jacob and Your Torah to Israel, it is they who shall place incense before Your presence, and burnt offerings of Your Altar. Bless, Lord, his resources, and favor his handiwork. Smash the lions of his foes, and his enemies that they may not rise again. To Benjamin he said: May the Lord's beloved dwell securely by Him. He hovers above him all day long, and rests His Presence among his hills.* **ISRAEL** *And to Joseph he said: His land is blessed by the Lord, with the heavenly bounty of dew, and with the deep waters crouching below, with the bounty of the sun's crops, and with the bounty of the moon's yield, with the quick-ripening crops of the ancient mountains, and with the bounty of eternally fertile hills;*

וּמִמֶּגֶד אֶרֶץ וּמְלֹאָהּ וּרְצוֹן שֹׁכְנִי סְנֶה תָּבוֹאתָה לְרֹאשׁ יוֹסֵף וּלְקָדְקֹד נְזִיר אֶחָיו: בְּכוֹר שׁוֹרוֹ הָדָר לוֹ וְקַרְנֵי רְאֵם קַרְנָיו בָּהֶם עַמִּים יְנַגַּח יַחְדָּו אַפְסֵי־אָרֶץ וְהֵם רִבְבוֹת אֶפְרַיִם וְהֵם אַלְפֵי מְנַשֶּׁה: *Fourth* וְלִזְבוּלֻן אָמַר שְׂמַח זְבוּלֻן בְּצֵאתֶךָ וְיִשָּׂשכָר בְּאֹהָלֶיךָ: עַמִּים הַר־יִקְרָאוּ שָׁם יִזְבְּחוּ זִבְחֵי־צֶדֶק כִּי שֶׁפַע יַמִּים יִינָקוּ וּשְׂפֻנֵי טְמוּנֵי חוֹל: וּלְגָד אָמַר בָּרוּךְ מַרְחִיב גָּד כְּלָבִיא שָׁכֵן וְטָרַף זְרוֹעַ אַף־קָדְקֹד: וַיַּרְא רֵאשִׁית לוֹ כִּי־שָׁם חֶלְקַת מְחֹקֵק סָפוּן וַיֵּתֵא רָאשֵׁי עָם צִדְקַת יְהֹוָה עָשָׂה וּמִשְׁפָּטָיו עִם־יִשְׂרָאֵל: *Fifth* וּלְדָן אָמַר דָּן גּוּר אַרְיֵה יְזַנֵּק מִן־הַבָּשָׁן: וּלְנַפְתָּלִי אָמַר נַפְתָּלִי שְׂבַע רָצוֹן וּמָלֵא בִּרְכַּת יְהֹוָה יָם וְדָרוֹם יְרָשָׁה: וּלְאָשֵׁר אָמַר בָּרוּךְ מִבָּנִים אָשֵׁר יְהִי רְצוּי אֶחָיו וְטֹבֵל בַּשֶּׁמֶן רַגְלוֹ: בַּרְזֶל וּנְחֹשֶׁת מִנְעָלֶךָ וּכְיָמֶיךָ דָּבְאֶךָ: אֵין כָּאֵל יְשֻׁרוּן רֹכֵב שָׁמַיִם בְּעֶזְרֶךָ וּבְגַאֲוָתוֹ שְׁחָקִים:

PERMISSION FOR CHATAN TORAH

,vehanora וְהַנּוֹרָא	hagibor הַגִּבּוֹר	hagadol הַגָּדוֹל	haEl הָאֵל	mershut מֵרְשׁוּת
,yekara יְקָרָה	umipninim וּמִפְּנִינִים	mipaz מִפָּז		omershut וּמֵרְשׁוּת
,vehatehora וְהַטְּהוֹרָה	hakedosha הַקְּדוֹשָׁה	sanhedrin סַנְהֶדְרִין		umershut וּמֵרְשׁוּת
,hatorah הַתּוֹרָה	ve'alufei וְאַלּוּפֵי	yeshivot יְשִׁיבוֹת	rashei רָאשֵׁי	vmershut וּמֵרְשׁוּת

with the bounty of the land and its fullness, and by the favor of Him Who rested upon the thorn bush. May this blessing rest upon Joseph's head, and upon the crown of him who was separated from his brothers. Sovereignty will go to his most distinguished, mighty descendant, and his glory will be like the horns of an oryx, with both of them together he shall gore nations to the ends of the earth; they are the myriads of Ephraim's victims, and the thousands of Manasseh's victims. **FOURTH** And to Zebulon he said: Rejoice, Zebulon in your excursions, and Issachar in your tents. The tribes will summon one another to the Temple Mount; there they will bring offerings of righteousness, for they will be nourished by the riches of the sea, and by the treasures concealed in the sand. And to Gad he said: Blessed is He Who broadens God's boundary, he dwells like a lion tearing off arm and even head. He chose the first portion as his own, for that is where the Lawgiver's plot is hidden. He marches at the head of the nations, carrying out the Lord's justice and His laws with Israel. **FIFTH** And to Dan he said: Dan is a lion cub, leaping forth from the Bashan. And to Naftali he said: Naftali, satiated with favor, and filled with the Lord's blessing, go possess the sea and its south shore. And to Asher he said: Asher is most blessed with children, he shall be pleasing to his brothers, and dip his feet in oil. May your borders be sealed like iron and copper, and like the days of your prime, so may your old age be. There is none like God [of] Yeshurun. He rides across Heaven to help you, and in His majesty through the Upper Heights." *(Deuteronomy 33:1-26)*

PERMISSION FOR CHATAN TORAH

With permission of the Great, Mighty, and Awesome God;
with permission of [the Torah] that is more precious than the finest gold and gems; with permission of the holy and refined Sanhedrin; with permission of head of academies and the nobles of the Torah,

umershut וּמֵרְשׁוּת zekenim זְקֵנִים un'arim וּנְעָרִים yoshvei יוֹשְׁבֵי shura שׁוּרָה,

eftach אֶפְתַּח pi פִּי beshira בְּשִׁירָה uvzimra וּבְזִמְרָה, lehodot לְהוֹדוֹת

ulhalel וּלְהַלֵּל ledar לְדָר binhora בִּנְהוֹרָא, shehecheyanu שֶׁהֶחֱיָנוּ vekiymanu וְקִיְּמָנוּ

beyir'ato בִּירְאָתוֹ hatehora הַטְּהוֹרָה, vehigi'anu וְהִגִּיעָנוּ lismo'ach לִשְׂמוֹחַ

beSimchat בְּשִׂמְחַת haTorah הַתּוֹרָה, hamesamachat הַמְשַׂמֵּחַת lev לֵב

ve'enayim וְעֵינַיִם me'ira מְאִירָה, notenet נוֹתֶנֶת osher עֹשֶׁר vechavod וְכָבוֹד

vechayim וְחַיִּים, vetif'ara וְתִפְאָרָה ma'arechet מַאֲרֶכֶת yamim יָמִים

umosefet וּמוֹסֶפֶת gevura גְּבוּרָה, le'ohaveha לְאוֹהֲבֶיהָ ulshomreha וּלְשׁוֹמְרֶיהָ

betzivuy בְּצִוּוּי ve'azhara וְאַזְהָרָה, uvchen וּבְכֵן yehi יְהִי ratzon רָצוֹן

milifnei מִלִּפְנֵי hagevura הַגְּבוּרָה, latet לָתֵת chayim וְחַיִּים vachesed וָחֶסֶד

va'atara וַעֲטָרָה, lerabi לְרַבִּי [name of the *Chatan Torah*] ben בֶּן [his father's name]

hanivchar הַנִּבְחָר lehashlim לְהַשְׁלִים hatorah הַתּוֹרָה: le'amtzo לְאַמְּצוֹ

levarcho לְבָרְכוֹ legadlo לְגַדְּלוֹ betalmud בְּתַלְמוּד torah תּוֹרָה,

ledorsho לְדָרְשׁוֹ lehadro לְהַדְּרוֹ leva'ado לְוַעֲדוֹ bechavura בְּחַבוּרָה,

lezarzo לְזָרְזוֹ lechasno לְחַסְּנוֹ letakso לְטַכְּסוֹ leyashro לְיַשְּׁרוֹ lechavdo לְכַבְּדוֹ

lelamdo לְלַמְּדוֹ lekach לְקַח usvara וּסְבָרָה, lemalto לְמַלְּטוֹ lenas'o לְנַשְּׂאוֹ

lesa'ado לְסַעֲדוֹ vesa'ad בְּסַעַד berura בְּרוּרָה, le'adno לְעַדְּנוֹ lefarneso לְפַרְנְסוֹ

letzadko לְצַדְּקוֹ ve'am בְּעַם nivra נִבְרָא, lekarvo לְקָרְבוֹ lerachamo לְרַחֲמוֹ

leshomro לְשָׁמְרוֹ mikol מִכָּל tzuka צוּקָה vetzara וְצָרָה, letakfo לְתָקְפוֹ

lesamcho לְסַמְּכוֹ letamcho לְתָמְכוֹ beru'ach בְּרוּחַ nishbara נִשְׁבָּרָה.

---

with permission of the elders and youths who sit in the ranks, I shall open my mouth with song and hymn to thank and praise Him Who dwells amid light, Who has kept us alive and sustained us through His pure reverence and has brought us to rejoice with the gladness of the Torah that gladdens the heart and enlightens the eyes; that provides life, prosperity, honor, and glory; that brings good fortune to those who walk its good and just paths; that lengthens days and increases strength of those who love Her and observe Her commandments and sanctions for those who occupy themselves with Her study and preserve Her with love and reverence. Therefore may it be the will of the Omnipotent that He bestow life, kindness, tiara and crown upon (name of the Chatan Torah) son of (his father's name), who has been chosen to complete the Torah; to strengthen, bless, and make him great in the study of the Torah; to seek him out for life, to glorify him, and to establish him in society; to grant him merit and life, and to assign him in the council of light; to grant him virtue and distinction, to teach him knowledge and logic; to let him escape danger, to raise him, to aid him with refined support; to delight him, to provide him, to make him righteous among the people for whom the world was created; to draw him near, to show him mercy, and to protect him against every distress and trouble; to strengthen and assist, and support him when he is broken spirited.

TORAH READING FOR SIMCHAT TORAH

עֲמֹד amod עֲמֹד amod עֲמֹד amod

רַבִּי rabi [name of the *Chatan Torah*] בֶּן ben [his father's name] וְזֹאת chatan תּוֹרָה torah,

וְתֵן veten כָּבוֹד kavvd לָאֵל leEl גָּדוֹל gadol וְנוֹרָא venora, וּבִשְׂכַר uvischar

זֶה ze תִּזְכֶּה tizke מֵאֵל meEl נוֹרָא nora, לִרְאוֹת lir'ot בָּנִים banim וּבְנֵי uvnei

בָנִים banim עוֹסְקִים oskim בַּתּוֹרָה batorah, וּמְקַיְמֵי umkaymei מִצְוֹת mitzvot

בְּתוֹךְ betoch עַם am יָפָה yafa וּבָרָה uvara, וְתִזְכֶּה vetizke לִשְׂמֹחַ lismo'ach

בְּשִׂמְוַֹת besimchat בֵּית bet הַבְּחִירָה habechira, וּפָנֶיךָ ufanecha לְהָאִיר leha'ir

בִּצְדָקָה bitzdaka בָּאַסְפַּקְלַרְיָא be'aspaklarya הַמְּאִירָה hame'ira, כְּנַבָּא keniba

יְשַׁעְיָהוּ Yesha'ayahu מָלֵא maleh רוּחַ ru'ach עֵצָה etza וּגְבוּרָה ugvura,

שִׂמְווּ simchu אֶת et יְרוּשָׁלַיִם Yerushalayim וְגִילוּ vegilu בָּהּ ba מְהֵרָה mehera,

שִׂישׂוּ sisu אִתָּהּ ita מָשׂוֹשׂ masos, כָּל chol הַמִּתְאַבְּלִים hamit'abelim

עָלֶיהָ aleha בְּאֶבְלָה be'evla וְצָרָה vetzara. עֲמֹד amod עֲמֹד amod עֲמֹד amod

וְזֹאת chatan בֶּן ben [name of the *Chatan Torah*] רַבִּי rabi

הַתּוֹרָה hatorah, בִּרְשׁוּת mershut כָּל kol הַקָּהָל hakahal הַקָּדוֹשׁ hakadosh

הַזֶּה hazeh וְהַשְׁלֵם vehashlem הַתּוֹרָה hatora: יַעֲמוֹד ya'amod

רַבִּי rabi [name of the *Chatan Torah*] בֶּן ben [his father's name] וְזֹאת chatan הַתּוֹרָה hatorah:

TORAH READING FOR CHATAN TORAH

מְעֹנָה אֱלֹהֵי קֶדֶם

וּמִתַּחַת זְרֹעֹת עוֹלָם וַיְגָרֶשׁ מִפָּנֶיךָ אוֹיֵב וַיֹּאמֶר הַשְׁמֵד: וַיִּשְׁכֹּן יִשְׂרָאֵל
בֶּטַח בָּדָד עֵין יַעֲקֹב אֶל־אֶרֶץ דָּגָן וְתִירוֹשׁ אַף־שָׁמָיו יַעַרְפוּ טָל:

Arise, arise, arise (name of the Chatan Torah) son of (his father's name), the groom of the Torah, and render honor to the great and awesome God, and in reward for this, may you be deemed worthy by the Awesome God to see children and grandchildren occupied with the Torah, and performing commandments among the beautiful and refined people. May you be worthy to rejoice in the gladness of the Chosen Temple; may your countenance give illumination with righteousness as through a clear lens, as Isaiah prophesied with a spirit of counsel and strength. Be glad with Jerusalem and exult with her speedily, rejoice in her joy, all who grieved for her with sorrow and distress. Arise, arise, arise (name of the Chatan Torah) son of (his father's name), the groom of the Torah, with the permission of this entire holy congregation, and conclude the Torah.
Arise (name of the Chatan Torah) son of (his father's name), the groom of the Torah.

TORAH READING FOR CHATAN TORAH

"The heavens are the abode of God immemorial, and below are the world's mighty ones, He drove away the enemy before you, urging you, "Destroy!" And Israel will dwell secure, solitary, in the likeness of Jacob's blessing, in a land of grain and wine. Even his Heavens shall drip with dew.

אַשְׁרֶיךָ יִשְׂרָאֵל מִי כָמוֹךָ עַם נוֹשַׁע בַּיהֹוָ‌אהדי‌אהדונהי מָגֵן עֶזְרֶךָ וַאֲשֶׁר־חֶרֶב

גַּאֲוָתֶךָ וְיִכָּחֲשׁוּ אֹיְבֶיךָ לָךְ וְאַתָּה עַל־בָּמוֹתֵימוֹ תִדְרֹךְ: וַיַּעַל מֹשֶׁה

מֵעַרְבֹת מוֹאָב אֶל־הַר נְבוֹ רֹאשׁ הַפִּסְגָּה אֲשֶׁר עַל־פְּנֵי יְרֵחוֹ וַיַּרְאֵהוּ

יְהֹוָ‌אהדי‌אהדונהי אֶת־כָּל־הָאָרֶץ אֶת־הַגִּלְעָד עַד־דָּן: וְאֵת כָּל־נַפְתָּלִי

וְאֶת־אֶרֶץ אֶפְרַיִם וּמְנַשֶּׁה וְאֵת כָּל־אֶרֶץ יְהוּדָה עַד הַיָּם הָאַחֲרוֹן:

וְאֶת־הַנֶּגֶב וְאֶת־הַכִּכָּר בִּקְעַת יְרֵחוֹ עִיר הַתְּמָרִים עַד־צֹעַר:

וַיֹּאמֶר יְהֹוָ‌אהדי‌אהדונהי אֵלָיו זֹאת הָאָרֶץ אֲשֶׁר נִשְׁבַּעְתִּי לְאַבְרָהָם לְיִצְחָק

וּלְיַעֲקֹב לֵאמֹר לְזַרְעֲךָ אֶתְּנֶנָּה הֶרְאִיתִיךָ בְעֵינֶיךָ וְשָׁמָּה לֹא תַעֲבֹר:

וַיָּמָת שָׁם מֹשֶׁה עֶבֶד־יְהֹוָ‌אהדי‌אהדונהי בְּאֶרֶץ מוֹאָב עַל־פִּי יְהֹוָ‌אהדי‌אהדונהי:

וַיִּקְבֹּר אֹתוֹ בַגַּיְ בְּאֶרֶץ מוֹאָב מוּל בֵּית פְּעוֹר וְלֹא־יָדַע אִישׁ אֶת־קְבֻרָתוֹ

עַד הַיּוֹם הַזֶּה: וּמֹשֶׁה בֶּן־מֵאָה וְעֶשְׂרִים שָׁנָה בְּמֹתוֹ לֹא־כָהֲתָה עֵינוֹ

וְלֹא־נָס לֵחֹה: וַיִּבְכּוּ בְנֵי יִשְׂרָאֵל אֶת־מֹשֶׁה בְּעַרְבֹת מוֹאָב שְׁלֹשִׁים יוֹם

וַיִּתְּמוּ יְמֵי בְכִי אֵבֶל מֹשֶׁה: וִיהוֹשֻׁעַ בִּן־נוּן מָלֵא רוּחַ חָכְמָה כִּי־סָמַךְ

מֹשֶׁה אֶת־יָדָיו עָלָיו וַיִּשְׁמְעוּ אֵלָיו בְּנֵי־יִשְׂרָאֵל וַיַּעֲשׂוּ כַּאֲשֶׁר צִוָּה

יְהֹוָ‌אהדי‌אהדונהי אֶת־מֹשֶׁה: וְלֹא־קָם נָבִיא עוֹד בְּיִשְׂרָאֵל כְּמֹשֶׁה אֲשֶׁר יְדָעוֹ

יְהֹוָ‌אהדי‌אהדונהי פָּנִים אֶל־פָּנִים: לְכָל־הָאֹתֹת וְהַמּוֹפְתִים אֲשֶׁר שְׁלָחוֹ

יְהֹוָ‌אהדי‌אהדונהי לַעֲשׂוֹת בְּאֶרֶץ מִצְרָיִם לְפַרְעֹה וּלְכָל־עֲבָדָיו וּלְכָל־אַרְצוֹ:

Praise be Israel, who is like you! Nation delivered by the Lord, the Shield of your help. Who is the Sward of your grandeur. Your foes will try to deceive you, but you will trample their haughty ones. And Moses ascended from the plains of Moab, to Mount Nebo, to the summit of the cliff, that faces Jericho, and the Lord showed him the entire land. The Gilead as far as Dan, all of Naphtali, and the land of Ephraim and Manasseh, the entire land of Judea as far as the last sea, the Negev, and the Plain, the valley of Jericho, city of date palms, as far as Zo'ar. And the Lord said to him: "This is the land of which I have sworn to Abraham, Isaac and Jacob, saying, 'I will give it to your offspring.' I have let you see it with your own eyes, but you shall not cross there." And Moses, servant of the Lord, died there, in the land of Moab, by the mouth of the Lord. He buried him in the depression, in the land of Moab, opposite Bet Pe'or, and no one knows his burial place to this very day. Moses was hundred and twenty years old when he died, his eyes had not dimmed, and his vigor had not diminished. And the children of Israel bewailed Moses in the plains of Moab for thirty days, then the days of tearful mourning for Moses came to an end. And Joshua son of Nun was filled with the spirit of wisdom, because Moses had laid his hands on him. The children of Israel therefore obeyed him. Doing as the Lord has commanded Moses. Never again has there arisen in Israel a prophet like Moses, whom the Lord has known face to face, as evidenced by all the signs and miracles that the Lord assigned him to perform in the land of Egypt, against Pharaoh and all his courtiers and all his land.

וּלְכֹל הַיָּד הַחֲזָקָה וּלְכֹל הַמּוֹרָא הַגָּדוֹל אֲשֶׁר עָשָׂה מֹשֶׁה לְעֵינֵי
כָּל־יִשְׂרָאֵל:

(We do not say Kaddish here)

Congregation then leader:

פהל chazak וֹזֹק (Left Column—*Gevurah*)   פהל chazak וֹזֹק (Right Column—*Chesed*)

venitchazek וְנִתְחֹזַק (*Malchut*)   פהל chazak וֹזֹק (Central Column—*Tiferet*)

PERMISSION FOR CHATAN BERESHEET

,veshira וְשִׁירָה beracha בְּרָכָה kol כָּל al עַל meromam מְרוֹמָם mershut מֵרְשׁוּת מֵרְשׁוּת

levav לְבַב chacham וְחַכֵּם ,vezimra וְזִמְרָה tehila תְּהִלָּה kol כָּל al עַל nora nora נוֹרָא

olam עוֹלָם umoshel וּמוֹשֵׁל ,ugvura וּגְבוּרָה ko'ach כֹּחַ ve'amitz וְאַמִּיץ וְאַמִּיץ

bat בַּת kevuda כְּבוּדָה umershut וּמֵרְשׁוּת ,yetzira יְצִירָה kol כָּל adon אָדוֹן

kinyano קִנְיָנוֹ reshit רֵאשִׁית ,atzura עֲצוּרָה penima פְּנִימָה melech מֶלֶךְ

meshivat מְשִׁיבַת temima תְּמִימָה bara בָּרָה ,atzura אֲצוּרָה alpayim אַלְפַּיִם

morasha מוֹרָשָׁה nitna נִתְּנָה Yeshurun יְשֻׁרוּן ,umachazira וּמַחֲזִירָהּ nefesh נֶפֶשׁ

ge'onei גְּאוֹנֵי melumadeha מְלֻמְּדֶיהָ ulshomra וּלְשָׁמְרָה le'ovda לְעָבְדָהּ

hod הוֹד kelil כְּלִיל ,ulsogra וּלְסָגְרָהּ lefotcha לְפָתְחָהּ Ya'akov יַעֲקֹב

midin מִדִּין al עַל yoshvei יוֹשְׁבֵי ,hamisra הַמִּשְׂרָה marbe מַרְבֵּה nasi נָשִׂיא

rashei רָאשֵׁי ,shara שַׁעְרָה milchama מִלְחָמָה meshivei מְשִׁיבֵי

umershut וּמֵרְשׁוּת •pezura פְּזוּרָה gola גּוֹלָה rashei רָאשֵׁי yeshivot יְשִׁיבוֹת

,hamushara הַמְּאֻשָּׁרָה eda עֵדָה tzedek צֶדֶק chavurat וְחֶבְרַת

,veshura וְשׁוּרָה shura שׁוּרָה bechol בְּכָל unarim וּנְעָרִים zekenim זְקֵנִים

And by all the mighty acts and awesome power that Moses performed before the eyes of all Israel."
(Deuteronomy 33:27-34:12)

Be strong! Be strong! Be strong! And let us strengthen ourselves.

PERMISSION FOR CHATAN BERESHEET

With permission of Him Who is exalted above every blessing and song, awesome above every praise and hymn, the wise-hearted, vigorously strong, Mighty One; Ruler of the World, Master of all Creation; and with permission of the Princess [the Torah] Whose glory is confined within; His prime possession that was treasured for two thousand generations; it is pure and perfect, refreshing the soul and restoring it; of Yeshurun of whom it was given as a heritage to perform and to observe; to be started and completed by its students, the great scholars of Jacob; of the totally glorious Nasi, who enjoys abundant dominion; of those who sit in judgment and bring the battles to the gates; the heads of the academies, the leaders of the dispersed exile; and with permission of the righteous company, the praiseworthy congregation; the elders and youths of every single rank,

קְבוּצִים kevutzim   פֹּה po   הַיּוֹם hayom   לְשִׂמְחַת lesimchat   תּוֹרָה torah,

וְנֶעֱצָרִים vene'etzarim   לְסַיֵּם lesayem   וּלְהָחֵל ulhachel   בְּגִיל begil

וּבְמוֹרָא uvmora,   אוֹתָהּ ota,   מְחַבְּבִים mechavevim   כְּיוֹם keyom   נְתִינָתָהּ netinata

בַּהֲדָרָהּ bahadara,   מְסַלְסְלִים mesalselim   בָּהּ ba   כַּחֲדָשָׁה kachadasha   וְלֹא velo

כְּיֶשָׁנָה kayshana   שֶׁעָבְרָה she'avra,   צְמֵאִים tzeme'im   לָמֹץ lamotz

וּלְהִתְעַנֵּג ulhitaneg   מִזִּיו miziv   יְקָרָה yekara,   מְשַׂמַּחַת mesamachat   לֵב lev

וְעֶצֶב ve'etzev   מְסִירָה mesira,   תַּנְחוּמֶיהָ tanchumeha   יְשַׁעְשְׁעוּ yesha'ashe'u

נַפְשָׁם nafsham   בָּהּ ba   לְהִתְפָּאֲרָה lehitpa'ara,   וְהוֹגִים vehogim   בְּמִקְרָא bemikra

וְהַגָּדָה vehagada   בְּמִשְׁנָה bemishna   וּגְמָרָא ugmara,   רָצִים ratzim

וּמְבִיאִים umvi'im   טַפָּם tapam   לְבֵית levet   הָעֲתִירָה ha'atira,   וְעוֹשִׂים ve'osim

גַּם gam   מַעֲשִׂים ma'asim   בְּאַזְהָרָה be'azhara,   לָכֵן lachen   גָּדוֹל gadol

שְׂכָרָם secharam   מֵאֵת me'et   הַגְּבוּרָה hagevura,   עַל al   רֹאשָׁם rosham

שִׂמְחַת simchat   עוֹלָם olam   קְשׁוּרָה keshura,   תְּאֵבִים te'evim   לִרְאוֹת lir'ot

בִּנְיַן binyan   בֵּית bet   הַבְּחִירָה habechira   וּבְכֵן uvechen   נִסְכַּמְתִּי niskamti

דַּעַת da'at   כֻּלָּם kulam   לִבְרֵרָה levarera,   בָּחוּר bachur   הֲרִימֹתִי harimoti

מֵעָם me'am   תּוֹךְ toch   הַחֲבוּרָה hachavura,   מְצָאתִיו metzativ   לֵב lev

נָבוֹן navon   לְהַסְבִּירָה lehasbira,   צֶדֶק tzedek   וָחֶסֶד vachesed   רוֹדֵף rodef

בְּאֹרַח be'orach   יְשָׁרָה yeshara,   וּנְשָׂאוֹ unsa'o   לִבּוֹ libo   וְנָדְבָה venadva

רוּחוֹ rucho   לְהִתְעוֹרְרָה lehit'orera,   תְּחִלָּה techila   וְרִאשׁוֹן verishon

הֱיוֹת heyot   לְהַתְחִיל lehatchil   הַתּוֹרָה hatorah,   וְעַתָּה ve'ata   קוּם kum   רַבִּי rabi

[name of the *Chatan Beresheet*] בֶּן ben [his father's name]   עֲמֹד amod   לְהִתְאַזְּרָה lehitazra,

בֹּא bo   וְהִתְיַצֵּב vehityatzev   וַעֲמֹד va'amod   לִימִינִי limini   וּקְרָא ukra,

---

who are gathered here for the gladness of the Torah; and remain to complete it and to begin it with joy and reverence. They adore it as on the day it was given majestically; they preen themselves with it as with a fresh treasure and not an old thing whose time has passed. They thirst to extract and to enjoy its precious radiance, which gladdens the heart and removes sadness. Their soul enjoys its consolations to glory themselves, and they discuss the Scripture and Aggadah, the Mishnah and Gemara. They run to bring their children to the house of prayer, and they do good deeds at their parent's bidding; therefore their reward from the Omnipotent One is great. Eternal joy is bound upon their head, for they long to see the rebuilding of the Chosen Temple. So now I assent to the unanimous decision to select a chosen one, exalted by the people from among the company, I have found him to have an understanding heart to comprehend; he pursues righteousness and kindness in a just manner and his heart has inspired him to begin to be the first to start the Torah. So now stand (name of the Chatan Beresheet) son of (his father's name), arise and gird yourself, come and stand erect, and arise to my right and read

bara בָּרָא • tzur צוּר lichvod לִכְבוֹד Bereshit בְּרֵאשִׁית ma'ase מַעֲשֵׂה

lehashlama לְהַשְׁלָמָה hatchala הַתְוֹזְלָה matkifin מַתְכִּיפִין zot זֹאת al עַל

zo זוֹ be'am בְּעַם yeragel יְרַגֵּל shelo שֶׁלֹּא ad עַד bitdira בִּתְדִירָה,

lemitzva לְמִצְוָה rishon רִאשׁוֹן na'aseta נַעֲשֵׂית ya'an יַעַן leshakra לְשַׁקְרָה,

umaskurtecha וּמַשְׂכֻּרְתֶּךָ tuvcha טוּבְךָ rav רַב ma מָה gemura גְּמוּרָה,

benidvatcha בְּנִדְבָתֶךָ tevorach תְּבוֹרַךְ ayin עַיִן tov טוֹב yetera יְתֵרָה,

tevorach תְּבוֹרַךְ vora'acha בּוֹרַאֲךָ umibirkot וּמִבִּרְכוֹת milatzra מִלְעָצְרָה,

shekol שֶׁכָּל va'avur בַּעֲבוּר milkatzra מִלְקַצְרָה, yadcha יָדְךָ

gufo גּוּפוֹ yehi יְהִי bitzfira בִּצְפִירָה, torah תּוֹרָה hamchabed הַמְכַבֵּד

amod עֲמֹד maher מַהֵר lehit'ashra לְהִתְאַשְּׁרָה, becho'ach בְּכֹחַ mechuvad מְכֻבָּד

amod עֲמֹד amod עֲמֹד rabi רַבִּי [name of the *Chatan Beresheet*] ben בֶּן [his father's name]

hakahal הַקָּהָל mershut מֵרְשׁוּת, bara בָּרָא Bereshit בְּרֵאשִׁית chatan וְזֹאת

venora וְנוֹרָא, gadol גָּדוֹל El אֵל levarech לְבָרֵךְ hazeh הַזֶּה hakadosh הַקָּדוֹשׁ

mehera מְהֵרָה: hakol הַכֹּל acharecha אַחֲרֶיךָ ya'anu יַעֲנוּ amen אָמֵן

[his father's name] ben בֶּן [name of the *Chatan Beresheet*] rabi רַבִּי ya'amod יַעֲמֹד

bereshit בְּרֵאשִׁית chatan וְזֹאת:

TORAH READING FOR CHATAN BERESHEET

בְּרֵאשִׁית בָּרָא אֱלֹהִים אֵת הַשָּׁמַיִם וְאֵת הָאָרֶץ: וְהָאָרֶץ הָיְתָה **CHESED**
תֹהוּ וָבֹהוּ וְחֹשֶׁךְ עַל־פְּנֵי תְהוֹם וְרוּחַ אֱלֹהִים מְרַחֶפֶת עַל־פְּנֵי הַמָּיִם:

---

the story of Creation in honor of Him Who formed and created. For this we always hurry to begin the Torah anew as soon as it is completed so that [Satan] cannot maliciously accuse the people. Since you are made for the first of this perfect precept, how abundant is your goodness and how fulsome your reward. Generous one, may you be blessed without your give being restrained and with your Creator's blessings may your hand be blessed that it never skimp, for whoever honors the Torah beautifully, may his body be honored powerfully to become strong. Quickly arise, arise, arise (name of the Chatan Beresheet) son of (his father's name), the groom of Beresheet Bara, with permission of this holy congregation, to bless the Great and Awesome God. Let all swiftly respond Amen after you.

Arise (name of Chatan Beresheet) son of (his father's name), the groom of Beresheet

TORAH READING FOR CHATAN BERESHEET

CHESED *"In the beginning God created the Heavens and the Earth, and the Earth was astonishingly empty, with darkness upon the surface of the deep, and the Divine Presence hovered upon the surface of the water.*

וַיֹּ֣אמֶר אֱלֹהִ֔ים יְהִ֣י א֑וֹר וַיְהִי־אֽוֹר: וַיַּ֧רְא אֱלֹהִ֛ים אֶת־הָא֖וֹר כִּי־ט֑וֹב וַיַּבְדֵּ֣ל
אֱלֹהִ֔ים בֵּ֥ין הָא֖וֹר וּבֵ֥ין הַחֹֽשֶׁךְ: וַיִּקְרָ֨א אֱלֹהִ֤ים ׀ לָאוֹר֙ י֔וֹם וְלַחֹ֖שֶׁךְ קָ֣רָא לָ֑יְלָה
וַֽיְהִי־עֶ֥רֶב וַֽיְהִי־בֹ֖קֶר י֥וֹם אֶחָֽד: **GEVURAH** וַיֹּ֣אמֶר אֱלֹהִ֔ים יְהִ֥י רָקִ֖יעַ בְּת֣וֹךְ
הַמָּ֑יִם וִיהִ֣י מַבְדִּ֔יל בֵּ֥ין מַ֖יִם לָמָֽיִם: וַיַּ֣עַשׂ אֱלֹהִים֮ אֶת־הָרָקִיעַ֒ וַיַּבְדֵּ֗ל בֵּ֤ין
הַמַּ֨יִם֙ אֲשֶׁר֙ מִתַּ֣חַת לָרָקִ֔יעַ וּבֵ֣ין הַמַּ֔יִם אֲשֶׁ֖ר מֵעַ֣ל לָרָקִ֑יעַ וַֽיְהִי־כֵֽן: וַיִּקְרָ֧א
אֱלֹהִ֛ים לָֽרָקִ֖יעַ שָׁמָ֑יִם וַֽיְהִי־עֶ֥רֶב וַֽיְהִי־בֹ֖קֶר י֥וֹם שֵׁנִֽי: **TIFERET** וַיֹּ֣אמֶר
אֱלֹהִ֗ים יִקָּו֨וּ הַמַּ֜יִם מִתַּ֤חַת הַשָּׁמַ֨יִם֙ אֶל־מָק֣וֹם אֶחָ֔ד וְתֵרָאֶ֖ה הַיַּבָּשָׁ֑ה
וַֽיְהִי־כֵֽן: וַיִּקְרָ֨א אֱלֹהִ֤ים ׀ לַיַּבָּשָׁה֙ אֶ֔רֶץ וּלְמִקְוֵ֥ה הַמַּ֖יִם קָרָ֣א יַמִּ֑ים וַיַּ֥רְא
אֱלֹהִ֖ים כִּי־טֽוֹב: וַיֹּ֣אמֶר אֱלֹהִ֗ים תַּֽדְשֵׁ֤א הָאָ֨רֶץ֙ דֶּ֗שֶׁא עֵ֚שֶׂב מַזְרִ֣יעַ זֶ֔רַע עֵ֣ץ
פְּרִ֞י עֹ֤שֶׂה פְּרִי֙ לְמִינ֔וֹ אֲשֶׁ֥ר זַרְעוֹ־ב֖וֹ עַל־הָאָ֑רֶץ וַֽיְהִי־כֵֽן: וַתּוֹצֵ֨א הָאָ֜רֶץ
דֶּ֠שֶׁא עֵ֣שֶׂב מַזְרִ֤יעַ זֶ֨רַע֙ לְמִינֵ֔הוּ וְעֵ֧ץ עֹֽשֶׂה־פְּרִ֛י אֲשֶׁ֥ר זַרְעוֹ־ב֖וֹ לְמִינֵ֑הוּ
וַיַּ֥רְא אֱלֹהִ֖ים כִּי־טֽוֹב: וַֽיְהִי־עֶ֥רֶב וַֽיְהִי־בֹ֖קֶר י֥וֹם שְׁלִישִֽׁי: **NETZACH** וַיֹּ֣אמֶר
אֱלֹהִ֗ים יְהִ֤י מְאֹרֹת֙ בִּרְקִ֣יעַ הַשָּׁמַ֔יִם לְהַבְדִּ֕יל בֵּ֥ין הַיּ֖וֹם וּבֵ֣ין הַלָּ֑יְלָה וְהָי֤וּ
לְאֹתֹת֙ וּלְמ֣וֹעֲדִ֔ים וּלְיָמִ֖ים וְשָׁנִֽים: וְהָי֤וּ לִמְאוֹרֹת֙ בִּרְקִ֣יעַ הַשָּׁמַ֔יִם לְהָאִ֖יר
עַל־הָאָ֑רֶץ וַֽיְהִי־כֵֽן: וַיַּ֣עַשׂ אֱלֹהִ֔ים אֶת־שְׁנֵ֥י הַמְּאֹרֹ֖ת הַגְּדֹלִ֑ים אֶת־הַמָּא֤וֹר
הַגָּדֹל֙ לְמֶמְשֶׁ֣לֶת הַיּ֔וֹם וְאֶת־הַמָּא֤וֹר הַקָּטֹן֙ לְמֶמְשֶׁ֣לֶת הַלַּ֔יְלָה וְאֵ֖ת הַכּוֹכָבִֽים:

And God said, 'Let there be light,' and there was light. And God saw that the light was good, and God separated between the light and the darkness. And God called the light 'Day,' and the darkness He called 'Night.' **And there was evening and there was morning, day one.**
GEVURAH *And God said: 'Let there be a firmament in the midst of the waters, and let it separate between water and water.' So God made the firmament, and separated between the waters which were beneath the firmament and the waters which were above the firmament. And it was so. And God called to the firmament: 'Heaven.'* **And there was evening and there was morning, a second day.**
TIFERET *And God said, 'Let the waters beneath the Heaven gather into one place, that the dry land may appear.' And it was so. And God called the dry land 'Earth,' and the gathering of water He called 'Seas.' And God saw that it was good. God said, 'Let the earth sprout vegetation, herbage yielding seed, fruit trees yielding fruit each after its kind, containing its own seed on the earth.' And it was so. And the earth brought forth vegetation: yielding seed after its kind and trees yielding fruit, each containing its seed after its kind. And God saw that it was good.* **And there was evening and there was morning, a third day.**
NETZACH *And God said, 'Let there be luminaries in the firmament of the Heaven to separate between the day and the night, and they shall serve as signs, and for holidays, and for days and years, and they shall serve as luminaries in the firmament of Heaven to shine upon the Earth.' And it was so. And God made the two great luminaries, the greater luminary to dominate the day ad the lesser luminary to dominate the night, and the stars.*

וַיִּתֵּן אֹתָם אֱלֹהִים בִּרְקִיעַ הַשָּׁמָיִם לְהָאִיר עַל־הָאָרֶץ: וְלִמְשֹׁל בַּיּוֹם

וּבַלַּיְלָה וּלְהַבְדִּיל בֵּין הָאוֹר וּבֵין הַחֹשֶׁךְ וַיַּרְא אֱלֹהִים כִּי־טוֹב: וַיְהִי־עֶרֶב

וַיְהִי־בֹקֶר יוֹם רְבִיעִי: **HOD** וַיֹּאמֶר אֱלֹהִים יִשְׁרְצוּ הַמַּיִם שֶׁרֶץ נֶפֶשׁ חַיָּה

וְעוֹף יְעוֹפֵף עַל־הָאָרֶץ עַל־פְּנֵי רְקִיעַ הַשָּׁמָיִם: וַיִּבְרָא אֱלֹהִים אֶת־הַתַּנִּינִם

הַגְּדֹלִים וְאֵת כָּל־נֶפֶשׁ הַחַיָּה | הָרֹמֶשֶׂת אֲשֶׁר שָׁרְצוּ הַמַּיִם לְמִינֵהֶם וְאֵת

כָּל־עוֹף כָּנָף לְמִינֵהוּ וַיַּרְא אֱלֹהִים כִּי־טוֹב: וַיְבָרֶךְ אֹתָם אֱלֹהִים לֵאמֹר פְּרוּ

וּרְבוּ וּמִלְאוּ אֶת־הַמַּיִם בַּיַּמִּים וְהָעוֹף יִרֶב בָּאָרֶץ: וַיְהִי־עֶרֶב וַיְהִי־בֹקֶר יוֹם

חֲמִישִׁי: **YESOD** וַיֹּאמֶר אֱלֹהִים תּוֹצֵא הָאָרֶץ נֶפֶשׁ חַיָּה לְמִינָהּ בְּהֵמָה וָרֶמֶשׂ

וְחַיְתוֹ־אֶרֶץ לְמִינָהּ וַיְהִי־כֵן: וַיַּעַשׂ אֱלֹהִים אֶת־חַיַּת הָאָרֶץ לְמִינָהּ

וְאֶת־הַבְּהֵמָה לְמִינָהּ וְאֵת כָּל־רֶמֶשׂ הָאֲדָמָה לְמִינֵהוּ וַיַּרְא אֱלֹהִים

כִּי־טוֹב: וַיֹּאמֶר אֱלֹהִים נַעֲשֶׂה אָדָם בְּצַלְמֵנוּ כִּדְמוּתֵנוּ וְיִרְדּוּ בִדְגַת הַיָּם

וּבְעוֹף הַשָּׁמַיִם וּבַבְּהֵמָה וּבְכָל־הָאָרֶץ וּבְכָל־הָרֶמֶשׂ הָרֹמֵשׂ עַל־הָאָרֶץ:

וַיִּבְרָא אֱלֹהִים | אֶת־הָאָדָם בְּצַלְמוֹ בְּצֶלֶם אֱלֹהִים בָּרָא אֹתוֹ זָכָר וּנְקֵבָה

בָּרָא אֹתָם: וַיְבָרֶךְ אֹתָם אֱלֹהִים וַיֹּאמֶר לָהֶם אֱלֹהִים פְּרוּ וּרְבוּ וּמִלְאוּ

אֶת־הָאָרֶץ וְכִבְשֻׁהָ וּרְדוּ בִּדְגַת הַיָּם וּבְעוֹף הַשָּׁמַיִם וּבְכָל־חַיָּה הָרֹמֶשֶׂת

עַל־הָאָרֶץ: וַיֹּאמֶר אֱלֹהִים הִנֵּה נָתַתִּי לָכֶם אֶת־כָּל־עֵשֶׂב | זֹרֵעַ זֶרַע אֲשֶׁר

עַל־פְּנֵי כָל־הָאָרֶץ וְאֶת־כָּל־הָעֵץ אֲשֶׁר־בּוֹ פְרִי־עֵץ זֹרֵעַ זָרַע לָכֶם יִהְיֶה

And God set them in the firmament of the Heaven to give light upon the Earth, to dominate by day and by night, and to separate between the light and between the darkness. And God saw that it was good. **And there was evening and there was morning, a fourth day.**

HOD *And God said, 'Let the water teem with creeping living creatures, and fowl that fly about over the Earth across the expanse of the Heavens.' And God created the big sea-giants and every living being that creeps, with which the waters teemed after their kinds, and all winged fowl of every kind. And God saw it was good. And God blessed them, saying, 'Be fruitful and multiply, and fill the waters in the seas, and the fowl shall increase on the earth.'* **And there was evening and there was morning, a fifth day.**

YESOD *And God said, 'Let the earth bring forth living creatures according to their kind. Cattle, and creeping things, and beasts of the land according to their kind.' And it was so. God made the beast of the land after its own kind, and the cattle after its own kind, and every creeping being of the ground after their kind. And God saw that it was good. And God said, 'Let us make man in Our image, after Our likeness. They shall rule over the fish of the sea, the birds of the sky, and over the cattle, the whole Earth, and every creeping thing that creeps upon the Earth.' So God created man in His image, in the image of God He created him, male and female He created them. And God blessed them and God said to them, 'Be fruitful and multiply, fill the Earth and subdue it, and rule over the fish of the sea, the bird of the sky, and every living thing that moves on Earth.' And God said, 'Behold, I have given to you all herbage yielding seed that is upon the entire Earth, and every tree that has seed-yielding fruit, it shall be your for food.*

לְאָכְלֶה: וּלְכָל־חַיַּת הָאָרֶץ וּלְכָל־עוֹף הַשָּׁמַיִם וּלְכֹל ׀ רוֹמֵשׂ עַל־הָאָרֶץ
אֲשֶׁר־בּוֹ נֶפֶשׁ חַיָּה אֶת־כָּל־יֶרֶק עֵשֶׂב לְאָכְלֶה וַיְהִי־כֵן: וַיַּרְא אֱלֹהִים
אֶת־כָּל־אֲשֶׁר עָשָׂה וְהִנֵּה־טוֹב מְאֹד וַיְהִי־עֶרֶב וַיְהִי־בֹקֶר יוֹם הַשִּׁשִּׁי:
MALCHUT וַיְכֻלּוּ הַשָּׁמַיִם וְהָאָרֶץ וְכָל־צְבָאָם: וַיְכַל אֱלֹהִים בַּיּוֹם הַשְּׁבִיעִי
מְלַאכְתּוֹ אֲשֶׁר עָשָׂה וַיִּשְׁבֹּת בַּיּוֹם הַשְּׁבִיעִי מִכָּל־מְלַאכְתּוֹ אֲשֶׁר עָשָׂה:
וַיְבָרֶךְ אֱלֹהִים אֶת־יוֹם הַשְּׁבִיעִי וַיְקַדֵּשׁ אֹתוֹ כִּי בוֹ שָׁבַת מִכָּל־מְלַאכְתּוֹ
אֲשֶׁר־בָּרָא אֱלֹהִים לַעֲשׂוֹת:

After the reading say the Half *Kaddish* on pages 501-502, and then read the *Maftir* below.

MAFTIR FOR SIMCHAT TORAH

בַּיּוֹם הַשְּׁמִינִי עֲצֶרֶת תִּהְיֶה לָכֶם כָּל־מְלֶאכֶת עֲבֹדָה לֹא תַעֲשׂוּ:
וְהִקְרַבְתֶּם עֹלָה אִשֵּׁה רֵיחַ נִיחֹחַ לַיהֹוָ֨ה אֲדֹנָי אֱלֹהֵנוּ פַּר אֶחָד אַיִל אֶחָד
כְּבָשִׂים בְּנֵי־שָׁנָה שִׁבְעָה תְּמִימִם: מִנְחָתָם וְנִסְכֵּיהֶם לַפָּר לָאַיִל וְלַכְּבָשִׂים
בְּמִסְפָּרָם כַּמִּשְׁפָּט: וּשְׂעִיר וְזֹּאת אֶחָד מִלְּבַד עֹלַת הַתָּמִיד וּמִנְחָתָהּ
וְנִסְכָּהּ: אֵלֶּה תַּעֲשׂוּ לַיהֹוָ֨ה אֲדֹנָי אֱלֹהֵנוּ בְּמוֹעֲדֵיכֶם לְבַד מִנִּדְרֵיכֶם וְנִדְבֹתֵיכֶם
לְעֹלֹתֵיכֶם וּלְמִנְחֹתֵיכֶם וּלְנִסְכֵּיכֶם וּלְשַׁלְמֵיכֶם:

And to every beast of the Earth, to every bird of the sky, and to everything that moves on Earth, within which there is a living soul, every green herb is for food.' And it was so. And God saw all that He made, and behold it was very good. **And there was evening and there was morning, the sixth day.** **MALCHUT** *And the Heaven and the Earth were finished, and all their array. By the seventh day God completed His work which He had done, and He abstained on the seventh day from all His work which He had done. God blessed the seventh day and hallowed it, because on it He abstained from all His work which God created to perfect." (Genesis 1:1-2:3)*

MAFTIR FOR SHIMCHAT TORAH

"The eighth day shall be an assembly for you, you may not do any laborious work. You are to offer an elevation-offering, a fire-offering, a satisfying aroma to the Lord, one bull, one ram. Seven lambs within their first years, they are all to be unblemished. Their meal-offerings and libations for the bull, the ram, and the lambs are to be in their proper numbers as required. And one he-goat for a sin-offering, aside from the continual elevation-offering, and its meal-offering and its libation. These are what you should offer to the Lord on your appointed holiday, aside from your vows and you free-will offering for your elevation-offerings, your meal-offerings, your libations, and your peace-offering. And Moses spoke to the children of Israel, according to everything that the Lord commanded Moses." (Numbers 29:35-39)

HAFTARAH FOR SIMCHAT TORAH

Say the blessing before the *Haftarah* on page 502, and then read the *Haftarah* below.

וַיְהִ֗י אַחֲרֵ֛י מ֥וֹת מֹשֶׁ֖ה עֶ֣בֶד יְהֹוָ֑ה וַיֹּ֤אמֶר יְהֹוָה֙ אֶל־יְהוֹשֻׁ֣עַ
בִּן־נ֔וּן מְשָׁרֵ֥ת מֹשֶׁ֖ה לֵאמֹֽר: מֹשֶׁ֥ה עַבְדִּ֖י מֵ֑ת וְעַתָּה֩ ק֨וּם עֲבֹ֜ר אֶת־הַיַּרְדֵּ֣ן
הַזֶּ֗ה אַתָּה֙ וְכׇל־הָעָ֣ם הַזֶּ֔ה אֶל־הָאָ֕רֶץ אֲשֶׁ֧ר אָנֹכִ֛י נֹתֵ֥ן לָהֶ֖ם לִבְנֵ֥י יִשְׂרָאֵֽל:
כׇּל־מָק֗וֹם אֲשֶׁ֨ר תִּדְרֹ֧ךְ כַּף־רַגְלְכֶ֛ם בּ֖וֹ לָכֶ֣ם נְתַתִּ֑יו כַּאֲשֶׁ֖ר דִּבַּ֥רְתִּי
אֶל־מֹשֶֽׁה: מֵהַמִּדְבָּ֣ר וְהַלְּבָנ֡וֹן הַזֶּה֩ וְעַד־הַנָּהָ֨ר הַגָּד֜וֹל נְהַר־פְּרָ֗ת כֹּ֚ל אֶ֣רֶץ
הַחִתִּ֔ים וְעַד־הַיָּ֥ם הַגָּד֖וֹל מְב֣וֹא הַשָּׁ֑מֶשׁ יִהְיֶ֖ה גְּבוּלְכֶֽם: לֹֽא־יִתְיַצֵּ֥ב אִישׁ֙
לְפָנֶ֔יךָ כֹּ֖ל יְמֵ֣י חַיֶּ֑יךָ כַּאֲשֶׁ֨ר הָיִ֤יתִי עִם־מֹשֶׁה֙ אֶהְיֶ֣ה עִמָּ֔ךְ לֹ֥א אַרְפְּךָ֖ וְלֹ֥א
אֶעֶזְבֶֽךָּ: חֲזַ֖ק וֶאֱמָ֑ץ כִּ֣י אַתָּ֗ה תַּנְחִיל֙ אֶת־הָעָ֣ם הַזֶּ֔ה אֶת־הָאָ֕רֶץ
אֲשֶׁר־נִשְׁבַּ֥עְתִּי לַאֲבוֹתָ֖ם לָתֵ֥ת לָהֶֽם: רַ֣ק חֲזַ֤ק וֶאֱמַץ֙ מְאֹ֔ד לִשְׁמֹ֤ר לַעֲשׂוֹת֙
כְּכׇל־הַתּוֹרָ֗ה אֲשֶׁ֤ר צִוְּךָ֙ מֹשֶׁ֣ה עַבְדִּ֔י אַל־תָּס֥וּר מִמֶּ֖נּוּ יָמִ֣ין וּשְׂמֹ֑אול לְמַ֣עַן
תַּשְׂכִּ֔יל בְּכֹ֖ל אֲשֶׁ֥ר תֵּלֵֽךְ: לֹֽא־יָמ֡וּשׁ סֵ֩פֶר֩ הַתּוֹרָ֨ה הַזֶּ֜ה מִפִּ֗יךָ וְהָגִ֤יתָ בּוֹ֙
יוֹמָ֣ם וָלַ֔יְלָה לְמַ֙עַן֙ תִּשְׁמֹ֣ר לַעֲשׂ֔וֹת כְּכׇל־הַכָּת֖וּב בּ֑וֹ כִּי־אָ֛ז תַּצְלִ֥יחַ
אֶת־דְּרָכֶ֖ךָ וְאָ֥ז תַּשְׂכִּֽיל: הֲל֤וֹא צִוִּיתִ֙יךָ֙ חֲזַ֣ק וֶאֱמָ֔ץ אַֽל־תַּעֲרֹ֖ץ וְאַל־תֵּחָ֑ת
כִּ֤י עִמְּךָ֙ יְהֹוָ֣ה אֱלֹהֶ֔יךָ בְּכֹ֖ל אֲשֶׁ֥ר תֵּלֵֽךְ: וַיְצַ֣ו יְהוֹשֻׁ֔עַ אֶת־שֹׁטְרֵ֥י
הָעָ֖ם לֵאמֹֽר: עִבְר֣וּ ׀ בְּקֶ֣רֶב הַֽמַּחֲנֶ֗ה וְצַוּ֤וּ אֶת־הָעָם֙ לֵאמֹ֔ר הָכִ֥ינוּ לָכֶ֖ם צֵידָ֑ה
כִּ֞י בְּע֣וֹד ׀ שְׁלֹ֣שֶׁת יָמִ֗ים אַתֶּם֙ עֹֽבְרִים֙ אֶת־הַיַּרְדֵּ֣ן הַזֶּ֔ה לָבוֹא֙
לָרֶ֣שֶׁת אֶת־הָאָ֔רֶץ אֲשֶׁר֙ יְהֹוָ֣ה אֱלֹֽהֵיכֶ֔ם נֹתֵ֥ן לָכֶ֖ם לְרִשְׁתָּֽהּ:

HAFTARAH FOR SHIMCHAT TORAH

"And it was after the death of Moses, servant of the Lord, that the Lord said to Joshua son of Nun, Moses attendant, saying, 'Moses My servant has died. Now, arise! Cross this Jordan, you and this entire people, to the land which I give to them, to the children of Israel. Every place upon which the sole of your foot will march I have given to you, as I have spoken to Moses. From the desert and this Lebanon to the great river, the Euphrates River, all the land of the Hittites to the Great Sea westward will be you boundary. No man will challenge you all the days of your life. As I was with Moses, so I will be with you; I will not fail you, nor forsake you. Strengthen yourself and persevere because you will cause this people to inherit the land which I have sworn to their fathers to give to them. That you will strengthen yourself and preserver very much in order to observe, to do, according to all of the Torah that Moses My servant has commanded you. Do not deviate from it to the right or to the left that you may succeed wherever you may go. This Book of the Torah is not to leave your mouth. You should contemplate it day and night in order to observe, to do, all that is written in it. For then you will make your ways successful, and then you will become understanding. In truth I commanded you, "Strengthen yourself and persevere." Do not fear and do not lose resolve, because the Lord, your God, is with you wherever you may go. Then Joshua commanded the officers of the people, saying: 'Pass through the midst of the camp, and command the people, saying: Prepare you victuals; for within three days you are to pass over this Jordan, to go in to possess the land, which the Lord, your God, give you to possess it.'

וְלָרֽאוּבֵנִי וְלַגָּדִי וְלַחֲצִי שֵׁבֶט הַמְנַשֶּׁה אָמַר יְהוֹשֻׁעַ לֵאמֹר: זָכוֹר

אֶת־הַדָּבָר אֲשֶׁר צִוָּה אֶתְכֶם מֹשֶׁה עֶבֶד־יְהוָׂוָׂהֱלֹהֵיֱאֲדֹנָי לֵאמֹר

יְהוָׂוָׂהֱלֹהֵיֱאֲדֹנָי אֱלֹהֵיכֶם מֵנִיחַ לָכֶם וְנָתַן לָכֶם אֶת־הָאָרֶץ הַזֹּאת: נְשֵׁיכֶם

טַפְּכֶם וּמִקְנֵיכֶם יֵשְׁבוּ בָּאָרֶץ אֲשֶׁר נָתַן לָכֶם מֹשֶׁה בְּעֵבֶר הַיַּרְדֵּן וְאַתֶּם

תַּעַבְרוּ חֲמֻשִׁים לִפְנֵי אֲחֵיכֶם כֹּל גִּבּוֹרֵי הַחַיִל וַעֲזַרְתֶּם אוֹתָם: עַד

אֲשֶׁר־יָנִיחַ יְהוָׂוָׂהֱלֹהֵיֱאֲדֹנָי | לַאֲחֵיכֶם כָּכֶם וְיָרְשׁוּ גַם־הֵמָּה אֶת־הָאָרֶץ

אֲשֶׁר־יְהוָׂוָׂהֱלֹהֵיֱאֲדֹנָי אֱלֹהֵיכֶם נֹתֵן לָהֶם וְשַׁבְתֶּם לְאֶרֶץ יְרֻשַּׁתְכֶם וִירִשְׁתֶּם

אוֹתָהּ אֲשֶׁר | נָתַן לָכֶם מֹשֶׁה עֶבֶד יְהוָׂוָׂהֱלֹהֵיֱאֲדֹנָי בְּעֵבֶר הַיַּרְדֵּן מִזְרַח

הַשָּׁמֶשׁ: וַיַּעֲנוּ אֶת־יְהוֹשֻׁעַ לֵאמֹר כֹּל אֲשֶׁר־צִוִּיתָנוּ נַעֲשֶׂה וְאֶל־כָּל־אֲשֶׁר

תִּשְׁלָחֵנוּ נֵלֵךְ: כְּכֹל אֲשֶׁר־שָׁמַעְנוּ אֶל־מֹשֶׁה כֵּן נִשְׁמַע אֵלֶיךָ רַק יִהְיֶה

יְהוָׂוָׂהֱלֹהֵיֱאֲדֹנָי אֱלֹהֶיךָ עִמָּךְ כַּאֲשֶׁר הָיָה עִם־מֹשֶׁה: כָּל־אִישׁ אֲשֶׁר־יַמְרֶה

אֶת־פִּיךָ וְלֹא־יִשְׁמַע אֶת־דְּבָרֶיךָ לְכֹל אֲשֶׁר־תְּצַוֶּנּוּ יוּמָת רַק חֲזַק וֶאֱמָץ:

Say the blessing after the *Haftarah* on pages 503-504.

And to the Reubenites, and to the Gadites, and to the half-tribe of Manasseh, spoke to Joshua, saying: 'Remember the word which Moses the servant of the Lord commanded, you, saying: The Lord your God give you rest, and will give you this land. Your wives, your little ones, and your cattle, shall abide in the land which Moses gave you beyond the Jordan; but you shall pass over before your brethren armed, all the mighty men of valor, and shall help them; until the Lord have given your brethren rest, as to you, and they also have possessed the land which the Lord your God give them; then you shall return to the land of your possession, and possess it, which Moses the servant of the Lord gave you beyond the Jordan toward the sun rising.' And they answered Joshua, saying: 'All that you have commanded us we will do, and where ever you send us we will go. According as we hearkened to Moses in all things, so will we hearken to you; only the Lord your God be with you, as He was with Moses. Whoever that shall rebel against your commandment, and shall not hearken to your words in all that you commanded him, he shall be put to death; only be strong and of good courage.'" (Joshua 1:1-18)

Simchat Torah and the Hakafot (Circling) – From The Rav

The *Zohar* asks why does this holiday have two names: *Shemini Atzeret* (Eighth Day of Assembly) and *Simchat Torah* (Happiness of the Torah) and why is it called *"zeman simchatenu"*—time of our rejoicing?

According to the principle that illuminates a light bulb, joy can be revealed only when everyone is taken care of. The positive and negative poles do indeed exist but without the resistance of the inner filament the revelation of Light will not be achieved. Light exists in the potential state at all times but it is not revealed without Central Column resistance. Therefore, it is written in the *Zohar* that Jacob, together with the other guests, is part and parcel of *Simchat Torah*, for Jacob is Central Column. Thus, Jacob and restriction already exist on *Simchat Torah*. And after working on restriction for the entire holiday, we can now enjoy the Light. This happiness is indiscriminate for it is the revelation of all of the Light.

On *Simchat Torah*, all the Light of the Torah is revealed (like it was on *Shavuot* when the Ten Utterances were given), even for people who were not stringent about fulfilling all the communications on *Rosh Hashanah*, *Yom Kippur*, and *Sukkot*. This is because of the presence of the Central Column. In this sense, *Simchat Torah* is like a wedding, it is a time when *Zeir Anpin* joins with *Malchut*. Everyone who comes to the wedding—even those who have not themselves prepared for the event can participate in the celebration; the bride, the groom, and their families have taken pains preparing for the event but all the guests can certainly enjoy the party. It is just like the person who turns on the light in a room; everyone who enters the room can enjoy the light for free. Everyone can receive, provided that they are conscious of being one with all those present, and are also willing to share.

There is no explanation in the Torah for the name *atzeret* (gathering or assembly), and there is no explicit reason for the celebration of this holiday. Only the *Zohar* explains that *atzeret* comes from the word *atzirah* (stopping). This refers to resistance, the Central Column, and Jacob. In addition, the meaning of the word *atzeret* is "gathering," for on this holiday all the Light assembles. Therefore, we first perform spiritual work during *Sukkot*. Later, on the eighth day, comes the holiday of the *Atzeret*, for the gathering and uncovering of all the Light. On the day of *Simchat Torah*, we receive Surrounding Light for the entire year. Only by letting go of what we now have is it possible to receive an entire year's portion of life. By holding on to what we have, we prevent the Light from entering our lives and are therefore destined to lose it all.

On *Simchat Torah*, Kabbalah teaches that we are given the ability to rid our lives of cancer and other grave diseases. How is this possible? We know that every illness exists only as long as the body is alive. Illnesses thrive on the life processes that take place in the body; therefore, the moment a person dies, all disease in his body ceases. This principle applies to all difficulties we encounter in life. If we could skip over the processes in the physical world and rise above the illusion of the time-space continuum, we would enter a postmortem state and thus bring immediate extinction to all manifestations of chaos in our lives. *Simchat Torah* is just such an opportunity. On this holiday, we rise above the illusion of time, for *Simchat Torah* is Surrounding Light—a union of past, present, and future—and therefore constitutes an unmatched opportunity to rid our lives of all chaos. To connect to the Surrounding Light we circle the *bimah* with the Torah scrolls on *Simchat Torah* night, morning and the night after (as the Ari used to do). The amount of circles equals the amount of connection to the Surrounding Light for the year.

Everything is there for us. We need only have certainty in its existence. When we tear away the illusions from ourselves, cancel all of our limiting presuppositions, abolish all prejudices and doubts we open up to let the Light in. This is important every day but especially on *Simchat Torah*.

HAKAFOT (CIRCLING) OF SIMCHAT TORAH

HAKAFOT (CIRCLING) OF SIMCHAT TORAH

hu **הוא** Adonai יְהֹוָוּאַדנִיאהדונהי ki **כִּי** lada'at **לָדַעַת** hor'eta **הָרְאֵתָ** Ata **אַתָּה**

od **עוֹד** en **אֵין** haElohim **הָאֱלֹהִים** אהיה אדני ; ילה ; ר"ת ; ה' הוא האלקים = ענו עג"כ

gedolot **גְּדֹלוֹת** nifla'ot **נִפְלָאוֹת** le'ose **לְעֹשֵׂה** מ"ב: milvado **מִלְּבַדּוֹ**

levado **לְבַדּוֹ** מ"ב ki **כִּי** le'olam **לְעוֹלָם** ריבוע ס"ג ו' אותיות chasdo **וְחַסְדּוֹ** ג' הויות,

vaElohim **בָאלֹהִים** kamocha **כָּמוֹךָ** en **אֵין** נגה = ר"ת ; מלא ; ילה ; אהיה אדני

chevod **כְּבוֹד** yehi **יְהִי** kema'asecha **כְּמַעֲשֶׂיךָ** ve'en **וְאֵין** ללה Adonai **אֲדֹנָי**

le'olam **לְעוֹלָם** ריבוע ס"ג ו' אותיות Adonai יְהֹוָוּאַדנִיאהדונהי כבוד יהוה = יוד הי ואו הה

yismach **יִשְׂמַח** משייזו ; לעולם ישמחו ע"ה = ריבוע קס"א Adonai יְהֹוָוּאַדנִיאהדונהי

bema'asav **בְּמַעֲשָׂיו** ה' במעשיו ע"ה = קס"א קנ"א קמ"ג ; הוזע ; ר"ת הפסוק = אמן (יאהדונהי) ע"ה:

yehi **יְהִי** shem **שֵׁם** Adonai יְהֹוָוּאַדנִיאהדונהי mevorach **מְבֹרָךְ** ר"ת = ריבוע ע"ב

ריבוע ס"ג ; ה' מבורך = רפ"ח (להעלות רפ"ח ניצוצות עופלו לקליפה דמוש באים התולואים)

me'ata **מֵעַתָּה** ve'ad **וְעַד** olam **עוֹלָם** ייל: yehi **יְהִי** Adonai יְהֹוָוּאַדנִיאהדונהי

Elohenu **אֱלֹהֵינוּ** ילה imanu **עִמָּנוּ** ka'asher **כַּאֲשֶׁר** haya **הָיָה** יהה im **עִם**

avotenu **אֲבֹתֵינוּ** al **אַל** ya'azvenu **יַעַזְבֵנוּ** ve'al **וְאַל** yiteshenu **יִטְּשֵׁנוּ:**

ve'imru **וְאִמְרוּ** hoshi'enu **הוֹשִׁיעֵנוּ** Elohei **אֱלֹהֵי** מילוי ע"ב, דמב ; ילה ;

yish'enu **יִשְׁעֵנוּ** vekabetzenu **וְקַבְּצֵנוּ** vehatzilenu **וְהַצִּילֵנוּ** min **מִן** vehagoyim **הַגּוֹיִם** hagoyim

lehodot **לְהֹדוֹת** leshem **לְשֵׁם** kadshecha **קָדְשֶׁךָ** lehishtabe'ach **לְהִשְׁתַּבֵּחַ**

bithilatecha **בִּתְהִלָּתֶךָ:** Adonai יְהֹוָוּאַדנִיאהדונהי melech **מֶלֶךְ**

Adonai יְהֹוָוּאַדנִיאהדונהי malach **מָלָךְ** Adonai יְהֹוָוּאַדנִיאהדונהי | yimloch **יִמְלֹךְ**

le'olam **לְעוֹלָם** ריבוע ס"ג ו' אותיות ; ר"ת ייל va'ed **וָעֶד:** מלך מלך ימלך = בז"זר, סנדלפון, ערי

HAKAFOT (CIRCLING) OF SIMCHAT TORAH

"You have shown to be known that the Lord is your God and there is none beside Him." (Deuteronomy 4:35) "To the One Who alone performs great wonders, for His kindness endures forever." (Psalms 136:4) "There is none like You among the deities Lord and there is nothing like Your works." (Psalms 86:8) "May the glory of the Lord last forever. May the Lord rejoice in His works." (Psalms 104:31) "May the Name of the Lord be blessed from now and for all eternity." (Psalms 113:2) May the Lord, our God, be with us as He was with our forefathers. May He not abandon or forsake us." (1 Kings 8:57) And say: Save us, God of our salvation; gather us and save us from all nations, to give thanks to Your Holy Name, and to be glorified in saying Your praise." (1 Chronicles 16:35) The Lord is King, the Lord has reigned, the Lord shall reign forever and for eternity.

יְהֹוָ֯אֲדֹנָיאהדונהי Adonai יִתֵּן֯ yiten לְעַמּוֹ le'amo עֹז oz יְהֹוָ֯אֲדֹנָיאהדונהי Adonai

יְבָרֵךְ yevarech עסמ"ב, הַבְּרָכָה (למחק את ז' המלכים שמתו) אֶת et עַמּוֹ amo

בַּשָּׁלוֹם vashalom ר"ת ע"ב: וְיִהְיֽוּ veyih'yu יא"י (מילוי דס"ג) נָא na אֲמָרֵינֽוּ amarenu

לִרְצוֹן leratzon מהע ע"ה, ע"ב בריבוע וקס"א ע"ה, אל שדי ע"ה, לִפְנֵי lefenei אֲדוֹן adon אני

וַיֹּאמֶר vayomer הָאָרֹן ha'aron בִּנְסֹעַ binso'a וַיְהִי vay'hi ילי: כֹּל kol

מֹשֶׁה Moshe מהע, ע"ב בריבוע וקס"א, אל שדי ע"ה, ד"פ אלהים ע"ה קוּמָה kuma קנ"א (מקוה)

יְהֹוָ֯אֲדֹנָיאהדונהי Adonai וְיָפֻצוּ veyafutzu אֹיְבֶיךָ oyvecha וְיָנֻסּוּ veyanusu

מְשַׂנְאֶיךָ meshanecha ס"ג מ"ה ב"ן: מִפָּנֶיךָ mipanecha קוּמָה kuma קנ"א (מקוה)

יְהֹוָ֯אֲדֹנָיאהדונהי Adonai לִמְנוּחָתֶךָ limnuchatecha אַתָּה Ata וַאֲרוֹן va'aron

עֻזֶּךָ uzecha: כֹּהֲנֶיךָ kohanecha יִלְבְּשׁוּ yilbeshu צֶדֶק tzedek

וַחֲסִידֶיךָ vachasidecha יְרַנֵּנֽוּ yeranenu: בַּעֲבוּר ba'avur דָּוִד David

עַבְדֶּךָ avdecha פרי, אל אדני, אל וכחמה בינה אַל al תָּשֵׁב tashev פְּנֵי penei

מְשִׁיחֶךָ meshichecha: וְאָמַר ve'amar בַּיּוֹם bayom ע"ה נגד, מזבוז, זן, אל יהוה

הַהוּא hahu הִנֵּה hineh אֱלֹהֵינוּ Elohenu ילה: זֶה ze קוִּינֽוּ kivinu

לוֹ lo וְיוֹשִׁיעֵֽנוּ veyoshi'enu זֶה ze יְהֹוָ֯אֲדֹנָיאהדונהי Adonai קוִּינֽוּ kivinu

לוֹ lo נָגִילָה nagila וְנִשְׂמְחָה venismecha בִּישׁוּעָתוֹ bishu'ato:

מַלְכוּתְךָ malchutcha מַלְכוּת malchut כֹּל kol ילי עֹלָמִים olamim

וּמֶמְשַׁלְתְּךָ umemshaltecha בְּכָל bechol ב"ן לכב דּוֹר dor וָדוֹר vador רי"ו:

כִּי ki מִצִּיּוֹן miTziyon יוסף, ר"פ יהוה, קנאה תֵּצֵא tetze תּוֹרָה torah

וּדְבַר udvar ראה יְהֹוָ֯אֲדֹנָיאהדונהי Adonai מִירוּשָׁלָֽיִם mirushalayim:

"May the Lord give strength to His people may the Lord bless His nation with peace." *(Psalms 29:11)* "When the Ark traveled forward, Moses would say: Arise, Lord. Let Your enemies be scattered and let those who hate You flee before You." *(Numbers 10:35)* "Arise Lord to Your resting place, You and the Ark of Your strength. Your priests don justice and your pious once shall sing. For the sake of David, Your servant, do not turn Your countenance away from Your anointed one." *(Psalms 132:8-10)* "And it shall be said in that day: 'Here is our God, for whom we waited, that He might save us; this is the Lord, for whom we waited, we will be glad and rejoice in His salvation." *(Isaiah 25:9)* "Yours is the Kingdom of all worlds and Your reign extends to each and every generation." *(Psalms 145:13)* "Because out of Zion shall the Torah emerge, and the Word of the Lord from Jerusalem." *(Isaiah 2:3)*

hu הוּא   berich בְּרִיךְ   kudesha קֻדְשָׁא   yichud יִחוּד   leshem לְשֵׁם

(יאההויהה,) ushchinte וּשְׁכִינְתֵּיה   bidchilu בִּדְחִילוּ (יאהדונהי)   urchimu וּרְחִימוּ,

shem שֵׁם   leyachada לְיַחֲדָא   udchilu וּדְחִילוּ (איההיוהה)   urchimu וּרְחִימוּ

(יהוה) shelim שְׁלִים   beyichuda בְּיִחוּדָא   kei קֵי   bevav בְּוא"ו   kei קֵי   yud יו"ד

anachnu אֲנַחְנוּ   hineh הִנֵּה   Yisrael יִשְׂרָאֵל   kol כָּל יִלי   beshem בְּשֵׁם

kedoshim קְדוֹשִׁים   Yisrael יִשְׂרָאֵל   minhag מִנְהַג   lekayem לְקַיֵּם   ba'im בָּאִים

sheba שֶׁבָּה   lateva לַתֵּיבָה   hakafot הַקָּפוֹת   shiv'a שִׁבְעָה   lehakif לְהַקִּיף

besimchat בְּשִׂמְחַת   ul'harbot וּלְהַרְבּוֹת   hatorah הַתּוֹרָה   sefer סֵפֶר

bemakom בִּמְקוֹם   shorshan שָׁרְשָׁן   et אֵת   letaken לְתַקֵּן   hatorah הַתּוֹרָה

elyon עֶלְיוֹן   vihi וִיהִי ratzon רָצוֹן

milfanecha מִלְּפָנֶיךָ   Adonai יְהֹוָה   Elohenu אֱלֹהֵינוּ

shebcho'ach שֶׁבְּכֹחַ   avotenu אֲבוֹתֵינוּ   velohei וֵאלֹהֵי

hakafot הַקָּפוֹת   chomat חוֹמַת   tipol תִּפֹּל   elu אֵלּוּ

levenecha לְבֵינֶיךָ   benenu בֵּינֵינוּ   hamafseket הַמַּפְסֶקֶת   barzel בַּרְזֶל

umitzvot וּמִצְוֹת   mitorah מִתּוֹרָה   mukafim מֻקָּפִים   venih'ye וְנִהְיֶה

venidavek וְנִדְבַּק   umichutz וּמִחוּץ   mibayit מִבַּיִת

becha בְּךָ   uvtorat'cha וּבְתוֹרָתְךָ   tamid תָּמִיד

zar'enu זַרְעֵנוּ   vezera וְזֶרַע   vezar'enu וְזַרְעֵנוּ   anachnu אֲנַחְנוּ

Elohenu אֱלֹהֵינוּ   Adonai אֲדֹנָי   no'am נֹעַם   vihi וִיהִי

alenu עָלֵינוּ   konena כּוֹנְנָה   yadenu יָדֵינוּ   uma'ase וּמַעֲשֵׂה   alenu עָלֵינוּ

konenehu כּוֹנְנֵהוּ:   yadenu יָדֵינוּ   uma'ase וּמַעֲשֵׂה

For the sake of unification of the Holy Blessed One and His Shechinah, with fear and love and with love and fear, in order to unify the Name Yud-Kei and Vav-Kei in perfect unity, and in the name of Israel, we have hereby come to perform the custom of Israel, the holy people, to complete seven circles around the bimah, upon which rests the Torah scroll, and rejoice exceedingly in the joy of the Torah, to correct its root in the Supernal Place. And may it be pleasing before You, Lord our God, and God of our fathers, that with the strength of these hakafot may there fall the iron wall that separates us and You. And may we be surrounded with Torah and precepts from within and without, and may we cleave to You and to Your Torah constantly, we and our offspring and our offspring's offspring. "And may the pleasantness of the Lord, our God, be upon us and may He establish the work of our hands for us and may the work of our hands establish Him." (Psalms 90:17)

דְּאָגָה אַהֲבָה, אוֹד, havu הָבוּ leDavid לְדָוִד mizmor מִזְמוֹר

= יַעֲקֹב בְּנֵי יהוה הבו elim אֵלִים הבל ר"ת benei בְּנֵי ladonai לַיהֹוָאדֹנָיאהדונהי

va'oz וָעֹז kavod כָּבוֹד ladonai לַיהֹוָאדֹנָיאהדונהי דְּאָגָה אַהֲבָה, אוֹד, havu הָבוּ

shemo שְׁמוֹ kevod כְּבוֹד ladonai לַיהֹוָאדֹנָיאהדונהי דְּאָגָה אַהֲבָה, אוֹד, havu הָבוּ

מֵהוֹי ע"ה, ע"ב בְּרִיבוּעַ וקס"א ע"ה, אל שדי ע"ה ; הבו יהוה כבוד שמו = אדם דוד מֵשִׁיחַ

הבל ר"ת behadrat בְּהַדְרַת ladonai לַיהֹוָאדֹנָיאהדונהי hishtachavu הִשְׁתַּחֲווּ

kol קוֹל (:קַבָּלָה לִלְמוֹד צָרִיךְ עוֹבֵת (עוֹבִים קַבָּלָה לְמִפְרָע ר"ת kodesh קֹדֶשׁ

רמוֹת עֹנִי וְאל – (חֶסֶד לָמֵד אֶלֶף = ר"ת hamayim הַמָּיִם al עַל Adonai יְהֹוָאדֹנָיאהדונהי

אֲדֹנָי ה"פ hir'im הִרְעִים לאו hakavod הַכָּבוֹד יא"י (מִילוּי דס"ג) El אֵל ◆ (בַּמִּילָה בַּהֶמְשֵׁךְ

(לְהַמְתִּיק שׁכ"ה דִּינִים) rabim רַבִּים mayim מָיִם al עַל Adonai יְהֹוָאדֹנָיאהדונהי

(לְעֵיל הָרְמוֹזִים א"ל שֵׁמוֹת ע"י נִמְתָּקִים דִּינִים העוֹכ"ה וְעֹנִי – דִּינִים (עוֹכ"ה ר"ת

יהוה אֲדֹנָי אהיה אֱלֹהִים, יב"ק ר"ת bako'ach בַּכֹּחַ Adonai יְהֹוָאדֹנָיאהדונהי kol קוֹל

:יהוה אֲדֹנָי אהיה אֱלֹהִים, יב"ק ר"ת behadar בֶּהָדָר Adonai יְהֹוָאדֹנָיאהדונהי kol קוֹל

vayshaber וַיְשַׁבֵּר arazim אֲרָזִים shover שֹׁבֵר Adonai יְהֹוָאדֹנָיאהדונהי kol קוֹל

:הָאָא ר"ת haLevanon הַלְּבָנוֹן arzei אַרְזֵי et אֶת Adonai יְהֹוָאדֹנָיאהדונהי

veSiryon וְשִׂרְיוֹן Levanon לְבָנוֹן egel עֵגֶל kemo כְּמוֹ vayarkidem וַיַּרְקִידֵם

Adonai יְהֹוָאדֹנָיאהדונהי kol קוֹל :re'emim רְאֵמִים ven בֶּן kemo כְּמוֹ

kol קוֹל :esh אֵשׁ lahavot לַהֲבוֹת הבל ס"ת chotzev חֹצֵב

yachil יָחִיל midbar מִדְבָּר אֲדֹנָי ללה, ס"ת yachil יָחִיל Adonai יְהֹוָאדֹנָיאהדונהי

:קַיִן = ר"ת kadesh קָדֵשׁ midbar מִדְבָּר Adonai יְהֹוָאדֹנָיאהדונהי

A Psalm of David: Render to the Lord, you sons of the powerful ones, render to the Lord honor and might. Render to the Lord honor worthy of His Name, prostrate yourselves before the Lord in the glory of His Holiness. The Voice of the Lord is upon the waters, The God of glory has thundered, Lord is upon vast waters. The Voice of the Lord is powerful. The Voice of the Lord is majesty. The Voice of the Lord breaks cedars, the Lord breaks the cedars of Lebanon. He makes them dance around like a calf, Lebanon and Sirion like a wild young ox. The Voice of the Lord cleaves the flames of fire. The Voice of the Lord convulses the wilderness; the Lord convulses the wilderness of Kadesh.

ayalot אַיָּלוֹת yecholel יְחוֹלֵל Adonai יְהֹוָאהדונהי kol קוֹל

omer אֹמֵר kulo כֻּלּוֹ uvhechalo וּבְהֵיכָלוֹ ye'arot יְעָרוֹת vayechesof וַיֶּחֱשׂף

ר"ת ילי yashav יָשָׁב lamabul לַמַּבּוּל Adonai יְהֹוָאהדונהי kavod כָּבוֹד:

le'olam לְעוֹלָם melech מֶלֶךְ Adonai יְהֹוָאהדונהי vayeshev וַיֵּשֶׁב וס"ת הבל

yiten יִתֵּן le'amo לְעַמּוֹ oz עֹז Adonai יְהֹוָאהדונהי ריבוע ס"ג י אותיות דס"ג:

יְהֹוָאהדונהי Adonai ycvarech יְבָרֵךְ עסמ"ב, הברכה (למתק את ז' המלכים שמחתו)

et אֶת- amo עַמּוֹ vashalom בְּשָׁלוֹם ר"ת ע"ב, ריבוע יהוה:

אל (ייא"י מילוי דס"ג) אותיות בפסוק דס"ג (Keter) haleluya הַלְלוּיָהּ אלהים, אהיה אדני ; ללה

bekodsho בְּקָדְשׁוֹ (דס"ג) (מילוי) ייא"י El אֵל halelu- הַלְלוּ

ס"ת = ע"ב בן: uzo עֻזּוֹ birki'a בִּרְקִיעַ (Chochmah) haleluhu הַלְלוּהוּ

(Chesed) haleluhu הַלְלוּהוּ vigvurotav בִּגְבוּרֹתָיו (Binah) haleluhu הַלְלוּהוּ

beteka בְּתֵקַע (Gevurah) haleluhu הַלְלוּהוּ :gudlo גֻּדְלוֹ kerov כְּרֹב

vechinor וְכִנּוֹר: benevel בְּנֵבֶל (Tiferet) haleluhu הַלְלוּהוּ shofar שׁוֹפָר

(Hod) haleluhu הַלְלוּהוּ umachol וּמָחוֹל betof בְּתֹף (Netzach) haleluhu הַלְלוּהוּ

vetziltzelei- בְצִלְצְלֵי (Yesod) haleluhu הַלְלוּהוּ :ve'ugav וְעֻגָב beminim בְּמִנִּים

teru'a תְּרוּעָה: betziltzelei בְּצִלְצְלֵי (Malchut) haleluhu הַלְלוּהוּ shama שָׁמַע

ר"ת כהת, משיזו בן דוד ע"ה tehalel תְּהַלֵּל haneshamah הַנְּשָׁמָה ילי kol כֹּל

אלהים, אהיה אדני ; ללה: haleluya הַלְלוּיָהּ Yah יָהּ

ר"ת כהת, משיזו בן דוד ע"ה tehalel תְּהַלֵּל haneshamah הַנְּשָׁמָה ילי kol כֹּל

אלהים, אהיה אדני ; ללה: haleluya הַלְלוּיָהּ Yah יָהּ

The Voice of the Lord frightens the hinds and strips the forests bare, and in His Temple all proclaim His Glory. The Lord sat at the deluge, and the Lord sits as King forever. The Lord gives might to His people. The Lord will bless His people with peace." (Psalms 29) "Praise the Lord! Praise Him in His Sanctuary; praise Him in the firmaments of His might; praise Him by His valorous deeds; praise Him according to His bountiful greatness; praise Him with blowing the Shofar; praise Him with lyre and harp; praise Him with drum and dance; praise Him with instruments and pipe; Praise Him with the sound of cymbals; praise Him with reverberating sounds. All the souls praise God. Praise Him! All the souls praise God. Praise Him!" (Psalms 150)

THE FIRST HAKAFAH (CIRCLING)—ABRAHAM—CHESED

:na **נָא** hoshi'a **הוֹשִׁיעָה** יהוה ע"ע נהורין Adonai **יְהוָֹואהדונהי** לכב ב"ן ana **אָנָּא**

:na **נָא** hatzlicha **הַצְלִיחָה** Adonai **יְהוָֹואהדונהי** לכב ב"ן ana **אָנָּא**

veyom **בְּיוֹם** anenu **עֲנֵנוּ** Adonai **יְהוָֹואהדונהי** לכב ב"ן ana **אָנָּא**

ע"ה נגד, מזבוז, זן, אל יהוה Elohei **אֱלֹהֵי** מילוי ע"ב, דמב ; ילה :kor'enu **קָרְאֵנוּ**

bochen **בּוֹחֵן** •na **נָא** נהורין ע"ע יהוה hoshi'a **הוֹשִׁיעָה** haruchot **הָרוּוֹת**

פהל chazak **וְזֵק** go'el **גּוֹאֵל** :na **נָא** hatzlicha **הַצְלִיחָה** levavot **לְבָבוֹת**

:kor'enu **קָרְאֵנוּ** אל יהוה זן, מזבוז, נגד ע"ה veyom **בְּיוֹם** anenu **עֲנֵנוּ**

meshoch **מְשׁוֹךְ** •harachaman **הָרַוֲמָן** av **אָב** nefesh **נֶפֶשׁ** yedid **יְדִיד**

yarutz **יָרוּץ** •retzonach **רְצוֹנָךְ** el **אֶל** אדני אל פוי, avdach **עַבְדָּךְ**

el **אֶל** yishtachave **יִשְׁתַּוֲזֶה** •ayal **אַיָּל** kemo **כְּמוֹ** אדני אל פוי, avdach **עַבְדָּךְ**

lo **לוֹ** ye'erav **יֶעֱרַב** •קס"א ס"ג יבק, ב"פ hadarach **הֲדָרָךְ** mul **מוּל**

:ta'am **טַעַם** vechol **וְכָל** tzuf **צוּף** minofet **מִנּוֹפֶת** •ילי ר"ת yedidutach **יְדִידוּתָךְ**

nafshi **נַפְשִׁי** •ha'olam **הָעוֹלָם** ziv **זִיו** na'e **נָאֶה** hadur **הָדוּר**

(מילוי דס"ג) יא"י El **אֵל** ב"ן ana **אָנָּא** •ahavatach **אַהֲבָתָךְ** cholat **וֹוֹלַת**

•(11-Letter Name for healing) lah **לָהּ** na **נָא** refa **רְפָא** na **נָא**

titchazek **תִּתְוַזֵּק** az **אָו** •zivach **זִיוָךְ** no'am **נוֹעַם** lah **לָהּ** behar'ot **בְּהַרְאוֹת**

:olam **עוֹלָם** simchat **שִׂמוַות** lah **לָהּ** vehayta **וְהָיְתָה** •vetitrape **וְתִתְרַפֵּא**

THE FIRST HAKAFAH (CIRCLING)—ABRAHAM—CHESED

"We beseech You, Lord, save us now. We beseech You, Lord, give us success now." (Psalms 118:25)
We beseech You, Lord, answer us on the day we call. God of the spirits, save us now.
Tester of hearts, bring success now. Powerful Redeemer, answer us on the day we call.

י *Beloved of the soul, Compassionate Father, draw Your servant to Your desire. Your servant will run like a hart, he will bow before Your majesty. Your friendship will be sweeter than the dripping of the honeycomb and any taste.* ה *Majestic, Beautiful, Radiance of the world, my soul pines for Your love. Please, God, heal her, by showing her the pleasantness of Your radiance. Then she will be strengthened and healed, and she will have the gladness of the world.*

נָא na   עַל al   בֵּן ben   יֶהֱמוּ yehemu   רַחֲמֶיךָ rachamecha◆   וְחוּסָה vechusa

כַּמָּה chame   נְכְסוֹף nichsof   נִכְסַף nichsaf◆   כִּי ki   זֶה ze

בְּתִפְאֶרֶת betiferet   עֻזָּךְ uzach◆   אָנָּא ana   ב"נ   אֵלִי Eli   וְחֶמְדַּת chemdat

לְרְאוֹת lir'ot

לִבִּי libi◆   וְחוּשָׁה chusha   נָא na   וְאַל ve'al   תִּתְעַלָּם tit'alam

הִגָּלֶה higale   נָא na   וּפְרוֹשׂ ufros   וְזִיב chaviv   חי   עָלַי alai◆   אֶת et   סֻכַּת sukat

שְׁלוֹמָךְ shelomach◆   תָּאִיר ta'ir   אֶרֶץ eretz   מִכְּבוֹדָךְ mikevodach   ב"נ, לכב◆

נָגִילָה nagila   וְנִשְׂמְחָה venismecha   בָּךְ vach◆   מַהֵר maher   אָהוּב ahuv

כִּי ki   בָּא va   מוֹעֵד mo'ed◆   וְחָנֵּנוּ vechonenu   כִּימֵי kimei   עוֹלָם olam

After the circling one should say:

יְמִין yemin   יְהֹוָאֲדֹנָי Adonai   רוֹמֵמָה romema ר"ת רי"י   יְמִין yemin

יְהֹוָאֲדֹנָי Adonai   עֹשָׂה osa רהע וְזִיל chayil ומב:

שְׁמַע shema   יִשְׂרָאֵל Yisrael   יְהֹוָאֲדֹנָי Adonai   אֱלֹהֵינוּ Elohenu ילה

יְהֹוָאֲדֹנָי Adonai | אֶחָד echad אהבה, דאגה:

יְהֹוָאֲדֹנָי Adonai   מֶלֶךְ melech   יְהֹוָאֲדֹנָי Adonai   מָלָךְ malach

יְהֹוָאֲדֹנָי Adonai | יִמְלֹךְ yimloch (מֶלֶךְ מָלַךְ יִמְלֹךְ = מנצפ"ך, סנדלפון, ערי)

לְעֹלָם le'olam   ריבוע דס"ג וי' אותיות ; ר"ת דס"ג ר"ת ייל וָעֶד va'ed:

אָנָּא ana ב"נ לכב   יְהֹוָאֲדֹנָי Adonai   הוֹשִׁיעָה hoshi'a יהוה ע"ש נהורין   נָא na:

אָנָּא ana ב"נ לכב   יְהֹוָאֲדֹנָי Adonai   הַצְלִיחָה hatzlicha   נָא na:

יְהִי yehi   וְחַסְדְּךָ chasdecha   יְהֹוָאֲדֹנָי Adonai   עָלֵינוּ alenu   כַּאֲשֶׁר ka'asher

יוֹחַלְנוּ yochalnu   יִחַלְנוּ yichalnu   סָאָל sa'al   לָךְ lach: קוּמָה kuma קנ"א (מקוה)   עֶזְרָתָה ezrata

לָנוּ lanu   אֱלֹהִים, אֶהְיֶה אֲדֹנָי   וּפְדֵנוּ ufdenu   לְמַעַן lema'an   וְחַסְדְּךָ chasdecha:

וֹ *All Worthy One, may Your mercy be aroused and please take pity on the sons of Your beloved, because it is so very long that I have yearned intensely, speedily to see the splendor of Your strength. Only these my heart desired, so please take pity and do not conceal Yourself.* הֹ *Reveal and spread upon me, my Beloved, the shelter of Your peace. Illuminate the world with Your glory that we may rejoice and be glad with You. Hasten, show love, for time has come, and show us grace as in days of old. "The right of the Lord is raised. The right of the Lord does mighty things." (Psalms 118:16) "Hear Israel, the Lord our God. The Lord is One." (Deuteronomy 6:4) The Lord is King, the Lord has reigned, the Lord shall reign forever and for eternity. We beseech You, Lord, save us now. We beseech You, Lord, give us success now." (Psalms 118:25) "Lord, may Your kindness be upon us as we have placed our hope in You." (Psalms 33:22) "Arise! Help us and redeem us for the sake of Your kindness." (Psalms 44:27)*

ve'ad וְעַד me'olam מֵעוֹלָם Adonai | יְהֹוָאדֹנָיאהדונהי ריבוע יהוה ע"ב, vechesed וְחֶסֶד

:vanim בָּנִים livnei לִבְנֵי vetzidkato וְצִדְקָתוֹ yere'av יְרֵאָיו al עַל olam עוֹלָם

yeminecha יְמִינֶךָ gedulat גְּדֻלַּת becho'ach בְּכֹחַ בן לכב ana אָנָּא

tatir תַּתִּיר tzerura צְרוּרָה: אבג יתץ

ratzon רָצוֹן מוהש ע"ה, ע"ב בריבוע וקס"א ע"ה, אל שדי ע"ה yehi יְהִי

milfanecha מִלְפָנֶיךָ ס"ג מ"ה בן יְהֹוָאדֹנָיאהדונהי Adonai Elohenu אֱלֹהֵינוּ ילה

velohei וֵאלֹהֵי לכב ; ע"ב, דמב מילוי ; ילה avotenu אֲבוֹתֵינוּ av אָב

harachamim הָרַחֲמִים שאה. shethe שֶׁתְּהֵא וְחָשׁוּבָה chashuva וּמְקֻבֶּלֶת umkubelet

urtzuya וּרְצוּיָה lefanecha לְפָנֶיךָ ס"ג מ"ה בן hakafa הַקָּפָה rishona רִאשׁוֹנָה

shehikafnu שֶׁהִקַּפְנוּ lateva לַתֵּיבָה besimchat בְּשִׂמְחַת toratcha תּוֹרָתֶךָ

haromezet הָרוֹמֶזֶת laChesed לַחֶסֶד ע"ב, ריבוע יהוה. ke'ilu כְּאִלּוּ kivanu כִּוַּנּוּ

bechol בְּכֹל לכב בן, hakavanot הַכַּוָּנוֹת hare'uyot הָרְאוּיוֹת lechaven לְכַוֵּן

veAta וְאַתָּה betuvcha בְּטוּבְךָ terachem תְּרַחֵם לאו ג"פ רי"ו ; אברהם, רי"ו אל,

alenu עָלֵינוּ רי"ו ול"ב נתיבות החכמה, רמ"ח (אברים), עסמ"ב וט"ו אותיות פשוטות yehi יְהִי

chasdecha חַסְדֶּךָ Adonai יְהֹוָאדֹנָיאהדונהי alenu עָלֵינוּ utzakenu וּתְזַכֵּנוּ

le'ovdecha לְעָבְדֶךָ beyir'a בְּיִרְאָה רי"ו, פוי, אל אדני ve'ahava וְאַהֲבָה אוזר, דאגה.

vetih'ye וְתִהְיֶה ahavatcha אַהֲבָתְךָ tekua תְּקוּעָה belibenu בְּלִבֵּנוּ tamid תָּמִיד

kol כָּל ע"ה קס"א קנ"א קמ"ג ילי yemei יְמֵי chayenu וְחַיֵּינוּ vetihye וְתִהְיֶה

yiratcha יִרְאָתֶךָ al עַל panenu פָּנֵינוּ levilti לְבִלְתִּי necheta נֶחֱטָא

uvchol וּבְכֹל בן, לכב mida מִדָּה umida וּמִדָּה shetimdod שֶׁתִּמְדֹד

lanu לָנוּ אלהים, אהיה אדני node נוֹדֶה lecha לְךָ bimod בְּמֹאד me'od מְאֹד

---

*"The kindness of the Lord is from forever
and ever upon those who fear Him, and His righteousness upon their children's children." (Psalms 103:17)*

אבג יתץ *We beseech You, with the power of Your great right, undo this entanglement.
May it be pleasing before You, Lord our God, God of our fathers, Merciful Father, that there be
deemed worthy and acceptable and favorable before You the first circling that we have circled the bimah
in the joy of Your Torah—which alludes to Kindness, as we have intended all the meanings that are
appropriate to propose. And You, in Your goodness, may You have mercy upon us. Lord, may Your
kindness be upon us; and may You cause us to merit to serve You with reverence and love. May Your love
be implanted in our heart constantly all the days of our lives, and may Your reverence be over us so that
we shall not sin. And with each and every measure that You mete out to us, let us praise You exceedingly.*

veligmol וְלִגְמוֹל   lehetiv לְהֵטִיב   lehaskil לְהַשְׂכִּיל   utzakenu וּתְזַכֵּנוּ

begufenu בְּגוּפֵנוּ   kochenu כֹּחֵנוּ, לכב   bechol בְּכָל ב"ן   Chesed חֶסֶד ע"ב, רִיבוּעַ יהוה

umamonenu וּבְמָמוֹנֵנוּ   belevav בְּלֵבָב בוכו   shalem שָׁלֵם   veyihyu וְיִהְיוּ יא"י (מילוי דס"ג)

chol כָּל ילי   ma'asenu מַעֲשֵׂינוּ   leshimcha לְשִׁמְךָ   ulzichrecha וּלְזִכְרֶךָ

ta'avat תַּאֲוַת   nefesh נֶפֶשׁ   utzakenu וּתְזַכֵּנוּ   lehitrachek לְהִתְרַחֵק

mehakin'a מֵהַקִּנְאָה יוסף, ציון, ר"פ יהוה   ve'achzariyut וְאַכְזָרִיּוּת   vacha'as וָכַעַס

bekinyan בְּקִנְיָן   haChesed הַחֶסֶד ע"ב, רִיבוּעַ יהוה   midot מִדּוֹת   veliknot וְלִקְנוֹת

hakedosha הַקְּדוֹשָׁה   toratcha תּוֹרָתְךָ   ulma'an וּלְמַעַן   gamur גָּמוּר

hanitenet הַנִּתֶּנֶת   bayamin בְּיָמִין   ulma'an וּלְמַעַן   Avraham אַבְרָהָם

ahuvecha אֲהוּבֶךָ   וז"פ אל, רי"ו ול"ב נתיבות החכמה, רמ"ח (אברים), עסמ"ב וט"ז אותיות פשוטות

ish אִישׁ   haChesed הַחֶסֶד ע"ב, רִיבוּעַ יהוה   temale תְּמַלֵּא   mish'alot מִשְׁאֲלוֹת

libenu לִבֵּנוּ   letova לְטוֹבָה אכא   yivada יֻוָּדַע   le'enei לְעֵינֵי רִיבוּעַ מ"ה

hakol הַכֹּל ילי   tuvcha טוּבְךָ   vechasdecha וְוַחְסְדְּךָ לאו   imanu עִמָּנוּ רִיבוּעַ ס"ג

Initials of *Chesed*—חסד.

chasdei חַסְדֵי   Adonai יְהֹוָהאהדונהי   olam עוֹלָם   ashira אָשִׁירָה   ledor לְדֹר

vador וָדֹר רי"ו   odia אוֹדִיעַ   emunatcha אֱמוּנָתְךָ   befi בְּפִי   sitri סִתְרִי ב"פ מצר

umagini וּמָגִנִּי   ata אַתָּה   lidvarcha לִדְבָרְךָ   yichalti יִחָלְתִּי   derachecha דְּרָכֶיךָ

Adonai יְהֹוָהאהדונהי   hodi'eni הוֹדִיעֵנִי   orchotecha אֹרְחוֹתֶיךָ   lamdeni לַמְּדֵנִי

There are 42 letters in the verse in the secret of *Ana Beko'ach*.

yihyu יִהְיוּ יא"י (מילוי דס"ג)   leratzon לְרָצוֹן מהטו ע"ה, ע"ב בריבוע וקס"א וקס"ה, אל שדי ע"ה

imrei אִמְרֵי ר"ת   fi פִי = אלף למד - שׂין יוד דלת ע"ה   vehegyon וְהֶגְיוֹן   libi לִבִּי אֶלֶף

lefanecha לְפָנֶיךָ ס"ג   Adonai יְהֹוָהאהדונהי ב"ן מ"ה   tzuri צוּרִי   vego'ali וְגֹאֲלִי

And cause us to merit to distinguish, to award good, and to bestow kindness with all our might, with our bodies and our possessions, wholeheartedly. And let all our actions be for Your Name and Your remembrance, as is the desire of our soul. And cause us to merit to be distanced from jealousy, cruelty and anger, and to acquire the attributes of kindness with complete attainment. And for the sake of Your Holy Torah, which was given with Your right arm, and for the sake of Abraham, Your beloved, the man of kindness, may You fulfill the requests of our heart for the good. Let it be known before the eyes of all, Your goodness and Your kindness with us. "Of the kindness of the Lord, I shall sing forever; to every generation I shall make known Your faith with my mouth." (Psalms 89:2) "My haven and my shield are You; I have longed for Your word." (Psalms 119:114) "Lord, let me know Your ways; teach me Your paths. (Psalms 25:4) "May the utterances of my mouth and the thoughts of my heart find favor before You, Lord, my Rock and my Redeemer." (Psalms 19:15)

THE SECOND HAKAFAH (CIRCLING)—ISAAC—GEVURAH

אָנָּא na: נָא נהורין ש״ע יהוה hoshia הוֹשִׁיעָה Adonai יְהֹוָה/אדני אלהים אדני לכב ב״ן ana אָנָּא

אָנָּא ana ב״ן לכב na: נָא אָנָּא na: נָא hatzlicha הַצְלִיחָה Adonai יְהֹוָה/אדני אלהים אדני לכב ב״ן ana אָנָּא

יְהֹוָה/אדני אלהים אדני אל יהוה זן, מזבוח, נגד ע״ה veyom בְּיוֹם anenu עֲנֵנוּ Adonai

קְרָאֵנוּ :kor'enu hoshi'a הוֹשִׁיעָה נהורין ש״ע יהוה tzedakot צְדָקוֹת dover דּוֹבֵר

נָא na: נָא וָתִיק vatik hatzlicha הַצְלִיחָה bilvusho בִּלְבוּשׁוֹ hadur הָדוּר הֶהָדוּר •

וְחָסִיד vechasid anenu עֲנֵנוּ veyom בְּיוֹם אל יהוה זן, מזבוח, נגד ע״ה anenu kor'enu: קְרָאֵנוּ

beshafrir בְּשַׁפְרִיר mistater מִסְתַּתֵּר (מילוי דס״ג) יי״א El אֵל *Keter*

וֻבְיוֹן chevyon, ילי hashechel הַשֵּׂכֶל hane'elam הַנֶּעְלָם mikol מִכָּל ,chevyon

רַעְיוֹן ra'ayon, ilat עִלַּת הָעִלּוֹת hailot muchtar מוּכְתָּר bechter בְּכֶתֶר ה׳ מלך

כֶּתֶר Keter ה׳ מלך elyon, עֶלְיוֹן אל גאל ובאתב״ע ועד לעולם ימלוך ה׳ מלך

Adonai♦ יְהֹוָה/אדני אלהים אדני lecha לְךָ yitnu יִתְּנוּ גאל ובאתב״ע ועד לעולם ימלוך ה׳ מלך

בְּרֵאשִׁית bereshit toratcha תּוֹרָתְךָ hakeduma, הַקְּדוּמָה *Chochmah*

רְשׁוּמָה reshuma, chochmatcha וְחָכְמָתְךָ hasetuma, הַסְּתוּמָה me'ayin מֵאַיִן,

רֵאשִׁית reshit ne'elama, נֶעְלָמָה vehi וְהִיא timatze תִּמָּצֵא

וְחָכְמָה Chochmah (מצוות) תרי״ג במילוי yir'at יִרְאַת יְהֹוָה/אדני אלהים אדני ♦Adonai

אֱמוּנָה emuna, nachalei נַחֲלֵי hanahar הַנָּהָר rechovot רְחוֹבוֹת *Binah*

תְּבוּנָה tevuna, ish אִישׁ yidlem יִדְלֵם amukim עֲמֻקִים mayim מַיִם

בִּינָה Binah sha'arei שַׁעֲרֵי chamisim וַחֲמִישִׁים totzoteha תּוֹצָאוֹתֶיהָ

ע״ה אהיה אהיה יהוה, ע״ה וזיין notzer נוֹצֵר emunim אֱמוּנִים יְהֹוָה/אדני אלהים אדני ♦Adonai

---

THE SECOND HAKAFAH (CIRCLING)—ISAAC—GEVURAH

"We beseech You, Lord, save us now. We beseech You, Lord, give us success now." (Psalms 118:25)
We beseech You, Lord, answer us on the day we call. Speaker of righteousness, save now.
Majestic One in has garb, bring success now. Faithful and Devout One, answer us on the day we call.

Keter - *God conceals Himself in a canopy of secrecy, the wisdom hidden from all notion. Cause of all causes, crowned with the Supernal Crown; they will give You a Crown, Lord.*

Chochmah - *In the beginning there was Your ancient Torah, inscribed with Your hidden wisdom, whence will she be found for she has disappeared? The source of wisdom is awe of the Lord.*

Binah - *The breadth of the river, like a stream of faith are deep waters drawn by a wise man, whose results are the fifty gates of Binah; the faithful are guarded by the Lord.*

Chesed **הָאֵל** haEl לאה, ייא״י (מילוי דס״ג) **הַגָּדוֹל** hagadol להוו, עם ד׳ אותיות מבה, יזל, אום

rav **רַב** enei ריבוע מ״ה **עֵינִי** negdecha ז, מזבוו, אל יהוה **נֶגְדְּךָ** chol **כֹּל** ילי ריבוע מ״ה

al **עַל** Chesed ע״ב, ריבוע יהוה gadol **גָּדוֹל** להוו, עם ד׳ אותיות מבה, יזל, אום **וְחֶסֶד** Chesed

הַשָּׁמַיִם hasamayim י״פ טל, י״פ כוו **וְחַסְדְּךָ** chasdecha, **אֱלֹהֵי** Elohei מילוי ע״ב, דמב ; ילה

אַבְרָהָם Avraham וז״פ אל, רי״ו ול״ב נתיבות הוזכמה, רמ״וז (אברים), עסמ״ב וט״ז אותיות פשוטות

chasdei **וְחַסְדֵּי** אל אדני פוי, יהי אור ע״ה קס״א, ע״ב zechor **זְכוֹר** le'avdecha **לְעַבְדְּךָ**

◆Adonai **יְהוָ֑ה**אדניאהדונהי tehilot **תְּהִלּוֹת** azkir **אַזְכִּיר** Adonai **יְהוָה**אדניאהדונהי ◆Adonai

uGvurah **וּגְבוּרָה** רי״י becho'ach **בְּכֹחַ** ne'edar **נֶאְדָּר** marom **מָרוֹם** Gevurah

pachad **פַּחַד**, temura **תְּמוּרָה** me'en **מֵאַיִן** ora **אוֹרָה** רו, א״ס motzi **מוֹצִיא**

ha'ira **הָאִירָה**, mishpatenu **מִשְׁפָּטֵינוּ** ע״ה ב״ן אלהים ה״פ ד״פ ב״ן Yitzchak **יִצְחָק**

◆Adonai **יְהוָה**אדניאהדונהי le'olam **לְעוֹלָם** ריבוע ס״ג עם י׳ אותיות gibor **גִּבּוֹר** Ata **אַתָּה**

After the circling one should say:

◇

yemin **יְמִין** Adonai **יְהוָה**אדניאהדונהי romema **רוֹמֵמָה** ר״ת ריי yemin **יְמִין**

osa **עֹשָׂה** רהע **וָזֶיל** chayil ומב: Adonai **יְהוָה**אדניאהדונהי **יְהוָה**אדניאהדונהי

Elohenu **אֱלֹהֵינוּ** ילה Adonai **יְהוָה**אדניאהדונהי Yisrael **יִשְׂרָאֵל** shema **שְׁמַע**

echad **אֶחָד** אהבה, דאגה: Adonai | **יְהוָה**אדניאהדונהי

malach **מָלַךְ** Adonai **יְהוָה**אדניאהדונהי melech **מֶלֶךְ** Adonai **יְהוָה**אדניאהדונהי

yimloch **יִמְלֹךְ** (מֶלֶךְ מָלַךְ יִמְלֹךְ = מנצ״ך, סנדלפון, ערי) | Adonai **יְהוָה**אדניאהדונהי

va'ed **וָעֶד:** ייל ר״ת ; דס״ג אותיות וי' דס״ג ריבוע le'olam **לְעוֹלָם**

na **נָא:** hoshi'a **הוֹשִׁיעָה** יהוה ע״ע נהורין Adonai **יְהוָה**אדניאהדונהי ב״ן לכב ana **אָנָּא**

na **נָא:** hatzlicha **הַצְלִיחָה** Adonai **יְהוָה**אדניאהדונהי לכב ב״ן ana **אָנָּא**

Chesed - Great God, all eyes are upon You, Teacher of great kindness, on the Heavens is Your kindness; God of Abraham, remember Your servant; God's benevolence I will proclaim in praises of the Lord.

Gevurah - The Supernal One is adorned in power and might, draws light from that which has no value. One feared by Isaac, illuminate our sentencing, Your might is forever, Lord. "The right of the Lord is raised.

The right of the Lord does mighty things." (Psalms 118:16) "Hear Israel, the Lord our God. The Lord is One." (Deuteronomy 6:4) The Lord is King, the Lord has reigned, the Lord shall reign forever and for eternity. We beseech You, Lord, save us now. We beseech You, Lord, give us success now." (Psalms 118:25)

עוֹרְרָה orera אֶת et גְּבוּרָתֶךָ gevuratecha וּלְכָה ulcha לִישֻׁעָתָה lishuata

לָנוּ lanu אלהים, אהיה אדני: im עִם zero'a זְרוֹעַ lecha לְךָ gevura גְּבוּרָה רי"ו תָעֹז ta'oz

יָדְךָ yadcha תָּרוּם tarum יְמִינֶךָ yeminecha: ata עַתָּה yadati יָדַעְתִּי ki כִּי

הוֹשִׁיעַ hoshi'a יְהוָֹה Adonai meshicho ר"ת מיה בִּישִׁיזוֹ ya'anehu יַעֲנֵהוּ

מִשְּׁמֵי mismei קָדְשׁוֹ kodsho בִּגְבֻרוֹת bigvurot יֵשַׁע yesha יְמִינוֹ yemino:

קַבֵּל kabel רִנַּת rinat עַמֶּךָ amecha שַׂגְּבֵנוּ sagevenu.

טַהֲרֵנוּ taharenu נוֹרָא nora: קְרַע שטן

יְהִי yehi רָצוֹן ratzon מהע ע"ה, ע"ב בריבוע וקס"א ע"ה, אל שדי ע"ה

מִלְּפָנֶיךָ milfanecha ס"ג מ"ה ב"ן יְהוָֹה Adonai אֱלֹהֵינוּ Elohenu ילה

וֵאלֹהֵי velohei לכב ; ע"ב, דמב ; מילוי ילה אֲבוֹתֵינוּ avotenu.

אָב av הָרַחֲמִים harachamim שאה. שֶׁתְּהֵא shethe שֶׁתְּהֵא shethe וְשׁוּבָה chashuva

וּמְקֻבֶּלֶת umkubelet וּרְצוּיָה urtzuya לְפָנֶיךָ lefanecha ס"ג מ"ה ב"ן הַקָּפָה hakafa

הַזֹּאת hazot הַשֵּׁנִית hasenit הָרוֹמֶזֶת haromezet לַגְּבוּרָה laGevurah רי"ו.

כְּאִלּוּ ke'ilu כִּוַּנּוּ kivanu בְּכָל bechol ב"ן לכב הַכַּוָּנוֹת hakavanot

הָרְאוּיוֹת hare'uyot לְכַוֵּן lechaven. וְאַתָּה veAta בְּטוּבְךָ betuvcha לאו

תְּרַחֵם terachem גי"פ רי"ו ; אברהם, וז"פ אל, רי"ו ול"ב נתיבות החכמה, רמ"ז (אברים), עסמ"ב וט"ו

עָלֵינוּ alenu וּתְזַכֵּנוּ utzakenu לְהִתְגַּבֵּר lehitgaber עַל al

יִצְרֵנוּ yitzrenu. וְתֶן veten בָּנוּ banu כּוֹן ko'ach לִכְבֹּשׁ lichbosh

תַּאֲוֹתֵינוּ ta'avotenu הַגּוּפָנִיּוֹת hagufniyot. וּלְמַעַן ulma'an יִצְחָק Yitzchak ד"פ ב"ן

עֲקֵדְךָ akedecha נֶאֱזָר ne'ezar בִּגְבוּרָה bigvura רי"ו. עוֹרְרָה orera אֶת et

גְּבוּרָתֶךָ gevuratecha וּלְכָה ulcha לִישֻׁעָתָה lishu'ata לָנוּ lanu אלהים, אהיה אדני:

"Awaken Your might and come to deliver us. Yours is the arm with power, You strengthen Your hand, Your right is raised up." (Psalms 89:14) "I now know that the Lord has delivered His anointed one; He shall answer him from His Holy Heavens, with the mighty deliverance of His right hand." (Psalms 20:7)

קְרַע שטן *Accept the singing of Your Nation. Strengthen and purify us, Awesome One.*

May it be pleasing before You, Lord our God, God of our fathers, Merciful Father that there be deemed worthy and acceptable and favorable before You this second circling, which alludes to Might, as if we had intended all the meanings that are appropriate to propose. And You, in Your goodness, may You have mercy upon us, and may You cause us to merit to overpower our inclination. And give us strength to suppress our corporeal desires; and in the merit of Isaac, Your bound one, girded in might, "awaken Your might and deliver us." (Psalms 80:3)

וּכְמוֹ uchmo שֶׁכָּבַשׁ shekavash אַבְרָהָם Avraham וז"פ אל, רי"ו ול"ב נתיבות החכמה,

רמ"ח (אברים), עסמ"ב וט"ז אותיות פשוטות אָבִינוּ avinu אֶת et רַחֲמָיו rachamav

לַעֲשׂוֹת la'asot רְצוֹנְךָ retzoncha בְּלֵבָב belevav בוכו שָׁלֵם shalem • כֵּן ken

יִכְבְּשׁוּ yichbeshu רַחֲמֶיךָ rachamecha אֶת et כַּעַסְךָ ka'asecha וְיִגֹּלּוּ veyigolu

רַחֲמֶיךָ rachamecha עַל al מִדּוֹתֶיךָ midotecha • וְתִתְנַהֵג vetitnaheg

עִמָּנוּ imanu ריבוע דס"ג יְהוָֹה Adonai (אהי)(אהיה)(אהדונהי) אֱלֹהֵינוּ Elohenu ילה

בְּמִדַּת bemidat הַחֶסֶד hachesed ע"ב, ריבוע יהוה וּבְמִדַּת uvmidat

הָרַחֲמִים harachamim • וְתִכָּנֵס vetikanes לָנוּ lanu אלהים, אהיה ארני

לִפְנִים lifnim מִשּׁוּרַת mishurat הַדִּין hadin • וּבְטוּבְךָ uvtuvcha לאו

הַגָּדוֹל hagadol להו, עם ד' אותיות מבה, יזל, אום יָשׁוּב yashuv וְזַרוֹן charon

אַפְּךָ apach מֵעַמְּךָ me'amach מֵעִירְךָ ume'irach וּמֵאַרְצָךְ ume'artzach

וּמִנַּחֲלָתָךְ uminachalatach • וּתְבַטֵּל utvatel מֵעָלֵינוּ me'alenu כָּל kol ילי

גְּזֵרוֹת gezerot קָשׁוֹת kashot • וְרָעוֹת vera'ot וְתִגְזֹר vetigzor

עָלֵינוּ alenu גְּזֵרוֹת gezerot טוֹבוֹת tovot כְּרֹב kerov רַחֲמֶיךָ rachamecha:

גַּם gam מִזֵּדִים mizedim וְְשַׁךְ chasoch עַבְדֶּךָ avdecha פוי, אל ארני אַל al

יִמְשְׁלוּ yimshelu בִי vi אָז az אֵיתָם etam וְנִקֵּיתִי veniketi מִפֶּשַׁע mipesha רַב rav:

בְּאֶבְרָתוֹ be'evrato יָסֵךְ yasech לָךְ lach וְתָחַת vetachat כְּנָפָיו kenafav

תֶּחְסֶה techse צִנָּה tzina וְסֹחֵרָה vesochera אֲמִתּוֹ amito: וַאֲנַחְנוּ va'anachnu

עַמְּךָ amcha וְצֹאן vetzon מַרְעִיתֶךָ maritecha נוֹדֶה node לְּךָ lecha לְעוֹלָם le'olam

נְסַפֵּר nesaper רי"ו וָדֹר vador רביע ס"ג עם י' אותיות לְדֹר ledor תְּהִלָּתֶךָ tehilatecha:

Just as our patriarch Abraham suppressed his compassion to do Your will wholeheartedly, so may Your compassion suppress Your anger, and may Your compassion be stirred over Your attributes. Deal with us Lord our God, with the attribute of kindness and the attribute of compassion, and enter on our behalf beyond the line of strict law. In Your great goodness, may Your anger be turned back from Your nation, from Your city, from Your land, and from Your heritage. And may You eliminate from us all harsh and evil decrees, and may You decree for us good decrees, in accordance with Your abundant mercies. "Restrain Your servant also from intentional sins—let them not rule over me; then will I be whole and be cleansed of great transgression." (Psalms 19:14) "He shall cover you with His pocket, and under His wing shall you find refuge, His truth being a shield and armor." (Psalms 91:4) "We, Your people, the sheep of Your pasture, shall give thanks to You forever; in each and every generation we shall recount Your praises." (Psalms 79:13)

ro'e רֹעֵה · Yisrael יִשְׂרָאֵל · ha'azina הַאֲזִינָה · noheg נֹהֵג · katzon כַּצֹּאן

Yosef יוֹסֵף צִיוֹן, רַ"פ יהוה, קִנְאָה · yoshev יֹשֵׁב · hakeruvim הַכְּרוּבִים · hofi'a הוֹפִיעָה:

horeni הוֹרֵנִי · Adonai יְהֹוָ‌ה‌אדניאהדונהי · darkecha דַּרְכֶּךָ · ahalech אֵהַלֵךְ

ba'amitecha בַּאֲמִתֶּךָ · yached יַחֵד · levavi לְבָבִי · leyir'a לְיִרְאָה רי"ו · shemecha שְׁמֶךָ:

There are 42 letters in the verse in the secret of *Ana Beko'ach*.

yih'yu יִהְיוּ (יי"א) מילוי דס"ג · leratzon לְרָצוֹן מהטע ע"ה, ע"ב בריבוע וקס"א וקס"א ע"ה, אל שדי ע"ה

imrei אִמְרֵי ר"ת אֶלֶף = אלף למד ▪ עין דלת יוד ע"ה · fi פִי · vehegyon וְהֶגְיוֹן · libi לִבִּי

lefanecha לְפָנֶיךָ ס"ג מ"ה בֶּ"ן · Adonai יְהֹוָ‌ה‌אדניאהדונהי · tzuri צוּרִי · vego'ali וְגֹאֲלִי:

THE THIRD HAKAFAH (CIRCLING)—JACOB—TIFERET

ana אָנָּא בֶּ"ן לכב · Adonai יְהֹוָ‌ה‌אדניאהדונהי יהוה ע"ע נהורין · hoshi'a הוֹשִׁיעָה · na נָא:

ana אָנָּא בֶּ"ן לכב · Adonai יְהֹוָ‌ה‌אדניאהדונהי · hatzlicha הַצְלִיחָה · na נָא:

ana אָנָּא בֶּ"ן לכב · Adonai יְהֹוָ‌ה‌אדניאהדונהי · anenu עֲנֵנוּ · veyom בְּיוֹם ע"ה נגד, מזבוח, זן,

kor'enu קָרְאֵנוּ · zach זָךְ יי · veyashar וְיָשָׁר · hoshi'a הוֹשִׁיעָה יהוה ע"ע נהורין אל יהוה

na נָא · tov טוֹב והו · hatzlicha הַצְלִיחָה · dalim דַּלִּים · chomel חוֹמֵל · na נָא ▪

umetiv וּמֵטִיב · anenu עֲנֵנוּ · veyom בְּיוֹם ע"ה נגד, מזבוח, זן, אל יהוה · kor'enu קָרְאֵנוּ:

Tiferet · mi מִי · El אֵל יא"י ילי (מילוי דס"ג) · kamocha כָּמוֹךָ

ose עוֹשֵׂה · gedolot גְּדוֹלוֹת להה, עם ד' אותיות מבה, יזל, אום, · avir אֲבִיר הרוח

Ya'akov יַעֲקֹב זפ יהוה, · nora נוֹרָא אידהנויה · tehilot תְּהִלּוֹת,

Tiferet תִּפְאֶרֶת · Yisrael יִשְׂרָאֵל · shome'a שׁוֹמֵעַ · tefilot תְּפִלּוֹת,

ki כִּי · shome'a שׁוֹמֵעַ · el אֶל · evyonim אֶבְיוֹנִים · Adonai יְהֹוָ‌ה‌אדניאהדונהי ◆

"Shepherd of Israel, hear, He Who leads Joseph like sheep;
He Who dwells atop the Cherubim, appear." (Psalms 80:2) "Teach me Your way, Lord, so that I may walk in Your truth; unify my heart to hear Your Name." (Psalms 86:11) "May the utterances of my mouth and the thoughts of my heart find favor before You, Lord, my Rock and my Redeemer." (Psalms 19:15)

THE THIRD HAKAFAH (CIRCLING)—JACOB—TIFERET

"We beseech You, Lord, save us now. We beseech You, Lord, give us success now." (Psalms 118:25)
We beseech You, Lord, answer us on the day we call. Pure and Just One, save now.
He Who pities the poor, bring success now. God and Beneficent One, answer us on the day we call.
Tiferet - Who is like You, He who performs greatness, Knight of Jacob of awesome praises.
The Splendor of Israel hears prayers, for the Lord hearkens to the prayers of the poor.

Netzach יָהּ Yah הההה zechut זְכוּת avot אָבוֹת yagen יָגֵן alenu עָלֵינוּ,

נֹצֵר Netzach יִשְׂרָאֵל Yisrael מִצָּרוֹתֵינוּ mitzarotenu גְּאָלֵנוּ ge'alenu,

וּמִבּוֹר umibor גָּלוּת galut דְּלֵנוּ delenu וְהַעֲלֵנוּ veha'alenu, לְנַצֵּחַ lenatze'ach

עַל al מְלֶאכֶת melechet בֵּית bet ב״פ ראה יְהֹוָאדְנִיאהדונהי Adonai ◆

Hod מִיָּמִין miyamin וּמִשְּׂמֹאל umismol יְנִיקַת yenikat הַנְּבִיאִים hanevi'im,

וְהוֹד vaHod הההה מֵהֶם mehem נִמְצָאִים nimtzaim,

יָכִין yachin וּבוֹעַז uvo'az בְּשֵׁם beshem נִקְרָאִים nikraim,

וְכֹל vechol ילי בָּנֶיךָ banayich לִמּוּדֵי limudei יְהֹוָאדְנִיאהדונהי Adonai ◆

Yesod יְסוֹד Yesod ההע צַדִּיק tzadik בְּשִׁבְעָה beshiv'a נֶעְלָם ne'elam,

אוֹת ot בְּרִית berit הוּא hu לְעוֹלָם le'olam רִיבוּע ס״ג עם י׳ אותיות,

יְסוֹד Yesod ההע צַדִּיק tzadik הַבְּרָכָה haberacha מַעְיָן me'en

עוֹלָם olam, צַדִּיק tzadik אַתָּה Ata יֻהֹוָוּהֹיאדְנִיאהדונהי Adonai ◆

Malchut נָא na הָקֵם hakem הקם מַלְכוּת malchut דָּוִד David

וּשְׁלֹמֹה uShlomo, בַּעֲטָרָה ba'atara שֶׁעִטְּרָה she'itra לּוֹ lo אִמּוֹ imo,

כְּנֶסֶת keneset יִשְׂרָאֵל Yisrael כַּלָּה kala קְרוּאָה keru'a בִּנְעִימָה bane'ima,

עֲטֶרֶת ateret תִּפְאֶרֶת Tiferet בְּיַד beyad יְהֹוָאדְנִיאהדונהי Adonai ◆

וְחֹזֶק chazak פהל מְיַחֵד meyached כְּאֶחָד ke'echad אהבה, דאגה ke'echad עֶשֶׂר eser

סְפִירוֹת sefirot, וּמְאֻחָד um'ached אַלּוּף aluf יִרְאֶה yir'e רי״ו

מְאוֹרוֹת me'orot, סַפִּיר sapir גְּזָרְתָם gizratam יוֹחַד yachad מְאִירוֹת me'irot,

תִּקְרַב tikrav רִנָּתִי rinati ס״ג מ״ה ב״ן לְפָנֶיךָ lefanecha יְהֹוָאדְנִיאהדונהי Adonai ◆

Netzach - *Yah, may the merit of our forefathers protect us, Israel's victor will redeem us from our troubles and from the pit of exile He will draw us and raise us up to be victorious in the service of the House of the lord.*
Hod - *From right and from left are the prophets nurtured, they are found in Netzach and Hod They are called by the names Yachin and Boaz, all of your children will learn of the Lord.*
Yesod - *The foundation of a righteous man is concealed in seven, he is the sign of the covenant for the world. A fountain of blessing – a tzaddik is the foundation for the world. You are the tzaddik, Lord.*
Malchut - *Restore the kingdoms of David and Solomon with the tiara by which his mother crowned him. Israel is called a bride in her pleasantness; she is a crown of beauty in the Lord's hand. Strength unifies us as one – the Ten Luminous Emanations, and unite the chief who will see lights. The lights together were carved from sapphire, draw my song near before You, Lord.*

After the circling one should say:

לְמִין yemin יְהֹוַאדְנִיאהדונהי yemin Adonai רוֹמֵמָ֫ה romema ר״ת רִיי לְמִין

יְהֹוַאדְנִיאהדונהי Adonai עֹשֶׂה osa רהע וְזִיל chayil ומב:

שְׁמַ֫ע shema Elohenu אֱלֹהֵ֫ינוּ Adonai יְהֹוַאדְנִיאהדונהי Yisrael יִשְׂרָאֵל Elohenu ילה

יְהֹוַאדְנִיאהדונהי Adonai אֶחָ֫ד echad אהבה, דאגה:

יְהֹוַאדְנִיאהדונהי Adonai מֶ֫לֶךְ melech Adonai יְהֹוַאדְנִיאהדונהי malach מֶ֫לֶךְ

יְהֹוַאדְנִיאהדונהי Adonai | יִמְלֹךְ yimloch (מֶלֶךְ מַלַךְ יִמְלֹךְ = מְנַצֵּחַ, סַנְדַלְפוֹן, עֲרִי)

לְעֹלָם le'olam רִיבוֹעַ דס״ג וי׳ אוֹתִיּוֹת דס״ג ; ר״ת ייל וָעֶד va'ed:

אָנָּא ana בּ״ן לכב יְהֹוַאדְנִיאהדונהי Adonai הוֹשִׁיעָה hoshi'a יהוה ע״ע נהורין נָּא na:

אָנָּא ana בּ״ן לכב יְהֹוַאדְנִיאהדונהי Adonai הַצְלִיחָה hatzlicha נָּא na:

כִּי ki תִּפְאֶ֫רֶת tiferet עֻזָּ֫מוֹ uzamo אַתָּה Ata וּבִרְצֹנְךָ uvirtzoncha

תָּרוּם tarum (כְּתִיב תָּרִים) קַרְנֵ֫נוּ karnenu: תִּתֵּן titen ב״פ כהת לְרֹאשְׁךָ lerosh'cha

לִוְיַת livyat חֵן chen וָז מוזי עֲטֶ֫רֶת ateret תִּפְאֶ֫רֶת tiferet תְּמַגְּנֶ֫ךָ temagneka:

אֲשֶׁר asher עָשָׂה asa כָּל kol יְלִי עַל al עֶלְיוֹן elyon ultitcha וּלְתִתְּךָ עֶלְיוֹן elyon עֲמם ; הַגּוֹיִם hagoyim

וּלְתִפְאָ֫רֶת ultif'aret וְלִהְיֹתְךָ velih'yotcha עַם am קָדֹשׁ kadosh ; אמת וּלְשֵׁם ulshem לִתְהִלָּה lit'hila ע״ה asa עָשָׂה asher

לַיהֹוַאדְנִיאהדונהי ladonai אֱלֹהֶ֫יךָ Elohecha ילה כַּאֲשֶׁר ka'asher דִּבֵּר diber ראה:

נָּא na גִּבּוֹר gibor ◆ יְזוּדֶךָ yichudecha דּוֹרְשֵׁי dorshei

כְּבָבַת kevavat שׁמְרֵם shomrem: נגד יכש

יְהִי yehi רָצוֹן ratzon מהשׁ ע״ה, ע״ב בריבוע וקס״א ע״ה, ע״ה, אל שׁדי ע״ה

מִלְּפָנֶ֫יךָ milfanecha ס״ג מ״ה בּ״ן יְהֹוַאדְנִיאהדונהי Adonai אֱלֹהֵ֫ינוּ Elohenu ילה

וֵאלֹהֵי velohei לכב ; מילוי ע״ב, דמב ; ילה אֲבוֹתֵ֫ינוּ avotenu ◆

The right of the Lord is raised.
The right of the Lord does mighty things." (Psalms 118:16) "Hear Israel, the Lord our God. The Lord is One." (Deuteronomy 6:4) The Lord is King, the Lord has reigned, the Lord shall reign forever and for eternity. We beseech You, Lord, save us now. We beseech You, Lord, give us success now." (Psalms 118:25) "For You are the pride of their power, and in Your favor shall our might be exalted. (Psalms 89:18) "Bestow upon your head an adornment of grace; a crown of glory it will bequeath you." (Proverbs 4:9) "And to make you supreme over all the nations that He has made; for praise, for fame and for glory; and so that you may be a holy nation unto the Lord your God, as He has spoken." (Deuteronomy 26:19)
נגד יכש *Please, Mighty One, those who seek Your unity, guard them like the pupil of the eye.*
May it be pleasing before You, Lord our God, God of our fathers,

אָב av   הָרַחֲמִים harachamim   שאה   שֶׁתְּהֵא shethe   וְשׁוּבָה chashuva

וּמְקֻבֶּלֶת umkubelet   וּרְצוּיָה urtzuya   ס״א מ״ה בן   לְפָנֶיךָ lefanecha   הַקָּפָה hakafa

שְׁלִישִׁית shelishit   הָרוֹמֶזֶת haromezet   לְתִפְאֶרֶת leTiferet   וּתְזַכֵּנוּ utzakenu

לִהְיוֹת lih'yot   מֵעֲבָדֶיךָ me'avadecha   הַנֶּאֱמַר hane'emar   עֲלֵיהֶם alehem

יִשְׂרָאֵל Yisrael   אֲשֶׁר asher   בְּךָ becha   אֶתְפָּאָר etpa'ar   וּתְזַכֵּנוּ utzakenu

לַעֲסֹק la'asok   בְּתוֹרָתְךָ betoratcha   הַקְּדוֹשָׁה hakedosha   תּוֹרַת torat   אֱמֶת emet

ל״פ יהוה, אהיה פ׳   לְעָבְדְךָ le'ovdecha   וּתְזַכֵּנוּ utzakenu   פו׳   בֶּאֱמֶת be'emet

מְגַמָּתֵנוּ megamatenu   ילי   כָּל kol   וְתִהְיֶה vetih'ye   אהיה פ׳ ל״פ יהוה

לְבַקֵּשׁ levakesh   הָאֱמֶת ha'emet   ל״פ יהוה, אהיה פ׳   וּתְחָנֵּנוּ ut'chonenu

לְמַעַן lema'an   דַּעַת da'at   אֲמִתּוּת amitut   דִּינֵי dinei   הַתּוֹרָה hatorah

וּתְזַכֵּנוּ utzakenu   לְהִתְרַוֹזֵק lehitrachek   מֵהַשֶׁקֶר mehaseker   וְהַכָּזָב vehakazav

עַל al   (ייא״י מילוי דס״ג) אל   יִהְיוּ yih'yu   שֶׁנִּפְנֶה shenifne   פִּנּוֹת pinot   ילי   וְכָל vechol

דְּבַר devar   ראה   אֱמֶת emet   ל״פ יהוה, אהיה פ׳   וּבִזְכוּת uvizchut   תּוֹרַת torat

אֱמֶת emet   ל״פ יהוה, אהיה פ׳   וּזְכוּת uzchut   יַעֲקֹב Ya'akov   ל״פ יהוה יאהדונהי אידהנויה

אָבִינוּ avinu   הֶחָתוּם hechatum   בְּתִפְאֶרֶת beTiferet   מִדַּת midat   אֱמֶת emet

ל״פ יהוה, אהיה פ׳ אהיה   וּכְתִיב uchtiv   תִּתֵּן titen   ב״פ כהת   אֱמֶת emet   ל״פ יהוה, אהיה

לְיַעֲקֹב leya'akov   ל״פ יהוה, יאהדונהי אידהנויה   תַּעֲנֵנוּ ta'anenu   וְתַעֲשֶׂה veta'ase   פ׳ אהיה

בַּקָשָׁתֵנוּ bakashatenu   וְנִקְרְאָה venikre'a   יְרוּשָׁלַיִם Yerushalayim   עִיר ir

הָאֱמֶת ha'emet   ל״פ יהוה, אהיה פ׳   עַל al   כֵּן ken   נְקַוֶּה nekave   בסזוזך, סנדלפון, ערי

לָךְ lach   יְהֹוָה וֹאדנ״יאהדונהי Adonai   אֱלֹהֵינוּ Elohenu   ילה   לִרְאוֹת lirot

מְהֵרָה mehera   בְּתִפְאֶרֶת betiferet   עֻזָּךְ uzach   ס״ת כהת, משיוז בן דוד ע״ה:

Merciful Father, that there be deemed worthy and acceptable and favorable before You this third circling, which alludes to Glory, as if we had intended all the meanings that are appropriate to propose. And You, in Your goodness, may You have mercy upon us, and may You cause us to merit to be Your servants about whom it is stated: "Israel, through you I will be glorified." (Isaiah 49:3) And may You cause us to merit to delve into Your Holy Torah, the Torah of truth; and may You cause us to merit to serve You with sincerity. And may our entire aim be to seek the truth; and may You graciously grant us so as to know the truth of the laws of the Torah. And may You cause us to merit to be distanced from falsehood and deceit; and any turns that we shall take, may they be for the truth. In the merit of the Torah of truth, and the merit of our patriarch Jacob, who is sealed with Glory, the attribute of truth, and it is written: "May You grant truth to Jacob." (Micha 7:20) may You answer us and may you fulfill our request. And let Jerusalem be called the city of Truth. Therefore, we place our hope in You, Lord our God, to see the glory of Your Might speedily.

Initials of *Tiferet*—תפארת.

תִּקְרַב tikrav רִנָּתִי rinati לְפָנֶיךָ lefanecha ס״ג מ״ה ב״ן יְהֹוָ֖ואדנילאהדונהי Adonai

כִּדְבָרְךָ kidvarcha הֲבִינֵנִי havineni: פְּעָמַי pe'amai הָכֵן hachen

בְּאִמְרָתֶךָ be'imratecha וְאַל ve'al תַשְׁלֶט tashlet בִּי bi כָל chol יִלִי אָוֶן aven:

אַשְׁרֵי ashrei אָדָם adam מ״ה עוֹז oz לוֹ lo בָךְ vach מְסִלּוֹת mesilot

בִּלְבָבָם bilvavam: רַחֲמֶיךָ rachamecha רַבִּים rabim יְהֹוָ֖ואדנילאהדונהי Adonai

כְּמִשְׁפָּטֶךָ kemishpatecha וַזֵּנִי chayeni: תְּהִלַּת tehilat יְהֹוָ֖ואדנילאהדונהי Adonai

יְדַבֵּר yedaber ראה פִּי pi וִיבָרֵךְ vivarech עסמ״ב כָל kol יִלִי בָשָׂר basar

שֵׁם shem קָדְשׁוֹ kodsho לְעוֹלָם le'olam ריבוע ס״ג עם י׳ אותיות וָעֶד va'ed:

There are 42 letters in the verse in the secret of *Ana Beko'ach*.

יְהִי֖וּ yihyu אל (ייא״י מילוי דס״ג) לְרָצוֹן leratzon מהע ע״ה, ע״ב בריבוע וקס״א ע״ה, אל עדי ע״ה

אִמְרֵי imrei פִּי fi ר״ת אֶלֶף = אלף למד ← עין דלת יוד ע״ה libi לְבִּי vehegyon וְהֶגְיוֹן

לְפָנֶיךָ lefanecha ס״ג מ״ה ב״ן יְהֹוָ֖ואדנילאהדונהי Adonai צוּרִי tzuri וְגֹאֲלִי vego'ali:

THE FOURTH HAKAFAH (CIRCLING)—MOSES—NETZACH

אָנָּא ana ב״ן לכב יְהֹוָ֖ואדנילאהדונהי Adonai הוֹשִׁיעָה hoshi'a יהוה ש״ע נהורין נָא na:

אָנָּא ana ב״ן לכב יְהֹוָ֖ואדנילאהדונהי Adonai הַצְלִיחָה hatzlicha נָא na: אָנָּא ana ב״ן לכב

יְהֹוָ֖ואדנילאהדונהי Adonai עֲנֵנוּ anenu בְיוֹם veyom ע״ה נגד, מזבוה, זן, אל יהוה

קָרְאֵנוּ kor'enu: יוֹדֵעַ yode'a מַחֲשָׁבוֹת machashavot הוֹשִׁיעָה hoshi'a יהוה ש״ע נהורין

נָא na• כַּבִּיר kabir וְנָאוֹר vena'or הַצְלִיוֹחָה hatzlicha נָא na: לוֹבֵשׁ lovesh

צְדָקוֹת tzedakot עֲנֵנוּ anenu בְיוֹם veyom ע״ה נגד, מזבוה, זן, אל יהוה קָרְאֵנוּ kor'enu:

"*May my prayer approach You, Lord: like Your word, allow me to understand.*" (Psalms 119:169) "*Set my steps in Your utterances, and let not any iniquity rule over me.*" (Psalms 119:133) "*Fortunate is the man whose stronghold is in You, and the pathways in their heart. Your compassion is great, Lord, preserve my life according to Your laws.*" (Psalms 119:156) "*My mouth shall speak the praise of the Lord, and all flesh shall bless His Holy Name forever and ever.*" (Psalms 145:21) "*May the utterances of my mouth and the thoughts of my heart find favor before You, Lord, my Rock and my Redeemer.*" (Psalms 19:15)*

THE FOURTH HAKAFAH (CIRCLING)—MOSES—NETZACH

"*We beseech You, Lord, save us now. We beseech You, Lord, give us success now.*" (Psalms 118:25)
We beseech You, Lord, answer us on the day we call. Knower of thoughts, save now. Powerful and Illustrious One, bring success now. He who garbs Himself in righteousness, answer us on the day we call.

olamim עוֹלָמִים lechai לְחַי	veha'emuna וְהָאֱמוּנָה	ha'aderet הָאַדֶּרֶת
olamim עוֹלָמִים lechai לְחַי	vehaberacha וְהַבְּרָכָה	habina הַבִּינָה
		בינה ע"ה = אהיה אהיה יהוה = וזיים
olamim עוֹלָמִים lechai לְחַי	vehagedula וְהַגְּדֻלָּה	haga'ava הַגַּאֲוָה
olamim עוֹלָמִים lechai לְחַי	vehadibur וְהַדִּבּוּר	hade'a הַדֵּעָה
olamim עוֹלָמִים lechai לְחַי	vehehadar וְהֶהָדָר	ההה hahod הַהוֹד
olamim עוֹלָמִים lechai לְחַי	vehavatikut וְהַוָּתִיקוּת	hava'ad הַוַּעַד
olamim עוֹלָמִים lechai לְחַי	vehazohar וְהַזֹּהַר	ייי hazach הַזָּךְ
olamim עוֹלָמִים lechai לְחַי	vehachosen וְהַחֹסֶן	ומב hachayil הַחַיִל
olamim עוֹלָמִים lechai לְחַי	vehatohar וְהַטֹּהַר	hateches הַטֶּכֶס
olamim עוֹלָמִים lechai לְחַי	רי"ו vehayir'a וְהַיִּרְאָה	hayichud הַיִּחוּד
olamim עוֹלָמִים lechai לְחַי	לאו vehakavod וְהַכָּבוֹד	haketer הַכֶּתֶר
		כתר = ה' מלך ה' מלך ה' ימלוך לעולם ועד ובאתב"ש גאל
olamim עוֹלָמִים lechai לְחַי	vehalibuv וְהַלִּבּוּב	halekach הַלֶּקַח
olamim עוֹלָמִים lechai לְחַי	vehamemshala וְהַמֶּמְשָׁלָה	hamelucha הַמְּלוּכָה
olamim עוֹלָמִים lechai לְחַי	vehanetzach וְהַנֶּצַח	hanoy הַנּוֹי
olamim עוֹלָמִים lechai לְחַי	vehasegev וְהַשֶּׂגֶב	hasiguy הַסִּגּוּי
olamim עוֹלָמִים lechai לְחַי	veha'anava וְהָעֲנָוָה	ha'oz הָעֹז
olamim עוֹלָמִים lechai לְחַי	vehape'er וְהַפְּאֵר	hapedut הַפְּדוּת

The strength and faithfulness to the One Who lives eternally. The discernment and blessing to the One Who lives eternally. The grandeur and greatness to the One Who lives eternally. The wisdom and speech to the One Who lives eternally. The glory and majesty to the One Who lives eternally .The convocation and authority to the One Who lives eternally. The refinement and radiance to the One Who lives eternally. The accomplishment and power to the One Who lives eternally. The adornment and purity to the One Who lives eternally. The oneness and reverence to the One Who lives eternally. The crown and honor to the One Who lives eternally. The study and insight to the One Who lives eternally. The kingship and dominion to the One Who lives eternally. The beauty and triumph to the One Who lives eternally. The eminence and supremacy to the One Who lives eternally. The might and modesty to the One Who lives eternally. The redemption and splendor to the One Who lives eternally.

olamim עוֹלָמִים lechai לְחֵי	vehatzedek וְהַצֶּדֶק	hatzevi הַצְּבִי
olamim עוֹלָמִים lechai לְחֵי	vehakedusha וְהַקְּדֻשָּׁה	hakeri'a הַקְּרִיאָה
olamim עוֹלָמִים lechai לְחֵי	veharomemot וְהָרוֹמְמוֹת	haron הָרוֹן
olamim עוֹלָמִים lechai לְחֵי	vehashevach וְהַשֶּׁבַח	hashir הַשִּׁיר
olamim עוֹלָמִים lechai לְחֵי	vehatiferet וְהַתִּפְאֶרֶת	hatehila הַתְּהִלָּה

תהלה ע"ה = אמת, אהיה פעמים אהיה, ז"פ ס"ג

After the circling one should say:

yemin יְמִין romema רוֹמְמָה Adonai יְהֹוָאֲדֹנָיהִ ר"ת רי"ו yemin יְמִין

יְהֹוָאֲדֹנָיהִ osa עֹשָׂה רה"ע Adonai וָזִיל chayil ומב:

שֶׁמַע shema י"לה Elohenu אֱלֹהֵינוּ Adonai יְהֹוָאֲדֹנָיהִ Yisrael יִשְׂרָאֵל

אֶזוֹד echad אהבה, דאגה: Adonai | יְהֹוָאֲדֹנָיהִ

malach מָלַךְ Adonai יְהֹוָאֲדֹנָיהִ melech מֶלֶךְ Adonai יְהֹוָאֲדֹנָיהִ

yimloch יִמְלֹךְ (מֶלֶךְ מָלַךְ יִמְלֹךְ = מנצפ"ך, סנדלפון, ערי) Adonai | יְהֹוָאֲדֹנָיהִ

le'olam לְעֹלָם ריבוע דס"ג וי' אותיות דס"ג ; ר"ת ייל va'ed וָעֶד:

ana אָנָא בן לכב יְהֹוָאֲדֹנָיהִ Adonai hoshi'a הוֹשִׁיעָה יהוה ע"ע נהורין na נָא:

ana אָנָא בן לכב יְהֹוָאֲדֹנָיהִ Adonai hatzlicha הַצְלִיחָה na נָא:

hashivenu הֲשִׁיבֵנוּ Tzeva'ot צְבָאוֹת ילה Elohim אֱלֹהִים Adonai יְהֹוָאֲדֹנָיהִ

haer הָאֵר panecha פָּנֶיךָ ס"ג מ"ה בן venivashe'a וְנִוָּשֵׁעָה: todi'eni תּוֹדִיעֵנִי

orach אֹרַח chayim וְחַיִּים אהיה אהיה יהוה, בינה ע"ה sova שֹׂבַע semachot שְׂמָחוֹת

et אֶת panecha פָּנֶיךָ ס"ג מ"ה בן ne'imot נְעִמוֹת bimincha בִּימִינְךָ netzach נֶצַח:

The desire and righteousness to the One Who lives eternally. The summons and sanctity to the One Who lives eternally. The exultation and exaltation to the One Who lives eternally. The song and praise to the One Who lives eternally. The lauding and magnificence to the One Who lives eternally. The right of the Lord is raised.

The right of the Lord does mighty things." (Psalms 118:16) "Hear Israel, the Lord our God. The Lord is One." (Deuteronomy 6:4) The Lord is King, the Lord has reigned, the Lord shall reign forever and for eternity. We beseech You, Lord, save us now. We beseech You, Lord, give us success now." (Psalms 118:25) Lord, God of hosts, bring us back; shine your countenance and we will be delivered. May You make known to me the path of life, satiated with joy in Your presence, the pleasantness that is in Your right hand eternally.

HAKAFOT (CIRCLING) OF SIMCHAT TORAH

780

בָּרְכֵם barchem טַהֲרֵם taharem ♦ רַחֲמֵי rachamei צִדְקָתְךָ tzidkatecha ♦

בטר צתג תָּמִיד tamid גָּמְלֵם gomlem: ♦

יְהִי yehi רָצוֹן ratzon מהע ע"ב בריבוע וקס"א ע"ה, ע"ב ע"ה, אל שדי ע"ה

מִלְּפָנֶיךָ milfanecha ס"ג מ"ה ב"ן יְהֹוָאדֹנָי Adonai אֱלֹהֵינוּ Elohenu ילה

וֵאלֹהֵי velohei לכב ; מילוי ע"ב, דמב ; ילה אֲבוֹתֵינוּ avotenu ♦

אָב av הָרַחֲמִים harachamim שאה♦ שֶׁתְּהֵא shethe וְחֲשׁוּבָה chashuva

וּמְקֻבֶּלֶת umkubelet וּרְצוּיָה urtzuya לְפָנֶיךָ lefanecha ס"ג מ"ה ב"ן הַהַקָּפָה hakafa

הָרְבִיעִית harevi'it הָרוֹמֶזֶת haromezet לְמִדַּת lemidat נֶצַח Netzach ♦

כְּאִלּוּ ke'ilu כִּוַּנּוּ kivanu בְּכָל bechol ב"ן לכב הַכַּוָּנוֹת hakavanot הָרְאוּיוֹת hare'uyot

לְכַוֵּן lechaven ♦ וְאַתָּה veAta בְּטוּבְךָ betuvcha לאו תְּרַחֵם terachem ג"פ רי"ו ;

עָלֵינוּ alenu ♦ אברהם, וז"פ אל, רי"ו ול"ב נתיבות החכמה, רמ"ז (אברים), עסמ"ב וט"ז אותיות פשוטות

וְרַחֲמֶיךָ verachamecha הָרַבִּים harabim אַל al יַעַזְבוּנוּ ya'azvunu נֶצַח netzach

סֶלָה sela וָעֶד va'ed ♦ וְנִשְׂמְחָה venismecha וְנִרְאֶה venir'e נְעִימוֹת ne'imot

בִּימִינְךָ bimincha נֶצַח Netzach ♦ וּתְזַכֵּנוּ utzakenu לְכָל lechol יה ארני

הַבְטָחוֹת havtachot וְנֶחָמוֹת venechamot שֶׁהִבְטַחְתָּנוּ shehivtachtanu עַל al

יְדֵי yedei נְבִיאֶיךָ nevi'echa הַקְּדוֹשִׁים hakedoshim ♦ וְגַם vegam נֶצַח netzach

יִשְׂרָאֵל Yisrael לֹא lo יְשַׁקֵּר yeshaker וְלֹא velo יִנָּחֵם yinachem ♦

וּתְחַזְּקֵנוּ ut'chazkenu וּתְאַמְּצֵנוּ ut'amtzenu לָנֶצַח lanetzach ♦ וּתְנַצֵּחַ utnatze'ach

אוֹיְבֵינוּ oyvenu ♦ וְתִסְתֹּם vetistom וְתַחְתֹּם vetachtom פֶּה pe מילה ;

עָלֵינוּ alenu ♦ הַמְקַטְרְגִים hamkatregim כָּל kol ילי ארני אהיה, אלהים, ע"ה

וּלְמַעַן ulma'an זְכוּת zechut מֹשֶׁה mshe מהע, ע"ב בריבוע קס"א, אל שדי, ד"פ אלהים ע"ה

בטר צתג *Bless them. Purify them. Your compassionate righteousness always grant them.*
May it be pleasing before You, Lord our God, God of our fathers, Merciful Father, that there be deemed worthy and acceptable and favorable before You this fourth circling, which alludes to Victory, as if we had intended all the meanings that are appropriate to propose. And You, in Your goodness, may You have mercy upon us; and Your great compassion, may it never leave us selah forever. And may we rejoice and may we see the pleasantness that is in Your right arm eternally. And may You cause us to merit all of the pledges and consolations that You promised us through Your holy prophets. Also, the Victorious One of Israel shall not deceive nor reconsider. May You strengthen us and fortify us for eternity; and may You vanquish our enemies. And may You close and seal the mouth of all who accuse us. And in the merit of Moses,

Raya רַעְיָא   Mehemna מְהֵימְנָא   hechatum הֲוָתוּם   bemidat בְּמִדַת

◆haNetzach הַנֶּצַח   ta'ir תָּאִיר   enenu עֵינֵינוּ ריבוע מ"ה   betoratecha בְּתוֹרָתֶךָ◆

ve'acharei וְאַחֲרֵי   mitzvotecha מִצְוֹתֶיךָ   tirdof תִּרְדֹף   nafshenu נַפְשֵׁנוּ◆

vetig'alenu וְתִגְאָלֵנוּ   ge'ulat גְּאֻלַּת   olam עוֹלָם   migalut מִגָּלוּת   hachel הָוֵל

hazeh הַזֶּה וְהוּ   bizchut בִּזְכוּת   Moshe מֹשֶׁה מהע, ע"ב בריבוע קס"א, אל שדי,

vetivne וְתִבְנֶה   Raya רַעְיָא ע"ה   Mehemna מְהֵימְנָא◆   אלהים ד"פ

◆beyamenu בְּיָמֵינוּ   bimhera בִּמְהֵרָה   hamikdash הַמִּקְדָּשׁ ראה ב"פ bet בֵּית

vekol וְקוֹל   ben בֶּן   Levi לֵוִי   tisov תָּסוֹב   al עַל   shira שִׁירָה   unvala וּנְבָלָה

imo עִמוֹ   kinor כִּנּוֹר   naim נָעִים   im עִם   navel נֵבֶל   lenatze'ach לְנַצֵּחַ

al עַל   melechet מְלֶאכֶת   bet בֵּית ב"פ ראה   Adonai יְהֹוָאדֹנָי:

Initials of Netzach—נצ"ח.

noda נוֹדָע   bihuda בִּיהוּדָה   Elohim אֱלֹהִים ילה   beYisrael בְּיִשְׂרָאֵל   gadol גָּדוֹל

shemo שְׁמוֹ אום, יזל, מהע"ה, ע"ב בריבוע וקס"א וקס"א ע"ה, אל שדי ע"ה: לההו, עם ד' אותיות מזבה,

tzedek צֶדֶק   lefanav לְפָנָיו   yehalech יְהַלֵּךְ   veyasem וְיָשֵׂם   lederech לְדֶרֶךְ ב"פ יב"ק

ekra אֶקְרָא   elecha אֵלֶיךָ   ki כִּי   Adonai אֲדֹנָי   chaneni וְחָנֵּנִי   pe'amav:פְּעָמָיו

kol כָּל   hayom הַיּוֹם נגד, מזבוח, זן, אל יהוה:

There are 42 letters in the verse in the secret of Ana Beko'ach.

yihyu יִהְיוּ אל (ייא"י מילוי דס"ג) מהע ע"ה, ע"ב בריבוע וקס"א וקס"א ע"ה, אל שדי ע"ה   leratzon לְרָצוֹן

imrei אִמְרֵי   fi פִּי ר"ת אֶלֶף = אלף למד ♦ עין דלת יוד ע"ה   vehegyon וְהֶגְיוֹן   libi לִבִּי

lefanecha לְפָנֶיךָ ס"ג מ"ה בן   Adonai יְהֹוָאדֹנָי   tzuri צוּרִי   vego'ali:וְגֹאֲלִי

---

the Faithful Shepherd who is sealed with the attribute of Victory, may You illuminate our eyes in Your Torah, and let our soul pursue Your commandments. Redeem us an everlasting redemption from this exile of the masses, in the merit of Moses, the Faithful Shepherd; and may You rebuild the Temple speedily in our days. And the voice of the Levite may You establish on the song and the harp of God with it, the pleasant harp together with the lyre, to administer the work of the House of the Lord. "God is renowned in Judah; his Name is great in Israel." (Psalms 76:2) "Righteousness walks before Him, and He places it on the path of His footsteps." (Psalms 85:14) "Be gracious to me, Lord, for it is to You that I call all day." (Psalms 86:3) "May the utterances of my mouth and the thoughts of my heart find favor before You, Lord, my Rock and my Redeemer." (Psalms 19:15)

THE FIFTH HAKAFAH (CIRCLING)—AARON—HOD

אָנָּ֑א na: נָ֫א ana ב"ן לכב יְהֹוֲֽאדֳנָיֲֽאהדונהי יהוה ע"ע נהורין hoshia הוֹשִׁ֫יעָ֖ה Adonai

אָנָּ֑א ana ב"ן לכב :na נָ֫א hatzlicha הַצְלִ֫יֲחָה Adonai יְהֹוֲֽאדֳנָיֲֽאהדונהי ana ב"ן לכב

יְהֹוֲֽאדֳנָיֲֽאהדונהי Adonai anenu עֲנֵ֫נוּ veyom בְּי֫וֹם ע"ה נגד, מזבח, זן, אל יהוה

קָרְאֵ֫נוּ :kor'enu melech מֶ֫לֶךְ olamim עוֹלָ֫מִים hoshia הוֹשִׁ֫יעָ֖ה יהוה ע"ע נהורין

נָ֫א na• נָ֫אוֹר na'or וְאַדִּ֫יר ve'adir הרי הַצְלִ֫יֲחָה hatzlicha נָ֫א na: סוֹמֵ֫ךְ somech כוך

נוֹפְלִים noflim anenu עֲנֵ֫נוּ veyom בְּי֫וֹם ע"ה נגד, מזבח, זן, אל יהוה kor'enu: קָרְאֵ֫נוּ

מִפִּי mipi El אֵל ייא•• El מִפִּי mipi El אֵל ייא•• yevarech יְבָרֵךְ עסמ"ב et אֶת־ יִשְׂרָאֵל :Yisrael

אֵין en adir אַדִּ֫יר הרי כִּיהֹוֲֽאדֳנָיֲֽאהדונהי kadonai• וְאֵין ve'en בָּרוּךְ baruch

כְּבֶן keven עֲמְרָם Amram• אֵין en גְּדוּלָה gedola להוו :katorah כַּתּוֹרָה katorah•

וְאֵין ve'en דּוֹרְשָׁהּ dorshah כְּיִשְׂרָאֵל keYisrael:

מִפִּי mipi El אֵל ייא•• El מִפִּי mipi yevarech יְבָרֵךְ עסמ"ב et אֶת־ יִשְׂרָאֵל :Yisrael

אֵין en הָדוּר hadur כִּיהֹוֲֽאדֳנָיֲֽאהדונהי kadonai• וְאֵין ve'en וְתִיק vatik

כְּבֶן keven עֲמְרָם Amram• אֵין en זַכָּאָה zaka'a כַּתּוֹרָה katorah•

וְאֵין ve'en וְזוֹמְדָהּ chomda כְּיִשְׂרָאֵל keYisrael:

מִפִּי mipi El אֵל ייא•• El מִפִּי mipi yevarech יְבָרֵךְ עסמ"ב et אֶת־ יִשְׂרָאֵל :Yisrael

אֵין en טָהוֹר tahor י"פ אכא כִּיהֹוֲֽאדֳנָיֲֽאהדונהי kadonai• וְאֵין ve'en יָשָׁר yashar

כְּבֶן keven עֲמְרָם Amram• אֵין en כְּבוּדָה kevuda :katorah כַּתּוֹרָה katorah•

וְאֵין ve'en לוֹמְדָהּ lomda כְּיִשְׂרָאֵל keYisrael:

מִפִּי mipi El אֵל ייא•• El מִפִּי mipi yevarech יְבָרֵךְ עסמ"ב et אֶת־ יִשְׂרָאֵל :Yisrael

---

THE FIFTH HAKAFAH (CIRCLING)—AARON—HOD

"We beseech You, Lord, save us now. We beseech You, Lord, give us success now." (Psalms 118:25)
We beseech You, Lord, answer us on the day we call. Eternal King, save now.
Illustrious and Mighty One, bring success now. Supporter of the fallen, answer us on the day we call.
There is none as powerful as the Lord. There is none as blessed as Amram's son. There is no greatness like the Torah; no one illustrates it like Israel. From God's mouth, from God's mouth, may Israel be blessed. There is none as majestic as the Lord. There is none as worthy as Amram's son. There is no merit like the Torah; it has no scholars like Israel. From God's mouth, from God's mouth, may Israel be blessed. There is none as pure as the Lord. There is none as straight as Amram's son. There is honor like the Torah; it has no students like Israel. From God's mouth, from God's mouth, may Israel be blessed.

אֵין en   מֶלֶךְ melech   כַּיְהֹוָה kadonai   וְאֵין ve'en   נָבִיא navi

כְּבֶן keven   עַמְרָם Amram   אֵין en   סוֹמְכָה somcha   כַּתּוֹרָה katorah

וְאֵין ve'en   עֹזְרָה ozra   כְּיִשְׂרָאֵל keYisrael

מִפִּי mipi   El   מִפִּי mipi   El   יְבָרֵךְ yevarech   אֶת et   יִשְׂרָאֵל Yisrael

אֵין en   פּוֹדֶה pode   כַּיְהֹוָה kadonai   וְאֵין ve'en   צַדִּיק tzadik

כְּבֶן keven   עַמְרָם Amram   אֵין en   קְדוֹשָׁה kedosha   כַּתּוֹרָה katorah

וְאֵין ve'en   רוֹזְעָה rochasha   כְּיִשְׂרָאֵל keYisrael

מִפִּי mipi   El   מִפִּי mipi   El   יְבָרֵךְ yevarech   אֶת et   יִשְׂרָאֵל Yisrael

אֵין en   שׁוֹמֵר shomer   כַּיְהֹוָה kadonai   וְאֵין ve'en   תָּמִים tamim

כְּבֶן keven   עַמְרָם Amram   אֵין en   תְּמִימָה temima   כַּתּוֹרָה katorah

וְאֵין ve'en   תּוֹמְכָה tomcha   כְּיִשְׂרָאֵל keYisrael

מִפִּי mipi   El   מִפִּי mipi   El   יְבָרֵךְ yevarech   אֶת et   יִשְׂרָאֵל Yisrael

After the circling one should say:

◇

יְמִין yemin   יְהֹוָה Adonai   רוֹמֵמָה romema   יְמִין yemin

יְהֹוָה Adonai   עֹשָׂה osa   חָיִל chayil

שְׁמַע shema   יִשְׂרָאֵל Yisrael   יְהֹוָה Adonai   אֱלֹהֵינוּ Elohenu

יְהֹוָה Adonai | אֶחָד echad

יְהֹוָה Adonai   מֶלֶךְ melech   יְהֹוָה Adonai   מָלַךְ malach

יְהֹוָה Adonai | יִמְלֹךְ yimloch

לְעֹלָם le'olam   וָעֶד va'ed

There is no king like the Lord. There is no prophet like Amram's son. There no treasure like the Torah; it has none involved with it like Israel. From God's mouth, from God's mouth, may Israel be blessed. There is none who redeems like the Lord. There is none as righteous as Amram's son. There is no holiness like the Torah; it has none who exalt it like Israel. From God's mouth, from God's mouth, may Israel be blessed. There is none as Holy as the Lord. There is none as merciful as Amram's son. There is no protection like the Torah; it has none who support it like Israel. From God's mouth, from God's mouth, may Israel be blessed. The right of the Lord is raised. The right of the Lord does mighty things." (Psalms 118:16) "Hear Israel, the Lord our God. The Lord is One." (Deuteronomy 6:4) The Lord is King, the Lord has reigned, the Lord shall reign forever and for eternity.

אָנָּא na: נהורין ע"ע יהוה הוֹשִׁיעָה hoshi'a אֲדֹנָיִאהדונהי Adonai לכב ב"ן ana אָנָּא

אָנָּא na: הַצְלִיחָה hatzlicha יְהֹוָאהדונהי Adonai לכב ב"ן ana אָנָּא

הרי adir אַדִּיר מ"ה ma מָה adonenu אֲדֹנֵינוּ יְהֹוָאהדונהי Adonai

asher אֲשֶׁר ha'aretz הָאָרֶץ אלהין דההין לכב ב"ן, bechol בְּכֹל shimcha שִׁמְךָ

תְּנָה tena י"פ טל, י"פ כוזו hasamayim הַשָּׁמַיִם קס"א קנ"א קמ"ג, נתה al עַל hodcha הוֹדְךָ

kevodo כְּבוֹדוֹ אום יזל, מבה, אותיות ד' עם להו, gadol גָּדוֹל

עָלָיו alav: teshave תְּשַׁוֶּה vehadar וְהָדָר ההה hod הוֹד bishu'atecha בִּישׁוּעָתֶךָ

וְחָסִין לאו tuvcha טוּבְךָ אהיה י"פ berov בְּרוֹב kadosh קָדוֹשׁ chasin

וְקֹבַ טנע adatecha עֲדָתֶךָ: nahel נַהֵל

יְהִי yehi ע"ה אל שדי ע"ה ratzon רָצוֹן מהשׁע ע"ה, ע"ב בריבוע וקס"א ע"ה, אל שדי ע"ה

מִלְּפָנֶיךָ milfanecha ס"ג מ"ה ב"ן Adonai יְהֹוָאהדונהי Elohenu אֱלֹהֵינוּ ילה

וֵאלֹהֵי velohei לכב ע"ב, דמב ; מילוי ע"ב, ילה avotenu אֲבוֹתֵינוּ av אָב

הָרַחֲמִים harachamim שאה. shethe שֶׁתְּהֵא chashuva וְחֲשׁוּבָה

וּמְקֻבֶּלֶת umkubelet urtzuya וּרְצוּיָה lefanecha לְפָנֶיךָ ס"ג מ"ה ב"ן hakafa הַקָּפָה

וּזְמִישִׁית chamishit haromezet הָרוֹמֶזֶת leHod לְהוֹד ההה. ke'ilu כְּאִלּוּ

כִּוַּנּוּ kivanu bechol בְּכֹל ב"ן לכב hakavanot הַכַּוָּנוֹת haruyot הָרְאוּיוֹת

lechaven לְכַוֵּן betuvcha בְּטוּבְךָ ve'ata וְאַתָּה terachem תְּרַחֵם לאו terachem ג"פ רי"ו ;

עָלֵינוּ alenu. אברהם, וז"פ אל, רי"ו ול"ב נתיבות החכמה, רמ"ז (אברים), עסמ"ב וט"ז אותיות פשוטות

וּתְזַכֵּנוּ utzakenu lechabed לְכַבֵּד hatorah הַתּוֹרָה velomdeha וְלוֹמְדֶיהָ.

ulhachazik וּלְהַחֲזִיק ulametz וּלְאַמֵּץ birkayim בִּרְכַּיִם koshlot כּוֹשְׁלוֹת

hanei הַנֵּי birkei בִּרְכֵּי derabanan דְּרַבָּנָן deshalhei דְּשָׁלְהֵי.

"We beseech You, Lord, save us now. We beseech You, Lord, give us success now." (Psalms 118:25) "Lord, our Master, how mighty is Your Name throughout the entire world, that You have spread Your splendor throughout the Heavens." (Psalms 8:2) "His honor is great through Your deliverance; splendor and majesty shall You place upon Him." (Psalms 21:6)

וְקֹבַ טנע Invincible and Mighty One, with the abundance of Your goodness, govern Your congregation. May it be pleasing before You, Lord our God, God of our fathers, Merciful Father, that there be deemed worthy and acceptable and favorable before You this fifth circling, which alludes to Splendor, as if we had intended all the meanings that are appropriate to propose. And You, in Your goodness, may You have mercy upon us; and may You cause us to merit to honor the Torah and those who study it, and to strengthen and fortify the weak knees, those weary knees of the scholars.

resha'im רְשָׁעִים ba'atzat בַּעֲצַת nelech נֵלֵךְ shelo שֶׁלֹא utzakenu וּתְזַכֵּנוּ

ulma'an וּלְמַעַן ♦rachil רָכִיל meholchei מְהוֹלְכֵי nih'ye נִהְיֶה velo וְלֹא

Adonai יְהֹוָהיֱאֱלֹהִיםיֱאֲדֹנָי kedosh קְדוֹשׁ Aharon אַהֲרֹן zechut זְכוּת

♦aka אַכָּא letova לְטוֹבָה ההה Hod הוֹד bemidat בְּמִדַּת hechatum הֶחָתוּם

shalom שָׁלוֹם ulvakesh וּלְבַקֵּשׁ shalom שָׁלוֹם lirdof לִרְדֹּף tezakenu תְּזַכֵּנוּ

shalom שָׁלוֹם ulharbot וּלְהַרְבּוֹת shalom שָׁלוֹם velasim וְלָשִׂים

♦deAharon דְּאַהֲרֹן ovada עוֹבָדָא ulme'ebad וּלְמֶעֱבַד ♦ba'olam בְּעוֹלָם

utvarchenu וּתְבָרְכֵנוּ ♦benenu בֵּינֵינוּ shalom שָׁלוֹם vetasim וְתָשִׂים

♦ulshalom וּלְשָׁלוֹם tovim טוֹבִים אהיה אהיה יהוה, בינה ע"ה lechayim לְחַיִּים

לההו, gadol גָּדוֹל ♦go'el גּוֹאֵל קנאה, ר"פ יהוה, יוסף leTziyon לְצִיּוֹן uva וּבָא

ההה Hod הוֹד bishu'atecha בִּישׁוּעָתֶךָ kevodo כְּבוֹדוֹ אום, יזל, עם ד' אותיות מבה teshave תְּשַׁוֶּה vehadar וְהָדָר

:beyamenu בְּיָמֵינוּ bimhera בִּמְהֵרָה alav עָלָיו

Initials of Hod—הוד.

velo וְלֹא אהיה אהיה יהוה, בינה ע"ה bachayim בַּחַיִּים nafshenu נַפְשֵׁנוּ hasham הַשָּׂם

li לִי Adonai יְהֹוָהיֱאֱלֹהִיםיֱאֲדֹנָי vayhi וַיְהִי :raglenu רַגְלֵנוּ lamot לַמּוֹט natan נָתַן

lemisgav לְמִשְׂגָּב מהטע, ע"ב ברבוע קס"א, אל אלהים ד"פ, אל עדי ע"ה velohai וֵאלֹהַי מילוי ע"ב,

דמב ; ילה derech דֶּרֶךְ :machsi מַחְסִי אלהים ההין ע"ה letzur לְצוּר

:libi לִבִּי tarchiv תַּרְחִיב ki כִּי arutz אָרוּץ mitzvotecha מִצְוֹתֶיךָ

There are 42 letters in the verse in the secret of Ana Beko'ach.

yihyu יִהְיוּ אל (ייא"י מילוי דס"ג) leratzon לְרָצוֹן מהטע ע"ה, ע"ב ברבוע וקס"א וקס"א ע"ה, אל שדי ע"ה

imrei אִמְרֵי fi פִי ר"ת אָלֶף = אלף למד ♦ שׁין דלת יוד ע"ה vehegyon וְהֶגְיוֹן libi לִבִּי

:vego'ali וְגֹאֲלִי tzuri צוּרִי Adonai יְהֹוָהיֱאֱלֹהִיםיֱאֲדֹנָי ס"ג מ"ה בן lefanecha לְפָנֶיךָ

And may You cause to merit that we not walk in the counsel of the wicked, and that we not be from those who bear slander. And in the merit of Aaron, the holy one of the Lord, who is sealed with the attribute of Splendor for goodness, may You cause us to merit to pursue peace, and to seek peace, and to establish peace, and to increase peace in the world, and to perform the deeds of Aaron. Establish peace among us, and bless us for a good life and for peace. And a redeemer shall come to Zion, his honor is great through Your deliverance; splendor and majesty shall You place upon him, speedily in our days. "He Who keeps us alive, and does not allow our feet to falter." (Psalms 66:9) "But the Lord was a strength for me and my God was the Rock of my refuge." (Psalms 94:22) "In the path of Your commandments I shall run, for You shall expand my heart." (Psalms 119:32) "May the utterances of my mouth and the thoughts of my heart find favor before You, Lord, my Rock and my Redeemer." (Psalms 19:15)

THE SIXTH HAKAFAH (CIRCLING)—JOSEPH—YESOD

na **נָא**: hoshi'a **הוֹשִׁיעָה** יהוה ע"ע נהורין Adonai **יְהֹוָואֲדֹנִיֵאהֱדֹוִנֵהִי** ב"ן לכב ana **אָנָּא**

לכב ב"ן ana **אָנָּא** na **נָא**: hatzlicha **הַצְלִיחָה** Adonai **יְהֹוָואֲדֹנִיֵאהֱדֹוִנֵהִי** ב"ן לכב ana **אָנָּא**

אל יהוה ז', מזבוח, נגד, ע"ה veyom **בְּיוֹם** anenu **עֲנֵנוּ** Adonai **יְהֹוָואֲדֹנִיֵאהֱדֹוִנֵהִי**

na **נָא**◆ hoshia **הוֹשִׁיעָה** יהוה ע"ע נהורין dalim **דַּלִּים** ozer **עוֹזֵר** kor'enu **קָרְאֵנוּ**:

tzur **צוּר** na **נָא**: hatzlicha **הַצְלִיחָה** הרי umatzil **וּמַצִּיל** pode **פּוֹדֶה** tzur **פּוֹדֶה**

kor'enu **קָרְאֵנוּ**: אל יהוה ז', מזבוח, נגד, ע"ה veyom **בְּיוֹם** anenu **עֲנֵנוּ** olamim **עוֹלָמִים**

ashrecha **אַשְׁרֶיךָ** nimshachta **נִמְשַׁחְתָּ** Yochai **יוֹחַאי** Bar **בַּר**

mechaverecha **מֵחֲבֵרֶיךָ**: sason **שָׂשׂוֹן** shemen **שֶׁמֶן**

Malchut

kodesh **קֹדֶשׁ**, mishchat **מִשְׁחַת** shemen **שֶׁמֶן** Yochai **יוֹחַאי** Bar **בַּר**

hakodesh **הַקֹּדֶשׁ** mimidat **מִמִּדַּת** nimshachta **נִמְשַׁחְתָּ**

hakodesh **הַקֹּדֶשׁ**, nezer **נֵזֶר** מנצ tzitz **צִיץ** nasata **נָשָׂאתָ**

Bar Yochai pe'erecha **פְּאֵרֶךָ**: roshcha **רֹאשְׁךָ** al **עַל** chavush **וְחָבוּשׁ**

Yesod

yashavta **יָשַׁבְתָּ**, והו tov **טוֹב** moshav **מוֹשַׁב** Yochai **יוֹחַאי** Bar **בַּר**

nasta **נַסְתָּ** יהוה אל ז', מזבוח, נגד, ע"ה yom **יוֹם**

barachta **בֵּרַכְתָּ** asher **אֲשֶׁר** יהוה אל ז', מזבוח, נגד, ע"ה yom **יוֹם**

sham **שָׁם** she'amadeta **שֶׁעָמַדְתָּ** tzurim **צוּרִים** bim'arat **בִּמְעָרַת**

Bar Yochai vahadarecha **וַהֲדָרֶךָ**: hodcha **הוֹדְךָ** kanita **קָנִיתָ**

THE SIXTH HAKAFAH (CIRCLING)—JOSEPH—YESOD

"We beseech You, Lord, save us now. We beseech You, Lord, give us success now." (Psalms 118:25)
We beseech You, Lord, answer us on the day we call. Helper of the destitute, save now.
Redeemer of rescuer, bring success now. Eternal Rock, answer us on the day we call.
Bar Yochai, you are anointed and praises, drawing the oil of happiness from your friends.

Malchut   Bar Yochai Holy oil anointed you from the Holy tribute.
You carried the tiara of the Holy Crown, on you head for beauty.

Yesod   Bar Yochai, you sat in good place, the day you run and escaped.
In the cave of rock you stood, to obtain your majesty and glory.

Netzach Hod

בַּר Bar · יוֹחַאי Yochai · עֲצֵי atzei · שִׁטִּים shitim · עוֹמְדִים omdim,

לִּמּוּדֵי limudei · יְהֹוָה Adonai · הֵם hem · לוֹמְדִים lomdim · אוֹר or [רו, א"ס]

מֻפְלָא mufla · הַיְקוֹד hayekod [or אוֹר, רו, א"ס] · הֵם hem · יוֹקְדִים yokdim,

הֲלֹא halo · הֵמָּה hema · יוֹרוּךְ yorucha · מוֹרֶךָ: morecha · *Bar Yochai*

Tiferet

בַּר Bar · יוֹחַאי Yochai · וְלִשְׂדֵה velisde · תַּפּוּחִים tapuchim,

עָלִיתָ alita · לִלְקוֹט lilkot · בּוֹ vo · מֶרְקָחִים merkachim,

סוֹד sod [מיכ, י"פ האא] · תּוֹרָה torah · כְּצִיצִים ketzitzim · וּפְרוּחִים ufrachim,

נַעֲשֶׂה na'ase · אָדָם adam · נֶאֱמַר ne'emar · בַּעֲבוּרֶךָ: ba'avurecha · *Bar Yochai*

Gevurah

בַּר bar · יוֹחַאי yochai · נֶאֱזַרְתָּ ne'ezarta · בִּגְבוּרָה bigvura [רי"י]

וּבְמִלְחֶמֶת uvmilchemet · אֵשׁ esh · דָּת dat · הַשַּׂעְרָה hasha'ra,

וְחֶרֶב vecherev [רי"י] · הוֹצֵאתָ hotzeta · מִתַּעְרָה mita'ra,

שָׁלַפְתָּ shalafta · נֶגֶד neged [מזבוח, זז, אל יהוה] · צוֹרְרֶךָ: tzorerecha · *Bar Yochai*

Chesed

בַּר bar · יוֹחַאי yochai · לִמְקוֹם limkom · אַבְנֵי avnei · שַׁיִשׁ shayish,

הִגַּעְתָּ higata · לִפְנֵי lifnei [וחכמה בינה] · אַרְיֵה arye · לַיִשׁ layish,

גַּם gam · גֻּלַת gulat · כּוֹתֶרֶת koteret · עַל al · עַיִשׁ ayish,

תָּשׁוּרִי tashuri · וּמִי umi [יל] · יְשׁוּרֶךָ: yeshurecha · *Bar Yochai*

Netzach Hod	*Bar Yochai, the acacia wood stands for you to study God's teachings. A wonderful, shining light is a glow, as your teachers taught you.*
Tiferet	*Bar Yochai, you came to a field of apples to gather potions. The secret of Torah is like buds and blossoms; "Let us create man" was stated with you in mind.*
Gevura	*Bar Yochai, you take courage with vigor, and fight with fire. You drew a sword out of its sheath against your opponent.*
Chesed	*Bar Yochai, to the place of marble stones, you arrived with lion's face. We will see even the headstone of lions, but who will see you?*

Binah

בַּר Bar   יוֹחַאי Yochai   בְּקֹדֶשׁ bekodesh   הַקֳּדָשִׁים hakodashim,

קַו kav   יָרֹק yarok   מְחַדֵּשׁ mechadesh   י"ב הויות, קס"א קנ"א   וָחֳדָשִׁים chodashim,

שֶׁבַע sheva   שַׁבָּתוֹת shabatot   סוֹד sod   מ"כ, י"פ האא   וַחֲמִשִׁים chamishim,

קָשַׁרְתָ kasharta   קִשְׁרֵי kishrei   שִׁי"ן shin   קְשָׁרֶיךָ kesharecha: *Bar Yochai*

Chochmah

בַּר Bar   יוֹחַאי Yochai   יו"ד yod   וְחָכְמָה chochmah   במילוי = תרי"ג (מצוות)

קְדוּמָה keduma,   הִשְׁקַפְתָ hishkafta   לִכְבוֹדוֹ lichvodo   פְּנִימָה penima

ל"ב lev   נְתִיבוֹת netivot   רֵאשִׁית reshit   תְּרוּמָה teruma,

אֶת at   כְּרוּב keruv   מִמְשַׁח mimshach   זִיו ziv   אוֹרֶךָ orecha: *Bar Yochai*

Keter

בַּר bar   יוֹחַאי yochai   אוֹר or   רו, א"ס   מֻפְלָא mufla   רוֹם rom   מַעְלָה ma'la,

יָרֵאתָ yareta   מִלְהַבִּיט milhabit   כִּי ki   רַב rav   לָהּ la,

תַּעֲלוּמָה ta'aluma   וְאַיִן ve'ayin   קוֹרֵא kore   לָהּ la,

נַמְתָ namta   עַיִן ayin   ריבוע דמ"ה   לֹא lo   תְּשׁוּרֶךָ teshurecha: *Bar Yochai*

בַּר Bar   יוֹחַאי Yochai   אַשְׁרֵי ashrei   יוֹלַדְתֶּךָ yoladetecha,

אַשְׁרֵי ashrei   הָעָם ha'am   הֵם hem   לוֹמְדֶךָ lomdecha

וְאַשְׁרֵי ve'ashrei   הָעוֹמְדִים ha'omdim   עַל al   סוֹדֶךָ sodecha   מ"כ, י"פ האא

לְבוּשֵׁי levushei   וְחֹשֶׁן choshen   תֻּמֶּיךָ tumeicha   וְאוּרֶךָ ve'urecha: *Bar Yochai*

בַּר bar   יוֹחַאי yochai   נִמְשַׁחְתָ nimshachta   אַשְׁרֶיךָ ashrecha,

שֶׁמֶן shemen   שָׂשׂוֹן sason   מֵחֲבֵרֶיךָ mechavereicha:

Binah   *Bar Yochai, in the Holy of Holies, a green line renews the months. Seven Shabbats are the secret of fifty, the letter Shins for your own connections.*

Chochmah   *Bar Yochai, the ancient Yud of Chochmah, you observed its inner honor. 32 paths are the beginning of offering; you are the Cherub from which brilliant light anoints.*

Keter   *Bar Yochai, a wonderful light of highest greatness, you feared looking to her greatness. A mystery no one can read, you sleep, and no eye can see you.*

Bar Yochai, praised be those who gave birth to you, praised be the people who study your writings. And praised be the people who can understand your secret, dress with armor of your breastplate and of your Urim and Tumim. Bar Yochai, you are anointed and praises, drawing the oil of happiness from your friends.

After the circling one should say:

יָמִין yemin יְהֹוָאדְנֵיאהדונהי Adonai רוֹמֵמָה romema ר"ת רי"י יָמִין yemin

יְהֹוָאדְנֵיאהדונהי Adonai עֹשָׂה osa רהע וָזָיל chayil ומב:

שֶׁמַע shema יִשְׂרָאֵל Yisrael יְהֹוָאדְנֵיאהדונהי Adonai אֱלֹהֵינוּ Elohenu ילה

יְהֹוָאדְנֵיאהדונהי Adonai | אֶחָד echad אהבה, דאגה:

malach מַלַךְ Adonai יְהֹוָאדְנֵיאהדונהי melech מֶלֶךְ Adonai יְהֹוָאדְנֵיאהדונהי

יְהֹוָאדְנֵיאהדונהי Adonai | yimloch יִמְלֹךְ (מֶלֶךְ מָלַךְ יִמְלֹךְ = מנצפ"ך, סנדלפון, ערי)

le'olam לְעֹלָם ריבוע דס"ג וי' אותיות דס"ג ; ר"ת ; ייל va'ed וָעֶד:

ana אָנָּא ב"ן לכב יְהֹוָאדְנֵיאהדונהי Adonai הוֹשִׁיעָה hoshi'a יהוה ש"ע נהורין na נָא:

ana אָנָּא ב"ן לכב יְהֹוָאדְנֵיאהדונהי Adonai הַצְלִיחָה hatzlicha na נָא:

tzadik צַדִּיק יְהֹוָאדְנֵיאהדונהי Adonai bechol בְּכֹל ב"ן, לכב דְּרָכָיו derachav

וְחָסִיד vechasid bechol בְּכֹל ב"ן, לכב מַעֲשָׂיו ma'asav: יָצָאתָ yatzata לְיֵשַׁע leyesha

amecha עַמֶּךָ leyesha לְיֵשַׁע et אֶת מְשִׁיחֶךָ meshichecha מָחַצְתָּ machatzta

rosh רֹאשׁ ריבוע אלהים ואלהים דיורין ע"ה mibet מִבֵּית ב"ה ראה

rasha רָשָׁע עָרוֹת arot יְסוֹד yesod ad עַד ההע tzavar צַוָּאר tzavar ad ... סֶלָה sela:

yachid יָחִיד ge'e גֵּאֶה ע"ב ס"ג. le'amcha לְעַמְּךָ pene פְּנֵה ע"ב ס"ג.

zochrei זוֹכְרֵי kedusatecha קְדוּשָׁתֶךָ: יגל פזק

yehi יְהִי ratzon רָצוֹן מהע ע"ה, ע"ב ברביעו וקס"א ע"ה, אל שדי ע"ה

milfanecha מִלְּפָנֶיךָ ס"ג מ"ה ב"ן יוהדונווהי Adonai יְהֹוָואדְנֵיאהדונהי Elohenu אֱלֹהֵינוּ ילה

velohei וֵאלֹהֵי לכב ; מ"ב, דמב ; ילה avotenu אֲבוֹתֵינוּ.

av אָב הָרַחֲמִים harachamim שאה. shethe שֶׁתְּהֵא chashuva וְחֲשׁוּבָה

The right of the Lord is raised. The right of the Lord does mighty things." (Psalms 118:16)
"Hear Israel, the Lord our God. The Lord is One." (Deuteronomy 6:4) *The Lord is King, the Lord has reigned, the Lord shall reign forever and for eternity. "We beseech You, Lord, save us now. We beseech You, Lord, give us success now."* (Psalms 118:25) *"The Lord is righteous in all His ways and magnanimous in all His Deeds."* (Psalms 145:17) *"You have gone forth to deliver Your people, to deliver Your anointed one; You have shattered the head of the house of the evil doers, unsheathing the foundation of the fortifications selah."*

יגל פזק *Sole and proud One, turn to Your people, those who remember Your sanctity.*
May it be pleasing before You, Lord our God, God of our fathers, Merciful Father, that there be deemed

וּמְקֻבֶּלֶת umkubelet · וּרְצוּיָה urtzuya · בֵּן מ"ה ס"ג lefanecha לְפָנֶיךָ · הַהַקָּפָה hakafa

הַשִּׁשִּׁית hasisit · הָרוֹמֶזֶת haromezet · לַיְסוֹד laYesod · ההע• · כְּאִלּוּ ke'ilu

כִּוַּנּוּ kivanu · בֵּן לכב בְּכָל bechol · הַכַּוָּנוֹת hakavanot · הָרְאוּיוֹת hare'uyot

לְכַוֵּן lechaven • · וְאַתָּה veAta · לאו בְּטוּבְךָ betuvcha · תְּרַחֵם terachem ג"פ רי"ו ;

עָלֵינוּ alenu• · אברהם, וז"פ אל, רי"ו ול"ב נתיבות החכמה, רמ"ח (אברים), עסמ"ב וט"ו אותיות פשוטות

וְעָוֹן ve'avon · וְחֵטְא chet ילי · מִכָּל mikol · וְתַצִּילֵנוּ vetatzilenu

וְהַרְהוּרִים vehirhurim · רָעִים ra'im • · וְאַתָּה veAta · בְּטוּבְךָ betuvcha לאו

הַגָּדוֹל hagadol לההו, עם ד' אותיות מבה, יזל, אום · תְּלַקֵּט telaket · אֲשֶׁר asher

פִּזַּרְנוּ pizarnu• · וּתְיַחֵד utyached · אֲשֶׁר asher · הִפְרַדְנוּ hifradnu•

וּתְתַקֵּן utetaken · אֲשֶׁר asher · עִוַּתְנוּ ivatnu• · וְתוֹצִיא vetotzi · לָאוֹר la'or רז, א"ס

כָּל kol ילי · הַנִּיצוֹצוֹת hanitzotzot · שֶׁל shel · קְדֻשָּׁה kedusa · אֲשֶׁר asher

נִטְמְעוּ nitme'u · בֵּין ben · הַקְּלִפּוֹת hakelipot• · וְ"חַיִל chayil ומב · בָּלָע bala

וַיְקִאֶנּוּ vayki'enu ר"ת וחבו ו- ילי · מִבִּטְנוֹ mibitno · יוֹרִישֶׁנּוּ yorishenu

אֵל El ייא"י (מלוי דס"ג) ; ס"ת וכל וּתְזַכֵּנוּ utzakenu • · לִשְׁמֹר lishmor · עַצְמֵנוּ atzmenu

וּדְרָכֵינוּ udrachenu · מִכָּל mikol ילי · וְחֵטְא chet• · וְלֹא velo · יִמָּצֵא yimatze

בָּנוּ banu · וְלֹא velo · בְּזַרְעֵנוּ bezarenu · שׁוּם shum · פְּגָם pegam•

וְיִהְיֶה veyihye יי" · כָּל kol ילי · זַרְעֵנוּ zarenu · זֶרַע zera · קֹדֶשׁ kodesh•

וּבִזְכוּת uvizchut · יוֹסֵף Yosef ציון, ר"פ יהוה, קנאה · צַדִּיקֶךָ tzadikecha

הֶחָתוּם hechatum · בְּמִדַּת bemidat · הַיְסוֹד haYesod ההע•

---

worthy and acceptable and favorable before You this sixth circling, which alludes to Foundation, as if we had intended all the meanings that are appropriate to propose. And You, in Your goodness, may You have mercy upon us; and rescue us from all sin and iniquity and evil thoughts. And You in Your great goodness, may You gather that which we have dispersed, and may You unify that which we have separated, and may You rectify that which we have corrupted, and may You bring to light all the sparks of holiness that have been plunged among the klipot. "He has devoured wealth, he shall vomit it from his stomach, God shall chase it out." (Job 20:15) May You cause us to merit to guard ourselves and our paths from all sin. And let there not be found in us nor in our offspring any blemish; and may all our progeny be holy seed. and in the merit of Joseph, Your righteous one, who is sealed in the attribute of Foundation,

תְּרַחֵם terachem ג'פ רי"ו ; אברהם, וז"פ אל, רי"ו ול"ב נתיבות החוכמה, רמ"וז (אברים), עסמ"ב וט"ז

אותיות פשוטות alenu עָלֵינוּ Shadai שַׁדָי מהע, ע"ב בריבוע קס"א, אל שדי, ד"פ אלהים ע"ה. El אֵל

teromamna תְּרוֹמַמְנָה Tziyon צִיּוֹן יוסף, ר"פ יהוה, קנאה. yesod יְסוֹד ההע yased יַסֵד

karnot קַרְנוֹת tzadik צַדִּיק uvizchut וּבִזְכוּת Yosef יוֹסֵף ציון, ר"פ יהוה, קנאה.

yosif יוֹסִיף Adonai אֲדֹנָי ללה shenit שֵׁנִית yado יָדוֹ veyig'alenu וְיִגְאָלֵנוּ

ge'ulat גְּאֻלַּת olam עוֹלָם bimhera בִּמְהֵרָה beyamenu בְּיָמֵינוּ:

Initials of Yesod—יסוד.

yisha יֵשַׁע veracha בְּרָכָה me'et מֵאֵת ר"ת יבמ Adonai יְהֹוָהאדנייאהדונהי

utzdaka וּצְדָקָה ע"ה ריבוע אלהים me'elohei מֵאֱלֹהֵי מילוי ע"ב, דמב ; ילה

yish'o יִשְׁעוֹ עכינה ע"ה ; ס"ת יהוה: sur סוּר mera מֵרַע va'ase וַעֲשֵׂה tov טוֹב והו

bakesh בַּקֵּשׁ shalom שָׁלוֹם verodfehu וְרָדְפֵהוּ: vehaya וְהָיָה יהה, יהוה

ke'etz כְּעֵץ shatul שָׁתוּל al עַל palgei פַּלְגֵי mayim מָיִם asher אֲשֶׁר

piryo פִּרְיוֹ yiten יִתֵּן be'ito בְּעִתּוֹ ve'alehu וְעָלֵהוּ lo לֹא yibol יִבּוֹל

vechol וְכֹל ילי asher אֲשֶׁר ya'ase יַעֲשֶׂה yatzli'ach יַצְלִיחַ:

derachai דְּרָכַי siparti סִפַּרְתִּי vata'aneni וַתַּעֲנֵנִי lamdeni לַמְּדֵנִי chukecha וְחֻקֶּיךָ:

There are 42 letters in the verse in the secret of *Ana Beko'ach*.

yihyu יִהְיוּ אל (יי"י מילוי דס"ג) leratzon לְרָצוֹן מהע ע"ה, ע"ב בריבוע וקס"א וקס"א ע"ה, אל שדי ע"ה

imrei אִמְרֵי fi פִי ר"ת אלף = אלף למד למד ד עין דלת יוד ע"ה vehegyon וְהֶגְיוֹן אלף למד ד עין דלת יוד ע"ה libi לִבִּי

lefanecha לְפָנֶיךָ ס"ג מ"ה ב"ן Adonai יְהֹוָהאדנייאהדונהי tzuri צוּרִי vego'ali וְגֹאֲלִי:

---

may You have mercy upon us. El Shaddai, reestablish the foundation of Zion; let the horns of the righteous be uplifted. And in the merit of Joseph, may the Lord extend His hand a second time, and may He redeem us an everlasting redemption, speedily in our days. "He shall receive blessing from the Lord, and beneficence from God of his salvation." (Psalms 24:5) "Turn away from evil and do good; seek peace and pursue it." (Psalms 34:15) "He will be like a tree that is planted at the brook of water that yields its fruit at its proper time, and whose leaves do not wither; in all that he does, he will succeed." (Psalms 1:3) "I have related my needs and You have answered me; teach me Your laws." (Psalms 119:26) "May the utterances of my mouth and the thoughts of my heart find favor before You, Lord, my Rock and my Redeemer." (Psalms 19:15)

THE SEVENTH HAKAFAH (CIRCLING)—DAVID—MALCHUT

na **נָא** נהורין ע״ע יהוה hoshi'a **הוֹשִׁיעָה** Adonai יְהֹוָאדנׁיאהדונהי לכב ב״ן ana **אָנָא**

לכב ב״ן ana **אָנָא** na **נָא** hatzlicha **הַצְלִיוָה** Adonai יְהֹוָאדנׁיאהדונהי לכב ב״ן ana **אָנָא**

אל יהוה זן, מזבח, נגד, ע״ה veyom **בְּיוֹם** anenu **עֲנֵנוּ** Adonai יְהֹוָאדנׁיאהדונהי

נהורין ע״ע יהוה hoshi'a **הוֹשִׁיעָה** venora **וְנוֹרָא** kadosh **קָדוֹשׁ** kor'enu **קָרְאֵנוּ**

na **נָא** hatzlicha **הַצְלִיוָה** vechanun **וְחַנּוּן** rachum **רַחוּם** na **נָא**

veyom **בְּיוֹם** anenu **עֲנֵנוּ** haberit **הַבְּרִית** יהוה פ כ״א shomer **שׁוֹמֵר**

temimim **תְּמִימִים** tomech **תּוֹמֵךְ** kor'enu **קָרְאֵנוּ** אל יהוה זן, מזבח, נגד, ע״ה

ב״ן ב״פ la'ad **לְעַד** takif **תַּקִיף** na **נָא** נהורין ע״ע יהוה hoshi'a **הוֹשִׁיעָה**

bema'asav **בְּמַעֲשָׂיו** tamim **תָּמִים** na **נָא** hatzlicha **הַצְלִיוָה**

kor'enu **קָרְאֵנוּ** אל יהוה זן, מזבח, נגד, ע״ה veyom **בְּיוֹם** anenu **עֲנֵנוּ**

After the circling one should say:

yemin **יְמִין** ר״ת רי יְמִין romema **רוֹמֵמָה** Adonai יְהֹוָאדנׁיאהדונהי yemin **יְמִין**

ומב: chayil **וָיִל** osa **עֹשָׂה** רהע Adonai יְהֹוָאדנׁיאהדונהי

ילה Elohenu **אֱלֹהֵינוּ** Adonai יְהֹוָאדנׁיאהדונהי Yisrael **יִשְׂרָאֵל** shema **שְׁמַע**

יְהֹוָאדנׁיאהדונהי echad **אֶחָד** Adonai | אהבה, דאה:

malach **מָלַךְ** Adonai יְהֹוָאדנׁיאהדונהי melech **מֶלֶךְ** Adonai יְהֹוָאדנׁיאהדונהי

עָרי, סנדלפון, מנצֿנֿר = יִמְלֹךְ מָלַךְ מֶלֶךְ yimloch **יִמְלֹךְ** Adonai | יְהֹוָאדנׁיאהדונהי

va'ed **וָעֶד** ייל ר״ת ; דס״ג וי אותיות דס״ג ריבוע le'olam **לְעֹלָם**

THE SEVENTH HAKAFAH (CIRCLING)—DAVID—MALCHUT
"We beseech You, Lord, save us now. We beseech You, Lord, give us success now." (Psalms 118:25)
We beseech You, Lord, answer us on the day we call. Holy and Awesome One, save now.
Merciful and Gracious One, bring success now. Keeper of the covenant, answer us on the day we call.
Supporter of the wholesome, save now.
Eternally strong One, bring success now. Perfect in His deeds, answer us on the day we call.
The right of the Lord is raised.
The right of the Lord does mighty things." (Psalms 118:16) "Hear Israel, the Lord our God. The Lord is One." (Deuteronomy 6:4) The Lord is King, the Lord has reigned, the Lord shall reign forever and for eternity.

אָנָּא na: נָּא נהורין ע״ע יהוה hoshi'a הוֹשִׁיעָה Adonai יְהֹוָאדֹנֵיאהדונהי לכב ב״ן ana אָנָּא

אָנָּא na: נָּא hatzlicha הַצְלִיחָה Adonai יְהֹוָאדֹנֵיאהדונהי לכב ב״ן ana אָנָּא

verav וְרַב ע״ב יהוה vesalach וְסָלַּח והו tov טוֹב ללה Adonai אֲדֹנָי Ata אַתָּה ki כִּי

malchutcha מַלְכוּתְךָ kor'echa קֹרְאֶיךָ: אדני יה lechol לְכֹל ריבוע יהוה ע״ב, chesed וְחֶסֶד

umemshaltecha וּמֶמְשַׁלְתְּךָ olamim עֹלָמִים ילי kol כָּל malchut מַלְכוּת

Adonai יְהֹוָאדֹנֵיאהדונהי lecha לְךָ: רי״ו vador וָדוֹר dor דּוֹר לכב ב״ן bechol בְּכָל

vehanetzach וְהַנֵּצַח vehatiferet וְהַתִּפְאֶרֶת רי״ו vehagevura וְהַגְּבוּרָה hagedula הַגְּדֻלָּה

basamayim בַּשָּׁמַיִם ילי chol כֹל ki כִּי ההה vehahod וְהַהוֹד

hamamlacha הַמַּמְלָכָה Adonai יְהֹוָאדֹנֵיאהדונהי lecha לְךָ uva'aretz וּבָאָרֶץ

vehamitnase וְהַמִּתְנַשֵּׂא lechol לְכֹל אדני יה lerosh לְרֹאשׁ:

tza'akatenu צַעֲקָתֵנוּ ushma וּשְׁמַע kabel קַבֵּל shav'atenu שַׁוְעָתֵנוּ

ta'alumot תַּעֲלוּמוֹת yode'a יוֹדֵעַ שׁקו צית

ratzon רָצוֹן מהשע ע״ה, בריבוע וקס״א ע״ב, מ״ה yehi יְהִי

Elohenu אֱלֹהֵינוּ Adonai יְהֹוָאדֹנֵיאהדונהי ב״ן מ״ה ס״ג milfanecha מִלְּפָנֶיךָ

El אֵל avotenu אֲבוֹתֵינוּ velohei וֵאלֹהֵי מילוי ע״ב, דמב ; ילה

lema'an לְמַעַן sheta'ase שֶׁתַּעֲשֶׂה rachamim רַחֲמִים maleh מָלֵא

umkubelet וּמְקֻבֶּלֶת chashuva וְחֲשׁוּבָה uthe וּתְהֵא rachamecha רַחֲמֶיךָ

shevi'it שְׁבִיעִית hakafa הַקָּפָה ס״ג מ״ה ב״ן lefanecha לְפָנֶיךָ urtzuya וּרְצוּיָה

kivanu כִּוַּנּוּ ke'ilu כְּאִלּוּ laMalchut לַמַּלְכוּת haromezet הָרוֹמֶזֶת

lechaven לְכַוֵּן hare'uyot הָרְאוּיוֹת hakavanot הַכַּוָּנוֹת לכב ב״ן bechol בְּכָל

"We beseech You, Lord, save us now. We beseech You,
Lord, give us success now." (Psalms 118:25) For You are the Lord, good and forgiving, and abundant in mercy
to all who call upon You. Your Kingdom is a kingdom of all the worlds and Your reign is in each and every
generation. (Psalms 145:13) "Yours, Lord, are the greatness, the might, the glory, the victory and the splendor,
for everything in the Heavens and Earth; Yours Lord is the reign and all those who ascend to lead.
שׁקו צית *Accept our cry and hear our wail, You that knows all that is hidden.*
May it be pleasing before You, Lord our God, God of our fathers,
Merciful Father, that there be deemed worthy and acceptable and favorable before You this seventh
circling, which alludes to Kingdom, as if we had intended all the meanings that are appropriate to propose.

וְאַתָּה veAta בְּטוּבְךָ betuvcha לאו תְּרוֹזֵם terachem ג"פ רי"ו ; אברהם, וז"פ אל, רי"ו ול"ב

וְתִגְלֶה vetigaleh ◆alenu עָלֵינוּ נתיבות החכמה, רמ"ח (אברים), עסמ"ב וט"ז אותיות פשוטות

וְתֵרָאֶה vetera'e מַלְכוּתְךָ malchutcha עָלֵינוּ alenu מְהֵרָה mehera◆

מְלֹךְ meloch עַל al כָּל kol ; עמם יְלִי הָעוֹלָם ha'olam כֻּלּוֹ kulo

בִּכְבוֹדֶךָ bichvodach ב"ן, לכב וְהָיְתָה vehayta לַיהֹוָה-אהדונהי ladonai

הַמְּלוּכָה hamelucha: יְהֹוָה-אהדונהי Adonai יִמְלֹךְ yimloch לְעֹלָם le'olam

יְהֹוָה-אהדונהי ha'aretz רביע ס"ג עם י' אותיות ; ר"ת ייל וְהָיָה vehaya יהה, יהוה וְנֶאֱמַר vene'emar: וְעֵד va'ed:

לִמְלֹךְ lemelech עַל al כָּל kol ; עמם ילי הָאָרֶץ ha'aretz

בַּיּוֹם bayom ע"ה נגד, מזבח, זן, אל יהוה ע"ה הַהוּא hahu יִהְיֶה yihye ייי

אֶחָד echad אהבה, דאגה מהש ע"ה, ע"ב ברביוע וּשְׁמוֹ ushmo יְהֹוָה-אהדונהי Adonai

לְמַעַן lema'an וְעָשֶׂה va'ase: דאגה, אהבה אֶחָד echad ע"ה עדי אל, וקס"א ע"ה

דָּוִד David הַמֶּלֶךְ hamelech עָלָיו alav הַשָּׁלוֹם hasalom הַוֹּזָתוּם hechatum

בְּמִדַת bemidat ◆malchut מַלְכוּת וְתִשְׁרֶה vetishre שְׁכִינָתְךָ shechinatcha

עָלֵינוּ alenu◆ יְהִי yehi יְהֹוָה-אהדונהי Adonai אֱלֹהֵינוּ Elohenu ילה

עִמָּנוּ imanu ריבוע ס"ג כַּאֲשֶׁר ka'asher הָיָה haya יהה עִם im

אֲבֹתֵינוּ avotenu אַל al יַעַזְבֵנוּ ya'azvenu וְאַל ve'al יִטְּשֵׁנוּ yitshenu:

Initials of *Malchut*—מלכות.

מְהֻלָּל mehulal אֶקְרָא ekra יְהֹוָה-אהדונהי Adonai וּמִן umin אֹיְבַי oyvai

אִוָּשֵׁעַ ivashe'a: לְעוֹלָם le'olam ריבוע ס"ג עם י' אותיות יְהֹוָה-אהדונהי Adonai

דְּבָרְךָ devarcha ראה נִצָּב nitzav בַּשָּׁמַיִם basamayim י"פ טל, י"פ כוזו:

כִּי ki וְחַסְדְּךָ chasdecha עם ד' אותיות מובה, יזל, אום חָדוֹל gadol להו,

עָלַי alai וְהִצַּלְתָּ vehitzalta נַפְשִׁי nafshi מִשְּׁאוֹל mishe'ol תַּחְתִּיָּה tachtiya:

And You, in Your goodness, may You have mercy upon us; and let your Kingdom be revealed and seen over us speedily. Reign over the entire universe with Your glory, and the Kingdom will be the Lords. The Lord will be King over the entire world. And it says: "on that day the Lord will be One and his Name will be One." (Zachariah 14:9) Act for the sake of King David, may peace be upon him, who is sealed with the attribute of Kingdom. And may Your Shechinah dwell upon us. "May the Lord, our God, be with us as He is with our forefathers, may He not abandon us nor forsake us." (1 Kings 8:57)
"Praises I shall call to the Lord and will I thus be saved from my enemies." (Psalms 18:4)
"Forever, Lord, your word is setteled in Heaven." (Psalms 119:89) "For Your kindness to me has been great, and You have rescued my soul from the deepest abyss." (Psalms 86:13)

וַאֲנִי va'ani אני | כְּזַיִת kezayit | רַעֲנָן ra'anan | בְּבֵית bevet ב"פ ראה | אֱלֹהִים Elohim ילה

בָּטַחְתִּי batachti | בְּחֶסֶד vechesed ע"ב, ריבוע יהוה | אֱלֹהִים Elohim ילה | עוֹלָם olam

וָעֶד :va'ed | תַּאֲוַת ta'avat | עֲנָוִים anavim | שָׁמַעְתָּ shamata | יְהֹוָה Adonai אלהיאהדונהי

תָּכִין tachin | לִבָּם libam | תַּקְשִׁיב takshiv | אָזְנֶךָ oznecha | יוד הי ואו הה:

רִבּוֹנוֹ ribono | שֶׁל shel | עוֹלָם olam◆ | הִנֵּה hineh | אֲנַוְנוּ anachnu

בָּאִים ba'im | בְּיִרְאָה beyir'a רי"ו ראה | וְאַהֲבָה ve'ahava אוזר, דאגה

וְשִׂמְחָה vesimcha | רַבָּה raba◆ | וּמוֹדִים umodim מאה ברכות | אֲנַוְנוּ anachnu

לָךְ lach | עַל al | אֲשֶׁר asher | קִדַּשְׁתָּנוּ kidashtanu | בְּמִצְוֹתֶיךָ bemitzvotecha

וּבָחַרְתָּ uvacharta | בָּנוּ banu | מִכָּל mikol | הָעַמִּים ha'amim◆ | אָהַבְתָּ ahavta

אוֹתָנוּ otanu | וְרָצִיתָ veratzita | בָּנוּ banu◆ | וַתִּתֶּן vatiten ב"פ כהת | לָנוּ lanu

אֶת et | תּוֹרָתְךָ toratcha | הַקְּדוֹשָׁה hakedosha | תּוֹרָה torah

שֶׁבִּכְתָב shebichtav | וְתוֹרָה vetorah | שֶׁבְּעַל shebal מילה | פֶּה pe | שֶׁבְּעַל

וְקֵרַבְתָּנוּ vekeravtanu◆ | לַעֲבוֹדָתֶךָ la'avodatecha◆ | מָה ma

אֲנַוְנוּ anachnu◆ | מָה ma | וְחַיֵּינוּ chayenu◆ | אֲשֶׁר asher | עָשִׂיתָ asita

עִמָּנוּ imanu | וְחֲסָדִים chasadim | גְּדוֹלִים gedolim | רַבִּים rabim

וַעֲצוּמִים va'atzumim | כָּאֵלֶּה ka'ele◆ | לְפִיכָךְ lefichach | אֲנַוְנוּ anachnu

וְחַיָּבִים chayavim | לְהוֹדוֹת lehodot | לָךְ lach | תָּמִיד tamid

וְלוֹמַר velomar | לְפָנֶיךָ lefanecha | שִׁירָה shira | בְּכָל bechol | יוֹם yom

יוֹם yom | אֵל יהוה | תָּמִיד tamid :

"I am like a fresh olive tree in the House of God; I have trused in the kindness of God forever and ever." (Psalms 52:10) *"The desires of the humble You hear, the Lord; may You prepare their heart, may Your ears hearken."* (Psalms 10:17) *Master of the World we hereby come with reverence and love and great joy, and we give thanks to You for that which You sanctified us with Your commandments, and You chose us from among all the nations. You loved us and You favored us and You gave us Your Holy Torah, the written Torah, and the oral Torah, and You drew us near to Your service. What are we? What is our life that You have performed for us many great and mighty kindnesses such as these. Therefore, we are duty bound to thank You constantly, and to express song before You, every day, constantly.*

amnam אָמְנָם	gadal גָּדַל	tza'arenu צַעֲרֵנוּ	beha'alotenu בְּהַעֲלוֹתֵנוּ
al עַל	levavenu לְבָבֵנוּ	kol כָּל ילי	asher אֲשֶׁר	nitrasalnu נִתְרַשַּׁלְנוּ
mila'asok מִלַּעֲסֹק	betoratcha בְּתוֹרָתְךָ	hakedosha הַקְּדוֹשָׁה ◆	vechol וְכָל ילי
asher אֲשֶׁר	pagamnu פָּגַמְנוּ	belimudenu בְּלִמּוּדֵנוּ ◆	hen הֵן	mitzad מִצַּד
limud לִמּוּד	lehitgadel לְהִתְגַּדֵּל,	hen הֵן	mitzad מִצַּד	shelo שֶׁלֹּא
lamadnu לָמַדְנוּ	bikdusha בִּקְדֻשָּׁה	vcyir'a וְיִרְאָה ראה ריי	kedat כְּדָת	ma בֹּה מ״ה
lehavin לְהָבִין	tarachnu טָרַחְנוּ	shelo שֶׁלֹּא	vehen וְהֵן	la'asot לַעֲשׂוֹת ◆
ve'omek וְעֹמֶק	hadin הַדִּין	mitzuy מִצּוּי,	buryo בּוּרְיוֹ	al עַל ראה	davar דָּבָר
malu'ach בְּמִלּוּי	katafnu קָטַפְנוּ	asher אֲשֶׁר	vehen וְהֵן	hahalacha הַהֲלָכָה ◆
tamachnu תְּמַכְנוּ	lo לֹא	asher אֲשֶׁר	vehen וְהֵן	si'ach שִׂיחַ ◆	alei עֲלֵי
imatznu אִמַּצְנוּ	velo וְלֹא	deshalhei דְּשַׁלְהֵי ◆	derabanan דְרַבָּנָן	birkei בִּרְכֵּי
vechazot וְכָזֹאת	vechazot וְכָזֹאת	koshlot כּוֹשְׁלוֹת ◆	birkayim בִּרְכַּיִם
toratecha תּוֹרָתְךָ ◆	otiyot אוֹתִיּוֹת	bechafbet בְּכַ״ב אבא	pagamnu פָּגַמְנוּ
nahagnu נָהַגְנוּ	velo וְלֹא ◆	uvhora'a וּבְהוֹרָאָה ◆	belimud בְּלִמּוּד	veta'inu וְטָעִינוּ
ve'od וְעוֹד ◆	chachamim וַחֲכָמִים	talmidei תַּלְמִידֵי	betachsis בְּטַכְסִיס
toratenu תּוֹרָתֵנוּ	nitzotzei נִיצוֹצֵי	naflu נָפְלוּ	asher אֲשֶׁר	acheret אַחֶרֶת,
vayishb וַיִּשְׁב	nishbarim נִשְׁבָּרִים	levorot לִבוֹרוֹת	umitzvotenu וּמִצְוֹתֵינוּ
boshnu בּוֹשְׁנוּ	hakol הַכֹּל ילי	al עַל	shevi שֶׁבִי ◆	mimenu מִמֶּנּוּ
nafshenu נַפְשֵׁנוּ ◆	tivke תִּבְכֶּה	uvamistarim וּבַמִּסְתָּרִים	venichlamnu וְנִכְלַמְנוּ

However our anguish is great when we consider in our heart all that we have been lax from delving into Your Holy Torah, and all that we have defiled in our study, whether due to study for the sake of honor or due to our not having studied with holiness and reverence, as is proper to act; or our not having exerted ourselves to understand the subject matter clearly, extract the law, and the depth of the law; or having plucked crabgrass leaves of trees; or for our not having supported and sustained the weary knees of the scholars, our not having strengthened knees. And in many similar ways we have caused defects in the twenty-two letters of Your Torah, and we have erred in study and in ruling and we have not conducted in the matter of Torah scholars. And yet another thing: that the sparks of our Torah and Precepts have fallen to depths that are ruptured and he has taken a captive from it. For everything we are ashamed and humiliated, and our soul weeps in private;

yir'a יִרְאָה רי"י   vara'ad וְרַעַד   yavo יָבֹא   banu בָּנוּ   vatchasenu וַתְּכַסֵּנוּ

palatzut פַּלָּצוּת   vehen וְהֵן   ata עַתָּה   bevoshet בְּבֹשֶׁת   panim פָּנִים

anachnu אֲנַחְנוּ   shavim שָׁבִים   umitchartim וּמִתְחָרְטִים   va'anachnu וַאֲנַחְנוּ

rotzim רוֹצִים   la'asot לַעֲשׂוֹת   retzoncha רְצוֹנְךָ   kirtzoncha כִּרְצוֹנְךָ   vihi וִיהִי

ratzon רָצוֹן   milfanecha מִלְּפָנֶיךָ

Adonai יְהֹוָה   Elohenu אֱלֹהֵינוּ   velohei וֵאלֹהֵי

avotenu אֲבוֹתֵינוּ   El אֵל   rachum רַחוּם   vechanun וְחַנּוּן

hatov הַטּוֹב   vehametiv וְהַמֵּטִיב   shetkabel שֶׁתְּקַבֵּל   kavanatenu כַּוָּנָתֵנוּ

ki כִּי   Ata אַתָּה   bochen בּוֹחֵן   libot לִבּוֹת   veyadata וְיָדַעְתָּ

sheretzonenu שֶׁרְצוֹנֵנוּ   la'asot לַעֲשׂוֹת   retzoncha רְצוֹנְךָ   vela'asok וְלַעֲסֹק

betoratcha בְּתוֹרָתְךָ   hakedosha הַקְּדוֹשָׁה   kedat כְּדָת   ma מַה

la'asot לַעֲשׂוֹת   veAta וְאַתָּה   hivtachtanu הִבְטַחְתָּנוּ   al עַל   yedei יְדֵי

avadecha עֲבָדֶיךָ   chachmei וְחַכְמֵי   Yisrael יִשְׂרָאֵל   haba הַבָּא   litaher לִטַּהֵר

mesay'in מְסַיְּעִין   oto אוֹתוֹ   uvchen וּבְכֵן   yehemu יֶהֱמוּ   na נָא

rachamecha רַחֲמֶיךָ   ur'e וּרְאֵה   ki כִּי   azlat אָזְלַת   yad יָד   ve'efes וְאָפֵס

atzur עָצוּר   ve'azuv וְעָזוּב   va'avir וַאֲוִיר   eretz אֶרֶץ   ha'amim הָעַמִּים

hatahora הַטָּהֳרָה   vetokef וְתֹקֶף   galut גָּלוּת   guf גּוּף   vanefesh וָנֶפֶשׁ   uvitul וּבִטּוּל

hen הֵן   hena הֵנָּה   hayu הָיוּ   be'ochrenu בְּעׇכְרֵנוּ   ki כִּי   gavar גָּבַר

oyev אוֹיֵב   yitzrenu יִצְרֵנוּ   hara הָרָע   ve'asa וְעָשָׂה   asher אֲשֶׁר   zamam זָמַם

lehadichenu לְהַדִּיחֵנוּ   mitoratcha מִתּוֹרָתְךָ   ume'avodatecha וּמֵעֲבוֹדָתְךָ

---

fear and trembling come upon us and we are covered with trepidation. And behold now, shamefaced, we repent and regret and we wish to do Your desire, as is Your will, Lord our God, God of our fathers, God, Compassionate One and Gracious One, Who is good and beneficent, that You accept our intention, for You examine hearts and You know that it is our desire to do Your will and to delve into Your Holy Torah, as is proper to act. And You promised us through Your servants, the sages of Israel: One who comes to be purified, they assist him. And thus, may Your compassion please be stirred, and see that the hands keep getting stronger and there are none to be led or helped. And the atmosphere of the land of the nations, and the end of purity, and the overwhelming exile of body and soul, it is they that have been our destruction, for the enemy has triumphed, our evil inclination, and he has carried out his design to push us away from Your Torah and from Your service.

vaharei וַהֲרֵי anachnu אֲנַוְזנוּ mekablim מְקַבְּלִים alenu עָלֵינוּ mitzvat מִצְוַת

aseh עֲשֵׂה shel שֶׁל hateshuva הַתְשׁוּבָה kakatuv כַּכָּתוּב batorah בַּתּוֹרָה׃

veshavta וְשַׁבְתָּ ad עַד Adonai יְהֹוָה Elohecha אֱלֹהֶיךָ

veshamata וְשָׁמַעְתָּ vekolo בְּקֹלוֹ vaharei וַהֲרֵי anachnu אֲנַוְזנוּ

mitchartim מִתְחָרְטִים al עַל asher אֲשֶׁר nitrashalnu נִתְרַשַּׁלְנוּ

mila'asok מִלַּעֲסֹק betoratcha בְּתוֹרָתְךָ hakedosha הַקְּדוֹשָׁה veAta וְאַתָּה

El אֵל chanun וְזַנּוּן verachum וְרַוֶזם hatov הַטּוֹב

vehametiv וְהַמֵּטִיב bochen בּוֹוֶזן libot לְבּוֹת uchlayot וּכְלָיוֹת galuy גָּלוּי

veyadu'a וְיָדוּעַ lefanecha לְפָנֶיךָ shertzonenu שֶׁרְצוֹנֵנוּ la'asot לַעֲשׂוֹת

retzoncha רְצוֹנְךָ vela'asok וְלַעֲסֹק betoratcha בְּתוֹרָתְךָ hakedosha הַקְּדוֹשָׁה

kedat כְּדָת ma מַה la'asot לַעֲשׂוֹת ela אֶלָּא sheyitzrenu שֶׁיִּצְרֵנוּ

hara הָרַע hu הוּא me'akev מְעַכֵּב׃ uvchen וּבְכֵן en אֵין

lanu לָנוּ go'el גּוֹאֵל umoshi'a וּמוֹשִׁיעַ biltecha בִּלְתְּךָ

haneshama הַנְּשָׁמָה lach לָךְ vehaguf וְהַגּוּף pa'olach פָּעְלָךְ chusa וְזוּסָה

al עַל amalach עֲמָלָךְ uvcho'ach וּבְכוֹוַז sheva שֶׁבַע hakafot הַקָּפוֹת

shehikafnu שֶׁהִקַּפְנוּ lateva לַתֵּיבָה sheba שֶׁבָּה sefer סֵפֶר hatorah הַתּוֹרָה

vesimachtanu וְשִׂמַוְזתָּנוּ lichvod לִכְבוֹד toratecha תּוֹרָתְךָ

titmale תִּתְמַלֵּא rachamim רַוֲזמִים alenu עָלֵינוּ hashivenu הֲשִׁיבֵנוּ

avinu אָבִינוּ letoratecha לְתוֹרָתְךָ vekarvenu וְקָרְבֵנוּ malkenu מַלְכֵּנוּ

la'avodatecha לַעֲבוֹדָתֶךָ veyitmatku וְיִתְמַתְּקוּ hadinim הַדִּינִים

We hereby accept upon ourselves the positive commandment of repentance, as is written in the Torah: "And you shall return unto the Lord, your God, and you shall hearken to His voice." (Deuteronomy 4:30) And we hereby regret our having been negligent from delving into Your Holy Torah. And You, Almighty God, Gracious One and Compassionate One, Who is good and beneficent, Who examines thoughts and emotions, it is revealed and known before You that it is our desire to do Your will and to delve into Your Holy Torah, as is proper to act, but our evil inclination prevents. And thus, we have no redeemer nor savior other than You. The soul is Yours and the body is Your work, take pity on Your labor. And with the power of the seven circlings that we have circled around the bima upon which is the Torah Scroll, and we have rejoiced for the honor of Your Torah, may You be filled with mercy for us. Bring us back, our Father, to Your Torah, and bring us near, our King, to Your service. May the Judgments be sweetened,

וְיִכְבְּשׁוּ veyichbeshu — רַחֲמֶיךָ rachamecha — אֶת et — כַּעַסְךָ ka'asecha

וְיִגֹּלוּ veyigolu — רַחֲמֶיךָ rachamecha — עַל al — בְּמִדּוֹתֶיךָ midotecha — וְתוֹצִיא vetotzi

לָאוֹר la'or — רז, א"ס — כָּל kol — יל׳ — נִיצוֹצֵי nitzotzei — תּוֹרָתֵנוּ toratenu

וּמִצְוֹתֵינוּ umitzotenu — וְיָשׁוּב veyashuv — הַכֹּל hakol — לְאֵיתָנוֹ le'etano

הָרִאשׁוֹן harishon — וְלֹא velo — יִדַּח yidach — מִמֶּנּוּ mimenu — נִדָּח nidach

וּתְזַכֵּנוּ utzakenu — לַעֲסֹק la'asok — בַּתּוֹרָה batorah — לִשְׁמָהּ lishmah — לִלְמֹד lilmod

וּלְלַמֵּד ulelamed — לִשְׁמוֹר lishmor — וְלַעֲשׂוֹת vela'asot — וּלְהוֹצִיא ulhotzi

לָאוֹר la'or — רז, א"ס — כָּל kol — יל׳ — וְחֶלְקֵי chelkei — פַּרְדֵּ"ס pardes

תּוֹרָתֵנוּ toratenu — הַשַּׁיָּכִים hasayachim — לְנַפְשֵׁנוּ lenafshenu — רוּחֵנוּ ruchenu

וְנִשְׁמָתֵנוּ venishmatenu — וּתְחָנֵּנוּ utchonenu — מֵאִתְּךָ me'itcha — וְחָכְמָה Chochmah

(מצוות) תרי"ג במילוי — בִּינָה Binah — ע"ה וזיים, ע"ה אהיה אהיה יהוה — וָדַעַת vaDa'at

לְחַדֵּשׁ lechadesh — י"ב הוויות, קס"א קנ"א — וְחִדּוּשִׁים chidushim — רַבִּים rabim

אֲמִתִּיִּים amitiyim — בְּפַרְדֵּ"ס befardes — תּוֹרָתְךָ toratcha — הַקְּדוֹשָׁה hakedosha

וְקוּשְׁיוֹת vekushyot — וְהַוָיוֹת vehavayot — וְיִשּׁוּבִים veyisuvim — אֲמִתִּיִּים amitiyim

וְחִדּוּשֵׁי vechidushei — דִּינִים dinim — לַאֲמִתָּהּ la'amita — שֶׁל shel — תּוֹרָה torah

וּבְרֹב uvrov — י"פ אהיה — רַחֲמֶיךָ rachamecha — תְּזַכֵּנוּ tezakenu — לְזֶרַע lezera

קֹדֶשׁ kodesh — בָּנִים banim — וַחֲכָמִים chachamim — וַחֲסִידִים vachasidim — זֶרַע zera

אֲנָשִׁים anashim — וּבְרִיא uvari — בְּמַזָּלַיְהוּ mazalayhu — וְלֹא velo — יִמָּצֵא yimatze

בָּנוּ banu — וְלֹא velo — בְּזַרְעֵנוּ bezar'enu — שׁוּם shum — פְּגַם pegam — וְשׁוּם veshum

פְּסוּל pisul — וְלֹא velo — יִכָּרֵת yikaret — זַרְעֵנוּ zar'enu — וְזַס chas — וְשָׁלוֹם veshalom

---

and may Your compassion suppress Your anger, and May Your compassion be stirred over Your attributes. And may You bring to the Light all the sparks of our Torah and our Precepts, and let everything return to its original strength, so that none should be totally banished. And may You cause us to merit to delve in the Torah for its own sake, to study and to teach, to keep and to do, and to bring to the Light all the parts of the Pardes (achrinym of the four levels of depth) of our Torah, which relate to our Nefesh (lower soul), Ruach (our spirit), and Neshamah (our higher soul). And graciously grant us from Yourself wisdom, understanding and knowledge, to innovation e many true chidushim in the Pardes of Your Holy Torah, questions and queries and true resolutions and new laws according to the truth of the Torah. And in Your abundant compassion, may You cause us to merit having holy offspring, wise and pious children, male children, with good fortune. And let there not be found in us not our offspring any blemish or any flaw, and may our seed not be cut off, Heaven forbid.

וְאַתָּה veAta   בְּרֹב berov   אהיה י"פ   רַחֲמֶיךָ rachamecha   תִּתֵּן titen   ב"פ כהת

בָּנוּ banu   כֹּחַ ko'ach   וּבְרִיאוּת uvri'ut   וִיכֹלֶת vicholet   מַסְפִּיק maspik

וָחֹזֶק vechozek   פהל וְאֹמֶץ ve'ometz   בְּאֵבָרֵינוּ be'evarenu   וְגִידֵינוּ vegidenu

וְגוּפֵנוּ vegufenu   לַעֲמֹד la'amod   עַל al   הַמִּשְׁמָר hamishmar   וְלֹא velo

יֶאֱרַע ye'era   לָנוּ lanu   אלהים, אהיה אדני   שׁוּם shum   מֵחוֹשׁ michush   וְשׁוּם veshum

כְּאֵב ke'ev   וְנִהְיֶה venihye   שְׂמֵחִים scmechim   וְטוֹבִים vetovim   וּבְרִיאִים uvri'im

לַעֲבוֹדָתֶךָ la'avodatecha   וְתַצִּילֵנוּ vetatzilenu   מִכָּל mikol   רָע ra

אָמֵן amen   יאהדונהי   כֵּן ken   מהש ע"ה, ע"ב בריבוע וקס"א ע"ה, אל שדי ע"ה   רָצוֹן ratzon   יְהִי yehi

אֱלֹהֵינוּ Elohenu   ילה וֵאלֹהֵי velohei   לכב ; מילוי ע"ב, דמב ; ילה   אֲבוֹתֵינוּ avotenu

מְלוֹךְ meloch   כֹּל kol   ילי עמם   עַל al   הָעוֹלָם ha'olam   כֻּלּוֹ kulo

בִּכְבוֹדֶךָ bichvodach   ב"ן, לכב   וְהִנָּשֵׂא vehinase   עַל al   כֹּל kol   ילי עמם

הָאָרֶץ ha'aretz   אלהים דההן ע"ה   בִּיקָרֶךְ bikarach   וְהוֹפַע vehofa   בַּהֲדַר bahadar

גְּאוֹן ge'on   עֻזֶּךְ uzach   עַל al   כֹּל kol   ילי עמם   יוֹשְׁבֵי yoshvei   תֵבֵל tevel   ב"פ ריו

אַרְצֶךָ artzach   וְיֵדַע veyeda   כֹּל kol   ילי   פָּעוּל pa'ul   (Asiyah)

כִּי ki   אַתָּה Ata   פְעַלְתּוֹ pe'alto   וְיָבִין veyavin   כֹּל kol   ילי   יְצוּר yetzur (Yetzirah)

כִּי ki   אַתָּה Ata   יְצַרְתּוֹ yetzarto   וְיֹאמַר veyomar   כֹּל kol   ילי

אֲשֶׁר asher   נְשָׁמָה neshama   (Beriah)   בְּאַפּוֹ ve'apo   יְהֹוָה Adonai   אדני יאהדונהי

אֱלֹהֵי Elohei   מילוי ע"ב, דמב ; ילה   יִשְׂרָאֵל Yisrael   תרי"ג (מצוות)

מֶלֶךְ malach   (מֶלֶךְ)   וּמַלְכוּתוֹ umalchuto   בַּכֹּל vakol   לכב, ב"ן   מָשָׁלָה mashala

---

And You, in Your abundant compassion,
may You infuse us strength and health and suitable ability and support and strength in our organs, our sinews,
and our body to stand at the watch; and let not any malady or any pain befall us. And may we be happy
and good and healthy for Your service; and may You rescue us from all evil. Amen, so may be Your will.

Our God and the God of our forefathers, cover the entire world with glory and be exalted over the entire
Earth in Your splendor, and reveal Yourself in the majestic grandeur of Your strength over all the dwellers
of the inhabited world, which is Your land. Then all that is made will know that You have made them
and all that is formed will realize that You have formed them and everything that has a soul in its
nostril shall proclaim: "The Lord, the God of Israel, had reigned and His Kingship rules over everything."

קַדְּשֵׁנוּ kadeshenu ◆vemitzvotecha בְּמִצְוֹתֶיךָ ten תֵּן ◆vemitzvotecha וְחֶלְקֵנוּ chelkenu

בְּתוֹרָתֶךָ vetoratach sabe'enu שַׂבְּעֵנוּ mituvach מִטּוּבָךְ לאו◆ same'ach שַׂמֵּחַ

נַפְשֵׁנוּ nafshenu ◆bishu'atach בִּישׁוּעָתֶךָ vetaher וְטַהֵר libenu לִבֵּנוּ

לְעָבְדְּךָ le'ovdecha ◆ve'emet בֶּאֱמֶת פיו, אל יהוה ve'emet אהיה פעמים אהיה, ז"פ ס"ג ve'al וְאַל

תַּדִּיחֵנוּ tadichenu mipnei מִפְּנֵי shum שׁוּם nivra נִבְרָא sheba'olam שֶׁבָּעוֹלָם◆

וְתַאֲרִיךְ veta'arich yamenu יָמֵינוּ batov בַּטּוֹב והו ushnotenu וּשְׁנוֹתֵינוּ

בַּנְּעִימִים bane'imim◆ umaleh וּמַלֵּא shenotenu שְׁנוֹתֵינוּ batov בַּטּוֹב והו◆

אֹרֶךְ orech yamim יָמִים נלך ushnot וּשְׁנוֹת chayim וַחַיִּים אהיה אהיה יהוה, בינה ע"ה

תּוֹסִיף tosif lanu לָנוּ ulchol וּלְכָל אלהים, אהיה ארני יה benei בְּנֵי ארני קס"א קנ"א

בֵּיתֵנוּ vetenu ב"פ ראה la'avodatecha לַעֲבוֹדָתֶךָ uvtzel וּבְצֵל kenafecha כְּנָפֶיךָ

תַּסְתִּירֵנוּ tastirenu◆ vetatzilenu וְתַצִּילֵנוּ mikol מִכָּל ילי gezerot גְּזֵרוֹת

קָשׁוֹת kashot vera'ot וְרָעוֹת utchadesh וּתְחַדֵּשׁ י"ב הויות, קס"א קנ"א

עָלֵינוּ alenu shana שָׁנָה tova טוֹבָה אכא◆ venihye וְנִהְיֶה sheketim שְׁקֵטִים

וְשַׁאֲנַנִּים vesha'ananim deshenim דְּשֵׁנִים vera'ananim וְרַעֲנַנִּים

לַעֲבוֹדָתֶךָ la'avodatecha ulyir'atecha וּלְיִרְאָתֶךָ ki כִּי imecha עִמְּךָ mekor מְקוֹר

וַחַיִּים chayim אהיה אהיה יהוה, בינה ע"ה be'orcha בְּאוֹרְךָ nir'e נִרְאֶה or אוֹר רז, א"ס:

Initials of the Name יהו.

יְהִי yehi chasdecha וְחַסְדֶּךָ Adonai יְהֹוָאדֹנָיאהדונהי alenu עָלֵינוּ ka'asher כַּאֲשֶׁר

יִחַלְנוּ yichalnu lach לָךְ harenu הַרְאֵנוּ: Adonai יְהֹוָאדֹנָיאהדונהי chasdecha וְחַסְדֶּךָ

וְיֶשְׁעֲךָ veyeshacha titen תִּתֶּן ב"פ כהת lanu לָנוּ אלהים, אהיה ארני:

Sanctify us with Your commandments; give us our portion in Your Torah; satiate us from Your goodness; gladden our soul in Your salvation; and purify our heart to serve You with sincerity. Do not cast us aside on account of any creature in the world. Lengthen our days in goodness and our years in pleasantness and fill our years with good. Long days and years of life may You increase for us and for all the members of our household for Your service. Hide us in the shade of Your wings, and rescue us form all harsh and evil decrees. And may You renew for us a good year, and may we be calm and peaceful, fulfilled and vigorous, for Your service and for Your reverence. For with You is the source of life, by Your Light shall we see light. (Psalms 36:10)

"Lord, may Your kindness be upon us as we have placed our hope in You." (Psalms 33:22)

"Show us Your kindness, Lord and grant us Your salvation" (Psalms 85:8)

וַאֲנִי va'ani אֲנִי בְּחַסְדְּךָ bechasdecha בָּטַחְתִּי vatachti יָגֵל yagel לְהוּ לִבִּי libi

בִּישׁוּעָתֶךָ bishu'atecha לַיהוָֹה ladonai ashira אָשִׁירָה ki כִּי gamal גָּמַל

עָלָי alai: הִנֵּה hineh אֵל el (מילוי דס"ג) יָא"י יְשׁוּעָתִי yeshu'ati אֶבְטַח evtach

וְלֹא velo אֶפְחָד efchad כִּי ki עָזִּי ozi אלהים ע"ה, אהיה אדני ע"ה וְזִמְרָת vezimrat

יָהּ Yah יְהוָֹה Adonai וַיְהִי vayhi לִּי li לִישׁוּעָה lishu'a:

קוֹל kol מְבַשֵּׂר mevasher מְבַשֵּׂר mevasher וְאוֹמֵר ve'omer: (X7)

רִבִּי ribi וַחֲנַנְיָה Chananya בֶּן ben עֲקַשְׁיָה Akashya אוֹמֵר omer:

רָצָה ratza הַקָּדוֹשׁ haKadosh בָּרוּךְ Baruch הוּא Hu לְזַכּוֹת lezakot

אֶת et יִשְׂרָאֵל Yisrael. לְפִיכָךְ lefichach הִרְבָּה hirba לָהֶם lahem תּוֹרָה torah

וּמִצְוֹת umitzvot שֶׁנֶּאֱמַר shene'emar: יְהוָֹה Adonai וָחָפֵץ chafetz

לְמַעַן lema'an צִדְקוֹ tzidko יַגְדִּיל yagdil תּוֹרָה torah וְיַאְדִּיר veya'adir:

Here we say *Kaddish Al Yisrael* on pages 260-262.

"As for me, I have trusted in Your kindness, my heart will therefore rejoice in Your salvations; I shall sing to the Lord for He has bestowed goodness upon me." (Psalms 13:6) "Behold, God is my salvation, I shall be secure and not fear, for the strength and cutting power of God, the Lord, were for me a salvation." (Isaiah 12:2)

A voice announces—announces and exclaims (X7)

"Rav Hananya ben Akashya says: The Holy One, blessed be He, desired to grant merit to Israel. He therefore gave them an abundance of Torah and Precepts, as it is stated: The Lord wished for the sake of his righteousness, He made the Torah great and gave strength." (Tractate Makkot, 23b)

3 *Binah* Left Brain יְהֹוָה	1 *Keter* Skull יְהֹוָה	2 *Chochmah* Right Brain יַהֲוָה
5 Left Eye יהוה יהוה יהוה יהוה יהוה	9 8 Nose אֵל אֱלֹ אֶל	4 Right Eye יהוה יהוה יהוה יהוה יהוה
7 Left Ear יוד הי ואו הה		6 Right Ear יוד הי ואו הה

10 Mouth **יוד הי ואו הי (אהיה)** אוזה"ע גיכ"ק דטלנ"ת וסער"ץ בומ"ף

12 *Gevurah* Left Arm יְהֹוָה	13 *Tiferet* Body יְהֹוָה	11 *Chesed* Right Arm יְהֹוָה
15 *Hod* Left Leg יְהֹוָה	16 *Yesod* Reproductive Organs יו הו וו הו	14 *Netzach* Right Leg יְהֹוָה

17 *Malchut* עטרה יְהֹוָאדני

יוֹם אָ - Sunday

יֱהֹוֵה

יוּד הֵי וְיו הֵי יֵוּד הֵי וָאו הֵי

אֵל שַׁדַּי יָאולדפההייִיאוּודההיי

אָנָּא בְּכֹחַ גְּדוּלַת יְמִינְךָ תַּתִּיר צְרוּרָה

אַבְגִיתַץ יְהֹוָה יְהֹוָה

סְמַטְיוּרִיָּה גְּזֵריֵאֵל וְעֲנָאֵל לְמוּאֵל

ר"ת סָגוֹל

יוֹם בְּ - Monday

יֵוּד הֵי וָאו הֵי וְיו יֵוּד הֵי וְאו הֵי וָאו הֵי יוּד הֵי וָאו הֵא

אֵל יְהֹוַה יָאולדפהההואאואיאוּודההאא

קַבֵּל רִנַּת עַמְּךָ שַׂגְּבֵנוּ טַהֲרֵנוּ נוֹרָא

קָרַעְשָׁטָן יֱהֵוָה יְהֹוָה

שַׂמְעִיאֵל בַּרְכִיאֵל אַהַנִיאֵל

ר"ת שׁוָא

יוֹם גָ - Tuesday

יוֹד הֵא וָאו הֵא יוֹד הֵא הֵה וָו הֵה

אֵל אֲדֹנָי יָאולדפהההואווּודההה

נָא גִבּוֹר דּוֹרְשֵׁי יְחוּדְךָ כְּבָבַת שָׁמְרֵם

נַגְדִיכַשׁ יֱהֵוַה יְהֹוָה

וַנִיאֵל לְהַדִיאֵל מוֹזְנִיאֵל

ר"ת חֹלָם

Wednesday - יוֹם דְ

יוֹד הֵא וֹאוֹ הֵא יוֹד הֵהַ וָו הֵהַ

אֵל אֲדֹנָי יאולדּהּפּהַהַהֹהַוּוֹדּהַהֹה

בֹּרכֶם טֹהֵרֵם רוֹזמֵי צִדְקֹתְךָ תָּמִיד גֹּמלֵם

בַּטְרֵצָתַג יַהֵוֹהַ יַהֵוֹהַ

וֹזקִיאֵל רֹהֹטִיאֵל קְדֹעִיאֵל

ר"ת וֹזרק

Thursday - יוֹם הְ

יַוּוּד הֵיַ וֵאַוּ הֵיַ יֵוֹד הֵיַ וֵאָוּ הֵיַ יוֹד הֵא וֹאוֹ הֵא

אֵל יַהֹוֹה יאולדּהּפּהַהֹאַאִיאֹוּאֹוֹדֹהַהֹאַא

וֹזסֹין קָדֹוֹעַ בֹּרוֹב טוֹבֹך נַהֹל עֹדתֹך

וֹזקְבֹטַנַע יַהֵוֹהַ יַהֵוֹהַ

שְׁמֹוֹעַאֵל רֹעַמִיאֵל קֹנַיאֵל

ר"ת עֹרק

(הַקְבֹּוּץ מֹלֹאכִיו בּר"ת עֹוּרק)

Friday - יוֹם וּו

יַוּוּד הֵיַ וִיוּ הֵיַ יַוּוּד הֵיַ וֵאָוּ הֵיַ

אֵל עֹדֹי יאולדּהּפּהַהֹיַיִיאֹוּוֹדֹהֹיַיִ

יוֹזִיד גָאַה לֹעַמֹך פַּנֵה זוֹכְרֵי קֹדֹוּשָׁתֹך

יַגֹּלֹפֹזֹק יַהֵוֹהָ יַהוֹוּוֹהוּ

עֹוּמֹוֹעֹוֹיַיִאַוּלוּ רוֹפֹוֹאַוֹלוּ קֹוּדֹיעֹוֹיַיִאוּלוּ

ר"ת עֹרק

Angels of Friday night

יוֹד הֵי וָאו הֵי   שׁוֹעָתֵנוּ קַבֵּל וּשְׁמַע צַעֲקָתֵנוּ יוֹדֵעַ תַּעֲלוּמוֹת

עֹקְוּצִית יְהֹוָה יְהֹוָה יְהֶוֶה יְהֹוֶה

שְׂמַעְאֵל בִּרְכִיאֵל אַהֲנִיאֵל

ר"ת שׁוֹא

סַמְטוֹרְיָה גַּזְרִיאֵל וְעַנָאֵל לְמֶוֶאֵל

ר"ת סָגוֹל

צוּרִיאֵל רְזִיאֵל יוֹפִיאֵל

ר"ת צִירִי

Angels of *Shabbat* (Saturday) Morning

יוֹד הֵי וָיו הֵי יוֹד הֵי וָיו הֵי

שׁוֹעָתֵנוּ קַבֵּל וּשְׁמַע צַעֲקָתֵנוּ יוֹדֵעַ תַּעֲלוּמוֹת

עֹקְוּצִית יְהֹוָה יְהֹוָה יְהֹוָה

שְׂמַעְאֵל בִּרְכִיאֵל אַהֲנִיאֵל

ר"ת שׁוֹא

קָדְמִיאֵל מַלְכִּיאֵל צוּרִיאֵל

ר"ת קָמַץ

Angels of Shabbat (Saturday) Afternoon

יוֹד הֵא וָאו הֵא יוֹד הֵא וָאו הֵא

שׁוֹעָתֵנוּ קַבֵּל וּשְׁמַע צַעֲקָתֵנוּ יוֹדֵעַ תַּעֲלוּמוֹת

עֹקְוּצִית יְהֹוָה יְהֹוָה יְהֹוָה

שְׂמַעְאֵל בִּרְכִיאֵל אַהֲנִיאֵל

ר"ת שׁוֹא

פַּדָאֵל תַּלְמִיאֵל (תּוּמִיאֵל) וְסַדְיאֵל

ר"ת פָּתוּוֹ